THE
GOOD
ENGLISH
GUIDE

THE

GOOD
ENGLISH
GUIDE

ENGLISH USAGE IN THE 1990s

compiled and written by
GODFREY HOWARD

M

First published 1993 by Pan Macmillan Publishers Limited
Cavaye Place London SW10 9PG
and Basingstoke

Associated companies throughout the world

ISBN 0-333-53867-6

2 4 6 8 10 9 7 5 3

A CIP catalogue record for this book is available from the British Library.

Typeset by Florencetype Ltd, Kewstoke, Avon
Printed by Mackays Ltd, Chatham, Kent

To Françoise
who shared every word
and for Mona and Lesley
who will enjoy most of them

Introduction

We should be lost without dictionaries. They chart the vast wilderness of words in which we wander all our lives. But words in a dictionary are like do-not-touch exhibits in a museum. It is only when we use them that they come to life. This book is planned to take over at the point where dictionaries leave off. It is about language in action. It sets out to put the reader in the driving-seat, opening up ways of negotiating the daily difficulties of arranging words in sentences, resolving grammatical doubts, distinguishing shades of meaning and responding to linguistic change.

Few things register more passion and outrage than English usage. For many people 'good English' is the English they learned at school ten, twenty, thirty or more years ago. William Safire, in *The New York Times*, warns that '. . . if sticking grimly to the rules of grammar makes you sound like a pompous pedant, you *are* a pompous pedant'. Not that changes are always for the better, for distinctions of meaning and points of style are sometimes lost on the way. But the language is alive and well, and we need to be in touch with the mainstream of its development.

There is no one who does not feel uncertain at times about English grammar, as we can never master all the complexities. English is a minefield, and there is hardly a writer, from the translators of the Bible to Dickens, E M Forster and Agatha Christie, who has not been picked on for making mistakes. The eccentricities of English spelling, loaded with multiple-choice options, belong to its antiquity and tangled roots. Yet most of us love the language, which remains as forceful and flexible as it was for Shakespeare and Milton, Eliot and Graham Greene. Hardliners who impose a comprehensive code of dos and don'ts are on the wrong path, for style and usage are not an exact science. Over a hundred years ago, Henry Alford wrote a book called *The Queen's English* (it was Queen Victoria of course). His style is old-worldly but his advice is as fresh as new paint:

> 'Aim at satisfying the common sense of those who read and hear, and then, though any one who has no better employment may pick holes in every third sentence, you will have written better English than one who suffers the tyranny of small critics to cramp the expression of his thoughts.'

For centuries English was in the frigid grip of Latin and Greek scholars. Even by the 1860s, the study of English did not count for much. There were no professors of modern English at Oxford or Cambridge; at Eton the English teacher ranked below the teacher of French and at Marlborough behind the dancing master! Grammar was based on Latin and Ancient Greek, marvellous languages, but dead ones with fossilized rules, which led to tired old commandments such as, never begin a sentence with the conjunctions *and* or *but*, never end a sentence with prepositions such as *with, on, to* or *for*, and never ever split an infinitive, even if you have to turn a double-somersault to avoid it.

All the evidence shows that English cannot be hemmed in for long. The Society for Pure English, formed in Oxford in 1913 to guide the use and development of the English language, has long since turned up its toes.The Advisory Committee on Spoken English, set up by the BBC in 1926, with Bernard Shaw, Robert Bridges (poet laureate 1913—30), Julian Huxley and Alistair Cooke as members, threw in the towel in 1938. Lord Reith, as director general of the BBC, spoke its epitaph: 'There are no experts, only users.'

Most Europeans think of the British as traditionalists. But when it comes to language, it is the other way round. English is constantly being stretched in new directions. We wake up every morning to new discoveries, new concepts and fresh demands on language to express what we think and feel. And all the time spoken English is lubricating the wheels of the written language, leaving it more easygoing. Recently the British government minister responsible for education warned that skills in English '. . . are vital not only for educational and cultural development but also for our economic development and competitiveness'. The emphasis on economic development is valid, for it is estimated that three-quarters of the world's mail and faxes are in English, as well as 80 per cent of all the data stored in computers. British Council figures show that English is used at some time every day by over 2,000 million people, two-fifths of the world's population.

Education advisers are agreed that English is the most important subject in the curriculum. It is also the most contentious. There is much talk of 'traditional values', without any agreement on how far back they should go. Language reflects society, illumines new understandings, and problems near the end of the 20th century cannot be frozen in a 19th century idiom. We have never thought so much before about the language we all use. To explain thought and ideas, we have to focus on the words and sentences that express them. Language may be as basic as mother's milk, but at the same time it has to encompass the exploration of outer space.

There are opposing attitudes towards the use of English, set apart by *prescriptive* and *permissive* as defining terms. The prescriptive approach seeks to lay down the law uncompromisingly, resisting to the last changes in grammar, spelling, pronunciation and the meaning of words. There are still grammarians who have some strange notion that English should be strictly logical, disregarding the fact that language holds up a mirror to life which constantly confounds logic. There is no place for a high retaining wall round the English language, and who should know better than James Murray, first editor of the original *Oxford English Dictionary*? When the first section was published in 1884, he noted '. . . there is absolutely no defining line in any direction: the circle of English has a well-defined centre but no discernible circumference'. In the 1990s, even Murray's 'well-defined centre' cannot be taken for granted. Antonia Byatt, winner of the 1990 Booker Prize, concludes that 'the language is provisional, shifting, in a state of flux, in a state of change'.

The permissive approach, at its best, responds to the way the language is changing, without opening the floodgates, for a language must have structure to survive. Good writers and speakers play a part in keeping the structure of English in place, but it is a light framework supporting the language not heavy chains that shackle it. There is freedom in the way we can use English but there is also order. *The Good English Guide* seeks to walk the tightrope in between. Recommendations on grammar, vocabulary, pronunciation and meaning are taken from a consensus of writers, editors, broadcasters and others for whom the English language is a tool in their daily work. A balance is held between conventional grammar and linguistic change. The entry on *who or whom*, for example, accepts there are many people who take a pride in using these forms with orthodox correctness, while others feel the distinction has no value and only preserves a grammatical museum piece. Advice and recommendations are offered to both lobbies.

Specialized terms and new expressions move quickly into everyday language and are often only hazily understood. Readers are helped to relate to confusing terms connected with technology, literature, music, the visual arts, religion, philosophy, psychology, sexology and social science. Linguistic savoir faire also requires an awareness of colloquial and slang usage. Here a line is drawn between words and expressions that are taking root and easy-come-easy-go expressions that are no more than leaves blown across the linguistic landscape.

Contrary to what is often believed, good slang is part of good English. Eric Partridge, who spent a lifetime studying slang, decided that an exact definition of it is impossible. A word considered slang at one time may move up in the world and eventually be accepted in formal writing. This book indicates when words are decidedly on one side of the tracks or the other, but allows for a generous grey area in between! For example, we all use *guts* to mean courage and determination, the way Philip Sidney used it in the 16th century for his version of the Psalms. Yet most dictionaries refuse to promote that use of guts beyond colloquial or informal. And there are many other times when we, not our dictionary, can decide to have the last word.

The Good English Guide is about British English, but American English and other varieties of English come into it many times, because there is an ever-increasing overlap. Nor is this cause for dismay. Immigrant influences, bouncing back at the language in ceaseless bombardment, have kept English on its toes as the most lively and adaptable language the world has ever known. And linguistic history shows English has an instinctive genius, absorbing or rejecting changes without losing its cadence and poetry.

Anyone who tries to write well discovers it is hard work, for good English demands respect for the language. Dag Hammarskjöld left us the message that 'Respect for the word – to employ it with scrupulous care and an incorruptible heart-felt love of truth – is essential if there is to be any growth in a society or in the human race.'*

G H

*From *Markings*, translated by W H Auden and Leif Sjöberg.

Acknowledgements

This book owes much to many examples and references taken from books, newspapers, magazines and broadcasts. It could hardly have been written without constant cross-checks with the work of lexicographers and other commentators on English usage. The following list covers mostly contemporary writers, broadcasters, academics and others in Britain and America who are the sources of short quotations, points of view and information. It also includes people who have generously offered suggestions and advice. If there are any accidental omissions or inaccuracies, please accept my apologies, and let me know for correction in future editions.

G H

Gilbert Adair (*The Independent*); Polly Adler, *A House Is Not a Home*; Kingsley Amis, *Take a Girl Like You* (Gollancz); Martin Amis, *London Fields* (Cape); Kenneth Anger; Lisa Armstrong (*The Independent*); Louis Armstrong; Josephine Bacon; Paul Bailey (*The Observer*); James Baker (BBC); Russell Baker (*The New York Times*); Lynn Barber (*The Independent*); H E Bates, *The Darling Buds of May* (Michael Joseph); Patricia Beer (*London Review of Books*); Alan Bennett, *Talking Heads* (BBC); *Beveridge Report* (HMSO); Lionel Blue (BBC); Pierre Boulez; Boutros Boutros-Ghali; Melvyn Bragg; Sally Brampton (*The Times*); Gilbert Brim; British Rail; Peter Brook, *The Shifting Point* (Methuen); Peter Brooks (*The Times Literary Supplement*); Anita Brookner, *Hôtel du Lac* (Cape); Ivor Brown, *A Word in Your Ear* (Cape); Bill Bryson, *Dictionary of Troublesome Words* (Penguin); BT publications; Alan Budd (BBC); David Budgen; Alan Bullock, *Bullock Report, Industrial Democracy* (HMSO); Robert Burchfield (*The Sunday Times*), *The English Language* (OUP), *The Spoken Word* (BBC); George Bush; Antonia Byatt (BBC); John Cage; Champagne Shippers' Association; Raymond Chandler; Jenny Cheshire (*English Today*, CUP); John Cole (BBC); Alex Comfort, *The Joy of Sex* (Quartet Books); Alistair Cooke, *Letter from America* (BBC); Jilly Cooper, *Class* (Eyre Methuen); Aaron Copland; Alan Coren (*The Times*); Susan Crosland (*The Sunday Times*); Martin Cutts, Plain English Campaign; David Dabydeen (*State of the Language 1990*, University of California & Faber); Siobhan Davies; Roger de Grey; *Debrett's Peerage*; Len Deighton, *The Ipcress File* (Cape); Jacques Delors; Ernest Dichter; David Dimbleby (BBC); Carl Djerassi (BBC); John Doherty (*The Times*); Peter Drucker; Duchess of York (BBC); John Foster Dulles; *The Economist*; David L Edwards; Willard R Espy, *Words at Play* (Clarkson N Potter, New York); Frederico Fellini, *La Dolce Vita*; Carl Felsenfeld (BBC); *Financial Times*; E M Forster, *A Room With a View* (Hutchinson); Brian Foster, *The Changing English Language* (Macmillan); Roy Foster; Roy Fuller; Zsa Zsa Gabor; John Kenneth Galbraith; Gerald Gardiner; Conor Gearty, *Terror* (Faber); John Georgiadis (BBC); Jonathan Glancy (*The Independent*); David Gold (*Language in Society*, CUP); Ernst Gombrich (BBC); Teresa Gorman; Ernest Gowers, *Plain Words*, and Bruce Fraser's revised edition (HMSO); Graham Greene, *A Gun for Sale, The End of the Affair* (Bodley Head); *The Green Consumer's Guide*;

Germaine Greer, *Sex and Destiny, The Change* (Hamish Hamilton); Elizabeth Grice (*The Sunday Times*); Valerie Grove (*The Sunday Times*); Mel Grundy (*The Independent*); Stephanie Gutman (*The Independent*); John Haffenden, *Poets in Conversation* (Faber); Dag Hammarskjöld, *Markings* (Faber); Charles Handy; *Harpers & Queen*; Robert Harris (*The Sunday Times*); Sophia Hartland; *Harvard Business Review*; John Harvey-Jones, *Making It Happen* (Collins); Roy Hattersley; Stephen Hawking, *A Brief History of Time* (Bantam Press); Health Education Council; Ernest Hemingway, *Death in the Afternoon* (Cape); Michael Heseltine; David Hockney; David Holloway (Whitechapel Art Gallery); Alastair Horne, *Harold Macmillan* (Macmillan); Lesley Howard; Philip Howard (*The Times*), *English Observed, Words Fail Me, Winged Words* (Hamish Hamilton); Geoffrey Howe (BBC); Douglas Hurd (BBC); Aldous Huxley, *The Doors of Perception, Proper Studies, Brave New World* (Chatto & Windus); Institute of Marketing; Kazuo Ishiguru, *The Remains of the Day* (Faber); A Lloyd James, *Broadcast English* (BBC); Simon Jenkins (*The Times*); Frank Johnston; Michael Jones (*The Sunday Times*); C G Jung, *Man and his symbols* (Aldus Books & W H Allen); Jack Kerouac; David Kessler; Arthur Koestler, *The Act of Creation* (Macmillan, New York); Aung San Suu Kyi, *Freedom from Fear and Other Writings* (Viking & Penguin), with thanks to Michael Aris; Philip Larkin, *High Windows* (Faber); D H Lawrence, *Lady Chatterley's Lover* (Penguin Books); Mark Lawson (*The Listener*); Timothy Leary, *Psychedelic Review*; Bernard Leach; Laurie Lee, *Cider with Rosie* (Hogarth Press); Adrienne Lehrer(*Language*); Alicja Lesniak (*The Sunday Times*); Bernard Levin (*The Times*); C S Lewis, *The Allegory of Love* (OUP); David Lodge; London School of Economics; Gerald Long (BBC); Graham Lucas (*The Times*); Alison Lurie, William Lutz (*State of the Language 1990*, University of California & Faber); Sue

MacGregor, *Today* (BBC); Brian Magee (BBC); Chrissie Maher, Plain English Campaign; John Major; Alan Maley (*English Today*, CUP); Antoni Marianski; Marks & Spencer; Masters & Johnson; Armistead Maupin, *Significant Others* (Chatto & Windus); Arthur Miller, *The Crucible*; Missouri University (School of Journalism); Nancy Mitford, *Noblesse Oblige* (Hamish Hamilton); H Montgomery Hyde, *The 'Lady Chatterley's Lover' Trial* (Bodley Head); Bel Mooney; Janet Morgan, *Edwina Mountbatten* (Harper Collins); Desmond Morris, *Manwatching* (Triad Panther); Elizabeth Murray, *Caught in the Web of Words* (Yale University Press); Jenni Murray, *Woman's Hour* (BBC); Vladimir Nabokov, *Lolita*; National Consumer Council: *Plain English for lawyers, Plain words for consumers, Gobbledegook*; National Union of Teachers; Bill Naughton; Andrew Neil; *Newsweek*; Dennis Norden; Oliver North; Norwegian National Tourist Office; Patrick O'Connor (*The Independent*); George Orwell, *Nineteen Eighty-Four, Animal Farm* (Secker & Warburg), *Politics and the English Language* (News of the World, 1946); P D Ouspensky, *A New Model of the Universe* (Routledge); Vance Packard, *The Hidden Persuaders* (Longmans, Green); Dorothy Parker; Northcote Parkinson; Passport Office; Pembroke College *Record*; S J Perelman; M F Perutz; Lawrence Peter; B A Phythian, *A Concise Dictionary of Correct English* (Hodder & Stoughton); Harold Pinter; Robert M Pirsig, *Zen and the Art of Motorcycle Maintenance* (Bodley Head); Jackson Pollock; Raymond Postgate (*The Listener*); Dennis Potter; Stephen Potter; Dilys Powell (*The Sunday Times*); Enoch Powell; *Private Eye*; Randolph Quirk (*State of the Language 1980*, University of California); Brian Redhead, *Today* (BBC); Mandy Rice-Davies, *Mandy* (Sphere Books); Mary Robinson; Richard Rogers (BBC); Anthony Rose; Alan S C Ross, *Linguistic Class-indicators* (*Neuphilologische mitteilungen*, Finland); Leo Rosten, *The Joys of Yiddish* (W H

Allen); Bernice Rubens; Robert Runcie (BBC); Damon Runyon, *Guys and Dolls*; Salman Rushdie, *The Satanic Verses* (Viking), lecture at ICA; Jonathan Sachs (BBC); Oliver Sacks; William Safire (*The New York Times*); Anthony Sampson (*The Independent*); Greg Sams; Kate Saunders (*The Sunday Times*); Michael Saward (*The Times*); Vernon Scannell, *Protest Poem* (lines quoted by permission of *New Statesman and Society*); Pierre Schaeffer; Norman Schwarzkopf; Paul Scott, *Jewel in the Crown* (Heinemann); Jacques Séguéla, *Ne dites pas à ma mère...* (Flammarion, Paris); Bernard Shaw, *Prefaces, Pygmalion, Man & Superman*; Clare Short; John Silverlight, *Words, More Words* (Macmillan); Joanna Simon (*The Sunday Times*); Susannah Simons (*The Sunday Times*); Clive Sinclair; Emma Soames (*The Sunday Times, The Tatler*); Alexander Solzhenitsyn, *The Gulag Archipelago* (Harvill); Susan Sontag; *The Spectator*; Fritz Spiegl (*The Listener*), *In-Words & Out-Words* (Elm Tree Books); Munni Srivastava; Nancy Stein (*The Independent*); Fred Sternfeld; Adlai Stevenson; Christopher Strachey (*Fontana Dictionary of Modern Thought*); Alan Sugar (*The Times*); Walter Sullivan (*The New York Times*); *The Sun*; Deborah Tannen; Tavistock Institute of Marital Relations; A J P Taylor (*New Statesman*); Norman Tebbit; Studs Terkel, *Working* (Avon Books, New York); John Tessimond, *The Collected Poems of A S J Tessimond* (The Whiteknights Press), lines quoted by permission of Hubert Nicholson; Margaret Thatcher; Paul Theroux (*The Independent*); James Thurber, *Men, Women and Dogs* (W H Allen); Michael Tippett; J R R Tolkein, *The Hobbit* (Allen & Unwin); Hugh Trevor-Roper; Guinevere Tuffnell; George Turner; University Teachers' Association; Marina Vaizey (*The Sunday Times*); John Wakeham; William Waldegrave; Keith Waterhouse, *Billy Liar, Bimbo* (Hodder & Stoughton); David Watt, Royal Institute of International Affairs; Evelyn Waugh, *The Loved One*; Casper Weinberger; E S C Weiner (*Oxford English*, OUP); Laurence Whistler, *The Initials in the Heart* (Hart-Davis); Mary Whitehouse (submission to Annan Committee on Broadcasting); Elie Wiesel; Andrew Wilkinson, *Spoken English* (Open University Press); Bernard Williams (BBC); Lewis Wolpert (BBC); Margaret Wright; H C Wyld, *A Short History of English* (John Murray); John Wyndham, *The Kraken Wakes* (Michael Joseph); Gerard Young; Michael Young, *The Rise of the Meritocracy* (Thames & Hudson).

Editorial comments – Macmillan: Julian Ashby, Penny Warren, Caroline Ball. Rupert Crew: Doreen Montgomery.

Dictionaries – Collins *Cobuild Dictionary*. B & C Evans, *A Dictionary of Contemporary American Usage* (Random House). *Fontana Dictionary of Modern Thought*. Longman: *Dictionary of the English Language; Dictionary of Pronunciation* (J C Wells). Macmillan: *Dictionary of American Slang; Dictionary of Business & Management; Dictionary of the Environment; Dictionary of Historical Terms; Dictionary of Information Technology; Dictionary of Marketing & Advertising; Dictionary of Modern Economics; Dictionary of Psychology*. Mozeley & Whiteley's *Law Dictionary* (Butterworth). Oxford University Press: *Oxford English Dictionary; Shorter Oxford; Concise Oxford* (1976 and 1990 editions); *Dictionary of English Etymology* (C T Onions); *Dictionary of Middle English* (Skeat); *American Dictionary; Dictionary for Writers & Editors; Modern English Usage* (H W Fowler, 1926 and revised edition by Ernest Gowers, 1965); *The King's English* (H W and F G Fowler, 1906). Eric Partridge: *Usage and Abusage, Smaller Slang Dictionary* (Hamish Hamilton); *A Dictionary of Catch Phrases* (Routledge). Smith's *Latin Dictionary* (Murray). Webster's *American Dictionary of the English Language* (1828).

Notes on use

The Good English Guide is designed to be user-friendly. The simple system of phonetics used for pronunciation of difficult words can be understood at sight. Grammatical terms are explained in entries under their names: the only ones used elsewhere are *noun* and *verb*, which present no problem to most readers.

A word in **bold** type in an entry indicates there is a separate entry for that word: turn to it for more information. Apart from obvious ones, the only other abbreviation that appears is **OED**: the *Oxford English Dictionary*, second edition 1989. For more information, see entry under **dictionaries**.

Although the book is arranged for easy reference, it is also written to be opened at any page and simply read, which it is hoped will add insights into English usage in the 1990s.

• A •

a or **an** For over four hundred years grammarians have called these 'indefinite articles', and the *Oxford English Dictionary* confounds us with 15,000 tightly packed words on *a* alone before, over 400 pages further on, taking a solemn lexicographical look at *an*, which is in fact the older form of *a*. All that may be gripping stuff for grammarians or suitable material for masochists, but for the rest of us here are the essential guidelines. We all know the basic rule: *a* before a consonant, *an* before a vowel. There are four things to look out for:

1 When a word begins with an 'h' which is not sounded (heir, hour, honest, honour), use *an*: an honest broker, an hourly rate. It is better not to write 'an hotel', 'an historian', 'an habitué', even if you drop the 'h' in speech, as in French, which some people still do: 'an 'otel'. That sounds dated now and is heard less and less, although Anita Brookner, whose *Hôtel du Lac* (1984) won the Booker Prize, insists on 'an hotel'.

2 When words begin with 'u' or 'eu' pronounced 'yoo', it's like a consonant. Use *a*: a union, a European.

3 Before abbreviations and letters listen to the *sound*: an A road, a B road, an FRS (Fellow of the Royal Society), a UN resolution.

4 Watch out for the figures 8, 80, etc, which begin with a vowel-sound. Use *an* in speech and also in writing: an £8 million contract.

a or **the** There is a not all that subtle difference between calling someone *a* something-or-other or *the* something-or-other. Anthony Burgess is '*the* writer', while it is reasonable to call Joe Bloggs, assuming he is unknown, '*a* writer'. But there are many cases in between where there are some writers who bridle at being called '*a* writer', particularly when being introduced to give an after-dinner speech. The dividing line is uncertain, but it is always flattering to use *the* whatever-they-are, even when it is not altogether justified.

a- A useful Greek prefix to remember because it guides us to the meaning of some words. It means 'not' or 'without': amoral, asexual, asymmetry, atheism, atypical. . . .

For some words the Old English prefix *un-* (related to Latin *in-*) conveys exactly the same meaning: unsymmetrical, untypical. . . . For a few words the *a-* prefix is a non-judgemental alternative: *immoral* suggests morally wrong or even depraved, whereas *amoral* implies something outside the scope of moral-

ity, just as *apolitical* could mean outside the scope of politics, whereas *unpolitical* could be taken to mean unwise from a political point of view.

The prefix *a-* is usually pronounced 'ay': 'aySEXual', 'ayMORal', 'aypoLITical', 'aysimMETrik'. . . . (For some words, the 'a' sound (as in h*a*t) is an acceptable alternative: 'amMORal', 'assimMETrik'.)

abbreviations It now seems heavy-going to put stops between the letters of most abbreviations: BBC, TUC, USA, MA, PhD, BLitt, MP, QC, OBE. . . . This also applies to stops after Mr, Mrs, Ms, Revd, St and even to stops between someone's initials: H G Wells (this has not become standard practice yet).

Numerical abbreviations do not need stops any more: 2nd, 3rd, 10th. Nor do abbreviations of counties (Northants, Bucks . . .), points of the compass (NW, SE, NWW . . .) and shortcuts such as co-op, demo, recap, repro.

It is not, of course, wrong to use stops and the great *OED* still solemnly places stops between the letters of some abbreviations, including B.B.C. The BBC, in its annual report, puts the *OED* in its place and leaves out the stops. Rules for proofreaders at the Oxford University Press require stops in some instances, such as *a.m.* and *p.m.*, abbreviations of days and months (Mon., Tues., Jan., Feb., etc) and abbreviations using combinations of capital and small letters (D. Phil., B. Litt., etc) but concede that these may be dropped 'to accord with an author's special wishes'.

Such things are a matter of style: the trend is to leave stops out and by the end of the century they are likely to be omitted from all abbreviations. Unexpectedly, Americans are inclined to retain stops in more instances than the British. If you don't mind looking like a retired compositor, go on using stops in abbreviations whenever you like, so long as you are consistent. Otherwise feel free to get up at 7*am*, on *Mon*, *7th Feb* when the temperature is only 3*C*, listen to the *BBC* on *VHF*, buy the *FT* (*Financial Times*), send a letter to *WC1* or to *Herts*, and take *Mr J F Fields PhD* from *NYC* and *Mlle F E* Legrand from the *SW* of France round *St* Paul's Cathedral – all without stops.

Most abbreviations form the plural in the usual way by adding *-s*, but the former custom of slipping in an apostrophe is old-fashioned: MPs, MAs, QCs . . . (not MP's . . .). A few plurals are formed by doubling up one letter: MS (manuscript), MSS (manuscripts); p7 (page 7), pp 7–9 (pages 7–9). Where an abbreviation is

1

used for the title of a book, it should be in italics or underlined, as it would be if the title were in full: *OED* (*Oxford English Dictionary*).

Abbreviations are often a jargon, shorthand in speech or writing for the initiated, but incomprehensible to anyone outside the circle. Be on guard against using abbreviations that many people are not familiar with: not everyone knows, for example, that 'Please return *asap*' means 'Please return as soon as possible', or that *aka* means 'also known as'. The sensible rhyming rule is – When in doubt – spell it out!

'ABdomen' or 'abDOMen'   Most of us stress the first syllable ('ABdomen'), but curiously doctors and surgeons often stress *dom*, perhaps because of the influence of 'abDOMinal', a word often used in medicine. Most dictionaries show 'ABdomen' as the only pronunciation, so maybe doctors should fall in line with their patients.

abet   Lawyers, who feel more secure when they double-up words (fit and proper, null and void . . .), still talk about 'aiding and abetting' an offender or an offence. But outside criminal courts, *abet* (from 14th-century Old French) is pompous in everyday language. See also **archaisms**

ability or capacity   An ability is an acquired skill: her *ability* to speak several languages. A capacity is more an innate talent: her *capacity* for learning languages. This is a useful distinction although the dividing line is becoming blurred.

It is preferable to write or say 'the ability *to* . . .' and 'the capacity *for* . . .', although this is not a fixed rule.

-able or -eable   When a verb ends in a silent *-e*, it is dropped, *except* after *c* or *g*: drive – *drivable*, move – *movable*, but renounce – *renounceable*, change – *changeable*. With occasional words (*movable* is one example) the *-eable* spelling is an accepted alternative, but is less common.

-able or -ible   Is it accessible or accessable, responsible or responsable? Because it is more usual, a common mistake is to use *-able* instead of *-ible* (*accessible* and *responsible* are correct). There is no reliable rule unless you can recognize words that derive from Old English, because these nearly always take *-able*: unforgettable, washable, bearable. . . . More recent and new formations are also likely to be *-able*: unget-at-able, clubbable, unbeatable. And there are a few words where you can choose *-able* or *-ible*: extendable (or -ible), discussable (or -ible).

Unless you know, the only way to be sure is to turn to a dictionary. Because there are fewer *-ible* words, it is worth noting the more common ones: accessible, admissible, audible, collapsible, compatible, comprehensible, contemptible, credible, defensible, destructible, divisible (but dividable), edible, eligible, fallible, feasible, flexible, forcible, gullible, indelible, intelligible, irresistible, legible, negligible, perceptible, permiss-

ible, plausible, possible, responsible, reversible, sensible, susceptible, tangible, visible.

able-bodied   At sea this has a precise meaning: an *able-bodied* seaman has served three years before the mast, at least one of them in a merchant ship, so he is able to carry out all duties on board. On dry land, *able-bodied* is used more generally for anyone, man or woman these days, who is fit, healthy and competent to see a job through: 'From today, only slim, able-bodied English speakers with no children may sit in the row of seats next to emergency exits on American airliners' (*The Times*).

It is also extended to provide an 'acceptable' opposite to 'disabled', as in PHAB, the Physically Handicapped and Able-Bodied Association.

abnormal or subnormal   People sometimes confuse them. *Abnormal* is anything different from normal; *subnormal* is anything below normal. When they are used about people, both words have a pathological sense, so in some cases it is gentler to use *not normal* or *below normal*. Above normal is also possible, and for something or someone out of this world, *supernormal* is recognized by most current dictionaries.

about, around or round   'The wheels go *round*', because *round* accords with the idea of something revolving. But we can look *around* the corner, or *round* it. London Transport has issued a book called *Country Walks Around London*. As you can see, it's something of a free-for-all, so you can usually say whatever comes naturally.

Many people are happy saying 'Come for a drink around seven o'clock' or 'There were around 30 people in the room'. Others complain that this is **American English**, and that we should say 'about seven o'clock', 'about thirty people'. If you want it both ways, you can say 'round about seven o'clock', but this is labouring the point. *Around* (or *round*), for about, is normal usage in America, and has settled down comfortably in Britain, helped by a successful 1980s film about the jazz saxophonist, Dexter Gordon, which was called *Round Midnight*.

(see) above   See **see above** . . .

above par   See **par**

abrasive   Sandpaper is abrasive and it would hurt to rub it over the back of your hand. Since the early 16th century, 'rub' has been used for upsetting people ('rub someone up the wrong way'), and for some years now *abrasive* has also been applied to people, as a slightly more polite way of saying that someone is aggressive or tactless. The problem is that if you are honest and say what you really think, it's likely to be *abrasive* to some people. Or perhaps it depends upon how you say it.

(in the) absence (of)   Some people feel it's more impressive to write or say *in the absence of* instead of 'without': 'in the absence of more details, we cannot deal with your complaint'. 'Without' does the same job – and does it better.

absolute This is used in many different senses. The key is the Latin source, meaning 'complete'. So when we demand *absolute proof*, we require proof that is complete and free from any reservations. *Absolute power* is dictatorship or tyranny, since it is power without questioning. *Absolute majority* is usually political, used after elections to mean the overall majority of the leading party against all other parties combined. If there is no absolute majority, a party can govern only with support from other parties. *The Absolute* is a more difficult concept: it is a philosophical God, the ultimate reality embracing 'all and everything'.

Absolute is not a term often found in science, since there are few absolutes, but *absolute zero* is used for the lowest attainable temperature theoretically. *Absolute age* comes up in news items about archaeological or geological finds. It is based on carbon dating, an estimate of the age of a fossil or other organic material by measuring the decay of radioactive carbon, which takes place at a determined rate after the death of the organism.

absolutely The conversational use of *absolutely* has become common as an emphatic way of saying 'Yes' or 'No': 'Isn't it a lovely day?' 'Absolutely!', 'Are you feeling tired?' 'Absolutely not!' Conversational it may be, but it relates to the Latin origin of the word (see previous entry), so we are *absolutely* justified in using it this way. See also **yes**

absorb or **adsorb** Unless you've studied chemistry, it's easy to be puzzled by *adsorb*, or to think it's a mistake for *absorb*. Both words come from the same Latin word meaning 'to swallow'. *Adsorb* is used when condensation of gases forms a film that clings to the surface of a solid or liquid. *Absorb* is the everyday word we use when a sponge absorbs water or for the way we take in information. To understand something, you should not only be reading it, but *absorbing* it.

abstract Because of **abstract art** (a term that became familiar in the 1920s), *abstract* in general use as a descriptive word has come to mean abstruse and obscure, usually pejorative: 'That point of view is too abstract', or even 'That's just abstract', meaning out of touch and without meaning (see also **academic**).

Abstract as a noun ('This is an abstract of what is said') or as a descriptive word (abstract art) is stressed on the first syllable: 'ABstract'. As a verb, the stress moves forward to the second syllable: 'abSTRACT papers from a file'.

abstract art This found a place as an attempt by artists to free themselves from the traditional European concept of art as a representation of what is perceived in the outer world, in order to arrive at a purer aesthetic, a personal inner vision.

Abstract art is used now in such vague imprecise ways, that we hardly know what it means any more. Almost any art that does not immediately relate to external appearances is loosely called *abstract*. The problem increased when *abstract expressionism* was used in America in the 1940s and 50s for spontaneous anything-goes painting, with the artist following the emotion of the moment wherever it leads. *Abstract impressionism* (said to have been first used in 1951 at the Arts Club, New York, by Elaine De Kooning, wife of the abstract expressionist, Willem De Kooning) was an even more confusing description.

Unless you're sure of your ground in all this, you may feel more comfortable talking about so-called *abstract art* as *non-figurative* or *non-representational*, as no one should argue with that. See also **figurative**

abstract nouns These represent states and concepts we are aware of in our minds but are one step back from tangible objects: aspect, factor, poverty, situation, truth. . . . Politicians and diplomats like using abstract nouns because they diffuse the directness of a statement, leaving room for negotiation and compromise: 'Our *perception* of the *situation* is that economic *factors* require the continued *application* of the high-interest rate *discipline*'.

When you want to lay it on the line and make sentences clear and immediate, cut out as many abstract nouns as possible: 'The way we see it, interest rates have to stay high'.

abstract of title You will hear this phrase from a solicitor when you're buying or selling a property, so it is not a bad thing to be able to nod knowingly. The original title deeds and documents that prove ownership are not passed over until binding contracts are exchanged, or all the money has been handed over. In the meantime, the purchaser's solicitor makes do with an *abstract of title*, written details of the title deeds, which can subsequently be compared with the originals.

absurd or **ridiculous** *Absurd* is a more serious word for something that is separated from reason and common sense. *Ridiculous* is a lighter more everyday word for something that is plain stupid: 'It's absurd to say that people are happy because they are poor'; 'It's ridiculous to judge a painting by the quality of its frame'.

Admittedly the words can seem interchangeable, and no one should make a fuss if you mix them up. But the *theatre of the absurd*, associated with writers such as Samuel Beckett and Harold Pinter, is profoundly serious, cutting across normal rational life to present a sharp and disturbing view of the human situation. If it were called 'theatre of the ridiculous', the idea would be much more superficial.

abysmal or **abyssal** Both words relate to 'abyss' (which helps us to remember there's only one *b*) and both meant of unfathomable depth. *Abyssal* is now confined mostly to oceanography, usually for depths below 300 fathoms. *Abysmal* has come to extend the idea of depth to qualities and conditions: abysmal ignorance, abysmal poverty. . . . By further extension, the weather can be abysmal, and if you pick the wrong restaurant, you can have an abysmal meal. Some dictionaries limit those last examples to conversational language, but there are many instances in serious writing of the use of *abysmal* for anything that is immeasurably bad. And why not? It's a good way of saying that something is rock-bottom.

AC See **appellation contrôlée**

ACA See **chartered accountant**

academic We no longer believe that intellectual concepts can solve the world's problems. Too often they have gone badly wrong. Already by the end of the 19th century, *academic interest* was being used to mean of no practical value. Now when we say 'his approach is academic' we usually mean it is up in the clouds and irrelevant. An *academic question* is of no real importance. When art critics say a painting is *academic*, they mean that it is formal, conventional and dull. This does not apply to *academic* as a noun, as this has become the standard word for anyone teaching at a university or college of higher education. Apart from that, if you use *academic* in the old Platonic sense of scholarly and wise, you will probably be misunderstood.

ACAS See **arbitration**

acceleration or **momentum** These are precise terms in Newtonian mechanics: *acceleration* is force ÷ mass, *momentum* is mass × velocity. In everyday use, *accelerate* and *acceleration* relate to a condition that develops more and more rapidly, and *momentum* to a building up of impetus and force: 'increased competition has accelerated the fall in sales'; 'the approaching election is giving momentum to environmental issues'.

accent or **accentuate** As a verb, *accent* is usually connected with sound and pronunciation: we accent a syllable in a word by stressing it. *Accentuate* is more often used in a general or a visual way, meaning to emphasize something or make it stand out: we might accentuate a point by banging the table, or the whiteness of a dress could be accentuated by a jet-black belt.

Accentuate may sound formal or even old-fashioned in the 1990s, as *highlight* has taken over. *High light* (as two words) goes back to the 17th century as a classic term in painting (and later in photography) for the brightest parts of a subject. But now we highlight a point by drawing attention to it in some way, or highlight a colour with a contrasting colour. And in the 1960s, a new item of stationery appeared on the scene, the *highlighter*, a felt pen that lays transparent bands of colour over words in a text – to *accentuate* them.

accents in print and writing Accents, used in foreign languages to mark the pronunciation of cer-

tain vowel sounds and consonants, are a nuisance in English, as they are not on standard typewriter or computer keyboards. So there is a tendency to drop them. Some persist: most dictionaries prefer *café* (although the word has been used in English for at least 100 years), and *pâté* guards its circumflex and acute accent, even though it is everyday supermarket language from Scunthorpe to Surbiton. Some people using the circumflex in *rôle* to show they know what's what, but most dictionaries now leave it out. Because they are used in English more than any other accents, **French accents** are dealt with in a separate entry.

The German *umlaut* (two dots over a vowel) shows up occasionally, mostly in German names of people and cities, such as Düsseldorf and Dürrenmatt (the Swiss dramatist). Further notes on this are under **diaeresis** . . . (the corresponding English term). The same accent appears in some Swedish names (Malmö) as well as in names in Finnish, Albanian and Hungarian.

Danish and Norwegian have replaced ö by ø (known as the *slashed o*), which has the vowel sound of 'turn'. Scandinavian languages also have a long *a* vowel, marked by a small circle above (å), often replaced in English by a double *aa* (Aalborg instead of Ålborg). It has the vowel sound of 'aw'. For the wavy line over *ñ* in Spanish and over *ã* and *õ* in Portuguese, see **tilde**.

Less familiar to the British are the round accent in Turkish over *ğ* (which modifies it into a *y* sound) and the v over certain letters in Czech. It is courteous to retain these in people's names (Dvořák, for example), but that's about all.

In general, accents are on their way out, and not only in English, since they are also gradually being dropped in some foreign languages. The reason is they do not readily adapt to modern communications technology and to computerized text. For example, accents do not reproduce well on hard-to-read text transmitted by **fax**.

accents in speech In 1912 Bernard Shaw wrote *Pygmalion*, which he described as an experiment to demonstrate that applied phonetics could undermine the British class system, partly held together by the way people speak. In 1990 the BBC broadcast a radio programme which showed that the class barrier is still largely a *sound* barrier, that it takes no more than a few vowels and consonants to signal the kind of school someone went to and the social background they come from. The signals are not always reliable but much of the time they convey remarkably accurate information.

How much has changed between the early years of the century and the last decade? There is a broader range of what 'educated English' sounds like. Even some of the younger members of the royal family, such as the Duchess of York and Prince Andrew, are more commonplace in the way they speak. Ted Hughes, the poet laureate, intones his poetry with a strong Yorkshire accent, and Dr C T Onions, the last surviving editor of the original *OED* and for many years the foremost authority on the English language, spoke with a flat ordinary accent.

There is also a **public school** accent, a plummy style of speaking picked up at some (but not all) public schools. Then there is the well articulated standard English spoken by most BBC and ITN newscasters and actors in the Royal Shakespeare Company. This range of accents, with variations, is known as **received pronunciation**, which is supposed to define 'educated speech' in the south of England. Alongside RP, educated Scottish, Irish and Welsh have an equal status.

In the 1990s, there is a wider concept of what it means to 'talk proper', which is good news. How much does it matter? If you do not speak in the 'right' way, it could affect the impression you make at an interview or on the telephone, your credibility as a defendant in court, even the way your doctor treats you. There remains a conspiracy of silence about all this, but in Britain, perhaps more than in any other country, people are still often assigned to a social and educational category, and even to a level of intelligence, partly because of their accent. See also **pronunciation**

accentuate   See accent or accentuate

access   This has become a key word in computer science, which makes use of *access* in a number of complex ways mostly connected with retrieving information stored on disks. As a result, we've become used, since the 1960s, to seeing *access* used not only as a noun ('access to a building'), but as a verb: you *access* data from a computer by entering the appropriate codes to call it up on to the screen. *Access time* is how long it takes between pressing the keys and the information coming up. But so far this use has not become extended: we do not *access* a word in a dictionary, we *look it up*.

accessible   There was a time when only objects or places were accessible, something or somewhere you can get at or to easily: 'It may seem remote but it's really very accessible'. It's fashionable now to use *accessible* about people, to mean they're available to discuss things with (especially by their clients, students or people who work for them), and about art or music or a theory to suggest that it can be readily appreciated or understood: 'For a contemporary composer, his music is remarkably accessible'. These extensions of meaning are useful and accepted by all recent dictionaries.

accessory or **accessary**   These used to be two separate words. *Accessary* was used in law for someone involved in a crime but who did not actually commit it. *Accessory* was something additional or extra, such as a radio fitted to a car or a matching stole for a dress. American English established *accessory* for both meanings and this is now standard usage in British English as well. Some dictionaries confuse us by showing *accessary* as an alternative spelling for *both* uses of the word. But most lawyers, fashion writers and motor car salesmen use – *accessory*.

access time   See access

accidentally   When you're speaking quickly, you have to keep your wits about you to give this word its full five syllables: 'acciDENT-e(r)ly'. Come what may, it should never be spelt 'accidently'.

accommodate and **accommodation**   For social workers, *alternative accommodation* is standard English for 'another home'. And other people, who are not social workers, will go up to the reception desk of a hotel and ask 'Do you have any accommodation?' instead of for 'a room'.

Some people spell these words wrongly, and many people are eager to point it out. Always *cc–mm*.

(in) **accordance with**   'In accordance with your instructions', 'in accordance with our agreement', etc are heavy-going ways of saying 'following your instructions', 'under our agreement', etc. Why bother?

according to   A phrase which may carry with it a hint of doubt or even suspicion: 'According to the chairman, the board has the situation under control' could be taken to imply 'But I'm not so sure about that!' It's more direct and less open to implied doubt to state simply: 'The chairman says the board has the situation under control'. Of course, if you don't think someone is telling the truth, and you don't want to come out in the open and say so, *according to* is a useful standby, even more so if you prefix it with a doubtful 'Well, according to . . .'.

account   An advertising agency talks about its 'accounts' rather than its 'clients': 'We've just won an important new account' means 'We've got a new client who is spending a lot of money'. On the UK Stock Exchange an *account* is the name of the official period, normally two weeks (ten working days), subject to agreement that all transactions carried out during that account are settled on the *account day*, a fixed number of days after the end of the period. This means that when dealers buy shares at the beginning of an account, they have that much longer before they have to settle up. See also next entry; **after-hours dealings** . . .

account, **invoice**, **statement** or **bill**   An *account* or a *bill* are general terms for a note stating how much you have to pay for goods or services supplied. *Bill* is down-to-earth, *account* more upmarket: Harrods sends an account, a plumber sends a bill.

Invoice and *statement* are more precise commercial terms. An invoice is usually a detailed note setting out a list of the goods or services supplied, with prices or charges alongside, VAT (if applicable) and any special discounts. An invoice is sent with the goods or soon afterwards: sometimes payment is required when you receive it, in other cases an invoice is not a request for payment but a confirmation of charges incurred, so you can check them.

Statement is short for *statement of account* and it can be like a page of bookkeeping, with columns itemizing all invoices submitted during the period, cheques received and credits allowed. The final balance is the amount due within the period specified on the statement. Follow-up statements are sent if you haven't paid on time, and these often have stickers on them with entreaties or increasingly sinister threats about what will happen if you don't pay soon.

See also **bill**, for the different use of this word in Britain and America.

accountable or **responsible** *Accountable* is a solemn word which signifies we can be called to account for our deeds: 'We are accountable for our sins at the Last Judgement'. *Responsible* means much the same but is a lighter word: 'They are responsible for not having done the washing-up'. It's preferable to use *accountable* only in relation to people, using *responsible* for people or things: 'Heavy rain was responsible for the delay'.

William Lutz, an American academic who campaigns against **doublespeak** in public affairs, sees an element of evasiveness in the way these two words are used. Someone may say they are responsible, but if they say 'I'm accountable', they come right into the open and admit they have to answer for something.

accountant Anyone can call themselves an accountant: in fact it has almost replaced the old-fashioned title 'bookkeeper', particularly since so many accounts now are not kept in books but on a computer. *Certified* or **chartered accountants** are something else: it is illegal to use these titles unless you are a member of the corresponding professional association.

account day See **account**

accursed The usual pronunciation is 'acCUR-sed', with *three* syllables. 'acCURST' (*two* syllables) is also heard and is an optional alternative: in fact at one time *accurst* was an accepted spelling but that would now look archaic. See also **cursed**

achieve and **achiever** There's an air of importance about these words so it's not surprising that business management and education have taken them up. Up-and-coming executives are described as *high-achievers*, and on job applications, especially in America, there's sometimes a panel headed 'Significant Achievements'. But any achievement is significant, for *achievement* is a noble word describing success after great effort. It's a distortion of this meaning to use the word in a negative way ('he achieved bankruptcy'), but perhaps sometimes it is in a good cause: failures may not feel so badly about it, when they're called *under-achievers*, even though it comes to the same thing.

Some people object when *achieve* is used about objects ('the car can achieve 160mph'), although this is a reasonable and common extension of use as a way of suggesting something outstanding.

acid What started off in the late 17th century as a term in chemistry for compounds of hydrogen, has

become an emotive word in the 1990s. *Acid* is the familiar name for LSD (lysergic acid diethylamide), the cult 'mind-blowing' drug of the 1960s. *Acidheads*, not often heard now, were addicts. Later *acid rock* came on the scene, describing long hypnotic passages of electronic music intended to induce hallucinations.

Acid house parties first made dramatic newspaper stories in the late 1980s, with thousands of young people blocking motorways on their way to dance all night in weird clothes to deafening psychedelic music. Moral outrage followed, hundreds of party-goers were arrested, and a bill was introduced in Parliament to make the parties illegal. Yet *The Independent* (3.3. 1990) suggested that acid house is 'the simplest and gentlest of youth manifestations'. And *acid house* refers more to the type of music played than to drugs.

Acid rain is another sinister use of *acid*, because it is said to be destroying forests and killing fish in rivers and lakes. All rain is acid to some extent, although so-called acid rain picks up pollutants from acid discharged into the atmosphere from factories and motor-vehicle exhausts.

There's nothing nasty about an *acid test*, unless it's being applied to some work we've done: the expression is a convenient adaptation of the use of nitric acid as a test for gold, to any test for quality, value or truth. In business an *acid test ratio* is the ratio of assets that can be converted to cash against money owed: it is the acid test of whether a company can pay its debts.

It's all a long way from the innocent *acid drops* (sweets made from sugar flavoured with tartaric acid) that we used to suck at school.

acknowledgement or **acknowledgment** Either, but *acknowledgement* is more usual. Compare abridgement, amazement: when **-ment** is added to a word ending in a silent -*e*, the -*e* usually stays. And while we're about it, it is less self-important to 'receive a letter' than to *acknowledge receipt* of it.

acoustic or **acoustical** They are often used interchangeably for qualities, characteristics or technology relating to sound. Generally *acoustic* is preferred for things or places: the *acoustic* qualities of a hall or an *acoustic* guitar (or other musical instrument) that relies upon its natural sound without electric amplification. *Acoustical* is usually reserved for people – an *acoustical* engineer – but is much less used.

Acoustics is or *acoustics are*? When it's a science, always singular: 'acoustics *is* an interesting subject'. When it's the qualities in a hall always plural: 'the acoustics of the new concert hall *are* good'.

acquiesce If you accept an arrangement, you acquiesce *in* it, which is considered better usage than acquiesce *to* or *with*, shown in some dictionaries. The 17th-century meaning of *acquiesce* was to remain quiet or submit, so to acquiesce in something carries with it the implication that you've agreed simply by saying nothing to object: 'Everyone kept quiet so it was assumed they acquiesced in the suggestion put forward'. *Agreeing to* something is more wholehearted than *acquiescing in* it.

acquire It is unnecessarily grand to *acquire* something when you can *buy* it, *win* it or *get* it in some other way.

acquisition This is the preferred term in business for a takeover: when a company makes a successful bid for another company, the board will talk about its *acquisition*. Perhaps this sounds less aggressive than 'takeover' or 'buyout', although the whole affair can be just as ruthless (see **merger**).

Of course, *acquisition* is anything acquired, although there's no need to use it all the time: 'Come and see our latest acquisition' is a pompous alternative to '. . . what we've just bought'.

acquisitive On the face of it, this simply means someone, such as a collector, who likes to acquire things. But it has now taken on the unpleasant meaning of being greedy and materialistic. It's better not to use it unless you intend to say something nasty about a person.

acre Most things to do with ownership of land are complicated. A statutory acre is 4840 square yards, which seems straightforward. But in Scotland and Ireland, as well as in some English counties, other measures may still be used: a *Scottish acre* can be approximately 1.27 and an *Irish acre* 1.62 English acres. *US acres* are the same as English ones.

British landowners feel more secure defining their land in acres, an Old English word going back to before the Norman Conquest, first used as a rough measure of what one man could plough in a day. Metric land measurements, *hectare* (pron: 'HECtaire') and *are* (pron: 'ahr'), both from Latin 'area', are much slower to take over than other metric measures. A hectare equals 100 ares, equivalent to 2.471 acres. 3 hectares 7 ares, for example, is expressed as 3ha 7a. But so far, landowners in the Shires aren't interested.

acronyms *Acronym* is a postwar formation, following the pattern of 'homonym' (see **synonym**). *Acro* is from a Greek word meaning 'end' or 'tip', and an *acronym* is a word formed from the first letters of other words.

The idea is not new: *Anzac* (Australian and New Zealand Army Corps) goes back to 1915. With the increase in international organizations, acronyms have become a verbal epidemic because they make names usable in all languages: *Unesco* (United Nations Educational, Scientific and Cultural Organization), *Nato* (North Atlantic Treaty Organization), *Unicef* (United Nations International Children's Emergency Fund), etc are established names, hardly thought of as abbreviations any more.

Other organizations followed this lead since it was clearly good public relations to have a sequence of initials that could be pronounced as one word: *Aslef* (Associated Society of Locomotive Engineers and Firemen), one of the British railway trade unions, **NASA** (National Aeronautics and Space Administration), the central US agency directing space exploration. Even the Oxford Dictionary Department joined the bandwagon and cashed in on the legendary wisdom of *OWLS* (Oxford Word and Language Service).

Some acronyms become so familiar that they lose even the initial capital letter and become ordinary words: **laser** (light amplication by stimulated emission of radiation). The acronym that takes centre-stage in the 1990s is **Aids** (acquired immune deficiency syndrome) which, according to one sufferer from the disease, has spawned over fifty related acronyms.

Convenient though they are, acronyms can be overdone and become a coded language for specialists, incomprehensible to the rest of us.

acrylic Chemists know what *acrylic* means, but for others it's usually just a word on labels of sweaters and blankets that seem too cheap to be made of wool. It describes material made by a chemical process using synthetic resins derived from acrylic acid.

In Los Angeles, as far back as the 1930s, artists were experimenting with plastic paints, although it was not until the 1950s that water-based *acrylics* were used more widely because they offered intense colours with a much quicker drying time than oil paint. 'Acrylic on canvas' took its place alongside oil and watercolour.

act or **action** These are not interchangeable words. An *act* is more a thing that is done, immediate and complete: an act of kindness, an act of war. . . . An *action* is continuous, the process of carrying out an act: go into action, killed in action, the action taken by the Bank of England to counter a fall in the value of the pound. . . . When in the 1950s, Jackson Pollock, the artist from Wyoming, hurled paint at his canvases, *action painting* was born.

action (as a verb) 'Action this report', 'Action this decision', meaning 'Do something about it!', looked as if it would become standard management language, because it had a go-getting ring to it. But it sounds rather dated now, perhaps because so many of the actions went wrong.

activate or **motivate** *Activate* is used mostly about things, often in chemistry or physics for a process that brings about a reaction: *activated carbon* is carbon heated to a very high temperature to increase its adsorption, particularly for use in reducing pollution.

Motivate is used mostly about people and has become one of the trendy words in business. The ways in which *motivate* and its associated words are now used is so much a part of the jargon of our time, that they are dealt with under a separate entry: **motivate, motivation and motivational**.

active and **passive voice** Most grammatical terms are very old because they were based on Latin and Ancient Greek. *Voice*, used to describe how nouns and verbs interact, goes back some 500 years, and you could win the Nobel Prize for Literature without knowing anything about it.

Active voice is when a noun relates to the verb directly: 'the dog bit the man'; 'the woman opened the door'. *Passive voice* is when sentences are turned round: 'the man was bitten by the dog'; 'the door was opened by the woman'.

Diplomats and lawyers often favour the passive voice because it's less direct and confrontational: 'It has been decided that . . .' is not as out in the open as 'I have decided . . .'. When William Lutz, an American academic, analysed Oliver North's testimony at congressional hearings of the Iran–Contra affair, he observed that North sidestepped personal responsibility by using passive constructions such as 'it was clearly indicated', 'it was already known', 'it was recognized'.

Jung believed that words 'gain life and meaning only when you take into account their relationship to the living individual': 'You are loved by me' (passive voice) may mean the same as 'I love you' (active voice), but it doesn't lift your heart in the same way.

activist   A 'revolutionary' harks back to the Bolsheviks or the sansculottes of the French Revolution. *Activist* is the modern equivalent for someone who believes in the use of direct action or force for political or social ends. The suffrage movement, the struggle for Indian independence, the civil rights movement all involved *activists*. But the power of the word has been watered down, and is often used now for someone who does little more than declaim publicly about something: a BBC news item referred to 'activists in the Brentwood and Ongar Conservative Association' – hardly all that dangerous or seditious. *Militant* (see **militancy**) still retains the meaning of activist in its extreme form.

act of God   There is nothing religious or divine about this expression: it is another way of saying 'an act of nature'. An act of God implies that no one is responsible, so it's a phrase used in some insurance contracts to exclude liability. Look out for it because the insurance concept of 'act of God' has been challenged in courts.

actor and actress   *Actor* is used now to cover both sexes, especially by people working in the theatre. When Judi Dench was made a Dame in the 1989 Birthday Honours List, *The Sunday Times* wrote about her 'unactorish life out of the limelight'. When women were first seen on the London stage after the Restoration in 1660, they were called *actors*: Pepys in his *Diary* entry for 27 December 1666 noted that the part of Doll Common in Ben Jonson's *The Alchemist* was played by 'an excellent actor'.

Feminists dislike *actress*, which dictionaries define as 'a woman actor', because they feel it implies that the standard is male: Actors' Equity, Actors' Studio, etc. But the *OED* is premature in writing off *actress* as 'obsolete', since many people go on using it. We can still choose, although by the end of the century, *actor* will have taken over altogether as the unisex word, the way *sculptor* and *poet* have done. When that

happens, *actress* will survive only in the time-honoured phrase 'As the actress said to the Bishop . . .'. See also **-ess forms**

acts   It's all too easy to allow *acts* to sound the same as 'axe'. But good speakers retain a hint of the sound of *t*.

actually   If you say 'We're going to get married actually', *actually* is merely a social **cliché**. But you can use it to give a sentence a 'How about that?' flavour: 'We're actually going to get married!' It depends upon where you position *actually*.

acute accent   The accent is used in several languages, including Polish and Serbo-Croat, but most familiar to us in words originating from French (where it changes the 'e' sound: café) and Spanish (where it indicates stress: Málaga). See **French accents**; **accents in print and writing**

AD   This is necessary only for dates near the traditional date of Christ's birth, the focal date for the calendar in worldwide use, or when BC (before Christ) dates come into the context. Because AD stands for anno Domini (in the year of the Lord) it should come *before* the year: AD 200 (in the year of the Lord 200), just as BC comes *after* the year: 200 BC. But usage such as 'the 5th century AD' is so well established that no one quarrels with it.

Followers of other religions sometimes prefer to use CE (Common Era) instead of AD for the Christian era date system: CE 200. CE does not appear often and many people wouldn't know what it means, so it cannot be recommended for general use.

adapter or adaptor   Although these words are used interchangeably, they can still denote different things. An *adapter* is a person, someone who adapts a book for television, or a piece of equipment to serve another purpose: an *adaptor* is an object, commonly an electrical fitting used to adapt one kind of plug to another kind of socket.

You can preserve this difference, but the tendency is to use *adaptor* for all meanings: most dictionaries have given up making the distinction, simply listing *adapter* as an alternative spelling.

addenda or addendums   For some Latin words ending in *-um* there are alternative plural forms: the Latin plural (changing *-um* to *-a*) and the usual English plural (formed by adding *-s*): memorandums (as well as memoranda), rectums (as well as recta). . . . For other words the Latin plural is the only correct form: one addendum, two or more addenda.

(in) addition (to)   English is rich in good simple words. *Besides* is Old English, has been in use for centuries, and is better and more direct than *in addition to*: 'Besides doing the washing-up, would you make the beds'. *In addition to* has a place in formal contexts, but don't lose sight of *besides*.

additives We rarely used this word before the 1980s, but it is now a clarion call for everybody who cares what they eat. The word simply means something added to something else to give it another quality, but perhaps the first meaning we think of now is *food additives*. That doesn't always mean anything sinister, for adding salt or pepper to food during cooking is using an additive. The trouble starts when food manufacturers use synthetic dyes, flavours and chemical preservatives to give food eye-appeal and **shelf-life**.

address This has become a fashionable word in politics and business: ministers talk about having to address an issue, chief executives address problems. It sounds self-important, but it is not as forceful as *facing up* to something, which conjures up a picture of determination, or as straightforward as *dealing* with whatever it is. See also **confront**. . . .

addresses The faster pace of life has led to more and more stops and commas being dropped from traditional uses (see **abbreviations**). In the 1990s envelopes are usually addressed like this:

> The Macmillan Press Ltd
> 4 Little Essex St
> London WC2R 3LF
> England

adequate, **enough** or **sufficient** There are differences between these words, although there's no need to get tangled up in them. *Enough* is Old English, pre-10th century, and on Churchill's principle that 'old words are best', we should use it in preference to alternatives. *Sufficient* is Old French, 14th century, and is more formal: 'Do you have sufficient money?', rather than 'Do you have enough money?', is the kind of caution you'd expect from a stern bank manager.

Adequate is from Latin and appeared in English during the 17th century. It carries with it a suggestion of just about enough: 'One bottle of wine is adequate for four people' doesn't sound lavish. And when you use *adequate* about quality it's even more grudging: 'The wine's adequate' means it's drinkable, if you're not fussy.

Lastly, there are people who believe that *sufficient* is more polite than *enough* ('Thank you, but I've had sufficient'). It is perfectly in order even for the best people to 'have had enough'.

adjacent or **adjoining** *Next to* is simpler than *adjacent* and means the same. 'Her house is adjacent (or next) to mine' suggests both houses are side by side (or very near each other), although they could be detached. *Adjoining* suggests actually touching: 'Her house adjoins mine' usually means the houses are next to each other in a terrace, or are semi-detached.

adjectives Grammarians resist any change to old Latinate grammatical terms: *adjective* goes back to the 14th century. Adjectives, as most people know,

describe **nouns** (a *lovely* day, an *economic* miracle), and we use such words perfectly well without ever thinking of them as adjectives, just as we don't think about how to ride a bicycle. In *The Good English Guide*, adjectives are called *descriptive words*.

More and more nouns are now used as adjectives, especially in newspaper headlines. We live with the '*world* situation' instead of the 'situation in the world' and we read about '*reactor design* problems' instead of 'problems over the design of reactors'. This is often a useful shortcut, but when there is a build-up of nouns as descriptive words, a sentence becomes awkward and more difficult to understand: 'We have to increase city-centre hospital building planning' is not as clear as 'We have to plan to build more hospitals in the centre of cities'.

But if we always insist on 'the population of the world' rather than 'world population', the 'crisis over balance of payments' rather than the 'balance of payments crisis', etc, our sentences will drag. It's a matter of what is clear, and reading a sentence aloud is often the best guide. It's all part of *fast-lane* living in the 1990s, to use yet another noun as an adjective.

Occasionally the same word as adjective and noun have different meanings. For example, *musical* describes something that is melodious or anything related to music, but *a musical* is more specific – it's short for a musical comedy or a musical film.

Some modern grammarians use the term *modifier* for a noun used as an adjective. Others use *modifier* as a more explanatory word in place of the traditional grammatical terms *adjective* and *adverb*. See also **grammatical terms**

adjoining See adjacent . . .

adjudge, **judge** or **adjudicate** *Adjudge* is generally confined to courts of law: judges judge or adjudge a case (it comes to the same thing). But when damages are awarded, these are *adjudged*.

Judge is the more general word: we judge a beauty contest or judge how long something might take. *Adjudicate* is the usual word for tribunals: they adjudicate over a dispute or adjudicate a claim. We cannot adjudicate a beauty contest but we can *adjudicate at* or *over* it (which is the same as *judging* it).

adman In Madison Avenue, traditional centre of advertising business in New York, they were talking about *admen* back in the 1920s. The word crossed the Atlantic some years ago and at least one Oxford dictionary accepts it as standard English, although most dictionaries label it informal. There's nothing derogatory about it and most male copywriters and executives in ad agencies are happy to be called admen. *Adwoman* and *adperson* have not yet arrived.

admass J B Priestley invented this word in his novel *Journey Down a Rainbow* (1955). Admass turns individuals into faceless **socio-economic** groups, whose lifestyle is manipulated by advertising, television and popular newspapers. Admass means much the same as consumer society, the 'never-had-it-so-good' syndrome that confuses a material standard of living with quality of life. See also **built-in obsolescence**

administer or **administrate**   You can administer the affairs of a business or administrate them. *Administer* is the original word (dating from the 14th century) but because of the influence of 'administration', a common word in business contexts, *administrate* has become the usual verb. *Administer* is now used mostly in law and religion: to administer justice or administer the rites of a sacrament.

(the) **administration**   In America *administration* is used for the government in power under a particular president, or for the period of office of a president: 'the administration has to make difficult decisions to get the US economy back on course'; 'the Gulf War was the notable event during President Bush's administration'.

admissible or **admissable**   *Admissible*. See **-able or -ible**

admission or **admittance**   Keep-out signs read NO ADMITTANCE. Welcoming signs read NO ADMISSION FEE (no one talks about 'an admittance fee'). If you want to join a society, you apply for admission, and it's an admission when you admit to something. To enter a building you can ask for admittance or admission as, in that sense, the words are interchangeable. If the indecision is an agony, there's always 'Can I come in?'

ado   'So he left without more ado' means 'so he left right away'. *Ado* is a 14th-century word from the north of England, meaning fuss or trouble. You don't hear it much in the 1990s, except perhaps from older people. Even Shakespeare's *Much Ado About Nothing* is not often staged.

adrenaline   A hormone that the body releases as an automatic response to fear or danger. It makes the heart beat faster, raises blood pressure and gets us ready to run for our lives or fight back. When something shakes us out of our lethargy and someone says 'That's got the adrenaline going', it could well be an accurate description of what is actually happening in our physical and nervous systems. (*Adrenalin* is an alternative spelling.)

adsorb   See absorb . . .

adult   This is a word to use with caution, because it is so imprecise. The age of legal accountability for our actions used to be 21 but in 1969 was brought down to 18. The right to vote in elections was reduced in that year from 21 to 18, but can Acts of Parliament change the age at which we reach maturity?

There is no reliable definition of *adult*, as legal rights and obligations are acquired at different stages: at 5

you can have a drink at home, but cannot legally purchase alcohol; at 10 you can stand trial for murder; at 14 you can go to the cinema alone, use a shotgun (if supervised), smoke (but not buy) cigarettes, and sit inside a pub (but not buy a drink); at 17 you can drive and go to prison; at 18 you can get married without parental consent.

The *Encyclopedia Americana* offers one of the more useful definitions of *adult*, as someone who ceases to depend on their parents for financial support, is able to earn a living and make decisions about money, work and social behaviour.

Adult education does not cover university education or 'further education' received after the age of sixteen: it refers to various activities for adults after their formal and full-time education has ceased.

Adult is manipulated as a nasty cover-up word for obscene films, books or magazines, strip-tease shows and so-called 'life-shows', a euphemism for joyless demonstrations of copulation for sad-faced voyeurs.

In British English, the preferred pronunciation is 'ADult' (stress on first syllable), with 'aDULT' as less acceptable. In American English, it's the other way round.

ad valorem   Some taxes or stamp duties are fixed, whatever the size of the transaction. Others go up and down depending upon how much money is involved: these are *ad valorem* (Latin for 'according to the value') taxes. VAT is an ad valorem tax since it is a percentage of the value of goods or services supplied. Pron: 'ad ve(r)LAWrem'.

advance   As a noun, *advance* is used in different ways. A specialized use is when a writer talks about an advance: it means a cheque from the publishers, when a contract is signed, paying out before the book is written a portion of the royalties the book is expected to earn. Still heard, although rather quaint in the 1990s, is a woman saying 'He made advances to me', meaning that a man suggested in one way or another that he wants to make love to her, or at least get to know her better: for another way of expressing this thought, see **proposition**.

adverbs   An adverb is to a verb what an **adjective** is to a noun: it adds something to the meaning of it. Just as 'the *yellow* dress' tells us about the dress, so 'they walked *slowly*' explains how they walked. But adverbs are much more complicated: they can also add to the meaning of other descriptive words ('she is *wonderfully* happy') and to other adverbs ('they walked *very* slowly'). And all manner of words can be classified as adverbs, words such as 'yes', 'no', 'however', 'therefore'. . . .

Before you worry about this, remember that it's most unlikely that the writer who wins the next Booker Prize would be able to identify accurately all the adverbs in their prizewinning novel.

adverse or **averse**   Even good writers occasionally mix up these two words. If you are *adverse* to something you are against it, its *adversary*: 'I am adverse to you getting married'. If you are *averse* to something, you have a strong distaste for it, an *aversion* for it. But there's no need for such a pompous expression as 'I'm not averse to a whisky'. If you want a drink, why not say so? Pron: 'ADverse', 'aVERSE'.

advertisement or **commercial** *Advertisements* (*ads* or *adverts*) are printed forms of advertising in newspapers, magazines, etc. In America, where radio and television have carried advertising from the beginning, a *commercial* has always been the word for advertising in those media. *Commercial* is now used in the same way in Britain, alongside advertisement: a TV ad during a commercial break. Short publicity films shown in cinemas are called *advertising films*, and the international festival for them (which includes television commercials) is officially called the Advertising Film Festival, to make it sound more like a real film festival.

advise We have all received letters beginning 'We are glad to advise you of . . .', 'I have to advise you that . . .', and they sound as if someone is looking over their pince-nez at us. *Inform* or *notify* are less pontifical or, if a more friendly word is called for, there's the short Old English word *tell*: 'We're glad to tell you . . .'.

adviser or **advisor** Dictionaries now show both spellings but *adviser* is preferred. In fact, many people consider *advisor* a wrong spelling, taken from the associated word 'advisory'.

advocate See **barrister**

ae or **æ**, **oe** or **œ** It was awkward (especially on a typewriter) when we had to use *ligatures*, the word for joining æ or œ together, in words derived from Latin and Greek: æsthetic, gynæcology, cæsarean, diarrhœa, etc. All that is over as dictionaries (except the *OED* which retains æ for certain words) show *ae* and *oe* as separate letters: aesthetic, gynaecology, caesarean, diarrhoea, etc. Some classical scholars still use the traditional ligatures, although they're thwarted if they use a wordprocessor.

In a few words (and the number is increasing), it has become easier still, as the simple *e* has replaced *ae* or *oe*: encyclopedia, medieval and **primeval** are the usual spellings now, with encyclopaedia, mediaeval and primaeval listed in some dictionaries as alternatives. In American English, *e* replaces *ae* and *oe* in many more words: archeology, gynecology, diarrhea, esthetic. . . .

aegis The word comes from *Aigis*, the name of the shield of Zeus in Greek mythology, and you're not likely to use it often. But you might want to say something is 'under the aegis of . . .', meaning under the responsibility or protection of a particular person or organization. (Pron: 'EEjis'.)

aerie See **eyrie** . . .

aerobic and **anaerobic** Starting in America, *aerobic* has been a buzzword for years among joggers and fitness experts. It is primarily a biological term, derived from Greek words meaning 'air' and 'life', describing micro-organisms that require oxygen to support life. The fashionable, if nonsensical, meaning of *aerobic* has taken over in general use, and is the primary meaning given in the latest dictionaries: steady, rather than violent and intermittent, exercise sustained long enough to induce a higher rate of heartbeat and respiration. The exercises are called *aerobics* (pron: 'airROHbics').

You sometimes hear of *anaerobic exercises*, which is turning the word upside down, because *anaerobic* describes organisms that can live without oxygen in the atmosphere, and unless you're a biologist, it is unlikely you'll ever need the word.

aerodrome See **airfield** . . .

aeronautics or **astronautics** The distinction will become increasingly common when travel in space becomes more common. *Aeronautics* covers the science and technology of flying aircraft; *astronautics* is the technology of space travel, from rocket propulsion to communications to human adaptation to weightlessness.

aeroplane See **aircraft** . . .

aerospace and **airspace** *Aerospace* is a word we shall hear more and more during the remaining years of this century because it includes both the earth's atmosphere and outer space. A journey in aerospace could cover a quick hop over to Brussels or a voyage to the moon.

Airspace is a comparatively recent word, the result of international law declaring that the air above a country comes under its sovereignty. But in the Outer Space Treaty of 1987, outer space, the universe beyond the earth's atmosphere, is not 'up for grabs', as no country can claim ownership of it. So part of aerospace comes within a country's domain, and the part beyond the earth's atmosphere does not.

aesthetic We use this word but the meaning is elusive. It comes from the Greek word 'aisthetikós', for things that are perceptible by the senses. *Aesthetic* describes a contemplative or mystical way of relating to things we see, hear or touch, at an altogether different level from their factual meaning or practical value. While *aesthetic* is not a religious word, it is concerned with a quality in the human situation that transcends everyday survival or scientific analysis. Because *aesthetic* seeks to penetrate the essential meaning of art and hence of life itself, it is not open to precise definition, and the best we can do is to intuit its meaning.

As a noun, *aesthetic* represents the principles of a form or a work of art. We can talk about 'the aesthetic of a painting', that is those qualities of technique that give it conviction and cohesion.

Pron: 'eesTHETik' although many people say 'essTHETik' (the usual pronunciation in America, where *esthetic* is an alternative spelling).

affect or **effect**   When these are used as verbs, there's not much problem. *Effect* means to accomplish or to make something happen: 'The bonus scheme effected a big increase in productivity'. *Affect* means to have an influence on something or somebody: 'She was much affected by what he said'; 'Outside work has been affected by the weather'. It can also be used in the sense of *assume* or *pretend*: 'He affected indifference'; 'She affected a foreign accent'.

As a noun, *effect* is always the word when you want to say the result, outcome or influence: 'What he said had a powerful *effect* on her'; 'The bonus scheme had a big *effect* on productivity'. A **knock-on effect**, often used in politics and economics, is a secondary effect that follows after the primary more obvious effect: 'The knock-on effect of high interest rates is bigger wage settlements'.

The noun *affect* is a clinical term in psychology for an emotion or a desire, and in this specialized use, the stress is on the first syllable: 'AFFect'. In all other uses the stress for both words is on the second syllable: 'afFECT', 'efFECT'.

affiliated   Although it derives from the Latin word *filius*, 'son', it can denote any loose connection, such as *affiliated clubs*, which may be separate organizations offering reciprocal facilities to each other's members. Or it can represent a much closer connection, such as an affiliated company, which is owned by another company, legally responsible for its activities. So when someone says 'we're affiliated' it may need searching questions to find out what it really means.

affinity *between*, *with*, *to* or *for*   An affinity is a natural relationship or attraction to someone or something. The doctrine is that it should be followed by *between* or *with*: 'There's an affinity between us'; 'I felt an affinity with the car the moment I was in the driving seat'. We are advised that good writers never have an affinity *to* or *for* people or things.

affluent   Affluent used to be a warm word, describing a generous flow (it is used by river authorities for a tributary stream flowing into a river). The extended meaning of rich or wealthy, which goes back to the 17th century, has become the primary meaning since the economist, John Kenneth Galbraith, used the phrase 'the Affluent Society' in 1958. Now *affluent* implies, for many people, too much of a good thing, a never-had-it-so-good smugness. When we say someone is affluent, we may mean very rich, or simply comfortably off. Thanks to Galbraith, this is a word to watch. See also **admass; consumer society**

afforestation   Concern about the world we live in has made us value trees instead of cutting them down recklessly to make paper and other products. *Afforestation* is one of the words that has moved

centre-stage: it means not only the planting of trees in a designated area, but also the control of an area to allow trees to seed themselves naturally and produce a forest. See also **deforestation**

aficionado   Thirty years ago *aficionado* did not have a place in many English dictionaries (although there are occasional examples of its use in the 19th century), but it is now well established in the English language. It's a Spanish word, originally for a passionate fan of bullfighting. But it's used in English for a devoted follower of any sport, or of anything else for that matter: a financial writer in *The Observer* commented on 'aficionados of unit trust savings schemes'. Note: never 'aficionadoes', even though you will sometimes see it spelt that way, and don't let the association with the word 'affection' mislead you into spelling it with two *ff*s. If you want to show off, you can use *aficionada* for a woman (as in Spanish), although *aficionado* is normally used in English for both sexes. Pron: 'afissioNAHdo'.

aforementioned and **aforesaid**   Your solicitor might write to you about the aforementioned or aforesaid lease, deed or whatever, although Clarity, an organization that campaigns for simpler legal language, would not approve. For the rest of us, we're better off saying 'the lease' or 'the deed' or, if it's clear what we mean, simply *it*.

African-American   See **black** . . .

African National Congress   See **ANC**

Afro-   *Afro-* is a relaxed abbreviation for 'African'. *Afro-American* or *Afro-Caribbean*, for example, are used about the culture of people of African descent living in America or the Caribbean. An Afro hairstyle is the frizzy bushy hairstyle that belongs naturally to many black women. Some people feel that *Afro-* may have racist connotations, but it is merely descriptive in the same way as **Anglo-** (an *Anthology of Afro-American Literature* has been published, for example).

after or **afterwards**   In conversation, it is quite usual to say: 'She made three telephone calls and went to bed immediately *after*'. In writing, this would be better: '. . . immediately *afterwards*'. But when we indicate how much time is involved, *after* or *afterwards* are both all right: 'She telephoned him three days after (or afterwards)'.

Afterwards is the British form; *afterward* is American usage. And 'a quarter after seven' is the American way of saying 'a quarter past seven'.

After- is a common prefix: *after-care*, *after-effect*, *after-hours*, *after-sales* and *after-taste* are better with a hyphen; *afterbirth*, *afterglow*, *afterlife*, *aftershave* and *afterthought* should be treated as single words.

after-hours and **new time dealings (stock exchange)**   *After-hours dealings* may sound rather shady but they are perfectly legitimate: the official close of the London stock exchange is 4.30pm: business transacted afterwards is called *after-hours dealings* (or *early bargains*). These count as the first dealings done on the next day of business. *New time dealings* are transacted by special arrangement during the last two days of the stock exchange account period; they are treated as if they fall within the subsequent account period, so that settlement is postponed (see **account**).

-age Words ending in *-age* usually come from French, and in that language the stress falls on the *-age* syllable. In English, the stress usually moves back to the preceding syllable: 'BARRage', 'DRESSage', MASSage', 'MIRage'. . . . In American English, the stress (as in French) is usually on the *-age* syllable: 'baRRAGE', 'maSSAGE'. . . .

Montage and *collage* are still thought of as French words so the stress is on the second syllable ('monTAGE', coLLAGE') on both sides of the Atlantic. See also **garage**

age, **era** or **period** These words, relating to sequences of time are confusing. *Period* is the vaguest of all, as it could cover centuries ('the period between Shakespeare and Dickens') or only a few minutes ('ten-minute rest period'). *Age* suggests a much longer time, and is the basic division of time in archaeology, characterized by a dominant culture: the Stone Age, the Iron Age, etc. The *golden age* (usually spelt without capitals now) is the period when life (or anything else) was supposedly at its best: 'the golden age of the Hollywood musical'.

Other than in archaeology (when an era is a shorter period than an age, such as the *palaeolithic era* of the *Stone Age*) and geology (where an era is the second largest division of time after the aeon), *era* and *age* are often used interchangeably. *Era* is preferable when it's a period of time given some unity by cultural or historical circumstances: the Victorian era, the era of silent films. This distinction is not always made, as you also read the Victorian age, or even the Victorian period.

When Margaret Thatcher resigned as Prime Minister in November 1990, commentators wrote about 'the end of an era'. Because of the dominant effect she had on life and society in Britain, 'the end of a period' would have seemed too slight, but it did not have the dimension to warrant 'the end of an age'. See also **epoch**

aged There are two meanings, and it depends upon how you say it. As *two* syllables ('AYjid') it means very old or infirm:

> Oh my *aged* Uncle Arly!
> Sitting on a heap of Barley . . .
> Edward Lear, *Nonsense Songs*

As *one* syllable ('ayjd') it's simply a way of saying someone's age ('She's aged seven') or to mean 'grow older' ('whisky is aged in casks', 'he has aged greatly since her death').

ageism As sexism is discrimination against women because of their sex, *ageism* is prejudice or discrimination against someone because they are 'old'. We're not even clear about what 'old' means any more: a news item will refer to an attack on an 'old person', and we read on to find they are 62, younger than many people actively involved in the affairs of the world.

'Old' is often used to mean written off and dependent on society, a view challenged by the Institute for Public Policy Research, which submits that society should 'maintain the principle of lifelong learning, and allow, indeed encourage people to contribute to the economic and cultural wealth of the country for as long as possible'.

You hear the word *ageism* more and more in the 1990s, as it emerges as a social and political issue in the way that sexism (see **feminism**) and **racism** have done.

agenda or **agendum** Occasionally a Latin scholar might prefer *agendum* for the singular and *agenda* for the plural, and if you were living in ancient Rome no one would argue. But in the 1990s that could be pedantic, as nearly everyone says and writes *agenda* for one and *agendas* for more than one. If your dictionary still shows *agendum* in current use, it's time you got a new one. See also **hidden agenda**

aggravate and **aggravation** They are derived from Latin *aggravare*, meaning 'to make heavy' (think of *gravity*). They mean to make a bad situation worse: 'her illness was aggravated by overwork'. The words are also commonly used as a way of saying to annoy or upset someone: 'the loud background music aggravated him and he left the restaurant'. But if you use *aggravate* or *aggravation* like that, be warned that some people may think you're uneducated, even if you point out that good writers have been using the words this way since the early 17th century. Take heart because recently a usage panel of writers and broadcasters voted on the use of *aggravate* to mean 'annoy' or 'irritate', and the majority no longer find it *aggravating*.

aggressive To call someone an **aggressor** is to say something odious about them: it means they have made a vicious attack without justification. *Aggressive* is used in that way as well, especially about people. But when it comes to attitudes or policies, *aggressive* is often used approvingly: 'an aggressive attitude' can mean resolute and determined, 'an aggressive stance', a fashionable phrase in politics and business, suggests a forceful dynamic approach to the situation, even if it does make us think of a Victorian pugilist taking up a formal two-fists-raised posture in the ring.

aggressor This has been called a 'question-begging' word. It assumes that the *aggressor* is in the wrong, that the attack is unjustified and unprovoked. But the person making the attack may see it as a legitimate protection of their interests. Before we can fairly call anyone an aggressor, we have to establish the facts. See also previous entry

agnostic or **atheist** In practice, the distinction between these two attitudes towards God and the supernatural is not as clear-cut as many people think. Taking the Greek word *gnosis*, meaning 'knowledge', the biologist Thomas Huxley formed the word *agnostic* in 1869, to express his conviction that we cannot know about anything beyond material phenomena as explained by science. Religious and mystical beliefs and experience come outside this range.

Atheism, derived from Greek *atheos* (without God), goes back to the 16th century and is a positive denial of God, linked to the impossibility of knowing anything beyond space and time.

Stephen Hawking, the physicist who holds Newton's chair as Lucasian Professor of Mathematics at Cambridge, believes we are within decades of arriving at the final set of equations that will explain the existence of the universe. This could be seen as the ultimate expression of atheism, as science would explain everything and God would no longer be necessary. Yet Stephen Hawking concludes that, when physics finds the final equation, 'it would be the ultimate triumph of human reason – for then we would know the mind of God' (*A Brief History of Time*). Is this empty rhetoric, for it has been suggested that Professor Hawking is an atheist who believes no such thing, or is he leaving the door open, as an agnostic who concedes that science could transcend the material world to lead us into the presence of God?

agony aunt and **agony column** Quotation marks or italics have dropped away and these are standard expressions now. *Agony columns* are the sections of a newspaper or magazine that give advice to readers who write in about their personal intimate problems. And an *agony aunt* is the journalist (of either sex), sometimes using a pseudonym, who writes the replies, giving advice on anything from acne to premature ejaculation.

AI See **artificial intelligence**

aid or **help** *Help* is more down-to-earth, deriving from Old English, and is the word we should use most of the time. *Aid* from French, dating from the 15th century, is a more official governmental word, usually for situations where money or resources are provided. It is solemn to use *aid* in everyday contexts (except *first aid*): to ask, for example, 'Will you aid me with the washing-up?' would sound as if you've been drafting too many **White Papers**.

aide or **assistant** *Aide* is short for *aide-de-camp* (an officer acting as personal assistant to a high-ranking officer) and is still used in military contexts. The use has become extended to hospitals (a nursing aide). Where British English would use *assistant* in a business or professional activity, Americans would quite often prefer the word *aide*.

aided recall This is the name of the technique, often used in market research, where people are prompted to remember something. If, for example, researchers are trying to find out how many people have seen a particular television commercial, they might play a snatch of the music used or show some visual reminder. In surveys or opinion polls, aided recall can sometimes be carried too far in order to prompt people into giving the answers wanted by the organizations paying for the research.

Aids Never before has a disease produced so much linguistic confusion. It is sometimes written in capitals, AIDS (especially by health authorities in America), but newspapers usually write *Aids*. Many people are not aware it's an abbreviation and many more could not say what the letters stand for.

In 1980 doctors in New York, Los Angeles and San Francisco became aware of a new disease. As the symptoms were identified, they were classified as a **syndrome**, a complex of symptoms that all relate to a malfunction of the body. In this case, the body lost its natural resistance to infections, some of which were fatal. It is hard to believe that 1992 was only the tenth anniversary of the year when federal health authorities in America defined the condition as 'acquired immune deficiency syndrome', which in no time became the familiar **acronym**, Aids.

The virus that causes the syndrome is called *HIV*, human immunodeficiency virus (unlike Aids, it is always referred to by the letters, never as 'hivv'). It is incorrect to refer to the *Aids virus*, because Aids is not a virus, but the mistake is so common in newspapers and on radio and television that *Aids virus* is drifting into general use. To refer to the *Aids syndrome* is also wrong, since the word 'syndrome' is part of the abbreviation. Nor should we talk about people being 'tested for Aids': they are tested for HIV.

The social implications of Aids have led to a whole new related language: one sufferer in America lists over fifty acronyms which 'one must recognize, to be included among the Aids cognoscenti'. When we use the word *Aids*, we trigger off fears and prejudices that go far beyond the name of the disease itself.

ain't *Aren't* is all right but *ain't* isn't. There's no good reason why, except custom. 'An't' goes back to the beginning of the 18th century as a contraction for 'are not', and the variant *ain't* developed from that. But although it has good antecedents, *ain't* has never crossed the railroad tracks and has remained lower class ('Fings ain't what they used to be'), although *aren't I?*, ungrammatical though it is, is the usual and acceptable contraction for 'am I not?'

aircraft, **aeroplane** or **airplane** They were first called 'flying machines' but *aeroplane* was already in use by the end of the 19th century. The word derives directly from the French *aéroplane*, although you'd get a funny look in France if you spoke about flying in an *aéroplane*, because the French word now is 'avion' (from Latin for a bird). But *aeroplane* has survived in English.

Which word you use depends upon whether you're

British, American or in the RAF. You take off from London's Heathrow airport, in an *aeroplane* but you land at Kennedy airport, New York, in an *airplane*.

The RAF fly *aircraft*, a useful word which is taking over in general use: *aircraft* is both singular and plural and also includes helicopters, which *aeroplane* and *airplane* do not. For many people *aircraft* has replaced *aeroplane* in all contexts.

airfield, **airport** or **aerodrome** *Aerodrome* is still in dictionaries but if you use it you will sound like a World War I pilot wearing a helmet and goggles. The words now are *airfield* (for landing places with limited facilities for take-off and maintenance) and *airport* (a complex of runways and buildings with full facilities for passengers and customs).

airplane See aircraft . . .

airport See airfield . . .

airspace See aerospace and airspace

à la . . . A la mode and à la carte are as at home in English as they are in French. *A la* . . . has also become detached in English, used to mean in the style of someone. We conveniently ignore the fact that *la* is feminine in French, so not only can a woman be a glamorous 60-year-old à la Elizabeth Taylor, but someone could exploit pension funds à la Robert Maxwell.

A la . . . has a place in **gastronomy** and **menu English**. It indicates the style in which a dish is prepared, sometimes relating it to a region: *tripes à la mode de Caen*, for example, is a way of cooking tripe that originated in that city in Normandy, a gastronomic adventure for the brave, for traditionally it is tripe cooked for 12 hours, with ox feet, onions, leeks, cider and calvados. Or *à la* . . . can be culinary fantasy, as in the hors-d'oeuvre *nymphes à l'aurore* ('virgins at daybreak' you might say). Nor is the recipe an anticlimax: frogs' legs poached in white wine, then covered in a gently warmed sauce, served on aspic jelly and sprinkled with tarragon.

à la carte or **table d'hôte** Usually the most expensive way to eat in a restaurant is to order *à la carte* ('according to the menu'), anything you want from the menu, including specialities. Where it is available, *table d'hôte* ('host's table') is cheaper: this is the set meal at a fixed price, usually offering a limited selection of dishes for each course. Both phrases are used on the restaurant scene in Britain, although they sound rather grand in the 1990s, when 'set menu' or 'special menu' is often used for *table d'hôte*.

à la mode Originally used mostly for fashions in clothes, *à la mode* can be used about almost anything now to mean it's the latest thing. If you cycle to the office, or eat vegetarian food, someone might say it's 'very à la mode'.

On menus, *à la mode* is used in different ways on opposite sides of the Atlantic. In British or French restaurants it usually means beef braised in wine; in America it's more likely to mean served with ice-cream. The phrase can be pronounced more or less as in French ('allaMAWD') or anglicized to 'allaMOHD'.

alas This word is a curious survival from the biblical English poem, *Cursor Mundi*, dating from the early 14th century. It comes from Old French, *a las* ('hélas' in Modern French), and although it is still used in English as an expression of dismay or anguish, it has an archaic melodramatic air about it. It is all right to use *alas* in the 1990s, if you don't mind sounding like a Victorian damsel in distress. Otherwise substitute 'unfortunately', 'sadly', 'tragically', 'disastrously', 'catastrophically', depending upon how bad it all is.

albeit This Chaucerian word has survived into the 1990s, so not surprisingly it has an antiquated air about it. It's a contraction of 'although it be that': 'they eventually arrived, albeit too late for dinner'. The word 'though' can always be used instead, albeit some people prefer the old-world sound of *albeit*. See also **archaisms**

alcohol abuse No more than fashionable sociological jargon for **alcoholism**. See also **drug abuse**

alcoholic or **dipsomaniac** As a noun, *alcoholic* is used primarily as a medical term for someone who cannot control how much beer, wine or spirits they drink. But it's sometimes used more generally now, even in a lighthearted way, for anyone who cannot get through the evening without a couple of gins. Nevertheless, *alcoholic* is linked to **alcoholism**, a dangerous addiction to drink, and the supportive organization, started in 1935 to offer therapy to addicts, is called *Alcoholics Anonymous*. So we should be careful about using the description too lightly.

Dipsomaniac, at one time the word for an acute alcoholic, is hardly used at all now. Instead, doctors and social workers use *alcoholic* for any case of serious addiction.

alcoholism The meaning of the word has not changed but it has a different significance. Alcoholism at one time meant 'demon drink' and a sin against society. It is now seen more now as an illness to be treated than a vice to be condemned, since the dependence on alcohol is both biochemical and psychiatric, like any other drug addiction.

ale or **beer** Even dictionaries disagree about the difference between *ale* and *beer*. If you look up *ale* in some dictionaries, they will simply say that it's beer. Other dictionaries will say that it's beer made without hops, which seems a contradiction, since beer is defined as an alcoholic drink 'flavoured with hops'.

The confusion is understandable, since only English has kept both words (Scandinavian languages use a word related to *ale*, and a word related to *beer* is used in other Germanic languages). *Ale*, a very old word in

English, going back to Old Saxon, originally meant liquor made from a fermentation of malt without any hops added, whereas *beer* in the 16th century was a malt liquor with hops.

Not everyone would make such a distinction now: if you go into a pub and ask for a pint of ale, and your friend asks for a pint of beer, you'd probably both get exactly the same.

alibi   Lawyers – and readers of detective stories – know that an *alibi* is when an accused person claims they could not have committed a crime because they can prove they were somewhere else at the time. That is the proper meaning, because the word in Latin means 'elsewhere'. But *alibi* is used so often now simply to mean an excuse ('I've a good alibi for being late for dinner'), that some dictionaries have capitulated and show this false meaning as acceptable, at least in conversation. But it is still better to use 'excuse' or 'defence' when you want to explain why something has gone wrong, and keep *alibi* to mean being somewhere else at the time.

alimony   See **maintenance . . .**

all alone   Fusspots criticize this, saying that *all* is unnecessary, since you are either alone or not alone. But language is more subtle than that, and if you want to stress how lonely or frightened you are, *all alone* is a good way of putting it, as Coleridge found in *The Ancient Mariner*:

> Alone, alone, all all alone,
> Alone on a wide, wide sea!

For some people, *lonesome* is a cosier word, and although it is sometimes attacked as an **Americanism**, it's been used in English since the 17th century. It can be used to mean both 'alone' and 'lonely'.

allegation and **allege**   Newspapers fall back on *allege* to avoid a libel action: when we read someone is *alleged* to have done something, it means there is no proof at least for the time being. But the smirch remains, for as Edward Gibbon with his talent for irony and epigram expressed it in the 18th century, 'where much is alleged, something must be true'.

An *allegation*, although usually an assertion that has not been proved, is also used as a forthright accusation: 'She made an allegation that he had attempted rape'. *Allege* and *allegation* are uneasy words, since they enable damaging suggestions to be made about someone, without proof.

alleluia or **hallelujah**   Both words come from Hebrew, *alleluia* through Greek, and *hallelujah* directly ('praise Jah', that is Jehovah). They mean 'God be praised'. *Alleluia* (sometimes spelt *alleluya*) is the more usual form now, although the triumphant close to Part II of Handel's *Messiah* is always called the *Hallelujah Chorus*.

allergic and **allergy**   These began as medical terms describing hypersensitivity to anything. If eggs make you ill or roses make you sneeze, you are allergic to them. The words came to be used loosely for almost anything we dislike intensely: 'the lady is allergic to turning', as somebody once wrote about Margaret Thatcher. We understand much more now that reactions to different foods and atmospheric conditions can cause many physical and psychological problems, and the clinical application of *allergic* and *allergy* are more familiar.

If you really can't stand something or someone, there's no reason why you shouldn't adapt the medical use and say you're allergic to them: it implies that they make you ill, which may well be the way it is. If you don't feel as strongly as that, there's always the simple word *dislike*.

'ALLied' or **'aLLIED'**   See '**ALLy**' or '**aLLY**'

all in, **all-in** and **all in all**   When you feel *all in*, you're totally exhausted: most dictionaries limit this use to conversational English, but when it finds its way into written English, as is happening more and more, there's no hyphen.

In industry, an *all-in* rate is a wage rate that includes bonuses and other extras. And this is extended to general use where an 'all-in price', an 'all-in rent' . . . includes all charges. Used in this way it takes a hyphen, as it does in 'all-in wrestling', wrestling with no holds barred. Everything considered or, to put it another way, *all in all* (no hyphens), that sums it up.

alliteration and **assonance**   *Alliteration* is a run of words beginning with the same consonantal sound in the same passage: '. . . the stuttering rifles' rapid rattle' (Wilfrid Owen, *Anthem for Doomed Youth*). It should be used with restraint, because although it can be effective, especially in poetry, it can also be irritating. Sometimes it is unavoidable: 'I may marry Mary'.

Assonance is a run of similar vowel sounds. When it is unintentional, the effect is clumsy: 'I should have *thought* they *ought* to *sort* out their ideas before taking action'. When you know what you're doing, the effect can be attractive: 'The *rains* in *Spain* stay *mainly* in the *plains*' stopped the show in *My Fair Lady*.

A combination of alliteration and assonance can create an intriguing rhythm:

> And the couples (bubbles burst) relapse from
>   tom-tom jubilation
> Into tit-for-tat back-chat and flat conversation.
>   John Tessimond, *Charleston*

all of   Some grammarians suggest that 'all of the time', 'all of the people' . . . should not be used in serious writing. Certainly in those phrases 'of' is unnecessary and 'all the time', 'all the people' . . . mean exactly the same. But *all of* is well established in phrases such as 'all of them', 'all of us' . . ., so the way is open to use *all of* whenever it suits you, but not, perhaps, all of the time.

allow or **allow of**   Either: 'our agreement allows two interpretations' or 'our agreement allows of two interpretations'.

all ready or **already**   In conversation, no one knows how you're spelling it. But in writing, *all ready* and *already* mean different things: 'we're all ready to leave' (everyone of us is ready); 'we're already leaving' (we're leaving at this very moment); 'we've told you already' (Why do you keep asking? We've told you before); 'I'm all ready' (I've got my coat on, packed my bag, or whatever is required to be ready for the next thing).

all right or **alright**   Although you see *alright*, even in *The Times* occasionally, it still seems an incorrect and uneducated form of *all right*. This is a pity, because the two spellings could make a useful distinction: 'the prices are all right' (every one of the prices is correct), and 'the prices are alright' (the prices are acceptable). Nevertheless, it's better to avoid *alright*, since most people think it's bad English – unless you want to make a fight for it because of **already**, **altogether**. . . . Of course, in a slang expression such as 'he's an alright guy', it's pedantic to fuss about whether *alright* or *all right* is all right.

all that   There's some argument about whether expressions such as 'it's not as far as all that', 'it's not as bad as all that' . . . , common in speech, are acceptable in writing. We can rephrase them as: 'it's not so far', 'it's not so bad' . . . , but they do not mean quite the same, for *all that* suggests we should not make too much fuss about whatever it is.

Written English and spoken English are constantly coming closer to each other, and if it comes naturally to write a sentence such as 'they do not see each other all that often', there's probably no need to worry all that much about it.

all together or **altogether**   They mean different things. *All together* is when a number of things are happening or a number of people are somewhere *at the same time*: 'The women arrived all together'; 'All together now – let's sing!' *Altogether* means totally, with nothing left out: 'It was an altogether different approach'; 'He has had three wives altogether'. (If he had three wives *all together*, it would be polygamous.) To be 'in the altogether' is something else: it is a prudish way of saying naked.

allude or **refer**   These are sometimes used interchangeably but they do not mean the same. When you *allude* to someone or something, you mention them indirectly. When you *refer* to them, it is more out in the open. In the weeks after Margaret Thatcher's resignation as Prime Minister, Labour members of the House of Commons (who for so long were obliged to *refer* to her as the 'Prime Minister') took delight in *alluding* to her as 'the right honourable member for Finchley'. It is normal practice in the Commons to *allude* to members as 'the right honourable member . . .', instead of *referring* to them by name.

'ALLY' or **'aLLY'**   As a *noun*, the stress is on the *first* syllable: 'America was Britain's ALLy during World War II'. As a *verb*, when you link two ideas or things together, the stress is on the *second* syllable: 'I hope our points of view will aLLY'. When things are connected, they can be either 'aLLIED' or 'ALLied': you can choose which you prefer, except in a military context when the stress is on the first syllable: 'ALLied forces'.

almanac or **almanack**   The usual spelling is *almanac*, which relates it to the medieval Latin word. But it's always *Whitaker's Almanack* and the *Oxford Almanack*, which follow the archaic spelling that Chaucer used.

alphabetical order   At some time or other we may have to write a list of items in alphabetical order. The best system to follow is that used in this book and in most dictionaries. This system keeps to *strict* alphabetical order, without taking into account capital letters, hyphens and spaces between two or more words:

> data
> databank
> database
> data flow chart
> data *is* or *are*
> data processing
> Data Protection Act

See also **Mac** . . .

alpine   Some naturalists and geographers apply *alpine* to the section of a mountain above the timberline and below the level of year-round snow. But this is too sharply defined for most of us, as we tend to use *alpine* for anything to do with high mountains: 'an alpine scene', 'alpine flowers'. 'Alpine skiing' differentiates downhill skiing from cross-country skiing, wherever it is to be found. With a capital A, Alpine relates specifically to the Alps, the highest range of mountains in Europe, extending through France, Italy, Switzerland and Austria.

already   See **all ready** . . .

alright   See **all right** . . .

alter or **change**   *Alter* may suggest a relatively slight change: you *alter* a skirt by having the waist taken in. But someone could *change* the course of history. When the words seem interchangeable, it's better to use *change*: change your mind rather than altering it, change plans, change a colour scheme. . . . *Alter* would do in those examples, but it doesn't fit in as well.

alternate or **alternative**   These are sometimes mixed up, particularly *alternately* and *alternatively*: 'You can come for lunch or *alternately* for dinner' really means you can come for lunch one day, dinner the next, lunch the next and so on! For *alternate* means in turn or every other, so odd or even numbers are alternate numbers: 1, 3, 5, or 2, 4, 6. . . . *Alternative* suggests a choice, so the above invitation should have been 'You can come for lunch or *alternatively* for dinner'. See also next entry

alternative In dictionaries before 1960, *alternative* was a straightforward word that kept to its Latin source, *alter*, meaning 'one of two': it was used for one of two things, and if it referred to one of several things, that was considered bad English. Since then, *alternative* has become a complex word with political, sociological and ideological force.

It started with the youth culture of the 1960s and the concept of an *alternative society*, a way of living that turned its back on technology, materialism and conventional morality, to seek universal love and liberated spiritual values in communes. That was the ideology, but in practice it often led to drug-abuse and disorder. Some individuals genuinely found another way of living, but no alternative structures to conventional society have emerged.

From then on, *alternative* became a 'save the world' word, describing a more enlightened way of doing things, a breakaway from the entrenched convictions of industrial society. *Alternative energy* rejects coal, petroleum, nuclear fuel, etc in favour of solar or wind power and other sources of energy that do not affect the earth's atmosphere. *Alternative technology* sets out to conserve resources and so reduce damage to the environment. *Alternative medicine* (see **complementary medicine**) brought different ways of approaching health and treatment of illness.

Even the other meaning of *alternative* has opened up: instead of being restricted to 'one of two', all dictionaries now accept we can have as many alternatives as we like ('there are a number of alternatives to consider').

As *alternative* became fashionable, it degenerated into jargon and clichés: sociologists talk about *alternative accommodation* instead of 'other places to live', people are offered *alternative employment* rather than 'new jobs', when plans are changed, *alternative arrangements* are made instead of 'other arrangements'. Before using *alternative* in such ways, see if 'other' or 'new' would do equally well: they are simpler and more direct words.

although or **though** Mostly it doesn't matter which one you use. *Although* is more formal and you might prefer it in certain contexts for that reason. There are a few cases where *although* cannot be used for *though*, as in the phrase 'as though' or a sentence such as 'He said he would pay, but he didn't, though'.

altogether See **all together** . . .

aluminium or **aluminum** *Aluminium* in Britain (pron: 'aluMINyum'). *Aluminum* in America (pron: 'aLOOminum').

alumnus This Latin word (the plural is *alumni* – pron: 'aLUMnye') is used in America for a former student of a college, and is also sometimes used in Britain, mostly by Oxford and Cambridge colleges. But there are sexist problems. The feminine word is *alumna* (plural *alumnae* – pron: 'aLUMnee'), and women who graduate from mixed colleges may object to being called *alumni*. The solution is to call them all 'graduates', which is all right in Britain but less satisfactory in America, where 'graduate' is used for someone completing a course of studies at a high school. As fewer people are learning Latin, we may be able to get away with *alumnus* and *alumni* for both sexes, but don't count on it, as women have more rights now than they did in ancient Rome.

amalgamation See **merger** . . .

amateur No one wants to be called an *amateur*. The exception is in games and athletics, where *amateur* has a different status altogether: it is the highest honour to be selected for the Olympic Games, amateur athletic contests. In most other contexts, *amateur* has come to mean below professional standards.

Everyone knows the word is connected with 'love' ('amator' is Latin for a lover), yet since the late 18th century, *amateur* is more often than not used in a derogatory way. Monet loved painting, but who would call him an amateur painter? Amateur theatre is endured rather than enjoyed. 'An amateur approach' is a scornful comment, the last thing we want, for example, from a plumber or a surgeon. *Amateurish* dismisses someone as bungling and incompetent.

The pronunciation has been all over the place, with the stress switching between the first and last syllables. It has settled down now and the established British way of saying it is 'AMe(r)te(r)' (the same as the last three syllables of 'parameter'), with 'AMe(r)ture' more usual in America.

amatory See **amorous** . . .

ambassador An *ambassador* is, of course, an accredited diplomat assigned to be representative of a State in a foreign country. The word is also now used loosely for anyone sent by anyone on a special mission.

Whatever they look like or whatever you think of them, an ambassador accredited to the Court of St James is addressed as 'Your Excellency', supposedly at least once in a conversation. But radio and television interviewers, self-conscious about using this Ruritanian form of address, often simply say *Ambassador*.

The husband or wife of an ambassador does not rate 'Your Excellency' and, if the occasion arises, you call them 'Sir' or 'Madam', as the case may be.

Ambassadress is shown in dictionaries for a woman ambassador but it is not used in diplomatic circles, although you do hear it sometimes for an ambassador's wife. There is no word for an ambassador's husband!

ambience or **ambiance** The French word is *ambiance*, which some people prefer to use in English, pronouncing it more or less as in French: 'AMbeeahns'. To others this sounds affected, as the English version *ambience* is the accepted form now and is always pronounced as in English: 'AMbee-e(r)ns'. It's a useful word because it covers not only the general surroundings of a place but the atmosphere as well.

ambient *Ambient* is used environmentally to describe the general quality present: ambient noise, ambient temperature. . . . In ordinary conversation or writing, 'background' does just as well: 'background noise', 'background temperature'.

ambiguity and **ambiguous** There is a tendency to consider these words as derogatory, implying that because a statement can be interpreted in different ways it must be devious. *Ambiguity* may indeed be underhand or an attempt to avoid commitment, but so much in the human situation and in the affairs of the world cannot be clearly defined, and ambiguity may sometimes be preferable to dogmatism or oversimplification. The theatre producer, Peter Brook, has said that some ideas can be 'all the more powerful because of their ambiguity'.

Ambiguous is not a synonym for vague or indecisive. Properly used, *ambiguous* tells us that a word or statement can have more than one meaning. Neither *ambiguity* nor *ambiguous* is in itself a good or bad word: it depends on the circumstances and the intention.

ambivalence and **ambivalent** When we say someone is *ambivalent* about something, we mean they cannot make up their minds how they feel one way or the other, and we usually mean it as a criticism. In fact *ambivalence* was a term first used in psychiatry, and in an extreme form: when opposing feelings takeover altogether, it is a symptom of schizophrenia. Yet most of us experience ambivalence about many things (see **love–hate**). A more neutral expression, without any implied criticism, is *mixed feelings*. We can all understand and accept that.

ambulance chaser This cynical expression is current in America for lawyers who go out of their way to encourage people injured in accidents to sue for compensation. It's a way of touting for legal business. In Britain, some solicitors have advertised for possible clients who might have a case for damages because of injury or illness. Someone whose health has been affected by smoking may be encouraged to take legal action against the cigarette manufacturer. As a result, *ambulance chaser* is finding its way into British news programmes.

amen At the end of a hymn in church, 'ahMEN' is easier to chant than 'ayMEN'. But if we use it in speech, either pronunciation is acceptable. Although it comes to us from Greek, it is a Hebrew word for certainty or truth.

amend or **emend** Nearly always the verb you want is *amend*, whether it is to make an improvement in a piece of writing or to correct errors in it: 'she amended the draft of the letter'; 'he amended the paragraph to make it easier to understand'.

Emend is a more limited technical word covering editing to remove errors in a text ('the figures in the accounts were emended by the auditors'), although it is also used for changes required for particular reasons: 'the draft agreement was emended to cover the new conditions'. The nouns are *amendment* and *emendation* (pron: 'eemenDAYshun'). See also next entry

amendment At an official meeting or a conference, *amendment* is the word used for a change in the wording of a resolution. But if it is something extra added at the end, it will be an **addendum**.

amenities At one time *amenity* always meant something pleasant (it relates to the Latin word for love) and we use it (usually in the plural) for attractive or useful features of a place: 'the amenities of a ski resort'. It has now slipped into being used for almost any facility, so that a sewage disposal system might be called an 'amenity'. Not many dictionaries have picked this up yet, so we must hope that the predominant use of *amenity* will remain for pleasant things, which would not include a sewage disposal system or a rubbish dump, which some local authorities call an 'amenity site'. Pron: 'aMEENity' (heard more often) or 'aMENNity'.

America, the States, US or **USA** These are all short versions for the *United States of America*. *America* is probably the most commonly used, especially in conversation, even though it can be taken to include Canada and the countries of Central and South America. But Simon Jenkins, when editor of *The Times*, commented, this 'is a small price to pay for not having to rewrite every reference as US'. On both sides of the Atlantic, *the States* is also commonly used, again usually in conversation. In writing, *US* is more formal; but in speech US doesn't sound right and it's better to say the *United States* or *America*. People say or write *USA* less (except when addressing envelopes), unless they want to be punctilious or ceremonial.

To sum up, all are acceptable, although when speaking it's probably better to avoid US. Reserve *USA* or *United States of America* for full-dress occasions.

American Citizens of the United States have appropriated the name *American*, although technically it could apply to any inhabitant of the American continent. All dictionaries accept that the first meaning of *American* concerns the United States and its people.

There have been in the past stalwart patriots in the United States who wanted to declare linguistic independence and call their language *American*. The State of Illinois even passed a law in 1923, declaring the language used in that state was officially American. Such affirmations are lost in the cobwebs of history, and if you ask Americans what language they speak, the answer will be *English*.

There was no need in any case to protest, for **American English** has found its own style and vocabulary, and has brought a transfusion of rich vigorous new blood to the language of Britain. As long ago as 1962, *The Times Literary Supplement* believed that without American influence, English might have become a language that belonged to 'a club for initiates, housing a subtle and exclusive language of gesture, understatement, unstatement'.

(the) American dream   The British hear this expression but are often vague about what it means. This is understandable for Americans themselves interpret it in different ways. *The American dream* (sometimes called *the great American dream*) is a hazy vision of freedom, the good life and the possibility of riches.

The American dream possesses a symbolism in America that it is not easy for outsiders to understand. It is believed that over 100 million Americans, about 40 per cent of the population, are related to someone who passed through the 'gateway to the American dream', the huge terminus on Ellis Island in New York Harbour, now an immigration museum. Alistair Cooke tells us that 'some Americans have tears in their eyes whenever they hear "the American dream": others throw up and want to leave for New Zealand'.

American English or Americanisms   The deep-rooted hostility of the British towards American English is focused in the word *Americanism*, which is often a term of linguistic abuse. **Fowler** proclaimed magisterially 'Americanisms are foreign words and should be so treated' (*The King's English*, 1906). Take that to heart and we throw out *gatecrasher*, *debunk*, *teenager*, *bulldoze*, *babysitter*, *crank*, *bluff*, *boom*, *slump*, *stunt*, *paperback* and so many other words that we would find it hard to live without. The BBC still gets sackfuls of letters complaining of announcers using Americanisms.

American English does not carry this stigma: generally it is an unbiased description of the English used in the United States (some include the English spoken in Canada). *General American* is a more technical description used in linguistics to define educated use of English in America, a style of speaking that is not markedly regional. It is the American equivalent of Standard English (see **British English**) and **received pronunciation** or RP.

For a very long time, the British variety was regarded as the standard all over the world, and even in the 1990s it is not unusual to find language schools in other countries advertising for teachers who speak 'the **Queen's English**'. Most people now recognize that the existence of two major forms of English does not mean there are two standards, one below the other. British dictionaries often now include American usage, spelling and pronunciation. It is common to hear an Israeli diplomat or a Japanese industrialist speaking American English, since many people learn English as a second language in America, or from a teacher who speaks American rather than British English. There are, after all, at least four times as many people using English in North America as there are in Britain.

There remain people in Britain who make the territorial claim that English belongs to England. Of course, the language had its origin here (see **English**), but since then other countries have established an equal claim to it. An Oxford sociologist has quoted approvingly a comment that 'When the American people get through with the English language it will look as if it has been run over by a musical comedy'. Let's enjoy the joke, so long as we remember that the attitude behind it is blinkered, out of touch with the real linguistic world.

'AMicable' or 'aMICable'   You hear 'aMICable' (stress on the second syllable) but never from the cognoscenti, who will always say 'AMicable'.

amid or amidst   Whichever you use – and both forms are correct – this is a rather flowery word. Perhaps the only everyday use is in relation to a background: 'he won the race amid (or amidst) roars of applause'. Otherwise reserve *amid* or *amidst* for talking to the local poetry society. See also **among or amongst**.

amok or amuck   A bull can either 'run amok' or 'run amuck', as both spellings are correct, with *amok* as the more usual one. They are both pronounced in the same way: 'aMUCK'. It is a Malay word meaning to fight in a homicidal frenzy, and it's used in English for running around out of control, wrecking everything in sight.

among or amongst   Although *amongst* could sound rather literary in New York, it's common in Britain, alongside *among*. Some people imagine there is a subtle difference of meaning between the two words but there isn't: choose whichever comes naturally, remembering that *among* is becoming the more usual variant. See also **between or among**

amoral and immoral   The difference between these words is important. An *amoral* person does not acknowledge or may not be aware of the concept of 'right' and 'wrong'. This would be true of babies and animals. In other cases, the psychiatrist, Dr Margaret Wright, says that to be *amoral* is a psychopathic state. It can also be a philosophical attitude.

To be *immoral* you have to *do* something that society considers evil, dissolute or depraved. The problem with immorality is that morals are not absolute, and can vary from one society to another, or at different periods. In sexual relationships, there are people who believe that even minor deviations are immoral. At the same time, the sexologist, Dr Alex Comfort, advises that 'the whole joy of sex-with-love is that there are no rules, so long as you enjoy, and the choice is practically unlimited'. *Immoral* is a word to used with caution.

Remember: *amoral* – one *m*: *immoral* – two *m*s. See also **deviant** . . .

amorous or **amatory**   It is hard to find a whisker of difference in meaning between these two words. They both relate to sexual love. *Amatory* (pron: 'AMe(r)tery') is rarely used, except in a literary way: 'amatory scenes in a novel'. *Amorous* is the usual word, and some people say they're 'feeling amorous', because they think it's less crude than 'feeling sexy'.

amount, **number** or **quantity**   *Amount* or *quantity* is used when what is referred to is *singular* ('an amount of money', 'a certain amount of influence', 'a quantity of sand'). In many cases we can use either – 'a large quantity (or amount) of food'. But if something is less tangible, *amount* is preferable: 'an amount of energy', 'an amount of time'.

Number is always used when what is referred to is plural: 'a number of words', 'a number of eggs'. When we have *any amount of* or *the right amount of* it's easy to go wrong and slip into 'any amount of eggs', 'the right amount of words'. As one aggrieved grammarian commented on those examples, 'The correct word, of course, is *number* and it doesn't take a large *amount* of education to know it'. See also **number of**

ampersand (&)   This looks like a learned word for what is often called 'the *and* sign', which is just as good a name for &. But it's not at all that scholarly, as it was cobbled together in the 19th century from 'and per se and', meaning '& by itself is and'. An ampersand is mostly used in business names, such as Marks & Spencer and S J Perelman's accountants, Whitelipt & Trembling. People use a variety of adaptations of the symbol in handwriting. Pron: 'AMpersand'.

A popular alternative to an ampersand is **'n** or **'n'**.

amphetamine, **purple heart** or **benze-drine**   *Amphetamine* is the correct chemical name (an abbreviation of **a**lpha-**m**ethyl **phen**ethyl**amine**) for one of the most common stimulant drugs. *Purple heart* is a familiar British name for a heart-shaped light blue tablet containing the drug (ironically taking the name of the oldest US military decoration, established by George Washington). Another version is *benzedrine* (properly, but not usually, spelt with a capital B, because it is a brand name), which is used loosely for any tablet containing a stimulant drug. *Uppers* is a general slang term for the whole lot.

ample   At a stuffy dinner party you might still hear someone use *ample* because they think it is a polite way of saying 'enough': 'No thank you, I've had ample'. *Ample* really means 'plenty': 'You've had ample time to consider this'. And in most sentences, *plenty* is perhaps a more direct word to use, unless you're referring to a distinguished lady having an 'ample bosom'.

amuck   See amok . . .

anaerobic   See aerobic . . .

analgesic, **painkiller** or **anodyne**   Doctors use *analgesic* (pron: 'analJEEZic') to cover a variety of painkilling drugs, usually of the narcotic group, which can be taken orally, by injection or inhalation. *Painkiller* (no longer hyphenated) is a popular every-day word, mostly for tablets, such as aspirin or para-cetamol, that relieve pain.

Anodyne can also be used about a drug that relieves pain or is soothing, but you are less likely to hear it from doctors. *Anodyne* is more commonly used now to dismiss something as being deliberately bland and unprovocative, that encourages an unthinking uncriti-cal response. A report on a controversial subject could be called an *anodyne* if it glosses over the real issues. And sentimental songs, such as 'I'm Dreaming of a White Christmas', have been called anodynes.

analog   See analogue . . .

analogous and **analogy**   One thing or an argu-ment is analogous 'to' or 'with' something else, mean-ing there are parallels between them: an orange is *analogous to* (or *with*) a lemon (they are both citrus fruits with fleshy skins). Another way of expressing the same idea is: there is an *analogy between* an orange and a lemon, or an orange has an *analogy to* or *with* a lemon.

Be on guard against a form of reasoning using *anal-ogous* or *analogy*, which draws conclusions from correct but selected facts, implying that other parallels also correspond. An orange and a lemon are certainly analogous to each other but they do not taste the same.

Because *analogy* is correctly pronounced 'e(r)-NALe(r)jee', it is easy to slip into saying 'e(r)NAL-e(r)jus' for *analogous*. The *g* is hard, as in '**gate**': 'e(r)NALe(r)gus'.

analogue or **digital**   Dictionaries earlier than 1970 would not be much help with these words as they are used in the 1990s. Technology has brought them into everyday use. *Analog* (which is how it is spelt in America and in computer language everywhere) and *digital* describe two contrasting systems of showing numerical information. A digit is any number below 10 and comes from Latin 'digitus' (finger or toe, a reminder of the way we first learn to count). It is piquant that *digital*, deriving from the most primitive approach to numbers, is used for sophisticated com-puter systematization.

Analogue and *digital* have come into our homes, our cars and on to our wrists, as digital watches blink at us continuously, as opposed to the calm sweep of the hands of analogue watches. The effect on us is differ-ent. Digital instruments, whether they are bathroom scales or the line-up of winking figures in a spaceship, present information in isolated numbers. Analogue in-struments based on a dial show information as part of a sequence. For example, the detached read-out on digital scales is a bald statement: the spinning pointer on the dial of analogue scales is a graphic represen-tation of what you weigh, which you can relate to what you would like to weigh!

For a time, digital instrumentation took over, as winking lights and flashing numbers seemed to represent space-age precision. But there are signs of a swing back to analogue presentation of information. Perhaps people need the continuity of a revolving pointer round a dial, such as the hands round a clock relating time to the past and the future.

analysand It is a way of showing you are familiar with psychoanalysis (see **psychiatry . . .**) if you use the word *analysand* (pron: 'e(r)NALLeesand'). It is the name used by the cognoscenti for the person who lies on a couch pouring out their unconscious to the supposedly all-wise impassive **psychoanalyst** sitting alongside them.

analyse or **analyze** Always *analyse* in Britain, always *analyze* in America.

analysis or **parsing** These are both names for an archaic or traditional (depending on the point of view) approach to teaching English grammar. Students were taught how to break down a sentence into separate grammatical components (*analysis*) and each word was in turn classified according to its function (*parsing*). This is essentially a Latinate discipline, which some argue is essential to understanding the structure of English, and which others believe has no relevance to the language.

For centuries English was in the frigid grip of Latin and Greek scholars who made the running. Even by 1870, the study of English, as English, didn't count for much. There were no professors of modern English at Oxford or Cambridge; at Eton the English teacher came below the teacher of French and at Marlborough – behind the dancing master! All grammar was based on Latin and Ancient Greek, perfect languages for grammarians, because they are dead languages and rules can be fixed.

Few school children now have heard of analysis or parsing. It has to be admitted that for many in the past it was a tedious rather pointless exercise, laboriously learned for examinations and then soon forgotten, a comment that may well result in a letter to the publishers of this book from **Disgusted, Tunbridge Wells**. See also **grammar; case (grammatical)**

(in the final) **analysis** This weighty expression is often out of all proportion to what follows: 'In the final analysis, I think it's better to go by train'. There are simple alternatives, such as 'when you think about it . . .', 'all in all . . .', 'in the end . . .'.

analyst At one time, especially in America, an *analyst* meant predominantly one thing – a **psychoanalyst**, who sits with rapt or bored attention, while a patient lies on a couch and talks about repressed fears and conflicts. In the 1990s, in the money markets of London and New York, the first meaning of *analyst* is an *investment analyst*, a highly paid consultant who specializes in the investment prospects of different sectors of financial markets.

analytic or **analytical** The difference between the meaning of these words is arguably too subtle to bother about. *Analytic* is the term generally used in philosophy and linguistics. An *analytic* statement in philosophy is true by definition ('a triangle has three sides'). In linguistics, *analytic* describes a language, such as English, where the relationship between words in a sentence is shown by the order in which they are used ('the dog bit the man') as opposed to an *inflected* language, such as Latin, where meaning is indicated by a change in the form of the words themselves rather than their order.

In other contexts, *analytical* is perhaps the more usual word: 'an analytical approach', 'an analytical method'.

analyze See analyse . . .

ANC The abbreviation is more familiar in news bulletins than the name in full: *African National Congress*, which dates from 1923. In 1990, when its most famous leader, Nelson Mandela, was released from prison, ANC moved centre-stage on the international scene, as the major opposition party in South Africa representing the rights of black inhabitants. See also **apartheid**

anchorman This is one of the good descriptive words in broadcasting that has crossed the Atlantic to Britain. It is the central person in a newscast on television or radio who holds the whole programme together, as outside interviews, recordings or film sequences are fed in. In television studios *anchorman* is also used for a woman, rather than 'anchorwoman' or 'anchorperson'. It is replacing 'compère' (an old-fashioned word now) and 'presenter'. The word appears, even in some recent dictionaries, as two words or hyphenated, but the one-word version is taking over. See also **continuity**

'ANchovy' or **'anCHOHvy'** It is 'ANchovy' (stress on first syllable) in the best circles.

ancient How old is *ancient*? *Ancient history* is correctly history before the fall of the Western Roman Empire in 476. Depending on your own age, a person might be *ancient*, if they are aged anywhere between 50 and 100. And if you have enjoyed uninterrupted light coming through a window for more than 20 years, that window is protected in English law against obstruction, under *ancient lights*. With the faster pace of change, *ancient* is becoming more and more recent, so something that happened last week might already be, in conversation at least, *ancient history*.

and Here is one of the simplest and oldest words in English, yet people can still hesitate over how to use it. These are three common difficulties:

1 Many of us were taught at school that we should never begin a sentence with *and*. That is a misguided linkage of English with Latin. The first page of the Authorized Version of the Bible, published in 1611 and

translated by some of the best scholars of the time, has a whole string of sentences and paragraphs beginning with *and*: '*And* the earth was without form and void . . . *And* the spirit of God moved upon the face of the Waters . . . *And* God saw the light, that it was good . . . *And* the evening and the morning were the first day . . .'. After that, need we worry any more about beginning a sentence, or even a paragraph, with that Old English word *and*? See also **but**.

2 When *and* comes in the middle of a sentence it has long been usual to precede it by a comma. This is a custom, rather than a rule. When what follows is a separate idea, a comma is helpful: 'she got out of bed, and decided to phone him'. But when what follows is immediate, a comma gets in the way: 'after dinner, he stood up and raised his glass'.

3 In a list of items, when *and* precedes the final item, some people prefer to use a comma before *and*: 'she bought a dress, shoes, a bag, and an umbrella'. It's a matter of preference and the comma after 'bag' could be left out. But when there's a risk of misunderstanding, a comma should go in: 'it's available in red, red and green, yellow and white, and blue'. Otherwise it would not be clear how many colour combinations are available.

and/or On forms or specifications *and/or* has a place to explain that items are a combination *or* alternatives: 'brass and/or steel screws'. But in letters and other forms of writing *and/or* is out of place, often unnecessary, usually making readers think twice about what it means. Try *and* or *or* on its own to see if that is satisfactory, or rewrite the sentence: 'brass or steel screws or a combination of both may be used'.

anecdotal evidence An *anecdote* is an account of a particular event, a one-off story. When there is so much news coverage, *anecdotal evidence* is the term now to distinguish between factual evidence, based on proper research, and a series of individual points of view which are neither statistically significant nor properly analysed. When someone says, for example, 'a number of people have commented . . .', 'many people have said . . .', 'our postbag confirms . . .', etc, we're dealing with *anecdotal evidence*. It may be used to support a view, but is in fact not real evidence at all. It is a straw in the wind, and it takes a large representative sample of straws to prove a point. See **cross-section . . .**

Angelinos Knowing a useful word or expression before everyone gets hold of it can help us to win the never-ending game of words. *Angelinos* are the people of Los Angeles, the volatile urban and industrial complex, the third largest population centre in the United States.

angle In geometry, an *angle* is the degree of inclination between the meeting point of two lines or planes. In fishing, *to angle* is to use a baited hook (an angled piece of wire), and because of that *angle* was adapted in the 17th century to mean persuade or catch

someone. Later Hollywood gangster films picked up that idea: 'What's your angle?', accompanied by a narrowing of the eyes, suggests an underhand motive. But there's nothing nasty about 'we have a new angle on . . .', meaning a new approach.

Anglican or **episcopalian** *Anglican* (usually spelt with a capital) or *episcopalian* (spelt with or without a capital) can mean the same, a member of or something related to the Church of England or one of the churches in communion with it. In America and Scotland and in some other countries, *episcopalian* is more likely to be used than *Anglican*, because the corresponding Church is called the Episcopal Church. The word comes from Latin for bishop, and can equally well be used for government of the Church by bishops.

Anglo- *Anglo-* sets all kinds of traps for us. It came into English, via Latin, from the Angles, a German tribe from the Angul district of Schleswig, who settled in central and northern parts of England during the 5th century.

For a long time it was safe enough to use *Anglo-* to embrace all of Britain, but that can now sometimes lead to misunderstanding or resentment. When Geoffrey Howe, as deputy Prime Minister, referred on radio to 'Anglo-Irish policy', he hastily changed it to 'British-Irish' – perhaps he was afraid of upsetting the Welsh and the Scots, or concerned that *Anglo-Irish* might, for some Irish, refer to the early settler-rulers of Ireland, a highly charged part of Irish history.

Anglo-Indian is even more uneasy: it is too connected with the British Raj and imperialist India to be used comfortably for current relations between India and Britain. Anglo-Indian is still used for the British who spent their working lives in India, governing the country. As these die out, Anglo-Indian is more commonly used for people of mixed British and Indian descent. Perhaps the best alternative, to avoid misunderstanding, is 'Indo-British'.

In many contexts, *Anglo-* is still used to cover the whole of Britain (an Anglo-Soviet agreement): but alongside that we use *Anglo-Welsh* or *Anglo-Scots*, which limits *Anglo-* to the English. When in doubt, consider replacing *Anglo-* by 'British-', as Geoffrey Howe did. See also **Anglo-Saxon**

Anglo-Saxon An indeterminate appellation because it can have different meanings. First of all, *Anglo-Saxon* is the name generally used for the Germanic tribes who arrived in Britain after the 5th century, and over a period settled in the country that now corresponds more or less to England. Among scholars, the English language before the mid-12th century was known as *Anglo-Saxon*, a linguistic term that has since been replaced by the more appropriate name **Old English**. There remains, by tradition, a Chair of Anglo-Saxon at Oxford University. Both terms refer to the same period (roughly 600 to 1150) of the English language.

After 1600, *Anglo-Saxon* came to be used as an alternative descriptive word for English, especially about culture, ethnic characteristics, heritage and attitudes. This is how Angus Wilson used it in the title of his satirical novel, *Anglo-Saxon Attitudes* (1956).

More recently, *Anglo-Saxon* is often used as a euphemism for so-called **four-letter words**, justifiably since some of these words do in fact go back to Old English.

angst It is not surprising that the German word for fear, which took up residence in England some years ago, is more and more in demand in the 1990s, since it describes a general feeling of anxiety about anything, but especially about the state of the world and the human condition. To experience angst (pronounced exactly as it is spelt), look at the news on television almost any evening or at the front page of any newspaper.

anima This word comes up sometimes in talks about art or psychology but unless you have studied the teachings of Jung, it is difficult to understand. Jung took the meaning of *anima* in Latin, 'soul' or 'inner being', and used it for the personification in a man's **psyche** of mystical feelings and the capacity for love. For Jung, the anima was symbolized as the image of a woman that every man carries within him, which has its first incarnation in his mother. The corresponding word for women, which Jung introduced later, is *animus*, representing the masculine force or influence operating within a woman.

More generally, *anima* is used for both sexes to represent the source of sensitivity and inspiration. We might compare it to the artist's muse, symbolized in mythology as a woman.

animal rights Since it was founded in 1824, the RSPCA (Royal Society for the Prevention of Cruelty to Animals) has sought to protect animals. After World War II, *animal rights* defined a new creed, that animals have rights on this planet and are not here merely for exploitation by humans. *Animal rights activists* make the headlines when they use violent or controversial methods to get their message across.

annex or **annexe** The verb is always *annex* ('one country tries to annex another when it occupies its territory'). The noun is usually *annexe* in Britain ('the hotel has extra accommodation in the annexe'), although *annex* (the spelling in America) is also found.

annual, **biennial** and **perennial** These words buzz round the Chelsea Flower Show, but less than passionate gardeners sometimes confuse them. An *annual* is a plant that grows and flowers in one year, and that's the end of its life cycle. A *biennial* completes its life cycle in two years (see also **biennial**). A *perennial* comes back to flower year after year for a number of years.

annual percentage rate See **APR**

annual report Anyone can make an annual report, that is an account of what has been going on in the previous year. But for a registered company in the UK, *annual report* has a statutory meaning. To start with, it is a legal requirement, and it has to include a balance sheet, profit and loss account and the auditors' and directors' report. For shareholders in companies, the annual report is essential reading.

annuity or **pension** A *pension* is usually an income you are entitled to, either because of a period of employment or service, or because of an injury, and as a rule it is paid weekly or monthly. An *annuity* may also be a form of pension, purchased by an employer putting down a lump sum. Or you can buy an annuity for yourself with a sum of money that guarantees you an annual payment for as long as you live. Strictly speaking, an annuity should be paid once a year, but in spite of that, some annuities are paid monthly. A *pension* implies that someone has retired from or been invalided out of full-time employment whereas an *annuity* can simply be a way of investing money to produce an income.

anodyne See **analgesic** . . .

anorexia This is short for *anorexia nervosa* (pron: 'annaREXia nerVOHse(r)'). Although described in medical writings over 100 years ago, this disorder came into the news in the 1960s. It is the grotesque condition of starving in the midst of plenty. Advertising and popular journalism encouraged women to believe that 'thin is beautiful, fat is ugly', and some young women (rarely men) become terrified of eating, almost to the point of death from starvation. Doctors have treated children as young as eight for what has become known as 'the slimmers' disease'. These victims of the pressures of society have, according to psychiatrists, an abnormal fear of growing up.

A N Other If there is a list of people and an extra one, as yet unnamed, is going to be added, they are sometimes included as *A N Other*, as if it is a person's name. It is a silly practice, as it would be easy to put 'one extra'.

answerphone Not many people knew this word until the 1980s, although Ansafone was registered as a proprietary name in the early 1960s. It's now an everyday method of 'putting a message in a bottle'. We record something that is played back to anyone telephoning when we're not in or don't want to answer the phone. Whoever is calling records their message to us, and maybe we call them back, or maybe we don't.

Antarctic See **Arctic** . . .

ante- or **anti-** *Ante-* comes from Latin and means 'before'. When you put up an *ante* in poker, you put down a stake *before* drawing cards. Hence antediluvian (see next entry), antenatal clinic. *Anti-* (much more common than *ante-*) is from Greek and means 'against' or 'opposite': antidote, anticlimax, anticlockwise, antiseptic, antisocial and many other words. Both are pronounced the same: 'ANti' (to rhyme with 'shanty'). (For *anti-*, many Americans prefer the pronunciation 'ANTeye'.)

antediluvian   You are not likely to want to describe the period before Noah's Ark and the Flood, which is what this word really means. It is also an emphatic way of saying that something is altogether out-of-date. In the 1990s, technology and ideas are changing so fast that even yesterday's way of doing something could seem *antediluvian*. (Pron: 'anty-diLOOvian'.)

antennae or **antennas**   It is *antennae* (pron: 'anTENee') when they are the sensitized feelers on the heads of some insects or, borrowing that idea, imaginary probes that some people think they have to help them pick up what is going on. Television aerials are *antennas*.

anti- or **ante-**   See ante- . . .

antibiotic   Penicillin, discovered by Alexander Fleming and used to treat infections during World War II, brought *antibiotic* into general use. Some people still believe that *antibiotic* is just another word for penicillin, but there is a whole group of antibiotics, which are medicaments derived from micro-organisms (or made synthetically) and used to destroy bacteria that are susceptible to them.

anticipate or **expect**   There can be no doubt that *anticipate* means to estimate something in advance: 'I cannot anticipate how she will respond'; 'A good driver tries to anticipate what will happen next'. But for 200 years people have been using *anticipate* to mean exactly the same as *expect*: 'I anticipate that she will agree'. There are people who pick on this as a misguided use of English. It helps to avoid this criticism if you never write or say 'anticipate that' (or use *anticipate* so that it could be followed by 'that'), as that always leads to the meaning of *expect*.

On the other hand, the use of *anticipate* for *expect* is so well established, and does not conflict with the other meaning of the word, that perhaps it's time it was accepted. If you agree, you might say 'That's just the kind of sensible approach I anticipated from this book'. Or you might think it's too soon to anticipate that everyone will use *anticipate* in that way.

anticlimax, **bathos** or **pathos**   *Bathos* (pron: 'BAYthos') is mostly used as a literary word, corresponding to the more everyday word *anticlimax*, a big build up to something that turns out to be trivial: 'I have something of the greatest import to announce – a coffee-break'.

Pathos (pron: 'PAYthos'), sometimes confused with *bathos*, is also more likely to be used in literary contexts ('it is a novel full of pathos'): the everyday words with a similar meaning are 'pity' or 'sadness'.

anticyclone or **high pressure area**   An anticyclone is a centre of high pressure in the atmosphere, where the air rotates anticyclonically, that is in the opposite direction from the rotation of the earth. This is why weathermen talk about either a *high pressure area* or an *anticyclone*, meaning more or less the same conditions.

anti-hero   The heroes in modern novels, films and plays are more likely to be *anti-heroes*. The classic idea of a **hero** (the word is now used for both sexes) is someone with noble qualities, courage and unselfishness. Heroes are admirable but they can also be boring. An *anti-hero* is more likely to come home drunk than kneel at a woman's feet. It is because anti-heroes are so much less than perfect, that we are more able to relate to them.

There is nothing new about the type or the description (*anti-hero* was first used in literary criticism in 1897 by a professor of poetry at Oxford). Satan in Milton's *Paradise Lost* is an anti-hero, so is Becky Sharp in Thackeray's *Vanity Fair*. Humphrey Bogart was the archetypal anti-hero in films, likeable because he was too human always to do the 'right thing'. The concept, and the expression *anti-hero*, really became talked about in the late 1950s through Jimmy Porter, in John Osborne's play *Look Back in Anger*.

anti-Semitism or **antisemitism**   Many dictionaries keep the hyphen and capital S. The reason is that Semite is the name of a group of people, supposedly descendants of Shem, son of Noah (see **Semitic**). But *antisemitism* is also written, following the precedent of 'antichristian'.

antiseptic, **aseptic** or **sterile**   In hospitals these words may also be used in more precise ways, but in general use *aseptic* and *sterile* both describe things, such as bandages or surgical instruments, that are free from germs or other micro-organisms. *Sterile* is the word used in operating theatres. *Sterile* also means unable to produce offspring, and there is the extended meaning of lifeless and lacking in imagination ('a sterile discussion'). *Antiseptic*, although it can be used in much the same way as *aseptic* or *sterile*, is usually applied to products that actually destroy germs ('an antiseptic cream').

antisocial, **unsociable**, **unsocial** or **nonsocial**   Although we may think of *antisocial* as a relatively recent word, it was used in the 18th century. Its original meaning of opposed to the principles of society has become blurred, and it is now used loosely to describe any behaviour that doesn't suit someone else. So if you smoke cigarettes or wake the neighbours with your loud music, you might well be accused of being *antisocial*.

If you always refuse invitations to parties, you might be called *unsociable*, because you don't want to mix with other people. *Unsocial* tends to be used for circumstances that exclude someone from normal social activity, as in *unsocial working hours*, for which people usually expect a higher rate of pay because their social life is affected.

Although *non-social* is sometimes used as a synonym for *unsocial*, it is a word that can generally be ignored, for few dictionaries include it.

antithesis See opposite . . .

antitrust Most industrialized countries are uneasy if groups of companies under the same control become too big or powerful, and in America *antitrust* laws (the hyphen, *anti-trust*, is dropped by most current dictionaries) are enacted to prevent this happening. In Britain similar control is exercised by the Monopolies and Mergers Commission (see **cartel** . . .).

antonym The word **synonym**, for a word that means the same as another, is more familiar than *antonym*, for a word that means the opposite: good and bad, hot and cold, rich and poor. . . .

anxious or **eager** 'I'm *anxious about* having dinner with you' means you are worried about it for some reason. That is the correct use of *anxious*. 'I'm *anxious to* have dinner with you' means there is nothing you want more. This use of *anxious*, for something we want very much, is so common now, that it is pointless to object to it, even if we don't like it. If you're still anxious about it, there are alternatives, such as 'eager to', 'want to', 'care about'. . . .

any . . . There is often doubt over whether *any* combines with a following word to make *one* word, or whether it should be kept separate. See **any more/ anymore; anyone/any one; any time/anytime; any way/anyway**

any or **any other** 'She is a better actress than *any* in the play' or '. . . *any other* . . .'? There is some objection to leaving out *other*, but it is an unnecessary fuss since the use of *any* on its own is both clear and well established.

any more or **anymore** You can make a distinction between *anymore* for time and *any more* for quantity: 'she doesn't work here anymore' but 'I don't have any more money'. But *anymore* is felt to be American usage and *any more* British, irrespective of sense.

anyone or **any one** Keep it as one word, unless it is one of a number: 'you can invite anyone' but 'you can do it in any one of six different ways'.

any place See anywhere . . .

any time or **anytime** *Anytime* is common in America but is not listed in most British dictionaries, because the words are usually kept separate in Britain.

any way or **anyway** When it is used as an alternative to 'in any case' or 'at all events': *anyway* (one word). When it's a way of going somewhere, it is better as two words: 'you can go any way, on the motorway, along the bypass or through the town'. If

it's a way of doing something, two words could help to avoid misunderstanding: 'you can do it any way' means whichever way you like, but 'you can do it anyway' could mean 'you can do it in any case'.

anywhere or **any place** The usual English word is *anywhere*, but there is nothing wrong with *any place* (always two words), at least in conversation, if you don't mind sounding slightly American. (Some Americans prefer *anywhere*, although *anyplace*, spelt as one word, is more common.)

AONB An Area of Outstanding Natural Beauty is not protected to the same extent as a **national park** or a nature reserve, but it is nevertheless a statutory designation that enables local authorities to control development.

apart from or **aside from** At one time *apart from* was British and *aside from* was used more often in America. But now you come across *aside from* in British English and you hear *apart from* in America. It doesn't matter which you use, wherever you are.

apartheid Dictionaries note that *apartheid* can be used for racial segregation anywhere in the world. But it's an Afrikaans word associated with racial discrimination laws in South Africa, and it avoids misunderstanding to use it only about that country. In countries other than South Africa, **segregation** is the equivalent word.
Pronunciation varies: 'aPAHThide' is commonly heard, because that's the way it's spelt. Nelson Mandela says 'aPAHThate', the recommended pronunciation, for when it comes to pronouncing *that* word correctly, he would know.

apartment The American word for 'flat' has become common in London. But don't use it if you live in a modest bedsitter.

apiary or **aviary** Think of 'aviation' and you will never get these words mixed up: you keep birds in an *aviary*, bees in an *apiary*.

aplenty or **galore** They both mean there is a lot of something, and they both come *after* the word they're describing. *Aplenty* is perhaps more restrained, *galore* (an adaptation of an Irish expression) more expansive: 'whisky galore', but maybe 'caviare aplenty'!

apogee and **perigee** Outside astronomy, these were rare words before satellite communications. They are now more familiar. When speaking of satellites, the *apogee* (pron: 'APPerjee') is the point in orbit when a satellite is at its maximum distance from the earth. The *perigee* (pron: 'PERidjee') is the point where a satellite is nearest the earth. *Apogee*, in particular, has also come to be used in the wider sense of 'pinnacle' or 'height': 'The graph of sales reached its apogee at £2.9m'; 'His career reached its apogee when he was made head of the marketing department'.

apoplexy and **apoplectic** For a note on these rather dated words, see **coronary** . . .

apostrophe The apostrophe has been called 'the great dilemma of the English language', but it's a dilemma that will one day be partly resolved. Sooner or later, at least some uses of the apostrophe will be relegated to the cobwebs of linguistic history. For the time being, it is considered uneducated not to know when and where to use an apostrophe. But take heart: one professor in America, who kept a record, complained that he had to insert over 50,000 apostrophes in his students' written work in one term alone, to say nothing of moving or removing almost the same number.

So it's better to keep it simple:

1 Every schoolchild is taught that an apostrophe is used to show *possession*. If the noun is singular, add *'s*: 'the *boy's* dog'. If it's plural ending in *s*, just add an apostrophe: 'the *boys'* dog' (a dog belonging to two or more boys). If it's plural, not ending in *s*, add *'s*: 'the women's husbands'.

Problems:

i Names ending in *s*. There is no reliable rule, only custom. 'Charles's office' is more usual than 'Charles' office', but it is always '*Jesus'* parables' ('*Jesus's* in speech or writing seems out of place). In spite of the accumulation of *ss*, it has to be 'the Joneses's house', 'the Birches's children', etc (in speech we can relax and say 'the Jones's house').

With other names, you just have to know which is right. The street off Piccadilly is called *St James's* Street; it is *Queen's* College, Oxford, but *Queens'* College, Cambridge; **Lord's** Cricket Ground but *Earls* Court; St *John's* Wood but All *Souls* College, Marks & *Spencer's* but the famous store founded by Henry Harrod lost its *apostrophe* in mysterious circumstances – it is simply *Harrods*. . . . The only safe guide in such cases is to look it up.

Where there are two names, it is more relaxed to place the apostrophe after the second name only: 'We are going to Jack and Jill's party', rather than 'Jack's and Jill's party', which is not incorrect but is rather laboured.

ii Expressions such as 'ten *years'* experience', 'seven *miles'* visibility'. Illogically they are supposed to take an apostrophe. But it is likely that the apostrophe will eventually be dropped. (When a journalist in Chicago wrote about a woman 'who is five *months'* pregnant', his editor commented 'Nice try, but no cigar!')

iii Drawn out descriptions. It's all right to *say* 'the woman I'm going to *marry's* name is Susan', but it looks silly in writing. Rephrase it: 'the name of the woman I'm going to marry is Susan'.

2 *Hers, yours, theirs, ours, its* never take an apostrophe, because they are already possessive: 'the book is *yours, theirs, hers, ours* . . .'. But distinguish between *its* (possessive) and *it's* (contraction for 'it is'), *theirs* (possessive) and *there's* (contraction for 'there is'). It is surprising how many people slip up over this.

3 Some people use an apostrophe for the plural of abbreviations (MP's, QC's . . .), or letters (a's, b's . . .) or years (the 1920's . . .). This is now old-fashioned: Parliament has *MPs*, there are *QCs* in courts, and in the *1990s*, you mind your *ps* and *qs*.

4 An apostrophe in contractions shows that letters are omitted, as in *can't, you've, they're* . . . (see **contracted forms**). But it is contrived to use one merely because letters are not sounded, as in 'he far'd well', 'her eyes were heavily mascara'd'.

5 For the shortening of *and* to *'n* or *'n'*, see **'n**.

apparatus It means, of course, a piece of equipment. But it is often used almost as a synonym for 'organization': 'we have all the apparatus we need to market this new product'.

appear When *appear* is followed by *to*, look out for the risk of confusion: 'she appeared to answer the questions that had arisen' can mean two quite different things. It could mean she arrived to answer the questions, or she seemed to answer them, with a suggestion that she had not really done so. In such cases, either 'arrive' or 'seem' should be used to make the meaning clear.

appellation controlée (AC) For wine buffs, *appellation controlée* is part of everyday conversation. If you've paid enough for a bottle of French wine, you will see these two words on the label, followed by the name of the region where the wine was made. Such wines are regulated by strict laws designed to maintain a high standard, even prescribing methods of cultivating and pruning vines. In practice, AC (as it is abbreviated) does not always provide an unfailing guarantee of quality, for some AC wines are not as enjoyable as simple French country wines not entitled to this top 'appellation'.

AC is the most well-known designation for wines. Others have more a place in a wine guide than here, where only brief notes are called for. France has less prestigious categories on wine labels, ending up with *vin de table* at the bottom of the scale. The top category in Italy is *DOC*, short for a polysyllabic Italian flourish that sounds like the title of an operatic aria: *denominazione di origine controllata*, literally 'controlled denomination of origin'. Germany uses a complicated system of five grades on labels, depending on ripeness of the grapes, from *Kabinett* at the bottom to the awesome *Trockenbeerenauslese* at the top. The Spanish system is post-war and is more concerned with defining areas of wine production.

appendices or **appendixes** The Latin plural *appendices* (pron: 'e(r)PENDe(r)seez') is beginning to sound self-conscious. It is not, of course, wrong but most people now are more at home saying *appendixes*. In operating theatres, surgeons have always taken out *appendixes*, never *appendices*.

Apple Mac See **raincoat** . . .

'APplicable' or **'apPLICable'** Because of *apply* (pron: 'apPLY'), many people find it easier to say 'apPLICable' (stress on second syllable), but arguably 'APplicable' remains the upmarket pronunciation.

applied . . . When a science is studied for its practical applications, it may be called 'applied . . .'. Applied mathematics is the use of abstract mathematics in the sciences or, more generally, the use of mathematics for calculation. Applied psychology relates academic or theoretical psychology to human problems. The developments of applied psychology have become so varied that they have been classified under separate names, such as clinical psychology, educational psychology and industrial psychology.

appoint, consult, engage or retain There is a certain professional etiquette about which word is used in which situation. Advertising agents, management consultants, etc are *appointed*. Doctors and medical specialists are *consulted*. Solicitors usually prefer to be *engaged*, accountants are *appointed* with a *letter of engagement*. Barristers are always *retained*. None of them would approve of down-to-earth words such as 'hire' or 'employ', although that's what it comes down to, since we pay out money in return for services.

appraise, assess or estimate *Appraise* in the 15th century meant to fix a price for something. This early meaning remains: when we appraise people or achievements, we decide upon their value. *Assess* is used to calculate the value of the amount of tax to be paid or the value of a property (an insurance assessor agrees the amount of a claim). But *assess* has a wider application, as it can be used for deciding the quality or weight or size of something. When *estimate* is used instead of *assess*, it usually suggests a more approximate judgement, more reliable than a guess, but not as authoritative as an assessment. See also **guesstimate**

appreciable This is such a vague word that it hardly means anything, and is often a sign that someone does not want to commit themselves: they don't write or say 'a lot of money' but 'an appreciable sum of money'. Used like this, *appreciable* is indeterminate. Unless you intend to be noncommittal, it's better to choose a more positive word, such as 'serious', 'significant', 'considerable'. . . .

appreciate The alternative meanings of *appreciate* are to go up in value, to be grateful for something, or to be fully aware of something: 'I appreciate your sympathy'; 'I appreciate just how difficult this is'. *Appreciate* has become a pompous cliché in **business English**: 'we should appreciate an early reply' instead of 'please reply as soon as you can'.

Before using *appreciate* in a letter, try out 'understand' or 'realize' to see if they are more direct: 'I understand the problem'; 'I realize how much this will upset you'.

apprehend or comprehend They both mean to understand something. *Comprehend* is used more

often and suggests more of a mental process: 'I comprehend how you intend to plan the campaign'. *Apprehend* suggests becoming aware of something without necessarily having thought about it: 'I apprehend why you are concerned'. The nouns for each of these words draw the meanings further apart: *comprehension* is 'understanding'; *apprehension* is 'concern'.

appropriation Apart from the usual meanings of appropriation, there is a specific business and financial use, which is to set aside a fixed sum of money for a particular purpose, such as 'an advertising appropriation'.

APR This abbreviation appears in many financial advertisements, especially those offering credit. It stands for annual percentage rate. An important provision, following the Consumer Credit Act 1974 in the UK, made it a statutory requirement, when lending money or offering credit, to quote the true annual rate of interest involved, so that it is not obscured by misleading figures. See also **flat rate**; **CAR** (compound annual rate)

a priori or prima facie Both *a priori* and *prima facie* suggest that the available evidence may not be conclusive, so it is not surprising that these two Latin expressions are sometimes confused, even in official statements. *A priori* (pron: 'ay pryeAWrye') is used about a method of reasoning: an *a priori conclusion* is a conjecture assuming that because one thing is true, something else follows from it: if the roads are icy and there is an accident, you assume it was caused by a skid, which may not be true.

Prima facie (pron: 'prime(r) FAYshee') means 'at first sight'. A lawyer or the police may talk about a *prima facie case*, meaning there is a sufficient case to proceed with, based on the available evidence.

If you want to avoid getting caught up in this, you can often substitute 'at first sight' or 'from what can be seen' for *prima facie*; and see if you can use a phrase with 'assume' or 'assumption' instead of *a priori*: 'because the roads were icy, it's an assumption (instead of an *a priori conclusion*) that the accident happened because of a skid'.

apropos or à propos *A propos* is French, *apropos* is English. The proper meaning of *apropos* is 'to the point' or 'strictly relevant': 'your comment is apropos'. It is also used to mean 'with reference to' or 'concerning', often followed by 'of', although that's not necessary: 'apropos of the problem' or 'apropos the problem'.

In conversation, *apropos* is used casually, simply to mean 'by the way': 'apropos, she's not coming to the party'. It is better not to use it that way in writing.

Apropos is often pronounced in a slightly French way, with the stress on the last syllable ('appre(r)-POH'), although many people take the stress back to the first syllable: 'APpre(r)poh'. Some current dictionaries show both pronunciations, usually now with a preference for stressing the first syllable.

apt, **liable** or **prone** *Apt* suggests a tendency, not necessarily good or bad: 'he's apt to look in for a drink on the way home'. *Liable* follows the meaning of 'liability' and suggests an undesirable tendency or a risk: 'he is liable to get drunk'; 'we are liable to lose money over this'. *Prone* is used mostly for bad effects on people, rather than on situations or things: 'if she gets wet, she is prone to colds'.

aquaplaning Aquaplaning can be an exciting sport, when you ride standing on a board pulled along by a speedboat, and remain afloat because of the hydrodynamic effect of the cushion of water building up under the board. *Aquaplaning* is also used for a dangerous phenomenon when someone is driving too fast in heavy rain: a film of water builds up between the tyres and the road, so steering has no effect and the car glides uncontrollably.

Arab, **Arabic**, **Arabian** or **Islamic** *Arab* is the word for nearly everything concerning the inhabitants of the Middle East generally; the countries that form the Arab League, including Morocco, Tunisia and Algeria: the Arab world, Arab traditions, Arab politics. . . .
Arabic is reserved mostly now for the script, language and literature of the Arabs. Where *Arabic art* was used at one time, the expression now is *Arab* for secular art, or *Islamic* especially for religious art. For *Islamic* relates to Islam (Arabic for 'submission', that is to God), the religion established by the prophet Mohammed. Islamic art pervades almost all design, from the ornamentation of mosques to illuminated manuscripts to the motifs of wonderful carpets.
Arabian does not occur often now, except in mythology and geographic references to parts of Arabia, the vast peninsula contained partly by the Red Sea in the West and the Persian Gulf in the East: Arabian Desert, Arabian Sea. . . .

arabic numerals These are the numbers we are all familiar with (1, 2, 3, 4 . . .), which replaced **roman numerals** (I, II, III, IV . . .) for most uses in the 12th century. They are based on the Arabic form of numerical notation, but the term can be spelt with either a capital or small *a*.

'ARbitrarily' or **'arbiTRARily'** The approved pronunciation is 'ARbitrarily' (with only the first syllable stressed); but a row of four unaccented syllables is awkward, so the usual American pronunciation, which puts the stress on the third syllable ('arbiTRARily'), is often heard in Britain and is generally accepted, although it's considered a downmarket pronunciation by some. See also **-arily**.

arbitration We may think of *arbitration* as a post-World War II word, but it was used in much the same way as it is now as far back as the early 17th century. But the Arbitration Acts in Britain of 1950, 1975 and 1980 have given *arbitration* a new currency. The 1975 Act gave birth to a new **acronym**, ACAS (pron: 'AYcass'), the Advisory Conciliation and Arbitration Service, a statutory body that is a buffer between trade unions and employers. A willingness or refusal to go to *arbitration* has become a symbol of reasonableness or hardline obstinacy in disputes.

arboretum This is sometimes used wrongly and pretentiously for any wooded area. In fact an *arboretum* describes a botanical garden given over to a collection of rare trees. (Pron: 'ahberREETum').

arcade See **mall** . . .

archaeology or **archeology** *Archaeology* remains the standard British spelling, with *archeology* used in America. But having noted that, the second *a* is being dropped in Britain as well, and *archeology* is already shown by some recent dictionaries as an accepted alternative. See also **ae** or **æ**.

archaisms Archaisms are the linguistic equivalent of pince-nez and high-button boots, words and expressions that are still used although, according to the Oxford lexicographer, Robert Burchfield, they are well past their **'sell-by** date'. Some *hark back* (an archaism derived from an old hunting call) to Shakespeare; others, especially the *-eth* ending, come from the Authorized Version of the Bible (at tea parties with vicars, cups still *runneth* over); some are ancient legalistic doubling-up to make doubly sure, such as 'aid and **abet**', 'let or hindrance'.
Dictionaries may put *arch* after certain words to show they are archaic, but this does not mean we should never use them, for archaisms can sometimes add flavour and poetic feeling to language, as when Bob Dylan sang of 'the times they are *a-changing*'. Snatches of poetry keep old words alive, so even in the 1990s we still echo Kipling's '*lest* we forget', to show our fervour and solemnity. But if we use too many archaisms, we end up sounding like linguistic dinosaurs, out of touch and out of date. See also **yesterday's words**

archetype or **prototype** The meaning of these words overlap: dictionaries define *prototype* as an *archetype*, and the other way round. So there is some confusion, added to because both words are used in different senses. *Proto-* is from the Greek word meaning 'first', and the primary meaning of *prototype* used to be the first or original example of something on which later examples are modelled. In literature, Homer's *Iliad* and *Odyssey* are the prototypal epics that led to other epics, from Virgil's *Aeneid* to Milton's *Paradise Lost*. But the more usual meaning now of *prototype* is for the first or trial model of a machine which can be tested and modified before going into production.
Arch- goes back to a Greek word meaning 'chief' (hence archangel, archbishop, etc), and *archetype* means the principal or primary pattern on which copies are based. *Archetype* is more likely to be used about ideas and principles rather than specific things: Macaulay called the House of Commons 'the archetype of all the representative assemblies'.

Jung adopted the word *archetype* and gave it another meaning to reflect his belief in the timeless and universal inheritance of the human condition. When, for example, on a cold day we sit by a log fire, it is not only the warmth that draws us but the *archetypal* response to a symbol of security (see also **collective unconscious**).

Arctic and **Antarctic**   Most of us do not find ourselves very often talking about the north and south polar regions. When we do, it's worth taking the trouble to pronounce *both* cs: 'ARKtic', 'anTARKtic'.

are (measure of land)   See acre

aren't I?   See ain't

Argentina or **the Argentine**   Both are used for the republic in South America, although Argentina (which the BBC prefers) is taking over as the more usual name. *Argentinians* or *Argentines* can be used for the people, with *Argentinian* as the more usual word. But it's always the *Argentine* (not *Argentinian*) Republic.

-arily   The pronunciation of words ending in *-arily* may present a problem. They are formed from three-syllable *-ary* words, with the stress on the *first* syllable: 'MOMentary', 'ORDinary', 'VOLuntary'. . . . When *-ly* is added and the words become four syllables, keeping the stress on the *first* syllable leads to an awkward flight of unaccented syllables: 'MOMentarily', 'ORDinarily', 'VOLuntarily'. . . . The temptation is to follow the American stress pattern and shift the stress forward to the third syllable: 'momentARily', 'ordinARily', 'voluntARily'. . . . Many people disapprove. The only way out is either to practise keeping the stress on the first syllable, or to recast the sentences, using phrases such as 'for the moment', 'in the ordinary way', 'on a voluntary basis'. . . . But it seems likely that sooner or later stress on the third syllable will become the normal pronunciation.

'ARistocrat' or **'aRIStocrat'**   'If you want to sound like one, you will put the stress on the first syllable: 'ARistocrat'. Stress on second syllable, the usual American pronunciation, is heard increasingly often in Britain, but might not go down so well in the House of Lords.

armed forces   Wars are fought with attacks by land, sea and air forces. 'Military forces' could be taken to mean the army only ('He's in the military' used to be a way of saying a man was in the army). *Armed forces* is the standard collective term that takes in all fighting units.

armed with   If you are going into a meeting you want to be *armed with* all the facts. That suggests you have everything you need to put up a good fight for the case you're presenting. Used in that way, the allusion to weapons is justified. But you also hear people saying

'I'm going to dinner armed with a bunch of flowers'. That doesn't make any sense.

arms control or **disarmament**   The talk after World War I was of *disarmament*. Since World War II, especially after the Strategic Arms Limitation Talks (SALT), 1969–79, *arms control* has become the general expression covering most aspects of arms limitation and the testing of nuclear weapons.

aroma, odour or **smell**   *Smell* is all-purpose and down-to-earth, as befits a word that goes back many centuries, probably to Old English. *Aroma* is more refined, a much later word from the 18th century. *Odour* is somewhere in-between, a more clinical or scientific word, perhaps.

A *smell* can be pleasant or nasty, and is the only one of the three words that can be also used as a verb ('a rose by any other name would smell as sweet'). *Aroma* is more subtle, always pleasant and stimulating: 'the aroma of fresh coffee'. *Odour* is more likely to be used about a chemical or a bad smell ('the odour of formaldehyde'; 'the odour of unwashed feet'), although it can be used about pleasant smells as well, in which case it sounds rather formal.

You can use *smell* or *aroma* in a good sense about food, (*aroma* sounds more complimentary!), but never *odour*. You can use *smell* or *odour* (but not *aroma*), about people but it is offensive, unless you make it clear that's not what you intend ('You smell lovely!').

Smell and *odour* are also used figuratively: 'in bad odour' (meaning unpopular or even in disgrace) and 'the sweet smell of success'.

Remember these words are not used for *wine*, which has a 'bouquet' or a 'nose'. For more about that, see **winespeak**.

around   See about . . .

arouse or **rouse**   These are simply alternative forms with no difference in meaning. Although it comes to the same thing, it sounds self-important to say 'Would you rouse (or arouse) me at 7 o'clock', rather than 'Wake me up at 7'. Music can be *rousing* (but not *arousing*) if it makes you feel alert and alive, but *arouse* (not *rouse*) is used commonly in an abstract way, as a lower-key alternative to 'excite': *arouse* curiosity or suspicion, sexually *aroused*. . . . See also **awake** and **wake**

arse   Most dictionaries say *arse* is 'vulgar' or 'coarse' or whatever other designation is used to discourage our using the word. Listen to Eric Partridge, a distinguished authority on English: 'Arse, an excellent Old English word, is no longer obscene'. Chaucer in *The Canterbury Tales*, uses *ers*, the early English form, with abandon: 'But with his mouth he kiste hir naked ers . . .' (*The Miller's Tale*). But people will argue that everyone knows Chaucer is bawdy.

In the end, you have to decide for yourself whether to sit on your bottom, behind, buttocks or your arse. Americans spell and pronounce the word 'ass' and are generally more relaxed over using it. Nevertheless, for many people, *arse* remains one of the taboo **four-letter words**.

art We go to *art* exhibitions, there is the *Arts Council of Great Britain* and the *Royal Academy of Dramatic Art*, yet it is next to impossible to be clear about what we mean by the word *art*. It is almost a religious word, as it relates to something eternal in the human spirit: Salman Rushdie believes that 'art has taken the place of faith in the secular world' and could be called 'a secular definition of transcendence' (lecture at the Institute of Contemporary Arts, 6.2.1990).

Unless *art* suggests a meditative quality, we are probably misusing the word: the German art historian, Werner Haftman, called Rothko's paintings 'meditation veils', 'tablets of contemplation'. The problem is that if God can be seen 'in a grain of sand', everything around us is material for meditation, so the frontiers of art cannot be drawn. Perhaps the best we can do is to reserve the word *art* for works of human creation that seem possessed of an eternal quality, beyond the nuts and bolts of daily life.

Arts subjects at universities in Britain separate subjects such as literature, history and languages from the sciences (see **humanities**). See also **aesthetic**

art deco and **art nouveau** As both these terms in art history are applied to decoration and ornament, from the design of buildings to table lamps and even ashtrays, they are occasionally mixed up. In fact, art deco was in some ways a natural development from art nouveau.

Art nouveau belongs to an earlier period, the last two decades of the 19th century, and in spite of its French name (which comes from the name of a shop in Paris), found its early expression mainly in London, through artists such as William Morris, Gabriel Rossetti and Aubrey Beardsley, before spreading to other countries in Europe. It is characterized by delicate, some would say decadent, intertwining flowing curves that follow the lines of plants and foliage.

Art deco belongs to the 1920s and started in Paris with the Exposition des Arts Décoratives in 1925. It was the decorative art of the 'brave new world', with angular shapes and geometric patterns to express the modern look, and used the newly developed materials, chrome, steel, aluminium and the synthetics **Bakelite** and **celluloid**. It was *art déco* to begin with, short for *art décorative*, but the accent is now usually dropped in English, along with the original French pronunciation: art historians now say: 'art DEKko'. But *art nouveau* should be pronounced with the best French accent you can muster, roughly 'ahr nooVOH'. Both terms are often spelt with capitals, but the tendency is to use small letters.

artefact or **artifact** Both spellings are acceptable, with *artefact* more usual in Britain and *artifact* in America. Although an artefact can be anything made by human craft and workmanship, the word is mostly reserved for archaeological finds of prehistoric objects.

articles (grammatical) See a or an; the

articulate or **enunciate** As a verb used about speech, *articulate* means pronouncing every syllable distinctly. *Enunciate* has the same meaning, but is used about whole words rather than separate syllables. Both verbs have similar extended meanings for expressing an idea clearly and precisely: 'I have already articulated (or enunciated) my opinion of this matter'.

Only *articulate* can be used as a descriptive word for someone who can speak readily, expressing ideas clearly and without hesitation.

artificial, **synthetic** or **man-made** *Artificial* is mostly used for something that is an imitation of the real thing, often made by hand with considerable skill: artificial flowers, artificial limbs. *Synthetic* suggests production in factories using chemical compounds. Before World War II, *artificial* was used about fabrics (artificial silk, abbreviated to 'art silk' to make it sound better!), but now *synthetic* is used for fabrics such as nylon. Both *artificial* and *synthetic* have taken on pejorative associations and are often replaced by *man-made* which, because it echoes 'handmade', can sound like a good thing. So you may see on a pair of shoes 'leather uppers, man-made soles'. Nonetheless, *man-made* is no more than a commercial variant for *synthetic*.

In passing, the German word, *ersatz* (replacement), has been used in English since the 19th century for an inferior imitation of the real thing. It was fashionable in World War II for available alternatives, such as 'ersatz coffee' (made from acorns and other grains). It is not often heard now, as it is more usual to attach the word 'substitute', which is likely to suggest that the alternative is healthier than the real thing (coffee-substitute, sugar-substitute . . .).

artificial intelligence (AI) In the 1990s we shall hear of artificial intelligence more and more often. But defining what it means is no easier. AI (as it's abbreviated) is part of computer science and information technology. It raises the question of whether machines can think. Behind that is another question, more profound and more important: do humans have independent minds and free will or are they no more than complex automatons 'programmed' in the way that computers are?

In 1990 a chess computer took a game off the former world chess champion, Anatoly Karpov. For some this proved that a machine can be 'intelligent'. Others passionately believe that **microchip** logic is not the same as human consciousness and human understanding, insight and imagination. When we use the words *artificial intelligence*, we may be touching the whole mystery of human existence, or we may use them simply as a convenient way of describing the capacity of computers to solve and relate to complex problems. See also **generation**

artiste *Artiste* (pron: 'arTEEST') is still used backstage for singers and dancers of either sex. But it's an old-style word with the smell of stale greasepaint about it. Producers are much more likely now to talk about 'singers' or 'dancers'.

art nouveau See art deco and art nouveau

art paper This is a technical description used in printing and desktop publishing. It is not very precise, as it can be used about any paper that is smooth-coated and good quality.

arts centre The whole complex of buildings on London's South Bank, including cinemas, theatres, concert halls and an art gallery, is a real *arts centre*. But it has become fashionable for any small local library that arranges an occasional exhibition or poetry reading, suddenly to become – *an arts centre*.

as For a short word, *as* can give a lot of problems, most of which depend upon abstract arguments about how *as* should be treated grammatically. These are the more common difficulties:

1 *as I/he/she/we/they* or *as me/him/her/us/them*? 'You can do it as well as I', 'she does it as well as he' sound too formal for some people, '. . . as well as *me*', '. . . as well as *him*', could be considered ungrammatical because 'can' is understood to follow in each of these examples, and '. . . as well as me can' is obviously wrong. But '. . . as me/him/her/us/them' are used so commonly now, even by good writers and speakers, that the old grammatical objection is losing its force. Whether you conform to 'as I . . .' or relax with 'as me . . .' depends upon how you feel about it.

2 *confused meaning.* 'She loves me as much as Helen' could mean 'she loves me as much as Helen loves me' or '. . . as much as she loves Helen'. Be on guard against this risk of confusion and when necessary spell out what you mean.

3 *as* or *like*? 'She did it perfectly *like* she always does' may not read or sound as good as '. . . *as* she always does'. Although *like* for *as* is used by writers such as Iris Murdoch and Patrick White, it is better for most of us to avoid it.

4 *equally as.* The only thing wrong with this is that *as* is unnecessary and gets in the way: 'both restaurants are equally good' is better than '. . . equally as good'.

5 *as* or *while*? 'As they were shouting, he came into the room' could mean he came into the room *because* they were shouting, or *while* they were shouting. It's all right to use *as* for *while*, but check the sentence to see if there's no risk of misunderstanding.

6 *so . . . as,* or *as . . . as*? Some people are careful to say or write 'he is not so clever as she is' because they think it is preferable to 'as clever as . . .'. Even hardline grammarians accept that there is no need to fuss about this any more: use 'as . . . as' or 'so . . . as', whichever comes naturally.

as and when and **if and when** It is easy to slip into one of these combinations ('we take on extra staff as and when required for handling new business'), even though *as, if,* or *when* alone is perfectly adequate. The only case for *as and when* is if something is going to happen in stages: 'we will warn you of regular increases in costs *as and when* they are unavoidable'.

If and when is sometimes justified on the grounds that *when* on its own implies a certainty that something will happen, and *if* on its own suggests it may never happen. It is doubtful whether anyone is going to work that out, so it is nearly always simpler to choose *as, if,* or *when* according to which comes closest to the intended meaning: 'we take on extra staff as required . . .'; '. . . increases in costs if they become unavoidable'; 'when this bloody war is over'.

as a result of Some people feel *as a result of* sounds more weighty than the simple word 'because': 'as a result of the increased price of petrol, we have to make extra charges for delivery'. 'Because petrol has gone up . . .' hits the nail more squarely on the head.

aseptic See antiseptic . . .

as follows or **as follow** 'The subjects discussed were as follows . . .'. Although 'subjects' is plural and a list of things may follow, it is always *as follows*, never *as follow*. As follows, according to the *OED*, is a detached invariable expression that does not depend on whether what comes before or after is singular or plural.

as from or **as of** *As from* followed by a date ('as from 7 July . . .') indicates a date or a point in time after which something, such as an increase in prices, will take place. *As of* is the exact American equivalent, and has now become more or less standard British English as well. *As of now* sounds like someone in a film trying to act tough. It's better to keep to 'from now' or simply 'now'.

Asian or **Asiatic** *Asiatic* is now usually regarded as a racist word: the direct parallel to European, African, etc is *Asian*, which should be used, except in scientific or geographical contexts, such as The Royal Asiatic Society. See also **Hindi** . . .

aside from See apart from . . .

as if or **as though** There is no difference between these phrases: when preceded by 'not', they both suggest that something is extremely unlikely ('it's not as if – or as though – you are rich'); or they can suggest make-believe ('behave as if you are rich'); or they can suggest that something may well be true: 'you look as if (or as though) you are rich'.

ask or **elicit** See elicit . . .

as of See as from . . .

as possible This is not so much a rule as a recommendation. *As possible* is much more effective when it is placed *immediately* after the noun it refers to. This may seem obvious but is so often overlooked. Compare: 'we should give as much time as possible to develop these new ideas' with 'we should give as much time to develop these new ideas as possible'. The first sentence lays it directly on the line, the second is fuzzy.

as regards   This is often no more than a self-important way of saying 'about': 'As regards your investments, . . .'. If you believe that plain English is best, use 'about': 'About your investments, . . .'.

ass   See **donkey** . . .

as seen on TV   This is at the same time the most sought-after and the most meaningless description tagged on to a person, product, play, film or anything else put in the shop-window for people to buy. There were always people who believed that if it's 'in print', it must be true. The equivalent in the 1990s is *as seen on TV*, which implies that someone or something is important or desirable.

assembly line   First associated with Henry Ford and his Model-T cars, the assembly line has become a symbol of depersonalized production, with workers performing a single mechanical operation, detached from purpose or meaning. If something – or someone – is turned out on the assembly line, it may suggest efficiency, but it could also imply run-of-the-mill uniformity.

assertive   For many business executives, this is considered a good word, suggesting a forceful positive approach from someone determined to succeed. If you are going to 'win that sale' or 'clinch that deal', you have to be *assertive*. At least, that's what they say on management courses. See also **aggressive**

assertiveness   *Assertiveness* courses are now a fashionable part of management training. Aggression and table-thumping are not supposed to be the same thing, because although they may bring about compliance, they do not get people on your side. Assertiveness, we are told, is not projecting our own ego, but getting the right response from someone else.

assess   See **appraise** . . .

asset   An *asset* is anything that is valuable. It is derived from an Old French word and relates to modern French 'assez' (enough). Business has a number of classifications of *asset* that we read about but may not clearly understand. *Fixed assets* are assets, such as a factory and machinery required to run the business. *Current asssets* are variable, such as money in the bank or money owed to the company. *Liquid assets* is the term for anything that can be quickly converted into cash. *Tangible assets* are things you can see and touch, such as equipment. *Intangible assets*,

although they cannot be seen, may be even more valuable, because they include reputation, copyrights, patents and the experience and skill of a company's employees. Shareholders now accept that most businesses are 'people' businesses, where some of the most valuable *intangible assets* go up and down in the lifts each day.

asset stripping   *Asset stripping* was a dirty expression in the 1960s, when financial **whizz-kids** made fortunes by buying up old-established businesses with undervalued **assets**, such as properties. The assets were sold off to make huge profits, after which the business was often closed down or 'rationalized', with no concern for the employees or public interest.

assign or **transfer**   More often than not, *assign* is used for a contractual transferring of rights or ownership. *Transfer* is generally a lighter word for passing over something to someone else: 'transferring a reservation'. A lease, for example, is assigned (rather than transferred) to the person who purchases it.

assignation or **assignment**   There is some overlap in meaning, as both words can be used for the act of assigning something from one person to another. Lawyers prefer *assignment* for legal transfers (assignment of a lease). An *assignment* can also refer to a job of work relegated to someone.
   Assignation is used for a meeting, with the suggestion that it is a secret meeting to plot something. Do not use *assignation* about a meeting between man and a woman, unless you mean to imply that they are secret lovers.

assistant   See **aide** . . .

associate or **partner**   In business, *partner* is a specific statutory definition in Britain under the Partnership Act 1890, and *partners* are usually jointly liable for any debts incurred.
   An *associate* suggests a less formal relationship, and is often used for groups of architects, or senior executives in public relations firms and advertising agents. It may mean someone working full time with the group, although not necessarily one of the owners of the firm, or no more than a specialist who gives advice from time to time.

assonance   See **alliteration** . . .

assume or **presume**   If you remember Stanley's famous greeting after his long search in Africa for the missing explorer ('Dr Livingstone, I presume'), you'll be sensitive to a subtle difference between *assume* and *presume*. We can *presume* something when it is a reasonable conclusion from the evidence in front of us: 'I presume they are satisfied, because they have sent another order'.
   When we *assume* something, there may be no evidence: 'I assume they are satisfied, although we haven't heard yet'.

But we cannot assume that this distinction of meaning is generally accepted, as many people use *assume* and *presume* almost interchangeably. What's more, *presume* is used in a critical way to mean unasked for advice or comments: 'Don't you presume to tell me what to do!'

The above applies equally to *assumption* and *presumption*.

assurance or **insurance** *Insurance* is for an event that may never happen, such as a burglary, accident or loss. *Assurance* pays out money against a certain event, such as death or the expiry of a fixed number of years. Insurance policies are for your car, home, holidays, etc but assurance policies are for your life. This is a technical and unnecessary distinction for most people, who use *insurance* in all cases, which is the way *insurance* is used in America.

assure, **ensure** or **insure** An insurance broker might say 'I *assure* you that I have *ensured* that you are fully *insured*'. That sets out the differences between these words. *Assure* is used from one person to another to mean 'promise' or 'guarantee' (see previous entry). *Ensure* means 'to make certain'. Finally, *insure* is restricted to financial protection through insurance.

asterisk or **star** *Asterisk* comes from the Greek word for 'star', and has been used since the 14th century for a star-shaped symbol to mark words or passages in texts. In fact, *star* is an alternative word, particularly in America: William Safire, who writes a column on language in *The New York Times*, comments, 'It conjures up a vision of an insect hitting my windshield and making a mark that has me looking for a footnote on my dashboard'.

Asterisks and stars are used for various purposes. As Safire mentioned, the most common use is to direct the reader to a relevant note at the bottom of the page. But reference books may also use asterisks for cross-references or for other reasons. This is irritating to readers, who have to remember different meanings of asterisks in different books.

A favourite use is to mark letters left out of **four-letter words** (*f**k*, *c**t*, etc). This thin veil of coyness is no more than hypocritical convention, for readers see the words in their minds.

Both *asterisk* and *star* are used as verbs as well as nouns: 'asterisk (or star) that word' means mark it with an asterisk.

as they say It is a superior attitude to put a slang expression in quotation marks to show you know full well that it is not good English. Another way of doing the same thing is *as they say*: it covers the use of any doubtful form of English and implies that it is not something you would say or write yourself. A BBC sports reporter, speaking to the Liverpool football manager about a player, said 'Saunders came good, *as they say*'. The effect is condescending.

asthma If you pronounce the *th*, it would sound as if you are lisping, because the normal pronunciation is 'ASSma' ('AZZma' in America).

as though See **as if** . . .

astronaut, **cosmonaut** or **spaceman** In Britain and America travellers in outer space are *astronauts*. Astronauts from the former Soviet Union are called *cosmonauts* (adapted from the Russian word, which uses as a prefix the Greek word for an ordered universe).

Some dictionaries make a distinction between *astronaut*, for someone trained to operate spacecraft, and *spaceman* or *spacewoman* (*spaceperson* has not yet appeared) for a traveller in space. But few people, other than editors of dictionaries, would separate the words in that way. See also **cosmic**; **space travel**

astronautics See **aeronautics** . . .

astronomical At one time *astronomical* was used only about the ancient science of astronomy, the study of celestial bodies. Then it was adapted to mean enormous numbers or distances. Then it was corrupted, so that a 10 per cent salary increase has been described as astronomical. When *astronomical* is used to compare something to the vastness of the universe, the amount of money, quantity, distance or whatever should at least be truly large.

astronomy or **cosmology** *Astronomy*, said to be the oldest exact science, is the study of the sun, moon, planets and stars. *Cosmology* treats the universe as a whole, and seeks to explain, with hypotheses such as the **big bang** theory or steady state theory how the universe came into being. *Astronomers* observe the stars and the planets: *cosmologists* are physicists and mathematicians, who try to solve the riddle of the universe through equations.

at call A business term that means the same as 'on demand': money is lent or deposited to earn interest on condition that it can be called on at any time, without notice.

at hand See **hand**

atheist See **agnostic** or **atheist**

athletics is or **are** Usually athletics *is*. Athletics in Britain covers track and field sports, but in America *athletics* is often used for any kind of sport. See also **-ics**

at it If you say that a couple were *at it*, nearly everyone will assume you mean they were making love. For more notes on this coy euphemism, see **make love**

atmospheric *Atmospheric* relates to atmosphere. But the word is also used in a vague way about music or art to suggest it has an emotional effect. To describe a concerto or a painting as 'very atmospheric' is almost meaningless, since this could apply to all music and art.

atom See **electron** . . .

atomic or **nuclear** The bomb that was dropped on Hiroshima, 6 August 1945, is referred to as the first *atomic* (or *atom*) bomb. But long since then, bombs, warheads, missiles involving *nuclear fission* (the splitting of the nucleus of an atom) or *nuclear fusion* (the fusion of light atoms to form heavier atoms) have been called *nuclear weapons*. *Atomic physics* deals with the structure of atoms; *nuclear physics* studies the central core of an atom, the nucleus, which contains most of the mass and the positive charge of energy.

Atomic and *nuclear* are close enough in meaning for it not to matter much, outside specialized contexts, which word is used. The United Kingdom has an Atomic Energy Authority and a Nuclear Installations Inspectorate; the United States has an Atomic Energy Commission and a Nuclear Regulatory Commission. But for most general purposes, *nuclear* has almost superseded the word *atomic*: the CND (Campaign for Nuclear Disarmament) was formed in 1958, nuclear reactors provide nuclear energy for power stations, nuclear waste has to be disposed of, and a nuclear war remains a threat.

Nuclear should not be pronounced as three distinct syllables ('nu-clee-ar'); instead pronounce the second part of the word the same as 'clear'.

at par See **par**

attempt . . . see **try**

at this moment in time and **at the end of the day** It is fashionable to criticize *at this moment in time* as a pretentious way of saying 'now' or 'at present'. Yet good writers and speakers like to use it occasionally because it has a certain cosmic ring to it. Why not use it, when it seems appropriate? But not so often that it becomes boring. The same applies to *at the end of the day* which, at the right moment and in the right place, has a quiet biblical flavour about it.

attitude, opinion or **taste** Our *attitude* is based on our personality, experience and prejudices. It is the right word to use when an opinion is firmly held. An *opinion* is not inborn but more a result of reflection. *Opinion polls* are sometimes called *attitude surveys*, since they reflect spontaneous answers to questions, rather than thought-out conclusions.

Opinion should always imply some thought (a *considered opinion* suggests a good deal of thought): an *attitude* may be based on reflection, but can also be no more than a **knee-jerk** reaction.

Taste is somewhere in between. It suggests the way we feel about something, just as our taste in food is personal. For example, the way we dress is largely a matter of taste, that is dependent on our feelings about it. When we say something is in *bad taste*, it is not an objective comment but an expression of our own feelings. What's more, a concept of bad taste changes: we are used now to accepting more open sexual scenes in plays, films and on television than before the 1960s. *Bad taste* can be a narrow-minded comment, or a snobbish observation reflecting what we feel is the right way to dress or decorate our homes.

attorney In Britain this can mean a person, not necessarily legally qualified, empowered to act and sign documents in legal and financial matters on behalf of another, who has given them *power of attorney* by executing a written deed. In America, *attorney* is often used for any qualified lawyer, especially when pleading on behalf of a client in court, usually the role of a **barrister** in Britain.

attractive *Attractive* of course means 'something which attracts', but has now lost its power and is a noncommittal word used about almost anything – a woman, a man, a restaurant, an idea . . . . It suggests that someone or something is pleasing or interesting, but it doesn't go overboard. *Attractive* is a useful standby, when you are not particularly impressed, but need to say something pleasant. See also **interesting**

at your convenience There is a story of someone offering to meet a man *at your convenience*, only to be told 'Oh, but I don't have a regular public lavatory!' (*convenience* is an old-fashioned euphemism for a lavatory). That puts *at your convenience* in its place as stuffy **business English** for 'as soon as you like' or 'whenever it's possible'. As for *at your earliest convenience*, what's wrong with 'as soon as possible'?

au fait or **au courant** Both these French expressions are used in English and often confused, because the meanings are similar. *Au fait* means 'informed' and is usually followed by 'with': 'I'm au fait with the arrangements that have been made'. *Au courant* stresses being up to date: 'I'm au courant with the new arrangements'. Both phrases have been used in English for so long, that the pronunciation is usually only an approximation of the original French, roughly: 'ohFAY', 'ohcooRAH(N)'.

au pair See **maid or servant**

Aussie This was a friendly name for Australian soldiers in World War I. Australians do not seem to mind it in any way, and it's now internationally recognized as a casual way to describe all things Australian, even 'Aussie wine'. It is pronounced with a *z* sound: 'OZZie'. See also **Oz**

Australian English There are no significant differences between the *written* language in Britain and in Australia. But when it comes to speaking, the gap is much wider. Spoken English in Australia has a roughneck energy about it. Australia began as a penal colony, with many of the early settlers speaking cockney English, and the echo of London vowels still resounds in the Australian accent.

Outside their own country, many Australians used to have a sense of inadequacy because of the way they spoke: a director of education in New South Wales commented in the mid-1920s that Australian English was a 'variation from the accepted standard . . . harsh, unmusical and unpleasant'. Even by the 1940s, Arthur Delbridge, an Australian professor of linguistics, tells us that the Australian Broadcasting Corporation preferred Englishmen as announcers.

All that has changed. Australian culture is more confident of its own roots. Australian theatre and films have had international success. Australians travelling to Europe are as self-assured linguistically as Americans. Professor Delbridge confirms that linguistic decisions in Australian broadcasting are now referred to an Australian dictionary rather than a British one. For Australians, their language in the 1990s is not a substandard form of English, but has its own standards and place alongside British English. See also **New Zealand English**

authentic, genuine or **real** These words are used interchangeably at times. *Authentic* is the strongest, and may even suggest proof or authority that something is genuine: perhaps it is safer to buy an 'authentic antique' than a 'genuine antique'! *Real* seems lower still down the scale of authenticity: it would be reassuring to know that a 'real antique' is authentic, or at least genuine. It is only fair to add that some people, including antique dealers, might claim all that is splitting hairs.

Genuine rhymes with 'feminine', never with 'swine', unless you are trying to be funny, and even then it's a tired old joke.

author See **writer** . . .

authoritarian Although this was a neutral word once, meaning a belief in the principle of authority, it now nearly always carries with it the meaning of tyrannical, rigid, prejudiced and opposed to individual freedom of action.

authority 'I have it on good authority' is too often used to give credibility to a statement. It should usually be countered by the question '*Who* is the authority?'. An *authority*, in this sense, should always be someone who can claim knowledge in depth: 'good authority' can be misleading, unless you know just how good the authority is.

auto- *Auto-*, from the Greek word for 'self', is a guide to the meaning of many words in English. Most of these were hyphenated, but now nearly all *auto*-formations are treated as one word: autoimmune, autopilot, autoradiograph. . . . A hyphen is usually preferred for a few combinations, such as *auto-erotic* and *auto-suggestion*.

autograph See **manuscript**

automated or **automatic** Both words are used about an appliance or machine that functions by itself, without anyone having to 'press the button' at each stage. *Automated* tends to be used for something on a larger scale, a manufacturing process or a factory controlled by computer technology. *Automatic* is used about even modest domestic appliances, such as a kettle that switches itself off when the water is boiling. And when people do something *automatically*, they do it spontaneously, without thinking about it.

auxiliary verbs See **verbs**

avant-garde See **experimental** . . .

average or **mean** It may be surprising to be told that many people are not immediately aware of the difference between *average* and *mean*. The *mean* is a midway figure between the highest and the lowest of a series of numbers: the mean of 10, 30, 50, 80, 100, 150 is 80, exactly halfway between 10 and 150. The *average* is all the figures added together and then divided by the number of figures: in the above example, there are six figures, with a total of 420. When that is divided by 6 (the number of figures), it comes to an average of 70, which is not, of course, the same as the mean.

It is worth remembering that a casual reader might well take *average* and *mean* to be the same. For that reason, unless you are dealing with statistics, or technical and scientific matters (when a calculation of the mean might be required), it is safer to work out the average, and use that word.

averse See **adverse or averse**

aviary See **apiary or aviary**

avuncular *Avuncular* was borrowed in the 19th century from Latin 'avunculus' (uncle). But it is used now, not about a real uncle, but to describe how any good uncle should behave, a kind, friendly, hand-on-shoulder approach. You don't have to be anyone's uncle any more to be avuncular. Aunts come off rather badly, because there is no corresponding word for them. Nor can a woman be avuncular: the nearest she can get to it is 'motherly', which conveys a different feeling.

awake and **wake** These ordinary words cause so much confusion that we can sympathize with Irving Berlin singing 'Oh how I hate to get up in the morning!' Were you *awakened* by the alarm clock, *awoken* by it, or *awoke, awaked, waked, waken, woken* or *woken up*? Any one of those versions could be justified, although some would sound odd and others would be criticized by grammarians. No one should object to *awakened, woken* or *woken up*.

Wake (or *wake up*) is the everyday verb: 'Quiet! You'll wake the baby' (only a heavily committed grammarian would 'waken or awaken the baby'). When you want an early call, you can say 'Wake me (up) at 7'. Or, if you prefer the grand manner, 'Awaken me at 7'. If it's all too much for you, just ask to be 'called'.

aware The normal use of *aware*, usually followed by 'of' or 'that', means informed: 'she is aware of the disagreement', or 'aware that there is a disagreement'.

A trendy use of *aware* is to suggest someone is enlightened, in tune with life, or with a particular situation: 'she's a very aware person'; 'he is politically aware'. There are mystical teachings that extend the meaning of *aware* even further, to suggest a higher state of consciousness. Some people feel these extended applications of *aware* are overdone and overused, nor are they recognized by all recent dictionaries. See also **consciousness** . . .

awful and **awfully** For over a hundred years these two words have been going downhill. At one time they related to 'awe' and were solemn and transcendent. But even for the Victorians, missing a train could be 'an awful nuisance' or a party 'awfully jolly'. We have to live with 'Thanks awfully'. There is no point any more in giving either word its powerful and portentous meaning, as no one would understand you.

At one time, 'AWfly' (two syllables) was an affected pronunciation, but it is now standard, more often heard than three syllables ('AW-ful-ly').

axis Mussolini did not make many contributions to the English language, but he did extend the meaning of *axis*: in a speech on 1 November 1936, he described the alliance of Fascist Italy with Nazi Germany as the *Axis*. This has become one of the accepted meanings of *axis* – an alliance between two or more countries that share a common objective or policy.

aye This **archaism** (in its earliest use, spelt *I*, probably to signify 'I agree') survives in parliament: when the 'yes' votes are in the majority, members are informed 'The ayes have it'. When voting takes place in some societies, they go in for 'All those in favour say Aye'. *Aye* was also a traditional response to an order in the Navy: but in the 1990s, it would sound odd to hear a sailor, ordered to launch a cruise missile, respond 'Aye aye, Sir!'

a year or **per annum** See **per**

· B ·

-babble, **-spiel** or **-speak** We can attach these to a number of words to describe a specialized jargon or a way of speaking (**Eurospeak**, **psychobabble**, etc). For further notes on this, see **-speak** . . .

babysitter An importation from America that has become as indispensable as 'teapot', and like that word, there is no need to hyphenate it, although it still appears that way in some dictionaries.

back burner or **on hold** Not all the latest dictionaries have caught up with *back burner*, although it has become a widely used expression in business and politics for something that is put on one side for future attention, instead of getting active consideration or action: the *Financial Times* has written about a company facing takeover as 'keeping competing bids on the back burner'. It's an expression that comes straight from the kitchen: you keep something you're frying at the front of the cooker and something that's stewing on a back burner.

Other than in the kitchen, a good alternative expression is 'keep it on hold'.

background At one time *background* was mostly used in art and photography for the setting or scenery behind the real subject. But *background* has moved more and more into the foreground, as a useful multi-purpose word: someone's background is their family, education, career; the phrase 'people with (or from) different backgrounds' usually refers to their position in society and is a welcome alternative to the uneasy word 'class'; 'the background of a problem' means all the facts leading up to it; 'against a background of . . .' means in relation to something that is specified.

Like other useful words, *background* can be used too often to avoid taking the trouble to think of a more precise expression, which might be 'experience and training', 'alongside' or 'in relation to'.

backlash In the 19th century *backlash* was used only about machinery to describe a sudden recoil when something goes wrong. Although it can still be used with that meaning, and some dictionaries give this as the only meaning, *backlash* is much more likely to be used now in social or racial situations, to describe a violent **knee-jerk** reaction against a change or a movement: we have read about the 'anti-gay backlash', 'the reactionary backlash in South Africa against the abolition of **apartheid**'.

backlog A useful word, borrowed from America, where its literal meaning is a large log put at the back of the fireplace to keep the fire going. It still has the meaning there of something in reserve, so an American businessman is happy to have a backlog of orders. In Britain, *backlog* has taken on a negative meaning, usually implying a pile up of work due to strikes or other problems. In America, you look cheerful about a backlog; in Britain, you have a long face.

backpack, **rucksack**, **knapsack**, **haversack** or **kitbag** *Backpack* is taking over from *rucksack*; it deserves to because 'back' is a much more familiar word than 'ruck' (from the German word for back). *Knapsack* and *haversack* belong more to the past than to the 1990s. But if you're in the army, you can still 'pack up your troubles in your old *kitbag*', which is different: it's a long cylinder of a bag, humped about on the shoulder, rather than carried on the back.

backup, **back-up** or **back up** *Backup*, as one word (or sometimes with a hyphen, but less often now), is a *noun* for technical support in handling new equipment, or moral support for an argument or principle, or (in computer language) the copy of data kept for security in case the original is lost.

Back up, as two words, is a *verb* for giving moral support (as above), or making a copy of data stored in a computer.

backward or **backwards** In London you are more likely to walk or look *backwards*: in New York they usually prefer to go *backward*. But for describing something, *backward* is more usual: a backward look, a backward movement.

bacteria See germ . . .

bad or **badly** The proper grammatical distinction requires *bad* to be used with nouns (the big bad wolf) and *badly* with verbs (he drove badly). But *bad* is usually preferable with the verb 'feel', especially in relation to health ('she feels very bad after the operation'). And when a verb can be replaced by 'am', 'is' or 'are', *bad* is also used: 'it looks bad'; 'things seem bad'. . . . Because of this, there is a tendency to use *bad* with other verbs as well: 'I want it bad'; 'they didn't do so bad'. . . . This might pass in casual conversation but it would be out of place in writing or a serious discussion.

bad debts   A *bad debt* is the traditional term in accountancy for money that is owed but is not going to be paid or recovered, because whoever owes it has gone bankrupt, has no resources – or has left the country in a hurry.

badlands   The term *badlands* has become more familiar in Britain as an environmental term. It was originally used about the barren tracts in South Dakota (the Bad Lands). As one word (without capitals), *badlands* is now used about any vast area of land that is impassable and cannot be cultivated.

bad language   *Bad language* has a double meaning. For most people, it means obscenities, **four-letter words** and milder words that children are told not to say in front of visitors. For a few schoolteachers and linguistic purists, bad language can be a **split infinitive**, beginning a sentence with **And**, or anything else that does not accord with their notion of what *good* English should be.

Both these concepts of bad language are subjective, based on a personal view of English, which others might disagree with.

badly or **bad**   See bad . . .

bad taste   See attitude . . .

bag   See handbag . . .

bag lady   The expression arose in the 1980s, when there were pictures on television of the homeless in London. A *bag lady* is a woman who lives out of plastic carrier bags which contain all her worldly possessions, or at least everything she needs for the day. The poet, Elizabeth Jennings, says she lives out of carrier bags, and Candida Crewe entitled an article about her 'Bag Lady of the Sonnets'.

bail or **bale**   There is no problem when you're *saying* these words, because they both sound alike, but in writing they can get mixed up. One of the sources is 'baille', Old French for a bucket, so it's logical to *bail* out water from a boat, yet an alternative spelling, with the same meaning, is *bale*. It is more usual to *bale* out from an aircraft with a parachute, but that can also be spelt *bail*. If it's a bundle of hay or other things, there's no choice – it is always *bale*. Lastly, it has to be *bail* for the security against the temporary release of someone who is waiting trial for an offence – and *bails* for the crosspieces over cricket stumps.

bail bandit   The expression came to the surface in early 1992, and it looks as if it is here to stay as one of the law and order problems of the 1990s. Kenneth Baker, Home Secretary at the time, spoke in the House of Commons about a 'crack-down on bail bandits'. He defined them as men between 17 and 20 who commit crimes while on bail.

Bakelite   This word is little used now, and many young people wouldn't have heard it, because it has become replaced by 'plastic'. Older people may still call any form of hard plastic *bakelite*, because that was one of the first synthetic resins. It should, in fact, be spelt with a capital B because it is a registered brand, named after Leo Baekeland, who invented it in 1908.

balance of nature or **ecological balance**
Balance of nature is the emotive term for the essential harmony of the basic elements of the Earth necessary for it to remain a stable, self-renewing system. *Ecological balance* is a more scientific term for the same concept. Whichever term is used, and it depends upon the audience and the context, the issue is central in the 1990s, as factors, such as pollution and **global warming**, may cause irreversible changes.

balance of payments or **balance of trade**   These are indicators of a nation's economic position. The usual meaning of *balance of payments* is the two sides of a country's trade with the rest of the world: money coming in from exports and so-called invisible earnings (services, shipping, tourism, etc), against money going out to pay for imports and other needs.

Balance of trade, a term that goes as far back as the 17th century, is the part of balance of payments dealing specifically with goods, excluding services and other factors: it is the difference between the value of imports of manufactured goods and raw materials, and corresponding exports.

In Britain, it is the balance of payments figures that are awaited anxiously each month. If more money has come in than has gone out, there's a *balance of payments surplus*, and the stock market has a good time; if it's the other way round, there is a *balance of payments deficit*, and if that is bigger than expected, there are long faces in the City.

balance of power   The principle of preserving peace because leading nations retain more or less equal military power goes back to the Greek city states. It dominated European politics for a long period, and was given a brief new life after World War II, in the cold war between the USSR and the US with its Western allies. But before long, it was clear that the term was outmoded, and a new phrase came into being, *balance of terror*, suggesting that nuclear capacity, leading to fear of retaliation by the other side, is the only effective deterrent.

balance of trade   See balance of payments . . .

balding   As well as saying that a man is becoming bald, *balding* carries with it a hint that he is showing his age and the stress of the job he is doing.

bale   See bail . . .

balk   See baulk . . .

ballgame   A ball game (two words) is any game played with a ball, which could include cricket. But *ballgame* is as American as popcorn, for more than anything else it means baseball. *Ballgame* also has an extended meaning, that was lively to begin with but has become a tired, worn-out cliché for a situation, project, or circumstances: 'it's a whole new ballgame'; 'that's a different ballgame altogether' . . . .

ballot box   Politicians feel it is trendy and democratic to use *ballot box* to mean a general election: 'Let the ballot box decide'; 'We'll leave that to the ballot box'.

ballpen, **ballpoint** or **biro**   For a long time it looked as if the Hungarian inventor, Laslo Biró, had achieved linguistic immortality. He invented the *ballpoint pen* with its own quick-drying ink supply in 1938, and for many years all *ballpens* were called *biros*. But this has become dated, as other kinds of pens have been developed, such as felt-tip pens and rollerball pens. The generic name for these is a *ballpoint*.

balls   It is difficult to know whether this 5-letter word comes into the **four-letter word** category. Even the most formal of men would hardly refer to his 'testicles'. A reporter on *Today*, the most popular BBC radio news programme, describing an effigy in a religious festival, and hooked on **alliteration**, said it had 'an erect penis and bulging balls'. No one telephoned to complain. A recent Oxford dictionary tut-tuts over *balls-up*, classifying it as 'coarse slang', yet it is used to mean a complete mess of something by so many people, including David Watt who, as director of the Royal Institute of International Affairs, said 'Harold Nicolson and Lord Robert Cecil felt that the great men were making a fearful balls-up, as indeed they were.' If someone makes a balls-up, it does not seem seriously offensive to say so in almost any company.

Balls, meaning rubbish or nonsense, can offend many people. Others use it freely as a way of writing off a stupid comment: 'What if a critic construes a poem in a way you felt you didn't mean?' asked John Haffenden, interviewing the poet Philip Larkin. Larkin replied, 'I should think he was talking balls.'

balmy or **barmy**   Apart from their literal meanings (*balm* – something that is soothing, *barm* – the froth of fermenting yeast), these friendly words have been in use interchangeably since the 17th century to mean slightly mad or daft (in this sense, the spelling *barmy* is more common). The most literate people use them that way, even in writing sometimes, so it seems barmy that some dictionaries, although not all, still regard them as 'slang'.

baloney   *Baloney* (also spelt *boloney*), the American slang word from the 1920s for rubbish or nonsense, was popular for a while in Britain. No one is sure of its origin: a 'bologna', used in America for a kind of sausage of smoked meats, is as good a suggestion as any.

Baloney is a middle-aged expression now and it would be surprising to hear young people use it. But it still comes naturally to an older generation: when Barbara Bush was told about the suggestion that the cost of running the White House was excessive, with its domestic staff of 40, including five florists and five calligraphers for writing 'personal' handwritten notes, her comment was 'Oh, baloney!'

banana skin   An expression that has become standard on the political scene, to describe awkward slip-ups, or bungling in handling a situation. See also **own goal**

Band Aid   *Band Aid* has replaced 'flower power' of the 1960s as a symbol, this time of practical compassion, among millions of young people, cutting across bureaucratic indifference to famine in Africa. Bob Geldof, the rock musician, gave birth to Band Aid in 1984, bringing together international pop musicians, who raised over £100m (much of it through the hit record 'Do They Know It's Christmas?') for famine relief in Ethiopia. (*Band Aid* works as a pun in America, where the term is used for a sticking plaster.)

bandit   Those who know that it comes from the Italian word 'bandito' might say 'banditti' for a gang of robbers. But that would be showing off, as nearly everybody says *bandits*.

bandwagon   In America a *bandwagon* is the cart at the head of a parade, carrying the band, which literally drums up support. To 'jump or climb on the bandwagon' began as a colourful American expression, meaning to join something when it is well under way and going well. The expression was too useful for the British not to jump on the same linguistic bandwagon and 'get in on the act' (which means exactly the same).

banger   It's easy to see why an old car that rattles along should be called a *banger*, and it's a good word for it. But no one has come up with a convincing reason why a sausage should also be a *banger*.

banister or **handrail**   How many people know a *banister* is strictly one of the uprights supporting a *handrail* along the side of a staircase? For most of us *banister* (more usually *banisters*) means the handrail as well as the uprights, or the handrail on its own: it's impossible to slide down uprights, but we slide down the *banisters*. It sounds as if it should be spelt with two *n*s, which is an alternative spelling but not the more usual one.

Banister is used only for indoor staircases; *handrail* can be used for indoors or outside.

bank clerk, **manager** and **official**   *Bank clerks*, who used to be behind open unprotected counters, were always men, steady types who stayed in the same branch for years and were regarded by the rest of the community as established as civil servants.

The term has disappeared, replaced by the common-sense name *cashiers*, working behind toughened-glass security screens, with much the same role in people's minds as assistants in shops.

Anyone working for a bank could at one time call themselves a *bank official*, which carried a certain status. That term has gone too. Banks are now money shops in the high street, doing their best to attract customers like any other shop. Even some *bank managers*, formerly a revered title, now call themselves *branch managers*, although this has not become general yet.

Is there anything left that we can bank on? See **bank on something**

bank draft or **banker's draft**   These are inter-changeable terms, and everyone involved in international trade knows all about them. But to others the terms may be obscure. A bank draft or a banker's draft is a cheque written out by the bank itself, on which payment is guaranteed.

banker's order   See **standing order** . . .

bank holidays   See **public holidays** . . .

bank manager   See **bank clerk** . . .

bank on something   Can we use *bank on* any more to mean rely on something, without thinking twice about it? The notion belongs to the time when banks looked imposing and solid, austere marble halls. Now they look more like social clubs, chatty and friendly, and the sobriety of earnest **bank clerks** in dark suits has given way to laid-back teenagers, with pin-on badges telling us they're 'Tracey' or 'Suzie' or 'Brian', who count out banknotes with casual indifference. As **Disgusted, Tunbridge Wells** might ask, if we cannot bank on banks any more, can we bank on anything else?

bank paper   *Bank paper* sounds as if it should be thick and impressive, paper you can **bank on** to give a good impression. In fact it is the reverse: bank paper is generally lightweight paper used for file copies.

bank, **base** or **minimum lending rate**
Bank rate used to be *the* bank rate, the declared rate of interest charged by the Bank of England. Since 1972, the term has been officially replaced by *minimum lending rate* (most often referred to as MLR), still fixed by the Bank of England, which affects the interest we all have to pay when we borrow money from a bank or building society. But financial institutions are slow to change their terminology, and *bank rate* still comes up at times, to refer to the MLR.

The equivalent in America to MLR is the *discount rate*, which operates in much the same way.

Base rate is what you are more likely to hear from a bank manager when you want to borrow money. It changes with MLR, but is set by the main banking groups, which arrange loans at a specified percentage

'over base rate', depending on particular circumstances. In this way base rate serves as a point of reference. Before 1971, base rate was a common standard agreed between the major UK banks, but since then each banking group sets its own base rate. The American equivalent is *prime lending rate*.

bankruptcy or **insolvency**   These are connected but they do not mean exactly the same. Someone or a business is *insolvent* if they cannot pay their debts, although given more time, they might be able to find the money to do so. *Bankruptcy* is more final, a legal adjudication by a court that there is no likelihood that the debts can ever be repaid in full. A dramatic extension of *bankruptcy* is when it is used about someone or an organization to suggest that they don't stand a chance of finding the qualities necessary to achieve something ('bankrupt of ideas'). See also **belly-up** . . .

barbaric or **barbarous**   To the ancient Greeks, a barbarian was someone who could not speak Greek, who spoke a language that might, as Philip Howard has suggested, have sounded to them like the bleating of sheep ('baa-baa'). Hence *barbaric* has come to mean uncivilized in style and manner, extending for some people to mean brutal and cruel: 'his treatment of her was barbaric'. Less commonly, *barbaric* is used to mean unspoilt and primitive, especially about art.

Although there is a tendency now to equate it with *barbaric*, *barbarous* is a much more severe word and can never have good connotations: it can only indicate extreme cruelty and harshness. Classical scholars, aware of the Greek origin of the word, will sometimes use *barbarous* about crude or clumsy use of English, and might say of a writer 'he writes barbarously'.

barbecue   *Barbecues* are so fashionable on patios in suburban stockbroker belts, that it's surprising to discover that the word in English, with much the same meaning, goes back to the 17th century. It comes through Spanish from a Haitian word for a framework of sticks. It is used for any open-air cooking, although usually of meat or fish, but there is at least one cookery book about vegetarian barbecues. The spelling 'bar-b-q', as in 'bar-b-q flavoured crisps', meaning spicy, is supermarket jargon cashing in on a trend.

bar chart and **pie chart**   Both are part of the language of business and other presentations. A *bar chart* is a visual way of comparing different sets of figures, such as sales of competing products. Vertical rectangles or bars, drawn to the same scale, are arranged side by side, so different values can immediately be related to each other.

A *pie chart* (or *pie diagram*) uses a circle representing a pie, divided up into slices showing how various ingredients make up the whole. For example, personal capital might have segments of different sizes showing what proportion should be in equities, fixed interest, building societies or kept available for emergencies.

barcode First developed in the 1960s, barcodes belong to computer terminology, although we see them all around us: they are the irregular black and white zebra stripes on the back of this book jacket and on almost everything else we buy anywhere in the industrialized world (they are called *universal product coding* in America). Barcodes contain information such as price and product codes which are 'read' at checkout counters by a **light pen** or other scanning system, linked to a computer. The computer instantly records the information, providing data for stock control and other records.

One problem is that barcodes stick out like a sore thumb and designers try to tuck them away, making it difficult for clerks and cashiers to 'machine-read' them. So in 1991, the Paris Ecole Supérieure des Arts Graphiques was called in to turn barcodes into abstract art. One day, perhaps, we shall see these designer barcodes on packaging in supermarkets: they are called, in an untranslatable French pun, *codes b'art*.

barely, **hardly** and **scarcely** People sometimes forget that these three words are already negative, meaning 'almost without' or 'almost none', so we should avoid a second negative creeping in: '*without barely* a sound, he left', 'I couldn*'t hardly* hear him', '*scarcely no* one understood'. Those should be: 'with barely a sound . . .', 'I could hardly . . .', 'scarcely anyone . . .'. See also **double negatives**

bargain On the Stock Exchange, any transaction, whether it is buying or selling shares, is called a *bargain*. That's as may be, but whether buying shares is a real bargain or not depends upon what happens to the stock market.

barmy See **balmy** . . .

baroque or **rococo** It is easy to be confused about *baroque* and *rococo*, because they are both used about elaborate or excessive decoration in design and architecture, both are also used about music, and *baroque* is extended to literature and to contemporary situations.

Up to the 19th century, *baroque* could mean grotesque, even absurd, and in some contexts there remains an echo of that earlier meaning. But when it is used about art or architecture, it is a description of a style, usually without implied criticism. The style is European, roughly between late 16th and early 18th centuries, characterized by ornate and extravagant design, yet with control and a sense of unity. Outside art criticism, *baroque* is applied to something that is tortuous and over-complicated, such as baroque politics or a baroque novel.

Rococo (pron: 're(r)COHcoh') could be described as a degeneration of baroque style in 18th-century France, decoration for the sake of decoration, without relating to the whole. But art historians are now more likely to use *rococo*, without the negative suggestion that it is overdone, about elaborate design using whirls and curls (*rococo* is associated with the French word 'rocaille' for fancy rockwork or shellwork).

Used about music, both are chronological labels: *baroque* from about 1600 up to the deaths of JS Bach (1750) and Handel (1759), with *rococo* from the mid-1700s up to the deaths of Mozart (1791) and Haydn (1809).

As general terms, it is reasonable to use *baroque* about any richly ornamented design using curves and flourishes, and *rococo* in much the same way, when shell patterns come into it.

barrage The particular use of *barrage* as a military term for concentrated gunfire has been usefully adapted to a verbal attack, such as a *barrage* of questions or a *barrage* of criticism. Because the word looks French, it is sometimes wrongly given a French stress pattern: 'barRAGE'. But the stress in British English should be on the first syllable: 'BARRage'. (American English moves the stress to the second syllable.)

barrel or **cask** You can roll out either a *barrel* or a *cask*, as they are both shaped like a cylinder, usually bulging in the middle, and they can both contain beer. But a *barrel* should be made of wooden staves, secured by metal hoops round them, whereas a *cask* could be made of wood, metal or even plastic. And a barrel (not a cask) can designate a specific measure of capacity, as in the oil industry, where the price of crude oil is quoted by the barrel, measured as 159 litres.

barrister, **advocate** or **counsel** The usual word for a person admitted to plead at the Bar in England or Wales is *barrister*. The equivalent in Scotland is *advocate*. But this more descriptive word is sometimes heard in the legal profession in England: the legal press has carried at least one advertisement from a firm of solicitors for 'a qualified advocate', so the solicitors can set up their own advocacy department.

Solicitors don't talk about 'getting a barrister's opinion'. They say 'We must take *counsel*'s opinion on this'. When a barrister is appointed to senior rank, they become a *Queen's Counsel* (QC) or *King's Counsel* (KC). QCs wear silk gowns in court, hence becoming a Queen's Counsel is known as *taking silk*. Finally, barristers are far too lofty to be 'employed' by whoever is paying them: they are 'retained'. See also **attorney; jurist; lawyer**

-based A hyphen should always be used when *-based* is added to the name of a city or a country where an organization is located: 'A Swiss-based corporation', 'the Brussels-based committee', 'the London-based institute'. . . . This indicates that the corporation, committee or institute may be international or, for that matter, British, American, Italian, etc, and simply located in a particular country or city.

base rate See **bank rate** . . .

bases When this is the plural of *base* it is pronounced 'BASE-iz'; when it is the plural of *basis*, it is 'BASE-eez'.

basic or **fundamental** The words are interchangeable and it is a matter of taste, or perhaps context, which one is used. They both relate to words meaning 'foundation'. *Basic* is a 19th-century formation from 'base', which is something that gives support from underneath or is the foundation of a structure. *Fundamental* is an older word with the same meaning, but more applicable to abstract ideas: 'the fundamental requirements of a sound economy'. This is more a question of style, than a rule.

Used about religion, *fundamentalism* is an extended meaning of the word (see **evangelical** . . .).

basis 'On the basis of . . .', 'on a something-or-other basis' and other such phrases using *basis* are usually roundabout expressions that are better avoided. Compare 'we shall charge on the basis of the amount of time the work takes' with 'we shall charge according to how much time it takes', or 'the new product is available on a strictly limited basis' with 'supplies of the new product are strictly limited'. Dropping the *basis* phrase makes the sentences more straightforward.

basket of currencies No one puts currencies in a basket. But a *basket of currencies* is often used, instead of a 'range of currencies', to show a broader value of sterling (or any other currency) by relating it to several currencies instead of just to, say, the US dollar or the German mark. See also **ECU** . . .

bastard and **illegitimate** A woman who wants the experience of motherhood but rejects the convention of marriage would rightly turn on someone who called her child a *bastard*. As far back as 1984, statistics in the UK showed that one in five babies in England and Wales was born to an unmarried mother. The figure is much higher now, especially if it includes babies born to parents who live together but are not formally married. The words *bastard* and *illegitimate*, to describe a child born outside legal marriage, are no longer acceptable, belonging as they do to a system of social values that many people do not accept. This feeling about using the word in that sense is underlined, because *bastard* is a term of abuse, often racial abuse. According to Jenni Murray, who presents the most famous of all radio programmes for women, *Woman's Hour* on the BBC, 'There is a strong argument for remaining an unmarried mother. There's no stigma any more.'

bathos See anticlimax . . .

battered wives and **babies** The expression *battered babies* appeared in medical journals in the early 1960s for babies subject to continual violence. It was later extended to *battered wives*, which evokes a dramatic picture of women with black eyes and bruises: it uncovered the human problem that has always existed of women exposed to violence by their partners. *Battered mothers* is an expression coming over the horizon, for mothers beaten up by their teenage sons.

battery or **broiler** These are both intensive methods of breeding chickens for eggs or meat.

Battery hens are kept in tightly packed cages, with collection of eggs automated. Broiler chickens are for producing poultry meat: they supposedly have more freedom, because they are not in cages, although they are also housed indoors under crowded conditions. Both systems are a near industrial approach in the way the birds are treated to produce food.

baulk or **balk** Some recommendations say *balk* should be used for the *verb* (meaning a drawing-back or refusal to do something: balk at tackling a problem), and *baulk* for the *noun* (a roughly-squared heavy wooden beam). But this is too fine a point, as both words are used for both meanings, with *baulk* the more usual spelling.

BBC See **Beeb**

BBC pronunciation See **pronunciation**

BC See **AD**

bear, bull and **stag (as Stock Exchange terms)** In pubs and restaurants near the Stock Exchange you hear comments such as 'The market was *bearish* this morning', 'How long can the *bull* market go on?', 'The *stags* are out!', We are told that *bear* comes from bear hunters making sure there is a market for the skins before going out shooting. On the Stock Exchange *bears* sell shares, often ones they have not yet paid for, because they expect the market to fall, so they can buy them back at a lower price. *Bulls* are investors charging in to do business, buying shares because they expect the market to rise. *Stags* (animals inclined to cut and run) are investors who buy shares in a new issue, intending to make a quick sale and a quick profit.

bearskin or **busby** The Guards call their ceremonial fur hats *bearskins* and it is offside to call them *busbies*, even if it does mean much the same thing.

beat Jack Kerouac, the American novelist, gave *beat* its post-World War II meaning in the phrase 'the beat generation', young people who turned their backs on social conventions and looked for a meaning in life through **Zen**, jazz, unrestrained sex and drugs. But *beat*, in that sense, like the beat generation, has middle-aged spread and is one of yesterday's words.

Beaufort scale See **blizzard** . . .

beaus or **beaux** You might hear 'ma belle' in French about a beautiful woman (*Beauty and the Beast* is *La Belle et la Bête*) but no one says 'mon beau'. *Beau* came into English after the Restoration (1660) and became used for a 'lady's suitor', the courtly 18th-century equivalent of boyfriend. It has survived in America, where some girls still talk about their *beau*, and then the plural would be *beaus*. But no one in Britain would be likely to use it.

In fact almost the only use of *beau* is in *beaux arts* (always with an *x*).

because There are two possible problems with *because*:

1 In a negative sentence, *because* can be ambiguous: 'She didn't marry him because he was rich' could mean 'She married him, but not because he was rich', or 'Because he was rich, she did not marry him'. When necessary, rephrase the sentence to avoid a risk of misunderstanding.

2 *Because* has a way of edging in when it is not required: 'the reason is because he is rich', 'one value of power steering is because it makes parking easier'. Leave out *because* and those sentences work just as well, or even better: 'the reason is he is rich', 'one value of power steering is it makes parking easier'.

bed and breakfast The Stock Exchange has made a takeover bid for this time-honoured welcome displayed on boards outside farmhouses in Britain. A *bed and breakfast deal* is when shares are sold one day and bought back a day or two later, usually to take advantage of capital gains tax allowances during a tax year.

Beeb People who have something to do with the BBC sometimes show they are 'in the know' by calling it the *Beeb*. This is rather like referring to Lawrence Olivier as 'Larry', implying an intimacy that might or might not have existed.

beer See ale . . .

before long See soon . . .

begrudge or **grudge** As verbs, *begrudge* is usually followed by a word that represents a person or something a person possesses, while *grudge* is usually followed by a word that represents an action or a condition. 'I begrudge him his success'; 'she begrudged John his happy marriage'; 'she begrudged his happiness'. But 'I grudge paying so much money for dinner'; 'she grudged giving him dinner'.

beg the question If someone says 'that begs the question', they may well mean that you have not given them a straight answer or have evaded the question. But *beg the question* does not mean either, as many people suppose, it means to reach a conclusion on the basis of an unproven assumption: 'The plan will fail because of his misguided policies.' That begs the question, unless you have proved the policies are misguided. See also **leading question**

behalf See on behalf of . . .

behove If you don't mind talking like a character in a Victorian novel, you can still use this word but it must always be preceded by 'it': 'It behoves you to take care how you speak to me'; 'It ill behoves you to speak to me like that'. It's less starchy to put it this way: 'You should be careful how you speak to me'; 'You shouldn't speak to me like that'. Americans spell it *behoove* and pronounce it that way. See **archaisms**

beige, **buff** or **fawn** They all mean a light brown colour: *beige* is lighter and has a yellowish tinge, while *fawn* has a greyish tinge, the colour of a fawn, a young deer, which is unlikely to be around when you want to make the comparison. It is oversubtle to work out the difference between *beige* and *buff*. It is more a matter of use: buff envelopes are usually the ones that contain bills; beige is more usual for women's clothes, buff for men's, but even that may be putting too fine a point on it.

Beijing or **Peking** Of all the new designations of place-names proposed by the United Nations, Beijing and Peking remain the most inconsistent in use. *Peking* is the traditional British name for the capital of the People's Republic of China, the name still used in most atlases and encyclopedias. *Beijing* (pron: 'bayDJING') is the transliteration of the Chinese name. The Foreign Office have taken *Beijing* on board, but Chris Patten, Governor of Hong Kong, favours *Peking*. The BBC officially use *Beijing*, while newspapers vary, some staying with *Peking*. See also **foreign place-names**

Being or **being** A *being* evades clear definition: it is generally considered a living thing that has intelligence and self-consciousness, not an animal but not necessarily a *human being*, in the sense that we understand that, because there could be beings in outer space.

With a capital B, *Being* belongs to existentialism, which could be called the philosophy and psychology of existence in the world. In this mystical sense, *Being* is the reality of an individual's existence to himself or herself and his or her relationship to the world. If we are to use *Being* to express these ideas, we need some familiarity with the thought of Kierkegaard and Sartre.

Being is sometimes used for 'being alive': 'What is the purpose of being (or Being)?' is another way of asking 'Why are we here?'

belly or **stomach** Raymond Postgate once wrote in *The Listener* about having to enter a low doorway by 'crawling on one's stomach'. He was accused of 'vulgar gentility' in a letter from a schoolmaster in Ramsgate, who added 'the *stomach* is an internal organ: what Mr Postgate means is "crawl on one's *belly*" '. Postgate apologized for his 'mealy-mouthedness', explaining he thought readers might not like the word *belly*. Gosh!

It is many years since any dictionary classified *belly* as vulgar. It is a good Old English word and useful too, because it includes the outside of the body and the internal organs as well, whereas *stomach*, as the schoolmaster pointed out, refers to one specific internal organ. So if anyone should criticize you for saying you have a *bellyache* or have had a *bellyful* of anything or anyone, the best thing to do is to have a *belly-laugh*.

(go) belly-up, **go to the wall** or **go bust** When a business *goes belly-up*, it goes bankrupt, a graphic description for it summons up an image of a dead fish floating upside down. The expression has been common in America since the 1960s at least. During the recession of the early 1990s, *belly-up* made a bid to cross the Atlantic to become part of the jargon of **business English** in Britain, as an alternative to *go to the wall*, or *go bust*, the down-to-earth term favoured in news programmes when listing companies going out of business.

(see) **below**   See **see above** . . .

below par   See **par**

benchmark and **hallmark**   Originally a benchmark (a symbol which looked like this: ↑) was cut by a surveyor in a wall or a pillar as a reference point for height above sea level, or a mark against which all other measurements of height were calculated. The term *benchmark* is now used for the standard against which the output of individual workers in the same industry is assessed, in computer technology as a reference point for comparing the performance of computers and related equipment. It is also used as the criterion for assessing quality and standards: 'How much money you make is not the benchmark for success as a human being'.
The statutory meaning of *hallmark* (Hallmarking Act 1973) is a mark made on gold, silver or platinum that guarantees its standard of fineness. The meaning of the word has been extended in two ways. In the 19th century it became used for the characteristic feature that marks out a special quality in a person or a concept: the hallmark of genius, the hallmark of great art. . . . It was also used for the design or emblem that represents a company or a brand: 'the company uses a lion as its hallmark'. This second use has been discarded: the word now is **logo**.

bended   See **bent or bended (past forms)**

benign and **malignant**   In medicine *benign* is used for an abnormal growth of tissue that is not cancerous. The opposite can be *malign*, but *malignant* is much more usual in a medical sense (*malign* is a more general word to mean malevolent or evil).

bent or **bended (past forms)**   The past form of the verb *bend* is *bent*, with only one exception: we go down on our *bended* knees.

bent and **straight**   Be wary of the slang use of *bent*, because it has *two* meanings. The older meaning is to be corrupt or dishonest. The second meaning, recognized by recent dictionaries, is to be homosexual. In the 1990s the second use is widespread and is taking over from the earlier slang meaning, so there is a risk of awkward misunderstandings. *Straight* is used as the opposite of both these senses:, as well as meaning honest, it is used by homosexuals about heterosexuals. In San Francisco married men and women are known to call themselves 'married straight couples'.

Be warned that 'to be straight' can mean different things to different people.

benzedrine   See **amphetamine** . . .

bereaved or **bereft**   These past versions of *bereave*, a verb that is rarely seen in the present, are used in different ways. 'I shall be *bereft* when you are gone' means I shall miss you very much when you have gone away; 'I shall be *bereaved* when you are gone' means I shall have lost a relative or a friend when you are dead. For *bereaved* is used about death; *bereft* about being deprived, sometimes of an abstract quality, when it is followed by 'of': 'bereft of hope', 'bereft of comfort'. *Bereft* can also stand on its own: to be utterly or totally bereft is to feel you have lost everything.

Berkeley   If you are listening to a nightingale in Berkeley Square, London, pronounce it 'BAHKley'. For students at Berkeley, the main campus of the University of California, the first syllable rhymes with 'Ber' in Berlin: 'BERKley'. (Ironically, it's named after the Irish philosopher George Berkeley, pron: 'BAHKley'.)

Bermuda Triangle   The *Bermuda Triangle* covers a vast area of nearly four million square kilometres between Bermuda and Puerto Rico, an area in which many ships and aircraft have disappeared without trace. Reasons given for these vary from mundanities, such as the great depth of the sea and exceptionally strong currents, to little green men from Mars and the site of Atlantis. . . . But the expression has been used in other contexts for a disaster that completely engulfs a person or an organization. When Norman Lamont presented his first Budget in March 1991, a political writer commented 'It has got the government out of the Bermuda Triangle of the poll tax'.

berserk   You can go *berserk* over the pronunciation of this word, as there are seven different pronunciations that could all claim to be acceptable. It is better to single out the one that is generally felt to be the most usual: 'berZURK' (second syllable rhyming with 'Turk').

BES   This abbreviation, born in the 1983 Finance Act, is often used in financial advertisements in newspapers. The Business Expansion Scheme was introduced to help small businesses to set up or expand by obtaining finance from private investors, who are allowed tax relief on the money they put in, up to certain limits.

beseeched   See **besought** . . .

beside or **besides**   *Beside* when it means alongside: 'I'll walk beside you'; 'put it beside me' . . . and if something is not relevant, it's 'beside the point'. *Besides* when it means 'as well as': 'Besides paying for dinner, I paid for the taxi'.

besought or **beseeched**   To beseech someone to do something is almost to beg them to do it. If it happened in the past, then you *besought* them (which is the more usual form) or *beseeched* them.

best before   See **sell by . . .**

better   'A better class of people live in this road' is bad English, as well as being snobbish. For *better* compares one thing with another: 'this is better than that'. 'A good class of people live in this road' is still snobbish but at least it's good English.

between or **among**   Many people and even some grammar books maintain that *between* should only be used about *two* persons or things, and that when there are more than two, *among* must be used. The *OED* contradicts this: 'In all senses, *between* has been, from its earliest appearance, extended to more than two . . .'. So if you want to divide a bill *between* all six of you, the *OED* gives you the green light. In fact, *between* is the only way to show how one thing relates to a number of other things individually: 'There is an understanding between Britain, America and France'.

Between also conveys the idea of separating, whereas *among* suggests right in the middle of, which is why we talk about 'putting the cat among the pigeons'.

Note also that *between* is a choice between one thing *and* other things, not 'or' other things: 'We have to decide between going to Florence *and* (not "or") going to Rome'.

between you and me   See **I or me**

bewitched or **hexed**   *Bewitched* is the normal word in British English: you are more likely to hear *hexed* in America, although *hexed* was used in a review of Arthur Miller's *The Crucible*, in *The Independent*, perhaps because it's a play about witchcraft in America.

bi-   *Biannual* means twice a year and there's no problem there. But *bimonthly* and *biweekly* (the hyphen is now usually dropped) can be taken to mean either every two months, every two weeks *or* twice a month, twice a week. So it is better to say what you mean: every two months, twice a month. . . . There is no problem over *bilateral* which always means two-sided: a bilateral decision. See also **biennial**

biased or **biassed**   It depends upon the **house** style of the publisher: some (such as Macmillan and Oxford University Press) prefer *biased*, others insist on *biassed*. Dictionaries leave us with the option, usually with a preference for *biased*. See also **focused**

bicycle   See **cycle . . .**

bid or **offer**   We *bid* for something at an auction, that is we *offer* a certain price. In the business world, either *bid* or *offer* is used for the price one company is prepared to pay to buy out another. *Bid price* has been adopted in unit trust investments to describe the price at which a unit trust management will buy back units, always a lower price than they *offer* to sell them. In everyday use, we're more likely to make an *offer* if we want to buy something below the asking price (although 'make a bid' would come to the same thing).

For the past form of *bid*, you still hear 'I *bade* him farewell': *bade* sounds curiously formal or pompous, as bid is the usual form.

bidet   In the 1990s this standard piece of French bathroom equipment is becoming well-known on the other side of the English Channel, yet there are still English plumbers who are embarrassed by the whole idea.

'Bidet' is French for a pony: the bathroom equipment has the same name because, it was said in an early 19th-century dictionary, 'ladies . . . bestride it like a French pony'. The pronunciation remains discreetly French, 'BEEday', but in the plural the *s* is sounded.

bid price   See **bid . . .**

biennial   *Biannual* is twice a year (see **bi-**) but *biennial* is every two years. The name of the famous international art show in Venice, which takes place every two years, is the *Biennale* (pron: 'bee-enNAHLay'). For *biennial* in the horticultural sense, see **annual**

Big Apple   Back in the 1930s jazz musicians used *apple* for a northern city in America (after the name of an animated dance). So for people in show business, and many outside it, New York remains the *Big Apple*, implying excitement, agitation, lights and action.

big band   Anyone old enough to remember Glenn Miller and his music of the late 1930s and 40s knows the *big band sound*. *Big band* is not used for symphony orchestras, but is reserved for large groups of musicians playing arranged jazz and popular dance music.

big bang   *Big bang* was originally used for the disputed theory of the origin of the universe, primordial matter at millions of degrees of heat exploding into the galaxies. The words have come to be applied to any momentous happening. The deregulation of the London Stock Exchange in October 1986, doing away with all restrictive practices, was called the *Big Bang* (with initial capitals). In 1990 newspapers described the government's plan to open up the television system as the 'big bang for TV'.

Big Brother   *Big Brother* was George Orwell's concept (in his nightmare vision, *Nineteen Eighty-Four*) of an all-powerful dictator, made to seem benign, whose control extended to every aspect of his subjects' lives: wherever they were, whatever they were doing, 'Big Brother was watching them'. The idea caught on and *Big Brother* is used about anyone who has too much authority, in school, in a company, in a family. . . .

Big deal! See deal

Big One *Big One* is fashionable earthquake language for talking about the major earthquake that may follow earlier earth tremors. As a result any development, from a stock market trend to an advertising campaign, might, or might not, be the Big One.

bike See cycle . . .

bikini This is the only happy by-product of nuclear experiments. Bikini is the atoll in the Pacific where the US staged an **atomic** explosion in 1946. A clever designer fastened on to the name to suggest the explosive effect on a man of a woman wearing such a minimal swimsuit, and *bikini* crossed every frontier to become an international word. When **topless** bathing for women arrived in the 1960s, *monokini* was tried, a brave if bizarre attempt to throw in a Greek prefix on the false assumption that the *bi-* of *bikini* meant 'two'. But it never caught on, so we are left with *bikini bottom*.

bill (American and British usage) If you've just had dinner in a New York restaurant, and ask the waiter for a *bill*, it's just possible he might think you are demanding a dollar. For Americans, *bill* means first of all a banknote, such as a ten-dollar bill. In the States, when you want a bill for something you've bought, it is better to ask for a *check*. In Britain you pay a *bill* with a **cheque**, although Americans might say they're paying with a *bill*. In America you could pay a *check* with another *check* (American spelling of cheque), if you don't have enough *bills* on you . . . it's all a matter of using the right words in the right place.

bill or **account** See account . . .

billboard See hoarding . . .

billboard art Admen have for some time claimed that advertising is an art form, especially when it is on posters. But an advertising poster does not exist in its own right: its job is to convey an urgent message – *Buy it!* – and its success depends on that alone.

In the 1990s, a new art form, or rather a new way of exhibiting art, appeared. The BBC Billboard Art project was launched: artists were commissioned to use space on poster sites donated by one of the leading hoarding companies. These were not selling anything, but opened exhibition space for contemporary artists in the streets of a number of cities.

See also hoarding . . .

billion and **trillion** *Billion* was always a *million million* in Britain, but a *thousand million* in America. The American definition has taken over in newspapers and as the first definition in recent dictionaries, so generally people will assume *billion* to mean a thousand million.

Trillion used to mean a *million million million*, but has taken over the old meaning of *billion*, so that it is now used for a million million.

bimbo As long ago as the 1920s *bimbo* was used in New York as a contemptuous word for a man, and by the late 1920s *bimbo* became slang for a prostitute. The word did not make much of an impression on British English until the 1980s. In Britain, although *bimbo* does not suggest a prostitute, it is not a complimentary word, even if it does derive, as is possible, from the friendly Italian word 'bambino', for a child. Kate Saunders, reviewing Keith Waterhouse's novel, *Bimbo*, in *The Sunday Times*, offers a definition: 'A big pair of tits and a brain the size of a chick-pea'.

bio- This Greek prefix, for life or living organisms, is part of the formation of an increasing number of words, and guides us to their meanings. *Biolinguistics*, still to find a place in most dictionaries, is a new branch of linguistics that studies the conditions necessary for man to develop the use of language. *Bioengineering* is the use of mechanical organs, such as an artificial kidney, to replace parts of the body that are not functioning. *Biochemistry* dates from the late 19th century and is a science that deals with the chemical processes affecting substances present in living organisms. *Biotechnology*, a much more recent formation from the 1960s, is **high tech**. It is applied *biochemistry*, that develops therapeutic agents, such as human growth hormone, substances to counter Aids, cancers and other disorders, as well as biological processes in industry, such as the manufacture of packaged food and wine-making. The trend is for the hyphen to be dropped between *bio-* and the following word, even when the latter begins with a vowel (*bioengineering*).

biodegradable Although included in dictionaries since the early 1980s, not many people were familiar with this word until the last years of that decade, when the **green** movement hit the headlines. *Biodegradable* means capable of being decomposed through the action of living organisms, such as bacteria.

For a long time, industry in every country treated the world as a vast free rubbish dump (See **industrial waste**), ignoring the problem of plastic packaging that remains inert for thousands of years. There are two alternatives. One is to use materials that can be recycled to slow down the pile-up of waste. The second is to use biodegradable materials that break down within a few days into harmless substances. An example is a biodegradable ballpen developed in Germany, with a casing made of cardboard that rots away naturally when it's discarded. See also **green**; **recycle**

biological parents See natural parents . . .

biological or **chemical weapons** These were the horrifying threats hovering over the Gulf War of 1991. *Biological weapons* employ dangerous microorganisms, such as the smallpox or anthrax viruses. *Chemical weapons* employ poison gas and other toxic chemicals to kill or disable people and pollute food and water.

biosphere   With the prediction that the population of the world will rise to more than 8 **billion** by the year 2025, the word *biosphere* is tipped to be in the news. It combines **bio-**, from the Greek word for life, and *sphere*, the Latin word (derived from Greek) for globe, and means the part of the surface of the Earth and its atmosphere that supports living beings.

birdie   We hear *birdie* in golfing commentaries. It seems that a certain A H Smith, playing at Atlantic City in 1903, holed out in one stroke under par, and declared, 'That was a bird of a shot'. Since then, a *birdie* is a score of one under **par** at any hole – with the imagery taken further with *eagle* (2 under par) and *albatross* (3 under par).

biro   See **ballpen** . . .

bisexual or **hermaphrodite**   *Hermaphrodite* comes from Greek mythology: according to Ovid, Hermaphroditos, the son of Hermes and Aphrodite, became joined in one body with the nymph Salmacis. *Hermaphrodite* is used (as well as *bisexual*, the usual term) in zoology about organisms having both male and female reproductive organs, or in botany about plants with both stamens and pistils in the same flower.

Unless you are a zoologist or a botanist, *bisexual* is the word you are likely to use, applying it to a man or a woman who finds persons of either sex physically attractive, and enjoys both heterosexual and homosexual eroticism. See also **unisex** . . .

bistro   For the French, 'bistro' (or 'bistrot') used to be the owner of a small café, then the café itself, at that time simple and inexpensive. Bistros in Paris are still usually simple, but sometimes now as a deliberate style, in which case they are no longer inexpensive. In London, some bistros (the alternative spelling 'bistrot' is not used in English) opened after World War II, and to begin with these were simple friendly French restaurants, serving simple food at low prices. But that has changed, and in the 1990s a bistro in Britain is likely to offer sophisticated food at equally sophisticated prices. See also **trattoria**

bit   You can make a bit of a fuss about this innocent word. To start with, some people claim that to use *bit* for 'a small amount' (a bit of cheese, etc) is slang. Others say that *bit* should only be used for solids and not for liquids, (a bit of cheese, but not a bit of wine). Everyone seems happy to talk about 'a bit of trouble' or 'a bit of a fuss'. If you're a bit worried about it, keep to the solids not liquids usage, or if you want to be even safer, ask for a 'small piece' of cake or whatever it is. If you think it doesn't matter a bit, go on using *bit* in whatever way comes naturally. But remember that *bit* is not always an innocent word: 'a bit of fluff' suggests a woman who is open to sexual advances; 'a

bit on the side' is extra money that someone is not entitled to.

bit (computer term)   See **byte**

bitten or **bit**   Whether you've been *bitten* or *bit* it's just as unpleasant, but grammatically it is better to be bitten: 'I've been bitten' (not 'I've been bit').

bitter-sweet   These seemingly contradictory words, usually linked together by a hyphen, are most familiar for dark plain chocolate that appeals to extremes of our taste buds. The *OED* tells us it is 'sweet with an admixture of aftertaste of bitterness'. More profoundly, the double sense of *bitter-sweet* weaves its way through the sound and fury of the human situation, from a love affair, to making love, to triumph, to getting old. The experience is universal and archetypal, and long ago Chaucer used the expression in the *Canterbury Tales* (about 1387). In passing, the French reverse the order ('douce-amère').

biweekly   See **bi-**

black or **blacken (as verbs)**   *Black* is used more about the actual colour, so we *black* shoes or *black* a grate. *Blacken* is used less specifically to suggest that something has become dark or dirty: the sky *blackens*; the walls were *blackened* by smoke; a person's character can be *blackened*.

black or **coloured**   *Coloured*, as a racial generalization, always suggested the disparagement of **nonwhite** and is associated with **apartheid**, as the official designation by the South African government for persons of mixed race. *Black* was at one time not liked by black people in America, until the proud and assured use of it in the late 1960s, when Martin Luther King launched a campaign with the slogan 'Black is beautiful'. Then *black* went beyond skin colour, to identify common cultural and life experiences that set black people apart from other groups. Since then *black* has replaced *coloured*, a word which should be avoided as a description of people.

Black is usually written without a capital, because many blacks feel that a capital B sets it aside from 'white'. But there are blacks who prefer the assertion of *Black* as a stronger symbol of their identity.

In the 1990s, there is a tendency for some American blacks to call themselves *African-Americans*, although blacks remains the generally accepted name.

black comedy or **black humour**   Jean Anouilh called some of his plays 'pièces noires' (black plays), which led to the literary term *black comedy*. This takes a painful or tragic story and focuses on the funny side, so we find ourselves laughing at something that would normally shock us or evoke our sympathy. The underlying attitude is essentially despairing, a loss of faith in humanity. Many things in life are tragicomic, so *black comedy* has slipped into use about everyday situations which are sad but present themselves in a way that makes us laugh.

Black humour is deliberately callous and spiteful, a rejection of compassion. It is sometimes called a **sick joke**, because it distorts human values. *Black comedy* reflects a philosophical attitude towards life; *black humour* displays cruelty.

Black days Any day of the week can be a *black day*: *Black Thursday* (24 October 1929), the beginning of the Wall Street crash that led to the Great Depression, *Black Monday* (19 October 1987), the major post-World War II slump on the New York Stock Exchange, *Black Wednesday* (16 September 1992), when the pound slumped out of the exchange rate mechanism. *Black Fridays*, in particular, have become so common (because it's the end of the working week and often a day when economic statistics are published) that we read about *black fridays*, without capitals. Any Friday can be a black friday, if it is the end of a week when things have gone badly wrong, and the political editor of *The Sunday Times* mixed it up with the shooting season, writing about the 'government facing a brace of black fridays'.

black economy This covers a wide range of buying and selling goods and services which are illegal because they involve tax evasion (see **tax avoidance**). It could be someone cleaning windows or someone offering a high level of professional service, so long as it is paid for in cash, because the *black economy* functions on a strictly cash basis, so that nothing passes through a bank, except maybe a Swiss bank account.

blackleg See **scab** . . .

black power It was given the force of initial capitals – Black Power – when it was used in the 1960s for the fight for civil rights and political power for **black** people, by the Black Panthers and other organizations. Black Power still means action to support those rights, but it is also written now with small letters as an assertion of black cultural identity, rather than a threat to the political order.

black tie, **dinner jacket** or **tuxedo** *Black tie*, which is downgraded by at least one recent Oxford dictionary as 'informal', is printed at the bottom of some of the most formal invitations as an indication that men should wear a *dinner jacket* or, to give it a truly informal name, a *DJ*. *Tuxedo* (pron: 'tuxSEEdo') has been the American equivalent since the late 19th century, named after a country club in Tuxedo Park, New York State, where presumably men had to dress for dinner.

blank cheque and **carte blanche** A *blank cheque* is not altogether blank: it has a signature on it, but no sum of money is written, so any amount could be filled in by whoever the cheque is payable to. And there is a useful extension of meaning: if someone is allowed to spend as much money as they like on a project, they are 'given a blank cheque'.

By further extension, giving someone 'a blank cheque' can be giving them complete freedom of action in a situation. That is the same meaning as *carte blanche*: this is French for a blank sheet of paper, usually (like a blank cheque) bearing a signature, so that anything written on it is authorized. When we give someone *carte blanche* (without 'a' in front), we give them freedom to act as they wish.

blanket . . . Because a blanket covers the whole bed, the word is used in an ever-increasing number of situations to express the idea of total coverage: a *blanket agreement*, usually in industrial relations, would apply to all firms in a particular industry; *blanket acceptance* is acceptance of all conditions or of all the facts in a report or statement; *blanket bombing* drops bombs over a wide area, rather than selecting specific targets. . . . But a *blanket bath* reverts to the literal meaning of *blanket*: it is an all-over wash given to a patient in bed.

blasphemy or **obscenity** *Blasphemy* (and *blasphemous*) should be restricted to the vulgar or coarse use of sacred words and names, especially God or Mohammed. But the violent conflict of opinion over Salman Rushdie's novel, *The Satanic Verses*, demonstrated there is not always agreement about what is blasphemous. There is even more disagreement over *obscenity*, which means coarse sexual language or pictures: it is defined by law as tending. '. . . if taken as a whole . . . to deprave and corrupt . . .' (Obscene Publications Act 1959). But only courts have the authority to make decisions about that. For the rest of us, it's 'all in the mind'. See also **obscene**; **pornography** . . .

blatant or **flagrant** *Blatant* was first used by Spenser in *The Faerie Queene* (1596) to describe a 1000-tongued monster, but this meaning of harsh insistent noise has almost disappeared, although we can still talk about 'a blatant salesman', meaning that he wouldn't stop talking. Generally, *blatant* and *flagrant* have become so similar in meaning that it is difficult to put a whisker between them: they both mean something is glaringly wrong, with no attempt to hide it: 'a blatant (or flagrant) misuse of public money'.

bleed The technical application of *bleed* in printing, which means to take an illustration to the edge of the paper, has moved into more common use: *bleed* is the instruction given when a photograph is to be printed with no border.

bleep At the beginning of the 1950s, an edgy high-pitched sound made its electronic debut. No one knows who first put together the word *bleep* as an imitation of the sound: perhaps it was picked up from 'blip', an earlier word for a sharp blow or popping sound.

Bleeps are an ever-increasing part of life in the 1990s: **answerphones** order us to 'Please speak after the bleep', computers bleep at us when they reject instructions, **pagers** bleep to summon us to the telephone. A *bleep* is the standard electronic equivalent of *Ready!*, *Lookout!*, *Not on your life!*, or *Oi!*

blessed In church, *blessed* usually has two syllables: the bless-ed saints, 'bless-ed be Thy name'. . . . Outside church, it is usually one syllable (he is blessed with good health), although when it comes just before a noun, two syllables are usual: a bless-ed occasion. So you have to be careful every *bless-ed* time you use the word *blessed*.

blimp and **blimpish** See **Colonel Blimp**

blitzkrieg In German *blitzkrieg* means 'lightning war', an all-out campaign aimed at overwhelming the enemy. *The Blitz*, the name given to the German air raids on London in 1940, might have been the wrong use of the word, but it sounded right, and *blitz* has survived, as a noun and a verb, for an intensive attack: 'blitz the kitchen', 'a blitz on the paperwork'. . . . It is notable that *blitzkrieg* was not used about the coalition's air attacks on Iraq during the 1991 Gulf War, perhaps because the associations were uneasy.

blizzard, **cyclone**, **gale**, **hurricane**, **tornado** or **typhoon** Storms have different names in different parts of the world, with the English word for them sometimes adapted from what they are called in the local language. Taking them in alphabetical order, a *blizzard* is a strong wind and a snowstorm occurring at the same time, with a blinding effect (hence a *blinding blizzard*). The origin of the word is obscure but it may be an imitation of the noise made by snow whipped up into the air.

A *cyclone* is essentially a centre of atmospheric low pressure caused by wind blowing in the same circular direction as the rotation of the Earth (anticlockwise in the northern, clockwise in the southern hemisphere). It derives from a Greek word meaning the coil of a snake. Cyclones give rise to violent winds in tropical areas.

Gale is a general word for any high wind. It goes back to the 16th century and no one knows how it arose. For meteorologists to talk about a gale, the wind has to reach a speed of at least 50kph (approx 32mph).

A *hurricane* is a cyclonic storm where the wind reaches at least 122kph (approx 76mph). They are more common at sea but when they pass over land, they cause major destruction. Although the word has been used about exceptionally high winds in Britain (such as the storms in 1987 and 1991), *hurricane* is the term usually reserved for such storms around the Caribbean Sea and the Gulf of Mexico, which can affect the Florida peninsula. The name, which also goes back to the 16th century, has its source in Spanish and

Portuguese words. Hurricanes, when they occur in the midwestern United States (and in some other parts of the world), are called *tornados*, also taken from a Spanish word.

A *typhoon* is a word for a hurricane that occurs in the China Sea. It derives from Chinese words meaning 'big wind', and has existed in English since the 16th century.

A British admiral, Sir Francis Beaufort (1774–1857), brought order into these various terms for storms, by classifying winds in terms of their speed. His name deservedly lives on, as it is regularly mentioned in weather forecasts for shipping. The *Beaufort scale* starts at 0, for a virtually windless day, to 12 for winds over 65 **knots** (approx 75mph).

bloc or **block** It is awkward that both *bloc* and *block* exist in English. *Bloc* is used for an alliance of political parties or governments: before the break-up of the Soviet Union, the *Communist bloc* or *Eastern bloc* described the USSR and all its **satellite** countries under communist rule. In most other cases (see, for example, next entry and **block vote**), *block* is the normal spelling.

block, **hang-up**, or **inhibition** *Block*, meaning a psychological or emotional impediment that prevents someone doing something or even thinking about it, goes back to American psychoanalytic **jargon** of the 1930s. *Hang-up*, meaning more or less the same, came later and is usually classified by dictionaries as slang or 'informal'. This is too conservative, since psychiatrists have been known to use *hang-up*, even in writing, and it is an effective expression for a block that impedes us from getting on with something.

In general use, an *inhibition* means the same as *block* or *hang-up*, but psychologists would usually restrict it to something that stifles the normal expression of an instinct. So in ascending order of formality, we should feel free to use *hang-up*, *block* or *inhibition* in much the same way. But that age-old affliction that most writers suffer from at one time or another is always called a *writer's block*.

blockbuster In London during World War II, *blockbuster* came into use as the name for a huge bomb dropped from German aircraft and capable of destroying a whole block of buildings. But it has only one use now, which is for a novel that sells a million, or for a film or musical that makes a million.

block or **card vote** At a trade union conference, *block* (occasionally *bloc*) *vote* describes the principle under which one delegate's vote has a value in proportion to the number of members the delegate represents. A handful of delegates may therefore be empowered to cast many thousands of votes. When the delegates vote by holding up a card on which is marked the number of voters they represent, it is called a *card vote*. The terms really mean the same.

bloke Nowadays a woman is more likely to say she is going out with a 'feller' rather than with a 'bloke'.

Bloke was a low-class word until about 1900, and then later on it became fashionable. But it has a dusty unused look about it now.

blond or **blonde** The title of an old Marilyn Monroe film was *Gentlemen Prefer Blondes*. Arbitrarily English has taken over the French masculine *and* feminine forms, so that fair women are *blondes* and fair men are *blonds*. This has not happened to **brunette**.

bloody On the 11th April 1914, Mrs Patrick Campbell, playing Eliza Doolittle in Bernard Shaw's *Pygmalion*, caused a sensation at the first night with the line 'Walk! Not bloody likely! I am going in a taxi'. A bishop demanded that the play should be banned and the Women's Purity League delivered a protest to 10 Downing Street. In the years since then, *bloody* has become almost as inoffensive as 'dear me'. As for *bloody-minded*, meaning deliberately obstructive and unhelpful, nearly everyone uses it anywhere. The literal use of *bloody* to mean 'covered in blood' is almost lost, unless the context makes it clear ('a bloody handkerchief'). See also **ruddy**

bloomers *Bloomers* were part of the women's liberation movement of the mid-19th century and were originally loose pants gathered at the ankles. Amelia Bloomer, an early American feminist, recommended them to free women from long cumbersome skirts. Her name will live on for ever, even if *bloomers* is only used now as a joke.

blooming When **bloody** was still considered an outrageous word, *blooming* was a polite substitute. But we have moved on to much stronger expletives, so *blooming* has reverted to its proper meaning, back in use at the Chelsea Flower Show.

blouse or **shirt** Unisex fashion has forced common names on women's and men's clothes, and feminists do not seem to object to the names of men's clothes taking over. *Blouse*, an early Victorian word, sounds rather quaint in the 1990s, and most younger women wear *shirts*, even letting the tails hang out to prove the point. For frilly or fancy shirts, *blouse* is taken out, dusted, and re-used.

But before we write off *blouse*, there are signs of it making a comeback with fashion writers. For some women it has never died out anyway.

blow up or **blow-up** You *blow up* (no hyphen) a photograph and the result is a *blow-up* (with a hyphen). Those were the fashionable words in the 1960s, but now photographers have gone back to 'enlarge' and 'enlargement'.

blue As far back as the 16th century, one of the meanings of *blue* was to be melancholy. This use of *blue*, at least in British English, has become old-fashioned, and someone is now more likely to feel 'low' or 'depressed'. People still *sing the blues* (songs which record black people's moods, history and struggle) but

are less likely to say they've *got the blues*. Although a new mother suffering from mild post-natal depression is said to have the *baby blues*.

blue berets and **blue helmets** See **peace-keeping**

Blue Books We hear about **Green Papers** and White Papers, although many people, other than politicians and political commentators, are hazy about what they are. The same applies to *Blue Books*, which may sound as if they are pornographic novels. It is in fact the usual term in Britain for government publications of official documents submitted to parliament. When the pile of papers becomes thick enough, it is bound in a blue cover.

blue-chip or **gilt-edged** These are both terms for Stock Exchange investments that provide a high level of security. *Gilt-edged* stock (or *gilts* as they are called informally) are supposedly 'as good as gold', issued by the government, who guarantees payment of interest and eventual repayment of the **face value** of the stock.

Blue-chip companies are those that are, in principle, never down, at least not for long. It is an imprecise term in investment **jargon** for major companies, such as ICI or Marks & Spencer, whose shares are almost as reliable as gilt-edged securities. In passing, the expression is said to come from gambling chips with the highest value, which are *blue*.

Both terms, more especially *gilt-edged*, are used about any proposition considered to be sound and reliable.

blueprint This word from engineering terminology (the copying process reproduced technical drawings on a *blue* background) is freely used now, some say too freely, to describe a plan for any project: 'The blueprint for a successful sales campaign'. But we should use it to mean a final detailed programme, not an outline scheme, because in engineering a blueprint marks the final stage of the design on the drawing-board.

blues See **blue**

blurb Because it is a funny word, *blurb* sounds like slang. But every dictionary classifies it as standard English and it is used in the most august literary circles to describe a publisher's description of a book. The blurb for *The Good English Guide* is on the inside flap of the jacket. By extension, *blurb* is also used for any short sales pitch in speech or writing. The word was invented in the 1920s by an American humorist, Gelett Burgess, and passed effortlessly into standard language on both sides of the Atlantic.

blush or **flush** The words mean the same, to go red in the face. Although men can *blush*, the word is used more for women, especially young girls, and always about embarrassment. *Flush* is used for either sex, and people can flush with anger, as well as because they've said the wrong thing, or made some other social gaffe.

(the) board _is_ or _are_ See **collective words**

boat, **ship** or **vessel** Sailors usually know which word to use but landlubbers are sometimes afraid of getting it wrong. Strictly speaking, a _boat_ is a small _ship_. But a fishing trawler, no matter how big, is always 'a fishing _boat_'. When cargo or passengers are carried it is usually in a ship. But passengers on cross-Channel ferries, some of which are large, sail on a cross-Channel _boat_. A millionaire's yacht, with wall-to-wall carpets and spacious luxury, remains a sailing _boat_, yet 'I spied three _ships_ come sailing by'.

In the Royal Navy, almost anything afloat is HMS – Her Majesty's Ship, unless it is a boat launched from a ship; and submarines are always _boats_. A flying ship would be a fantasy but aircraft that landed on water were quaintly called _flying boats_. Even in the smallest boat, everything should be _ship-shape_. These notes will help you to steer the right course, but if in doubt you can fall back on the word _vessel_, a fine old word from the 13th century, that can be used in almost any context for a boat or ship.

boatswain, **bosun** or **bo'sun** Whichever spelling you use, and all three are acceptable, with _boatswain_ as the most usual, there is only one way to pronounce it: 'BOHsun'.

bobby See **cop** . . .

body clock In the 1950s, the concept of an inner body clock was introduced, a human biological clock that registers the time for a person irrespective of what the clocks outside say. When we jet across time zones the body clock loses synchronization with local time. On long journeys, the body clock can take up to 24 hours to reset itself, and during that period it may be telling us to go to bed, instead of attending an important meeting.

body language Politicians and business executives learn about _body language_ at self-presentation courses or courses on communication skills. The theory is that how we sit, our eye movements, gestures and almost everything else the human body can get up to, reveal what we're thinking and feeling, and unconsciously affect other people's responses. When we learn to 'read' another person's body language, we can, we are taught, stay one jump ahead. To prove the point, Alan Ayckbourn called his play, produced in 1990, _Body Language_ – but to make the point, he had to use a lot of words. So perhaps what we say and how we say it count for most.

If you dislike the expression _body language_, as some people do, you can call it _paralanguage_ (see **para-**). See also **neurolinguistic programming**

body politic See **political**

boffin _Boffin_ was popular during World War II for backroom scientists working on new military developments. It is a dated word now, since more and more scientists have emerged from their 'back rooms' to give expert opinions on television or to choose eight records they would take with them on a desert island.

bogey or **bogy** This can be spelt either way to mean an awkward obstacle (_bogeyman_ or _bogyman_ is the imaginary person conjured up to frighten children).

Bogey (not _bogy_) is the word used in golf, at one time for the number of strokes a good player should go round the course in. Apparently, the term was first used in 1891, when someone called such players _bogey men_. It is now in disuse in that sense, but returned in the 1960s, when Americans began using _bogey_ for a score of one stroke more than the standard scratch score for a hole.

'boLEro' or 'BOlero' If it is the Spanish dance, the stress is on the second syllable: 'boLEro'. Ravel's sensuous, compulsive piece of music is pronounced the same, but takes an acute accent: 'Boléro'. If it is the short open jacket, the stress is on the first syllable: 'BOLero'.

bollocks It may be useful to know that if you have to write this word (as William Rushton did in _The Listener_, 10.5.1990), you can spell it _ballocks_, which was the earlier spelling, meticulously listed as an alternative spelling in the latest Oxford dictionary. _Bollocks_ is not often used for testicles, as it was for centuries, but as an exclamation to mean something is a load of rubbish: 'Oh bollocks!', to quote William Rushton. Perhaps because of the coarse sound of the word, 'Bollocks!' may be more likely to offend some people than '**Balls!**' – or is that just a load of . . .?

boloney See **baloney**

bolshie The Bolsheviks were the most radical faction of the Russian revolutionary party, and seized power in 1917. The flavour of that period in history is kept alive by _bolshie_ (or _bolshy_, an alternative spelling), still often used, without any political implication, about anyone obstinate or difficult, from an uncooperative trade union leader to a man who refuses to help with the washing-up.

bona fide or **bona fides** It is not one _bona fide_, two or more _bona fides_.

Bona fides is a _singular_ noun meaning genuine and with honest intentions. So 'their bona fides _is_ unquestionable' is correct. That sounds wrong to many people, so 'their bona fides _are_ unquestionable', and especially 'their bona fides _are_ in order', have become usual, although we may prefer to avoid making this mistake ourselves.

Bona fide describes something that has _bona fides_: 'a bona fide offer', 'a bona fide scheme'. . . .

bona fide or **good faith** These Latin and English phrases mean the same but by tradition _bona_ *fide* is used for a provision in contract law: when someone enters into a contract they are required to disclose all facts that are material to it, so that it is a *bona fide* contract. In general use, 'in good faith', 'genuine' or 'sincere' are usually preferable, because they are easily understood: 'this is a genuine proposition' rather than 'a bona fide proposition'. See also previous entry.

bonanza *Bonanza* was taken up in America in the mid 19th century from a Spanish word meaning fair weather at sea. It soon became a slang word for a rich output from a mine.

Bonanza has long been accepted as standard English in Britain and America, for a windfall or big profits that come in without much effort. There is a flavour of 'money for jam' about the word.

bon appétit When a French visitor raised his glass at dinner and said 'Good appetite!', everyone looked startled. This familiar French phrase doesn't work in English. So if those are your sentiments, it is better to say it in French – *Bon appétit!* See also **bon voyage**

bond *Bond* has a number of meanings in law and stockmarket transactions, but in the UK the most familiar use is for securities issued by the government or local authorities (*premium bonds*, for example). We read about 'shorts', 'mediums' or 'longs', depending upon how long they have to be held before they are redeemed – up to 5 years, 5 to 15 years, over 15 years respectively. Since the 16th century, a bond in English law has been a written deed that irrevocably commits someone, which led to the expression, not used perhaps with such conviction now as it used to be, 'An Englishman's word is his bond'.

bondage It is rare for *bondage* to be used in its primary meaning of serfdom or slavery. The more likely meaning now, for some people, is what Dr Alex Comfort, in *The Joy of Sex*, calls 'the gentle art of tying up your sex partner – not to overcome reluctance but to boost orgasm'.

bonded . . . Imported goods on which duty has not been paid are *bonded goods*. Such goods are stored in a *bonded warehouse* until duty has been paid or they are re-exported; *bonded stores* are for use on board ship and are free from duty; *bonded cellars* are where wines and spirits are stored before duty is paid.

bond paper This printing term for a standard of paper goes on being used in stationery shops, although it doesn't mean much to most people. In fact, bond paper is simply good quality writing paper.

bone china See **china . . .**

bonkers This British slang word for crazy (probably from the idea of *bonking* someone on the head) has been exported: *Newsweek*, the US magazine, has commented: 'Folks are going slightly bonkers these days . . .'; and Bob Hawke, as Australian Prime Minister, announced in February 1990 that to delay the election would send the country 'collectively bonkers'.

bonus or **windfall** A *bonus* is often the outcome of something that has been expected: it can be extra payment to workers for achieving a production target, or a special dividend paid to shareholders because a company has done well. A *windfall* comes out of the blue, such as an unexpected legacy from an uncle you haven't seen for years. A company benefits from a *windfall profit* if an increase in tax enables it to sell goods, on which a lower rate of tax has been paid, at the higher price.

bon voyage It wouldn't be affected to speed parting guests with *Bon voyage*, because this French phrase has almost moved into English as a way of saying 'have a good journey'. See also **bon appétit**

boobs This is a word many women and men use for breasts. Although dictionaries classify *boobs* as slang, none of them considers it vulgar. As a result, 'breast' has become rather formal and ladylike, which is a pity, because it's an attractive word. See also **bosom . . .**

boogie-woogie It is not worth trying to define *boogie-woogie* too precisely. It began as a kind of primitive blues piano-playing, but now almost anything played on the piano with an insistent bass rhythm could be called boogie-woogie.

book value A technical term used by financial journalists and accountants, which often has nothing to do with the real value of anything. It is a value of assets or even of the whole business shown in the accounts of a company – a value that is arranged, in accordance with accepted rules, for tax purposes, or presentation to shareholders, or for some other reason, rather than based on the actual market value.

boom A *boom* is described as 'a period of rapid growth in output, bringing with it growth in employment and an increase in living standards' (*Macmillan Dictionary of Business and Management*). Politicians sit back and say 'You've never had it so good'. For the rest of us it's a *boom* (a word used in that way in America as long ago as the late 19th century) and we enjoy it as long as it goes on, forgetting that a boom always seems to be followed by a *bust*. See **overheating**

bordeaux or **claret** The British have long called the wines from the Bordeaux region in France *claret*. Although *claret* is an Old French word, meaning clear and bright, it does not exist in modern French, and in France these wines are called *bordeaux*. Most members of clubs in Pall Mall still insist on drinking claret, and wine writers may still use *claret* from time to time. But generally *bordeaux* has become the standard term in the wine trade.

born or **borne** We were *born* into this world, but *borne* by our mothers. And if it's all too much to bear, then it's too much to be *borne*. That should sort it out.

born again In the late 1970s President Jimmy Carter announced that he had become a *born again Christian*, and the phrase became popular in America, soon arriving in Britain. It signifies a mature decision to take or retake Christian vows, a spiritual rebirth. Inevitably the idea has spread to other things, usually with the cynical implication of an expedient reconversion to an old allegiance ('a born again monetarist').

borne See **born or borne**

borrowed time There is a sinister ring to *borrowed time*: it is extra time to live or to deal with a crisis, extra time that at any moment could be cut short. The front pages of newspapers show that living on borrowed time is part of life in the 1990s. *Borrowed time* is present-day idiom for 'the sands are running out', with the suggestion that they already have.

borrow *from*, *of* or **off** We *lend to* and *borrow from*, rather than *of* or *off*, which are not considered good English.

bosom or **breasts** If she doesn't say **boobs**, a woman would talk about her breasts rather than her bosom. When *bosom* is used, it is about clothes (the bosom of a dress) or as a centre of emotions (a bosom friend, the bosom of the family). Men are not supposed to have bosoms or breasts, at least none to speak of: they have chests, although tailors talk about the *breast pocket* on a man's jacket.

boss Some dictionaries still classify *boss* in the sense of 'person in charge' as informal or even slang, although it has been in English since the early 19th century. Other dictionaries rightly treat *boss* as standard English, for it is the most convenient word for someone who is in charge and able to give orders. In America *boss* has a negative aspect, especially when used for the boss of a union or of a political organization. It is still preferable to keep *boss* as a *verb* ('to boss someone about') for conversation or casual writing, rather than formal letters or documents.

bosun See **boatswain** . . .

both There are four points to bear in mind:

1 *Both* should be used about *two* things or people, so it is wrong to say 'both John, Mary and Helen are coming to dinner'. To emphasize a number that is more than two, use *all*: 'John, Mary and Helen are all coming to dinner'.

2 The use of *both* for 'each' is criticized because, it is claimed, 'there is a chemist on both sides of the street' could mean the chemist straddles the street. This is nit-picking, because *both* is so often used this way and the meaning is usually completely clear.

3 Be careful to put *both* in the place where you want

it to work in the sentence: 'she loves both men and money' rather than 'she both loves men and money'.

4 Look out for a confusion of meaning: 'both directors and their secretaries were at the meeting' could mean two directors plus their secretaries, or a number of directors with their secretaries. It has to be spelt out: 'the two directors and their secretaries . . .' or simply 'the directors and their secretaries . . .'.

bottleneck *Bottleneck* is good word creation, because visually it conjures up the meaning of the word. Long ago *bottleneck* became a word in its own right and it is silly to object to phrases such as 'a serious bottleneck' or 'deal with the bottleneck' because, according to some authorities, you cannot use words like 'serious' or 'dealing with' about the neck of a bottle.

bottle sizes A standard bottle of wine, under EC regulations, must be 75cl. A double bottle is a *magnum*. But although *magnum* comes from Latin 'magnus' (great), bottles of wine can be much greater still, and then they are dignified with the awe-inspiring names of Old Testament personages: a *jeroboam* is a double magnum (4 ordinary bottles), a *methuselah* is the equivalent of 8 bottles, a *salmanazar* is 12 bottles, a *balthazar* is 16 bottles, and the king who built the hanging gardens of Babylon bestows his name on a gigantic bottle, a nebuchadnezzar, the equivalent of 20 standard bottles.

bottom line Americans use *bottom line* for **nitty-gritty**. This is happening in British English as well, for *bottom line* is being used, not only for the final cost of something or the realistic profit, often shown in the last line of a set of figures, but also for what a negotiation, problem, discussion, etc really mean: to look at the bottom line is to get down to the nitty-gritty. *The Times*, in a leading article on John Major's approach to the European Community, concluded, 'His bottom line is obscure'. This gives *bottom line* another slant, as a way of saying a final arrangement from a difficult negotiation.

boulevard A boulevard is usually a wide avenue lined with trees and it is a word used more often in French than in English: *les grands boulevards* sweep across Paris, whereas London has no boulevards to speak of, save the Mall, Park Lane and a stretch of the Embankment. In America, *boulevard* is used about any wide avenue, even when there isn't a tree in sight.

Boulevard should be pronounced with three syllables ('BOOL-er-vahd'), which is the usual way in America, or with two syllables (as in French): 'BOOLvahd'.

bourbon If you have a taste for American whiskey (see **whisky**), known as *bourbon*, after Bourbon County in Kentucky, where it originated, remember that the first syllable rhymes with 'purr': 'BURbon'.

bourgeois See **middle class** . . .

bourse There is the Stock Exchange in London, Wall Street in New York, the *Bourse* in Paris. The *bourse* (with a small *b*) is used for Stock Exchanges in other European countries as well. (Pron: 'boors'.)

boutique   There is no good reason why this French word for a small shop became so popular in English. During the 'swinging sixties', Carnaby Street in London, the place of pilgrimage for the latest clothes, latched on to the word, and for a while any ordinary clothes shop, as far from Paris as the Western Isles, called itself a *boutique*. But nowadays the word is gathering dust.

boxers, **shorts**, **pants** or **briefs**   It would sound very elderly to go into a shop and ask for 'underpants'. *Pants* is the standard word used by men and (sometimes via the diminutive *panties*) by women. As pants are 'an undergarment that covers the crotch and hips and that may extend to the waist and partly down each leg' (*Longman Dictionary*, 1984 edition), it is not surprising that many young people switched to *briefs* or, if they are longer in the leg, to *shorts*. *Boxers* (because they're a similar cut to the shorts boxers wear in the ring) is a more fashionable name for shorts worn as an undergarment. Some men and women in Britain use *pants*, as Americans do, for **trousers**. In the 1990s, **knickers** must also be taken into account.

box in   At one time only printers used this term for enclosing a section of text in a ruled square or rectangle. Now it is familiar to many other people, since wordprocessors will do it to order.

boy   In London clubs you still occasionally hear 'Hallo, old boy' or 'I say, dear boy', but generally after a certain age (17 or 18 maybe, but getting younger), it could sound derogatory to call a man a *boy*, unless you're talking about your school, in which case you remain an *old boy* until you die.

As soon as men in the armed forces go overseas, some politicians in Britain and America call them 'our boys'. This is a supposedly affectionate but in fact a patronizing and cloying word for men who are fighting a war. See also **old boy network**; **girl**

boycott   It was the Irish Land League who used social and economic sanctions against Captain Boycott (1832–97). The word *boycott* is now used not so much for social ostracism but mostly for a trade embargo against a company in order to force it to accept certain conditions, such as minimum pay for employees.

boyfriend and **girlfriend**   In the 1970s there was a great deal of fuss about *boyfriend* and *girlfriend*, words that we had taken for granted for years. In those days a shocked or discreet silence still prevailed when a couple lived together without getting married. But as this became almost as much the rule as the exception, everyone felt at a loss for a substitute word for 'husband' or 'wife'. *Lover*, too ardent for some people, implied an extramarital relationship, and *sweetheart* seemed old-fashioned, or more appropriate to young love.

Some women made (and still do) a distinction between 'a boyfriend' (for a man who is a friend) and 'my boyfriend' (for a sexual relationship). Philip Howard, as literary editor of *The Times*, devoted a whole chapter to this sociolinguistic problem in his appropriately named book, *Words Fail Me* (1980). Following up variants in America, he found that some maternity hospitals informed women that they may have present at delivery 'a significant other person'. The phrase caught on. Armistead Maupin called his novel, first published in the mid-1980s, *Significant Others*, and to show what he meant, began it with a man waking up in bed next to his naked wife.

In Britain and America most women are relaxed about using *girlfriend* for any woman friend, and it usually carries no hint of a sexual relationship. But cohabiting males, not at ease with *boyfriend*, needed another word for each other, to use on forms, etc.

The whole business seems to have settled down in the 1990s, as two men or two women living together, or a woman and a man living in unmarried bliss, are not any more worth the twitching of lace curtains. And another word, that was waiting in the wings all the time, has come out to fill the gap: *partner*. Popular magazine quizzes ask 'After a one-night fling, do you tell your partner?'; the US census includes *partner* as an official category. Nevertheless, there remain some situations where we have to fall back on *boyfriend* and *girlfriend* for a steady, presumably sexual, relationship, because no other words seem satisfactory.

boyish and **girlish**   To use *boyish* about a man is on the whole complimentary, suggesting that he is youthful and charming: but to say a woman is *girlish* suggests she is silly and behaving in a way that is much younger than her age. *Girlie* is positively offensive, as it is so often used about pornographic magazines and photographs. Admittedly it is unfair and sexist, but language has its own way. See also **effeminate . . .**

boyo   A friendly Irish or Welsh greeting, but it can be used in a patronizing way. A leading article in *The Independent* (3.4.1991) was critical of some newspapers for calling Neil Kinnock 'a pugnacious boyo from the valleys'. Generally *boyo* should be left to the Welsh and the Irish, who are at home with it.

bra or **brassière**   At least one dictionary states solemnly that *bra* is 'a slang abbreviation of *brassière*'. The truth is that only a sedate dowager duchess would dream of calling a brassière anything else but – a *bra*, which has been standard English for years.

brackets or **parentheses**   Printers call ( ), *parentheses* (pron: 'perRENthe(r)seez'), to distinguish them from square brackets [ ]. In everyday English, both words are used, but *brackets* is more usual, for either round or square brackets. *Parentheses* is the usual word in America. *Parenthesis*, the singular form (from Greek 'put in beside'), is used for the actual words within the brackets (this is a parenthesis).

Brackets are useful for including a piece of background information, without holding up the flow of the sentence. The same job can be done by **commas** or **dashes**, with varying degrees of separation:

Commas, you could say, mark off the least separation.

Dashes – which are like an aside in the theatre – come next up the scale, and are useful – when the fancy takes you – for a humorous or dramatic effect.

Brackets mark off a complete separation from the main sentence.

How does punctuation work with brackets? If the parenthesis comes in the middle of a sentence, punctuation of the main sentence belongs *outside* the brackets: 'He was late (over two hours), but we waited for him'; 'She believed his excuse (she did every time), unlikely though it was'. A sentence should still make sense if the words in brackets are omitted.

Even when the parenthesis is a complete sentence within the main sentence, it does not need an initial capital or a stop: 'He arrived late (this is what he told me later) and left early'; 'They made love that night (it was a tradition on Saturdays). Not (. . . on Saturdays.).

A sentence standing on its own in brackets is treated as an ordinary sentence: 'She believed his excuse. (That is how it always was.)' When ellipses (a row of dots) come within brackets they do not double up as a stop: 'Any hard cheese can be used (cheddar, gruyère, gouda . . .).'

Exclamation marks and question marks that belong to the parenthesis come within the brackets and do not affect punctuation outside: 'She believed his excuse (she is that kind of a woman!).'; 'They said they were married (but were they?).' Exclamation and question marks relating to the main sentence are kept outside the brackets: 'Would you like another glass (it's very good wine)?'

Square brackets are a convention to separate a comment by someone else inserted into a quotation: 'To be or not to be? [Indecision reigns supreme!] That is the question'.

If you are indicating the idea of brackets in what someone has said, *parenthetic* and *parenthetically* are useful: 'his comment was parenthetic', or 'said parenthetically', suggests that the comment was outside the main theme.

After all that, you might like to reflect, next time you use ( ), that *bracket* derives from the French word 'braguette' for a codpiece, because the shape reminded people of the reinforced flap sewn into the front of men's breeches to protect their genitals.

brain death   The precise definition of death is arguable, since the heart can be kept beating with a mechanical aid. *Brain death*, which is irreversible brain damage rendering unaided respiration impossible, is usually regarded as the clinical definition of death.

brain drain   Near the end of her period as Prime Minister, Margaret Thatcher received a petition from more than 1600 British scientists working abroad calling on her to reverse the brain drain caused by starving British science of money. *Brain drain* is used mostly about scientists emigrating from Britain to other countries because, as the dean of science at a University in Texas said, commenting on British universities, 'There are a lot of big brains on very small salaries'.

brainstorm   *Brainstorm* has two different meanings. The first meaning is a sudden fever of emotional excitement brought about by a disturbance in the brain. But *brainstorm* can also suggest a flash of inspiration, a brilliant idea. This is the usual meaning in America, and taking over in Britain. *Brainstorming* is a technique for dealing with problems by bringing a group of experts together and encouraging as many ideas as possible, no matter how far-fetched, to come to the surface.

brainwashing   We should never forget this word, first heard in the early 1950s. It is an imitation of the Chinese phrase describing psychological techniques practised in China on political prisoners and prisoners of war, whereby mental attitudes were completely reshaped. In the West, we need to be on guard against brainwashing, usually of a less sinister nature, in advertising and political campaigns. These can play on our fears and insecurities, trapping us into accepting unproven claims and assertions.

Subliminal advertising is even closer to brainwashing. It is illegal to project images in an advertisement or television commercial that we do not see at a conscious level, but which influence us unconsciously. An American observer, Vance Packard, summed up this uneasy business in the title of his book, *The Hidden Persuaders* (1957). See also **conditioning**; **image**; **psycholinguistics**

branchless banking   Since in the late 1980s market research revealed that one in five people had not visited their bank in the previous month, ideas continue to be developed to see whether all those costly money-shops in the high street are essential. As a result the term *branchless banking* has come into English: with the Firstdirect Bank, customers arrange all their banking requirements by telephone, with a service available 24 hours a day, so they can check their balance in the middle of the night, even on Christmas Day. See also **home banking**

brand image   See **image**

brand name or **proprietary name** *Proprietary name*, for a registered name that no one else can use, is almost completely replaced by *brand* or *brand name*. Hence a *brand manager* is the executive in charge of marketing a particular product sold under a registered name; *brand leader* is the best-known and top-selling product in its category; *brand loyalty* is the extent to which people will go on buying a particular brand, even if other brands cost less or are more heavily advertised.

brandy or **cognac**   *Brandy* is a spirit distilled from grapes or any other fruit. For a brandy to be called *cognac*, it must be made from grapes grown and distilled in the region round Cognac, a city in Charente in western France. The word *brandy* on its own implies that it is a grape brandy, otherwise it would be called cherry brandy, apricot brandy, etc.

Brandy and *cognac* are used interchangeably, but only up to a point: all cognacs are brandies – but all brandies are not cognacs, as they could be made anywhere in the world. You have to look at the label to know whether the brandy you are drinking is cognac, unless you know from the taste. See also **VSOP**

brasserie, **café** or **restaurant**   *Café* often comes across as a downmarket word, not quite shaking off the idea of 'workman's café'. A few exceptions stand out, such as the legendary Café Royal in London, but *café* has come down in the world since the *café society* at the turn of the century, and cafés are now more modest places serving teas, snacks or simple meals. Although both *café* and *restaurant* both retain echoes of French pronunciation, the Michelin inspectors award coveted stars, their orders of merit, to *restaurants* (rather than cafés).

Brasserie is the French word for a brewery, later extended to a beer-saloon and thence to a restaurant serving a limited number of dishes throughout the day. It is not often used in Britain but has a place at times, when 'snack bar' is too basic and 'wine bar' too limiting. As British an institution as the National Gallery had to fall back on *brasserie* for the bar-cum-restaurant in the new Sainsbury Wing opened in 1991, to distinguish it from the more ordinary *café* in the main building. Presumably they chose the word because service is continuous throughout the day, in the tradition of brasseries, whereas *restaurant* suggests meals at conventional times.

brassière   See **bra** . . .

bravado and **bravura**   As both words describe a style rather than real bravery, they sometimes get mixed up. *Bravado* is putting on a show of bravery or confidence, with the suggestion that there is a touch of swaggering about it. *Bravura* is used more than anything else about a musician or a singer performing a difficult piece with showy virtuosity. *Bravura* deserves an appreciative 'Bravo!', which does not apply to *bravado*.

brave new world   Shakespeare invented the phrase, which Miranda used with innocent idealism in *The Tempest* (Act V Sc i): 'Oh brave new world, that has such people in't!'. Aldous Huxley lifted it for the title of his novel, *Brave New World*, written in 1932, but used it despairingly: his fable is about a future world state which achieves a society free from conflict and want, but only at the expense of enslaving the human spirit.

We are left with both visions: *brave new world* can be used ironically and without hope, or with faith that the world will one day be a better place. Inevitably, it is Huxley's disillusionment that seems more likely to take over: 'It's a brave new world where millions diet to lose weight and millions of others die from hunger'.

bravura   See **bravado** . . .

break   *Break* is a very old word in English, going back centuries, earlier than the Conquest. But it adapts itself to life in the last years of the 20th century: television picked it up and instead of interrupting programmes for advertisements, there is a 'pause for a *commercial break*'; travel agents find a *winter break* more inviting than a package holiday; *break* is an indispensable word in snooker. We never give this hardworking word a break.

breakdown or **break down**   As one word *breakdown* is the *noun*: as *two* words it's the *verb*: to break down sales by regions.

The two meanings of *breakdown* can cause misunderstanding. One meaning is a total failure to function or to make progress: a nervous breakdown, a breakdown of negotiations, a marriage breakdown. The other meaning is analysis or division into categories: a breakdown of sales region by region. But someone could get the wrong idea from 'a breakdown of the business' or 'a breakdown of hospital patients by sex'. In those examples 'analysis' or 'classification' would be better.

break-even   *Break-even* is indispensable as a quick way of saying we haven't made a profit but we haven't made a loss either. A *break-even point* is the point where all costs have been recovered: from then on you're making a profit.

break-up value   The term is used about assets of a business, when the *break-up value* is the value of assets at the price they can be sold for cash.

breasts   See **bosom** . . .

breath or **breathe**   The first is a noun, the second a verb: 'Take a deep *breath* and then *breathe* out'.

Breathalyser   It should be spelt with a capital B because *Breathalyser* is a registered name for the device that measures the amount of alcohol in the breath. But many people are not aware of this, so *breathalyser* often appears in newspapers. Since verbs do not have capital letters, a driver is *breathalysed*.

Brechtian   *Brechtian* first described the style of the German playwright Bertolt Brecht (1898–1956). Brecht rejected the illusion of the theatre and the need to engage the audience's emotions: his uncompromisingly drab plays demand a reasoned and intelligent view.

Brechtian is now used about any theatrical production that is uncompromisingly grey and cold, and the word is showing signs of being used about a real life situation that has a typically Brechtian social realism, underlined by greed and corruption.

brethren or **brothers**   It depends upon whether you are a vicar, an abbot or a trade unionist. Vicars are accustomed to using *brethren* in church for members of the Christian community, quaintly taking in women as well: 'Dearly beloved brethren . . .'. An abbot may use *brethren* in chapel for monks who are members of the order, but outside chapel he would be more likely to call them *brothers*. For trade unionists, members of their unions are *brothers*.

briefs (as underwear)   See **boxers** . . .

bright or **brightly**   Grammatically, the moon shines *brightly*. But the poetic use of *bright* for *brightly* ('Tiger! Tiger! burning bright . . .') is transferred to prose. So 'the moon shines bright', 'a candle burns *bright*' and similar expressions are as acceptable as '. . . shines brightly', '. . . burns brightly'.

bring, **fetch** or **take**   We can think of these three words as arrows. *Bring* is an arrow pointing *towards* the speaker and the word 'me' is implied: 'bring a bottle of wine' means 'bring me . . .'. *Take* is an arrow pointing *away* from the speaker: 'take me to your leader' means 'take me from here . . .'. *Fetch* is a *double-headed* arrow, since it means go away and come back: 'fetch a bottle of wine' suggests go away and come back with a bottle. Those examples preserve the correct distinction between the three words but we can relax about it in conversational use: a taxi can *bring*, *fetch* or *take* you.

brinkmanship or **sabre-rattling**   *Sabre-rattling* is more swashbuckling, but in a way both expressions mean the same, a cliffhanger policy that goes right to the limit, so that the others lose their nerve. In 1956, John Foster Dulles, at the time US Secretary of State, spoke about the diplomatic skill of going 'to the brink' of war, and was accused by Adlai Stevenson of *brinkmanship*, apparently the first use of the word. *Brinkmanship* can be used in any situation where you are calling someone's bluff or 'testing the temperature of the water'.

Brinkmanship, accepted as standard English by dictionaries, could be foreign policy in some situations; *sabre-rattling* is more for braggarts and was used about Saddam Hussein in the build-up to the 1991 Gulf War.

Brit, **Britisher** and **Briton**   Some British people do not like being called *Brits* but generally it is not felt to be pejorative. Harold Walker, British ambassador in Baghdad at the beginning of the 1991 Gulf War, was altogether at ease talking about 'the Brits in Iraq'. Americans often use *Britishers*, an alternative not generally heard in Britain.

The British rarely call themselves *Britons* (unless they're singing *Rule Britannia!*), although journalists find it a useful shorthand term: TWO BRITONS WIN GOLD MEDALS! *Ancient Britons* is usually an expression for the inhabitants of England before the Norman Conquest. The word, itself, is an echo of Old French 'Breton', which today applies to inhabitants of Brittany.

Britain, **Great Britain**, **British Isles** and **United Kingdom**   Many foreigners, and some British, are not aware that *Britain*, short for *Great Britain*, includes England, Scotland and Wales, but leaves out Northern Ireland. *British Isles* is geographical and not political: it includes the whole of Ireland as well as all the adjacent islands, the Hebrides, Shetlands, Channel Islands, etc. *United Kingdom* is political, short for the *United Kingdom of Great Britain and Northern Ireland* (a designation in use since 1922, following the creation of the Irish Republic), and does not include the Channel Islands and the Isle of Man, which have their own legislatures and taxation systems.

In spite of the ambiguity, *British* is generally taken to mean the inhabitants of and anything to do with the whole of the United Kingdom. See also next entry

British and **English**   For a long time, *English* was often synonymous with *British* and the habit has not altogether disappeared, although in official use everyone is more careful now to avoid offending the Irish, Scottish and Welsh. The French, less sensitive about such matters, are still likely to talk about *les anglais*, meaning the *British*. But *Made in England*, a valued legend on labels all over the world, has been replaced by *Made in Britain* or *Made in the UK*.

British can refer to Great Britain (which excludes Northern Ireland) or to the United Kingdom (see previous entry). There was a time when members of the British Commonwealth called themselves British, but that belongs more to the days of the British Empire.

It could be considered an anachronism to describe the inhabitants of England before the Act of Union (1707) as *British*, although the designation Great Britain had been in use since 1603, when James VI of Scotland became James I of England (including Wales). See also **Brit**

British or **Standard English**   In 1913 the philologist, Henry Cecil Wyld, defined *Standard English* as 'the "best" type of spoken English . . .', with *Modified Standard* as 'the various vulgar forms of this heard among the inferior ranks of the population' (*Standard English and its Varieties*). In 1985 Robert Burchfield, at the time chief editor of Oxford English dictionaries, regarded Standard English as 'the variety considered most suitable for use on the spoken channels of our broadcasting systems emanating from London'.

About many words and expressions, there is general agreement. About others, even dictionaries take different views on whether a word or a phrase is slang or Standard English, how to pronounce some words and on what is good grammar. Outside linguistics, few people use the term Standard English; in any case, it seems more valid to spell it with a small *s*, as in *The*

Good English Guide, to suggest generally accepted good use of English instead of a prescriptive decree laid down by an absolute authority, since such authority does not exist.

In books on linguistics, *British English* has been used since the late 19th century. But many people in Britain would consider the term unnecessary, as they would share Enoch Powell's sentiment that 'others may speak English . . . but it is our language not theirs'. *The Times Literary Supplement* has long taken a more liberal view: 'West African writers . . . regard English as a language which is theirs to use and which they are entitled to mould and pound and batter into any shape they please' (10.8.1962).

Up to the 1980s, dictionaries used *British English* mostly to distinguish the language of the UK from the language of the US. In the 1990s, dictionaries regard British English as the English spoken in the UK, as against other varieties of English, with their own standards, used in different parts of the world. See also **English; Queen's English; received pronunciation**

Britisher   See **Brit**

British Isles, **Great Britain**, **Britain** or **United Kingdom**   Many foreigners, and some British, are uncertain over the proper distinction between these names. To be sure of using them correctly, see **Britain** . . .

Britishisms   Just as the British talk about **Americanisms**, until these become completely at home in **British English** (stunt, room-mate, paperback, babysitter and thousands of other examples), Americans talk about *Britishisms* (or *Briticisms*).

There are obvious ones that Americans learn on their first day in London, such as *underground* for 'subway', *pavement* for 'sidewalk', *petrol* for 'gas', *tap* for 'faucet'. Others come as a shock, as when an American couple moving house in England were greeted by the *removal men*: in America 'movers' shift furniture, while removal men do a more sombre job – they work for undertakers.

Briton   See **Brit** . . .

broad   There was a time when, thanks to Humphrey Bogart, *broad*, as a word for a woman, generally but not always used offensively, looked as if it might settle down in British English. But it has not survived, except as an echo of old Hollywood gangster films, leaving Americans to raise their eyebrows when an Englishman says he's going to 'have a holiday on the Broads'. 'Broad in the beam' is different. A beam is the width of a ship where it curves out most and the expression has been used in English for many years about a woman's (but unfairly, not a man's) hips.

broad or **wide**   They are very close to each other in meaning, and dictionaries define both as indicating that something is large from side to side. *Broad* is

more general (a broad expanse) and a word that is used about people (broad shoulders, broad hips). *Wide* is more specific and tangible (a wide pavement, a wide entrance, a board two metres wide). A *broad* view of something is a general overall view, without focusing on detail; a *wide* view suggests taking as many other things as possible into account.

broadcast or **broadcasted**   English is littered with relics of alternative past forms of verbs. Sometimes one form eventually takes over, but there is no reliable pattern: *broadcast* is now the usual past form, but 'fitted' won out over 'fit', 'dived' over 'dove' but 'strove' has scored over 'strived' (note 'fit' and 'dove' are retained in America). Although *broadcast* covers radio and television, it is more associated with radio, with *telecast* available for television.

broadsheets and **tabloids**   Journalists and programme presenters, when referring to newspapers, talk about the *broadsheets* and the *tabloids*. These are both printing terms: a *broadsheet* is a sheet of paper in its uncut form and a *tabloid* is a sheet of paper cut to half that size. Among newspapers, broadsheets are the large, serious-looking, so-called 'quality' papers, *The Times*, *The Independent*, etc. They are sometimes called the 'heavyweights', although it is undisclosed whether this refers to the weight of paper or the long words in the editorials. *Tabloids* are the easy-to-read, easy-to-handle, small-format newspapers with sensational headlines and nubile **page three** pin-ups, the so-called *popular press*. (The word *tabloid* began as a brand name registered in 1884 of a small pharmaceutical tablet.) See also **Fleet Street**

broiler   See **battery** . . .

broke   *Broke* is an old past form of the verb *break*, but nowadays cups and hearts get *broken*. *Broke* still has a place in certain expressions: if you have spent all your money, you are broke, and when you *go for broke*, you gamble everything on an all-out effort. *Go for broke* was given an airing and a punning twist on the other use of *broke* in the summer of 1991, with the Conservative anti-Labour poster campaign, 'Labour's going for broke again'.

broker or **dealer**   A *broker* is a middleman, a go-between, who arranges sales without ever owning the goods, by bringing together buyers and sellers. A *stockbroker* (officially a *broker-dealer*, after the London Stock Exchange reforms in 1986) buys and sells shares, *insurance brokers* buy insurance – in both cases not usually for themselves but for their clients. Usually brokers take no risk, but receive a commission on every deal they negotiate whether it makes money or not.

A *dealer* also buys and sells, but usually takes legal possession of the goods expecting to sell them at a profit, taking the risk of not being able to. A *wheeler-dealer* is a special kind of dealer who deals in anything on hand, or is someone who arranges a deal in business, politics or international affairs, by **lobbying** the right people. A more informal name for this second kind of wheeler-dealer is a *fixer*, and perhaps that's a better name, because it's a reminder that some of the things they 'fix' come unstuck.

brothers See **brethren** . . .

brouhaha There is some doubt whether *brouhaha* is a real word, or a conversational noise to indicate a commotion or fuss. It is regarded as standard English and shows up in the leader columns of serious newspapers. Although it doesn't sound like it, *brouhaha* is a French word, although not used as often in that language as it is in English. Pron: 'BREWhahhah'.

brunch Formally admitted as standard English by recent dictionaries (instead of 'informal' or 'colloquial') and about time too, because what other word is there for a late-morning meal that serves for both *br*eakfast and *l*unch, so useful when you get up late?

brunette Unlike **blond(e)**, English has taken over only the feminine form of this French word. Some dictionaries also include 'brunet' but the word is never used: a man is called 'dark-haired'. *Brunette* means dark brown, but is also used in English about a woman with black hair.

brusque People hesitate over whether to say 'broosk' (*oo* as in 'foot'), 'broohsk' (*ooh* as in 'moon') or 'brusk' (to rhyme with 'rusk'). You can choose, as all three are acceptable, with a preference for 'broosk', because it is nearer to the French pronunciation.

BTU Since nearly everyone has central heating these days, nearly everyone hears about BTUs, because that is how boilers are usually rated, but not everyone knows what the letters stand for, let alone what they mean. A British thermal unit is the energy necessary to increase the temperature of one pound of water by 1°F.

bubbly See **champagne**

bucket shop Bucket shops began in America in the 1880s, as unofficial traders speculating by buying and selling grain in buckets. Later the expression was used for places selling liquor of doubtful quality, also in buckets. Then bucket shop was extended to cover crooked stockbrokers using their clients' money to gamble on stocks. But now, for anyone who has ever tried to get an air ticket for less than the official rate, *bucket shop* has only one meaning, accepted by recent British dictionaries as standard English: a travel agent who specializes in doing deals for cheap travel with airlines, sometimes perfectly legitimate, sometimes outside the regulations.

Buddhism *Buddhism* has been a fashionable word in the West since the 1960s, often with little awareness that it is one of the most profound religions of the world, predating Christianity by five centuries (the Buddha taught in India in the 5th century BC). A Buddhist's view of life centres on an inner detachment, difficult to comprehend in Western terms, leading to **nirvana**, another word that is often used glibly. *Buddha* is a title (from the Sanskrit word for enlightened), not a name, and was bestowed most recently on Gautama (about 563–483BC). It is customary to refer to Gautama as *the* Buddha and to use *a* Buddha for a statue or other representation. See also **Enlightenment**; **Zen**

budget *Budget* has become a way of saying 'cheap', without it sounding like it. *Budget* clothes, *budget* holidays, *budget* anything you can think of can mean cheap and nasty, or reasonably priced for people who can't afford the earth.

With a capital B, the *Budget* is the national financial statement presented by the Chancellor of the Exchequer. See also next entry

budget account A *budget account* is a polite way of implying that you cannot afford to pay big bills, such as telephone or electricity accounts, in one go. They enable payment to be made by monthly instalments, often in the form of **standing orders**. Department stores picked up the term *budget account* to encourage customers to pay so much a month. This enables them to buy goods at the store up to an agreed limit, which is part of the 'enjoy today, pay tomorrow' syndrome that has been affecting the economy for decades.

buff In the early 19th century, *buff* overcoats were supplied to volunteers in New York City who loved helping to put out fires. Those long-forgotten amateur firemen are recalled by the use of *buff* for an enthusiast about anything: film buff, railway buff, computer buff. . . .

For the difference in colour between *buff*, *fawn* or *beige*, see **beige**. . . .

buffer state Buffers on a train function like bumpers on a car, giving some protection against an impact. A *buffer state* is a neat adaptation of the word in international politics, for a small independent state sandwiched between two hostile states, reducing the risk of clashes on the border between them.

buffet A *buffet* is the French word for sideboard and when it is used that way in English, the first syllable rhymes with 'buff'. When *buffet* is a serve-yourself meal or a snack bar, the first syllable has the same sound as the *oo* in 'foot': 'BOOFFay'. But if you pronounce *buffet* either way for either meaning no one is likely to notice.

Buffet, the noun and verb for a blow (pron: 'BUFF-it'), is a much older word from 13th-century Old French. It does not double the *t* in its other forms: buffeted, buffeting.

bug Since the 14th century, *bug*, which probably has some connection with the word **bogy**, has meant something unpleasant. It continues to be used like that: in computer science, a bug is a hidden defect that makes a program go wrong; in international or commercial intrigue, bugging a room or a telephone is hiding a miniature microphone so that the enemy can listen in. And if something *bugs* a machine or a plan (a useful slang use that may move up into standard English), it is a fault or a miscalculation that makes it go wrong.

To *bug* a person, that is to annoy someone, is likely to remain slang, as good alternatives are available.

bugger   Dictionaries do not classify *bugger*, in its literal meaning, as 'vulgar', yet it would disgust some people, either because they are not quite sure what it means or because anal intercourse is shocking to them. *Bugger* has been a term of abuse since the 16th century, yet curiously it is also used in a friendly way, even with a hint of admiration: 'You old bugger!' It all depends upon how you say it.

Buggerall, as in 'there's buggerall to do here', is slang but not generally regarded as offensive. Dylan Thomas called the first version of *Under Milk Wood*, *Llareggub* (*buggerall* backwards).

bugging   See bug

built environment   See environment

built-in and **planned obsolescence**   The terms relate to the **consumer society** (see also **admass**). In order to maintain demand, the life-span of goods is deliberately limited, either by the materials used in manufacturing them or by engaging journalism and advertising to manipulate changes in fashion. *Built-in* and *planned obsolescence* are alternative terms for this principle (or lack of principles) of maintaining a needless demand for new products.

(the) **bulk of**   There is a view that *the bulk of* should apply to quantity, not to number, that 'the bulk of the work' is correct but 'the bulk of the workers' should be avoided. But *the bulk of* is so often used for 'the greater number of', and by good writers, that it seems fussy to object to it. If it bothers you, use **majority** instead about numbers ('the majority of the workers').

bull (as Stock Exchange term)   See bear . . .

bulldoze   Long before heavy *bulldozers* cleared earth and rubble to prepare the ground for a new supermarket, office block, or some other development, a 'bulldose' in America in the 19th century meant a 'dose' of flogging, possibly with a whip made out of bullhide. No one knows how *bulldozer* became connected in the early 1930s with the tractor-based mechanical workhorse for clearing ground. *Bulldoze* is still an ugly word, used also for shoving aside ruthlessly everyone else's opinions and feelings to force through some proposal, or to *bulldoze* your way to the top.

When we use *bulldoze* in that way, we can recall the way it was used all those years ago in America.

bullion or **gold**   Bullion is gold in bulk form, gleaming bars of the yellow metal, rather than gold coins or other treasures. We read about *gold bullion*, because *bullion* is also used for silver, although we can generally assume that bullion means gold, especially when it's a bullion robbery.

bull and **bullet points**   This recent adaptation of the aggressive qualities of a bull has not yet found its way into most dictionaries. The *bull points* of a campaign, a sales message, or a person are the dynamic advantages, the most telling pluses. During the 1990 election contest for the leadership of the Conservative Party, *The Independent* compared John Major's, Douglas Hurd's and Michael Heseltine's *bull points*. In a book such key points are often marked by *bullets* (●) and may be called bullet points.

bull's-eye or **bullseye**   Some people, in their worthy desire to get rid of unnecessary hyphens, forget that this expression means the eye of a bull. It has to be written *bull's*, which makes the hyphen unavoidable: *bull's-eye*.

bum   Even the most refined dictionary does not put a 'coarse' or 'vulgar' tag on the word *bum*. It has been used for the **buttocks** since the 14th century but continues to be regarded as slang. Nor is it a contraction of 'bottom', as some people believe. In fact, the origin of the word is unknown. It comes into Shakespeare's plays a number of times, and later became a mildly daring word. But now *bum* sounds twee, a word used to children.

The American use of *bum* for a layabout or good-for-nothing is known in Britain but has never caught on, except when used as a verb: 'As a student he spent his summers bumming round Europe'.

bumf   Because it is an abbreviation of 'bum-fodder' (lavatory paper), *bumf* is not a bad word for a stack of unnecessary paperwork. But it has become dated, perhaps because so much *bumf* is now stored on disks.

bumping along the bottom or **a corrugated phase**   *Bumping along the bottom* became a regular phrase during the recession of the early 1990s. It indicated small insignificant ups and downs, with no real change or improvement in the economy. In mid-1992, an alternative expression was heard, 'the economy is in *a corrugated phase*'. If you look at corrugated cardboard, with its small ridges, a corrugated phase comes to exactly the same thing as bumping along the bottom.

bureaucracy   As autocracy is power exercised by one person, *bureaucracy* is power exerted over people's lives by faceless officials from their offices or 'bureaux'. Bureaucracy is attractive to big organizations, because responsibilities, rules and procedures can be clearly defined. But therein lie its defects – insensitivity, inflexibility and avoidance of clear-cut decisions. *Bureaucracy* and its attendant words *bureaucrat* and *bureaucratic* always suggest wasteful, frustrating inefficiency.

bureaus or **bureaux**　*Bureau* is, of course, a French word, first of all meaning a desk, but now the standard word for an office. In English, *bureau* is an old-fashioned name for a particular kind of desk with lots of drawers. The French use also exists in English for an official government office dealing with specific business, and this usage has become familiar through local Citizens' Advice Bureaux.

The French plural, *bureaux*, is usually preferred but *bureaus* also occurs. Either way, whether the plural is formed with *x* or *s*, it is pronounced in English with a final *z* sound: 'BYOORohz'.

-burger　Hamburger appeared in American English in the early 1900s. It had nothing to do with ham but was a fried or grilled round of minced beef in a soft roll, something like a one-time speciality of Hamburg in Germany. After the war, the fast-food business cornered the suffix *-burger*, using it for any fried food that could be slipped into a soft roll (*beefburger*, *chickenburger*, *fishburger*, even, for vegetarians, a *nutburger*). Inevitably, *burger* began to stand on its own as a separate word, useful when whatever is stuffed into the roll defies description.

burglary, **housebreaking** or **robbery**　*Housebreaking* has ceased to be a statutory term in English law: in 1968 it was officially replaced by *burglary*, for the crime that involves breaking into a building in order to steal property. *Robbery* is less specific: it is stealing from someone, at one time suggesting the use of force or threats (*highway robbery*), but this implication does not always apply now. If your pocket has been picked, it is robbery, not burglary.

burned or **burnt**　These are alternative past forms of the verb *burn*. Either can be used but generally *burnt* is preferred in sentences such as 'she burnt the letter', 'the toast was burnt'. *Burned* is more usual when it is describing how something was burning: 'the candle burned brightly', 'the fire burned fiercely'. This is not a fixed rule, merely a guideline for anyone who wants to take the trouble to choose between *burned* and *burnt*.

busby　See **bearskin** . . .

buses or **busses**　*Busses*, the usual plural form in America, appears occasionally in British English, but is not considered correct, as *buses* is the standard form. When schoolchildren are taken to school, they are sometimes said to be *bussed*.

Bushspeak　Every president and prime minister has personal turns of phrase, sometimes dictated by their own nature and their ability to use English, some-

times by political and diplomatic constraints. During his presidency, George Bush seemed anxious at times to avoid being too clearly understood, and *Bushspeak* was characterized by him 'stumbling with his script', as Peter Jenkins of *The Independent* put it, agonizing over the syntax of hesitant sentences.

The 1991 Gulf War did present Bush with many linguistic problems, since every one of his utterances would be nit-picked over for diplomatic gain. So in the early days, while relentless bombing of Baghdad continued, *Bushspeak* declared that US forces in the region had a 'wholly defensive' role. Speaking one Sunday from his holiday home at Kennebunkport, Maine, George Bush, himself, had the last word on *Bushspeak*: 'No point in getting into all these semantics'. See also **Reaganisms**

business or **trade**　Both involve buying and selling. *Business* has a general meaning covering everything to do with commercial activities from ICI to a corner shop. *Trade* is often used about wholesale and international dealings: for example, the *jewellery trade* suggests Hatton Garden, while a *jewellery business* suggests a high street shop. But there are expressions, such as the *rag trade*, which covers all aspects of the fashion business. At the same time, *trade* is the more formal word, as in Department of Trade and Industry.

business English　In business letters people used to be thanked for their *esteemed enquiry* and assured of *best attention at all times*. In the last 30 years this starched-white-collar language has loosened its tie a good deal, and is likely to become even more relaxed by the end of the century. Here's a real-life example of the way business English is going. Rosie is a copywriter in an advertising agency. Her husband has his own business, and she does letters for him in the evening. In one case, she changed:

'We acknowledge receipt of your first order, but regret that we are unable to deliver by the date specified. The 27 June is the earliest we can manage.'

to:

'We were very glad to get your order and welcome you as a new customer. So you can imagine how much we hate saying we cannot make your delivery date. Can you possibly wait until 27 June? If you can, we'll bust a gut to get it to you by then.'

'You can't say things like that,' her husband said.
'Why not?'
'Because people don't write like that in business letters.'
'What's so special about a business letter? It's just one person talking to another.'

Although business English should not become too chatty, for business is serious business, Rosie's heart is in the right place.

businessman and **businesswoman**　*Businessperson* is an awkward unisex word and is not used often, so the separate words *businessman* and *businesswoman* remain. *Business people* is the most convenient way to describe a gathering of women and men in business.

business and **industrial parks** There is usually no pasture or woodland about these parks. It is simply a case of the gracious word 'park' being eagerly taken up by property developers since the 1970s, to use for developments on the edge of towns, providing office accommodation (a *business park*) or small workshops and other units for light industrial use (an *industrial park*).

(go) **bust** See **belly-up** . . .

bust or **chest** Both men and women have chest X-rays but when it comes to clothes, men are measured round the *chest*, women round the *bust*. A woman has a chest but is more likely to call it her bust, except when she has a cold on her *chest*. See also **bosom** . . .

-busters The suffix was used in the title of the film, *The Dambusters*, about the low-flying Lancaster bombers, led by Guy Gibson in 1943 to destroy the dams and power stations in the Ruhr valley. After the war, *-buster* stayed on, debased as commercial and journalistic jargon: shops with sales call themselves *pricebusters*, scientists working on new discoveries are headlined as *mythbusters*. As a worn-out cliché, *-busters* is best avoided.

busy See **engaged** . . .

but *But* can give a few problems and it is no help to be told that it's 'an adverbial conjunction and a pronominal preposition'.

1 It is still taught that *but* should not be used to begin a sentence. *But* there are many examples in the *OED* to dispute that. You can even use *but* to begin a paragraph. (See also **and**.)

2 Should it be 'but I/she/he' or 'but me/her/him'? If you want to make the distinction, complete the sentence: 'No one *but I* (can do it)'; 'No one *but she* (could have written this)'. But 'There's no one here *but her*'.

It must be added that some writers use 'but me/her/ him' in all cases: 'Who can do it? No one *but me*'. If you prefer to be careful, follow the above rule.

3 *But* is a double-edged word: it can put people on guard or it can encourage them. 'It's very good but . . .' will produce a reaction of caution; 'It will be very difficult but . . .', gives some hope. Be especially careful of 'Yes, but . . .', which often means *No*.

butch It is often indecisive whether a word is slang or good respectable English. At least two reputable dictionaries classify *butch*, for a mannish-looking woman (also used about a male homosexual who is aggressively masculine), as standard English. The word is probably taken from 'butcher'.

buttocks You'd only use this word in the singular to refer, for some reason, to either your left or right

buttock. In the plural, *buttocks* is a useful word for anyone who finds **arse** too crude, **bum** too prissy, rump and backside too much like a cut of beef, and bottom or behind too prudish. So the nearest we can get to calling a spade a spade, without upsetting anyone, is that 13th-century word *buttocks*.

buyers' and **sellers' market** These two expressions are manifestations of the archetypal economic principle of supply and demand. In a situation where there are too many goods chasing too few customers, it is a *buyers' market*, because buyers can call the tune. When there's a lot of money about and not enough goods, it is a *sellers' market*, because sellers have a field-day.

buzz and **buzzword** If a place is *buzzing* with something it means everyone is talking about it. The expression goes back to the 17th century (in *Hamlet*, Shakespeare wrote about the 'pestilent speeches' of *buzzers*). Since the 1980s, *buzz* has become the fashionable word for anything that's all the rage: 'Dance is the buzz cultural form in France today . . .' (*The Listener* 27.4.1989).

Buzzwords is a more lively expression than *voguewords*, which is what some writers on English call them, catchwords that the media and people in the know feel good about using, even if it's not altogether clear what they mean. It is easy to sound out of touch if you use a buzzword from a year or two back. Because they're overexposed, buzzwords suffer from the wearout factor and usually stop buzzing after a period. For examples, see **designer** and **state-of-the-art**

by or **bye** Many of us have to think which to use in different circumstances. It's a *bye* in cricket (a run scored from a ball not hit), and in golf (remaining holes not played after the match is decided). A *by*-election and *by*-laws are now preferable to *bye*-election and *bye*-laws, with the older forms going out of use. And it is bygone, bypass, bypath, byroad, bystander, byway, byword (all now without hyphens).

And *by the bye* (the usual spelling for the expression meaning 'by the way'), it is always **goodbye** (except in America where it can be *goodby*) because that's a contraction of 'God be with ye'.

by or **in comparison** See **comparison**

bye-bye See **goodbye** . . .

By jingo! See **jingoism**

byte *Byte* is part of the language of computers, understood by schoolchildren in the 1990s, but not always by their parents. Bytes are the units used to define how much information a computer can store or how much information capacity is required to perform a particular task. A byte is a group of *bits* (the smallest information unit held in a computer) stored as one unit of **data**. The word *byte* is probably a mixture of 'bit' and 'bite'.

The memory capacity of computers is given in *kilobytes* (abbreviated K), one of which equals 1024 bytes, roughly two pages of A4 text. A *megabyte* is equal to 1,048,576 bytes.

Byzantine   Thanks to package holidays in Greece and Turkey, *Byzantine* is now sprinkled liberally in travel brochures and guidebooks. This very old rich word, from the ancient Greek city of Byzantium (now Istanbul), founded in the 7th century BC on the shores of the Bosphorus, is used in as many different ways as it is pronounced.

Unless you study it in depth, it is safer to use *Byzantine* above all for religious art, the architecture of churches that makes use of the round arch, the dome dominating a cross with the four arms of equal length, and lavish stylized mosaics against a background of gold. The great period was the 4th, 5th and 6th centuries, and the renowned example is Santa Sophia in Istanbul.

Because the politics of Byzantium were complicated, *Byzantine* is used also to describe obscure or devious situations (it came in for a lot of use during Richard Nixon's presidency).

The pronunciation favoured by some classical scholars is 'BIZZantyne', but 'bizzANtyne' or 'byeZANtyne' is generally preferred.

· C ·

CA See chartered accountant

cabinet government Outside books on political science, most electors had never heard the term *cabinet government*, until Margaret Thatcher became Prime Minister. In one of her early speeches she introduced a new term, *conviction government*: 'It must be a conviction government. As Prime Minister I could not waste time with any internal arguments'. This, we were told, effectively abolished government by the committee of senior ministers who form the Cabinet. The cry 'Bring back cabinet government!' was heard in the land. See also **consensus politics**

cad Even in the 1990s, one dictionary defines *cad* as 'a person capable of ungentlemanly conduct'. But does anyone call anyone a *cad* any more?

caddie or **caddy** When it is a box for keeping tea, the word is *caddy*, an adaptation of 'catty', the name of a weight in Malay. An 18th-century word for a porter was *caddie*, which is the usual spelling for someone who carries golf clubs around for players, unless they have two-wheeled trolleys known as *caddie-cars*.

café See **brasserie**; **accents in print and writing**

calculate In Britain, 'I calculate the train will arrive at 5 o'clock' suggests 'I have worked out from the timetable that it will arrive at that time'. In America, it usually means 'I suppose it will arrive then'.

calendar or **calender** Some people have to think twice about the spelling. Pirelli Tyres were famous for their *calendars* (now collectors' pieces), with photographs of beautiful women, and which in passing also showed dates. A *calender* is an uncommon word, the name of a machine in which paper is pressed by rollers.

calorie Many people count calories but few know what the word means. It is a term from physics, now used mainly to describe the energy-producing value of different foods. One calorie is the amount of energy required to raise the temperature of 1 kilogram of water by 1°C. Will that help next time you eat a cream cake?

Cambodia or **Kampuchea** See **foreign place-names**

cameo or **intaglio** They are both carved stones, often forming part of a ring. An *intaglio* (pronounced in the Italian way, without sounding the *g*: 'inTALLyoh') can be used as a seal, because the stone is carved out, leaving a sunken image that would make an impression in wax. A *cameo* is the other way round: it is carved in relief.

camera-ready Now that nearly all printing is based on photographic reproduction, *camera-ready* is an everyday term for publishers and others. When the last stages of design and editing are completed and the text and other material are prepared for reproduction, everything is *camera-ready*.

camp *Camp*, as a word to describe a homosexual style, is more or less replaced by **gay**. But *camp* remains theatrical slang in Britain and America for an outrageously exaggerated style, either on the stage or in real life: 'a marvellous piece of high camp'. It belongs to the theatre, going back to the 16th century (possibly from the French 'campagne', the country, where itinerant actors gave performances) long before it had anything to do with homosexuals.

Camp David *Camp David* is associated with US presidents almost as much as the White House: it provides a weekend change of scene, a retreat in the Appalachian Mountains, Maryland, that can double as a conference centre.

Camp David is sometimes used to describe a diplomatic coup ('a kind of Camp David deal'), particularly related to the Middle East since 1978, when Jimmy Carter brought together the President of Egypt and the Prime Minister of Israel at Camp David.

campus Americans use *campus* (Latin for a field or a plain) for the area occupied by a university or one of its departments. *Campus* is rarely, if ever, used at Oxford and Cambridge, but after World War II the new universities in Britain, some of them in a landscaped setting, adopted *campus* to describe the whole university site. The plural is *campuses*.

can or **may** *Can* means ability to do something: 'I can help you' means I know how to. *May* suggests possibility rather than certainty: 'I may help you' leaves the option open. Both *can* and *may* are also used interchangeably to express permission: 'You can (or may) go now' means it is in order for you to go. Of the two, *may* is more formal, *can* more relaxed: 'Subject to certain conditions, you may proceed' as against 'You can go ahead'. 'May I have another drink?' is more polite (or more old-fashioned) than 'Can I . . .?' The two meanings of *may* could cause confusion: 'I *may* help you' can suggest possibility (as above), but could also mean I have permission to help you. In practice, the 'possibility' meaning might be assumed. Nevertheless it is worth being on the lookout for the risk of misunderstanding.

can or **tin**   A *can* is any metal container (a petrol can, etc) and *tin* specifies what it is made of. The two words became separated by the Atlantic Ocean, with a 'can of beans' as American and a 'tin of beans' British. But since beer was canned, *can* has become the more modern word in Britain, with *tin* sounding almost old-fashioned – whoever heard a British film director say 'It's in the *tin*'?

Canadian English   Spoken Canadian English is considerably affected by the spoken English of the United States, and the Canadian accent has a lot in common with the accent on the other side of the border. But the *written* language retains more allegiance to British English. Some US spellings (honor, program, tire . . .) have been adopted but not all. For example, Canadians write out 'cheques', rather than 'checks', and look through 'catalogues' instead of 'catalogs'. With vocabulary, it's anyone's guess: inevitably Canadians fill their cars with 'gas', but they keep their trousers up with 'braces' (not 'suspenders') and turn on 'taps' (not 'faucets').

candelabra, **candelabrum** or **chandelier**   *Candelabrum*, the Latin singular word (from 'candela', candle) for a majestic multi-branched candlestick, with *candelabra* for the plural form, are shown as standard even by the most recent dictionaries. But many people find this is pedantic and would use *candelabra* for the singular and *candelabras* for the plural. It remains a matter of choice.
Chandelier (from French 'chandelle', candle) became the fashionable name in the early 18th century. Now there is a distinction: *candelabra* (or *candelabrum*) for the standing version and *chandelier* for the suspended kind. And the same words apply whether they hold candles or electric light bulbs.

cannabis, **marijuana**, **pot**, **grass**, **dope** or **hashish**   Illicit drugs are a worldwide operation running into millions of pounds. These six terms for the most common drugs are confusing even to addicts. The difference between them is perhaps not all that important, since they are all terms for drugs derived from the flowers, bark, leaves and twigs of the hemp plant which yield a narcotic resin.
Marijuana (also spelt *marihuana*), made from the

dried leaves, flowers and stems, is the name for the preparation smoked as cigarettes; *cannabis* is more or less the same as marijuana, but more often used for the preparation that is eaten. Its name comes from the plant's botanical name (*Cannabis sativa*).
Pot and *grass* are popular slang names for marijuana, when rolled into cigarettes. *Dope* is a loosely used slang word for any narcotic drug, although perhaps more especially for cannabis and marijuana. *Hashish* (from the Arabic name for powdered hemp leaves) is properly applied to the resin obtained from the tender leaves at the top of hemp plants, which can be chewed or used for smoking.

cannon or **canon**   One *n* or two *n*s is sometimes a question. A *cannon* is the majestic museum-piece of a gun mounted on a carriage, often on display outside artillery barracks. In modern warfare, cannon is only used for the automatic guns firing shells that are fitted to aircraft. More peacefully, a *cannon* is the shot in billiards when a ball is made to *cannon* off two other balls in succession.
With one *n*, *canon* has a number of meanings: the most common are the title of a priest appointed as a member of a cathedral (a canon of Westminster), a church decree that regulates practice (the canons of the church), the list of works of an author (the Shakespeare canon), and a piece of music in which the same theme is taken up in successive parts (Tallis' 'Canon').

can't   See **contracted forms**

canvas or **canvass**   *Canvas* (rarely used as a verb) is the noun for the cotton or jute material; *canvass* (rarely used as a noun) is the verb for trying to win votes or orders or to seek opinions. To call an oil painting a *canvas*, because it is painted on canvas, is to show you're in the know in the art world, and the more usual plural would be *canvases*, although *canvasses* is also acceptable.

capacity   See **ability . . .**

capital . . .   *Capital* is all the money tied up in a business, whether it is in buildings, stock or equipment. A person's capital can be one of two things: it can represent the amount of money they have available or the total value of all their possessions. *Capital* is such a life-and-death factor that it is attached to a whole string of business and financial terms, such as *capital allowance*, for the amount a company is permitted to write off against tax to cover loss in value of equipment, etc; *capital equipment*, a general term for expensive equipment used in manufacturing the products a company sells; *capital gains*, the increase in value of a person's or a company's property, shares, etc, which becomes real when the items are sold and are subject to *capital gains tax*.

capitalism and **capitalist**   Not so long ago it was all right to call someone a capitalist. Recent dictionaries still define *capitalist* as someone who possesses capital and uses it in business, which applies to a lot of people. But Marxists won the battle for this word as, outside economic and political theory (where *capitalism* remains an unemotional word for a system based on private capital, as opposed to public ownership), *capitalist* and *capitalism* mean for many people exploitation of workers by those who control the means of production. In the 1990s, capitalists prefer to be called **industrialists**, developers or investors. When the former Soviet Union began to change over to a system that allowed for private ownership, *capitalism*, so heavily loaded with history, was replaced by the neutral term – **market economy**.

Capitalism and *capitalist* should be pronounced now with the stress on the first syllable: 'CAPitalist', 'CAPitalism', although some dictionaries still show stress on the second syllable as an alternative ('caPITalist'), but they are out of date about that.

CAPITAL LETTERS There was a time when most titles and institutions were dignified with initial capital letters: Managing Director, Bank Manager, the Bank, the Police, a Civil Servant, my daughter's Headmistress, our Solicitor. As society has become more egalitarian and authority less awesome, capital letters for most titles have dropped out of use. John Harvey-Jones writes about himself as the 'former chairman of ICI' and about the 'board' and the 'balance sheet', all without capitals. *The Times* believes that capitals 'make pompous what need not be' and have downgraded the four top cabinet posts to prime minister, chancellor of the exchequer, foreign secretary and home secretary, as well as calling President Bush the president, right on the front page (14.9.1990). This is going too far for most of us, although it's a pointer to the way the wind is blowing.

If you use capitals for too many titles, it will now seem heavy-going: if you use small letters for personages, such as the Archbishop of Canterbury, it will look out of order. The golden rule is be consistent: don't write Foreign Secretary followed by home secretary. But even this rule can be broken when the sense requires it. For example, it's helpful to use an initial capital for a specific dignitary in a general context: 'The Bishop gave an address to the assembly of bishops'; 'Edward Heath was the Prime Minister who took the UK into the EEC, a decision that was supported by prime ministers who succeeded him'.

The four seasons (spring, summer, etc) long ago lost their capitals. God still takes a capital (but not gods) and so does the Queen.

Abbreviations formed by initials are still usually in capitals: BBC, CBS, UNESCO. But where **acronyms** (words formed from initial letters of abbreviations) have become words in their own right, they may lose their capitals: **laser** (light amplification by stimulated emission of radiation). Sometimes they retain an initial capital for a while to remind us it's an abbreviation: **Aids** (acquired immune deficiency syndrome).

Titles of books, plays, chapters, newspapers and so on usually have a capital for the first and last words and

all other important words, but not for short words such as 'a', 'the', 'to', 'for', 'of', 'in': *The Taming of the Shrew, The Man Born to be King*.

Points of the compass take capitals and also when part of an established geographical name or defining a region: NW (North-West), NNE (North-North-East), Northern Ireland, South America, unemployment in the North. But if you are driving south or exposed to a cold north wind, or visiting western Scotland, use small letters.

There are not many rules left about the use of capitals. It's mostly convention and the conventions are changing. The National Consumer Council, in *Plain English for Lawyers*, advises 'avoid too many capital letters in a sequence. They are difficult to read'.

With terms, such as F/french window, V/venetian blind, capitals are optional, although the tendency is not to use them. When registered names, such as Hoover, Thermos, etc, are used in a general way, capitals are not used: we hoover the carpet. Lastly, it is no disrespect to the Duke of Wellington, to put on our wellingtons! See also (names of) **wines**

capital or *corporal* **punishment** 'Capitalis' is a Latin word relating to the head or life (a capital letter is at the head of a word); 'corpus' is Latin for body (a corpse is a dead one). Hence *capital punishment* is a sentence of death, and *corporal punishment* is inflicted on the body, usually by beating.

Capitol or **capitol** With a capital C, the Capitol is one of two buildings: the temple of ancient Rome dedicated to Jupiter in 509BC, and the building in Washington, DC where the US Congress meets, the cornerstone of which was laid by George Washington in 1793. With a small *c*, a *capitol* is the building in each state of the US where the State legislature meets. Either way, the *tol* is not stressed and *capitol* is pronounced in the same way as 'capital'.

capping (of expenditure) During the 1980s and early 90s, *rate capping* and later *charge capping* became controversial terms associated with the Conservative government. Capping is a limit of expenditure in a fiscal year imposed by central government on certain local authorities, with the object of reducing the level of the proposed local rate, community charge (see **poll tax**) or council charge set by those authorities. The objection is that capping results in cuts in social and education services.

caption or **subtitle** Both words mean the same: explanatory notes printed below illustrations or superimposed at the bottom of films. *Subtitle* has taken over altogether for film use ('English subtitles on a foreign film'), with *caption* the usual word in print. When a title is printed *above* the illustration, *caption* is the only possible word.

CAR This is a recent abbreviation used by banks and building societies when they pay interest monthly or at other intervals, instead of in one sum at the end of the year. CAR stands for compound annual rate, and is intended to show the true rate over 12 months when interest is left in the account to add to **capital** earning interest. See also **APR** (annual percentage rate).

carbon dating   See **absolute** (age)

car-boot sale   The expression appeared in the mid-1980s and has become established enough to have found a place in a headline in the business section of *The Times*. Anyone can take part by piling unwanted domestic junk into the boot of a car and driving to an established car-boot sale, which could be anywhere from a school playing field to the station car park at Brighton.

car clocking   Dictionaries are slow to catch up with *car clocking*, although it has been in use for some years in the motor trade, and defrauded buyers of secondhand cars soon learn it. Car clocking is the illegal practice of altering the mileage reading on the speedometer of a car so that it shows a lower figure than the true reading.

cardboard city   Not yet in dictionaries, *cardboard city* has become established, first by journalists and then by government ministers, to describe the plight of the homeless, particularly in London. They **sleep rough** (another journalistic and ministerial phrase), keeping as warm as they can using the insulation of cardboard carton 'walls' huddled together in a *cardboard city*, an underworld of poverty, **as seen on TV** by viewers in centrally heated houses and flats.

card vote   See **block vote** . . .

career woman   Women justifiably comment that there is no parallel description 'career man' and that *career woman* carries with it a 'judgement of feminine abnormality' (Ann Oakley, *Subject Woman*, 1982). Forecasts indicate that by the end of the century women will make up over half the workforce in Britain, and in the United States it is said that half of all accountants are now women and so are more than 25 per cent of Wall Street **high-fliers**. As the balance shifts from men towards their wives, girlfriends, daughters and sisters, *career woman* will become an old-fashioned term belonging to outmoded attitudes.

carefree or **careless**   There is an important distinction now. *Carefree* is a happy state, free from care or anxiety. *Careless* at one time meant the same: '. . . he never could recapture, The first fine careless rapture!' (Robert Browning, 1812–89, *Home Thoughts from Abroad*). But now *careless* is nearly always used in a negative way, to mean not bothering, not giving a damn.

carelessness   See **negligence** . . .

carillon or **peal**   When a bell or bells are rung it is a *peal*. When it is a tune played on bells or the effect of

bells created on a keyboard instrument, such as an organ, it can be called a *carillon* (pron: 'kerRILLion' or, less commonly, with the stress on the first syllable: 'KARRillion').

caring   Many people accused Margaret Thatcher of being *uncaring*, because of cuts in the health and social services, so *caring* became one of the most important words for every political party. No one quite knows what it means or who is being taken care of: the important thing is to have caring policies, to be in one of the caring professions, to have a caring attitude. A good word has become a political catchphrase and has lost its heart. See also **community**

carte blanche   See **blank cheque** . . .

cartel or **monopoly**   Both words have a lot in common as they describe the control of a market for a product or group of products, by fixing prices that no one can argue with, because competition is prevented. A *cartel* is an 'oligopoly', a word that only an economist would be likely to use, a group of companies who carve up the market between them, manipulating prices, production and advertising. A *monopoly* has the same effect, but with one organization controlling production and the market. Most countries try to prevent monopolies and cartels: there is the Monopolies and Mergers Commission in the UK and **antitrust** laws in America. See also **combine**

cartridge or **cassette**   *Cartridge* is used much more often now in **information technology** than it is about firearms. Computers, cameras, tape recorders, typewriters all use *cartridges*, plastic packs of film, disks, magnetic tape, or printing ribbon, ready for quick insertion and immediate use. *Cassette* is a parallel word, usually preferred instead of *cartridge*, for magnetic tape wound on spools for insertion into a *cassette-player*, and for 35mm film that slots into a camera.

case (grammatical)   Other than language teachers and classicists, how many people understand the *case-system* of language? And how much does it contribute to the good use of English? Some would claim that it is an essential part of English grammar, while others, for whom *case* is little more than a distant echo from their schooldays, would dismiss it as irrelevant.

Case defines the grammatical relationship of certain words in a sentence. For anyone who is interested, or needs to refresh their memory, look at this sentence: She sent him Mary's letter.

'She' does the action and is in the *nominative* (or *subjective*) *case*; 'letter' is the object of the action and is in the *accusative* (or *objective*) *case*; 'him' is the recipient of the action and is in the *dative case*; 'Mary's' denotes possession and is in the *genitive* (or *possessive*) *case*.

Old English, the language before roughly the mid 12th century, had a *case-system* as complex as Latin and Greek, with different forms of words depending on how they related to other words in the sentence. But nearly all that system has dropped away and no one misses it. Even what is left of case in modern English is often arguable. Because the verb 'to be', for example, is a verb of 'being', it should properly be followed by the nominative case (I, she, he, etc). Most grammarians concede that 'it's me', 'this is him' . . . sound natural when we are speaking, but require the nominative case ('it is I', 'this is he' . . .) in writing. This is reasonable in formal writing but does written English always have to be so stiff-necked? There is also much argument about whether 'as' is followed by the accusative case ('as me') or the nominative case ('as I'). See **as**. This applies to the words following 'than' (see **than _I_ or _me_**), to say nothing of the notorious 'between you and I' (see **I or me**).

In the future development of English, case may well become increasingly irrelevant, although for the foreseeable future careful writers will continue to observe at least some of the rules. But if you spend too much time worrying about it you can end up as a suitable *case* for treatment. See also **direct and indirect object**

cash . . . *Cash* is a focal word in business and leads to a number of compound terms. A *cash book* records all in-and-out transactions in a company's bank account; a *cash cow* is one of a company's products in a reliable market, that generates a steady regular income which can be 'milked' to support new products or to develop new markets; *cash flow* is the money flowing in and out, and it is important that there is enough cash flow to support daily needs (a business that carries considerable stocks or gives long-term credit may be sound financially but have serious *cash-flow problems*); *cash limit* is a British fiscal term to define a limit set on government departments' spending, to prevent total government expenditure getting out of control (the system of cash limits is criticized because it often obstructs or delays valuable projects that may be important socially or may generate additional income or economies); *cash ratio* is the critical reserve a company or a bank keeps available to meet demands, such as, in the case of a bank, customers coming in to *cash* cheques.

cask See **barrel** . . .

casket You have to be careful using *casket* in America, where most people will assume you mean a coffin.

cassette See **cartridge** . . .

-cast *Cast* is related to an Old Norse word for something thrown up, and has been in English since the 13th century, giving birth to a number of compound words, such as broadcast, forecast, overcast, etc.

cast or **throw** See **throw** . . .

caste This is associated with the rigid traditional social separation among Hindus. But the 'caste system' is also used in Western society as a comment on divisions in society based on family background and inherited wealth. See also **accents (in speech)**

caster See **castor** . . .

Castilian and **Catalan** *Castilian* is another name for the official Spanish language. It developed from the language spoken in Castile, the former kingdom in the central plateau of Spain that has dominated politics and culture in the country since 1479, when its union with Aragon, the kingdom in NE Spain, led to the formation of the Spanish state.

Although the Spanish is 'castellano', in English *Castile* has only one *l*. Catalan is the language of Catalonia, the region of NE Spain bordering France. It is related to Castilian, but different enough to be confusing to people who have learned standard Spanish: The survival of Catalan as a language (it is spoken by over five million people in Catalonia) has helped to maintain the strong tradition of **separatism** in Spain, so *Catalan* is a word that has political connotations as well as linguistic ones.

casting couch Even if the practice goes on, *casting couches* are now museum pieces. They go back to the time when some film producers and impresarios kept a couch in their office in order to claim an immediate return for giving a young actress a part in a film or show. According to Kenneth Anger, the film director and Hollywood archivist, the original casting couch was in the office of Mack Sennett (1884–1960), who produced Keystone Cops and Charlie Chaplin comedies.

castor or **caster** *Castor* is the usual spelling for the swivelled wheels on armchairs and sofas, and for white sugar more finely ground than granulated sugar. In both those meanings, *caster* is, for the time being, an alternative spelling but less common. *Castor* is the only spelling for *castor oil* (probably because the origin may go back to 'castoreum', an oil essence obtained from beavers and used as a drug).

casual *Casual* suggests something that has happened in passing ('a casual affair') or that no one has bothered about ('she was casual about it, as if she didn't care much'). In this sense *casual* and *careless* (see **carefree** . . .) are close to each other. *Casual* has also come to be the standard English equivalent of **laid-back**, relaxed and easy-going, which makes it close to **carefree**. Casual clothes, or casuals, are as carefully designed – and as expensive – as the most formal clothes. In fact, designers put a lot of hard work into making clothes look casual.

casualty The *casualty department* of a hospital deals with victims of accidents and disasters. But *casualty* is now used in a much wider context about anyone or anything that has suffered as a result of some action: 'The first casualty of war is truth', as a war correspondent wrote early in the 1991 Gulf War.

Catalan See **Castilian and Catalan**

catalyst To use this fashionable word effectively it helps to understand what a *catalyst* means in chemistry: a substance, whose composition remains unchanged, that brings about by its presence a chemical change in something else. The extension of this meaning in everyday language is for something or somebody who does or says very little but changes a situation or brings about an understanding, simply by being involved: a counsellor can act as a catalyst in a difficult marital situation. But it is senseless to use *catalyst* simply to mean making something happen: 'Lack of planning was a catalyst in the failure of the project'. The proper words in that context are '. . . was a factor . . .' or '. . . caused . . .'.

catalytic Before the late 1980s, few motorists had heard of a *catalytic converter*, but by the end of the 1990s every car may be required by law to have one fitted. It is a device fitted to the exhaust system that incorporates a **catalyst** which converts pollutants, such as carbon monoxide, into harmless emissions.

catamite Most people had never heard of the word until the very first sentence of Anthony Burgess's novel, *Earthly Powers* (1980), sent them rushing to their dictionaries: 'It was the afternoon of my eighty-first birthday, and I was in bed with my catamite when Ali announced that the archbishop had come to see me'.

In the Middle Ages, Ganymede, Jupiter's cup-bearer, was a symbol of homosexuality, and in the late 16th century the name was adapted as *catamite*, to mean a boy kept by a man for sex. *Catamite* has continued to be included in dictionaries, although rarely used, waiting for Anthony Burgess to summon it up.

catchphrase or **slogan** *Catchphrase* was probably taken from 'catchword', used in party politics in the early 1800s. A catchphrase is now more likely to be called a *slogan*, a Scottish battle cry from the 16th century. Slogans are used now, not to rally the troops, as they once were, but to boost a political party or to sell anything from toothpaste to an airline.

catch-22 Useful shorthand to describe a 'heads I lose – tails you win' situation. It is in dictionaries now and some class it as standard English. It comes from Joseph Heller's book, *Catch-22* (1961), in which a US Air Force captain asks to be grounded because he is insane. But the proposed flight mission was suicidal and it was good sense to try to get out of it, so how could he be insane? Suppose your boss asks you to come up with a brilliant new idea. You do just that, but then he asks 'But how do we know it will work – we've never tried anything like it before?' The characteristic of *catch-22* is that the case for both sides is so reasonable, there's no way out.

categorical or **unconditional** It is not sufficient any more to have a denial, it has to be a *categorical* denial, we cannot just state something, it has to be a *categorical* statement. *Categorical* is used so often to mean absolute or without argument, that it has lost its power. The 1991 Gulf War offered a simpler and more direct word, when the United Nations' resolution demanded from Iraq an *unconditional* withdrawal.

cathartic It is not uncommon for people to talk about a *cathartic experience*, meaning a profound experience. This is a misunderstanding of *catharsis*, which is from the Greek word for purification, a concept that Aristotle (384–322BC) in *Poetics* saw as the function of Greek tragedy: to purge the psyche of excessive emotions by arousing those same emotions in the audience. 20th-century psychoanalysis uses the same principle to release suppressed fears and complexes by bringing up the events that caused them. For an experience to be truly cathartic, it must apply the 'hair of the dog' principle, freeing someone of a fear that has haunted them, through arousing the emotion that was the source of the problem.

Catholic or **catholic** *Catholic* with a capital C is religious, referring to the *Roman Catholic* religion and its adherents. As an ordinary word, *catholic* is a secular application of the Greek word 'holos', whole (see also **holistic**), to mean a wide range of tastes and interests: if you have, for example, a catholic taste in music, it suggests you enjoy anything from Bach to Bebop.

catsup See **ketchup** . . .

Caucasian The Caucasus Mountains between the Black Sea and the Caspian Sea is where white races are supposed to have originated, and *Caucasian* (pron: 'kawKAYzhan') is used in scientific contexts as a term for white or light-skinned races. On a BBC programme a doctor described research being carried out on Caucasians to see if their response to specific drugs was different from Africans'. While it is unquestionable, of course, to use *Caucasian* for inhabitants of the Caucasus, in ordinary contexts it is preferable to use 'white people' or 'whites' for the white races of the world.

cause or **causation** *Causation* is more likely to be used in a medical context to describe why certain symptoms appear. *Cause* is the general word for someone or something that makes an event occur. Used in that way the word *cause* says it all, and there is no need to add 'because of', 'due to' or any other linking phrase: 'the cause of the government's defeat was because of the poll tax'. Leave out 'because of' and the sentence is sharper and more direct.

caustic or **sarcastic** *Caustic* comes from a Greek word that means burning (caustic soda or sodium hydroxide are alkaline crystals that burn the skin on contact). A caustic comment or remark has the same effect, so to speak, because it is sharp and hurtful.

Sarcastic comes from a different Greek word with an

equally unpleasant meaning – to tear flesh. A sarcastic comment is double-edged, achieving its effect by a cutting comment that is intended to mean the opposite. If someone comes to stay for the weekend, bringing as an offering a packet of crisps, a caustic comment would be 'Thank you for nothing!': a sarcastic one would be 'Thank you for being so very generous!' See also **ironic** . . .

cavalcade or **motorcade**   Just as cavalry is a section of an army on horseback, so a cavalcade has been, since the 17th century, a procession of horsemen or horse-drawn carriages. By extension *cavalcade* has come to be used for a sequence of connected historical events (Noel Coward called his patriotic play about the courage of the British, *Cavalcade*). For want of another word, a procession of cars was called a cavalcade, but *motorcade* is the usual word now, which is more appropriate.

caveat emptor   This Latin motto, often quoted as a principle in common law, should be over the entrance to every supermarket. It means 'let the buyer beware' and is a reminder that when we buy anything it is our responsibility to decide that it is worth the money. Pron: 'CAV-ee-at-EMPTor'.

caveat subscriptor   Just as you are on the point of signing a contract, this is the Latin phrase to call to mind. It means 'let the signer beware'. Admittedly it is not used very much now, but it could be useful to bring it out when someone complains that you are taking too long over reading the **small print**. Pron: 'CAV-ee-at subSCRIPTor'.

caviare or **caviar**   The authentic caviare is black, the roe of a sturgeon, which is what it was as far back as the 16th century. The red roe of a salmon is also called caviare, but while not exactly downmarket, a **tsar** would only have eaten it on off-days, if at all. The authentic spelling is *caviare*, with *caviar* as an alternative.

CBI   The Confederation of British Industry (formed in 1965 to represent the major industrial employers in the UK) is often in the news, as the most important non-governmental economic indicator. The 11-syllable name in full is something of a mouthful and it is nearly always referred to as the CBI.

cc   At the bottom of some business letters, the abbreviation *cc* is still sometimes seen to indicate that copies of the letters have been sent to other people ('*cc* John Brown, Mary Smith . . .'). People have forgotten, or never knew, that the letters *cc* stand for 'carbon copies', so are now as out of date as carbon paper itself. Alternatives that have been proposed are *wpc* (wordprocessed copy), *p/o* (printout), or simply – *copy to*. . . .

CD   See **compact disc**

CE   See **AD**

cease   See **stop** . . .

cedilla   The little squiggle which, when used below a *c* in French (ç), changes it from a *k* to an *s* sound. It has also been adopted as a 'softening accent' in a few other languages such as Turkish. See **French accents**

Ceefax   See **videotex(t)**

ceiling   It is easy to make a fool of yourself when using this word to indicate the upper limit of something. A sales director, anxious to maintain prices, declared 'I am determined to stick to the ceiling'. Philip Howard in *Words Fail Me* reminds us that Hugh Dalton once announced 'a ceiling price on carpets'. You have been warned.

celibacy or **chastity**   The two words overlap. Strictly speaking, *celibacy* is the state of being unmarried ('célibataire' is the French word for a bachelor, or, less commonly, an unmarried woman). That is how the *OED* defines *celibacy*. When Michael Saward, a canon of St Paul's Cathedral, wrote that the Roman Catholic Church should not be allowed 'to foist clerical celibacy on the rest of us as a necessary requirement for Christian ministry' (*The Times* 9.5.1991), he was using the word to mean abstention from marriage.

But *celibacy* has come to be used so often for abstention from sexual relations, that most current dictionaries now usually show that as the first meaning of the word. So a married man might talk about 'a month of enforced celibacy' because his wife is away.

Chastity is unambiguous: it can only mean abstention from sex. Although it is available for use about both sexes, it tends to be used more about women. The descriptive word *chaste* is less clear: it describes chastity, total abstention from sex, but it is also used sometimes for not indulging in sex outside marriage.

cellphone   Telephones are now more for people than for places: by the end of the century, it is believed that portable phones will be in the hands of 15 million people in Britain. *Cellphones* are part of this revolution: they are radio-telephones installed permanently in cars, or portable, small enough to fit in a briefcase or even a pocket. The *cellular system* uses a network of base stations across the country, with special channels. Calls are transmitted to the nearest station (or cell) which links up with an exchange connected to the worldwide telephone network.

cellulite   The cause and cure of this condition are subject to much controversy, both in medical circles and among women themselves. The French seem to have invented this name for the 'orange peel thighs' sighed over by so many women of all shapes and sizes, and lead the market in special creams, pills, surgical techniques and expensive courses of exercises, each lauded as The Cure.

celluloid   It is surprising to find out that the name of this first commercial plastic material dates from 1871. It is highly flammable, which made cinema film so dangerous when it was made of celluloid. Film technicians still talk about 'putting it on celluloid' to mean filming the scene, but the term is obsolete for film and is only used as film jargon, to show you're in the know.

Celsius or **centigrade** In 1985 the BBC switched from giving temperatures in weather forecasts as X° *centigrade* to X° *Celsius*. Anders Celsius (1701–44) was the Swedish astronomer who devised the logical *centigrade scale* at which water freezes at 0° and boils at 100°. *Celsius* (with a capital C, pron: 'SELsyus') is the international name for this scale and has now been adopted in the UK. There is nothing else to learn, because 20° Celsius is exactly the same as 20° centigrade and both are abbreviated 20°C (no stop). Most people, other than **meteorologists**, still say *centigrade*.

Celt, **Celtic**, **Gaelic** or **Gallic** There were a number of *Celtic* tribes, which included the pre-Roman inhabitants of Britain. The present-day Irish, Scottish, Welsh and Bretons all, at times, call themselves *Celts*, and so do the people of Cornwall and the Isle of Man. *Celtic* is a general descriptive word for anything relating to the Celts and is the name of the group of languages that belong to them, which includes Cornish, Welsh, Irish and Breton. *Celt* and *Celtic* can begin with an *s* sound ('selt', 'SELtic'), but a *k* sound is usually preferred: 'kelt', 'KELtic'. An exception is the Scottish football team, Celtic, always pronounced 'SELtic'.

Gaelic, as a descriptive word, can be used in the same way as *Celtic*, but is usually reserved for the *languages* of the Celts, especially the forms spoken in Ireland, Scotland and the Isle of Man. Pron: 'GAYlic' (rather than 'GALLic').

Gallic is a different word altogether. It relates to Gaul, an ancient region of Europe that included France, and is now used to describe anything that has a particularly *French* style, from the worldly way a Frenchman gestures (a Gallic shrug) to the way Parisiennes walk (a Gallic swing of the hips).

cement, **concrete** or **Portland cement** *Cement* is the grey powder, a mixture of limestone and clay. When it is mixed, either by hand or in a *cement-mixer*, with water and sand, it hardens into *concrete*, the most common of all building materials. *Portland cement* is not a brand of cement, as some people suppose, but the most commonly used cement mixture, which includes chalk, so-called because it hardens to the colour of Portland stone quarried on the Isle of Portland, Dorset.

censorship or **restrictions** In World War II, *censorship* was freely used when news was edited for reasons of military security. But the word has become increasingly uneasy, suggesting the withholding of information for political and propaganda purposes. In the 1991 Gulf War, the word *censorship* was hardly ever used: the broadcasts of allied reporters in Baghdad were subject to 'restrictions'. In this context, *restrictions* means exactly the same as *censorship*, but apparently sounds more diplomatic.

census, **consensus** or **concensus** *Concensus* is not in dictionaries because it is a common misspelling of *consensus*. The mistake is easily avoided by remembering that *consent* and *consensus* have the same origin, the latter meaning general consent and agreement about a decision or point of view. See also **consensus of opinion; consensus politics**

Census, a different word, was used by Gibbon in *The Decline and Fall of the Roman Empire* (1776–88) for the count of the population, which is how it is still used. The plural is *censuses*.

centenary or **centennial** A centenary is the hundredth anniversary of an event; *centennial* describes something that relates to a hundred years or takes place every hundred years. It gets confusing when Americans celebrate an important centennial, because that means for them exactly the same as a British centenary.

centigrade See **Celsius** . . .

central processor Nearly all the administration in our lives, from the cradle to the grave, is registered and regulated by *central processors*, otherwise known as *central processing units* or *CPUs*. These are the master minds of computers, housing the circuits that execute commands and resolve arithmetical and logical problems. All other computer functions, such as **keyboards**, **VDUs**, printers, etc, are subservient to the central processors. In the 1990s, the defence, control, communications of civilization are dependent upon the central processors of the world. See also **computer**

centre A *centre* is used to mean an important group of buildings and facilities for certain activities, such as the Barbican Centre in London or the Lincoln Center (American spelling) in New York. But now any poky backstreet shop seems to have the presumption to call itself 'The Cycle Centre', 'The Travel Centre' (if it's a travel agent), or whatever.

Linguistic purists object to 'centre *around*' or '. . . *about*' ('the discussion centred around the proposed merger'), insisting on 'centre *on*' or '. . . *in*'. Perhaps they have a case, but centre 'around', or 'about' is common usage, and useful to suggest touching on different aspects of something rather than focusing on one central detail.

centre ground (in politics) The *centre ground* was the political catchphrase at one time used about the Social Democratic Party when it was formed in 1981, to suggest its belief in limited state intervention combined with decentralization of authority, so-called moderate policies between the Left and Right parties. It is an uncertain political term in the 1990s, when the main political parties have many members advocating middle-of-the-road policies. See **Left and Right** . . .

centurion A centurion was the commander of a Roman legion of a hundred men. So you might have a double take when you first hear a commentator of a test match talk about *centurions*: they have borrowed the word to mean a player who has scored a hundred runs.

century *Century* used to be spelt with a capital C, but no longer, not in the 20th *century*. Even when it is an abbreviation, a small *c* is usually used (19thc). But 19C is also seen, particularly in guide books closely packed with historical facts and dates. Perhaps this is why *century* is still so often seen, incorrectly, with a capital C.

ceramic or **pottery** *Ceramic* can include a wide range of articles made out of a baked clay mixture, such as tiles, earthenware, china and porcelain. *Pottery* could include most ceramics, but not, by custom, **china** or **porcelain**. Since pottery in Britain, under the influence of potters such as Bernard Leach (1887–1979), has been used not only for utilitarian objects but as an art form, as it was in ancient Greece, there has been a tendency to call it *ceramics*, perhaps because the word comes from the Greek word for pottery, 'keramikós', whereas *pottery* is a more earthy Old English word. *Pottery* should be used about everyday pots and jugs, *ceramic* reserved for pottery that sets out to be art, although it must be added that the dividing line is often arguable (we talk of ceramic tiles, not pottery tiles, lining the bathroom walls). It seems affected to call someone a *ceramist* (pron: 'SERR-e(r)mist') rather than a *potter*, the word Bernard Leach used about himself.

ceremonial or **ceremonious** *Ceremonial* is used about occasions of pomp and splendour. *Ceremonious* is used about people and behaviour and is not usually complimentary, as it suggests an exaggerated and fussy formality: 'after the feast, there were ceremonial dances'; 'before speaking, he gave a ceremonious bow'.

ceremonial English See **formal English** . . .

certain *Certain* can mean *un*certain, which can at times lead to misunderstanding: 'she has a certain talent for cooking' could mean you might eat well – if you're lucky, or that you're bound to eat well. In speech, it is usually clear by the way someone says it: emphasis means *certain*, a slight hesitation implies *un*certain. In writing it is better to put your cards on the table: 'an undoubted talent', 'a real talent' or 'a modest talent', 'a limited talent'.

cervical *Cervical* is an anatomical word relating to the neck. But for most women it is a word used about the womb, as they are familiar with the *cervical smear* test, a specimen taken from the neck (or cervix) of the womb, which is examined for early detection of cancer.
    In medical circles, *cervical* is likely to be pronounced 'serVYCal' (stress on second syllable, rhyming with 'cycle'), but not, as is often heard, 'serVY-ACal'. 'SERvical' (stress on first syllable, rhyming with 'bicycle') is the pronunciation most other people find more natural. Dictionaries offer both alternatives.

CFCs CFCs are in the news, on the agendas of international conferences, but how many government ministers (**pace** former research chemist Margaret Thatcher) could write down what the letters stand for? Chlorofluorocarbons (pron: 'KLAWro–floohro–CAHbe(r)ns') are a range of gaseous mixtures, mainly, as the name suggests, of carbon, chlorine and fluorine, which are used in the cooling systems of refrigerators and air conditioners, in **aerosols**, cleaning agents, plastic foams, and other industrial and domestic applications. They have the chemical advantage of being stable and non-toxic but have been identified as the chemicals that thin the **ozone** layer, contributing to **global warming** and increasing the worldwide risk of skin cancer.

chagrin It is a French word and some people still copy the French pronunciation, making the second syllable slightly nasal. But this seems affected now as the standard pronunciation is anglicized: 'SHAgrin'. If it's pronounced 'shaGREEN' (not unheard of), it's another word altogether (shagreen is a form of leather with a rough surface).

chain reaction A popular term borrowed from chemistry and nuclear physics, where it describes a ripple effect, with one reaction causing another or a series of similar reactions, sometimes controlled, as in a nuclear reactor, sometimes uncontrolled, as in an explosion. Outside science, *chain reaction* is used for a number of inevitable consequences brought about by one event, and are usually uncontrollable. In this sense, *chain reaction* is identical with **knock-on effect**.

chain store See **multiple** . . .

chairman, **chairperson** or **the chair** *Chairman* was one of the first victims of the campaign against sexist language. Up to that time, *chairwoman* or the old-worldly 'Madam Chairman' was used. Then *chairperson* became standard on the BBC. But since then the BBC have adopted *chair*, which has become the most usual unisex word, although it has led to such absurdities as 'this is the chair's chair'. ICI and most other big institutions still prefer to have a chairman, and *The Sunday Times Business News* has described Ms Jan Hall as 'chairman of the Design Business Association'. *Chairperson* remains in use but *chair* is gaining ground among many writers and speakers. See also **-person**

chaise longue Whereas in Britain or America a sexual scandal can still cause a government minister to resign, the French would look at the offender not only with sympathy but with admiration. It is not by chance that the *chaise longue* was invented in Paris and that in the 1820s the French name for this accommodating sofa, unrestricted because there is a backrest at only one end and a low armrest along the side, was adopted in London. The proper plural is *chaises longues*, although some dictionaries concede *chaise longues* as an alternative. But either way, to pronounce the final *s* ('shezz long*z*'), although regrettably also regarded as an alternative, sounds decidedly downmarket. See also **couch** . . .

chamber or **lodging**   These are archaic words that survive in special ways. A *chamber* (from Latin 'camera', the current Italian word for a bedroom) is a room or a hall, and by extension the organization that meets in it: the London Chamber of Commerce. Barristers would not dream of having 'rooms' or 'offices' in one of the Inns of Court: they have *chambers*.

Lodgings is now an upmarket word too: if you take lodgings in a town, it suggests you are engaged in some cultural or diplomatic mission; and the gracious accommodation occupied by heads of Oxford colleges is traditionally called their lodgings. On the other hand, a *lodger* moves a long way downmarket: if you take in lodgers, you are letting bedsitters to any Tom, Dick or Mary, to make ends meet.

chamois   For some obscure reason, when it is a goat antelope, it is pronounced 'SHAMwah' but when it is the soft leather for washing cars or windows we say 'SHAMmee' (and sometimes even spell it 'shammy', although it is better not to). In passing, the plural remains *chamois*, pronounced the same as the singular or with a final *z* sound: 'SHAMwahz'.

champagne   To begin with and long ago, the bubbles were present in champagne as an unwanted by-product of secondary fermentation. Then (so the legend goes) a local monk, called Dom Pérignon, saw the possibilities. From then on the bubbles gave this hitherto modest white wine from the Champagne region of France star billing. By law, only the sparkling wine produced in the officially designated area around Reims and Epernay, to the east of Paris, can be called *champagne*. Sparkling wines from other regions are said to be *méthode champenoise*. Other wine-producing countries call their sparkling wine by another name: Italy calls it *asti spumante* (pron: 'asti-spooMANtee'); Germany has *sekt*; Spain, *cava* (pron: 'CAHva').

Champagne is associated with celebration and luxury and at different times has attracted pet names. *Bubbly* harks back to the roaring twenties and the charleston. Those in the know advise that *champers* (pron: 'SHAMperz') should be shunned, as a Hooray Henry vulgarism. The in-word now is *fizz*, used by serious wine writers, even in *The Times*. *Fizz* comes nearer to imitating the sound of effervescence in a glass, but remember it is used not only for champagne, but for any sparkling wine, even if it hasn't been within

a thousand miles of Reims or Epernay. See also **marque**; (names of) **wines**

chandelier   See **candelabra** . . .

change   See **alter** . . .

(the) **change**   See **menopause** . . .

channel or **frequency**   At one time *channel* related to 'canal' (both words come from Latin 'canalis') and referred to some kind of waterway. But now, outside seafaring contexts, *channel* is used more often about communication, sometimes in a general way: 'please keep in touch through the usual channels' usually means going through the same intermediaries. In radio and television a channel is a band or range of frequencies between defined limits, over which the station transmits: it is also used for the name of the station itself ('Channel Four', 'switch to another channel').

A *frequency* is the specific rate at which electromagnetic waves (or sound waves) vibrate, measured in *hertz* units, abbreviated Hz (named after Heinrich Hertz, the German physicist who in 1888 first detected radio waves), which are one cycle per second. For optimum reception, a receiver has to be tuned to the most suitable frequency for a particular location, within the waveband available for that *channel*. See also **FM**

Channel tunnel, **Chunnel**, **Eurotunnel** or **Le Shuttle**   On 1 December 1990, construction workers from the British and French sides met in the middle of the English Channel: Malcolm Rifkind, British minister for transport at the time, announced this was the first time since the Ice Age that Britain was joined to Europe.

Eurotunnel is the name of the consortium who, in January 1986, won the concession to build the *Channel tunnel*. *Chunnel*, the telescoping of *Ch*annel *tunnel*, bid fair to become the popular name, but there was an Anglo-French wrangle over it. Market researchers came up with a new name, a mishmash of **franglais** – *Le Shuttle*. In 1992, *Eurotunnel* announced this as the name for the cross-Channel shuttle-coach service.

If the French are happy to take *Le Shuttle* to England for 'le weekend', perhaps it's not asking too much for the British to show some entente cordiale and accept the name as well.

chaos   *Chaos* is a cosmic word used to describe the state that existed before the creation of the universe when 'the earth was without form and void' (*Genesis*). *Utter chaos* should not perhaps be used lightly about, say, an untidy collection of papers on someone's desk.

chap   *Chap* (formerly an abbreviation for 'chapman', a travelling salesman) is a dated word, although some older people still use it. But do women go out with *chaps* any more? *Old chap* now sounds patronizing, and *chappie* is arch.

chaperon or **chaperone**   Both spellings are all right, with *chaperon* as the usual one. *Chaperon* is less likely to be used now as it used to be, for an older woman who accompanies a girl to protect her reputation and virtue, but more generally for a woman in charge of a group of young people on an outing. There's no reason why a man should not be called a chaperon(e), but it's less usual. The alternative spellings also apply to the verb.

character, **personality** or **persona** Human beings defy ultimate analysis and these three words attempt to separate different aspects of a person, which are easily confused. *Character* should apply to someone's inner strength, mental, emotional and moral qualities that set the standards of their behaviour.

Personality describes the qualities a person projects outwards, their force, style, humour. Someone may have a strong character but not necessarily a strong personality, in that they could be self-effacing. More common, is someone with a strong personality who does not have a strong character, in that their steadfastness cannot be relied upon.

In Latin, a *persona* is a mask, especially worn by actors to show the roles they are playing. Jung used *persona* as a psychological term for the ways people present themselves to the world, their attempt to adapt to society and life. A persona is a role acted out in real life: we cannot truly know the person, until we look behind the mask.

characteristic, **representative** or **symptomatic** Each of these words can describe something that fits into a pattern. If we say of a novel, for example, that it is *characteristic* of a particular writer, it suggests that it is in keeping with previous novels by the same person. To say it is *representative* is almost the same, with the added suggestion that the novel contains examples of characters, turns of plot, etc that have been used in previous novels by the writer.

When something is *symptomatic*, it is an example of a problem or difficulty that occurs regularly in the same context: 'the character of Helen in the novel is symptomatic of his failure to understand how a woman feels'. *Symptomatic* relates to the medical sense of *symptom*, a physical or mental indication of a disorder. It should not be used, as it sometimes is, about something good, as in 'this is symptomatic of his ability to handle a complex plot'. The word there should be *characteristic*.

charge account See credit account

charge card See credit card . . .

chargehand or **foreman** These are both supervisors in factories or on sites, responsible for a group of workers. A *chargehand* (a British term, usually now one word rather than two or hyphenated) is usually in charge of a smaller group and carries less responsibility. A *foreman*, used in Britain and America, could be in charge of a whole team of workers on a project.

charisma and **charismatic** In the last ten years these words have moved into such popular use

that they have lost contact with 'kharisma', the original New Testament Greek word meaning the gift of grace, a quality conferred by God. *Charisma* has become a **designer** tag for anyone or anything a little out of the ordinary, from a politician to an athlete or a fashionable restaurant. Nevertheless it is better to reserve the word for people, for some extraordinary quality that sets them apart and enables them to have exceptional influence on others. There are people like that, but not as many as the frequent use of the words suggests. Pron: 'kaRISma', 'karisMATic'.

charlady, **charwoman** or **cleaner** *Char* is a much earlier version of 'chore', a tedious job of work, and in the 16th century *woman* was tagged on to it to make *charwoman*. When charwomen became hard to find, they moved up to *charladies*, leading to such anomalies as 'I am a woman barrister's *charlady*'. But both have almost dropped out of use, and notices in newsagents' windows are now headed: '*Cleaner* wanted'.

Some people talk about their *daily*, an inaccurate word for a cleaner who comes in once a week! *Home help* was a popular genteelism, but less so now, since it is a term used by social services for helpers sent to do things for people unable to look after themselves.

charter or **hire** Generally *charter* is used about a means of transport: ships are chartered, a charter flight is on an aircraft chartered by a travel company. *Hire* is used for people, objects and places: hiring a dance band, a hall, equipment. Exceptions are taxis, which are 'for hire', and cars, which are hired.

chartered accountant CA after an accountant's name denotes membership of the Institute of Chartered Accountants in Scotland, the oldest of the professional bodies, which received its royal charter in 1854. ACA denotes associate membership of the corresponding Institute in England and Wales or the separate Institute in Ireland. FCA after someone's name shows they have achieved fellowship of either Institute, but this is not a higher degree, as fellowship is automatically awarded ten years after first qualifying. All it indicates is more experience – and more grey hairs.

(the) **charts** *The charts* are holy writ in the world of pop music: they are the lists produced weekly of the best-selling records and albums. To get *in the charts* is the equivalent in the theatre of having your name up in lights: it means you've arrived.

charwoman See charlady . . .

chastity See celibacy . . .

chat show or **discussion programme** A *chat show* is an ego-trip on radio or television: people, more or less well-known, are invited by an interviewer, who has been more or less briefed about them, to expound on their work, their lives, their plans, their hopes, as if the future of the world depends upon it. A *discussion programme* is an exchange of views between experts or other people, more or less informed, about almost anything under the sun. Both *chat shows* and *discussion programmes* demand compulsive talk without reflection: the ineffable is unacceptable, since unless we can talk about everything without hesitation, we are inarticulate, ineffective and no use on radio or television. Yet the quality of response to art or to any experience is inevitably cheapened if there is an overriding obligation to say something about it right away. See also **chattering classes**

chattels Derived in the 13th century from medieval Latin, *chattels* survives mostly only in legal use, to describe possessions that can be moved, as opposed to land and buildings. It is usually doubled with an Old English word, so that everyone can understand: *goods and chattels*.

chattering classes No one is quite sure who are the *chattering classes*. The description was first used derisively about the verbal activists who attacked Margaret Thatcher's policies on news and discussion programmes. Since then the term has become conversational and journalistic shorthand to write off self-proclaimed pundits, whether they are writers, political journalists, presenters of current affairs programmes or the more articulate academics, who have access to airtime on radio and television. The chattering classes are 'talking heads' (to borrow Alan Bennett's title for his monologues) dedicated to being seen and heard as often as they can, usually cloaking commonplace opinions with the appearance of insight. See also **chat show** . . .

chauvinism and **chauvinist** Nicholas Chauvin, a soldier in Napoleon's army, acquired an inglorious immortality. His simple-minded unquestioning devotion to his leader led to his name surviving as the word for dangerous unthinking patriotism: my country, my party, my cause – right or wrong. See also **jingoism**.

In the 1960s, the women's liberation movement adopted the word and *male chauvinists* was used angrily for men who assumed as if by right their superiority over women. First in America and then in Britain, *male chauvinist pig* became a passionate term of abuse, for after years of being 'chicks', 'cows' and 'dogs', women turned the tables and animalized men.

cheap or **cheaply** When it comes to buying and selling, *cheaply* is more formal ('we must buy as cheaply as we can'), *cheap* is more usual: 'we must buy as cheap as we can'. Apart from that, *cheap* is a word to use with caution: it has for centuries meant low in price and good value, but has also come to mean worthless and shoddy. As the context does not usually make it clear which meaning is intended, it is often worth adding an extra phrase: 'we must buy as cheap as we can, so long as the quality is first class'.

cheap money A political and economic expression much used about the 1980s. Money is cheap when banks are falling over themselves to lend money, and interest rates are low. Governments may encourage a *cheap money policy* to stimulate the economy, increase production and reduce unemployment. But such good things come to an end in a 'boom and bust' cycle. See also **affluent**; **consumer society**

check See **bill**

check, **check up on** or **check out** Everyone agrees that it's all right to *check* something. Some nit-pickers object to *check up on* as unnecessary extra words, but people like using *check up on* to imply checking extra carefully because there is doubt. And in the 1990s to *check out* something, meaning to look into something or somewhere to see if it is suitable, has become as much at home in Britain as in America.

Cheers! *Cheer* is associated with the Latin word for 'face', and in the 13th century it was used for the expression on the face. This led to *Cheer up!* as an encouragement to someone looking downcast, and to the cry of goodwill: *Three cheers for . . .!* By this linguistic route, *Cheers!* became the most usual salutation in English when people drink together.

More recently, for some unexplained reason, *Cheers!* has been turned into an all-purpose expression, particularly with younger people, instead of 'Goodbye' or 'Thank you'.

chemical weapons See **biological weapons** . . .

chemist or **pharmacy** Most people in Britain go to the *chemist* for medical goods and toiletries, or to have a prescription made up. But many chemists now prefer *pharmacy*, a more distinguished name since it goes back to the Greek word for the practice of a person trained in the use of drugs. But it is slow to catch on with their customers. In America the usual word is 'druggist'.

chemistry *Chemistry* is the science concerned with the qualities and interaction between thousands of natural and synthetic substances. An interesting extension is the use of chemistry about people, the interaction between different temperaments and personalities, which can cause good or bad business, professional, social and sexual relationships. The use of *chemistry* in this way has a certain logic, since an encounter between one person and another is dependent on the interaction of so many fears, anxieties, memories, dreams and longings.

cherubs or **cherubim** Cupid is the most familiar example of a cherub, a classical portrayal of a fat-cheeked child with wings. The usual plural is *cherubs*; the plural *cherubim* is only used when it is an order of angels in a biblical context or painting.

chest See **bust** . . .

chesterfield   The names of clothes have a way of commemorating people (see **bloomers**, **mackintosh**). Perhaps only traditional tailors would be likely to know now what a *chesterfield* is: it is a straight-cut overcoat with a velvet collar, presumably the style worn by the Earl of Chesterfield in the 19th century. And presumably the Earl sat on a *chesterfield*, a sofa with arms the same height as the back, to make a low upholstered wall on three sides. See also **couch**

chic   *Chic*, which may originate from artists' slang in the 19th century, is a peculiarly French word, adopted by English because there is no other way of expressing quite the same thing. It summons up a certain kind of attractiveness which is self-assured and seemingly effortless. *Chic* of course means elegant and distinguished. But the word is now also used about a different style, for those women who look calculatedly and provocatively dishevelled, as if they have just got out of bed. It is a look that is achieved by a cleverly contrived disorder. When years ago jeans came over from America, before long designers in Paris were cutting them in a way that turned jeans into casual high fashion. **Jeans** became chic.

chicory or **endive**   What to call the elongated white salad vegetable with smooth tight leaves causes no end of problems in greengrocers. The British with holiday homes in France become used to buying *endive* but when they come back to Britain they have to ask for *chicory*. If they cross the Atlantic, they have to go back to *endive* again, because that's the name in America. *Endive* in Britain can be a curly-leaved lettuce-type salad vegetable, which the French call *frisée*, a name becoming used in Britain as well. This confusion is being sorted out, as British greengrocers hear more and more people using *endive* for the same salad vegetable as the French and Americans, pronouncing it either 'ENNdeeve' or nearer the French way, 'AHNdeeve'.

chief executive or **managing director**   The Post Office led the way in 1969, giving up the frock-coated title Postmaster General, for Chairman and Chief Executive of the Post Office Board. Many British companies have changed over from *managing director* to *chief executive*, as the more trendy title for the senior management executive with ultimate responsibility for decisions. See also **executive**

childish or **childlike**   It is a pity to mix up these words, as often happens, since to be *childlike* is to have the natural innocence and openness of a child, a quality that makes every day an adventure, whereas to be *childish*, unless it is used about a child, is to be immature, spoilt and stupid.

chilled, **cool** or **frappé**   All three words are used about drinks. *Cool* or *chilled* are the usual words for serving wine, *cool* being less cold than *chilled*. *Frappé* is colder still, too cold for wine, but used for a liqueur or fruit juice poured into a glass full of crushed ice.

china or **porcelain**   You have to work at it to distinguish between *china* and *porcelain*, as dictionaries include *porcelain* as part of the definition of *china*. The Portuguese in the 16th century introduced into Europe a fine glazed ceramic from China, where it had been developed about AD900. They called it *porcelain* (from a similar word in Portuguese) but it also became known as *chinaware*, later shortened to *china*.

Porcelain now distinguishes a fine mixture of china clay or kaolin with hard minerals, glazed during firing at about 1400°C. With china the clay is mixed with various materials, such as sand and lime, soda, etc and fired at a lower temperature, with glazing applied during a second firing. But this distinction is too rarefied for most people, particularly since sanitary ware is now called *porcelain* (in her book, *Class*, Jilly Cooper has Howard Weybridge asking euphemistically if he can go and 'point Percy at the porcelain').

Bone china (often called *English bone china*, wherever it is made, because it was developed in England during the 18th century), uses a mixture of bone ash and china clay. See also **ceramic . . .**

Chinese or **Chinamen**   *Chinese* is the only word to use now for the people of China: *Chinaman*, while not as offensive as *Chink*, is old-fashioned and condescending, to say nothing of landing us, sooner or later, with 'Chinaperson'.

Chink   See previous entry

chinless wonder   See **Hooray Henry**

chip   See **microchip . . .**

chips or **French fried potatoes**   It was many years ago in Paris that long thin sections of potato first sizzled in boiling oil and came out as 'frites', destined to lead one day to the chips-with-everything cult from Clacton to the Costa Brava. Although you do hear people taking the precaution of saying 'I mean the chips you eat – not the ones in computers', there is little risk of potato chips and **microchips** occurring in the same context.

French fried potatoes (which Americans call 'French fries') is perhaps little more than an attempt to add a gastronomic gloss, since *frites* are thinner and crisper than the chunky British variety. The other thing to remember is that in America chips are potato crisps.

chiropodist   The *sh* sound ('shIROPodist') is heard often, although not shown in all dictionaries as an alternative pronunciation. 'Chiro-' is from a Greek word with an initial *k* sound, and 'kiROPodist' was the original pronunciation, and the one preferred by most chiropodists.

(the) choir is or **are**   See **collective words**

cholesterol   Until the 1960s, *cholesterol* hardly appeared in dictionaries. Then it became the focus of dietary concern, especially among middle-aged business executives, warned that high levels of cholesterol, a normal fatty constituent in the blood and most tissues, increased the risk of heart disease. Cholesterol continues to come up in the news, usually because there is a continuing cholesterol controversy, with medical opinion divided over whether cholesterol is the killer it was once supposed to be.

choose or **opt for**   Why should we *opt for* something instead of *choosing* it? *Opt* could be taken to suggest a flip-of-a-coin decision as against a considered choice, a useful distinction for an inconsequential matter: 'she opted for a meal out rather than a film at the local'.

Opt out of is a sharper way of expressing a negative decision than *choose not to*: 'We could make no contribution, so we opted out of going to the meeting'.

choosy or **choosey**   These are not alternative spellings, as is sometimes believed: only *choosy* is correct.

chop or **cutlet**   You know where you stand with a chop: it is always meat, usually pork, lamb or mutton, a thick slice cut from the ribs, with a bone as part of it. You're less certain with a *cutlet*, except that it is usually boneless: it is often used for a piece of veal but also for almost anything else, from minced meat to fish, or even for a chopped nut mixture formed into flat cakes for frying.

chord or **cord**   There is no doubt that a *chord* is the musical term and *cord* is tightly twisted string. But because the voice is associated with music, some people hesitate over *vocal cords* (not chords), so-called because they are cord-like tissues that vibrate to produce sounds.

choreograph   *Graph* is from the Greek word for writing (auto*graph*, bio*graphy*, etc) and *choreography* was first limited to the writing down of the patterns or steps of a dance. But it is now used for the art of devising the steps and movements, and even for creating the whole visual scene that is presented to the audience.

Christian   *Christian* relates to the religion founded on the life and teachings of Jesus Christ. There is some criticism of the use of *Christian* to describe a kind and compassionate attitude, because it implies this is exclusive to Christianity. After all, a Jew or a Buddhist can behave just as compassionately and it would be presumptuous to call either of them *a good Christian*. The word *Christian* is debased when it is used, as it often is, in a smug way to mean respectable, decent, or even voting for the Conservative Party. See also **first or Christian name . . .**

Christian name   See **first name . . .**

Christmas or **Xmas**   Capital X is the first letter of *Christ* in the Greek alphabet, and *Xmas* for

Christmas goes back to the 18th century, with variations much earlier still. Because *Xmas* has become so associated with commercial exploitation of Christmas, there's a hint of something shoddy and cheap about it. It's better to write *Christmas* and leave *Xmas* to the tinsel displays in shop windows.

chrome and **chromium**   *Chrome* and *chromium* are words of the 1920s and 30s, recalling the shiny chromium-plate radiator grills and bumpers on cars. The words seem dated now, although chromite (the ore containing chromium) is still mined, because plastic and other synthetic non-metallic materials are used in many of the applications that were formerly chromium.

chromosomes   See **genes . . .**

Chunnel   See **Channel tunnel . . .**

Churchillian   Winston Churchill was a hard act to follow, so who or what can be described as *Churchillian*? It must suggest an outstanding quality of leadership, informed by a sense of history, matched by a power of oratory that rises to any occasion. It is not a word to use lightly.

chutzpah   Everyone is expected to know what the Yiddish word *chutzpah* means (pronounce it 'HOOTZ-pah', giving the first *h* a gutteral sound as in 'loch'). *Chutzpah* is used in *The Times*, on news programmes, and appeared in large print in a poster campaign. So what does it mean? It suggests a cheek that knows no bounds. Alistair Cooke once explained *chutzpah* to the uninitiated, by telling the story of a man who killed his mother and father, and then asked the court for mercy because he was an orphan. Admittedly *effrontery* means the same as *chutzpah*, but sounds so restrained in comparison.

cinema, **films** or **pictures**   When characters on film seemed to move, Americans called them 'moving pictures' and then 'movies'. The word crossed the Atlantic even before World War I but never settled down in Britain. For a long time the British went to the *pictures* or the *cinema*: run-down flea-pits were called *picture palaces* and given regal names, such as The Majestic. Some older people still go to the *pictures* or the *cinema*, but younger people usually go to the *films*, the word that has now taken over. The art form is called *film*, the critics are *film critics*. *Cinematograph* survives only in the name of the trade union, the Association of Cinematograph and Television Technicians, but its members say they are 'in films' or 'in the film industry'.

The American 'movie-theater' has also been resisted in Britain, where *cinema* remains the usual word for the place where films are shown (classically correct since it comes from Greek 'kinema' meaning movement). But the official film complex in London looks across to Hollywood and calls itself The National Film *Theatre*. See also **motion pictures**

cinematheque   Using as a model 'bibliothèque', French for a library, the word 'cinémathèque' was put together in France to describe a film library or archive. The word is now used in English without the accents (pron: 'SINNematek'), for a small cinema that shows classic or non-commercial experimental films.

cinematic *Cinematic* is no longer used only about the cinema: it is applied now to any narrative form, such as a novel or a play, that uses a style that has something in common with film realism.

cinéma-vérité See **documentary** . . .

cipher See **code** . . . ; **logo** . . .

circulation See **coverage** . . .

circumflex This is most commonly found over French vowels (â, ô), but may not be destined to live forever. See **French accents**; **accents in print and writing**

(**in** or **under** the) **circumstances** A few pedants argue that *under the circumstances* is illogical and only *in the circumstances* will do, because 'circum' in Latin means 'round', and something is *in* not *under* a circle. **Fowler** dismissed the rule as stupid. Language, created in the daily illogical lives of people, is not logical and it is good English to do something *under* or *in the circumstances*.

CIS (Commonwealth of Independent States) See **Russian and Soviet**

citation or **quotation** See **quotation** . . .

cite or **quote** See **quote** . . .

citizen The word *citizen* has been with us in English for six hundred years, but in 1992 it was put up in lights. The main three political parties in the UK queued up to publish *citizens' charters*. Suddenly, we were all aware of being citizens.

Citizen has a militant ring to it, because 'Aux armes, citoyens!' ('Take up arms, citizens!') is part of the revolutionary French national anthem. But on behalf of the Conservative Party, John Major challenged left-wing monopoly of the word. Under his Citizens' Charter, a citizen is a consumer with rights of redress when rubbish is not collected, trains run late and waiting-lists at hospitals are too long. *Citizen* is beginning to return to its original meaning of a privileged inhabitant of a city state.

(the) **City** *The City* is the self-assured name for the *City of London*, sometimes also known as the *square mile*: it is the square mile that forms the old city of London and is now the financial centre of Britain, containing the Bank of England, the Stock Exchange, Lloyds and head offices of the major banks. Before World War II, bowler-hatted men in black suits, on trains up to London from **stockbroker belts**, were described by their awed neighbours as 'something in

the City'. That would be a joke now: the men and women working in the electronic money markets of the 1990s could be under 30 and living in **Dockland**. See also **Wall Street**

city or **town** The distinction between *city* and *town* is not always clear-cut, although strictly a *city* in Britain is established by royal charter. But in general use, any large town may be called a *city*: the official sign at the approach to the new town in Buckinghamshire reads THE CITY OF MILTON KEYNES. In some circumstances, a city is called a town: people in the country visiting London go 'up to town', just as in New York you can be 'on the town' or 'work **downtown**'.

A town is distinctly larger than a village and would be expected to have at least one important shopping street, a large church and at least a modest town hall plus a mayor and a town council. But there are borderline cases where it is uncertain whether a place is a village or a town.

Lastly, the *city of London* is not the same as the City of London. See also **hamlet or village**; **township**

City of London See (the) **City**

civil disobedience *Civil disobedience* describes non-violent protests against the law or a regime: Gandhi gave the strategy currency in the 1930s when he sought to discredit the British rule in India by mass obstruction and refusal to comply with laws. In the 1990s, mass demonstrations, processions and sit-ins in protest against government policy are manifestations of civil disobedience.

civil or **human rights** There is a considerable overlap between the meanings of these two descriptions of the rights of man. *Civil rights* are the rights of **citizens** under the law of the land. In America, where civil rights are enshrined in the constitution, they were particularly associated with the right of blacks to be treated equally. In Britain, civil rights are often related to the rights of immigrant communities as UK citizens.

Human rights go beyond the statute book to what might be called natural law, the rights of an individual as a human being. At one time, these were known as the 'rights of man', which were set out in the US Declaration of Independence (1776). The term *human rights* was given currency by the UN Charter of 1945 and the UN Universal Declaration of Human Rights (1948). These rights include liberty, freedom from persecution and from imprisonment without trial, and economic and political rights. Human rights transcend national boundaries, as they are the legitimate concern of every civilized country.

claim The earlier meaning of *claim* was to assert a right, such as 'to claim compensation'. But it has become extended to mean 'state' or 'contend': 'he claims that he was not there at the time'. Used in this way, *claim* often seems to throw doubt on what is claimed:

'he claims that he was not there at the time (but I wonder . . .)'.

clairvoyance See **parapsychology** . . .

clandestine If you are having a *clandestine* relationship, keep the stress on the second syllable and make the last syllable rhyme with 'tin' ('clanDEStin'), and at least your pronunciation will be beyond reproach. 'CLANdestyne' is an accepted alternative pronunciation in dictionaries, but sometimes frowned upon.

claret See **bordeaux** . . .

clarinettist or **clarinetist** *Clarinettist* is correct at the Royal Festival Hall in London, but use *clarinetist* (American spelling) at Carnegie Hall, New York.

class There will always be class distinctions but the word *class* is a throwback to the past. A few trade union leaders may still use *working class* as a rallying cry; and Emma Soames (Sir Winston Churchill's granddaughter), when editor of *The Tatler*, said it was a magazine 'for and about rich *upper-class* people', but the terms are increasingly rare and used self-consciously. The BBC use 'top social bracket' and 'lower income group' to sidestep the terms *upper class* and *working class*. *Middle class* remains in use but more as a description of society at large: when John Major became Prime Minister and looked forward to a *classless* society, he meant a universal middle class of homeowners in centrally heated houses.

In 1990 the Market Research Society publication, *Occupational Groupings* (in effect a guide to class in Britain), the word *class* was replaced by *socio-economic groups*, a measure of the prestige and financial rewards of different occupations, starting with A (which includes the Chief Rabbi, admirals and chiropodists with more than five staff), down the scale to D (which includes bingo-callers, dustmen and rat-catchers).

Americans have an aristocracy of their own, even though George Bush, during his first presidential campaign, declared that 'class is for European democracies . . . not for the United States of America'. But he was hooked on the *word* not the reality, for in America, as in Britain and everywhere else, there are haves and have-nots, the enlightened and the benighted, the rich and the poor.

Just as the aristocracy is being replaced by the **meritocracy**, so by the end of the century *class* will be largely replaced by **status**, a reflection of someone's occupation, money, success and **lifestyle**, rather than social origins. By then the word *class* may perhaps still be whispered in drawing-rooms in the Shires, or shouted defiantly by old-fashioned trade unionists, but it will have a dying fall about it. See also **accents in speech**; **class language**

(the) **class** *is* or *are* See **collective words**

classic or **classical** Understanding the different ways in which *classic* and *classical* are used is one indicator of cultural awareness. *Classics*, as a noun in the plural, is the easiest word. With one exception, *the classics* usually refers to literature, either ancient Greek and Latin literature or by association later works of literature not precisely defined, probably written before the 20th century and considered good prose or poetry: the writings of Chaucer, Shakespeare, Milton, Jane Austen. . . . The exception is the five famous flat races in England, *the classics*: the Derby, the Oaks, the St Leger and the Two Thousand and One Thousand Guineas.

For centuries the great writers of ancient Greece and Rome were supreme, so *classic* came to be the descriptive word for the highest level of achievement in anything (a classic performance, a classic example, even a classic crime), an outstanding or perfect example of its kind. As this embodies the idea of timelessness, *classic* became used about clothes that transcend passing fashion, so a *classic dress* is that simple (usually black) dress, inoffensive and unostentatious, that at one time every woman was required to keep in her wardrobe.

Classical is the accepted descriptive word for art and architecture, firstly for the art and architecture of ancient Greece and Rome. For later art, *classical* is used in two ways. The first is for art of any period that is inspired by the style and form of ancient classical art. The second makes a distinction between classical restraint and the expressive or emotional romantic approach, so that *classical* is opposed to **romantic**: in contemporary literature, for example, W H Auden is considered classical, Dylan Thomas romantic.

In music, *classical* is sometimes treated as a chronological term, music from about 1750 up to the death of Beethoven (1827) and Schubert (1828). But in general use, classical music is music of any period, including the 1990s, that is considered 'serious', rather than light popular music. This use of *classical* could be considered plebeian, because it is so vague. It is certainly arguable, since there could be disagreement over whether certain music is or is not classical.

classics *is* or *are* Nouns ending in *-ics* often present this problem. See **-ics**

classified or **sensitive** The two meanings of *classified* sometimes get mixed up. The most common meaning is divided up into classes or categories (classified advertisements, a classified list, etc). But be careful of the term *classified information*: it could mean, as above, information divided into categories, but could also mean *classified* in its other sense: information that must not be published, because it could affect military, national or commercial security.

Sensitive, with its primary meaning of something that is keenly responsive to stimuli, was extended some time in the 1950s to matters that could affect security, more or less synonymous with *classified*, somewhere between **confidential** and 'top secret'. *Classified* is an official category, with *sensitive* used more generally.

class language Of all European languages, English is one of the most riddled with class-distinction. Shaw observed in the Preface to *Pygmalion*, written just before World War I: 'Every time an Englishman opens his mouth another Englishman despises him'. This was a comment not only on accent and pronunciation but on the choice of words. Although she had learned to speak with an upper-class accent, it was a giveaway when Eliza Doolittle declared about her aunt, '. . . they done the old woman in.' (*Pygmalion*, Act III), instead of 'they murdered the old lady'. Not so much has changed since then. Jilly Cooper, in her book, *Class* (1979), found many examples of expressions and words that 'are so crucial for determining your class'.

'Thanks ever so' or 'Thanking you' puts you on one side of the tracks, 'Thank you so much' establishes you on the other. It is downmarket to sit on a *settee*, middle-class to sit on a *couch* or *sofa*. The right thing is to have a *drawing-room* or *sitting-room*, less so to have a *lounge* (unless you own a hotel). *Serviette* may seem a gracious word, but those in the know treat it with disdain, wiping their lips on a down-to-earth *napkin*. And there are people who would rather die than call their midday meal *dinner*, instead of *lunch*.

The above examples and other aspects of 'posh lingo', as it is called in Nancy Mitford's *Noblesse Oblige*, are looked at more closely under **accents in speech; couch . . . ; dinner . . . ; goodbye . . . ; lavatory . . . ; napkin . . . ; sitting-room . . . ; U and Non-U English.**

clean or **cleanse** *Clean* is the word we use most, to mean removing dirt: we clean the floor or a wound, etc. *Cleanse* has a spiritual meaning suggesting purification and is usually followed by 'of': to cleanse someone of their sins. But by custom that *cleans* the skin is a *cleansing* cream.

cleaner See **charlady** . . .

clean-living An upper-class phrase which belongs to the past with its opposite term 'bounder'.

Clean-living was always used about men, nearly always Englishmen, for who could expect foreigners to be clean-living? It had nothing to do with taking a shower every morning: clean-living meant moral uprightness, doing the right thing, not having too many sexual affairs, and then only with white women. In 1991, 'clean-living Englishmen' turned up in *Edwina Mountbatten*, Janet Morgan's biography. As an expression loaded with smugness and double standards, *clean-living* should not be exhumed, even in books about the British Raj.

cleanse See **clean** . . .

clear or **clearly** *Clearly* is usually the correct form: 'I can see clearly now', 'Will you say it clearly?'. One exception is the combination 'loud and clear': 'Will you say it loud and clear?'

clear or **plain** When used about language, *clear* and *plain* often mean exactly the same. But perhaps *plain* implies 'simple', with *clear* suggesting free from obscurity or ambiguity, even though the language may not be *plain*. *Plain* is the preferred word for good, easy-to-understand language: the book for officials on the use of English is called *Plain Words*, there is a Campaign for **Plain English** and the National Consumer Council publishes notes on plain language for lawyers and consumers.

clearing bank Now that it is possible to have cheque accounts with many different organizations, the term *clearing bank* takes on a new significance. It is limited to those banks that have access to a central *clearing house*, which allows them the facility to settle the huge number of daily inter-bank transactions by means of single large cheques.

cleavage *Cleavage*, which has a geological meaning for the splitting of rocks under pressure, is at last accepted as standard English by most dictionaries for the hollow between a woman's breasts. There is no other word for it anyway.

clementines See **tangerines** . . .

(the) clergy (forms of address) In the Church of England, *archbishops* are written to as: The Most Reverend and Rt Hon the Lord Archbishop of . . ., and letters begin *Dear Archbishop*. They are spoken to as *Your Grace*, or less formally as *Archbishop*.

Bishops are: The Right Reverend the Lord Bishop of . . . (only the Bishop of London rates: The Right Reverend and Rt Hon the Lord Bishop of London), and letters begin *Dear Bishop*. They are spoken to as *My Lord* or *Bishop*.

Lower down the hierarchy: The Very Reverend the Dean of . . ., The Venerable the Archdeacon of . . ., The Reverend Canon John Brown, and letters begin *Dear Dean, Dear Archdeacon* or *Dear Canon*. They are spoken to as *Dean, Archdeacon* or *Canon*.

Vicars are: The Revd John Brown, followed by *Dear vicar* or *Dear Mr Brown*.

Wives, even of an archbishop, are simply *Dear Mrs.* . . .

Starting high up in the Roman Catholic Church: His Eminence the Cardinal Archbishop of . . . and His Eminence Cardinal . . ., and letters begin *Your Eminence* or *My Lord Cardinal*. They are spoken to as *Your Eminence*, or less formally as *Cardinal*.

Roman Catholic priests are: The Revd John Brown, followed by *Dear Father Brown*. See also **minister . . . or priest**

clerical *Clerical* work can be the activities of clergymen or of **clerks** in offices, but only the former wear *clerical* collars (see **dog-collar**). A *clerical error* is less likely to be a clergyman's misdemeanour than an error made in copying something or an error in accounting or administration.

clerk In the 11th century, a *clerk* was a man in holy orders, then by association a scholar (the Clerk of

Oxford in Chaucer's *Canterbury Tales*, c1387), and by the 16th century, a bookkeeper or someone doing paperwork in an office. It is an old-fashioned word now, surviving in a few titles such as *clerk of the course* (the official in charge of a horse-race or motor-race), *clerk of the works* (the man in charge of major building works). Cashiers in banks do not like to be called **bank clerks**, as they once were, and *clerks* would sound out of place for people sitting in front of computers in offices. In America, *clerk* is often the word for a shop assistant.

Curiously, although the commercial world has now dismissed the label *clerk* as mundane and lowly, certain prestigious offices retain it: the Queen's Clerk of the Closet is a bishop in the Ecclesiastical Household.

The pronunciation is 'clahk', with 'clerk' (rhyming with 'jerk') as a downmarket variant in Britain but the usual pronunciation in America. See also **executive**

clever *Clever* was a good word once, when it meant a quick lively mind able to solve problems. But it is double-edged now and can mean cunning or superficial. 'That's a clever idea' would probably be taken as a compliment, but 'That's just a clever idea' writes it off as having no real value. Be on the lookout for a misunderstanding over the meaning of *clever*. And don't be surprised, especially in Australia or the East End, if someone says they are 'not too clever': it is not saying they are stupid, but simply they are not feeling well.

cliché *Cliché* comes from the French verb 'clicher', meaning to stereotype, and has been used in English since the late 19th century for a penny-in-the-slot expression, a word or phrase that has become used too often by too many. The sad thing about a cliché is it takes words

> . . . that once were strong and fine,
> Primal as sun and moon and bread and wine,
> True, honourable, honoured, clear and clean,
> And leaves them shabby, worn, diminished,
>   mean.
>   John Tessimond, *The ad-man* (1957)

Suppose you wrote this: I 'have seen better days', am 'poor but honest' and 'haven't slept a wink' because someone has 'made me mad'; if something is 'all Greek to you' or simply 'neither here nor there'; when 'there is method in your madness' and 'last but not least', 'to tell the truth and shame the devil', 'your heart's desire' is to 'have a charmed life' and to be 'as sound as a bell', because it is 'cold comfort' to be told 'you can only die once' . . . you could be accused of using a whole string of clichés. Yet every one of those phrases was written by Shakespeare. Do we now have to discard them? We do have to be careful about using them, because custom has made them stale.

client, **customer** or **clientele** Solicitors, accountants, advertising agencies, insurance brokers, etc all have *clients*, so do hairdressers (the posh ones

have a *clientele*). Shops have *customers* although couturiers and the grander dress-shops give themselves airs by having *clients*. Social workers have picked up the idea and talk of the people they deal with as *clients*. As Eric Partridge (a campaigner for honest English) asked: 'What's wrong with *customer*, anyway?'.

climacteric See menopause . . .

climatology or **meteorology** *Climatology* is the scientific study of weather trends, such as temperature, rainfall and hours of sunshine, over a large number of years. *Meteorology* is the short-term approach to the same subject and is the basis of weather forecasts for the next few days, or even for later the same day. See also **meteorologist** . . .

climax Some scholars fight established usage, arguing that *climax* comes from the Greek word meaning 'ladder' and should only be used for an advancing sequence. But everyone and all dictionaries take it now to mean the most dramatic or most critical point in a situation. *Climax* as a verb (meaning to bring about a climax) is not generally used in Britain, where 'reach a climax' is preferred. But both American and British English use *climax* as a verb for having a sexual **orgasm**.

climb up and **climb down** Linguistic nitpickers object to *climb up*, because *climb* already means upwards. But to *climb up* emphasizes the direction and effort. After all, if we accept *climb down*, as we have to, because everybody climbs down ladders, mountains and from attitudes, what's so wrong with *climb up*? When we climb down from something we have insisted on, the result is a *climb-down* (with a hyphen). Social climbing is never climbing down – it is always **upwardly mobile**.

clinic or **hospital** They are both *hospitals*, but the word *clinic* is often used for a smaller hospital to which only private patients are admitted, or for a building with consulting and treatment rooms, where patients are given specialized treatment or advice, such as a *fertility clinic*. A hospital may include several clinics, to which out-patients come.

clinical *Clinical* is from the Greek word for 'bed', which explains terms such as *clinical psychology* and *clinical medicine*. In those contexts, *clinical* distinguishes the academic study from the application to practical problems of dealing with patients. A clinical psychologist works in a hospital (see also **psychiatry** or **psychology**); clinical medicine is concerned with the actual treatment of patients, as against research. *Clinical*, a good word in medicine since it is about helping people who are ill, has in general use a negative meaning, suggesting cold and unfeeling: 'a clinical way to look at a human problem'.

clitoral and **vaginal orgasm** See orgasm . . .

clock in, on, off or **out** Employees who record the time they start and finish work with a card punched by a time-clock can *clock in* or *on*, for starting, and *off* or *out* for finishing. But for some reason, *clock in* and *clock out* are preferred in general use, simply as a way of saying what time you start or finish work: even the chairman of a company has been known to say 'I clock in every morning at 8'.

clones and **cloning** Both these words from genetic science have moved into popular use. *Cloning* is producing identical copies of a gene for experiment; the copies are *clones*. Outside science, *clones* and *cloning* are used, often with a derogatory implication, for producing imitations of anything for commercial, political or other purposes. See also **lookalike**; **genes** . . .

close or **shut** Is there any difference between *closing* a door and *shutting* it? It is hard to see any. In other cases, it is more a matter of custom whether *close* or *shut* is used: we *shut* or *close* our eyes or a window, we may *shut* up *shop* but the sign on the door reads *Closed*. The last example suggests that *close* is a more formal or polite word, *shut* more down-to-earth: it is one thing to close your mouth but another to shut up.

close company This is a technical term which appears in the business section of newspapers and is not always understood. A close company is under the control of no more than five directors or shareholders, even though a limited amount of shares may be held by other people, who have no say in how the company is run.

closed shop Although we say a **close company**, it is a *closed shop*, the restrictive practice that enforces all employees of a company to belong to a particular trade union.

close proximity Think of a couple making love and the man saying to the woman: 'It's marvellous to be *in close proximity* to you darling!' After that, could we ever use *close proximity* as a pompous way of saying 'near'?

close scrutiny Is the word *close* really necessary? Logic says no; good sense justifies it. See **scrutiny**

closet Since the 17th century, *closet* has been a word in English for a cupboard, yet it is only used that way now in America. In Britain, *closet* used to be a word for a lavatory (*water-closet*), but no one asks 'Where's the closet?' any more. In the 1990s, *closet*, in Britain and America, is used increasingly for something kept secret: a recent headline announced: THE NEW FASHIONS COME OUT OF THE CLOSET, meaning the new fashions are revealed. See also next entry

closet gay First used in America, *closet gay* now gets into the headlines in Britain. It is used about men,

particularly well-known men, who conceal their homosexuality, and echoes the old British expression 'a skeleton in the cupboard'. See also **gay** . . .; **outing**

cloud-cuckoo-land The expression goes back nearly 2500 years, as it is a translation of the name of the idealistic realm in Aristophanes' play *Birds* (414BC), a place where everything goes according to plan. It survives in the 1990s, when politicians accuse other politicians of living in cloud-cuckoo-land. There is a more up-to-date way of saying the same thing: 'You are not living in the real world'.

(on) **cloud nine** To be marvellously happy is such a rare state that it is like being in a remote inaccessible place. One such place is *on cloud nine*, although for Americans it is more likely to be *on cloud seven*. Either way, it is a good place to get to whenever possible.

co or **co-** See **hyphens/6**

coarse See **vulgar** . . .

cocaine and **heroin** Because these are both dangerous drugs and are at the same time related to drugs used medicinally, they are sometimes confused. *Cocaine* (from which **crack** is derived) is produced either synthetically or from the dried leaves of the coca plant, grown mostly in South America. *Heroin* is a by-product of morphine, which is produced from opium.

coccyx The small bone at the base of the spine is easily bruised and if this happens, you soon learn that it has a strange name, *coccyx* (pron: 'COKsix'), which comes, through Latin, from the Greek word for 'cuckoo', because the bone is supposed to look like a cuckoo's bill.

cock The Latin names for sexual organs are the polite ones: **penis** for the male organ or self-importantly, 'membrum virile', Latin for 'male member', which explains why some men still refer to the penis as their 'member'. *Cock* is classified as 'vulgar' or 'coarse' by dictionaries, yet the word has a long and innocent history. Since the 14th century it has meant a male bird, more particularly a domestic fowl, and perhaps because of the stance taken by a fighting cock, *cock* came to be used for something that sticks up stiffly, such as the cocking hammer of a gun and a penis.

Cock may be a **four-letter word** to lexicographers, but it is the word most commonly used by men, and by many women, for a penis, although a few people may find it mildly offensive. If a man and woman are in bed together, and the subject comes up, it is the most natural word to use, even for a lexicographer.

For some subtle reason, a *cock-up*, meaning a complete mess of something, is more acceptable to dictionaries than a **balls**-up. But *talking cock*, meaning nonsense, is level pegging with *talking balls*, both classified as vulgar, coarse or taboo.

code or **cipher** Both words can mean a secret way of writing or transmitting messages. *Code* is the more up-to-date word, and the word used in data security and in business ('the code-name for a new product'). And *codes* is the term commonly used in computer practice for the ways of generating the different features of a **program**.

Cipher is a word which has a number of different meanings and, perhaps because of this, is seldom used for any of them. Perhaps the sense in which it is most often used (and that not often) is to mean 'a nonentity', 'a nothing', in expressions such as 'he was a cipher in the organization'. (The alternative spelling *cypher* is rare now.)

Decipher is used where *decode* would not mean quite the same thing. Secret messages are decoded or deciphered, but bad handwriting is *deciphered* (unless it is indecipherable!). See also **logo** . . .

coding In computer technology, *coding* is the preparation of detailed instructions to enable a computer to carry out a task.

coed Since coeducational colleges or schools have become the rule rather than the exception, *coed* for a mixed school is not much needed now. In America, *coeds* are women students, not the college.

coercion or **inducement** There is argument in philosophy and in political theory about what constitutes *coercion*, persuasion by force. It is clear that if you are made to do something at the point of a gun, that is coercion. But when there is, for example, high unemployment, someone might be forced to take less than a fair wage for a job, which could be regarded as a less blatant form of coercion. Governments in particular use coercion, not only by totalitarian force, but in democracies, by imposing punitive penalties. *Inducement* is a different kind of persuasion, usually through offering concessions or extra money. But there are times when the line between coercion and inducement is such a thin one that it is worth thinking about which is the appropriate word to use.

coexistence or **cohabitation** *Coexistence* is a passive being together, more or less putting up with each other, notwithstanding major differences. It was used a lot after Stalin's death (1953) in connection with the relations between the communist USSR and the capitalist powers in the West. *Cohabitation* is an active state, used most commonly about an unmarried couple living together as man and wife. But *cohabitation* can be used in a more general way: when François Mitterrand, a socialist president, had to work with Jacques Chirac, a right-wing prime minister, the French delighted in calling it *cohabitation*, a piquant word, which suggests **living in sin**.

coffee-table book This goes back to publishing trends in the 1960s, when impressively large books full of colour illustrations had a statutory place on people's coffee-tables, more to be glanced at rather than read,

and to impress guests. At the turn of the century they were called 'grand piano books'.

cognac See **brandy** . . .

cognition or **cognizance** *Cognizance*, a formal word for 'knowing', is also used in a specific legal sense for the authority of a court to deal with a particular matter. *Cognition* is more than knowing, since it implies an intuitive perception and awareness: 'my cognition of her situation enables me to help her'. *Cognitive*, however, has become more than anything else a technical term, especially in psychology. *Cognitive psychology*, in simple terms, is concerned with the processes of acquiring and the organization of knowledge. *Cognitive dissonance* is useful for describing a common human condition, the conflict arising out of beliefs that are incompatible with desires.

cognoscente The word has been used in English since the late 18th century, although even some recent dictionaries, still self-conscious about it being Italian, print it in italics. It is more commonly used in the plural (*cognoscenti*) to mean those in the know, especially about literary and cultural matters.

If you want to sound like one, remember that both the singular and the plural are pronounced the same: 'konnye(r)SHENtee'.

cohabitation See **coexistence** . . .

cold call Every salesman knows what a *cold call* is. It is a foot-in-the-door visit, calling out of the blue on a new customer, who has not been made responsive by a letter or advance information. Most cold calls now are telephone calls: someone sits down with a long list of numbers of people in an area, in an appropriate business, or supplied by an agency, and telephones each one of them, hoping to interest someone in life assurance, double glazing, dance lessons. . . .

cold war It seems that *cold war* is a term that may now belong to history books about the period after World War II. First used in 1947, it described the state of near-war, conducted by snarling and growling, plus subversive actions on both sides, between the USSR and the Western allies. It lasted until 1985, when Mikhail **Gorbachev** became first secretary of the Soviet Communist Party, and a Russian word, full of hope, passed into other languages – **perestroika**.

collaborate See **cooperate**

collage or **montage** These two terms in the visual arts overlap. *Collage*, the French word for glueing, is the universal name of the art form that goes back to Picasso in the early 20th century, when he used scraps of wallpaper and other materials to make a 'painting'. Any combination of cut-outs, tear-offs, or three-dimensional objects, pasted up on a backing can be called a *collage*, even if it is combined with the use of paint, although the art gallery term for that is **mixed**

media. *Montage* (or *photomontage*), the French word for mounting a photograph, is used for a collage made up of fragments of photographs and other illustrations; by extension, any assembly of words or music to form a composite whole is also called a *montage*.

Montage, the French term used for editing a film, is occasionally also used in English as an arty word for film editing.

collateral or **security** When someone borrows money and deposits with the lender assets as a guarantee of repayment, the standard term is *security*. *Collateral* is more American, and unlikely to be used by a British bank manager.

colleague This is the only general purpose blanket word available for someone working in the same organization. 'Fellow-worker' sounds Marxist, 'mate' is too chummy and belongs to plumbers anyway, and **associate** has other meanings.

collective bargaining This is a term in industrial relations. *Collective bargaining* is balancing the power that a large organization has to sack an employee against the power of a trade union to impose sanctions on behalf of the total workforce. *Collective bargaining* is used mostly about negotiations over pay but can extend to all other working conditions.

collective unconscious The psychologist, Carl Gustav Jung, used *collective unconscious* to describe his theory of the universal inheritance of the human condition. Just as the human body has a long evolutionary history, Jung believed that our reactions, feelings and functioning are a combination of the *collective unconscious*, a psychological evolution going back to the beginning of the human species, and linked to each individual's experience of life. See also **archetype**; **unconscious** . . .

collective words Words, such as *board*, *company*, *committee*, *collection*, *family*, *orchestra*, cover groups of separate people or things. The problem is whether to treat these words as *singular* or *plural*. In many cases it is often better to treat them as *singular*: 'the committee *is* having a meeting'. But you cannot have it both ways: 'the committee *is* having a meeting and will give *their* decision'. If you start off with *is*, it must be followed by '*its* decision'. The *government* (and, in the US, the **administration**) are treated as singular, since governments always have to keep up the illusion of being undivided.

When it is clearly about individual members, it is more natural to treat such words as *plural*: 'the orchestra *are* having coffee'. Otherwise it sounds silly: 'the orchestra *is* having coffee'.

When necessary, a collective word must be followed by *which* when it is *singular*, but *who* when it is *plural*: 'the orchestra *which is* giving the concert'; 'the orchestra *who are* having coffee'.

college, **school** or **university** These three words are used in different and confusing ways in Britain and America. When an American says 'I'm at school' it is generally the equivalent in Britain of 'I'm at university'. For in America, the medieval sense of *school*, for the teaching department of a subject at a university, is preserved.

'I'm at college' in Britain means a place of higher education other than a university. For an American it will often mean this, too, but may also refer to a department within a university specializing in a particular subject. While there are *colleges* in some British universities, a student at an Oxford college, for example, would not say 'I'm at college', but 'I'm at university' ('I'm at Oxford' would, in fact, be more likely!) But a British student at a *sixth-form college* is still 'at school'.

By long tradition, anyone studying art, whether they're British or American, enjoys the cachet of being at art *school*, following the tradition of the *Ecole* des Beaux-Arts in Paris.

collision course Two cars going flat out towards each other on the same side of the road, approaching a blind corner, is a graphic representation of a *collision course*. The expression is used in international, political or industrial relations about decisions or actions by two parties that are destined to lead to a conflict.

colloquial or **demotic** See demotic . . .

colloquial, **informal**, **slang** and **non-standard** Dictionaries set out to draw a precise line between what is and what is not standard English, and these are four terms used for words and expressions on the wrong side of the tracks.

Non-standard is a presumptuous umbrella word for anything a linguistic expert disapproves of.

Colloquial (colloq) and *informal* (inf) mean the same, language freely used in relaxed conversation or casual writing. *Slang* (sl) is considered on the fringe of respectability. Such decisions are subjective: for example, the seventh edition of *The Concise Oxford Dictionary* (1982) leaves 'booze' without a usage label, the eighth edition (1990, under a different editor) labels 'booze' *colloquial*, and *Longman Dictionary* (1984) writes it down as *slang*. At best, the lines dividing the categories keep moving. *Colloq* today may become standard English tomorrow, this year's *sl* can move up to *colloq* next year.

Because of radio and television, spoken English is lubricating the wheels of written English, making it more easygoing. The poet, Roy Fuller, tells us '. . . written English has changed so much . . . slang is now accepted, even expected, in almost all kinds of imaginative literature'. Many old-established linguistic traditions are on the blink (*sl*) and there is scope now for a wider range of personal choice in the use of English. But here is a warning: many people suffer from hardening of the linguistic arteries, and are very uptight (*colloq*) about the slightest deviation from what they learned at school. There is no need to try to be trendy (*colloq*) if that is not your style, but an overcareful use of language takes the guts (*colloq*) out of it.

Lastly, *colloquial* and *informal* are lexicographers' terms. *Conversational English* is preferred in *The Good English Guide* as a better term for words and expressions used in intelligent everyday conversation, but which might not be considered to have a place in formal writing. At the same time, Churchill advised 'Let us not shrink from using the short expressive phrase even when it is conversational'. See also **formal English** . . .

collusion   See **cooperation**

colon (:) and **semicolon (;)**   There are few rules about **punctuation;** mostly it is a matter of recommendations. Of all punctuation marks, the colon and semicolon are the most esoteric. Some people think they are obsolete: the National Consumer Council, giving advice in *Plain English for Lawyers*, states 'colons and semicolons are meaningless blobs to many people'. But it would be a pity to discard them altogether, as a semicolon has a touch of class about it and a colon an air of authority.

Generally, a *semicolon* is like a heavy-duty **comma**. When a comma does not seem a sufficient break, a semicolon can be used instead. Look at the first sentence of this entry. A comma in the middle would have done, but a *semicolon* is more effective in separating the two statements.

In **lists of names or things**, a comma is usual between the items: 'In Oxford Street, there are many famous shops, such as Selfridges, John Lewis, Marks & Spencer, . . .'. But when necessary a semicolon makes a more definite separation: 'In Oxford Street, there is Selfridges, the first department store to be opened in Britain; John Lewis, part of the John Lewis Partnership; Marks & Spencer, perhaps the best loved of all stores; . . .'.

A *colon* is useful:

1 As a shorthand symbol for 'as follows', that is to lead on to a quotation, a list of things or of separate points, which is how it is used above. It does not need to be followed by a **dash** (:—)

2 When a statement follows on from or explains a preceding one: it is a just war: naked aggression must not be allowed to triumph.

3 To contrast two opposing statements, when it works like a gentle clash of cymbals: Sometimes I sit and think: sometimes I just sit!

Colonel Blimp   *Blimp*, a word from World War II, has survived into the 1990s, and because there will always be blimps among us, it will probably be here for ever. The political cartoonist, David Low (1891–1963), created Colonel Blimp, a portly, pettifogging, pompous character, out of date and out of touch. But although he was an imaginary character, his counterparts existed in real life, so *Colonel Blimp* (or *blimp* or *blimpish*) became used during the war, as it still is, for anyone who is ultra-conservative or reactionary.

colony and **colonial**   These are now uneasy words, reeking of **imperialism** and exploitation. Instead, colonies are now called 'dependent territories', which may come to the same thing.

colophon   A *colophon* (pron: 'COLe(r)fon') is a bookish name for a publisher's **logo** at the bottom of the title page of a book. The bold **M** on the title page of *The Good English Guide* is Macmillan's colophon.

colossal, **gigantic**, **huge** or **vast**   Choosing one of these descriptions of great size is more a matter of literary style than of relative dimensions. *Colossal* suggests classical grandeur as well as size: the word comes from the Colossus of Rhodes, a statue of the sun god, so awesome that it was counted one of the wonders of the ancient world. *Gigantic* carries with it a hint of the grotesque, like a giant (a gigantic birthday cake). *Huge* is a more everyday word (a huge breakfast), and *vast* is more suitable for space or expanse (the vast loneliness of the desert). See also **gargantuan** . . .

coloured or **black**   See **black** . . .

colour *negative* or ***transparency***   These are indispensable terms, not only for professional photographers, but for millions of others who take colour photographs. A *colour transparency* is a positive image with direct colour values, on a transparent film base intended for projection on to a screen, as well as for making colour prints. *Diapositive* is an alternative word, but too technical to be used often.

A *colour negative* is a colour film image on photographic emulsion in which colours and tones are reversed, and which is intended only for making prints.

combine   As a verb, the stress is on the second syllable ('comBINE'); as a *noun*, it moves back to the first syllable ('COMbine'). Agriculture is an exception: farmers COMbine crops using a COMbine harvester.

In most senses, when things are combined, the result is a *combination*. But in business, when companies combine for commercial purposes, such as maintaining prices, the result is a *combine* ('COMbine'). See also **cartel; conglomerate**

come (sexual use)   *Come* is a bisexual verb for having an **orgasm**, and in bed is the most popular word used in this way. But is it offensive? A recent Oxford dictionary considers it 'coarse slang' and a Collins dictionary rates it 'taboo'; but Longman and Collins Cobuild dictionaries find it no worse than 'informal'. In any case, language between lovers is a personal matter, not guided by dictionaries. And Cressida (in Shakespeare's play) acknowledged both meanings of the word:

My lord, *come* you again into my chamber:
You smile and mock me as if I meant naughtily.
(*Troilus and Cressida*, Act IV Sc ii)

comedian or **comic** These words overlap in use but generally a *comedian* is an actor who plays comedy roles in plays or films. You expect a *comic* to be broader, more of a clown. Like **actor**, *comedian* and *comic* have become unisex words, although it is still usual to call a woman a *comedienne*.

comedy or **humour** *Comedy* suggests a funny dramatic situation in a play, a film, or in real life. *Humour* is more abstract, the expression of comedy in literature, a painting, a situation, or a remark.

comic See **comedian** . . .

comic or **comical** The distinction between *comic* and *comical* is a reflection of life itself. *Comic* suggests something that is contrived to be funny, such as comic verse or a comic opera. *Comical* describes the funny side of life, comedy that happens inadvertently: it is comical when someone slips on a banana skin, at least to the onlooker.

comma (,) Even the greatest writers agonize at times over whether to put a comma in or leave it out, or having put one in, decide to take it out again later. For commas are in a no man's land of punctuation, where few routes are charted and mostly we have to find our own way. It was easier before World War II, when commas could be used all over the place. But the style now is to use them as sparingly as possible, so there is more reason to hesitate before slipping one in. Here are some guidelines:

1 **Addresses** and **dates**: the old custom of putting a comma after the house number and the month was dropped some years ago. It is now 10 Downing Street, 25th March 1993 (not 10, Downing Street, 25th March, 1993).

2 In letters, commas after 'Dear Sir', 'Dear Lesley' and so on, or after signing-offs such as 'Yours sincerely', are no longer the rule and are often omitted.

3 Commas separate items in a list but not usually between the last but one item and the 'and' leading on to the last item: history, literature, politics and economics. But there are times when a comma before the 'and' helps, particularly when there are descriptive words: Roman history, English literature, international politics, and economics. Leaving out the comma after 'politics' could mean that international economics were also on the agenda. (See also **lists of names or things**).

In some instances, it is better to use a *semicolon*(;) between items, instead of a comma (see **colon and semicolon**).

4 *Commas* between descriptive words: a long, well-written, imaginative book. There is a tendency to leave out the *commas* (a long well-written imaginative book), which is equally correct. But the use of commas is sometimes preferable to separate the descriptive words, particularly if there are more than two.

5 A comma before 'and' when it divides a sentence into two parts: see **and/2**

6 It used to be invariable practice to sandwich 'perhaps' and 'of course' between commas, as well as words such as 'however' or 'therefore'. This can now seem heavygoing, although necessary at times to avoid misunderstanding: 'I am going away, perhaps, with my wife'. Take out one comma and the sentence takes on a different meaning: 'I am going away, perhaps with my wife'; take out both and it becomes ambiguous.

7 The most important reason for using commas is to make a sentence easier to understand. One of the best guides to whether a comma should go in is to read the sentence aloud. If it works just as well without one, it is often safe to leave out the comma. But be on guard: 'butt' is American slang for 'buttocks', and James Thurber once mentioned the legend of how the editor of the *New Yorker* slipped in a prudent *comma* after the third word in the sentence, 'I saw her but a moment'.

command From the beginning, computers seemed to have robot-like qualities, so the word *command* was used for operating the appropriate keys to make a computer carry out a function. *Command language* is part of computer technology, describing procedural operations that instruct a computer to execute 'orders'.

command economy See **market economy** . . .

commander or **commandant** *Commander* is a specific rank in the Royal Navy, the US Navy and the police. But *commander* can also be used in all the services for a commanding officer of any rank in charge of a unit or a military establishment. In this latter sense, *commandant* is an alternative word, more usually for the officer in charge of an establishment rather than in the field, again in all the services and without signifying a particular rank.

commence or **start** *Commence* is a formal word, *start* an everyday word: proceedings or a ceremony might commence, but we start dinner, start work, start a fight. . . .

comment or **commentate** 'Would you please comment on this' means would you explain it or make a few remarks about it. 'Would you please commentate on this' means would you take the role of a *commentator*, giving a running *commentary* on something taking place at that moment. If you are being interviewed on radio or television, you might be asked to *comment* on something, which is giving your opinion. If you work for a radio or television company you might *commentate* on an event, which is doing your best to give the audience a sense of actually being there.

commerce There used to be university degrees in commerce, such as a bachelor or master of commerce (*BCom*, *MCom*) and some universities may still grant them. But generally *commerce* has become a fusty word, replaced by *business* or, at universities and colleges, by *business studies*. Harvard, the oldest university in the US, includes the Harvard Business

School, which publishes the *Harvard Business Review*. Universities now grant **MBA** degrees (Master of Business Administration). See also **business or trade**

commercial Of course this word has a perfectly harmless and legitimate use, but in the 1990s it often carries with it the suggestion of being more interested in profits than in quality and integrity: 'the commercial theatre', 'too commercial'. It was a master-stroke of public relations to call the commercial television service in the UK 'independent television', but the advertising agencies missed a trick when they did not call commercials 'announcements' (see **advertisement** . . .). *Commercial* is a word to be careful about.

commercial traveller See salesman . . .

commie See Communist . . .

commission or **committee** A *commission* suggests an authority to take action: a *committee* could be limited to discussion and giving recommendations. *Commission* is the title favoured by the government for a body set up to deal with a problem and given legal powers, such as the Commission for Racial Equality.

commitment and **committed** Outside its ordinary meaning of a pledge or a promise, *commitment* has acquired, post-World War II, a spiritual and philosophical application not taken into account by most dictionaries. Used in this way, *commitment* suggests an inner dedication to certain principles or beliefs. If, for example, we say that someone is a committed Christian, the implication is that the tenets and morality of Christianity inform everything they do. To be socially committed is to be dedicated to improving conditions in society, a committed doctor is not only professional, but cares deeply about patients. This kind of commitment is a way of life.

committee or **commission** See commission . . .

(the) **committee** *is* or *are* See collective words

commodity A commodity is anything tangible that can be bought or sold. But in investment markets, *commodity* has a more limited meaning: raw materials and foodstuffs, such as tin, copper, coffee and wheat, that are traded internationally in *commodity markets*, as well organized and controlled as Stock Exchanges.

common See vulgar . . .

common or **joint** See joint . . .

common or **mutual** *Common* and *mutual* should properly be used in different ways. *Mutual* means reciprocal, from one person to another: our mutual love, a mutual agreement . . . . *Common* means to share something: a common point of view, a common

objective . . . . But because *common* also has the meanings of **vulgar** or cheap and nasty, as well as ordinary and everyday, there is a problem over expressions such as 'our common friend'. To avoid misunderstanding, Charles Dickens called his novel *Our Mutual Friend*. Perhaps we should follow his lead and call friends we have in common, our *mutual* friends, because if we say our *common* friends, someone may think we mean our gorblimey friends!

Common Era See AD

common land Environmental issues have brought the term *common land* into more frequent use and it is often misunderstood. Common land is not the same as a 'common', which is an area of public land, usually in a village or a town, over which no one has rights of ownership. *Common land* is often, in fact, owned privately, but subject to other people having *rights in common*, for example to graze cattle or to have access for other purposes.

common law The principle of common law (not spelt with capitals) is puzzling to some people outside the legal profession, because it seems to run parallel to the law laid down by Acts of Parliament. *Common law* is the interpretation of those Acts, the record over centuries of judgements given in courts. These judgements become the 'common law of the land', which is why a counsel will quote in court a judgement given in a similar case of 'so-and-so versus so-and-so', to request that it should be taken into account in considering the case in court at that moment.

common-law wife This label for a woman living with a man but not married to him has lost much of the derogatory overtones it once had, but it seems altogether out of place now that so many women and men are living together without the sanction of legal marriage. The meaning was never clear anyway: Lord Denning, the High Court judge who became Master of the Rolls, submitted that 'no such woman was known to the common law'. Nor is there a statutory requirement of how long a couple have to live together to achieve 'common-law marriage'. In America, a common-law wife may in fact be a legally married woman in those states that recognize a marriage without a licence.

It is a complicated business and the best advice is to avoid using the term (or *common-law husband* for that matter) because it means different things to different people, and still often carries with it a moral judgement that is no longer acceptable to society.

common man and **common woman** Most dictionaries leave out the expression *common woman*, perhaps because editors dare not include it. A common woman used to be a disparaging description of a prostitute or of any woman who was sexually promiscuous. But it is blatantly sexist, as *common man* carries with it the suggestion of a certain noble simplicity: it was all right for the composer Aaron Copland to write *Fanfare* *for the Common Man*, but he would never have written one for the Common Woman. The expression is hardly used any more, even behind twitched lace curtains.

Common Market See EC . . .

commonsense or **common sense** When it is descriptive, it is better as *one* word: a commonsense approach. When it is a noun, it is better as *two* words: the approach is common sense. When it comes to what it means, it is not so easy: *common sense* carries with it the assumption that something is unquestionable. But what is common sense to one person may not be common sense to another: some of the greatest minds have approached commonsense assertions with considerable doubts. When someone says 'it's common sense', there is no need always to be lulled into nodding in agreement. See also **lateral thinking**

commonwealth, **confederation** or **federal union** The difference of meaning and implication between these words for an association of independent states is an area of contention in the European Community (see **EC** . . .).

In the 17th century, the *Commonwealth* was the name given to the republican government in England under Cromwell, between the execution of Charles I, 30 January 1649, and the restoration of the monarchy, 8 May 1660.

As a term at the present time, the model for a commonwealth is the *British Commonwealth*, the free association of independent nations that replaced the old British Empire. The term now applies to a loose association of countries with their own legislatures, linked together in mutual interest but usually without a clearly defined charter. The *Commonwealth of Independent States* was the term chosen towards the end of 1991 to describe the association of some of the newly independent states that were once part of the Soviet Union (see **Russian and Soviet**).

A *confederation* is a more clearly defined and regulated alliance. Certain powers are vested in the central government, especially concerning defence and trade, although the separate states retain their identities and legislative authority where it affects their citizens.

A *federal union* or *federation* is usually an indissoluble political union of states, devolving considerable powers over the citizens to a central government. There is a written constitution that sets out the division of powers between central government and the separate states. The biggest federal union is the USA. Others include Australia and Canada. 'Federal' is the word that gave so many headaches at the Maastricht summit of the European Community in December 1991. See **Federal** . . .

common woman See **common man and common woman**

communal and **commune** With *communal* the stress is on the first syllable in Britain: 'COMmunal'. Stress on the second syllable ('comMUNal'), which is usual (although not invariable) in America, is felt to be downmarket in Britain. If you live on a commune, call it a 'COMmune', but if you commune with nature, you can either 'COMmune' or 'comMUNE' with it (the latter is more usual and preferable).

commune (as a noun) See **cooperative** . . .

communication and **communications** Michael Tippett called communication a 'primeval miracle'. For centuries it was called 'speaking and writing' but now the word *communication* has taken over: there are vice-presidents in charge of *communication*, and politicians and executives in every country are taking courses in – *communication*. But no one is quite sure what it means.

Communication, caught up in the human psyche, is a strange thing and defies ultimate analysis. Dictionaries sidestep the mystery by using some such phrase as 'the process of imparting', which is typical of the way writers of dictionaries explain the inexplicable.

The 'process of imparting' is supposed to cover anything from someone tapping you on the shoulder to attract your attention, to the marvel of Michelangelo's ceiling in the Sistine Chapel, to the mastery of a late Beethoven quartet, to lovers holding hands, to a frustrated lorry-driver winding down his window and shouting 'Fuck off!'

According to **image** consultants, everything about us communicates something about us. *Communication* may refer to every detail of the impact we as individuals, or a business, political party, or other organization makes on the world at large. It could include the clothes we wear, the cars we drive, the way we enter a room, even our eye movements and the way we sit down (see **body language**). These are 'ways of communication', never 'communications'. *Communications*, as the plural form, is used about the new technology of communication, such as computers, telecommunications, satellite systems, microelectronic processing, storage and dissemination of data, otherwise known as **information technology** (IT).

In organizations, *communications* may have another meaning: a recent advertisement for a director of communications specified responsibility for 'media relations, public awareness, publications, public affairs and information'.

Communist, **communist** or **Marxist** Someone who believes in the ideology of a classless society and common ownership, based primarily on the teachings of Karl Marx (1818–83), is a *communist* or a *Marxist*. If they are also a member of the Communist Party, they might be called a *Communist* (with a capital C). At one time, *commie* was a term of abuse for a member of the Communist Party, or loosely for almost anyone with even moderately radical ideas.

In 1991, the events in Eastern Europe discredited the name *Communist*. The iron hammer and sickle became a rusty symbol of the past, and the Communist Party of Great Britain, at a congress on 22 November 1991, formally decided to bury them, with a tattered

red flag as a shroud. A new name for the party was proposed, the Democratic Left. See also **Red**

community *Community* used to mean, more than anything else, a group of people living in the same village or part of a town, many of whom would know each other, at least by sight. The word has warm human overtones, built up by associations, such as Christian community, community singing. . . . At some time, it seems in the 1950s, *community* was discovered as a word to make people feel good about things, first perhaps in a vaguely socialist way, then spreading to every possible context. It might have begun with the Treaty of Rome (1957), which left aside words, such as union, association, consortium, to settle for the cosy, sociable alternative, the European Community (see **EC**).

Community soon became the word of the **welfare state**, suggesting a benevolent attitude by those in charge towards those in need. It had the advantage of being woolly and noncommittal and could be prefixed to all manner of words to imply a caring, compassionate do-goodness: community action, community health, community relations. . . . Politicians, who are no slouches when it comes to jumping on verbal **bandwagons**, cornered the word in the late 1980s, to soften the edges of the new local tax: whatever the truth, the **community charge** at least sounded cuddly and fair . . . while it lasted.

community charge See **poll tax** . . .

commuter In America a *commuter* became the word for someone who held a commutation-ticket (season ticket). The word crossed the Atlantic to be used in Britain for people who work in large cities and have to travel some distance to get in, by rail, bus or car.

compact, **small** or **petite** *Compact* always implies convenience because of an efficient use of space, such as a *compact camera*, in which an extraordinary number of photographic functions are contained in a very small appliance. *Small* refers to size only and does not suggest either convenience or efficiency. *Petite* is a complimentary word to use about a small woman, suggesting well-proportioned rather than dumpy.

compact disc (CD) Seventy-eights (the original gramophone records that revolved at 78 revolutions per minute) were succeeded by LPs (long playing records that revolved at 33rpm) which in turn gave way to CDs (compact discs, making use of **laser** beams). But how compact is *compact*? We are awaiting the name for a new disc forecast by the Japanese, which will be the size of a 10p coin, on which can be recorded all Beethoven's nine symphonies.

Compact discs are also used for high-capacity storage of computer data, but the English spelling is arbitrarily retained in this instance, although in all other computer applications **disk** is standard.

company or **firm** In a legal sense, a *company* is a business registered under the Companies Acts, in which case the name of the company is followed by 'Limited', 'Ltd' or **plc**. But *company* is also used in a general way for any business, usually with at least a handful of employees. Such businesses, not necessarily companies in a legal sense, may call themselves 'Robinson and Company', or whatever, which has no legal significance.

Firm is interchangeable with the general use of *company*, used about any business, whether it is a legally registered company or not ('Robinson and Sons Ltd might be described as 'a family firm'). *Firm* is not used about really big companies (it would be unexpected to refer to ICI, for example, as a *firm*).

(the) company is or **are** See **collective words**

company secretary A company secretary is a statutory title for the person in a business, registered as a **company** under the Companies Acts, who is held responsible for carrying out the legal requirements of registration.

'COMparable' or **'comPARable'** Keep the stress on the *first* syllable: 'COMp(e)rable'. Because of 'comPARE', 'comPARable' is often heard but is usually considered a downmarket variant, even though it is heard on the BBC.

comparative or **relative** These are not always interchangeable as descriptive words. *Comparative* puts one thing alongside others: *comparative religion* is the study of different faiths in the world, *comparative linguistics* studies the common characteristics of different language groups. *Relative* (usually followed by 'to') looks at something as it is affected by or affects something else: 'profit is relative to productivity', 'the facts relative to the subject under discussion'.

comparatively and **relatively** It is all right to say 'out of the million pound advertising campaign, a comparatively (or relatively) large amount was spent on television', because there is an implied comparison between how much was spent on television and in other media. But both words are often used without making any comparison: 'he is comparatively rich'; 'she is relatively happy'. In that way, the words suggest an in-between state, rather than truly relating one thing to another, so it is generally better to use 'fairly', 'reasonably', 'more or less', whichever shade of meaning you intend: 'he is fairly rich'; 'she is reasonably happy'; 'it was more or less successful'. As for doing something within 'a relatively (or comparatively) short time', that is simply a blank cheque for taking as long as you like.

compare or **contrast** Both words offer an easy way out for writers of examination questions: 'compare so-and-so with such-and-such', 'contrast such-and-such with so-and-so'. *Compare* is an invitation to look for similarities, as in the opening line of Shakespeare's most famous sonnet: 'Shall I compare thee to a summer's day?' (In effect, Shakespeare answers *No* to his question, since he suggests there is no comparison, only differences.) *Contrast* is to point up differences: 'Contrast a summer's day in London with a summer's day in the country'. Contrast as a noun has the stress on the first syllable ('CONtrast'), but as a verb, on the second syllable ('conTRAST'). See also next entry

compare *to* or ***with*** For some writers there is a distinction of meaning. *Compare to* can stress things in common: 'He compared the flavour of young beaujolais *to* the taste of wild blackberries' (suggesting the taste is similar). **Compare with** puts more stress on differences: 'He compared the flavour of young beaujolais *with* that of mature claret'; 'Compare the driver's evidence *with* the evidence given by the witness'.

This is a useful distinction worth preserving, although it is probably a lost cause, since not enough people observe it for it to be a reliable rule. The *OED* quotes examples showing that *compare to* and *compare with* are often used interchangeably.

With passive constructions, which are often negative, the rule is to use *compare with*: 'Young beaujolais cannot be compared *with* mature claret'; 'Beethoven cannot be compared *with* bebop'.

(*in* or *by*) **comparison** There is no difference between *in* or *by* comparison, but it should always be followed by *with* (not *to*): 'air transport is expensive in (or by) comparison with road transport'.

(points of the) **compass** See **abbreviations; CAPITAL LETTERS**

compatible and **compatibility** For a long time *compatible* was used mostly about men and women who could get on well together. But both words have moved from human relationships to computer technology: if systems or equipment can be interchanged between different computers they are said to be *compatible*.

compel or **impel** Both words are associated with the same Latin word meaning 'drive'. *Compel* suggests external force and *impel* is more likely to be a force from within us: 'the minister was compelled to resign'; 'the minister felt impelled to object'.

compelling or **compulsive** The meanings of both words are very close to each other. But *compelling* is usually a good word: a compelling novel is one you cannot put down because the story or style holds you from page to page; a compelling argument sweeps away all objections; a compelling man or woman has a personality that is irresistibly attractive.

Compulsive usually carries with it some of the meaning of a *compulsion* in psychiatry, an impulse that is an obsessional mental disorder: a compulsive gambler, a compulsive eater, etc. *Compelling* viewing on television is a programme that holds our attention because it is so interesting; *compulsive* viewing could be a

programme we watch almost against our will because it has a morbid fascination.

compère See **anchorman**

competence or **competency** The two words mean the same, usually the ability of someone to carry out a particular task ('you can rely on his competence as a plumber') or to cope with things in general ('she has a lot of competence'). *Competency* could replace *competence* in each of these examples, but is becoming old-fashioned and is not used much now. The use of *competence* (or *competency*) to mean an income that is enough to live on ('she is paid a competence') also has an old-fashioned ring to it. But *competence* is still used in law to confirm that a court or a magistrate has the jurisdiction to deal with a specified matter.

competitive Look out for the increasing use of *competitive* as a **euphemism** for 'cheap', when it may also mean something of inferior quality. A truly *competitive price* should mean a price that is lower than average for something of comparable quality.

compilation Because of 'compile', the second syllable of *compilation* is sometimes pronounced 'pyle'. It is preferable to let it rhyme with 'pill': 'comPILL-ation'.

complacent or **complaisant** The meanings of these similar-sounding words are completely different, although the words are often confused. *Complacent* means smug and pleased with yourself; *complaisant* suggests an over willingness to please other people.

The last syllable of *complacent* has an *s* sound ('comPLAYsnt'); *complaisant* a *z* sound ('comPLAYznt').

complementary or **alternative medicine** For a long time *alternative medicine* (at one time also called *fringe medicine*) was used for a whole range of unorthodox treatments, such as **osteopathy**, acupuncture, hypnosis, meditation, outside the mainstream of medical practice. For patients, alternative medicine offered other ways of being cured, some using their own self-healing potential, rather than surgery or drugs.

Patients and some orthodox practitioners became increasingly interested in these methods of treatment. One result is that alternative medicine has come to be called *complementary medicine*, implying a partnership with traditional medicine. The Research Council for Complementary Medicine has been established, which confirms that *complementary medicine* is the term to use now. See also **holistic**

complete It is rightly said that *complete* is an absolute quality, so something cannot be 'more complete' than something else. But it is pedantic to fuss too much about this, as in some situations it is acceptable to have degrees of completeness: 'this is the most complete account of what has happened'. It is better to avoid saying that something is 'very complete', as that makes nonsense of the word.

complex (as a noun) In psychology, a complex is an interacting group of unconscious tendencies that affects our responses and behaviour and causes mental disorders. The word became familiar when the psychiatrist, Alfred Adler, invented the term **inferiority complex**. Before long, people were using *complex* for any marked tendency or strong feeling in ourself or someone else, without it being necessarily morbid or neurotic: 'you've got a complex about being on time'. **Hang-up** is a good alternative, although some dictionaries write it off as 'slang'.

Complex has also become the standard word for an arrangement of buildings within a contained area (a shopping complex, an arts complex), which is reasonable since *complex* implies an interrelationship.

complex or complicated Dictionaries are not much help in separating these two words, especially as some define *complex* as 'complicated' and *complicated* as 'complex'.

Complex is often used in a complimentary way: if someone says a wine is complex, they mean it is subtle, with depth and character. 'A complex novel' suggests that it offers an insight at different levels. *Complicated*, on the other hand, is often a term of criticism, meaning that something is mixed up and confused: 'a complicated novel' could suggest that the writer has not thought through his ideas properly. It has been said that the human condition is marvellously *complex* – 'What a piece of work is a man!' as Shakespeare saw it (*Hamlet* Act II Sc ii) – but it is we who make it *complicated*.

compose, comprise, consist or include *Comprise, consist of* and *is composed of* all mean the same: 'the orchestra consists of (or is composed of) 60 musicians' or 'the orchestra comprises 60 musicians' (*comprise* is not followed by 'of'). These terms must be followed by *all* the parts that make up the whole: it is wrong to say 'the orchestra comprises (consists of or is composed of) 20 violins', unless that is the complete orchestra. Otherwise use *include*: 'the orchestra includes 20 violins' refers to part of the string section only.

This leaves a disputed point of usage. One argument is that *comprise* must always be preceded by the collective word: we must say 'the orchestra comprises 60 musicians' (not '60 musicians comprise . . .'). But *comprise* has been used to mean *compose* since the 18th century, which sanctions '60 musicians comprise the orchestra'. Take your choice.

There is a difference between *consist of* and *consist in*. *Consist of* describes what something is composed of: 'an omelette consists of eggs and whatever filling you choose to put in'. *Consists in* describes the essence of something, as in Shaw's cynical observation, 'All enjoyment consists in undetected sinning'.

Lastly, we include someone *in* a group but never the other way round. Even Sam Goldwyn saw the light

about that: 'For years I have been known for saying *include me out*, but today I am giving it up for ever' (from an address at Balliol College, Oxford).

composite In general use *composite* is used for something made up of different things. But there are some specialized uses of this word that can be confusing. A *composite motion*, at a meeting or conference, is used for the grouping together of a number of motions all relating to the same subject. A *composite photograph* is not a **montage** of fragments of photographs pasted up, but a photograph made in the darkroom by superimposing images from other photographs.

The stress is on the *first* syllable in Britain ('COMposite'), on the *second* in America ('comPOSite').

compositor See **typesetter** . . .

compound To 'compound a felony' is a formal legal charge that you have deliberately concealed a crime, or refrained from prosecuting in the case of a crime. This led to *compound* being used in the wrong way, to mean adding to or making something worse: 'you have compounded the mistake by making another mistake'. The mistaken use of *compound* has become so general that dictionaries now accept it, so unless you are a lawyer, you can use *compound* to mean aggravate, add to, worsen, etc, although some people may criticize you for it. But there are many examples in English of the wrong use of a word eventually becoming accepted.

Compound, as a verb (see above), has the stress on the second syllable ('comPOUND'); but as a noun (a compound of several substances) or as a descriptive word (a compound fracture), the stress moves to the first syllable ('COMpound').

comprehend or apprehend See **apprehend** . . .

comprise See **compose** . . .

compromise The usual meaning of *compromise* is a give-and-take arrangement when all parties involved in a dispute make concessions. But since the 19th century, *compromise* has been used for damaging a woman's reputation.

In Victorian times and well into the 20th century, a woman was *compromised* if she had dinner or even lunch with a man in his flat. Now a woman can invite a man to have dinner in her flat, or even to spend the night, without being compromised. To use *compromise* now about a woman exposing herself to scandal or disrepute belongs to *Lady Windermere's Fan* and has nothing to do with the 1990s.

Compromise, coming from Latin not Greek, is always spelt *-ise* (never *-ize*).

comptroller See **controller** . . .

compulsive See **compelling** . . .

computer In the second half of this century, the word *computer* has come to carry with it an image of ultimate authority, able to reach superhuman conclusions that cannot be denied. Computers touch almost every aspect of our lives, as the next few entries illustrate.

A computer is dependent on the information fed into it. Christopher Strachey, a former professor of computation at Oxford, believed that if the assumptions are wrong, conclusions 'would bear only a tenuous resemblance to . . . the real world' (*Fontana Dictionary of Modern Thought*). A computer is a marvellous tool, but it is in human hands.

computer-aided This descriptive compound is applied to a number of different processes which make use of a visual display screen linked to a computer. The two that occur most often are *computer-aided design* (designs are made directly on a screen instead of on paper, so they can be adapted and changed electronically), and *computer-aided manufacturing* (which uses computers to control ordering raw materials, production scheduling, stock control and other stages of manufacture).

computer crime This is so-called 'white collar' crime involving unauthorized use of a computer system. Computer crime is electronic forgery, sometimes used to carry out fraudulent fund transfers, sometimes to manipulate **data** or to gain access to confidential information. See also **data protection**; **hacker**

computer graphics See **graphics**

computer and **wordprocessing language**
The vocabulary of computer technology is settling down. Children, for whom computers are as familiar as exercise books, grow up with the basic terms as daily classroom language. As more and more adults use computers and wordprocessors for keeping records and writing letters, the more common terms have become familiar. For others, who want to keep in touch, comments on the more common terms used in computer technology and wordprocessing are included alphabetically in this book: **access** (+ *access time*), *analog* (see **analogue**), **artificial intelligence (AI)**, **backup**, **box in**, **bug**, **byte** (+ *bit*), **central processor**, *chip* (see **microchip**), **command** (+ *command language*), **compatible**, **computer**, **computer-aided**, **computer crime**, *computer graphics* (see **graphics**), *computer literate* (see **literate**), **computer science**, **continuous stationery**, *CPU* (see **central processor**), **cursor**, **cut and paste**, **daisy-wheel**, **data**, **databank/database**, **data processing**, **debug**, **dedicated**, *digital* (see **analogue**), **desktop computer**, **desktop publishing**, *disk* (see **disc**), **display**, **document**, **document retrieval**, **DOS**, **dot matrix**, **draft quality**, **fail-safe**, *fifth-generation* (see **generation**), **file**, **floppy disk**, **format**, *fourth generation* (see **generation**), **generation**, **hacker**, *hard copy* (see **printout**), *hard disk* (see **floppy disk**), **hardware**, **IBM**, **information technology**, **input**, **interface**, *IT* (see **information technology**), **justify**, **keyboard/keypad**, *kilobyte* (see **byte**), **laptop**, **letter quality**, **mainframe**, *megabyte* (see **byte**), **memory**, **menu**, **microchip**, *microcomputer* (see **desktop computer**), **modem**, **mouse**, **off-line/on-line**, *output* (see **input**), *personal computer* (see **desktop computer**), **printout**, **program**, **RAM**, *retrieve* (see **recall**), **save**, **scroll**, *software* (see **hardware**), **user-friendly**, **users' group**, **VDU**, **virus**, **wordprocessor**, **wraparound**, **WYSIWYG**.

computer-literate See **literate**

computer music See **electronic music**

computer *science* or *technology* A science requires fundamental laws and principles. In the study of the operations and applications of computers, not many laws and principles stay constant for long, so there is a good case for claiming that *computer technology* is a more suitable description than *computer science*. Nevertheless, *computer science* is the fashionable name for the subject and the one computer experts prefer – but then they would, wouldn't they?

comrade *Comrade*, from the Latin word for a room (cf *chamber*), has been used since the 16th century to mean a companion. The army took over the word for soldiers fighting alongside each other. Then the communists moved in on it, as *comrade* became the form of address between everyone engaged in the Marxist class struggle. After the discrediting of the Communist Party in the Soviet Union and the Baltic Republics, *comrade*, in a political sense, is old history. Nevertheless it can still be heard at highly-charged moments during trade union meetings, as a nostalgic attempt to keep the red flag flying. It was reported that Roy Hattersley, then deputy leader of the British Labour Party, had revived *comrade* at the 1991 conference of the Party, not to reaffirm the Socialist Revolution, but as a friendly apolitical greeting, which is about all that is left for *comrade* in the 1990s.

con and **con man** In the 1980s, Oxford dictionaries recorded *con* and *con man* (for the practice and the practitioner of making money by deceiving others) as 'colloquial'. The first Oxford dictionary of the 1990s downgraded the two words to 'slang', which seems severe since *con* and *con man* are used at boardroom meetings in the world of high finance. What is more, *confidence man*, recorded as standard English by dictionaries, seems curiously formal, since everybody everywhere uses *con man*.

conceal or **hide** *Conceal* comes from a Latin word and *hide* is from Old English. So as you would expect, *conceal* is the more formal alternative, used particularly about abstract qualities: 'she concealed her embarrassment'. *Hide* is more down-to-earth: 'she hid the letter under the pillow'. This is a matter of style.

concensus or **consensus** *Consensus*. But see also **census** . . .

concept *Concept* was once a serious term in philosophy for a theory based on observed instances. Now it is used all the time to make banal ideas seem significant and important, such as 'a new concept in potato crisps'. Do not be taken in by it, for *concept* is used in such inconsequential ways.

concerned 'As far as this matter is concerned . . .'; 'This is important as far as our customers are concerned . . .'; 'As far as I am concerned . . .'; and hundreds of other such roundabout expressions belong to old-fashioned **business English**. Better alternatives are 'About this matter . . .', 'This is important to our customers . . .', 'As for me . . .'.

concert or **recital** Just as it takes two to tango, a *concert* requires a number of musicians. A *recital* is a performance by a soloist (a piano recital) or a small group, such as a quartet. But there are no recitals of pop music: even if it is only one singer, it is always a *concert*.

concerto or **sonata** Musical terms have often been used loosely, with different meanings at different times in the history of music. Since the latter part of the 18th century, a *concerto* has usually meant a piece of music written for a virtuoso performance by a soloist, accompanied by an orchestra. A *concerto grosso* ('big concerto') is a composition for a group of solo instruments and orchestra.

A *sonata* (from the Italian 'sonare', to sound) has been used, also since the late 18th century, for compositions for one instrument on its own, or for an instrument with a piano accompaniment.

The plural of *sonata* is straightforward – *sonatas*. The plural of *concerto grosso* is *concerti grossi* (pron: 'conTCHERtee GROSSee'). But for the plural of *concerto*, most people use *concertos*, although *concerti* is shown in dictionaries as an alternative plural form.

concrete See cement . . .

conditional or **dependent** *Conditional* usually suggests that something is subject to requirements imposed, and could have a legal bearing in an agreement: for example, an order may be given conditional on a specified delivery date being met, so that if the date were not met, the order could be cancelled. *Dependent* suggests a connection with outside circumstances: a price can be quoted dependent on the cost of raw materials at the time the order is placed. Both words are usually followed by 'on'.

conditioning In the sense of moulding opinion, *conditioning* may sound an innocent word, and a political party would talk about *conditioning* the electorate to accept a particular policy. It is worth remembering that in psychology, *conditioning* is the systematic process controlling someone's behaviour, not so far away from **brainwashing**. See also **image**; **psycholinguistics**

condole See console . . .

condom, **sheath** or **French letter** By the 1980s, these words were covered in the dust of history. The device they represented had been rendered almost obsolete by the contraceptive **pill** and had become a quaint relic, almost unheard of in the easygoing sexual life of teenagers. The spread of **Aids** produced a dramatic turnaround: until a cure is found, a *sheath* over the penis during intercourse is the only way to help prevent this fatal disease becoming an epidemic.

What do we call them, now they are out in the open? *French letter* is confusing (how many people know that *letter* was an Old English word meaning hinder or prevent?), and unjustified (in the 18th century they were imported by France from England, hence the French name 'capote anglaise' – 'English bonnet'). *Sheath* sounds clinical. *Condom* is the only contender. The word had been discreetly omitted from some dictionaries before 1960, but now they are advertised on television, and bought by women as well as men without embarrassment. Do not believe any of the stories about the origin of the word: some say it was invented in the 18th century by a Dr Condom, others talk about Colonel Cundum, a British Guards officer. The editors of the *OED* agree that the word dates from the 18th century but the origin is unknown. See also **rubber** or **eraser**

conduit See pipe . . .

confederation See commonwealth . . .

confidant or **confident** Some people have to think twice about which is which, although the meanings are completely different. *Confidant* is a noun for someone you *confide* in, to whom you tell your innermost secrets. If it is a woman it can be spelt *confidante* (following the French pattern of adding *-e* to form the feminine), but with the trend towards unisex words, this is no longer necessary. Either way, the pronunciation is the same, with the stress on the *last* syllable: 'confiDANT'.

Confident (pron: 'CONfident') is the descriptive word meaning sure of yourself.

confidential, **secret**, **personal** or **private** *Confidential* and *secret* describe things that should not be disclosed to others. *Confidential* is the usual word in business matters, the word you might put on an envelope or at the top of a letter. *Secret* is the more powerful word, the word used by the military about information that could help the enemy, a word that might appear at the top of a file. To say something is secret suggests that it should not be revealed to anyone; you might feel free to share a confidential matter with others who are directly involved. But this distinction is not clear-cut. *Secret* is also the more intimate word: lovers have secret meetings, people have secret longings.

Personal covers matters that someone might not want others to know about. Bank statements are often sent in envelopes marked 'Personal', because many people feel that way about their financial affairs.

Private is often used as an alternative to *personal*, when a matter is not intimate but nevertheless concerns only a few people. 'Private and Confidential', which also appears on envelopes, is simply a belt and braces approach.

It is in order to put 'Confidential' at the top of a letter to indicate that it should not be left casually where anyone could see it. There's not the same point in putting *personal* on a letter (as well as the envelope), because the person it's written to can see that.

If you write to someone in an organization and mark the envelope 'Confidential' or 'Private', a secretary might be entitled to open it. If it is marked 'Personal', only the person named on the envelope should have that right.

Lastly, 'Confidential' and 'Private and Confidential' are often misused now, on routine circulars from banks and similar organizations.

conflict or **war** There is a tendency in international disputes to avoid the word *war* and use *conflict* instead, particularly when war has not been officially declared. During the battle in 1982 to recapture the Falkland Islands, it was referred to throughout as the Falklands *conflict*. Perhaps this is because *war* is a drastic word, a commitment, whereas *conflict* does not seem to go quite as far. For anyone engaged in the fighting it comes to the same thing.

conform *to* or **with** Some dictionaries note that we should *conform to* regulations or *to* what is usual, and *conform with* what is suitable or convenient. But few people bother to work that out any more, and the general view is that *conform to* or *with* are simply alternatives.

confront or **face** *Confront* suggests an aggressive or defiant attitude: 'we must confront the problem and fight back'. If we confront someone it is usually an aggressive challenge: 'she will confront him with new evidence'. *Face* is a more neutral word and may mean no more than dealing with something: 'we must face the difficulties in the best way we can'. The fashionable word now is **address**, which is neither one thing nor the other.

confrontation This has become a fashionable word for journalists to use about relations between trade unions and the government or employers: 'there is a confrontation between the workforce and management over extra payment for working unsocial hours'. But journalists need good stories and we should not always take *confrontation* too seriously: it may mean anything from a disagreement that can be resolved to a real eyeball-to-eyeball clash.

congenital, **hereditary** or **genetic** There is a good deal of overlap between these three descriptive words for an illness or an organic malfunction. *Congenital* means a condition that was present at birth. Such a condition may or may not be *hereditary*, that is an illness or weakness that exists in someone's family

and is passed on. *Genetic* is the more usual word now to describe a hereditary disease, for genes are transmitted across generations of a family and genetic research is now in the forefront of medical science (see also **genes . . .**).

conglomerate *Conglomerate* has replaced the word **combine** (now usually used with a different sense) for a very large business, with subsidiaries operating in different fields, and possessing great financial and industrial power. Most conglomerates are the result of mergers and takeovers, so *conglomerate* is a good word, since it derives from the Latin word for a globe and means a rounded mass made up of different parts. See also **merger . . .**

Congress, House of Representatives and **Senate** Even some British MPs are not always sure-footed over the difference between these three names relating to the legislature of the USA. *Congress* is the equivalent of the British Parliament, in that it includes both the upper house (the *Senate*) and the lower house (the *House of Representatives*). *Senators* (there are a hundred, two for each of the 50 states, elected for a six-year term) are members of the upper house, with *representatives* (elected for a two-year term from particular districts of each state) the members of the lower house.

congressman, congresswoman, representative or **senator** Dictionaries define a *congressman* and a *congresswoman* as a member of the US **Congress**, which is, of course, unarguable. But in practice a member of the US upper house is nearly always called a *senator* and *congressman* and *congresswoman* are used for members of the lower house. *Representative* is an alternative name for members of the lower house, and has the advantage of clearly not including senators, as well as being unisex.

Whether you use initial capital letters for these titles is a matter of taste: the tendency is not to (see **CAPITAL LETTERS**).

'CONjugal' or **'conJUGal'** Marital problems are bad enough, but at least we can be clear about how to pronounce *conjugal*, the word for the relationship between husband and wife. Stress is on the first syllable: 'CONjoogle'.

conjugation *Conjugation* is another of those Latinate (from 'conjugare', to link together) grammatical terms that are a hangover from the time when English grammar was entirely based on Latin and Greek. The conjugation of a verb lists the different forms the verb takes, such as I love, she loves, they have loved. . . . This exercise has much more relevance to Latin, a highly inflected language in which a whole range of different meanings is expressed by different suffixes added to nouns and verbs, than it has to English. Most of us don't give a thought to it, as we get on with the business of loving and living.

conjunctions This is a Latinate grammatical term for those short words, such as *and* and *but*, that link two words or two groups of words together: 'Jack *and* Jill went up the hill'; 'Jack is clever *but* Jill is pretty'; 'Do you want tea *or* coffee?'. See also **and**

connection or **connexion** Either, although *connexion* is becoming increasingly rare and may eventually become obsolete. Always *connection* in American English.

(*in*) connection with and **in this connection** 'I am writing to you in connection with . . .'; 'in this connection, I have decided. . .'. These are stuffy long-winded ways of saying 'about': 'I am writing to you about . . .'; 'about this, I have decided . . .'.

connive Remember *connive* has two meanings. It can mean being an accessory to a wrongdoing by knowing about it and not reporting it: 'The accountants connived at the tax evasion, because they knew the facts but kept quiet about them'. As a criminal offence, the formal legal charge is 'compound a felony' (see **compound**). *Connive* can also mean taking an active part in the wrongdoing: 'The accountants and the directors of the company connived together to evade tax'.

connote or **denote** *Connote* is often used in *The Good English Guide* because it refers to other meanings that people associate with words, in many cases meanings that dictionaries have not yet caught up with. *Denote* is the straightforward two-dimensional definition of a word. For example, **mankind** denotes the human race in general; for some women, 'mankind' connotes sexism, the domination of the affairs of the world by men.

Sometimes the connotative meaning of a word obscures the original denotative meaning: **manipulate** used to be a harmless word, meaning to handle something skilfully, but the predominant meaning now is sinister, suggesting exerting a cunning influence on someone or in a situation.

consciousness or **awareness** As well as their straightforward meanings, both words have been fashionable, since the **gurus** and mystical cults of the 1960s, in an esoteric sense, referring to higher states of being, sometimes brought about by **meditation**, sometimes by drugs. There are *consciousness-raising* groups, people working together to increase awareness of themselves, or as part of the women's movement to help women to become aware of their unconscious acceptance of and submission to male domination in society.

consensual sex See **date rape**; **rape or seduction**

consensus See **census** . . .

consensus of opinion This expression is used so often ('the consensus of opinion is this is the best restaurant in town') that it is perhaps unreasonable to object to it. But since *consensus* already means a

general agreement about something, there is no need to add *of opinion*: 'the consensus is this is the best restaurant in town'.

consensus politics In the 1960s, *consensus politics* was used about supposedly common commitments by the Conservative and Labour governments towards certain policies, such as the maintenance of the **welfare state**. Under Margaret Thatcher as Prime Minister, *consensus politics* was at times used in another way, for an approach to government that takes into account the collective opinion of the party, as opposed to conviction government, the authoritarian control of policy by the Prime Minister. See also **cabinet government**

(as a) consequence 'As a consequence, we cannot come to dinner' means the same as 'So we cannot come to dinner'. Then why not say *so*?

consequent or **consequential** Some dictionaries equate *consequential* with *consequent*, both meaning something which follows as a result. But *consequent* usually means as a *direct* result, while *consequential* implies an *indirect* result, and is mostly restricted to legal and insurance matters. For example, if there is a fire in a factory, there is a direct loss consequent on machinery being damaged or destroyed. There could also be an indirect loss, a *consequential loss*, as it is often expressed in insurance policies, because production is interrupted. *Consequential* can also mean significant or important: a consequential matter.

conservation or **preservation** Conservation in connection with forests, and even the expression *conservation of energy*, had already been heard well before the end of the 19th century. But it was not until the 1950s that *conservation*, beginning to be seen by then as a global problem, was finding its place as a key word in the future of this planet. It takes in the planned and efficient use of natural resources, such as **fossil fuels**, so that life on earth can be sustained into the future. When *conservation* is used about art treasures, architecture or historic monuments, it carries with it the belief in a cultural heritage that belongs by right to generations to come. The word now embraces a wider concept, looking further ahead than *preservation*, a more general word for protecting things from deterioration and damage.

Conservative or **conservative** A headline in *The Independent* (23.6.1990) read 'Conservative leads Russian party voting', which suggested that a member of the British Conservative Party was ahead in the leadership election in Russia. The news story referred to 'a noted conservative', meaning someone of moderate views. When the broadcaster, Sue MacGregor, was interviewing Dr Jonathan Sachs, the Chief Rabbi, she commented 'you are not as conservative – with a *small c* – as your predecessor'. She was anxious to make it clear that she was not alluding to his political allegiance.

Conservative with a capital C relates to the Conservative Party; conservative with a small *c* is a descriptive word for moderate or traditional views. Confusion may arise, as Sue MacGregor realized, when we are speaking, or, as in the headline of *The Independent*, when *conservative* is the first word in a sentence.

Conservative or **Tory** In the 17th century, a *tory* was an Irish bandit, which led to it becoming an abusive name for a Catholic. Linked with that use, *Tory* first took on a political colouring as the name given to the party in the 1680s that did not want to exclude James from succession to the throne because he had become a Catholic. The Tory Party remained the name for the party that supported the King and the established order, until it was renamed the Conservative Party in the 1830s.

Tory is more likely to be used now in London clubland, and is convenient, because of its brevity, in newspaper headlines (TOP TORIES is a favourite alliteration). For young people, *Tory* is an old-fashioned name for a *Conservative*. Others find it useful as a two-syllable alternative, and for some political opponents, *Tory* has a built-in sneer about it.

In American history, a Tory was a colonist who remained loyal to England during the American Revolution.

conservatory, **orangery** or **gazebo** In the 17th century, a *gazebo* (pron: 'ge(r)ZEEboh') was a turret or other structure that gave an all-round view. The word was probably formed as a pun on the word 'gaze'. It was adopted in America for a summerhouse in a garden, and is often used in the same way in Britain, although it never seems at home here. A *conservatory* is properly for protecting fragile plants, and is usually a glass-fronted structure with direct access from the house. But it has become a pretentious fashionable word for any small greenhouse or for the back-extension of a suburban house facing the garden.

An *orangery*, originally for cultivating orange-trees, is a grander building, large enough for people to walk up and down in. Some people retain the French pronunciation ('orRAHNzhery') but the English form is more accepted, following the normal pronunciation of 'orange': 'ORRinzhery'.

conserve See jam . . .

conserving See conservation . . .

consider or **consider as** There is a difference. Read these two statements: 'I consider Mary a friend'; 'I consider Mary *as* a friend'. The first means I believe Mary is a friend; the second means I take her into account as a friend, that is I behave to her accordingly. This may seem subtle, and you can take it or leave it.

consideration In law, the word *consideration* is necessary. Contracts often state 'In consideration of

. . .': one party agrees to do something because of a *consideration*, which could be a payment of money, or the agreement to do something or not to do something in return. Outside law, it is unnecessary, unless you want to be evasive, to write or say 'I'll do this for a consideration' when what you mean is 'I'll do it if you pay me'.

consist See compose . . .

consistent or **persistent** For Arnold Bennett, the *consistent* sound of a distant violin playing 'six bars – no more – of an air of Verdi's over and over again . . . was the most melancholy thing I have ever heard' (*Sketches for Autobiography*). If it had been a *persistent* sound, it might have been the most irritating thing he had ever heard. For *consistent* suggests unvarying, without change, whereas *persistent* is a calculated or relentless going-on that drives you mad.

consist in or **of** See compose

console or **condole** Because these two words are used in the same kind of situation, they are often confused. *Condole* is used less often. It means to express sympathy and is always followed by 'with': 'I condoled with her on the loss of her child'. *Console* is the word we usually want. It means to comfort and support: 'I tried to console her. . .'.

consonant, **vowel** or **letter** What is said to be the first alphabet, devised more than 3500 years ago by a Semitic people, contained only *consonants*. With the addition of vowels in the Greek alphabet, written language came closer to representing spoken language. When we refer, for example, to the consonants *b* or *d* or the vowels *a* or *i*, it is an allusion to the speech sounds. If we mean written characters, it is better to use the word *letters*.

consortium This is the usual name now for a group of companies or individuals forming an association to find the money, or the drive, or the political influence, to carry out a project, such as submitting an application for a television franchise, or building a new industrial centre. The Latin plural, *consortia*, is more generally used, but the anglicized plural, *consortiums*, is also acceptable.

constitute Other than in legal use, where *constitute* is used about a law or a court or a decision ('this does not constitute a precedent'), it is often heavy-going to use *constitute* in everyday writing or speaking: 'Does this constitute an offer?'. 'Is this an offer?' or 'Is this a formal offer?' is more direct. It is different, of course, if you're being funny: 'Does this handful of lettuce leaves constitute dinner?'

constrained or **limited** Both words are similar in meaning. But some people feel there is a difference of emphasis, in that *constrained* suggests working within certain definitions, which may well be a creative challenge, whereas *limited* may imply a cramping of style and possibilities. When the architect, Richard Rogers, was asked about being *limited* by his clients' requirements, he preferred the word *constrained*, suggesting for him a discipline that focused rather than inhibited his work.

consult or **consult** *with*   In Britain we can consult our lawyer or our doctor without *with* getting in the way. Americans often prefer *consult with*. Some recent British dictionaries have come to accept *consult with*, but although this is now heard in Britain, it does not come naturally.

consult, **engage**, **retain** or **appoint**   There is a certain professional etiquette about which word is used in which situation. See **appoint** . . .

consultant   At one time *consultant* was used mostly for medical specialists in hospitals and **Harley Street**, but now the word has run amok. Everywhere people are setting themselves up as consultants about anything: if you want to invest money, choose a holiday, get a mortgage, get on better with your spouse, lose weight, get rid of moles, you go to a *consultant*.

consulting room or **surgery**   See **doctor** . . .

consumer   Before World War II, when we bought things we were 'customers'. We are now *consumers*, the **admass** word that has turned us into faceless **socio-economic** groups. Consumers are at the other end of the see-saw from producers and if it gets out of balance, there are problems with the economy. See also next entry

consumerism   When customers were called **consumers**, it gave them a collective sense of their rights, and some time in the 1970s a new -*ism* was born – *consumerism*. It describes the increasingly organized pressure by people buying goods over quality, guarantees, prices. . . . Consumerism seeks to turn the old but often hollow the-customer-is-always-right maxim into a reality in the marketplace. *Consumerism* is also used in another way, as an economic principle that the basis for a sound economy is for consumption of goods to increase in line with production.

consumer society   See **admass**

consummate   With the stress on the second syllable ('conSUMMut'), it means perfect or masterly: a consummate performance. With the stress on the first syllable ('CONsumayt'), it means to make complete: a marriage is consummated by sexual intercourse.

contact   A few die-hards are still left who say you cannot *contact* anyone, you can only *make a contact*. Ivor Brown took a more sensible view as far back as the early 1940s (*A Word in Your Ear*): 'There is no other word which covers approach by telephone, letter and speech, and *contact* is self-explanatory and concise'. All dictionaries now give us permission to use *contact* as a verb, and to have *contacts* in Paris, New York or anywhere we like.

contagious or **infectious**   The usual distinction is that a *contagious* disease is one that can be caught only by direct physical contact with someone or something, and that an *infectious* disease is transmitted through micro-organisms in air or water. But this distinction is not always clear-cut: Dr M F Perutz, a joint winner of a Nobel Prize for Chemistry (1962), has countered the belief that **Aids**, for example, is not infectious, quoting the criteria for an infectious disease as one that can be transmitted 'from person to person either directly or through a carrier, and the existence of a . . . micro-organism or a virus that can be demonstrated to cause the disease'.

Apart from disease, the words are used interchangeably: 'his enthusiasm was contagious'; 'her laughter was infectious'.

The everyday word for the same meaning in almost all circumstances is *catching*, but no doctor would stoop to using it!

container   In international trade, this has become a word with a new meaning. It is used for the stowing of goods into packing cases of standard shapes and sizes so they can be handled mechanically by standard loading and unloading equipment, for transferring from one form of transport to another at maximum speed and minimum cost. Hard on the heels of this use of *container* came a new word – *containerization*.

contemplative, **meditative** or **reflective**
There are interesting shades of difference between these three words. *Contemplative* carries with it a feeling of timelessness, a withdrawal to an inner state. Aristotle made a distinction between the contemplative life and the active life. *Meditative* is more focused, a conscious directing of thought towards the human condition, often as a spiritual excercise. *Reflective* is nearer the surface: it suggests a thoughtful nature, a habit of mind, rather than a way of life, or it could mean an approach to a specific matter (a reflective attitude towards a problem). See also **meditation**

contemporary or **modern**   *Contemporary* relates to 'tempus', Latin for time, and strictly it means present during the same period. As a descriptive word it is used about style, fashion, art, architecture, ideas . . . that reflect the time we are living in: for example, the Pompidou Centre in Paris, which opened in 1977, officially France's national centre for contemporary art. The building itself reflects a contemporary faith in function, with pipes, ventilator shafts and escalators on the outside.

Modern is such a confusing word, with so many qualifications, that it requires a separate entry.

Even rules about how *contemporary* should be used are not reliable. For a time, it was reasonable to use the word for post-World War II styles and ideas, but by now many of those are out of date. Perhaps the best thing is to use *contemporary* to relate to the 1990s. If that does not fit a particular situation, consider **experimental**, progressive, 'belonging to the 1990s', or looking forward to the 21st century'. For additional guidelines on this, and for the distinction between *contemporary* and *modern architecture*, see **modern**.

contemptible or **contemptuous** It would be embarrassing to confuse these two words. 'I am contemptible' means I deserve contempt; 'I am contemptuous' means I feel contempt for somebody else or for something they have done. The following two examples should prevent you saying the wrong thing: 'the way he treats her is contemptible'; 'she is contemptuous of the way he treats her'. *Contemptuous* is usually followed by 'of', 'about' or 'towards', and it doesn't matter which.

content or **happy** See happy . . .

content *by* or *with* When *content* is used as a verb, it should be followed by *with* (not *by*). It is easy to slip up when other words come in between: 'she contented herself for the time being *with* saying no more about it'.

context, **framework** and **setting** There is a primary meaning to all three words. *Context* is the flow of words that relate to other words in the same passage. If something is quoted *out of context*, it might have an altogether different meaning: 'I found it fascinating', splashed across a theatre poster, might have been lifted out of a review that said 'I found it fascinating to work out why *anybody* should come to see this play'!

A *framework* is the structure that supports something. A *setting* is the surrounding scenery or the place and time against which something takes place.

All three words (and some others as well) have become woolly clichés that obscure what is being said or written: 'this could only be possible in the context (or within the framework, or against the setting) of a sound economic policy'. The writer means '. . . *if* there is a sound economic policy'. 'We must consider this within the context (or the framework, or the setting) of the peace terms that are agreed'. The writer means 'against' or 'alongside' the peace terms.

continental See European . . .

contingency The word has spread from specialized use in philosophy and theology to business and financial forecasting, where it provides a cushion (or an excuse) against something unexpected or a miscalculation. Hence *contingency planning*, open-ended forward planning to allow for almost anything that could happen; a *contingency fund*, money kept in reserve in case something goes wrong.

continual or **continuous** There is a useful distinction. *Continual* refers to something that is going on all the time but with interruptions. *Continuous* is

going on all the time without interruption. It is hardly possible to argue continuously all day as you have to stop sometimes. A bee can give a continuous buzz, but a dog is more likely to bark continually.

continuance or **continuation** *Continuance* is usually about a state, circumstances or a condition: continuance after death, continuance of Stonehenge, continuance of the same economic policy. *Continuation* applies more to an action, an event, an occurrence: continuation of the war, continuation of the game, continuation of the takeover bid. See also next entry

continuity *Continuity* refers to the state of being continuous, rather than to the action of continuing. On television an **anchorman** is responsible for the continuity of the programme, that is for holding it together as a logical continuous sequence (you could say that the engineers are responsible for the *continuation* of the programme, that is keeping it on the air). *Continuity girls* in a film studio (no one ever talks about a 'continuity woman' and 'continuity men' are rare) make sure that all details are consistent, so that the film has a continuous flow: a man leaving for work in the morning must arrive at the office wearing the same clothes, even if several days elapse between the two scenes being filmed.

continuous See continual . . .

continuous stationery Wordprocessing and computer printouts have brought this term into everyday use. Continuous stationery is a long roll of paper, perforated into page-length divisions, so that it feeds continuously into a printer.

contracted forms *I'm, I'll, you're, you'll, isn't, it's, can't, don't, he's, she's, they're* . . . we all use them in conversation but some people hesitate to use them in writing. Written English and spoken English are much closer to each other now and these contracted forms appear in official letters from government departments, solicitors, MPs and from many others who would not have used them before the 1960s. Novelists, such as William Trevor, Saul Bellow and Kingsley Amis, use them, not only in dialogue where they are natural, but also in descriptive passages. When it seems laboured to write these forms out in full all the time, the way is now open to use the contractions. But remember that if you overdo it, it can seem too casual. *I'd, you'd*, etc sound perfectly all right when we say them but look a little odd in print so, although there's no rule about it, they're not used in writing as often as the other *contracted forms*. *Shan't* and *won't* are conversational forms and have no place in writing, except when recording dialogue. And dialogue is the only place to find such extreme contractions as *would've, I'd've, Mary'll*.

Newscasters on radio and television often make a point, when asking questions, of saying 'is it not?', 'are you not?', rather than 'isn't it?', 'aren't you?' This has become almost a mannerism, but perhaps they feel it gives more weight to questions. See also **ain't**; **elision**

contract killing This is commercial assassination. Businessmen, or lovers with a grudge, hire *hitmen* to carry out murders for them, sometimes for vast fees. This kind of crime, we are told, is on the increase. Graham Greene wrote about it in *A Gun For Sale* (1936): 'Murder didn't mean much to Raven. It was just a new job'. See also **hit-list**

contract out If a manufacturer cannot handle a particular job, they might *contract out* the work, that is arrange for another manufacturer to do it. If the manufacturer decides not to take on or go on with a job, they will *contract out*, that is withdraw and have nothing more to do with it. In practice these two different meanings of *contract out* should not get in the way of each other.

contradiction or **paradox** *Contradiction* is the simpler word, which helps us to understand the more complex nature of a *paradox*.

A *contradiction* is two opposing statements, points of view or pieces of information that clearly cannot both be true: 'it is a contradiction to say that the business is doing well and to give figures of falling sales and profits'. A *contradiction in terms* renders a statement meaningless, because one part of it negates the other: 'How can you fall in love rationally? It's a contradiction in terms'.

A *paradox* seems contradictory on the face of it but may in fact have a sound basis. The classic example is the statement 'I am lying'. If it is true, then the person is not lying; if it is false, the person is telling the truth. Paradoxes can take us deep into philosophy, logic and mathematics. When it comes to using the word to explain something, its value is to describe an apparently contradictory situation that nevertheless contains a truth: 'the paradox she often experiences is to feel intensely lonely when surrounded by people at a party'.

'CONtrary' or **'conTRARY'** When it's 'on the contrary', most people get it right, putting the stress on the first syllable ('CONtrary'). But a 'CONtrary' point of view, for example, means an opposite viewpoint, whereas a 'conTRARY' point of view is an obstinate or perverse attitude. The nursery rhyme is a reminder of the difference: 'Mary, Mary, quite contrary . . .'.

contrast (meaning and pronunciation) See **compare** . . .

'conTRIBute' or **'CONtribute'** More and more people stress the first syllable ('CONtribute'), which is almost an accepted alternative. But perhaps not yet as the standard pronunciation puts the stress on the second syllable: 'conTRIBute'.

contributory negligence See **negligence** . . .

control *Control* is used in a particular way in experimental work in different fields. A control, in this sense, is not exposed to whatever is being tested but kept as a neutral standard for comparison. For example, a *control group* in psychology would be chosen as the closest parallel with the group being tested. The control group is given exactly the same tests, although not subjected to the special factor under observation, such as alcohol, fatigue, time of day. . . . In that way any difference in results between the two groups could presumably be ascribed to that factor.

controller or **comptroller** *Comptroller* is an old-fashioned word, based on a mistaken spelling (through a wrong association with Latin 'computus'), that caught on 400 years ago. It survives in some official titles, 'Comptroller-General of the National Debt Office'. Although it sounds grand, don't be impressed because it means exactly the same and is pronounced exactly the same as *controller*.

'CONtroversy' or **'conTROVersy'** Feelings run high about whether to put the stress on the *first* or *second* syllable. British dictionaries show both pronunciations, usually with the stress on the *first* syllable as preferable. Some people consider 'conTROVersy' ill-educated, others feel that 'CONtroversy' is affected. You have to make up your own mind, or emigrate to America, where the stress is always on the first syllable, the pronunciation recommended by *The Good English Guide*.

conurbation A 20th-century word, linked with the Latin 'urbs' for 'city', that is increasingly useful because it describes the sprawl of a city as it spreads out in **suburban** development, absorbing outlying villages.

convenience Someone once put that stuffy expression 'at your convenience' in its place. In reply to a letter offering to meet him 'at your convenience', he replied 'my nearest convenience is in Paradise Row' (*convenience* being a genteelism for a public lavatory). The moral is replace 'at your convenience' by 'whenever it suits you', and 'at your earliest convenience' by 'as soon as possible'. And if you need a lavatory, don't mince matters.

convenor *Convenor* (also spelt 'convener') belongs to the language of trade unions. It is the leader elected by shop stewards (see **shop-floor**) to act as their representative in dealings with employers and at meetings of the **Trades Union** Congress. Pron: 'konVEENe(r)'.

conventional In general, *conventional* means conforming to what is generally accepted and expected, not necessarily a bad thing. But *conventional* has also taken on another colour and is often used to mean dull, boring, unimaginative: 'it was a conventional dinner party and I was bored out of my mind'. At a time when society is looking for innovation and new points of departure, *conventional* is increasingly used for a dull stick-in-the-mud approach, and this is likely eventually to become the primary meaning of the word. For *conventional weapons*, see **war (language of)**.

conversational English See colloquial . . .

converse See opposite . . .

convey To use *convey* instead of 'give', 'take', 'pass on' . . ., is to carry formality to the edge of pompousness: 'Please convey my good wishes to your father'; 'Please convey this lady to the station'; 'Would you convey my suggestion to the minister?' Substitute 'give', 'take', 'pass on' in those three sentences and it takes the stuffiness out of them.

conviction government See cabinet government; consensus politics

cool (of drinks) See chilled . . .

cool or **laid-back** The use of *cool* by American jazz musicians in the late 1940s, to mean unrestrained, relaxed or unemotional (as opposed to the 'hot' sweaty involvement of traditional jazz), soon crossed the Atlantic. The more recent slang expression that means exactly the same is *laid-back*, which has the advantage of conjuring up an appropriate picture. No one knows how the term arose: it may have alluded to smoking cannabis or the semi-reclining position of some motorcyclists. But now, according to BBC reports, even the director-general of the CBI and the Chancellor of the Exchequer can be *laid-back*.

cooling-off This is a useful way of describing a prudent period of waiting, sometimes imposed by law, so that something might be reconsidered before action is taken or a definite commitment is made. In industrial disputes, a cooling-off period gives both sides the chance to think again before the workforce goes out on strike. With certain investments, investors are entitled by law to a cooling-off period, allowing them time to change their minds within a specified number of days.

cooperate or **collaborate** It is worth deciding which word to use, as the meanings divide. *Collaborate* suggests working together ('collaborate on a book'); *cooperate* is a more passive word for offering advice and information. But the distinction becomes blurred at times. Although *collaborator* has an innocent meaning, describing a co-author, for example, it also has a nasty meaning of a traitor who cooperates with an enemy in occupation. See also next entry

cooperation or **collusion** Avoid using *collusion* in a good sense: 'the two scientists are working in collusion on the experiments'. The proper word there is *cooperation*, because *collusion* is always used about something dishonest or fraudulent: 'the directors were in collusion over falsifying the accounts'. See also previous entry

(a) cooperative or **a commune** Both words, which describe associations of people, are sometimes confused. *Cooperatives* stem from economic movements in Britain and France during the 19th century: they are voluntary organizations sharing common facilities and arrangements, such as processing and packing machinery, purchasing and marketing, run by the workers who share all profits on an agreed basis. There are now cooperatives all over the world, especially in activities, such as farming, wine production and crafts.

A *commune* (for pronunciation, see **communal**) is a way of living rather than an economic arrangement, usually based on idealistic or political convictions. Generally members own no property as individuals, sharing living accommodation and often pooling all the income from their work. The **kibbutzim** in Israel, on which even the bringing up of children is communal, are well-known examples of *communes*.

coordinates As far as anyone knows, *coordinates* was first used about clothes in an advertisement in *Vogue* in 1959. Before then it was mainly a mathematical term for magnitudes used to define the position of other magnitudes or for map references. Now the most modest clothes shops tucked away in back streets have adopted *coordinates* for a matching skirt and shirt or socks and braces, or for any other different pieces of clothing that are designed to be sold together.

cop, **copper**, **bobby** or **policeman** Elderly people in Britain might still use *bobby* (after Sir Robert Peel who established the London police force in 1829). *Copper*, also British English, is not used so much now, as *cop*, familiar in American films, has become the most usual word. Although *cop* is considered slang by some dictionaries, a survey showed that the police themselves like it. What's more, it has a respectable connection with Latin 'capare' (cf 'capture'). Note also that the formal name *policeman* is making a comeback.

copier A copier used to be a scribe who copies documents. But not any more. A *copier*, standard equipment in offices, is now a machine that makes copies, using **xerography**, a **laser** printer or whatever other process is next in the pipeline.

copper See cop . . .

copy As a noun, *copy* means different things in different situations. Some publishers still talk about a **manuscript**, meaning the text supplied by the author, but many would now call it the copy. For a journalist, copy is the information available for a news story ('political scandals are good copy'). Printers call anything they have to reproduce the copy, even if it is only a name and an address on a visiting card. In advertising agencies, the copy is the words, written by a *copywriter*, that go into an advertisement, not including, at that stage, illustrations. And in offices, a copy is the photocopy that glides neatly out of a **copier**.

cord or **chord** See chord . . .

cordless Used as far back as the beginning of the century about telephone switchboards, where connections are made with plugs, *cordless* took off in the late 1960s, when telephones and more and more electrical appliances were able to function without being connected to the power by wire. By that time the word 'wireless' was not available to describe them, as it had already been used for **radio**.

corn *Cornflakes*, *cornflour* and *sweet corn*, all normal British English, relate to the American and Australian meaning of *corn*, which is maize. Otherwise, *corn* in Britain refers to wheat, oats or barley.

corner shop and **high street shop** *Corner shop* has become newscasting idiom for any small local privately owned shop, whether it is on a corner or not. It contrasts with *high street shop*, used for big shops and stores, usually part of groups. See also **high street** . . .

coronary, **stroke** or **heart attack** Causes of death and serious illness are in the open now and these terms are used freely, sometimes with misunderstanding. A *coronary* (stress is on the *first* syllable: 'CORronery') is short for *coronary thrombosis*, loosely called a *heart attack*, the most common form of heart disease. It is a blood clot in one of the coronary arteries, which supply blood to the heart.

A *stroke* is a blood clot in one of the arteries that supply blood to the brain, or a rupture of one of the blood vessels in the brain, which usually causes partial paralysis. A stroke used to be called *apoplexy* but that term has dropped out of use: *apoplectic*, used for someone going red in the face with fury, also sounds dated, although you still hear it from older people.

corporate A *corporation* (from Latin 'corpus' for a body) is a ponderous word for a big business (a 'body' of people), but *corporate*, especially since the 1960s, has become the self-important fashionable word for the overall approach that a company takes on certain matters. A big business now yearns for a *corporate image*, a strong unified impression on the world at large. *Corporate strategy* is long-term planning, taking into account the resources of the company and the projected requirements of world markets. A more recent corporate creed is *corporate culture*, 'the way you do things', according to management consultants, which seems to be an attempt to direct the work and attitudes of a company's employees so that everything reflects the same purpose.

corps Although it derives from Latin, *corps* came into English from French and is pronounced in the French way: 'caw'. Otherwise it would get mixed up with 'corpse'. *Corps* (It is the same in the singular and plural) is used for a group of people with particular duties, such as the Royal Army Medical Corps, diplomatic corps, press corps.

The French connection is retained in some French phrases used in English, such as *corps de ballet* (the general group of dancers in a ballet company), and in *CD* (*corps diplomatique*) plates seen on cars in capital cities all over the world.

corpus The Latin word for a body (see **corporate** and **corps**) survives intact in this word, not used often now, for a collection of writings and texts, usually by a major author: the corpus of Graham Greene's novels, the corpus of Shakespeare's writings. . . . But unless you are wearing academic robes, and want to sound like it, you might just as well say 'the novels of . . .', or 'the complete works of . . .'. See **work or oeuvre**

correspond to or **with** Some people make this distinction. When *correspond* is used to mean 'it comes to the same thing', it is followed by *to*: 'although there are minor differences, this corresponds to what we wanted'. When *correspond* means in agreement with something, it can be followed by *to* or *with*: 'this corresponds to (or with) our general policy'. It must be added that most people regard that distinction as unnecessary and use whichever they prefer in all circumstances (except when it's about writing letters, in which case it is always correspond *with*).

corridors of power See (the) **Establishment**

(a) corrugated phase See **bumping along the bottom** . . .

cosmetic Noble words are often downgraded. *Cosmetic*, linked to the awe-inspiring Greek word 'kosmos', which encompasses the whole order of the universe, has the trivial meaning of 'superficial appearance'. Used about lipstick, powder and other make-up products, cosmetic has been extended as an attack on any proposal or change that has no real effect but only makes something look better. Political parties often use it about opposition parties' ideas. See also **face-lift**

cosmetic surgery See **plastic surgery** . . .

cosmic Centuries ago, *cosmic* pertained to this world but that meaning has long been obsolete. Now the primary meaning of *cosmic* is for the universe apart from this world. So it has become a word for space travel, which has brought *cosmic*, once confined to philosophers and visionaries, into more everyday use.

cosmonaut See **astronaut** . . .

cosmopolitan or **international** Since the mid-19th century, *cosmopolitan* has meant belonging to or knowing about different parts of the world. It underwent a change of emphasis in the 1960s: it now has a flavour of the **jet set** about it, implying worldly, fashionable, sophisticated, rich. The American magazine *Cosmopolitan* latched on to this idea and used it as the title to suggest success, wit, worldly wisdom and female sexual gratification.

International is a more political, cultural and economic word for matters involving different countries: an international gathering suggests statesmen, business executives, scientists . . . , whereas a cosmopolitan gathering would be less serious, more social and pleasure-seeking.

cost or **cost** *out* The American form *cost out* is heard more and more in Britain, especially in government departments and business. As a result, *cost out* has become a more sophisticated alternative to *cost*: a local builder will still *cost* a job, that is work out an estimate for the work, but a minister or a chief executive would be more likely to ask someone to *cost out* a project or a proposal.

cost or **price** In general use, we might ask the *cost* or the *price* of something, both meaning how much do we have to pay for it. In business, the words usually mean two different things: the *cost* could represent what something cost to produce, and the *price* how much it could be sold for. The price, in that sense, could be based on a fair profit or on 'what the market will stand', that is how much people would be willing to pay for it. Oscar Wilde reflected this in his definition of a cynic: 'A man who knows the price of everything, and the value of nothing' (*Lady Windermere's Fan*, Act III).

Cost is usually preferred for services and abstractions, such as cost of living, cost of phone calls, cost of war.

cost-benefit In economics or business *cost-benefit* is useful shorthand for comparing the cost of a project or an action with the profit or saving it is expected to produce. A *cost-benefit analysis* sets it out in figures, like a balance sheet. But remember this is an accountant's way of looking at a proposal and may leave out environmental or social considerations, since it is difficult to put a figure against such things.

cost-effective *Cost-effective* means doing something at a cost that makes good sense in relation to what is achieved: 'this is a cost-effective way of introducing the new model'. It should imply good value for money, but look at it carefully because it can cover up a waste of money: something can be called cost-effective, in that the result is worthwhile, but it still may cost more than is necessary.

cost of living index See index

cost out See cost . . .

cosy No one knows about the origin of this word, except that it comes from Scotland (Robert Burns, 1759–96, used it). Look out for a tendency to use *cosy* in a nasty way to mean smug and self-satisfied:

'she's very cosy about marrying a rich man'. Some recent dictionaries have picked this up. As for the spelling, you are *cosy* in Britain, but *cozy* in America.

Côte d'Azur See **South of France** . . .

couch, sofa or **settee** *Couch* is the oldest of these words, going back to the 14th century, when it was also a verb meaning to lie down, a suggestion that lingers on. There is really no difference between a couch and a *sofa*, as they both can have a back and two arms. But a couch may have a rest at only one end, making it easy to lie on, which is why some film producers (see **casting couch**) and most psychoanalysts have couches, although for different purposes.

Another word for a sofa or a couch is a *settee* (although, to be precise, a settee need not have arms). For some reason, perhaps because it sounds affected, *settee* has become a downmarket word, unlikely to be heard in manor houses. If you want to be completely sure of what you're sitting on, see also **chaise longue; chesterfield**.

could or **might** Some grammarians make the following point. 'The sun *might* shine tomorrow' is the correct way to express uncertainty: 'The sun *could* shine tomorrow' is a statement of the obvious, because of course the sun *could* shine, if it wants to. The use of *could* for *might* in such contexts has become so widespread, that if you argue against it, people *could* say you are being pedantic, and they *might* be right.

council or **counsel** *Council* can only be a noun for an official body of people, sometimes with executive powers (a *town council*), sometimes acting only in an advisory capacity. *Counsel*, as a noun, means advice on some important matter, or a **barrister** in England, or a lawyer in America. Note that a *counsel of perfection*, sometimes misunderstood, means advising someone of the perfect thing to do in a situation, but it is advice that is rarely possible to carry out.

As a verb, *counsel* means the same as 'advise', but is more formal, and is usually applied to a professional adviser. See also **councillor or counsellor**

council housing See **public housing** . . .

(the) council *is* or ***are*** See **collective words**

councillor or **counsellor** It doesn't matter when you are talking, because they both sound the same. In writing, you have to be careful. A *councillor* is a member of a council, often in local government. A *counsellor* is someone who gives advice (marriage-guidance *counsellor*). **Barristers** are *counsels*, not counsellors (although a lawyer in America may be called a *counselor-at-law* – note spelling with one l).

council tax See **poll tax** . . .

counsel See **barrister; council or counsel**

counselling Before World War II, the word *counselling* was not used all that often; 'advising' was the more usual word. Now *counselling* is a **buzzword** and half the western world seems to be counselling the other half. There are call-in counselling programmes on television and radio, a counselling telephone service on the widest range of problems, from impotence to impetigo, and the number of psychotherapists in private practice has increased five times since the early 1980s, all providing expensive counselling sessions. As a result of all this, *counselling* relates almost exclusively now to traumatic personal problems.

counsellor   See **councillor or counsellor**

countdown   *Countdown* is the word used in space and nuclear technology for counting second by second backwards to zero. The method was invented by the German film director, Fritz Lang (1890–1976), to heighten suspense. It is logical because it tells us how many seconds we have left.

The most unnerving *countdown* is the Génitron, the digital clock outside the Pompidou Centre in Paris, counting down the seconds to the end of the **millennium**, midnight, 31 December 1999.

counter-productive   When you take measures to achieve something and they produce the opposite result, that's *counter-productive* and very discouraging.

coup   Although it derives from medieval Latin, *coup* is as French (it means a blow) as the Eiffel Tower, but it has been used in English for centuries, pronounced more or less as in French: 'koo'. In the plural (*coups*) it is acceptable to say 'cooz' in English, although many people choose not to pronounce the *s*.

Coup is used in English for a brilliantly successful move or feat in a game, the power game, politics. . . . There are at least two associated French phrases for which there is no good English alternative: *coup d'état* (pron: 'koodayTAH'), for an overnight seizure of power in a country by force, and *coup de grâce* (pron: 'kooderGRAHSS'), for a final blow that finishes off an animal or a person and spares them more suffering.

(a) couple *is* or *are*   For people and objects it is better to treat *a couple* as plural: 'a couple of people *are* here'; 'a young couple *have* bought the house'; 'a couple of books *are* on the table'. With units of time, it often sounds more natural to use a singular verb: 'a couple of hours *is* quite long enough'.

coupon   It should always be pronounced 'KOOpon'. 'KYOUpon' is considered vulgar, even though some broadcasters say it that way.

courage or fearlessness   The distinction between these two words is part of understanding the human situation. In one of her essays, Aung San Suu Kyi, former leader of Burma's National League for Democracy and winner of the 1992 Nobel Peace Prize, focused on the difference:

Fearlessness may be a gift but perhaps more precious is the courage acquired through endeavour, courage that comes from cultivating the habit of refusing to let fear dictate one's actions, courage that could be described as 'grace under pressure'.

(*Freedom from Fear and Other Writings*, 1991)

(of) course   See **of course**

course or seminar   *Seminars* were confined to universities at one time, particularly in America, for a small group of advanced students in a class conducted by a professor. American business took up the word in the 1940s, and it soon became the **buzzword** for any short course for senior managers. Going on a *course* is kids' stuff, but going on a *seminar* is something you can impress your friends with.

Seminar soon crossed over to Britain, as the fashionable word for almost any course of instruction. Business executives like it because it sounds learned and important. For the same reason, *seminar* is almost the standard word for courses in esoteric quasi-mystical subjects, so there are aromatherapy seminars, rebirth seminars, meditation seminars. . . .

Now that *seminar* has become such an everyday word, there is, or could be, a useful distinction between a course and a seminar: *seminar* could be reserved for a short intensive course from one day up to a week or so, while *course* can cover any period (a degree course, for example, which usually takes three years).

cousins   Everyone knows that the children of brothers or sisters are *cousins* (or *first cousins*) to each other. But beyond that it gets more complicated. Your *second cousin* is a child of a first cousin of either of your parents. Your *first cousin once removed* is a child of one of your first cousins or the first cousin of one of your parents. Your *first cousin twice removed* is a grandchild of your first cousin, or a first cousin of one of your grandparents.

You can take this further on still but enough is enough.

couturier or dressmaker   It depends upon whether it is a woman round the corner with a sewing-machine or someone with an expensive shop in London, Paris, New York. . . . A *dressmaker* may design clothes as well as make them, or simply make up your own material to your own pattern. A *couturier* (pron: 'kooTCHOOReeay') always designs clothes as well as having them made in their workshops, or at least supervising them being made by *dressmakers* working at home.

Strictly, a *couturier* is a man and the feminine equivalent is *couturière*, but in practice *couturier* is often used for a fashion designer of either sex.

covenant   *Covenant* has certain uses for taxation purposes in connection with regular payments to charities or to provide funds for the education of children. Apart from that, an area of confusion can arise because *covenant* can be used to mean a formal legal agreement, or a single clause or condition in such agreement. For example, it is usual to call the conditions and stipulations in a lease *covenants* rather than clauses.

coverage, viewership, circulation or **readership** In radio and television, *coverage* is the number of people within range of the transmissions from a station, that is the maximum possible audience (advertisers are more interested in *viewership*, the number of people who watch a particular programme). For a newspaper or a magazine, *coverage* is a greater number than the total number of copies sold, the figure known as *circulation*: it is the number of people who read or at least look at a copy, since one copy may be seen by two or more people. Newspapers and magazines like to call this coverage figure, their *readership*, which is misleading because it suggests someone reading from cover to cover, although it includes anyone merely flicking through the pages. In public relations, *coverage* is the total amount of 'free' publicity a product, person, show, or a story receives in newspapers and magazines and on radio and television.

cover charge *Cover charge*, once common on the menus of restaurants, appears much less often now in Britain. The French, who used to lay down the law for **restaurateurs**, call a place-setting at a table a 'couvert' (a 'cover'), and many restaurants in France still have a fixed charge for every customer, in addition to the cost of the meal. This covers bread and overheads, such as the tablecloth, supplying cutlery and washing-up. A cover charge in a British or American restaurant, where it still exists, follows this practice.

cowboy At one time we knew where we stood with *cowboys*. They were the heroes of Hollywood westerns, marvellous horsemen, displaying courage and chivalry, beating black-hatted evil men to the draw, and riding off into **Technicolor** sunsets, choosing a life on the open range rather than settling down with the blue-eyed blonde they had rescued from a 'fate worse than death'.

Since then, how they have come down in the world! A *cowboy* now could mean a reckless lorry driver on a motorway, or anyone who makes a botch of something because of carelessness or incompetence, or to make some money on the quick, especially by anything to do with building, plumbing, etc. While this use of *cowboy* is treated as slang by dictionaries, it is used so widely that it's probably on its way to becoming standard English.

How did the cowboy fall from grace? It has long meant a maverick character without much regard for order (the original *OED* entry of 1893 considered cowboys 'rough and wild'), and as the old-style romantic westerns gave way to more realistic films showing the plight of the American Indians, we began to see the historic cowboy in a different light.

cozy See cosy . . .

CPU See **central processor**

crack Since the mid-1980s, *crack* has acquired a powerful and sinister new meaning. Drug addicts, impatient for quicker results, found that when cocaine hydrochloride, the form in which it is most widely sold, was converted into a cocaine base, it could be smoked directly instead of inhaled, which gives a much quicker and far more intense 'high'. It came to be called *crack*, apparently from the noise it makes during smoking. Recent dictionaries include *crack*, writing it down as slang. But the word has been used by doctors, government ministers and others in public broadcasts in nearly every country, so it must now be regarded as the standard word for this form of cocaine.

craft As a noun, *craft* goes back centuries in English, a good word suggesting skill and knowledge acquired over years. As a verb, there is an increasing tendency to use *craft* in a crafty way to suggest that something is made by hand with traditional skill and care ('specially crafted'), even though whatever it is was produced on a production line. Don't be taken in by it.

crap In 1900 Thomas Crapper produced the 'Valveless Water Waste Preventer' or as we know it, a **lavatory**, loo, toilet or whatever. (In passing, his biography, when it came to be written, was called – wait for it! – *Flushed With Pride*). But in spite of popular belief, Thomas Crapper had nothing whatsoever to do with the use of *crap* for excrement and excreting, since *crap* comes from an early Dutch word and has been used in English since the 15th century for different kinds of waste matter. Nevertheless, all dictionaries condemn *crap* as a **four-letter word**, coarse and taboo. So instead of going for a you-know-what, we're supposed to go to the *toilet*.

crash The difference between a *crash programme* and a 'short' programme is that *crash* promises results by putting on the pressure. After a *crash course* in Japanese, we're supposed to be able to speak the language to some extent, whereas a 'short' course might leave us with only a smattering. A better word than *crash*, in this sense, is 'intensive'.

crayfish or **crawfish** Both words are used for different kinds of shellfish, especially thin spiny lobsters. *Crayfish* is more usual in Britain with *crawfish* more often used in America. Grander restaurants prefer the French name *langouste* (pron: 'lahn-GOOST') for the spiny lobster, not to be confused with *langoustines*, which are not baby lobsters, as some people believe, but large so-called Dublin Bay or 'king-sized' prawns, which when fried make that ubiquitous Italian dish *scampi*.

creative or **imaginative** The two words have something in common, as you cannot be *creative* without being *imaginative*. But *creative* encompasses much more. It is an amalgam of different intellectual abilities, involving 'the whole personality, down to unverbalized and unconscious layers' (*The Act of Creation*, Arthur Koestler, 1905–83). The result is a bringing forth, a synthesis, and something new emerges ('God created the heaven and the earth').

Imaginative is a slighter word, suggesting forming a mental image or making a mental connection. An imaginative idea might lead to a solution to a practical problem; a creative idea brings something into being that did not exist before, as when Coleridge awakened from an opium-induced trance with *Kubla Khan* fully formed in his mind. *Imaginative* describes a spark jumping across; *creative* describes an explosion.

crèche See nursery . . .

credibility *Credibility* means being believable. Some time in the 1950s, the expression *credibility gap* was conjured up in defence circles in Washington, as a measure of whether the pile of long-range nuclear weapons would look convincing enough to deter the **USSR** and the **NATO** allies from thinking it was a bluff.

Since then, this use of *credibility* has moved into politics and business as an indication of whether a party, a company, an individual really look as if they will do what they claim, or whether a promise or an undertaking will really be carried out.

Credibility gap has also taken on another meaning, as linguistic shorthand for saying there is a difference between what is being said and what seem to be the facts, a diplomatic way of suggesting something may be a lie.

credible or **credulous** Someone or something can be *credible*, that is you can believe them or it: 'what she says is credible'. Only a person can be *credulous*, too ready to believe something, too easily taken in: 'she must think him credulous to believe what she says'. For *creditable*, see next entry

credit Other than in business and finance, *credit* has always meant something good: we give someone *credit* for doing something well; we claim *credit* for having been the first to think of a good idea. But newscasters have come to use *credit* in the opposite way, about something bad: 'the IRA claims credit for the bomb attack'; 'he claims credit for deceiving the police'. Even some recent dictionaries have not recorded this confusing use of *credit*, confusing because it could sound as if a bomb attack or deceiving the police are creditable.

See also **credit and debit**

credit or **charge account** They are both the same, an arrangement whereby someone can buy goods and pay for them at a later date instead of on the spot. *Charge account* is the usual term in America,

although it is becoming more common in Britain, with *credit account* (or simply *account*) still the more familiar British equivalent. See also next entry

credit and **debit** These words are like mother's milk to accountants, but many other people may have to think twice when they receive a notice that a sum of money has been *debited* to their account. *Debit* comes from the Latin word for 'debt', so when a sum is debited to you, you are in debt and owe the money, or the sum has been taken off money you have in a bank account. To be *in debit* is the same as being overdrawn, more money has gone out than has come in. When your bank account is *credited* or *in credit*, it means money is paid to you. The terms belong to old double-entry bookkeeping. The left side of a page in an accounts ledger book is the *debit* side for goods you receive, and for which you have to pay. The *credit* side is on the right which shows money you have paid out.

To simplify this, it's a good thing when your account is *credited*, because money has been paid into it. Not so good when it's *debited*, because money has been taken out. Good when you're *in credit*, because that's money in the bank: bad when you're *in debit*, because you owe the bank money.

credit, charge and **debit card** A *credit card* enables people to buy things and pay a few weeks later, either in full or in part, interest being charged on the outstanding balance: Barclaycard and Access are well-known examples. To begin with, a *charge card* (American Express is an example) enabled goods to be charged against a central account, and had to be paid off in full at the end of the period of credit. Now that some charge card companies are also allowing part-payment, charging interest on the outstanding balance, the terms are becoming used interchangeably. *Charge card* is now more likely to be used as an alternative to account card for a charge account held with a particular shop or chain (see **credit account** . . .).

A *debit card* may look very similar to a credit card, but is a form of 'plastic cheque': the amount is debited to your bank account straight away, without any period of credit. Switch is an example of a debit card.

The terms credit and debit are often confused: see previous entry. See also **plastic money**

credit squeeze This descriptive term for restrictions imposed by a government on the lending of money is not used as often as it used to be, perhaps because it sounds too much like doctrinaire interference with market forces. But the reality still exists, since raising interest rates has much the same effect.

credulous See credible . . .

Creole See pidgin . . .

crepe or **crêpe** *Crepe* is always pronounced in the French way ('krayp') but there is no rule about whether the **circumflex** (ˆ) should be used or not. It is usually dropped when *crepe* means the fine wrinkled material. It is more likely to be retained when *crêpe* is used for a thin pancake, probably because of the association with *crêpe suzette* (the orange-flavoured pancake doused with liqueur and set fire to with a flourish).

crescendo *Crescendo* is a musical term for a gradual increase in loudness, a progression, not the peak of loudness. Expressions such as 'reach a crescendo', 'rise to a crescendo' are using the word wrongly in place of **climax**. But the wrong use ('the shouting reached a crescendo') is so common now, that it seems stuffy to object to it any longer. Whichever way we use it, *crescendo* should at least be reserved for sound, and should not be extended, as it sometimes is, to other things, as in 'the crescendo of his achievement'. Only words such as 'climax' or 'peak' are possible in that sense. See also **apogee**

crevasse or **crevice** Once you've seen a *crevasse* (pron: kre(r)VASSE'), you could never confuse it with a *crevice*: it is an awesome opening with a sheer drop, in a glacier or in ice. A *crevice* (pron: 'KREViss') is a narrow crack or split in a rock or in the wall of a building.

criteria or **criterions** Use the Greek plural form: one *criterion*, two or more *criteria*.

critical path analysis This can be an impressive title to a report, or used by management consultants. It is a technique of analysis that breaks down each phase of a complicated project, estimating time required for each stage. As work progresses, hold-ups can be seen in advance and the cost of disruption of the total programme reduced to the minimum, by rescheduling in advance. See also **flow chart**

A critical path analysis may start with a date everything must be completed by and work back from that, sometimes revealing that the whole thing should have been started months or even years ago.

criticism, **critique**, **notice** or **review** All four words can cover articles written about books, films, plays, music. . . . The problem with *criticism* is that it can imply pointing out the bad things: 'Have you read the criticism of the play?' could suggest a condemnation of it, although the *criticism* might have said it was marvellous. A *critique* is an analysis, without any suggestion of good or bad, but it sounds pretentious (unless it is used about the philosophy of Kant). *Critique* has been adapted, especially in New York, as an awkward verb ('he has critiqued the play'), but is not often used that way by British critics.

Notice is used mostly about plays, rather than films, books, art or music: 'the play has good notices'. *Review* remains the best all-round word that can cover anything from a pop concert to a tone poem.

cropping This word from printing and photographic terminology has come more into everyday use

with **desktop publishing**. *Cropping* cuts out parts of a photograph or a design, so that only the remaining section is printed, enlarged if required to fill the space available.

cross-check or **verify** A *cross-check*, or *to cross-check* something, is to check a result using an alternative method: a very simple example would be to *cross-check* that 3 times 7 equals 21 by dividing 21 by 3, to see if it gives the answer 7. We could cross-check that Mary Robinson is going to a meeting, as she agreed, by telephoning her secretary.

Verify is much more far-reaching: it means to establish the truth or correctness of something. You can cross-check a calculation by doing it another way, as in the example above, but a lot of research might be necessary to verify that the figures themselves are the right ones to be using.

crosses or **ticks** See ticks . . .

cross-section or **sample** During an election, interviews are often recorded with a *sample* of the people who will be voting. These provide some individual points of view that may be interesting but offer no guide to the outcome. For an indication of the way things are going, a *cross-section* of the electorate must be interviewed, because this takes into account age, sex, income and as many other factors as possible, so that the people interviewed represent to some extent the total electorate. Public opinion polls often use *sample* to describe a survey, sometimes distinguishing between a *random sample* and a *representative sample*, which should be chosen in the correct proportions based on the actual proportions of the different factors in the whole population. Only then is it a true *cross-section*. See also **anecdotal evidence**

(the) **crowd is** or **are** See collective words

crucial *Crucial* comes from 'crux', the Latin word for a cross, suggesting the possibility of different directions. It means that something will have a decisive effect one way or another: 'accurate strategic bombing was crucial to the success of the land offensive'. It is not good practice to use *crucial* merely to mean 'important': 'we have to discuss a crucial matter'.

crude As a technical term, *crude* is material in its raw state, such as *crude oil*, which is petroleum in the form it is extracted. So *crude* can be a descriptive word, without implying judgement: 'these are crude figures' simply means the figures are approximate and have not yet been properly worked out. The other use of *crude*, to mean offensive and lacking in refinement, can lead to misunderstanding. At a business meeting, a comment that 'these are crude proposals' would normally be taken to mean that they have not been worked out in detail as yet: but in a social situation, 'a crude suggestion', particularly from a man to a woman, would have another meaning altogether.

crustacés See seafood . . .

cryonics   *Cryonics* (pron: 'kryONics') is still to be picked up by most dictionaries. The word relates to cryogenics, which deals with the use of very low temperatures. *Cryonics* is a macabre technique of freezing corpses in liquid nitrogen to −360°F, to preserve them until some future date when medical science is sufficiently advanced to bring them back to life. There is an American Cryonics Society offering this hope of eternal life, meantime patiently waiting for *cryonics* to be accepted, at least by dictionaries.

CS gas . . .   See **tear gas**

cubic or **cubical**   For measurements, it is always *cubic*: a cubic yard, a cubic metre. . . . We can use *cubical* to describe something that is shaped like a *cube* (a cubical structure), but many people are more comfortable saying 'a cubic structure', which leaves *cubical* as an alternative that is not used so often.

cuckold   As a noun, *cuckold* is a man whose wife is having sexual intercourse with another man; as a verb, they can both be said to *cuckold* him. It comes from 'cuckoo', the bird that takes over another bird's nest. But *cuckold* is more at home in Restoration comedy of the early 18th century, than in Surbiton or East Cheam of the 1990s.

cult or **fashion**   *Cult* comes from the Latin word 'cultus', worship. The use that comes closest to that is for a group of people who follow a creed and carry out its rituals, often in a particular locality, such as a commune, and usually focused on a charismatic or compelling leader. It is still often used in this way, but since the late 19th century, the meaning of *cult* has become diluted to mean a devotion to anybody or almost anything, such as a particular writer (the Beckett cult), or a style (the cult of violence in films), or a way of thinking (the small-is-beautiful cult).

Post-World War II, *cult* has been used increasingly as a descriptive word (a cult film, a cult designer) to say that whatever or whoever it is has a particular following. About the same time, *cult* was diluted still further to mean no more than a fashion picked up and followed by a section of society, such as business executives (the dark grey suit cult). Even with this use, it is better to restrict *cult* to a specific group, which at least keeps it closer to the original meaning. If a style is widespread, *fashion* is the better word: 'the miniskirt *fashion* is returning'.

cultivated   See **cultured** . . .

cultural   While **culture** is used broadly to refer to customs, traditions and lifestyle, *cultural*, as a descriptive word, usually relates to recognized art forms. The concept of *cultural capital* places a high value on an accepted artistic and literary inheritance, passed on through education, travel and the 'right' kind of books, pictures and music.

Cultural pluralism is a rejection of such accepted standards in a particular society: ethnic groups, instead of accepting the melting-pot concept where everyone becomes all-British or all-American, rediscover their own culture and traditions, and even their own language. The broadcaster Alistair Cooke tells the story of a New York taxi driver complaining to him, 'You need *two* languages to get on in this town – and one of them sure ain't English!'

cultural capital   See preceding entry

cultural pluralism   See **cultural**

culture   There are different meanings to the word *culture*, depending on whether you are an anthropologist, an archaeologist, a historian, a sociologist. . . . At best it is an elusive word to define, which is why T S Eliot promised no more in the title of his book on the subject than *Notes towards the Definition of Culture* (1948).

One particular misunderstanding stands out: 'Australian culture', for example, can mean the arts in Australia, or it could mean the pattern of behaviour, thoughts, institutions and the rest, that make up the Australian way of living. Where there is a risk of misunderstanding, use 'cultural scene' for the arts, and 'institutions', 'lifestyle' or 'attitudes' for other things. *Culture* is also coming to be used about almost anything, to mean nothing more than 'accepted custom': a bizarre example was a professor of local government writing a paper called *The Culture of Non-Payment of the Poll Tax*.

For the use of *culture* in business, see **corporate**.

cultured or **cultivated**   The *OED* does not distinguish between these two words, defining both as tilling the land to grow crops and, by extension, the development of the mind by education and reading. We can still say that someone is *cultivated*, meaning with a wide knowledge of the arts, but to some of us that may sound precious, as we prefer to keep *cultivated* for growing crops on the land, using *cultured* about a person.

culture shock   *Culture shock* is a serious term for the traumatic disorientation experienced by people who find themselves in an environment completely out of keeping with their understanding and points of reference. It could apply to emigrants, or social workers exposed to conditions of extreme squalor. But *culture shock* is also used flippantly (or snobbishly) by someone who feels superior to the situation they find themselves in: 'It was a real *culture shock* to go on a package holiday!'

cum   *Cum* is Latin for 'with' and is used in English as an elegant alternative to a stroke (/): kitchen-cum-dining-room (kitchen/dining-room). It appears in early English place-names, such as Horton-cum-Studley in Oxfordshire.

It is also used about the price of shares: when the price is quoted as *cum dividend* (abbreviated *cum div*) the buyer is entitled to receive the next dividend payment (as opposed to *ex div*, when the next dividend is not included). In America, *cum laude* (pron: 'kum LOWdee'), literally 'with praise', on diplomas and examination results, is the equivalent in Britain of 'with credit'.

cum div or **ex div**   See previous entry

cunnilingus or **fellatio**   These are refined words, adapted from Latin, for sexual practices that some people consider disgusting and others as natural. Refined they may be, but they were prudishly left out of most dictionaries until the 1960s, and even in the 1990s a few dictionaries still turn a blind eye to them. *Cunnilingus* (pron: 'kunnyLINgus') and *fellatio* (pron: 'feLAYSHeeyou') are different forms of **oral sex**, and if you're not clear about which is which, the Latin sources explain it. *Cunnilingus* combines 'cunnus', the external female genitals, with 'lingere', to lick; *fellatio* is derived from 'fellare', to suck. The psychologist, Dr Joyce Brothers, expressed it openly in *What Every Woman Should Know About Men*: 'fellatio is what you do to him and cunnilingus is what he does to you'.

cunt   See **four-letter words**

cupfuls or **cupsful**   See **-ful**

curate's egg   Few cartoons have contributed to the English language, but this one did: it was drawn by George du Maurier and appeared in *Punch*, 9 November 1895. At breakfast, the Right Reverend Host apologizes to the curate, who is his guest: 'I'm afraid you've got a bad egg, Mr Jones!' The curate, anxious not to make a fuss, replies 'Oh no, my Lord, I assure you! Parts of it are excellent!' From then on a *curate's egg* became the expression for something that is partly good and partly bad. That old issue of *Punch* belongs to the archives: 'good in parts' or 'partly good, partly bad' are better than saying 'It's like a curate's egg', which not everyone understands.

curb or **kerb**   As a *noun*, meaning the edge of a pavement or path, *kerb* is the usual spelling in Britain (with *curb*, the American spelling, a less familiar alternative). As a verb, meaning to hold back or restrain, it is always *curb*, which also applies to the noun with that meaning (to put a curb on spending).

currently   There seems no good reason for saying 'I am currently working on a new book', when we can use simple words, such as 'now' or 'at present' instead.

curricula or **curriculums**   Some dictionaries only accept the Latin plural *curricula*, which overlooks the fact that many people now use the anglicized plural *curriculums*. Other dictionaries show both forms. If you are a headteacher, perhaps you should stay with *curricula*, because that might be expected of you.

curriculum vitae   See **cv**

curriculums   See **curricula** . . .

(the) curse   See **period** . . .

cursed   Before a noun, it is two syllables: 'this is a cursed ("curs-ed") business'. After a noun, it is one syllable: 'the whole business was cursed'. See also **accursed**

cursor   How many people remember that a *cursor* is the transparent panel, with a marker line down the middle, that slides along a slide-rule? Its only meaning now for nearly everyone is the flashing symbol on a computer or wordprocessor screen that indicates where the next character will appear.

custom-built   *Custom* and *customer* both come from the same source. Something that is *custom-built* should be made to the requirements of the customer who ordered it. The term is used often now to suggest something individual or personal, even if it is 'off the peg', made by people who have no idea who the customer is going to be. *Customize* (a word imported from America after World War II) is more specific, as it means something made, or at least modified, for an individual customer.

customer   See **client** . . .

cut and paste   This was the old way of composing text and illustrations: sections were *cut out* and *pasted* on a sheet of paper, to make up the page. The term for this rudimentary technique has been carried over into sophisticated **desktop publishing** and **wordprocessing**: *cut and paste* is used for arranging text and illustrations on a display screen, or taking out one section of text and positioning it in another place. But although most of the time a keyboard is used now, there are many designers still working away with a pair of scissors and pot of paste.

cutback or **cut back**   There is a *cutback* (one word) in production but production has been *cut back* (two words). You could say, as some do, that *back* is unnecessary as it's enough to say there is a cut, or that production (or whatever it is) has been cut. Nevertheless, *back* has a value because it emphasizes the negative aspect of a *cutback*.

cute   Unless you want to sound like an ingenuous American tourist, goggle-eyed at European customs, it would be better not to use this word.

cutlet   See **chop** . . .

cut-price   See **low-cost** . . .

cv   The abbreviation is used in writing, and also in speaking, more often than the expression in full: most people talk about a 'seevee' rather than 'curriculum vitae' (pron: 'kerRIKyoolum VEEtye'), Latin for 'course of life'. A cv is a brief statement of someone's education, qualifications, experience and positions held. Although it is an abbreviation, it is often written with small letters as an alternative to capitals. In

America, cv is not used: the corresponding term is *résumé* (with or without accents).

cycle, bicycle or **bike**   When two-wheeled velocipedes (as scholars called them) or 'boneshakers' (as the riders called them) were invented in the 19th century, they were called *bicycles*, combining the prefix *bi* (for two) with *cycle*, from the Greek word 'kuklos' for a wheel. By the 1990s, *bicycle* has come to sound rather elderly: the **Yellow Pages** list 'cycle shops', the unemployed were exhorted to 'get on your bikes' and look for jobs elsewhere. Either *cycle* or *bike* are the usual words now, remembering that *bike* is also the most common word for a motor cycle, whereas *cycle* is usually assumed to mean a bicycle. Their riders are *bikers* and cyclists respectively. See also **mountain bike**

cyclone   See **blizzard . . . ; depression . . .**

cypher   See **code . . .**

Cyrillic or **Russian**   *Cyrillic* is the alphabet used in the Russian language, and also for Bulgarian and some other Slavonic languages. It was developed from the Greek alphabet in the 9th century, reputedly by the Greek missionary, St Cyril, hence its name. *Russian* is the spoken and written language.

czar   See **tsar . . .**

· D ·

dago In the late 19th century, *dago* was used harmlessly in America for a Latin-American (*Diego* is the Spanish equivalent of James). Then it deteriorated into an abusive slang name for almost any foreigner, but especially for Spaniards and Portuguese. *Dago* has no place in the internationalism of the 1990s: do not use it unless you want a fight.

Dáil *Dáil* is Irish for an assembly, and with a capital D it is the name of the elected assembly of the Republic of Ireland (*Dáil Eireann* in full). For non-Irish speakers, the nearest we can get to the proper pronunciation is 'doyl'.

daily See charlady . . .

daily or **diurnal** *Daily* is obviously the usual word for the daily round, daily papers, daily chores and for anything else that happens every day. *Diurnal* has a place in science for cycles that occur at daily intervals, applied, for example, to animals active only in the daytime, plants that open during the day. *Diurnal* is also the opposite of 'nocturnal', used for the daytime period of an activity that also continues during the night.

dais See platform . . .

daisy-wheel This is one kind of printer used with computers and wordprocessors. The characters are at the end of spokes radiating from a central hub. One advantage is that one daisy-wheel can easily be exchanged for another to change the typeface; a disadvantage is it prints more slowly than **dot matrix** or **laser** printers. A daisy-wheel disc doesn't look much like a daisy, except perhaps to a computer freak.

dame or **Dame** Some men, especially in America, may still talk about 'having dinner with a dame' but it sounds dated, unless you are having dinner with a *Dame*, who in the UK is a woman with the rank of Knight Commander or has been awarded an order of chivalry. The title must always precede her first name, Dame Judi Dench, for example (never 'Dame Dench').

damn This used to be a very offensive word: after all, in theology to damn someone was to condemn them to hell. For centuries, it was even printed 'd—n'

or 'd***' to avoid giving offence. It would hardly upset anyone now, unless you call them a *damfool* (when *damn* becomes 'dam', as in *dammit*). No recent dictionary regards *damn* as vulgar, and most treat it as normal English, rather than slang. This is as it should be, since *damn* occurs in standard everyday phrases, such as 'to damn with faint praise', 'damning evidence'; and even a bishop, caught off guard in astonishment, might say 'Well, I'll be damned!' Not that he would mean it literally.

dance or **dancing** Modern *dance* is the art form, usually choreographed; modern *dancing* is usually a pastime. African dance is treating it as serious ethnic culture; African dancing is dancing in an African style. You learn dancing but you study dance.

dashes Dashes should be used sparingly. They have four useful functions:

1 Dashes (like **commas** or **brackets**) can separate a comment from the rest of the sentence: 'I was leaving for the office – early that morning as it happens – when the telephone rang'.

2 A dash can lead to a follow-up: 'It was one of the kindest things you could have done – to ask me out to dinner that evening'.

3 A dash can gather up a list of things and lead on to a general statement about them: 'Income tax, a mortgage, instalments on the car, renting a TV – by the time you've paid all those, there's not much left'.

4 A dash can replace a **colon** (:) before a follow-on statement or a list – 'Here are the things you need – a passport, airline ticket, money. A colon would have done after 'list' and 'need', but a dash is sharper, more energetic. There is no need to use a colon *and* a dash (:–), as either does the job.

data Computer technology makes so much use of *data*, that in other contexts it is often more precise to use an alternative word. For example, 'the survey provides useful data' is indeterminate: 'the survey provides useful information (or facts or figures or statistics)' is more selective.

Strictly, *data* is the plural of *datum* and some people, who remember their Latin lessons, insist on following it by 'are', 'have'. . . . But it is usual to treat *data* as a collective singular noun: 'this *is* all the data we need'; 'what data *is* available?' (See also **collective words**) By the end of the century, *datum*, like **agendum**, is likely to become obsolete, except as a technical term for a point of reference (a datum point or a datum line).

The accepted pronunciation is 'DAYta', rather than 'DATTa' or 'DAHta', which are also heard.

databank or **database** The two terms are often used interchangeably for an extensive record of information classified for a particular purpose. A distinction is sometimes made when *databank* is used for an elaborate set of statistics, and *database* for textual information. It would normally be assumed, unless otherwise stated, that a databank or a database is stored in a computer system.

data *is* or **are** See **data**

data processing This covers the use of computers to store a mass of information and to utilize it for routine requirements, such as the payment of salaries. As with **wordprocessing**, there is a tendency for *dataprocessing* to be treated as one word.

data *protection* or **security** Personal details about everyone of us is stored, generally without our knowledge or consent, on computers all over the place. *Data protection* is concerned with protecting us against the wrong use of such information, or its being disclosed for unauthorized purposes. There is a UK Data Protection Act 1984, which sets out principles of protection following recommendations of the Council of Europe. You could say that data protection has slipped every time you receive an unsolicited sales brochure, because that usually means some organization has had access to information about you.

Data security is concerned with **computer crime**, which is the manipulation of data either maliciously or for personal gain, such as fraudulent transfers of funds. See also **hacker**

date rape This term was first used in America in 1989 by Dr Mary Koss, a professor of psychiatry at the University of Arizona. Dr Koss believed that many women are exposed to rape or attempted rape when they are out on a date with men they know well. *Date rape* became familiar during the William Kennedy Smith rape trial in 1991 and the Mike Tyson trial in 1992, and is now used in Britain. At these and similar trials the question was not whether intercourse had taken place, but whether it was *consensual sex* (see **rape or seduction**).

dates The old way of writing a date was: 21st May, 1993. This style has become superseded by: 21 May 1993 (no *th* or *st* and no *comma*). When dates are expressed entirely as figures, there could be a misunderstanding because of varying conventions in different countries: 7.5.1993 would mean 7 May 1993 in Britain, but in some countries, including America, it would be taken to mean 5 July 1993. See also **AD**

datum See **data**

daughters-in-law or **daughter-in-laws** *Daughters-in-law*.

dawn raid When it's used in the world of big business, a *dawn raid* has nothing to do with an early morning attack across enemy lines: it is the term used when a company instructs brokers to buy up all the shares possible, in another company it wants to takeover, the moment the Stock Exchange opens for business.

de or **De** It is nearly always *de* in French names: Charles de Gaulle. But it may be *De* in some Italian names (Vittorio De Sica, the film director), and in some Dutch names (Hugo De Vries, the botanist). In English names, when it is established as a surname, it is often De: Cecil B De Mille (the American film producer), Geoffrey De Havilland (the aircraft designer), but Olivia *de* Havilland (the film actress).

de- and **dis- words** *De-* has been used for centuries to make a verb mean the opposite but this has now become an epidemic, as convenient shorthand that suits bureaucratic pomposity. You can go into hospital and be 'hospitalized', and then when you're cured, *de-*hospitalized. Nationalized industries can be 'privatized', and then the opposition threatens to *de-*privatize them, possibly because it seems more like 'talking tough' than 're-nationalize'.

You can jump on the **bandwagon** and invent new *de-* words for yourself: *The Times* has referred to *de-*educate (presumably unlearning something), an MP has said he will *de-*resign (that is withdraw his resignation) and an actress, who didn't like the idea of a divorce, announced she was going to get *de-*married.

When a *de-*word becomes familiar, the hyphen is often dropped, as in *declassify* (to take something off the secret list), *defrost*, *decode*. The *de-*prefix is useful when there's need to emphasize that something is undone: *decontaminate* and *derestrict*, for example, are more precise than 'cleanse' and 'free'. But there's no need to use *de-* when a good alternative exists, such as 'unlearn' or 'divorce', instead of *de-*educate and *de-*marry in two of the examples above.

Dis- is another prefix, that has been used since the 15th century to give a verb or a noun the opposite meaning. *Dis-* is the alternative to *de-*, sometimes because the word it is joined to begins with a vowel (*disown, disestablish, disunion, disallow . . .*), sometimes because it sounds better (*displease, disservice, discourteous . . .*), sometimes because of custom (*disrobe, disconnect, discontent . . .*).

If you find there is the need for a new *de-* or *dis-* word, check with an up-to-date dictionary to make sure that someone has not already thought of it and has established a prefix. If not, choose whichever sounds better when attached to the word that follows.

dead beat *Dead beat*, meaning completely exhausted, is classified as colloquial or informal by most dictionaries, but is nonetheless used in serious writing. So perhaps it's time that lexicographers looked at it again. There's a risk of confusion with *dead-beat* (or *deadbeat*) in America, where it can mean a good-for-nothing, or a sponger who borrows money from friends and never pays it back.

deadline In the 19th century this was a line round a military prison beyond which a prisoner might be shot. In its more recent and useful meaning of an absolute time-limit, it is now one of the words on which the fate of the world may hang. When someone gives you a deadline by which something must be ready or agreed, you know they mean business.

deadly or **deathly** Something that is *deadly* can kill you (a deadly poison). *Deathly* is used when something resembles death: 'a deathly silence' (as quiet as the grave) or 'a deathly pallor'. At cricket, a left-handed West Indies spinner delivers *deadly* bowling; and something can be *deadly* dull (so dull it almost bores you to death).

deadpan, **dispassionate**, **impassive** or **poker-faced** Many people think *deadpan* is slang and that *impassive* is the respectable equivalent. *Deadpan* may have a hint of American English about it, but British dictionaries treat it as standard English: it describes someone's face not showing any emotion or reaction, no matter how they feel. It is the precise equivalent of *poker-faced*. *Impassive* also means not displaying emotion, but suggests that someone is unaffected by feelings.

Dictionaries are not usually much help over the difference between *impassive* and *dispassionate*. *Dispassionate* suggests not feeling anything about a particular matter, not cold, but genuinely calm or objective: 'he remained dispassionate about the accusation'.

deal Generally a *deal* is any kind of transaction or agreement. On the Stock Exchange, a deal is a particular term for a single transaction involving selling or buying shares. Although *deal* is an Old English word, its use in the present day sense for a transaction started with American usage in the 19th century. A *big deal* can mean what it says, an important transaction with a lot of money involved. On the other hand, if someone says about anything 'Big deal!' they mean emphatically that it is *not* a big deal.

dealer See broker . . .

Dear Sir or **Madam** *Dear Sir* or *Dear Madam* were standard openings to letters, even when the person addressed was known. In cases of uncertainty, there were instances of 'Dear Sir or Madam (as the case may be)'! Such openings are now only used when the writer doesn't know the other person's name. Otherwise, Dear Mrs Robinson, Dear Mr Russell . . . are standard, even if the letter that follows is abusive! *My dear Sir* now sounds Dickensian, and *My dear Mr*

Russell sounds patronizing, although *My dear Mary* is affectionate. At one time, *My dear Jones*, *My dear Smith*, etc (using a man's surname) was an established way of showing regard between social equals, but it is old-fashioned now and could be misconstrued. Some people prefer to avoid the formality of *Dear Mr* . . . by using the name in full: Dear Godfrey Howard. This device can backfire if it seems overfamiliar. See also **letter endings**

deathly See deadly . . .

death squad This is a new and sinister term for the age-old practice of getting rid of opponents by assassination. Death squads (the expression was probably first used in connection with the repressive regime in El Salvador) are gangs of thugs, officially 'unofficial', who carry out killings of people who speak out against the regime in power.

deb Does anyone talk about a *deb* any more? In British society it was short for a *debutante* (and if you were one in those days, you would have included an **acute accent** (débutante), still defined in dictionaries as a rich young woman being presented at court or to society. Something of the sort may still go on but even a dowager duchess would look nervously over her shoulder before using the word. The description *debby* lingers on, still used for a young woman with a particularly middle-class look and manner.

debacle At the beginning of the 19th century, the meaning of *debacle* was a deluge of water that carries along with it anything that gets in the way. Geologists might still use the word in that sense, but for most people it is the extended meaning that has taken over. This is a complete failure or defeat, a shambles when everything goes wrong and disorder takes over: 'the vote was a debacle for the government'. It is pedantic to use the French accents (débâcle). The pronunciation is half anglicized: 'dayBAHke(r)l'.

debar or **disbar** *Debar*, instead of meaning the opposite of the verb 'bar', means almost the same, which is to exclude someone or to prevent them doing something. It is usually followed by 'from': 'because he was not suitably dressed, he was debarred from entering'; 'we shall debar her from serving on the local committee because she lives outside the area'.

Disbar is mostly used in the legal sense of taking away the right of **barristers** to practise, or expelling them from the Bar.

debatable or **questionable** *Debatable* suggests that there are arguments on both sides; *questionable* suggests that something is untrue, or even downright dishonest. *Debatable* keeps the door open by inviting discussion; *questionable* can be a tactful way of saying that something is wrong.

debenture 'An issue of debentures' or 'debenture stock' often comes into business sections of newspapers. A debenture is, in effect, a formal document setting out the terms of a loan to a company. Debenture holders take precedence over ordinary shareholders.

You may also see *debenture* used in a quite different context. By buying a debenture at Wimbledon (or Ascot, the opera or many other social and sporting occasions), you are entitled to the use of the seats or box for life.

debit See credit . . .

debit card See credit card . . .

debug RAF pilots from World War II remember 'gremlins', mysterious sprites that were blamed if something went wrong with equipment. They were also called 'bugs', hence *debug*, used for the final check of an aircraft before it went into service. *Debug* has lived on with two separate meanings. In computer technology *debug* is to locate an error in the system. In international and industrial espionage, *debug* is to check a conference room or a hotel bedroom for hidden microphones, which could transmit or record secret information. There is even the word *debugger*, which could cause raised eyebrows if someone didn't know it is no more unwholesome than a computer program devised to help the user trace errors.

debut or **début** The French pronunciation remains, 'DAY-byoo', with 'DEBB-yoo' as an alternative. But the **acute accent** over the *e* is no longer necessary, and some dictionaries now omit it. *Debut* is much less likely to be used any more about a young woman being introduced to society, than for the first public performance of a soloist or a conductor, or for the first appearance of a player in an international game.

Debuts is the plural form and, unless you want to show off your French, the *s* is pronounced in English: 'DAY-byooz'.

DECade or **deCADE** The stress on the second syllable is heard more and more often but many people consider it wrong. The recommendation is stress the *first* syllable: 'DECade'.

decadence *Decadence* is a judgemental word and as such is dependent upon a point of view. Anything outside narrow conventional morality and manners has been called decadence. In the early 1960s, men wearing their hair down to their shoulders was declared by some to be an example of decadence.

The last decades of the 19th century saw *decadence* as a term in art and literature: *the decadents* was a movement in France linked with writers in England, who included Oscar Wilde, Aubrey Beardsley and Arthur Symons. The scandal of Wilde's relationship with Lord Alfred Douglas, which led to the Wilde–Queensberry trial, confirmed in many people's minds the name of the group, for at the time nothing was

more decadent than homosexuality. Decadence became synonymous with self-indulgence. But the line between self-indulgence and self-expression is a fine one.

decent *Decent* is a loaded word. It can mean 'doing the right thing', behaving 'in the right way', conforming to the 'right standards'. But what is 'right'? 'A decent film' is one that neither disturbs nor offends; 'a decent man' is one who can be relied upon not to say or do anything out of line with our own standards. This is not to say that we should never use the word *decent*, but that we should see it as having a meaning relative to a particular way of looking at life.

decidedly or **decisively** In some sentences these two words can appear interchangeable, although they suggest different things. 'High interest rates had a decidedly depressing effect on the company's business' means there is no doubt that the business was badly affected; '. . . a decisively depressing effect . . .' could suggest that the company went out of business as a result. *Decidedly* means positively and without question; *decisively* means conclusively, settling something finally. When we speak *decidedly* against something, there's no doubt that we are completely against it: to speak *decisively* against it is more final, as it implies that our arguments are conclusive.

decimal currency The accepted practice is to express sums less than a pound as: 25p, 50p . . . (no stop after *p*), rather than £0.25, £0.50. . . . For sums over a pound, the *p* is usually dropped: £20.25, £35.50. . . .

decimate There are some who believe that *decimate* means to destroy an army or other body of people so that only one-tenth remains. The original meaning is to kill off one in every ten. This has come to mean through general (some would claim uneducated) use to kill a large unspecified proportion. Although there are people who object strongly to *decimate* being used as loosely as this, that is how it is now understood.

(*make* or *take* a) **decision** At one time it was more usual to *take* a decision but now it seems to be more common to *make* one. There's no need to *make* or *take* a decision about which to use, since there's no rule about it.

decisively See decidedly . . .

deck See hi-fi . . .

deckle-edged When paper was made by hand, a deckle was a guide that controlled the size of a sheet, leaving a rough uncut edge. This ragged edge is now imitated by special machines to make paper look handmade, and people who have never heard of a deckle may specify *deckle-edged* paper for invitations to weddings, barmitzvahs or to any other reception where they want to cut a dash.

décollage, **décolletage** and **décolleté**
Even fashion writers, who should know better, have been known to mix up *décollage* with *décolletage*. *Décollage* (pron: 'daykuLAHDJ') is French for 'unsticking', and the word is used for a form of **collage**, strips of which have been roughly pulled off so that it looks like a torn poster. *Décolletage* (pronounce with three syllables: 'daykollTAHDJ') is the neckline of a dress cut low to reveal a woman's **cleavage**. Finally, *décolleté* (also three syllables: 'dayKOLLtay') is the descriptive word for a dress that has a décolletage.

decoy As a noun, for a person or an object used to trap someone or an animal, the stress can be on the first or second syllable: 'DEEkoy' or 'deeKOY'. The same applies to the verb, meaning to trap someone by using a decoy. The balance of opinion is in favour of stressing the *first* syllable for the noun and the *second* for the verb.

dedicated Clive Sinclair believes that computers will be the slaves of the future, which is why words used about people are applied to the machines. *Dedicated* is one of them: it means that a piece of equipment is designed specially for one type of application. A dedicated **wordprocessor**, for example, is a computer that is designed and programed specially for reproduction of text.

deed *Deed* is one of the oldest words in English, going back beyond Old English to Indo-European. The antiquity of the word bestows a solemnity on it: in law, certain contracts are not binding unless made by deed. The *deeds of a house*, the most familiar use of the word, is the document that confirms ownership of it.
Deed is the noun relating to the verb 'do', which makes 'I do', the response given at a marriage service, a solemn declaration.

deem *Deem* has a place in letters from lawyers and in legal documents: it can give the right of assumption of something. When, for example, you sign a **credit card**, you may be *deemed* to have accepted the conditions under which it was issued, even if you haven't read them. This is the point of **caveat subscriptor** ('let the signer beware'): if you sign a contract you are deemed to have read it.
To use *deem* outside these special applications is a pontifical, pompous, pretentious substitute for the word 'think': 'I deem this to be a useful suggestion' instead of 'I think this is a good idea'.

deep sea or **high seas** *Deep sea* is an indeterminate term, sometimes taken to be the ocean beyond the continental shelf, the sea area surrounding continents, taken to be 370 kilometres (230 miles) from the coast. But generally this definition is not intended and

deep sea is simply used for the deep waters of the oceans, without reference to distance from the coast.
High seas is also at times used loosely about the sea in general, but it does have a specific legal meaning: it is used for the sea beyond a range of 12 nautical miles from the coast, which is not subject to any country's jurisdiction and is open to any ship.

defect As a *noun*, some dictionaries recommend 'DEEfekt' (stress on first syllable) for the pronunciation, others 'diFEKT' (stress on second syllable). Others give you the choice, which in fact you have, although stress on the first syllable is becoming standard. The second pronunciation ('diFEKT') is the only one for the *verb* describing someone leaving a political party or a country to ally themselves with another ('he defected to the West'). *Defector* also has the stress on the second syllable: 'diFEKtor'.

defective or **deficient** It is preferable to use *defective* to describe something that does not work properly, and *deficient* for when an essential part is missing, even though most dictionaries are woolly about this distinction (a recent dictionary defines *defective* as 'lacking or deficient'). 'Supply' is a good word to illustrate the difference. A *defective* supply (of water, etc) means something has gone wrong with it: a *deficient* supply means there is not enough. With qualities, the words are often interchangeable: bad sight or hearing, for example, can be defective or deficient.

defector See defect

defence or **defense** *Defence* is English and *defense* is American. But wherever we are, we should use the American spelling for official US posts and institutions: the US Secretary of Defense, the US Department of Defense.

deficient See defective . . .

deficit or **shortfall** *Deficit* (pron: 'DEFicit') derives from a Latin word spelt in the same way and meaning 'there is a wanting'. This is exactly the same as *shortfall*, and is used particularly in relation to accounts, as it has been since the 18th century, where more money is going out than coming in: a **balance of payments** deficit in UK trade figures is gloomy financial news. A *deficit* in accounts can also mean that liabilities exceed assets.
Shortfall is a much more recent word, from the late 1940s, and is not generally used about official figures. *Shortfall* is used particularly when not enough money has been raised or is available for a specific purpose, or when production has not reached the target set.
Deficit is the more formal and official word, *shortfall* the more everyday word.

definite and **definitely** The wrong spelling 'definate' is a surprisingly common mistake. *Definite* means clear and well defined: a definite proposal. It is often used, especially in conversation, to mean positively, sure about something: 'Do you love me?' 'Definitely!'; 'I definitely think . . .'. This does not stray far from the meaning of *definite*, so does it matter? Some would say 'Definitely not!' But there's no need to overdo it: most of the time we can use **Yes** instead of 'definitely', and **No** instead of 'definitely not'.

definite or **definitive** *Definitive* is often used instead of *definite*, perhaps because it sounds more impressive. But the words do not mean the same and the distinction between them is important, because it can change the whole meaning of a statement. *Definitive* always suggests finality: a definitive answer is a final answer and that's that. A *definite* offer is a positive offer, clear and unmistakable, whereas a *definitive* offer is a final offer – not a penny more. (But they may be bluffing of course!)

deflation and **disinflation** See **inflation**

deflower It seems strange in the 1990s to use this old-worldly 14th-century expression, but it is still a way to describe the act of taking away a woman's virginity. The implication is that something beautiful and innocent has been lost.

deforestation *Deforestation* is now part of the vocabulary of environmental and green issues: it is used for the permanent destruction of forests for industrial or housing development, or for other commercial purposes.

defuse or **diffuse** The words are occasionally confused. A bomb is *defused* (pron: 'diFYOOZD'), light or other things are *diffused* (pron: 'diFYOOSSD'), that is spread out widely. Writing or speech can also be *diffuse*, when it is rambling and imprecise.

(to a) **degree** Dictionaries, even some published in the 1990s, classify *to a degree* as colloquial, rather than literary. Yet the expression seems literary enough, since it was used by Sheridan in his comedy, *The Rivals* (1775), and by Fanny Burney in her novel, *Cecilia* (1782). It is short for *to the Nth degree* or *to the last degree*, meaning all the way.

If someone has made you angry *to a degree*, it means you were really furious. But there is confusion over this: one recent dictionary gives only one meaning for *to a degree*, which is 'somewhat, up to a point', which is an alternative meaning: 'we can do it *to a degree*' doesn't mean we can go all the way, but only to some extent. If you want to make sure that everyone understands you, it would be better to specify 'to the Nth degree' or 'to the last degree', if that's what you mean, or 'to some degree' if you mean 'just so far'.

deify and **deity** The question is whether the first syllables have an *ay* or an *ee* sound. Some people insist that only 'DEEify' and 'DEEity' are acceptable. But

they're in the minority since most speakers prefer 'DAYify' and 'DAYity'.

déjà vu The normal meaning is expressed by dictionaries as the illusion of having experienced something before, although the event or feeling is happening at that moment. *Déjà vu* is also used in another way, to describe a boring 'seen-it-all-before' impression: 'it may be a new film but it seems all too déjà vu to me'. This may be the wrong use of *déjà vu*, but it is understandable since the phrase does mean 'already seen'. The pronunciation can be as French as you choose, approx: 'DAYdjah VOO'.

delicatessen We can go into the **etymology** of *delicatessen*, tracing it to German, Dutch or French, but it tells us nothing of the smells, agitation, the gallimaufry of bagels and bortsch, chopped liver and gefilte fish in the Jewish **corner shops** that opened up in New York and London after the late 19th-century exodus of Jewish refugees from Eastern Europe. A few archetypal delicatessens may remain, but the word has been watered down, along with the flavour of the food. Supermarkets have delicatessen counters, refrigerated cabinets containing some token black olives, liver pâtés and smoked fish, flanked by breeze-blocks of anonymous cheddar.

deliver 'But can they deliver the goods?' is not necessarily asking if they can send the goods to your door. It could well mean can whoever it is fulfil their promise or agreement. 'Can they deliver?' is a shorter way of asking the same question. This use of *deliver* (or *deliver the goods*) is well-established now, although some dictionaries are hesitant to accept it, and is available for use when you need the sharpshooting language of business or politics: 'Expansion plans are one thing, but will they deliver the promised increase in profits?'

deliverance or **delivery** Both words mean the same, but *deliverance* is more at home coming from a pulpit, with *delivery* the more down-to-earth word of the milk round.

delivery or **labour room** Although women still 'go into labour', when contractions start in childbirth, most maternity hospitals are now talking of the *delivery room* rather than the *labour room*.

delusion or **illusion** A *delusion* is a feeling of certainty that something false is true ('to labour under a delusion'). An *illusion* is something imaginary, not founded on reality. Both words are similar in meaning, although delusions can be more dangerous, and in extreme cases can be a form of madness. Most of us have some illusions, and it would be hard to live without them. In practice it is not likely to matter much if you mix these words up, but be careful: 'he has so many *delusions*' means he is wrong about so many things, with the implication that this could do harm; 'he has so many *illusions'* means he lives in **cloud-cuckoo-land** and is probably harmless. There is no point in saying that something is a *false illusion*, because all illusions are false.

de luxe   *De luxe* used to mean the height of luxury, no expense spared, but it has gone downhill. House agents use *de luxe* about any ordinary semi-detached house, just because it has a tiled bathroom. There are de luxe coaches, de luxe hamburgers, de luxe ice-cream. The term is still used in its former glory in some guidebooks to hotels and restaurants, but we can no longer take it for granted.

De luxe is two words in British English, as in French, but usually one word in America. The usual English pronunciation is 'deLUKS', rather than 'deLOOKS' (which some dictionaries show as an alternative).

demand   *Demand* is the most critical word in the economics of industrialized society. It is the desire to purchase goods or obtain services at the ruling prices. It is *demand*, in this sense, that makes the business world go round, the balance of *supply and demand*.

demand *from*, *of* or *on*   It doesn't make any difference whether we *demand* something *from* or *of* someone: 'he demanded some money *from* (or *of*) me'. Demand *from* is perhaps more usual. But if we *make* a demand, it is always *on* someone: 'she makes too many demands *on* him'.

demanding   The way *demanding* is used now, the meaning can be uncertain. If a person is demanding, it can mean they are always thinking of themselves and what they want, or that it takes a lot of energy to deal with them, for one reason or another. We can distinguish between the two by alternatives, such as 'makes a lot of demands' or 'needs a lot of attention (or care)'.

If a task or a situation is demanding, it can mean stretching us to our limits, or tiring. We can distinguish between the two by using alternatives such as 'challenging' or 'exhausting'.

demand *of*, *from* or *on*   See demand *from* . . .

demean   In theory, the two meanings of *demean* can cause problems. One meaning relates to 'demeanour', how we conduct ourselves in front of other people: 'she demeaned herself well at the interview'. The other meaning, which relates to the word 'mean', is to lose self-respect or dignity: 'she demeans herself by accepting the money'. In practice, the use of *demean* for our bearing in public is so rare now, that it is almost disappearing.

demi-, hemi- or **semi-**   These three prefixes all mean 'half': *semi-* and *demi-* are from Latin, *hemi-* from Greek, and the origin usually dictates which prefix is

used with which word. *Demi-* is probably the least used: *demigod*: part god, part human (or more loosely, someone of exceptional beauty or authority); *demi-pension*: half-board (bedroom, breakfast and either lunch or dinner).

Hemi-, as you would expect from its Greek origin, is used for scientific words, such as *hemiplegia* (paralysis of one side of the body) and *hemisphere*.

Semi- is the prefix used in most formations, sometimes with a hyphen (*semi-basement, semi-detached, semi-skilled* . . .), but often without (*semicircle, semicolon, semitone* . . .). Nearly all later or new formations make use of *semi-* (*semi-autobiographical, semi-independent, semi-invalid* . . .). For the record, all three prefixes line up in one word, a musical term, *hemidemisemiquaver*, a note of the value of one-eighth of a quaver (♪).

demise   *Demise* is a legal term for the transfer of property, and by extension is used for the most common reason that brings about the transfer, that is the death of someone. Hence a lawyer talking to a client might say 'on your demise', where the rest of us would say 'when you die'. Pron: 'dimMYZE'.

democracy   *Democracy* is a classical word pertaining to the ancient Greek city states, combining the Greek words for citizenry and rule. Lincoln's famous definition was 'government of the people, by the people, for the people' (Gettysburg Address, 19 November 1863), fine words, like the word *democracy*. But when we look closer, *democracy* seems more an ideal than a reality. 'What is democracy?' Byron asked, '. . . an aristocracy of blackguards' he concluded (*Diary*, May 1821). For without regular **referendums**, democracy is vested, not in the people, but in their elected representatives.

In a broadcast, Alistair Cooke, made the point another way when he urged universities to establish 'schools of comparative democracy'.

Democrat or **democrat**   With a capital D, a *Democrat* is a member of the Democratic Party, one of the two major political parties in the US, thought of as more left wing and progressive than the **Republican** Party. With the word *democratic*, a lot hangs on the capital D: all US presidents are democratic, but with Bill Clinton, the US now has a Democratic president.

Democrats is also an informal name for the Liberal Democrats in Britain (see **Liberal** . . .), which is discouraged by the party. With a small d, *democrat* can mean two things. The political meaning is someone who believes in democracy. It can also be used for someone who believes in the absence of hereditary class distinction and the influence of wealth. Many people who are democrats in the political sense are far from being democrats in the other sense of the word.

democratic   The proper meaning describes the practice of **democracy** or someone who believes in and advocates that principle. But it is also used about someone who believes in or at least puts on a show of social equality: 'the chairman is democratic in the way he explains company policy to the workforce'.

In business, democratic management involves all employees in making important decisions. Inevitably *democratic* has joined the **process** bandwagon: politicians talk about the *democratic process*, by which they mean the machinery of democracy, free elections, one person–one vote and so on.

demographic As governments need to have more and more detailed information about society, *demographic* will become an everyday word. It combines two Greek words, one meaning the people (see **democracy**), and the other meaning writing. *Demographic* describes statistical charting of births, deaths, health, employment, spending and every other aspect of the population of a country.

'DEMonstrable' or 'deMONstrable' There's no hesitation in America: the stress goes on the second syllable ('deMONstrable'). In Britain, stress on the first syllable ('DEMonstrable') is still considered the more educated pronunciation. But far more people put the stress on the second syllable, which is easier to say, and this pronunciation is likely to take over in time. Until then, dictionaries give both alternatives, usually toeing the line by showing preference for stress on the first syllable.

demonstration The two meanings of *demonstration* have existed side by side at least since the mid-19th century: one is for showing how something is done or how something works, the other for a public protest against something or somebody. The second kind of demonstration is seen by millions on television, so that meaning is becoming uppermost in people's minds. The two meanings are not, in fact, likely to get mixed up with each other, although you never know: Fritz Spiegl quotes 'demonstrations by active homosexuals in St Peter's, Rome' (*In-words and Out-words*, 1987).

demotic or **colloquial** *Demotic* is the Greek equivalent of *colloquial*, a word based on Latin. But *colloquial* refers more to conversational language and *demotic* to the current everyday language of people, used particularly about classical languages: Demotic Greek is the language you read and hear in modern Greece, as against the language of classical Greek literature. No one refers to demotic English, since there is no classical form of English (Shakespeare used the language of the people, not a literary version of it).

denationalization See privatization . . .

denims See jeans . . .

denote See connote . . .

denouement or **dénouement** Although it is pronounced in a French manner ('dayNOOmah(n)'), the **acute accent** over the first *e* can be dropped. After all, the word has been at home in English since the mid-18th century, used in the same way for the final clarification of a story, a play or other work of fiction, or the resolution of a complicated situation in real life.

deny, **refute** or **rebut** *Refute* is often wrongly used as an aggressive word meaning to deny something emphatically: 'I refute that statement'. *Refute*, when it is properly used, means that conclusive evidence has been produced to show that something is wrong: 'Here are the facts that *refute* that statement'. Such conclusive evidence is *irrefutable*.

Dictionaries show *rebut* as an alternative to *refute* but it is possible to use *rebut* to mean argue against, without necessarily disproving something: 'I shall rebut that statement, and if you are not convinced, I'll produce evidence to refute it'.

Neither word should be used as a synonym for *deny*, that is simply saying something is not true. It must be added that this error is so common now that some current dictionaries are showing *deny* as one of the meanings of *refute*, with a warning that this is not accepted by everyone.

depend, **depend on** or **upon** Does it *depend* what we think, or *on* or *upon* what we think? In conversation *on* or *upon* are often omitted and it would be unreasonable to criticize that, although some people regard it as careless. In writing, it is preferable to follow *depend* by *on* or *upon*: it doesn't matter which, although *upon* is more formal.

dependant or **dependent** It's this way round: you claim tax relief for a *dependant*, but the rate of relief may be *dependent* on your income.

dependence or **dependency** *Dependence* is used about someone being dependent or reliant on someone or something: 'I'm sorry about her dependence on him for so many things'. The main use of *dependency* is for a territory that comes under the control of another country or a larger administrative centre: the island of South Georgia is a dependency of the Falkland Islands.

dependent See conditional . . .

depend on See depend . . .

depositary, **depository** or **repository** Dictionaries concede such a range of alternative uses of these three words that the best way is to take a simple line, in order to be consistent.

Depository should be used only about a *place* where things, most commonly furniture (a furniture depository), are stored. *Depositary* should be used only about a *person*, such as a trustee, to whom documents, money or anything else, including personal secrets, are entrusted.

Repository can be used for either a place, a person or an object: furniture can be stored in a repository, someone can be a repository of information on a subject (although not usually our personal secrets), a book can be a repository of wisdom, an urn a repository of someone's ashes.

These are not hard and fast rules but a reliable way out of confusion. At least you can be sure of one thing – there's no such word as 'repos*itary*'.

depreciation or **wear and tear**   Both mean the loss in value of something through being used or because time has elapsed. *Wear and tear* is the more old-fashioned term, and accountants use *depreciation* about assets, in the accounts of a business. On the other hand, some insurance policies retain *wear and tear* for the loss in value of property through use. And it is a good expression about people, describing what Dickens called 'the wear and tear of daily life'.

(The *-sh-* sound ('dePREESHiation') is preferable to the *-ss-* sound ('dePREESSiation'), although they are considered alternative pronunciations.)

depression, **cyclone** or **low-pressure area**   In **meteorology** they all mean barometric low pressure around which air circulates *cyclonically*, that is in the same direction as the rotation of the Earth. Weather forecasters are more likely to use *depression* or *low-pressure area*, because *cyclone* also means a violent storm (see **blizzard**).

depression, **downturn**, **recession** or **slump**   They all mean a reduction in business and economic activity, but each has its own effect on business confidence. *Slump* is reserved for the most severe cases: Alan Budd of the London Business School commented early in 1991 that 'it isn't a slump as in the 1930s but a severe recession'. *Depression* is an emotive word, a reminder of the soup kitchens of the 1930s. Economists define a *recession* as a drop in national output (**GDP**) for two three-monthly periods in succession. *Downturn* is a mild word, suggesting a minor or temporary fluctuation: John Major made a point of using the word *downturn* (House of Commons 12.11.1990) about the economic situation, an understatement as it turned out.

deprived   *Deprived* is one of those fashionable evasive words for the **poor**, suffering, maltreated, loveless. See also **underprivileged**

(in) **depth**   See **in depth**

derisive or **derisory**   A comment or a remark can be either *derisive* or *derisory*, meaning scornful or suggesting that something is ridiculous. But for some reason, only *derisory* is used about something that is absurdly small or unimportant: pay-offs and financial settlements can only be derisory (not derisive).

derivative   *Derivative* simply means that something comes from another source, and it is also a mathematical term used in calculus. In everyday language, *derivative* is usually derogatory, especially about art, music, literature, or ideas in general, suggesting that something is a pale shadow of an original concept.

descendant or **descendent**   *Descendent* is a word rarely used: it is a descriptive word (a son is descendent from his father). The more usual way of expressing this is 'a son is descended from his father'. *Descendant* is the noun: a son is a descendant of his father.

description *of* or *about*   A *description*, the process of describing, is always *of* someone or something, never *about* them.

desert or **dessert**   In case there are some people who hesitate over which is which, a *desert* is a sandy wasteland and the stress is on the first syllable ('DEZZert'). So we have *desert boots*, *desert rats* (the armoured division that fought in the 1942 campaign in the North African desert) and *desert islands* (islands that are deserted, not necessarily desert-like). When wives and husbands *desert* one another and villains get (or should get) their *just deserts* the stress is on the second syllable: 'dezZERT'. (The last use is a noun corresponding to the verb 'deserve'.)

Only after dinner does the double *-ss-* appear, for the sweet course: see **dessert or pudding**.

designer   The word goes back to the mid-17th century, as a noun for someone who devises a plan. But in the 1960s it was given a new status. The labels on clothes, identifying the name of the person or group who designed them, took on the cachet of the signature on a painting. *Designer* was reborn as a descriptive word: a *designer* whatever-it-was came to mean clothes that were special, produced in a limited series, distinguished and certainly expensive, because you were 'paying for the name'. By the end of the 60s *designer* was being applied to almost anything as a way of saying it was not off the production line.

The word was too good not to be taken up in all contexts: the 1980s saw a flood of designer jeans, designer potatoes, designer violence, designer babies (for which, among other things, a child's sex could be chosen in advance). *Designer stubble*, sported by Bob Geldof, Don Johnson and others, became the fashionable unshaven look, an indication of more important things to think of than shaving every day.

Designer lives on as a trendy, cryptic, overworked word to attach to many things that work hard at being new and different.

desirable   *Desirable* is a favourite word with estate agents: 'this highly desirable residence', 'in a desirable area'. . . . It means a good thing to have, something that people want. As a courtly word that a man might use about a woman to mean she is attractive or sexy, *desirable* belongs more to the 1890s than the 1990s.

desire, want or **wish** Nowadays even an assistant at Harrods would hardly ask 'And what does Madam desire?' There are a few situations when it might be more gracious to use *desire* rather than the more obvious word *want*, but they are thin on the ground.

Wish is more deferential than *want*, not as pompous as *desire*: 'Do you *wish* for some more wine?' might be all right coming from a waiter in a grand restaurant, but in almost any other context it would sound silly. If *want* is too direct, 'Would you like . . .?' is the usual way of putting it. Of course *wish* is still the usual verb when we wish someone every happiness or success, or on postcards from faraway places: 'I wish you were here!'

desk research A management consultant or business executive might say 'I've done some desk research on this'. It is a useful term to describe analysing written reports and other published material, rather than going out and finding new information. It is the opposite of **field research**.

desktop, micro, mini, or **personal computer** *Desktop* is perhaps a better, certainly a more descriptive name for what is more commonly called a *personal computer* (or PC). These are computers designed to be used by one person, rather than a shared facility, and include a **processor**, screen, **keyboard** and often a printer as well. For many people the word computer is synonymous with a personal computer.

A *microcomputer* is a more general name for any small computer used in a variety of applications, such as small businesses, schools, cash-dispensing machines. . . . The name is less indicative of performance than it was to begin with, since microcomputers have become increasingly powerful, in some cases going beyond the capacity of some of the early **mainframe** computers. The term *microcomputer* is also used for computer technology used in equipment, such as washing machines, telephones. . . .

There is no clear distinction between a *microcomputer* and a *minicomputer*, which was the name first used when smaller computers were developed. Some computer technologists use *minicomputer* for a more sophisticated microcomputer, in terms of capacity and speed of operation.

desktop publishing The term *desktop publishing* (or DTP) originated some time in the 1980s. Not so long before, printing required molten lead and movable type, techniques which still had some kind of connection with Gutenberg and Caxton, the pioneers of printing in the 15th century. *Desktop publishing* was a total break with that tradition, arranging the text and graphics on a page by using a keyboard and screen linked to a computer. It became possible when **laser**

printers were developed offering high quality, reproduction.

despatch See **dispatch** . . .

'deSPICable' or **'DESpicable'** Stress on the first syllable ('DESpicable') used to be the accepted pronunciation but it sounds wrong to many people now, as stress on the second syllable ('deSPICable') has become the general way of saying it. Some dictionaries continue to list 'DESpicable' as the preferred pronunciation, others have changed to 'deSPICable', which is likely to become the only accepted pronunciation in the future, except for a few of the old guard, who will continue to regard it as 'DESpicable'.

despite, despite of or **in spite of** *In spite of* and *despite* are correct: 'in spite of his money, he never travels first class'. *Despite of* is a vulgarism, for *despite* stands on its own: 'despite his money . . .'.

Dictionaries define *despite* as *in spite of*, so there isn't a whisker between them. If anything, *despite* is a more literary word.

dessert or **pudding** A *dessert course*, which comes at the end of a meal, gets its name from the French verb 'desservir', an old-fashioned word for clearing the table (which takes place before the dessert is served).

A *pudding* is properly a cooked, often hot sweet dish (plum pudding, rice pudding, etc), but it has become the trendy name for any dessert, even ice-cream. The kind of restaurant that lists **hors-d'oeuvres** as *starters* will go on to list desserts as *puddings*.

A *dessert wine* is the sweet wine that accompanies a dessert or fruit and nuts at the end of a meal. It has become nauseatingly fashionable in recent years to call such wines *pudding wines*. Even the distinguished wine merchants, Berry Brothers & Rudd of St James's Street, London, have written about a 'revival of interest in pudding wines'. Tut-tut!

('Dessert' is a common misspelling for 'desert' in such phrases as 'just deserts': see **desert or dessert**.)

desultory Stress on the first syllable ('DEZultry') is the only accepted pronunciation and 'deZULtry' (stress on second syllable) would make many people wrinkle their noses. *Desultory* describes a half-hearted, unthinking way of going about anything.

détente *Détente* has been used in English since the early 20th century for the easing of strained relations. After World War II it was used almost exclusively about the relationship between the US and the USSR. When they were talking to one another, there was – *détente*. Since the breakup of the Soviet empire in 1991, *détente* has become part of the history of the **cold war**, and applied to similar historical situations. (Pron: 'dayTAHNT'.)

detergent It is surprising to discover that *detergent* has been used in English for a cleansing agent since the 17th century. Strictly speaking, detergents are any agents that remove dirt and grease, which makes ordinary soap a detergent. But during the second half of the 20th century the word has come to mean only detergents composed of synthetic compounds.

deteriorate or **worsen** Something good, such as fresh food or good health, can *deteriorate*. But only something bad can *worsen*. It is a mistake to write: 'a bottle of good wine will worsen if left near a radiator'. *Deteriorate* should be pronounced with its full *five* syllables: 'dee-TEER-ree-er-rayt' and it is careless to contract it to four syllables, as often happens.

determine or **find out** Among its other meanings, *determine* is not just a formal alternative to *find out*: it carries with it the idea of precision, as in the geometric use of *determine*, to fix exactly the position of a point. 'We have to determine how production will be affected' suggests a detailed analysis: 'We have to find out how production will be affected' means that the problem must be looked into, but maybe in a more general way.

When *determine* is used in law, it relates to the word 'terminate', to end: an agreement is determined, that is brought to an end so that it is no longer in force, either on a fixed date or when certain other events, such as death, occur. We should hesitate to apply this legal meaning of *determine* in non-legal matters, because not everyone understands it: instead of 'this dispute will be determined when terms are agreed', it may be preferable to say 'this dispute will end (or come to an end) . . .'.

deterrence or **deterrent** *Deterrence* is a noun: 'the high unemployment figures will be a deterrence in the new wage-bargaining round'. *Deterrent* is the corresponding descriptive word: 'we must apply deterrent sanctions'. But *deterrent* is also used as a noun, especially in connection with military or defence matters: nuclear weapons are called a *deterrent*. Because it is so often used in this context, *deterrent* has become the more usual noun in general use, with *deterrence* as a less common alternative.

detour The pronunciation 'DAYtour' goes back to the time when it was usual to put an **acute accent** over the *e*, as in French (*détour*). That's out of date: the standard pronunciation now is 'DEEtour' and most recent dictionaries do not allow an alternative.

deus ex machina This is a useful phrase in these times of ever-impending doom. When you are at the end of the line with no hope, and something turns up to save the situation, it can seem like divine intervention. That's a *deus ex machina* (pron: 'DAYus ex MAKina'). Gods were always intervening in ancient Greek tragedy and were suspended above the stage, lowered by machinery at the critical moment. *Deus ex machina* is the direct Latin translation of the Greek phrase, 'god from the machinery'. The phrase usually relates to a providential intervention in a play or a novel, but there's no reason why it should not be used in a real life situation as well. Keep it in mind for when something unexpected saves the day!

Deutschmark or **Deutsche Mark** Either will do but the tendency is to write it as one word and say it with two syllables ('DOYTSH-mahk'), rather than three syllables: 'DOY-tsher-mahk'.

develop *Develop* means something happening gradually, in stages: a situation can develop over years; a town develops as the population increases. Something cannot develop 'suddenly' or 'overnight'. But this way of using *develop* and *development* is so common that many people would think it is fussing to argue against it. If you want to hold back for as long as possible the flood of misuse, you can replace 'suddenly developed' or 'just developed' by 'suddenly occurred', 'just happened' or 'suddenly arisen'.

developing or **underdeveloped country** Both terms are euphemisms for countries, particularly in Africa, South America and parts of Asia, where there is widespread poverty and in many cases hopelessly inadequate provision for education and health. They are indeterminate terms for poor or primitive countries relying on agriculture, crafts and raw materials.

Underdeveloped country is now regarded as a pejorative term, and the more euphemistic *developing country* is used by the United Nations. In some cases, but not necessarily, that implies the process of changing over to an industrial base. See also **economic development; poor; Third World**

development area *Development area* is a designation for regions within which investment grants and concessions are made by central government to industries, in order to counteract a higher than average level of unemployment.

deviant or **perverted** Both words are used about sexual practices, and both often carry with them condemnation or judgement. For some people, the words mean the same, although *perverted* is usually more censorious. The two reports on sexual behaviour by the American psychologist, Alfred Kinsey (1948 and 1953), and the work of Masters and Johnson (*Human Sexual Response*, 1966) have extended ideas about what is 'normal', and for some people at least, *perverted* would not be used, for example, about such practices as **oral sex**.

Deviant can also describe any behaviour considered a departure from normal, but the word has become so associated with psychosexual disorders, that we have to be careful about using it in other contexts.

devil's advocate It is easy to see why this expression, still much used, is often misunderstood. The devil's advocate was the official in the papal court who found objections to someone being declared a saint (and was used in this way as the title of a book by Morris West). In everyday use, it means someone who picks holes in something that is positive and constructive. Suppose you are planning to present proposals to a client. A colleague might say 'Let me be the devil's advocate', and proceed to put all possible objections to your proposals, so that when you face the client you will be ready with the answers.

devolution or **separatism** *Devolution* remains a word that continues to be brought forward on political agendas, especially relating to Ireland, Scotland and Wales. It represents the transfer of legislative power from the parliament in London to an assembly set up in another region. (Compare **subsidiarity**.)

Separatism is similar to devolution, but more nationalistic. It reflects a movement for a breakaway by an ancient national group with its own customs and traditions, sometimes with its own language, from a central sovereignty. The Basque separatists in Spain are often in the news. Nearer home, Scottish separatists demand secession from the Westminster parliament and the establishment of independence not just devolution for Scotland. See also **subsidiarity**

dexterous or **dextrous** These were alternative spellings but *dextrous* has fallen into disuse, although recent dictionaries continue to show it as a variant. But dictionaries, like railway timetables, can be out of date.

Dexterous has been used since the 17th century for both manual and mental skills in handling something. It comes from the Latin word meaning the right-hand side, implying at one time that right-handed people were more *adroit* (another suggestion of the superiority of right-handedness, since it comes from French 'à droit', on the right). But of course left-handed people can be equally dexterous (the original Latin equivalent, *sinister*, for left-hand side, having long ago taken on an entirely different meaning).

diabolic or **diabolical** In principle, you should believe in the Devil to use *diabolic*, because the word has a theological flavour, used more about the attributes of the Devil himself. *Diabolical* is more for human beings who behave like the devil: 'his treatment of her is diabolical'. In practice, *diabolic* and *diabolical* are often used interchangeably.

To use the words about food, the weather or anything else we're fed up with, is usual enough in conversation or casual writing, but should not cross the line into formal English.

diaeresis or **umlaut** They both look the same, two dots over a vowel. A diaeresis (pron: 'dye-EHR-re(r)sis') is used at times over a vowel in English to indicate that it is pronounced separately: *naïve*, *Chloë*. This used to be quite common, with words such as

'aerate' and 'cooperate' having a diaeresis (*aërate*, *coöperate*) to show they are pronounced with three and four syllables respectively. In those words and in most others the diaeresis is omitted now. As it often has to be put in by hand on printouts from wordprocessors, the *diaeresis* in English will eventually become obsolete, except possibly for names, such as *Brontë*.

The German word *umlaut* (pron: 'oomLOWT') is used for the same two-dot symbol in German to show a change in the sound of a vowel: *mädchen* (girl), *schön* (beautiful), *Köln* (Cologne). Even in that language, the umlaut is often replaced by adding *-e* after the vowel. With names, Germans spell some with or without an umlaut depending on family convention. It is wrong, for example, to write to a Herr *Müller* as Herr *Mueller*, or to someone who spells his name *Mueller*, as *Müller*.

diagnosis or **prognosis** When these medical terms are used more generally, they are sometimes misunderstood. A doctor *diagnoses* a disease by discovering what is wrong with the patient, and the result is a *diagnosis*. The doctor's *prognosis* is a forecast of how the disease will develop. Likewise the *diagnosis* of a problem in business, or any other sphere, is finding out the real cause. The *prognosis* might be that it will sort itself out or that the business will go bankrupt. The plurals are *diagnoses* and *prognoses*, the last syllables pronounced 'seez'.

diagnostics In medicine the *diagnostics* of a disease is the science of diagnosing it, and it is treated as singular: 'the diagnostics of this disease *is* . . .'. In computer language, *diagnostics* are programs and techniques for detecting errors, and treated as plural: 'diagnostics *are* available . . .'.

dial Telephones have keypads now and telephones with dials belong to museums. Americans may talk of 'punching a number' but the British still *dial* a number, even if they are in fact pressing buttons. The words *dial* and *dialling* survive and are likely to continue being used, linguistic hangers-on from a non-computerized past.

dialect or **patois** Many people would be put out to be told they speak a *dialect*, but in fact we all speak one. The word means a form and style of speaking related to a particular class or region (it derives from a Greek word meaning 'a way of speaking'). A dialect is not an inferior form of language and may have a great deal of antiquity and tradition behind it: it simply does not conform to the language used by the majority, and is none the worse for that.

A *patois* (it is a French word pronounced in the French way: 'PATwah') is another form of dialect, more likely to be used of a peasant language (*patois* in French means rough speech). *Patois* is not used about varieties of English spoken in Britain, but more about varieties of foreign languages spoken in other countries. Unlike a dialect, a patois usually has no literature and would generally be thought of as an uncultured version of the language it relates to.

At a time of ever-increasing standardization, a new value is seen in preserving minority languages and endemic culture, so we should not use *dialect* or *patois* in a way that could be interpreted as patronizing.

dialogue A *dialogue* is any number of people speaking together, not just two, as is often supposed. The word for a conversation between just two people is *duologue*, but it would sound odd to ask for a duologue with someone: the word is more or less reserved for the theatre, for a play or a scene in a play with only two people on stage. See also **monologue** . . .

The fashionable use of *dialogue* for an exchange of views is overdone and often not necessary: 'Can we have a dialogue about this?', instead of 'Can we talk about it?' Perhaps *dialogue* has a place in diplomatic and political situations, especially where there is hostility: to say there is a dialogue between opposing factions means at least they're not shooting at each other.

diapositive See **colour negative** . . .

diary or **journal** In previous centuries, people were more likely to keep a *journal* as a record of what happened during the day, although Pepys started his famous *Diary* on 1 January 1660. Both words, with the meaning of a record of daily events, go back to the 17th century, but in the 1990s, keeping a journal would sound old-fashioned or literary, so we keep a diary.

Although *journal* derives from Latin 'diurnalis' (during the day) and was used in the 18th century for a daily newspaper, it now applies to any periodical, even one that comes out once a quarter, which is probably why *diary* has become the more usual word for a personal record day by day. Anyone of us can be a *diarist*, but you have to belong to a trade union to be a *journalist*.

Dickensian The word can be used in a literary sense about the style and form of the novels of Charles Dickens (1812–70). Or it can be a descriptive word for slums and bad social and working conditions (which Dickens often described). A *Dickensian character* is someone who is grotesquely old-fashioned or comic, reminiscent of the curmudgeon Scrooge in *A Christmas Carol* or Mrs Gummidge in *David Copperfield*, or other comical or unpleasant characters that Dickens created.

Note that the expression of surprise, as in 'What the dickens are you up to?' has nothing to do with Charles Dickens: it goes back to the 16th century, and *dickens* is probably a euphemism for the Devil.

'DICtate' or **'dicTATE'** As often in English, the stress is different when the word is used as a noun or a verb: with a *verb* the stress is on the *second* syllable;

the *noun* is stressed on the *first* syllable. We 'dicTATE' letters and follow the 'DICtates' of conscience.

dictionaries There was no comprehensive and authoritative dictionary for Shakespeare, which enabled him to twist and stretch words to make them do what he wanted, without anyone challenging him by 'looking it up'. Some limited attempts to list and explain selections of words were published in the 17th century but Samuel Johnson's *Dictionary*, published in 1755, was the first to be accepted as having stature and authority. It is still known as the *Dictionary* and still in print (a facsimile edition was published in 1990).

Johnson's *Dictionary* remained an authority on English for well over a hundred years until the *New* (later called *The Oxford*) *English Dictionary* appeared in 12 volumes between 1884 and 1928. James Murray, the Scottish schoolmaster who was the first editor, set himself the awesome task of recording the entire vocabulary of the English language from about 1150 up to his own time. The *OED* is the cornerstone of every English dictionary published ever since. The second edition, published in 1989, extends to 20 volumes and weighs over 50 kilos. Everyone who uses English should be grateful to the lexicographers of Oxford, and *The Good English Guide* takes this opportunity to salute them.

Sooner or later all dictionaries have to accept as good English what the majority of people say and write. If anyone argues with that, you can quote Robert Burchfield, at the time chief editor of Oxford English Dictionaries: 'It is the duty of lexicographers to record actual usage as shown by collected examples, not to express moral approval or disapproval of usage'. But since the late 1980s, editors of dictionaries have become wary of criticism and hedge some entries with a new qualification: **disp**, short for *disputed*, meaning that there are many people who reject the way certain words are used or pronounced.

Dictionaries, like railway timetables, become out of date. The meanings of words change and affect us in new ways. Elizabeth Barrett Browning wrote in a letter, when she was on honeymoon in 1846: 'After two months of uninterrupted intercourse he loves me better every day . . . and my health improves too'. She would hardly write that now! English is on the move all the time, leaving your dictionary behind. A new word or the new use of a word is not wrong just because it is not in the dictionary.

The status of words changes too. A word considered slang a few years ago may by now have moved up into standard English, suitable for use in formal writing. (See **colloquial, informal, slang** or **nonstandard**.) During the transition period dictionaries often disagree on whether a word has crossed over, and we have to make up our own minds, or better still, take note of how good writers and speakers are using it.

Etymology in dictionaries is often indisputable, thanks to the scholarship of the great *OED*. But meanings and usage of words reflect the opinions of editors, which is why dictionaries disagree in some cases over sense, usage or pronunciation. Editors' decisions are valuable as guidance but not always final: there are times when we – not our dictionary – can decide to have the last word. See also **lexicography; meaning**

didactic See **pedantic** . . .

didn't See **contracted forms**

die of or **from** It is more usual to die *of* an illness, old age. . . . Die *from* is equally correct but less commonly used.

diet Whatever we habitually eat, whether it is good or bad for us, is our *diet*, for that is the meaning of the word. But most people assume, if you talk about 'your *diet*', that it is limited to certain foods for medical reasons or more usually to lose weight. We can make a distinction by saying someone is *on a diet*, which may suggest it is for a special purpose and possibly only for a period: or we can say they *follow* a *diet*, which could be held to suggest it is a committed way of life. But we cannot be sure that the difference would be interpreted in this way.

In passing, the *diet* (or *Diet*), as the name for the legislative assemblies in some countries, or of a session of court in Scotland, has the same pronunciation ('DYEe(r)t').

dietetics or **nutrition** *Dietetics* embraces the scientific study of both the food that is or should be eaten. *Nutrition* is the branch of physiology that deals with the values of food and the way carbohydrates, fats, proteins, minerals, etc are utilized by the physical organism.

Note that *dietetics* is nearly always regarded as singular.

dietitian or **dietician** Both spellings are used. Most dictionaries prefer *dietitian*, putting *dietician* in brackets as an alternative. But that doesn't settle the matter because many dietitians prefer the spelling *dietician*.

differences or **differentials** It is unnecessary to use *differentials* simply because it sounds more important than *differences*: 'salaries should relate to the differentials of corresponding skills'. Why not *differences*?

Differential has become the standard term in industrial relations for established different levels of pay for different categories of jobs. As a descriptive word, it singles out this factor: 'differential pay settlements' indicates more than 'different pay settlements'. It links agreements specifically to levels of pay already established for different jobs.

different This word has a way of slipping in where it's not wanted: 'he has had three different wives',

'he looked it up in six different books'. In such sentences, *different* adds nothing.

different from, to or **than** Can anyone say anything new about this old grammatical shibboleth? We (*The Good English Guide*, that is) must first put our cards on the table: all three forms are available. For some people, different *from* is the only acceptable form and they object even to different *to*, although current dictionaries list it as good English, and it has been used by good writers from George Eliot to Evelyn Waugh.

Different *than*, which makes people even more hot under the collar, is dismissed as an ungrammatical Americanism, unjustifiably because many British writers have used it (Defoe, Coleridge, Trollope, Carlyle, Goldsmith, John Maynard Keynes . . .). *Than* is particularly useful after *differently*: 'they do things differently in New York *than* in London'. Which form you use, or whether you use all three, depends upon how much you mind some people criticizing your grammar, even though you have the *OED* and other good authorities on your side. If it keeps you awake at night, put your money on *different from*, which is gilt-edged and irreproachable.

differentials See **differences** . . .

differentiate or **distinguish** The two words are close to each other in meaning the ability to recognize differences. If anything, *differentiate* may suggest an especially slight difference, and is usually followed by 'between': 'the colours are so similar that I cannot differentiate between them'. *Differentiate* also has more of a place in scientific matters, such as *differentiating* between different botanical species.

differ from or **with** When people or things are not the same as each other, they *differ from*: Italian wines differ from French wines. When people hold different opinions, they usually *differ with* each other, although they can also differ *from* each other. Because of this, be on the lookout for a misunderstanding: 'she differs *from* her brother' could mean she is different from him or that they hold different opinions. It can be made clear by adding either 'in some ways' (to mean they are different from each other), or 'over some things' to cover a difference of opinion.

diffuse or **defuse** See **defuse** . . .

'Digest' or **'diGEST'** We 'diGEST' food and 'diGEST' information because the verb has the stress on the *second* syllable. We read or write a 'DIgest', as the noun (meaning a synopsis of a book, article, or a compendium of books or articles) has the stress on the *first* syllable.

digital See **analogue** . . .

dike See **dyke** . . .

dilapidated The word strictly applies to buildings ('lapis' is the Latin word for stone) and is used by surveyors about a structure in a bad state of disrepair. But it is accepted as standard English now to apply *dilapidated* to, say, an armchair, a car, a person or to almost anything else that has seen better days.

dilemma You have not understood this word if you say 'We're in a dilemma about where to go for our holiday'. To be in a *dilemma* is to be between the devil and the deep blue sea, that is to be faced by nasty alternatives: 'I'm in a dilemma over whether to pay the telephone bill or have it cut off'. Because the prefix *di-* is from the Greek word for 'two', it should strictly only apply to *two* decisions: as with the word **alternative**, it is often extended now to cover any number, although most dictionaries still restrict *dilemma* to two. To be on the *horns of a dilemma* also stresses *two*: whichever you choose, one of them will spear you. There is a choice of pronunciation: either 'dilLEMMa' (first syllable rhymes with 'pill') or 'dyeLEMMa', with a preference for the former.

dimension It is customary for writers on English usage to tut-tut over the use of *dimension*, a term for denoting area or volume, in a general context to mean another factor: 'having a child adds another dimension to our lives'. Yet the word works well when it is used, not just as an unnecessary synonym for 'increase' ('parking restrictions add another dimension to the problems of driving in London'), but to emphasize the addition of a significant new factor or influence, as in the first example above.

There are alternative pronunciations for the first syllable of the word: 'dyeMENshun' or 'dimMENshun', with a preference for 'dye'.

dinghy or **dingy** These are two different words. *Dinghy* is taken from a Hindi word for a rowing-boat and is often used in English for any small boat, especially one carried by a ship. *Dingy* probably goes back to the Old English word for dung and appropriately describes something that looks dirty or drab. The pronunciations are different: *dinghy* – 'DINgee' (*g* as in 'get'); *dingy* – 'DINjee'.

dinner, **lunch**, **luncheon** or **supper** Dictionaries define *dinner* as the main meal of the day, eaten at either midday or in the evening. Yet many people would rather be seen dead than call their midday meal *dinner*! The *Shorter OED* (1959 reprint) reminds us that dinner was originally eaten about midday 'but now, by the fashionable class, in the evening'. This is a curious example of linguistic class and regional distinction.

The working class often use *dinner* for their midday meal, even if it's only sandwiches. For the middle class the midday meal is always *lunch* and the evening meal *dinner* (hence a *dinner* jacket). *Supper* for the working class could well be a meal at 6pm, whereas for the middle class *supper* is more likely to be after 9pm

('supper after the theatre'). In Scotland, *high tea* is often the equivalent of working-class *supper* in England, a cooked meal about 6pm. In the North of England, *tea* is not uncommon for the evening meal.

As noted above, most dictionaries take an admirably classless attitude towards the whole question, yet the facts remain: a plumber will usually eat sandwiches for *dinner* at midday and go home for *supper* in the evening, while a barrister will go out for *lunch* about 1 o'clock and go home for *dinner*.

As for *luncheon*, that is pretentious other than for formal or official lunches. Where *luncheon meat* and *luncheon vouchers* fit in is anybody's guess.

dinner jacket See black tie . . .

diocese The clergy will not hesitate over the pronunciation of this word for a district under the authority of a bishop, but other people may be unsure. The singular *diocese* is pronounced 'DYEe(r)sis', and the plural *dioceses*, either 'DYEe(r)seez' (which is easier to say) or 'DYE-e(r)-sis-iz' (which is more difficult). There's no easy alternative with *diocesan*: 'dyeOSS-isse(r)n'.

diphthong Unlike *diphtheria* (where a *p* sound is an alternative) *diphthong* always has an *f* sound: 'DIFFthong'.

diplomacy Officially diplomacy is the skill of handling international relations by representatives of countries. Since the mid-19th century it has been extended to include personal relationships of all kinds, especially where there is a problem. *Diplomacy* means tact and skill in negotiations, but sometimes with a hint of deviousness as well: Sir Henry Wotton's (1568–1639) famous definition of an ambassador, which he wrote in Latin, out of diplomacy, was translated (by Izaak Walton) as 'an honest man, sent to lie abroad for the good of his country'. See also **shuttle diplomacy**

dipsomaniac See alcoholic . . .

direct, **direction**, **director** and **directory** Current dictionaries give a choice of pronunciation: you can go 'dirREKT' (the first syllable rhyming with the first syllable of '*mirror*') or you can pronounce it 'dyeR-EKT'. You have the same choice when you go off in any *direction*, if you are the *director* of a company or look something up in a *directory*. There is no discernible preference one way or the other. With *indirect*, 'in*dye*REKT' is usually preferred.

direct or **directly** In some cases either can be used: 'You can go direct to the river' means there is a more or less straight path there: 'you can go directly to the river' could mean the same thing, but it could also mean that you can go immediately. When there is a risk of misunderstanding, it's better, in the latter sense, to replace *directly* by at once, immediately, straightaway, without delay. . . .

direct debit See **standing order** . . .

directly See **direct** . . .

direct mail A most unlikely marketing genius, an American railway clerk named Richard Sears, invented selling by post. About a century ago, in 1891, he set out, as an essay in moonlighting, to sell watches by writing to people about them. The floodgates opened, and before long the Sears and Roebuck catalogue, a thousand pages thick, was selling almost anything you could think of by post – ploughs, printing-presses and cure-alls, as well as watches, of course. The bandwagon has never stopped, and in the 1990s the *direct-mail* industry has become the fastest growing form of sales promotion in the world.

Direct mail is the advertising and marketing term for those leaflets, letters, catalogues and cajolements that thump on to our doormats. The trade call them *direct-mail shots* (also called *mailing shots* or *mail shots*), an unconscious suggestion that they are attacks and incursions. The fact that the other name for direct mail is *junk mail* (first used, it is believed, by *The Economist* in 1967, and now treated by dictionaries as standard English), tells us something else.

direct and **indirect object** Arguably it is not necessary to understand this grammatical distinction in order to write good English. But it is useful when it comes to reading grammatical explanations. For anyone who is not clear, a *direct object* is someone or something directly in line with the action of a verb: 'he sent *a letter*'; 'she spoke *the truth*' (*letter* and *truth* are direct objects).

An *indirect object* is someone or something one stage removed: 'he sent a letter to *Mary*' (or 'he sent *Mary* a letter'); 'she spoke the truth to *him*' (*Mary* and *him* are indirect objects). See also **case**

direct and **indirect speech** These are stylistic terms to describe two different ways of reporting what someone has said. *Direct speech* encloses within quotation marks the actual words that are said: 'Will you come to dinner?' he asked her.

Indirect speech describes what has been said, without using the actual words that were spoken: He asked her if she would come to dinner. Note that a question in indirect speech (as in the last example) is not followed by a question mark.

director, **directory (pronunciation)** See direct . . .

director general This august Ruritanian title is usually reserved for the head of large official organizations, such as the BBC or the CBI. In effect, it doesn't mean anything more than the director, chief executive, or – the **boss**.

dirty tricks A *dirty trick* is something dishonourable and underhand, rather than necessarily dishonest. But now *dirty tricks* (in the plural) has become a political catchphrase for the not uncommon practice of a political party using any piece of scandal, half-information or misinformation to discredit an opponent. Politicians even talk about the *dirty tricks department*, as if the other party has unofficially appointed a gang of members to plan and execute dirty tricks. In America, the nasty business was given a false legitimacy by calling it *negative campaigning*, a term that came to the fore in Britain during the 1992 election campaign.

dirty words Because humankind finds it difficult to reconcile its higher intelligence with its animal functions, the ordinary words for those functions are labelled *dirty words*. Add to that the hangover from Victorian repressiveness and we are left hedged in on all sides whenever we want to talk about our bodily activities. Havelock Ellis's *Studies in the Psychology of Sex* was declared 'lewd and obscene' by the courts in 1897; nearly a century later, the English language still maintains much the same conspiracy of silence. The ways women and men make love to each other remain shrouded in the evasive respectability of euphemisms and the moment we attempt to lift the veil, we have to use either cumbersome Latinisms or so-called 'dirty words'. Whether we go along with this game or take a more open linguistic attitude depends upon our hang-ups or how much we care about offending others. See also **four-letter words**

dis- words See de- words . . .

disability or **inability** Generally *disability* should only be used in connection with a physical or mental handicap, because that is what most people would assume is meant. *Inability* is for someone who cannot do something because they do not have the knowledge, the skill, the intelligence, or the resources.

disadvantage (as a verb) Current dictionaries give us permission to use *disadvantage* as a verb, as well as a noun. The director general of the **CBI** commented that 'high interest rates should not be allowed to disadvantage business . . .', which is quicker and more direct than saying '. . . to put business at a disadvantage'.

disadvantaged (as a noun) *Disadvantaged* is one of those fashionable evasive words for the **poor**, suffering, maltreated, loveless. See also **underprivileged**

disappointed at, **by**, **in** or **with** If it is a *person*, we can be disappointed in or with them, meaning a disappointment in what they are like or how they act: 'they were disappointed *in* (or *with*) their son's behaviour'. If we are disappointed *by* them, it is because of something specific they have done or not done: 'she was disappointed *by* his late arrival'. If it is an *object*, we can be disappointed *with* it. If it is a *result* or an *occurrence*, we can be disappointed *by*, *with* or (less usually) *in* it: 'she was disappointed *by*, *with* or *in* dinner'. (If she was disappointed *at* dinner, it would mean that while she was having dinner, something happened to disappoint her.)

disapprove or **disapprove of** The distinction is important: if someone *disapproves of* a plan, it means they don't like it, but if they *disapprove* a plan, they have turned it down. Perhaps in the end it often comes to the same thing, but not always: someone may disapprove of your plan but still let you go ahead with it, whereas if they disapprove your plan, it's a dead duck.

disarmament See arms control . . .

disassociate See dissociate . . .

disastrous or **disasterous** *Disastrous*. (See -erous or -rous.)

disbar See debar . . .

disc or **disk** Before the 1960s, some dictionaries recommended *disk*. This has now been reversed and *disc* is standard in British English, with *disk* the American spelling. But *disk* is used in English everywhere in connection with computers. See also **compact disc**; **floppy disk** . . .

disc or **record** In spite of *disc-jockeys*, *disc* never really replaced *record* in Britain, for a gramophone record. But **compact discs** have changed that. People who have a collection of seventy-eights or LPs are still likely to call them *records*.

discernible or **discernable** If your dictionary shows *discernable* as an alternative spelling, and a few still do, it is better to ignore it. *Discernible* has become the only accepted spelling, and most dictionaries now offer no alternative.

disclose or **reveal** Although *disclose* and *reveal* mean no more than to make something known, they often carry the suggestion that it was hidden for dubious reasons: 'he disclosed his motives'; 'the facts were revealed'. Unless something of this kind is intended, or there is no risk of misunderstanding, it is often better to use words, such as 'show', 'explain', 'announce', which are less likely to imply that anything undercover has been going on. Compare 'he explained his motives', 'the facts were given' with the examples quoted earlier, and you'll see there is a different nuance.

discomfit or **discomfort** *Discomfit* was at one time a much stronger word, meaning seriously frustrated or disturbed by something. *Discomfort* is a mild

word. Hence 'she was discomforted by his remark' means she was a little put out by it; 'she was discomfited . . .' could suggest she was very upset. In practice, few people would recognize the difference.

discontinue See stop . . .

discount The Stock Exchange uses *discount* as a verb in a particular way, not recorded in all dictionaries. It is used to mean anticipate or take into account beforehand: when some good or bad financial news is expected, share prices may go up or down in advance, that is to say the news is *discounted*, so when the event happens, prices are hardly affected. For pronunciation, see next entry.

'DIScount' or **'disCOUNT'** A letter in *The Times* complained about BBC newsreaders who 'DIScount' the possibility, instead of 'disCOUNTing' it, as if they were talking about a cut-price shop. The writer has a case: we 'disCOUNT' something when we write it off as being untrue or unimportant; but when we buy something for less than the going rate, we get a 'DIScount'. The *verb* is stressed on the *second*, the *noun* on the *first* syllable.

discount rate See bank rate . . .

discover or **identify** Management consultants seek to justify high fees by *identifying* a problem, rather than finding out or *discovering* what the trouble is. They then go on to *identify* the best method of dealing with it, instead of 'working it out'. On the other hand, 'the problem was discovered' could suggest it came to light more or less by chance: 'the problem was identified' suggests an effort was made to define it. But in many cases *identify* is often used where ordinary down-to-earth words would be more to the point.

discover or **invent** This is a distinction of meaning that we all think we know about, but which still throws up uncertainty at times. We can only *discover* something that is already there but unknown to us: it could be a star, a writer, an island. . . . We *invent* something that did not exist before, such as a new piece of equipment. When it is a **concept**, a new way of looking at something, or a technique, a new way of doing something, do we *discover* or *invent* it? Either word can be used, although it is more usual to choose *discover*, perhaps because an *invention* can only be patented when it is a tangible construction: we cannot patent a concept or a technique, only the device required to apply it.

discreet or **discrete** The problem with these two words is not so much that people get the meanings confused, but that *discreet* is sometimes wrongly spelt *discrete*, for both words are pronounced exactly the same. *Discrete* means separate and distinct: for example, pointillism is the technique in impressionist painting that uses *discrete* (ie individually separate) dots of pure colours.

Discreet is the word we use more, meaning sensitive and careful in not doing or saying the wrong thing: 'you can tell her anything as she is very discreet'.

discrepancy or **divergence** Use *discrepancy* when things should agree but do not, especially when it concerns figures: a discrepancy in accounts. Use *divergence* about things that happen to be different, usually not in a marked way: a divergence of opinion.

discrete See discreet . . .

discrimination Before the 1960s, *discrimination* was usually a good word, suggesting judgement, the ability to distinguish between what is fine and the run-of-the-mill. That meaning still exists, of course, but now the *first* meaning is narrow prejudice because of race, colour or sex. There is a *Sex Discrimination Act* on the statute-book (1975), which requires women to be treated on the same basis as men. People now are likely to think of *discrimination* as a bad thing, and we need to be careful when using it in a good sense. This is so much the case that, to avoid misunderstanding, a new term has arisen: *positive discrimination* (see **positive** . . .), for preferential treatment given to **underprivileged** groups in society.

discussion programme See chat-show . . .

disease or **illness** The words are often interchangeable: 'he has an illness (or a disease)'. *Disease* is preferred for infection: we catch a disease from polluted water. *Illness* is usually preferred for common diseases, such as a cold. *Illness*, rather than *disease*, is the word used about mental disorders: a mental illness.

Some people believe that *disease* only applies to **contagious or infectious** conditions. But *disease* need not be restricted in that way. When the nature of an illness is specified, *disease* is usually the appropriate word: Parkinson's disease, heart disease, a rare eye disease. . . .

The descriptive word *diseased* means that someone has a disease, just as *ill* means they have an illness; but we should be careful how we use *diseased* since it has acquired such a strong connotation of abnormality: 'he is diseased' sounds much more sinister than 'he is ill'. See also ill . . .

disenfranchise or **disfranchise** These are alternative words for depriving people of the right to vote. *Disfranchise* is the earlier form, going back to the 15th century, but *disenfranchise* is perhaps the more usual word now.

disgusted *at*, *by* or **with** We can be *disgusted at* or *by* something that has happened (see next entry). If it were a person who upset us, we would be *disgusted at* or *with* them. This is considered proper usage: *at* or *with* about a person, *at* or *by* about an occurrence. But it is difficult to justify this as a hard and fast rule: there seems no good reason, except custom, why you should not be disgusted *with* the weather, or *by* your neighbour.

Disgusted, Tunbridge Wells By long tradition, angry letters to the editor of *The Times* about any subject, from so-called explicit sex scenes on television to the price of caviare in the food department of Harrods, are symbolically signed *Disgusted, Tunbridge Wells*. Perhaps at one time there was a disproportionate number of choleric retired colonels living in that town, or perhaps there really was living there a letter-writer to *The Times*, who remained anonymous by using the appellation *Disgusted*. Either way, the legend has passed into everyday language.

dish In the second half of the 1980s, *dish* became for all of us, not only a container for serving food, but the familiar word for *satellite dish*, a concave aerial designed to receive the low-power signals from communication **satellites**. From then on, dishes had a place on rooftops as well as in kitchens.

disinflation See inflation

disinformation, misinformation or **propaganda** Until 1933, when Goebbels was appointed Minister of Propaganda by Hitler, *propaganda* was a neutral word for the giving out of information. It was officially used by the Church for the spreading of the gospels. Goebbels changed that: his unscrupulous manipulation of facts turned *propaganda* into a sinister word, meaning selecting or distorting information for political or commercial ends. *Propaganda* is a collective singular noun and has no plural: 'the propaganda *is* confusing people'.

Disinformation is the up-to-date word for the same process, official lies or half-truths given out to the media. *Misinformation* can be used in the same way but does not necessarily mean that the wrong facts were given deliberately: an inaccurate map can give misinformation.

disingenuous See ingenious . . .

disinterested See uninterested . . .

disk or **disc** See disc . . .

dislike While we can like *to* go to the theatre, like *to* travel, like *to* meet friends, and so on, we cannot dislike *to* do anything. The correct construction is *dislike going* to the theatre, *travelling*, *meeting* friends. . . .

dismiss, sack, fire or **make redundant** It is less common now for employers to *dismiss* or *sack* people from their jobs. Instead they *make them redundant*, which sounds even worse, since it points to the scrap heap. Journalists still like the down-to-earthiness of *sack*, especially in headlines, so prime ministers sack other ministers and boards sack their chairmen. Dictionaries still consider *sack*, in this sense, colloquial or informal, which is too conservative as the word has been used this way since the 19th century, and even appears in academic writing.

Fire still has an American ring to it. For a while, it was gaining ground in Britain as a popular word to replace *sack* as a verb, which was beginning to sound old-fashioned. This is no longer true: *fire* is not used so often now and *sack* is back in, almost a **buzzword** during the recession of the early 1990s.

There is an important legal difference between *dismiss/sack/fire* and **make redundant**. *Wrongful dismissal* is the legal term for sacking an employee in breach of a contract of service or before the end of the required period of notice. *Unfair dismissal* is sacking someone without proper cause, and could lead to reinstatement or compensation under the Employment Protection Act 1978. When an employee is made redundant, they cannot be replaced since, technically, it is the job which is made redundant. See also **golden-** for *golden handshake*

disoriented or **disorientated** Both are correct although some people feel *disoriented* is American. Nevertheless *disoriented* is often used in Britain, because it's easier to say. Remember the words have two shades of meaning: to lose a sense of physical direction ('the familiar landmarks had gone and she was *disorientated*, not knowing which road to take'), and to be mentally off balance ('she was *disorientated* by the bright lights and loud music').

disp (disputed) Oxford dictionaries, and some others, have come up with a new cautionary label: *disp*, short for *disputed*. This is a warning that a particular definition, usage, or pronunciation might be objected to by some people, even though it may follow general practice. As time goes by and new editions of dictionaries appear, editors have to decide whether every *disp* label is still justified. Serious users of English have to make the same decision: at what point do we accept that a departure from correct usage has become standard? For when most reasonable and literary writers and speakers accept a usage as normal, the fact that a few linguistic **Colonel Blimps** continue to make a song and dance about it hardly warrants a *disp*.

dispassionate See deadpan . . .

dispatch or **despatch** The spelling *despatch* appeared in Johnson's famous *Dictionary* (1755), although he chose to use *dispatch* in his other writings. Johnson had so much authority that *despatch* continues to be listed as a variant spelling. The *OED* prefers *dispatch*, which is the spelling most used now. Whatever the spelling, the pronunciation remains 'disPATCH'.

displace, **replace** or **substitute** *Replace* is a less emotive word than *displace*, for sooner or later everybody and most things have to be *replaced*. The word is used especially when something new or up-to-date supersedes something worn out or lost: employees are replaced when they retire, batteries are replaced when they are spent, possessions are replaced when they are lost.

Displace is more highly charged because it suggests removing by force: governments are displaced by military coups, people are displaced by machines, ministers are displaced when they are sacked but *replaced* when they resign.

With *replace* there is something else to look out for. When, for example, you replace things on a desk, it could mean putting back the same things, or different things altogether. In some cases, you have to spell it out to make sure everyone knows which you mean, or simply use the words 'put back' or *substitute*.

display In this age of visual communication, *display* is the all-purpose word for any visual presentation of information, whether it is on a blackboard, flip-chart or overhead projector, although it is used most of all for information on screens linked to computers.

disposal or **disposition** *Disposal* is the noun corresponding to 'dispose of', used (other than in particular applications, such as 'the disposal of property under a will') for getting rid of or getting out of the way: *disposal* of rubbish, waste *disposal*. . . . *Disposition* is the noun corresponding to 'dispose', meaning to arrange or put in order. When everything is arranged in a room, it is the disposition of the furniture. When furniture is sold or stored, it is the disposal of it.

At your disposal and *at your disposition*, are used to mean available whenever you need someone or something: 'I am at your disposal, should you need further advice'; 'the funds are at your disposition'. 'At your disposal' is the more usual form now, although both expressions are somewhat old-worldly, more appropriate to courtly firms of family solicitors.

'disPUTE' or 'DISpute' With some words, such as **defect**, different syllables are stressed depending on whether it is a *noun* or a *verb*. Most speakers agree that this does not apply to *dispute*: it should always be 'disPUTE', whether it's a dispute with someone or you dispute something. Some dictionaries do show stress on the *first* syllable as an alternative for the *noun*, but it is more acceptable to keep the stress on the *second* syllable for both noun and verb. (It should be noted that most trade union leaders, who make a special claim to this of all words, prefer 'DISpute'.)

disquieting, **disturbing** or **upsetting** These all describe states of anxiety and distress but the subtleties of difference contribute to sensitivity of expression. Examples cannot be precise but the following are indications of degree, which individuals can evaluate for themselves: it could be *disquieting* if we mislay an important letter or someone is late; *disturbing* if we lose our wallet or a friend is unhappy; *upsetting* if our car has been stolen or a friend has been taken seriously ill. Although not everyone will agree with those gradations, they are based on the views of a number of careful and experienced writers and broadcasters, and are intended as a guide.

dissatisfied or **unsatisfied**   *Dissatisfied* is a state of mind, when something has not come up to expectations; *unsatisfied* is when there isn't enough and a need has not been met. We are dissatisfied by dinner when the food is disappointing: we are unsatisfied if we are still hungry!

dissertation or **thesis**   In British universities a *thesis* is the more solemn word: it goes back to the Greek word for a proposition, and is usually a long detailed exposition on a subject, presented for a doctorate. A *dissertation* is from the Latin word, to discuss, and is usually a more modest treatment of a subject, submitted as part of the requirements at some universities for a first degree, at others for a higher degree.

dissident   *Dissident* has been used since the 18th century for a person who makes a stand against generally agreed policy or opinion. It became used, particularly after World War II, for opponents of the communist regime in the USSR, notably Alexander Solzhenitsyn and Andrei Sakharov. It has since become a term in British politics as well for anyone refusing to toe the party political line. In this context, it is used more about the Labour than the Conservative Party: Conservatives seem to prefer 'Tory *rebels*', suggesting opposition to certain policies, rather than an independent idealism, which *dissident* suggests.

dissociate or **disassociate**   *Dissociate* is not a more recent adaptation, as is often supposed, because the Latin word is 'dissociare'. Most dictionaries allow both forms, but *dissociate* is the one to use, as *disassociate* is on its way to becoming obsolete, which is just as well because a string of *s* sounds is awkward.

distance (as a verb)   Political journalists fall back on *distance* as a way of saying that a minister or a party sidesteps embarrassment by behaving as if they have nothing to do with an extremist point of view, a **maverick** party member, or with anything else that might require an awkward explanation. They are said to *distance* themselves from whoever or whatever it is.

distinct or **distinctive**   The line between *distinct* and *distinctive* can be uncertain. A soap may have a *distinct* smell of roses, that is a definite, perhaps even strong rose scent; soap with a *distinctive* smell of roses has a scent easily identified as belonging to roses (rather than to any other flowers). If something is not *distinct* it means we cannot be sure what it is; if it

is not *distinctive*, it means it does not seem truly characteristic of what it is supposed to be.

distingué(e)   See distinguished . . .

distinguish   See differentiate . . .

distinguished or **distinguished-looking**   'Look at that *distinguished* woman', someone might say, which could mean one of two things. It is a way of saying that she is a famous and eminent woman, or that the woman *looks* as if she is eminent, that is *distinguished-looking*. In a straight statement, such as 'he is very distinguished', there is only one interpretation, which is that the man is truly eminent. Otherwise we should say *distinguished-looking*, or *distingué* (*distinguée* for a woman). This French word (pron: 'diSTANgay'), has been part of English since the early 19th century; for many of us, it goes with a monocle or lorgnette as an affected alternative to *distinguished-looking*.

distrait or **distraught**   If you are *distrait* (pron: 'disTRAY'), your mind is elsewhere because you are worried about something. Some Francophiles follow French grammar, using *distraite* (pron: 'disTRETT') about a woman, and there are current dictionaries that support this distinction. But generally *distrait* is now a unisex word in English.
  Distraught (pron: 'disTRAWT') is a stronger word, suggesting extreme worry and agitation.

'disTRIBute' or **'DIStribute'**   Dictionaries offer stress on the *first* syllable as an alternative pronunciation. It is better avoided, as many people consider it wrong.

distributor or **distributer**   It is wrong to use a different spelling for a person or company dealing in certain specified brands and the device in an engine for relaying electric current to sparking plugs. Both end in *-or*. (The word *distributer* does not exist.)

distrust or **mistrust**   In most cases it doesn't matter in the slightest which word is used about a person, an organization, motives, intentions. . . . But if it is about ability, *mistrust* is the more usual alternative: 'I mistrust my ability to see this through'; 'I mistrust his understanding of the situation'.

disturbing   See disquieting . . .

diurnal   See daily . . .

divergence   See discrepancy . . .

diverse or **divers**   *Diverse* is the only word we need be concerned with to describe different or varied qualities ('she has diverse talents'). *Divers* used to have a similar meaning, as well as meaning 'several' or 'some', but is now labelled by dictionaries as archaic or literary, and so out of place in everyday language.

diversification Before World War II, a company usually remained in the same line of business seemingly from here to eternity. Since then, the rate of technological change, movements in public needs and taste, the development of new world markets have turned many old-established businesses into dodos, with demand for their products or services shrinking. *Diversification* became the new word in industry for moving into completely different areas of trading, usually by acquisitions of other businesses, sometimes by the development of new resources within the same company.

dividend or **yield** Both terms represent the financial return received from shares, but the difference is important. *Dividend* is straightforward: it is the payment, usually paid annually, to holders of shares and expressed as a percentage of the *nominal value* (see **face value** . . .) of the shares (see also **cum**). *Yield* expresses the dividend as a percentage of the price paid for the shares. As an example, a dividend of 10 per cent on a share with a nominal value of £100 would be £10, but if someone paid £200 for the share, that same dividend represents a *yield* of 5 per cent.

division of words The division of a word, with part at the end of one line and the rest at the beginning of the next, is always a nuisance to readers. If it is unavoidable, the aim should be to disrupt the flow for readers as little as possible. Here are some useful principles:

1 Keep prefixes and suffixes intact: aero- space, atmo- sphere, bio- degradable, para- military, re- invest, xero- graphy. . . .

2 When consonants and vowels are pronounced as one sound, keep them together: de*bt*- ors, o*ph*- thalmology, wa*sh*- ability, b*eau*- tiful, s*ou*- venir. . . .

3 The following endings can be carried over:

-cial(ly)	(ra- *cially*)
-ing	(develop- *ing*)
-ism	(commun- *ism*)
-ist	(activ- *ist*)
-logy	(psycho- *logy*)
-logist	(bio- *logist*)

4 Words with similar beginnings do not necessarily break in the same place – check on pronunciation and sense: man- gonel but mango- steen; tran- scend but trans- port.

5 Look out for parts of words left in embarrassing isolation. Here are some unfelicitous examples that have appeared: reap- pear, the- rapist, leg- end.

6 It is awkward, if unavoidable sometimes, to break a word at the end of a line, but inexcusable (even if it happens in this book!) to divide a word at the bottom of a page and continue it on the next. Readers may not have a union to protect them, but they still have rights.

divorcee or **divorcé(e)** To use the French words, *divorcé* for a man, *divorcée* for a woman, goes back to the time when divorce was a scandal, so un-British that it required a French word, accents and all. In the 1990s, when almost one in three marriages in Britain end in divorce, a unisex word is called for – *divorcee*.

DNA See **genes** . . .

DNA profiling This is the term in forensic medicine for what popular journalism calls *genetic fingerprinting*. See **genes** . . .

DOC (Italian wines) See **appellation controlée**

dockland or **Dockland** The *dockland* is the area of wharfs, warehouses and usually run-down buildings near the docks of a city. Americans refer to it as the **waterfront**. With a capital D, *Dockland* was born in the mid-1980s: it is the spectacular development of office blocks and expensive houses and flats, replacing the slums of London's dockland.

docter or **physician** Fifty years ago, a *doctor* would have been assumed to be a medical practitioner, for in Britain it was not considered good form for holders of non-medical doctorates, such as PhD, DSc, etc, to use the title other than in academic circles. In most other countries, *doctor* has always been used for anyone with a doctorate in any subject. Britain has now followed suit: there are doctors all over the place, most of whom know nothing about 'coughs and sneezes and all kinds of diseases'. Anyone who gains a doctorate now expects to be introduced as Dr So-and-so, even if they are sometimes asked 'Are you a *real* doctor?' For most of us still associate *doctor* with a man or woman with a stethoscope.

A medical practitioner is called *doctor* even if they only hold a bachelor's degree in medicine. Paradoxically, a *doctor* of medicine becomes *Mr*, *Mrs* or *Ms* when they take up a post as a surgeon in a hospital, which is a peculiar kind of inverted medical class-distinction. To complicate it further, every medical practitioner in Britain has to qualify as a surgeon, which explains why they call their consulting room a **surgery**.

Lastly, anyone legally qualified to practise medicine or surgery is a *physician*. But in practice the term *physician* is usually reserved for medical specialists, who see patients in their consulting rooms, rather than their surgeries.

The medical profession is loaded with linguistic protocol, and patients, who pay the bills, are firmly put in their place if they get the terminology wrong.

document A *document* is a solemn word for an important record on paper of evidence or an agreement. It has been taken over by **wordprocessing** for any section of text, even a few short lines, treated as a single unit.

documentary or **cinéma-vérité** These two approaches to making films are very similar but the terms should not be used interchangeably. *Cinéma-vérité* (literally 'cinema truth') is applied to an ideal style of recording actuality, even if it is reconstructed, not using professional actors and allowing the camera to record free from interruption and contrivance. *Documentary*, a term first used by John Grierson, the leading British director of documentary films in the 1930s, uses film techniques, including actors sometimes, to give a factual, if dramatized, account of an aspect of human life or of a social or political issue.

A *fly-on-the-wall documentary* expresses exactly what it is: a documentary made without script or recourse to reconstruction, with the camera a supposedly unobtrusive 'fly on the wall'. *Cinéma-vérité* is a particular approach to film, *documentary* is using film for a particular purpose.

document retrieval Computer language for locating and displaying on the screen the complete text of an item stored in the system.

DoE Some unexplained quirk decrees that in the UK Ministry of Defence is abbreviated to MOD, but the Department of the Environment is *DoE*, with a small *o*. The DoE extends the meaning of **environment** beyond its usual limits, since its responsibilities include the relationship between national and local government.

doesn't See **contracted forms**

dog-collar *Dog-collar* for a clerical collar is friendly, rather than disrespectful, and clergymen often use it among themselves. But it is becoming an old-fashioned term, not used as often as it used to be.

dogged Pronounced as *one* syllable ('doggd') it is the past form of the verb meaning to follow closely or pursue, in the way of a hunting dog ('their every move was dogged by misfortune'): as *two* syllables ('dog-ged') it is the descriptive word meaning determined or persistent (*dogged* pursuit).

dogma and **dogmatic** Originally *dogma* was a valid term in the Christian Church for the tenets of the faith, religious truths beyond question, and it is still used that way in theology. But the bad meaning of *dogma* and *dogmatic* have taken over: in any context it is likely that the words would be taken to mean narrow, rigid, arrogantly authoritative.

(la) dolce vita Using foreign expressions unnecessarily can sound affected, but this one, which we learned in the 1960s from Fellini's film, *La Dolce Vita* ('the sweet life'), is justified because there's no good alternative in English. The 'good life' suggests a life of quality and happiness, whereas *la dolce vita* is out-and-out self-indulgence. Fellini's film opens with a helicopter jaunt over the ancient ruins of Rome. Women in bikinis wave from a roof garden; from the helicopter Marcello Mastroianni shouts for their telephone numbers . . . all part of la dolce vita. (Pron: 'DOHLtchay VEEtah'.)

(the) dole The *dole*, for something doled out, goes back to the 14th century. It was first used soon after World War I for relief paid to people out of work. The dole has never been replaced by the camouflage of euphemisms, such as 'social security' and 'unemployment benefit', and remains the most popular of all expressions, especially among people in *dole queues*.

domiciliary visit This is bureaucratic window-dressing for a 'home visit' by doctors or social workers.

don *Don*, from Latin 'dominus', lord, and a Spanish title (*Don* Juan), was first used for senior fellows of Oxford and Cambridge colleges in the 17th century. The word is rarely used for the teaching staff of other universities, and while it is still heard in the *High* at Oxford or by the *Backs* at Cambridge, dons are now more likely to be called *fellows* (when it applies) at **Oxbridge**, or **academics**, the word for professors and lecturers at universities anywhere in the world.

donkey, ass or **mule** Zoologists may use *ass* for the wild African and Asian varieties, and *donkey* for the domestic animal. But in general use, *donkey* and *ass* are used for the same long-eared animal of the horse family, with *donkey* as the usual name, particularly with children. Both words are also used to mean a fool ('a silly ass', 'a stupid donkey').

A *mule* is different: correctly this is the offspring of a male donkey and a female horse, although it is often used for any cross-breed of a horse and donkey. Like *ass* and *donkey*, there are human mules too: obstinate people are *mulish*.

don't See **contracted forms**

doodle Few films have made a permanent contribution to the English language. When Gary Cooper scribbled absentmindedly in a court scene in *Mr Deeds Goes to Town* (1936), and called it *doodling*, the word soon passed into dictionaries as standard English on both sides of the Atlantic. Doodles are the scribbles or drawings we make while on the telephone, when we're trying to think of something, or at any time we're bored, nervous or preoccupied.

doorkeeper, doorman, porter or **janitor** All four words can be used for a man posted near the door of a building to usher people in and prevent unauthorized persons from entering. *Doorman* and *doorkeeper* derive from Old English; *porter* relates to Latin 'porta', a city-gate (the other meaning of *porter* derives from Latin 'portare', to carry), and *janitor* comes from 'janua', Latin for door.

Which word is used depends on tradition and custom. The Ritz has a *doorman*, a factory is more likely to have a *doorkeeper* and so does the stage door of a theatre. Oxford and Cambridge colleges and clubs in Pall Mall have *porters*. *Janitor* has been used for a doorkeeper since the 17th century, but if used now in British English, is most likely to be in the American sense of the caretaker of a building.

dope See **cannabis** . . .

DOS In computer language DOS (an **acronym**, so pronounced 'doss') is used for any disk operating system which is the basis of handling information on disks (see **disc**). The initials of the particular system usually precede DOS, as in MS/DOS (**M**icrosoft **D**isk **O**perating **S**ystem).

dot matrix A dot matrix printer is one of the types of printer that can be linked to a computer. The characters are formed by a pattern of dots, which gives more flexibility but a less sharp definition. See also **daisywheel; laser**

dots (. . .) A row of dots (traditionally three) is a linguistic device to help out in a number of situations. Here is a key to them:

1 In the middle of a quotation, . . . shows that one or more words, or a sentence, or even a paragraph, is omitted. This may be to make the quotation shorter, or to leave out something that does not make the required point. They enable whoever is quoting to leave out whatever they like, without reproach, but it can enable the context to be concealed, which is in its way a form of misquoting.

2 . . . is frequently used in *The Good English Guide* to show that a list continues, a typographical alternative to 'etc': 'a variety of vegetables, carrots, peas, beans, spinach . . . .

3 . . . can mark a pause in dialogue: 'Come up for a drink . . . don't worry, there are no strings attached!' During a rehearsal of his play, *The Homecoming*, Harold Pinter, whose plays are known, among other things, for dramatic pauses, reprimanded an actor, 'You're playing *two* dots; if you check in the script you'll find it's *three*'.

4 If a **four-letter word** is considered so obscene as to be unusable, it is apparently in order to write the first letter and place a typographical veil over the next three letters: c . . ., f . . . . This device is still used, although full frontal exposure is more usual now. Bernard Levin, in his column in *The Times*, scorned the notion that a handful of dots could leave the most obscene and licentious words 'entirely robbed of their dreadful power, able to be read by the most sensitive souls without harm or danger'.

The literary name for three dots used in this way is an *ellipsis*.

double-barrelled It is easy to see why *double-barrelled* should be used about shotguns, but more puzzling why it came to be used about two names linked with a hyphen. The *double-barrel* treatment (which apparently did not exist before the 18th century) can give very ordinary names, such as Jones or Smith, a snob value (Harvey-Jones, Smith-Cresswell . . .). Some women are giving another angle to double-barrelled names: when they marry they link their own and their husband's surnames together, sometimes putting one first, sometimes the other, to create for themselves and their children a new double-barrelled name. When their daughters eventually marry, we might even see triple-barrelled names. Somewhere along the line, it would have to stop.

double entendre This linguistic curiosity is French, of course, but is not used in France, where they say 'double entente'. It appeared in English in the 17th century and is established, useful for describing an expression that sounds innocent but which has an unmistakable sexual innuendo.

Double entendres are not always intentional: during an official visit to London by Mikhail Gorbachev, John Wakeham, then Leader of the House of Commons, was asked to list the Prime Minister's engagements. He read out his brief: 'She is making herself available to the Soviet leader'. File that away as a copybook example of an off-the-cuff double entendre.

double helix See **genes** . . .

double negatives At one time two negatives were used in English, as they still are in some other languages, to intensify a negative meaning. But the *double negative* is now regarded as a stock example of uneducated speech: 'I did*n't* do *nothing*'; 'He do*n't* know *nothing* about it'. Those are obvious examples, but *double negatives* have a way of creeping in unnoticed: see **barely**, **hardly** and **scarcely**, negative words easily and mistakenly combined with a second negative.

'I shouldn't wonder if . . .' and 'I shouldn't be surprised if . . .' are so often followed by a second negative, even in educated speech, that perhaps it is fussing to object: 'I should*n't* be surprised if it did*n't* rain' is correct without the second negative: 'I shouldn't be surprised if it did rain'.

There are times when a double negative is not only correct but useful in order to provide an in-between meaning: '*not infrequently*' is not quite the same as 'frequently' but somewhere between 'frequently' and 'infrequently'. There is further discussion of this under **meiosis**.

In other cases, two negatives are deliberately used to create a positive, at the same time avoiding a questionable direct statement. In 1991, a new brand of margarine was introduced, called *I Can't Believe It's Not Butter*. That says, in effect, 'I believe it's butter'.

Double negatives have a place in the good use of English, when you know how to handle them to achieve a particular nuance or effect. At other times, they can be a linguistic deadly sin.

double-page spread In printing, a double-page spread is two facing pages considered as a single unit, from the left of the left-hand page to the right of the right-hand page. Advertisers can buy a double-page spread in a newspaper or magazine so that their advertisement has greater impact by filling two pages facing each other.

doublespeak, doubletalk, doublethink, gobbledygook or newspeak Words have always been used not only to reveal the truth but to cover it up, or to dress up banal ideas in impressive language. *Gobbledygook* was one of the first words to be invented to describe the process. *The Shorter Oxford English Dictionary* is convinced it was conjured up by Maury Maverick from Texas. Others claim it was President Roosevelt's brainchild. *Gobbledygook* does not necessarily mean the devious use of language: it is official or academic writing and speaking that buries meaning under polysyllabic incomprehensibility. In case that sounds like *gobbledygook*, all it means is – using too many long words.

Doublespeak and *doubletalk* are more sinister: they are double-dealing in words, using language to doublecross people. *Doublespeak* is used when it is written or spoken, *doubletalk* is more for spoken language. They do not mean unintelligent use of language, as *gobbledygook* might. They are words carefully chosen and contrived in 'defence of the indefensible ... to make lies sound truthful and murder respectable, and to give an appearance of solidity to pure wind' (George Orwell, *Politics and the English Language*, 1946). George Orwell's novel, *Nineteen Eighty-Four* (1949), extended the idea to *doublethink*, describing the ability to believe in two concepts, even though they contradict each other, demonstrating it with the slogan 'War is Peace'. *Newspeak* is also **Orwellian**, from the same novel, official state language designed to re-present facts to suit the party line. *Newspeak* has become a term for doublespeak used at press briefings, when information is carefully doctored to obscure what is really happening. See also **disinformation; euphemism** ...; **plain English;** (language of) **war; politically correct**

doubling final letter before -ed and -ing Some people have to think twice whether, for example, it is developed, developing or 'developped', 'developping', particularly as American practice often differs from British English (traveled, traveling instead of travelled, travelling). The following simple rules are worth reading through to save unnecessary checking with a dictionary. *Note*: 3 is the most useful rule, since it covers many words that people often hesitate over.

1 Most words of *one syllable*, ending with a single consonant, *double* the consonant before *-ed* or *-ing*. It is usually obvious from the pronunciation: fit – fitted, fitting; pit – pitted, pitting; ship – shipped, shipping. . . .

2 With words of *more than one* syllable, ending with *one* consonant, listen to the stress pattern. If the *final* syllable is stressed, the consonant is usually doubled: allot ('aLOT') – allotted, allotting; omit ('oMIT') – omitted, omitting; remit ('reMIT') – remitted, remitting. . . . But with words ending in more than one consonant, the second one is not usually doubled: repent ('rePENT') – repented, repenting; suggest ('sugGEST') – suggested, suggesting. . . .

3 With words of more than one syllable, *not* stressed on the last syllable, the final consonant is not usually doubled – unless it is *l*: ballot ('BALlot') – balloted, balloting; bracket ('BRACket') – bracketed, bracketing; focus ('FOcus') – focused, focusing (but see entry for **focus**), profit ('PROfit') – profited, profiting. . . .

4 Most words ending in *l* double the *l*, wherever the stress falls: bedevil – bedevilled, bedevilling; cancel – cancelled, cancelling; rebel – rebelled, rebelling (in American English most words ending in *l* like this do not double the *l*: bedeviled, traveling, canceling, labeling, etc.) Look out for **parallel**, which is the most common exception – paralleled, unparalleled.

doubt if, that or whether The prescribed distinction is as follows. *Whether* or *if* should be used in positive statements when there is doubt: 'I doubt *whether* (or *if*) she will marry him', meaning it is possible that she will but I don't think so. *That* should only follow a negative statement, and implies certainty: 'I have *no doubt* (or I *don't* doubt) *that* she will marry him', meaning I am sure she will.

There is no doubt that *that* should always follow negative statements, as above, but with positive statements, it may be too punctilious to insist on *whether* or *if* and exclude *that*. 'I doubt that' is the usual form in American English, and is now so common in British English, that it is doubtful *whether*, *if* or *that* the distinction can be justified any longer.

dour This should be pronounced as *one* syllable, rhyming with 'moor', rather than making it sound like 'dow-er'. It is a 14th-century Scottish word, meaning severe or stern, so if you can say it with a Scottish accent, it will sound even more authentic.

douse or dowse *Douse* is the usual spelling for the verb meaning to throw water over something (douse a fire). Some dictionaries show *dowse* as an alternative spelling, but this is rare. It could also lead to confusion, since *dowse* is the verb for water-divining, searching for hidden springs by holding a divining-rod, also known as a dowsing-rod.

doves and hawks Doves make a soft cooing sound and have been a symbol of peace since one brought back tidings to Noah that the Flood had subsided. So the name has been borrowed for politicians who prefer diplomacy and restraint in foreign affairs, as against *hawks*, for politicians who are trigger-happy. (Thomas Jefferson used *'war hawks'*, in 1798, for Americans overeager to declare war on France.)

doves or **pigeons**   Doves and pigeons belong to the same family of birds. *Pigeons* is the usual name for the wild birds, *doves* for domesticated pigeons, kept in *dovecots*.

Dow-Jones Index   This is a figure based on a selection of typical share prices on the New York Stock Exchange. It goes up and down as unpredictably as a nervous yo-yo, but is nevertheless taken to be one of the key financial indicators of the world. *Dow-Jones* is correctly hyphenated, since it combines and commemorates the names of two American statisticians, Charles H Dow (died 1902) and Edward D Jones (died 1920).

downmarket and **upmarket**   These are words bandied about in advertising agencies to describe products or advertising aimed at the lower or upper social ends of the market. Both terms have become extended beyond marketing, as ways to describe styles, fashions, habits. So a dinner-party might be called *upmarket* if caviare, or even smoked salmon, is served, or *downmarket* if it's sausages and mash.

downside   Even recent dictionaries are slow to catch up with *downside*, a word frequently used in connection with investments. The *downside risk* is an estimate of the most you can lose, so you know where you stand even if things go badly wrong.

downstage or **upstage**   When an actor moves *upstage*, that is towards the back of the stage, other actors have to turn their backs on the audience: they are *upstaged*. Outside the theatre, *upstage* is a good way to describe someone stealing the show in any situation and by any trick: 'her fantastic dress upstaged every other woman at the reception'.

Downstage in the theatre is the front of the stage near the footlights. Unlike *upstage*, it is used mostly in stage directions, rather than in other situations.

down to or **up to**   1 *Direction*: travelling from London to Edinburgh, for example, is undeniably going *up* to Edinburgh. But the custom is to go *up* to London, whichever direction you're travelling in, perhaps because it's the capital. This is usage rather than a rule, and if you live in the North of England and prefer to go *down* to London, so be it.

Oxbridge is a special case. To go *up* to Oxford or Cambridge is to enter the university. No matter which direction they are travelling, members of those universities will say they're going *up*. This is an old tradition, with a touch of intellectual arrogance about it, for the idea of going *down* to Oxford, even from John o'Groat's, is unthinkable!

2 *To express responsibility*: the usual idiom is 'it's *up to* so-and-so to decide'. For some reason, it has become trendy to reverse it: younger people are quite likely to say 'in the end, it's *down to* you to decide'. Whatever the explanation for this, it seems that we have a choice now of expressing responsibility for something as being *up to* someone or *down to* them.

downtown, **midtown** or **uptown**   These terms for different parts of a city are still American and have not made a serious bid to cross the Atlantic. They are familiar words from American films, songs and books but not often understood. *Downtown* is the commercial part of a city, where most of the important offices are found. *Uptown* is more residential, but not as far out as the suburbs. *Midtown*, as you would expect, is somewhere in between, and includes the central shopping streets.

downturn   See **depression** . . .

down under   *Down under* used to be a common expression for Australia, when that country seemed to be at the edge of the world. With the development of instant communication and fast regular air services, making Australia as much a part of the world scene as any country in Europe, *down under* has become a quaint term from the past, used whimsically on occasions.

downward or **downwards**   *Downward* is better as the descriptive word: a downward trend. *Downwards* is better after a verb: it leads downwards.

dowry   Men used to expect a bride to bring with her a *dowry*, property or money bestowed by her father. It still happens, but it is less likely now to be called a dowry. After all, in some cases, a bride's dowry may well be her flat or house, which her husband moves into.

doyen and **doyenne**   *Doyen* relates to the old 14th-century title of 'dean' as head of a cathedral chapter, and has been used for centuries to refer to the senior member within a group of official bodies, such as the senior ambassador in a country. Since the 19th century, *doyen* and the feminine equivalent *doyenne* have been used more generally for the most longstanding and respected of any group of people, such as 'the doyenne of London literary agents', 'the doyen of advisers on foreign policy'.

Doyen is pronounced 'DOYenne', or with the near-French pronunciation 'DWAHyeh(n)'. *Doyenne* follows the same pattern: 'DOYenne' or 'DWAHyenne'.

doze or **snooze**   *Doze* is standard English (probably of Scandinavian origin), going back to the 17th century. *Snooze* is unreasonably classed as colloquial by dictionaries, although it has been in use since the 18th century (it sounds like a fusing of 'snore' and 'doze'). What's more, it's the *snooze* button, not the *doze* button, on digital alarm clocks that allows you to snatch a few minutes extra in bed before you really have to get up.

draft or **draught** It is easy to be confused over which to use. In Britain we *draft* legal documents, treaties, a letter, a preliminary sketch for a design or a plan for carrying out a project. The legal document, treaty, etc becomes a *draft*. But we drink *draught* beer and do not like sitting in a *draught*. In America *draft* is the usual spelling for *all* those uses. A *draftsman* or *draftswoman* draws up legal documents, and a *draughtsman* or *draughtswoman* does drawings. It sounds complicated but the above guidelines are reliable, even though there are variations on both sides of the Atlantic. One last point: a game of *draughts* in Britain is a game of 'checkers' in America.

draft quality The term is usually applied to **dot matrix** printers. When switched to *draft quality*, the printer operates at maximum speed with a loss of printing quality, although the result is adequate for copies used for comment or amendment. See also **letter quality**

drag The slang meanings may seem puzzling. A man in woman's clothing is in *drag* – but *not* the other way round. This usage goes back further than people think: in the mid-19th century, *drag* referred to the long petticoats which dragged along the ground, worn by actors in women's roles. When someone or something is a *drag*, they are boring and heavy-going, good slang because the word sounds like its meaning.

dramatic or **poetic licence** *Dramatic licence* relates to telling a story, and is used to justify embellishing the facts to make the story more interesting or exciting. The expression is sometimes used as a half-apologetic excuse for adorning the actual event with more fiction than facts. It should not go as far, as it sometimes does, as justifying distortion of the truth for an ulterior motive.

Poetic licence is the privilege of a writer or artist to depart from established usage of words or forms in the pursuit of creativity. The expression is sometimes used, with a half-smile, to justify exaggerating about anything for any reason. Even poets and painters have used *poetic licence* to try to get away with a literary or artistic confidence trick.

drank, **drunk** or **drunken** 'I *drink* today, I *drank* yesterday, and when I have *drunk* too much, I am *drunk*'. The main use of *drunken* is as a descriptive word: 'What shall we do with the drunken sailor?' But note that *drunken* suggests habitual drunkenness (his drunken ways), so it is often better to use *drunk* as the descriptive word: 'the drunk sailors lurched back to their ship'. See also **drink-driving** . . .

draught See draft . . .

drawer We open a drawer (*one* syllable, the same sound as 'draw'). Drawer, for a person who writes out a cheque or does drawings, has *two* syllables ('drawer'). See also **intrusive *r* sound**

drawing-room See sitting-room . . .

dreamt or **dreamed** Either will do: 'I dreamt last night' or 'I dreamed last night'. Some people feel *dreamt* is the more educated form, and it is shown as the preferred alternative by some dictionaries.

dream ticket *Dream ticket* began as a political expression for the ideal leadership combination that offers party unity and the prospect of winning the next election. It was used in 1983, when Neil Kinnock became leader of the Labour Party and Roy Hattersley became deputy leader, a balancing act between the left and right of the Party, and was used again about the leadership election for the Labour Party in 1992, for John Smith as leader and Margaret Beckett as deputy. *Dream ticket* is also used about combinations outside politics that promise success.

The opposite of a *dream ticket* is a **nightmare scenario**.

dress or **frock** *Frock* has had a good innings, as it was used for a garment with a skirt as far back as the 14th century. *Dress* has taken over now, leaving *frock* on the shelf, likely to become obsolete by the end of the century. But clergymen are still *defrocked*.

dressmaker See couturier . . .

drier or **dryer** Some dictionaries give *drier* as the spelling, with *dryer* as a variant, others reverse that order. So either spelling can be used, whether it means an appliance that dries something, such as a hair *drier*, or to say that something is *drier* than something else. If anything, there seems to be a slight preference for *drier*. A useful distinction (not recognized by most dictionaries) is to use *dryer* for an appliance, and *drier* as a descriptive word: 'this is a drier wine'.

drily or **dryly** Either spelling is acceptable but there is a distinct preference for *drily*, at least in British English.

drink-driving or **drunk-driving** These two clumsy expressions are interchangeable as the common term for the offence of driving with over the legal limit of alcohol in the blood: 'convicted of drink-driving (or drunk-driving)'. The descriptive term *drink-drive* usually means '*anti*-drink-driving': 'the police's latest drink-drive campaign'.

drizzle or **shower** A *drizzle* is fine rain that goes on continuously for some time; a *shower* can be quite heavy, even sleet or hail, but is brief or intermittent. A *drizzle* is more likely to stop play at cricket, a *shower* more likely to hold it up.

drop a clanger See faux pas . . .

drop out and **drop-out** Timothy Leary, a former professor at Harvard, gave *drop out* a particular meaning. He started a cult in America in the 1960s, promoting spiritual enlightenment through the use of **LSD**, with the slogan, 'Turn on, tune in and drop out'. A *drop-out* became someone who followed that advice. The expressions are no longer associated with drugs: people who decide not to continue a degree course, or to give up a well-paid career, or to change a conventional way of life in order to farm in Wales, take up thatching, join a commune, etc may be said to drop out, but are seldom any longer called *drop-outs*.

The verb *drop out* and the noun *drop-out* are still vaguely pejorative for a lot of people, suggesting living on social security and shirking responsibilities. That may be true of many *drop-outs*, but others may be free spirits refusing to be engulfed by the tidal wave of conformity.

drug abuse *Drug abuse* is the fashionable sociological jargon for drug addiction. Like *alcohol abuse*, it has become the preferred term used by health authorities and the media. The term is also used for taking steroids or other drugs by athletes in order to improve performance.

drugs or **narcotics** *Drugs* are chemical compounds that disturb the normal functioning of the body. Many drugs can be bought over the counter in a chemist: analgesics, such as aspirin, are mild drugs. There are so-called 'social drugs', such as caffeine (in tea, coffee and chocolate) or nicotine (in cigarettes). But in general use, the word *drugs* is reserved for the illegal drugs, notably **cannabis, cocaine and heroin**. (It should be noted that some doctors regard smoking cigarettes or heavy drinking as forms of drug addiction.)

Narcotics is often used in an indeterminate way for any dangerous addictive drug. In fact, *narcotic* (which comes from the Greek word meaning 'to make numb') is a drug that induces sleep or a trance-like state, or relieves pain. Morphine is one of the familiar narcotics in medical use: the word *narcotic* was at one time used particularly about opium, which for much of the 19th century was freely available in almost any grocer's shop in Britain. See also **crack**

drunk, drunken See drank . . .

drunk-driving See drink-driving . . .

dry, medium or **medium dry (wines)** It is strange to describe wine and sherry, which are liquids, as *dry*, but it is a more sophisticated word than 'non-sweet'. *Medium dry* does not indicate a flavour halfway between non-sweet and sweet, as defined by most

dictionaries: it usually means a flavour more in the direction of dry, with a suggestion of sweetness. *Medium* is the usual way of describing the halfway taste. But describing flavour in words is always subject to personal taste, and there is often disagreement about what is *dry, medium* or *medium dry*.

dryer See drier . . .

dryly See drily . . .

DTP See **desktop publishing**

due to or **owing to** Countless words have been written in grammar books to explain that *due to* must always be used as an **adjective**, and that instead of saying 'Due to illness he was absent', we must say 'His absence was due to illness', so that *due to* 'qualifies' the word 'absence'.

This grammatical argument is not easy for everyone to follow, and there are good writers who feel nothing important is lost if they use *due to* in the same way as *owing to*: 'play was stopped due to rain'; 'due to a breakdown in negotiations, the strike started'. Some people consider those sentences ungrammatical, and would insist on 'the stoppage of play was due to . . .' or 'owing to a breakdown . . .'.

The grammatical debate over *due to* seems for many irrelevant, and they use *due to* as it suits them, knowing they are in good company. Others meticulously follow the grammarians' rules. If you are worried, you can always fall back on 'because of', as no one will ever throw a grammar book at you for that.

duffel *Duffel* (sometimes spelt 'duffle') was the name of a coarse woollen cloth made in the 17th century in Duffel, a town in the north of Belgium. A *duffel coat* became a worker's overcoat, warm, cheap and complete with a hood, as well as uniform in the Royal Navy. *Duffel* is moving upmarket, with *duffels* now in mock-fur and gunmetal satin, materials undreamt of by the worthy burghers of Duffel.

duly At one time letters and people *duly* arrived, cheques were *duly* sent, matters *duly* dealt with. . . . *Duly* hardly meant anything in such sentences, except to make them sound starchy and important. In the 1990s the word has been *duly* put away in the attic.

dumping As well as its other meanings, *dumping* is a trading term for selling goods cheaply in overseas markets, even below the production cost in the home market. This is sometimes ruthless opportunism, which can damage the economy of the importing country, hence *dumping*, never the most gracious of terms, is more often than not used in a bad sense.

durable goods *Durable goods* is used in marketing and consumer statistics for equipment in the home, such as cookers and washing machines, which are intended to last a long time. But see also **built-in obsolescence**

Durex or **durex**   The best-known brand name of **condom** in Britain is *Durex*. Because of this, *durex* (with a small *d*) has come to be used as a word for any condom. To save Australian readers writing to the publishers of *The Good English Guide*, it should be added that in Australia, *durex* is sometimes used for sticky tape, because Durex in that country is a well-known brand name for such a product.

duty   See tax . . .

duvet, **eiderdown** or **quilt**   A *quilt* is any padded bed-covering. Long ago, an *eiderdown* was a quilt stuffed with the soft down from the breast of an eider duck, and was thought of in Britain as continental and rather peculiar. The British used *eiderdown* for a satin-covered decorative quilt thrown over the blankets on a bed. They are no longer called *eiderdowns* much now, except perhaps by some older people.

In the 1950s, the so-called *continental quilt* began to catch on in Britain, a quilt with a zip-on cover that made bed-making so much easier because it replaced both the top sheet and blankets. Later, the name 'continental quilt' was replaced by the French word *duvet* (pron: 'DOOvay'). Surprisingly, duvets became all the rage, and thousands of blankets were stored away in chests or given to appeals for the homeless. Duvets may still be filled with feathers but can now also have synthetic foam stuffing, light-years away from the breast of an eider.

dwarfs or **dwarves**   Dictionaries show both as alternative plural forms, usually indicating (by listing it first) that *dwarfs* is the more usual. J R R Tolkien, the professor of English language at Oxford who wrote *The Hobbit*, a fantasy about dwarfs, commented, in a letter to his publisher, Stanley Unwin, '. . . I use throughout the "incorrect" plural *dwarves*. I am afraid it is just a piece of private bad grammar, rather shocking in a philologist; but I shall have to go on with it'.

dyke or **dike**   *Dyke* is the usual spelling for a low wall or bank built to prevent water flooding over, or for a ditch used for drainage. *Dike* is shown as a variant spelling in most dictionaries. *Dyke* was also a slang word for a lesbian, but not used much now.

dynamic(s)   *Dynamic* derives ultimately from a Greek word meaning power, so it should not be used lightly about a person, action, or a policy. It should suggest a driving motivation, forceful and effective: 'this is a dynamic policy that will sweep aside everything that obstructs it'. *Dynamics*, whether it is used about Newtonian mechanics or about human action, is usually treated as singular: 'the dynamics of this policy is . . .'.

dynasty   Because this is the title of one of the most popular American television series shown in Britain, the American pronunciation 'DINEasty' is increasingly heard. Nevertheless, the British pronunciation still prevails on this side of the Atlantic: 'DINNasty'.

dys-   See **Greek roots**

dyslexic or **dyslectic**   Dyslexia is now a much more familiar condition than it used to be (the word is not listed in most dictionaries published before 1960). It is a cause of writing and reading problems but, contrary to earlier beliefs, is in no way related to intelligence. Leonardo da Vinci, Edison and Einstein are all believed to have been *dyslectics*, which brings us to the next point. Some dictionaries are vague about the distinction between *dyslexic* and *dyslectic*, others only list *dyslexic*. *Dyslexic* is usually preferred for the descriptive word: a dyslexic student. Either form can be used for the noun: the student is a dyslectic (or a dyslexic).

· E ·

-eable   See **-able or -eable**

each   If you are uncertain about whether *each* is singular (each *has* . . .) or plural (each *have* . . .), here is a simple rule. When *each* comes *before* the word it relates to, treat it as singular: 'each of them *has* . . .', 'each of the players *was* . . .'. When *each* comes *after* the word it refers to, it should be plural: 'they each *were* . . .', 'London and New York each *have* many good restaurants'.
   Each one is always singular: 'each one of the women *is* . . .'. See also next entry; **either/5**

each and every   The textbook argument is that *each and every* should always be avoided, because 'each' *or* 'every' is sufficient on its own. That is true, although most people are quite happy about *over and above*. When we want to make something doubly clear, extra emphasis doesn't do any harm: 'Visitors have to pay an entrance fee each and every time they come here'. But most of the time choose either 'each' *or* 'every', and reserve *each and every* for when you want to thump the table.

each other or **one another**   Most authorities believe there is no justification for the old rule that *each other* refers to *two* persons or things, and *one another* to more than two: we can say 'they love each other' or 'they love one another'. The possessive is *each other's* (not *each others*'): 'we like each other's friends'.

eager   See **anxious** . . .

early bargains   See **after-hours dealings**

earned or **earnt**   A computer or sub-editor on *The Independent* should have picked up this mistake in an article about John Major (19.7.1991): 'His subsequent refusal to be hurried into announcing a replacement for the poll tax *earnt* him a reputation for "dithering" '. With the verb 'learn', there is a choice for the past form (see **learned or learnt**), but with 'earn' there is only one possible past form: *earned*.

Earth or **earth**   It is a useful distinction in some contexts to use *Earth* for the planet we occupy and *earth* for soil or the ground: 'we must protect the Earth we live on' but 'the seed was buried in the earth'. This is not obligatory, nor is it a rule followed by the Bible: 'The earth is the Lord's and the fulness thereof' (Psalm 24), and it hardly applies to everyday phrases, such as 'What on earth . . .?'; 'You look like nothing on earth!'

earth or **world**   The *earth* (or *Earth*) only refers to our planet, but we talk about other *worlds* in outer space, which usually implies planets that are inhabited by some form of life. In many cases it is custom that decides whether *earth* or *world* is used. *Earth* is more appropriate in connection with the **environment**, and in astronomical or spiritual senses: Friends of the Earth; the Earth Summit in Rio de Janeiro in 1992; the Earth orbits the sun. *World* is more for human activities, international affairs, and in geographical and political contexts: 'All the world's a stage' (*As You Like It*, Act II Sc vii); the nations of the world; the leaders of the world. . . .
   Earth is the more poetic word: 'the ends of the earth'; 'heaven on earth'; 'At the round earth's imagined corners . . .' (John Donne, *Holy Sonnets*). *World* is more materialistic: workers of the world; all the money in the world; the way of the world.
   On earth and *in the world* are often interchangeable: 'the greatest show on earth (or in the world)'. *On earth* is more transcendent and timeless: 'Mozart was the greatest composer on earth'. *In the world* is more specific, more here and now: 'he is the greatest tennis player in the world'. These are aspects of style, not rules of usage. See also previous entry

earthly or **earthy**   It is not unknown for *earthly* to be used when *earthy* is intended. *Earthly* relates to this earth as a planet: Anthony Burgess's novel, *Earthly Powers* (1980), is an international panorama of people running the world. *Earthy* is about the soil (earthy hands, that is hands with earth on them). By extension, *earthy* also means basic or crude (an earthy attitude, an earthy remark).

earthquakes   The terminology of earthquakes is used when they are reported, but rarely explained. The *epicentre* is the precise location on the surface of the earth directly above the centre of disturbance underground. (*Epicentre* is also used for the point directly above or below a nuclear explosion.) Charles Richter (1900–85), a Californian seismologist, achieved immortality, because his name is mentioned every time there is an earthquake anywhere in the world: the *Richter scale* (usually pronounced 'RIKter') devised in 1935 is the standard measurement for the magnitude of an earthquake. It is based on the highest reading recorded 100 kilometres from the epicentre: 7 is taken as a major earthquake, and the highest measurement ever recorded is 8.6.

earthy or **earthly**   See earthly . . .

easement   This 14th-century word survives in the 1990s mostly in property deeds or in discussions with neighbours. It is, in effect, another word for 'right of way' over someone else's land, which could include access to a path or a road, or the right to run pipes, etc under adjoining land.

East or **east**   See North, South, East, West . . .

east or **eastern**   See north or northern . . .

Eastern or **eastern**   With a small *e*, *eastern* is used for a general direction, instead of 'east': eastern France, the eastern shores of a lake. With a capital E, *Eastern* is often used about the spiritual teachings of India, China and Japan (Eastern religions). In other contexts *Eastern* can be ambiguous, as it could refer to the Near, Middle or Far East: it is better to avoid expressions, such as 'Eastern politics' or 'Eastern attitudes', and to choose a more specific description.

A capital or a small letter is used for the half of the world that includes Europe, Asia, and Africa: Eastern (or eastern) hemisphere. The time zones in the *eastern* United States, in *eastern* Canada and *eastern* Australia are known in those countries as *Eastern Time*.

eastward, **eastwards** or **easterly**   See northward, northwards or northerly . . .

eatable or **edible**   *Edible* means safe to eat (an edible mushroom); *eatable* implies that the taste is good enough. Something that is edible, if badly cooked, may not be eatable. Not everyone makes this distinction, although it is a useful one. It should always be observed for **inedible** and uneatable.

-eau   For the plural form of words with this ending, see French words ending in -eau.

EC, EEC, Common Market or **single market**   The *EEC* (*European Economic Community*) came first, with the avowed purpose of free trade, free movement of labour and capital, and common social and economic policies. On 25 March 1957, *the Six*, as they were called (Belgium, France, the German Federal Republic, Italy, Luxembourg and the Netherlands), signed the Treaty of Rome, which brought the EEC into being on 1 January 1958. Britain became a member on 1 January 1973. The *Common Market* was the popular name for the EEC; both names occur less often in the 1990s. As from midnight, 31 December 1992, when the remaining trade barriers came down, *single market* (without capitals) is the standard name, covering 320 million Euro-consumers, a third larger than the US market and more than twice the size of the market in Japan.

EC can have two meanings, which is sometimes confusing. The *European Community*, established in 1967, groups together a number of executive arms of the EEC and, through the Council of Ministers representing all member nations, is the main decision-making authority. The *European Commission* in Brussels is the policy-making and power-centre of the Community. Commissioners are the top *Eurocrats*, answerable to the European Parliament, members of which are elected in the separate member countries. See also **Eurospeak**

echelon   Even as late as the 1960s, there was still some objection to the use of *echelon* for levels of rank, importance, or social class (the upper echelon of society). The first meaning of *echelon* was a formation of aircraft, ships or troops in parallel lines, narrow at the front and widening out in the rear (a flight in echelon is triangular, with one aircraft leading).

Perhaps it is unnecessary to refer to the higher echelons in the army, instead of 'higher ranks', or the top echelons in a company, instead of directors and senior executives, but the use is so general that it is now given as the first meaning of the word in most current dictionaries. The word comes from French ('échelon' is the rung of a ladder).

echoes or **echos**   *Echos* used to be an alternative plural form but no longer. *Echoes* is the only plural now.

eclectic psychology   The three pre-eminent schools of psychoanalysis are **Freudian, Jungian** and Adlerian. There are some psychoanalysts who describe themselves as *eclectic psychologists*, that is they do not adhere to any one school but accept and use different teachings and approaches.

ecological balance   See balance of nature . . .

ecology or **environment**   When one of John Wyndham's characters said '. . . *ecology* – whatever that is' (*The Kraken Wakes*, 1953), the term was little known outside science. It was first used in the late 19th century for those aspects of biology dealing with the relationship between humans, animals and plants and their surroundings. Now, *ecology* is a **buzzword** for the *environment*, that is describing the physical surroundings of living things, rather than the relationship between them. There is a Faculty of the Environment at the Polytechnic of Central London, which offers postgraduate courses in architecture, structural engineering and town planning, which are now sometimes called the *built environment*.

Ecology properly relates surroundings to living organisms, hence courses of study, such as *botanical ecology* (the effect of changes in the environment on plants), *human ecology* (ways in which people are affected by the physical world around them), *behavioural ecology* (relating psychology to the environment).

Disasters, such as the nuclear fall-out arising from the accident in 1986 at the nuclear reactor in Chernobyl, or the burning of the oil wells during the 1991 Gulf War, are rightly called environmental disasters: the effects on people and agriculture are ecological issues.

To complicate it further, *environment* is used increasingly in trivial ways. 'We live in a nice environment' means no more than a pleasant road; and there's the little girl (quoted in Ernest Gowers' *Plain Words*) accusing her baby brother, who had wet his pants, of 'polluting his environment again'.

It is well worth keeping *ecology* and *environment* separate, *Environment* should be used for the **green** issues on the political agenda; *ecology* reserved for the study of and concern over how those issues affect life on earth.

economic or **economical**   When it's cheap at the price, or at least good value, use *economical*. Otherwise the proper word is *economic*. *Economical* is to do with stretching pounds or dollars as far as possible (an economical car); *Economic* relates to *economics*, the science of the production and distribution of wealth. An *economic summit* is a conference of heads of states on the international economy; an economical summit, if one ever took place, would still be a gathering of presidents and prime ministers, but done on the cheap, with beer and sandwiches instead of champagne and banquets.

The same distinction can apply to *uneconomic* and *uneconomical*, although both words usually mean the opposite of *economical*, that is to say wasteful or bad value for money. *Uneconomic* is more applicable to important projects, *uneconomical* an everyday word for small matters.

There is a choice of pronunciation of the first *e*: it can be pronounced *ee* ('eekoNOMic'), or like the *e* in 'egg' ('eckoNOMic'). Preference is for the *ee* sound, which may eventually take over.

economic sanctions   This is a diplomatic term for economic warfare, for it involves hostile measures. *Economic sanctions* are imposed when a country or an organization of countries, such as the United Nations, takes action against another country, disrupting or even destroying its economy by restricting or cutting off altogether imports and exports. Economic sanctions used against South Africa and against Iraq were as powerful in their way as tanks.

economics is or **are**   When it is the name for the academic theory or study, it is appropriate to treat it as singular, since it relates to 'the science of economics': 'economics is an important subject'; 'economics *does* not always provide an answer to a political problem'. When it describes practical applications, it is usually plural: 'the economics of this policy *are* . . .'; 'the economics of running a business *are* complicated'.

ecstasy or **extasy**   The Latin source is spelt with an *x* and 'extasie' was an earlier form in English. But now it is always *ecstasy*. *Ecstasy* has had various meanings in the past, including a state of religious possession, but it usually describes a transcendent feeling of joy.

With a capital E, *Ecstasy* became in the late 1980s the popular name for the so-called '**designer** drug' or 'love drug' that produces an intense sensation of loving everybody and everything about the world. In the long term, it can lead to paranoia, psychosis and death.

ECU, Ecu or **ecu**   Until there are freely available banknotes and coins, the ECU (European Currency Unit) exists only on cheques and in financial documents. In anticipation of the time when the ECU becomes a currency in its own right, as part of the European Monetary System (**EMS**), it has become an **acronym** (pron: 'ECKcue'), with either a capital or small *e*.

The name *Ecu* owes much to the influence of Valéry Giscard d'Estaing, at the time President of France, who wanted to give the name of the proposed European currency a predominantly French flavour. An *écu* was an old French silver coin, and Giscard d'Estaing had commemorative silver coins minted, with the European Community coat of arms on one side and the design of the old French *écu* on the other.

The *Ecu* is a **basket of currencies**, with the value made up by averaging out specific proportions of the currencies of the **EC** member countries. According to John Major, during his brief tenure as Chancellor of the Exchequer, the Ecu could 'In the very long term, if peoples and governments so choose, develop into a single European currency'. When it becomes real money, used for paying taxis and buying newspapers, the capital E will go, as ecus will be an alternative to pounds, francs, pesetas. . . . There are straws in the wind. Portuguese stamps already show the value in ecus as well as escudos, and there is talk in France of some newspapers carrying the ecu price alongside the price in francs.

ecumenical   This is a confusing word to many people because the meaning has implied different things. The earlier spelling, *oecumenical* (with *ecumenical* as an American variant) is still shown in some dictionaries, but is obsolete. *Ecumenical* used to describe the universal Christian Church, but is now taken to mean the movement to re-establish worldwide Christian unity, after the Reformation and other divisions. More than anything, *ecumenical* is associated with the World Council of Churches founded in 1948, and the belief that the way ahead must be bridges across denominational divides.

A clear example of the use of *ecumenical* in 1992 arose from the building of the new church in Milton Keynes in Buckinghamshire. It is owned jointly by the Baptist Union of Great Britain, the Church of England and the Methodist, Roman Catholic and United Reformed churches, and is described as the *ecumenical* equivalent of a cathedral. The name of the church is a symbol of the ecumenical principle: 'Christ the Cornerstone'.

-ed In the 15th century, *-ed* was nearly always pronounced as a separate syllable, and with a few words this has lingered on. When one lawyer wants to sneer at another, he calls him 'my *learn-ed* friend' (two syllables). If you have spent a lifetime studying, you are also entitled to two syllables, because you are *learn-ed*. After a *t* sound, pronunciation requires *-ed* to be separate: fat-ed, rat-ed, slat-ed. . . .

In poetry, but not otherwise, a **grave accent** is sometimes used to show the *-ed* is required by the metre to be treated as an extra syllable (adorèd).

eddy or **whirlpool** The difference is one of power. An *eddy* is a current in water that moves in a contrary direction to the main flow, usually creating a rotary motion. A *whirlpool* is the same, but is always rotary and so powerful that it sucks things down into the centre.

edible See eatable . . .

edifice An *edifice* is an imposing building, such as a great church, and dictionaries dutifully record this as the meaning. But to use the word in that sense now is either formal or literary ('St Pancras Station, that great Victorian edifice so beloved by John Betjeman'), or a joke about, say, a semi-detached house in a suburban road. *Edifice* has come to be used more often for a structure of conventions or a system of beliefs: 'Western civilization rests on a whole edifice of accepted conventions'.

Edinburgh Gazette See gazetted

editing (films) See collage . . .

editor In journalism, at some time in the past, an *editor* could only be the person in charge of the whole presentation of a newspaper or magazine, writing the **editorial**, the leading article on an important issue. Under the editor came *sub-editors* and reporters. At most, there might also have been a *literary editor* in charge of book reviews.

But the word has been downgraded, and now, according to Philip Howard, when *literary editor* of *The Times*, 'any rag worth its 35p has at least 30 editors, with responsibilities ranging from pop to knickers'.

Editors not only work on newspapers and magazines. Publishers have editors, people who work on the text of a book in preparation for publication: this is a legitimate use of the word, going back to the 18th century, relating to 'edition', the printing of a literary work ('éditeur' is the French word for a publisher). Early on, the film industry adopted the word for the technician who arranges the different film scenes into a continuous sequence. Television has this sort of editor, but also uses *editor* in the same way as newspapers, for people in charge of different sections of news presentation (*political editor, diplomatic editor* . . .).

The result of all this is that *editor* is now so ill-defined, it has to be explained: a *newspaper editor* usually means the person in charge; *sports editor, fashion editor*, etc are the journalists responsible for those sections of a paper. A *book editor* is not a *literary editor*, which is a newspaper title (see above), but works in a book publishing house. A *film editor* works in a cutting room, assembling film.

Finally, do not use the word *editress* to a woman editor, unless you want to get a black look.

editorial or **leader** *Editorial* was first used in mid-19th century for an article that reflected the opinion of a newspaper on an important issue of the day. At that time, it was written by the editor himself. *Editorial* is still used that way but the more usual word now, for British newspapers, is *leader*, short for 'leading article', likely to be written, with the approval of the editor, by special *leader writers*. *Leader* is not used in America, where *editorial* remains the usual word for the central article expounding a newspaper's policy on a political or international issue.

editress See editor; -ess forms

educational *Educational* has become an open-ended word capable of being used about so many different things that the important meaning of the word is diluted. There are educational toys, educational tours, educational television programmes, educational experiences, suggesting anything from vaguely cultural to the development of practical skills.

educationist or **educationalist** Both words exist but *educationist* is usually preferred, because it is shorter and more logical, to describe someone who is a specialist in methods of teaching.

-ee This can be a useful suffix that enables one word to be used instead of three or four: examinee (someone who is examined), absentee (someone who is absent), trainee (someone being trained). . . . It is particularly convenient in legal terminology so that opposites can be paralleled: assignor and assignee, lessor and lessee, etc. But *-ee* words are often unattractive and there is no point in coining new ones when the more usual suffixes *-er* and *-or* are available ('escaper' is better than 'escapee').

EEC See EC . . .

effect or **affect** See affect . . .

effeminate or **effete** *Effete* is sometimes used about a man, when the intended meaning is *effeminate*. A man who minces, gestures and speaks in a feminine way is *effeminate*, and the word is always uncomplimentary.

A woman is never called *effeminate*: if she behaves in an exaggeratedly coy manner, she might be called **girlish**, also uncomplimentary. If she displays attractive womanly qualities, she is *feminine*, a word generally used admiringly about a woman, but if used about a man means the same as *effeminate*. For some women, *feminine* is a condescending word used by men, and might not be welcomed as a compliment. Attitudes between the two sexes are still passing through a period of transition, and we can no longer take for granted previously accepted meanings of some words.

Although *effete* comes from a Latin word meaning worn out through child-bearing, it is used more about men, to mean weak, ineffectual and lacking in virility. See also **boyish**; **feminism**

efficacy The first syllable should be stressed ('EFFikersy'), not the second ('efFIKersy').

'effing' By convention, 'fucking' is an obscene word, rejected by polite society (although not by everyone), while *effing* (an evasive variant of 'fucking') is considered no worse than 'slang' in some dictionaries and is more or less acceptable. Words, like people, can have double standards. See **fuck**

EFL In Paris, Rome, Tokyo, Warsaw, Moscow, Tel Aviv and in every other major city, teaching English is big business. Alan Maley, who has encouraged the teaching of English in his work for the British Council, tells us that in every country 'English is worn as a badge of modernity, carried as a passport to well-paid jobs'. This vast business is called by teachers in language schools, by writers and publishers of textbooks (but not by students themselves) *EFL* (English as a foreign language).

EFTA EFTA (pron: 'EFFta') is such a familiar **acronym** that a surprising number of people have forgotten what the letters stand for. The European Free Trade Association was formed in 1959 by Austria, Britain, Denmark, Portugal, Sweden and Switzerland to encourage a free trade area between themselves and the EC. As members join the EC, they withdraw from EFTA. Britain left in 1973.

eg or **ie** These Latinate abbreviations are, of course, a common part of English, although they get sometimes confused with each other. *Eg* (Latin: *exempli gratia*) is shorthand for 'for example' and is preceded by a comma: 'there is a wide choice on the menu, *eg* steak, trout and chicken'. *Ie* (Latin: *id est*), also preceded by a comma, is shorthand for 'that is': 'there are only three dishes on the menu, *ie* steak, trout and chicken'. See also **ie or viz**

egalitarian This emotive word has an uncertain meaning. In some religions, it means 'equal in the sight of God'. In the US Declaration of Independence, it means equal rights to 'life, liberty and the pursuit of happiness'. Marxists might see the egalitarian economic ideal as an equal distribution of wealth.

People will offer lip-service to egalitarian principles because it is unfashionable, unchristian or racist not to, although they may share Aldous Huxley's contention 'That all men are equal is a proposition to which, at ordinary times, no sane individual has ever given his assent' (*Proper Studies*).

In the 1990s, when we talk about an *egalitarian society*, it is likely to mean for most people equality of opportunity, rather than the elimination of inherited wealth or the refusal to accept unequal individual endowments. See also **equal opportunities**

egghead or **highbrow** As with many words, it is arguable whether *egghead* and *highbrow* are standard English: they *are* in some dictionaries, others label them colloquial or informal. The words are similar in meaning but not the same. *Egghead* is often associated with scientists and with arcane knowledge and remoteness from everyday life, and derives from the old-fashioned belief that intellectuals are bald and have high foreheads. *Highbrow* is more about someone's erudite taste in the arts, especially in music and literature. Both words seem dated now, as abstract ideas and tastes in all kinds of music and literature are more widespread. See also **intellectual . . .**; **middlebrow**

egis See **aegis . . .**

ego *Ego* in the teaching of Freud and in psychoanalysis in general is a complex term related to someone's awareness of self and reality. In general use, *ego* means self-estime ('his ego was badly dented'). As for an *ego-trip*, that is usually derogatory, suggesting an activity that is self-indulgent. The first syllable has the same sound as 'eager', rather than 'egg': 'EEgoh'. The plural of *ego* is *egos* (not *egoes*).

egocentric, **egoistic** or **egotistic** Books on English carefully point out that an *egoist* is someone who only thinks of themselves, while an *egotist* is someone who is always talking about themselves. The earlier word was *egoism*, a term in philosophy for the belief that nothing exists except in our own thoughts, and in ethics for the theory that self-interest is the basis of all action. *Egotism* was a later formation, with the *t* slipped in probably to help with pronunciation.

In general use now the distinction between *egoistic* and *egotistic* is at best arbitrary: they are both used about someone who is full of themselves, conceited, self-opinionated. If we are contrasting this attitude with *altruistic*, that is putting other people first, *egoistic* is the better word to use.

Egocentric, a late 19th-century formation, is tending to supplant both *egoistic* and *egotistic*, and has the same meaning.

The first syllable of all three words has an *ee* sound (not *e* as in 'egg').

eiderdown See **duvet . . .**

Eire or **Southern Ireland** The various names used for different parts of Ireland can be confusing. Guidelines are given under **Ireland . . .**

either *Either* is a minefield of difficulties:
1 Take care where you place it: 'we shall *go to either* Paris or Rome' is better than 'we shall *either go to* Paris or Rome'.

2 Is *either* singular or plural? If *both* words after *either* are singular, treat as *singular*: 'Either pilot error or mechanical failure *was* to blame'. But if either of the words is plural, *either* becomes *plural*: 'Either pilot error or the flight controllers *were* to blame'.

3 In other cases, always look at the *second* word related to *either*: 'Either he or *I am* to blame', 'Either she or *you are*. . .'.

4 It is not correct, as is sometimes stated, that *either* can only be used for *two* choices: 'it is available in either red, blue or green'.

5 Notwithstanding edicts in some grammar books, good writers often use *either* as an alternative to **each** about pairs of things: 'there is a chemist on either (or each) side of the street'; 'at either (or each) end of the table'.

6 There is no need to repeat 'at', 'for', 'of' or 'with', when one of those words precedes *either*, although it is all right to do so: 'we can deal with this *at* either a board meeting or (at) an informal discussion'; 'candidates must be fluent *in* either French or (in) German'; 'we must pay the price *of* either a long delay or (of) working long hours'.

7 After all that, is it 'EYEther' or 'EEther'? Either! Dictionaries show both as correct, although 'EYEther' is preferred. (In America it is usually 'EEther'.)

eke out *Eke* derives from an Old English word meaning increase, and is properly used, followed by 'with' or 'by', to mean something inadequate was made sufficient by the addition of something else: 'she eked out her housekeeping money by (or with) a part-time job'. But *eke* has long since come to be used to mean just about managing to earn a living or to support existence, a meaning accepted by current dictionaries: 'she eked out a living by freelance journalism'.

elapse or **lapse** Time *elapses*, that is passes by, just as hours or days can *elapse* before we get down to work. The 1990s is a period when many customs and traditions *lapse*, that is fall into disuse because nobody bothers with them any more. An insurance policy can *lapse* if you don't pay the premium.

elder or **older** The rule was that *elder* and *eldest* were the proper words for members of a family, with *elder* as the correct form for one of two (the elder of two brothers). This is often disregarded now, with *older* becoming the more usual word: she has an older (or elder) sister. And many people use *eldest* when only two people are involved: 'Her eldest sister is helping her' no longer necessarily implies she has more than one sister, but 'her oldest sister' does. In practice now, it is easier to forget *elder* and *eldest*, and use *older* for one of two, and *oldest* when there are more than two.

Outside family relationships, *older* has always been the normal word for people and things: an older friend, an older MP, an older dress. . . . *Elder* survives in some traditional terms, including *elder statesman*, often used now apart from politics for a senior experienced person in any organization.

elderly or **old** It is considered impolite now to call someone *old*: old people are *elderly* (an elderly woman, my elderly father . . .). We can have an old car, old wine, old friends, old habits, etc, but people are not supposed to be *old* any more. Perhaps *old-age pensioners* do prefer to be given the respect of **senior citizens**: certainly **OAP** seems to write them off. On the other hand, a one-line letter to *The New York Times* objected to all this euphemistic **namby-pamby**: 'Don't call me a senior citizen,' it began. 'Just call me a *little old lady*'.

electric or **electrical** Most people do not question the difference between these two words. Often it is a matter of custom which is used. An appliance that uses electricity to function is an *electric* whatever-it-is: an electric motor, electric light. . . . *Electrical* is more abstract, relating to electricity as a form of energy: an electrical breakdown, an electrical system. . . . Used by extension to describe a mood or an impact, *electric* is more common, although *electrical* can also apply: a situation or an effect can be electric or electrical.

For the difference between *electric* and *electronic*, see **electronic**.

electron or **atom** *Electron* is a technical term that frequently comes up in scientific news items, an everyday word for physicists but often mystifying to others. An electron is not the same as an *atom*: it is a basic constituent of matter, part of every atom but much smaller. Electrons are agents for the conduction of electricity, which has made **electronic** part of our everyday life.

electronic *Electronic* is not a post-World War II word: it was a term used in physics by the end of the 19th century. But since the war it has become a word used about everyday equipment. In physics, the word describes the movement of **electrons**. In general use, it describes the technology of using so-called semiconductors (crystalline material that conducts electricity as it warms up) in circuits, such as transistors and **microchips**. It is the impact of this technology on the development of a vast range of equipment, from computers, telephones, typewriters, videos, to dishwashers and electric toasters, that has made *electronic* literally a household word.

electronic mail Electronic mail will become ever more commonplace as we reach the end of the century. It is simply a term for sending communications, which can be printed out if required, between terminals of linked computers.

electronic music, **computer music** or **musique concrète** These names for different kinds of synthetic music are often confused. *Musique concrète* ('concrete music') was used for the first time in the late 1940s by Pierre Schaeffer for music that takes real sounds, the human voice and other natural sounds, or sounds made with musical instruments, and feeds them into tape-recorders. They are then treated in various ways, playing them faster or slower, or backwards, mixing the results to build up a montage of musical sequences. Messiaen and John Cage are two well-known composers who worked with these techniques.

Electronic music is loosely applied to any music created on electronic equipment, whether it is using natural sounds or not. But the term is applied by purists only to sequences of sounds that are created in the first place electronically.

Computer music is in another category and covers a wide range of music for which computers are used, either linked to synthesizers, or programmed to create different sounds. Computer music is an attempt to probe into the future, to discover the sounds of music to come in the 21st century. Pierre Boulez, who has established in Paris the most advanced centre for experimental music, describes it as 'forms of musical expression right to the limits of possibility'.

electronics is or **are** Nouns ending in *-ics* often present this problem. See *-ics*

elementary or **simple** Sherlock Holmes's catchphrase might just as well have been '*Simple*, my dear Watson', but Arthur Conan Doyle's archetypal private eye was created in 1887, when 'Elementary, my dear Watson' sounded more impressive. When we mean, as Holmes did, that something is easy to understand, *simple* is the right word to use. *Elementary* has a place to describe first or basic steps: elementary German lessons, elementary precautions. . . .

elevator *Elevator* is often trotted out as an example of how American English is unnecessarily complicated. What's wrong, it is demanded, with that good old 13th-century word 'lift'? But Americans can come back, claiming that their *sidewalk* and *subway* are better words than British **pavement** and **underground**. So if we want to go to the top floor of Saks Fifth Avenue, we'd better take the *elevator*, and keep quiet about it.

elicit or **ask** To *elicit* information implies a certain degree of pressure on someone, or skill in asking the right questions in order to get at the facts. It is a misuse of the word to say, for example, 'Let us *elicit* what is on the menu'. We *elicit* the truth or the facts: we *ask* the time or the way.

The first syllable of *elicit* has the sound of 'ill': 'illLISSit', but the spelling should not be confused with **illicit**.

elision *Elision* is the linguistic term for leaving out a letter (usually a vowel) or syllable, when speaking: *I'm, can't, she's, Mary's* done it. . . . Some writers use elisions all the time, others slip one in from time to time to add a touch of spontaneity or friendliness. There is no rule about this but we can expect to see elisions used more and more as a reflection of life in the **fast lanes** of the 1990s. For a fuller account, see **contracted forms**

(the) **élite**, **élitist** See (the) **Establishment** . . .

ellipsis See dots (. . .)

em Many of us now have to be familiar with this old printing term because it comes into **desktop publishing**. *Em* is the name of the letter M, used as the standard measurement of the width of a single letter in a particular typeface. This enables the space taken up by a line of printed matter to be given in *ems*.

embargo An *embargo* originally prohibited ships within a country's ports from leaving, usually in anticipation of war. This has since been extended to cover the prohibition of any action, such as trade between countries (a trade embargo), or the release, before a stated date, of information given to the media (an embargo on a news story). The correct plural form is *embargoes* not *embargos*.

embattled *Embattled*, at one time a military term for an army in a state of readiness for battle, is now a fashionable word with financial journalists, so we have embattled chairmen of companies under pressure by their board or shareholders, or embattled companies facing a hostile takeover bid. Anybody or any organization up against it is now called *embattled*.

emblem See **logo** . . .

embryo or **embryonic** The use of *embryo*, a biological and botanical term for an offspring before birth (in the case of humans, in the first eight weeks after conception), or a plant contained in the seed, has since the late 17th century been extended as a descriptive word: it is applied to anything in a preliminary or underdeveloped stage. Either *embryo* or *embryonic* can be used in this way: the plan is in embryo, or the plan is embryonic. (Pron: 'EMbreeoh', 'embreeONic').

embryology See **reproductive technology**

emend See **amend** . . .

emigrant, **immigrant** or **émigré** It is important to get these sensitive words right. The same person is usually both – at different times. When people leave their own country for another, they are *emigrants*; when they arrive in the new country, they are *immigrants*. *Immigrants* is occasionally heard for British citizens who clearly have non-British ethnic origins, even if their families have been in Britain for many years. This is both offensive and the wrong use of the word.

An *émigré* is an old-fashioned word for a refugee, someone forced to leave their country by war or oppression.

emoluments See **pay** . . .

emotional or **emotive** Most dictionaries are not much help in separating these two words, which relate to the emotions. *Emotional* is when emotion is displayed: an emotional woman is always showing her feelings; an emotional situation is one where a sense of joy or sadness is openly expressed or felt. *Emotive* is when emotion is aroused: **racism** is an emotive word; an issue is emotive when it makes people feel strongly about it one way or another.

A book or a piece of music is *emotional* if it is full of passion and feeling: Tchaikovsky's symphony, the *Pathétique*, is an example. If a book or music is *emotive* it arouses feelings in other people, although it may not be *emotional* itself: Salman Rushdie's *The Satanic Verses* (1988) is a dramatic example.

empathy or **sympathy** *Empathy* is a word that more people are using now. It was coined early this century and used by the English psychologist, Edward Titchener, to translate the German word 'einfuhling', literally a 'feeling into'. *Empathy* is the capacity to enter, in one's imagination, into someone else's feelings or into the whole mood and quality of literature, music or a painting. *Sympathy* is similar but always embraces compassion for suffering or distress. You have *empathy*, rather than sympathy, for a painting or a piece of music, and you may have empathy for someone in love, although sympathy could come in too, if you believe they are in love with the wrong person. Keep these words apart because the distinction between them can be expressive.

Empathetic exists to describe a feeling of empathy, but is rarely used.

emphasis When there is more than one *emphasis*, the plural is *emphases* (pron: 'EMFaseez'). (Try saying 'emphasises' aloud and you'll see why.)

emphasizing or **talking up** *Emphasizing* something is giving prominence to it, stressing its importance; *talking up* implies bringing a subject to the fore out of expediency, without really caring all that much about it. For example, the pressure group, Friends of the Earth, have complained about politicians talking up environmental issues.

empiric, **empirical** or **pragmatic** All three words are opposed to *theoretical*, which is the method of arriving at a solution by conjecture or thinking about it in abstract. *Empiric* is an alternative word for *empirical*, a trial and error approach, putting ideas into practice to see if they work, sometimes coarsely called the 'suck it and see' method. (*Empiricism* is the theory in philosophy that definitions of knowledge depend on experience.)

Pragmatic has a different emphasis: it is using a method that is seen to meet the requirements. An *empiric* or *empirical* approach carries out experiments until one is found to work; a *pragmatic* approach follows a line that is from the outset demonstrably practical and effective.

EMS and **EMU** As with many **Euro-** abbreviations, EMS is used more often than the name in full: the European Monetary System was introduced in March 1979 to create exchange rate stability among members of the European Economic Community. Members of the EMS agree to keep fluctuations in exchange rates between prescribed limits. The EMS is seen as a movement towards eventually creating a single European currency, with *economic and monetary union*: the abbreviation for this, EMU, is already an **acronym** ('EEmew'). See also **EC** . . . ; **ECU** . . .

enclave The proposal during 1991 for a safe **haven** for the Kurds in Iraq brought up the pronunciation of *enclave*, the word for part of a territory of one state contained within the territory of another. *Enclave* is from a French word and some people preserve the French sound in the first syllable: 'AHNclayve'. It is more usual to anglicize it: 'ENNclayve'.

enclose or **inclose** *Inclose* as a variant of *enclose* is more or less obsolete.

enclosure or **inclosure** *Enclosure* is standard now for anything enclosed with a letter. *Inclosure* is old-fashioned, except for the inclosure of land, in which sense this variant spelling is still often used.

encyclopaedia or **encyclopedia** See **æ** or **ae**

endangered A project can be *endangered* when it is exposed to danger or put at risk in some way. The more recent use of the word by conservationists, particularly in the term *endangered species*, is common now. When there is the risk of animals, birds or plants becoming extinct because of commercial exploitation or because their habitats are so reduced, they are endangered.

endeavour We might have more confidence when someone says they will try to help us, rather than *endeavour* to. Even as a noun, *endeavour* is usually over the top in formality: if 'make a good try' sounds too conversational, the word 'attempt' is usually preferable to *endeavour*.

ended or **ending** When it is a period in the future, it is logical to use *ending* rather than *ended*: the tax year ending April next year. When it is a period in the past, *ended* is more usual (although it would be fussing to object to *ending*): the tax year *ended* last April.

endemic or **epidemic** There is sometimes confusion over the difference between an *endemic* disease and an *epidemic*. *Endemic* describes a condition that habitually goes with a certain group of people, a particular area, or a set of circumstances: an *epidemic* is a disease that runs riot anywhere and lasts until it clears up, after which it may never recur. *Pandemic* is perhaps the more appropriate word when an epidemic extends to a whole country or even the whole world.

ending a sentence with a preposition
See **prepositions**

endive See **chicory** . . .

endogenous or **indigenous** *Endo-* is from a Greek word meaning within. The word *endogenous*, as well as being a general descriptive word for something originating or developing from its own sources, has become a standard economic term for anything arising from the forces within the economic system. For example, *endogenous money supply* is not regulated by the government or a central bank, but is left to the influence of factors within the free economy, such as interest rates and industrial output.

Indigenous is used for animals and plants belonging naturally to a place, about people born in a region (the indigenous population), or about anything that has a traditional place in a country (indigenous culture).

endorse or **indorse** Well after its sell-by date has expired, most dictionaries continue to include *indorse* as an accepted variant of *endorse*. But *indorse* is rarely used and most people would now think it is a spelling mistake for *endorse*.

endorsement When we sign the back of a cheque as an *endorsement*, we are endorsing a use of the word that dates from the 16th century, as well as acknowledging the Latin source, which means 'back' (compare the word 'dorsal'). A much more recent use of the word is for the commercial practice of famous people giving their backing – or endorsement – to a brand by being seen to use it, wear it or its insignia, or talking about it on television.

end papers The traditional bookbinding term for the sheets of paper folded, with half pasted on the inside of the front and back covers of a book. In the 1990s, **desktop publishing** is bringing the term into common use.

energy It is *energy* that makes the world go round, gets aircraft into the air and presidents and prime ministers out of bed. Since the 1950s, the word *energy* has taken on an increasing political significance, as it was forced on the world that the price of using energy is pollution from exhaust fumes of cars or the burning of gases in industrial processes, and that sources of energy could not be taken for granted as a bottomless pit. The word *energy* has become used not only for the power generated by fuels but for the fuels themselves. We hear about the *cost of energy* meaning the price of gas, electricity, petrol, etc.

engage, **consult**, **retain** or **appoint** There is a certain professional etiquette about which word is used in which situation. See **appoint** . . .

engaged or **busy** American telephone operators say a line is *busy*; their English counterparts say it's *engaged*. Americans visiting Britain learn that soon

enough. But other telephone idioms can come as a shock: an American politician staying at a famous hotel in London was given a nasty turn when he was told by the operator, as he was connected, 'You're through!' (To an American that means 'You're done for!'.) See **through**

engine or **motor** *Engine* is a very old word, used for a mechanical contraption as far back as the 14th century. *Motor* is much more recent, dating from the 19th century. Both words describe a machine that converts fuel into energy in order to do work or provide locomotion. Smaller engines are likely to be called *motors*, so we have railway *engines* but *motor*-bikes. On the other hand, since the 'horseless carriages' that appeared in the late 19th century were powered by internal-combustion engines, even the smallest car can boast an engine, although it is called a motor car; and although ships have engine-rooms, even big vessels are called motor launches. Nevertheless, the most reliable guide to which word to use is size: *engine* for a big and powerful machine and *motor* for a smaller engine.

English It is hardly possible to find a definition of *English* that all users of the language would agree with. The magisterial H W **Fowler** proclaimed 'Americanisms are foreign words and should be so treated'. (See **American English.** . . .) Does that mean *teenager, babysitter, bluff, boom, slump* and thousands of other words that have crossed the Atlantic are not English? Enoch Powell, addressing the Royal Society of St George, declared 'Others may speak English – more or less – but it is our language not theirs'. Does that suggest **Australian English** is not English? In 1990 a judge in London asked for an interpreter because he could not understand the language spoken by a witness from Glasgow. But the Glaswegian was speaking English.

English started as a modest dialect brought to England in the 5th century AD by Germanic tribes. Some time before the 9th century, *Englisc* was the name used for the various dialects spoken in Britain by the descendants of those original Germanic peoples. The Norman Conquest, after the Battle of Hastings in 1066 (the one history date everyone remembers), brought English into the mainstream of European languages, as the vocabulary took on shiploads of words from Norman French, most of which had descended from Latin.

William Caxton and his printing press at Westminster, set up about 1476, took English a step forward, as from then on books could be produced faster and cheaper than manuscripts. A hundred years later and on into the 17th century, English basked and stretched in the warmth and glory of Elizabethan England, making and being made by Shakespeare and the Authorized Version of the Bible.

The 18th century, with its scientific outlook, disciplined and polished English, as it became a language of reason and philosophy. Imperial expansion of British power in the 19th century carried English all over the world. The language had arrived, and in smug Victorian England was settling down complacently, the worst thing that can happen to any language. But before this hardening of the arteries set in, along came a transfusion of rich vigorous new blood from America, a linguistic lease-lend of young colourful words that has been shaking up the language ever since. More than any other language, English has been kept on its toes and has become the most lively and adaptable language the world has ever known.

All the people all over the world who learn English care little about such matters of linguistic history. For most of them, this is what really counts: English comes first by a long way at doing the very thing for which language came into being – to communicate with other people. No other language is understood by such a diversity of people in so many different countries. English is the first language for worldwide communication. At the opening of the Middle East peace conference in October 1991, at the Royal Palace in Madrid, both Yitzhak Shamir for Israel, and Haider Abdelshaft for the Palestinian delegation, chose to speak in *English*, because they wanted the whole world to listen.

Hungary, Italy, Japan, Mexico, Peru, and on into over half the other countries of the world, are adding more and more English words to their vocabularies. In Panama, a puncture is called a *flataya*, at dry-cleaners in Madrid you can ask for *el pressing* and they will know what you mean. In Tokyo, *Japlish* has turned someone who works for a business into a *salaryman*. As for France, so many English words have moved in that the hybrid language is called **franglais**.

In so many expected and unexpected places, from the Australian outback to the road to Katmandu, there are people who speak English, although it may be very different from the language of Stoke-on-Trent and Stoke Newington, of Old Sodbury and the Old Kent Road, forms of English which in turn are different from the language of Oxford dons, Wiltshire farmers, the Archbishop of Canterbury, or the language you hear on the New York subway or the Mississippi River. For many people all over the world, who have American teachers, English is *American* English.

In the end, perhaps the only way to define English, is any language that corresponds in some recognizable way to the language spoken in traditionally anglophone countries. See also **British English**

English or **British**   See British . . .

English bone china   See china . . .

engraving, **etching** or **print**   Anyone who has been to art school could be expected to know the difference between these three terms, but many others are uncertain. *Print* is an umbrella word for any reproduction of a work of art by any process. Even a photograph of a painting could be called a *print*, although that could be misleading, since *print* usually implies a graphic technique as well as a process.

Engraving can also cover a variety of processes used for reproduction, such as woodcuts and linocuts, but in practice, an *engraving* is usually taken to mean a reproduction made from a metal plate, with the design incised by one of several different techniques. An *etching* is specific. It is a type of engraving, whereby a print is made from a design bitten into a metal plate by means of acid.

The tendency in the art world now is to use the term *print* for etchings and any other kind of engravings, which is technically correct, although the term is used more loosely outside art circles.

Enlightenment   *Enlightenment* became a catchphrase in the 1960s for every Asian mystic setting up shop in the West. It was said we were approaching the Age of Enlightenment. An earlier movement called the Enlightenment, in the 18th century, meant something altogether different: it was a philosophy which stressed reason, replacing old traditions and beliefs by the new precepts of science, underlined by a belief in individuality.

Enlightenment in the 20th century is at the opposite end of the philosophical spectrum: it is identified with Eastern mysticism, especially the ancient spiritual teachings of **Buddhism** ('Buddha' comes from a Sanskrit word meaning 'enlightened') and Hinduism. This Enlightenment is the attainment of *nirvana*, a Sanskrit word for freedom from self, from the agonized holding on to individuality and desires.

enormity   When in February 1985, Neil Kinnock spoke of the enormity of the unemployment total in the UK, we weren't sure what he meant. It might have been the monstrousness, the sheer wickedness of the size of the figures, because that is the true meaning of *enormity* ('the full enormity of a crime'). Or he might have been following a more recent usage to refer to the 'enormousness' of the total. This misusage, as in 'the enormity of the building', is understandable and is now common. Some people criticize it, recent dictionaries warn that it is still a disputed usage, but by the end of the century it's unlikely that anyone will fuss about it. In the meantime, there are alternatives: 'enormousness' (an awkward word), or, 'great size', 'vastness' or 'hugeness'.

enough   See adequate . . .

enquire or **inquire**   In Britain these words have been moving apart in recent years. To *enquire* or to make an *enquiry* refers more now to asking for information. *Inquire* and *inquiry* refer to an investigation in some depth. (In America, *inquire* and *inquiry* have taken over for both meanings.)

enquiry or **inquiry**   See previous entry

ensemble   An *ensemble* is a collection of parts taken together as a whole. It is used in English mostly about different items of women's clothes designed to be worn together, and in the artistic sense of a small group of musicians or actors performing together. A composition for such a group is also called an *ensemble*.

Although the word derives in the first place from Latin, *ensemble* is as French as *crêpes suzettes*, and used to be pronounced in a French manner ('ahn-SAHMbl'). Saleswomen in the more expensive clothes shops are still likely to pronounce it this way, but the last syllable is now usually anglicized, with announcers of BBC music programmes saying 'ahnSAHMbul' (the last syllable with the same sound as the final syllable of 'resem*ble*').

ensure   See **assure** . . .

enterprise   It is rather old-fashioned to refer to a company or a business as an *enterprise*, although *enterprise zones* is the official designation for inner-city areas in Britain where the government is encouraging businesses to start up by offering grants, tax concessions and other bonuses.

Enterprise culture is a phrase that arose during the 1980s to describe a society that encourages people to break away from the mould of their birth, education, family background, and to express personal ambition by making careers for themselves in new fields.

Because *enterprise* derives from Latin, not Greek, it is always spelt (in Britain and America) with *-ise* (see **-ise or -ize**).

enterprise culture   See previous entry

enterprise zone   See enterprise

enthral or enthrall   These used to be alternative spellings but most current dictionaries now show *enthral* as the only acceptable form (*enthrall* is the usual spelling in America). In both countries the other forms are *enthralled* and *enthralling*.

enthuse   This verb formed from *enthusiasm* to mean either to make someone enthusiastic ('the project enthused her') or to show enthusiasm ('she enthused about the project') is regarded by some dictionaries as 'informal' and by others as standard English. In time, dictionaries will probably drop the 'informal' label, as the verb becomes generally accepted. In the meantime, some people find *enthuse* brash, and prefer to 'be enthusiastic about' something, to 'show enthusiasm', or 'be filled with enthusiasm'.

entomology   See etymology or entomology

entrée   In the days when eight-course dinners were usual, an *entrée* (pron: 'AHNtray') was a mere aside, served between the fish and meat courses. It may still be used that way on menus for formal banquets. Grand restaurants may use *entrées* in a different way, as the heading for the list of *main* courses on the menu. But in general, *entrée*, as a gastronomic term, belongs more to a past world. See also **pièce de résistance**, which was the classic name for the main course of an important meal.

The other use of *entrée* is more common now, for the right of admission to an exclusive group: 'Marriage to Lady Hermione was his entrée into titled society'.

entrepreneur   In French an entrepreneur is a contractor (an *'entrepreneur* en bâtiments' equals a building contractor), but in English the most common meaning was for someone who had the enterprise to start a new kind of business, risking their own or other people's money. The word is used more now in books by economists than in the real business world of the 1990s. The word has an anglicized French pronunciation, with the stress on the last syllable: 'ahntre(r)pre(r)NER'.

entrust or intrust   Although the variant *intrust* is still included, even in some of the latest dictionaries, it is more or less obsolete and could be regarded as an archaic spelling of *entrust*.

enunciate   See articulate . . .

envelope   The pronunciation 'AHNvelope', still often heard, is an echo from the time when the word was self-consciously French. Most younger people say 'ENNvelope', which is the pronunciation BBC announcers are asked to use.

envious, enviable or jealous   It is clear that *jealous* and *jealousy* are the words when it comes to love and affection: Othello was a jealous husband, and killed Desdemona out of jealousy. But when it comes to feelings of resentment because another person has qualities or possessions, or has achieved something you want for yourself, *envious* and *jealous* come close to each other in meaning. Both words mean you desire what someone else has. Perhaps *envious* includes admiration, while *jealous* is more grudging and spiteful: 'I am envious of your success' suggests I admire you for it and would like it for myself, whereas 'I am jealous of your success' suggests I hate you for it, because *I* want it.

Enviable and *envious* are sometimes confused. People are *envious* because the qualities, possessions or achievements of another person are *enviable*: 'her success is enviable'; 'he is envious of her success'. *Enviably* and *enviously* are particularly easy to confuse: we look at someone enviously because they do something enviably well.

environment   See ecology . . .

environmental tobacco smoke   See passive smoking

ephemeral   The preferred pronunciation is 'ifFEMMeral', although 'ifFEEMeral' is an accepted alternative.

epic or saga   Homer's *Odyssey*, Virgil's *Aeneid*, Milton's *Paradise Lost* are *epics*, monumental narrations in verse, celebrating heroic achievements and eternal truths. Hollywood film producers latched on to the word for almost any film lasting more than a couple of hours. Then *epic* was taken up for long, involved and complicated novels. The use of the word for such things remains a commercial and journalistic vulgarism. Perhaps *saga* would be more acceptable. *Saga*, an Old Norse word for long legendary narratives, is used in English about drawn-out stories, and does not have the same association with the great *epics* of classical literature.

epicentre See **earthquakes**

epidemic See **endemic or epidemic**

episcopalian See **Anglican . . .**

epoch An *epoch* is an event of such magnitude that things are never the same again. An epoch ushers in a new era (see **age . . .**). As with other portentous words, *epoch* is often trivialized in such journalistic comments as 'a new epoch in women's hairstyle'. Epochs, in the real sense, are extremely rare, and there are other adequate words for less consequential changes: departure, development, transition, turning-point. . . .

This applies equally to *epoch-making*. Not many discoveries are as epoch-making as headlines would have us believe. They may be notable, important, significant, newsworthy, or even breath-taking, without being momentous, earth-shaking or world-shattering, which is, after all, what *epoch-making* suggests.

epoch-making See previous entry

eponym and **eponymous** Inventing something or devising a technique that everyone uses can be the best way to be remembered for ever, for your name might become an *eponym* (from the Greek word meaning name), the name of anything called after a real or imaginary person.

The blind will always use *braille* to read (invented by Louis Braille, 1809–52); thousands of *sandwich* bars celebrate the 4th Earl of Sandwich (1718–92), who devised this way of eating (see **fast food**); and every day, as children are told to put on their *wellies*, the 1st Duke of Wellington (1769–1852) rides again. These names and many others are *eponymous*. The word can also be used in business: for example, Laura Ashley was the *eponymous* founder of the international company that bears her name. When an eponym is a brand name, it takes a capital, although sometimes when the name is used as a generic word, the capital is dropped (see **Hoover . . .**, for example).

equal The double-dealing decree in *Animal Farm*, George Orwell's satirical fable about the corruption of power, is 'All animals are equal but some animals are more equal than others'. *Equal* is an absolute measurement, so strictly speaking *more equal* makes no sense. But there are times when irony (as in George Orwell's maxim) or emphasis justifies *more*

equal or *exactly equal*. But usually *equal* should stand on its own without qualification. See also **equal opportunities**

equally as See **as/4**

equal opportunities There is an Equal Opportunities Commission, whose terms of reference are to ensure that no one is excluded from consideration for a job on the grounds of sex, creed, colour or race. In some job advertisements, a footnote declares 'We are an Equal Opportunities employer'. But women, blacks and others have learned that some opportunities are a good deal *less equal* than others (see **equal**).

equerry An *equerry* (a personal assistant to a member of the British royal family) puts the stress on the second syllable: 'iKWERRy'. That was the stress pattern in Old French (compare 'esquire'). In less exalted circles, which include dictionaries, stress on the first syllable is preferred (although the other pronunciation may be shown as an alternative): 'EKwery'.

equity In the 14th century, *equity* meant fair dealing, a meaning that survives as the name of a section of British law that takes precedence over statute and **common law**. *In all equity* is an old-fashioned expression used to mean in all fairness. The more familiar use of *equity* is short for *equity capital*, capital raised by issuing shares. The traditional reason for the term was the acceptance as fair, that investors who take the greatest risk should be entitled to profits and reserves after prior obligations have been met.

If someone asks you to join them in business, they may offer you a share of the *equity* (ie shares in the business) instead of a straight salary. Stock markets are called equity markets because they buy and sell shares in companies. Spelt with a capital, *Equity* is the name of the trade union for actors.

equity capital See previous entry

er . . . *Er . . .* is the usual way of representing in written English this peculiarly British sound of hesitation and uncertainty. Why bother to include it in *The Good English Guide*? Well er . . . at least three current dictionaries (*The Concise Oxford, Collins Concise* and *Longman Dictionary*) see fit to include it as well.

-er or **-re** See **-re . . .**

era See **age . . .**

eraser See **rubber . . .**

erection Physiologically an *erection* can refer to any erectile tissue becoming enlarged, a use that goes back to the end of the 16th century. Because the most usual meaning now is for an erect penis, the word *erection* is loaded with symbols of aggression and power, and fantasies and fears. It is one of the few sexual words that is clinical enough to be at home in a doctor's consulting room, yet natural enough to be used in bed.

ergonomic, **ergonomy**   See **user-friendly** . . .

erogenous, **eros**, **erotic**, **erotica**, **eroticism**, **erotogenic**   Eros, the god of love in Greek mythology, has given birth to some of the more respectable words for sexual responses. The word *eros*, in **Freudian** psychology, evokes the whole power of sexual love and the **life-force** that flows from it. *Erogenous* describes something that arouses sexual desire and excitement. *Erotogenic* is an earlier form of *erogenous* and means exactly the same. It is used less often now. Both words apply particularly to parts of the body responsive to sexual stimulation (*erogenous* or *erotogenic* zones). *Erotic* has a similar meaning, but relates to *eroticism*, sexual expression in art, literature and religion.

But *erotic* and *eroticism*, while in the language of art criticism, were long ago trivialized to take in provocative lingerie and soft-core **pornography**. *Erotica*, once pure Kamasutra (the ancient Sanskrit treatise on love), and used only about esoteric and aesthetic sexual imagery, is now used for the kind of things sold over the counters of sex shops. *Erotic* and *erotica* are still available for, say the buttocky busty women in Rubens' paintings or for Picasso's blatantly sexual drawings, but the same words may now be used in a sleazy underworld to sell joyless demonstrations of copulation.

The word *eros* requires further consideration. For disciples of Jung, it has a deeper meaning than Freudian sexual drive or libido. C S Lewis separated *eros* from sex, and for him it evoked other things (*The Four Loves*, 1960). This **Jungian** aspect of eros, although difficult to define, is a vital part of psychic experience. It is perhaps an irradiating love of life, engendered by a love of God, that animates the whole organism.

Eros or **eros**   See previous entry

erotogenic   See **erogenous** . . .

-erous or **-rous**   The usual ending is *-erous*: boisterous, murderous, slanderous . . . *Disastrous* and *wondrous* are the most common exceptions ('disasterous' and 'wonderous' are not alternative spellings).

erratum and **errata**   When there are mistakes in a book, a directory or a report that are picked up at the last moment, they may be listed at the end. It is usual practice to head the list *Errata* (pron: 'irRAHta'), the plural of Latin *erratum*. There is no need for readers to be any more forgiving, as this heading is no better than saying mistakes, blunders or cock-ups.

ersatz   See **artificial** . . .

Erse   See **Irish** . . .

erstwhile   It is wrong to write off *erstwhile* as pompous or archaic, because there are examples when its formality might seem appropriate. 'My erstwhile charwoman' sounds ridiculous, but 'my erstwhile husband' may sound better than 'my **ex**'. Nevertheless, there has to be a good case for using *erstwhile* rather than 'former'. See also **archaisms**

escalate   The word *escalade* is no longer used, except in history books, since it describes the dangerous technique of attacking fortified walls by scaling them with ladders. In the 20th century, *escalator* was formed from the word in America. Later, the verb *escalate*, first used as a warring term for the way a conflict builds up as each side puts on more pressure, was then applied far too often to anything else, from the price of butter to divorce statistics. 'Develop', 'expand' or 'increase' are often more direct words to use, although *escalate* does suggest a rapid movement: 'the price of shares escalated as soon as the takeover bid was announced'. But even there, 'shot up' or 'soared' are better alternatives.

escape clause   Like an 'escape route', an *escape clause* is a way out when the going gets rough. It is used about contracts which include a condition that allows one or both parties to break the terms under certain conditions.

ESP   See **parapsychology** . . .

especially or **specially**   Earlier this century *especial* had a different meaning from *special*: it meant exceptional (an especial wine) as opposed to something for a particular purpose (a special wine to go with cheese). Although it remains included in dictionaries, *especial* has all but disappeared from use, as *special* covers both meanings. *Very special* or *remarkably special* are required to indicate that something is outstanding rather than for a particular purpose.

The distinction between *especially* and *specially* still remains. *Especially* suggests outstanding (this is especially good); *specially* suggests designed for a purpose (specially designed for handicapped people). It must be added that writers preserve this distinction less and less and by the end of the century, *especially* may be put out to grass, alongside *especial*.

More especially is likely to survive, because it has become so popular, which is a pity, since it uses two words when one does the job: 'There may be problems in the company, (more) especially with the new chairman'. Leave out 'more' and nothing is lost.

espresso or **expresso**   This strong shot-in-the-arm Italian coffee took off in London in the 1960s (although the machines were being imported even before World War I), and has remained popular. Since the machine sounds like an old steam express train, some people call it *expresso*. It is *espresso*, both for the machine and the coffee it makes. The plural in Italian is 'espressi' but in English it's *espressos*.

esprit de l'escalier   If you are not familiar with this French expression, used in English, which means literally 'spirit of the stairs', it's worth taking it on board. There is nothing else that conveys the same meaning so wryly. We have all experienced that idea for a flash of wit or for a sharp retort that comes to us too late – while we are going down the stairs on the way out: that is an *esprit de l'escalier* (pron: 'esPREE-de-leSKALLyee-ay').

Esq *Esquire* belongs to the days of chivalry, when it was the title conferred on a young aspirant to knighthood, acting as an aide-de-camp to a knight. Later it became a title of rank, with a number of disputed complications about who was entitled to use it. Then it lost its status and was used as the standard form of address on a letter or envelope for any man. It has almost, but not quite, died out, replaced by plain 'Mr' or just nothing: Mr John Brown, or John Brown, rather than John Brown, Esq.

Esquire may still show up in country villages as a facetious form of cap-doffing – 'Evening, squire!'

-ess forms Linguistic differentiation between the sexes is woven throughout English in so many different ways that it seems impossible to unravel it. With animals, *-ess* forms are taken for granted, and no one feels that a lioness or a tigress is a substandard lion or tiger. But with humans, it is different. Many women feel that to be a something-or-other-*ess* makes them a kind of afterthought in the shadow of the male counterpart.

At times this may confuse differentiation with discrimination. It is occasionally relevant to know whether a noun represents a man or a woman, and there is a loss in abandoning all *-ess* forms. On the other hand, some have never existed: directors, doctors, surgeons, solicitors, barristers, conductors (of orchestras), prime ministers have always been unisex words, although it must be added that for a very long time it was assumed without question that those job-titles referred to men.

The situation is fluid now and the best we can do is to avoid *-ess* forms that are not liked by a significant number of women. **Actor** is standard in the theatre for both sexes and the *OED* considers *actress* 'obsolete', although many people go on using it. Women who are authors, poets or sculptors would scorn the alternative forms, *authoress*, *poetess* and *sculptress*. *Hostess* remains in use without any noticeable fuss. Mistress is usually interpreted as someone different from a female **master**, and it would be difficult for even the most ardent feminist to claim that *seductress* and *heiress* are discriminatory.

No one calls one of the few women who conduct orchestras a *conductress*, which is also dropping out of use for women conductors of buses. Heads of departments in business are **managers**, whatever their sex: a woman in charge of, say, a laundrette might still be a **manageress**, but probably not for much longer, as the word sounds old-fashioned. And who has ever called in to see a *bank manageress*? The most recent dictionaries still include *Jewess*, usually without comment, although *Collins Cobuild Dictionary* warns that 'many people consider this to be an offensive word' for a Jewish woman.

Linguistic habits are difficult to change but younger generations brought up with unisex words have an increasing influence, and it is likely that the whole concept of *-ess* forms will eventually become archaic. See also **feminine forms**; **-person**; **sexist language**

(the) Establishment or the élite There is an account in Trotsky's autobiography of how Lenin pointed out to him the sights of London, declaring 'That's *their* Westminster Abbey! That's *their* Houses of Parliament!' By *their* he did not mean 'the British' but the 'ruling classes'. The *Establishment* is a vague umbrella term that covers Lenin's *their*: it was devised by the historian A J P Taylor in 1953, in an article in the *New Statesman*.

There is considerable overlap between the Establishment (usually but not always with a capital E) and the *élite*, an equally general term, first used over a century earlier for the upper-crust of the aristocracy. The question is do the leaders of the government, the **mandarins** of the Civil Service, the Foreign Office, archbishops, half a dozen of the 'top' public schools, a selection of Oxford and Cambridge colleges link up to form a loosely knit but recognizable social and political network of power that controls the affairs of Britain?

Another historian, Hugh Trevor-Roper, demonstrates his doubts by spelling the word with a small *e*, as well as putting it in quotation marks. But the American economist, John Kenneth Galbraith, believes the word *Establishment* 'gained currency because it describes something'. When people talk about *friends in high places* they are echoing the same belief. There is no doubt that there are a number of separate *corridors of power*, not all related to each other clearly enough to form a coherent network, yet with labyrinthine links that give some credence to the idea.

The Establishment implies power and influence, while the élite is more a level of superiority within society, because of rank and social background. As suggested earlier, the two overlap.

The word *élite* now has a pejorative resonance because *élitist* has become a term of angry abuse hurled at members of a small group enjoying seemingly unfair privileges. The word *establishment* has been borrowed to cover cores of people in authority in different fields, who use their power to maintain conformity to established canons. There is the musical establishment, the literary establishment, the legal establishment . . ., all said to be concerned with keeping out people who might 'rock the boat'.

estate or house agent The name *estate agent* for offices in the high street selling houses and flats is an old association with the legal term *real estate* (see **property . . .**), used in matters of inheritance for possessions that are immovable. Although *estate agent* remains the most usual name, there is an increasing tendency for these businesses to call themselves *house agents*, which makes more sense in the 1990s.

estimate See **appraise** . . .

ET *ET* may appear in newspaper headlines any morning. The abbreviation, which means extraterrestrial, also embraces *extraterrestrial intelligence*. On 12 October 1992, which not coincidentally was the 500th anniversary of the day Columbus landed on Watling Island (now San Salvadore Island in the Bahamas), scientists at **NASA** officially started a project to monitor radio waves sent by beings in extraterrestrial worlds. NASA has promised that within 48 hours of confirming a positive contact, it will be announced to the world. If that happens, *ET* will no longer belong exclusively to science fiction.

etc *Etc* is the abbreviation for *et cetera*, 'and the other (things)'. In a list of items separated by commas, it is usual to include a final comma before *etc*, because it's easier to take in: 'the room was furnished with tables, chairs, bookshelves, etc'. There is an argument for omitting the comma before *etc*, especially when there is only one item ('chairs etc'), but it is easier on the eye to put one in. The alternative *&c.* (as used by **Fowler**) is old-fashioned. To write *etc* without a stop looks wrong to many people, but the prevailing practice is to leave out stops in **abbreviations**.

It is offhand to follow a list of people with *etc* (bishops, archdeacons, canons, etc), and preferable to use a phrase, such as 'and others (of the same kind)'. In speaking, it's careless to slip into 'exSETera', instead of 'etSETera', although even newscasters are guilty of this sometimes.

etching See **engraving** . . .

ethical This word, relating to the rightness and wrongness of action, is causing a number of problems, as many more people are working transnationally. Research has been carried out by the Centre for International Business Studies in the Netherlands: 10,000 business managers in 24 industrialized countries were asked about ethical questions, such as the willingness to lie under oath to protect a friend. The results show that what is ethical to people in one country may not be the same in another. We need to consider the word *ethical*, in the sense of correct and honourable in social and business relationships, as more relative than we believed.

ethics *is* or ***are*** As a branch of philosophy, *ethics* is treated as singular. As a quality that someone manifests, or as a code of conduct, it is plural: 'their ethics *are* different from ours'. See also **-ics**

ethnic This is an uneasy word, capable of being used anthropologically, politically, or patronizingly. It comes from the Greek word for people or nation, and its ecclesiastical meaning corresponded to Hebrew 'goyim' (see **goy**), which means non-Jewish. In 15th-century English, it was used about people who were neither Christian nor Jewish, and so regarded as pagan or heathen. It could be logically related to *ethnology*, the scientific comparison of peoples in different regions of the world.

It is used now with different connotations and implications. Every one of us has an ethnic origin, that is our roots deriving from the origin of our parents, rather than nationality. Since World War II, immigration has given the word a strong political colouring, and *ethnic minorities* are associated with the problem of integrating concentrations of Asians or blacks in **inner city** areas.

Ethnic is important as a descriptive word for regional, ancestral, cultural and lingual identities, but it is not easy to separate the word from the other associations it has acquired. The useful noun that embraces both ethnic considerations and ethnic qualities is *ethnicity* (pron: 'ethNISSity'). See also next entry

ethnic cleansing We first heard this cold clinical term in the middle of 1992, about the war in what was Yugoslavia. It is a Serbian description of driving out local Muslims with ruthless brutality. It was the *ethnic cleansing* of large areas of Bosnia which created the largest refugee crisis in Europe since World War II.

etiquette Is the word *etiquette* still used about so-called rules of behaviour? Certainly attitudes have changed since George IV rejected Sir Robert Peel, the Prime Minister, complaining 'He divides his coat tails when he sits down'. The 'what is done' and 'not done' concept still exists and *Debrett's Peerage*, founded in 1769, continues to publish books on the subject, but the word *etiquette*, now considered dainty and snobbish, is usually replaced by 'modern manners' or 'correct form'. The leading guide in America is called *The Guide to Excruciatingly Correct Behaviour*.

etymological fallacy See next entry

etymology or **entomology** *Entomology* has nothing to do with *The Good English Guide*, since it means the study of insects. But every time an entry in this book refers to a Greek, Latin or other source of a word, it is dealing with *etymology*, the branch of linguistics covering the origins of words and the development of their meanings.

Etymology is not always clear-cut. There is no **carbon dating** of words. C T Onions, the last of the editors of the original *OED*, said that some words '. . . going back to Old English are as old as time . . .' (introduction to *The Oxford Dictionary of English Etymology*).

There are some scholars who find it difficult to accept that while etymology can tell us what a word meant at the beginning, and at different periods in its history, it can never dictate what it means *now*. It is pedantic to pursue the lost cause of objecting to the way a word is used in the 1990s on the grounds that the original meaning in Latin, Greek or Old English was different. This is known as an *etymological fallacy*.

eugenics See genetics . . .

euphemism or **genteelism** A *euphemism* is an overall word for a whole range of motives and methods of avoiding calling a spade a spade. If this is for snobbish reasons, to use a word 'less soiled by the lips of the common herd' (H W **Fowler**, *Modern English Usage*, 1926), it could be called a *genteelism*: 'perspire' instead of 'sweat', 'unpleasant odour' instead of a 'stink'. . . . But if it is to avoid upsetting someone, *euphemism* is a better word: 'handicapped' is kinder and less harsh than 'crippled', 'senior citizens' may be kinder for some people than 'old age pensioners' (but see **elderly . . .**).

When it is political evasiveness (as when a Chancellor of the Exchequer stated there will be a 'zero pay-rise', or when the poor are called 'those in lower-income brackets'), **doublespeak** nails it down. When it is a sinister attempt to conceal horrors, such as referring to civilian casualties in a nuclear war as 'collateral damage', **smokescreen words** is a good description. See also **war (language of)**

European or **continental** If you talk about going to the *Continent* every time you cross the English Channel, it could mean you were born well before World War II. If you talk about a *Continental*, meaning someone who is French, German, Italian and so on, you will sound as if your world is bounded by a high-backed leather armchair in a club in Pall Mall or St James's. *Mainland Europe* is the normal way now to distinguish between the British Isles and the rest of Europe (although Americans do not usually make that distinction – it's all *Europe* to them).

The front page of any newspaper for 1 January 1993 should convince anyone that the British are *Europeans*. *European* remains a descriptive word for anyone or anything belonging to the continent of Europe, but it is far more likely now to be a political or economic term relating to the European Community (see **EC**).

The quaint expression *continental breakfast* lives on in hotels – but it's only coffee and rolls.

European Commission See **EC** . . .

European Community or **European Economic Community** See **EC** . . .

European Currency Unit See **ECU** . . .

European Economic Community See **EC** . . .

Europeanism Surprisingly, *Europeanism* is not a new word. It goes back to the early 19th century when it meant adopting European styles and manners. In the 1990s, it has a different meaning altogether. It is used for the approach to integration with Europe, as

enshrined in the ideals of the European Community (see **EC**).

Eurospeak 'Europe' was a Greek word that meant the central area of Greece and later the continental tract of land behind that country. In English, the use of *European* goes back to the beginning of the 17th century, when the word had its present meaning of belonging to the continent of Europe (see **European . . .**).

Euro-, the omnipresent political, economic and commercial prefix of the 1990s, started with the Treaty of Rome which established the European Economic Community in 1957 (see **EC . . .**). Since then *Euro*- has appeared in front of many words as the need arises or the fancy of Eurocrats dictates (hyphens were used early on but are now usually omitted). Dictionaries cannot keep up with the flood of Eurowords. Anyone has the right to add to the list, and many of the terms are ill-defined. What follows are some examples of basic Eurospeak:

Eurobond: These function, in effect, like shares, and are issued by international companies to raise capital in European markets.

Eurocrat: The term is applied mostly to senior executives working for the European Commission (see **EC . . .**). It carries with it the suggestion of bureaucrat and is usually not complimentary.

Eurocurrency: An umbrella term for any currency of the members of the European Community (see **EC . . .**) which is held in a bank outside the country to which the currency belongs (eg German marks held in France).

Eurodollar: These form part of the Eurocurrency market and are funds in US dollars held in European banks.

Euroman: The term is loosely applied to any senior executive working in Europe for a multinational company. Euromen are said to be identified by their **designer** clothes, from a Burberry trenchcoat, to an Italian lightweight suit, down to Gucci shoes.

Euromanager: Companies setting up in Europe look for Euromanagers, men or women with a knowledge of the languages and social attitudes of the main members of the EC, with a European outlook and European business and political savoir faire.

Europerson: An attempt to create a unisex word. It has not caught on and *Euroman* or *Eurowoman* are more usual.

Europhile: Anyone passionately dedicated to the cause of European **federalism**, with all its confusion of different meanings.

Eurospeak: This is a coded language of **acronyms**, Eurowords and politico-economic technical terms used by Eurocrats.

Eurowoman: See *Europerson*

For the difference between Eurospeak, Eurospiel and Eurogabble, see **-speak . . .**

Eurotunnel See **Channel tunnel . . .**

euthanasia *Euthanasia* first meant a quiet easy death, without suffering. The word is now used for inducing death through drugs administered by doctors to the incurably ill. More recently, euthanasia has been separated into three categories. *Voluntary euthanasia* is requested by the sufferer; *involuntary euthanasia* is when the decision is made by someone else, in the case of infants or people suffering from severe mental disorders; *passive euthanasia* is not a deliberate administering of a lethal dose but withdrawing treatment or switching off a life-support machine. The practice is fraught with ethical and legal difficulties. *Mercy killing* is an accepted, if somewhat journalistic, alternative term for euthanasia.

evangelical or **fundamentalist** *Evangelical* has become a confusing word to many people. On the one hand it describes the teaching of the gospel (Matthew, Mark, Luke and John, the writers of the Gospels, are the *evangelists*) and the work of missionaries. In a more recent use, *evangelical* has become synonymous with Christian fundamentalism.

Fundamentalism was used in America in the 1920s for the reactionary movement against the subversion of orthodox Christian beliefs by science and sociology. It reasserted a belief in the revelations of the Bible, rejecting the contention that religious texts must be reinterpreted in the light of a new society and new knowledge. *Evangelical*, in this sense, places the same emphasis on the authority of the Bible and on unquestioning acceptance of miracles, such as the virgin birth and the corporeal resurrection.

In the last decades of the 20th century, *fundamentalist* has become strongly identified with the power of *Islamic fundamentalism*, the strict adherence to the revelations in the Koran, which has given the words at times the suggestion of religious extremism. Conor Cruise O'Brien, the Irish diplomat who was editor of *The Observer*, commented that 'Muslim fanatics . . . are politely referred to as fundamentalists in the West'. This has in turn rubbed off, to some extent, on the word *evangelical*, which, unlike *fundamentalist*, can only be used about the Christian religion.

even With the word **only**, the context usually explains the meaning, but with *even*, the whole sense of a sentence depends on its position. Take these three sentences:

1. I did not *even* see Mary yesterday.
2. I did not see *even* Mary yesterday.
3. I did not see Mary *even* yesterday.

The first suggests that although I had expected to have a conversation with Mary yesterday, I did not manage to see her at all. The second suggests that I saw no one yesterday, although normally I would have seen Mary on that day. And the third suggests that yesterday was the usual day when I would expect to see Mary, but didn't.

In speaking, the meaning can be conveyed by stressing the appropriate word: 'I did not even see Mary yesterday' can have all the above three meanings, depending on whether the stress comes on *see*, *Mary*, or *yesterday*. But in writing, it all depends on where *even* is placed.

(in the) event See **in the event**

-ever There is a case for following the rule that when *-ever* is linked to a *wh-* word as part of a question, it should be kept separate: *When ever* are we leaving? *Where ever* did you put it? *What ever* did you do? *Which ever* will you choose? *Who ever* did this?

When it is part of a proposition qualifying a statement, *-ever* and the *wh-* word should be written as one word: *Whenever* we leave, we must take a taxi; *Wherever* it is, we'll find it; *Whatever* you do, be careful; *Whichever* you choose, I hope it goes well; *Whoever* did this will regret it. This also applies to **how ever** (*How ever* will you do it? *However* you do it, take care). *Whatever* is one word when it comes before a noun: *whatever* reason, *whatever* subject.

This distinction is a grammatical nicety that is often ignored. It only shows in writing and it makes no difference to the sense. Some people are careful to observe it, others write *whenever, whatever, whoever* . . . every time. See also **forever** . . .

ever so *Ever so*, as an alternative to 'very', to stress a point, strikes a downmarket note. Ernest Gowers, in his revised edition of *Modern English Usage* (1965), expresses it with characteristic urbanity, listing three expressions as examples of 'progressive vulgarization': 'Thank you *ever so* much', 'He's *ever so* nice', 'I've enjoyed myself *ever so*'.

every The verb after *every* should always be *singular*, even when *every* is combined with a plural noun: '*every* one of the *women has* the right to vote'.

everybody See **unisex grammar**

every day or **everyday** Milk is delivered *every day*, which makes it an *everyday* (that is unremarkable) occurrence. See also next entry

everyday or **ordinary** The two words are similar in meaning. But an *ordinary* dress, *ordinary* wine, etc writes off the dress and the wine as dull and uninteresting. An *everyday* dress, an *everyday* wine does not dismiss them in the same way: it suggests that the dress or the wine may be quite pleasant, all right for those times when something special is not called for. It is interesting that in France the description 'vin ordinaire' had become so derogatory that it has been replaced by 'vin de table', best translated as 'everyday wine'.

every one or **everyone** *Everyone* is for people: 'Everyone turned up'. *Every one* is for things: 'Every one of the glasses was broken'. Use it also for a number of specific people: 'Every one of the bishops turned up'.

The dilemma over whether *everyone* should be followed by 'his' or 'his or her', when necessary, is dealt with under **unisex grammar**.

evince or **evoke** The two words are sometimes confused with each other. *Evince* means to reveal a hitherto hidden quality: 'he evinced a generosity that was altogether unexpected'. *Evoke* is to call up a response or an emotion: 'the accusation evoked an immediate denial'; 'his generosity evoked her gratitude'.

evolution See development . . .

ex *Ex* was the word in America for a former husband or wife. Now that relationships are less formalized and more diverse, *ex* is freely used in America and Britain for a former partner in any relationship, married or not, heterosexual or homosexual. 'My ex' may imply a friendliness and lack of rancour, but not always. See also next entry; **erstwhile**

ex-, **late** or **former** At the time of writing, Richard Nixon is an *ex*-president, or a *former* president of the United States. When he dies, he will be the *late* president for a few years, for *late* is used about someone who has died recently.

Note that an *ex*- or a *former* whatever-it-is remains that for life. We cannot say, of John Major for example, he *was* a former Foreign Secretary. Even though he became Prime Minister, he *is* a former Foreign Secretary. Only after he is dead, can we say 'When he became Prime Minister, he *was* a *former* Foreign Secretary'.

When a woman or a man is talking about a husband or a wife who is no longer alive, no matter how long they have been dead, they remain 'my late husband' or 'late wife' (former or ex-husband implies they are divorced). See also previous entry

exactly equal See equal

excellent Is it all right to say 'Thank you for a *most excellent* dinner'? *Excellent* is absolute and things cannot be *more* excellent or, the argument continues, *most* excellent, although *quite* excellent is in order, because this is not comparative. Perhaps this is linguistic hair-splitting. In 1892 William Watson wrote *Lachrymae Musarum*, a long poem in which every stanza ended with the line 'The things that are more excellent', which doesn't prove anything but does suggest that there are occasions when *more excellent* or *most excellent* could fit the bill.

except or **excepting** *Excepting* only applies to negative constructions: 'all the senior ministers were present, *not* excepting the Prime Minister'. This is using a **double negative** to make a positive, so it means, of course, that the Prime Minister *was* present, otherwise it would be '. . . *except* the Prime Minister'. It is an awkward turn of phrase and '. . . including the Prime Minister' or '. . . even the Prime Minister' communicates more directly.

In passing, *with the exception of* has twice as many syllables as *except for*, so why use it?

exceptionable, **exceptional**, **unexceptionable** and **unexceptional** Surprisingly often something outstanding is described as *exceptionable* instead of *exceptional*. *Exceptionable* means something that can be objected to, that we can *take exception to*. But the word should be used with care, since some people would misunderstand it and take 'this is exceptionable' to mean 'this is exceptional'.

The negative forms can also be confusing. *Unexceptionable* means there is nothing that can be criticized: *unexceptional* means ordinary or unremarkable. 'The statement is unexceptionable' is praising it; 'the statement is unexceptional' is dismissing it.

(in) excess (of) See in excess of

excitable or **exciting** A BBC political correspondent once said about a member of parliament that he was 'not the most excitable of politicians, so the House was empty when he rose to speak'. The word should, of course, have been *exciting*, meaning someone or something that arouses feelings of excitement in other people. *Excitable* can only be used about people or animals, since it means easily becoming excited.

exclamation See interjection . . .

exclamation mark (!) An exclamation mark is properly used as a form of punctuation after an **interjection** or a word or phrase said in passion. At times it can be as wrong to omit it as it is to leave out a question mark after a question: How good this is! God save the Queen! 'Waik! Not bloody likely!' (Eliza Doolittle in Shaw's *Pygmalion*).

It is questionable whether an exclamation mark should be used to show superiority or to indicate that a comment is funny: 'He went to the Ritz in a T-shirt and jeans!'; 'A funny thing happened to me on the way to the opera!' The words in such statements stand on their own. On the other hand, there are times when an exclamation mark is justified to show surprise or anger, that would not obviously follow from the words themselves: 'He said that to you!'; 'It doesn't matter what you say!'

Exclamation marks can be arch, coy, or a heavy-handed way of saying to a reader 'That's a joke, see?' Nor is there much reason to use an exclamation mark in brackets (!) to show something is unexpected or funny. If there's a case for an exclamation mark, use one – but not too often, or they lose their effect. Using double or treble exclamation marks (!!!) is labouring the point.

exclusive *Exclusive* has become one of the most popular words with **estate agents**: 'an exclusive house for sale' could mean it excludes anyone who cannot afford the price, or doesn't like a tawdry imitation of Georgian architecture, or doesn't want a double garage with automatic doors. . . . But that's not what the estate agent means: *exclusive* is meant to suggest snobbish, upmarket and designed to impress friends.

excreta or **faeces** These are the two most formal words for **shit**, but the meanings do not exactly coincide. *Excreta*, which is singular, includes urine as well as waste matter from the bowels. *Faeces* (pron: 'FEEseez'), which is plural, relates to the bowels only. There are few occasions when the words are used, as alternatives usually come to mind first.

ex div See **cum**

executive There used to be a distinction between **clerical** and *executive*: *clerical* described employees who did routine work, such as bookkeeping and filing, while *executive* was a higher grade, with more responsibilities for decisions. In government, the executive deals with the administration of laws. As the word **clerk** became old-fashioned and everyone in offices wanted to be called an executive, the word became devalued and almost meaningless. Paradoxically, at the same time *executive* became a snob word, encouraged perhaps by the fashion for calling managing directors **chief executives**.

Everyone climbed on the bandwagon. Estate agents joined in, with executive houses, and a caption under a *New Yorker* cartoon read: 'This is my executive suite and this my executive vice-president, Ralph Anderson, and my executive secretary, Adele Eades, and my executive desk and my executive carpet and my executive waste-paper basket and my executive ashtray . . .'. For *executive class*, see **first class** . . .

(object of the) **exercise** See **object** . . .

ex gratia The literal meaning of this Latin phrase is 'out of kindness' or 'as a favour'. It is used in English to suggest that a payment is made, not out of a legal obligation, but as a gesture of goodwill. But there are instances, when the question of legal obligation has not been tested, that an ex gratia payment is made or offered in the hope that it will be the end of the matter. That is less 'out of kindness' or 'as a favour' than 'trying it on'. (Pron: 'exGRAYsher'.)

exhausting or **exhaustive** *Exhausting* describes an activity that leaves you exhausted; *exhaustive* describes the treatment of a subject that is thorough, detailed and comprehensive. There is no real overlap in meaning, except that an exhaustive explanation or report may at the same time be exhausting to listen to or read.

exhibitionist A word with two meanings, one irritating but not especially harmful, the other a manifestation of a psychosexual disorder. The first kind of exhibitionist is a show-off, someone who behaves in an exaggerated way in order to attract attention. The second kind is a person, usually a man, who has a compulsive desire to expose his genitals in public in front of women, a practice known in law as 'indecent exposure'. Women, especially younger ones, are likely to call this kind of exhibitionist by a colourful slang word – a *flasher*.

exit poll Exit polls are last-minute news at election time. It seems that no one can wait, even for a few hours, to know the result of an election, so pollsters are waiting outside polling booths to ask people who are leaving how they voted. The figures are averaged out into an *exit poll*.

exorbitant An intrusive *h* creeps into this word from time to time ('exhorbitant'), probably because of some unconscious association with 'exhort'. Even *The Times* has commented on 'exhorbitant interest charges', which Bill Bryson, deputy chief sub-editor of that paper, justifiably calls 'inhexcusable' (*Penguin Dictionary of Troublesome Words*).

exotic *Exotic* comes from a Greek word meaning outside, and should really be used for something coming from another country. In botany, *exotic* is applied to plants found in a region where they are not **indigenous**. Nowadays every supermarket has exotic fruits, fruits from faraway places. But the way the word is used about people is different: it describes what they look like, not where they come from. Any woman born and bred in Surbiton or Scunthorpe could be called exotic, if she has dyed her hair green or has worked hard in other ways at looking bizarre.

expatriate The musicologist, Fritz Spiegl, picked on the magazine, *Classical Music*, for unintentionally defaming the Irish flautist, James Galway, by referring to him as an 'expatriot'. That could only mean someone who is no longer prepared to support or defend their country. The mistake is understandable, since the word the magazine intended, *expatriate*, is often pronounced in exactly the same way ('exPATrie(r)t'). This makes out a case for adopting the alternative but less common pronunciation: 'exPAYtrie(r)t'. An expatriate is someone who lives abroad, and in expatriate circles, is shortened to *expat*.

expect *Expect* means to assume that something is going to happen: 'they expect to get married later in the year'. There is still an objection to the use of *expect* to mean suppose or believe, or that an event is probable: 'I expect the train will be late as usual'; 'I expect they've arrived by now'. Some current dictionaries still label this as colloquial. This use of *expect* is so well established, that we can hardly expect people to pay any attention to the purists who still make a fuss about it. See also **anticipate** . . .

expectant See **pregnant** . . .

experimental, **avant-garde** or **progressive** All three words can apply to innovators and innovation in art, literature and music. In France, *avant-garde* is still used as a military term for a unit sent out in advance. In 19th-century France, it was adopted as the cultural expression for artists and writers who took the risk of defying established conventions by leading new movements. It became equally popular in English: the avant-garde theatre, an avant-garde exhibition. *Avant-garde* is also used as a noun: an exhibition of the avant-garde.

It seems that now *avant-garde* is old-fashioned, even an anachronistic term, since modern trends are so widely accepted: the BBC regularly broadcasts new and unorthodox music, and even the Royal Academy, according to Roger de Grey, as president, has 'embraced modernism . . . an evolution which would have been unthinkable ten years ago' (introduction to the RA's 1990 Summer Exhibition).

Progressive is also used much less now about art forms, and is more often applied in politics to parties and policies aimed at social reform, or used in business about companies employing new and more efficient methods of management, or is a term for schools and educational methods that break away from traditional attitudes.

Experimental remains as a seemingly indispensable word in art, literature and music: almost anything in art galleries, concert halls or theatres that defies expectations and shocks sensibilities is labelled *experimental*. In this sense, the word is noncommittal, suggesting we have no idea what it means: it may be a load of rubbish or possibly a work of genius, so we'd better be careful what we say about it. See also **contemporary** . . .; **modern**

explicit or **express**   These are often used interchangeably, since they both mean that something has been put clearly into words. But there is a useful distinction. *Explicit* suggests that everything has been set out clearly and in some detail: 'it is an explicit offer, leaving no doubt about the conditions'. *Express* suggests definite and positive, with no room for argument: 'although details are still to be agreed, it is an express offer'.

Explicit has a more recent and more dubious meaning: it is short for *sexually explicit*. 'Explicit scenes' in films or novels is sometimes no more than a commercial euphemism for **pornographic**.

exploit   Since the mid-18th century *exploit* has been a double-edged verb. On the one hand, it is perfectly all right to exploit an opportunity, meaning to make the most of it, or to exploit resources, that is to get the maximum benefit from them. But to exploit a situation is to use it ruthlessly for one's own ends, and to exploit a person is to take advantage of their weakness or vulnerability. It is a verb to be used with care now, since the unpleasant meaning of *exploit* is taking precedence and may be colouring the meaning of the word in all senses.

Similarly, the noun *exploitation* is usually positive when referring to resources or business opportunities (exploitation of North Sea oil), but negative when used about people (exploitation of women). *Exploitative* is nearly always a strong negative word, describing someone or a situation that takes ruthless advantage of people.

exposed and **exposure to**   It is usually a bad thing to be *exposed to* anything, just as *exposure to* is usually unpleasant: exposed to danger; exposure to the cold. But the expressions are increasingly used now about good things as well: 'we need someone who has had exposure to European ways of doing business'; 'I was exposed to valuable new ideas'. There is some objection to this extended use, although the meaning is clear enough, so perhaps it is pedantic to make an issue over it. There are ready alternatives, such as 'come into contact with'. Choose whichever seems appropriate, so long as you don't mind being exposed to occasional criticism for wrong usage.

express   See **explicit** . . .

expresso   See **espresso** . . .

'EXquisite' or **'exQUIsite'**   For the right effect, the stress should be on the first syllable: 'EXquisite'. Stress on the second syllable ('exQUIsite') is now a recognized alternative, but for many people it lets the side down.

extempore, **impromptu** or **extemporaneous**   'Ex tempore' in Latin is literally 'out of time', and hence on the spur of the moment. 'In promptu' is Latin for 'in readiness'. At one time *extempore* in English was used for a speech thought out briefly in advance, with maybe just a few notes on hand, while *impromptu* meant a speech with no preparation at all. But both words are used in the same way now, for a speech or performance off the cuff, just as it comes. The only verb available is *extemporize*.

Extemporaneous is a later form of *extempore* (pron: 'ikSTEMpery') and has exactly the same meaning.

extended or **extensive**   'It was an extended assignment because the work was so much more extensive than anticipated': *extended* is when something is drawn out or added to, whereas *extensive* is long, wide-ranging, far-reaching.

extension or **extention**   There is no such word as 'extention': it is a spelling mistake. Remember 'extensive' and there should be no problem.

extensive   See **extended** . . .

extention   See **extension** . . .

exterior or **external**   *Exterior* is appropriate where there is clearly a corresponding interior. *External* simply means outside. An *exterior* door, for example, suggests there is a double door, an inner door as well as an outer one; an *external* door is simply any outside door of a building.

There are exterior paints, that is paints used for the outside of buildings, corresponding to paints for interior decoration. Some lotions carry a warning 'for external use only' (not *exterior*, for the inner organs of the body cannot be said to correspond to the skin).

extraordinary   The first *a* should not be pronounced, leaving the word with five syllables: 'ekSTRAWdinery'. While 'extra-ordinary' (six syllables) is still listed by dictionaries as an alternative pronunciation, to say it that way sounds exaggerated.

Extraordinary means out of the ordinary. When a company convenes an *extraordinary general meeting*, it is a special meeting to deal with a particular matter, as opposed to the customary annual general meeting. Placed *after* a noun, *extraordinary* may be used in diplomatic affairs for someone with a special assignment, such as an *envoy extraordinary*, but it has come to be used in that position to imply exceptional distinction: Nelson Mandela, before his release, was referred to as a 'prisoner–celebrity extraordinary'.

extrasensory perception See **parapsychology** . . .

extraterrestrial intelligence See **ET**

extremist *Extremist* is part of post-World War II language of terrorism. It is usually applied to someone who not only holds drastic, possibly fanatical, political or religious views, but is prepared to use violence in support of them. But an extremist from one point of view, may be a *freedom fighter* from another (see **terrorism**).

extrovert or **outgoing** An extrovert (*extravert* is an alternative but less usual spelling) is a psychological type: *extroversion* was Jung's term for the state of evading feelings and sensitivities by focusing attention on others. The word is used loosely for anyone who is friendly and sociable. In principle, it is better to leave *extrovert* in the domain of psychology and to choose the simpler, less loaded word *outgoing* about someone who is good company and easy to be with. See also **introvert**

eye contact *Eye contact* is part of the folklore of courses on public speaking and business presentations. The idea is that instead of looking down at your notes or over the heads of the audience, you make a point of looking directly at as many of them as you can, even if only for a split-second, so they feel you are talking to *them*. Politicians have all been on the courses, and when they are speaking they dutifully look from side to side, making eye contact.

eyrie or **aerie** The most recent dictionaries continue to include the older spelling *aerie*, as an alternative, but it would be eccentric to use it now (although it is still seen in America). Nearly every recorded use shows *eyrie*. There are also various alternative pronunciations, but the most usual one makes it rhyme with 'eerie'. The primary meaning is the nest, usually of an eagle, high up and remote, and by extension, *eyrie* is used about a dwelling-place, out of the way on a hill or mountain, or, to bring it more down-to-earth, a study–bedroom built into the roof space of a semi-detached house in the suburbs.

· F ·

fable or **parable** The words are close to each other, because a fable and a parable both contain a lesson. A *fable* usually illustrates the lesson by a story about animals that reflects an everyday aspect of human nature: for example, the fable of the tortoise and the hare teaches us that steady progress is more likely to win in the end than showy flashes of brilliance. The lesson contained in a *parable* is moral or spiritual, rather than practical, and is inherent in the story rather than explicitly stated. Compare the parable of the prodigal son with the fable of the tortoise and the hare.

fabulous Dictionaries have capitulated to the popular use of *fabulous*. Not many years back, the primary meaning was shown as legendary, as recounted in fables, which is what it meant in the 15th century. But since the 1980s, most dictionaries have moved that meaning to the bottom of the list, giving the first meaning as 'beyond belief', followed by colloquial meanings that can range from 'marvellous' to 'beautiful'.

The word has lost its magic, cheapened by advertising ('Don't miss this fabulous offer!'), show business ('Fifty fabulous girls!'), and anyone who talks about a 'fabulous meal', a 'fabulous man', 'fabulous weather', or to say in response to the most ordinary suggestion – *Fabulous*!

To use *fabulous* any longer in its original meaning is likely to be misunderstood, unless it is made clear in the context: 'the tapestries depicted fabulous beasts that do not exist in reality'.

façade or **facade** Most current dictionaries show the **cedilla** under the *c* as optional, although some people insist on it to show they know what's what. It may disappear even in French one day. Meantime, it may be safer to use *façade*, to avoid anyone thinking you've made a mistake. See also **accents (in print)**

face See confront . . .

face or **face up to** Purists object to *face up to* as unnecessary because *face*, as a verb, can stand on its own. Yet to *face up to* something does suggest courage and a stiffening of resolve, so the phrase is useful. If anyone criticizes it, say it was used as long ago as 1920, by Sir Walter Raleigh, professor of English at Oxford, no less.

face-lift *Face-lift* is an expression that goes back to the early 1920s, when discreet clinics in Switzerland surgically removed wrinkles and sagging skin to make a person look younger. After World War II, the term was extended to include modernizing or cleaning up buildings, statues or almost anything. Even a business can be given a face-lift by bringing in new management.

Face-lift can, in some contexts, suggest a superficial change simply to make something look good, rather than a thorough overhaul (see **cosmetic**): 'the government's policies were given a face-lift before the election'. See also **plastic surgery** . . .

face to face or **tête-à-tête** *Face to face* describes a personal conversation between two people, sometimes implying a certain degree of confrontation: 'Instead of writing letters, let's meet face to face over this'. *Tête-à-tête* (literally 'head-to-head') suggests a confidential or intimate discussion or meeting. It can be used as a descriptive word or as a noun: 'Let's have a tête-à-tête discussion . . .', or simply 'Let's have a tête-à-tête'. *Face to face* should be used about negotiation; *tête-à-tête* has more of a hand-on-shoulder feeling about it . . . or a candlelit dinner.

face, **intrinsic**, **market** or **nominal value**
Face and *nominal value* amount to the same thing in Stock Exchange terminology: it is the sum recorded on a share certificate or other negotiable document. The *market value* of the same security could be very different: it is the price that a buyer will pay for it, which could be much more, especially in the case of shares, if the company is doing well, or much less, if circumstances are different. *Intrinsic value* is the basic measurable value of the material.

A gold sovereign can demonstrate all four values: the face or nominal value is £1, the sum engraved on it; the intrinsic value depends on the value of gold at the time and the weight of the coin, that is what it would fetch melted down; the market value is what a buyer will pay for the coin as a collector's item, which would depend on its rarity.

Intrinsic value is often used in a less specific way, to mean an inherent quality or interest: 'this painting has an intrinsic value because the artist gave it to us as a wedding present'. See also **street value**

facile Although *facile* means easy and without effort, it *always* carries with it the negative meaning of superficial and without real value: a facile argument is one that has not been thought out. *Facile* should never be used in a complimentary sense.

facsimile   See fax . . .

faction   *Faction* is a trouble-making group within an organization, usually in a political party. It tends to imply disruptive and destructive intentions and, for that reason, should not be used in a good sense.

Faction, as a literary term, was coined in the 1970s for a book, play or film that purports to be based on facts or real events, but mixes them up with fiction. The problem is to separate the two, so the result can be a distorted view of history that becomes accepted. There is nothing new about the idea of faction, which could apply to Shakespeare's historical plays. It is an unfortunate literary term, because it sounds dismissive, neither one thing nor another, although it is not usually intended that way.

factitious or **fictitious**   The similarity of meaning between these two words causes confusion, particularly as both words can be used with the same noun. Anything *factitious*, although seemingly genuine, is deliberately contrived for an ulterior motive: spreading a rumour about a takeover bid could create a factitious demand for shares, which would push up the price; to hint that an unsigned drawing is by Picasso gives it a factitious value.

Fictitious is imaginary or unreal: a fictitious demand for shares means there was no demand at all; a fictitious value could be given to a worthless painting by putting it in a beautiful frame. As in the last example, sometimes it is necessary to think carefully about which is the right word to use.

factor   *Factor* is used so loosely and so often that it is easy to forget it has a precise meaning, which is something that contributes directly to a result: 'the unpopular tax was a factor in the defeat of the government at the by-election'. For *factor* has become in many situations a vague substitute for a more precise word: 'the factors in this dispute' (instead of 'disagreements' or 'issues'): 'the factors we must take into account . . .' (instead of 'considerations'); 'whatever the factors are . . .' (instead of 'circumstances').

faculty   See facility . . .

faeces   See excreta . . .

fag   *Fag*, as a British slang word with strong class distinctions, is going through a transition. Its use for a cigarette, predominantly working-class, is much less common than it used to be. The upper-class use of *fag* at some public schools, for a junior boy at the beck and call of a senior, if not obsolete, now sounds out of place. The latter use may derive from 'fatigue', which also applies to *fag* for a tedious job of work, a colloquial use that is as popular as ever.

In America, *fag* for a cigarette was recorded in the late 19th century but would be rare now, when it is more likely to be an offensive slang term for a male homosexual, which, it has been suggested, may be connected with the use of *fag* in British public schools.

fail and **failure**   Some authorities criticize the use of these words in sentences such as 'it failed to happen . . .'; 'his failure to turn up . . .'. While *fail* and *failure* mean trying but not succeeding, they are freely used simply to mean something not happening, that should happen, as in the above examples. After all, no one argues about *without fail*, a common expression used to stress the importance of doing something: 'it must be done without fail'.

fail-safe   *Fail-safe* is when something is made to *fail* in order to make other things *safe*. Technically, this functions as an automatic cut-out in the event of a component breaking down, so that no damage is done. In computer use, *fail-safe* automatically protects a processing system by switching off when a failure is detected.

In non-technical use, *fail-safe* has become a useful term for a plan or system, worked out in such a way that if part of it goes wrong, reserve procedures automatically take over. In technology, this principle is covered by the post-World War II use of the word **redundant** for an extra component built in to take over if another one fails.

failure or **unsuccess**   The difference between *failure* and *unsuccess* may come near to splitting hairs, but it can be useful: *unsuccess* does not go as far as *failure*, perhaps only halfway. Graham Greene makes the point in *The End of the Affair* (1951), by using *unsuccess* about a writer. See also **un- words**

fair   Be on guard when you see the word *fair*, because it can be used to disarm criticism, or at best is often dependent on a particular point of view. A *fair offer* should be fair to all parties, rather than fair only to the person making it. In law, *fair comment* can be a defence against an action for defamation, claiming that whatever was written or said was reasonable in the circumstances. Such actions can be fiercely contested, which proves that no one has exclusive right to interpret the word *fair*.

fairy   This is one of the slang words in Britain and America for a homosexual that has almost dropped out of use since homosexual relationships have become more accepted. Fairies have gone back to their proper place at the bottom of gardens or on Christmas trees. See also **gay, queen, queer**

faith or **religion**   Both words reflect a system of beliefs concerning the purpose of life. But the distinction is fundamental, and there is a tension between the two concepts. *Religion* usually refers to an organized external structure, with institutions proclaiming and regulating doctrines and procedure. *Faith* is essentially personal, an inner belief, which may or may not be linked to an established religion. We can follow the

Christian or Jewish religion, or any other religion, for social or family reasons, and as a consequence say we are of the Christian or Jewish faith. That is no more than using the word *faith* to mean religion. The real meaning of the word does not relate to external conformity. We cannot take possession of faith: it has to take possession of us.

faithfulness   See **fidelity** . . .

fall   The **Fowler** brothers regretted (*The King's English*, 1906) the loss of this American word for 'autumn', which had been used long ago in Britain, as early as the 14th century. And there are others who would like to see British English once again adopt this more poetic and descriptive name for the 'season of mists and mellow fruitfulness'. But there is no sign of this happening.

fallacy or **falsehood**   *Fallacy* is often wrongly used to mean a falsehood, or even a **lie**, as in 'She was sacked, and it is a fallacy to say she resigned'. *Fallacy* is a term in logic for a slip-up in reasoning that makes an argument invalid. *Fallacy* and *fallacious* should carry with them the suggestion of a wrong inference: 'It is a fallacy that high inflation leads to high unemployment'; 'The argument that low interest rates always leads to high inflation is fallacious'. *Falsehood* (and *false*) suggests more a deliberate attempt to mislead than illogical reasoning.

fall guy   See **scapegoat** . . .

fall out or **fallout**   To *fall out* with someone is to have a row with them. *Fallout*, as one word, is more sinister, because it usually means airborne radioactive debris from a nuclear explosion, or an accident in a nuclear reactor. As one word, it is also used for almost any kind of side-effect, good or bad: *Newsweek* wrote about the 'literary fallout' from the war, meaning books written about it.

falsehood   See **fallacy** . . .; **lie** . . .

false illusion   See **delusion** . . .

(the) **family *is*** or ***are***   See **collective words**

family man   This ambiguous journalistic expression is also in general use. It is not intended to mean simply a man with a wife and children, but a man who gives them as high a priority in his life as his work and other interests. For the time being, the corresponding expression, *family woman*, does not exist, since a woman's priority is taken for granted, but as more women pursue ambitious careers and independent lives, we may before long hear about *family women* as well.

fancy   *Fancy* has a number of different meanings. Three of these are worth looking at more closely. Used as a verb, you can fancy a drink (or anything else) or you can fancy yourself (be pleased with the way you look). But to fancy a man or a woman means you find them sexually attractive. This was formerly working-class slang but is now classless.

As a descriptive word, *fancy* has moved up from colloquial to standard English, as a way of saying exaggerated or pretentious: fancy shops, as you would expect, charge fancy prices.

The poetic use of *fancy* as a noun, to mean imagination ('Tell me where is fancy bred, Or in the heart or in the head?', *Merchant of Venice*, Act III Sc ii) is sadly perhaps too literary now for everyday use.

fanny   This slang word, classed in Britain as vulgar or coarse, means a woman's genitals, and according to Eric Partridge, may go back to 1794. That year, a classic on life in a brothel was published, *The Memoirs of Fanny Hill*. This origin is disputed by the latest Oxford dictionary, which places the word in the 20th century, with its origin unknown.

Fanny is used, without seeming vulgar, by both men and women, and is surrounded by legends. There is the story of BBC technicians falling about, as the announcer, winding up a cookery demonstration by Fanny Cradock, said blandly 'Well, that's all we have time for, and I hope *your* doughnuts will look like Fanny's!' When the residents of Fanny Road in Barnes, London, were unable to stand the jokes any more, they had their road renamed 'St Hilda's Road'. Such is the power of language. In America, *fanny* is everyday slang, not considered vulgar, for the backside, and is used for both sexes.

fantasy or **phantasy**   These are alternative spellings of the same word. *Fantasy* is taking over, probably because of the influence of 'fantastic', and the spelling *phantasy* is beginning to look archaic, although it is still used in psychology. Note that *phantasmagoria* and *phantasmagorical* are always spelt *ph-*.

far away or **faraway**   This is usually two words ('it isn't far away from here'), but becomes one word when used as a descriptive word in front of a noun (faraway places).

farm fresh   *Farm fresh* is meaningless jargon in the food industry, cashing in on two evocative words. Food in supermarkets does not usually come straight from a farm, and even if it did, why should that, in itself, be a guarantee of freshness?

fart   Although treated seriously, as an early English word going back to the 13th century, by C T Onions (*The Oxford Dictionary of English Etymology*), *fart* remains prudishly classified as vulgar or coarse slang by dictionaries.

What alternative is there? To 'break wind', which was at one time an attempt to be polite about something that doesn't lend itself to politeness, now sounds quaint. So we can either treat the manifestation as unmentionable, or refer to it in some roundabout way, such as 'the release through the anus of wind from the intestines' (fourteen syllables as against one).

farther or **further** Some authorities advise that because *farther* is the comparative of 'far' it should always be used for distance: 'Is there much farther to go?' But there is no general agreement over this, and in practice there is only one difference between the two variants to remember. Either can be used about distance: 'Rome is farther (or further) from London than it is from Brussels'). But when it comes to time, something additional, or symbolic distance, only *further* should be used: until further notice; a further payment on account; can we take this further?

Fascist or **Nazi** Long after the fall of Mussolini in Italy and Hitler in Germany, *Fascist* and *Nazi* are kept alive as terms of abuse for someone supporting extreme nationalistic, coercive or undemocratic policies. *Fascism* derives from Latin 'fasces' (a bundle of rods round an axe), the name of the ancient symbol of authority of the Roman state. It was used about the movement Mussolini led to power in Italy in 1922, later becoming a word associated with the Nazi movement in Germany under Hitler.

The term *Nazi* (phonetic spelling of the first part of Nationalsozialist, the German socialist party) is also hurled at someone who advocates extreme racist and authoritarian measures. *Fascist* and *Fascism* have become symbolic words to attack any form of dictatorship: it is ironic that on 19 August 1991, the day the coup by hardline Communists deposed President Gorbachev, the cry went up in the streets of Moscow: '*No* to Fascism!'

fashion See cult . . .

fast, **quick** or **swift** In order of speed, *fast* and *swift* are about equal, and *quick* perhaps a little way behind, hence the *fast lane* on a motorway. In at least a couple of phrases, *quick* catches up: 'quick as a flash'; 'quick as lightning'. *Swift* is a more literary word ('swift as an arrow').

fast food Arguably, the concept was invented by the 4th Earl of Sandwich (1718–92), to enable him to stay at the gaming table, without breaking for meals. But rather than a **snack** or a sandwich, *fast food* means a complete meal, usually hamburgers or fried chicken, served up before you can say knife and fork.

fast lane The term *fast lane* on motorways, the outside lane used to overtake or to drive at high speed, has become part of competitive life in the 1990s. Anyone who wants to get to the top has to live in the fast lane, leaving others behind. Some companies have fast-lane management training schemes. In America they call it *fast track*.

fat cat A slang expression that spread to Britain in the 1980s from America, where it goes back to the 1920s. It is used derisively about a rich person in power, over-eating at the most expensive restaurants, driven about by a chauffeur, and completely out of touch with the problems of ordinary people.

fatherly or **patriarchal** *Patriarchal* is a biblical and ecclesiastical word of authority. It is, of course, exclusively male, which is why for some women it describes the institutions of male domination, political, economic and coercive. To say a man is patriarchal may mean no more to some people than he takes up a role of paternal authority: to feminists it is identified with sexual and economic oppression. Other than in connection with the Roman Catholic and Eastern Orthodox Church, *patriarchal* is a word to use with caution, because of what it may symbolize.

Fatherly is a much more affectionate word, usually meaning supporting, helping or comforting a woman or a younger man. See also **motherly or matriarchal**

fathers-in-law or **father-in-laws** *Fathers-in-law*.

fatwa It is through Salman Rushdie, the British writer born in India, that this Arabic word is now included in all current English dictionaries. Ayatollah Khomeini, the religious leader in Iran, issued a fatwa, condemning Salman Rushdie to death, because his novel, *The Satanic Verses* (1988), was seen as blasphemous. A *fatwa* is not a death sentence, as some newspapers have said, but any decree on a spiritual matter. There are still some newspapers that slip *fatwa* between inverted commas to mark its foreignness, but this is hardly necessary.

faultline Until the autumn of 1992, *faultline* was a geological and engineering term. In a general sense, it had appeared in a very few dictionaries. It was brought to the fore during the currency crisis in September 1992. Norman Lamont, as Chancellor of the Exchequer, spoke about the *faultline* in the European exchange rate mechanism (see **EMS**). The word was quickly taken up by other politicians and commentators. It is, in fact, a useful word, suggesting not so much a fault, but a weakness in an arrangement that makes it liable to give way under stress. For Los Angelinos *faultline* remains first and foremost connected with the geological fault on which their city is built.

faux pas See gaffe . . .

fawn See beige . . .

fax or **facsimile** *Facsimile* has been used in English since the 17th century: it combines two Latin words, meaning 'to make like'. The first recorded use of *fax* goes back to 1948, when *Time* magazine in America used it for *facsimile*, in the early days of photocopying machines. In the last years of the 1980s, fax shot into everyday language in every country in the world, as 'plug-in-and-go' technology used ordinary telephone lines to send and receive letters, drawings and diagrams. Overnight, fax revolutionized intercity and international communications. At the end of the 1980s, *fax art* was unveiled when, on 10 November 1989, David Hockney transmitted from his studio in Los Angeles 144 sections of a giant painting, to be assembled on the wall of a gallery near Bradford.

Although **phone** is curiously still classified as 'colloquial' by some dictionaries, *fax* has immediately become standard English. No one ever says *facsimile*, as *fax* is too neat and all-purpose, doubling as a noun ('send a fax') or a verb ('*fax* it'). *Facsimile* remains, of course, the standard word outside telecommunications for something that is an exact reproduction of a book, a manuscript, document, etc.

fax art   See previous entry

FCA   See **chartered accountant**

fearful or **fearsome**   *Fearful* is used far more often, always followed by 'of' or 'that': 'he is fearful *of* being made redundant'; 'she is fearful *that* he will get hurt'. *Fearsome* is a more literary word, more applicable to appearance: a fearsome spectacle; a fearsome ogre. . . .

fearless or **unafraid**   Dictionaries do not usually point out the subtle but important difference between these two words. *Fearless* describes an admirable quality that some people possess, to be brave and without fear in the face of danger: 'she will do what she believes to be right, fearless of the risks involved'.

To be *unafraid* is a right that belongs to living in a civilized society, to be able to go about our daily life without fear of oppression, unfair discrimination, or violence. The writer, Salman Rushdie, who can surely claim to speak with feeling about this, has declared that 'liberty is to be unafraid'. For the distinction between *courage* and *fearlessness*, see **courage** . . .

fearsome   See **fearful** . . .

feature   *Feature* has been used since the late 17th century for a prominent part of something. The film industry took a liking to the word: films feature well-known actors, and at the time when two films were usually shown in one programme, the *feature film* was the main one, preceded by a *second-feature* film, a fill-in made on the cheap.

As a verb, the word has become overused in publicity: 'the fixed-price dinner features three courses and coffee'; 'the weekend visit features an evening at the opera'. This is no more than a pretentious substitute for 'includes'.

February   The pronunciation 'FEByoo-ery' is downmarket, although it is easy for anyone to slip into it at times. But it has been criticized so often that most people are careful to pronounce the word as it is spelt: 'FEBroo-ery'.

feckless or **reckless**   Reckless driving may also be feckless, that is unthinking, without attention. But *reckless* carries with it the implication of knowing what you are doing, deliberately taking risks, rather than acting stupidly, because you don't know any better, which is nearer to the meaning of *feckless*. That's why the police use the charge *reckless* driving.

federal and **federalism**   A *federation* is a group of states, each of which retains a certain independence in their internal affairs but devolve principal powers to a central government. The word was first used in a political sense about the United States, and Andrew Jackson, Democratic president 1829–37, referred in a famous toast to 'Our Federal Union'. From the early days of the European Economic Community (see **EC**) *federal* and *federalism* were part of the vocabulary: Jean Monnet (1888–1979), the French statesman who did much to establish the EEC, proclaimed 'Les Etats-Unis d'Europe ont commencé'.

The term *federal* remained in the realms of political science until the early months of 1991, when suddenly it became a linguistic cause célèbre in Europe. The **broadsheets** ran leading articles about the word and its meaning, John Major in the House of Commons called it 'That *word!*' (25.6.1991). The fuss was about the inclusion of *federal* in the proposed Treaty of European Union.

Two words were creating a European Tower of Babel, because *federal* and *federalism* have different meanings in different countries, from a benevolent interpretation in France, where it suggests a devolution of power to regions, to a direct threat, according to some politicians on the other side of the Channel, to British sovereignty, and hence to the Queen herself.

Although it was a linguistic problem, lexicographers were powerless to help, nor could dictionaries clear up the mess. The *f-word*, as it came to be called in the run-up to the Maastricht summit in December 1991, had become as taboo as the four-letter f-word. In the end, the onus was on the European Commission in Brussels to find new unambiguous terms. *Confederation* could be a contender. Unlike a central *federal* government, a *confederation* would have no power over the citizens of the individual countries. *Commonwealth*, a good word for an open association of independent countries, is a term that is too loose and indeterminate for the European Community, and might be seen as a peculiarly British word. The debate continues, with *federal* still a linguistic hot potato. For *federal union* and *confederation*, see **commonwealth**

feedback   *Feedback* is both a technical term and a fashionable word in general use. Technically, it is the return of part of a mechanical output that automatically makes corrections to the functioning of a machine. A simple example is a thermostatic shower: if the water is too hot, the 'output' information is *fed back* to the 'control', which automatically adjusts the balance between hot and cold supply, to keep the water at the pre-set temperature.

In everyday use, *feedback* is almost synonymous with the word 'response', although it should link with the technical application of the word by suggesting that information coming back brings about a regulating change of output. For example, a television station seeks feedback from viewers and uses the information to change programme policy.

Positive and negative feedback have complex economic applications. In simple terms, for example, *positive feedback* from inflation increases pay-settlements, which pushes up prices, which in turn increases inflation. *Negative feedback* has a modifying effect: high unemployment, for example, reduces pay-settlements, which brings down prices and leads to lower inflation. In general use, particularly in advertising and public opinion polls, the terms mean little more than people liking or approving of someone or something (positive feedback), or disapproving (negative feedback).

feel or think 'I *feel*' is a less confrontational way of saying 'this is what I *think*'. Perhaps 'I feel you should not drink so much' is more tactful than 'I think . . .'. At least, it's worth trying.

feel-good factor Political commentators talked about the *feel-good factor* during the pre-election campaign early in 1992. No politician used the phrase, at least in public, for it is such a blatant admission of the selfish motives of voters standing in front of the ballot-box: the supposition is that people *feel good* when they have more money in their pockets, which is an argument for tax-cuts or any other kind of **sweetener** in a pre-election budget. Few other expressions are such a raw display of political cynicism as the feel-good factor.

feet or foot Just as 'a 20-mile journey', 'a 10-pound note' use the singular forms, it is customary to use *foot* when it is hyphenated as a unit of measurement: a six-foot man, a three-foot rule. Foot is also preferable in measurements, such as 'two foot three'. But when 'inches' follows, *feet* should be used (to correspond to the plural 'inches'): two feet three inches.

fellatio See **cunnilingus** . . .

fellow There is no rule about whether *fellow* should or should not be hyphenated in combination with another noun. The following are usually hyphenated: fellow-countryman, fellow-creature, fellow-feeling, fellow-officer. The following are usually kept as two separate words: fellow author, fellow passenger, fellow sufferer, fellow soldier. *Fellow traveller* are separate words for two people travelling together; the hyphenated version (*fellow-traveller*) is the now outdated term for a person who secretly supports the Communist Party.

There is no feminine equivalent of *fellow*, which would be useful as an alternative to **girl**, which some women object to. Women are, willy-nilly, fellows of colleges or of learned or professional societies.

fellow-traveller See previous entry

female See **lady** . . .

feminine See **effeminate** . . .

feminine forms This is a **sociolinguistic** problem. Many women feel that to define people because of

their sex is as discriminatory as defining them on account of colour, race or religion, that 'woman barrister', 'lady doctor', 'headmistress' are as invidious as 'black barrister', 'Asian doctor', 'Jewish teacher'. The argument is that separate classification for women implies the standard is male, which is no better than suggesting the standard is white or Christian.

More and more feminine forms are falling into disuse, as younger generations brought up with unisex words have increasing influence. Eventually the whole situation will settle down, as everyone becomes relaxed about the situation and more unisex forms come into normal use.

Specific examples of feminine forms are dealt with under separate entries in *The Good English Guide*. The principal ones are: **-ess forms; he or they; Ms; -person; unisex grammar**

feminism or sexism There is sometimes uncertainty over how these two words relate to each other. *Feminism* is a stand taken by women: *sexism* is a masculine attitude, sometimes conscious, sometimes unconscious. *Feminism* and *feminist* are not post-World War II words: before the end of the 19th century, there were already examples of them being used about the rights of women. Neither word was used by the women who campaigned, in the 20th century, for the rights of women to vote: instead they took up the name *suffragette* (coined in 1906 in the *Daily Mail*, by adding a feminine suffix to 'suffrage').

In the late 1960s, *feminism* and *feminist* became passionate campaigning words in politics and society. By then, women had long since achieved *political* equality with men (1920 in the US, 1928 in Britain), and *feminism* became identified with issues across the whole social spectrum, from equality of pay and opportunity, the right to abortion, stereotyped attitudes, the trivialization of women in the media, to the age-old masculine bias in the English language.

Sexism and *sexist* were new words, battle-cries in the women's liberation movement of the time. They were deliberately formed on the models of **racism** and racist, to describe social, institutional and economic discrimination against women.

For some people, the terms are less relevant now. In Britain, the Equal Pay Act 1970 and the Sex Discrimination Act 1975 are on the statute book, and by the end of the 1980s, a newspaper headline announced there are more and more 'WOMEN KNOCKING AT BOARDROOM DOORS', not to take in morning-coffee but to sit round the table. In America, the percentages of women lawyers and architects quintupled in two decades, and women make up more than a quarter of Wall Street high-fliers. At the same time, feminism and sexism remain for many women vital terms, still high on the agenda in the 1990s.

feminist See previous entry

femininity *Femininity* is not a straightforward word. For some it means the attractive qualities associated with women, such as gentleness, grace and sensitivity. Some women see it as a meaningless word, claiming that it signifies whatever men want it to mean. Mary Wolistonecraft in *A Vindication of the Rights of Women* (1792) described it as 'weak ellegancy of mind, exquisite sensibility, and sweet docility of manner'. It is a word to watch, to see how new meanings emerge. In the meantime, *femininity* should be used with awareness that it could be interpreted in different ways, not all of which are complimentary.

ferment or **foment** *Fermentation* is the action of yeasts, as in wine- or beer-making, causing agitation and unsettlement. *Fomentation* is the drawing out with heat, mainly used for a hot compress applied to a wound or infection, which is why both verbs can be used to mean stirring up trouble or disorder: 'he fermented (or fomented) trouble among the workforce'.

Ferment (but not 'foment', which doesn't exist) can be used as a noun to mean a stirring up, an excitement: 'the workforce is in ferment over the change of policy'.

Ferment as a verb has the stress on the second syllable ('ferMENT') but as a noun on the first syllable ('FERment').

fetch, **take** or **bring** See bring . . .

fête or **fete** Even in English the **circumflex** sits firmly over the *e* and it seems wrong to drop it, perhaps because the pronunciation still has a hint of the French sound: fête rhymes with 'fate'.

fetish The word has two different meanings. To an anthropologist, a fetish is an inanimate object worshipped by a primitive tribe because it is believed to enshrine a spirit. It is the psychiatrist's use of *fetish* that has become more common: an object, an unexpected part of the body, or a piece of clothing that arouses feverish sexual excitement in someone.

As an extension of the anthropological meaning, *fetish* can be used about almost anything that excites an irrational or compulsive belief or need. There are linguistic fetishes too: see, for example, **hopefully**, **ongoing**, **split infinitive**.

fever . . . See **temperature** . . .

fewer or **less** There is usually someone waiting to pounce on the wrong use of these words, often *less* when it should be *fewer*. There is a simple rule. Use *fewer* when the associated noun is *plural* and *less* when it is *singular*: 'there were fewer *men* than women'; 'fewer *miles* to the gallon'; '*less* butter means *fewer* calories'. An exception is '*less* than 20 *miles* away', since '20 miles' is taken as a distance, rather than separate miles in the plural.

As a piquant postscript, Marks & Spencer discovered there was a surprising number of grammarians among their customers. For years, quick-service check-out points in their food departments were labelled FIVE ITEMS OR LESS. On 7 November 1991, thousands of amended notices appeared: FIVE ITEMS OR FEWER. Henry **Fowler** rides again!

fewest or **least** *Least* is often used wrongly: 'he had the least votes of all the candidates' (*fewest* is the right word there). For an easy rule, see previous entry.

fiancé and **fiancée** These words are archaic for some people, for whom the institution of marriage is outmoded. But many couples still get engaged, and when the words are called for, the traditional masculine (*fiancé*) and feminine (*fiancée*) forms are required, complete with **acute accents** and, presumably, an engagement ring.

At one time, a woman who was engaged used to talk about my *intended*, meaning the man she was going to marry, but it always seemed a genteel expression. **Fowler** made a plea for 'my betrothed' to be revived (*Modern English Usage*, 1926). But the word has sunk into oblivion, lost beyond recall.

fiascos or **fiascoes** One fiasco at a time is usually enough, but when the plural is required, *fiascos* is indicated by most dictionaries, with *fiascoes* as the more usual American spelling.

fibre The word *fibre* has a number of meanings, but the one that comes out on top now is the dietary use, encouraging people to eat wholemeal bread, brown rice and more vegetables and fruit. Because *fibre* is the part of plants that cannot be digested, it enables food to pass more quickly through the alimentary canal, helping to prevent degenerative diseases.

fibreglass or **glass fibre** The words can mean the same thing. *Fibreglass* is the more usual one for the fibre made from glass and used for insulation. The same word is used when it is bonded with resin as a lightweight construction material used in various ways, such as a material for car bodies and boats. *Glass fibre* is preferred for another application, which is glass filaments woven into a fabric.

fictional or **fictitious** There are a few instances where either word can be used, such as a fictional or fictitious country in a novel. But generally *fictitious* carries with it the pejorative meaning of false or sham, or a downright lie: 'his fictitious excuse didn't convince anyone'. *Fictional* describes the imaginary, a character, event, place, etc that exist in a novel, play or film, and is the better word to choose for those meanings (although both words can be used with that sense), since it avoids the negative associations of *fictitious*.

fictitious or **factitious** See factitious . . .

fiddle See violin . . .

fidelity or **faithfulness** A use of *fidelity*, that goes back to the late 17th century, has unexpectedly remained one of the main uses of the word in the 1990s: *fidelity* is preferred, as a noun, to *faithfulness*, for someone never having sexual affairs outside marriage or another stable relationship.

Fidelity has other meanings, especially for an accurate representation of the truth or facts: *high fidelity* is, or should be, a close reproduction of the original sound in a recording (see **hi-fi**).

field, **province** or **sphere**   All three words are to some extent interchangeable when they are used to describe an area of knowledge or activity: we can say that a barrister's field, province or sphere is divorce law. *Field* is preferable in that context, since it suggests specialization within a narrow aspect of a wider subject. A *sphere* tends to apply to a general area of influence, interest or action: 'he has achieved a great deal in the sphere of politics'.

field research   *Field research* is using on-the-spot (that is to say, in-the-field) surveys or interviews to collect information on a subject. It is the opposite of **desk research**.

fifth   It is easy to drop the second *f* and say 'fith', but it's worth making the effort to pronounce it.

fifth column   *Fifth column* seems a strange expression to use about a subversive group in a country or an organization. It arose in the Spanish Civil War (1936–9). A Nationalist general is said to have claimed, during the siege of Madrid in 1936: 'I have four columns advancing on Madrid – and a fifth inside the city'. Members of so-called fifth columns are called *fifth-columnists*, a term extended to cover any traitor operating secretly from within: someone in a company passing on confidential trade information to a competitor might be called a fifth-columnist.

fifth-generation (computers)   See **generation**

figurative or **representational**   As art terms, *figurative* and *representational* mean the same and are equally imprecise: they are applied to any work of art in which the appearance of people or objects can be discerned. This could range from a realistic portrait, landscape or **still life** to an allusive impressionistic portrayal in which the elements from the real outside world are hardly recognizable. When a painting or sculpture is beyond that limit and cannot be related to external appearances, except in the imagination, it becomes **abstract**, *non-figurative* or *non-representational*.

Artists generally prefer the terms *figurative* and *non-figurative* to the other alternatives.

figures, **numbers** or **numerals**   Although the British Standards Institution prefers the term *numerals* for both arabic and roman forms (BS 2961), most people are more at home with the alternatives, *figures* or *numbers*.

How *numbers* are expressed in writing is often a matter of taste. The golden rule is consistency: whatever guidelines are followed, keep to them throughout the same piece of writing.

These are the most common guidelines recommended, although there are variations:
Use figures for:
Numbers over 10 (some authorities specify over 20, others over 100).
Time and other measurements (4 o'clock, 8°F, 5 per cent or 5%, 3 km), although time and distance can be expressed in words when used in a general way, and the actual measurement is not being stressed ('let's meet at six'; 'the house is about five miles away').
-Year-old ('a 4-year-old girl', but 'my daughter is four years old').
House numbers and most street numbers (but see exceptions below).
Dates (the title of George Orwell's *Nineteen Eighty-Four* is a rare exception).
Use words for:
Numbers below 11 (or 21, or 101 – see above)
Fifth Avenue, Third Avenue, etc, where such street numbers have become names.
Legal contexts (when it is usual for any figure to be expressed in both words and numbers to avoid error).
Numbers at the beginning of sentences, if the sentence cannot be turned round to avoid it ('. Seventeen guests came to dinner' looks better than '. 17 guests . . .').
When there is a *series of quantities* it often helps to use words for one set of items and figures for another. This can take over sometimes from the above/below 10 rule: 'There were eight groups of 5 men, ten groups of 15 men and fifteen groups of 35 men'.
Separating thousands: the old rule was to mark off *thousands* with a comma (3,000; 60,500 . . .). There is a tendency now to leave out the comma on figures from 1000 to 9999, and reserve commas for figures over 9999: 7277; 70,277. In scientific and foreign-language contexts spaces should be used instead of commas: 10 000; 1 700 300.
Millions: 7 million or 7m.
Ranges: when writing about a range of figures or dates, remember that *between* must be followed by *and*, and *from* by *to* or *until*, not just a dash: rows 18–20 are at the back, William Somerset Maugham (1874–1965) but 'All ages are welcome, *from* 18 *to* 80', 'Queen Victoria reigned *between* 1837 *and* 1901'.
See also **billion**; **money**; **roman numerals**

file   *File* is related to the French word 'fil', a thread, and as early as the 16th century it was used for a wire on which papers were kept for reference. By the early 17th century, *file* was used for any collection of papers arranged in order, which is the way it is still used. By the end of this century, the most common use of *file* will be for related data held on a disk within a computer system. To ask for the file on something will more often than not be a request for the information to be called up on the screen of a **desktop computer**.

Filipino or **Philippino**   *Philippine* describes anything to do with the Philippine Islands and their people, but anyone who comes from those islands is a

Filipino (plural *Filipinos*). There is a feminine form, *Filipina*, shown in some dictionaries, although it doesn't come in for much use.

film buff   Why *buff* for an enthusiast about films? It recalls long-forgotten amateur firemen in New York. See **buff**.

filmography   As far as is known, the word appeared for the first time in the 1960s. It was formed on the model of biography, and is now used by film historians for the list of films of an important director, cameraman, or actor. When Marlene Dietrich died (6 May 1992), the obituary by Gilbert Adair in *The Independent* commented, in a felicitous phrase, that her 'langorous eroticism far exceeded the confines of her . . . filmography'.

films   See **cinema** . . .

filmscript   See **scenario** . . .

Filofax   Filofax is one of those brand names, such as **Hoover**, that has achieved the fame of being included in dictionaries as part of the English language. A Filofax was a symbol of success in the 1980s, implying that its owner had so many connections, contacts and appointments that this portable personal filing system in a loose-leaf ring-binder was essential to get through the day. Many high-fliers (see **flyer**) in the 1990s have switched to 'filing their facts' on pocket computers. See also **organizer**

finalize   Many -ize, -ization words have invaded English. Even if we don't like them, they are useful shortcuts (**liquidize, pressurize, hospitalize** . . .). Some people have taken a violent turn against *finalize* because they dislike the sound of it, and because there are already the verbs 'finish' and 'complete'. For others, it is stronger than 'complete', as it implies working through all relevant details. Whatever we think, dictionaries now accept *finalize* as standard English.

finance   There are two ways to say this word: 'FINE-ance' (stress on first syllable) or 'finn-NANCE' (stress on second syllable). The former is generally favoured in Britain, with the alternative, 'finn-NANCE', in America.

financial, fiscal or **monetary**   All three words are used about money. *Financial* is commercial or personal; *fiscal* is governmental, since it refers to public expenditure and taxation. A company has a financial policy and a financial year, whereas a government has a fiscal policy and a fiscal year. *Monetary* relates to currency, the tangible money in circulation.

While *monetary* is a 19th-century term, *monetarism* is an economic **-ism** dating from the late 1960s. There is some disagreement over what the term means, although broadly it is about the theory that regulating the supply of money in circulation is the most effective way to control the economy.

Financial, fiscal and *monetary* are clearly defined terms. But *monetarism* and *monetarist* should be used more cautiously, especially if you are not an economist, since they open up considerable areas of disagreement over their precise meanings.

financier, magnate or **tycoon**   The word *financier*, which sums up an image of a remote figure smoking a fat cigar and manipulating vast sums of money, may seem out of place in the 1990s. Large-scale financial operations are now more likely to be conducted by banks, merchant banks or consortia, but when it is an individual operating personally, and on a large enough scale, *financier* remains the appropriate word.

Journalists like the word *magnate*, but this is for a man of great wealth and power, who controls big businesses (so far, it is rarely, if ever, used about a woman), especially in combinations, such as *oil magnate* or *shipping magnate*.

Tycoon, which has the same ring to it of a man wielding supreme power over many enterprises, reverts to the 19th century, when *tycoon* was coined on the model of the Japanese word for a hereditary general. *Tycoon* was brought out by the media as the most appropriate word to use when Robert Maxwell, the high-powered owner of the *Daily Mirror*, died in November 1991.

find or **locate**   *Locate* derives from 'locus', the Latin word for place, and should be used for finding the exact place where someone or something is: we can locate the hotel where a person is staying, locate the site where treasure is buried. It is both pompous and incorrect to use *locate* simply as a grander alternative to *find*: if we lose contact with someone, or mislay something, we try to find them. If it is a fault in a system, for example, we want to locate it, that is to look for the precise place where it occurs.

find out   See **determine** . . .

fiord or **fjord**   Both spellings are current in English for this word taken from Norwegian, for a narrow inlet of sea between precipitous cliffs. The Norwegian National Tourist Office prefers *fjord*, since the slogan for low-cost holidays in that country is 'Affordable Norway!'.

fire   See **dismiss** . . .

firm   See **company** . . .

first   See **former** . . .

first or **firstly, etc**   The once hotly debated grammatical rumpus over this has at last fizzled out, and no one now seems to mind whether it's *firstly, secondly, thirdly* . . . or *first, second, third* . . ., which seems more in keeping with the 1990s. Fowler considered all along that it was a lot of fuss about nothing (*Modern English Usage*, 1926). See also **last or lastly**

first, second and **third class** These terms were traditionally used in travel. *First class* is still used on trains and ships, but some air services have replaced *first class* by *executive class*, acknowledging that most people who pay extra are travelling on expenses.

The Post Office is one of the few organizations using the term *second class*, for a cheaper and slower postal service. Universities award 1st, 2nd, 3rd (some even 4th) class honours degrees. In other contexts, second and third class have acquired such derogatory associations (second-class citizen, third-class work . . .), that organizations fall over backwards to find alternative descriptions. British Rail replaced *second class* by *standard class* (whose or what standard?), airlines are more likely to use 'tourist class' or some other fancy euphemism to cover up varying degrees of discomfort.

firstly See **first or firstly, etc**

first or **Christian name** A *Christian name* is strictly a name given at baptism, admission to the Christian Church. At one time, a request for Christian names was standard on official forms, and even if your *first name* happened to be Isaac, Rachel or Mohammed, down it went as your Christian name. In America *given name* is used for any name other than the surname, but this has never been taken up in Britain, where it is standard practice now for forms to request surname and *first names* or *other names*. The British Passport Office tries a balancing act by putting on their forms *Christian names or forenames*.

fiscal See **financial** . . .

fix or **repair** To say in Britain, 'I'll fix you a meal', is trying to sound as if you are just in from New York. 'I'll fix it', meaning to put something right, is normal British usage, but to 'get the car fixed' is not quite as usual, since *repair* remains more usual in British English. Dictionaries are slow to catch up with **quick fix**, although it is standard English for a papering-over-the-cracks solution to a political problem. To be 'in a fix', meaning to be in trouble over something, is as much at home in the East End of London as on East Side, New York.

fixer See **broker** . . .

fizz See **champagne**

fjord See **fiord** . . .

flaccid Dictionaries show 'FLAKsid' and 'FLAS-Sid' as alternative pronunciations, in that order of preference. *Flaccid* comes from a Latin word meaning 'flabby', and is used more often now for the state of being lifeless and lacklustre: 'he is so flaccid about it that I don't believe he will do anything'.

flag of convenience This euphemistic term describes the business of registering a merchant ship in a country such as Costa Rica and Panama (instead of the country the ship belongs to), in order to avoid taxes, minimum wages for seamen and other expenses. The merchant ship then flies a *flag of convenience*, the flag of the country where it is registered.

flagrant See **blatant** . . .

flagship In the navy, a flagship is the ship with the admiral on board. More recently, this naval term has become extended to commercial and other contexts. A manufacturer's most important brand name is called its *flagship*. Even the Oxford University Press has joined in, calling *The Concise Oxford Dictionary* its flagship, meaning its leading title.

flak *Flak* (sometimes wrongly spelt 'flack') is the wartime word for bursting shrapnel: it is an **acronym** of a polysyllabic German word for an anti-aircraft gun. It is now accepted as standard English for particularly hostile criticism: 'his proposals came in for a lot of flak'. This is a good lively use of the word, in line with the next stage, which would be: 'his proposals were shot down', meaning thrown out.

flameproof See **next entry**

flammable, inflammable or **inflammatory** These three words are in disorder. In the 14th century, *inflame* meant to set fire to something. That literal meaning survives mostly as a culinary term, as when a pyromaniac waiter inflames (or flames) a dish at the table.

As a result, the connection between *inflame* and *inflammable* has faded, so that the latter word is sometimes taken as a negative, meaning unable to burn, a dangerous mistake. There is an attempt to introduce the invented word *flammable*, to avoid misunderstanding, but this is not completely accepted. Instead, labels may carry the words *highly inflammable* to make doubly sure.

The true negatives of *inflammable* are *non-inflammable* or *non-flammable* (preferable because it is easier to say). But generally *flameproof* is used because the meaning is immediately clear.

Inflammatory cannot be used in the literal sense of easily set on fire, only in a symbolic way about words, action or a situation: 'his speech was inflammatory and aroused the audience'. *Inflammable* has a similar symbolic meaning, but only about people who are easily excited or aroused. A crowd, for example, can be inflammable (not inflammatory): 'it was dangerous to make that speech before such an *inflammable* audience'.

flan see **tart**

flasher See **exhibitionist**

flat rate This term used about a rate of interest can be misleading, because the word *flat* suggests that it is low. In fact, it works out higher in the long run, because a *flat rate* of interest is paid on the *full* sum of money that is borrowed, throughout the period of the loan. That is, it does not take into account that the sum is gradually being paid off. One of the provisions that followed from the Consumer Credit Act 1974 in the UK made it a statutory requirement to show the true annual percentage rate (more commonly known as the **APR**) in agreements for loans.

Flat rate is also used for the basic rates of contribution to National Insurance in the UK and for benefits payable under that scheme.

flaunt or **flout** Journalists in particular have a tendency to use these words the wrong way round: a headline in *The Independent* read: CHINESE ARMS DEALERS FLAUNT UN EMBARGO. A president of the United States made the same mistake, when Jimmy Carter spoke about Iran not being allowed to 'flaunt the law of the world community'. In both cases, the word should have been *flout*, because that means to disregard openly and contemptuously.

Flaunt means to show off something, and is nearly always pejorative since it implies arrogance: 'he flaunts himself in a Rolls-Royce to show how much money he's made'.

Political parties regularly accuse their rivals of flaunting the truth. They should all know better and use *flout*, instead of *flaunting* their ignorance.

flautist or **flutist** The Italian word for a flute is 'flauto', and the player is a 'flautista'. While *flute* remains the name of the instrument in English, as it has been since the 14th century, *flautist* was adopted in the mid-19th century for the name of the player, because Italian musical terms were fashionable. Unlike the Italian word, the stress in English is on the first syllable: 'FLAWtist'. Americans use the older name *flutist*.

floe See fly . . .

Fleet Street It would be an anachronism to use *Fleet Street*, as it was used before the 1980s, to mean the London newspapers ('What does Fleet Street say?'). Nearly all the leading London papers have moved away and, although Reuters and some other news agencies remain, Fleet Street has become a place of sentimental pilgrimage for veteran newspapermen. Instead of referring to 'Fleet Street', newscasters on radio and television talk about the **broadsheets and tabloids** for the national daily papers.

fleshly or **fleshy** *Fleshy* is about the physical flesh, whether it is human or otherwise. Hands can be fleshy, that is plump and fat, so can fruit when the texture is reminiscent of flesh. *Fleshly* can only be used about worldly, sensual tastes of human beings: 'he is too concerned with fleshly satisfactions to give much time to things of the spirit'.

flexitime This term will become increasingly common in the 1990s as computer-links and advanced telecommunications increase the percentage of the workforce freed from time and geographical restraints. *Flexitime*, short for flexible working hours, is the principle that enables employees to choose working periods during the day to make up an agreed total number of working hours in a week. See also **work sharing**

filer See flyer . . .

flip-chart Every **executive** and **salesman** knows all about flip-charts: they are either using them or looking at other executives or salesmen turning the pages. For a flip-chart is a giant-size pad on a stand, so that one page can be turned at a time to reveal the next key sales point or persuasive statistic. The great advantage is there are no technical problems, no switches, bulbs or fuses to go wrong.

Usually the pages are prepared in advance, but there are clever presenters who have their flip-charts arranged with lightly pencilled-in outlines, which the audience cannot see, and so are dazzled by the assurance and skill of the executive, who seemingly draws brilliant visuals free-hand with a felt pen.

float *Float* has many meanings in different situations. Companies are floated on the Stock Exchange, when their shares are offered for sale. A more recent use is in EC monetary contexts, where *float*, as a verb, is used about a currency that is allowed to find its own exchange rate through market forces, without intervention by the country's central bank.

floor or **storey** *Storey* (for one level in a building) and *story* (for an anecdote) come from the same Latin word 'historia' (a narrative of past events, which in Anglo-Latin came to mean a picture). The double meaning probably arose from tiers of stained glass windows depicting scenes. The word 'clerestory', the row of windows high up in the wall of a church, is a reminder. (Pron: KLEERstery).

In Britain a typical *two-storey* house has living-rooms on the *ground floor* and bedrooms upstairs on the *first floor*. A *three-storey* building has a second floor above the first floor, and so on.

In America, the terminology is more logical: the *ground* floor becomes what it really is, the *first floor*, with the *second floor* (the British *first floor*) above it, and so on. As a result, the top floor of a 30-*story* (the earlier spelling which is still used in America) building in Manhattan is the 30th floor, whereas in London it would be the 29th floor.

It is usual to refer to a ten-*storey* building, rather than a ten-*floor* building, but to have a flat on the tenth *floor*, rather than the tenth *storey*.

floppy or **hard disk** These are two kinds of disk used in the storage systems of computers. *Floppy disks* are made of thin magnetic-coated flexible plastic, and because they are cheap and easily removed from computers for filing, they are particularly convenient for **desktop computers**. *Hard disks* are rigid, with greater storage capacity, able to function at higher speeds but, unlike floppy disks, they remain in the disk drive of the computer.

flotsam and **jetsam** These were technically shipping terms and meant different things: *flotsam* (which relates to 'float') is part of the wreckage of a ship found floating in the sea, while *jetsam* (which relates to 'jettison') is anything thrown overboard to lighten the load of a ship in distress, which is then washed ashore. The definition in the Royal Navy used to be *flotsam* for wreckage under six foot long, *jetsam* for over six foot.

The two words have since become a double-act, rarely used separately, and are no longer confined to shipwrecks. *Flotsam and jetsam* can mean any kind of junk or rubbish, and are even extended to cover human wreckage, down-and-outs sleeping rough.

flout See flaunt . . .

flow chart *Flow chart* began as a term in management consultancy and has become popular and useful in business, with a number of applications. A flow chart is basically a graphic method of showing a process at its different stages: it could be the movement of raw materials in a manufacturing company, the chain of decision-making in an organization, or the movement of goods from production to consumers.

flu, **'flu** or **influenza** Hardly anyone says *influenza* any more. *Flu* has become the standard word, nor is it necessary to write *'flu*, just as it's old-fashioned to write *'bus*, *'phone* or *'plane*.

fluke In the 19th century this was slang for a lucky shot in billiards. *Fluke* is now used for anything successful that happens by chance, rather than through judgement or skill, either in a game or in life. Nor is it slang any more: you read it in leading articles in the **broadsheets** and hear it used by judges.

flurried, **flustered** or **fuddled** The distinction between these words is subtle but worth preserving. *Flurried* is when someone doesn't know where to turn next, because there are too many matters to deal with: 'she was flurried because she was trying to cook dinner and the telephone kept ringing'. To be *flustered* is to be in a state of nervous confusion, because something unexpected has happened: 'she was flustered because her guests arrived an hour earlier than expected'.

In the 15th century one of the meanings of *flustered* was confused by drink, and there are current dictionaries that still include that meaning, although it is rarely used in that way now. If someone is unsteady because of too much to drink, *fuddled* is by far the best word, as

ever since the 16th century, the word has been associated with being drunk.

flush See blush . . .

flushing See reproductive technology

flustered See flurried . . .

flutist See flautist . . .

fly a kite The symbolic meaning of *flying a kite* is trying out an idea to see what people think. It corresponds to the go-getting expression of the 1960s in Madison Avenue, one-time location of the leading New York advertising agencies: 'Let's run it up on the flagpole and see who salutes it!' To *fly a kite* is still current but the flagpole expression belongs to the archives of old advertising jargon.

flyer or **flier** The word is not often used any longer for someone flying an aircraft, but when it is, *flyer* is the usual spelling in Britain, with *flier* in America. The most regular use of the word in the 1990s is in the combination *high-flier* (arguably a replacement term for **yuppie**), for a young person in business on their way up to the top ('a Wall Street high-flier'). Because the expression started in New York, *high-flier* is often spelt that way in Britain.

flying pickets and **secondary picketing**
Flying pickets is part of the language of trade unions, not used as often as it was in the 1980s, particularly during the miners' strike in Britain of 1984–5, but still lurking below the surface. It describes a group of pickets ready to move round the country at short notice, to counter attempts by a firm in an industrial dispute to switch production to another plant.

Secondary picketing is a similar practice, but it extends to strikers picketing associated companies, such as firms making components, whose employees are not involved in the dispute. Both practices were greatly restricted by the Employment Acts of 1980 and 1982.

fly-on-the-wall documentary See documentary

focal point *Focal point* is a precise technical term in optics and electromagnetic communications. It is unnecessary to use it in general expressions, such as 'the focal point of all this . . .', or 'he is the focal point of her life'. Either the word 'point' or 'focus' is perfectly adequate on its own: 'the point of all this . . .'; 'he is the focus of her life'.

foci or **focuses** See focused . . .

fo'c'sle See forecastle . . .

focused or **focussed** Dictionaries show both spellings for other forms of the verb *focus*. Most newspapers now use -ss- (focussed, focussing), but many books (including this one) prefer -s- (focused, focusing, focuses).

The plural of the noun 'focus' never doubles -s and is always spelt *focuses*, or there is the alternative, now uncommon but still in use, *foci* (pron: 'FOHsye').

focuses See previous entry

folk The word *folk* is an ancient one. The plural form *folks* sounds more American, as in Britain we tend to talk about 'the old folk', or 'Would you folk like a drink?' *Folksy* is usually pejorative, used about someone who tries too hard to seem simple and unsophisticated, or about artefacts that are self-conscious imitations of *folk art*.

follows or **follow** See as follows . . .

foment See ferment . . .

foodie *Foodie* has become the slang synonym for a 'gourmet', a person who seems to think of nothing but the best restaurants and the most exquisite food. The word is probably modelled on **junkie**, for food, carried that far, becomes an addiction.

fool's gold The 1944 edition of the *Shorter Oxford English Dictionary* wrote off this archaic mining expression as obsolete, so where did John Major pick it up as a catchphrase for his 1992 election campaign? He used it to mean something that looks valuable, but is in reality worthless.

foot or **feet** See feet . . .

foot or **foot-** Nearly always when *foot* is combined with another word, the compound has become one word and there is no need for a hyphen: football, foothills, foothold, footlights, footbath, footbrake, footbridge, footprint, footstep, footnote and most of the others. A foot-fault in tennis, foot-rule, foot-soldier and a few others still take a hyphen.

Footsie or **footsie** Give it a capital and *Footsie* is an abbreviation, used by financial journalists and everyone connected with stock exchanges, for the *Financial Times Stock Exchange 100 index of companies' shares*, taken as a measure of general ups and downs in the market. A typical comment on financial pages of British newspapers is 'By the close Footsie was nursing a 5.8 fall'.

With a small *f*, *footsie* is much more irreverent: it is slang for the sexy games people play with each other's feet under the dining table, unobserved by the other guests.

for (and on behalf of) See pp (per pro) . . .

forbade or **forbad** *Forbad*, as the past form of 'forbid', is old-fashioned; *forbade* is more usual now. At the same time, it is more usual to pronounce *forbade*

'forBAD', although 'forBAYD' is an accepted alternative pronunciation.

forbear or **forebear** These are different words. *Forbear* (pron: 'forBEAR') is a verb (*forbore* is the past form), meaning restrain: 'please forbear from interrupting until I have finished'. *Forebear* (pron: 'FORbear') is a noun meaning ancestor: 'some of his forebears were parliamentarians'.

force and **military intervention** In diplomatic language, *force* is now the standard word for sending in tanks and dropping bombs on a country that refuses to comply with a decree: 'if economic sanctions are not effective, the next stage is to use force'. And nowadays UN language requires a government to take *military intervention*, instead of 'sending in the troops'.

forceful or **forcible** There has long been debate over the distinction between these two words. It is not all that complicated: *forceful* is possessing force, *forcible* is using it physically. An argument or a person can be forceful, meaning powerfully persuasive, but an action is forcible. A *forceful* entry is a person entering a room with presence and making an impact; a forcible entry is breaking in using force, which, in passing, is usually referred to as a *forced entry*.

forecastle or **fo'c'sle** The spelling *fo'c'sle*, for the forward part of a ship, can best be left to Horatio Hornblower. *Forecastle* is the standard spelling. Either way, the pronunciation is 'FOHKsl'. The word comes from the castellated tower, at one time in the bow of ships, used for keeping a look-out and attacking the enemy.

forego or **forgo** As a verb the word required is nearly always *forgo*, meaning to do without something: 'he will forgo a holiday this year'. Although some dictionaries show *forego* as an alternative spelling for that meaning, it is so rare as to be considered a mistake.

The spelling *forego* is a reminder that the meaning connects with *before*. It is found mostly in the descriptive forms *foregoing* and *foregone*: the foregoing statement (the statement that has gone before); a foregone conclusion (a result that can be seen in advance or before).

forehead There are two pronunciations: 'FORRid' is by far the more usual and the safer one to use. But an alternative pronunciation is shown in most dictionaries, which follows the spelling: 'FOREhead'.

foreign place-names The old British arrogance of pronouncing foreign place-names in the English manner is giving way to internationalism. The pronunciation of many place-names has been brought into line with a closer approximation to the way they are said in the countries they belong to. Nowadays, for example, it would seem unworldly, if not downright uneducated, to say anything other than 'LEEonn' for

Lyons (instead of letting it rhyme with 'lions'), and 'mahSAY' for *Marseille* (instead of 'mahSAYLZ'). Since the English spelling *Majorca* is being replaced by the Spanish *Mallorca*, the pronunciation is changing from 'maJORKa' to 'maYORKa'. Not everyone agrees with all this, and a plaintive letter to *The Times* asked 'Why can't I say "Lyons" as in "pride of" without sounding a complete wally?'

Some place-names resolutely hold on to their Englishness: it would be arch to say 'Paree' for Paris, 'Napoli' for Naples, and *Bruxelles* has been resisted even by the most ardent Europeanists, perhaps because the Flemish name is *Brussel* (or because of Brussels sprouts . . .?).

The names of some cities have a historical context. Ancient Byzantium was renamed *Constantinople* in 330, when the emperor Constantine made it the capital of the Eastern Roman Empire, then renamed *Istanbul* when it was captured by the Ottoman Turks in 1453. St Petersburg, founded by Peter the Great in 1703, was secularized to *Petrograd* in 1914, renamed *Leningrad* in 1924, reverting to *St Petersburg* after the downfall of the Communists in 1991.

The best way to keep abreast of changing fashions in pronouncing place-names, as well as dealing with the more obscure places in the news, is to listen to newscasters. They rehearse pronunciations carefully to be sure of saying any name that comes up with a cosmopolitan nonchalance. New spellings are laid down by a UN group of experts and pronunciations are recommended by the BBC pronunciation unit. We can defy them if we wish, and insist on saying, for example, *Peking*, rather than **Beijing** (see entry), for the capital of the People's Republic of China, or *Cambodia* instead of *Kampuchea*, the official name for the republic since 1979. But our children, or at least our grandchildren, may not understand us.

foreign pronunciations It is pedantic to pronounce familiar foreign words in the middle of an English sentence, with an impeccable accent in the language they belong to. The usual practice is to acknowledge the origin of the words by an adaptation of normal English sounds to the foreign language. For example, *éminence grise* (the French term used in English for a person not officially holding office but exercising considerable power behind the scenes) is pronounced with anglicized French sounds: 'aymin-NAHNS GREEZ'. This applies to words clearly not part of standard English. When it comes to naturalized words, such as *spaghetti* or *minestrone*, even some Italian waiters in Britain make them sound as English as Yorkshire pudding. See also next entry

foreign words and phrases Some of these, such as **blitz**, matador, piazza, have settled down in English and hardly seem foreign any more. Thousands more, such as *restaurant, bungalow, hotel*, are rightly taken for granted as English words. There are other foreign expressions which are not readily understood by many people, and using these is inconsiderate and affected. A distinguished British administrator in India,

Gerard Young, defined the purpose of language as 'to get an idea as exactly as possible out of one mind into another': a foreign word or phrase can be justified if it expresses an idea in the way that no English expression quite reaches, provided it is reasonable to assume the other person will understand it. There is, after all, such a thing as the *mot juste*. And with so much travel and international communication technology, foreignness gets less foreign with every passing year. For the custom of printing foreign words and phrases in italics, see **italics**. See also previous entry

foreman   See **chargehand** . . .

forever or **for ever**   There is a useful distinction between *for ever*, meaning for all time ('I will love you for ever') and *forever*, meaning persistently ('he's forever saying that'). In America, *forever* is always one word, whatever the meaning, and this is becoming more common in Britain: 'Kidnappers to close hostage file forever' (*The Times*).

foreword, **preface** or **introduction**   *Foreword* is the 19th-century English alternative to the Latinate *preface* and means the same thing, usually a short explanation at the beginning of a book of its subject and purpose. Some publishers make a distinction, using *preface* when it is written by the author of the book, and *foreword* when it is by someone else, but it is doubtful whether many readers are aware of this subtlety. (It is not unknown for someone to write 'forward', instead of *foreword*, but inexcusable since *foreword* clearly describes *words* that come be*fore*.)

An *introduction* is longer and more detailed than a foreword or preface, usually written with the purpose of helping readers to approach the book in the way the author intended.

forgo   See **forego** . . .

formal and **informal English**   There are occasions, such as the Queen's speech at the opening of parliament, when language is required to have dignity and solemnity, and certain perfectly good words and expressions are excluded because they seem too casual. Perhaps the description *ceremonial English* is more appropriate for such language, just as ceremonial robes are worn.

Although there are still different levels of formality appropriate to different situations, these are less easily defined in the 1990s. The trend is for English to be more relaxed, conversational and human in letters and public address, where at one time a more stern and formal tone would have been obligatory. The concept of what is or is not *formal English* in particular situations is changing all the time. There is some loss, since language can no longer always be relied upon to reflect seriousness and human dignity.

Even the word *formal* means different things to different people. Dr John Doherty, as the local doctor in tropical north Queensland, was confronted by this dilemma, when he was requested to be present at 'a formal occasion'. 'Anxious not to offend', he wrote in a letter to The Times, 'I enquired what this implied. "No bare feet, mate," came the crisp response'. See also **colloquial**, **informal**, **slang** and **non-standard**

format Once restricted to typography and printing, *format* is now used for the arrangement or layout of almost anything: 'the format of a TV show'; 'the format of a sales conference'. In computer language, *format* is the arrangement of data on the screen.

former and **latter** It is a temptation to use *former* and *latter* to save trouble, and they are useful from time to time. They can only be used for one of *two* things previously mentioned; if there are three or more, *first* or *last* are required. These devices should be used sparingly, and only in writing. Even then, they oblige readers to glance back to see which is the former and which is the latter. In speech, keep in mind that listeners have to remember which is which, while the speaker goes on talking.

former See ex-...

'FORmidable' or **'forMIDable'** There is almost equal preference over whether the stress should be on the first or second syllable. Nevertheless the more educated pronunciation usually puts the stress on the first syllable ('FORmidable'), with stress on the second syllable considered by some to be downmarket.

forms of address There are whole books written about what are irreverently called *handles*, how we have to write to or speak to dignitaries, the ennobled and holders of various offices. A selection of useful forms of address are given under the following headings: **ambassador; clergy; royalty**

formulae or **formulas** Mathematicians and scientists are more likely to say *formulae* (pron: 'FORmulee') for more than one formula. Otherwise, it is usual to say *formulas*, the now accepted English plural in non-scientific contexts, such as 'here are some formulas for success'.

forte *Forte* has for centuries been an all-purpose word for anything a person is good at: 'her forte is soufflés'; 'his forte is an ability to think clearly in a crisis'. 'Speciality' and 'strength' are more precise words in those contexts.

In spite of the pronunciation, the final *e* never takes an **acute accent**: the reason is *forte* is the feminine form of the French word 'fort' ('strong'), wrongly used in English since the mid-17th century, and later pronounced with two syllables ('FAWtay'), perhaps on the model of the Italian musical term ('forte', marking a passage to be performed loudly).

forthwith See immediately...

fortuitous or **fortunate** *Fortuitous* is used so often as if it meant lucky or *fortunate*, that the time

may come when dictionaries have to accept that as one of the meanings. This is an example of the wrong use: 'It was a fortuitous time to buy shares in the company, because the following week there was a takeover bid'. In fact, it was a *fortunate* time, for since the 17th century, *fortuitous* has meant the result of chance but not necessarily a lucky chance. Fortune is so often implied, that the word has become confused with *fortunate*, as in the above example.

Here is an example of the correct use of the word: 'It was not fortuitous that he bought shares in the company, as he had inside information'.

forward or **forwards** The old distinction, which some people preserve, is that when there is a physical movement, *forwards* should be used: 'she went forwards towards him'; 'the car moved slowly forwards'. But we look forward to something, bring forward a date, and use *forward* as a descriptive word in front of a noun: *forward price* (the price fixed for buying or selling at a future date), *forward dealings* (agreements to buy or sell commodities, currencies or shares at a fixed price at an agreed date in the future).

It is no bad thing to retain *forwards* for physical movement, as indicated above, if for no other reason than *backwards and forwards* is an invariable expression. Otherwise, use *forward* in all cases.

Lastly, when it comes to *forward* as a verb, it is commercial jargon to forward anything to anyone (see **business English**), unless it means redirect it to a new address. Otherwise, just *send* it.

for or **in years** At one time *for years* was usual in Britain and *in years* in America. But now both expressions are equally at home in Britain: 'she hasn't seen him for years (or in years)'.

for your information and **need to know** *For your information* reassures the reader that it is merely to keep them in the picture, and there's no need to *do* anything. It is bad practice to use the phrase when action *is* required: 'For your information, unless a cheque is received within seven days, we shall take legal action'. After all, that's not a reassurance but a threat.

In government circles, *need to know* is sometimes used: 'This information is sent to you on a need to know basis'. It is a diplomatic way of saying you can do nothing about it, but we do not want to be accused at some future date of not having told you!

fossil fuel So-called **green** issues have brought this term into everyday use. A fossil is a form of mineralized bones and other solid matter which are traces of animal or organic plant life from a past geological age. A *fossil fuel* is derived from such primeval remains: the most common examples are coal, crude oil and natural gas. These fuels are, in relation to a human time scale, **non-renewable** resources, since they can only be replaced in a geological time scale measured in millions of years.

The environmental concerns are that fossil fuels are

being used up at a much faster rate than they can be replaced, and that their combustion is causing **global warming**.

foundation or **underpinning** This is not concerned with the construction industry but with the fashionable use of *underpinning* in general contexts, especially by academics: 'Writers, such as Heidegger and Sartre, have provided the philosophical and literary *underpinnings* for a psychology . . .' (*Group Therapy in Britain*, ed. Mark Aveline and Windy Dryden, 1988). At best this is an awkward substitute for the more accepted word *foundation*. At worst it is the compulsive use of a trendy word, where a simpler word, such as 'support', or a more relevant word, such as 'background', are both less polysyllabic and more immediate. *Underpinning* is best left to builders and structural surveyors for whom it has a precise meaning.

four-letter words These words are a deep-rooted **sociolinguistic** fetish, loaded with double standards. For many years rigorously excluded from books, newspapers and even dictionaries, the door was at last opened to them in 1960, when Penguin Books published the full version of D H Lawrence's *Lady Chatterley's Lover*. They were brought to trial at the Old Bailey in London, eminent literary critics gave evidence for them, and Gerald Gardiner, the defence counsel, assured the jury that Mellors and Lady Chatterley enjoyed a 'healthy, beautiful, normal relationship', with nothing 'unclean' about it. Penguin Books won the case.

That verdict heralded the 'swinging sixties', a more open freedom to explore human experience and the linguistic reverberations from that. More than 20 years later, the 1982 edition of the *Concise Oxford Dictionary* solemnly maintained that *four-letter words* are 'used only by those who have no wish to be thought either polite or educated'. That was a slap in the face for the BBC, a number of leading novelists on both sides of the Atlantic (including one Nobel Prizewinner for Literature), many critics and journalists, good poets such as Philip Larkin, the compiler of *The Good English Guide* and no doubt many of its readers.

Eric Partridge, a respected lexicographer, considered that some of these words 'belong to the aristocracy of the language'. Gerald Long, at the time managing director of Times Newspapers, cheerfully used 'turd' and 'shit' in a talk for the BBC, and similar words in *English Observed*, by Philip Howard, when literary editor of *The Times*, were included in extracts specially chosen for a reading on radio.

There is a descending scale of supposed degradation in *four-letter words*. 'Piss' and '**shit**', while not heard commonly at royal garden parties, hardly shock any more. '**Fuck**' still causes a tightening of the lips among many people, although a survey revealed that during the 18 months to 30 November 1989, it was printed in full twice in the *Financial Times*, four times in *The Times* and 45 times in *The Guardian*.

'Cunt' produces the greatest verbal shock: newspapers that spell out other *four-letter words* use coy typographical devices, from 'c***' to 'c-word' to avoid printing it in full. But there are double standards. 'Cunt' has broken through the television barrier, with the approval of the Independent Broadcasting Authority: Melvyn Bragg believes that David Hockney was the first to use the word on television, when he was drawing viewers' attention to the focus of interest in a sketch by Picasso.

In the 1990s we have to decide for ourselves whether to toe the linguistic line, which is not all that clearly defined now anyway, or use the language that belongs to us in ways that are natural and appropriate to the situation.

fourth generation (computers) See **generation**

Fourth World See **Third World**

Fowler There are still many people who want to settle a linguistic dispute with 'But Fowler says . . .'. Fowler's *Modern English Usage* is a classic, as much as anything for his magisterial idiosyncratic style, and it does not diminish it to say that, like the rest of us, he had personal prejudices and quirks about the use of English.

Henry Watson Fowler died in 1933 (his book was re-edited by Ernest Gowers some 40 years after its first publication in 1926, and there will be a new edition by Robert Burchfield in the 1990s). His linguistic edicts are not divine commandments, true for all time. English changes to keep up with the lives of the people who are using it. This should not be a free-for-all, and Fowler has played a part in keeping the structure of the language in place. But it remains a light framework, not heavy chains that shackle the language. See also **Hart's Rules**

fraction, **percentage** or **proportion** The objection to the use of *fraction* to mean a small part of something ('only a *fraction* of the debt has been repaid') may be logical, inasmuch as $9/10$ is also a fraction, but it is pedantic. The usage is so common that everyone knows what it means, particularly when it is preceded by 'only', as in the above example.

The same does not apply to *percentage*. 'A percentage of the debt has been repaid' is so vague as to be almost useless, since all it tells us is that the debt has not been repaid in full. At the least, it should be defined as a 'small' or 'large' percentage, if the precise figure cannot be given. (See also **per cent . . .**).

This applies equally to *proportion*: 'only a proportion of . . .' says no more than 'not the total amount': 'only some . . .' says the same thing. *Proportion* properly relates a quantity to the whole: '£10,000 pa for rent is too high a proportion out of a total income of £20,000'.

framework See **context . . .**

franchise In the 15th century, *franchise* was used for a district in which a person had certain rights and privileges. Post-World War II, this feudal concept and the word that describes it were adopted commercially on a wide scale: *franchise* describes exclusive rights to sell a particular range of goods or supply certain services under an established and advertised trade name. The *franchisor* arranges for the products to be packaged and supplied, or the special equipment required for the service to be installed. The *franchisee* has independence within conditions laid down by the franchisor. *Franchises* can cover setting up anything from fast food restaurants to laundrettes, printing services and driving schools.

The extensive use of *franchise* commercially has led to an extended meaning of the word, to mean an exclusive right to a particular quality: 'no political party has a franchise for social reform'. Note the difference between the expression *lose the franchise* (meaning losing commercial rights as described above) and *disenfranchise* or *disfranchise* (meaning to deprive people of the right to vote).

franglais Anglo-French, a hybrid of the English and French languages, came into being after the Norman Conquest, the invasion of England following the Battle of Hastings in 1066. At the Restoration in 1660, when Charles II and his court returned from exile in France, there was another influx of French words into English. After World War II, particularly since the 1960s, the tide flowed the other way: Anglo-American culture broke through the floodgates erected by the Académie Française, official guardians of the language of Racine and Molière, Balzac and Flaubert. The French language was swamped by words, such as *le fast-food*, *le businessman*, *les covergirls* and – inevitably – *le jogging*. To make the point, a French newspaper commented 'L'anglais est un véritable *bouldozeur!*'

In 1964 a French scholar, René Etiemble, attacked this linguistic invasion in his book called *Parlez-vous franglais?* Ironically the French called his book *un bestseller*, passing yet another word into the ever-growing franglais vocabulary.

frappé See chilled . . .

fraud or **larceny** From a legal point of view, the word *larceny* is obsolete. It was never an alternative word for *fraud*, as some people believe, but meant the theft of property from an individual. In 1968, the statutory crime in English law became known as 'theft', and 'larceny' fell into disuse. *Fraud* is deception that is a criminal offence, inasmuch as it involves false statements deliberately made in order to gain a dishonest financial or personal advantage.

freebie Although the *OED* notes the arrival in Britain of this unattractive word from America as long ago as 1942, it did not become current until the 1960s, as an alternative to **perk**, the colloquial British abbreviation for *perquisite*. These are supposedly free offerings to journalists, customers, politicians or to anyone else who is in a position to do something in return. Banks have tumbled over themselves to offer freebies, such as diaries, pens, overdrafts without interest to students, to encourage them to open accounts, and at least one bank openly refers to them as 'bank freebies'.

Freebies are invariably followed up by hints that products, books, restaurants or whatever should be mentioned in newspapers or on television, or for some other kind of 'favour'. It usually turns out that freebies are not so free after all.

freedom fighter See terrorism; guerrilla; resistance

freelance This is such an everyday word, that we forget its chivalrous associations. It was first used in the early 19th century about soldiers of fortune in the Middle Ages who offered their services (bear a lance) to any country at war. It has long since been adapted for anyone working on a temporary basis, as a film director, copy-editor, business consultant, etc, who would just about know one end of a lance from another. But we have not extended *freelance* to dailies, plumbers, gardeners, etc.

Most dictionaries now show *freelance* as one word in all uses (freelance cameraman, she freelances for a living, he's a freelance). It is easy to slip in an unwanted *r* at the end of the word: 'he's a freelancer'; 'they employ freelancers to do the work'. The correct forms are *freelance* and *freelances*.

free market or **trade** The term *free market* is mixed up in some people's minds with *free trade*. They are not the same. *Free trade* is international trade between countries, allowed to operate without import and export taxes, quotas or other restrictions. *Free market* can be the internal domestic trade of a country, which is left to operate without any government intervention, such as subsidies or credit restrictions, so that supply and demand and the impact of competition are the only factors involved.

freight or **goods** In America *freight* covers merchandise transported by train, road, sea or air. In Britain the custom is to use *goods* when they are transported by land, and *freight* when transported by sea or air. The use of **containers** is cutting across this distinction, because these are transferred from one form of transport to another: they are called *freight* throughout.

French accents The forty members of the Académie Française, the official repository of French wisdom and enlightenment, have been debating French spelling reforms for years, and the use of accents has come into question. There are plans to phase out accents for certain words but this has met with storms of protest from French traditionalists. In English, on typewritten text and wordprocessor printouts, accents have to be put in by hand and people don't always bother. Others hesitate to leave them out in case it looks uneducated. The tendency will be to omit more of them, although Francophiles may regard that as distinctly déclassé.

The accents used in French are:

Acute accent (´): This is the mark over the letter *é* to show the quality of the vowel, or if it is pronounced. For example, *rose* (meaning 'a rose', or 'pink') has only one syllable, but *rosé* (meaning 'rosy' as in *vin rosé*) has two syllables.

In English, the French *é* is pronounced 'ay': *risqué* ('RISkay'), *blazé* ('BLAHzay'), *soigné* ('SWUNyay') . . . and it sounds affected to pronounce *é* exactly as in French (see **foreign pronunciations**). There are a number of words in English where the acute accent is now left out: for example, most dictionaries show *seance* as the usual spelling, with *séance* as an alternative.

In France, it is considered correct to retain the acute accent over a capital *E* (*Élisabeth*), although some printers omit it.

Cedilla (˛): The cedilla is the tiny squiggle under the letter *ç*, to indicate that it has an *s* sound. The custom is followed in English, with *façade* for example, to show it is pronounced 'faSAHD'. This has become optional, according to some dictionaries. Cedillas will tend to be omitted in English, although the habit will doubtless remain for anyone who reads or writes French regularly.

Circumflex (ˆ): The circumflex is the inverted *v* over a vowel to show it has a longer sound or some other different quality. It shows up in some words in English (such as *pâté*) and is optional on others (such as *rôle* or *role*). In France there was a move to abolish the circumflex to make spelling easier, but they seem to have had second thoughts, deciding to keep use of the circumflex optional, at least for a time.

Grave accent (`): This is used over *è* or *à*, either to modify the sound or indicate a difference of meaning. It is the accent used least in English. A few words, such as *première* retain it, and *à propos*, when it is used as a French expression, although **apropos** is the accepted form in English. Unlike the acute accent, French printers do not use the grave accent over capital letters.

See also **accents in print and writing**

French expressions See **foreign words and phrases**

French fried potatoes See **chips** . . .

French letter See **condom** . . .

French names ending in -s and -x There is a problem over the possessive form in English of French names ending in *-s* or *-x*. The safest rule is always to add *'s* in writing but not to pronounce it as an extra *s* sound, since *-s* and *-x* are not pronounced at the end of the name in French. For example, write Alexandre Dumas's novels, Delacroix's paintings, but pronounce them 'DJOOmaz' novels, 'DELLercrwahz' paintings (not 'DJOOmazez' and 'DELLercrwahzez'). See also next entry

French words ending in -eau The plural form of these words (*gateau, plateau* . . .) in English is

ambivalent. It is formed either in the English way by adding *-s* (*gateaus, plateaus* . . .), or in the French way with an *-x* (*gateaux, plateaux* . . .), which is usually preferred. Either way, the words are pronounced with a final *z* sound: 'GATohz', 'PLATohz'. . . .

frequency See **channel** . . .

fresh or **new** At one time, BBC newscasters were advised against talking about 'fresh fighting breaking out' or 'fresh talks taking place', and to use the word *new* instead. But they ignored that advice and *fresh* is the standard overused journalistic word for anything *new* that is happening. In most contexts the words *new* (or *renewed*) are better: 'a new attempt'; 'a renewed effort'.

Freudian and **Jungian** Freud's work in psychoanalysis changed the way we look at human nature, and his name has become part of the English language, used and misused in the loosest way to suggest that a remark, gesture or attitude has its origin in sexuality. For example, someone might see a woman eating a banana and remark 'That's very Freudian!' A *Freudian slip* is any kind of unintentional mistake in speaking or action that supposedly reveals some unconscious motive or feeling.

Jung collaborated with Freud for a period as an equal pioneer in the development of psychoanalysis and the understanding of the unconscious. But it is the word *Freudian* that has entered popular language. *Jungian* is more likely to be used by people who have studied Jung's theories and beliefs, or have undergone Jungian analysis.

FRG See **Germany**

friendly fire The American forces introduced us to this paradoxical term during the 1991 Gulf War. When coalition forces suffered casualties or attacks by mistake from their own allies, that was called *friendly fire*. It is a misleading description, because whoever is behind the guns, when they're pointing at you, the fire is anything but friendly. See also (language of) **war**

friends in high places See (the) **Establishment** . . .

fringe So-called *fringe events* started to take place at the Edinburgh Festival in the late 1950s, unofficial plays and concerts that sometimes attract more comment than the **establishment** shows in the main festival. A few years later, someone had the clever idea of taking it further by calling a brilliant sideshow at Edinburgh, *Beyond the Fringe*, the show that launched Jonathan Miller, Alan Bennett, Peter Cook and Dudley Moore. It did much to bring *fringe* into wide use for anything outside or additional to what is standard: *fringe benefits* (rewards to employees in addition to pay, such as medical insurance and low-interest mortgages), *fringe theatre* (experimental plays in small noncommercial theatres, known in New York as 'Off-

Broadway'), *fringe medicine* (see **complementary medicine . . .**).

Further out, truly 'beyond the fringe', comes the *lunatic fringe*, fanatics or nutcases at the edge of society or politics (see **loony left**). *Beyond the fringe* in New York theatre has become 'off Off-Broadway'.

frisée See **chicory . . .**

frisson To refer to a 'slight frisson' is wrong. *Frisson* is always slight, a tremor of nervous excitement that someone or a group of people experience. Sometimes it is printed in italics as a French word, even by current dictionaries, but it can be accepted now as standard English, although still pronounced in the French manner: 'FREESsonn'.

front man The term can be perfectly innocent, meaning a well-known person who is appointed as a figurehead to represent an organization, to give it prestige or authority. But the pejorative use of the word *front*, to mean a seemingly respectable organization used as a cover-up for an illegal or subversive activity, has rubbed off: *front man* is also used now for someone acting as a cover for something sinister: 'he is the front man for a vast gunrunning cartel'.

frontrunner As two words this is used in horse-racing for a horse which runs at its best when in the lead. It is more likely to be used now (often as one word) for the favourite in a race, or in an election, or for a commercial product or plan on which most hopes are pinned: 'she is the frontrunner in the selection contest for a new candidate'.

fruition When linguistic errors become absorbed into a language, there is no point in arguing about them any more. In the 19th century, *fruition* was wrongly associated with the word 'fruit', instead of with the Latin word 'frui', to enjoy. Up to that time, it was possible to say 'I am glad to have the fruition of your company'. But the wrong use has taken over completely now, and when plans come to *fruition*, it means they reach a successful conclusion. Even some current dictionaries continue to list 'enjoyment' as a possible alternative meaning of fruition, but that's flogging a dead horse.

fuck Once the most notorious of **four-letter words** and strictly forbidden, *fuck* now turns up regularly in speech and print. When D H Lawrence defied the taboo over the word in his last novel, *Lady Chatterley's Lover* (1928), the book was banned for obscenity. It took five years after that ban was lifted in 1960, before *fuck* was heard on the BBC. The critic, Kenneth Tynan, made linguistic history on 13 November 1965 when he said *fuck* on a television programme. Consternation and panic followed.

The floodgates opened: now *fuck* is heard on television and radio in plays, readings from books, even in interviews. It is printed in the best newspapers, used in serious poetry published by Faber and Faber and

given full frontal exposure in dictionaries. Yet there remain double standards over this old word, that goes back as far as the early 16th century. Newspapers that print it on inside pages, draw back from using it on the front page: *The Sunday Times*, reporting on the row between Mike Gatting, the England cricket captain, with Shakoor Rana, the Pakistani umpire, wrote that the umpire had allegedly called him 'You f—ing cheating b——!' Perhaps it was not cricket to spell the words out in full.

Double standards continue. In January 1992, the literary magazine, *Granta*, used in advertisements its cover, on which was quoted the first line of the famous poem by Philip Larkin: 'They fuck you up, your mum and dad'. When the advertisement appeared in newspapers, letters from readers piled up on editorial desks, and the Advertising Standards Authority upheld a complaint. Yet the poem was on the A-level syllabus.

No one is sure of the origin of the word: it may be related to the German *ficken* or the French *fourtre*, which Harrap's *French and English Dictionary* (1980 reprint) translates prudishly as *f—k*. There is no doubt that *fuck* is out in the open. Writers are more relaxed about using it than editors are about printing it, and old circumlocutions, f**k, f*** or the *f-word* still appear. There are times when not to use the word, in speech or writing, is pussyfooting. But always remember *fuck* can still give great offence, so be prepared for the shock waves. See also **dirty words; dots/4; effing**

fuddled See **flurried . . .**

fudge During the 1980s, *fudge* became one of the most popular verbal attacks in British politics. Politicians on opposite sides regularly accused one another of fudging an issue. The meaning has not been clearly defined but is something like dodging the real problem with **doublespeak**, or dealing with something in a dishonest way, papering over the cracks, using a makeshift solution (see **quick fix**).

It is uncertain how this use has come about. In the late 17th century, *fudge* meant, among other things, to 'cook the books', to fake accounts, but it is unlikely that British politicians are so tuned in to word origins to have picked that up. The present use of *fudge*, hurled aggressively across the floor of the House of Commons, could come from old journalistic jargon: fudge was part of a column space left blank, usually on the back page of evening newspapers, into which the latest City prices or racing results could be stamped at the last moment.

-ful There is often reason to hesitate over how to form the plural of nouns ending in *-ful*, such as *spoonful, handful, basketful*, etc. Are there *spoonfuls* or *spoonsful, handfuls* or *handsful*? **Fowler** had no doubt, contemptuously dismissing *handsful*, etc in favour of *handfuls*. Some cookery books prefer to take *cupsful* and *tablespoonsful* for recipes but this can be regarded as culinary licence, not to be taken outside the kitchen.

fulfil or **fulfill**   The ending with one *l* is standard in British English, two *l*s in American English. *Fulfilled* and *fulfilling* double the *l*, but the corresponding noun has the separate spellings, *fulfilment* in Britain, *fulfillment* in America.

full stop, **stop** or **period**   Americans often use earlier forms of English. They prefer *period*, which was a 16th-century word for a *full stop*. In Britain, *full stop* was the usual name but now more often than not, it is simply *stop*.

Stops mark the end of sentences, and the style in the 1990s is to use fewer **commas** and more stops, as sentences become shorter in keeping with the fast pace of life. No one should lay down a rule about this. It is a matter of **style** and the principle must always be to make a piece of writing comfortable and intelligible for readers. But more than ever, people are under pressure, with too much to read, and shorter sentences make less demands. At the same time, an interplay between mostly shorter and occasional longer sentences gives prose variety and rhythm. See also **abbreviations; punctuation; stops in titles**

fulsome   People will sometimes use *fulsome* in a complimentary way to mean generous and lavish, which is close to its original meaning. But that no longer holds: *fulsome* should now always taken to as pejorative, meaning over the top, cloying with excess. A fulsome vote of thanks goes further than is required, to describe something in fulsome detail is laboured and boring.

fun   *Fun* is a noun, as in *fun and games*. It is increasingly used in Britain in the American way, as a descriptive word for anything lighthearted, not to be taken seriously: 'it was a fun thing to do'; 'a fun dinner party'. Some recent dictionaries include this as a legitimate use, others label it **disp**, meaning that some people object to it. In time, it may well become standard English, as no other descriptive word serves quite the same purpose. There are many examples in English of nouns doubling as descriptive words, and sooner or later many of them become accepted.

function (as a verb)   In the 19th century, *function* followed the tendency that has gone on for centuries, of nouns being adapted as verbs. In our **high tech** society, *function* has become overused, possibly because it seems a more technical word than 'work': 'How does this function?'; 'the system doesn't function'; 'the new machine functions well'. In those three examples, at least, the word 'work' would *function* better than the word 'function'.

fundamental   See basic . . .

fundamentalism and **fundamentalist**   See evangelical . . .

funds or **money**   Organizations, local authorities or projects run out of funds but individuals run out of money. *Funds* is the grander word, appropriately used about large sums of money, especially when allocated for a particular purpose. *Money* is the everyday equivalent, which is why children are given pocket money rather than funds.

funeral director, undertaker or **mortician**   Ever since the late 17th century, it was good enough for people to be buried by *undertakers*. But now undertakers in Britain prefer to be called *funeral directors*. In America they go further, taking 'mortis', the Latin word for death, to form *mortician*, as the name for the sombrely dressed men who sit professionally sad-faced in hearses.

fungi or **funguses**   Both plural forms are recognized but *funguses* might sound wrong to many people, so it is better to stay with *fungi*. The older pronunciation, 'FUNjye', also sounds odd now, as 'FUNghee' has become the standard way of saying it.

funny   It was Ian Hay (1876–1952), in his play, *The Housemaster*, who found the perfect way of expressing the double meaning of *funny*: 'What do you mean, funny? Funny-peculiar or funny-ha-ha?' Dictionaries recognize the word has two meanings: a funny situation can be amusing or it can be strange and difficult to explain. Where there's a doubt, it is better to make clear which meaning is intended, by using alternative words, such as 'amusing' or 'comical' on the one hand, or 'peculiar' or 'perplexing' on the other.

furore   A *furore* (meaning an uproar) has *three* syllables ('fewRAWree'), although the American two-syllable pronunciation is occasionally heard ('fewRAW').

further   See farther . . .

future   Future has a way of creeping in when it is not needed: 'he would not reveal his future intentions', 'their future plan is to live in New Zealand'; 'What are the future prospects?' Leave out the word *future* from those sentences and the meaning remains unaltered. As for 'in the near future' and, even worse, 'in the not too distant future', this is pompous officialese, which should be replaced by '**soon**' and 'fairly soon' respectively.

futurology   There is big money in making long-range predictions of the course of social and economic change. In the late 1940s, this uncertain business was given scientific status by calling it *futurology*. Now there are practitioners called futurologists, specializing in looking as far ahead as possible.

Futurology does not meet the criteria for a science, in that at best it can hardly be more than calculated speculation based on trends and statistical probabilities. It has been argued that **science fiction** is a more honest term.

· G ·

Gaelic   See Celt . . .

gaffe or **faux pas**   In French, a *faux pas* is a false step, and the expression is also used to mean a blunder. In 17th-century English, *faux pas* came to be used for a woman's sexual indiscretion, and later for any kind of social bad taste.

By now, *faux pas* in English is perhaps less used, although it is still heard. *Gaffe* is the more customary word for eating peas off a knife or any other indiscretion or lapse from good taste. (It is also French: 'faire une gaffe' means to put one's foot in it.) An equivalent slang expression is to *drop a clanger*.

gaffer   This odd word has become familiar to millions who have no idea what it means, since it appears on film and television credits. It is the usual term in the film business for the chief electrician working with a production unit. But it goes back much further, to the 16th century, when it was used, as it still is, for an old man, especially one leaning on the bar of a country pub. *Gaffer* is also used in the building industry for the site foreman, and in some parts of the country by farmworkers about the farm owner.

The origin of *gaffer* is uncertain. It is thought to be some kind of corruption of 'godfather', a piquant reflection, as we watch it on television credits rolling up the screen.

gage   See gauge . . .

gainsay   The trouble with *gainsay* is that if you write or say something 'cannot be gainsaid', probably half your readers or listeners will be uncertain of what you mean. *Gainsay* means to go against or deny, and was often used in the negative past form, as above. But this elegant expression, that goes back to the 13th century, is now literary, and C T Onions (*Oxford Dictionary of English Etymology*, 1966) called it 'slightly archaic'.

gale   See blizzard . . .

gallant   There was a time when a woman would acknowledge an act of kindness from a man by saying 'That was very gallant of you', and he might have doffed his hat and bowed. Men may still open doors for women or help them over stiles, but *gallant* in the old sense has little place left for it in the sexual equality of the 1990s, except perhaps for some older women.

An act of selfless courage could still be called a gallant act, an especially fine ship could be a gallant ship, and a brave horse a gallant horse. But there are not many other ways in which *gallant* can be used now, without it sounding old-worldly.

galleys   See proofs . . .

Gallic   See Celt . . .

gallimaufry   A useful word to keep in reserve as a colourful alternative to 'hodgepodge' or 'jumble', which is how it has been used since the 16th century. No etymologist has discovered the origin of this strange word, which gives it an added appeal. (Pron: 'gallyMAWfree'.)

gallon   Petrol pumps at most garages in Britain now show the price in litres, not readily convertible by motorists into the price per gallon, which they are more at home with. Gallon is, in fact, short for *imperial gallon*, eight pints or 4.546 litres. An *American gallon* is less, 3.785 litres.

Gallup poll   As early as the 13th century, *poll* meant a human head, and a *Gallup poll* is a counting of heads, a sounding of public opinion carried out by one of the companies founded by Horace Gallup (1901–84). He is the American who devised a statistical method, using a so-called 'representative sample' of the population, for assessing public attitudes about anything from a detergent to voting in an election. A Gallup poll is now sometimes used loosely for any public opinion survey, whether or not carried out by the Gallup organization. Some years ago, the word *pollster*, for someone conducting a public opinion poll, became accepted by dictionaries.

galore   See aplenty . . .

galumph   Dictionaries sometimes copy one another unthinkingly, so even the latest ones write down *galumph* as colloquial or informal. Well over a hundred years ago, Lewis Carroll invented it by combining syllables of 'gallop' and 'triumphant', and the word now deserves to be accepted as standard English. It means moving along heavily and clumsily but energetically, and has the hallmark of a good word, because it sounds like what it means.

gambit   The extended use of *gambit* has become much more common than the original meaning, which was an opening move in chess where you sacrifice a pawn or piece to secure an advantage. Now a calculated move in any situation, that makes things go your way, is called a clever or shrewd *gambit*. An *opening gambit* (it is argued that 'opening' is unnecessary since a gambit is an opening move anyway) is a preliminary comment carefully calculated to win support. It is wrong to use it for any clever remark.

gaol See **prison** . . .

gaoler See **jailer** . . .

garage Two different pronunciations have become recognized, at least by some recent dictionaries; 'GArahj' and 'GAridge'. But for many people only 'GArahj' is correct, and the alternative 'GAridge', which is heard more and more, is on the wrong side of the railway tracks.

garden flat No one says any more 'I live in a basement'. *Garden flat*, which began as an estate agents' euphemism, has taken over. And even when there is no garden, basement flats are now 'at garden level'.

gargantuan or **gigantic** Rabelais's satire, *Gargantua* (1534), about a giant, brought *gargantuan* into English. It is usually pejorative, suggesting something grotesquely large, and is often used for a huge meal or portion of food, since Rabelais's giant had an enormous mouth. *Gigantic* is a usually uncritical word for anything that is huge. See also **colossal** . . .

gas Although you can *step on the gas* and even *run out of gas* in Britain, *gas* has never become an accepted word for 'petrol', as it is in America, where it is the abbreviation of 'gasoline'. See also **petrol**

(language of) **gastronomy** Long ago, but well within living memory, it used to be considered bad taste in Britain to pass any comment on the food being eaten. The French, on the contrary, talk of nothing else, and this obsession with food has crossed the English Channel. It is now not only in order to mention the *coquilles Saint-Jacques* or the *fegato alla milanese* or whatever other dish the cook has slaved over a hot stove to produce, but it would be ungracious not to.

In the 1990s the vocabulary of food is worldwide. As new editions of English dictionaries appear, more and more culinary terms from different countries are included, such as, to name only two examples, the Arab *falafel* (deep-fried balls of minced chick-peas and herbs) or the Indonesian *sate* or *satay* (barbecued bamboo skewers of spiced meat). Many such dishes are almost as familiar in Britain as *shepherd's pie* or *toad in the hole*, and the names of them have become well digested by the English language. **Menu English** is something else.

-gate Watergate is a complex of buildings in Washington, DC, that encompasses a hotel and offices.

It includes the Democrats' political campaign headquarters, where during the night of 17 June 1972, five men were arrested, caught removing microphones and recording equipment that had been hidden there. The ensuing scandal became known as *Watergate*.

The *-gate* suffix entered the language for every new political skulduggery that was exposed. The exposé of the millions of dollars raised for the Nicaraguan Contras rebels, by overcharging Iran for arms, became *Irangate*; the collapse of the BCCI banking combine in 1991 was spoken about as *BCCIgate*. The same year came *Inkathagate*, the revelation that the state police in South Africa had been secretly funding the Inkatha Freedom Party. Politics will at times be a dirty business, and the Watergate Hotel in Washington will continue to get free, if dubious, publicity for years to come.

gauge or **gage** As a noun for a measuring instrument, or a verb meaning to measure or calculate, the spelling is *gauge* in Britain, usually *gage* in America. *Gage* does have other meanings in British English: a fruit, a pledge deposited as a guarantee, a symbol of a challenge to a duel (traditionally a glove thrown down).

gay, homosexual or **lesbian** Notwithstanding its classical components, *homosexuality* is not an old word. Some time in the latter part of the 19th century, the Greek word *homo*, meaning same, was combined with *sexus*, the Latin word for sex, to describe physical attraction between people of the same sex, men or women. The new word came to be mostly associated with men, perhaps because the 'homo' prefix was mistakenly taken to be the Latin word for a man: the pronunciation has shifted from the correct 'hommo-SEXual' to 'hohmoSEXual', now generally preferred. Women who have sexual relationships with each other usually choose to call themselves *lesbians*, after the Greek island of Lesbos, home in the 6th century BC of the poet Sappho and her lovers.

The word *gay* goes back to the 13th century, when it meant cheerful and lively, and later, by association, brightly coloured. By the 17th century, *gay* had acquired connotations of sexual abandon. Francis Grose in his *Classical Dictionary of the Vulgar Tongue* (1785) records 'gaying instrument' as slang for the penis.

So the word was waiting in the wings, ready to be taken over by homosexuals in New York, as the name for the *Gay Liberation* movement in the late 1960s. Here are a few lines from an epitaph on the word *gay*, as it was once known, taken from *Protest Poem* by Vernon Scannell, printed in the *New Statesman*, 9 June 1978:

> It was a good word once, a little sparkler,
> Simple, innocent even, like a hedgerow
>   flower . . .
> A good word once, and I'm disconsolate
> And angered by this simple syllable's fate:
> A small innocence gone, a little Fall.
> I grieve the loss. I am not gay at all.

There are some dictionaries, even in the 1990s, that are reluctant to accept the demise of the old meanings of *gay* and continue to define it, first and foremost, as lighthearted, joyful, showy, brilliantly colourful. But Vernon Scannell was right to lament the loss for ever of those meanings. It is no longer possible to say, with the old meanings in mind, 'I feel gay this evening' or 'You look so gay', without inviting misunderstanding.

Although the terms *gay men* and *gay women* are used, *gay*, like *homosexual*, is primarily associated with men, and *lesbian* remains the usual word for women. There is, for example, the London Lesbian and Gay Centre, and Ian McKellen, a prominent advocate of gay rights, makes the point of distinguishing between *gays* and *lesbians*. See also **closet gays**; **homophobia**; **outing**

gazebo   See **conservatory** . . .

gazetted   The *London Gazette* is a uniquely English institution. It started as the *Oxford Gazette*, 16 November 1665, when Charles II and his entourage moved to Oxford because of the Plague, becoming the *London Gazette* the following year. Now published by **HMSO** on Tuesdays and Fridays, notifications published in it are announcements to the world at large, which no one can deny knowledge of, whether or not they have seen them. Such notices might include changes of names of companies or individuals, special meetings, such as meetings of creditors, official appointments and certain other items that are actually required by law to be *gazetted*. The equivalent in Scotland is the *Edinburgh Gazette*.

gazump   How did anyone buying or selling a house manage without this word, which was on everyone's lips during the housing boom of the 1970s? The origin of the word is uncertain, but it may well be another of those colourful enrichments of English from Yiddish (see **Hebrew**). It is used mostly in connection with buying and selling property and means raising the price after accepting an offer, before contracts are exchanged. But *gazump* is being adapted to wider use for going back on any agreement: a headline in *The Times* claimed 'Major tells Tory rebels not to gazump treaty'.

GCSE   Successive governments in Britain have sought to reform national educational examinations. First examinations for the GCSE (General Certificate of Secondary Education) were set in the summer of 1988, replacing the long-standing GCE O-level examinations and the CSE (Certificate of Secondary Education).

GDP or GNP   The *GNP* figure is the one more often in the news: the gross national product is the total value of all business activities, at home and internationally, including production, investments and services. The *GDP*, gross domestic product, is the part of that figure limited to business activities within the home country.

GDR   See **Germany**

gearing   With gears, a large cogged wheel is linked to a smaller one, driving it at a faster speed. One turn of the larger wheel produces many more turns of the smaller wheel. *Gearing* is used for the financial application of that principle. When you invest money on the understanding that you pay only a small percentage of the sum to begin with and the rest later on, that is gearing: a small sum is doing the work of a larger sum. If the investment goes up in value before the full sum is due, you can sell and make a high percentage profit on the initial outlay. But gearing is not surefire: if the investment goes down in value, and you do not have the funds to pay the balance, you are in trouble.

Gearing in business is an application of the principle: a lesser amount of money is used to finance a correspondingly bigger project, usually by raising loan capital. And the same risks are present: if the project fails, there is no profit available to repay interest on the debt.

gender or sex   For centuries, *gender* was a term used in grammar rather than in real life. And English grammarians didn't need to use it much, for in English gender is commonsense: man, boy, husband, etc are masculine gender; woman, girl, wife, etc are feminine gender; person, pupil, worker, etc are common gender (either men or women); book, bed, table, etc are neuter (ie devoid of sex). None of that has much relevance to using English, except when it comes to words such as *her*, *him*, *its*. But in many other languages, we have to learn about gender because it is an essential part of grammatical form.

Two considerations have brought *gender* into use outside grammar. Some people find the word *sex* too steamy, and resort to *gender* as a euphemism ('I enjoy the company of someone of the opposite gender'). That should be dismissed with the contempt it deserves, as **Fowler** did: '*Gender*', he declared, 'is a grammatical term only' (*Modern English Usage*, 1926). But as women have taken more significant roles in the activities of the world, there has been a correspondingly increased focus on the dichotomy of feminine and masculine characteristics. The word *sex* is not always appropriate to express psychological and cultural differences. Take this sentence by John Cole, when BBC political editor: 'Margaret Thatcher's gender did not indelibly mark her style of government'. He is using *gender* to define the characteristics and qualities of a woman, and in that context it may be a useful word.

It is likely that *gender* and *sex* will be used increasingly with this distinction: *sex* for physical and social aspects, *gender* more related to cultural and psychological differences. But *gender* needs to be watched, so that it does not slip into use as a pretentious sheepish synonym for *sex*. For example, it is reported that a Senate committee of the US Congress plans to define rape as a 'gender-based hate crime'. That stands the word on its head.

-general   It is standard practice to form the plural of military titles by adding *-s* to *general*: lieutenant-generals. . . . With legal and organizational titles, the old practice was to use the plural of the preceding word: attorneys-general, directors-general. . . . But this is now changing to the more logical plural form of attorney-generals, director-generals. . . . For the time being, both plural forms are alternatives, with the expectation that 'attorneys-general', etc will eventually drop out of use.

General American This is a technical term used in linguistics. See **American English . . .**

generalissimo or **supremo** *Generalissimo*, at home in Italian, is too flamboyant to sit comfortably in English. But it is used at times for the supreme commander of different armies working together, or of a combined army, navy and air force. It is also occasionally used for the boss of a big organization, such as one of the multinational companies. *Supremo*, an equivalent word from Spanish, is used in the same way, especially in non-military contexts: *The Times* used the headline 'South Bank *supremo*' about the appointment of a chief executive for London's South Bank arts centre.

Both words are masculine in the languages they belong to, but are unisex in English, although so far they are rarely used for a woman. The plurals are anglicized: *generalissimos, supremos*.

generation Some of the terms used in **computer technology** suggest that the machines have near-human qualities. Early on, *generation*, a word used for the offspring of human beings, was applied to computers, to classify the advancing stages in electronic technology, from valves in the *first generation*, to transistors in the *second*, with integrated circuits in the *third*. *Fourth-generation* computers date from the mid-1970s and were a major advance requiring new terms, ever more closely related to the way humans function, such as **user-friendly** (a word invented in America in the late 1970s). *Fifth-generation* computers belong to the 1990s, a complete departure from earlier techniques, leading to machines of enormous power and sophistication, capable of responding to involved spoken instructions, and claimed by some experts to be the first stage of **artificial intelligence**.

generation gap The phrase represents an apparent difference of attitudes and ways of seeing life between older and younger people. No generally agreed definition exists about how many years it requires for there to be a generation gap. Thirty years used to be considered the period of time for children to grow up and form the next generation. But now teenagers have been known to talk about the generation gap between themselves and people in their late 20s.

genes, chromosomes, DNA or **genomes** Every germ cell in the human organism contains 46 *chromosomes*, wormlike compositions only visible under a powerful microscope. A chromosome is a formation of two filaments of **d**eoxyribo**n**ucleic acid. This made the headlines as *DNA* in 1953, when the

Cambridge scientists, Crick and Watson, determined its molecular form and structure, which they described as a *double helix* (a helix is a spiral shaped like a corkscrew).

Genes are ranged along the coils of the DNA and reveal a detailed chart of an individual's characteristics, from the colour of eyes and hair to predisposition to malfunctions and diseases.

The term *genome*, likely to become a more familiar everyday word, is a linguistic combination of *gene* and *chromosome*, and is useful because it covers the total genetic organization, taking in chromosomes, DNA and genes, just as *genetic* is a general all-embracing descriptive word.

Genetic research means, more than anything else, identifying the particular genes within the chromosomes, said to be some hundred thousand, isolating genes that relate to certain diseases, weaknesses, predilections, in fact almost everything that defines a person.

Genetic screening is an analysis of all the information that genes can supply about an individual, particularly inherited disorders and tendencies. It poses complex social and even financial problems. For example, it could lead to discrimination by employers against people with negative predispositions. Or if screening reveals that people will die at an early age, they could take out life insurance to protect their families. These social and legal dilemmas have yet to be confronted.

Genetic fingerprinting, a term from popular journalism for what forensic scientists call *DNA profiling*, provides positive identification of an individual. Blood samples, samples of hair or any other part of the body are all that is necessary for this genetic information to be charted. Fears have been expressed by the National Council of Civil Liberties in Britain that the police may build up a DNA **database**, which could undermine the principles of **data protection** rules.

Genetic engineering is the most controversial area of genetic research. It is controlled alteration of a section of DNA by adding new genes or changing one gene for another. At present, this is confined mostly to experimental work in laboratories, and forebodings over where it could lead, with talk of '**designer** people', are for the foreseeable future sinister science fiction.

genetic See congenital . . .

genetic engineering, fingerprinting, research, screening See genes . . .

genetics or **eugenics** *Eugenics* is a term rarely used now: it is related to Charles Darwin's theory of evolution, and was in fact a word coined in the 19th century by Francis Galton, Darwin's cousin. It describes a concept of improving the human species by selective breeding in order to reproduce the most desirable inherited qualities.

In the 20th century, *genetics* has superseded eugenics, as a possible way of manipulating hereditary factors in the development of the human race. (See *genetic engineering* under **genes . . .**)

genetics is or **are** Nouns ending in *-ics* often present this problem. See **-ics**

genitive case See **possessive case** . . .

genius For some time there has been a tendency to dilute the special quality of this word for someone with truly exalted powers as an artist, scientist or thinker. *Genius* doubles more and more now for mere aptitude or talent: 'She has a genius for making soufflés'. If we use it that way, what word do we have left for Mozart or Einstein? There aren't many *geniuses*, but when it is needed, that is the plural form. 'Genii' is only used for the plural of 'genie', a goblin or attendant spirit.

genocide It was the **Holocaust**, the attempt by Nazi Germany to exterminate the Jews, that gave rise to the word *genocide*, devised towards the end of World War II by an American lawyer, Raphael Lemkin. He used the word 'homicide' as the basis, substituting the Greek word 'genos', race, intending the word to describe the crime of deliberately exterminating a whole race of people. *Genocide*, a word for murder on a vast scale, is sometimes used by journalists too lightly, about ethnic killing in a village, for example. See also **ethnic cleansing**

genomes See **genes** . . .

genre This French word has been in English since the late 18th century. There is perhaps no exact alternative, especially when *genre* is used about literature, art or music. *Genre* can be translated as 'kind', 'sort', 'style', but none of those words go far enough, for *genre* suggests something is within the same artistic tradition, inspired by the same creative outlook.

The pronunciation is a problem. Nothing less than the full French treatment sounds right: something like 'ZHAHN-r'. But for some people that makes *genre* seem pretentious. There is no way out, except not to use the word at all.

genteelism See **euphemism** . . .

gentleman or **man** The word *gentleman* is kept alive by after-dinner speakers ('Ladies and gentlemen . . .'), MPs, even if they don't mean it, ('The honourable gentleman . . .'), signs outside lavatories in some of the more gracious hotels (assuming they have not been replaced by the ubiquitous symbolic outline), a few titles, such as *gentleman-at-arms* (a member of the Queen's bodyguard), and perhaps the term *gentlemen's agreement* (although it is wiser these days to have it in writing).

Otherwise the word *gentleman* is on the shelf, awkward and often out of place in the egalitarian 1990s. To describe someone as 'an old gentleman' is kinder perhaps than calling him 'an old man', although it depends on the circumstances. But for a woman to talk about 'her gentleman friend' would sound arch. The situation is at times uneasy. There are people who feel that to

say, for example, 'There's a man to see you', is impolite. Waiters and the few surviving butlers still feel obliged to say *gentleman*, as do the owners of pubs ('Time gentlemen, please!'). But in the years to come, *gentleman* will sound increasingly musty and fusty. Even the traditional title of the cricket match, Gentlemen v Players, has been replaced. And Anna Ford had no hesitation about entitling her symposium of masculine attitudes, which included conversations with bishops and cabinet ministers, with the simple monosyllable *Men*. The situation with **lady** is not the same.

gentlewoman The word is redundant, motheaten and superannuated, which is what anyone would sound like if they used it.

gentrification The word became used after World War II about the rebuilding or restoration of run-down inner-city areas, and was also applied when humble working-class cottages on the fringes of fashionable districts were transformed into tiny but luxurious houses for the affluent classes. *Gentrification* carries with it the slur of class-distinction and the eviction of the poor, and even estate agents hesitate to use it, preferring such euphemisms as 'beautifully converted', 'a rapidly improving area'.

gentry The word belongs to English social history, when it roughly corresponds to what might now be called the 'upper middle class', the class below the aristocracy. It has no place in other contexts.

genuine See **authentic** . . .

geo- Ge or Gaea, a goddess in Greek legend, personifying the earth, gave her name to this prefix, which is a useful guide to the meaning of certain words, such as *geobotany* (the study of the distribution of plants throughout the earth), *geophysics* (the study of physical forces relating to the earth, which includes meteorology and oceanography), *geopolitics* (the effect of the features of the earth's surface on politics), *geostrophic* (about winds caused by the rotation of the earth). . . .

Ernest Gowers, in his revision of Fowler's *Modern English Usage* (1965), issued a warning, worth repeating, against the sloppy pronunciation of the prefix *geo-* as 'jog' in *geography* (instead of 'jeeOGraphy'), and 'jom' in *geometry* (instead of 'jeeOMMetry').

geographical or **geographic** Both words mean the same. *Geographical* is the main entry in dictionaries now, with *geographic* shown as a variant, an indication that the longer form is preferred.

geometric or **geometrical** These follow the opposite pattern to **geographical** (see previous entry), and architects and designers usually refer to geometric features, geometric patterns, rather than geometrical.

geriatric *Geriatric* should relate to the medical treatment of old people (a geriatric ward in a hospital), since it combines two Greek words, one meaning old age and the other a physician. But the word has become for many people a synonym for an old person, possibly with the suggestion of infirmity ('geriatrics sitting on a park bench'). The latest dictionaries are divided: some show the primary meaning of *geriatric* as 'an old person', others insist on linking it to *geriatrics*, the branch of medicine dealing with the treatment of diseases suffered by the aged.

While the association with medical care remains a valuable definition, in the same way as 'paediatrics' refers to medical treatment of children, the way things are going, *geriatric* is likely to become, by the end of the century, just another word for the old, except perhaps when used by doctors and nurses.

germ, **microbe**, **bacteria** or **virus**   The popular use of these words does not coincide with their precise scientific meanings. In general use, they are all associated with micro-organisms that cause disease. A *germ* is, in fact, any microscopic organism, not necessarily harmful ones (*wheatgerm*, for example, is a food supplement). A *microbe* is the same as a germ, that is a micro-organism. The French bacteriologist, Louis Pasteur (1822–95), brought the word *microbe* into everyday use, and through him it is nearly always associated with harmful germs.

Bacteria is the plural of *bacterium*, the singular form that even bacteriologists do not have cause to use often. Although in many ways another term for germs or microbes, bacteria covers the whole range of micro-organisms present everywhere. Many of these are part of the normal living process, some are even essential for good health, although the science of *bacteriology* is primarily concerned with bacteria that cause diseases.

A *virus*, wrongly defined by some dictionaries as a term for bacteria, is different. It derives from the Latin word for poison, and is not a living organism, but a crystalline particle that infects the cells of living organisms, causing them to multiply rapidly, leading to such serious diseases and epidemics as smallpox and polio.

In ordinary non-medical use, it is reasonable to use *germ* or *microbe* about micro-organisms that cause diseases, with the reservation that *germ* is also used for harmless living seeds that contribute to good health. *Bacteria* should be kept as a general-purpose word for all micro-organisms, specifying, when necessary, whether they are dangerous or harmless. *Virus* needs to be used more cautiously by people without medical knowledge, usually in relation to certain epidemic diseases. To call the disease itself a virus ('he is suffering from a virus') is mistaken, but this is heard so often that we have become used to it.

See also **virus (computers)**

Germany   After World War II, Germany was divided into two separate states: East Germany became the *German Democratic Republic* (GDR), with West Germany as the *Federal Republic of Germany* (FRG). At midnight, 2 October 1990, German reunification took place, and the whole country became officially the Federal Republic of Germany. The abbreviation GDR, like the Berlin Wall, was relegated to history books.

gerund   *Gerund* is a convenient grammatical term for defining a particular form of verbs. It is the form ending in *-ing*, which serves as a noun: 'I enjoy *eating*'; '*swimming* is good exercise'.

Because a gerund is a verbal noun, the word that precedes it should often be in the possessive form. 'I do not like *his* drinking so much' is correct; 'I do not like *him* drinking so much' is technically ungrammatical. Similarly, 'she resented *John's* having dinner with another woman' is correct; 'she resented *John* having dinner with another woman' could be considered grammatically incorrect. Authorities on grammar disagree over this, some defining *John having* as a combined noun. The argument seems remote from the need to use language to express ideas. In any case, the form 'she resented John having dinner . . .' is so common that it is unreasonable to object to it, at least when it is used in conversation. To many people it sounds more natural than the 'correct' form.

Gestapo   The Gestapo was part of Hitler's regime in Germany: it was an **acronym** for **G**eheime **Sta**atspolizei, literally the 'secret state police'. The word survives in English, outside history books, as an abusive and often unjust descriptive word for any violent, seemingly brutal action by the police when they are dealing with public disorder ('Gestapo tactics').

gibe or **jibe**   *Gibe* is the usual spelling, with *jibe* as a variant for both the verb, meaning to jeer or taunt, or the noun meaning a provocative taunting remark. As the sailing term, *gybe* is the usual spelling in Britain with *gibe* (the American spelling) as a variant. It describes a change of tack when the wind is behind the centre line of the boat, catching the sail on the wrong side and making it jump across.

gift (as a verb)   It still sounds strange to hear *gift* used as a verb: 'she gifts a number of shares each year to her children, to avoid paying inheritance tax'. The use is accepted by current dictionaries. It does not mean quite the same as 'give', but suggests making a formal gift of money or property for tax reasons or other statutory purposes. It is pointless to use *gift* as a verb in ordinary contexts as an alternative to 'give'.

gigantic   See **gargantuan . . .; colossal**

gigolo   See **toy boy**

gilt-edged   See **blue chip . . .**

gimmick   Television and the other media are greedy for new words: *gimmick*, already current in America in the 1920s, which rocketed to fame in Britain in the 1950s, is becoming dated. Yet it will stay with us because it is useful, in a world of cheap publicity tricks, to describe something that has no real purpose except to get attention.

No one seems to know the origin of *gimmick*, although it is thought to be linked with 'gimcrack', another word for something that is cheap, showy and nasty.

gipsy   See gypsy . . .

girl   The latest dictionaries have picked up that feminists consider this simple innocent word is sexist. A few years ago this was a typical definition of *girl*: 'woman working in office, shop, factory, etc, woman secretary or other assistant . . .'. Recent dictionaries are more sensitive and use definitions such as 'a female child', 'a young unmarried woman', sometimes adding that *girl* for an older woman is 'informal'. Some women argue that we would not call a man over 18 a *boy*, so why call a grown woman a *girl*, with its belittling implication of immaturity and lack of importance? They believe that deep-seated attitudes will change only when we consciously change words that reflect them. Other women find all this exaggerated. It is certainly a long-established habit for both sexes to talk about women as *girls*. But we should be aware that, in the 1990s, there are many women who object to this. You still hear *old girl* used affectionately by some men to their wives or women friends, although it does sound like yesterday's language. *Girlie* is the most offensive of all, as it is used about soft porn magazines and photographs. See also **boyish** . . .; **sexist language**

girl Friday   Advertisements for a *girl Friday*, meaning a woman to act as a general dogsbody to a man, making coffee, running errands, etc, have almost disappeared from Situations Vacant columns. The idea was taken from Man Friday in Defoe's *Robinson Crusoe*, although no one ever advertised for a 'man Friday'.

Perhaps employers have come to recognize that the expression is demeaning, or perhaps advertising for a girl Friday, or a man Friday for that matter, is a contravention of the Sex Discrimination Act.

girlfriend   See boyfriend . . .

girlie   See boyish . . .; girl

girlish   See boyish . . .

given name   See first or Christian name

glacier   The recommended pronunciation is 'GLASSier', rather than 'GLAYssier', which some dictionaries show as an alternative.

glamorous   The word was trounced in the early 1970s by the lexicographer, Eric Partridge, as 'the dubious privilege of boss-driven copywriters' (*Usage and Abusage*). The origin of *glamour* is unexpected: it was an 18th-century form of 'grammar' (a subject that is far from glamorous), possibly connected with medieval esoteric teachings. Perhaps because it was overused in advertising at one time, as Partridge

complained, *glamorous* sounds rather dated to describe a love-affair, a person, an occasion or anything else that has enchantment and magic. In America, unlike most **-our** words, the spellings *glamour* and *glamor* are alternatives, but the descriptive word everywhere is *glamorous*.

glasnost   It was like a ray of sunshine for the world in 1985 when Mikhail Gorbachev took over as first secretary of the Soviet Communist Party. Unlike his solemn predecessors, Khrushchev and Brezhnev, here was a Soviet leader who wore a trilby hat and walked among the people of his country. Life on earth became a little more lighthearted, and a Russian word, serious and full of hope, passed into other major languages – *glasnost*. It means literally 'openness', the freedom to debate in public and criticize Soviet society and its government. See also **perestroika**

glass ceiling   In the 1980s, American management consultants invented this expression to describe the invisible, not-spoken-about barrier between women and the top jobs in big companies. It caught on in Britain, where, as the 1980s ended, a survey, *Women in Management in Great Britain*, revealed only eight women as directors of the UK's top hundred companies, and not one woman as the boss. Women executives talk about breaking through the *glass ceiling*.

glass fibre   See fibreglass . . .

glitzy   As *ritzy* (see **Ritz**) was going into the archives as an out-of-date colloquialism, it was combined with 'glitter' to make a new slang word, *glitzy*. That's as good an etymological explanation as any to account for the word, which appeared in the 1960s. *Glitzy* is a show-business word for something that is extravagant, showy and, so to speak, diamond-studded – with artificial diamonds, that is.

global warming or greenhouse effect   *Greenhouse effect* is the cause; *global warming* is the result. A greenhouse on a summer's day is stifling and humid, and the concept was borrowed to illustrate the effect of the layer formed by carbon dioxide derived from burning **fossil fuels**, and so-called *greenhouse gases* used in aerosols, foam-plastics, refrigerators and other products. This layer allows heat and radiation from the sun to pass through, trapping it in the Earth's atmosphere. The result is global warming. The 1980s was the warmest decade on Earth since records began, according to climatologists at the British Meteorological Office. The doomsday scenarios predict storms, failure of crops through drought, and floods from rising sea levels. The dangers have been known about since the industrial revolution in the 19th century, and the term *greenhouse effect* had been used back in the late 1930s. But when environmental issues moved centre-stage, everyone talked about the greenhouse effect as if it had just been discovered.

glossies   Imported from America in the 1950s, the word *glossies* (nearly always used in the plural) is accepted by now as standard English by most British dictionaries. It is a useful word to describe those showy expensive-looking magazines, printed on coated paper. And *glossies* sums them up, because a 'gloss' is only a surface shine that wears off quickly, just as the magazines are full of superficial sensations and ideas, soon forgotten.

glueing or **gluing** Dictionaries allow both spellings, usually listing *gluing* first. But in fact, *glueing* looks right, so many people prefer that spelling.

glue-sniffing See **solvent abuse** . . .

GNP See GDP . . .

gobbledygook See **doublespeak** . . .

God or **god** In the text of religious services or prayers, *God* is always spelt with a capital G. This also applies when there is the implication of the supreme being of monotheistic religions, as in: Thank God!, God knows, God forbid!, God bless you, Good God!

When the word is used more generally, or refers to a number of gods, a small *g* is appropriate: 'money is his god'; 'she treats him like a god'; 'Thou shalt have no other gods before me' (*Exodus*).

goddaughter See **grandad** . . .

(the) **godfather** In America, this benign word is used for the all-powerful boss or bosses of dominant criminal organizations. The word is becoming used in Britain about, for example, 'the godfathers' of paramilitary organizations in Northern Ireland. For further notes, see **Mafia**.

go for broke See **broke**

going into the Church See **ordained** . . .

gold See **bullion** . . .

gold or **golden** It is *gold* when an object is made of the yellow metal: a gold ring, a gold coin. . . . It is *golden* when it is used for the colour or quality of gold:

> Golden lads and girls all must,
> As chimney-sweepers, come to dust.
> *Cymbeline*, Act IV Sc ii

Goldfinch and *goldfish* are two exceptions to the rule! See also next entry

golden Down the ages, gold has had a magic quality, and *golden* is continually being prefixed to new words to suggest something special or enticing:
Golden age is a period when life (or anything else) was supposedly at its best (the golden age of the Hollywood musical).
Golden handcuffs is a sum of money paid to a director or executive to prevent them taking a job with another company.

Golden handshake is the opposite to *golden handcuffs*. It is a lump sum of money paid to a director or executive to encourage them to leave the company without making a fuss. This is often the result of a takeover or a struggle for power in the boardroom.
Golden hello is a sum paid to a person, in addition to salary, as an extra inducement to persuade them to join a company.
Golden scenario is a more recent *golden* term, which most dictionaries have not yet caught up with. It is the opposite of **nightmare scenario**, and describes a perfect arrangement, the cards falling in just the right way: 'Mr Heseltine's supporters regard a challenge from Sir Geoffrey as the *golden scenario*' (*The Independent*, 11.11.1990).

golf course or **golf links** The origin of the word *golf* has never properly come to light, as the attempt to relate it to an early Dutch word, 'kolf' or 'colve' for a club or bat, is unconvincing. It is certainly a Scottish word and can be traced back to the 15th century. The affected pronunciation 'goff' is not often heard now, and was never anything more than a poor attempt by the English to imitate the Scottish sound.

Links comes from an Old English word for sandy ground by the sea, which is how *golf links* arose (the Royal and Ancient, the most famous golf course in the world, is by the sea at St Andrews). *Golf course* has become the international name, although *links course* is heard to describe the qualities of a seaside sandy course with close-cropped grass.

goodbye, **bye-bye** or **ta-ta** *Bye-bye*, while not as downmarket as *ta-ta* (they are both childish forms), was nevertheless written off by Alan S C Ross and Nancy Mitford as decidedly *Non-U* (see **class language**; **U and Non-U**).

Americans often use the spelling *goodby*, but it should always be *goodbye* in British English (it's short for 'God be with ye').

good faith See **bona fide** . . .

goodies When the 1990 *Record* of Pembroke College, Oxford, described a distinguished scholar as having collected a drawer full of 'academic goodies', it was difficult to determine whether *goodies* had moved into literary English or whether the writer was trying to be trendy. The same can be said of the director-general of the **CBI**, who talked about 'goodies, such as tax cuts'.

Goodies sounds childish but some recent dictionaries no longer label it 'colloquial', which might have come to the notice of the Oxford college and the CBI director-general.

good-looking or **looking good** *Good-looking* is unequivocal; *looking good* may imply 'for your age'. It was the scriptwriter, Dennis Norden, who pointed out that the difference between *good-looking* and *looking good* is about 20 years.

goods See **freight** . . .

goodwill The word has two different meanings. In business, *goodwill* has the specific meaning of an intangible asset, impossible to define precisely but certainly worth money. It represents the reputation of a company, as perceived by its customers, and their loyalty towards it. When it comes to selling a business, goodwill can have a high commercial value.

In private life, goodwill is less mercenary: it is a friendly cooperative feeling between one person and another, valuable when one of them needs help or support, but not bought and sold.

go-slow or **work-to-rule** These are both forms of **industrial action** that stop short of workers going on strike. The difference between them is perhaps more a matter of terminology than practical reality. *Go-slow* is simply working more slowly than normal, but not so slowly that employees could be accused of not doing their jobs properly.

Work-to-rule is keeping strictly to rules agreed with employers, nonetheless a **restrictive practice** that causes disruption, in that it allows none of the flexibility usually essential for the efficient running of an organization.

got Some people think the word is ugly. It is sometimes unnecessary, which does not make it wrong, as is often claimed. Shakespeare, Swift, Ruskin and Dr Johnson all used *got*. **Fowler** maintained (*Modern English Usage*, 1926) that *have got* for 'have' or 'possess' is not 'good literary English'. But Ernest Gowers, in his revision of Fowler's book (1965), reverses that recommendation. 'I haven't got it in stock' is down-to-earth; 'I don't have it in stock' is more formal. With that difference in mind, use *got* whenever it suits you. In America, 'I haven't got' would be rare, as it's usually 'I don't have'. But Americans retain *gotten* in the sense of obtain ('I have gotten it for you'). This used to be British usage as well, but no longer, except in 'ill-gotten gains'.

go to the wall See belly-up . . .

gourmand or **gourmet** A gourmand eats like a pig; a gourmet eats with discrimination and refinement. *Gourmand*, for some people, is not derogatory and is almost a synonym for *gourmet*, with no more than a hint of someone enjoying food rather too much. But the word is linked in some dictionaries to gluttony, so it's better not used unless criticism is intended. If there is a comparison between eating and sex, as Lévi-Strauss, the French anthropologist, suggested, it could be said that a gourmand has an orgy, while a gourmet makes love. The pronunciations echo the French sound of the words: 'GOORmahn(d)' and 'GOORmay'.

governance The word *governing* is the normal one to use. *Governance* is not obsolete, for Harold Wilson called one of his books, *The Governance of Britain* (1976), but should be used only rarely in contexts where a ceremonial solemnity is appropriate.

Government or **government** At one time *government* was always given the dignity of a capital G. But the general tendency to avoid **capital letters** has affected the word and, except in formal contexts (Her Majesty's Government), it is very common now to use a small *g*.

This relaxed attitude should not affect the pronunciation: it is careless not to sound the *n* in the second syllable ('GUVernment').

(the) government is or **are** Usually *the government* is treated as singular (the government *is* . . .), as a collective body making laws and dealing with administration. See also **collective words**

Governors-General or **Governor-Generals** See **-general**

goy This Yiddish word, derived from **Hebrew** and meaning a Gentile, has to some extent passed into English. Some dictionaries show it as derogatory, which is not always true. You occasionally hear even non-Jews using it about themselves in a good-humoured way. And some Jews might use *goy* warmly to and about their non-Jewish friends. Any linguistic change that diminishes racism is good news, which is why *goy* has a place in this book.

graduate *Graduate* in Britain is confined to the award of academic degrees at universities. In America, it is used more generally, not only for universities, but for students who have completed a course at secondary schools.

graffiti These are what Randolph Quirk, as president of the British Academy, called 'spray-gun obscenities flagrantly unignorable on walls in Chicago or London' (*The State of the Language*, 1980). Graffiti can also be political or funny. They can be on the fringe of art forms, in some people's view brightening dreary urban landscapes. And it is an ancient tradition, for there are graffiti on the walls at Pompeii. *Graffiti art* (or *subway art*, as it has been called in New York) was exhibited in January 1992 at the Whitechapel Gallery in London. Dave Holloway, the organizer of that exhibition, explained, 'The psychology of graffiti art is deep and complex, hinging on powerlessness, a plea for recognition'. Although *graffiti* is standard English now, the word is as Italian as spaghetti, and is plural ('The graffiti *are* . . .'). The singular *graffito* is not usually used in English, except by people trying to show off their Italian. Pron: 'graFEEtee'.

gram or **gramme** See **metric**

grammar Attitudes towards grammar are ambivalent. The very name *grammar school* is a reminder that at one time grammar was almost synonymous with learning. But the grammar schools founded in the 15th and 16th centuries were so called because they taught Latin grammar, which was for centuries the model for English grammar.

There are still upholders of traditional prescriptive grammar for English, based to a great extent on the precepts of Latin grammar, but the more enlightened view now is that the fossilized laws of a dead language are a meaningless straitjacket to impose on English. The National Union of Teachers in Britain has stated a conviction that formal grammar teaching would 'run counter to everything which is known about language development'. Yet if grammar, as a form of moral compulsion, as once taught by a Mr Chips or a Miss Trump, is no longer sustainable, an awareness of the principles of structure and organization of a language (which is another way of saying *grammar*) is necessary in order to use it for clear expression of ideas and information.

The balance is uneasy and few things arouse more passion and outrage than changes to the English language. Bernice Rubens, the first woman writer to win the Booker Prize (in 1969, for her novel, *The Elected Member*), has expressed her own ambivalence towards grammar:

> Grammar to a writer is a total irrelevance. If I start thinking about grammar, I get caught up in the *how* instead of the *what* . . . grammar is a stranglehold on passion! But before a writer discards grammar, he must know it intimately. He must at one time have loved it. He must always respect it. Only then is its irrelevance clear and logical.

In the 1990s, education in Britain has become a major political issue, with declarations of intent to return to 'traditional values'. It is possible there could be a backlash against linguistic permissiveness, with 19th-century grammatical orthodoxy becoming fashionable. But at present this seems unlikely. See also **permissive or prescriptive (in linguistics)**

grammatical terms A complete list of *grammatical terms*, including such arcane ones as *ablative absolute* and *nonfinite subordination*, has no place in a guide to English in the 1990s. Mostly it is only grammarians who are aware of them: for many others they are, at best, echoes of distant thunder from their schooldays. This is not to say they do not have a place in the academic study of form and structure of language, but it is to say they are not part of using English creatively and effectively.

It is useful to be clear about what are referred to as the eight *parts of speech*, for one of these terms applies to nearly every word we use, and they provide the rudiments for talking about language. Those in **bold** type in the following list have a more detailed entry in *The Good English Guide*:

A **noun** is a word for a person, an object, a place, an action or a concept: *woman, book, town, walking, imagination*. . . .

A *verb* is a word for any kind of action or activity: *walk, talk, think, love*. . . .

An **adjective** is referred to in *The Good English Guide* as a *descriptive word*, because it describes a noun: *good, bad, large, small, beautiful*. . . .

An **adverb** is to a verb what an adjective is to a noun, that is it describes an action: to walk *slowly*, to think *quickly*, to do *well*. . . .

A **pronoun** takes the place of a noun. The most common ones are *she, he, it*: 'I saw the woman, as *she* left the house'; 'the train was late but *it* arrived eventually'.

A **preposition** is a word defining the relationship between two other parts of speech: 'she went *into* the house'; 'he stood *before* her'; 'wine goes well *with* cheese'.

A *conjunction* links two words or two groups of words together. The most common one is *and*: 'Jack *and* Jill went up the hill'; 'Jack is clever *but* Jill is pretty'; 'Do you want tea *or* coffee?'

An *interjection* is anything from a howl (*Ouch!*), to a greeting (*Hello!*), to any word used to express irritation, frustration or any other emotion (*Oh dear!*, *Ha! Ha!*). A more logical term is *exclamation*, since interjections are always followed by exclamation marks.

gramophone See hi-fi . . .

grand (for £1000) See K

grandad, granddaughter, grandmother, etc *Grandad*, if you ever have occasion to write it, should be spelt that way, rather than 'granddad'. *Granddaughter* and *goddaughter* retain the double *d*, but require no hyphen.

Nor is it necessary to make the effort to pronounce the *-d-* in *grandmother, grandfather, grandson, grandchild*, as it is in order to say 'GRANmother', 'GRANfather', etc. In fact, dictionaries show 'GRANDmother', 'GRANDfather', etc as the less usual pronunciation.

grande marque See marque

granny flat Statistically, grandmothers live longer than grandfathers, so 'granpy' flats do not exist. *Granny flat* appeared as estate agents' jargon in the mid-1960s, meeting the increasing social need to look after elderly relatives. The expression is used for a part of a house separated into self-contained accommodation, where a mother-in-law, grandmother or any other old person in the family can be kept comfortable and warm, but not too intrusive, or intruded upon.

graphics The word is used in films and other visual presentations to cover titles, diagrams, charts, graphs, etc. *Computer graphics* refers to the presentation of data in the form of drawings, diagrams, illustrations, etc.

grass See cannabis . . .

grasslands This useful generic word for fertile plains covered in rough grass can be used in place of specific names for particular regions, such as the *steppes* in Russia, the *prairies* in America, the *pampas* of South America, the *veldt* in South Africa, the *savannah* in the regions south of the Sahara in North Africa. In Britain, where grassy plains are much smaller, the usual words are *field* or *meadow*.

grassroots *Grassroots* has become such a regular word in the political vocabulary that it is now usually spelt as one word. Political parties think of the anonymous faceless mass of their supporters as the grassroots. So-called *grassroot opinion* is assessed arbitrarily by MPs going back to their constituencies and chatting to the local party organization. Nobody quite knows how to define *grassroots*, except perhaps as typical loyal supporters of the Conservative or Labour parties. One BBC political commentator, acknowledging the vagueness of the term, referred to the 'grassroots, whoever they may be'.

gratuitous The two senses of the word, one meaning something that is done without charge, and the other for something altogether uncalled for, do not generally lead to misunderstandings. The reason is that *gratuitous*, in the sense of uncalled for, is used about unpleasant things: a gratuitous remark would be taken to mean an insult or unnecessary criticism. This is by far the more common use of the word now, as in 'gratuitous damage to property', 'gratuitous acts of violence'. . . .

gratuity See tip . . .

grave accent This accent (`) is used to modify vowel sounds, mostly in French and Italian. See **French accents**; **accents in print and writing**

gravy or **sauce** *Gravy*, dating from the 14th century as possibly an imitation of an old French word, only applies to meat: it is properly used for the juices coming from a joint during cooking, usually thickened with flour. *Sauce*, also a French word going back to about the same period, should imply that it has been prepared from various ingredients to add flavour to any dish whether it's meat, fish or vegetables.

The words have attracted many slang uses in Britain and America. In both countries, *gravy* is often used for something that comes easily or is a bonus ('When we've covered our costs, everything else is *gravy*'). A *gravy train*, heard both in boardrooms and back streets, is slang for any scheme that provides easy money. The use of *sauce* for impudence or cheek, and *saucy* for a sexual innuendo, both common at one time, are now rather old-fashioned.

gray See grey . . .

great Who is a *great* writer, a *great* artist, a *great* man, a *great* woman? At Oxford University, *Greats* is traditionally used for the honours course in Greek and Latin classics, meaning the great writers and thinkers. Other than that, the word is bandied about so freely that it is in danger of becoming banal.

Graham Greene was widely regarded, it is said, as the greatest living writer in English, and when he died

in 1991, the question arose: who should now wear the mantle? There was no consensus, but two useful suggestions emerged: the word *great* should be reserved for the real giants, Shakespeare, Newton, Beethoven . . ., and is better left until after their death. Those opinions are offered here, not as a guideline, even less as an authoritative rule, but to reflect on the next time you use the word *great* about anyone. 'One of the greats' is a favourite phrase with sports commentators and there is nothing wrong with it in that context.

Great Britain, **Britain**, **United Kingdom** or **British Isles** Many foreigners, and some British, are uncertain over the proper distinction between these names. To be sure of using them correctly, see **Britain** . . .

Greek, **Grecian** or **Hellenic** The three descriptive words for anything Greek have their own particular places. *Greek* (an Old English word) is, of course, the normal word for the people, the language, the food, wine, islands . . . . *Grecian* (coming from medieval Latin) is retained for architectural elements (Grecian columns), archaeological finds (Grecian urns), facial features (Grecian noses) and a few other selected uses. *Hellenic* (pron: 'heLENNik'), close to the Greek word for 'a Greek', is the academic word related to Hellenism (pron: 'HELLinizm'), the spirit and culture of ancient Greek civilization and its influence. It has come into wider use, so that a tour of the archaeological sites in Greece can be called a Hellenic tour, a cruise round the Aegean, focused on history and art, a Hellenic cruise.

Greek prefixes and suffixes The hundreds of Greek roots that survive in English contain the seeds of meaning of many words, in spite of adaptation over the centuries. An awareness of the transliteration of Greek roots can not only save recourse to a dictionary, but add to the romance and delight of using English. As examples, here are a few Greek roots embodied in some of the more common prefixes and suffixes:

dys-, abnormal or diseased: dysentery, dysfunction, dyslexia. . . .
hyper-, excessive or above: hyperactive, hyperbole, hypercritical, hypermarket, hypersensitive. . . .
hypo-, below or abnormally low: hypodermic, hypotension. . . .
-iatric and *-iatry*, medical treatment: **geriatric**, psychiatric, psychiatry. . . .
-itis, inflammation: appendicitis, arthritis, laryngitis. . . .
mega-, a million or large: megabyte, megalith, megastar. . . .
micro-, small: *microchip, microfilm, micromesh*. . . .
pan-, all or the whole: *pandemic, panorama*. . . .
-logy, science: *biology, philology, psychology*. . . .
-nomy, a field of knowledge: *astronomy, economy*. . . .
-onym, name or word: **acronym**, antonym, synonym. . . .

-phile, fondness or liking: bibliophile, Francophile. . . .
-philia, abnormal attraction or tendency: *necrophilia, haemophilia*. . . .
-phobia, fear: *claustrophobia, xenophobia*. . . .
-phone, sound: *microphone, saxophone, telephone*. . . .
-physio, nature: *physiology, physiotherapy*. . . .
-psycho, life, soul: *psychoanalysis, psychopath, psychosexual*. . . .
-scope, looking through: *kaleidoscope, microscope*. . . .
-stat, stationary or fixed: *rheostat, thermostat*. . . .
tele-, at a distance: *telecommunication, telephoto*. . . .

green Up to the mid-1980s, the political and environmental meanings of *green* still seemed linked to pacifism, vegetarianism and fringe groups, such as the *Green Party*, started in Britain in 1973, and the *Greenpeace* organization founded two years earlier. Since then, the major political parties, multinationals from Coca-Cola to IBM, and even investment schemes have seen the light, or the political expedience, of proclaiming that green is good.

The alternative meanings of *green* have almost eclipsed the simple use of the word for the colour. If you say you are wearing green clothes, a not insignificant number of people would think you mean a dress or shirt made from fabric free from petro-chemicals or other non-renewable resources, or that your jeans are made out of cloth washed with pumice stones, rather than contaminating the environment through the use of chlorinated bleach.

Green is used about so many aspects of life, politics and society in the 1990s, that it is at times almost meaningless, a word to trigger vague fears and emotions. *The Green Consumer's Guide* offers a definition: green products should 'not cause significant damage to the environment or consume disproportionate amounts of energy, when made, used or thrown away'. The traditional British milk bottle, still left on doorsteps as we move towards the end of the 20th century, is cited as the perfect example: 'It looks good. It does the job . . . it can be re-used and recycled'. Milk bottles are green!

The word *green* has been recycled, just as everything else must be recycled to conserve the world's resources. All this is good news for everyone living on this planet, even if it has played havoc with the meaning of the word *green*. See also **biodegradable; pollution; recycle**

green audit The term first appeared towards the end of 1990, and is tipped to become part of the language of industry. A *green audit* is carried out by a specialist in environmental and pollution problems, who analyses the **green** performance of a manufacturing business, from the supplies it uses, to the disposal of waste products, to the efficiency of **recycling**.

greenhouse effect and **greenhouse gases** See global warming . . .

Green Paper and **White Paper** These are both British terms used for government reports. A *Green Paper* is the preliminary report of proposals for general discussion, before they are embodied in formal legislation. A *White Paper* is a statement of the government's policy on a particular issue. See also **Blue Book**

Greens *The Greens* is the collective name for the Green Parties of Britain, France, Germany and some other countries. Although clearly they stand for measures to protect the environment (see **green**), their aims may extend to other ideals, such as redistribution of wealth and restriction of economic growth in favour of self-sufficiency.

grey or **gray** These were alternatives, but now *gray* seems affected, except in America where it is the normal spelling.

grey area *Grey area* is used in different situations to indicate an uncertain, ill-defined policy, attitude or ruling. Lawyers will sometimes talk about a dispute being in a grey area, when the law does not offer clear guidelines on which a judgement can be based. Carl Djerassi, professor of chemistry at Stanford University, California, commented 'Grey is the political colour of this century', suggesting that solutions cannot be black or white any more.

grill or **grille** *Grill* is the only possible spelling for the appliance or part of a cooker that grills meat or fish. *Grille* is more usual than *grill* for the latticed metal screen erected for security in various situations, often for protecting people handling cash in public places.

grisly or **grizzly** Both words sound the same, so they are easily mixed up. *Grisly* means gruesome and ghastly ('a grisly apparition'). *Grizzly* is grey-haired, now used more about bears than people.

grocer The number of grocers is on the decline, as so many of their customers prefer to push trolleys round supermarkets. Before they all disappear, it is worth recording that the word goes back to the 15th century, and was used because grocers bought the provisions they sold 'by the gross' or 'in gross', that is wholesale. An echo of the original meaning of the word survives in the Worshipful Company of Grocers in the City of London: members do not work behind the counter selling tea, sugar, spices, etc but are bankers, businessmen and the like, successors to the prosperous wholesale merchants of the 15th century.

groper This is a nasty slang word for the kind of man who, whenever he gets the chance, will clumsily grab a woman's breast or put his hand up her skirt. It has found its way even into a headline in *The Times* about an item on sexual **harassment**: HOW TO DEAL WITH THE WORKPLACE GROPER.

gross *domestic* or **gross *national* product** See GDP . . .

grotty Still recorded by lexicographers as a slang word, *grotty* is likely to move up one day to standard

English. For it is a good word, a neat abbreviated form of 'grotesque', and sounds rather like what it means, which is shabby, rundown, unlovely.

ground or **grounds** We can have ground or grounds for a complaint, ground or grounds for suspicion, ground or grounds for satisfaction. *Grounds* is possibly more usual.

ground floor To be 'in on the ground floor' means to be involved early on in some profitable or important project. Illogically the expression originated in America, where the entrance level of a building is usually called the *first*, not the *ground* floor (for more on this, see **floor . . .**).

group *Group* has become a seemingly indispensable word in politics, economics, business and marketing. The poor are, as always, still with us, but now as the 'lower-income groups'; a handful or more people speaking out against government policy becomes a 'pressure group'; advertisers launching a new product no longer plan on selling it to a particular class but to a **socio-economic** group; executives, working for one of a number of subsidiary companies, talk self-importantly about 'the group'. Society, fearing that individuality might lead to anarchy, protects itself by grouping as many individuals as it can into – *groups*.

(the) **group** *is* or *are* See **collective words**

growth *Growth* has to be something getting bigger, and it is contradictory to force it into use about something getting smaller. It is all right, of course, to talk about *growth* in output, but the absurd paradox *negative growth* in output is turning the word upside down. There are good alternatives, such as 'reduction', or those simple easy words 'drop' or 'fall'.

grudge See **begrudge . . .**

(Mrs) Grundy Mrs Grundy is an off-stage character, who never appears, in Thomas Morton's play, *Speed the Plough* (1798). She is constantly referred to, and 'What will Mrs Grundy say?' became the equivalent of 'What will the neighbours say?' The play is hardly known now, but *Mrs Grundy* survives as a symbol of conventional morality: a Mrs Grundy attitude, a Mrs Grundy remark suggests prudishness and primness or, if you like, *Grundyism*.

gsm This is one of the printing abbreviations that **desktop publishing** has brought into more general use. The letters stand for *grams per square metre*, a standard scale used for the weight of paper. There is no general agreement over when lightweight paper becomes medium- or heavyweight. As a guide, 70/80gsm could be considered lightweight, 80/90gsm medium-weight and 90/100gsm heavyweight.

guarantee, **guaranty** or **warranty** It is easy to be uncertain about whether to write *guarantee* or

guaranty. There is sometimes an attempt to distinguish between *guarantee* for the verb, and *guaranty* for the piece of paper, the noun, but this is an unnecessary confusion. *Guaranty* is sometimes preferred in a legal context, for a person or a written undertaking accepting financial responsibility for a debt or a commitment entered into by someone else. But even for that use, *guarantee* is shown by a recent legal dictionary. In effect, forget the problem (and the spelling *guaranty*) and use *guarantee* in every situation.

Warranty is an alternative word for *guarantee*, as a noun, but is another unnecessary confusion. *Warranty* does have a more specific meaning in law, where it can imply that certain statements made in connection with a transaction are true, such as the ownership of something being sold, or that it is suitable and safe for a particular use. In most other contexts, *guarantee* is the straightforward word to use.

guerrilla The practice is as old as war itself, but the word *guerrilla* came into English through the Spanish Civil War (1936–9). Guerrilla warfare is harassment of established forces by independent groups, and the fighters, themselves, are called guerrillas (the original Spanish name was 'guerrillos').

The word sounds the same as 'gorilla', which some people prefer to avoid by slightly stressing the *e* sound (as in 'get'): 'gehRILLer'. But the approved pronunciation in English is 'gerRILLer'. Two spellings occur, with one *r* or two, but two *rs* are preferred, because it follows the source of the word from Spanish 'guerra', war.

Because of sympathy for the International Brigade during the Spanish Civil War, guerrillas summon up a picture of brave men fighting against superior odds. But it is a word that can be manipulated to suit a particular point of view: they might also be called **terrorists** or *freedom fighters*. See also **resistance**

guesstimate This invented word makes some people wince. But it tells you where you stand: the figure quoted is so rough that it's only one step up from a guess. In fact, when the final bill arrives, many 'estimates' turn out to have been guesstimates. Spell it with -ss- (although *guestimate* is an accepted alternative) to make it look more like a *guess* than an estimate. See also **appraise . . .**; **notional**

guest Words related to *guest* occur in a number of languages. It existed in Old English, and in the 13th century meant a person who is received in someone's house or eats at their table. By the early 18th century, *guest* was used for anyone who paid for food and accommodation at an inn, which eventually led to *paying-guest* as a decorous substitute for 'lodger'.

Chat shows on radio and television also like the word: 'My guest this week is . . .'. And there are guest professors at universities, guest speakers at conferences, guest conductors of orchestras, all of whom get paid well for being a guest.

guilt *Guilty* is still the descriptive word used in the original sense, meaning responsibility for committing a crime or a sin, and *guilt* is the corresponding noun. But psychology uses *guilt*, rather than *guilty*, as a descriptive word, where it no longer has any connection with crime or misdemeanour. Used in this way, it describes a suppressed feeling of being inadequate, not able to live up to expectations of behaviour in one way or another. This is what guilt feelings are about, and a guilt complex or a guilt obsession.

Gulag Glasnost put an end to *Gulags*, an **acronym** for Russian words meaning 'state administration for corrective labour camps'. It has joined another abbreviation, *Stalags*, the hated Nazi prisoner-of-war camps of World War II, in the history books. *Gulag* became an international word as a result of Alexander Solzhenitsyn's book *The Gulag Archipelago* (1974): the title presented a picture of the Soviet Union at the time as a sea studded with evil prison camps.

With a small *g*, *gulag* remains as a symbolic name for a repressive state system in any country used to prevent dissidents speaking out.

gumshoe A gumshoe in America is a shoe with a rubber sole. Because this suggests walking stealthily, *gumshoe* is the colourful American slang alternative to **private eye**: *The Independent* described a former New York assistant district attorney, who opened his own private detective agency, as 'the world's leading gumshoe'.

gung-ho An all-American expression for a trigger-happy attitude towards fighting. It is said that it comes from the abbreviation of Chinese Industrial Cooperative Association, and in the mysterious ways language interacts, it was taken up as the battle cry in World War II by the US Marines.

Gung-ho seems too American to be used comfortably about British forces, as it was in the press during the Falklands War of 1982, although it must be admitted that it has found its way into British English, meaning 'raring to go' about anything: 'the board is gung-ho about the takeover'. As a caution, it should be added that *gung-ho* is often taken to be pejorative, suggesting an unthinking, devil-may-care approach.

gunwale or **gunnel** The nautical word for the top edge of the side of a ship relates to its use at one time to support guns. Sailors usually prefer the spelling *gunwale*, but *gunnel* is an accepted alternative. Either way, there is only one pronunciation: 'GUNNe(r)l'.

guru This Sanskrit word travelled to the West in the 1960s, when the Beatles and some others, satiated with the pleasures of materialism, looked to gurus in

India for another meaning to life. In Hinduism, a guru is a personal spiritual teacher and guide. Since then, the West has corrupted the word: there is a 'Golden Guru' award for the best economic forecast, 'boardroom gurus', the Conservative Party apparently has its 'favourite advertising guru', all of which are light-years away from spiritual **enlightenment**.

gut reaction A tough-speaking macho synonym for an instinctive feeling.

gutsy This informal word has two meanings: gluttonous and greedy, or full of courage. Make sure the context makes perfectly clear which is intended.

guy This conversational word for a man is classless. You hear it at all levels of society, especially in America, where 'you guys' can mean a group of men and women. For Damon Runyon, who wrote *Guys and Dolls* (1932), *guy* was underworld poetry. Some people dislike the word because it sounds American, but if it comes naturally to you, why not say someone's a nice guy or you're meeting a guy for dinner? After all, *guy* is said to derive from Guy Fawkes, who was British enough.

gymnasiums or **gymnasia** Dictionaries may show both as alternative plural forms of *gymnasium*, but it is nonetheless pushing a knowledge of Latin to use *gymnasia*.

gymnastics *is* or ***are*** Nouns ending in *-ics* often present this problem. See **-ics**

gynaecologist or **obstetrician** They are both doctors dealing only with women, but the words do not mean the same. A *gynaecologist* (from the Greek word for 'woman') treats diseases and malfunctions particularly of the breasts and genital organs of women. An *obstetrician* (from the Latin word for 'midwife') does not necessarily deal with diseases, but looks after a woman during pregnancy and childbirth.

But for many women, obstetrician is an old-fashioned clinical term, and the only name they have for the doctor who looks after their functioning as women, whether or not they are pregnant, is their gynaecologist.

gypsy or **gipsy** Dictionaries accept both spellings, but since the name is connected with 'Egypt', where gypsies were supposed to have originated, *gypsy* is preferable. When the people or their language is meant, a capital G is appropriate, but not to describe someone or something, as in 'a gypsy way of life'.

· H ·

hacker From the early days, *hack* was computer slang in America with various meanings, usually connected in some way with being clever at working with a **program**. This is a curious reversal of meaning, for a hack journalist means a third-rate writer, a legal hack a run-of-the-mill lawyer, uses that probably came from the word *hack* for a horse for everyday riding. In the 1980s *hacker* became the word for someone committing **computer crime** by gaining unauthorized access to a computer system. *Hacker* is now part of English legal language, no longer slang, but the recognized word for a computer criminal.

haggle or **wrangle** *Haggle* involves money, when someone argues over the price and tries to get it reduced. Although it exists as a noun, it is more likely to be used as a verb: 'Although they agreed a price, when it came to settling, they haggled over the bill'. *Wrangle* is any kind of aggressive argument or dispute. Although it exists as a verb, it is more likely to be used as a noun: 'There was a long wrangle before anything was agreed'.

halal *Halal* (pron: 'hahLAHL') is an Arabic word heard in English for the slaughtering of animals and the preparation of meat according to the laws of Islam. It does not extend to overall dietary laws in the way that **Kosher** does in the Jewish religion, nor has English taken it on board with the same gusto, but halal butchers are to be found in many high streets.

half There are four areas of difficulty over this word:
1 Which is correct: 'three metres and a half' or 'three and a half metres', 'a year and a half' or 'one and a half years' . . .? In such cases, either will do, but because figures replace words so often now (3½ metres, 1½ years), people are more likely to choose 'three and a half metres', 'one and a half years'. . . .
2 Should it be 'a half-dozen' or 'half a dozen'? Some dictionaries record these expressions as colloquial forms of *six*, but these are standard usage to most people. Either will do, with perhaps 'half a dozen' as more usual.
3 When there is 'one and a half' of anything, the noun is in the *plural* but the verb is correctly in the *singular*: 'one and a half *weeks is* long enough'; 'one and a half *litres is* all that's left'.
4 Watch out for an unnecessary *a* creeping in before 'half a(n)': 'it will take a half an hour'; 'it weighs a half a ton'. The *a* has no place in such sentences.

For combining *half* with other nouns, see next entry.

half or **half-** As so often with **hyphens**, for many *half* combinations this is more a matter of custom and taste than rules. The following list represents a consensus, although there are dictionaries that take a different line in some cases: halfback, half-baked, half-blue (for sports at Oxford and Cambridge), half-brother and half-sister, half cock but half-cocked, half-hearted, half-hour, half-light, half-mast, half measures, half moon, half-past seven etc, half-price before a noun, half price after a noun (a half-price ticket, a ticket for half price), half-term, half-time, half-tone, half-truth, halfway, halfwit.

half-caste, **mulatto** or **Creole** *Half-caste* is considered racist. It was used mostly by the British Raj about a child of a European father and an Indian mother, but should now be avoided. Although *mulatto*, for a child of white and black parents, is not derogatory, it is not generally liked. In the highly sensitive area of **racist words**, 'of mixed blood', or 'mixed parentage' are more acceptable alternatives.
   Creole (not always with a capital) is used about people in confusing ways. For example, for a white person whose origin belongs to the French settlers in Louisiania, or for someone of mixed European and African origin. In general, it is safer for *Creole* to refer to someone of European (usually Spanish) descent, born in the West Indies or Central or South America. For the linguistic meaning of *Creole*, see **pidgin.** . . .

hallelujah See **alleluia** . . .

hallmark See **benchmark** . . .

hallo See **hello** . . .

hallucinogenic This is not as fashionable a word as it was in the 1960s, when Timothy Leary, a former professor at Harvard, started a cult in America to promote a shortcut to spiritual enlightenment through the use of **LSD** and mescaline. These are hallucinogenic drugs, in that they induce hallucinations and visions. Pron: 'haLUCEinoJENic'. See also **psychedelic**

haloes or **halos** This is not a plural form we need all that often. But just in case, *haloes* is the correct spelling, not that a heavenly host could object to *halos*, for some dictionaries show it as an alternative.

hamburger   See -burger

hamlet   See village . . .

hammered   It was an old custom on the Stock Exchange to call for silence with three bangs of a hammer. The word has carried over, and when the name of a member is announced on the floor of the Stock Exchange as not being able to meet their commitments, they are said to be *hammered*.

(*at*, *on* or *to*) **hand**   You have to work hard to separate the meanings of *at hand*, *on hand* and *to hand*. They all suggest something is on the spot, immediately available: 'he used it because it was at (or on or to) hand'. *To hand* is used after the verb *come*: 'he used it because it came to hand'. *At hand* is used about an event, meaning about to happen: 'Victory is *at hand*'. *At hand* or *on hand* are used about a person: 'she is at (or on) hand'.

handbag, **bag** or **purse**   Notwithstanding Lady Bracknell's famous outburst (on learning where her daughter's suitor was found as a baby): 'A *handbag*?' (*The Importance of Being Earnest*, Act I), *bag* is the more fashionable word. Alan S C Ross and Nancy Mitford wrote down *handbag* as 'not what the best people say' (see **U and Non-U**). Of course *hand-baggage* (which is what Lady Bracknell meant, but the word was not in use at the time) is something else: it is a holdall small enough to be carried by a passenger on to an aircraft.
  A *purse* in England is a small pouch or container for keeping money in, especially coins. But in America, *purse* is the usual word for a *handbag*.
  The special association of *handbag* for the **European Community** must also be mentioned: it is an echo from the period when Margaret Thatcher was Prime Minister, and refers to her so-called 'swinging *handbag*' with which she belaboured European ministers for not toeing her line.

handbook or **manual**   *Handbook* is an Old English translation of Latin 'manualis' (that which can be held in the hand). *Manual*, in this sense, was in the 15th century a small book for use by the clergy in church. By the 19th century *handbook*, following the similar German word, became used for a ready-to-hand book on practical matters.
  There is in effect no difference between the two words, and it is more custom which dictates which one is used. *Manual* is the usual word for instruction books for operating a machine: cars and computers are supplied with manuals. *Handbook* is the usual word for a book of tabulated information on a particular subject: *The Writer's Handbook* (Macmillan) gives details of markets for writers, such as lists of publishers, newspapers and magazines. Why books on the techniques of

making love are known as *sex manuals* is anyone's guess.

handfuls or **handsful**   See -ful

handkerchiefs or **handkerchieves**   *Hankerchiefs*. *Hankerchieves* looks and sounds peculiar, although it is shown as an alternative plural form in most dictionaries.

handle   A *handle* is the irreverent slang word for what people are called, from plain *Mr* to *The Most Reverend and Right Honourable The Lord Archbishop*. See **ambassador; clergy; royalty**

handrail   See banister . . .

hands-free   This descriptive word belongs to telecommunications and first appeared in this sense in the late 1980s. It is used about a telephone with a built-in loudspeaker, that enables calls to be made without using the handset, so both hands are left free for making notes or looking up something.

handshaking   Computer language uses many terms to show a belief in the near-human intelligence of the machines. *Handshaking*, previously reserved for humans, is the standard word for a connection made across an **interface**, often between two computers operating at a distance from each other.

hanged or **hung**   You *hang* a picture or wallpaper, *hang* your coat up, and an executioner can *hang* a person. If it happened yesterday, the picture and the coat were *hung*, but the person was *hanged*. In passing, that strange malediction or exclamation of surprise is 'I'll be hanged!'

hanger-on   A *hanger-on* always carries with it the derogatory suggestion of someone not genuinely involved or part of the scene, but behaving as if they are in order to claim some of the credit or fame. The plural is *hangers-on*.

hangover   Some dictionaries have at last upgraded *hangover* from slang or colloquial to standard English, so it's sanctioned for use in formal writing. About time too, because what other word is there to describe that unspeakable morning-after feeling? *Hangover* is extended to cover anything from the past that still affects the present, such as 'a hangover from the war'.

hang-up   See block . . .

hapless   *Hapless* goes back to the 16th century and perhaps it now has a literary flavour about it. But it is not obsolete, as some people feel, and remains a good word to describe someone who is unlucky and can never put a foot right.

happening   A *happening*, in the sense it became used in the 1960s, is difficult to define. It has been called 'an assemblage of events which also includes people'. *Happenings* of this kind first took place in New York, as a kind of anything-goes **pop art**.

happy, **satisfied** or **content**   *Happy* in the sense of *satisfied* has been in use to some extent since the 16th century. After all, when we're satisfied we're inclined to smile, which also expresses happiness. But this use of *happy* has increased so much now, that *satisfied* has become almost a formal word, meaning to verify that something is true: 'I'm satisfied that the conditions are right for the experiment'.

Of course we can still be *satisfied* with a result, with a job that has been done, or with the bill for it (as well as being *happy about* or *with* those things). There is a possible line to be drawn: *satisfied* suggests a preparedness to accept something, whereas *happy* goes further, suggesting that it has worked out better than expected. *Content* is almost synonymous with *satisfied*, but adds a note of resignation in accepting something.

hara-kiri   With Japanese films being shown in the West, this word has come more into use, and is often misspelt and mispronounced 'hari-kari'. It is ritual suicide by a **samurai** when faced with defeat or disgrace. Pron: 'harra-KIRri'.

harassment   In the 1990s, the social and legal meanings predominate: *police harassment* is unwarranted interference by the police in people's lives, and *racial harassment* is persecution of people because of their race. *Sexual harassment* is the most difficult to define, as men are not always sure when they are transgressing the barrier between friendly banter or admiration of a woman's looks, and behaviour that women rightly object to. This takes us into the most uncharted territory in human nature.

A survey carried out in 1989 by the London School of Economics, using a definition on the lines of unwanted sexual remarks, looking at a woman lasciviously and brushing up against her whenever possible, revealed that one woman in seven at work (which goes up to one in five among professional women) has been subjected to what *Newsweek* called 'the boss's dirty little fringe benefit'.

In Britain stress is on the first syllable: 'HARassment'. Stress on the second syllable ('haRASSment'), usual in America, is heard increasingly in Britain and some dictionaries now accept it as an alternative pronunciation. See also **rape or seduction**

hard-   For some reason this simple Old English word is constantly in demand for making new terms and slang expressions. To take only a few examples, computer technology has had recourse to it in a number of ways, such as *hard copy* (the output of a computer printed on paper or, less commonly, recorded on microfilm), and *hard disk* (a rigid magnetic disk used in the storage system of computers, see **floppy disk**). In finance there is *hard cash* (which probably derives from an old use of *hard* to distinguish gold from paper

currency), adapted after World War II as **hard currency**. In politics there are *hardliners* (members of a party who take an unyielding line on policy). Businessmen can be *hardnosed* (ruthless and uncompromising).

Hard is also constantly adding to slang and colloquialisms, from *hard cheese* (originally bad luck at billiards, but now a synonym for *hard luck* in any situation), *hard rock* (rock and roll music with a driving beat) to *hard porn* (see **pornography**), and that slang sexual expression, endearing to men on both sides of the Atlantic, and familiar since the 19th century, a *hard-on* for an erection. The Irish and Americans, in particular, talk about the *hard stuff*, strong spirits as opposed to beer or wine. And the Beatles sang about 'a hard day's night'.

hard copy   See **printout** . . .

hard-core pornography   See **pornography** . . .

hard, **soft** or **reserve** **currency**   *Hard currency* is a term used in trade between countries. It can be taken as any currency in which business is confident, a currency that seems stable and likely to maintain its value. In general, the currencies of the industrialized nations can be included, but not, as you would expect, currencies from Eastern Europe and developing countries. The latter, and any other currency not considered reliable for political or economic reasons, are *soft currencies*.

A *reserve currency* has to meet more exacting standards than a hard currency. It is a term used for a foreign currency which a government will hold as part of foreign exchange reserves. Such a currency must enjoy considerable confidence and be readily convertible into other currencies, since it is used to finance international trade. Among the usual *reserve currencies* are the British pound, the US dollar, the Deutschmark and the Swiss franc. At times a question mark may hover over the pound and the dollar, or for that matter over any currency considered as a *reserve currency*, when there is doubt about its long-term stability.

hard disk   See **floppy disk** . . .

hardliners   See **hard-**

hardly   See **barely** . . .; **double negatives**

hard-on   See **hard-**

hard and **soft sell**   These American advertising terms came over long ago to Britain, and have since spread to other kinds of selling. *Hard sell* is aggressive marketing and foot-in-the-door, never-take-no-for-an-answer selling. *Soft sell*, which often comes to the same thing, is heavily disguised to look fair, reasonable and low-key. Don't be taken in by *soft sell*, for there is a knife under the velvet cloak.

hardware   *Hardware* for ironmongery goes back to the early 16th century. But the first meaning that now comes to mind is much more recent: in the 1960s *hardware* became the standard term for the electronic items of computers, usually the processing units and printers, as against *software*, which covers **programs**, instruction books, ribbons, etc.

Military hardware is a 19th-century term for weapons but is now used mostly for big guns, tanks and other heavy fighting equipment.

It is too soon to say whether the name *hardware shop* will eventually fade out but it already sounds out of place. There is a case for bringing back *ironmonger*, which is what hardware dealers were called as far back as the 14th century.

Harley Street   Although not used as often as it was at one time, *Harley Street* is still a general name for medical specialists who have mahogany-panelled or flock-wallpapered consulting rooms in the Harley Street area of the West End of London. So-called *Harley Street doctors* do not need to be in Harley Street itself, so long as they have put up their brass plates on one of the Georgian doors within, say half a mile. The expression conveys the idea of exclusive and expensive private medicine.

Hart's Rules   The editorial cognoscenti know, or should know, about *Hart's Rules*. Horace Hart was printer to Oxford University 1883–1915. In 1864 he began to compile notes on alternative spellings, problems of typesetting certain words and other matters that caused indecision and stress to compositors and proofreaders. The first private edition was printed in 1893 but it was not until the 15th edition in 1904 that it went on sale generally. By that time, James Murray and Henry Bradley, editors of the *OED*, had been through it and, in the words of Horace Hart, the book bore 'the stamp of their sanction'.

Hart's Rules lives on, now in its 38th edition, a slim soberly covered book, with admirably measured judgements on such sequestered topics as how to differentiate between the exclamations *O!* and *Oh!*, the printing of thorn, eth, wyn and yogh in Old English texts, and the division at the end of a line of words in Welsh. *The Good English Guide* and many other scholarly books owe something to the ghost of Horace Hart looking over the compilers' shoulders.

hashish   See **cannabis** . . .

hassle   *Hassle* began as post-World War II American slang for any kind of difficulty or argument over getting something done ('filling in tax forms is a hassle'), and soon crossed the Atlantic to become popular in Britain. The origin is uncertain: one dictionary suggests it's a combination of 'haggle' and 'tussle', plausible maybe, but no more than a guess. Although at times life in the 1990s is even more of a *hassle*, the word is not as popular as it used to be.

haven   *Haven* is a very old word that can be traced back to the 11th century. It has always meant a harbour or a cove where ships can take shelter from storms, and the word is enshrined in place-names, such as Newhaven. Later *haven* came to be used for any refuge where people could be safe. The word came into the news after the 1991 Gulf War, when John Major showed his concern for the Kurds in Iraq by proposing a *safe haven* for them. The expression was criticized, and one journalistic wit commented that the redundant word 'safe' implied that 'there are a lot of dodgy havens about these days'. At all events, *safe haven* seems to have become an established term: by the end of 1991 official pronouncements referred to *safe havens* for the Serbs in Croatia. Tautologous it may be, but John Major has added *safe haven* to the language. *Haven* on its own hardly seems sufficient any more, except for *tax haven*, which gets by. (A tax haven is a country where wealthy people might choose to keep their money. If they go and live there, they become **tax exiles**.)

haven't   See **contracted forms**

haversack   See **backpack** . . .

haves and **have-nots**   Not exactly the same as the rich and the poor, as it used to be. In the 1990s, *have-nots* are the truly underprivileged, perhaps without a job or somewhere to live, while the *haves* are not necessarily rich – they may simply have a microwave and a video recorder.

hawker, pedlar or **peddler**   *Hawkers* and *pedlars* (*peddler* is the American spelling) were the old door-to-door salesmen, 'vendors of small wares', as they are quaintly defined by one dictionary. The words are old-fashioned now: the Hawkers Act 1888 disappeared from the statute book in 1966, and most of the NO HAWKERS OR PEDLARS notices on tin plates fixed to doors and gates, have long ago rusted away.

hawks and **doves**   See **doves** . . .

he or she   Leases and other legal documents may still say 'words importing the masculine gender shall be deemed to include females', or some other expression of male smugness. For centuries *he* in certain contexts was taken to include *she*. The 1975 Sex Discrimination Act makes that less comfortable, and in some situations it could now be a breach of the law. Jenny Cheshire, a lecturer in applied linguistics at Birkbeck College, London, commented that if we use *he or she* to deal with this problem, perhaps we should keep the balance by occasionally writing *she or he*. The awkward alternative used in some books is *s/he*. For further advice, see **unisex grammar**

he or **they**   The problem arises in a sentence such as 'No one expects you, does *he* (or *they*)?' The trouble with *he* is that it would seem to exclude women: the problem with *they* is that it is plural following the singular 'no one'. For a resolution of this difficulty, see **unisex grammar**.

headhunters   *Headhunters* (the hyphen is hardly required any longer, although most dictionaries still show it) were fierce warriors who beheaded their slain enemies in order to flaunt their heads as trophies. Now there are *headhunters* in London, New York and all other major business centres, less sinister but just as aggressive. Their job is to recruit directors and top-level executives, usually by 'poaching' them, as it used to be called, from other organizations. People are glad to use the term about themselves ('I was head-hunted'), as it is one of the hallmarks of a high-**flier**.

headline inflation   See **inflation**

headlines   Newspaper and advertising headlines have a deformed language of their own, and perhaps it is unreasonable to complain about their lapses from style and grammar. Their job is to catch the eye, sell the paper or the product, lead readers into news items, articles, or advertising copy, and all other considerations go to the winds.

Puns, which can be at the rock-bottom of literary style, find a regular place in headlines, where they may mildly amuse or make a point. Here are some examples, which in any other context would make us wince, but are more or less acceptable even in serious newspapers. *The Times* headlined a piece comparing the auction of television franchises with a **soap opera**: SOAPS IN A LATHER; a health club in Wall Street, the financial area of New York, advertises its services with the headline: WE SPECIALIZE IN STOCKY BROKERS; and the French mineral water, Perrier, was presumably intentionally unfunny with punning captions, such as 'Eau, I say'.

Like the writers of **T-shirt** legends, headline writers may use the language of Shakespeare and Milton but the words are cobbled together, ending up as flashy catchphrases.

headmaster and **headmistress**   See head-teacher . . .

headquartered (as a verb)   Sentences such as 'the organization is headquartered in New York' are more common in American English. In British English, it seems preferable to say '. . . has its headquarters in . . .'. At the same time, *headquartered*, using the word as a verb, is useful, even if we're not used to it yet.

headquarters *are* or *is*   We can choose between headquarters *is* or *are*. *Headquarters are* has the advantage of avoiding the awkward *ziz* sound.

headteacher, **headmaster** or **headmistress**   More and more words are being replaced by words that do not specify a woman or a man. *Headteacher* has become the usual word for the head of most schools now, although it would raise a few eyebrows to refer to the headmaster of famous boys' schools, such as Eton or Westminster, as the *headteacher*, or to use that title for the headmistress of girls' schools, such as Roedean or Benenden. Perhaps there is some discrimination, with *headteacher* used for

the heads of local authority schools and *headmaster* or *headmistress* retained for independent schools.

head-up device   See **sincerity machine**

healthfood,   **wholefood**   and   **organic**   *Healthfood* and *wholefood* are words from the 1960s, and in those days usually went with dirndl skirts or patched jeans, with perhaps some chanting on the side. It was not by chance that the pioneer healthfood restaurant in London at the time was called *Cranks*, and located in Carnaby Street, famous for breakaway clothes for nonconformists.

All that has changed. Instead of staying a fringe cult, *healthfood* and *wholefood* became **buzzwords** in the high street, and big business with a turnover of millions of pounds a year. Wimpy has introduced a 'beanburger', McDonald's a healthfood salad, supermarkets sell 'healthfood loaves', and in the Palace of Westminster, the House of Commons restaurant has a healthfood 'alternative' menu.

There is no real difference between *healthfood* and *wholefood*: they are both rather vague words, suggesting fruit and vegetables, dietary supplements, such as seaweed and yeast, lentils and almost any food that can be eaten raw. *Wholefood* is perhaps nearer in meaning to *organic*, which should properly describe food grown or meat and poultry fed on natural feed, using manure or compost, rather than industrially produced fertilizers or pesticides. It should follow the principles for organic farming set out by the Soil Association in Britain. Note that the negative of organic farming is not *inorganic* (which has a different meaning in chemistry) but *non-organic* farming.

Healthfood, *wholefood* and *organic* are no longer offbeat terms but have become respectably middle-class. The last word can be left to Greg Sams, who founded the Whole Earth company: 'Now we're selling frozen vege-burgers and convenience wholefood in cellophane wrappers. Nobody has to wear sandals or chant any more'. See also **macrobiotic**

heart attack   See **coronary** . . .

heath or **moor**   As topographical words, there is nothing much to distinguish between a heath and a moor, as both are rough uncultivated uplands, usually covered with rough grass and shrubs. *Moors* are usually associated with Yorkshire and Scotland and also with heather, as well as being a particular word for shooting reserves (*grouse moors*, for example).

heaved or **hove**   Heavy objects are *heaved* about and sighs are *heaved*, which is the usual past form of the verb. It is different at sea: 'the boat was hove to' (brought to a standstill), and 'another ship hove into sight', a seafaring expression now also used on land. But because old salts call out *heave-ho!* when raising the anchor, anchors are heaved (rather than hove) overboard.

Heaven or **heaven**   When *heaven* is a synonym for God, use a capital: 'for Heaven's sake', 'in Heaven's name'. But not otherwise: 'move heaven and earth'.

heavy-breathing As well as meaning breathing heavily, *heavy-breathing* has become an expressive synonym for sexy. For example, the famous recording, *Je t'aime, moi non plus*, made by Serge Gainsbourg and Jane Birkin, was called the heavy-breathing duet: in fact, breathing was so heavy that the BBC banned it at one time. The expression also has the more sinister association with menacing telephone calls, usually to women, when all they hear at the other end of the line is *heavy breathing*.

Hebrew, **Yiddish** and **Yinglish** The lexicographer, Eric Partridge, commented in *Usage and Abusage* on a misconception that Yiddish is a conversational or dialectal variant of Hebrew. This may be because Yiddish, occasionally written phonetically in the **Roman alphabet**, is traditionally written right-to-left in Hebrew characters, and is also a language of literature (most of the works of Isaac Bashevis Singer, winner of the Nobel Prize for Literature in 1978, are written in Yiddish, using Hebrew script).

Hebrew and Yiddish are completely different languages. *Hebrew* is thousands of years older, a Semitic language in the same group as Arabic. For centuries after it ceased to be a conversational language, it was kept alive by liturgy. Towards the end of the 19th century, there was an attempt to revive Hebrew as a language of daily life, and it was given a place on the agenda of the First Zionist Congress in 1897. When the State of Israel was proclaimed in 1948, Modern Hebrew was established as an official language, the beginning of an extraordinary linguistic project, described by David L Gold of the University of Haifa as 'the largest and most successful attempt at language planning in human history'.

Hebrew became the language of government, contemporary writing from popular paperbacks to serious literature, and the first language of new generations in Israel. Modern Hebrew remains rooted in the biblical language, arguably not much further removed than modern English is from the language of Shakespeare, although the time span for Hebrew is thousands of years greater.

Yiddish belongs to the mainstream of European languages. It existed in its earliest form in the 11th century, beginning as a West German dialect taken to Poland and the Baltic countries by Jewish refugees during the pogroms of the late Middle Ages. Later it developed into a **gallimaufry** of German, Russian, Polish, Hebrew plus an admixture of old forms of French and Italian, with variations in different countries. There are signs of a revival of the language, with courses in Yiddish at universities in Britain and America, as well as in Israel.

Yiddish warrants a place in *The Good English Guide*, because it has channelled so many colourful words and phrases into the English language, mostly via New York. As it merged with English, a hybrid language was born, affectionately known as *Yinglish* (Yiddish English), a term recorded in the *OED*. Many *Yiddishisms* (and it is linguistic **chutzpah** to add the Latin suffix **-ism** to the word *Yiddish*!) have become so much a part of English that we almost forget their origin. A few examples are **nosh, kosher, gazump**. In addition, there are hundreds of expressions influenced by a peculiarly wry or contemptuous Yiddish turn of phrase: 'I should have such luck!', 'it shouldn't happen to a dog', 'need it like a hole in the head', 'it's OK by me', but . . . 'enough is enough, already!' Philip Howard, as literary editor of *The Times*, used a Yiddish reversal of word order to demand of his readers: 'For liking Yinglish, I should apologize?'!

hectare See acre

he'd See contracted forms

he'd have See I'd have

hedge or **hedging** Everyone is familiar with the use of *hedge* as a protective or limiting barrier formed by a row of bushes, but the transferred use as a verb, in financial matters, is sometimes misunderstood. It is concerned with limiting the risk of loss through taking one action, by taking another action that would compensate. For example, in currency dealing, a hedge against falling interest rates, which would decrease the value of a particular currency, could be to put some funds in a currency where interest rates are expected to rise. This is *hedging* an investment. A graphic expression for hedging is a *belt and braces* policy: if one of them fails, trousers still stay up.

hedonist There are philosophical and psychological interpretations of this word which can lead us into deep waters. But in general use, *hedonist* is usually considered a pejorative word for someone concerned only with their own pleasure and self-satisfaction, no matter who else suffers in the process. Oscar Wilde's way of expressing it was 'I can resist everything except temptation' (*Lady Windermere's Fan*, Act I). There are alternative pronunciations for the first syllable: 'HEEDonist' or 'HEDonist'. Most dictionaries prefer the former.

heir apparent or **heir presumptive** These are used primarily about rights of accession to the throne of a monarchy, and come into the news from time to time. An *heir apparent* has an absolute right to inherit and nothing can interfere with it. An *heir presumptive* has a right that can be superseded: for example, the younger brother of a king or queen without children is heir presumptive. But if the monarch then has a child, the brother's status is lost, because the child becomes *heir apparent*.

Hellenic See Greek . . .

hello, hallo or **hullo** In the 16th century, *Hollo!* or *Holla!* (they probably come from 'holler', to shout) would have been used to attract attention. By the 19th century, *hallo* was the usual spelling. Now, for no apparent reason, dictionaries put *hello* first, with *hallo* and *hullo* as variant spellings. The recommended pronunciation is usually 'he(r)LOH' (rather than 'halLOH' or 'hulLOH'), but there's no need to stay awake at night worrying about it, as few people would notice the difference.

help   See aid . . .

hemi-   See demi- . . .

here- words   *Herein, hereof, hereto, hereunder, herewith* and so on appear much less frequently than they used to in business letters and letters from government departments. This is a good thing because they are pompous words and should hereafter be avoided whenever possible.

here *are* or **here *is***   Clearly in written English it should be *are* before a plural noun: here are some flowers, here are some sweets. . . . But it would be fussing to pick someone up for saying 'Here's some flowers', 'Here's some sweets', because that comes naturally in casual conversation.

hereditary   See congenital . . .

heritage or **inheritance**   The tendency now is to use *inheritance* about material things, especially things inherited under a will, or a title by succession. *Heritage* is less personal and specific: 'Our art treasures are a national heritage'. When it comes to personal qualities, either word is used: 'an ear for music is a heritage (or an inheritance) from my father'.

hermaphrodite   See bisexual . . .

hero and **heroine**   While *heroine* is still the more usual word for a woman, *hero* has joined the list of unisex words and is accepted by some recent dictionaries for a woman as well as a man, although many people find this uncomfortable. The plural is *heroes* (not 'heros').

heroin   See cocaine . . .; drugs . . .

heroine   See hero . . .

Herr, Frau and **Fräulein**   When Germans are in England, do we introduce them as *Herr* Schmidt, *Fräulein* Brandt, etc or *Mr* Schmidt, *Miss* (or *Ms*) Brandt? For the use of foreign courtesy titles in an English context, see Mr, Mrs . . .

hers or **her's**   *Her's* is *always* wrong.

hertz (Hz)   See channel or frequency

he's   See contracted forms

heterosexual   *Heterosexual* is such a familiar word now that it is surprising to find it was not included in a number of dictionaries published before 1980. The prefix *hetero-* comes from the Greek word meaning other or different. *Heterosexual* is, in fact, recorded in use at the beginning of the century, but there seemed little need for it, as heterosexuality, the attraction to people of the opposite sex, was a state taken for granted. But as homosexuality came out into the open in the 1960s (see **gay** . . .), there was a need for a word to describe sexual relationships between men and women. *Heterosexism* is recorded, as an alternative to *heterosexuality*, but is hardly ever used; because of *sexism* and *racism* it could be taken to mean hostility to or discrimination against heterosexuals.

heuristics   Most people know *Eureka!*, supposedly exclaimed by Archimedes when he got into a bath and the water overflowed, leading him to discover Archimedes' principle (loss of weight of a body can be measured by comparing the weight of liquid displaced). We still use the same exclamation when we stumble across a solution by chance. *Heuristics* comes from the same Greek root, but did not come in for much use until it was applied to techniques in computing, methods of solving problems by trial and error, using basic rules of thumb learned through experience. (Pron: 'hyooRISTiks'.)

'He would, wouldn't he?'   Although *He would, wouldn't he?* had long been a cockney retort, Mandy Rice-Davies made it classless. It was during the early stages of the Profumo affair in 1963, and she was in the dock at Marylebone Magistrates Court, London. Counsel challenged her account of her relations with Lord Astor, stating that Lord Astor had emphatically denied anything had taken place. Her reply entered dictionaries of quotations: 'Well – he would, wouldn't he?' She said it not as a cheeky remark but in all seriousness, which gave it a sharper point, and even the magistrate struggled to keep a straight face.

In the intervening years the riposte has been used frequently in politics about a minister denying anything to his party's disadvantage, and about anyone else who denies something they would hardly admit to. There are people who have laboured all their lives to make a remark half as memorable as Mandy Rice-Davies' off-the-cuff reply.

hexed   See bewitched . . .

hiccup or **hiccough**   The *OED* considers the variant spelling *hiccough* a popular error. Since the word is pronounced 'HIKup' it's unnecessary to spell it in any other way than *hiccup*.

hidden agenda   As the media expose to public gaze the stratagems of international diplomacy and big business deals, *hidden agenda* has become an indispensable term for aims and intentions not openly declared. For example, a BBC newscaster commented that 'a possible hidden agenda' lay behind the American Secretary of State's mission to Saddam Hussein at the beginning of December 1990, which was an unexpressed intention to avoid war.

Although there are at times perfectly valid reasons for not putting all the cards on the table, it's as well to remember that *hidden agenda* may often carry with it an undertone of intrigue or deviousness.

hide See conceal . . .

hi-fi, music centre, deck, record-player or **gramophone** If you listen to records on a machine with a large horn emerging from it, you could still call it a *gramophone*, a word that belongs to the 1880s and the invention of the first machine for reproducing sounds. The word is replaced by *record-player*, *deck*, or *music centre*. Of those terms, *record-player* is outdated by '**CD** player', *deck* is more a technician's term, which leaves *music centre*, the grand expression thought up by the manufacturers, as the most common description, alongside *hi-fi*, the collective term that covers an assembly of equipment, such as a radio, speakers and machines for playing **cassettes**, CDs and anything new that is developed. See also **fidelity** . . .

highbrow See egghead . . .

high-flier See flyer . . .

highjack See hijack . . .

highlight See accent or accentuate

high noon *High Noon* was the title of a famous Hollywood western made in 1952, and the phrase has remained as a dramatic term for the critical point in a dangerous confrontation. This is the moment when the chips are down and it has to go one way or the other, the shoot-out at high noon. Compare **moment of truth**

high-powered This is no longer always complimentary, as there is less confidence that driving force is altogether admirable. When *high-powered* is used now about a man or woman to mean thrusting and dynamic, it may carry with it the hint of ruthless ambition.

high pressure area See anticyclone . . .

high rise See tower block . . .

high seas See deep sea . . .

high street or **main street** *High street* in Britain is the equivalent of *main street* in America. *Main street* is now heard in Britain as well ('Where's the main street?'), but *high street* remains more usual, as *High Street* is sometimes the actual name of the road. *High street shops, high street banks*, etc are financial commentators' terms for the major banks and multiple stores (as against **corner shops**).

high tech *High tech*, short for *high technology*, is an imprecise journalistic umbrella term that is applied to almost any electronic or computerized equipment or gadget. It is an extension of terms, such as 'high fashion' and 'high finance', often used superficially, when it is more likely to be spelt *hi-tech*: during October 1991 in America, Judge Clarence Thomas described televised Senate hearings for his nomination to the Supreme Court, which held the world spellbound listening to allegations of sexual harassment by a woman professor of law, as 'a hi-tech lynching'.

In design, *high tech* (or *hi-tech*) is used equally loosely about anything from a wrist watch to an electric drill that has a look about it of space-age technology. In architecture, *high tech* relates to a style that uses materials, such as stainless steel, glass or plastic, in a visibly functional way, or that exposes the mechanics of a building: examples are the Pompidou Centre in Paris or the Lloyd's building in London (both designed by the same architect, Richard Rogers) with brightly coloured pipes, ventilator shafts, air ducts and escalators enclosed in glass tubes, all as part of the external elevation. See also **low tech**

hijack or **highjack** *Hijack* has become the standard spelling and some recent dictionaries no longer show *highjack* as an alternative. The origin of the word is obscure: it certainly goes back to the 1920s, as American slang for holding up a lorry and driving off with its load. It is now a standard noun and verb, with *hijacker* for the person responsible, mostly for the taking control by force of an aircraft in flight, although it is still used about hold-ups of lorries. It is also extended to situations where someone steals the show: 'She hijacked the programme with her wit'.

Himalayas Up to the 1970s there was no problem over the pronunciation of the name of this range of mountains in Nepal: 'himme(r)LAYe(r)z', with the stress on the third syllable. The name comes from Sanskrit, which may have led to a fashionable alternative pronunciation: 'himMAHLie(r)z'. This alternative pronunciation extends to the descriptive name *Himalayan* and, to confuse things further, it is also fashionable to refer to the range of mountains with the singular generic name *Himalaya*, also with the stress on the second syllable. This form and the alternative pronunciations are not the first listings in current dictionaries and gazetteers but they do seem to go down well with experienced travellers giving talks at local institutes.

Hindi, Hindu, Hindustani, Indian or **Asian** Before the Republics of India and Pakistan were established in 1947, *Hindu* was often used vaguely to describe anyone who belonged to the subcontinent. This was offensive to people of other religions, for a Hindu is a follower of Hinduism, one of the world's great religions, with an unbroken tradition of some 5000 years. In much the same way, *Indian* was loosely used in Britain for anyone belonging to the subcontinent. An Indian now is properly a citizen of the Republic of India. The correct generic name for someone whose ethnic origins go back to India, Pakistan, Bangladesh or Sri Lanka is **Asian**.

Hindustani was a northern Indian dialect made up of other dialects from all over the subcontinent. The word comes from *Hindustan*, an old name for India. Hindustani was used during the British Raj for communication with the 'natives'. The memsahib would bawl out her unfortunate cook in Hindustani, a term that educated Indians understandably prefer to consign to the past.

Modern *Hindi* has its origin in a northern Indian dialect and is one of the 15 official languages of the Indian Union, each state having its own language (Bengali, Gujarati, Tamil, etc). Hindi is the most well-known of these, for it is the language most commonly used in government and public affairs.

hippie *Hippie* moved from American slang to the edge of standard English. Its origin is debatable but the most likely source is jazz slang from the 1920s, when *hip* or *hep* meant cool, hence in touch. (Louis Armstrong explains: 'By running with the older boys I soon began to get *hep*'.) The media and the middle classes took up the word and attached labels to it of lawlessness, long-hair, dirtiness, drug-addiction and anything else that disturbed complacency. *Hippies* is still heard from older people as a vague put down of groups who turn their backs on respectable society, but the word truly belongs to a past period.

hippopotamus For most of us, one of the more dispensable bits of linguistic information is that the plural of *hippopotamus* can be either *hippopotamuses* or *hippopotami*.

hire See charter . . .

his own man When someone is *his own man* it means he is strong and independently minded, able to make his own decisions, do things in his own way, without being under the influence of anyone else. It became a political catchphrase the moment John Major became Prime Minister in the last months of 1990. Conservative MPs were overanxious to tell the world that John Major was *his own man*, and that Margaret Thatcher was not pulling his coat-tails.

Hispanic See Latino . . .

historic or historical Something that makes history is *historic*: 'That was a historic event'. Something that belongs to history is historical: 'Here's a *historical* account of the event'. 'For historic reasons', commonly heard, should be 'for historical reasons' (for reasons related to history). But note that the financial world refers to *historic cost* (the cost of an item at the time it was produced), an incorrect use which is accepted – for *historical* reasons (because the usage is now part of history).

historic cost See previous entry

hi-tech See high tech

hitherto There is a trap in using this word: it means up to *this* time, not up to *that* time. That is, it should only be used about the present: 'We must deal with this using a hitherto untried approach'. It should not be used about the past, so it would be wrong to say: 'Ten years ago we dealt with this using a hitherto untried approach'. That should be changed to: 'a previously untried approach' or 'an approach untried at that time'.

hit-list *Hit-list* is a sinister word that came into use after World War II when **terrorism** became an organized form of warfare. It is a list of individuals chosen for assassination for political purposes. See also **contract killing**

hit-man See **contract killing**

HIV See **Aids**

HMSO or the Stationery Office Her Majesty's Stationery Office is also known by the basic but imposing title *the Stationery Office*. Although it supplies most of the stationery for government needs, it is known more as a publisher and bookseller, the official publisher to the Crown, producing nearly all government publications, such as Hansard, Acts of Parliament, the *London Gazette* (see **gazetted**) and books on a number of subjects. The name goes back to medieval Latin when *stationer* was used for a tradesman, usually a bookseller or publisher, with premises rather than travelling about selling goods. For although *stationery* and *stationary* now have different spellings, both words come from the same Latin source.

hoard or horde They both sound the same so the spellings sometimes get mixed up. *Hoard* is to accumulate things or the accumulation itself: a miser hoards money and his money is a hoard. *Horde*, at one time a rare word used about hostile nomadic tribes, now means a disorderly crowd: a horde of football hooligans.

hoarding or billboard Outdoor advertising posters appear on *hoardings* in Britain and on *billboards* in America. Ogden Nash lamented: 'I think that I shall never see/A billboard lovely as a tree' (*Song of the Open Road*). Of the two, billboard is the more descriptive, and so probably the better word, and some people in Britain use it. In the 1990s, the term **billboard art** arose in Britain for poster sites as a form of public art exhibition ('hoarding art', as a term, would have been ambiguous). Perhaps Ogden Nash may yet be proved wrong.

Hobson's choice *Hobson's choice* does not mean, as it is sometimes used, a difficult choice to make. On the contrary, it means no choice at all: 'there was only one restaurant open, so if you wanted dinner, it was Hobson's choice'. The expression has given Thomas Hobson a linguistic immortality. In the early 16th century he hired out horses in Cambridge, but there was no question of choosing one you liked the look of: it had to be the horse by the stable door – which was Hobson's choice.

hoi polloi While there is nothing derogatory about expressions, such as 'the **common man**' or 'the man in the street', to mean ordinary people, *hoi polloi* is as disdainful as the 'common herd', implying the unintelligent, uncultured masses.

These Greek words mean 'the many', so it is not necessary to refer to 'the' hoi polloi, but it sounds wrong to leave out 'the' in English. Either way, the expression is a sneering one and should be avoided.

holding or ***parent*** **company** Both terms mean the same, a company which may not carry out much business itself, but exists to control a number of subsidiary companies, usually appointing the boards of directors and having the authority to make financial decisions. The term *parent company* is used less often now, since *holding company* is usual in law and financial journalism.

holistic By a roundabout route, *holistic* has become a cult word. First of all, it reverts to an earlier spelling of 'whole', for the *w* was not added until the 16th century. *Holism* (occasionally spelt 'wholism') appeared in the title of a book in the 1920s by General Smuts, the South African statesman, which expounded the philosophical theory that the whole is more important than its parts.

Holistic now is more associated with medicine than with anything else. *Holistic medicine* (or *holism*) takes as its point of departure that physical disease is a manifestation of psychological, social and spiritual factors, that the whole person must be treated, not just the symptoms that are apparent. The holistic approach ranges very widely, taking in **homoeopathy** and acupuncture, as well as other methods that have the purpose of mobilizing the therapeutic power of the mind and spirit. See also **complementary medicine**

Holland or **The Netherlands** *The Netherlands* is the proper name for the whole country, and *Holland* is the correct name only for the NW region, the two provinces known as *North Holland* (which includes Amsterdam) and *South Holland* (which includes The Hague). Those are the facts, but most people feel more at home using the name *Holland* for any part of the country, or for the country as a whole, which is generally accepted outside official contexts.

The people are, of course, *Dutch*: the name *Hollander*, which goes back to the 16th century when it was used also for a Dutch ship, is still heard but is rare.

Holocaust or **holocaust** The word derives from Greek words meaning 'whole' and 'fire', and meant complete destruction by fire. It is still used for total devastation, especially by nuclear war, or the wholesale slaughter of people. The American human rights campaigner, Elie Wiesel, first used Holocaust (with a capital H) for the murder of millions of Jews by the Nazis. This is what The Holocaust will always mean in history books.

home or **house** If you live in a house that is also your home, the words amount to the same thing. But the feeling is different: *home* is personal and warm ('home is where the heart is'), a *house* is constructed by builders and needs a *house-warming* before it becomes a *home*. Usually we know instinctively which word we want to use. The difference was expressed neatly in the title of a famous book written by Polly Adler, a former 'madam' of a New York brothel: *A House Is Not a Home*.

home banking We shall hear this term more and more by the end of the century, as **viewdata** links become almost as commonplace as the telephone, enabling nearly all banking transactions to be done from home.

home help See **charlady** . . .

homely *Homely* is the most often cited example of how misunderstandings can arise through different meanings of words on either side of the Atlantic. In Britain, *homely*, used about a person, may not be complimentary, but it is not an insult, because all it means is simple and friendly. In America, to say a woman is *homely* (the word is rarely used about men) means she is unattractive or downright ugly.

homo- The prefix *homo-* (or *homoeo-*), which comes from the Greek word for 'same', explains the meaning of a number of words in English. Examples are: **homogeneous** (of the same kind), **homographs** (words spelt the same), **homophones** (words with the same sound) and **homoeopathy** (treating like with like – see next entry).

The first syllable of *homo-* words should rhyme with 'Tom' rather than with 'tome'. An exception now is *homosexual* (see **gay** . . .).

homoeopathy or **naturopathy** These two forms of **complementary medicine** are not similar, as is sometimes believed. *Homoeopathy* (the American spelling *homeopathy* is seen in Britain but not in medical circles) was developed in the early 19th century by a German physician who first used the word. It is carried out mostly by qualified doctors, is available on the National Health Service in Britain and has a specialist hospital, The Royal Homoeopathic Hospital in London. It is a form of treatment based on the 'hair of the dog' principle, that is it administers minute doses of remedies that are directly linked to the same symptoms the patient is suffering from, with the purpose of activating the natural healing powers of the body.

Naturopathy is not a branch of medical science, and is perhaps a pretentious name for what used to be called 'nature cures', describing almost any form of non-medical treatment, such as the use of herbs, special baths, exercise, diet. . . .

homogeneous or **homogenous** *Homogeneous* is used for different things composed of similar or identical elements, or about something of a uniform and consistent composition: 'homogeneous materials, such as different kinds of plastics'; 'Conservative members of parliament are not homogeneous in their lifestyle'.

Homogenous is the descriptive word relating to *homogeny*, a biological term for similarity of organisms because of common descent and ancestry.

Because the meanings of the two words have something in common, *homogenous* is often used in exactly the same way as *homogeneous*. This is an error, but is so common that some dictionaries now accept that the two words have become interchangeable in most senses. To avoid criticism, it may be better to forget *homogenous*, since its correct use is very limited, and keep to *homogeneous* for the senses described earlier.

The words are pronounced differently. *Homogeneous* has the stress on the third syllable, and the last three syllables rhyme with 'genius': 'hommo-GEENious'; *homogenous* has the stress on the second syllable: 'he(r)MODGEe(r)ne(r)s'.

homographs This is a linguistic term for words with the same spelling but different meanings. There are many of these in English. Here are two examples. *Fair*: fair hair, fair and square, an antique fair, 'None but the brave deserves the fair' (Dryden, *Alexander's Feast*); *close*: a close shave, close the door, 'There's a breathless hush in the Close tonight' (Newbolt, *Vitae Lampada*).

homonym See synonym . . .

homophobia, **homophobic** and **homophobe** These words hardly existed before the 1980s but are shown in recent dictionaries. The Greek suffix *-phobia* (an abnormal fear) was latched on to *homo* (the colloquial word for a homosexual, before *gay* superseded it) to form *homophobia*. It means fear of and hostility towards homosexuals, with the associated words *homophobic*, describing the tendency, and *homophobe* for someone who manifests it. Regrettably, the feeling exists in both countries, but the words are used more often in America than in Britain.

homophones This is a linguistic term for words that sound exactly the same but have no connection with each other: *bear* and *bare*, *saw* and *sore*, *thyme* and *time*, *hoarse* and *horse*. In practice they rarely cause confusion, but they can be a nuisance when they force us to repeat the same sound in a phrase (see **repetition**). See also **synonym**

homosexual See gay . . .

hoofs See hooves . . .

hooker *Hooker*, the most common American slang word for a prostitute, caught on in Britain through American films. For Hollywood, a prostitute walked the streets and sold sex, but 'the hooker with a heart of gold' became a dream girl, promising mystery and everlasting potency.

Hooray Henry In the 1960s *Hooray Henry* took over from *chinless wonder* as the slang name for an upper-class young man with plenty of money, conventional attitudes, weak, ineffectual and boring. The expression is still used (there is a men's clothing shop in London called *Hooray Henry*), but not so often now, as perhaps there are fewer *Hooray Henries* around. The nearest equivalent for a woman is **Sloane Ranger**.

Hoover or hoover Even if the Hoover vacuum cleaner company ever went out of business, the name of its founder, W H Hoover, will never die, as so many people will go on talking about getting out the hoover and hoovering up, that is running a vacuum cleaner over the carpets, no matter what make of cleaner it might be. See also **eponyms**

hooves or hoofs All dictionaries agree that either plural form can be used but disagree over which is the more usual. So horses can have *hooves* or *hoofs*, with perhaps a preference for *hooves*.

hopefully This was the Great Linguistic Bore of the 1980s. People foamed at the mouth over what they declared angrily was the wrong use of *hopefully*, 'the final descent into darkness for the English language', as one grammarian declared. The first meaning is 'full of hope', as in Robert Louis Stevenson's famous line, 'To travel hopefully is a better thing than to arrive'. The new use meant 'it is hoped': 'Hopefully business will pick up'. There is a technical grammatical objection to this, but 'happily', 'regrettably', 'thankfully' and other words are used in the same way: 'Happily they were able to agree'.

Because it is useful, the alternative use of *hopefully* gained so much ground that people who hated it at one time often find themselves using it this way. There are objections, more because of ambiguity than grammar, as in a sentence such as 'We'll set off hopefully tomorrow' (do we hope to set off or shall we be setting off full of hope?). We should be aware of this risk and occasionally substitute 'we hope to' or 'full of hope', to make the meaning clear. But the fuss over this word has died down, and *hopefully* this will be the last word on the subject.

horde See hoard . . .

horns of a dilemma See dilemma

horrible, horrid and **horrific** These were all strong words once (linked with a Latin word suggesting hair standing on end). But the first two have had the guts taken out of them because they are used in trivial ways to mean no more than unpleasant: 'it was a horrible meal'; 'horrid weather'. *Horrific* (and *horrifying*) still retain power and their full meaning, for use about something that is truly blood-curdling: a *horrific* (or *horrifying*) accident.

hors-d'oeuvre or starter Grander, and even some modest, restaurants still put *hors-d'oeuvres* on the menu, as part of the classic language of **gastronomy**. It means literally 'outside of the work' and covers small dishes served to begin with to stimulate the appetite and arouse expectancy. The plural is anglicized, *hors-d'oeuvres*, with the final *s* pronounced ('orDE(R)VZ').

Many restaurants have switched to *starters*, easy to understand, even if it does sound vulgar. The media have picked up this word from menus, and will follow an opening joke or comment with 'How's that for starters?' It's not an elegant turn of phrase but we have to live with it.

horsepower Early in the Industrial Revolution it seemed natural to measure the capacity of engines by comparing them to horses, hence the use of *horsepower* in the 19th century. What is more surprising is that this primitive term continued in use up to World War II, as an imperial unit of power used to denote the capacity of the engines of motor cars. The measurement of engine power has long since gone metric, designated now in cubic centimetres, and only the begoggled owners of **veteran or vintage** cars still talk about horsepower.

horsy or **horsey** Either spelling is used. Unfairly, when used about a person, it seems to be reserved more for women than men, implying unfeminine and **galumphing**.

hosier The word had a long innings, from the 15th century up to about the mid-1900s. Although strictly it meant a shop selling stockings and socks, it was used for shops selling men's clothes, including shirts, ties, etc. Some of the men's shops in Jermyn Street, London, put on airs by still calling themselves *hosiers*, but generally the word is on the shelf.

'HOSpitable' or **'hosPITable'** It seems to come more naturally to put the stress on the second syllable ('hosPITable'), and this has become the more usual pronunciation, although considered by some to be downmarket. Stress on the first syllable keeps the word in line with 'hospital', and is preferred by most dictionaries.

hospital See **clinic** . . .

hospitalize This is one of the post-war **-ize** (or -ise) words that many people disliked. It is taken for granted now, accepted by current dictionaries as the standard term for 'admit to hospital'.

host To *host* a dinner-party, meaning 'to be the host at', is not a usage that everyone finds comfortable, although it's usual media-speak on television programmes (to host a chat show). Current dictionaries also accept the usage, and commentators are happy to talk about 'the Prime Minister hosting a meeting at Chequers', so by now we should all feel free to use *host* as a verb.

hostage The word has played a dramatic part in politics and diplomacy in the 1980s and 1990s, especially in connection with the Middle East, where people were seized by rival factions so they could be used for bargaining. *Hostage-taking* became the name for this activity, shorter and more direct than 'the taking of hostages'.

In passing, the expression *hostage to fortune* is not always understood. A hostage to fortune can be a person, but also anything else, such as a financial arrangement, that is at risk because there is a chance of something unexpected happening.

hotel or **inn** *Inn* is an Old English word, which from the early 16th century to the 19th century was the usual word for places that provided accommodation for travellers. It has been replaced by the word *hotel* (the Innkeepers Act of 1878 was amended by the Hotel Proprietors Act of 1956).

Inn is kept alive now because it sounds personal and welcoming, with associations of log fires in winter. Big chains of hotels, such as Holiday Inn, have taken up the word because of this image, although they belong to a very different world from the rustic travellers' inns of the past.

In the 1930s, motor cars brought with them *motor hotels*, simple places for an overnight stop, where there was room for parking cars. After World War II the name was compressed to *motels*, drive-in drive-out hotels which in America acquired the reputation for overnight sexual affairs. The name has been taken up in Britain, simply for hotels with plenty of parking space, usually located beside main roads, used more by businessmen than clandestine lovers.

hotline *Hotline* (often spelt as one word, which is likely to become standard) was used after World War II for the direct telephone line between the **White House** and the Kremlin. This awesome lifeline of last-minute communication, on which the peace of the world might have depended, has long since been trivialized. *Hotline* is used now for any telephone number you can ring, credit card in hand, to order anything from a theatre seat to a case of wine, or to give money to a charity appeal on television.

hot money In the underworld *hot money* is the term for stolen or forged banknotes. In the financial world it is used for funds shunted at short notice from country to country to catch the highest rates of interest.

hot seat The *hot seat* was originally American slang for the electric chair. The meanings are less sinister now: *hot seat* is used for the situation where someone has to answer searching questions, or for a position of demanding responsibilities where decisions cannot be sidestepped. The last meaning was summed up in a trenchant notice said to be on President Truman's desk: it read THE BUCK STOPS HERE.

house Since the 16th century, *house* has been used for a building where a body of people assemble for a particular purpose. This meaning is used in business, and in certain contexts *house* has become a synonym for 'company': a *house magazine* is a magazine published by a business for circulation among its employees; publishers have a *house style*, preferred spellings, hyphenations and other matters intended to make all publications consistent; *in-house* is used for jobs, such as research or translations, carried out using the resources of a company's own staff, rather than calling in outside services.

Colleges of a university are called *houses*, especially at Oxford and Cambridge. Perhaps the most high-handed use of the word is by Christ Church, Oxford, which simply calls itself *the House*, assuming the same status as three august institutions using that simple imposing title: the House of Commons, the House of Lords and the House of Representatives, members of which bask in the prestige of 'going to the House'.

house or **home** See home . . .

house agent See estate agent . . .

housebreaking See burglary . . .

House of Representatives See Congress . . .

house style See house

housewife It was usual at one time for many women to give their occupation as *housewife*. In the 1990s, the word is uneasy. Some women, who do not have independent occupations, prefer 'wife and mother', others are not sure. Established social ideas are changing, and in some cases English has not caught up. In the meantime, *housewife*, at one time said (by *men*) to be 'the noblest calling in the world', is beginning to sound like one of yesterday's words. No one, not even elderly recluses, uses the old pronunciation 'huzziff', except as an old-fashioned name for a small sewing-kit, which is apparently still current in the navy.

hove See heaved . . .

hovercraft or **hydrofoil** They are not the same, although one name is sometimes wrongly used for the other. The first *hovercraft* was built in 1959. Although they look like ships, the crews talk about being 'airborne', because hovercrafts rise on a cushion of air which enables them to operate over land or sea. In motion it looks as though it is supported up by a huge rubber ring.

The first *hydrofoil* was built in 1906 and is essentially a ship. Drag is cut down because a foil or curved surface at the front lifts the hull out of the water as the hydrofoil gathers speed, so the ship appears to be water-skiing.

How do you do? or **Pleased to meet you**
Logically, *Pleased to meet you* seems a friendly

greeting, particularly accompanied by shaking hands with the other person, and *How do you do?* is silly (How do you do – *what?*). But custom has it that *Pleased to meet you* is a downmarket vulgarism, while *How do you do?*, as a formal greeting, shows you have been properly brought up.

The shortening of *How do you do?* to *Howdy!* does not go down well in the best circles in Britain or America, except in the Wild West.

Except on formal occasions or best-behaviour situations in the Shires, the usual way of greeting someone in the 1990s is **Hello** or *Good morning*, etc.

however The distinction between *how ever* and *however* is dealt with under **-ever**. One other point remains, which is the use of *however* as a stuffy extra word to insert for no other reason than to sound self-important.

Examples are: 'We must consider, however, another point of view'; 'You must remember, however, that he is her husband'. In most sentences where *however* has a comma on either side of it, it's better to leave out the word.

HRT HRT has become everyday parlance among women and in doctors' surgeries, as fashionable and controversial as the **Pill** was in the 1960s. The letters stand for hormone replacement therapy, prescribed to replace the natural hormones, progestogen and oestrogen, which a woman's body ceases to produce when she undergoes the **menopause**.

huge See colossal . . .

hullo See hello . . .

humanist and **humanistic** These are difficult words to use. When they were put to a panel of well-informed people, a number of confusing interpretations came up. Over the centuries, one meaning has led to another, and in the 19th century, the words became associated with *humanism*, which in turn embraced different dimensions of thought and belief.

To go back to the 16th century, a *humanist* was someone who studied the Greek and Roman poets and philosophers (the **humanities**, as they are called), 'human' writings as opposed to the scriptures and other divine revelations. An echo of this remains, and a classical scholar is still called a humanist, although this meaning is becoming arcane and obscure.

An absorption with secular literature was seemingly a turning away from the Church, so *humanist* came to mean a freethinker, who rejects religious dogma in favour of a belief in a vague spiritual self-sufficiency. The words continue to reflect a belief in the central importance of human experience as the point of departure for knowledge and understanding of the human condition.

In this sense, we might talk about a *humanistic* film, in that the scenes are a celebration of the joy and pain of life, or *humanistic* art which seeks to reveal the essence of being alive. Following this meaning, a *humanist* does not look beyond human experience, which is seen as inherently fulfilling and the basis of moral values.

humanities The word is used in two ways. Originally it covered the writings of the ancient Greek and Roman poets and philosophers, *human* writings as opposed to scriptures and religious texts (see previous entry). The *humanities* is now often extended to include all literature, as well as history and other arts subjects, as against science and technology. The Americans use the term *liberal arts* to cover all the humanities but also extend it to include certain sciences, but not applied sciences, professional studies and technology.

humankind or **mankind** There is nothing new about *humankind* as a unisex word, as it is recorded in the mid-17th century. It is used more self-consciously now, to avoid the masculine bias of *mankind*, and is often heard in religious broadcasts. Some people find *humankind* awkward or silly, but there is no need to be inflexible, as there are many examples of the use of words changing to avoid sexism or racism. See also **-person**

human resources or **personnel** In business, *human resources* is now the usual replacement term for *personnel*, that aspect of management dealing with the people working in a company, recruitment, training, working conditions, etc. British companies have 'human-resources managers' and American corporations appoint 'vice-presidents of human resources'. This is a recognition that many businesses are 'people' businesses, where some of the most valuable assets go up and down in the lifts each day, the company's human resources. See also **human skills**

human rights See **civil rights** . . .

human skills This is a management term that emerged in the 1980s, as a parallel to technical skills. It is different from the old concept of managing people: it is learning to understand them, to relate to them and to get the best from them. In the 1990s management consultants give human skills as much space in recommendations as cost-per-unit efficiency and marketing, and it forms part of the studies for **MBA** degrees. Even some high-tech businesses in America have replaced élitist titles, such as 'manager', by 'team leader' or 'project head', titles that suggest working together.

The aim of human skills is to make working 'a search, too, for daily meaning as well as daily bread . . . for a sort of life rather than a Monday-through-Friday sort of dying' (Studs Terkel, *Working*).

humour See **comedy** . . .

hung or **hanged** See **hanged** . . .

hurricane See **blizzard** . . .

hydrofoil See **hovercraft** . . .

hydrospace *Space* is the leading word for new areas of exploration, and *hydrospace* is appearing as the new word for undersea exploration. Few dictionaries have noted *hydrospace* as yet, but the word has a popular appeal that will help it to become established.

hyper- or **hypo-** These two prefixes, which derive from Greek, are used medically and in some other contexts to describe opposite conditions. *Hyper-* means over, above or excessive, while *hypo-* is below and lacking: *hypertension* is high blood pressure, *hypotension* low blood pressure. Often in the news during winter months is *hypothermia*, an abnormally low body temperature brought about, especially in old people, by insufficient heating in the home.

hyperinflation See **inflation**

hyphens If you are bothered by hyphens, you are not alone. An old style book of the Oxford University Press is quoted as saying 'If you take hyphens seriously you will surely go mad'. Churchill growled to the civil servant who corrected his proofs, 'I am in revolt about your hyphens'. And more recently Philip Howard, as literary editor of *The Times*, alliterated 'Hyphens are hell'. Even the best dictionaries disagree with one another in many cases over whether a hyphen should go in or not.

There are some reasonable guidelines (a word hyphenated before the 1980s but no longer). Admittedly these will not solve every hyphenic (believed to be the first recorded use of this word!) problem but they do offer a life-raft (hyphenated in some dictionaries but separate words in others):

1 Hyphens should be used (or omitted) with the reader in mind, that is to avoid confusion of meaning: 'three-inch nails' is one thing, 'three inch-nails' is something else; **Fowler** wondered whether 'the Acting-British Consul at Shiraz' was only pretending to be British (*Modern English Usage*, 1926 edition); 'extra marital sex' is ambiguous, whereas 'extra-marital sex' or 'extra marital-sex' lays it on the line.

2 The ever-increasing tendency is to drop the hyphen when a compound word becomes familiar, and write it as one word. *Week-end* had universally become *weekend* by the 1960s, and there are many other examples of words fused together: *airstrip, breakthrough, bypass, teapot, subcommittee, takeover* (not all dictionaries agree), *wordprocessor* (some dictionaries show *word-processor* but surely not for very much longer).

Where both hyphenated and one-word forms exist, you can assume that it's only a matter of time before the hyphen fades out: *healthfood, lifeforce, marketplace, shopwindow* . . . are examples of words hyphenated in some dictionaries but shown as one word in others. In this free-for-all situation it is not always necessary to wait for your dictionary to catch up, as they often lag behind general usage when it comes to hyphens.

3 We should be more liberal with hyphens in compounds coming before a noun, as they combine separate elements into one descriptive word. 'The figures have been brought up to date', but 'the *up-to-date* figures'; 'a concert in the open air', but 'an *open-air* concert'; 'we must investigate this in depth', but an '*in-depth* investigation'.

4 When verbs plus linking words are used as *nouns*, hyphens are necessary for cohesion. We run through a procedure and the result is a *run-through*; when things are mixed up they become a mix-up; burglars break in and a break-in occurs. . . .

5 With *re-* words, the hyphen is now usually left out, even when the resultant word looks odd: *redo, reread, rerun, restructure*. . . . But when the following word begins with an *e*, the hyphen is retained to help with pronunciation: *re-elect, re-educate, re-entry, re-establish*. . . . A hyphen is also useful to separate some nouns from verbs: *refund/re-fund, reform/re-form, recount/re-count*. . . . There are a few cases where hyphenated and one-word forms coexist, because there are two different meanings: *reserve* and *re-serve, recover* and *re-cover* (recover an umbrella that has been re-covered).

6 Most *co* words do not need a hyphen any more. Dictionaries now drop the hyphen (or show it as an alternative spelling) in *cooperate* and *coordinate* (both

logical because for years *uncooperative* and *uncoordinated* have been written without hyphens). A *co-op* shop keeps its hyphen as does *co-opt*, because it helps with the pronunciation. *Co-pilot* is losing the hyphen, but *Co-author* and *co-star* retain hyphens, for the time being, again to help with pronunciation.

7 Many compound words are formed with *over-*. Some dictionaries now show every one as a complete word, without a hyphen: *overanxious, overblown, overcapacity, overconfident, oversight, overwrite*. . . . Other dictionaries select a few arbitrarily for hyphenation: *overact* but *over-active, over-produce, over-subscribe*. . . . The tendency is to drop the hyphen, so if in doubt, leave it out.

8 Guidelines for breaking words with a hyphen, at the end of a line, are given under **division of words**.

9 The golden rule, as always, is to be consistent. If a hyphen is used (or not used) in a compound, the die is cast, at least for the whole of that text, as the same form must be used whenever the compound recurs.

Either *hyphen* or *hyphenate* can be used for the verb. Fowler preferred to hyphen words, but it is now more usual to hyphenate them.

hypo- See **hyper-** . . .

· I ·

I or **me**   Case, which defines the grammatical function of certain words, together with terms such as *nominative* and *accusative*, are useful for explaining the structure of sentences but are not always readily understood. And a living language tends to force its way out of the straightjacket imposed by grammar.

Verbs and prepositions (short words, such as *to, for, after, between, from,* that relate one word to another) are followed by *me, him, her* and so on (accusative case), rather than *I, he, she* (nominative case): 'I did it for him', 'give it to her'; 'there's an understanding between her and me'. . . . Yet there are educated people who lapse happily into the false grammar of 'between you and *I*', 'for you and *I*'. . . . So upmarket is this error, that *between you and I* has been called the 'nob's phrase'.

This has been going on for centuries: Shakespeare wrote 'All debts are cleared between you and I'; and for Pepys (1633–1703), kind words were exchanged 'between my poor wife and I'. In our own time many distinguished interviewers and newscasters have given us 'from you and I', 'from she and I'. No wonder that Robert Burchfield, a former chief editor of Oxford English Dictionaries, regrets that the 'nob's' ungrammatical *between you and I* is 'racing away into general, even educated use'. Nevertheless, 'between you and I', 'from you and I', 'for you and I', etc should be avoided, even in speech, because for many of us they are ungrammatical and slipshod.

When *I* or *me, she* or *her, he* or *him*, etc stand alone, they should strictly take the same form as if a verb is present: 'Who did this? *I* (did)'; 'Which of them did you speak to? *Her* (ie I spoke to *her*)'. But in the first example, *me* sounds more natural. If you prefer to avoid this dilemma, follow *I, he,* etc by the appropriate verb: 'Who did this? I did'; 'Who will light the fire? I will'.

These recommendations are subject to review at the end of the century, if not sooner, by which time *between you and I,* etc may have become accepted usage, whatever we think. We cannot dispute this has long been the **Queen's English**, since in 1954 Her Majesty pronounced on her return from a Commonwealth tour, 'This is a wonderful moment for my husband and I'.

i* before *e* except after *c   This is the one spelling rule that all schoolchildren learn. Later they find there are exceptions, and get discouraged. They should be taught the full verse:

I before *e*
Except after *c*
Or when sounded like *ay*
As in freight, weigh and sleigh.

That covers most of the exceptions, although still leaves out 'foreign', 'forfeit', etc. But then an infallible rule for English spelling is inconceivable.

ibid and **op cit**   These Latin abbreviations are often used in academic and reference books but, other than the diminishing band of Latinists, many people are uncertain of the difference between them.

Ibid (or *ib*), short for *ibidem*, means 'in the same place', and is used after a quotation to indicate that it comes from the preceding book that has been quoted from: *ibid* (or *ib*) is all that is required, but a page or line number is sometimes added.

Op cit, short for *opere citato*, means 'in the work already quoted from', and is used after a writer's name (Stephen Hawking, *op cit*) to refer back to a book that has been mentioned earlier, when books by other writers have been mentioned in between. The use of *op cit* singles out the book by that particular writer. Be careful not to use it when more than one book by the same author has been quoted from.

IBM   The abbreviation for International Business Machines, the largest manufacturer of computers in the world, has become a standard term in computer technology. *IBM-compatible* is applied to personal computers made by any company, which have comparable facilities and can use **programs** developed for IBM computers.

-ible or **-able**   See -able . . .

-ics   This ending, derived through French or Latin from a Greek suffix for an art, science or area of activity, forms many words in English: athletics, classics, dynamics, electronics, gymnastics, linguistics, physics, statistics. . . .

The problem is whether to treat these words as *singular* or *plural*. The logical approach is to regard them as singular when they are used about the science, subject, or area of influence, which is often when the word is followed by a singular noun: 'gymnastics *is* her favourite sport'; 'statistics *is* an important part of the course'.

When the words are used more generally about different aspects or effects, they are better treated as plural: 'to solve this problem, mental gymnastics *are* required'; 'the statistics relating to this *are* difficult to follow'.

Ethics, **economics** and **politics** warrant special consideration and are dealt with under the separate headings.

I'd See **contracted forms**

identify See **discover** . . .

ideolect The word is a sociolinguistic term that combines two Greek roots meaning 'own' and 'dialect', and represents an individual personal way of using language. Each one of us has our own ideolect, preferences or hobby-horses about certain words, pronunciations or grammatical forms. Some people are very upset when they see or hear a **split infinitive**, for example, another person may discover a cult word, such as 'existential', and will use it whenever possible. *The Good English Guide* is about ideolects, seeking to draw a line between acceptable personal choice in the use of language and what is confusing, obscure, ungrammatical and out of touch with what is considered good English in the 1990s.

ideology or **philosophy** In ordinary use, both words have been demystified. *Ideology* was an aspect of *philosophy*, a word for the science of ideas. It is used more often than not now for the body of concepts and practical beliefs behind a theory, or on which a person's or a group's attitudes and actions are based. Political parties have *ideologies*, just as an economic theory can have an *ideology* (Keynesian ideology). Behind this, is sometimes a suggestion of narrow-mindedness, even intolerance ('But does he have the right *ideology* for the job?').

Philosophy can be used in a similar way, but without negative implications. This august word for the pursuit of wisdom, that brings to mind some of the greatest thinkers who have ever lived, has been turned into an ordinary everyday word, used for the principles or just a point of view about anything: 'What is the marketing philosophy behind the scheme?', 'My philosophy about pruning roses . . .'. A noble word has fallen into banality.

I'd have . . . When *I'd*, *you'd*, *he'd*, etc are short for 'I had', 'you had', 'he had', etc, it is a mistake to add *have* after the contraction: 'if I'd have known you were coming . . .'; 'if you'd have been there . . .'; 'if he'd have seen this . . .' are, in effect, saying 'if I had have . . .', etc. The correct forms are 'if I'd known . . .'; 'if you'd been here . . .'; 'if he'd seen this . . .'.

This mistake is so common in conversation that it doesn't matter much, but it should be avoided in writing.

idiom *Idiom* and *idiomatic* are open-ended linguistic terms. They can be used to explain why certain ungrammatical forms are acceptable, or why, for example, a telephone line is 'engaged' rather than 'occupied', and for that matter, why Americans say it's 'busy'. **Fowler**'s insular definition of idiom, for the purpose of *Modern English Usage* (1926), was '. . . any form of expression . . . preferred by Englishmen . . .'. That still stands, for *idiom*, which derives ultimately from a Greek word meaning 'own' or 'private', covers words and expressions habitually used by a group of people.

Idiom supersedes grammar and even common sense, for when a turn of phrase is in general use by most people, it is pointless to criticize it for being ungrammatical or illogical: examples are 'it's me' (instead of 'it is I' – see **I or me**); 'I only want one drink' (instead of '. . . only one drink' – see **only**). Idiom justifies such expressions as 'head over heels in love' (head over heels is the *normal* way round!); to put someone's 'nose out of joint' (there aren't any joints in the nose).

If there are enough of us, the way we use English will sooner or later drive a coach and horses through grammatical rules, for what we say or write will become idiom, that is generally accepted good use of the language. But there's a **grey area** where certain expressions are heard, but are still recognized by a significant number of people as bad English.

idiosyncrasy or **idiosyncracy** These are not alternative spellings. Only *idiosyncrasy* is correct, for the word does not belong to the same pattern as autocracy, bureaucracy, etc.

ie or **eg** See **eg** . . .

ie or **viz** Some Latinists distinguish between these two abbreviations for *id est* (that is) and *videlicet* (namely). They use *viz* to present a list of items or a definition of something alluded to, and *ie* to express something in other words: 'there are three principles, *viz* faith, hope and charity'; 'the person I care most about, *viz* my husband'; but 'there are three principles, *ie* guidelines to daily behaviour'.

This distinction is so subtle at times, that the tendency is to use *ie* and *viz* interchangeably. See also **eg or ie**

if or **provided** See **provided** . . .

if or **whether** See **whether** . . .

if and when See **as and when** . . .

if I was or **if I were** This involves the *subjunctive*, a grammatical form of verbs not easy to understand and not altogether at home in English any longer. The subjunctive mood of verbs expresses doubt, desire or a hypothesis: If it *come* to that; I wish it *were* all over; If I *were* you.

A detailed analysis of the subjunctive mood has no place here since it survives mostly in ceremonial, poetic or archaic English: 'Though Her Majesty *decide* to recall Parliament'; 'If music *be* the food of love' (*Twelfth Night*, Act I Sc i); 'Thy kingdom *come*'. In practice, we can happily use familiar turns of phrase, such as 'so *be* it', '*come* what may', 'far *be* it from me', 'God *save* the Queen!', without having to be aware of using the subjunctive. In most other cases, where there is doubt over whether the subjunctive form should be used, the problem can be avoided simply by putting 'should' before the verb in question: 'If Her Majesty *should decide* to recall Parliament'; 'The European Commission requires that Britain *should introduce* new legislation'.

This entry comes under *if I was or if I were* because the past subjunctive form *were* is the one that occurs most often now. When *if* introduces something that is clearly not true or is unlikely or poses a hypothesis, the subjunctive is still considered good educated usage: 'if I *were* you'; 'if she *were* married to someone else'; 'if the weather *were* always reliable'. Such sentences are followed by 'would' or 'would not': 'if I were you, I *wouldn't* have another drink'; 'if she were married to someone else, she would be happier'. But when *if* introduces something that is or could well be true, the subjunctive is not required and the conditional *would* does not follow: 'if I arrive in time, I *will* . . .'; 'if she marries him, she *will* be rich'; 'if the weather is good tomorrow, we *shall* eat out of doors'.

As you can see, it takes some working out, and there is a tendency to use 'If I was . . .', 'If she was . . .', etc in all contexts. This may eventually prevail, but at present, for many good writers and speakers, the 'If I were' usage has a grammatical nuance they would not want to lose.

if you like *If you like* is sometimes criticized as an unnecessary phrase that is slipped in out of habit: 'This, if you like, is a good example of . . .'; 'Many investments are, if you like, just another form of gambling'. Both those sentences mean the same when *if you like* is deleted. But the phrase does soften what could otherwise seem categorical statements, adding a nuance suggesting this is a particular or personal point of view. There's no need to be put off using *if you like*, when it comes naturally, so long as it does not become a mannerism.

ignorant *of* or *about* There is no rule about this, but 'ignorant *of*' flows more easily and could be considered better usage: 'I am ignorant of the arguments that led to this decision'.

ilk Every book on English usage has a go at the wrong use of *ilk* south of the Border. It is used in Scotland to mean 'of the same name' or 'of the place of that name'. The Scots seem to find it necessary at times to say 'McTavish of that *ilk*', meaning 'McTavish of McTavish', confirming it is the authentic McTavishes, or of the McTavish estate.

Since the 19th century, *ilk* has become commonly used to mean of the same family or of the same kind, in the latter sense often in a derogatory way: 'statisticians and others of that ilk are always telling us what we think'. The use of *ilk* in this casual, sardonic or humorous way is so established now that it's not all that important, except perhaps to the Scots.

ill or **sick** The usual British way was to use *ill* for 'not well' ('she cannot come because she's ill') and *sick* for vomiting ('I was sick after the meal'). In America it is more common to use *sick* to mean 'not well', although it is also used for vomiting.

In British English the distinction has become uncertain because of standard phrases, such as *sick pay* and *sick leave*. Although *sick* is the usual descriptive word ('a sick person'), 'an ill person' is also heard, as well as sentences such as 'she's away sick'. To avoid misunderstanding, the separate meanings should be retained after the verb 'feel': 'I feel ill' means 'not well', 'I feel sick' means 'I feel I might vomit'. See also **disease** . . .

The use of *sick* for a joke about something that is tragic or distressing ('That was a really sick thing to say!'; 'a sick joke') long ago reached Britain from America but is regarded as slang. In this sense, it is similar in meaning to **morbid**, but with the added implication of bad taste.

I'll See **contracted forms**

illegal or **illicit** The meanings of the two words overlap, but the distinction is important. *Illegal* relates to the statutory law of the land, codified and ultimately subject to the decision of a court. *Illicit* is less specific. It could be synonymous with *illegal*, describing an act that is against the law (illicit dealings in shares), but could also be used for something against general custom, or breaking the rules of a particular organization. An act that is illegal is illicit, but that is not always true the other way round. An illicit love affair, for example, may contravene the conventional moral code, but would not usually be breaking the law.

illegible or **unreadable** *Illegible* is a fact: something is impossible to read because, for example, the handwriting is so bad or the print is blurred. *Unreadable* is a matter of opinion: something is too dull, technical or heavy-going to read. If a book is illegible, the printers are usually to blame: if it is unreadable, the writer is always to blame. See also **legible** . . .

illegitimate See **bastard** . . .

illicit See **illegal** . . .

ill-informed, **misinformed** or **uninformed** Both *ill-informed* and *misinformed* mean that the wrong information has been given. *Ill-informed* could mean no more than that the facts are not correct, with no suggestion of dishonesty: 'because the timetable was out of date, she was ill-informed about the times of the trains'. *Misinformed* suggests that the wrong information was given to mislead: 'she was misinformed about the time of the last train, because he wanted her to have to stay the night'. *Uninformed* is simply not knowing, not being in the picture: 'she had to telephone the station, because she was uninformed about the times of the trains'.

illiterate, uneducated or **unlettered** The first meaning of *illiterate* remains 'unable to read'. But the word is often used loosely to mean uneducated or even not well read, often in an exaggerated way: 'If you haven't read that book, you're illiterate!' Both *illiterate* and *illiteracy* have come to be used for a lack of knowledge in a particular area: 'he's a political illiterate'; 'computer illiteracy'.

Unless the word is qualified, as in the last two examples, it is better not to use *illiterate* other than in its primary meaning of unable to read, retaining *uneducated* for someone who has had little or no education.

Unlettered was a gentler way of saying uneducated or illiterate, but is an old-fashioned word now. See also **literacy; literate**

illness See **disease** . . .

illusion See **delusion** . . .

I'm See **contracted forms**

image 'We must do something about our image'. When the head of a company or of a political party says that, they do not mean they must be more honest, do a better job, offer better value, but that they must *look* as if they are doing those things. It is the job of advertising and public relations to create an *image*, which need have nothing to do with reality but is good for business, getting votes. . . . A prime minister must have the right *public image*, a product must have a *brand image*, a big business has its *corporate image* (see **corporate**). Advertising, which creates images for clients, is often careless about its own image. Nowhere is this summed up in a more telling way than in the long title of a book by Jacques Séguéla, head of a successful advertising agency in Paris: *Ne dites pas à ma mère que je suis dans la publicité . . . Elle me croit pianiste dans un bordel* ('Don't tell my mother I am in advertising . . . She thinks I am a pianist in a brothel').

imaginative See **creative** . . .

imbue or **infuse** These two words are often used the wrong way round, because their meanings are close to each other. In fact, some dictionaries define *infuse* as meaning 'imbue'.

Imbue comes from a Latin word meaning to moisten, and was used to describe saturation. Someone or a group of people are *imbued* (or filled) with a quality, such as confidence or a sense of purpose: 'the captain imbued the team with a determination to win'. In the same way that tea is infused, that is allowed to permeate the water, it is a quality that is *infused* into a person (not the person who is *infused*): 'the captain infused a determination to win into the team'.

The best way to separate the two words is to follow *imbue* by the person or people who are affected and *infuse* by the quality that is affecting them (as in the above examples).

immanent or **imminent** There is hardly a whisker of difference in pronunciation, but the meanings are altogether apart. *Immanent* is a quality that is indwelling, an undeniable inner force: 'sexual drive is immanent throughout nature'. *Imminent* is something threatening that is about to happen: 'he is in imminent danger of being made redundant'.

immediately, forthwith or **straightaway** While it is too soon to write off *forthwith* as obsolete, it does have one foot in the grave. It's better to ask someone to do whatever it is *immediately* or simply – now. *Straightaway* (sometimes spelt as two words – *straight away* – but the one-word version has more attack) is a good word to convey a heightened sense of urgency.

Immediately means 'at once' and is not always appropriate when something else has to happen first: 'Please send the order *as soon as* you have supplies' (rather than '. . . *immediately* you have supplies').

immigrant See **emigrant** . . .

immoral See **amoral** . . .

immovable, unmovable or **irremovable** *Immovable* (also but less commonly spelt *immoveable*) is clearly something that cannot be moved, either because it is too heavy or is a permanent fixture. The word is extended for a person whose opinion or decision cannot be changed ('once he has made up his mind, he is immovable') or shows no emotion.

Unmovable (also but less commonly spelt *unmoveable*) is more likely to be used about people (in the senses described above) than about objects.

Irremovable ('irremoveable' is *not* an alternative spelling) is the only word to use for someone who cannot be forced out of office: 'since he owns most of the shares, the chairman is irremovable'.

impartial or **neutral** The distinction between the two words is significant. *Impartial* describes an attitude that is genuinely unprejudiced; *neutral* is not allowing a prejudiced attitude to affect actions. 'We are impartial over this question, ready to listen to both parties in the dispute, and make an honest judgement'; 'Although we have definite feelings about who is in the right, we have decided to remain neutral, not supporting either side'.

impasse Both a French and an anglicized pronunciation are acceptable: 'amPASSE' or 'imPASSE'. The preference is to acknowledge the French origin of the word.

impassive See **deadpan** . . .

impel See **compel** . . .

imperial The word belongs more to the halcyon days of the British Empire, when it was extended to describe an autocratic and eccentric system of weights and measures decreed by statute in 1838, with its 12 inches to one foot, 12 pennies to a shilling, etc. The internationally used metric system has taken over, and even the *imperial* **gallon**, with its eight pints, still used in many garages up to the end of the 1980s, has given way to litres.

The *imperial pint* remains enshrined in millions of milk bottles left on British doorsteps and in tankards of beer served in pubs. Otherwise *imperial* is more likely now to be used in a Gilbertian style for majestic pomp or ceremony ('imperial robes') or about someone who is particularly *august* (a truly imperial word derived from the name of Augustus, 63BC–AD14, the first Roman emperor). See also next entry

imperialism and **imperialist**   Both words were used without any awkwardness in the 19th century, alongside words such as *colonialism* (see **colony** . . .), often with a sense of patriotism and pride in carrying 'the white man's burden'. *Imperialism* and *imperialist* are now irrevocably bad words, carrying with them connotations of territorial expansion through conquest, and subjugation of the inhabitants of a country by force, or the extension of influence through economic power.

implants   The word has several meanings: for some women, the one that comes first is the surgical use of silicone implants to produce a generous **cleavage**. These were devised in the 1960s by an American plastic surgeon, since when it is believed that two million operations have been carried out in America and 100,000 in Britain. Some of these have been to remodel breasts after mastectomy, but many were cosmetic.

A radio commentator, during the 1992 election campaign in Britain, seized on the word to make a bizarre analogy: he compared a political proposal to 'an implant in the sagging bosom of democracy'.

implicit or **tacit**   In some contexts these words are interchangeable, with both describing an arrangement that has not been explicitly spelt out but is accepted as being in existence. It is sometimes a matter of custom which word is used in particular contexts. Lawyers are more likely to refer to 'implied contracts', implicit conditions under which certain things are done, embodying certain conditions to which the parties are assumed to have agreed. In more general use, *implicit* means clearly apparent, without it being mentioned: 'it was implicit from her manner that she was not going to agree'; 'there is an implicit violence in racialism'. *Tacit*, because it comes from the Latin word for silent, usually relates to feelings or understanding between people that are not put into words: 'there was a tacit feeling that nothing more could be done for the time being'; 'there was a tacit consent that their love affair was over'.

imply or **infer**   A speaker or a writer *implies* when they suggest or hint at something. When we read or listen, we *infer*, that is we 'read between the lines' and pick up what was really intended. 'Do you infer that I am wrong?' is a common mistake. It should be 'Do you imply. . . '. Someone infers from what someone else implies.

important or **importantly**   *More importantly* is trendy and seems to give some people a nice sense of self-importance, so they prefer it to *more important*, especially when speaking on radio and television. There are grammatical arguments for both forms. William Safire, who was Richard Nixon's speechwriter, gives this advice: 'More *important* is my preference, but if more *importantly* turns you on, go ahead and use it'. That's where *The Good English Guide* stands too. It must be added that a lot of people now make a point of saying *more importantly*. As this continues, there's a risk of *more important* being written off as ungrammatical.

impracticable, **impractical** or **unpractical**   There's an important distinction. If you are no good at doing the everyday things in life, you are *unpractical* or *impractical*. If something isn't worth doing because, for example, it's too complicated or not worth the expense, that is also *impractical* or *unpractical*. As you can see, they mean exactly the same. Perhaps *impractical* is better for ideas and things, with *unpractical* better for people.

If something is *impracticable* it means it cannot be done, or is an idea that could not possibly be carried out: 'not only is the plan impractical, because the risks are too great, but it is impracticable because there is no way in which it could go ahead'. See also **practicable**

impresario or **impressario**   'Impressario' may look right to some people. But the word is *impresario*.

imprint or **imprimatur**   *Imprimatur* is sometimes used wrongly for *imprint*. It is Latin for 'let it be printed' and was used in the 17th century, especially in the Roman Catholic Church, for an official licence to print a religious text. It has since come to be used rather generally for official approval of anything. So a scheme could be said to have the government's imprimatur, or a marketing plan has the chairman's imprimatur. Different pronunciations are heard: the most usual one is probably 'impriMAHTer'.

William Caxton (*c*1422–91) used *imprint* for an impressed mark and by the 18th century it had come to mean the publisher's name or symbol on the title page of a book. It is also a way of saying a book is issued by a particular publisher, that is under that publisher's imprint.

impromptu   See **extempore** . . .

impulse buying   The term belongs to 'live for today' consumer society and **credit-card** buying. It describes the tendency to buy without thinking, and is the real purpose behind appealing window and counter displays and the arrangement of certain goods just by check-out cash points.

in, **into** or **in to**   It is occasionally necessary to think twice about which of these three forms to use:

In is for location in a place: 'she was in the room'; 'dinner in the oven – love mum'.

Although *in* can be used where movement is involved ('she went in the room'; 'put the dinner in the oven'), *into* is usually preferable: 'Come into the garden, Maud' (Tennyson, *Maud*).

A common mistake is to write *into* (as one word), when the words should be separate. Here is a simple rule that works in most cases. When it is impossible to use *in* on its own, *in to* should usually be *two* words: 'Send her in to see me'; 'Shall we go in to see the play?', but 'Shall we go into the theatre?'; 'They went in to dinner', but 'They went *into* the dining-room'. Some exceptions: a book is turned *into* a film, we bump *into* something and look *into* a matter.

There's also the trendy use of *into* (as one word) to mean caught up with or enthusiastic about: 'she's into Japanese flower arrangement'. This is conversational rather than written usage. See also **onto or on to**

in or **on**   Saks, the famous department store in New York, is *on* Fifth Avenue. In London, Harrods is *in* Knightsbridge. The British are usually *in* town, while Americans tend to be *on* the town.

Others may sail *on* a ship, but the Royal Navy sails and serves *in* ships, which is why Noel Coward's wartime film was called 'In Which We Serve'.

There are signs that houses and shops in Britain are turning up on streets, instead of in them: *The Independent* mentioned 'Habitat and Heals on Tottenham Court Road'. At times, this avoids an awkward repetition of *in*: 'it's a shop *on* Sloane Street *in* London'.

in-, un- or **non-**   There is no reliable set of rules to tell us whether it is *un*detectable or *in*detectable, *in*experienced or *un*experienced and so on (*undetectable* and *inexperienced* are correct). It is true that *in-* is a Latin prefix and should be attached to words derived from Latin, while *un-* is English and should go with words of English origin. But we have to know which is which, and even then there are too many exceptions to make this a useful guide. When in doubt over *in-* or *un-*, it is best to turn to a dictionary.

There are a few words which take either *in-* or *un-*. Five common ones are:

inadvisable/unadvisable (Note that *unadvisable* can have an alternative meaning, describing a person who will not listen to or take advice.)
indecipherable/undecipherable
indisciplined/undisciplined
inessential/unessential
inescapable/unescapable

The tendency is for the *in-* forms to take over and the alternative *un-* forms may eventually become obsolete (except for the separate meaning of *unadvisable*).

Non- is not simply an alternative prefix to *in-* or *un-*: it can carry a different meaning. For *non-* often means no more than something is not so, without any suggestion of criticism, whereas *in-* or *un-* often carry a pejorative meaning: it is a statement of fact that a Jew or a Moslem is a *non-Christian*, but to call them

unchristian suggests they do not care about other people; a form of treatment that is *non-medical* does not belong to recognized medical practice, but to call it *unmedical* suggests it is contrary to medical advice and knowledge; *non-scientific* is not connected with science, but *unscientific* can mean slipshod or misguided because science has not been taken into account.

On the other hand, some words have been coined, particularly since World War II, using *non-* as a strong put down: there is nothing neutral about a *non-starter*, for example. It can refer to a listed horse that does not run, but usually means someone or something that doesn't stand a chance.

inability   See disability . . .

inadvisable or **unadvisable**   Either, but see in-, un- or non-.

inasmuch as, **insofar as** or **insomuch as**
These starchy phrases can have some purpose when used to mean 'to the extent that': 'the sales figures are acceptable but only inasmuch as they are no worse than last year's'. *Insomuch* can be followed by 'that', with perhaps a subtle change of meaning, suggesting 'only so far': 'the new treatment can be followed insomuch that there is evidence it can be effective in certain cases'. In general, all three expressions are best left to formal texts where heavy-going pompous language is tolerated, even if it does make us yawn.

in between times   See in the meantime . . .

incidentally   In normal conversation *incidentally* is so often pronounced with four syllables ('inciDENTly') that this is almost the standard way of saying the word. But that is no excuse for the spelling 'incidently', which appears at times. *Incidentally* may have some use in speech as a buffer word to create a pause before an aside, although 'by the way' or 'in passing' serves just as well. But in writing it often gets in the way: 'incidentally we should also consider . . .'; 'incidentally there is another way of . . .'. It is always worth seeing what a sentence is like with *incidentally* deleted: it will usually be more to the point.

incline   To be *inclined* to think or to do something is valid where a final decision has not yet been made: 'I am inclined to think we should publish this book, but am waiting for the reader's report'; 'I am inclined to buy a new computer, but need more advice'. Otherwise it is pointless shilly-shallying: 'I am inclined to have another drink'; 'I am inclined to go to Glasgow for the weekend'.

inclose   See enclose . . .

inclosure   See enclosure . . .

include   See compose . . .

income or **revenue**   *Income* usually covers the amount of money a person receives from various sources ('my monthly income from investments is . . .'). Hence *income tax* is usually taken to be tax on the earnings of individuals, and *incomes policy* relates to government control over wage increases paid to people.

Revenue could be more suitable when it is a very large sum of money: 'his revenue from holding a number of directorships is over £200,000 a year'. *Revenue* is also the normal word in public finance, while companies and other organizations are more likely to use *income*.

'inCOMparable' or **'incomPARable'**   The second syllable is stressed. Although some dictionaries show stress on the *third* syllable as an alternative, this is usually considered a downmarket mistake.

in or ***by* comparison**   See *(in* or *by)* comparison

in connection with   See connection

inconsequential or **inconsequent**   Some dictionaries distinguish between the meanings of these two words, suggesting that *inconsequent* means not following logically and *inconsequential* means irrelevant and of no importance. But few people make this distinction, and the general meaning of both words is trivial or unimportant, that is of no consequence. *Inconsequential* seems to be taking over and *inconsequent* is heard less and less often.

incredible, unbelievable or **incredulous**   *Incredible* is a synonym for *unbelievable*. Both words are also used to mean something or someone so amazing that it is hard to believe: an incredible achievement, an incredible person. Dictionaries are too cautious in writing down this extended meaning as informal. *Incredulous* is used about people, or the way they look at someone or the tone in their voice: 'He is always incredulous and questions everything you say'.

indecipherable or **undecipherable**   Either: *indecipherable* is perhaps more usual. See also **in-, un-** or **non-**

indefinitely   Although the literal meaning of *indefinitely* is without limits one way or the other, it is pedantic to maintain, as some purists do, that *indefinitely* should not be used simply to mean a very long time. That's how nearly everybody does use the word, and no one complains about 'interminable' being used for tediously long, although the literal meaning is without end. It is also claimed that the phrase *almost indefinitely* makes no sense, which again is only true if the words are taken literally. But most people are happy to say or write *almost indefinitely*, meaning for a long period ('celebrations will go on almost indefinitely') and everybody knows what is meant. That is what **idiom** is about.

independent or **independant**   Unlike **dependant and dependent**, *independent* is the only form and serves as both the noun and descriptive word. There is no such word as 'independant'.

independent school   See **public school** . . .

in-depth   *In-depth* is the fashionable alternative to 'thorough' or 'detailed', as in an 'in-depth review', 'in-depth research', 'an in-depth examination'. Although it is sometimes criticized, *in-depth* seems a good expression, since it points clearly to something much more than a surface approach.

index   *Index* has a number of meanings. In calculations, it is short for *index number*, which is a figure showing changes against a chosen base number. The *Retail Price Index* (or *RPI*) is a UK index number measuring changes in the cost of a range of goods and services supposedly purchased regularly by the average family. This is used as a measure of **inflation**, and was formerly called the *cost of living index*.

Wages, pensions, investments or anything else are *indexed* when they are automatically adjusted to take into account a rise or fall in the RPI. They are then *index-linked*. *Indexation*, a more recent word for *index-linking*, is the only way to guarantee the purchasing power of money.

indexes or **indices**   It is not wrong to use the plural form *indexes* in any context, but it would be pedantic to use the plural *indices* (pron: 'INDiseez') for say the indexes of books, or for card indexes. In mathematical and economic contexts, *indices* is the accepted, perhaps the more usual, plural: retail price indices, etc.

Indian   See **Hindi** . . .

Indian English   It is believed that no more than 3 or 4 per cent of the inhabitants of India speak English fluently. This is a small percentage, but out of a population of about 800 million it adds up to 24–32 million people: the only countries that have more English-speakers are Britain and the USA. English was introduced in India as the language of administration and law, as part of British colonialism from the late 18th century until 1947, when the Republic of India was established. Under the constitution of independent India, English was recognized as one of the official languages.

Indian English has a distinct sound, immediately recognizable, since the pronunciation and rhythm have particular characteristics that are altogether different from British English. Some linguistic scholars have even suggested that the influence of other languages spoken on the subcontinent, and the drive towards a national linguistic identity, may in the future encourage *Indian English* to develop so many further changes that it could arrive at a point where it would no longer be understood by people living in other anglophone countries. On the other hand, films and television exert a pull in the direction of standardization.

There is said to be a linguistic **generation gap** among

educated Indians. **American English** is seen by some young people at universities as modern and smart, free from the old Raj connotations. Perhaps the familiar modulations of English as spoken in India will in the future change to a style closer to American English. As in other countries that are finding a separate identity, the eventual form and sound of English, as spoken in India, is still in the melting-pot.

indicate or **suggest** *Indicate* is the more positive word, whereas *suggest* leaves the question open. News and current affairs programmes, which have to be extra careful to show political impartiality, say that opinion polls *suggest* a lead by one party over another, that is leaving open the possibility of doubt.

indices See indexes . . .

indict or **indite** Both words are connected to the same Latin source 'dictare' (to declare). *Indict* was spelt 'indite' until the 17th century when the spelling was modified, but the old pronunciation ('inDYTE') remained, which sometimes results in the word being spelt wrongly. It has the legal sense of charging with a crime: an *indictment* (pron: 'inDYTEment') is a formal written accusation.
    Indite, an old-fashioned, almost obsolete word meaning to put something in writing, has retained the earlier spelling.

indifference and **indifferent** There are recent dictionaries that give the first meaning of *indifferent* as of average quality, that is neither good nor bad. In fact, the word, in the way it is used now, is decidedly pejorative: an indifferent dinner usually means a bad dinner; to say something was done indifferently is likely to mean it was done badly. The old sense of *indifference*, which was impartiality, taking no sides, a meaning still included in current dictionaries, is hardly recognized any more. To say 'it's a matter of indifference to me' would not be taken as an expression of objective impartiality, but more as a formal alternative to that chilling sentiment 'I couldn't care less'.

indigenous See endogenous . . .

indirect While there are alternative pronunciations for the first syllable of *direct* (either rhyming with the first syllable of 'mirror' or with the same sound as 'dye'), the accepted pronunciation of *indirect* keeps the 'dye' sound: 'indyeREKT'.

indirect object See direct object . . .

indirect speech See direct speech . . .

indisciplined or **undisciplined** Either: *undisciplined* is perhaps more usual. See also **in-**, **un-** or **non-**

indiscriminate and **undiscriminating** These are the only correct forms of the two words in British English (*indiscriminating* is the usual form in America). Both words mean unable to distinguish between different things, usually between good and poor quality: 'many television viewers are indiscriminate (or undiscriminating) over the programmes they watch'. *Indiscriminate* has a further meaning (not shared by *undiscriminating*), which is random and without selection: an indiscriminate collection of books, indiscriminate bombing. Some dictionaries choose not to include *undiscriminating* as a separate entry, treating it as an unlisted negative form of 'discriminate'. The word is a valid, if less common alternative to *indiscriminate*, in the sense of lacking in judgement to choose between things.

'indisPUTable' or **'inDISputable'** At one time it was considered correct to put the stress on the second syllable and some people still prefer this. It sounds wrong now, since the standard pronunciation has moved the stress to the third syllable, making the word easier to say: 'indisPUTable'.

indite See indict . . .

individual Back in the 1920s, **Fowler** attacked the stupidity of using *individual* as merely another word for a person, but it still goes on: 'he is a strange individual'; 'there were a number of individuals in the room'. The word is correctly used when it sets one person alongside society or a large group of people: 'The worth of a State, in the long run, is the worth of the individuals composing it' (John Stuart Mill, *On Liberty*); or as Bernard Shaw is supposed to have said at the end of one of his plays, when the entire audience was clapping but one person was booing, 'I agree with you Sir, but what can two individuals do against so many?'

Indonesian The alternative pronunciations are: 'indoNEEzian', 'indoNEEsian' and 'indoNEEshan'.

indorse See endorse . . .

inducement See coercion . . .

industrial Although there are a few instances of its use earlier, *industrial*, as a descriptive word for the production of goods by workers in factories, started with the 19th century. The *Industrial Revolution* (first used in English by the political philosopher Friedrich Engels, 1820–95) became the historical name for the development of Britain as an industrial nation during the late 18th and the 19th centuries. In the 20th century, and especially since World War II, *industrial* has become applied as an all-purpose descriptive word in a range of contexts. Some of the most important examples are covered by the following entries.

industrial action The word *strike*, first noted in this sense in a 1768 annual return, seems to have become old-fashioned, except for long-lasting all-out affairs, such as the miners' strike of 1984–5. Generally the trade unions and the media prefer the more white-collar expression *industrial action*, a vague euphemism that covers anything from bashing the boss, an overtime ban, full strike action or **restrictive practices**, such as **go-slow** or work-to-rule.

Industrial action is an unsatisfactory term because it is so imprecise, and also inaccurate, since it is used for action in a dispute with employers taken by people, such as air-traffic controllers and teachers, whose work is hardly part of industry.

industrial archaeology The term appeared in the 1950s in connection with old machines, disused factories, mills, coal mines, railway trains and other memorabilia that could be used to study the Industrial Revolution. It has since been extended to include artefacts, such as early aeroplanes, film projectors, typewriters, in fact all the nuts and bolts of an **industrial society**.

industrial democracy This was the title of a report published in 1977 by a committee of inquiry under the chairmanship of Alan Bullock. Since then the term has been used generally to describe various approaches in industry that seek to involve employees in the planning, management and key decisions of the companies they work for.

industrial diseases This is a public health term for illnesses, such as silicosis, dermatitis, backache, caused by the environment in which people work. At one time certain of these diseases were treated by law as industrial injuries.

industrial espionage This broad term covers organized stealing of valuable confidential information between businesses, such as work on the development of new products, proposed sales campaigns and financial plans. It can involve most of the methods of traditional espionage, from telephone tapping to planting spies in the workforce. The thriller writer, Len Deighton, first used the expression in *The Ipcress File* (1962).

industrialist In the 19th century, an *industrialist* was anyone working in manufacturing, so there is no need to be impressed if people call themselves industrialists, since it covers anyone making anything from tin cans to tanks.

industrial park See **business park** . . .

industrial psychology This is the name for applied psychology used in industry. It is not a new term as it goes back to the early 1900s. Since World War II it has become increasingly prominent. Research is carried out by psychologists in offices and factories into boredom, fatigue, stress and other factors, so that efficiency and **job satisfaction** can be improved.

industrial relations For centuries the approach of management, or the 'bosses' as they were called, was based on using fear of the sack to discipline and drive workers. Since then, trade unions and legislation have developed codes of conduct and negotiation between employers and employees. The general name for this is *industrial relations*, a term that goes back to the beginning of the century. In the 1990s, the trendy catchphrase in management is **human skills**, which, in the words of John Harvey-Jones, a former chairman of ICI, seeks to involve the 'hearts and minds' of employees. See also **human resources**

industrial society This description has replaced the loaded term 'capitalist society' (see **capitalism** . . .). In effect it comes to the same thing, an economy based on the production and sale of goods, which requires a working class, and seems not far removed from the old Marxist class conflict. As the former communist societies of Eastern Europe looked to Western models to rebuild their desperate economies, the term *industrial society* was pushed aside by another term, **market economy**, which not only seemed to be part of the modern world but was also free from old associations.

industrial waste *Industrial waste* covers anything from ordinary rubbish from commercial and industrial premises to smoke belching out of factory chimneys and other toxic or dangerous waste materials. During the 1980s, industrial waste moved up into the headlines as an emotive word in **green** issues, as people became aware that industry was treating the world as a vast free rubbish dump. See also **biodegradable**

inedible or **uneatable** To say something is *inedible* is a statement of fact: it means it should not be eaten because it is poisonous or not suitable in other ways for human consumption. To say something is *uneatable* is more an expression of opinion: it means you cannot stand the taste. *Inedible* is often used when *uneatable* is intended, perhaps with some justification, since if you don't like something, it could make you ill. See also **eatable** . . .

inertia selling The term was coined to describe aggressive selling by sending goods to people who have not ordered them. If whoever has received the goods cannot be bothered to return them, an invoice follows.

inescapable or **unescapable** Either, with a preference for *inescapable*. See also **in-, un- or non-**

inessential or **unessential** Either, but *inessential* is more usual. See also **in-, un- or non-**

inevitable and **inevitably** *Inevitable* uses the negative prefix *in-* with a derivative from Latin, 'evitabilis' (avoidable), to describe something that is certain to follow. In this sense, *inevitable* is absolute and it is superfluous to write 'completely inevitable'. The same applies to *inevitably*. *Must inevitably*, often used ('this must inevitably cause problems'), is unnecessary, since *must* or *inevitably* are strong enough on their own: 'this must cause problems' or 'this inevitably causes problems'.

There is also the sardonic use of *inevitable* to mean 'that's the way it is': 'cheap restaurants with the inevitable smell of overcooked vegetables'. Some dictionaries regard this as colloquial, but it is used in serious writing for a wry effect.

in excess of   Why not 'more than'?

inexpensive   See **low-cost** . . .

infamous or **notorious**   They both mean of ill repute. *Infamous* stresses the evil or shocking nature of a deed or person: 'infamous behaviour', 'an infamous event', 'an infamous criminal'. *Notorious* stresses that the person, deed or event is well-known for bad or evil qualities.

infant or **minor**   In British law, an infant or a minor is a person under the age of 18. The Family Law Reform Act 1969 appears to suggest that the word *minor* should be preferred. *Infant* is also a term in the British educational system for a child between five and seven or eight.

infectious   See **contagious** . . .

infer   See **imply** . . .

inferiority complex   The term was formulated by the psychiatrist Alfred Adler (1870–1937) for a **complex** of feelings and thoughts of personal inadequacy. For some people this produces a drive for greater achievements, for others it can lead to paranoia, for most, it is part of the human condition: a famous American cartoon showed a psychoanalyst telling his patient: 'You haven't got an inferiority complex – you *are* inferior'.

infinite and **infinitely**   Only a few die-hards still criticize the use of these words to mean a great quantity or effort, or a great distance, etc. Long ago, Francis Fowler (Henry **Fowler**'s brother, who died in 1918), noted that this is acceptable as 'any other deliberate exaggeration'. By now, it is *infinitely* ridiculous to continue to make a fuss about such phrases as 'infinitely hard work', 'an infinitely long distance', 'an infinite amount of . . .'.

infinitive   The *infinitive* is a form of the verb which, as its name indicates, is not restricted to singular or plural, or past, present or future. In English, the *infinitive* is often the *to* form of the verb ('I want *to* dance') but not always ('Let them *dance*'). See also **split infinitive**

inflammable   See **flammable** . . .

inflation   Between World War I and World War II, this word was heard most often about other countries, notably Germany, where at one time in the early 1920s inflation was up to 50 per cent a day. Since the 1950s, inflation is always in the news as part of the scene in Britain. It is an alarming word. Visualize a balloon being inflated and transfer the effect to the prices we have to pay for everyday necessities. Visualize another balloon deflating and transfer the effect to the value of money in our pockets and bank accounts.

Inflation has spawned a number of associated words: *Deflation* means prices are going down. The word had its heyday during the Great Depression, the economic collapse of the 1930s. It has not been heard much since, although governments use what are called *deflationary policies*, such as high interest rates, to exert a downward pressure on prices.

Disinflation is a smokescreen word, because it suggests good news. For example, if inflation is 7 per cent this month, whereas last month it was 10 per cent, that is disinflation. But prices are still going up, although at a slower rate, which is what the word means.

Headline inflation is a term that emerged in the 1980s, and is a warning that the measurement of inflation is controversial. It is the rate of inflation based on the Retail Price Index (see **index**) and is usually the one on which indexation is based. See also *underlying inflation* below.

Hyperinflation is a runaway rate of inflation. No figure is laid down, although some economists define it as an annual rate of at least 20 per cent.

Inflation accounting is a technique for presenting the accounts of a business so that profit margins, value of assets, etc are not distorted by a high rate of inflation. For example, an increase in profits might in fact conceal a decrease in the real value of profits, when inflation is taken into account.

Stagflation combines 'stagnant' with inflation: prices are going up while industrial output remains stagnant.

Underlying inflation is a different figure from *headline inflation* (see above), because it excludes mortgage interest.

inflection or **inflexion**   Dictionaries allow both spellings, although *inflexion* looks odd to some people. It's better to keep to *inflection* (the only spelling used in America).

influenza   See **flu** . . .

informal English   See **colloquial, informal, slang** or **non-standard; formal** and **informal English**

informant or **informer**   The distinction is important. An *informant* is an innocent word for anyone who supplies information: 'we have a reliable informant to keep us up to date about prices charged by local restaurants'. An *informer* gives the police information about suspects, and is known in the underworld as a *stool-pigeon* or *copper's nark*.

(for your) information   See **for your information**

information technology (IT) *Information technology* is the lifeblood of most of the world's activities. Make an enquiry in person or by telephone, and the chances are someone will tap it into a computer and read the answer off a screen. Information technology can bring the whole world almost instantly to our desks, or in fact to anywhere we happen to be. For cars, trains and even aircraft have become mobile work centres, from which executives can dictate reports direct to central wordprocessing units, send facsimile documents and tap into **mainframe** computers.

So ubiquitous is information technology, that it's usual now to refer to it as IT. *The Macmillan Dictionary of Information Technology* (Dennis Longley and Michael Shain, 1985) defines IT as 'The acquisition, processing, storage and dissemination of vocal, pictorial, textual and numerical information by a microelectronics-based combination of computing, telecommunications and video'. Or more simply, every form of press-button communication.

infrastructure This is the post-World War II word for the essential underlying framework of a country. *Infrastructure* includes roads, bridges, drains and almost all the construction and development of transport and communications systems that enable society to function. *Infrastructure* is often used as a conveniently vague word: when a politician says we must spend more on the infrastructure, it sounds as if he hasn't worked out clearly where the real priorities are. Margaret Thatcher put the word in its place in a comment she made in 1985, 'You and I come by road or rail, but economists travel on infrastructure'.

infuse See imbue . . .

ingenious or **ingenuous** *Ingenious* is always a positive word, meaning that someone or something is clever, resourceful or original. Except when used about children, *ingenuous* is usually a negative word, implying that someone or something is oversimple or lacking in worldliness. *Disingenuous* is not a straight opposite of *ingenuous*: it means appearing to be innocent and open, but in fact cunning and devious.

ingénue This is more than anything else a theatrical term for a particular kind of role in a play: an innocent, unworldly young woman. It is less likely to be used outside the theatre: in real life, we'd say unsophisticated, inexperienced, naive or ingenuous (see previous entry).

ingenuous See ingenious . . .

inherent, **innate** or **intrinsic** The three words are so close to each other in meaning that it needs clear thinking to decide which one comes closest to what is intended. A quality in a person or a situation can be all these things. *Inherent* means underlying, ever-present: 'the nobility of a human being, inherent in all Shakespeare's tragedies, always comes through at the end of his plays'. *Innate* means interwoven, not

easily eradicated, even if it is not always apparent: 'there is an innate nobility in Shakespeare's heroes that reveals itself in moments of crisis'. *Intrinsic* describes something that is a basic or irreducible part of a larger scheme: 'the intrinsic nobility of Shakespeare's heroes is never diminished by the ebb and flow of their reactions to events'. For the particular sense of *intrinsic value*, see **face value**.

The second syllable of *inherent* can be pronounced as in 'heritage' or as in 'here'. The 'heritage' sound is more usual.

inheritance See heritage . . .

inhibition See block . . .

initiate and **initiation** It is always *people* who are *initiated*, at an *initiation* ceremony or ritual, into membership of a society or group, such as the House of Lords, or as a disciple of a master. Ideas and knowledge are not initiated – they are instilled or inculcated: 'the secret knowledge was instilled into him before he was initiated into the Freemasonry'. Business jargon *initiates* new sales campaigns, new schemes, new approaches. In such cases, *initiate* is a needlessly self-important word, usually better replaced by 'begin' or 'start'.

injunction or **interdict** An *injunction* in ordinary language is a stern warning usually not to do something, such as the injunction parents give to their children about not taking sweets from strangers. In law, an injunction is a court order to do or refrain from doing something. *Interdict* has the same meaning but is not often used, except for a sentence imposed by the Roman Catholic Church excluding a person from certain privileges or rights, and as the legal term in Scotland for an injunction.

-in-law Canon law, a compilation of ecclesiastical laws, prohibited marriage within certain relationships, and *-in-law* derives from that. It covered a wider range of relationships at one time, but now is used for relationships through one's husband or wife (*mother-in-law*, *brother-in-law*, etc) or with one's children's spouses (*son-in-law*, *daughter-in-law*). *-in-law* never takes an *s*, so the plural forms are sons-in-law, sisters-in-law, etc.

in lieu of See lieu

in love See love

inn See hotel . . .

innate See inherent . . .

inner city or **slums** *Slum* is a solid early 19th-century word, slang to begin with, that evokes a picture of squalid **Dickensian** streets and miserable living conditions. Although it is by no means obsolete, it has fallen into disuse as part of the trend to sidestep calling a spade a spade. The current term for run-down living areas, at least with politicians and the media, is *inner city*. It was used in America for parts of cities where blacks lived in overcrowded conditions and is now sociological jargon in Britain.

innings or **inning** It is not cricket to talk about *an* inning, for *innings* is both the singular and plural form in that game. Baseball players do talk about *an inning*, meaning one turn at bat for *both* teams.

innovation There is nothing new about the word: it was already being used in the 16th century for the introduction of new ideas. In the present high-tech age, it is often reserved for the application of new technological developments for use in business and industry. There are two descriptive words, *innovative* and *innovatory*, which mean the same thing and can be used about a person or proposals that introduce new approaches and ways of thinking. *Innovative* is perhaps the more common word. Both words are pronounced with the stress on the *first* syllable, and a light stress on the *third* syllable: 'INN-oh-*vay*-tiv' and 'INN-oh-*vay*-tery'.

innuendo The word should only be used for a derogatory implication: 'the remark contained an innuendo that he had bungled the matter'. We cannot say 'it was an innuendo that he had done well' – the word in that sense is 'implication'. Dictionaries show both plural forms, *innuendoes* or *innuendos*, some favouring one, some the other.

innumerate See **literacy and numeracy**

inoculate or **vaccinate** *Vaccinate* is the usual verb for protection against smallpox (the word comes from Latin 'vacca', a cow, and the cowpox virus was at one time used for the vaccination). But since a vaccine is used to inoculate people against any disease, *inoculate* and *vaccinate* have become interchangeable words. It is an understandably common mistake to spell *inoculate* and *inoculation* with a double *n*.

inorganic or **non-organic** *Inorganic* is a term used in chemistry; *non-organic* usually applies to farming methods (see **healthfood . . .**).

input and **output** In computer technology, *input* is data fed into a computer, and *output* is data produced. Some authorities believe these words should not be used outside technical contexts. But there is nothing new in technology passing on useful words into everyday language. No one complains if the economy is given a *kick-start*! *Input* and *output* are convenient shorthand terms in other contexts: publishers talk about putting their input into a book, that is making a contribution through suggestions to the writer or by editing. *Output* is a word for production in any industry, for the creative work of an artist, and so on. Provided they are not overused, the two words make a useful *input* into language in the 1990s.

inquire See **enquire . . .**

inquiry or **investigation** *Inquiry* is a neutral word for looking into a matter; *investigation* implies that there could be reason to suspect something is amiss. For example, Oliver North rejected the word *investigation* in connection with his part in the Iran–Contra affair, in favour of 'fact-finding inquiry'. And during the hearings there was a tendency for his supporters to say *inquiry*, while those on the other side were more likely to use the word *investigation*. See also **enquire**

inquorate and **quorate** See **quorum**

. . . in residence A concept that started in the 1960s is for universities, schools and other institutions to have a poet, novelist, quartet or some other creative person *in residence*. In-residence posts are sometimes advertised, and provide those who are appointed with a stipend for a period, which enables them to write poems, compose, etc, while they offer a cultural facility to students.

insensible or **insensitive** There is little discernible difference when the words are used to mean indifferent or unconcerned with a person's feelings or sufferings. Perhaps *insensitive* suggests unable to feel anything, whereas *insensible* may imply a deliberate callousness. *Insensible* also has the separate meaning of being physically unconscious ('she was knocked insensible by the blow').

insider The word **outsider** has social, philosophical and psychological meanings, but *insider* is usually related to the possession of information not available to others. That is how it was used as far back as the late 19th century. In the 1980s, the word became linked with dealings on Stock Exchanges: *insider dealing* is buying or selling shares through possessing confidential information that indicates the price will go up or go down. It is said that anyone working in the financial markets, or who has just returned from a so-called 'analysis' lunch', is an insider.

insinuate It is not possible to *insinuate* anything good. The word is always pejorative, so the question 'What are you insinuating?' is asking what *nasty* thing is being suggested. If someone insinuates themselves into a group, it is always for some underhand reason.

in situ 'In this place' is usually preferable to the Latin *in situ*, which means exactly the same thing. Exceptions are in archaeological or geological contexts, where *in situ* is used for the actual place where fossils, minerals or rocks were formed or deposited.

insofar as See **inasmuch as . . .**

insolvency See **bankruptcy . . .**

insomuch as See **inasmuch as . . .**

insouciance or **nonchalance** There is a useful distinction between these words. 'Souci' is French for worry or anxiety: *insouciance* (and *insouciant*) in English means carefree, without concern: 'where most people are nervous on their wedding day, she seemed insouciant'. Both words can be pronounced as in English ('innSOOsee-enss', 'innSOOsee-ent'), or in a French style ('annSOOsee-ahns', 'annSOOsee-ahnt'). The English pronunciation is taking over.

Nonchalance (and *nonchalant*), also from a French word, implies indifference, a casual attitude: to say 'she was nonchalant about her wedding day' could suggest she was not taking it seriously. The words are pronounced as in English, except that the French *sh* sound is preserved: 'NONshe(r)le(r)nt', 'NONshe(r)le(r)ns'.

in spite of   See despite . . .

inst and **ult**   Does even the most stuffy solicitor or bank manager still thank clients for their letter of the 10th *inst* (of this month) or the 15th *ult* (of last month)? These Latin abbreviations belong to stiff-necked **business English** of the past, now happily superseded by simply writing the name of the month, which is clearer anyway: 10 February, 15 January. . . .

install or **instal**   *Install* is the usual spelling now. Although dictionaries continue to show *instal* as an alternative spelling, this is becoming rare, which is convenient, since the other forms of the verb are invariable: *installed, installing*. But note that we pay *instalments* (one *l*). *Installments* are paid in America.)

instinct or **intuition**   *Instinct* is now used in so many different ways that it has become non-scientific, of little use any more in psychology and anthropology. In general use it covers any spontaneous response not thought out in advance, from jamming on the brakes in an emergency to a sexual impulse. Those last two examples illustrate the difference between *instinct* and *intuition*. *Instinct* leads to an action or a physical reaction; *intuition* involves the mind, something we understand, perceive or know without working it out: 'her intuition told her not to trust him'. *Instinct* is a knee-jerk reaction; *intuition* is a sixth sense.

institute or **institution**   It is more a matter of custom than anything else whether an organization is called an *institute* or an *institution*. *Institute* is by far the more usual word in a title, and applied to most professional bodies: Institute of Chartered Accountants, Institute of Actuaries, Institute of Chiropodists. . . . Learned societies also usually prefer to be institutes: Institute of Historical Research, Institute of Latin American Studies, Institute of Zoology. . . . For some unexplained reason, many engineering and allied societies prefer the dignity of *institution*: Institution of Civil Engineers, Institution of Mechanical Engineers, Institution of

Structural Engineers, Royal Institution of Chartered Surveyors . . . .

insurance   See assurance . . .

insure   See assure . . .

intaglio   See cameo . . .

intangible assets   See assets

'INtegral' or **'inTEGral'**   The stress is on the first syllable, not the second: 'INtegral'.

integrate   *Integrate* is no longer so fashionable as an all-purpose word that sounds more important than simple alternatives, such as join, bring together, combine. . . . That is to be welcomed as a step in the direction of using **plain English**. It is also less common now to talk about a man or a woman being *integrated*, meaning able to accommodate without stress the conflicting aspects of their personality. That is also a good thing, since words such as balanced, well-adjusted, calm, composed, are both more precise and less pretentious.

intellectual or **intelligent**   The word *intelligent* is in the clear: it unarguably describes a person as having a high level of mental ability, or an idea or concept as being well thought out. It is hard to imagine the word used other than in a good sense.

The word *intellectual* is loaded with confusing and conflicting social and political associations. It was originally as out in the open as *intelligent*, and meant someone with a high level of understanding and reasoning, or described an approach that revealed those qualities. For Milton, an 'intellectual being' possessed 'Those thoughts that wander through eternity' (*Paradise Lost*). Thomas Arnold (1795–1842) included 'intellectual ability' among the qualities he expected from his scholars at Rugby. Dictionaries continue to offer these definitions of *intellectual*, but the reality is that *intellectual* is often used disdainfully, to describe someone out of touch with feelings and ordinary people.

The word has become tainted by the old class associations of *intelligentsia*, originally a term for the educated class involved in the revolutionary movement. (A hangover from it is *left-wing intellectual*.) An article by an American academic, Peter Brooks, in *The Times Literary Supplement*, suggested that we 'are not quite sure what intellectuals are' and are more at home with the words 'writers, scholars, experts, pundits'.

After all that, it is difficult to know where the word stands now. To be called an *intellectual* might be taken as a compliment to one's intelligence and insight. Or it could be writing us down as arrogant, unbalanced and out of focus with life. If we want to play safe, we'd better describe a book, idea, argument, etc as intelligent or profound, rather than intellectual. When it comes to a person, there are Peter Brooks' alternatives, writer, scholar, expert, pundit, to which we can add savant, polymath and luminary.

intelligence quotient   See IQ

intelligent   See intellectual . . .

intelligentsia   See intellectual . . .

(my) **intended**   See fiancé . . .

inter   Hyphens are no longer used in the many words formed using the Latin prefix *inter* (between or among): intercontinental, interpersonal, interplanetary, interrelate. . . .

interact and **interaction**   These have become **buzzwords** in a wide range of contexts. People *interact* with each other, meaning respond to each other or simply work together; situations *interact*, meaning one has an effect on the other. In fact, the whole world, physical, commercial and human, depends on *interaction* more than anything else. At the same time, it is often worthwhile looking for a more precise word, such as cooperate, communicate, support, or simply get on well with each other. See also **interface** . . .

inter alia   In most cases there is nothing to be said for using this Latin phrase (pron: 'interAYlia'). After all, *among other things* has the same number of syllables and is the exact English equivalent.

intercourse   Although dictionaries still give the primary meaning as communication between people, it invites misunderstanding now to use *intercourse* in that way. When Elizabeth Barrett Browning was on honeymoon in 1846, she wrote: 'After two months of uninterrupted intercourse he loves me better every day . . . and my health improves too'. We cannot read that now without a double take. In 1908, E M Forster wrote 'I do detest conventional intercourse' (*A Room with a View*). Could we say that now, unless we intended it in another sense altogether? For *intercourse* has lost its innocence and the first meaning that comes to mind is *sexual intercourse*.

interdict   See injunction . . .

interesting   It should, of course, mean the opposite of boring. But *interesting* has become a standard noncommittal comment on anything we do not understand, are not sure of, or don't like. If we are looking at a painting, and don't want to make a fool of ourselves or offend our friend who has just bought it, we fall back on 'It's very interesting'. The trouble is no one is taken in by it any more. Here's an example of how cool and unconvincing the word has become. When Margaret Thatcher attacked, in her speech in The Hague on 15 May 1992, some of John Major's ideas for the future of European cooperation, the Prime Minister had one word to say about it – *interesting*!

interface or **interact**   There is a human interface laboratory at the University of Washington, Seattle that carries out research into the way people relate to technology. *Interface* has become a word used in so many different contexts that it is not always clear what is meant. In physics an *interface* is a common boundary between two compositions. The most common use of *interface* for computers is a complex plug-socket connection that enables separate pieces of equipment to function together. In general use now, an *interface* is the point where two systems come into contact with each other, and the word in this sense can be used as a noun or a verb. Many subjects can have an *interface* (or *interface* with each other), so students of history, for example, may need to attend lectures on economics and literature.

There is no need to use *interface* as a pretentious high-tech substitute for cooperate or work together: 'as chief executive, she has to interface successfully with production and marketing departments'. If 'work together' seems too ordinary an expression in a particular context, it is better to use *interact*, than to misuse *interface*.

interfere or **intervene**   To *interfere* with or in something always suggests a degree of obstruction or getting in the way: 'the withdrawal of a grant interfered with work on the project'. *Intervene* can suggest a helpful constructive contribution: 'as an honest broker, he intervened in the dispute in order to resolve difficulties'. Even the purpose of *armed intervention* is usually to liberate a country or restore peace.

inter-governmental conference   See summit

(in the) **interim**   See in the meantime . . .

interjection or **exclamation**   Grammarians prefer the term *interjection* as one of the so-called eight parts of speech (see **grammatical terms**). But an *interjection* and an *exclamation* are the same thing, anything from a grunt (Ugh!, Yuck!), a cry (Ouch!), a greeting (Hello!), to any word or sound used to express irritation, frustration or any other emotion.

intermezzi or **intermezzos**   The plural *intermezzos* is just as much at home now in English as the correct Italian plural *intermezzi*. As it is mostly used about music (for a short composition performed between acts, or simply a short piece for a solo instrument), the cognoscenti prefer *intermezzi*.

intermission   See interval . . .

internal politics   See political

international   See cosmopolitan . . .

international company   See multinational . . .

International Phonetic Alphabet   This was developed in the late 19th century as an attempt to represent every human speech sound by a combination of conventional letters, symbols and marks. It has been modified since, to add sounds in languages not previously included. The International Phonetic Alphabet is the most comprehensive guide available to identify sounds in languages and is used by most dictionaries to indicate pronunciation. There are two problems. Most people need to refer to a complicated table of letters and symbols in order to identify the sounds, and ideally the alphabet should be learned from a teacher of voice production.

The Good English Guide uses a simple phonetic system to show pronunciation where necessary. This is not nearly as comprehensive as the International Phonetic Alphabet, but is offered as an approximate guide to enable English speakers to pick up the pronunciation of a word at sight, without reference to a separate code of symbols.

internecine An *internecine* war inflicts heavy casualties on both sides, for the word derives from Latin 'necare' (to kill) and means mutually destructive. But with present usage, there can be an internecine dispute within an organization without any suggestion of carnage, although it should always imply a serious and damaging difference: 'there is an internecine conflict in the company, with senior executives divided over policy'. (Pron: 'interNEEsyne'.)

interpretative or **interpretive** Both forms are now considered correct. *Interpretive* is convenient and easier to say but *interpretative* is the more orthodox form.

It is a useful word, not used as often as it might be, to describe a comment or a statement that goes beyond being explanatory to seek to bring out an underlying meaning. Even the accounts of a company can provide material for an interpretative review, but the word is more commonly used about literature, music or art.

interval or **intermission** *Inter* means between, and properly used an *interval* is a distance or a period between things or events: 'three months was a long interval between sending a bill and receiving the cheque'. It is slipshod to use the word as a synonym for a period of time, without relating it to two events: 'three months was a long interval to wait for a cheque'. In that sentence, 'time' is clearly the right word.

Intermission, the American word for the interval in a play or other performance in a theatre, is heard more and more in Britain, especially on television, and recent dictionaries now include it, in this sense, without marking it as specifically American.

intervene See interfere . . .

intestinal The recommended pronunciation puts the stress on the second syllable ('inTEStinal'). But most British dictionaries also allow the pronunciation 'intesTINE-al'.

in or **under the circumstances** See circumstances

in the event *In the event of* has a place for important declarations: 'in the event of war . . .'; 'in the event of the terms of this contract not being adhered to . . .'. *In the event that* is usually no more than 5-syllable long-windedness for 'if': 'in the event that you are late . . .'; 'in the event that the board agrees on this matter . . .'. *In the event*, meaning 'as it turned out', is a valid use: 'In the event, they reached an agreement'.

in the meantime, **in the interim** or **in between times** *Interim* has its place in official language to describe something that is provisional or a stopgap: companies issue *interim* reports to shareholders to keep them in touch until the final annual report is available, and if they are lucky this could be accompanied by an *interim* dividend. Outside such contexts, *in the meantime* is more natural: 'in the meantime, she had gone to live in Cornwall'. *In between times* is useful for a longer period than *in the meantime* suggests: 'in between times, she married and had two children'.

in the neighbourhood of See neighbourhood

in the not too distant future See soon . . .

in the world or **on earth** See earth or world

in this connection See connection

intimate At one time the word had an embarrassing double meaning. The *News of the World* used to delight in expressions such as 'intimacy took place' or 'the couple were intimate', meaning there was sexual intercourse. Such squeamish circumlocutions are as old-fashioned as saying a couple 'had carnal knowledge' of each other. So these days *intimate* is more or less in the clear, and we can call someone an intimate friend without much risk of misunderstanding.

in to or **into** See in . . .

intonation There are short cuts to expressing something in speech that are not available in writing. *Intonation* is a way of conveying meaning by the pitch and tone of the voice. Take the simple word *really*: depending on the way it's said, it can mean anything from 'I don't believe a word of that' to 'That's marvellous'. Intonation can, to some extent, be expressed in writing: ' "Really?", she asked in utter disbelief'; ' "Really!", she said full of wonder'. Occasionally intonation can be indicated just by the choice between a question mark and an exclamation mark: 'Really?' suggests a tone of doubt, whereas 'Really!' suggests shock or amazement.

in toto This is Latin for completely or entirely, and there is no reason why it should not be replaced by one of those words: 'I reject the proposition in toto (or "completely" or "entirely")'. Because *in toto* sounds like 'in total' it is often wrongly used to mean that: 'the profits of the group of companies in toto are a record' ('in total' is right there).

'INtricacy' or 'inTRICacy' Although there is a tendency to move the stress forward to the second syllable, this is resisted by careful speakers, who keep it where it belongs, on the first syllable: 'INtricacy'.

intrigue As a verb, *intrigue* has given a lot of trouble in its day. The original meaning was to plot and scheme, which remains the main meaning of intrigue as a noun ('an intrigue to bring down the government'). There was a fuss when the verb came to be used to mean fascinate, puzzle, attract, arouse interest ('the idea intrigues me'; 'the first time they met, he intrigued her'). By now this use of *intrigue* is included in all dictionaries. In fact, some show it as the first meaning. Nevertheless, in this sense it is an indeterminate word, and 'mystify', 'fascinate', 'enchant', 'dazzle' are among a number of words that can focus more precisely on the intended meaning.

A recent dictionary considers it is archaic to use the noun *intrigue* for a secret love affair. But some women, although rarely men, still like the expression, especially about past love affairs: 'I had several intrigues at that time in my life'.

intrinsic See inherent . . .

intrinsic value See face value . . .

introduction See foreword . . .

introspective, introverted or withdrawn
Introspective is often used in a narrow pejorative way, suggesting a person is too wrapped up in themselves. There is another side to the word, for without introspection, a heightened awareness of self, human consciousness becomes little more than a mindless flow of sensations.

Introverted is a different word. It comes within the field of psychiatry and describes abnormal preoccupation with the self that inhibits normal relationships with other people. While *withdrawn* is a general rather than a psychological word, it does carry with it the unwholesome implication of being unsociable or abnormally retiring.

introvert As a word for turning the mind inwards, *introversion* existed in the mid-17th century. In the 20th century, Jung introduced the word into psychology when he developed the concept of **extrovert** and introvert types. The introvert is characterized by a withdrawal, a subjectivity. But *introvert* does not necessarily carry with it the implication of a personality disorder, in the way that *introverted* does (see previous entry).

Outside Jungian psychology, *introvert* is often used for a person who is quiet and thoughtful. Most psychological terms are loaded since they are used for morbid disorders of personality, so in principle it is better to avoid *introvert* in general use, in favour of alternatives, such as 'reflective' or 'meditative'.

intrusive *r* sound Other than phoneticians, few people are aware of the *intrusive r*, a light *r* sound creeping in where it is not called for. Lynn Barber wrote in *The Independent* that she finds herself 'banging on about *Laura Norder*', that popular character with politicians, who often impersonates **law and order**. In everyday rapid conversation the intrusive *r* is common, even with careful speakers. Be aware of it but don't let it keep you awake at night.

intrust See entrust . . .

intuition See instinct . . .

'INvalid' or 'inVALid' Whether it is a noun or a verb referring to a person who cannot move about because of illness, the stress is on the *first* syllable. When used as a verb ('as a result of injuries, we shall invalid him out of the service'), the last syllable has a 'leed' sound: 'INvaleed'. As a descriptive word meaning the opposite of 'valid', the stress is on the second syllable: 'inVALid'.

invaluable or valuable *Invaluable* is more valuable than *valuable*: it is beyond value, priceless. For this reason, it is a word that should not be devalued by using it too casually, almost as a synonym for useful ('that's an invaluable idea').

invariable and invariably *Invariable* should only be used for a factor that is a constant, something that never changes. Strictly, the same applies to *invariably*, but the word is often used more loosely: 'the train is invariably late'. That is probably not true, since even the legendary 8.20am train occasionally arrives on time. But no harm is done by the informal use of *invariably* to mean 'nearly always'.

invent See discover . . .

inventory The stress is on the first syllable ('INventory'), and to move it forward to the second syllable is not an option but a vulgarism. The word is pronounced with three syllables, rhyming with 'infantry'.

inverse or obverse Outside philosophical and technical contexts, *inverse* is not used much, except in two phrases: *inverse proportion* and *inverse snobbery*. *Inverse proportion* is a relation between two quantities in that one gets bigger as the other gets less: 'the cost of a meal in a restaurant can be in inverse proportion to how much we enjoy it' (that is, the more you pay, the less you might enjoy it). An example of *inverse snobbery* is an educated person speaking in a gorblimey accent or eating peas off a knife, as a kind of joke.

Obverse is another word that does not come in for much general use. To coin collectors it is the 'head' side of a coin, and is extended to refer to the counterpart of a statement or a fact: 'to live in a beautiful house with lovely objects, adds to the quality of life, and the obverse is also true'.

inverted commas or **quotation marks** These are the same thing but the term *inverted commas* has almost dropped out of use: strictly speaking it only applies to the comma or commas *before* a quotation as the commas after are not inverted ("and"). Some modern typefaces replace commas by identical diagonal dashes before and after quotations. All of that is an argument for referring to *inverted commas* as *quotation marks*. For detailed notes about using them, see **quotation marks**.

investigation See **inquiry** . . .

investigative journalism Reporting is by nature a process of investigation, but the term *investigative journalism* is particularly applied to journalists probing into intrigues in high places in government. The expression originated in America, and came to the forefront during the 1972 presidential campaign, when two reporters on the *Washington Post* delved into the burglary at the headquarters of the Democratic Party, the affair that became known all over the world as *Watergate* (see **-gate**).

invitation or **invite** Even after centuries, some words stay on the wrong side of the tracks. *Invite*, as a shortened version of *invitation*, has been in the language since the end of the 16th century, but is still classified by dictionaries at best as colloquial and at worst as vulgar. Nevertheless, in the last few years *invite* has been edging its way into respectability. But for the time being, it is better to send out *invitations*.

invoice See **account** . . .

inward or **inwards** As a descriptive word coming in front of a noun it has to be *inward*: 'an inward direction'. In other uses either *inward* or *inwards* will do: 'the direction is inwards (or inward)'; 'move it inwards (or inward)'. *Inwards* is more usual.

in years See **for years** . . .

IOU This abbreviation for 'I owe you' has been in use since the early 17th century. It is still occasionally put at the head of a note confirming a debt from one person to another, particularly a gambling debt. It cannot be used in a serious sense now, since its legal validity is uncertain.

IQ The abbreviation is used more often than the words in full: *intelligence quotient*. The term dates from the early 1920s, and different tests have been constructed to measure it. These are usually worked out so that the average IQ is 100. The value of IQ ratings is often questioned: Alicja Lesniak, as financial director of one of the largest advertising groups, commented 'How do you value the punchline in an ad? You have to measure genius as well as time. I'd love to be able to develop a formula for that!'

IRA, **Provisionals** and **Sinn Fein** All three names relate to the revolutionary movement in Ireland. The IRA is the paramilitary organization: the name in full, Irish Republican Army, is not often heard, perhaps because it might be seen to bestow official status. Although it has descended from revolutionary groups going back to the mid-19th century, the IRA dates from 1919, when it fought a successful war against British forces occupying Ireland. Its cause is the unification of the country into a single republic, rejecting the partition imposed by the Anglo-Irish treaty of 6 December 1921. The command structure is based in Dublin.

The *Provisional IRA*, a breakaway wing known as the *Provisionals* (or *Provos*), was formed in 1970. Based in Belfast, its aim is to force the British out of Ulster.

Sinn Fein (pron: 'shinnFAYN'), Irish for 'we ourselves', is the name of the political party established early in the 20th century, which was dedicated to achieving independence from British rule. Sinn Fein has become in effect the political arm of the Provisional IRA, with members who stand in local government elections in Northern Ireland, as well as in national UK elections.

Ireland, **Eire**, **Ulster**, **Northern Ireland** and **Southern Ireland** It is easy to get into deep water over the names for the different parts of the second largest island in the British Isles. *Ireland* is unarguably the English name for the whole island, and does not take into account political boundaries.

In Gaelic, *Eire* (pron: 'AIRer') means *Ireland*, and in 1937 replaced the *Irish Free State* as the official name for the part of Ireland independent of the UK. The *Republic of Ireland* (as proclaimed on 18 April 1949) replaced Eire as the official name, with the *Irish Republic* as the shorter form, and *Southern Ireland* an accepted everyday name. Older people may still use 'Eire' for the Republic out of habit, others to make a point, but it has now been superseded politically: its linguistic standing is as the Gaelic name for the island of Ireland.

Northern Ireland is the official name for the NE part of the country that remained with the United Kingdom after partition was proclaimed in 1921. It has its separate parliament at Stormont and limited self-government. *Ulster* has three different meanings. Historically it was one of the five kingdoms into which the island was divided, an area that would now comprise Northern Ireland and a province of the Irish Republic. Ulster is also the modern name for the northern province of the Republic, comprising the three counties Cavan, Monaghan and Donegal. Lastly, Ulster is the familiar name for Northern Ireland, which formed part of the old Kingdom.

To sum up, *Northern Ireland* and the *Republic of Ireland* (or the *Irish Republic*) should always be used in official language for the two parts of the country. In general use, outside historical contexts, *Ulster* will usually be taken to mean Northern Ireland, and *Southern Ireland* the Irish Republic.

Irene When it is the Greek goddess of peace, the name has three syllables: 'iREEnee'. If it is a woman's name, it has more often than not become two syllables, on the model of Doreen and Eileen. But if a woman with that name prefers the three-syllable version, it is not an affectation, as some people suppose, but the correct Greek pronunciation.

Irish or Erse In the 14th-century *Erse* was used for the Gaelic dialect spoken in the Highlands of Scotland. Later it became more associated with Irish Gaelic. In Ireland now, the usual name for the language is *Irish*, which is what it is officially called in the Irish Republic (see **Ireland** . . .). In passing, it is quite usual in that country to ask 'Do you have Irish?', rather than 'Do you speak Irish?' For the Irish writer, Roy Foster, this conveys the idea of the native language as a possession 'ripped away and painfully restored'. See also **Celtic** . . .

Irish Free State See **Ireland** . . .

iron curtain Although it seems he did not invent the phrase, it was Winston Churchill who gave it currency as a telling metaphor for the divide that separated the Communist bloc from the rest of the world. It now belongs to history books.

ironic or ironical Either can be used to describe a situation or event that has *irony*. The words should only be used when there is a twist in what has happened, so that it is the wrong way round: 'it was ironic (or ironical) that as well as giving me a big order, he paid for dinner'. To use the word to mean no more than surprising or unexpected misses the point: 'ironically, the train was on time' would only be ironic if you had brought sandwiches and a book, expecting the train to be late!

irradiation An *irradiated* chicken is not a chicken that is lit up with joy but a cooked chicken that has been treated by a radioactive process or by electrons in order to give it longer **shelf-life**. The word is likely to be more in the news as the debate is entered over whether irradiation is the answer to many concerns over the safety of food, or whether there are as yet unknown long-term risks in people eating a lot of irradiated foods, or whether the foods themselves are nutritionally deficient.

'irREFutable' or 'irreFUTable' For the time being, stress on the second syllable remains the more distinguished pronunciation, although third-syllable stress is an accepted alternative. But in time the standard pronunciation of **refutable** ('reFUTable') will encourage 'irreFUTable' to take over as standard.

irregardless See **regardless** . . .

irreligious, nonreligious, sacrilegious or unreligious There is nothing subtle about the differences between these four words. *Irreligious* is anti-religion: 'their irreligious behaviour in church was offensive'. *Nonreligious* is neutral, not taking religion into account: 'the Church should treat homosexuality as a nonreligious matter'. *Sacrilegious* describes an irreligious deed, and is a word of condemnation for the violation of something that is sacred. It comes via Old French from a Latin word that combines two words, 'sacri' (which explains the *-ri-* spelling), meaning sacred, and 'legere' (to take), and meant someone who steals sacred objects. Because *unreligious* is astride *irreligious* and *nonreligious*, in that it can have either meaning, it is usually better avoided. See also **profane** . . .

irremovable See **immovable** . . .

irreparable See **repairable** . . .

'irREVocable' or 'irreVOCable' In normal use, stress on the second syllable is the only acceptable pronunciation: 'irREVocable'. In legal matters, where the word is used for an agreement or powers of appointment that may not be revoked, the third syllable is sometimes stressed: 'irreVOCable'.

-ise or -ize See **-ize** . . .

Islamic See **Arab** . . .

-isms The suffix *-ism*, from the Greek form '-ismos', has long been used for creating new nouns, and in the 17th century *ism* became a word in its own right for a creed, principle or theory. It is more likely now to be used in a dismissive way: 'he is always chasing after new isms'. Post-World War II, there has been increasing use of *-ism* to denote prejudice and discrimination, with words such as sexism (see **feminism**) and **ageism**. Among other recent *-isms*, *long-termism* and *short-termism* are clumsy formations, needlessly replacing 'long-term and short-term policies'. The new meaning of **pluralism** is useful in a multi-racial society. In politics, *-ism* is a popular tag with historians and journalists for converting a president's or prime minister's name into a concept: *Stalinism*, **Thatcherism**, **Reaganism** . . .

-is nouns The plural of a number of nouns ending in *-is* is formed by changing the *-is* to *-es* (pron: 'eez'). These are the more common ones: analysis (pl: *analyses*), antithesis (pl: *antitheses*), basis (pl: *bases*), crisis, hypothesis, metamorphosis, oasis, parenthesis, synopsis, thesis. The reason is partly because of the Greek origin of the words and partly because of pronunciation, which can be demonstrated by trying to say 'synopsises'.

isn't See **contracted forms**

issue Two pronunciations are heard and both are generally acceptable: either 'ISHoo' or 'ISSyou'. The

-sh- sound is considered preferable and is the only pronunciation in American English.

IT See **information technology**

italics It is not only editors and printers who have to make up their minds about which words and phrases should be put into *italics*, but anyone who uses, or dictates to someone using, a **wordprocessor**. This facility encourages some people to indulge in what **Fowler** condemned as 'a mosaic of roman and italic type' (*Modern English Usage*, 1926). Reference books, such as this one, have a special need for *italics* to help readers to pick out points quickly. Otherwise *italics* should be used sparingly, or they lose their effect and become an irritation. Here are four basic guidelines:

1 *Titles* of books, plays, operas, works of art, etc should go into *italics* to single them out. The word *The* is sometimes a problem: if it is part of the title, it should also be in *italics*, but in the flow of a sentence it does no harm at times to leave out *The* altogether: 'Shakespeare's *Tempest* and *Merchant of Venice* were written at different periods'.

With newspapers and periodicals, some consider *The* part of the title and require it to be in italics. In general, this applies more to the **broadsheets** (*The Times*, *The Independent*, *The Observer*, etc) than the tabloids (*Daily Mirror*, *Daily Express*, etc), and to the more heavyweight magazines (*The Lancet*, *The Musical Times*, etc). There is no reliable rule: the *Financial Times*, for example, has dropped *The* from its title. If you are writing about a newspaper or magazine, it is a courtesy to enquire whether they like *The* included as part of the title.

2 *Stress* in speech can be marked by italics in print: 'Did he really say *that*?'; 'Marry *him*!'

3 It is helpful to pick out a word in italics when attention is being focused on it, but it is often unnecessary and condescending to use italics to stress a point: 'It is not grammatically *wrong* to begin a sentence with *And*' (*italics* for *And* are justified but are laboured for 'wrong').

4 At one time almost any word or phrase that seemed foreign was put in italics. Even now most dictionaries are inconsistent over this. If a foreign word or phrase is considered familiar, it is left in roman, but if it is considered too foreign to be admitted, it goes into italics: ad infinitum but *ad hominem*, bon voyage but *bon vivant*, borscht but *perestroika*, hors-d'oeuvre but *hors de combat*, à la mode but *de rigueur*. (The examples come from *Collins Concise Dictionary Plus*, 1989 edition, but similar ones can be found in nearly all current dictionaries.) The rule is too arbitrary to make much sense, so *The Times* has decided to print all foreign words and expressions, even recent ones appearing in English, in standard roman type. This is a sensible rule in the linguistic internationalism of the 1990s.

its or **it's** It is not unknown for these two forms to be used wrongly. *Its* is the possessive form ('a book has its title on the spine'); *it's* is a **contracted form**, short for 'it is' ('it's a good title for a book').

it stands to reason See (it stands to) **reason**

I've See **contracted forms**

Ivy League *Ivy League* in America has something in common with **Oxbridge** in Britain. It comes from a late 19th-century conference for intercollegiate sports that was known as the Ivy League, and the name became attached to a group of universities in Eastern America, such as Harvard, Yale and Princeton. Although students at these colleges now come from mixed social backgrounds, the prestige of the Ivy League remains, and a certain kind of shirt, with a button-down collar, often worn by high-fliers in the professions and business, is still known as an Ivy League shirt. While the names of the colleges are associated with academic standards, the expression *Ivy League* is more linked with class and social position.

-ization nouns *Nominalization* is the term for the process of forming nouns from a verb or some other word. It has been going on for centuries and never stops. Verbs ending in -*ize* (or -*ise*) are often converted to nouns by the -*ization* (or -*isation*) ending. Many such nouns have their place, of course, but using too many of them is heavy-going. Often simple verbs or phrases are much easier to take in than -*ization* formations: 'the utilization of the new equipment' compared with 'using the new equipment'; 'legalization will take place' compared with 'it will be made legal'; 'hospitalization of patients' compared to 'admitting patients to hospital'.

-ize or **-ise** The classic rule is to use -*ize* when it relates to the Greek *zeta* root: *organize*, *realize*, *trivialize*. . . . An easier rule is to use -*ise* in all cases, for that will never be wrong (with the exception of *capsize*). Most newspapers now follow the second rule: in 1990 *The Times*, one of the last to hold out for the orthodox use of -*ize*, reluctantly gave in to using -*ise* right across the board. So much, commented the editor at the time, Simon Jenkins, for 'Thou whoreson zed! Thou unnecessary letter!', as Kent called it in *King Lear*.

All current British dictionaries follow this principle: where -*ize* is correct, that spelling is usually given first, which indicates preference, with -*ise* shown as an alternative. Many writers and books (including *The Good English Guide*) also prefer to acknowledge the Greek origin of words, where it applies, by using -*ize*. For anyone who wants to maintain this standard, here is a list of the most common words where -*ise* must be used, (and -*ize* is not an alternative): advertise, advise, apprise, arise, chastise, comprise, compromise, despise, devise, disguise, enterprise, excise, exercise, expertise, franchise, improvise, merchandise, supervise, surmise, surprise, televise.

With most other words, -*ise* and -*ize* are alternative spellings.

The -*ize* (or -*ise*) ending is perhaps too readily on

hand for forming new verbs as shorthand for longer phrases. **Hospitalize**, containerize (see **container**), personalize, **privatize** (following the rule given earlier, these can all be spelt *-ise*) are among well-established examples. And more recently, British Rail has decided to *prioritize* certain train services. The process of forming words this way, though convenient, can get out of hand. See also **-ization nouns**; **-yse**

· J ·

Jacuzzi Jacuzzis have become so common in health clubs, that it is often spelt with a small *j*. But it is the name of the inventor of the apparatus that provides massage by powerful jets of water in a bath, and as such is also a registered trademark.

jail See **prison** . . .

jailer or **gaoler** It makes no difference when they're being said, because they are both pronounced the same ('DJAYler'). *Gaoler*, a reminder of an old pronunciation in English, has remained an alternative spelling in Britain, although it is becoming less common. See also **prison** . . .

jam, conserve or **preserve** *Jam* is the normal word for what is spread on bread and butter for tea. *Conserve* is hardly more than a posh name that some jam manufacturers like to put on their decorative labels. A *preserve* can be something different, chunks or sections of fruit preserved by boiling with sugar. In the end, all three are not precisely defined and can be used more or less interchangeably, depending on how grand the tea party. But when it comes to easy money, it has to be *money for jam*.

jam or **jamb** *Jam* is a verb and noun with a number of meanings, such as a fruit conserve (see previous entry), what happens to traffic in the rush hour and (informally) for the kind of mess or predicament we try not to get into. *Jamb* can only be a noun, and is an architectural term for the sidepost of a doorway or window frame.

janitor See **doorkeeper** . . .

Japs There is some argument about whether *Japs* is a racist word for the Japanese. Some dictionaries label it offensive, others give no guidance. Some Japanese, when questioned, say they find it harmless, and it is heard on the BBC. Where there is this uncertainty, it is better to use *Japanese*, both for the descriptive word (a Japanese restaurant) and for the people.

jargon The day of the **Renaissance man**, able to encompass all available knowledge, has long since passed. Now experts in increasingly narrow fields talk to other experts in *jargon*, an esoteric language more or less incomprehensible to other people. Even between experts, jargon is used to cover up half-baked thoughts or to make the commonplace sound important and significant.

Jargon properly used as expert-to-expert language saves a lot of time, and communication would almost break down without it. But good jargon in one place becomes bad jargon in another, when a specialist is speaking to or writing for people who do not hold the key to the language, or when it becomes a built-in habit of avoiding **plain English**. 'Low-dependency care', for example, is effective communication between doctor and nurse, but it could be alarming to the patient, who deserves a clear explanation of what is involved.

The test for *jargon* is to ask if it is useful shorthand that communicates quickly and clearly to the people at the receiving end. It fails the test if it uses complicated words, when simple ones will do, or when the other people do not understand.

jazz or **ragtime** *Jazz*, as a word, emerged in the early years of this century, a slang name to begin with for the ethnic music of African-Americans in the southern states of the US. There is no reliable evidence for the origin of the word. You can take your pick: possibilities are that it was the nickname for a black musician, others say it comes from African dialect, and others are convinced it is connected in some way with the male orgasm (jazz was predominantly male and is arguably the sexyist of all music). In the 20th century, jazz has conquered the world and the same word is used everywhere for a wide range of different styles of music characterized by a compulsive rhythm and various degrees of improvisation.

The name *ragtime* predates jazz, but not by long, for it was the immediate forerunner. It seems to have been first used for lively rhythmic piano–banjo duets, which was taken up by larger musical combinations, developing a pounding *oom-pah-pah* beat. The term is now used for piano music more than anything else, because the pianist Scott Joplin (1868–1917) made ragtime famous with his playing and compositions.

jealous See **envious** . . .

jeans or **denims** *Jean* (in various spellings), as the name of a cotton twill associated with Genoa in Italy, goes back to the 16th century, and by the mid-19th century, *jeans* was being used for trousers made of the material. After World War II, jeans became the standard bisexual teenage uniform, one of the let-it-all-hang-out symbols of the 'swinging 60s'. Before long, designers in Paris were cutting these hard-wearing westerns in a way that turned them into casual high fashion. Since then, the design pendulum has swung between wide 'heave-ho' bell-bottoms, which the manufacturers preferred to call 'flares', and skin-tight trousers you have to lie on the floor to prise yourself into. *Jean-aged* even became a synonym for 'teenaged', although by now jeans have broken through all age barriers.

Denims runs parallel as an alternative word for jeans, but has kept its original meaning as the name of the material (*serge de Nîmes* is the name of a functional cloth made in that town in southern France). So *denims* is also freely used for jackets, skirts, overalls and anything else made from that kind of cloth.

jerry building No one seems to know of a cheap-jack builder named Jerry, so the origin of *jerry building* for badly constructed houses has never been ascer-tained. It goes back to the boom years of the industrial revolution, and has survived into the 1990s for specu-lative building of houses of inferior quality.

jet- The *jet engine*, developed in Britain in the 1930s by Frank Whittle, sprouted a number of verbal combi-nations after it was used to power aircraft in the 1940s. By the 1960s the *jet age* had arrived: the *jet set* had become the media word for the rich and famous, *jetting* around the world. In the early 1960s, *jet lag* came to light, muzziness in the head and disorientation experi-enced after long flights.

Most of the *jet* combinations have become dated by now, as package tours and charter flights have made jetting commonplace. *Jet lag* is the one to survive, as executives and politicians still find themselves going into important meetings, dazed and confused because their bodies and minds are out of synchronization with local time (see **body clock**).

jetsam See flotsam . . .

Jew Whether we like it or not, racism is rooted in language. Some expressions are so much at home that the **racist** aspect has disappeared altogether. To **welsh** on someone, meaning not to pay a debt or carry out a promise, is not even spelt with a capital W. Nor do we feel it is an insult to other nations to talk about French leave, Dutch courage or the luck of the Irish.

While these usages are included in dictionaries with-out comment, Jew as a noun meaning someone who is mean or drives a hard bargain, or as a verb meaning to swindle, is labelled by current dictionaries as 'offen-sive'. In the early 1970s, a Jewish businessman issued a writ against an Oxford dictionary for such disparaging definitions of the word *Jew*, on the grounds it was hurtful to the Jewish people. The editors won the case, claiming it is the duty of lexicographers to record usage. But dictionaries have been careful ever since.

Nevertheless, it is good to report that these deroga-tory uses of *Jew*, which echo the historical role of Jews as moneylenders, have become much rarer, and may eventually become obsolete. When that happens,

lexicographers will be glad to forget them. See also next entry

Jew or **Jewish** There is the story of a man being asked in a radio interview whether he was a Jew, and replying 'Jewish actually'. The implication is that a *Jew* is a believer in Judaism, whereas *Jewish* refers more to the race, its history and outlook. Alan Sugar, who built up the Amstrad computer company, has a similar point of view: according to *The Times*, he maintains he is an atheist, but *Jewish*, explaining, 'That's different, that's a culture, a way of life'. The dividing line, if there is one, is not widely acknowledged. Some Jewish people are less comfortable with the word *Jew* because of its associations, and prefer the descriptive word *Jewish*, as less rabbinical and nationalistic. Others strongly reject any such distinction. For Jewess, see **-ess forms**

jewel in the crown *Jewels in the crown* was an expression used in the 19th century for the colonies of the British Empire. It was revived as the title of a book about India by Paul Scott, and took off when that was adapted as a popular television series in the mid-1980s. Since then any modest achievement has been called a *jewel in the crown*: after the local council elections in May 1990, the *Sunday Times* called three election victories as 'the three brightest jewels in the Tory crown'.

jewellery In Bond Street, home of such lordly diamond merchants as Cartier and Asprey, you will hear 'JEW-el-ry'. In the East End, you might hear 'JEW-ler-y'. Most downmarket of all is 'JOOLry'. *Jewelry* is an accepted but less common alternative spelling in Britain and the standard spelling in America.

Jewess See **-ess forms**

jibe See gibe . . .

jihad This Arabic word (pron: 'djeeHAD') for a struggle, especially one to promote the faith of Islam, came to be the name for a holy war. It had already appeared in English by the late 19th century but was little known until the 1991 Gulf War. Saddam Hussein summoned Muslim fanaticism to his aid by preaching that the war was a jihad, on the grounds that the holy places were in danger because of infidel forces in the region. *Jihad* is a word in the Middle East that stokes up blazing fires.

jingoism In the 17th century, *Jingo!* was an invented word used by conjurers, like 'Hey presto!' In 1888 it came up in a popular music hall song:

We don't want to fight, yet by Jingo! if we do,
We've got the ships, we've got the men, and
   got the money too!

Since then *jingoism* has become a word for sabre-rattling patriotism, the made-in-England equivalent of **chauvinism**. The word was becoming as oldfashioned as the blimpish (see **Colonel Blimp**) exclamation *By Jingo!* but was given a new life during the Falklands war of 1982.

Some people are uneasy with the jingoistic last night of the promenade concerts at the Albert Hall in London, when Union Jacks are flourished and the audience bellows lines such as 'God who made thee mighty . . .', 'Britannia rule the waves'. For many others it would not be the same without James Thomson's exhortation to Britannia and Elgar's *Pomp and Circumstance* setting of A C Benson's swashbuckling verse.

JIT See **just-in-time**

job, **situation**, **occupation**, **position** or **profession** *Job*, for a piece of work, goes back to the 17th century, but by the 20th century it was felt to be a lower-class word: a working man looked for a *job*, whereas a gentleman sought a *position*. Jobs were advertised in newspapers under Situations Vacant. But since the 1960s, *job* has become fashionable. Some newspapers use the heading Top Jobs, which might include advertisements for managing directors; the old employment exchanges have become *job centres*; *job satisfaction* is a fashionable catchphrase with doctors and psychologists engaged in occupational stress studies at all levels; someone is appointed to the job of Chancellor of the Exchequer or Foreign Secretary. In fact, *position* and *situation* have almost become euphemisms for the down-to-earth word *job*.

Many forms have a space for *Occupation*, by which is meant someone's job. They don't like to call it *job* in case it upsets bishops, barristers, professors, etc. Yet *occupation* is such a vague word, suggesting something done to pass the time. Passport applications and some other forms cover themselves by asking *Occupation or Profession*.

Profession used to be a solemn word restricted to occupations that required the profession of an oath (the Hippocratic oath at one time taken by doctors, vows taken on entering holy orders, etc). Now *profession* is hardly more than a synonym for *job*: the advertising profession, the acting profession, 'a shop manager by profession' . . . the 'oldest profession in the world', which topples the word off its prestigious pedestal.

In social conversation, the usual way of asking the question is 'What do you do?', which, although it often gets the required response, could invite all kinds of answers ('I eat, drink, make love . . .').

jobber or **stockbroker** Before the deregulation of the London Stock Exchange in October 1986, a *jobber* was a firm or individual who owned shares and acted as a kind of wholesaler, dealing with *stockbrokers*, who in turn bought and sold for members of the public. But the distinction has disappeared and jobber is simply a less formal name now for a stockbroker. In America, a jobber is a wholesaler in a general sense, buying from manufacturers and selling to retailers, or a pieceworker, or someone who does odd jobs.

jobbery This was originally a Stock Exchange word for crooked dealings. It is not used much now, but when it is, it covers sharp practice in any business.

jobless A media word. No one ever says 'I'm jobless'.

job satisfaction See **job . . .**; **human skills**; **industrial psychology**

jobs for the boys The phrase, a political extension of **old boy network**, means political preferment for supporters of the party. But political parties are too much in the glare of the media to go in for it as much as they used to. The idea survives in honours lists, described by *The Independent* as 'the means by which political parties dispense patronage to industrialists who contribute to their funds, to newspaper editors who slant the news in their favour, to backbench MPs who do not trouble the Whips . . .'. No doubt there are other handouts, and an unpublished survey claims that the government in office can influence the appointment of 40,000 individuals.

job sharing Job sharing no longer means sharing the workload to make it easier for others. It is two or more people sharing the same job, to avoid making one of them redundant, or to suit people who want or need to work part time.

Joe Bloggs and **John Doe** *Joe Bloggs* probably comes from a sympathetic nickname for a foot-soldier in the British army, and is now used in Britain for any ordinary, anonymous man, the man-in-the-street. *John Doe* is an equivalent name in America: it started as the name used in legal proceedings for an unidentified person and is now extended for what an American might call 'any ordinary guy'. *Jane Doe* is sometimes used for women.

jogging There is nothing new about the word. The verb *jog* appeared in Langland's *Piers Plowman*, written in the second half of the 14th century. People have been jogging on horses for centuries, and by the early 1700s they were called *joggers*. But the words were given a new meaning with the keep-fit craze of the 1960s that spread throughout the world. They jog in Central Park, Hyde Park, on Hampstead Heath, round the Villa Borghese in Rome and in the Parc Monceau in Paris, where the French have the same word for it – *le jogging*.

John Doe See **Joe Bloggs . . .**

John Thomas This old-fashioned name for a penis dates from the mid-19th century. It was one of the expressions that shocked people so much in D H Lawrence's *Lady Chatterley's Lover*. With the full frontal exposure of the 1990s, it sounds quaintly polite.

joint or **common** They often mean the same thing, which is something shared by two or more people. *Joint* is the word preferred in law, finance and administration: people have joint bank accounts, undertake joint ventures, apply for a joint mortgage.... *Common* tends to be the more abstract word: people have a common aim, a common purpose, common point of view. See also **common** or **mutual**

joint and several If you are sharing a responsibility with other people, this is not a phrase to treat lightly if it appears in the written agreement. It carries with it the legal weight of making you responsible, as one individual, for the total liability should the other parties fail for any reason to meet their obligations. Where *joint and several* is written into a contract, there is no safety in numbers.

join together Linguistic nit-pickers object to this combination, because *join* on its own means bringing people or objects *together*. But the phrase has a certain reassuring ring to it, probably because of the marriage service in The Book of Common Prayer: 'Those whom God hath joined together let no man put asunder'. The same applies to *link together*.

jollification or **jollity** Both words mean that people are making merry, eating and drinking. If anything, *jollification* suggests heavy drinking and raucousness, but perhaps this is putting too fine a point on it, since *jollity* hardly indicates restraint.

Jones We occasionally need a plural form of the name *Jones*, especially if we live in Wales. It is considered preferable to have the *Joneses* to dinner rather than the 'Jones'. See also **names ending in *s* . . .**

journal See **diary** . . .

journalese The word dates from the 1880s, when it was in fact used in a journal (the *Pall Mall Gazette*). Journalese can be applied to language used in all the media: it arises from the pressure on reporters to write stories in a hurry and falling back on **clichés** or exaggeration to attract attention: 'Chancellor slashes taxes', 'Jobless figures soar', 'Shares plummet'.... The readers of popular newspapers expect and require the flashy catchphrases of journalese, as these are familiar and easy to take in without effort. It is hard for journalism to be literature: as long ago as 1710, when life was slower and quieter, Steele and Addison acknowledged in *The Tatler*, 'The great art . . . is to catch the reader's attention'. See also **headlines**

judge See **adjudge** . . .

judgement or **judgment** Either will do but *judgement* is taking over as the more usual spelling in Britain, with *judgment* as standard spelling in America. In law and courtroom practice, the traditional spelling has been *judgment*. Although this is not always adhered to now, *judgment* remains the spelling for many lawyers and is used even in recent legal books.

judgemental While on the surface *judgemental* (less commonly spelt *judgmental*) means using the power of judgement, it has come, particularly since the 1960s, to have the pejorative meaning of condemnation based on prejudice. If we say someone is judgemental about a situation or other people's behaviour, we are probably implying an unhelpful holier-than-thou attitude, rather than an objective appraisal.

jump-start A *jump-start* is starting a motor car by pushing it, or using jump-leads connected to the battery of another car. The extended use in the 1990s, not yet picked up by all dictionaries, is to give a boost to business activities. British Airways spoke of giving a jump-start to the air travel market by cutting transatlantic fares, and during recessions chancellors of the exchequer try to give a jump-start to the economy. *Kick-start* (the kick-down device on a motor cycle to start the engine) is used in the same way. Boris Yeltsin was described in *The Listener* as giving a 'kick-start to the engine of change' in Russia.

Jungian See **Freudian** . . .

junk- This word, which may have been connected with the Chinese name for a basic type of sailing boat, and at one time meant old rope (as in 'money for old rope'), came in the early 20th century to mean rubbish. Since World War II it has become a prefix for anything that in reality is worthless: **junk bond**, **junk food**, junk mail, etc.

junk bond An investment term that arose in Wall Street in the late 1970s. *Bonds* is the usual word in America for what is called loan stock in Britain. When a high rate of interest is offered, but the security of the loan is uncertain because the assets of the company issuing the bond may turn out to be inadequate, investment banks call them *junk bonds*. The term can be misleading, because it does not always mean that the bonds are worthless. Far from it in some cases, because there are junk bonds issued by well-established companies, where the risk involved is very small in comparison with the high rate of return.

junk food An indeterminate term for food that contains more artificial colouring, synthetic flavours and chemical preservatives than nutritional value. See also **additives**

junkie Originally American slang in the 1920s for a drug addict, *junkie* is now just as familiar in Britain. It is apparently wrong to restrict the word any longer to the fringe of an underworld society: Dr Graham Lucas, as a consultant psychiatrist at King's College Hospital, London, uses *junkie* about someone who might be 'that neat man with his 2.4 children, his 2.4 Jag and his 2.4 acres . . . it could be the consultant surgeon as well as the porter'.

junk mail See **direct mail**

jurist or **juror** The two words are completely different. A *juror* is a member of a jury. A *jurist* is a rather academic word in Britain for a legal scholar, but an everyday word in America for an expert in law, or for a judge or a **lawyer**.

(the) **jury *is*** or ***are*** See **collective words**

(the) **jury is out** Apart from the literal meaning of the expression for a jury that has retired to consider its verdict, the phrase is becoming increasingly used in any context to mean that a final assessment cannot yet be made: 'the jury is out over the quality of this year's vintage in Bordeaux'.

just There are three points:

1 *Just not* and *not just* can be confusing. They mean different things. 'She's just not experienced enough' means she almost has enough experience but perhaps not quite enough. *Not just* is the equivalent of *not only*. To write or say 'she's not just experienced enough . . .' requires a further positive comment: 'she's not just experienced enough, she's also available immediately'.

2 Some people feel that 'we just had dinner', 'the post just arrived' . . . is American usage, and that British English requires 'we *have just had* dinner', 'the post *has just* arrived'. But the American form is now so common in Britain, that it is unreasonable to object to it, except in formal contexts.

3 Television and radio interviewers often put *just* at the beginning of a question to make it sharper. The difference between 'What do you mean by that?' and 'Just what do you mean by that?' is that the second question is more aggressive, or at least demands a less evasive answer.

justify *Justify* is a term used in printing and word-processing. It is lining up a block of text so that the margin on one side or on both sides is even. An uneven margin is *unjustified* or 'ragged'.

just-in-time This is an up-to-date management term for a system of production intended to encourage a smooth flow of work through a factory by reducing bottlenecks and unwieldy inventories. It was first developed in Japan and aims to keep the perfect balance between stocks maintained, deliveries by suppliers and small batches of production units. Those really in the know refer to it as JIT.

juvenile or **puerile** The meanings of the two words overlap, as either can be a synonym for 'childish': 'that's a juvenile (or puerile) attitude'. But *juvenile* can also be a harmless, if rather formal, alternative to the word 'young': 'the juvenile section of a library'.

· K ·

K or **grand** *Grand*, for a thousand dollars, originated in the American underworld of the early 1900s. Later we heard it in American gangster films, and after World War II it became the smart word to use for £1000 among go-getting advertising executives in Britain: 'We'll spend a hundred grand on the campaign'. It is dated idiom now, as smart business talk in the 1990s is European, taking up the metric K, the abbreviation for *kilo*: executives may ask for a salary of 60K (£60,000) or talk about a 500K (£500,000) advertising campaign. The expression is not used much other than for salaries and budgets. Since the recession of the early 1990s, there has been a tendency to shift back to rows of noughts, perhaps because it makes thousands look like thousands. See also **money**

Kabinett See appellation controlée

Kafkaesque People use *Kafkaesque* (pron: 'kafke(r)ESK') without ever having read a word of *The Trial*, *Metamorphosis* or *America*, novels by Franz Kafka (1883–1924), the German novelist of Czech origin. The word is used for a nightmarish situation in which the individual is threatened and helpless, swept along, lonely and bewildered, by the impersonal power of conformity to bureaucratic society. The poet, John Tessimond, encapsulated the feeling in the title of a book of his poems, *Voices in a giant city*, and in the lines:

I am the man too busy with living to live . . .
I am the led, the easily-fed,
The tool, the not-quite fool . . .

Kafkaesque is a valuable word at the present time to describe the sense of loss of identity in a world in which we see, on television screens, everything that is going on, but have a feeling of knowing nothing, a world that seems at the same time inevitable and crazy.

kamikaze This was the name (literally 'divine wind') for the Japanese 'suicide pilots' in World War II who deliberately crashed their aircraft on to enemy ships. You hear it used for any kind of reckless irresponsible decision: 'To spend so much on the scheme would be kamikaze'. (Pron: 'kamiKAHzy'.)

Kampuchea or **Cambodia** See foreign place-names

kangaroo *Kangaroo court*, an American (rather than Australian) expression from the mid-1800s, is trial by a group of people, with no proper constitution or legal authority, of anyone who steps out of line with what is required. No one seems to know why the name of these endearing long-eared jumping animals from **down under** came to be used. More logically, *kangaroos* is a Stock Exchange expression heard in Britain for shares in one of the Australian land, mining or tobacco companies.

kerb See **curb** . . .

kerb-crawling *Kerb-crawling* seems to have begun as a slang expression in the late 1940s for men driving a car slowly near the kerb and soliciting women. It has passed into standard English, used in the House of Commons in 1990 in connection with one of the provisions of a proposed Sexual Offences bill.

ketchup Long before Heinz cornered the word, *ketchup* had already appeared by the early 18th century, apparently adapted from a Chinese word. The alternative word *catchup* was also in use at the time, but is rarely heard now (but the variant *catsup* often occurs in America).

keyboard or **keypad** *Keyboard* is the standard word for the input control buttons of a computer. *Keypad* is used for a smaller, sometimes handheld, adaptation of a keyboard, or the panel of buttons on telephones. Typewriters also have keyboards and so do pianos.

Keynes and **Keynesian** John Maynard Keynes (1883–1946), the British economist, and *Keynesian* theories are often referred to as an argument against **monetarist** practice. It's a gaffe to say 'Keenz', instead of 'Kaynz', but note that Milton Keynes, the new town in north Buckinghamshire, is pronounced 'Keenz'.

kibbutz *Kibbutz*, the Israeli name for a cooperative farming settlement run on communal principles, is a modern Hebrew word, and the plural is *kibbutzim* (pron: 'kiBUTzim').

kick-start See **jump-start**

kids There are examples of *kid* being used for a child as far back as the early 1700s, but the *OED* suggests it was considered low-class slang until the 19th century, when it became used more generally. Yet somehow it has never been upgraded to standard English, and some of the latest dictionaries still write it down as slang.

kilobyte (K) See byte

kilometre 'SpeeDOMeter', 'baROMeter', so why not '*kiLOMetre*'? The answer is 'KILometre' keeps it in line with 'MILLimetre', 'CENTimetre', 'KILogram'. But most people say 'kiLOMetre' in America, and that pronunciation is becoming so common in Britain that recent dictionaries show it as an alternative. For the time being, it's better to keep to the traditional British pronunciation 'KILometre'. No stop is needed after the abbreviation (km, for singular and plural) and note American spellings kilometer, millimeter, etc. See also **metric**

kind or **sort** These two words present three problems:

  1 Both words are clearly singular, so it should be '*this* kind of argument', '*that* sort of person'. . . . But even good writers slip into phrases, such as '*those* kind of arguments . . .', '*these* sort of people'. . . . All that can be said is that, in writing at least, that kind of thing is wrong.

  2 It is unnecessary, and considered bad usage, to follow *a kind of* and *a sort of* by an additional *a* (a kind of a dinner, a sort of a novel), although in speaking, the extra *a* can change the meaning altogether. Before you start dinner, it is not unreasonable to ask 'What kind of dinner is this?' Once you have eaten it, you may feel like asking 'What kind of a dinner is this?', suggesting the meal hardly lived up to the name.

  3 In speech, *kind of* is too often allowed to degenerate into 'kinda'.

kinship *Kin*, an ancient word for family or race going back to Old English, meant a relationship by blood, including in a wider sense, relationships based on marriage (hence 'next of kin'). *Kinship* implies the same familial relationship, but the word is now used more freely about any relationship with other people based on a similarity of interests, or simply sharing the human situation: 'Let us show our kinship with those who are suffering from hunger and disease by donating as much as we can afford'.

kir At one time, a kir (pron: 'keer') was an aperitif only heard of in the South of France. But now kirs are served in wine bars everywhere, on patios in Pimlico, in drawing-rooms in Dulwich, and the word has passed effortlessly into English. In the parish church of Alesie in Burgundy there is a bust of Canon Felix Kir, who died as recently as 1968, and is said to have invented this combination of crème de cassis (blackcurrant liqueur) and dry white wine.

KISS This abbreviation for an adage used in computing could well be applied in many other contexts. It means keep it simple stupid.

kitbag See **backpack** . . .

kitchen cabinet Someone in the US used the expression *kitchen cabinet* back in the 1830s for backstage influential advisers to the President. And soon after it was used in the same way in British politics. It is still a useful, slightly edgy term: Harold Wilson's *kitchen cabinet* was much talked about, and *The Times* described Judith Chaplin, who 'advised on speeches, tours and potential political **banana skins**' as 'part of Mr Major's kitchen cabinet'.

kitsch A word, borrowed from German, used in art galleries about sentimental or pretentious paintings, etc that have no real quality or feeling. More recently, it is also used about novels, poetry and films that pretend to be profound but are really aiming at popular success. Debatable taste in design is also accused of being kitsch, and there are people who find it fashionable to buy something for that very reason. Terence Conran, who developed the Habitat style in the 1970s, with simple white porcelain pots and plain pine furniture, has been called the *kitsch-killer*. (Pron: 'kitch'.)

knapsack See **backpack** . . .

knee-jerk Most of us are familiar with this medical test of our reactions, a light blow on the tendon just below the knee that produces an involuntary kick. *Knee-jerk reaction* became a vivid and popular media expression in the 1980s for any automatic, unthinking response. Homosexuality, Aids, Europeanism, the ordination of women, and even English grammar and usage are some of the issues that give rise to knee-jerk bigotry, a reaction that is usually not thought through clearly and fairly. See also **reflex**

kneeled or **knelt** *Knelt* is the more usual past form in Britain, *kneeled* in America. But both forms are used in both countries.

Knesset With the ever-present threat to world peace from the explosive political situation in the Middle East, *Knesset* occurs more and more often in the news. It comes from a modern Hebrew word meaning a gathering and is the name of the Israeli parliament. This is a single chamber of 120 members, who are elected for four years. The K is sounded: 'KNESSit'.

knickerbockers or **plus-fours** See next entry

knickers The origin of the word is curious. George Cruikshank, who illustrated some of Dickens' books, did the illustrations for Washington Irving's *A History of New York*, showing men wearing Dutch baggy trousers, known as *knickerbockers*, from the

Dutch name. *Knickers* is still the word in America for men's loose-fitting breeches, gathered below the knee, which in the 20th century became known in Britain as *plus-fours*, because they came down four inches below the knee. By the late 19th century, Victorian ladies were recommended to wear flannel *knickers* in the winter, instead of a petticoat: the word had come to be used in Britain, but not in America, for women's underpants. Later, knickers became risqué with the arrival of wide-bottomed *French knickers*.

After World War II, knickers was put on the shelf alongside **bloomers**, as women bought pants, panties or briefs (see **boxers . . .**). And now, in the 1990s, the word is making a comeback as a trendy word for women's pants or briefs: '. . . at a Buckingham Palace garden party, at the women's caucus of Militant in Liverpool, at a chocolate factory in York or a nurse's hostel in Bristol – you can say with a conviction bordering on certainty that one in three of the women present is wearing M & S knickers' (*The Independent*, 28.7.1991).

knight- The *knight-* combinations are not required often outside heraldry and history books. The *-s* of the plural forms is added to the word *knight*: knights bachelor, knights errant, Knights Templar. . . .

knocking copy *Knocking copy* is a familiar term in advertising agencies. It means advertising that runs down a competitive product. For years this was regarded as unethical, and prohibited by self-imposed regulations in the advertising business. But now advertisements openly compare one product with another brand, particularly comparing the advantages of one make of motor car over other named makes. There is nothing new about knocking copy in political campaigns, especially in the build-up to elections. The only difference is that the knocking becomes harder and more strident.

knock-on effect A *knock-on effect* has a similar meaning to **chain reaction**, except that the follow-on effects are secondary and indirect. It is often used in political and economic contexts, where an action produces a series of cumulative effects: 'High interest rates resulted in many more businesses going into liquidation, with the knock-on effect of increased unemployment'. The expression is not slang, as some people believe, and is treated as standard English by current dictionaries.

knock up To *knock up* someone in Britain usually means to wake them up by banging on the door. Americans, who are familiar with the British meaning, sometimes use it as a **double entendre**, because in America the usual meaning is slang for making a woman pregnant.

knot Only landlubbers would ever dream of saying 'knots per hour', for *knots*, the standard way of defining the speed of ships, already means nautical miles *per hour*. It arose from the old method of measuring speed at sea by dropping a knotted line from the bows of a ship and counting the seconds as the knots pass the stern. At one time, the speed of aircraft was also given in knots, but miles per hour is now standard. (A nautical mile is 1852 metres or about 2025 yards.)

know-how or **savoir faire** *Know-how* isn't as modern as it might seem: it was already being used in America during the first half of the 19th century and had appeared in British English by the end of that century. But it became current after World War II, and has been regarded as standard English by dictionaries for some years. *Know-how* is the term for a blend of knowledge, ability, experience and lessons learned by trial and error. It is used particularly in practical, business and technical applications. *Savoir faire* (literally 'to know how to do') is more sophisticated, and refers to the ability to handle any situation that comes up, especially social situations, from speaking to the Queen, to dealing with an awe-inspiring wine waiter at the Tour d'Argent.

American know-how had a special meaning: it was a supremely confident expression used in America to describe their overwhelming superiority in business and production. The expression tip-toed out of the vocabulary in the 1960s or 70s, when Japanese technology started to dominate the world.

kosher This Yiddish word, derived from Hebrew, is used for food conforming to Jewish dietary laws. In New York, *kosher* has long had an extended use, and not only by Jewish people, for something that is legitimate or authentic: a kosher deal is a straightforward arrangement, a kosher Picasso is properly authenticated. Show business brought this use of *kosher* to Britain, where most dictionaries now include it, showing both the formal and extended meaning. Leo Rosten, whose knowledge of such matters is undeniably kosher, considers the word to be 'the most resourceful Yiddish word in the English language' (*The Joys of Yiddish*). See also **halal**

Kremlinology The cataclysmic breakup at the end of 1991 of the old Soviet empire has given a number of words unexpected retirement. *Kremlinology* used to denote the study of the **Byzantine** machinations of Soviet politics, for the Kremlin in Moscow contained within its 15th-century walls the headquarters of the USSR government. Academics and other experts in Soviet affairs, who had basked in the splendour of the title, *Kremlinologists*, have to look round for a new name, if they too are not to become redundant. See also **Russian . . .**

kudos To say 'she hasn't received the kudos that *are* her due' shows ignorance that *kudos* is a singular Greek word meaning fame or glory. It has to be '. . . the kudos that *is* her due'. A few dictionaries still insist on classifying *kudos* as 'colloquial', although it has been in English at least since Coleridge used it in the late 18th century, and was used by Disraeli and Darwin. It is reasonable to regard it as standard English. 'KOOdos', closer to the Greek pronunciation, is acceptable in English, but 'KYOOdos' is considered preferable.

· L ·

-l- or -ll- The basic rule is that words ending in *-l* double the *l* when endings such as *-ed*, *-ing*, *-er* are added. In American English, the single *-l-* is usually retained. For examples of both, see **doubling final letter** . . .

There are some exceptions. For example, the verbs *appal* and *distil*, correctly spelt with one *-l* in British English, are *apall* and *distill* in America, so the other forms on both sides of the Atlantic are appalled, appalling and distilled, distilling. See also entries for **install**; **fulfil**

labels Labels are stuck or tied on to things to identify them. Since the mid-19th century, the extended use has been to attach labels to people and concepts -- not real labels of course, but preconceived, automatic responses. The use of the word *label* in this way has increased a great deal since World War II, and has become a term for prejudice or **knee-jerk** reactions. Feminists, homosexuals, lesbians, blacks, the police, to take some examples, have many different characteristics and qualities as individuals, but the moment we attach, in our minds, a *label* to one of those groups, we direct an indiscriminating narrow-mindedness towards it. Labels are properly used for baggage and other objects, but society needs to be constantly on guard against attaching them to people.

'laBORatory' or 'LABoratory' The correct pronunciation in British English used to put the stress on the first syllable, but the long flight of unaccented syllables that followed is difficult to say, so now the accepted way is to stress the second syllable: 'LaBORatory'.

labourer See workman . . .

labour-intensive Before the Industrial Revolution, this descriptive term did not exist, because everything was *labour-intensive*, that is it required the time and energy of men and women. Now the term singles out industries or operations that cannot be done by machines, but require a good deal of human involvement.

Labour or Socialist Party The *Labour Party* has been the official name of the political party since 1906. For a long period, many members of the party called themselves *Socialists*, since they believed in a social system based on nationalization and to a greater

or lesser extent on the ideas of Marx and Engels. As the historical meaning of *socialism* became less relevant, and the leading members of the party bought their suits from the same kind of tailors as the Conservatives, the term *Socialist* was used less and less. During the election campaign of 1992, the Labour Party never spoke about socialist principles, and the word was used mostly by Conservatives as an alarmist echo of the origins of the Labour Party.

It is rare now to hear anyone call the British Labour Party the *Socialist Party*. Some trade unionists continue to talk about socialists and socialism, but the official party line is to sport a red rose in well-cut lapels, and refer to *Labour* policies.

labour room See **delivery room** . . .

lad Do we say to a young man who is annoying us: 'Now look here, my lad!'? Do we still describe a high-spirited man as 'Quite a lad'? If we do, then we sound elderly. *Lad* is not used much any more, except possibly as a defiant expression of male togetherness: 'Having a few jars with the lads'. And like the word **lass**, *lad* is still often heard in the North of England.

lady, woman or female In the 1990s, the word *lady* has uncertain status. The Queen still has ladies-in-waiting, and a woman MP is on occasions addressed as 'the honourable lady'. There are cleaning ladies and tea ladies, but women doctors and women barristers. Wimbledon still calls it *ladies'* tennis, which seems curiously out of place for Steffi Graf's power on the Centre Court. In a restaurant, when a waiter asks 'Who's the duck for?', a man might answer rather lamely 'It's for the lady', because he doesn't know what else to say. It still feels right to call a woman who is very old, 'an old lady', because 'an old woman' sounds ungracious. Apart from those situations and a few others, most of us are more comfortable now talking about 'the woman next door', 'an interesting woman', just as D H Lawrence called his novel, *Women in Love*.

Professional women are usually relaxed about using *woman* to describe themselves. We hear about 'The Woman of the Year', and the BBC called a television series about Flora Robson, Janet Vaughan, Barbara Wootton and others 'Women of our Century'. Back in 1973, Margaret Thatcher made the mistake of the century, when she said 'I don't think there will be a *woman* prime minister in my lifetime'.

It is clear by now that the old 13th-century word

237

lady has got itself into a mess. Nor is *female* a safe alternative, since as a noun it may carry with it a derogatory implication, especially when used by a man: 'So I said to this *female* . . .'. This does not extend to *female* as a descriptive word: a conference in London had the title 'Targeting the Female Buyer', And there are some publications that prefer *female* to *woman*, as in 'female doctors', 'female MPs'. . . .

The whole situation is much easier in America, where there's a relaxed tendency to use *ladies* for all women, without any uneasiness: 'Have a nice day, lady', 'A whole lot of crazy ladies are in charge', and Gershwin's song, *Lady, be good*! Perhaps this is encouraging a comeback of the word in Britain, at least in a particular sense. For even feminists like to use *lady* in such contexts as 'she's a very clever lady'.

This entry is more a report on a linguistic dilemma, than a set of rules. Much of the time, we hover between offending a 'lady' by calling her a *woman*, or sounding genteel, or even ridiculous sometimes, by saying *lady*. We have to decide for ourselves when to use *lady*, *woman* or *female*, and hope not to upset anybody. See also **girl**

Lady Mayor See mayor . . .

lager lout It means a young person who is a nuisance because of too much to drink, and neatly combines *lager* from the German 'lagerbier', a beer brewed so that it will keep, with *lout*, a 16th-century word that may well go back to Old English.

laid With **desktop publishing**, many of us have to be familiar with arcane printing terms. *Laid* is an old word used in papermaking: it comes from wires being 'laid' across a frame, which leave a watermark pattern of parallel lines. Few people know the origin of the term, and generally laid paper now simply means a good-quality paper.

laid-back See cool . . .

laissez-faire The expression (pron: 'lessay-FAIR') that belonged to classical economics of the 19th century is not used much in the 1990s, because it has acquired a derogatory undertone of the rich getting richer at the expense of the poor. The theory behind *laissez-faire* is that the State should not interfere in economic affairs, because left alone the economy finds its own peak of efficiency. Current expressions that lean in the same direction are **market economy** and **market forces**. Outside economics, *laissez-faire* is used in a general way about attitudes, again usually with a derogatory implication of not exercising proper control.

lame duck In the 19th century, a lame duck was appropriately a damaged ship at sea. Since then it has been used in less logical ways, on the Stock Exchange for a member who cannot meet commitments, for someone who is physically handicapped or does not pull their weight at work. More recently, a *lame duck*

company is one that does not make a contribution to profits of a group. The most common use in politics now is for a business that cannot balance its books and relies on government subsidy to keep going.

'LAMentable' or 'laMENTable' Stress on the first syllable ('LAMentable') is the only pronunciation considered correct.

laminate A laminate, in printing and in **desktop publishing**, is paper coated with a thin layer of plastic, which makes it stronger and gives it a glossy finish.

landscape Not everyone is sure what *landscape* means when it is used about a format in art, photography or printing. Because the eye sees the countryside that way, a painting of a landscape is nearly always wider from left to right than the height from top to bottom. From this, *landscape* has come to be used for any painting, photograph, book, printing of illustrations or tables, where the width is greater than the height. The American term, perhaps more self-evident in meaning but less picturesque, is *horizontal format*. The opposite of *landscape* is *portrait*.

landslide Landslide has become the first **cliché** that comes to hand for commentators on elections. The moment a party looks like gaining a modest number of seats, headlines tell us 'it's heading for a landslide'. A *landslide* is properly the falling away of a great mass of land. It is a cataclysmic event, and if the word is to be used about elections, it should at least be reserved for a party winning an overwhelming majority, no less.

langouste and **langoustine** See crayfish . . .

language or **tongue** With exception of the expression *mother tongue*, the use of the word *tongue* for *language* is archaic and biblical ('Though I speak with the tongues of men and of angels . . .', *Corinthians*). To say, for example, 'they were speaking a strange tongue' is literary to the point of affectation. In passing, it is interesting that French uses 'la langue' as the everyday word for the organ in the mouth and also for *language*.

language laboratory The term was devised in the 1940s, using the word *laboratory* as it is used in schools, for a room where science subjects are taught. A *language laboratory* is a room where foreign languages are taught, using tape recorders which the teacher can plug into to check on a student's progress.

languid or **limpid** More than one novelist has written 'she raised a limpid hand', or some other phrase misusing the word. The writer intended *languid*, the word for feeble or limp. *Limpid* is a more attractive word, used mostly about water or eyes when they are clear and free from muddiness: a pool can be limpid, so can innocent blue eyes. The word is also used, by extension, of a literary style that flows effortlessly.

lapse See elapse . . .

laptop First came the **desktop** computer, designed to be used by one person, small enough to be kept on a desk. Then **microchips** enabled computers to be made even smaller and battery-powered, carried in a briefcase and used on trains and planes. More often than not, these are simply called *laptops*.

larceny See fraud . . .

laser The word was devised at the beginning of the 1960s for a new invention that harnessed a powerful concentration of the energy of light. It has so many applications now, from providing high-quality **printouts** from computers, in surgery, reading **barcodes** in supermarkets, to playing **compact discs** and giving audiences a thrilling light show at rock concerts. It is almost forgotten that the word is an **acronym** for light amplification of stimulated emission of radiation.

lass This old dialectal word from the North of England, going back to the 13th century, was at one time being used more freely in the south of the country. It became familiar through Gracie Fields (1898–1979) calling herself 'a lass from Lancashire'. It is still current in everyday speech in the North, but in the South has a poetic or archaic ring ('It was a lover and his lass . . .', *As You Like It*, Act V Sc iii).

last or **first** See **former or latter**

last or **lastly** Much of the entry on **first or firstly** applies to *last* or *lastly*. Some people feel that *lastly* is grammatically correct ('. . . and lastly I have this to say. . . .'), but this is arguable, and *last* is sharper and more direct. After all, no one ever says 'lastly but not leastly'.

last or **latest** There are times when we should choose carefully between *last* and *latest*: 'This is my last word on the subject' means the subject is now closed, whereas 'This is my latest word on the subject' leaves the door open for further thoughts. But it is common to use *last* to mean the most recent: 'last year' is an everyday expression, not a warning of an approaching apocalypse, and Oscar Hammerstein expected to see Paris again, when he wrote 'The Last Time I Saw Paris'.

last or **latter** See **former or latter**

latchkey children Social workers use this expression for children who let themselves into an empty house when they come back from school, because their parents are out at work.

late See ex- . . .

lateral and **vertical thinking** The term and concept *lateral thinking* were originated by Edward de Bono in 1966, since when it has entered a number of dictionaries. The principle behind it is that when we look at a problem, we are often stuck at a traditional point of departure. *Lateral thinking* moves that point sideways, which encourages a new approach. Edward de Bono gives, as an example, a child pulling the decorations off a Christmas tree. His father is about to put the child in a playpen, when his wife suggests putting the playpen round the tree, that is keeping the tree away from the child, rather than the other way round. *Vertical thinking* has a fixed starting point, proceeding from A to B to C, etc following a predetermined line. For this reason, *vertical thinking* is a term sometimes used to criticize an approach that is rigid and inflexible.

latest or **last** See last . . .

Latin As well as referring to the language of ancient Rome (named after Latium, the plain near that city), *Latin* is used to identify people from different nations by the language they speak. If that language has its roots in Latin, the people are *Latins*. These include French, Italians, Spanish and Portuguese. Hence *Latin America*, the countries of Central and South America where so-called Latin languages, Spanish or Portuguese, are spoken. Although Latins have different national characteristics, they are often lumped together, as they were in the alliterative title of a book claiming to destroy a popular belief, *Latins are Lousy Lovers*.

Latinisms A *Latinism* is one of the many traditional phrases in Latin that are long-established in English, especially in law and medicine, such as *ultra vires* (beyond someone's legal powers), *ipso facto* (by the very act), *sub judice* (literally 'under a judge', meaning under consideration by a court). Many people who use Latinisms have long since forgotten the Latin they learned at school, if they learned any at all. They have simply fastened on to certain Latin tags, which they trot out on occasions, usually to impress people. But other than for lawyers, for whom many Latin expressions are woven into the fabric of the law itself, Latinisms have become more often than not out of place and pedantic. See also **foreign words and phrases**

Latino or **Hispanic** *Hispanic* used to be the usual word in America for a Latin-American inhabitant of the US. But now *Latino* is the popular name ('the Latino population of San Antonio'). British dictionaries are slow to catch up with *Latino*, although it's been in use in America for some years. Generally *Latino* carries no derogatory or racist suggestion.

Latin roots There are two sources for most English words that derive from Latin. The Romans were imperialists and administrators, and their conquests carried their language with them, displacing the native languages of the countries they invaded. Britain did not suffer this linguistic takeover, because the islands were too remote and unattractive for the Roman overlords to want to assimilate into. So English remained a Germanic language, which absorbed only a few ecclesiastical Latin words.

In 1066, the Norman Conquest changed that. Not that it happened right away. For nearly two hundred years, the indigenous language existed alongside Norman French, the language of the conquerors. But by the 14th century, social integration was having a linguistic effect and the native language was taking on board vast shiploads of new words, mostly derived from Latin. The works of Chaucer, written in the second half of the 14th century, are far more comprehensible to the present-day reader than, for example, the great Old English epic *Beowulf*, preserved in a late 10th-century manuscript.

The second process of Latinization of English was the rise of classical scholarship with the Renaissance, that gigantic transition in the mainstream of European thought between the 14th and 17th centuries. This latter process has never come to an end, as *Latin roots* continue to be called on for many new word formations, from *computer* (Latin 'computare', to reckon up) to *nuclear* (Latin 'nucleus', a nut or a kernel). The number of Latinate words in English is constantly increasing, so that probably half the words in a current English dictionary have traces of Latin origin.

latter See former . . .

laudable or **laudatory** These are rather grandiloquent words, but if they are to be used, they should not be mixed up. Someone or something that is *laudable* is praiseworthy ('it was a laudable suggestion'). Only a form of words expressing praise can be *laudatory* (pron: 'LAWDitery): 'Her laudatory speech singled out each of the members for praise'.

laundering It was in the early 1970s that *laundering* was used about money. Vast sums made illegally out of drugs or by robbing banks are fed into the international money markets through a number of bank accounts, so that the money comes out 'clean', with less risk of questions being asked.

lavatory, **toilet** or **loo** Earlier this century, *WC* (a Victorian euphemism for the already euphemistic *water-closet*) and *urinal* were words in common use. They would seem quaint now, and there's even a chance they would not be understood. Then *lavatory* (a word that goes back to the 14th century for a vessel used for washing) took over. It is still often heard, although used more by older people. *Toilet*, at one time considered middle-class prudery, has become the standard formal word (with *toilet* roll and *toilet* paper): when there was a debate on the subject this decade in the House of Lords, the noble peers settled for '*toilet* facilities'.

Loo began as an upper-class expression and soon spread like wildfire. Its derivation is obscure: some link it to the French 'l'eau' (water), others with

'Waterloo', as a jocular form of *water-closet*. However it began, *loo* is undoubtedly the most common informal word now in use.

Cloakroom is imprecise, because it might lead you to a place where you can only leave your coat; *powder-room*, although heard in the grandest hotels as well as in dancehalls, is a coy euphemism, and *little boys'* (or *girls'*) *room* makes you cringe. In America, the usual word in public places is *rest room* (a misnomer, as the writer Bel Mooney complained, when someone in Chicago banged on the door, shouting 'You finished, lady?').

law and order The expression is very much in use among politicians in the 1990s, especially in an election campaign. It is intended to cover the preservation of conformity to law, with reducing the number of crimes, such as theft and violence, by providing adequate funds for the police, and ensuring proper penalties are meted out to offenders. The breakdown of *law and order* is a threat to society and ultimately to civilization. See also **intrusive *r* sound**

lawful or **legal** *Lawful* is a general word meaning within the law, that is in accordance with what is recognized by the law, as against an act that is a breach of the law. *Legal* is a more precise word for following the specific requirements of the law. A procedure or a request may be *lawful* because it is based on *legal* principles or rights which could be quoted in court.

lawyer or **solicitor** *Lawyer* is a general word that covers **barristers** (or advocates in Scotland) and *solicitors*. Usually if someone tells you they're a *lawyer*, it's more likely to mean a solicitor, since barristers and advocates would make a point of using those specific titles. *Lawyer* may become an increasingly useful word in Britain if, as is predicted, there will be in the future less of a division between the Bar and firms of solicitors.

In America, *lawyer* is another word for an **attorney**, which corresponds in some ways to a solicitor in Britain.

lay or **lie** It is easy to be uncertain about which of the different forms to use. When *lay* or *lie* refers to people, the following forms are correct: 'if you are tired, *lie* down' (present) . . . 'yesterday she was tired and *lay* down' (past) . . . 'he has *lain* in bed all day' (past form after *has* or *have*) . . . 'the ship *lay* at anchor for a week' (ships take the same forms as people).

When they concern objects (other than ships), the forms are different: 'it is fragile so please *lay* it down carefully' (present) . . . 'because it was fragile, he *laid* it down carefully' (past) . . . 'he has already *laid* it down' (past form after *has* or *have*).

The most common mistake: 'Go and lay down', 'Tell her to lay down'. . . . Use *lie* in such sentences (see first example above).

lay off The standard use of *lay off* is in industry, when it covers discharging workers because production has to be temporarily suspended for reasons other than a dispute with the workforce. This could be a shortage of supplies or labour disputes in other companies that affect the chain of supply. As a noun, it takes a hyphen: a *lay-off*.

The slang use of *lay off* is to stop causing problems or annoyance, usually as an angry retort: 'Lay off!' Or to give something up: 'The doctor told him to lay off booze'.

LCD Most people know what an *LCD* is, without knowing what the letters stand for: liquid-crystal display. This is the usual visual presentation in pocket calculators, watches and most portable equipment using **information technology**. Two glass plates hold liquid between them, which is transparent until rendered opaque by an electric current, which serves to delineate figures or letters.

leader See **editorial** . . .

leading In printing, this is pronounced 'LEDDing', because it comes from the strips of lead which in former printing techniques were inserted to separate lines of type. The word is still used even in present technology, simply to refer to space added between lines of type.

leading question Outside courts of law, *leading question* is often used wrongly to mean a question that is awkward or embarrassing: 'Ah – that's a leading question and you can't expect me to answer it'. What it really means is a question that prompts you (or *leads* you on) to give the answer that is wanted: 'When you came home, he was already there, wasn't he?' (instead of 'Was he there when you came home?'). For this reason, a judge will often pick up a barrister for asking a witness a leading question. See also **beg the question**

leafs or **leaves** There are autumn *leaves* but 'she *leafs* through the pages of the book'.

leak or **trail (information)** As verbs, both words are used for passing on advance or confidential information to the media. *Leak* implies that the process was surreptitious, off-the-cuff telephone calls to editors, or a casual remark dropped over a drink. *Trail* suggests that it was openly disclosed, even by a press release, in order to get advance publicity for a statement or publication planned in the next few days.

leaned or **leant** Both forms are correct for the past form of the verb *to lean*, with a preference for *leaned*, the only form used in American English.

leaped or **leapt** In both British and American English *leaped* has become the more common form. Pronunciation is either 'leept' or 'lept'.

learned (pronunciation) See **-ed**

learned or **learnt** Either in Britain, with a preference for *learned*, the standard form in American English.

least See **fewest** . . .

leave or **let** '*Let* go of the rope' is better English than '*Leave* go of the rope', which is often heard. 'Leave me alone' and 'Let me alone' can mean different things. They can both mean 'stop driving me mad'. But 'leave me alone' can also be a way of saying 'I want to be alone'.

leaves See **leafs** . . .

leaves a lot to be desired This stuffy, dusty expression still comes up, an echo from old-fashioned school reports, as a way of avoiding coming out into the open and saying: not good enough by a long way, well below standard, or simply – bad.

lecher It is no longer always men who set the pace sexually, and while there are still *lechers* in the world, the word itself seems old-fashioned in a more permissive society. It has had a long innings, since the 13th century. The slang noun and verb *lech*, particularly about older men ('he's an old lech'), remain current.

lectern You sometimes hear it said that a speaker 'mounted the lectern'. With a great deal of agility, that might just be possible if it is one of the massive lecterns in a cathedral. But lecterns are not for mounting: they are reading stands on which a Bible is rested, from which the lessons are read in church, or on which a speaker rests notes or the text of a discourse. See also **podium** . . .

leeward and **windward** At sea *leeward* is pronounced 'LOOerd', but on dry land it is 'LEEwerd'. The *leeward* side of a boat is the side sheltered from the wind, just as the *windward* (pron: 'WINDwerd', both at sea and on land) is the side from which the wind is blowing. Both words are invariable and the forms 'leewards' and 'windwards' do not exist. (In passing, the *Leeward Islands* and their southern neighbours, the *Windward Islands*, make up the long string of the Lesser Antilles, stretching from Puerto Rico to the coast of Venezuela.)

left and **right banks of rivers** The bank of a river is taken as *left* or *right*, always from looking *downstream*. The most famous left bank is the *Left Bank* of the Seine in Paris, the *Rive Gauche*. About that city, *Left Bank* is used not only for direction, but to mean the intellectual and artistic life of Paris.

Left and **Right in politics** As political terms, these have been used in so many different ways at different times and in different countries, that they cannot be said to define political realities. They mean what we want them to mean, although somehow continue to be useful to express attitudes and policies towards social change and social equality.

The expressions arose from the seating plan of the French Estates General, which represented the nobility, higher clergy and commoners, summoned by Louis XVI in 1789. The aristocracy had the position of honour on the King's *right*, with the so-called Third Estate, the commoners, on his *left*. As soon as it met, the Third Estate defied the monarchy and declared itself a National Assembly. The Bastille was stormed, the French Revolution had begun, and the Left–Right divide was no longer ceremonial but political.

The *Left* was identified with change and social reform, the *Right* with preservation of existing order. In the 20th century, there have been so many contradictions in the use of these terms, that they ceased to be clear-cut definitions. The Right, or *extreme Right*, has been used about authoritarian coercive and racist movements, such as Nazism. The Left, or *extreme Left*, has been identified with the red flag of communism. Others see different interpretations.

Where do the terms stand now? In Britain, the Left indicates a more determined policy of social equality and a more even distribution of wealth through taxation, with the Right, while pursuing social reform, maintaining the status quo of private capital and privilege. To blur the terminology even more, there are expressions such as *right of centre* and *left of centre*, which again mean different things to different people.

All the above applies equally to such terms as *left-wing* and *right-wing*. See also **centre ground (in politics); loony left**

leftward or **leftwards** There are no formal rules, but as a descriptive word, it is better as *leftward* ('he went off in a leftward direction'). *Leftwards* is preferable when it indicates direction after a verb ('he went leftwards').

left-wing See **Left and Right in politics**

legal See **lawful . . .**

legal English The drafting of legal documents has little to do with good English. The most important consideration is that no one should ever be able to persuade a judge that the words could possibly have any other meaning than what was intended. Nevertheless, lawyers do sometimes get carried away by it all, and we are faced with language that is needlessly archaic and obscure, with unnecessary doubling to make doubly sure, such as 'bequeath and devise', '**let or hindrance**', 'null and void'. This age-long practice is being challenged.

In Britain, some leading insurance companies are presenting policies in straightforward language. In America, New York and other states have enacted **plain English** laws. Carl Felsenfeld, as a vice-president of Citibank, tells us, 'Lawyers writing consumer contracts in New York today do so with simplicity and communicativeness as prime legal goals'. *Clarity* is an organization, formed by British lawyers to promote

clearer, more readily understandable drafting of legal documents. Let's wish it well – after all, we should all be able to understand what we are signing. See also **Latin terms**; (length of) **sentences**

legend or **myth** The words are so close to each other in meaning that they are often lumped together. There is a valid distinction. A *legend* may stem from some historical truth ('the legend of Napoleon's invincibility'). A *myth* is entirely imaginary, and may even be a downright lie ('he was sacked and it is a myth to say he resigned'). *Myth* is used about the stories of classical literature (Greek myths). Anthropologists use the word, in preference to *legend*, because there is often a psychological reality underlying the myths of a society, since they arise from the unconscious, rather than history. See also **fable or parable**

legendary It is often debatable whether a person is *legendary*. Perhaps the best criterion is that it should be someone whose life or accomplishments fire our imagination. Winston Churchill, for example, has a claim to be called *legendary*. At a different level, Marilyn Monroe was a person about whom a case could be made for calling *legendary*. Perhaps those examples are arguable: the point is made here in order to preserve the particular quality of *legendary*, and to discourage the unthinking journalistic use of the word about any pop star with a talent for getting in the news.

legible or **readable** As with **illegible**, *legible* is a fact: it means that it is possible to read something because the print is large enough or the handwriting decipherable. *Readable* is a matter of opinion: a trite romantic novel is readable to some people, that is interesting to read, but not readable to others, who find it boring. A common mistake, to be avoided, is to use *readable* about an inscription that has been worn away: 'the letters are hardly readable', instead of '. . . hardly legible'.

legislation or **legislature** *Legislation*, which is the actual making of laws, is the function of the *legislature*, the assembly of people who make them: this is Parliament in Britain, the Congress in the United States, the Knesset in Israel, or whatever a country calls its assembly that enacts legislation.

legitimate theatre Surprisingly, the expressions *legitimate theatre* and *legitimate drama*, were used as early as the late 18th century to describe classical plays. In the 20th century, the *legitimate theatre* was used for any play in the theatre as against a musical comedy, a revue or films. An actor would say (more likely in America than in Britain) 'I'm in the legitimate theatre (or "in legit")', 'I'm a legit actor', meaning not working in vaudeville or in the movies. Since television, the term has become rather old-fashioned, as most actors work in all the dramatic media. Nor is legitimate theatre any longer accepted as having more prestige than films or television.

lend or **loan** 'Will you *loan* me a pen?' sounds affected, as *lend* is more usual. *Loan* was used that way in the 16th century, and has remained normal usage in America. In Britain, *loan* is more appropriate than *lend* where large sums of money are involved: 'The Government is loaning money to finance further exploration for North Sea oil'.

length Remember the word 'long' and sound the *g* lightly in *length*. It is slipshod to say 'lenth'.

length of sentences See **sentences**

lengthways or **lengthwise** Either word can be used in a sentence such as 'lengthwise (or lengthways) it is four metres'. *Lengthwise* is the usual word in America, which is probably also true for Britain.

lengthy or **long** A *long* letter or a report is what it says, a text running into a number of pages. A *lengthy* letter or report suggests that it is *too* long, because it is boring and heavy-going. The distinction is not always kept to but is worth bearing in mind: if you comment that a report is lengthy, simply meaning long, the writer of it could take offence.

Leonardo Certain artists are traditionally known and listed in dictionaries of art by their first names, and their surnames are unknown to most people. *Michelangelo* Buonarroti (1475–1564) and *Raphael* Sanzio (1483–1520) are examples. The full name of Leonardo da Vinci (1452–1519) is familiar but he is known, almost affectionately, as *Leonardo* (the Leonardo cartoon in the National Gallery in London). This may be because Leonardo da Vinci is the symbolic figure of the **Renaissance man**.

Not all 'one-name' artists are known by their real first names. In some cases it is a nickname that has taken over. The Venetian painter Jacobo Robusti (1518–94) is always called *Tintoretto*. It means 'little dyer' (his father was a dyer of silk). Paulo Caliari (1528–88) is established as *Veronese*, because he came from Verona. The French painter Henri Rousseau (1844–1910) is often referred to by the cognoscenti in the art world as *Le Douanier* (the customs officer), because he had a job with the department of customs and excise.

lesbian See **gay** . . .

Le Shuttle See **Channel tunnel** . . .

-less The suffix *-less* can be added to almost any noun to create a word meaning that whatever-it-is is not present. *Childless, friendless, mindless, senseless* are common examples: *carless, husbandless, paperless, sexless* are less familiar formations that have appeared. There is no need for a hyphen when *-less* is added, unless it results in three *l*s coming together: *railless, soulless*, etc, but *shell-less, smell-less*. . . .

less See **fewer** . . .

lest If the word *lest* is not archaic, it is certainly literary or ceremonial, as in the last line of Kipling's

Recessional: 'Lest we forget – lest we forget!' While *lest* can be followed by 'should' ('lest she should be upset by his presence'), formal use requires the **subjunctive**, a rare form of the verb in English: 'lest she *be* upset by his presence'. This is another reason why *lest* does not belong in everyday language, where 'in case' is more usual: 'in case she is upset . . .'.

let or hindrance *Let* was an Old English word meaning to prevent or hinder, and the meaning survives in 'French letter' for a **condom**. *Let or hindrance* is an archaic form of legal doubling to make doubly sure. It still appears occasionally in contracts and leases, but most lawyers now use 'without interference' or 'without impediment'.

let or **leave** See **leave** . . .

letter See **consonant** . . .

letter endings Signing off at the end of a letter used to be a matter of epistolary etiquette. 'Dear Sir' or 'Dear Madam' was followed by *Yours faithfully*, 'Dear Mr or Mrs Jones' by *Yours truly*, 'Dear John' or 'Dear Mary' by *Yours sincerely*. *Yours very truly* was supposed to be more formal than *Yours truly*, *Yours very sincerely* more intimate than *Yours sincerely*, with some subtle difference when the words were reversed (*Sincerely yours*). But how many people are still aware of these old rules of the game?

These valedictory nuances have all but disappeared. Most business letters end *Yours sincerely*, even if you've never met the writer, even if the letter is demanding settlement of an account, with threats of God-knows-what if you don't.

Letters to editors of newspapers (at least to the editor of *The Times*) traditionally end *Yours faithfully*, and there are diplomatic formulas for ending official letters to and from ambassadors. But generally in the 1990s, *Yours sincerely* can be regarded as the standard pay-off to nearly all letters. Some people now prefer to leave out these endings altogether, signing off *Kind regards* or *Good wishes* (unless the letter is abusive). Americans are keen on *Cordially* as an ending.

None of this applies, of course, to letters between friends or lovers. *As ever* and *Yours ever* are considered friendly but restrained. Otherwise, the door is wide open for any ending that takes your fancy, from the simple *Love*, the more expansive *All my love*, to going overboard with *Love and kisses*. See also **Dear Sir** . . . For forms of address see **ambassador; clergy; royalty**

letter quality The term is used in wordprocessing. *Letter quality* describes the best quality of print that can be produced by certain kinds of printers linked to a computer. Such printers can also print out at a faster speed with less definition, known as **draft quality**.

lexicography, lexicology, lexical and **lexist** *Lexicography* is the art and technique of compiling a dictionary. Even using computers, this is still very laborious and painstaking work, living up to Dr Johnson's famous definition of a lexicographer as 'A writer of dictionaries, a harmless drudge' (*Dictionary of the English Language*, 1755). *Lexicology* is the study of the form and properties of words. In order to write a dictionary, a *lexicographer* is of necessity a *lexicologist*. But lexicologists need not be lexicographers, in that they can be carrying out research into the way words are and have been used, without using the results in the compilation of a dictionary.

Two useful associated words are *lexical*, a descriptive term for the words in a language, as against the grammar ('four-letter words are no longer a lexical no-go area'), and *lexist*, a trendy word for a lexicographer.

liable See apt . . .

liaise and **liaison** Not long ago, the most common meaning of *liaison*, apart from technical meanings to do with phonetics and military matters, was for a secret sexual relationship. Although dictionaries still give this as one of the primary meanings of the word, we are much more likely to say now that the couple are having an affair. This leaves *liaison* available for any close bond or connection between organizations, ministers of governments or others in touch over a particular problem.

libel or **slander** Lawyers know the difference but some other people are unsure. *Libel* is something *written* that is untrue and damages a person's reputation. The evidence is the written or printed document. Since the Defamation Act 1952, something said on radio or television is regarded as publication and subject to the law of *libel*. *Slander* is *spoken*, in a less public way, and a witness is required to prove it.

Liberal or **liberal** With a capital L, *Liberal* in Britain used to mean a member of the *Liberal Party*, the political grouping that developed in the second half of the 19th century out of the so-called Whigs. The Liberal Party dominated politics until the early 1920s, under prime ministers such as Gladstone, Asquith and Lloyd George. Later the power of the party declined. In the 1980s, Liberal became mixed up with other names. In 1981, the Liberal Party formed an alliance with the Social Democratic Party as the *Liberal–SDP Alliance*. In 1988, it emerged with a new name, the *Social and Liberal Democratic Party* (the **SLD**). In 1989, after a ballot of members, this name was officially changed to *Liberal Democrats*. Some members of the party call themselves Liberals, although there is hardly any link with the historical meaning of the word.

With a small *l*, *liberal* may represent a rather indeterminate creed or political standpoint, connected with a long tradition of advocating freedom of the individual in politics, religion and art, accompanied by a leaning towards moderate social reform. Something associated with this feeling is meant in expressions such as 'a liberal point of view'. The descriptive word *liberal*

continues to mean, of course, generous, particularly with regard to donations of money.

For *liberal arts* see **humanities**

Liberal arts See **humanities**

liberated woman The expression first appeared in America in the early 1970s. It has no precise definition, and Susan Sontag has called it a contradiction in terms. It can be taken to mean a woman who earns her own living and has her own flat or house. But generally it would extend to a refusal to be bound by old traditional sexual and social roles imposed on women by custom and male attitudes.

libido You do not have to be a psychoanalyst to use this term: *libido* is a useful word to describe that vital inner energy or **life-force** that drives us. It is thought to derive from primitive sexual energy, and the early **Freudian** school of psychology used *libido* only about the sexual drive in humans, but Jungians use *libido* as described at the beginning of this entry. (Pron: 'LiBEEdoh'.)

library Even when you're in a hurry, give it *three* syllables ('LYBE-rer-ree').

libretti or **librettos** *Librettos* is being used more and more as the plural form of 'libretto', especially about musicals. But when it comes to operas, the cognoscenti wouldn't be seen dead saying anything other than *libretti*.

licence or **license** You may have a driving *licence* or a *licence* to sell wine. These mean that you are *licensed* to drive or *licensed* to sell wine in your *licensed* restaurant. That is, *licence* is the noun, *license* the verb, and *licensed* the descriptive word (occasionally you see 'licenced premises' as a form of 'premises with a licence'). In America, *license* covers all uses of the word.

licorice See **liquorice** . . .

lie, **falsehood** or **untruth** The word *lie* is considered offensive, and an MP using it in parliament, about something another member has said, would be requested by the Speaker to withdraw the remark. The point about a *lie* or *lying* is that it is intentional, with full knowledge that what is said or written is not the truth. Expressions, such as 'a deliberate lie' or 'she was lying and knew it', make no sense, because they apply to all lies and lying by definition. *Falsehood* and *untruth* are more likely to be overlooked by the Speaker in parliament, as they could just about be taken to suggest that something is an error rather than a *lie*. But don't assume everyone would see it that way!

The most polysyllabic alternative to *lie* was coined by young Winston Churchill in a speech to the House of Commons in 1906, when he spoke of *terminological inexactitude*. This is revived from time to time, with tongue in cheek, as it was for the heading of a leading article in *The Independent* (24.2.1990) about a prime minister's cabinet secretary admitting to a court that he had been 'economical with the truth', the ultimate euphemism, first used by Edmund Burke (1729–97).

lie or **lay** See lay . . .

lien In general, a *lien* is a right over someone else's property in certain cases where a debt has not been paid. The word is better left to lawyers, because the law relating to lien is not only complex but can vary with particular circumstances. It is useful, at least, to know how to pronounce it: 'LEEe(r)n'.

(in) **lieu (of)** It is difficult to think of any good reason why *in lieu of* should be used instead of 'in place of' or 'instead of', which are the obvious words. But for anyone who insists on the expression in conversation, there is a choice of pronunciation: 'lyoo' or 'loo'.

lieutenant In the army, you're a 'lefTENant', in the navy, a 'l-TENant'. In America, it's always 'looTENant'. The spelling stays the same in all cases.

life-cycle This useful term has several applications. In zoology and botany, the life-cycle of a species is the complete span of developments it undergoes from the beginning of its life until the end. In marketing, some manufactured products are said to have a *life-cycle*, which represents four stages: the development stage before a product goes on the market, the build-up of sales after it has been launched, the point at which sales reach a peak, and the time when sales begin to decline, leading eventually to the product being withdrawn.

life-force The term describes the mysterious dynamism that makes us climb mountains, write books or at least get out of bed in the morning. Behind it is a theory that every living organism is driven unconsciously by a psycho-biological force. Bernard Shaw developed the idea in *Man and Superman* (1903), at the same time bringing Life Force (he spelt it with initial capitals) into popular use. Later, for D H Lawrence, life-force was the will of God. Dilys Powell, reviewing the film *Zorba the Greek* in *The Sunday Times*, questioned the whole concept 'that the world consists of a male sky bending over a female earth; that existence should be conducted in a general uproar and that I ought to make a bonfire of my library'.

lifelong Looked at literally, *lifelong* means from the cradle to the grave, and there have been comments that 'a lifelong study of . . .', 'a lifelong interest in . . .', etc make no sense. But this is nit-picking, for the use of *lifelong* to mean a large part of someone's life is well established and understood.

life sciences See **natural sciences** . . .

life-size or **life-sized** Either form can be used, with *life-size* being perhaps the more usual. Although it seems unnecessary, for the words have been in use for a long time, most dictionaries prefer to retain the hyphen.

lifestyle *Lifestyle* began as a psychological term for the essential qualities of a person that are formed early in childhood. This meaning is overlaid by the more popular use for the way someone or a group of people live, which includes the kind of house they live in, the clothes they wear, the food they eat, the way they spend their time and so on almost without limit. Advertising agencies make particular use of the word, seeing *lifestyle* as the most important guide to which people will respond to a new product. Market research into so-called *lifestyle psychology* leads to recommendations for new products, which will appeal by creating a demand that is based more on **image** than usefulness. That is, you have to buy something because it is part of your *lifestyle*.

ligatures See ae or æ

lighted or **lit** Either form can be used. Most people prefer *lit*, as in 'the fire was lit', 'the torch was lit', and use *lighted* to describe something: 'the lighted fire', 'the lighted torch'.

lightening or **lightning** *Lightning* goes with thunder. *Lightening* is to make lighter, either literally or metaphorically (lightening a dark area, a lightening of burdens, the lightening of a situation).

light pen A *light pen* is a pen-like device that has a photosensitive tip that can be used with a computer to create shapes on the screen. The most familiar use of light pens is at checkout points of supermarkets, where they 'read' **barcodes**, registering price and product details.

light-years 'We needn't worry about it yet, as it will be light-years before it happens'. Perhaps it doesn't matter much, but that frequent use of *light-years* makes some people wince. A light-year is used in astronomy, not for time but as a measure of the distance light travels in one solar year (about six million million miles). On the other hand, there is a precedent for using *light-years* about time: we do say 'at this *distance* in *time*'.

like Some people believe it is ungrammatical to use *like* to mean 'in the same way as': 'Some girls change their lovers like they change their clothes' (Graham Greene), or in the old song, 'If you knew Susie like I know Susie'. This remains condemned by some recent grammar books, although it is general enough by now to be regarded as standard, used not only by Graham Greene but by Iris Murdoch ('Everything went wrong . . . like it does in dreams'), Martin Amis ('They didn't talk like other people talked') and other good writers. If it bothers you, replace *like* by 'the way' ('. . . the way they change their clothes', '. . . the way it does in dreams').

To use *like* to mean 'as if' still sounds ungrammatical

in Britain, although it is usual enough in America: 'she spends money like there's no tomorrow'. In Britain, 'as if . . .' is more educated usage.

It is also less acceptable to use *like* instead of 'such as': 'She enjoys games like tennis and squash'. Many people consider that a sloppy use of English, and in writing at least, it might be better to change it to 'such as tennis or squash'.

Yet *like* and *such as* are often used interchangeably, which generally seems perfectly all right, even though there is some ambiguity. Kingsley Amis, who is careful over linguistic points, had no hesitation in calling his novel *Take a Girl Like You*, even though it could mean 'like you, for example' *or* 'similar to you'. In formal use, that ambiguity should be avoided: *such as* should precede examples ('the great squares in Paris, such as the Place de la Concorde and the Place des Vosges . . .'), with *like* meaning similar ('there is no other square in the world *like* the Piazza San Marco in Venice'). No one should ever complain when you use *like* to mean 'similar to' or 'characteristic of', because that is what it does mean, as Irving Berlin knew: 'There's No Business Like Show Business'.

-like Many words are formed by adding *-like*, and there is no rule about whether a hyphen should be used or not, although the tendency now is to omit it. With new or less familiar formations, a hyphen is still appropriate: *boat-like, monk-like, pen-like*. . . . With established words formed with the suffix, the hyphen drops away: *childlike, ladylike, lifelike*. . . . In the rare cases when adding *-like* results in three *l*s coming together, a hyphen should always be used: *bell-like*.

likeable or likable These are accepted by dictionaries as alternative spellings, with a marginal preference for *likeable*. *Likable* is the normal spelling in America.

likewise *Likewise* is simply a shortened version of 'in like wise', meaning in the same way or the same thing: 'if you like what she is doing, why not do likewise?' It is a vulgarism, heard quite often in speech, to use *likewise* as a substitute for 'and', 'as well as', 'including', 'in addition to', etc: 'there are many problems, late delivery, higher prices, likewise a demand for immediate payment'. Any of the alternatives shown should be used, or simply 'plus' ('. . . plus the demand for . . .').

limited Something that is *limited* is restricted, that is a *limit* is imposed: 'his overdraft is limited to £500'. A *limited company* is one in which directors have *limited liability*. *Limited* is also often used to mean 'small' ('he has only a limited income', 'it is of only limited value'). This is so established that it is silly to object to it, although often the simple words 'small' and 'few' will do just as well.

limited See constrained . . .

limpid See languid . . .

linage or lineage The two words are sometimes confused with one another, because they both relate to 'line'. They have different meanings and different pronunciations. *Linage* is the number of lines on a printed page or in a complete printed text. It has two syllables: 'LYNE-idge'. *Lineage* is another word for ancestry, the line of descendants. It has three syllables: 'LIN-ee-idge'.

line The use of *line* to mean a sphere of activity or a type of work was particularly popular some years ago, because of a television quiz programme called *What's My Line?* It sounds dated now, and the question is more likely to be 'What's your job?', 'What business are you in?', 'What's your field?' See also **job** . . .

lineage See linage . . .

lineament or liniment The two words have no connection with each other. *Lineament* (pron: 'LINNye(r)me(r)nt') comes from a Latin word for 'line': it is nearly always used in the plural, mostly about facial features: the lineaments of a face. *Liniment* (pron: 'LINNyme(r)nt') comes from a Latin word for 'smear': it is a liquid, usually emulsified, for massaging strained muscles.

line management *Line management* is management by delegation. An executive is responsible to the next executive higher up in the line of management, so there is a clear structure of responsibility from one executive to the next, right up the *line*.

lingerie The word is not used so often now, mostly found in 'the lingerie department' in a store. Otherwise women talk about nightdresses, bras, pants or (a word now back in fashion) **knickers**. The pronunciation has never lost its French connection: 'LANGE-eree' (first syllable rhyming with 'flange').

lingo The image of the British as not being good at learning foreign languages has probably been exaggerated. It is changing in the 1990s under pressure of **Europeanism**. *Lingo* has been used at least since the late 17th century as a disdainful way of referring to any incomprehensible foreign language. It's a distortion of Latin 'lingua' (language), and even after 300 years has not been admitted to standard English (dictionaries still classify *lingo* as colloquial or informal). It has a hint of **Colonel Blimp** about it ('they were speaking some kind of foreign lingo').

lingual or linguistic There is a useful distinction, not always followed through. *Lingual* is a descriptive word for speech or language in general: 'the lingual characteristics of a region'. *Linguistic* should be used for the study or science of language, as in 'linguistic research'. In practice, the word *lingual* does not come in for much use, as *linguistic* usually serves for both senses. See also next entry

linguistics or philology Up to about the late 1950s, *philology* was the word most often used at

British universities: C T Onions (1873–1965), the Oxford lexicographer, taught philology. Since then, *linguistics* has more or less taken over as the word for that subject: Noam Chomsky (born 1928) became a famous name in this field as professor of modern languages and *linguistics* at the Massachusetts Institute of Technology (**MIT**). Linguistics has a number of branches. *Diachronic* or *historical* covers change in language. *The Good English Guide* is primarily concerned with *synchronic linguistics*, which is the present state of the language. The psychological, philosophical, sociological, anthropological and other aspects of language are usually grouped together under *general linguistics*.

linguistics *is* or *are* Nouns ending in *-ics* often present this problem. See **-ics**

liniment See lineament . . .

link or **linkage** The *link* or *linkage* between two objects or considerations seems to amount to the same thing. But during the crisis in the Middle East after the invasion of Kuwait in 1990, there was constant denial by the Western powers of any linkage between the invasion and the Israeli-Palestinian question. The word *linkage* was deliberately chosen. Perhaps this is because *linkage* implies the leverage or effect that one thing has on another, whereas *link* is simply a connection. The distinction seems subtle, but *linkage* has remained as the preferred word for different factors that may influence one another.

link together See join together

liqueur or **liquor** The word *liquor* is used less in Britain than in America, where it often covers any alcoholic drink, including wine. In Britain, *liquor* is usually (although not necessarily) confined to distilled spirits, such as whisky and gin. The word is used in both countries in a culinary sense for the juices produced in cooking, especially in meat dishes. *Liqueur* is a sweet spirit usually drunk after a meal. No matter how impeccable your French accent, the pronunciation in Britain is thoroughly anglicized: 'li-CURE'.

liquid Because liquid flows easily, the word is used in business for the cash situation of a company, that is how much ready money can be made to flow into its bank account at short notice, without borrowing. This is known as the *liquidity* of a company (see **assets**), and includes not only money in the bank but all those things that can easily and quickly be sold to produce cash. A broker who deals with investment in top vintage wines warns clients that such investments are paradoxically *not* liquid assets, inasmuch as they cannot be sold to raise cash quickly.

liquid assets See assets

liquidate Since the latter part of the 19th century, *liquidate* has been used in business for the closing

down of a company by selling off assets to meet liabilities. In the 20th century, the word was used for killing political opponents, and became popular in American gangster films as a way of ordering someone to be murdered ('I want him liquidated. Get it?'). It seems odd that gangsters should bother with **euphemisms**, but perhaps it was just a word that caught on.

liquidity See liquid

liquidize or **liquefy** *Liquidize* is the word used in the kitchen for reducing food to liquid state in a *liquidizer*. *Liquefy* means the same thing, but is the word preferred in chemistry or technical processes.

liquor See liqueur . . .

liquorice or **licorice** British dictionaries show *licorice* as a variant spelling; American dictionaries show only one spelling – *licorice*. The most well-known British manufacturer of sweets using this root extract calls them 'liquorice all-sorts'.

Most children say 'LIKerish', shown by British dictionaries as an alternative pronunciation, with 'LIKeriss', the more logical pronunciation, given preference.

lire or **liras** *Lira* is the monetary unit of Italy. The plural in Italian is *lire*, which is the official plural form in English when exchange rates are quoted. The anglicized plural, *liras*, is also commonly used and shown in some dictionaries as an alternative. But British owners of villas in Tuscany would regard the plural *liras* with disdain. What is clearly uninformed is to use the singular *lira* for the plural form, as is often done ('we came home because we were running out of lira').

listed and **unlisted companies** A *listed company* is one whose securities have been admitted to the London Stock Exchange (hence *listed securities*), and is consequently bound by the official regulations. Unlisted companies, not on the Stock Exchange list, may be admitted to the *unlisted securities market*, known as the USM, in which case they are bound by an undertaking given to the Stock Exchange to comply with certain regulations.

list price or **recommended retail price (RRP)** Shops will use these terms interchangeably, especially when showing reductions during a sale. A *list price* can have another meaning than the standard price charged to customers, and that is the wholesale price on a trade list. Unless there is a specific agreement, a manufacturer cannot usually enforce a price on a retailer, although they often suggest a price, known in the trade as the *recommended retail price* (RRP). This doesn't mean much in law but, as with *list price*, it is made full use of in shop windows, when the RRP is crossed out and a lower price put alongside.

lists of names or things Commas are the usual way to separate names or items in a list, with the comma omitted between the last but one item and the 'and' preceding it: 'in Oxford Street, there are many famous shops, including Selfridges, John Lewis, Marks & Spencer and BHS'. But there are times when a comma before the 'and' helps to avoid confusion: 'on the ground floor are the fashion, fabrics, and jewellery and accessory departments' makes it clear that three, not four, departments are mentioned. (See also **comma**)

When necessary, a **semicolon** makes a more definite separation, especially where items in a list have additional comments: 'in Oxford Street, there are many famous shops, such as Selfridges, the first department store to be opened in Britain; John Lewis, part of the John Lewis Partnership; Marks & Spencer, perhaps the best loved of all stores; . . .'.

lit See **lighted** . . .

litany or **liturgy** These two words for forms of worship in church have different meanings, which follow the Greek words from which they ultimately derive. *Litany* relates to the word for prayer and is a series of invocations usually recited by the minister taking the service, and responded to by the congregation with a repetitive affirmation. *Liturgy* relates to the word for public worship and is an order of service as officially laid down.

literacy and **numeracy** These are equivalent terms: *literacy* relates to words, *numeracy* to numbers. What is strange is that everyone accepts without question that literacy is part of being educated, but this does not apply equally to numeracy. Highly educated and intelligent people are quite likely to say with a certain smugness, 'Oh, I'm not good with figures', which is the same as saying 'I'm innumerate'. Yet to be illiterate would be shameful.

Literacy means being able to read and write, but the word implies more than that: it suggests being able to understand written language and able to organize it. Similarly, *numeracy* goes beyond mere counting: it implies the ability to understand the meaning of things and to organize them. A pocket calculator, which does difficult calculations more quickly than any mathematician, does not render numeracy redundant, any more than a **wordprocessor** replaces literacy. *Literacy*, in its broadest sense, remains the hallmark of any educated person, while *numeracy* is still at times felt to be the province of accountants, statisticians, etc.

literal See **misprint** . . .

literally It is difficult to know what to do about *literally*, as it is used so often to mean the opposite of its real meaning. *Literally* is taking a word or expression in its true and proper sense: if a knife is literally as sharp as a razor, it should be possible to shave with it. But *literally* is so often used to mean, not in reality but in a manner of speaking: 'dinner at that restaurant literally costs the earth'. Such use of *literally* to mean *not literally* is far too common to make much fuss about it, but we might prefer to be careful

ourselves to use *literally* only when we mean in reality: 'he is so rich that he could literally write out a cheque for £1,000,000'. When we are deliberately exaggerating for effect, nothing is lost by leaving out *literally*: 'dinner in that restaurant cost the earth'.

literary editor See **editor**

literate The first meaning of literate shown in most current dictionaries is able to read and write. But in the 15th century the word was used to mean educated and well read, which is the way it is often used now: 'she is highly literate'. It can also be used to mean well informed in a particular field: 'he is scientifically literate' or 'literate in science'. In fact, only when the context makes it clear is it safe to use *literate* in the primary meaning shown in dictionaries: 'most children in Britain are literate by the age of five'. *Computer literate* is the usual way of describing the ability to use a computer. See also **literacy** . . .

literature The plays of Shakespeare, the poems of Milton and so on are *literature*. But for nearly a hundred years, *literature* has been used about anything in print: people write to travel agents for literature about holidays on the Costa Brava, we are told there is a lot of literature written about house plants, and there are shops that sell 'pornographic literature'. We may regret that *literature*, a word that was reserved for poetry and prose of beauty, universal insight and value, is used increasingly in such banal ways, but there is nothing we can do about it.

lithograph The first syllable can be pronounced to rhyme with 'myth', or the *i* can have the same sound as 'eye': 'LITHe(r)graf' or 'LYTHE-e(r)graf'. The *lith* sound is considered preferable. The abbreviated form *litho* (pron: 'LYE-tho') is used more by printers than by artists.

litotes *Litotes* (pron: 'lyTOHteez') is a literary term for an understatement, often by a negative suggesting a positive ('she will *not be altogether unhappy* when the whole business is over', instead of 'she will be glad . . .'). Another term for this is **meiosis**, and this linguistic mannerism is dealt with more fully under that word.

(a) **little** . . . When Dr Johnson was asked if he would like 'a little wine', he snapped back that he would like a lot or none at all! To offer *a little* of anything is not only ungenerous, but a **namby-pamby** genteelism.

liturgy See **litany** . . .

living in sin When Victorians said a couple were *living in sin*, it was a severe moral condemnation of a man and a woman living together without the sanction of marriage. There are parents now who say jokingly *living in sin* in order to appear lighthearted about their children's relationships. In the 1990s, even a Mrs

Grundy would hesitate before using the expression seriously.

living-room   See **sitting-room** . . .

Lloyd's   A group of insurance underwriters, the people who carry the risk for insurance losses, used to carry on their business during the late 17th century in a coffee-house in London owned by one Edward Lloyd. His name lives on, not as a brand of coffee, but as the title of the most famous syndicate of insurers in the world, which explains why it is always *Lloyd's* (not *Lloyds*).

loan   See **lend** . . .

loath, **loth**   *Loath* and *loth* are alternative spellings of the word meaning reluctant to do something. Dictionaries show *loath* as the preferred spelling, with *loth* as a variant. The important thing is that whichever spelling is used, the word should be pronounced so that it rhymes with 'both', not with 'clothe'. *Loathe* (which *does* rhyme with 'clothe') is another word altogether, meaning hate or detest. Note also that *loathsome* keeps the same *th* sound as *loathe*.

lobbying   *Lobbying* is speaking to someone important in the lobby of the House of Commons or in one of the corridors of power in business or elsewhere, and persuading them to support some project or cause. The word was first used this way in America as long ago as the mid-1800s. We are told that some MPs have set themselves up as 'government affairs consultants', which sounds like a **euphemism** for *lobbyists*, which in turn could be considered another word for *fixers* (see **broker** . . .)

locale, **locality** or **location**   All three words relate to 'locus', the Latin word for place, but are used in different contexts. *Locale* (the *e* is added to show stress is on the *second* syllable: 'lohKAHL') is a place where something happens or is arranged: 'Madrid was the *locale* of the 1991 Middle East peace conference'. *Locality* is a more general word for a place, usually referring to an area not precisely defined: 'the people living in this locality'. *Location* often defines a precise position: 'the location chosen for the site of the new factory'. The word was borrowed in the early days of the cinema for scenes shot *on location*, that is in the actual place or real life setting, instead of using sets in a studio.

There is one final point about *locality*: it is often used unnecessarily as a rather pompous substitute for 'place': 'Let's see what the locality is like'.

locate   See **find** . . .

loch or **lough**   Loch Lomond is the largest lake in Scotland, and there are people who swear there's a monster in Loch Ness, also in Scotland. For *loch* is the Scottish word for *lake*. In Ireland, the river Erne flows across the border through Lough Erne. For *lough* is the equivalent Irish word.

Both *loch* and *lough* are pronounced in the same way, with a final guttural *ch* sound. This can often be arrived at by a gentle gargling. But to help out English people who cannot handle it, most dictionaries, as a concession, offer the alternative pronunciation 'lok'.

lockout   Fortunately the word does not come in for much use now, as the practice it describes is uncommon in industrial disputes. *Lockout* was a threat that hung over the heads of employees in the 19th century, when they were deprived of work because employers prevented access to the factories, until workers agreed to certain conditions. The term still represents an ugly and uncompromising confrontation between employers and the workforce.

logistics   The word was in use in the late 19th century to describe the organization, accommodation and arrangements for moving troops. In World War II, *logistics* was used frequently, especially in America, in connection with what was required to mount a particular military operation. The word is now used more widely in industry and business for the step-by-step planning required to carry out any project, such as launching a new product or marketing scheme, which could include allocation of funds, preparation of advertising, sales conferences, etc.

logo, **cipher**, **emblem**, **symbol** or **trademark**   Before the 1960s, *trademark* (abbreviated TM) was the usual word for the distinctive emblem of a company or product. It remains the legal term, since there is a Trade Marks Act 1938, and trademarks can be officially registered with the Patent Office. The name of a product is in itself a trademark, as well as the style in which it is displayed. This sometimes presents confusion when the name becomes used about any other product with the same function (see **Hoover** . . .). Some years ago when everyone was busy 'taking a xerox' or 'xeroxing a document', Xerox reminded the world in advertisements that the word is a trademark, which must be spelt with a capital X (see **Xerox**).

Although there is no reason why they should not be, *emblem* and *symbol* are not generally alternative words for *trademark*. They are used more often about a heraldic design for a person or institution, or about an object chosen to represent something: the British Labour Party uses a red rose as its *emblem* or *symbol*. (*Symbol* can have a much wider meaning in psychology and anthropology – Jung gave *symbol* a deep archetypal significance in understanding the unconscious.)

A design on interwoven initials is one of the meanings of **cipher**. But it is not a fashionable term, and is reserved mostly for ceremonial or heraldic use: the emblem on Royal Mail vans is the Royal Cipher. When interwoven initials are used as a trademark, it is more likely to be called a *logo*.

Since World War II, *logo* has become used most of all in business for the trademark of a company or a product, or the graphic design that represents the corporate identity of an organization. The word *logo* is constantly in use, because there is a craze for them, with vast sums being spent on what often seem inconsequential designs. British Petroleum are said to have spent a million pounds on research and design for their new logo based on the letters BP, to give them 'a fresh new identity for the 1990s'. British Telecom animate an ethereal trumpeting figure at the end of their television commercials, and display it on telephone boxes and vans. *Logo* is now a cult word in business, and even the most modest organization has to have one. The plural is *logos* (not *-oes*).

-logue or **-log** The suffix derives from the Greek root 'logos' (word) and forms nouns connected with speech and reason. It is *-logue* in British English, but often simplified to the phonetic form *-log* in American English: *analogue/analog, catalogue/catalog, dialogue/dialog, travelogue/travelog*. For a few words, some American dictionaries show both endings as alternative spellings, with a preference for *-logue* for *ideologue* and *monologue*, for example.

-logy See Greek roots

Lolita See nymph . . .

London Gazette See gazetted

lonely hearts *Lonely-hearted* was already used in the 19th century about someone living a solitary life. In the 1990s, *lonely hearts* are women or men living on their own and wanting to meet someone as a companion or to marry. They place advertisements in the *lonely hearts columns* of newspapers and magazines, asking to meet other men and women. They go to introduction agencies, sometimes called *lonely hearts clubs*, computerized now and catering for a huge market.

lonesome See all alone

long See lengthy . . .

long-distance or **trunk call** The trunk is the central part of a tree, from which stem the branches. By analogy, a *trunk line* on a telephone network is a main line. For many years, a telephone call in Britain outside the local charge area was known as a *trunk call*. The equivalent in America was always a *long-distance call*, which has now become the usual term in Britain as well. But with telephone numbers almost anywhere in the world available by pressing buttons, the expression *long-distance call* doesn't come in for all that much use any more: people are more likely to say they are calling Tokyo, New York, Moscow or wherever it is.

longhand Samuel Pepys is recorded as the first to use the word *longhand*. It was in an entry in his *Diary* for 17 November 1666. The *Diary* was written in a system of shorthand, and Pepys referred to longhand as opposed to that. Since then, *longhand* has come to mean ordinary handwriting, without reference to

shorthand: 'it was written in longhand' simply means it was written by hand, instead of typed or printed. This was, of course, the original meaning of **manuscript**, but no longer.

long-range *Long-range* is used about distance, particularly for intercontinental missiles. It is also used about time. *Long-range* planning is part of business strategy, working out objectives for years ahead. A weather prediction that looks ahead for a month or more justifies the name *long-range forecast*.

long- and **short-termism** These are clumsy formations, needlessly replacing 'long-term and short-term policies'. See also **-isms**

loo See lavatory . . .

lookalike *Lookalike* began as slang in America in the late 1940s. It is well established as standard English now, since journalists and broadcasters on both sides of the Atlantic find it a useful way of saying that something or somebody is an imitation of the real thing. The word can be a noun ('a Princess Di lookalike') or a descriptive word ('a lookalike Princess Di').

lookers-on or **looker-ons** *Lookers-on*.

looking good See good-looking . . .

lookout or **look out** It is always one word as a noun, meaning someone whose job it is to keep watch, as in the phrase 'on the lookout for'; when it is a bad prospect in view ('a poor lookout'); or in the colloquial use meaning it's someone else's problem ('that's her lookout'). The verb is always two words: 'Look out for trouble!'

loony left Even most of the latest dictionaries have overlooked this derisive term that has come into British politics. The *loony left* is not a political party, but an assortment of disorganized individuals advocating a radical extreme leftism that seeks to overthrow the whole structure of society, or even world order. Their vaguely idealistic revolutionary doctrinaire ideas are too inconsistent and dispersed to be called policies. See also **Left and Right in politics**; **militant**

loose or **lose** As verbs, these are occasionally confused. *Loose* has several different meanings as a verb, all connected with releasing or setting free: a boat can be loosed from its moorings, dogs can be loosed when they are taken off their leads, a gun is loosed when it is fired. . . . *Lose* also has a number of meanings, mostly related in some way to no longer having something or to being deprived: we can lose money, lose our nerve, lose a game, lose ground. . . . *Loose* rhymes with 'noose'; *lose* rhymes with 'cruise'.

Lord Mayor See mayor . . .

Lords or **Lord's** The most famous cricket ground in the world is in St John's Wood in London, where it has been since 1814. It was founded by one Thomas Lord and is known as *Lord's* (short for *Lord's cricket ground*). There are over a thousand lords in the House of Lords, the upper chamber of the British parliament, so it is known as *the Lords*.

lorry or **truck**   The word *lorry* does not have a place in American dictionaries for it is a peculiarly British word for a heavy motor vehicle used for transporting goods. The word dates from the 19th century, when it referred to baggage or goods containers on the railways. No one seems to know its origin. A heavy goods vehicle in America is a *truck*, which has also come into use in Britain, as an alternative to *lorry*. But *truck* has another meaning in British English, which is a *railway truck* used for carrying goods.

lose or **loose**   See loose . . .

lose no time   It is worth remembering that the expression *lose no time* can mean two different things, and it is not far-fetched to suggest that in some situations there could be a serious misunderstanding. 'Lose no time doing this' could mean get started on it without delay, or it is a waste of time doing it. Where there could be any doubt, it's better to use alternatives that lay on the line what is intended: for example, 'Get on with it right away', or 'Don't waste your time on it'.

loss-leader   This is a standard term in marketing and retailing. A particular product or service is sold at a rock-bottom price, even at a loss, in order to attract clients who might then use other services, or to bring customers into the shop. The trick for buyers is to snap up the *loss-leader* and get out of the shop without buying anything else!

(a) **lot**, (a) **lot of** and **lots of**   Some authorities suggest that *a lot*, *a lot of* or *lots of*, to mean 'many' or 'a great deal', are informal and not suitable for serious writing: 'ten people are a lot'; 'a lot of people turned up'; 'lots of people attended'. This is being too restrictive about expressions that are used such *a lot*. If anything, *lots of* ('lots of money') is more conversational than *a lot of*, so there is a case for avoiding *lots of* in official writing. But this cannot reasonably also apply to *a lot* or *a lot of* ('he paid a lot for it'; 'a lot of money').

loth   See loath . . .

loud or **loudly**   'Not so loud please!' is perfectly good English. 'Not so loudly please!' is also correct, of course, but sounds self-conscious, as if someone believes 'not so loud' is ungrammatical, which it isn't.

lough   See loch . . .

lounge   See sitting-room . . .

lovable or **loveable**   British dictionaries offer both spellings as alternatives: most American dictionaries list *lovable* as the only spelling. Since *lovable* is by far the most usual spelling in Britain as well, the best thing is to forget *loveable* altogether (although don't correct anyone else for spelling it that way).

love   The plaintive refrain of a romantic song demanded 'What is this thing called love?' The *OED* devotes 15 tightly packed columns to answering that question, but we are still left in the dark. For *love*, both as a word and an emotion, defies definition and classification, although Stuart Sutherland, professor of experimental psychology at the University of Sussex, settled for 'A form of mental illness not yet recognized in any of the standard diagnostic manuals' (*Macmillan Dictionary of Psychology*, 1989). C S Lewis divided love into four categories, which are altruistic, affectionate, companionate and erotic (*The Allegory of Love*, 1936). Dr Alex Comfort, more concerned with erotic love, tells us 'Love has been defined as the harmony of two souls and the contact of two epidermes' (*The Joy of Sex*, 1972). Certainly, *love* is used a great deal in connection with sex, although there is no doubt that the two can exist independently of one another. There is a distinction between *loving* and being *in love*. *Loving* is a deeper expression of feeling between people, while *in love* suggests a temporary infatuation.

When we have said all that, *love* remains one of the most mixed-up words in English: we love strawberries, love our children, fall in love, make love, say 'thank you, love (or luv)', become over-confident at tennis when the score is 40-love . . . and each time mean something altogether different by the word *love*. Yet even in the 1990s, *love* remains a magical disturbing word, evoking a state of happiness, distrusted and yearned for at the same time, alongside which most other things seem but a shadow.

loveable   See lovable . . .

loved ones   So many people on radio and television are using *loved ones*, instead of 'relatives', or perhaps 'nearest and dearest', that it has become a tedious **cliché**. Evelyn Waugh satirized it in the title of his book *The Loved One* (1948), a **black comedy** about bizarre funeral practices in California. Nevertheless, *loved ones* remains a favourite expression with politicians, who want to sound **caring**.

love-hate   A psychological concept that seems the only way to describe this contradictory emotional response that nearly everyone has experienced, when attraction and repulsion seem to alternate: 'a love-hate relationship'. An **oxymoron** is the stylisitc term for such an expression in which seemingly contradictory words are used together.

lover or **mistress**   In the past, when married people had other sexual relationships, women had *lovers* and men *mistresses*. *Lover* is now used freely by both men and women, whether they are married or not, about someone they are having an affair with. Even the British, who during the 19th and 20th centuries were more reticent about sexual relationships, have taken to the word. For those for whom *lover* is too ardent, most of the alternatives are unsatisfactory: they are reviewed under **boyfriend** . . .

The word *mistress* is hardly still available, for it is on its way into oblivion. In the 16th century, it could mean a woman a man loved, but not necessarily made love to ('O mistress mine! Where are you roaming?', *Twelfth Night*, Act II Sc iii). In the 19th century, a mistress was a 'kept woman'. But now no one wants to use the word any more, even innocently: a Mrs Mop would hardly call the woman she cleans for 'her mistress', and prim starchy *schoolmistress* has long since given way to 'woman teacher'. See also **Other Woman**

low-cost, **low-budget**, **cut-price** or **inexpensive** 'Cheap' is an ancient word going back to Old English, and is a perfectly good word for something that is good value for money. But 'cheap' does carry with it innuendoes: cheap labour, a cheap joke, dirt-cheap, cheap and nasty . . . . *Low-cost* is a reasonable euphemism for 'cheap', but some shops and advertisers are even more evasive, and prefer the face-saving euphemism *low-budget*. *Cut-price* means, or should mean, that the original price has been reduced, which does not apply to *low-cost* and *low-budget*. *Inexpensive* is a more middle-class expression, and is entirely relative to how much money you have: a diamond bracelet could cost the lifetime's savings for one person yet be inexpensive to another.

low-key In the late 19th century, there were examples of *low-key* being used to mean in low spirits. But *low-key* has come into use in a wider range of contexts, particularly since World War II. Perhaps *low-key* lighting, a term used in films and the theatre, encourage the use of the expression for almost anything that is restrained, whether it is an approach to a problem, a statement about the economy, or advertising that is seemingly quiet and modest. *Low-key* is not necessarily derogatory: on the contrary, it can suggest creating an effect by understatement. But when it is used about a person, it usually implies depressed or dull, as in 'she was very low-key this evening'. In some contexts *soft sell* (see **hard-**) is an alternative to *low-key*, adding the implication that a low-key approach is cunningly contrived. See also **soft-pedal**

low-pressure area See **depression** . . .

low tech *Low tech* is not heard nearly as often as **high tech**. But it is useful at times to describe a practical everyday way of dealing with something that would normally require a sophisticated high tech solution. A leading heart specialist, commenting on the discovery that taking an ordinary aspirin once a day reduces the incidence of heart-attacks, described it as *low tech* medicine. This contrasts it with the advanced surgical technology of bypass operations.

LSD This proud and ancient abbreviation, soberly punctuated (L.S.D.) and taken from Latin 'librae', 'solidi', 'denarii', for British pounds, shillings and pence, belongs, with the British Empire, to history. The abbreviation has only one meaning now, and a very different one: lysergic acid diethylamide, a **hallucinogenic** drug. See also **pound** . . .

Ltd or **plc** Before the 1980s, it was a statutory requirement to add *Ltd* (the abbreviation for *limited liability*) to the name of all companies registered under the Companies Acts. Now it is a statutory requirement to distinguish between a public limited company, quoted on the Stock Exchange, by adding *plc* after the name, and private limited companies which add *Ltd*.

For some reason, *Ltd* retains its capital, but *plc* is written in small letters.

lunch See **dinner** . . .

lush *Lush* is an American slang word of unknown origin from the late 19th century. It is used for a heavy drinker and is heard more and more in Britain: Lynn Barber, interviewing Melvyn Bragg for *The Independent*, explained that he did not drink alcohol for the first week of every month, 'not that he is a lush, but he works in a profession where alcoholism is almost an occupational hazard'.

-ly or **-lily** The problem arises when descriptive words, such as *friendly, holy, silly*, etc are used after verbs, and we are landed with the awkward forms *friendlily, holily, sillily* . . .: 'she spoke holily'; 'he grinned sillily'. Nearly always it is better to rephrase the sentence or use another word: 'she spoke in a holy way'; 'he grinned stupidly'.

lyric and **lyrical** Both words relate to the Greek use for verses sung to the accompaniment of a lyre. In English, the connection between *lyric* and music was lost, and the word became used about poems, usually short ones that are romantic and full of emotion. By the late 19th century, *lyric* was being used for the words of popular songs, and this restored relationship of the word to music has developed in the 20th century. At the same time, *lyric* moved downmarket into tin-pan alley: it is more associated with pop music than with lieder or opera. Curiously, the word is used more often in the plural, even for the words of one song ('the lyrics of the new song in the charts').

Lyric, as a descriptive word, is still mostly reserved for poetry, as in lyric poets, lyric drama, etc. *Lyrical* can mean poetic ('he described it in such a lyrical way'), but more usually means being carried away by enthusiasm: 'he was lyrical about his holiday on a Greek island'.

· M ·

Mac, Mc or **Mack** These familiar prefixes to many Scottish and Irish family names are variants of the Gaelic word for 'son', the equivalent of the French 'de' and the German 'von'. Whether it is *Mac*, *Mc* or *Mack* depends on what is customary in a particular family, and there is no rule to help the uninitiated, except to ask. The same name can be spelt using different forms: *Macmillan* or *McMillan*. After *Mc*, the family name usually begins with a capital (McArthur, McDonald . . .), but after *Mac* or *Mack*, this does not always apply (*Macauley, Mactavish*).

When it comes to alphabetical order, the standard practice followed by directories is to treat all three prefixes as *Mac*, with the next letter in the name determining the position in an alphabetical list: McArthur, MacHuish, McVicar, Madigan.

Mac is sometimes used as a nickname for any Scotsman, but they don't always like it. In America, *Mac* is heard as a conversational form of address for any man, sometimes friendly ('Have a drink, Mac?'), but often slightly aggressive ('Take it easy, Mac!').

mac See **raincoat** . . .

macabre The recognized pronunciation is 'me(r)-KAHbr', but the light *r* sound at the end is often dropped: 'me(r)KAHB'.

machination The word is often in the news because it means a plot or intrigue to do something nasty, and there's a lot of that going on in the world. The *-ch-* has a *k* sound (not like 'machine'): 'makiNAYshun'.

machismo and **macho** Both words describe heavy-going masculinity, all brawn and no brain. The Spanish word *macho*, a shorter form of *machismo*, can also be a noun for a man who is showing off his *machismo*. Neither word is generally complimentary.

The preferred pronunciation is 'me(r)TCHIZmoh' and 'MATCHoh', which are nearer to the Spanish sound than 'me(r)KISmoh' and 'MAKoh'. Zsa Zsa Gabor offered an easy way to remember that: 'Men who try too hard to be macho are generally not mucho'.

macintosh See **raincoat** . . .

macro- The prefix, derived from the Greek word for 'large', is used in some technical terms, such as *macromolecule* (a molecule that consists of great numbers of atoms), *macrolinguistics* (the study of overall patterns in the use of language). *Macro-* is sometimes used pretentiously to give a pseudo-scientific authority to a concept, as in *macromarketing*, where 'large-scale', 'national' or 'global' would be more straightforward.

A hyphen is not necessary to link *macro-* to the word it is joined to, even when that begins with a vowel, as in *macroeconomics* (the study of the aggregation of all economic factors).

macrobiotic *Macro* means large (see previous entry), and *macrobiotic* relates to ancient Chinese dietary teachings intended to keep the mind and body in harmony, not only with this planet, but with the greater cosmos. It is based on a complicated balance between *yin* (the passive feminine principle) and *yang* (the active masculine principle). But the term *macrobiotic* has come to be used so loosely, that some dictionaries equate it with almost any vegetarian diet that includes brown rice, lentils, etc.

mad The word properly means mentally deranged: *madhouses* were forerunners of what are now called psychiatric hospitals. But *mad* has come to be used in such casual ways, that doctors would never use it in connection with mental illness. At the end of the 16th century, Shakespeare was writing 'He made me mad', meaning furious (Henry IV Part 1, Act I Sc iii). 400 years later, Robert Harris, writing in *The Sunday Times*, (29.10.1989), submitted 'mad is not an unfair description of the present occupant of 10 Downing Street', explaining that he was using the word in the sense of 'unbalanced judgement, delusions of grandeur . . . instability'. Clearly *mad* is a subjective description of someone, not a clinical definition. It is even used in light-hearted ways, to mean no more than silly, wrong about something quite trivial, being in love, or liking icecream. In fact, *mad*, derived from Old English and going back centuries, has come to mean almost whatever we want.

Madam, madam or **madame** There is little problem in France, where the French use *madame* all the time when addressing a woman. *Madame* has no place in English, except as an affected pronunciation ('me(r)DAHM') for *madam*.

In letters, *Dear Madam* is the equivalent of **Dear Sir**, and is the only way to write to a woman when we don't know her name, unless we fall back on 'Dear customer', 'Dear colleague', etc. Apart from that, few people use the word *madam* any more, except waiters ('Would madam like a dessert?') and shop assistants ('Can I help you madam?'). 'Madam chairman' is still occasionally heard at committee meetings, but is courtly and old-fashioned (see **chairman . . .**). That leaves one other use of *madam*, which goes back at least to the 17th century: the woman in charge of a brothel is the *madam*.

Made in England   See British . . .

maestro   *Maestro* is used mostly for great conductors, but also extended to cover anyone who does almost anything in a masterly way. It's the Italian word for master, so the proper plural is *maestri*. That is the form shown first in most dictionaries, but it sounds self-conscious in English, as most people say *maestros*. (Pron: 'MYStro'.)

Mafia   The word is Sicilian dialect, and is used for a secret organized network of criminals in that country, so dominant as to be an alternative authority with its own hierarchy. Links were established among the Italian community in America, where powerful criminal groups were built up, using murder and extortion as a code of practice. A member of the Mafia is a *Mafioso* (pron: 'maffeeOHsoh'). The supreme boss of one of the organizations in America is known as the '*Godfather*', a name that is familiar in Britain through publicity of Mafia trials but mostly because of Mario Puzo's novel, *The Godfather* (1969), and the compelling performance of Marlon Brando in the film made from it (1972).

The word *mafia* (with a small *m*) has been extended in English, usually scathingly, about any tightly knit group of people capable of exerting influence to suit themselves. At a High Court hearing of a libel case in January 1990, the editor of *The Sunday Times* spoke of the 'Garrick Club mafia', meaning an influential clique who were members of that famous London club. Influential art dealers and galleries have been accused of forming an 'international art mafia', by dictating which art is important.

Mafioso   See previous entry

magazine or **periodical**   Joseph Addison was one of the first to use the word *periodical* for a publication that comes out at regular intervals. Together with Richard Steele, he ran *The Spectator*, known as a periodical, which appeared daily for a short time in the early 18th century. If *periodical* is used now, it would not be used for a daily paper but for a publication that appears at weekly or longer intervals. But it is more a librarian's word, rather formal for everyday use: *magazine* is more usual. See also **glossies**

Magdalen or **Magdalene**   This is a name that sorts out those in the know about certain matters. It is spelt with a final -*e* when it is St Mary Magdalene of Magdala in Galilee (*Luke* 8:2), or one of the churches

named after her. The name is usually pronounced with three syllables ('MAGde(r)lin'), but some people prefer four syllables ('MAGde(r)lin-e(r)'), in accord with the name in Greek and ecclesiastical Latin. There is a final -*e* in Magdalene College, Cambridge, but not in Magdalen College, Oxford. The names of the colleges in both universities are pronounced with two syllables: 'MAWDlin'.

magisterial or **magistral**   When the word is used to describe a person who speaks and bears themselves with great authority, it should be *magisterial* (pron: 'madge-i-STEERial'). *Magistral* (pron: 'maJIStre(r)l') is a descriptive word for someone who is a master with great knowledge. Someone can be magisterial in manner but not necessarily magistral. Or the same person can be both.

magnate   See financier . . .

maharishi   Derived from Sanskrit, *Maharishi* is used for a Hindu holy man, and means a great and inspired sage. It has been more familiar in the West since the 1960s, when the Beatles became interested in Eastern mysticism, and accepted initiation from Maharishi Mahesh Yogi, who devised a technique for **meditation** under the registered 'brand name' of *Transcendental Meditation* or TM.

maid or **servant**   The answer is neither. In the egalitarian society of the 1990s both *maid* and *servant* seem unacceptable words, although *maid* is still used in a relaxed way in America. It is perfectly all right to send compliments to the 'cook', if you are rich enough to employ someone to slave over a hot stove in the kitchen, or to have a 'housekeeper', that is a kind of major-domo who looks after everything in the house, or to have a 'nanny' to look after the children. But no one talks about maids or servants any more (other than hotel *chambermaids* or *maids of honour* attending a queen or princess). The nearest is an *au pair*, a living-in young woman (and by law specifically a woman) who helps with housework or looking after children, in return for her room, food and a modest wage, with enough time to attend the local language school to learn English. *Au pair* are French words, of course, but they are used far more in Britain, as an introduction or explanation for the tall Scandinavian blonde who joins the family and guests at dinner. After all, *au pair* means 'on an equal footing'. See also **charlady . . .**

maiden name   Even the most recent dictionaries continue to include *maiden name*, without labelling it obsolete, peculiar or sexist. It was the term for a woman's family name before she was married. Many women still use it, although it's usual now to refer to a woman's *single name*, as opposed to her married name. More and more women retain their single name after marriage, and would give you a funny look if you asked what their maiden name is.

mail or **post**   You *mail* a letter in America and *post* it in Britain. In Britain, we always received the *post*, but it's not uncommon now to hear 'Has the mail come yet?' After all, post office vans have *Royal Mail* on the side, and advertisers have **direct mail** campaigns, sending out tons of *junk mail*. Although it's unthinkable that we shall ever give up *postmen* and *postwomen*, the choice between *mail* and *post* is in the balance, with it shifting, if anything, towards *mail*.

mail(ing) shots   See **direct mail**

mainframe   This computer term describes a large computer system linked to a number of computer outlets for handling the work of a big organization. In the early days, all computers were mainframe computers, vast installations costing a great deal of money. Modern microcomputers, which can sit on a desk, have developed so that their capacity goes beyond the early huge mainframe computers. See also **desktop computer** . . .

mainstream   Before the 1950s, *mainstream* referred to the prevailing current of a river. Then the word was taken up in America for middle-of-the-road jazz, neither the traditional style of the early 20th century nor unmelodic abstract jazz. Later *mainstream* was extended as a useful word to describe the dominant trend in almost anything from philosophy to fashion, somewhere between **experimental** and conservative.

main street   See **high street** . . .

maintenance or **alimony**   *Alimony* (from the Latin word 'alimonia', nourishment or food) is still the usual word in America for the allowance awarded by divorce courts between a husband and wife. In Britain, *alimony* has become an old-fashioned term, no longer used in law, where the standard word now is *maintenance*. See also **palimony**

Majorca or **Mallorca**   See **foreign place-names**

majority and **minority** (*is* or *are*)   Although these are both singular words, they represent a number of people or things, and it nearly always sounds wrong when they are treated as singular: 'The majority of us *does* not agree'; 'A minority of MPs *has* voted against the Bill'. 'The majority of us *do* not agree' and '. . . *have* voted against . . .' sit more comfortably. See also next entry

majority of or **most of**   The *majority of* should only be used when it is the larger number of two measurable things. When it is an indeterminate number or something that is unspecified, *most of* is appropriate: 'the majority of the members have agreed', but 'she writes most of the letters', 'he does most of the work'. As for that tired old **cliché**, *the vast majority of*, it is much more to the point to write or say 'nearly all'. See also previous entry

make or **take a decision**   See **decision**

make love   Of the many respectable, slang and vulgar alternatives to 'copulate', the one that is used by far the most is *make love*. It may be a vague euphemism, but Hamlet used it about what went on in bed between his mother and Claudius, his father's brother: '. . . corruption, honeying and making love . . .' (*Hamlet*, Act III Sc iv). For those who cannot bring themselves to use any of the down-to-earth alternatives, *make love* is the way out, alongside evasive expressions, such as 'go to bed together', 'sleep together' (see **sleep with someone**), among others.

When it comes to talking about other people making love, if you say they were *at it*, nearly everyone will know what you mean. The *at it* euphemism may be coy, but does not seem either vulgar or offensive.

make redundant   See **dismiss** . . .

malapropism and **spoonerism**   These -*isms* are different kinds of linguistic jokes, and both are named after people. Mrs Malaprop was a character in Sheridan's *The Rivals* (1775), who was always getting a long word slightly wrong, so that the sentence became ridiculous: '. . . as headstrong as an allegory on the banks of the Nile'. As a result, she became, according to **Fowler**, 'the matron saint of all those who go wordfowling with a blunderbuss' (*Modern English Usage*, 1926).

W A Spooner (1844–1930), sometime Warden of New College, Oxford, used to enliven conversation at High Table by transposing the sounds of two words: he would turn 'a well-oiled bicycle' into 'a well-boiled icicle', 'Conquering kings their titles take' into 'Kinquering congs their titles take'. Presumably the other dons fell about. The more literary term for a spoonerism is *metathesis* (pron: 'meTATHesis').

male or **masculine**   There was a time when these words had their own place in different contexts. *Male* was generally used in biological, zoological or botanical senses to denote the male species, capable of fertilization and insemination. *Masculine* was used about humans to describe such qualities and characteristics properly belonging to men.

Since the feminist movement of the 1960s, *male* has come to be used, especially by women, as a shorter, crisper and angry alternative to *masculine*, about sexist attitudes and behaviour: male **chauvinist**, male prejudice, male superiority. . . . Women tend now to use *male* as a word of attack and *masculine* as a word of admiration. For notes about *female*, see **lady** . . .

male chauvinism   See **chauvinism**

malignant   See **benign** . . .

mall or **arcade**   *Mall* is an old-fashioned word now in Britain for a shopping precinct, not open to vehicles. An *arcade* is also an enclosed area, usually with shops, but it is covered, traditionally with an arched roof (*arcade* relates to Italian 'arcata', arched). Burlington Arcade off Piccadilly in London is an example. The pronunciation 'mawl' is shown as an alternative in dictionaries but should never be used for the London place-names: The Mall, Pall Mall and Chiswick Mall. For those, *Mall* always rhymes with the first syllable of 'Sally'.

Mallorca or **Majorca**   See **foreign place-names**

man   See **gentleman or man . . .**; **his own man**

-man   See **-person . . .**

management   Although the word had been used for a long time in connection with controlling the affairs of organizations and enterprises, the principles were more or less taken for granted until after World War II. Then it became fashionable to talk about *management skills*, *management science*, and different techniques of management were invented, or at least given names: examples are *management by crisis* (an approach that deals with short-term problems as they come up, rather than looking for underlying causes), *management by objectives* (a technique that defines specific personal objectives for everyone involved). There is nothing new about management, except the way it is now studied in depth, and the use of the word as a management **buzzword**.

management buyout (MBO)   The term is so often in the financial and business news, that it has its own abbreviation: MBO. A management buyout is the purchase of a business from its private owners or shareholders by the executives who are running it. Much has been made of how management buyouts give executives new incentive and revive old businesses that are in a decline.

manageress   See **-ess forms**

managing director   See **chief executive . . .**

mandarin   The word has been used in English since the 16th century. It is oriental, with its root in Sanskrit, and meant a Chinese official. Its main use now, often in the expression 'the mandarins of Whitehall', is disparaging, describing remote permanent senior members of the civil service, shadowy figures supposedly running the country by influencing government ministers.

mandarin(e)s   See **tangerines . . .**

mandate or **proxy**   The two words have something in common in that they are both a legal authority given to one person to act on someone else's behalf. A *mandate* can cover a wide range of things: for example, a mandate is given to directors or to a company secretary to sign cheques on behalf of the company, sometimes with a limit on the maximum amount. A *proxy* is customarily used for a person deputed to vote in the place of someone else. At company meetings, for

example, shareholders who cannot attend are usually asked to appoint the chairman of the company as their proxy, with authority to vote for them on specified resolutions. See also **attorney** for *power of attorney*.

mandatory or **obligatory**   When something is *mandatory*, it is *obligatory* because of a law or command from a higher authority: 'It is mandatory to advertise vacancies to persons of either sex'. *Obligatory* is a less legalistic word, which could apply to the rules of a club, for example ('it is obligatory for men to wear ties at dinner') and to moral obligations as well, which is not the way *mandatory* could be used. The preferred pronunciation is 'MANditery' ('manDAYtery' is considered non-standard).

man Friday   See **girl Friday**

mangoes or **mangos**   Either, with a preference for *mangoes*. See also **-oes or -os**

mania or **phobia**   Psychiatrists use both these words about the symptoms of mental illnesses, with *mania* describing a pathological overexcitement and *phobia* for an uncontrollable, often incapacitating, fear. In everyday use, *mania* can be used about a harmless craze that gets mildly out of hand, anything from collecting old cars to jogging. In a similar way, a *phobia* in everyday language can mean an excessive but not necessarily morbid fear of anything from flying to spiders.

manic   The word relates to *mania* (see previous entry), but outside psychiatry, has come to be used in trivial ways. For example, to say someone is manic about cleaning a new car means no more than they're always washing it. A film critic once described the Marx Brothers as having a 'manic transatlantic zing', and who could argue with that?

Manic-depression and *manic-depressive* should not be used lightly, as they sometimes are: they relate to severe psychiatric disorders in which a patient swings unpredictably between dangerous extremes of mood.

manifestos or **manifestoes**   Some dictionaries show these as alternative plural forms of *manifesto*, while others list only *manifestos*, the more usual form. See also **-oes or -os**

manifold   There is some argument about whether *manifold* should be treated as 'many-fold' and used simply to mean 'many', in the way that tenfold means ten times: 'the new system will result in manifold savings of time and money'. The matter is hardly worth pursuing, since *manifold* in that sense is a pointless substitute for 'many'.

The proper use of the word is for things of different and various kinds, so a piece of equipment can have manifold applications. The *manifold* on an engine is so called because it takes the exhaust gases from the range of cylinders.

manipulate   The word is used always in a good sense about things, and always in a bad sense about people. To manipulate a piece of equipment, for example, is to handle it with skill. To manipulate a situation or, even worse, to manipulate people, implies exerting a clever influence on them for personal advantage.

mankind See humankind . . .

man-made See artificial . . .

mannequin See model . . .

manoeuvre For the -ed and -ing forms of the verb, it is easy to slip in an incorrect e. The correct spellings are *manoeuvred* and *manoeuvring* (not 'manoeuvered' . . .). (The American spelling is *maneuver*.)

manpower *Manpower* had already occurred by the late 19th century, used in comparison with **horsepower**. The word came into use more specifically in the 1960s, as a term for the workforce in an industrial organization. The Manpower Services Commission was set up by the Employment Training Act 1973 to regulate employment and training, and to help with the problem of long-term unemployment. *Manpower* covers both sexes, and 'personpower' has not arisen as a unisex alternative.

manqué or **might have been** The French past form of the verb 'manquer' (lack or fall short of) has been used in English since before the mid-1800s, yet it is still placed, in the French word-order, *after* the noun: 'a cabinet minister manqué'. There is no one English word that means the same, something a person might have achieved but didn't make it, and the only alternative is to rephrase the sentence: 'he might have been a cabinet minister'. But the flavour of *manquée* is caught better by hyphenating *might have been* and using it descriptively: 'a might-have-been cabinet minister'.

When *manqué* is used about a woman, it should, following French grammar, be the feminine form *manquée*, but this rule is not usually followed in English: 'she is a writer *manqué*'.

-manship As a suffix, -*manship*, to mean the qualities required in relation to a particular skill, has been in use for a long time (*horsemanship*, for example), goes back to the 16th century). It was given a fillip in the 1940s and 50s by Stephen Potter (1900–70), who invented new -*manship* words, two of which some dictionaries include as standard English: *gamesmanship* (the art of winning games by unnerving your opponent) and *one-upmanship* (the art of being one jump ahead). Having a deliberate paroxysm of coughing just as a fellow golfer is teeing-off, is gamesmanship; making sure the head waiter of the expensive restaurant where you are being taken for lunch knows your name, is one-upmanship. This led to other -*manship* words, notably **brinkmanship**. But it seems that the fashion for coining new -*manship* words has passed.

mantra This Sanskrit word for a Hindu or Buddhist sacred chant has become familiar since the 1960s, as the term for incantations used in techniques of meditation. But it is out of place to use *mantra* as a smart alternative to 'slogan' or 'catchphrase', as 'Cash is trash, is the new Wall Street mantra' (*The New York Times*).

manual See handbook . . .

manuscript Most dictionaries continue to give as the first meaning of *manuscript* something like 'the text of a book written by hand'. That is what the word meant until the 20th century. But now, when writers, publishers or literary agents refer to a manuscript, they mean the text of a book typed or printed out by a **wordprocessor**. The connection with the Latin 'manus' (a hand) has disappeared. *Manuscript* in the true sense usually applies to music scores, for composers and copyists still mostly write these by hand. No computer can produce an *autograph*, for as well as being a signature, it is the word for a manuscript written in a composer's or writer's own hand.

The old abbreviations, MS and MSS, for the singular and plural of *manuscript*, are still used, mostly by publishers and literary agents. Archivists are more likely to use the words in full and only for texts written by hand.

many a . . . is or **are** While, for example, 'many women' is, obviously plural, *many a . . .* is illogically always followed by a singular verb: 'many a woman *has* to put up with . . .'.

marathon There were two famous long-distance runs in the battle of Marathon (490BC) in Ancient Greece: a messenger ran the 150 miles from Athens to Sparta to ask for reinforcements, and a soldier ran 'hot from the battle', according to Plutarch, 22 miles to announce the victory in Athens. It does not demean *marathon* when it is used for the long-distance race in the Olympic Games or for other long-distance runs, such as the London Marathon, of at least the prescribed distance of 42.195km (26 miles 385 yards). It is a reasonable, if arguable, extension of the word to describe any great task as a marathon, even one performed sitting down, like translating *War and Peace*. But it is debasing *marathon* beyond recognition to use it, as is often done now, about trivial tasks, such as washing up a big pile of dirty dishes.

marchioness See marquess . . .

margarine In English, *g* before *a* is pronounced as it is in Margaret, and there are hardly any exceptions. So the correct pronunciation of *margarine* followed the same pattern. But some time in the 1920s, *marge* became a derogatory slang variant ('all we could afford was bread-and-marge'). Manufacturers fought a rearguard action to break this downmarket association by insisting on the hard *g* sound, while nearly everyone else made the first syllable rhyme with 'barge'. No one bothers much now with either *marge* or *margarine*, as heavy advertising has made brand names take over.

marginal, minimal or **small** As a descriptive word, *marginal* means a lower limit, something that can hardly be registered: a marginal profit is only just about making a profit. Used in this way, *minimal* means the same, and there is little point in distinguishing between the two words. Neither word means quite the same as *small*, although they are often used casually to mean that: 'a small improvement', while not something to write home about, is mildly encouraging; 'a marginal (or minimal) improvement' is neither here nor there. It is worth taking the trouble to choose the word most suitable to a situation. In politics, *marginal* has a particular use. A marginal seat or a marginal constituency is one held by an MP with a relatively small majority of votes, so the seat is at risk at the next election.

Minimal art, the work of *minimalists*, terms that arose in the 1960s, leaves many people bewildered. It can mean simple geometric forms in painting and sculpture, in which there is the minimum of imagery and feeling, or massive primary structures or shapes, or any arrangement of everyday objects chosen to be exhibited. The fact that it is on display almost becomes the criterion. It has been commented that if it looks like art, it is not minimal art.

marginalize Most dictionaries leave out *marginalize*, for the old meaning of making notes in the margin is very rare now. Since the 1980s, a more significant use for the verb has emerged. When a matter or a person or a minority are marginalized, it means they are, so to speak, moved out to the margin, that is on to one side, treated as having no importance or relevance: 'Public concern has forced the question of immigration on the government's attention, and it can no longer be marginalized'.

marijuana See **cannabis** . . .

marionette See **puppet** . . .

mark-down and **mark-up** They are both trade terms in the retailing business that have passed into more general use. A *mark-down* is a price reduction, either to clear certain stocks or in a sale. Customers have become familiar with the term, and may well ask if a price can be *marked down*, instead of 'reduced'.

A *mark-up* can have two meanings. One is an increase in price because of inflation or extra costs. The more usual meaning is the amount added to the cost of something to cover overheads and profit. As nouns, the words are hyphenated; as verbs, they are separate.

market *Market* is a very old word that can be traced back to the 12th century. And it was a very simple word meaning a 'gathering of people for buying and selling' (C T Onions, *The Oxford Dictionary of English Etymology*). In the second half of the 20th century, the term *market* has become much more sophisticated. As the political and economic spotlight focused on the word, *market* turned into the buzzword of business and international trade. Government ministers talk about a **market economy**, and are solemn over the effect of **market forces**. The *financial markets* (or simply, *the markets*) is the usual name now for the world's stock and currency exchanges. On 25 March 1957, the Treaty of Rome brought the European Economic Community into being, and the popular name for it ever since is the *Common Market* (see **EC** . . .).

As an extension to all this, the word **marketing** has become a key term in its own right in industry and business. *Marketing director, marketing policy, marketing research* were terms that hardly existed before the 1960s.

market or **command economy** The term *market economy* is fashionable. We are frequently told that it is the only economy that can sustain growth and a high standard of living. Almost the first demand made by the liberated countries of Eastern Europe was for a *market economy*. When you look into it, it is not easy to distinguish *market economy* from the discredited term **capitalism**. For a market economy frees resources, production and prices from state control, and allows decisions to be made by private ownership of the means of production. It is an economy that is decentralized and to a great extent regulated by **market forces**. The opposite is a *command economy*, where resources, production and prices are dictated by government. See also **mixed economy**

marketeer, marketer or **marketor** The director-general of the Chartered Institute of Marketing prefers *marketer* as the standard term for marketing directors or senior executives working in marketing departments or consultancies: he considers *marketeer* 'a bit slick', and that *marketor* 'goes with professor and doctor'. The appointments columns of newspapers confirm that *marketer* is the usual word.

Marketeer does have another meaning, which is a good reason for not mixing it up with *marketer*: a marketeer is the name for someone supporting Britain's membership of the European Community. It sounds pejorative (from association with 'black marketeer' or 'racketeer') but it isn't – unless you are strongly opposed to the **EC**.

market forces This has become a favourite term with chancellors of the exchequer, as an off-the-peg explanation and justification of ups and downs in the **balance of trade**, interest rates, employment figures or whatever else goes off in the wrong direction. In effect, *market forces* is little more than an official pontifical term for the age-old law of supply and demand.

marketing The indispensable umbrella word for selling, taking in packaging, promotion, advertising, research, distribution and everything else in the long distance between dreaming up a new product and a 'consumer' taking it off the shelf in a supermarket. In the 1990s, it would seem almost crude to talk about mere 'selling'. See also **market**

marketing and advertising language
Marketing and advertising have a go-getting language, first used by shirt-sleeved executives in the conference rooms of Madison Avenue advertising agencies. Now it is just as familiar in Britain, where **admen** take a 'creative' idea (although they no longer 'run it up the flagpole to see who salutes it'), slot 'consumers' into **socio-economic groups**, 'package' products to 'position' them in the market and to give them 'shelf-appeal', hype them in television commercials, hoping that they will end up as 'brand leaders' rather than 'me-too' products, to quote but a handful of the jargonistic expressions of the business.

marketplace The word is used less now for the open space in a town where markets are held than for the general world of buying and selling: 'Let's try it out in the marketplace'.

market or **marketing research** The term heard more often is *market research*, which describes social and economic research and surveys into people's preferences, in order to identify and quantify the market for products or services.
Marketing research, according to the Institute of Marketing, has a separate meaning. It may take the findings of market research, and use them to study the practical business of actual selling, such as which products should be distributed to particular areas, how advertising should be planned, in fact everything connected with getting goods off shelves and into homes.

market value See face value . . .

mark-up See mark-down . . .

marque The French word for brand or trademark shows up in English in two contexts. One is in the language of motor car enthusiasts, who might use it for the make of a car, as against a specific model: 'Rover cars won more accolades than any other marque'. The other use is by wine writers for the brand of a **champagne**, particularly as *grande marque*, referring to one of the leading brands: according to the chairman of the Champagne Shippers' Association, 'a grande marque makes a statement about your personality'.

marquess or **marquis** A *marquess* is a rank in British nobility between a duke and an earl. A *marquis* is used about nobility in other countries for a rank between a duke and a count. A *marchioness* is the feminine equivalent of a marquess (for a wife or widow, or a woman holding the rank herself) with *marquise* as the feminine equivalent of a marquis.

marriage We all know that a marriage is the legal union between a man and a woman whereby there is a contractual basis for them living together. A *marriage certificate* is the evidential proof, and is the second major documentary landmark in life, between those other milestones, a birth certificate and a death certificate.

But the word *marriage* has other meanings. For Mary Wollstonecraft, the 18th-century English feminist, marriage was 'legal prostitution', a description that has been used many times since; the American writer, Dorothy Parker (1893–1967), called it an 'obscene travesty of a dance'. In the 1990s, the word *marriage* is wide open to individual interpretation, far beyond the range of till-death-do-us-part definitions in dictionaries.

marriage certificate or **marriage lines** It is traditional after a wedding ceremony for the registrar to present the bride with the *marriage certificate*, as if it were her property. At one time, she would refer to the document as her *marriage lines* (a man never talked about 'his' marriage lines). *Marriage lines* is not much used any more, except perhaps as a joke.

Marxist See Communist . . .

masculine See male . . .

masochism and **sadism** *Masochism* is when someone gets pleasure from being hurt or humiliated. *Sadism* is to get pleasure from hurting or humiliating someone else. Both words are **eponyms**: Sacher-Masoch was a 19th-century Austrian novelist who described instances of masochism, and the Marquis de Sade (1740–1814) was a French novelist whose books are full of sexual sadism. Both words relate particularly to forms of sexual perversion.

mass- One of the early *mass-* expressions was *mass-production*, first developed in the motor car industry by Henry Ford. *Mass-produced* used to mean things of indifferent quality churned out in factories, as against things made individually or by hand. *Mass-production* is not a term that is used much any more, since this is the standard method of production now for nearly everything we buy.
In the 20th century, most of the *mass-* combinations are to do with people. It started with the word *masses*, which Gladstone is thought to have used for the first time in the late 19th century, to parallel the word 'classes', meaning the ruling classes. *The masses* is still used disparagingly to suggest faceless unknowing and undiscriminating millions. This association is attached to *mass-* expressions, such as *mass culture*, used about pappy popular entertainment in all its forms, and a *mass-market* product suggests it is designed for the generality of supermarket shoppers (compare **admass**).
Saddam Hussein's regime in Iraq gave new force to the term 'weapons of mass destruction', never clearly defined, but presumably meaning missiles, warheads, poison gas and chemical and biological weapons.
Mass- words are generally not hyphenated (*mass-market* is one of the exceptions), except when used before a noun: the *mass-culture* media.

massacre This is one of the few words ending in -re that does not become -er in American usage.

Massacre is the only spelling used on both sides of the Atlantic.

massage Governments are always being accused of 'massaging unemployment figures'. This expressive use of *massage* suggests that figures, if not actually falsified, are 'pushed around' to make them look better. Even in the medical sense, the meaning of *massage* can be stretched: 'An attractive blonde with a great sense of fun offers interesting massage in her well-equipped apartment . . .' (from an advertisement): that may be straightforward physiotherapy but it doesn't sound like it. The first syllable is stressed in Britain ('MASSage'), the second in America ('massAGE').

(the) masses See mass-

master and mistress When a woman first became head of a college that traditionally had a *master*, there might have been a linguistic hiatus. But it has long since been sorted out. Once a college has a master, it always has one, which is why Baroness Tessa Blackstone, for example, is the Master of Birkbeck College, London. And if Malcolm Williamson should be succeeded by a woman composer, she too will be the Master of the Queen's Music. Similarly there are only **Masters of Wine**.

It does not work the other way round. It would take some living down if a man, appointed as head of a woman's college, found himself called the Mistress. See also **-ess forms; headteacher . . .**

master class Some time in the 1950s, it became fashionable for soloists who gave lessons to groups of young gifted musicians, to call these sessions *master classes*. The idea was too good for it not to be taken up: now hairdressers give master classes, and that grand description has even been used for demonstrations by cooks, gardeners and plumbers.

masterful or masterly This used to be the rule, and it is still given in some current books. *Masterly* means skilful and accomplished, in the manner of a master: 'he is masterly at handling difficult situations in the boardroom'. *Masterful* means bossy and domineering: 'he is so masterful with her, always telling her what to do'. In practice, *masterful* is used so often now to mean the same as *masterly* that most dictionaries accept that the words are interchangeable in that sense. This is convenient, particularly when a verb is described: 'he played that stroke masterfully' sounds much more natural than '. . . masterly'.

Only *masterful* can convey the meaning of dictatorial, so when there is risk of misunderstanding, use *masterly* when the meaning is adroit or skilful: 'he is *masterful* at handling difficult situations in the boardroom' could be misinterpreted.

Master of Business Administration See MBA

Master of Wine (MW) Because the name of this qualification in wine studies is still not familiar to many people (in 1992 there were only some 150 MWs), the words are often spelt out in full, but the abbreviation is, like any other degree, used after someone's name: Jancis Robinson, MW. When they want a more classical name, Masters of Wine call themselves *oenologists* (see **oeno-**).

mat or matt Dictionaries show these as alternative spellings for the word describing something with a dull rather than a shiny finish. *Mat* is the usual spelling, with *matt* as a variant. In America, it's the other way round. A third variant, *matte*, is the least common of all.

material or relevant What is the difference between 'this is material to the matter we were discussing yesterday' and 'this is relevant to the matter . . .'? *Material* is the stronger word, implying that something is essential or of real significance, while *relevant* does not go beyond suggesting that whatever it is is connected with or has some bearing on the matter.

mathematics *is* or *are* Nouns ending in *-ics* often present this problem. See **-ics**

matriarchal See motherly . . .

matt See mat . . .

mature *Mature* has come to be used in ambivalent ways about people. The familiar expression *mature students* does not mean wiser and more experienced: all they need to be is half a dozen or more years older than most of the other students. An 'older student' would be a better description. To say a person is 'very mature' does not mean their development as a human being is complete: it suggests a balanced attitude and a certain understanding of life, qualities that might or might not be present irrespective of age or intelligence.

matzo This Yiddish word, derived from Hebrew, is familiar to people who are not Jewish, for *matzos* are sold in many supermarkets. They are large flat unsweetened biscuits, which are unleavened to commemorate the headlong exodus of the Jews from Egypt, when there was no time for the dough to rise.

Most dictionaries offer the pronunciation 'MATsoh', but Leo Rosten (author of *The Joys of Yiddish*) scorns that, saying it should rhyme with 'lotsa'. Dictionaries offer the alternative plural *matzoth*, but you can ignore that too: Leo Rosten prefers *matzos*, which must surely guarantee that plural form is **kosher**!

maverick In the 19th century, Samuel Maverick owned a ranch in Texas. He broke with general practice by not branding his cattle. An unbranded calf became known as a *maverick*, and the word is still used among cattle-owners in America for a stray calf or yearling that cannot be identified because it is not branded with its owner's mark.

It wasn't long before the word was applied to people who would not join the general herd. In politics, *maverick* is often used pejoratively about someone who rocks the boat by being too outspoken against the party line. And outside politics, the word is not always complimentary, as it suggests someone who makes problems by running counter to what is generally agreed. At other times, *maverick* can be used admiringly, acknowledging a person's courage in standing out against established opinions.

maximize and **minimize** Both words are so convenient ('we must maximize our effort'; 'we must minimize our losses'), that they are given too much exposure. There are various ways to ring the changes: '. . . make the greatest possible effort . . .'; 'keep our losses at rock-bottom. . . '.

Maximize and *minimize* mean to take something up to the top limit, or take it down to the lowest limit. No degree is involved, so we cannot 'greatly' maximize or minimize anything, even though such expressions are often heard.

maximum and **minimum (plural forms)** Some dictionaries are strict about the plural forms, admitting only the Latin plurals *maxima* and *minima*. Others allow *maximums* and *minimums* as alternatives. These anglicized plurals are very commonly used, and to say 'these are the minima required' could, to some people, sound affected.

may or **can** See can . . .

may or **might** According to some authorities, *may* and *might* can express such fine shades of uncertainty and doubt, politeness and deference, that we need a chart to guide us as to what is intended. For example, it is suggested that 'I may go to see him' expresses a possible intention, while 'I might go to see him' indicates a possible doubt, that 'Might I come in?' is more deferential than 'May I come in?' Although these comments can be supported, they are stretching language beyond reasonable limits. It takes two to communicate, and it is asking a great deal of the other person to pick up such reading-between-the-lines nuances.

Some useful *may or might* rules can be extracted from the complexities:

1 *May* usually refers to the present, *might* to the past: 'it may happen any moment now'; 'it might never have happened'.

2 *May* is correct in a direct statement in the present, *might* is correct when something is reported: 'it may rain'; 'the weatherman said it might rain'.

3 After *if* statements, *might* should be used: 'if she had married someone else, she might have been happier'. This also applies generally to statements of uncertainty: 'without her help, he might not succeed'.

4 Conversationally, *might* is often a polite way of making a request, or alternatively a resentful complaint. 'While you're out, you might post these letters for me', and that classic reproach of the pre-dishwasher era, 'You might help with the washing-up!'

maybe or **may be** One word when it is an alternative to 'perhaps': 'Maybe it is true'. Otherwise it is two words: 'It may be true'.

mayor or **mayoress** Even current dictionaries tell you that a *mayoress* is a woman holding the office of mayor. But if you call a woman, elected as mayor, the *mayoress*, you deserve to be rapped over the knuckles with the mayoral mace. The first woman mayor was elected as long ago as 1908 (Elizabeth Garrett Anderson, mayor of Aldeburgh), and since then there have been other women mayors, all of whom objected strongly to the discriminatory title *mayoress*.

The 753rd mayor of Chester is a woman. When the status of the office in that city was raised to Lord Mayor in 1992, she gently rebuked a BBC interviewer for calling her *Lady Mayor*: irrespective of sex, a Lord Mayor is a *Lord* Mayor.

Mayoress is properly used for the wife of a mayor. There is no form for a mayor's husband. 'Mr Mayor' and 'Mayor's consort', tried out on place-cards at mayoral banquets, have not gone down well. The only safe way out is 'Mr' followed by his name.

MBA The old BCom (Bachelor of Commerce) degree never had much prestige, and was abandoned by the University of London after World War II. **Commerce**, in that sense, has become an outdated word. An MBA (Master of Business Administration) is a post-graduate degree awarded by universities in Britain and America. It is taken so seriously by industry, that even Oxford, long reluctant to admit business studies as a proper academic course, opens its doors to MBA students in 1994, although they will be discreetly tucked away at Templeton College, far beyond the fringe of the university, on the wrong side of the ring road.

MBO See **management buyout**

Mc, **Mack** or **Mac** See Mac . . .

me or **I** See I or me

(no) **mean** . . . See no mean . . .

mean or **average** See average . . .

mean, **stingy** or **tightwad** These are all words for someone who is ungenerous over money, counting every penny. *Stingy* is arguably sharper than *mean*. The alternative *pinchpenny* is rather old-fashioned. *Mean* is also used about small-minded attitudes or squalid streets and houses. *Mean* has another use as well, which is for spiteful or unkind. A *wad* is conversational American English for a big bundle of dollar bills, so *tightwad* is someone who keeps it tightly rolled. *Tightwad* is mostly used in America, but is occasionally heard in Britain as well.

meaning Most of the time *meaning* cannot exist without language. 'How can I know what I think till I see what I say?' demanded the little girl in Graham Wallas's *The Art of Thought*. Bernard Williams, professor of philosophy at Berkeley, California, warns 'We have a responsibility to make our words express what we mean . . . Our sentences *are* our meanings'. Those comments concern the use of language to understand our own meaning. When it comes to communicating that meaning to other people, the difficulties multiply.

In **communication**, the meanings of words are what people understand them to mean, which is not always exactly the same as meanings in **dictionaries**. This does not devalue dictionaries: we should be lost without them, and need them at every turn. But dictionaries leave words lifeless on the pages, and there is a great divide to cross before they can be animated into sentences that pass on our meaning to other people. *The Good English Guide* is an attempt to throw a bridge across the void.

means is or **are**   *Means*, for the way in which something can be brought about, is a plural noun, and there is no singular form with that meaning. So it is treated as singular or plural: '*this is* the means to an end', '*these are* the means to an end'. When the word is used about someone's financial resources, it is always plural: 'now she is on her own, her means *are* reduced'. But that use of *means* is formal and old-worldly: it is more natural to say '. . . she has less money'.

meantime or **meanwhile**   There is no discernible difference in the way these two words are used. We can do something 'in the meantime' or 'in the meanwhile'.

Mecca or **mecca**   With a capital M, Mecca is the holy city of Islam, where **Mohammed** was born, and the place to which every **Muslim** must try to make a pilgrimage. When the word is used in a general way for a place that a particular group of people is drawn to, it is still often spelt with a capital M, but *mecca* is possibly less offensive to Muslims: 'there is a shop in Milan that is the mecca of fashionable women'.

mechanics   *Mechanics* is properly the branch of physics dealing with motion and force. In the 20th century, the word is increasingly used in a loose way for the components of any operation that are required to make it work. We can, for example, talk about the mechanics of a marketing scheme, the mechanics of a takeover bid, the mechanics of a problem, even the mechanics of a plot on which a novel is based.

mechanics is or **are**   Nouns ending in -*ics* often present this problem. See -ics

mechanization or **technology**   *Mechanization* is as old as the wheel: it describes any way of making work easier by mechanical means, such as windmills and watermills, levers, pulleys – and the wheel. In the 20th century, mechanization is so much

taken for granted, that the word seems to belong to the Industrial Revolution: it is largely replaced by *technology*, the all-purpose word for the use of applied sciences in mechanical processes. See also **high tech**; **science** . . .

media   In the 1920s, the word was used mostly in advertising agencies about newspapers and magazines. Since World War II, it has become the ubiquitous umbrella word covering all means of communication with the public, especially newspapers, television and radio. Terry Waite, the former hostage, called it 'the media circus'. It is plural: 'the media *are* . . .' is unquestionably correct. But there are sentences where *media* functions as a collective noun, when a singular verb seems more natural: 'A media bound by restrictions is unable to speak the truth'. The singular form is *medium*: 'Which advertising medium was used?' The answer to that could be 'All the media'. See also **mixed media; mediums**

medieval or **mediaeval**   See ae or æ

mediocre   The proper meaning of the word is an in-between quality, neither good nor bad, a quality that might be acceptable. But in nearly all cases, *mediocre* has a pejorative sense of second-rate or poor quality. So much so, that it is better to describe something that is moderately good, or at least not bad, as 'average' or 'middling'.

meditate and **meditation**   If someone asks 'Do you meditate?', they probably no longer mean do you think long and hard about things. The other meaning of *meditation* has superseded the general meaning. Meditation now usually refers to a spiritual exercise, a turning attention away from our own consciousness, beyond thoughts or images, allowing oneself to be deeply silent. The discipline spread to the West through *transcendental meditation* (or TM). This is the registered brand name of one particular technique, over-publicized and commercially promoted, developed by the **maharishi** who was for a time the Beatles' **guru**. See also **Zen**

meditative   See contemplative . . .

medium (of wines)   See dry (wines)

mediums or **media**   In Noel Coward's *Blithe Spirit*, everyone sat round a table, and Madame Arcati asked 'Is there anyone there who wishes to talk to anyone here?' The plural of that kind of medium is *mediums*, spiritualists who believe they can communicate with the dead ('One rap for *Yes*, two raps for *No* . . .'). When *medium*, as a noun, is used in nearly all other ways, the plural is **media**.

medium-term   In business this term can have different meanings. *Medium-term liabilities* are liabilities that have to be discharged usually within a maximum period of three years; *medium-term capital* covers funds raised usually for a period of up to five years; *medium-term planning* can mean business development over a period of five to ten years. When people use *medium-term*, it is no bad thing to ask how many years is meant, otherwise it can remain an open-ended description of a period of time.

meet with and **meet up with** Both phrases have an American ring, although are heard increasingly often in Britain. For some people they go a little further than the word *meet*, suggesting meeting by arrangement, rather than by chance: 'we should meet with (or meet up with) them over this' could mean 'we should arrange to have a meeting with them'. Nevertheless, the expressions are unnecessary, nor are they liked in Britain, where 'boy meets girl' remains good enough.

mega- See **Greek prefixes . . .**

megabuck In America, *megabuck* is a slang word for a million dollars. So far, we do not have 'mega-pounds' in Britain.

megabyte See **byte**

megalomania To a psychiatrist, the word represents a pathological mental disorder that manifests itself as a delusion of grandeur, an overriding belief in one's importance and infallibility. But the word is used more casually about anyone who is big-headed: when Stuart Sutherland, professor of experimental psychology at the University of Sussex, defines *megalomania* as 'extreme overestimation of one's own importance and worth, endemic in politicians' (*Macmillan Dictionary of Psychology*), it is unlikely that he means politicians are clinically pathological.

meiosis We are concerned here with the literary, not the biological, meaning of this term. As a description of style, a *meiosis* (pron: 'myOHsis') is used for an understatement, often by expressing the positive by stating a negative. *Litotes* (pron: 'lyTOHteez') is another term for this linguistic mannerism. It can take many forms: 'I would not be truthful if I denied . . .'; 'it could not be said that she was always faithful to him'. *Not un-* is the most common form of meiosis: 'it is *not unreasonable* to ask . . .'; 'I am *not unwilling* . . .'; 'the matter is *not unimportant*'.

A meiosis (or litotes) is a way of avoiding coming out in the open with a direct statement. At times it can be justified because it is kinder or more tactful ('it would not be unfair to say she did not look her best'), but more often than not it is mealy-mouthed. George Orwell exposed the *not un-* ploy for its evasiveness: 'A not unblack dog was chasing a not unsmall rabbit across a not ungreen field' (*Politics and the English Language*, 1946). See also **periphrasis**; **un- words**

member bank The term in America is more or less the equivalent of a *clearing bank* in Britain, that is a bank that is part of a network of banks through which cheques are settled by joint arrangement.

mementoes or **mementos** Either.

memo or **memorandum** Even some recent dictionaries insist that the short form *memo* is colloquial. Other dictionaries accept it as standard. *Memo* is now used so often, in writing as well as speech, that *memorandum* has become the formal word, only strictly necessary in official reports. *Memo* has only one plural form: *memos*. The plural of *memorandum* can be either *memoranda* or *memorandums*. Because *memorandum* is formal anyway, you might as well go all the way and use the Latinate plural *memoranda*.

memory Computers have supposedly near-human attributes, and the word *memory*, previously reserved for the ability to retain knowledge in the mind, is the standard term for the facility of computer systems to hold data for subsequent recall, which in computer language is *retrieval*.

ménage This French word (pron: 'mayNAHZH') is used in English because there is no satisfactory equivalent. *Ménage* means rather more than 'household', the usual dictionary translation: it refers to how matters are arranged under the domestic roof. The most common use of *ménage* in English is *ménage à trois*, previously nearly always a man and two women living together, usually his wife and his lover, but nowadays a *ménage à trois* is sometimes two men and one woman. (*Vive l'égalité!*)

menopause, **climacteric**, **the change** or **midlife crisis** *Menopause* combines two Greek words, one for 'month' and the other for 'stop'. It was coined by a doctor in the late 19th century, but not used much before the 20th century, when it was recognized that this time in a woman's life, when menstruation ceases, presents physical and psychological difficulties.

Climacteric, which also stems from a Greek word, meaning a 'critical period', is a much earlier word, going back to the 16th century when it was used for any time of crisis in human life. Although, according to dictionaries, the word can be used about both men and women for the time when sexual activity declines, it has become so identified with the menopause in women, that it would seem odd to use it about a man.

The *change of life* was an expression used by a doctor in the early 19th century, before the word *menopause* had been coined. Shortened to *the change*, it became the most familiar of all expressions for this time in a woman's life. But now *the change* comes in for much less use, as women dislike the suggestion of being written off as ageing and less vital. In 1991 *the change* was given renewed currency as the title of Germaine Greer's book, *The Change: Women, Ageing and the Menopause*.

In the 1950s, an apparent *male menopause* was discovered. It was intended to explain an emotional crisis of confidence that men are supposed to experience at a certain age. In the 1960s, a more fashionable name for this arose, the *midlife crisis*. It was first used for men, then extended to women, and is said to occur as early as the mid-thirties, when ambitions may seem no longer attainable.

Midlife crisis became the popular diagnosis for anything from the boom in ballroom dancing, sales of fast cars to older men, to the increased divorce rate. In America the cult of youth can bring on midlife crises in people by their late twenties. An American specialist in this problem, Dr Gilbert Brim, had another explanation: 'It may be that what everybody calls a midlife crisis is nothing more than a need to sort out the psychological garbage accumulated over four decades of living'.

-ment The suffix should be added to the *complete* verb, retaining any final *e*: abridge – abridgement, amaze – amazement, excite – excitement. . . . Possible exceptions are *acknowledge* and *judge*: although *acknowledgment* and *judgment* are accepted alternatives, **acknowledgement** and **judgement** are preferred, so the rule can be said to hold.

mental age *Mental age* is used about adults who are mentally retarded. A person, say in their twenties, might be said to have a mental age of 12. This assessment is based on intelligence tests given to children in order to establish what is normal at different ages.

mental telepathy People often say, when some inexplicable communication occurs, 'it was mental telepathy'. But *all* telepathy is mental, because the word means extrasensory communication of thoughts.

menu Since the early 19th century, *menu* has meant the card showing the different dishes that can be ordered in a restaurant or that will be served at a banquet. Since the late 1960s, *menu* has also meant a list of options shown on a visual display unit (see **VDU**), listing the different choices available on a computer, with the appropriate method of selecting the one required.

menu English The language of **gastronomy** covers the range of accepted descriptions in various languages for a wide variety of dishes. *Menu English* is something else. It is the private jargon of individual restaurateurs, often French, with so many enigmatic descriptions devised by the chefs themselves, that there is no shame in asking for explanations. For example, a something-or-other *surprise* (with 'surprise' placed after the noun in French word-order, and pronounced 'syoor-PREEZ') is *menu English*: it usually means a chef's desperate last-minute bid to find a way of using left-overs, and allowing for some notable exceptions, it should be treated with caution. And a 'plate of cheese' does not sound impressive enough, so it has to be the cheese *platter*.

merchandise (as a verb) This old 13th-century word for goods that are bought and sold has another meaning in modern **marketing**. When a product is *merchandised*, sales are promoted through advertising, special displays and so on. *Merchandising* can be used to cover the whole spectrum of marketing from consumer research to planning advertising campaigns. Always *-ise* (never -ize).

merchant bank The term, in general use since the 1920s, describes British banks that specialize in dealing with big business ventures, rather than with individuals. Among other activities, merchant banks make financial arrangements for the launch of new companies and for mergers.

mercy killing See **euthanasia**

merger, amalgamation or **takeover** In business, *merger* and *amalgamation* are a coming together of two companies to form one business. *Amalgamation* is a rather old-fashioned word for this and *merger*, first used in this way in America in the 19th century, is the usual term now. Both terms imply that the arrangement is friendly and by mutual consent. *Takeover*, in a business sense, is more recent, dating from the 1950s. It usually suggests that a company has been acquired aggressively, often by buying a majority shareholding, or by making an offer to shareholders that encourages them to vote for the deal to go through. A takeover bid is described as *hostile* when it has not been invited.

meritocracy The word was invented, as a parallel to 'aristocracy', by Michael Young, and used in the title of his book, *The Rise of the Meritocracy* (1958). Meritocracy is a combination of intelligence, drive and ambition, irrespective of social background. *Meritocrats* often featured in honours lists during Margaret Thatcher's period as Prime Minister. Neither word is used so often now, as the principle of the best person for the job is more or less taken for granted (not that the **old boy network** and **jobs for the boys** have disappeared altogether). See also **technocrat**; **upwardly mobile**

meshuga Few dictionaries deign to include this Hebrew-Yiddish word that means 'crazy', 'nutty as a fruitcake'. This is a pity, for *meshuga* and its associated noun, *meshugener*, have an impressive ring to them, have appeared in English writing since the late 19th century (James Joyce used *meshuggah* in *Ulysses*), and the *OED* gives the words generous coverage. Variant spellings abound (*meshugga*, *meshuggah*, *meshuger* . . .), but what else would you expect from a word like this? (Pron: 'meSHOO(r)ger'.)

Messrs This is the plural of **Mr**, and at one time was always used before the name of a firm, as a form of address: Messrs Marks & Spencer. Sedate firms of solicitors may still use *Messrs*, but for most of us it belongs with wing-collars and high-button boots.

metal fatigue The expression occurs in news items about inexplicable aircraft crashes. Metal that has been exposed even to small stresses for a long period may become imperceptibly weaker, with the risk of breaking up. Fatigue is usually associated with humans, but there are early precedents for its use in connection with inert materials: *fatigue* was used centuries ago about the masts of sailing ships.

metaphor or **simile**   These are literary words for describing something by relating it to something else, with which it has no realistic connection: 'his ideas are a *load of old rubbish*'; 'the takeover bid became a *dog-eat-dog* situation'; 'she made a *song and dance* about it'. Those examples are *metaphors*. A *simile* works in the same way, but uses the word *like* to link the comparison: 'she was dressed up like a dog's dinner'; 'he was like a bull in a china shop'. Dictionaries attempt to sort out *metaphors* and *similes* into standard English, colloquial or informal, and slang. But this is even more arbitrary than the usual divisions between these categories.

Metaphors and similes are the imagery of poetry, and can add colour to everyday language. But they soon become **clichés**, weary and banal. George Orwell warned against using any metaphor or simile we are used to seeing or hearing (*Politics and the English Language*, 1946). *Mixed metaphors* should be avoided as they easily become ridiculous: 'You must put your foot down with a firm hand'.

metaphysical   *Metaphysics* is the title of a treatise by the Greek philosopher, Aristotle (384–322BC), in which he dealt with the ultimate nature of being. Dryden and Johnson used the label *metaphysical* about certain 17th-century poets, including John Donne, because they were using convoluted imagery to express an underlying meaning.

Meta is the Greek word for 'after', and Aristotle's treatise came after his works on physics. Nevertheless, *methaphysical* came to be misused to describe ideas and revelations that transcend the external physical world, almost as a synonym for 'mystical'. Outside academic philosophy, this is how *metaphysical* is often used now, for concepts that are intangible, which relate to another kind of reality, more real, some believe, than the seeming reality of the world around us. It is unfortunate and confusing that *metaphysical* is also used pejoratively about ideas that are too abstract to make sense or to be of any use.

metathesis   See **malapropism** . . .

meteorologist or **weatherman**   *Meteorologists* chart atmospheric phenomena in order to forecast the weather. When they do this on television, standing in front of electronically animated maps, they are more likely to be called *weathermen*. *Weatherman* has become a unisex word, for 'weatherperson' or 'weatherwoman' sounds silly.

meteorology   See **climatology** . . .

meter or **metre**   Both spellings are used in Britain for different purposes. *Meters* are gauges for measuring things: barometer, speedometer, thermometer. . . . *Metre* is used in all metric measurements: metre, **kilometre**. . . . In America, *meter* is the only spelling, whatever the meaning.

method or **technique**   When it comes to carrying out a process or an operation, the words are often used interchangeably, with *technique* as the fashionable alternative, since *technology* is a **buzzword**. In some ways, the words can have slightly different meanings. *Method* suggests a procedure that has been developed; *technique* is more of a surface word, for the way of doing something quickly and efficiently. Compare: 'he has worked out a method for assessing when to order new stocks' with 'she has a technique for dealing with complaints'.

methodology   The word is sometimes criticized as an unnecessary *-ology* word that means no more than 'method'. But methodology goes further, suggesting a detailed analysis of principles and a scientific approach: 'the methodology of statistical analysis'.

meticulous   Its proper meaning is fussy and pernickety, an over-attention to detail: 'A meticulous examination of the proposals wastes everyone's time'. But dictionaries accept that *meticulous* is often used now in a good sense, to mean careful and thorough. As a result, *over-meticulous* has to be used for the original meaning.

métier   The French word *métier* used to be a pretentious way of describing someone's job ('What is your métier?'). If *métier* is used now, it is more likely to refer to a particular skill or knowledge: 'his métier is using statistics to make accurate sales forecasts'.

metre   See **meter** . . .

metric   Most measurements in Britain are now metric, but there are a number of old-established expressions that continue to keep the old imperial units alive. Willard R Espy (*Words at Play*) quotes Walter Sullivan in *The New York Times*: 'Will angry men ever cry "I'll beat you to within a centimetre of your life"? Or "Give him a millimetre and he'll take a kilometre"?'

As part of life in a metric world, remember that the stop after km, cm, kg, ml, etc is often omitted now (see **abbreviations**) and that they do not take an *-s* in the plural (17km, 57ml . . .). *Gramme* is French for one-thousandth of a kilogram, but *gram* is the usual spelling in English (dictionaries show *gramme* as an alternative, but it looks out of place). The abbreviation in singular and plural is g (not 'gm').

metro   See **underground** . . .

mews   *Mew* is an old verb for putting hawks in cages, and *mews* first became the name for the royal stables at Charing Cross in London, which were built in the place where at one time hawks were *mewed*. Hence *mews* came to mean a courtyard for stabling. In fashionable parts of London, most of these have long since been converted into small expensive houses, or flats over garages. A mews in Mayfair or in Kensington can be a prestigious address.

Although *mews* is a plural noun, it is normally treated as singular, as if it were a road or a street: 'Hays Mews *is* only a couple of minutes' walk from Berkeley Square'.

mezzo-giorno *Mezzo-giorno* is Italian for midday, and it is the name sometimes used in Italy for the southern part of the country ('the land of the intense midday sun'). Because this part of Italy is poor and economically deprived, *mezzo-giorno* has come to be used in both Italian and English to highlight the problems of the Italian south, because of its social and economic deprivation.

micro *Micro* is the familiar name used for any kind of microcomputer (see **desktop computer . . .**). *Micro* is also used as shorthand for a microprocessor, which serves as the **central processing unit** of a computer.

micro- This Greek prefix for 'small' has been called on increasingly since World War II to formulate new words, such as *microcomputer* (see **desktop computer . . .**), *microfilm* (a film print of *microcopies* of documents, etc), *microsurgery* (complex surgical operations using miniature precision instruments), *microlinguistics* (a study of particular aspects of language, rather than the overall pattern). . . . See also **macro-**

Conversationally, *micro-* takes over when **mini-** doesn't seem small enough ('This café serves microportions of cake')!

microbe See germ . . .

microchip or **silicon chip** In general use they come to the same thing. A *microchip* is a minute wafer processed to form an integrated circuit. This has led to the phenomenal development of the electronics industry. Microchips are usually made from *silicon*, a semiconductive element. Santa Clara in California is known as Silicon Valley because of its concentration of manufacturers of microelectronic components.

micro computer See **desktop computer . . .**

microwave *Microwave* has been in use since the 1930s for micromagnetic wavelengths at the lower end of the spectrum. In the 1970s *microwave* took on a new meaning as the everyday word in millions of kitchens for a microwave oven.

middle age There is no general agreement when youth ends and *middle age* begins. As people stay active and healthy for longer, the onset of *middle age* is delayed, and it continues into what used to be called old age. The start of *middle age* used to be considered 40 ('Life begins at 40' was the consolation), but it is now often postponed until 50.

middlebrow *Middlebrow* has an unexciting feeling about it: it suggests dull, middle-of-the-road, middle-aged, nothing too jarring and certainly nothing remotely obscure. Some of that is unfair, for *middlebrow*, in music, for example, would include some of the compositions of the great composers, as well as George Gershwin and *West Side Story*. . . . On the other hand, it would exclude most music written before the 17th century, not to mention early Chinese folk songs.

middle class or **bourgeois** The terms have less in common than they once did. In fact, *bourgeois* is not used often now in English, which is just as well for people were often not clear what they meant by it. For the French, a bourgeois was first of all a citizen (the word is related to the English 'borough'), then later a shopkeeper or tradesman, and now one of the materialistic middle class. This last meaning carried over into English, where *bourgeois* came to mean rigidly conventional in attitudes, opinions and even in sexual habits. (It should be pronounced more or less as in French, roughly: 'BOORZHwah').

Middle class was never such a loaded term as *bourgeois*, although it did at one time suggest a rather colourless in-between section of society, churchgoing and never wavering from voting Conservative. But now many people who would have been called **working class** enjoy privileges that previously belonged to the middle class. The result is that *middle class* has become more of a universal class of homeowners in centrally heated houses, with two cars, dishwashers, microwave cookers, video machines and children at universities. It is said by sociologists that this new middle class in Britain will very likely take in half the population by the end of the century.

In America *middle class* has long had a wider application. The 19th-century writer, Matthew Arnold, observed 'That which in England we call the middle class is in America virtually the nation'. Certainly most Americans have what could be called a *middle-class attitude* in not accepting the idea of a lower rung on the social ladder. On the other hand, using the measure of income, there is evidence in the 1990s from the US Census Bureau, that the percentage of middle-income families is declining.

On both sides of the Atlantic *middle class* is taking on more of an economic meaning than a description of social origin, occupation and **lifestyle**. See also **class**

middleman In theory a *middleman* is anyone who comes between the producer of goods and the people buying them, which would include wholesalers and retailers. At one time, it was possible to buy many products from the people who produced them, so *middleman* had a certain pejorative ring, suggesting an unnecessary extra person to make a profit and so push up prices. Now society is altogether dependent on the distribution of goods, involving a chain of middlemen. As a result, the term has lost most of its significance and comes in for less use.

middle manager A *middle manager* in business is, or perhaps was, comparable to a sergeant or warrant-officer in the army, that is someone who does not make important decisions or spend large sums of money, but puts into operation what is passed down by senior management. That is changing. In the 1970s, the management consultant, Peter Drucker, forecast that **information technology** would turn most people in business into 'knowledge workers', since their **desktop computers** would give them access to a great deal of data, previously only available to senior management.

As a result, in many companies, middle managers are no longer cogs on the gearwheel, confined to a subordinate place in the hierarchy. Now they might have a finger on the steering-wheel through initiating ideas that influence senior management, and with control of very large sums of money.

midlife crisis   See **menopause** . . .

midtown   See **downtown** . . .

midwifery   Some people put the stress on the first syllable, giving the word three syllables: 'MID-wiff-ry'. But the tendency now is to move the stress to the second syllable, and to give the word four syllables: 'mid-WIFF-er-y'. Both pronunciations are acceptable, with 'midWIFFery' likely to take over.

miffed   This is often seen as an American slang word, meaning to be put out by something: 'he was miffed when she brought an unexpected guest for dinner'. Most dictionaries label *miffed* colloquial or informal. The word has been used in this sense since the early 19th century, and is good enough for *The Times Literary Supplement*. Admittedly, it is used more in America, but no one should be *miffed* if it is used in Britain.

might or **could**   See **could** . . .

might or **may**   See **may** . . .

might have been   See **manqué** . . .

migraine   Two pronunciations are heard in Britain, 'MEEgrain' or 'MYEgrain', and some dictionaries offer them as alternatives. 'MEEgrain' is more usual.

'Migratory' or **'miGRATory'**   The stress can be on the first or the second syllable. But some people consider the latter is a mispronunciation and that only 'MIgratory' is correct.

mileage   *Mileage* is, of course, the number of miles travelled. This meaning has been extended to cover the extent of usefulness or profitability of a product or an event: 'We want to get as much mileage as possible out of the advertising'. This seems a slick go-getting use of *mileage*, and words such as 'value', 'use' or 'profit' are more natural.

The spelling *milage* is given as an alternative in dictionaries, but *mileage* has become so much more usual, that *milage* looks like a mistake.

milieu   *Milieu* properly means social surroundings rather than social class. But these often go together, so it can be useful to fall back on *milieu* when the word **class** might cause uneasiness or resentment. At the same time, *milieu* can also cover environmental surroundings, such as town or country ('lieu' is French for 'place').

Dictionaries usually show both the French plural (*milieux*) and the anglicized form (*milieus*) as alternatives. Anglicization is justified because the word has been used in English for 150 years at least.

militancy, **Militant** or **militant**   The terms *militancy* and *militant* were used in the mid-19th century in non-military senses for political and industrial groups using action, such as demonstrations and strikes, to bring about political and social change. Both words came into use about the suffragette movement early in the 20th century.

With a capital M, *Militant* is short for *Militant Tendency*, the extreme political movement, an unofficial faction that emerged from within the Labour Party during the 1970s, whose ultimate aim seemed to be nothing less than the overthrow of the existing social order. The newspaper of the group is called *Militant*, which led to the name being taken up by the media. In the early 1980s, the Labour Party denounced Militant, seeing it as an electoral liability. See also **activist**

'MILitarily' or **'miliTARily'**   The orthodox pronunciation puts the stress on the first syllable but the flight of unaccented syllables that follows is awkward. During the 1991 Gulf War, correspondents, under stress reporting from the battlefront, were often inclined to take it easy and say 'miliTARily', and it is likely that stress on the third syllable will become usual.

military hardware   See **hardware**

military intervention   See **force** . . .

militate or **mitigate**   *Mitigate* is sometimes used wrongly instead of *militate*. The two words are different. When something is *mitigated*, the bad effects are lessened: 'the effects of the famine will be mitigated by worldwide aid'. *Militate* is connected with the word 'military' and means to 'go against something': 'his casual appearance militated against people taking him seriously'. It's a good rule never to write or say *mitigate against*, as it is only possible to *militate* against something.

millennium   We shall all get tired of this word, as broadcasters, newscasters and pundits use it ceaselessly as the year 2000 gets nearer. A *millennium* is 1000 years. Two *millennia* or two *millenniums* are 2000 years, and so on. Both plural forms are accepted: *millennia* to some people sounds more learned, while *millenniums* could sound as if you don't know any better. It is easy to slip up and spell it with one *-n-*, which would look really ignorant.

milliard The word is still included in British dictionaries (it has never been an American word), although it is now obsolete, and many people would not know what it means. It meant one thousand million, but in nearly all cases, **billion** is now used for that number.

milliner The word comes from Milan, and milliners as far back as the early 15th century used to sell Milanese hats, gloves and other accessories. Although *milliner* sounds if it belongs to a Jane Austen novel, it remains the most usual word for someone making or selling hats, and every year comes in for a fair share of use in June, during Ascot week.

mini- It could be said that *mini* had been waiting in the wings since the 17th century as part of that sedate word *miniature*. In 1932 W G Eavestaff patented a compact piano for people living in flats, registering the name as *Minipiano*. 1959 brought the *Mini*, Alec Issigonis' innovatory car design. But it took Mary Quant's sexy symbol of the 1960s, the *miniskirt*, to make *mini-* take off as the indispensable prefix to attach to anything that is a smaller version of the real thing. Since then it has never stopped: chancellors of the exchequer present *mini-budgets* between their main budgets, privatized industries issue *mini-prospectuses*, travel agents offer *mini-breaks* (which used to be called weekends), and a politician on television has accused an opponent of being out of his *mini-mind*.

Mini- remains available to all of us to attach to any noun, sometimes with a hyphen (which *miniskirt* sported to begin with), sometimes without (*minibus*, *minicab*, *minicomputer*), which is usually when the compound word is in everyday use. For *minicomputer* see **desktop computer**

minimal and **minimal art** See marginal . . .

minimize See maximize . . .

minimum (plural forms) See maximum . . .

minimum lending rate (MLR) See bank rate . . .

minister, parson, priest, rector or **vicar** Ecclesiastical regulations and customs surround these words, and even long-serving churchwardens can get bogged down over the differences between them.

Minister is short for *minister of religion*: it can refer to a Protestant clergyman who is authorized to administer sacraments and conduct religious services. It is also a convenient name for nonconformist clergy for whom the alternative titles might not be applicable. The word can extend to the Jewish faith, where a rabbi can be called a minister.

Parson is a very old word (a parson related one of Chaucer's *Canterbury Tales*, in the late 14th century), and was used for any holder of a parochial benefice. It became extended in popular use for anyone wearing a

dog-collar, particularly when they were the butt of music-hall jokes. Generally *parson* should be avoided, as it could sound disrespectful.

Priest is one of the orders of ministry in the Anglican, Roman Catholic and Orthodox Churches. But the word can also be used about a minister in other religions of the world: we can talk about a Tibetan priest or a Buddhist priest, for example (but not a Jewish priest).

At one time there was a distinction between a *rector* and a *vicar*: in the Church of England a rector would receive directly all tithes, that is taxes imposed for the support of the Church, whereas a vicar would not have that entitlement. This distinction is preserved only by the name **rectory** or vicarage in particular parishes.

These notes apply to most everyday situations, but it should be added that within the different churches, there are additional theological subtleties in the way titles are used. See also **pastor; rabbi**

minor See infant . . .

minorities In the 20th century the word *minority* has been turned upside down. At one time it would have meant the upper crust of society, the small group of privileged people at the top: it is now usually taken to mean the **underprivileged** at the bottom. For *minorities* are groups of people set apart, by their physical appearance, their dress, religion, culture or language, from the mainstream of society in the country they live in. Exploitation of these minorities was long accepted as normal. But the cry **human rights** is heard everywhere, and the word *minorities* now has an explosive political charge in nearly every country in the world.

minority See majority . . .

minuscule or **miniscule** Because of the pull of the prefix **mini-**, *minuscule* is often misspelt 'miniscule'. *The Independent* commented that a Bill going through Parliament was subjected to 'marginal amendments involving miniscule technical matters', and *The Observer* noted that a certain organization would lose 'a not-so-miniscule £20 million'. Tut-tut!

mis- There are not many rules about hyphens that can be relied upon, so make the most of this one. Words formed with the prefix *mis-* never take a hyphen. There are no exceptions, and you can ignore older or more obstinate dictionaries that show hyphens in such words as 'mis-shape'. From now on, you can *mishandle* something, *misremember* your *misspent* youth, and make as many *misstatements* as you like – all without hyphens.

mise en scène See set . . .

mishmash There are people who think *mishmash* is a slang word. It is nothing more than a repetition of the Old English word *mash* (as in 'sausage and mash'), with a change of vowel sound, and has been in use since the 15th century. *Mishmash* is respectable English, as good as if not better than many other words: '. . . ill-considered mishmash of pseudo-Nietzschean and other ideas . . .' (*Fontana Dictionary of Modern Thought*). Leo Rosten considers *mishmash* (which he pronounces 'mishmosh', the pronunciation demanded by Groucho Marx – and who would know better?) 'A triumph of **onomatopoeia**'. There is certainly no other word that describes total confusion and disorder with such immediacy.

The hyphen is usually in evidence, but some of the latest dictionaries spell it as one word, which makes it look even more of a mishmash.

misinformation   See **disinformation** . . .

misprint, **literal** or **typo**   These are all words for a printing error. *Misprint* is the most common word used by people not involved in publishing or printing. *Literal* (short for *literal error*, that is a mistake in letters) is the word most in use by writers, publishers and proofreaders. Printers often use the word *typo*.

Miss   See **Mr, Mrs,** and **Miss; Ms** . . .

missile   The American Secretary of State pronounces it 'MISSle' (rhyming with 'whistle'); the British Foreign Secretary says 'MISS-yle' (last syllable rhyming with 'mile'). The American pronunciation has better antecedents, since that is how it was pronounced in Britain in the 17th century.

missionary position   Extraordinary as it seems, missionaries are said to have preached to primitive peoples that the only moral position for sexual intercourse is for the woman to lie on her back with the man on top facing her. *The Daily Telegraph* once reported that in some states in America a woman could get a divorce if her husband made love to her in any other way than the *missionary position*. This expression has become used for straightforward 'no-nonsense' sex, with the implication that it's dull and uninteresting. The words are being applied to other things to suggest they are conventional and banal: 'This is a mind in the missionary position' (*The Sunday Times*); 'it is an example of architecture in the missionary position' (BBC).

mistakable or **mistakeable**   These used to be alternative spellings but most current dictionaries show only *mistakable*.

mistral   Although there are similar winds in other regions, *mistral* (pron: 'MISStrahl') should only be used about the wind in southern France, the dry cold wind that blows from the north down the Rhône valley into Provence. See also **sirocco**

mistress   See **-ess forms; lover** . . .; **master** . . .

mistrust   See **distrust** . . .

MIT   The Massachusetts Institute of Technology is such a polysyllabic name that it is usually referred to as MIT. It is a university, rather than an institute, that was founded in Boston in 1891, moving to its present site in 1916. Among other things, it is famous for its work in **linguistics**, largely because of the influence of Noam Chomsky, professor of linguistics at MIT.

mitigate   See **militate** . . .

mixed economy   A *mixed economy* does not refer to an economy depending on both industry and agriculture, but to an economy with a system that allows **market forces** to have their effect, alongside a degree of government control. See also **market economy**

mixed feelings   See **ambivalence** . . .

mixed media   *Mixed media* describes an art form that combines different forms of expression to achieve an effect. Although an early use of the term was about Andy Warhol's exhibitions in the 1960s, which linked projected colours and patterns with music and film, there is nothing new in the idea: opera, for example, with a combination of lighting effects, design, music and dance has long made use of mixed media. Nevertheless, an awareness of *mixed media* techniques is having an effect in the theatre, where plays sometimes make use of film or slide projection as part of the drama. Art galleries also use the term *mixed media* for a combination of a **collage** and a painting.

mixed metaphor   See **metaphor** . . .

MLR (minimum lending rate)   See **bank rate** . . .

model   Models, as three-dimensional representations of objects, usually on a smaller scale, are familiar (a model car, a model of the Taj Mahal, etc). But a model can also be abstract: the word can be used for an outline description of a system or of a concept, which by eliminating non-essential details enables something to be more easily understood. *Model* can also be used on a much grander scale for an intellectual or philosophical synthesis: P D Ouspensky called his exposition of the use of psychological method to explain science, religion and art, *A New Model of the Universe* (1931).

model or **mannequin**   Sometime after World War II, *mannequins* made their last appearance on the catwalks at fashion shows, as the word became replaced by *models*. This was probably because *model* is an all-purpose word that covers not only showing off clothes, but also posing for photographs in advertising and appearing in television commercials. It also covers men and women, although, as a rare linguistic instance of men being in the secondary role, a model is often assumed to be a woman, unless *male model* is specified.

In the old days of *mannequins*, some people clung to the French pronunciation, although it was usually anglicized: 'MANNikin'.

modem The word, often used in computer technology, was put together from the first syllables of **mod**ulator and **dem**odulator. In non-technical terms, it is a device that can connect computers to a telephone system so that data can be transmitted.

modern The word *modern* has always meant different things to different people at different times and in different contexts. The problem with *modern* is that 'it is always receding into the past' (*Fontana Dictionary of Modern Thought*, 1988).

Although *modern* comes from the Latin word for 'just now', in **linguistics**, *modern English* is taken to be the language from the death of Chaucer in 1400, or a hundred years later, from about 1500. Yet English has changed so much since then.

Modern art is essentially 20th-century art, for some art historians starting with Picasso and Braque finding their way into cubism in the early 1900s, for others beginning with **abstract** art of the 1920s. Other people will use *modern art* as a term of abuse for any art they cannot come to terms with: Winston Churchill showed his displeasure at Graham Sutherland's portrait of him by calling it 'This remarkable example of modern art!'

Modern architecture in Britain is said to start with the 'brave new world' architecture of the 1930s, which at the time seemed the shape of things to come, and now seems as curiously out of touch as 1930s Buicks and Chryslers. With architecture, it is better to separate *modern architecture*, as a stylistic or historical term, from **contemporary** architecture, architecture of our time, which could mean post-World War II, or the 1980s and 90s.

In general use, *modern* at one time meant simply anything that was recent and not old-fashioned. But the word *modern*, itself, has become in some ways out of date, superseded by terms such as **experimental**, *progressive* or *innovatory*. Leaving aside art, architecture, **modern dance** and technology, if we are to use *modern* in a general way, we can hardly do better than accept Alan Bullock's broad definition, which is to relate *modern* to the 20th century as a whole.

modern or **contemporary architecture** See previous entry

modern art See modern

modern dance Choreographers would not always agree on a definition of *modern dance*. Frederick Ashton's (1904–88) work for the Royal Ballet, although contemporary, is too rooted in classical tradition to be included. In one sense, Jerome Robbins' dance arrangements for *West Side Story* are *modern dance*: from another point of view, they make too many concessions to story-telling and entertainment. For although *modern dance* has to be an open-ended term, it is usually associated with an abstract style that has social and psychological content, and is intellectual, making no concessions to entertainment. It was Martha Graham (1893–1991), the American dancer and choreographer, who more than anyone else revealed that dance could be socially committed, and set the style for modern dance, not only in America but in Europe.

modern English See modern

Modern English Usage See Fowler

modifier (grammar) See adjectives

module and **modular** *Modular* is the modish descriptive word for prefabrication. Traditional building methods make use of a number of components that only have a purpose in the complete assembly. A modular system uses *modules*, standardized units that exist in their own right, which can be combined with other modules in different ways to make, for example, a complete kitchen, or even a factory, which can be designed to meet individual requirements by selection and arrangement of modules.

The word and the concept are extended to cover certain university courses: a student is given a choice of modules, set areas of study for prescribed periods, which can be combined at will to make up a total course eligible for a degree.

modus vivendi and **modus operandi** The Latin *modus vivendi* means literally 'way of living'. The orthodox use of the phrase is for a temporary compromise whereby parties in dispute with one another (a trade union and employers, for example) can work together until a proper agreement is arrived at. The phrase is also used in another way, accepted by some dictionaries, for a personal adaptation to a difficult situation: 'they were not happy together, but she has found her own modus vivendi'. That is a convenient way to apply the expression, but some people feel it is the wrong use of it.

Modus operandi (Latin for 'way of operating') is a useful term for describing the way something functions, particularly as a contribution to a system, or the way a person handles a matter: 'Her modus operandi, when faced with opposition over a proposal, is to present pages of so-called facts and figures, headed "There Is No Alternative"!' (Pron: 'MOHdus viVENdee', 'MOHdus opeRANdee'.)

Mohammed, **Mahomet** or **Muhammad** *Mahomet* has become an archaic form. The usual spelling now is *Mohammed*: the central boulevard in Marrakech is named Mohammed V (after the former king), and this is the spelling used in many books. Islamic scholars prefer the spelling *Muhammad*, which is also the spelling used in the *OED*. See also Muslim . . .

Mohammedan See Muslim . . .

moisten or **moisturize** *Moisten* has been in the language since the 16th century. *Moisturize* is a fancy word dreamt up by advertising agencies in the 1940s. In fairness to them, perhaps they wanted a word with a different meaning: *moisten* means to make slightly wet, whereas *moisturize* could suggest relieving dryness. That may be splitting hairs, as *moisten* is the normal word, with *moisturize* best left to television commercials and the labels on cosmetic products.

mole In the world of espionage, a *mole* is an undercover agent working in an enemy country. Since the 1970s, *mole* has been used more widely about anyone in industry or in government departments, who has access to confidential information and betrays it to the competition or the opposition.

'MOMentarily' or **'momenTARily'** It is still considered preferable to put the stress on the first syllable, although it leads to an awkward flight of unaccented syllables. Some British dictionaries accept as an alternative the American pronunciation which puts the stress on the *tar* syllable ('momenTARily'), but many people disapprove of this.

moment of truth The *moment of truth* is a situation when the chips are down and bluffing will get you nowhere. It is a good phrase, translated from the Spanish *el momento de la verdad*, the moment in a bullfight described by Ernest Hemingway as '. . . the final sword thrust, the actual encounter between the man and the animal' (*Death in the Afternoon*, 1932). Compare **high noon**

momentum See **acceleration** . . .

mommy track See **pregnancy discrimination**

monetarism and **monetarist** See **financial** . . .

monetary See **financial** . . .

money It is usual now to write even small amounts of money in figures: £3 (rather than *three pounds*). When it is a round sum of £100 or £1000, these figures are not preceded by 'a', which only applies if words are used: 'it costs *a* hundred pounds' but 'it costs £100'.

In the heady years of the 1980s, when salaries of senior jobs were going up and up, it became trendy to use the metric K (abbreviation for *kilo*) for salaries in advertisements: £30K (£30,000pa). But this practice does not usually apply to jobs carrying more modest salaries: no one advertises in the local paper for a gardener, offering £12K!

With worldwide inflation over the years, *millions* and even *billions* are more frequently seen in writing. The rows of naughts were becoming daunting, and these vast sums of money are now usually expressed in other ways: £100m or £100 million (instead of £100,000,000); £100bn (instead of £100,000,000,000). (For the different definitions of **billion**, see entry.)

money or **funds** See **funds** . . .

monitoring The word was first used in the 1920s for keeping a check on technical sequences. Later it was applied in a medical context, for observing and noting the progress of patients. It has now become extended still further. Any operation or scheme, such as a marketing plan or an election campaign, can be *monitored*, that is checks taken at intervals to make sure that the expected developments and progress are taking place at the right time.

monokini See **bikini**

monologue or **soliloquy** They are both primarily words used in the theatre for a character talking alone, and derive from Greek and Latin respectively. *Monologue* is the word generally used now, when an actor talks directly to the audience. A play that consists of only one actor speaking is a *monologue*. A *soliloquy* is a character thinking out loud, while the audience listen, almost as if by chance. The most famous soliloquy in English drama is Hamlet's 'To be or not to be' speech (Act III Sc i). Present-day actors are more likely to use *monologue* rather than *soliloquy* about modern plays, such as Alan Bennett's series, *Talking Heads*.

monopoly See **cartel** . . .

monseigneur or **monsignor** *Monseigneur* is French, a title formerly used for princely ranks in the aristocracy, and now accorded to French bishops and certain other prelates. *Monsignor* is the Italian version of the title, which is accorded to certain senior Roman Catholic priests, as well as to some officers at the Vatican.

Monsieur, Madame and **Mademoiselle** When French people are in England, do we introduce them as *Monsieur* Dupont, *Mademoiselle* Legrand, etc or *Mr* Dupont, *Miss* (or *Ms*) Legrand? For the use of foreign courtesy titles in an English context, see **Mr, Mrs, etc.**

montage See **collage** . . .

mood (in grammar) The *mood* of a verb is the way it is used to express meaning. The term was an alternative to 'mode', from Latin 'modus' (measure, or the way something is done), which would make more sense as the grammatical term. Mood only has relevance in formal grammar where four moods are catalogued:
The *indicative mood* is the straightforward use of a verb to express action: 'the dog *bit* the man'.
The *infinitive mood* is usually (but not always) the 'to' form of the verb: 'the dog wants *to bite* the man'.
The *imperative mood* is when a verb is used imperiously, that is to give a command: '*Tell* your dog to leave me alone'.
The *subjunctive mood* expresses doubt, desire, or a hypothesis: 'if your dog *were* to bite me . . .'; 'if it *come* to that . . .'. For a further explanation of the subjunctive, see **if I** *was* . . .

moonlight or **moonlit**   The best way in most cases is to use *moonlight* as the noun and *moonlit* as the descriptive word: 'Ill met by moonlight, proud Titania' (*A Midsummer Night's Dream*, Act II Sc i), but 'a moonlit night'. But when it is something taking place at night, happening during the time when the moon could be up, *moonlight* becomes the descriptive word: 'a moonlight flit' or 'a moonlight party'.

moonlighting   A poetic word used since the 1960s to describe the practice of doing a second job, usually in the evening, in addition to holding down a full-time job. The illicit flavour of *moonlighting* does not mean the second job is illegal, merely that it is during the evening or outside normal working hours.

moonlit   See moonlight . . .

moor   See heath . . .

morbid   The medical and psychological use of *morbid* exists alongside a general use. The word derives from the Latin word for 'disease', and a physical condition is morbid when it indicates a disease. *Morbid anatomy* is the study of diseased parts of the body. In the 19th century this was adapted to describe anyone who is preoccupied with death or disaster. Later, *morbid* also came to be used about a remark or an atmosphere that seems to focus on depression and gloom. In this sense, it is similar at times to the conversational or slang use of the word *sick*. A 'morbid joke' is a more literary way of saying a 'sick joke'. See also ill . . .

more or less   *More or less* is a useful way of indicating that a statement may not be altogether accurate, but is sufficiently so for it to be worth making: 'we have more or less agreed terms' means we have gone a long way towards agreeing them, but there are still some outstanding points to be cleared up. If we are told that 'this is more or less what it will cost', we have every right to expect that the estimate is not far out, although, depending on the circumstances, it could be naive to take that for granted. *More or less* should really mean rather more than less, which is no guarantee that someone might not use it to mean rather less than more.

more or **most**   *More* is used when there is a comparison between two standards: 'the students from this school are more advanced than the other first-year students'. When more than two are involved, *most* is used: 'taking the students from all five schools, these are the most advanced'. When it is a straight statement, rather than a comparison, the choice between *more* and *most* is often a question of personal style: 'the most (or more) expensive wines on the list'; 'the days that were most (or more) peaceful'.

more equal   See equal

more excellent   See excellent

more importantly   See important . . .

mores   *Mores* is a much stronger word than custom or convention: it suggests a code of behaviour that is deep-rooted and founded on moral attitudes, or at least on beliefs about the right way to do things. While not following the usual custom or convention might, in some circumstances, be tolerated, flouting *mores* would cause deep offence. The usual pronunciation is 'MAWrayz' but 'MAWreez' is an accepted alternative.

more than or **over**   See over . . .

more than one *is* or **are**   See one

morgue or **mortuary**   The words are synonymous. Hospitals usually have *mortuaries*, while municipal authorities have *morgues*, where dead bodies await identification or autopsies.

morphia or **morphine**   These are both words for the narcotic drug derived from opium. *Morphia* is the general word, while *morphine* is used in medicine when the drug is administered to relieve pain.

mortgage   The word relates to the Latin word for death (compare French 'mort'), and meant a 'dead pledge': the reason for the term apparently is that once the money is repaid, the pledge is, in effect, 'dead'. The word was originally spelt 'morgage' until lawyers underlined the meaning by adding the Latinate *t*, which is not pronounced: 'MAWgidge'.

mortgagee, **mortgager** or **mortgagor**   A *mortgagee*, usually but not necessarily a building society or a bank, lends the money for the purchase of a property, and retains the title deeds as security. The *mortgager* is the person borrowing the money, and in legal documents this is usually spelt *mortgagor*.

mortician   See funeral director . . .

mortuary   See morgue . . .

Moscow   The British can never get used to Americans making the second syllable of the name of this city rhyme with 'cow': Americans find it equally strange that the British pronounce it 'koh'. Neither is all that close to the name in Russian, so does it matter? A better transliteration is used for the river on which Moscow stands – the Moskva.

Moslem   See Muslim . . .

mosquitoes or **mosquitos**   Some dictionaries show both plural forms as alternatives. Others show only *mosquitoes*, which is more usual.

most   See more . . .

most excellent   See excellent

most of   See majority of . . .

motel   See hotel . . .

motherly or **matriarchal** *Matriarchal* is a word that denotes the authority of a woman as head of a family, a tribe or a nation: it was used about Golda Meir as Prime Minister of Israel (1969–74). *Motherly* is a more human word, carrying with it the idea of mother-love and womanly tenderness and care. See also **fatherly** . . .

motion pictures The British go to the *cinema*, *films* or the *pictures* (see **cinema**), the Americans go to the *movies*, but no one goes to the *motion pictures*. This was a silly term dreamt up in Hollywood to give the film business respectability and self-importance. It survives in America, where people involved may still talk solemnly about the *motion picture industry*.

motivate See activate . . .

motivate, motivation and **motivational** There is nothing new about the way *motivate* and *motivation* are used, except that they are being over-used: teachers have to motivate their students, instead of encouraging them; people at work must have motivation, instead of wanting to do the job; we ask 'What motivated you?' instead of 'Why did you do it?'. . . . Management consultants give *motivation* as much space in recommendations as cost-per-unit efficiency. The Xerox company motivates staff not only with a bonus, but with a badge inscribed 'You Deserve An X Today' (as you would expect, X at Xerox is the most important letter in the alphabet). *Motivate* and *motivation* are fashionable words. They do in fact acknowledge an enlightened principle, which is that if people are to give of their best, their hearts must be involved.

Motivational is a descriptive word now used mostly in advertising. It arrived from America in the 1950s. Not far from New York, 600 feet up overlooking the Hudson River, was the Institute for Motivational Research. It was never an academic institute, but a successful business that helped advertisers to understand the unconscious reasons why people buy their products. According to Ernest Dichter, who founded the so-called institute, and who was earlier in his career a psychoanalyst in Vienna, motivational research 'takes the social sciences out of the seminar and into the supermarket'. Vance Packard explored examples of deep-seated psychological motivation in advertising, and gave his book about it the sinister title *Hidden Persuaders* (1957).

mot juste The French phrase *mot juste* is used in English because there is no perfect English expression that has the same force: the 'right word' or 'appropriate expression' are half-hearted in comparison. For *mot juste* means hitting a verbal bull's-eye or ringing the bell on a wordprocessor.

motley Chaucer was using *motley* in the 14th century to mean varied colours. Shakespeare used it in the late 16th century for the patchwork colours of the traditional jester's or clown's costume. This meaning has survived almost unchanged into the 1990s: motley colours mean a mixture of different colours.

Another meaning has also come through. In the 17th century a group of people wearing clothes of different colours were called a motley assembly. This was later applied to any ill-assorted combination of people or objects. In this last sense, *motley* has become mildly pejorative: to talk about a 'motley crew' or a 'motley collection' is on the whole disparaging.

motor See engine . . .

motorcade See cavalcade . . .

mottoes or **mottos** Either, with a preference for *mottoes*.

mould In Britain, all the meanings of the noun (a hollow shape used to create a form by pouring in liquid that sets, a growth of fungus on food, topsoil, etc) are spelt *mould*. So is the verb, meaning to shape something in a particular way, or to direct or influence ideas. In America, *mold* is the spelling for all meanings of the word.

S J Perelman, who wrote scripts for Marx Brothers films, once conceived an epitaph for himself: 'After they made S J Perelman,' he wrote, 'they broke the mold'.

mountain bike Dictionaries are slow to catch up with *mountain bike*, although these light rugged bikes, with bulbous heavy-duty tyres, straight no-nonsense handlebars and at least 15 gears, now account for half of all bicycle sales in Britain. To begin with, mountain bikes had nothing to do with mountains. They were developed for the lifestyle of southern California, where surfers used them for riding over sand-dunes. Mountain bikes are the push-bike equivalent of Land-Rovers: in fact, they were first called *all-terrain bikes*.

mouse It is easy to see why this computer accessory was called a *mouse*: it is a small rounded **user-friendly** box, with a 'tail' linked to a **desktop computer**. The operator rolls it around the desk as it guides a pointer on the screen to whatever item is required. Once this is selected, a button on the mouse is pressed, and the computer does the rest.

moustache or **mustache** The Atlantic separates the two different spellings and pronunciations. In Britain it is *moustache*, pronounced 'me(r)STAHSH'; in America it is usually spelt *mustache*, and usually pronounced 'MUSStash' (although very occasionally the British spelling and pronunciation are also used).

movable or **moveable** Feasts can be *movable* or *moveable*, with a definite preference for *movable*. See also **-able** . . .

movies See cinema . . .

moving average The term is heard in statistics for a method of pointing up trends over a period.

Instead of taking the average over, say 20 years, an average is worked out for the first few years, which is then adjusted by adding another year or two at a time, until the whole period is covered. In theory, the *moving average* that is revealed by this series of averages should reveal the general tendency.

MP (Member of Parliament) The letters are often placed after the written name of a member of parliament: Henry Smith, MP. But MP is neither an award nor a degree, so Henry Smith, CBE, MP, or Henry Smith, DPhil, MP, etc does not look right. The way round this is to write Henry Smith, CBE, Member of Parliament.

Mr, Mrs and Miss *Mr*, the abbreviated form of *mister*, dates from the 16th century. *Mister* as a courtesy title was an adaptation of 'master', a title of respect for a man in authority. *Mrs* and *Miss* both began as abbreviations for *mistress*. Before the 20th century, it was quite usual for a woman to address her husband as Mr . . ., just as a man would introduce his wife as Mrs. . . . But now everyone wants to appear relaxed and informal: we are invited in brochures and advertisements to ring **freefone** numbers and ask for 'Shirley' or 'Karen', and the **chattering classes** are immediately on first-name terms with professors, bishops and other dignitaries.

In the 1990s it is not always easy to know when to use *Mr*, *Mrs*, etc without sounding over-formal and stuffy. Even with important people, there is a tendency to use just their first names plus surnames; 'John Major slapped down Margaret Thatcher's attack . . .' began a story in *The Independent*, and in the headline there was even less formality: 'Major hits back at Thatcher'. At other times, *Mr* is used when it seems quaintly inappropriate: a news item in the same newspaper about a man who ran amok with a large pistol reported: 'Mr Dryden opened fire at random on the crowd . . .'.

Mr, Mrs, etc are useful when introducing people whose first names are unknown, although if they're wearing T-shirts and jeans, it can sound silly. To announce oneself, as some people do on the telephone, as Mrs Whoever-it-is or Mr So-and-so is now distinctly downmarket.

These titles have not by any means dropped out of use, and still have a place when a certain level of formality is in order. On other occasions, they can seem old-worldly. There are people who still prefer to use Mr, Mrs or Miss on their business cards or even typed below their signature, but the general custom now is to use first name plus surname. As you can see, it is difficult to lay down rules and principles about these courtesy titles.

Keeping those comments in mind, here are some guidelines. When using someone's name in full, it is often in order to leave out courtesy titles, unless the person is much older than you are, or holds a position of particular importance. For people of ill-repute, courtesy titles can seem ridiculous (see the news item quoted earlier about Mr Dryden opening fire at

random). As people get older, they are more inclined to expect them to be used. Otherwise, it is a matter of keeping a balance between being overfamiliar with people who might not like it and being in touch with the style of the 1990s.

Mr, Mrs, etc or Monsieur, Frau, etc What courtesy titles should be used for referring to foreigners in an English context? If we insist on using foreign titles, it can become laboured: 'Mr Brown welcomed Frau Brandt to the meeting, and they were later joined by Monsieur Dupont, Signor Fradeletto and Señora González'. Television and radio announcers are inclined to use *Mr*, *Mrs*, etc throughout, irrespective of nationality, although they are not consistent about this, and most newspapers follow the same rule, to avoid complications. For some reason, an exception is sometimes made by retaining *Madame* for French married women.

On ceremonial occasions, diplomats and toastmasters, who are well-versed in such matters, usually prefer foreign courtesy titles, where these are appropriate. But apart from situations where protocol must be observed, it gives fewer difficulties to use the English forms of address. No one is offended by this, and it can save awkwardness: titles such as *Mademoiselle*, *Senorita* . . ., in particular, can seem arch and out of place, since these titles are not always used in the same way as *Miss* or *Ms* are. Wimbledon tennis is British and no nonsense: scoreboards and umpires keep to *Mrs* and *Miss* for all women players, no matter where they come from.

Mrs Mary Smith or Mrs John Smith It used to be considered correct to refer to *Mrs John Smith*, if her husband was alive, But if she was divorced, or if she was a widow, she became *Mrs Mary Smith*. Most women now do not consider themselves appendages of their husbands, and it would have been very odd, before she was ennobled, to have introduced the first woman prime minister as 'Mrs Denis Thatcher'!

There remains the problem of announcing a husband and wife: *Mr and Mrs John Smith* is still the general rule, since 'Mr John Smith and Mrs Mary Smith' does not make the relationship clear. But it is an uneasy compromise that not all women are happy to accept.

Ms The title was devised in America in the early 1950s. The purpose was to replace 'Mrs' and 'Miss' so that women, like men, should have a form of address not linked to their marital status. *Ms* made little impact in Britain until the mid-1960s, and to begin with it had a hostile reception: B A Phythian, in his *Dictionary of Correct English* (1979), proclaimed, 'The word is foolish, ugly, meaningless and almost unpronounceable, and deserves oblivion'. Since then, Ms has gained increasing acceptance. In 1974 the Passport Office conceded the right of women to use Ms on passports 'if they so choose'; the House of Commons officially accepted it for women MPs, once again 'if they wish to use it'; *The Times* states that 'the title Ms will be used "when requested" '.

Ms has proved useful for writing to women, and the old question 'Is it Mrs or Miss?' is no longer necessary. It must be added that many women do not want to be called Ms, and object strongly when it is used without their permission. And a few bastions of resistance still hold out, such as scoreboard displays at Wimbledon ('Miss M Navratilova', 'Miss J Capriati').

Nevertheless, Ms is here to stay and should be used to address women who prefer it, although it is uncertain how much more progress it will make towards becoming the standard form of address. The accepted pronunciations are 'mizz' or 'merz', with 'mizz' taking the lead.

MS and **MSS**   See **manuscript**

mugging   In the 19th century, *mug* was already boxing-ring slang for punching someone. After World War II, *mugging* became the usual expression, to begin with often in connection with Central Park, New York, for someone beaten up and robbed. Sadly, the word in this sense is now equally at home in Britain, and it is a sign of the times that British dictionaries treat it as a standard part of the language.

Muhammad   See **Mohammed** . . .

mulatto   See **half-caste** . . .

mule   See **donkey** . . .

multi-   In nearly all *multi-* formations the hyphen is now dropped: *multicultural, multidirectional, multiprocessing, multiracial*. . . . It is usually retained in *multi-storey* and *multi-purpose*.

multinational or **international company**
A *multinational* is a powerful commercial conglomerate, such as the Coca-Cola Corporation or IBM, whose organization is worldwide. A multinational treats the whole world as a single market, having strategic operational and production centres, with distribution networks in different countries, and using a global marketing strategy. An *international company* is simply one that sells its products in a number of countries, while remaining based in its country of origin.

multiple or **chain store**   These are both terms for a group of retail shops under the same management and selling the same kind of goods. *Chain store* is the more usual term in America. Both are used in Britain, but *multiple* is the term preferred by the Central Statistical Office, which classes companies with ten or more branches as 'multiple retailers'.

municipal   Stress the second syllable not the first: 'mewNISSsiple'.

muscle   'Muscle-men' are thugs whose job it is to throw their weight around and intimidate people. Perhaps from that use, *muscle* has become extended

to cover the heavyweight power to make things happen. We hear, for example, of the *marketing muscle* of companies and the *political muscle* of influential politicians. Big businesses can *muscle* aside competition.

musical wallpaper   See **Muzak** . . .

music centre   See **hi-fi** . . .

musicology and **musicologist**   *Musicology* is an **-ology** that dates from the early years of the 20th century. It was after World War II that the term became fashionable and recognized increasingly as an important subject. It is perhaps an unnecessarily scientific name for 'music history', although *musicologists* argue that it goes further, taking in the study of related documents, manuscripts of scores, printed music, as well as interpretation of music. But it could be said that the term 'art history' is concerned with the same corresponding aspects related to visual art.

music concrète   See **electronic music**

Muslim, **Moslem** or **Mohammedan**   These are names for a follower of the faith of Islam. The only one that should be used is *Muslim* (with a capital M). Many Muslims consider *Mohammedan* offensive and patronizing, nor is *Moslem* liked. *Followers of Islam*, in the plural, is an acceptable alternative. When speaking about culture or history, *Islamic* should be used, as in 'Islamic art' (see **Arab** . . .). See also **Mohammed** . . .
 Muslim can be pronounced 'MOOZlim' (the first syllable with the vowel sound of 'good'), usually considered preferable, or 'MUZZlim'.

must (as a noun)   To describe anything as *a must*, meaning something we need, is commercial vulgarization. What's more, it covers a broad band of meaning. It is better to use 'necessary', 'important', 'essential', 'vital', 'something we really need', etc.

mustache   See **moustache** . . .

mutual   See **common** . . .

Muzak or **piped music**   Both expressions are used for the intrusion of bland atmospheric music in lifts, airports, supermarkets, and now even finding its way into operating theatres in hospitals. *Muzak* is a brand name registered in 1938, apparently as a combination of 'music' and 'Kodak'. With a small *m*, *muzak* is used in a general way for what is also known as *piped music*, which suggests that background music is as indispensable as plumbing. It has also been called *musical wallpaper*.

MW   See **Master of Wine**

myself   *Myself* is often used pretentiously, when all that is needed is a simple 'I' or 'me': 'please contact myself over this', 'my wife and myself will be glad to come to dinner'. Why not 'please contact me . . .', 'my wife and I . . .'?

mystical or **occult**   The two words overlap in that they both relate to hidden knowledge, but the feeling behind them is quite different. *Mystical* is concerned with divine revelation (it derives ultimately from a Greek word for a person who is initiated). Since the 1960s, when it became fashionable to search for enlightenment in India, there has been a tendency to think of *mystics* as Eastern spiritual teachers. It is important to remember that the word is universal, and touches the concept of someone who has transcended this life to find an ultimate reality, wherever they are – and whatever clothes they are wearing.

Occult also refers to hidden knowledge: it derives from a Latin word for concealment, and in astronomy is a verb for a greater heavenly body hiding another by passing in front of it. *Occult* carries with it the feeling of magic and mysterious, rather than spiritual and divine. It is used particularly in such areas as spiritualism, clairvoyance and hypnotism. While the word does not necessarily imply an evil quality, it is also used about witchcraft and voodoo. *Occult* is stressed on the first syllable, when it is used as a noun or a descriptive word ('OCCult'); used in astronomy as a verb (see above), the stress moves to the second syllable ('oCCULT').

mystique   *Mystique* is now a doubled-edged word. It retains its original meaning that relates to *mystic*, that is a quality of mystery outside the apparent world. But now it often suggests the illusion of something special and remarkable that has been created by the media and public relations. Some experts enhance their reputations (and their fees) by implying a mystique about their abilities. See also **charisma**

myth or **legend**   See legend . . .

my wife or **the wife**   This opens up a social divide. A middle-class husband would refer to his wife, when she is not present, as *my wife* ('My wife is spending the weekend with her mother'). To talk about *the wife* ('The wife is taking the weekend off') is very downmarket. The latter may be an echo of the old cockney rhyming slang expression for a wife – 'the trouble and strife', which may explain why there is no equivalent 'the husband'.

· N ·

'n and 'n' Using *'n* or *'n'* for *and* started as fashion and *fast food* jargon in America: *mix 'n' match* was an invitation to women to choose skirts and shirts that went together, while *ham 'n' eggs*, *cheese 'n' tomato*, written on the windows of snack bars, gave an impression of quick service. Rock 'n' roll became universal. Later travel agents picked up the idea with combinations such as *sun 'n' sea, sea 'n' sky*. . . .

In casual speech the word *and* has long been shortened to *'n* (man 'n' boy) and perhaps the commercial exploitation of *'n'*, although it seems cheap and nasty to many of us, is understandable. It has even been taken up in the catalogue of an educational publisher: 'Do your students acquire their knowledge by *chalk 'n talk*?'

nadir and zenith In their extended use, these two words are sometimes used the wrong way round. They were astronomical terms originally for opposing points in the celestial sphere: the *nadir* is the point directly below the observer, *zenith* the point directly overhead. Both words have long since been adapted for the ups and downs in the lives of men and women, of governments, of the economy, or about anything where there is a wheel of fortune: *zenith* is the time when something is at its peak, *nadir* (pron: 'NAYdeer' or 'NADDeer') when it hits rock bottom. 'Tories reach election nadir' was a headline in February 1992, when bad unemployment figures, a deepening crisis in home repossessions and a setback in the fall of inflation were all announced on the same day. See also *apogee* . . .

naff *Naff* was bawdy slang before the mid-19th century, but it faded out. After World War II, *naff* appeared in a novel (Keith Waterhouse's *Billy Liar*, 1959) and in television programmes, as *Naff off!* In 1982 the *Daily Express* called it the 'newest four-letter word', and the following year it received 'by appointment' endorsement when Princess Anne told persistent press photographers to 'Naff off!' *Naff* had arrived as an upper-class expletive. About the same time, *naff* became a fashionable descriptive word for anything that is dowdy, unattractive or in bad taste.

The origin of the word is uncertain. Some suggest a connection with NAAFI, the canteens run for servicemen.

naive *Naïf* and *naïve* are the masculine and feminine forms of this descriptive word in French, and both words were used in English as long ago as the late 16th century. Only *naive* is used now in English. Sooner or later, the *diaeresis* (dots over the *i*) will go but it is still often retained to mark the separate pronunciation of *a* and *i*. Meantime, dictionaries show *i* and *ï* as alternative spellings.

Naive can have the harmless meaning of innocent and childlike, but the tendency is for the word to be used in a disparaging way to mean simple-minded, guileless or gullible.

As a term in art, *naive* is not pejorative. It corresponds to *primitive*, used appreciatively about native art unaffected by self-consciousness and Western academic tradition.

namby-pamby Some people are uncertain whether *namby-pamby* has a place in written English, or is simply a conversational expression. Ambrose Philips (c1675–1749) wrote a collection of gushing verses addressed to 'all ages and characters, from Walpole . . . to Miss Pulteney in the nursery'. The writer Henry Carey (who, in passing, wrote the words and music of *Sally in our Alley*) dismissed Ambrose Philips' poetry as 'Namby Pamby's little rhymes'. *Namby-pamby* has survived as a standard expression for anything that is insipid, half-hearted, mealy-mouthed, effeminate or, to revive that scathing 1980s' word for a middle-of-the-road Conservative politician, *wet*.

name of the game This slick expression is used about any kind of complicated situation to describe a ploy or an approach that has been worked out. During the 1991 Gulf War, an American war correspondent, speaking about American tactics, commented 'The name of the game is keeping Saddam Hussein's aircraft on the ground'.

The expression is heard in boardrooms, at sales conferences, or anywhere else where someone wants a go-getting confident-sounding alternative to the sober word 'policy'.

names Much of the time, we are clear about what to call someone, depending on how well we know them. In many situations, we can be on first name terms the moment we meet a person. And this can apply now even to the telephone, with someone we've never met and never will meet face to face. At other times, any one of us can hesitate over how to address someone: should it be 'Mary Robinson', 'Mary' or 'Mrs Robinson'? Guidance on the use of courtesy titles comes under **Mr, Mrs or Miss**; the beginnings of letters are dealt with under **Dear Sir** . . .

At meetings of committees, etc, unless protocol or a greater degree of formality has to be observed, we would use either first names ('I'll ask *Chris* to deal with that question'), or first names plus surnames ('I'll ask *Chris Robinson* . . .'). The first-plus-surname approach is particularly useful on radio to identify speakers to listeners.

names ending in -s, -ch, -sh You will never keep up with them if you say you had the *Jones* for dinner. The prescribed way of saying or writing the plural of Jones, Charles and most other names ending in *-s* is to add *-es*: *Joneses, Charleses*. . . . The same applies to names ending in *-ch* or *-sh*: the Birches, the Fishes. . . . And the *-es* is not lost for the possessive (the Joneses' house): see **apostrophe/1**, problem (i).

napkin or serviette Words, like clothes, go out of fashion, and for some perverse reason the elegant word *serviette* is now considered vulgar, probably because it sounds too refined. People in the know use the down-to-earth 15th-century word *napkin*.

narcotics See **drugs** . . .

NASA The BBC once called NASA 'the organization that put the first man on the moon'. The letters are an *acronym* for National Aeronautics and Space Administration, the central US agency dealing with exploration of outer space.

national *National* has a number of meanings. It can be geographical: a national advertising campaign, national distribution, a national survey, national radio, etc. All those projects extend over the whole country. *National* can also be a synonym for governmental: the National Health Service is organized and financed by central government, the national debt is the total indebtedness of government, National Insurance is personal insurance, such as sickness benefit, unemployment pay, etc, for which the government is responsible.

National Front See next entry

nationalism or patriotism Speaking about *patriotism* and *nationalism* on the BBC, Lord Tebbitt commented, 'one is good, one is bad'. That sums it up. *Patriotism* is love of one's country, a readiness to support and defend it. *Nationalism* has not always carried with it negative connotations: in the early 19th century, it was a force that gave countries identity, and in the 20th century, the word was associated with anti-colonial movements and the right of subjugated countries to self-determination. But now more often than not, *nationalism* means an extreme bigoted 'my country right or wrong' attitude that leads to *racism*. The *National Front* demonstrates this meaning of nationalism with its extreme anti-immigrant, antisemitic racist declarations. See also **chauvinism** . . .

national park or nature reserve All over the world, the description *national park* should represent a bastion against encroachment of an area by industry or urbanization. It should cover a big expanse of land largely in its natural state, unaffected by human enterprise, and which is preserved for all time by government restrictions. National Parks in England and Wales come under the Countryside Commission, with more limited protection. The Lake District National Park is England's largest.

A *nature reserve* can be an area of land or water, or a combination of both, which is managed and protected specifically to safeguard the flora and fauna, and also the physical features. In Britain, some nature reserves are designated by the Department of the Environment, others by local authorities.

nation is or are A nation must be regarded as a composite unit and always treated as singular.

native Although anyone is a *native* of somewhere, whether it is London or Houston, the word has old colonial associations with tribal war-dances, cannibals and what were regarded as inferior races ('the natives were friendly'). While no one should be upset at being called a native of East Cheam, if that's where they come from, if the word is used carelessly about inhabitants of former colonies, *native* could understandably give offence.

NATO The **acronym** represents the most important permanent military alliance since World War II, the North Atlantic Treaty Organization. It was formed in 1949 between a number of European countries and the USA and Canada.

natural or real Artificial substitutes have become the norm for so many things, that we now often have to use *natural* or *real* to emphasize that we want the real thing: a natural sponge, natural wood, real coffee, real cotton. Purists criticize this, arguing that wood is wood, cotton is cotton, etc, but at times we need protection against the commercial exploitation of words.

As a noun, a *natural* is someone who does something, from playing football to acting, as effortlessly as breathing. This expressive usage is still regarded as colloquial but it bids fair to being accepted one day as standard English. It is worn-out slang to call a scheme or a product *a natural*, meaning it is bound to succeed.

naturalist See **naturist** . . .

natural or biological parents When a man is infertile, and artificial insemination enables his wife to have a baby, there are two fathers. The woman's husband is, for social and legal purposes, the father. But what do we call the usually anonymous donor who provided the semen? To call him the 'real father' is both uneasy and ambiguous. The same question arises about how to distinguish linguistically between the actual and adopted parents of children.

There is a choice of terms. Traditionally, children born out of wedlock were called *natural* sons and daughters, and the father their *natural* father. Some people find this an outdated term and prefer the more precise description, *biological* father, and *biological* parents in the case of adopted children.

An officially recognized British organization calls itself the Natural Parents' Support Group. Nevertheless, the term *biological parents* seems more in keeping with social mores in the 1990s.

natural, **social** and **life sciences** What these three categories cover is partly convention, partly historical association (physics was for a long time called 'natural philosophy'), and there is no general agreement over how the different sciences are classified. The *natural sciences* (or *natural science*) are broadly considered as the sciences involving the physical world, which include physics and chemistry, as well as biology, botany and geology. The *social sciences* (or *social science*) embrace all the sciences that involve human society and relationships between people: these include sociology, anthropology, economics, certain linguistic studies and aspects of psychology that are connected with the interaction of the individual with the social world.

Life sciences is a term commonly used in America, but much less so in Britain. It covers those natural sciences that are related to biology, such as botany, physiology and of course biology itself.

As suggested, there are different views about the categorization outlined above, and with the traditional sciences being divided up into ever-increasing new branches, these divisions have uncertain significance, except as academic convenience.

natural wastage This is a curious expression, which became familiar in the 1980s, to use about human beings. When there is a need for an organization to reduce staff levels, it can be done through making redundancies (see **dismiss** . . .), or through *natural wastage*, that is allowing retirement and resignations for various reasons to take place without replacing the employees involved, so reducing staff numbers 'naturally'.

. . . nature . . . *Nature* is a word that slips in pointlessly in some contexts, when we're looking the other way, and clutters up what could be a straightforward statement: 'raising something of this nature in public will cause embarrassment'; 'problems of this nature are difficult to overcome'; 'because of the sensitive nature of this information, it must be kept confidential'. Resist the temptation to use *nature*, and the sentences immediately become more direct: 'raising something like this . . .'; 'problems like these . . .'; 'because this information is sensitive . . .'.

nature reserve See national park . . .

naturist, **nudist** or **naturalist** The word *nudist* is not used much in the 1990s because, as a

BBC reporter said, 'nude rhymes with lewd, rude and crude'. If you enjoy walking around naked, the word now is *naturist* (pron: 'ɴᴀʏcherist'), which has a comfortable feeling of living naturally and simply. No one cares if it makes all the rest of us 'unnaturists'. But when naturists call themselves *naturalists*, as some have done, that is going too far, since it's a different word altogether. *Naturalist* has certain uses in art, literature and philosophy, but generally it means a specialist in natural history, the study of plants and animals.

naturopathy See homoeopathy . . .

naught See nought . . .

naughty Curiously, what seems a nasty use of *naughty*, for striptease shows, women's frilly underwear or suggestive postcards, has a sound linguistic foundation: in the 16th century *naughty* meant immoral, as well as a word for a wayward child. It was also a much stronger word, conveying evil: ' 'tis a naughty night to swim in' says Lear's Fool at the height of the storm (Act III Sc iv). The word is used properly now only about children. No matter what it meant 400 years ago, it is prudish and coy to use *naughty*, as some women and men do, about a suggestive remark or a tentative sexual approach. The last word on this usage can be left to the *Longman Dictionary* (1984 edition), which gives as an example, 'don't forget to scrub your naughty bits'!

nauseated or **nauseous** *Nauseous* has three meanings: it describes something that makes people sick, such as a nauseous gas, or it describes a particularly unpleasant taste or smell, or anyone or anything that is disgusting ('his behaviour was nauseous'). *Nauseated* is used about a person who is feeling sick ('she was nauseated by the sight of so much blood'), or for someone who is disgusted, usually 'at' something: 'she was nauseated at his behaviour'.

A common mistake is 'I feel nauseous': it is possible to *be* nauseous, that is disgusting (although no one would be likely to admit it), but we can only *feel* nauseated, that is sick. One dictionary has slipped into defining 'feeling nauseous' as 'feeling sick', which, for a dictionary, could truly be called – *nauseous*.

nautical mile See knot

navvy See workman . . .

Nazi See Fascist . . .

nearby or **near by** When it comes before a noun, it is always one word: 'we stayed at a nearby hotel'. When it comes after a verb, it can be one word or two, usually one: 'we stayed nearby (or near by)'.

near disaster This is a peculiar mistake that keeps cropping up, even with good writers: 'we were saved from a near disaster'. You can *have* a near disaster, that is something that just stops short of being a disaster, but if you were saved in time, you were, in fact, 'saved from a disaster', not a *near* disaster.

'NECessarily' or **'necesSARily'**   Current dictionaries offer the choice between putting the stress on the first syllable, traditionally correct in Britain, and the American stress pattern which is on the third syllable. 'NecesSARily' is easier to say, but to some people in Britain, 'NECessarily' shows you know what's what.

neck   Three of the slang or conversational uses of *neck* have become elderly, and it's a giveaway of our age if we're still using them. One is the use of *neck* to mean a cheek ('He's got a neck asking me to do it for nothing!'); the second is 'neck of the woods', meaning a remote place ('Why are you living in this neck of the woods?'); most dated of all is *neck* as a verb to mean kissing and cuddling. But in America, these uses of *neck* still seem quite common among people of all ages.

Two other conversational uses remain current: it is no joke to *get it in the neck*, meaning to be blamed or punished for doing something, and we can be *up to our neck* in something, meaning overworked or totally involved in a task.

need or **require**   The words are often interchangeable. *Need* is usually the more direct word ('We need more time'), *require* more formal. *Require* is also a way of issuing a command: 'We need you to be present' means we need your advice or agreement, but 'We require you to be present' is, in effect, giving an order.

needless to say and **not to mention**   It has been argued that if anything is preceded by *needless to say* or *not to mention*, why say it or mention it? Language has turns of phrase as well as logical sequences, and *needless to say* and *not to mention*, or, for that matter, *to say nothing of* and *it goes without saying*, are ways of making a point by a kind of understatement. There are times when the obvious needs to be stated in case it's not obvious to the other person!

need to know   See for your information . . .

negative and **positive**   For the ways these words are being used now in new contexts, see **positive** . . .

negative campaigning   See **dirty tricks**

negative equity   An expression that seems to have been born during the slump in the housing market of the early 1990s. Many homeowners were caught in the so-called *negative equity trap*, which meant that the value of a house had fallen below the money outstanding on the mortgage. That is the depressing situation

of owing more money on your home than the property is worth.

negative feedback   See **feedback**

negatives   See **double negatives**

négligé, **negligée** or **negligee**   If you're going to use this rather dated word in English for a thin diaphanous dressing-gown, you might as well spell it in the correct French way: *négligé*. Not many people do: *negligée* is the most common spelling, arbitrarily with only one acute accent and adding an extra *-e* (the word is masculine in French), both hangovers from the 18th century. Another variant is to leave the accents out altogether, which is the standard form in America, where the word is more current.

The pronunciation remains more or less French: 'NEGlizhay'.

negligence or **carelessness**   In some everyday contexts, *negligence* and *carelessness* can be almost the same. *Negligence* puts the stress on not doing something that should have been done, or not giving enough care where it was clearly required. *Carelessness* is a lighter word, usually suggesting sloppiness or someone not thinking about what they are doing. In law, *negligence* is a much more serious word that implies a culpable failure to perform a duty that is a legal responsibility, with the result that someone sustains injury or loss. *Contributory negligence* is a legal expression that describes a person contributing, by their own failure to take proper care, to an accident that has been caused by others. As a result, the injured person might receive only partial compensation.

negotiate   At one time, authorities agreed that either the *sh* or the *s* sound was an acceptable pronunciation, but the latest dictionaries show only the *sh* alternative: 'neGOHshiate'. That does not stop some people saying 'neGOHsiate', because they think it sounds more educated.

Negro and **Negress**   These were legitimate names for members of black African races. For a long time now they have been considered offensive, and should be avoided, except for *Negro spirituals*, the accepted name for the traditional hymns originally sung by black people in the southern states of America. See **black** . . .

neighbourhood   This Old English word has always had warm associations. By the early 17th century it was being used in the sense of a community of people. Since the 1950s, *neighbourhood* has been taken up by urban planners and sociologists, as a word for decentralized sectors of towns, which have their own social and cultural facilities. The sign *Neighbourhood Watch*, which appears on many houses now, means organized vigilance by people, usually living in the same street, to protect property against crime. Those are worthwhile uses of a good Old English word. But in the mid-19th century a roundabout phrase was born, *in the neighbourhood of*, as a high-sounding substitute for the simple word 'about': 'the cost will be in the neighbourhood of . . .'. There is nothing to be said for using six syllables when two do the job better.

neither *is* or ***are*** The straightforward rule is that *neither* is singular: 'neither of us *is* ready yet'; 'neither of the women *has* arrived'; 'neither *costs* more than £10'. We have to bear in mind that for centuries good writers and speakers had been notoriously lax about keeping to this rule, and there are many examples of *neither* followed by *are*, *were*, *have*, etc. Nevertheless, the rule given is undoubtedly correct. See also next entry

neither . . . nor These are the rules:

1 *Neither . . . nor* is correct: 'neither . . . or' is always wrong.

2 It is not true, as some books lay down, that *neither . . . nor* should be used about only two alternatives. You can say 'Neither Mary, *nor* John, *nor* Harry, *nor* Susan was present'.

3 The verb after *neither . . . nor* can be singular or plural: it takes its cue from the noun that follows *nor*: 'neither the solicitors nor their *client is* available'; 'neither Mary nor her *solicitors are* available'; 'neither this book nor the *others are* suitable'; 'neither these books nor that *one is* suitable'.

neither (pronunciation) Although dictionaries show the alternative pronunciations 'NYEther' and 'NEEther', the *ee* sound in the first syllable jars on many people. It is the other way round in America.

neo- *Neo-* can be prefixed to philosophies, schools, of thought, ideas, styles of art and architecture, and to almost anything else to indicate a revival, or a revised or adapted version. The hyphen is usually omitted unless the following word begins with a vowel or a capital letter; neoclassical, neocolonial, neorealism, but neo-imperialism, neo-Nazis, neo-Marxism. . . .

neologism or **nonce-word** Few people use the phrase *for the nonce* any more, to mean for the time being ('Let us leave it at that for the nonce'). *Nonce* has a long history going back to the 12th century, when it meant something that applied to a particular occasion. The first editors of the *OED* coined *nonce-word* for a word that was dreamt up for a one-off use. Lewis Carroll was a prolific inventor of nonce-words, combining, for example, 'fair' and 'joyous' to give 'Oh *frabjous* day!' (*Through the Looking-glass*).

When a nonce-word outlives the occasion for which it was invented, it becomes a *neologism* (pron: 'neeOLLe(r)djizm'), that is a new word in the language: *frabjous*, as an example, now appears in some dictionaries, and has even found its way into the *New Yorker*. Eventually such words become too long in the tooth to be called neologisms: they are just words. For young people, neologisms hardly exist, as they take most new words on board without question. For conserva-

tive and older users of the language, words may remain neologisms long after most people have taken them for granted. The fact is English users are signally productive in devising neologisms, and lexicographers cannot keep up with us.

nephew In spite of the *ph*, the traditional British pronunciation is 'NEVyou'. But because of the spelling, 'NEFyou' is becoming more usual. Dictionaries show both alternatives.

nerd or **square** The American slang word *nerd*, which dates from about the 1950s, is now popular in Britain, even with *The Times*. It means a dull, conventional, unimaginative person, similar but not quite the same as the now dated slang expression a *square*. You might, for example, have been labelled *a square* for not approving of rock music, but *nerdy* would arguably be the right word if you sing *The Blue Danube* in your bath! But what is nerdy changes with fashion and points of view.

nerve-racking or **nerve-wracking** Rack, in the sense of straining, can also be spelt *wrack*, but this is becoming rare. Hence *nerve-racking*, straining the nerves, is now the accepted spelling, just as we *rack* (not *wrack*) our brains. See also *rack* . . .

net or **nett** When it is to do with sums of money, after all deductions have been made, or to do with weight excluding packing materials, etc, *net* is now the standard spelling. *Nett*, still shown in dictionaries as an alternative, is obsolete. *Net* derives from French and relates to 'neat', tidy and clear of deductions or additions.

Netherlands See Holland . . .

network What began in the 16th century as a simple word meaning an arrangement of cords or threads in the pattern of a net, has become a key word in industry, business and communication, continually being extended to cover new uses. It started in the 19th century, when *network* was the term for a complex system of railway communication, and later for an arrangement of cables for supplying electricity. In the early part of the 20th century, *network* became the standard term for a group of radio transmitters that could be linked.

It was not until after World War II that *network* became widely used for people and organizations (a network of personal contacts (see **Old Boy Network**), a network of factories). Then computer science took over the word, and prefixed *network* to a long series of terms (network database, network structure, network timing . . .) for aspects of data communication that relate to a chain of interconnected computers.

neurolinguistic programming This is the awesome name given to the study of how we reveal what we are thinking and feeling by how we behave, how we sit, the words we use, our eye movements, breathing, gestures and almost everything else the human body can manifest. See also **body language**

neurolinguistics In the 1990s the study of how language relates to human beings goes far beyond **lexicography** and **etymology**. Few dictionaries have caught up with *neurolinguistics*, a new branch of linguistics that applies the study of neurology to research into the development and use of language. See previous entry

neurotic or **psychotic** *Neurotic* is properly the descriptive word related to *neurosis* (short for *psychoneurosis*), a mental illness that manifests itself in chronic anxiety, obsessions and phobias. Instead of leaving *neurotic* to doctors, many people use it casually about anyone over-anxious or worried, or about the mildest of hang-ups. 'The meaning of neurotic has become so vague', according to the consultant, Dr Margaret Wright, 'that psychiatrists seldom use it any more'.

Psychotic is both a noun and the descriptive word related to *psychosis*. The words should never be used lightly: *psychosis* is a severe mental disorder (manic-depression and schizophrenia are examples) in which the sufferer loses contact at times with reality, as delusions and hallucinations take over.

neutral See **impartial** . . .

nevertheless or **nonetheless** These are alternative one-word ways of saying 'in spite of all that', 'no matter what the outcome', 'taking everything into account', etc. There is no difference in meaning between *nevertheless* and *nonetheless*, but perhaps *nonetheless* is more common, possibly because it has only three syllables. Some reference books insist on *none the less* as three separate words, at the same time accepting *nevertheless* as one word. You can please yourself, but there is no good case for not running *nonetheless* together.

new The *OED* devotes three pages to this simple Old English word, recording a use of an early form of it in the 9th century. Yet *new* remains fresh, still with the same old magic: it attracts our attention in headlines, shop-windows and advertisements (one advertiser in America liked the word so much that he tried to copyright it!). Linguistic pundits are in the habit of tutt-tutting over the unnecessary use of *new*: 'a new discovery', 'a new speed record', 'a new breakthrough'. Logically, *new* is not necessary in such phrases, but it stresses the point and captures our imagination. Like any other word, *new* should not be overused, but nor is it necessary to be po-faced about using it, just because newness is implied in the following noun. As Arthur Koestler once remarked, 'Moderation – in moderation – is the right approach'. See also **fresh** . . .

New Age As the 1980s came to an end, it was reported that a *New Age* was dawning when, according to believers, 'the heartless materialists of the Eighties

will be transformed into the caring global citizens of the Nineties' (*The Sunday Times* 29.10.1989). *New Age* is used to cover almost any aspect of alternative living and esoteric mystery, from astrology to **ESP**. Robert Runcie,as Archbishop of Canterbury, told us 'It's difficult to define the New Age . . . it is an umbrella title covering mysticism, ecology, meditation, even being a vegetarian'.

There is a difference between New Age values and the flower children and **hippies** of the 1960s. New Age people may be more affluent, with hairstyles by expensive hairdressers in London or New York, spiritual white robes designed by couturiers, and meditation rooms in white-walled penthouses. The journalist, Kate Saunders, expressed it neatly: 'This is hanging loose without dropping out'.

By the early 1990s, New Age was running out of steam, fragmented into too many cults, and subdued by the economic recession. Groups of people who seemed a new generation of hippies, and who called themselves *New Age travellers*, moved round Britain in convoys of buses, holding festivals and camping out, until evicted by the police.

newscast In the 1930s, a journalist had the idea of adapting the word 'broadcast' to form *newscast* for a news programme on radio. It caught on, much later in Britain than in America, and *newscast* has become the standard word for news reports on radio and television. And a new profession was born – *newscaster*.

newsflash *Newsflash* was a good **neologism** when it first appeared, because it tied in with a flash of lightning, to describe a sudden interruption of a radio, television or even a cinema programme to announce a startling event somewhere in the world. There is a striking example: it is well known that nearly everyone who saw or heard the *newsflash* on 22 November 1963, announcing the assassination of John Kennedy, remembers exactly where they were at the time.

Newspeak See **doublespeak** . . .

new time (Stock Exchange term) See **after-hours dealing** . . .

new words See **neologism** . . .

New World The New World has never been precisely defined geographically: in the 19th century it was generally taken to be North and South America, or sometimes the United States. (Dvořák's symphony, *From the New World*, 1893, was given that title because at the time he was director of the National Conservatory in New York.) For others it would have included Australia and New Zealand. In any case, in the 20th century the term became quaint and old-fashioned.

New World was revived in the late 1980s by wine dealers, as a way of defining the wines of the West Coast of the US, Australia, New Zealand and Chile. These wine regions all shared recent developments in cultivation of vines and wine-making techniques, producing wines that compare well with those made in the classic 'Old World' regions of Europe.

The expression *New World* is back to stay now, with a permanent place in the pages of wine lists.

New Zealand English There was little difference between New Zealand English and **Australian English** before the Australian confederation in 1901. Some differences of vocabulary had long been present, since New Zealand adopted words of Maori origin while Australia was open to linguistic influence from the Aboriginals. As far as accent is concerned, for years New Zealanders abroad have had the mildly irritating experience of being asked if they were Australians.

This is changing. New Zealanders are increasingly concerned with expressing their separateness from their dominant neighbour, and as so often, language is seen as a symbol of national self-assertion. According to George Turner of Adelaide University, vowel sounds in New Zealand are moving in new directions. Just as New Zealand wines have found a distinctive quality and worldwide reputation, so the spoken language of the country is becoming audibly different from Australian English, softer perhaps, with the vowel sounds more ironed out, at least to the ears of people in Britain.

nice It has been customary for a long time to condemn *nice* as an overused, noncommittal word for anything that is pleasant or agreeable. Perhaps it started with Henry Tilney in Jane Austen's *Northanger Abbey*: 'Oh, it is a very nice word indeed! It does for everything'. And so it does, for it is true that people use this maid-of-all-work word too often. It is usually more complimentary to take the trouble to choose a word more carefully: 'It was a delicious dinner', '. . . a fascinating evening', '. . . an attractive dress'. . . . But we shouldn't fuss too much about this: sometimes it is a nice day because someone has been 'nice to us'. And no one objects to the use of nice to mean subtle or finely balanced, as in 'a nice distinction', or a 'nice point'.

nickname or **sobriquet** The two words mean the same. *Nickname* is down-to-earth and friendly; *sobriquet* (pron: 'SOHbrikay') is more la-di-da. *Sobriquet* is called for perhaps if it is referring to a distinguished and important person: 'General Montgomery and General Eisenhower were known by the sobriquets "Monty" and "Ike" '.

nigger Everyone knows by now that *nigger* is a deeply offensive word to black people. One American dictionary in the 1960s even deleted the word altogether, which was going too far, for as a leading article in *The Times* commented on the omission: 'A dictionary's job is to map the language, not pass judgement on it'.

When it comes to the old description of a colour as *nigger brown*, most of us are now alerted, and we

substitute 'chocolate brown'. But *nigger in the woodpile* can still trip off the tongue when we're off guard. And it's insulting to switch to 'you-know-what in the woodpile', as was done at a political meeting in London. A black barrister in the audience was right to object. Alternatives to keep in reserve are 'troublemaker' and 'odd man out'.

night or **night-** Up to the 1980s, *night* was often hyphenated when joined to another word. Examples from the *Concise Oxford Dictionary* (1982 edition) are *night-club, night-dress, night-spot*; in the 1990 edition of the same dictionary these are fused into one word. *Night-time* usually keeps its hyphen because of the two *t*s, so does *night-watchman, night-light, night-long*, among the more common *night* combinations. *Night safe, night school* and *night nurse* are three combinations usually written as separate words without a hyphen.

If in doubt, it is not often wrong to slip in a hyphen, even when it's unnecessary, except at *nightfall* or when you have a *nightmare*.

nightmare scenario Few dictionaries have caught up with *nightmare scenario*. The expression came into prominence during the leadership election for the Conservative Party in November 1990. Political commentators used it for an outcome that left Margaret Thatcher winning by only a few votes, and remaining as leader without authority. During the 1991 Gulf War, the expression was revived: the nightmare scenario was for Saddam Hussein to withdraw from Kuwait without a battle, keeping his nuclear and chemical warfare capacity intact.

A nightmare scenario is any situation with a possible outcome that would lead to much more serious problems. The opposite of a nightmare scenario is a **dream ticket**. See also **scenario**

nihilist The word is sometimes used loosely for anyone who criticizes destructively an idea or an established belief. In reality, *nihilism* goes much deeper than that, and perhaps the word should not be used casually. In philosophical terms, a *nihilist* rejects all values in life on the basis that every truth is false because there is no reality or meaningful purpose. It is not for nothing that *nihilist* has its root in the Latin word for 'nothing'. Historically, *nihilist* was used in the late 19th century for extremist members of the Russian revolutionary party. (Pron: 'NYEilist'.)

-nik This Russian suffix was carried by Yiddish into American English, and thence back across the Atlantic to Britain. It gathered momentum when Russia launched the first artificial satellite in October 1957, and named it Sputnik ('travelling companion'). In the 1960s, *-nik* became a multipurpose suffix to attach to a noun, verb or descriptive word (with never a glimpse of a hyphen), as a name for someone who loves something, believes in something, or is closely linked to an attitude, or way of life: *beatnik, peacenik, refusenik*. Used for Jews in Russia, who were refused permission to emigrate to Israel, *refusenik* was later, tongue-in-cheek, attached to people, such as Peter Jay and Shirley Williams, who had refused honours. *The Independent* took *-nik* into outer space again, when its literary editor welcomed Stephen Hawking's best-seller, *A Brief History of Time*, as written by 'a space-nik who spoke English'.

No discussion of this expressive suffix can leave out *no-goodnik*, the New York equivalent of 'good-for-nothing', someone who is unreliable, does not earn an honest living, or is a cheapjack crook. Admittedly, *no-goodnik* does not rate inclusion in most British dictionaries, but that's their loss.

The *-nik* suffix should be used with restraint (*The New York Times* was going over the top to call lovers of Bach cantatas *Bachniks*), or it becomes a mannerism. Nevertheless, *-nik* remains on standby for anyone who can make good use of it.

nirvana   See **Enlightenment**

nitty-gritty   No one knows the origin of this 20th-century expression. When you get down to the *nitty-gritty*, there is a narrowing of the eyes, a squaring of the jaw, because polite conversation is over and you are about to deal with the hard facts, whether people like them or not. As well as being useful, *nitty-gritty* has the sound of what it means, and you can't ask more from language than that. See also **bottom line**

no   It has been said that *no* is one of the most useful words in English, yet people go on finding ways to avoid using it. We find *no* embarrassingly direct, and look for evasive alternatives: 'I am reluctant to accept the terms you offer'; 'I prefer not to do what you ask'; 'I can't go along with what has been suggested'; 'Thank you, but I'd rather not'. There are occasions, of course, when it is friendly to soften the harshness of *no*, but there is no need to drop the word altogether. After all, *no* means what it says and avoids misunderstanding, which roundabout alternatives may sometimes invite.

No is a problem word for women in sexual interplay with men, for male folklore has it that, when it is about sex, a woman's *no* can mean 'yes'. A judge, as part of his direction to a jury at a rape trial in 1982, advised them that 'Women who say No do not always mean No'. In fact, the word *no* is the key word in defining what is now known as consensual sex (see **date rape**).

nobody   'Nobody has made up *his* mind yet' is all right if it is a group of indecisive men, but what if it includes women? See **unisex grammar**

nom de plume   See **pseudonym** . . .

no mean . . .   When St Paul called himself 'A citizen of no mean city' (*Acts of the Apostles*, 21:39), he introduced an expression that has lived on as classic British understatement for someone who is highly creditable. It is no mean achievement to warrant people saying about you 'she's no mean artist', 'he's no

mean batsman'. The expression still has a ring to it. But the effect is spoilt if an incorrect *a* is slipped in: 'a no mean . . .' is ungrammatical.

nominalization   See **-ization nouns**

nominal value   See **face value** . . .

non- or **non**   When *non-* is joined to another word to give it a negative meaning, in nearly every case a hyphen provides the link: *non-alcoholic*, *non-breakable*, *non-communicating*, *non-delivery*, *non-effective*, *non-fiction*, *non-slip*. There are a few examples where *non* forms a word with its own meaning, and these are always one word: *noncommittal* is not the opposite of 'committal', but an altogether different word meaning not committed to an action or opinion; *nonconformist* relates to not conforming to the doctrine of the established Church, and is not the opposite of the usual meaning of 'conformist'. See also **in-** . . .

nonce-word   See **neologism** . . .

nonchalance   See **insouciance** . . .

none is or **none are**   Many people are convinced that *none* is short for 'not one' and must always be singular: 'None of the members *is* present'. Nearly all authorities argue against this: the *OED* states that *none* usually means 'no persons' and that 'not one' is the singular form. Since many radio and television announcers make a careful point of saying *none is*, as if they know what's right, *none are* is beginning to sound wrong. But we should not be bullied out of using *none are*: there are times when it is useful to treat *none* as plural to get us off the 'his or her' hook: 'None of the members *have* cast *their* votes yet'.

The best advice is to use whichever seems right in a particular sentence, and if anyone objects, throw all 20 volumes of the *OED* at them.

nonetheless   See **nevertheless** . . .

non-event   In the 1960s, when everything had to be 'swinging', *non-event* became a scathing write-off for anything that was supposed to be important, epoch-making, or at least interesting, and turned out to be ordinary. *Non-event* is still with us as more of a put-down than anticlimax, disappointing or damp squib.

non-executive   People are sometimes puzzled by what *non-executive* chairmen or *non-executive* directors do. They are on the board of a company, but are not employees and do not take any part in the daily running of the business. What then *do* they do? Sometimes nothing at all: they may be on the board because the name of an ex-cabinet minister, a retired admiral, a former ambassador, etc looks good on the letterhead. Or non-executive directors may have valuable specialized knowledge or business connections, in which case they are called on to give advice at board meetings. Other non-executive directors could be members of the family of the founders of the business, who are significant shareholders.

non-figurative See figurative . . .

non-flammable See flammable . . .

non-organic or **inorganic** *Non-organic* usually applies to farming methods (see **healthfood . . .**). *Inorganic* is a term mostly used in chemistry for compounds based on minerals.

non-religious See irreligious . . .

non-renewable This is a key environmental term: a *non-renewable resource* is 'A natural resource which, in terms of human time scales, is contained within the Earth in a fixed quantity and therefore can be used once only in the foreseeable future (although it may be recycled after its first use)' (from the *Macmillan Dictionary of the Environment*). See also **fossil fuel**

non-social See antisocial . . .

non-standard English See colloquial . . .

Non-U See U and Non-U English

non-white We refer to *white* people or *black* people, or *whites* or *blacks*. In some contexts, *non-white* is useful as a collective term, but many people consider it racist, since it implies the standard is white. At the same time, *black* cannot be used to cover Asians, so we need to take care in a multi-racial group. See also **black . . .**; **white . . .**

no one, **no-one** or **noone** It is tempting to write *noone*, on the lines of 'everyone', but it looks wrong. The hyphenated form is used, but the standard recommendation is to keep the words separate. One other point arises: 'no one has made up *his* mind yet' is all right when it is a group of dithering men, but what if it includes women? See **unisex grammar**

no problem *The Economist* included *no problem* in a list of the most universal English expressions. *No problem* is not used so much in Britain, as in almost every other country in the world, by anyone who has the merest smattering of English. It is, of course, meant to be reassuring, but people who have been taken in by *no problem* have often lived to regret it.

no question Be careful with 'there's no question', for the meaning may not be clear: 'there's no question we can give you a discount' could be taken to mean either 'of course we can give you a discount' or 'there's no hope of a discount'. Change to 'but that we can' or 'of giving' after *question* and it becomes clear.

'There's no question about it' usually means 'it is certain', just as 'there's no question of it' means 'it's impossible'. Misunderstandings can be avoided by replacing *no question about* by either 'there's no doubt' or 'there's no question of', depending on the intention.

nor or **or** and **nor** or **neither** When *neither* or *either* is part of the sentence, there is no problem: *neither* is always followed by *nor* (see **neither . . . nor**), **either** by *or*. In other cases, the choice between *nor* and *or* and *nor . . . neither* is often disputed. Here are two guidelines:

1 When *not* or any other negative comes after a verb, *nor* must follow, since the negative needs to be extended to each of the succeeding nouns: 'it will not be ready by tomorrow, *nor* by next week, *nor* even by next month'.

2 Some people maintain that *neither*, rather than *nor*, should be used after a negative statement, but this is more a matter of style than grammar: 'I don't like it, nor (or neither) does my friend'; 'it is not good value, nor (or neither) is it good quality'.

Nordic or **Scandinavian** *Scandinavian* is used both about the people and the language of Denmark, Norway, Sweden, Iceland, sometimes including Finland as well. *Nordic* is usually reserved for the physical appearance of the people, tall and blond.

norm *Norm* can have two distinct meanings, and people do not usually say which one they intend. The *norm* for many people is a subjective opinion of what is considered the right kind of social behaviour. The other meaning of *norm* is based on statistical evidence about what is usual in a particular set of circumstances. There are contexts where it is worth pressing the point by asking for a definition of *norm*. See also next entry

normal When *normal* has a clinical or technical meaning (normal temperature, normal dose, normal output . . .), there is usually little room for argument. In other contexts, particularly in relation to the social behaviour and psychological reactions of human beings, *normal* can cover up a standard that is imposed by society or a psychiatrist. In that sense, what is normal in one group may not be normal in another. *Normal* is often a word to watch, particularly when it carries with it an implied claim to rightness or goodness that is rooted in questionable beliefs and attitudes.

normalize Many people dislike this as yet another new *-ize* verb, but *normalize* has been in use since the late 19th century. The word does sound like jargon, and the alternatives 'make normal', 'bring back to normal', etc are more natural in everyday contexts.

normal sex The term *normal sex* is hardly new, but it has been given a new and different meaning since the spread of **Aids**. When newspapers ask questions like 'Just how safe is normal sex?', normal sex is equated with heterosexual sex. For many others, normal sex is a personal view, in some cases very restricted, and in others pushing the border back to the full range of eroticism offered by the *Kama Sutra*.

Norman or **Romanesque** For architecture, both words describe the style from about 900 to 1200, which is generally recognized by round arches and powerful vaulted roofs. *Norman* is the term used for cathedrals and churches of this style and period in Britain, notably Durham Cathedral, Ely Cathedral and the crypt of Canterbury Cathedral. *Romanesque* is used for the same style when it is found in France and elsewhere in Europe. There is a tendency now for art historians to use *Romanesque* wherever the style is found.

North, **South**, **East**, **West** or **north**, **south**, **east**, **west** You can go *south* or face a *north* wind, watch the sun rise in the *east* and set in the *west*, journey from *north* to *south*, without using capitals. Whenever a region or a political or social divide is indicated, use a capital: 'the ballet dancer, Mikhail Baryshnikov, now lives in the *West*'; 'house prices in the *South*'; 'trade barriers between *East* and *West*'; 'the economic split between *North* and *South*'.

north or **northern, etc** *North, South*, etc (with initial capitals – see previous entry) are usually geographical, administrative, or political: North Yorkshire, East Anglia, the South Downs, the West Bank, etc.

Northern, southern, etc are more general and indeterminate, hence often spelt without a capital: northern Europe, southern Spain, etc. There are exceptions to the above principle, notably Northern Ireland, the Western Isles, Western Australia. Note also that *north, south*, etc, rather than *northern, southern*, etc, are used about cities, with a small letter when direction is indicated (west London, north Oxford), or with a capital letter when it becomes the name of part of the city (the West End, East Side, New York). Finally, the most long-lasting genre of Hollywood films, with heroic cowboys riding off into Technicolor sunsets, is traditionally spelt with a small *w* – *westerns*.

Northern Ireland or **Ulster** Guidelines for using the various names for different parts of Ireland are given under **Ireland**. . . .

northward, northwards or **northerly, etc** *Northward, northwards, northerly*, and corresponding forms for the other directions, can all be used as descriptive words before a noun, or after a verb, to indicate direction: a northward (northwards or northerly) journey; they travelled southward (southwards or southerly). As a point of style, the *-ward* or *-ly* forms are usually better before *nouns* and *-wards* after *verbs*: an eastward or easterly direction, but 'she looked westwards'. Only *northerly, southerly*, etc can be used as nouns for a wind: a strong northerly.

nosey or **nosy** Alternative spellings in most dictionaries.

nosh This Yiddish word has crossed so many frontiers, that even a bishop might use it – off-duty. Originally it meant something tasty between meals,

but now it simply means anything to eat. A *nosh-up* means a lot to eat. No modern dictionary can leave out *nosh*, the most popular slang word that Yiddish has donated to English.

not We often need to be on guard over this word:

1 In what seems natural stressing of a negative, many good writers have slipped in an extra *not*, the old bugbear of the **double negative**. To present-day ears this nearly always sounds uneducated ('I do*n't* know *nothing* about it').

2 When *not* is linked to 'all', it should be positioned carefully, or the meaning changes. 'All is not well . . .' could mean that everything is out of order; 'Not all is well . . .' suggests that only something has gone wrong. On the other hand, 'all is not well' is often used to cover both those meanings.

3 When *not* is linked to 'because', there is a problem of ambiguity. What does this mean: 'I did not telephone her because she was ill'? Was the telephone call made, not because she was ill, but for another reason? Or was it *not* made, because she was ill? The sentence has to be rewritten: 'I telephoned her, not because she was ill, but because I needed to speak to her' or 'Because she was ill, I did not telephone her'.

notary This old word for a legal official goes back to the 14th century, and still appears on brass plates outside the offices of some solicitors. It is derived from French (a 'notaire' in France is, with some differences, the equivalent of a British solicitor), and the French word-order is preserved for the term in full: *notary public*. These are usually solicitors authorized to draw up legal documents and attest them to make them valid in other countries.

notice See **criticism** . . .

not in- and **not un-** Combinations such as *not infrequent, not unhappy*, etc are useful to express in-between meanings: 'her visits to him are not infrequent'. See also **meiosis**; **un- words**; **double negatives**

notional People are sometimes unclear about the significance of this word in phrases, such as 'a notional sum has been included for extra costs', 'a notional rent has been allowed for'. *Notional* in this sense is hypothetical, a figure that is included because it should be taken into account, but which is more of a **guesstimate** than a careful estimate.

In linguistics, *notional* may be used about formalized grammar regardless of the way language is used in real life.

notorious See **infamous** . . .

not to mention See **needless to say** . . .

not un- See **not in-** . . .

nought, naught, oh or **zero** The *o* and *a* spellings for *nought* and *naught* existed in Old English, and both have survived, leaving a confusing situation. In Britain, *nought* is the spelling when the word is used for *zero*; in America, the spelling is *naught*. In both countries, hopes, expectations, promises, etc may come to *naught*, the spelling when the word means 'nothing'. The same spelling is used when, as is the case now, there is naught left to say about this.

When reading out figures, such as telephone numbers, the most usual way in Britain of expressing 0 is *oh* (6107 = six-one-oh-seven); Americans say 'six-one-zero-seven'. Children are taught to use *nought* ('noughts and crosses'). Accountants and statisticians now often prefer *zero* (VAT regulations use *zero-rated* for certain goods and services).

The usual plural of *zero* is *zeros* (some dictionaries show *zeroes* as an alternative).

nouns Grammarians divide nouns into four categories:
proper nouns are always spelt with a capital letter, because they are names of people, places, etc: Mary, Paris, the Derby. . . .
common nouns are any ordinary nouns: book, language, letter. . . .
collective nouns are groups of people, animals or objects: herd, committee, orchestra . . . (see **collective words**).
abstract nouns are words for qualities, actions, states, etc: doubt, fear, honesty. . . .
See also **grammatical terms**

nouns as adjectives See adjectives

nouns as verbs In the 1930s, A P Herbert fumed over the use of the noun 'service' as a verb ('to service a car', etc). Everyone takes it for granted now. But many people continue to object to nouns being pressed into service as verbs (to première a film, for example). Yet there is nothing new in this: when Antony saw Cleopatra enthroned in her resplendent royal ship, Shakespeare verbalized a noun as an unforgettable way of saying 'indescribable': 'It *beggared* all description' (*Antony and Cleopatra*, Act II Sc ii).

nouveau and **nouvelle** In most cases, there is no need to use *nouveau* (or the feminine form, *nouvelle*) in English, instead of 'new'. Even *nouvelle vague*, the new style in French films in the early 1960s, can just as well be called the 'new wave'. But there are at least three expressions where *nouveau* and *nouvelle* do not translate: *nouveau riche* (plural *nouveaux riches*) for someone ostentatiously showing off when they have recently acquired a lot of money; the gastronomic term, *nouvelle cuisine*, invented in the 1970s by the French food commentators, Gault and Millau, for the breakaway from traditional rich sauces and classic cooking; and no wine-buff could call that first arrival from France, in November each year, from the current year's vintage, anything other than *beaujolais nouveau* (*nouveau* comes after the noun in order to stress the newness).

no way Many people in Britain dislike *no way* as a shortening of 'there is no way' and 'in no way', or as an emphatic negative: 'Can you give us a discount? No way'; 'Would you go there again? No way!'. Even in America, where *no way* is frequently used like this and often spelt as one word, it is considered conversational, rather than written English.

nowhere Even people who are careful have been known to slip in an extra negative before *nowhere*, ending up with a **double negative**: 'wherever we looked, we couldn't find it *nowhere*'. This comes from the habit of using *nowhere* as an inversion of a normal negative: 'we could find it nowhere', instead of 'we could not find it anywhere'. There is nothing wrong with this, unless that extra negative creeps in.

nubile Most dictionaries continue to show as the first meaning of *nubile* something like 'ready for marriage', meaning that a woman is old enough and mature enough, reflecting its derivation from Latin 'nubilis' ('marriageable'). But hardly anyone would use the word in that way now. When people talk about 'a nubile young woman', they nearly always mean a woman in her teens or twenties with a shapely figure and sexually attractive.

nuclear See atomic . . .

nuclear and **post-nuclear family** When people try to connect *nuclear family* with nuclear energy or nuclear weapons, they are confused. *Nuclear* is the descriptive word in all contexts for the noun 'nucleus', which is a central core to which other things relate. *Nuclear family* is a sociological term, first used in the late 1940s, for the basic family unit of a married couple and their children, which forms the core of industrialized societies. It is an unsatisfactory term because of the predominantly technological and sinister associations of the word *nuclear*.

The term *post-nuclear family*, not yet included in most dictionaries, belongs to the 1990s, and suggests departures from the traditional family unit, such as single-parent families or an unmarried couple living together with children.

nucleus See atomic . . .

nudge-nudge wink-wink This gossipy expression is a verbal substitute for the gesture of a sly prod with the elbow and a wink that accompany a suggestive remark: 'All I can tell you is – nudge-nudge wink-wink – I heard a man's voice, and she came to the door in her dressing-gown'. It is insinuating and nasty.

nudist See naturist . . .

number See amount . . .; figures

number of . . . is or **are** 'A number of books *is* on the table' or '*are* on the table'? There is an easy rule. *A number* is plural, followed by *are, have,* etc; *the number* is singular, followed by *is, has,* etc: 'a number of women *are* coming tonight'; 'the number of women who will be here *is* small'.

It is easy to overlook this rule when a sentence begins with 'There', and a word comes between *a* and *number*: 'There *was a* small number of women unable to be present' should be 'There *were a* small number . . .'.

When 'who' (or another word) comes in between, think extra carefully. We have to write, for example, 'The number of women who *are* . . .', but the above rule still holds, as a singular verb follows: 'The number of women who are coming tonight *is* small'.

All the same rules apply to *total of.* . . .

numeracy See **literacy** . . .

numerals See **figures** . . .

nutrition See **dietetics** . . .

nymph or **nymphet** *Nymphs* belong to classical mythology: they are nature sprites, associated with woods and springs, always portrayed as beautiful maidens, and often gambolling with shepherds. From Homer onwards nymphs have shown up regularly in art and literature.

A *nymphet* was originally a young nymph. But Vladimir Nabokov transformed the word in his novel *Lolita* (1955). From then on a nymphet was a precociously sexy young girl, usually knowingly but not always. Nabokov set the ages of 9 to 14 for his nymphets. Nabokov's novel brought *lolita* into the language, as another word for a teenaged nymphet, particularly one who gets involved with a middle-aged man.

nymphomaniac and **satyromaniac** *Nymphomaniac* is at times used unfairly by men about a woman who likes more sex than her partner can supply, or about any woman who is sexually uninhibited. It is very rare for the male equivalent, *satyromaniac,* to be used for a man who demands more sex than is thought decent. *Satyromania* or *satyriasis* (pron: 'sate(r)RYE-e(r)sis') are hardly known as the terms for lust in men.

It seems that nymphomania is an extremely uncommon clinical condition, and it would be hard to find a doctor who has ever been called upon to deal with it. But it should be added that *nymphomania* was cited in 1991 by an American lawyer as a mitigating circumstance in the case of a woman charged with prostitution. A journalist commented: 'This must be the cheekiest defence one profession has ever brought forward for another' (*The Independent*, 6.10.1991).

· O ·

O or **Oh**   For an invocation or a prayer, it is *O*, not usually followed by a comma or an exclamation mark: 'O God our help . . .'. When it is an exclamation of dismay or surprise, it is *Oh*, followed by an exclamation mark: 'Oh my God!'; 'Oh dear me!'; 'Oh! Do you really think so?' When it is a lead-in to something that follows, it is Oh, followed by a comma: '*Oh*, if it's going to rain, we'd better cancel the match'.

OAP or **senior citizen**   The abbreviation OAP for *old-age pensioner* is so well established that it is hard to believe it will ever give way altogether to the euphemism *senior citizen*, which originated in America just before World War II and reached Britain in the 1960s. OAP is not always accurate since pensionable ages are not considered old, nor are all OAPs in receipt of a pension. *Senior citizen* has become an acceptable alternative, now we are getting used to it, although it does not lend itself to a convenient abbreviation. See also **elderly**

OAPEC   See OPEC . . .

oasis   The normal meaning is, of course, a place in the desert where water is found. This is extended to include a place or period of time where something rare is available: 'in an area of cheap cafés, this restaurant is an oasis of good food'; 'during the heat and dust of the takeover battle, there was an oasis of calm, while the chairman was on holiday'.
   The only plural form is *oases* (pron: 'ohAYseez').

obiter dictum   This Latinism is best left to lawyers, who use it for an observation by a judge on a matter not directly concerned with the case in court. In other contexts we are better off changing 'he made an obiter dictum' to '. . . a passing comment' or '. . . an aside'. (Pron: 'obite(r) DIKte(r)m'.)

object or **objective**   In the sense of purpose, aim or intention, *objective* has become the fashionable word in most contexts: 'our objective is to secure the film rights before anyone else does'; 'the objective is to achieve lower production costs'. *Object* is a perfectly satisfactory word in such sentences, but *objective* sounds grander and more important, which is why it tends to be used at conferences and in reports. Regrettably, one of the most common uses of *object* is that military expression from World War II, which has lived on as a boring cliché, *the object of the exercise*.

There is no reason to use it instead of 'the intention', 'the purpose', or simply – 'the object'.

object (grammatical)   See **direct and indirect object**

(the) **object of the exercise**   See object . . .

objet d'art   An *objet d'art* can cover almost anything small, finely worked, antique and expensive, from a Georgian snuffbox to an ivory powder-horn. It is not used for paintings in miniature or about jewellery. Generally *objet d'art* is best for an antique object that no longer has a practical use, but is a beautiful thing to have on a table or in a showcase. The plural is *objets d'art*, pronounced the same as the singular ('obdjayDAH').

obligate   See oblige . . .

obligatory   See mandatory . . .

oblige or **obligate**   *Obligate* suggests a legal or moral duty: 'they are obligated by the lease to have the outside of the building painted every five years'. *Oblige* is a more general word for something that has to be done for any reason: 'she is obliged to visit her mother at least once a week'. The expression 'I am obliged (or much obliged) to you for . . .' is no more than an old-worldly way of saying 'Thank you for . . .'.

oblivious of or **to**   Two rules about *oblivious* have given way to established usage. The first is that *oblivious* should always relate to forgetful, so we cannot be oblivious of something we have never known about. Now the most usual sense of the word is to be totally unaware of something: 'she continued reading with rapt attention, oblivious of (or to) the knocking on the door'.
   The second rule was that *oblivious* must be followed by 'of' rather than 'to'. This applies logically only when the word is used as a synonym for 'forgetful': 'she continued reading oblivious of her coffee getting cold'. When *oblivious* is used to mean 'unaware', it can be followed by 'of' or 'to', as in the first example above.

oboist or **oboeist**   *Oboist.*

obscene   The word is used in different ways about something that is offensive or indecent. It is sometimes confused with 'blasphemous' (see **blasphemy . . .**), and sometimes used as a synonym for 'pornographic' (see **pornography . . .**). Although *obscene* is now often connected with sexual morality, in the 16th century it was used more generally about something that was disgusting. This old meaning has been unconsciously revived, as *obscene* is now often used about almost anything someone resents or dislikes: 'It's obscene that the train is over an hour late'; 'That's an obscene amount of money to spend on a dress'.

obscenity See blasphemy . . .; pornography

obsession Psychiatrists use *obsession* for a mental disorder marked by an emotion that dominates consciousness. In everyday use, the word can mean an excessive concern about something trivial, or a passion for a person, a quality or a belief. An example is the series of television programmes shown in 1992 by the BBC about British writers and the things that are important to them: the programmes were called *Obsessions*. There is a case for not using the word too lightly: 'he has an obsession about keeping his desk tidy' can just as well be expressed as 'he makes a fuss about . . .'.

Obsession can be followed by 'about' or 'with'.

obsolescent or **obsolete** There is a fine line between the meaning of the two words. Many pieces of equipment in use are *obsolescent*, inasmuch as they are superseded by new models that are more efficient. In the meantime, this obsolescent equipment may function adequately, with spare parts still available. Eventually it may become *obsolete*, that is altogether out of date, no longer able to meet present-day demands, and unable to be properly maintained. *Obsolescent* is a stage on the way to becoming *obsolete*.

For some reason, *obsolescent* is not generally used about language, although it would serve a purpose: for example, *actress* is not yet obsolete, because it is still used by many people, but it is falling into disuse, which makes it obsolescent (see **actor**). See also **built-in obsolescence . . .**

obstetrician See gynaecologist . . .

obtain It is difficult to think of a good reason why anyone should say 'Can you obtain this for me?' instead of 'Can you get this for me?' Perhaps there are still people who think that the short simple word *get* is slightly vulgar.

The other use of the verb *obtain*, to mean valid, in force, relevant, is useful in certain contexts: 'What are the conditions that obtain?' requires a more specific answer than 'What are present conditions?', which is more general.

obverse See inverse . . .

occult See mystical . . .

occupation See job . . .

ocean or **sea** There is more of a distinction for geographers than in general use. *Ocean*, which derives from medieval Latin, is used about one of the five expanses of water surrounding the continents: the Atlantic, Pacific, Arctic, Antarctic and Indian Oceans. In other contexts it can have a poetic exalted use ('A life on the ocean wave . . .'). *Oceanic* is the corresponding descriptive word, used, for example, about an *oceanic climate*, that is a climate affected by the ocean. More technically, *oceanic* is applied to regions of the oceans beyond the continental shelf, of greater depth than 200 metres.

Sea is the everyday word derived from Old English. It is used for maritime traffic and commerce ('They that go down to the sea in ships, that do business in great waters', *Psalm 107*), and for the lesser expanses of water, such as the North Sea, China Sea. . . .

o'clock Since this is short for 'of the clock', it should be a small *o*: 7 o'clock. Some stylebooks recommend that o'clock should be written close up to the figure, but it is logical to leave a space.

oculist See optician . . .

odd Compare these two sentences to see how a well-placed **hyphen** can avoid a possible misunderstanding: 'there were some 50 odd people present', 'there were some 50-odd people present'.

odour See aroma . . .

oe or **œ** See ae or æ . . .

OED The *Oxford English Dictionary*. See **dictionaries**

Oedipus In Greek mythology, Oedipus unknowingly killed his father and married his mother. In the 5th century BC, Sophocles used the story for his tragedy, *Oedipus Rex*. In the 20th century, Freud used *Oedipus complex* for his psychoanalytic theory about the sexual attraction felt by a child for a parent of the opposite sex (usually taken to be that of a son for his mother). Sam Goldwyn allegedly dismissed the whole business ('Oedipus . . . Schmoedipus . . . What does it matter so long as he loves his mother?'). (Pron: 'EEdipus'.)

oeno- The prefix *oeno-* is from the Greek word for 'wine', and if wine buffs are looking for a more classical name, they can call themselves *oenophiles* (pron: 'EENe(r)fylz'). *Oenology* (pron: 'EEnole(r)djee') is the study of wines. See also **Master of Wine**

-oes or **-os** **Fowler** complained 'The Englishman has a legitimate grievance against the words in -*o*' (*Modern English Usage*, 1926). There is no consistent rule for forming the plural of nouns ending in -*o*: sometimes it is -*oes*, sometimes -*os*, sometimes either ending can be used: mosquito(e)s, motto(e)s, for example.

As guidelines, here are the usual plural forms of

some common words ending in *-o*: cargoes, commandos, concertos (or concerti), curios, echoes, egos, frescos, heroes, medicos, potatoes, scenarios, tomatoes, zeros.

oeuvre See work . . .

of There are three points to look out for:

1 *Of* is out of order if a sequence starts with 'for' or 'to': 'The conditions *for* signing the contract, paying the balance due and *of* completing the sale . . .'. That should read '*for* completing the sale . . .'.

2 Unnecessary *of*s are hiccups in a sentence: 'We are thinking *of* signing the contract, *of* paying the balance due and *of* completing the sale . . .'. Leave out the second two *of*s, and it flows much better.

3 Omitting *of* when it *is* required can confuse the meaning: 'the prevention of completing the sale and signing the contract the next day caused many problems' could suggest that the contract was signed even though completion was prevented. 'The prevention of completing the sale and *of* signing the contract . . .' leaves no doubt that both were held up.

of all time Hollywood film trailers brought *of all time* into everyday hyperbole. We have long ago lost count of how many 'greatest films of all time' there have been. *Of all time* has a cosmic dimension, and there is a good case for using it very rarely indeed.

of course *Of course* is useful at times to avoid suggesting someone is ignorant or stupid, when you tell them something they ought to know but you're not sure: 'Washington, not New York, is of course the capital of the United States'. *Of course* is not used in *The Good English Guide* every time something obvious to some readers is spelt out. This, of course, is to avoid repetition, and no offence is intended.

Be on guard against the devious use of *of course* to suggest something can be taken for granted, when it really should be looked into carefully: 'At this price, it is of course incredible value'; 'You know, of course, that I love you'.

It was standard practice at one time to put a comma on either side of *of course*. Sometimes this is necessary, as in the last example above, but it is not always obligatory.

off Do not take anything *off of* anything since the one word *off* is enough. In restaurants, *off* can be ambiguous: 'the fish is off' may put you off the fish, or may simply be short for 'off the menu'.

offbeat or **off-key** *Offbeat*, which musically means out of rhythm, describes anyone or anything, often interesting and amusing, that is not in line with the usual order of things. *Off-key*, which in music is the same as 'out of tune', is also used for something that is unexpected or out of line, but in an unpleasant jarring way. An offbeat approach may be worth looking at because it is original; an off-key approach is out of place, unsuitable, or in bad taste.

The most recent dictionaries treat *offbeat* as one word but still require a hyphen for *off-key*.

Off-Broadway See fringe

offer See bid . . .

office boy See executive

officer In the armed services an *officer* holds a commission and has authority over the other ranks. Everyone in the police force is a 'police officer', and it used to be polite (or conciliatory) to address a policeman as *officer* ('I'm sorry officer, I didn't notice how fast I was driving'). The custom is less common now, and would seem old-fashioned to young people.

An officer of a limited company, a term used in law, can be a director, the company secretary and in certain cases, anyone acting on behalf of and with the authority of the board.

off-key See offbeat . . .

off-line and **on-line** *On-line* has different applications in computer technology. The most familiar reference is to a computer system where individual computers and peripheral equipment are connected to a central **mainframe** processing unit. *Off-line* is a computer work station within a network that is functioning unconnected to the **central processor**.

off of See off

offshore For *offshore* winds, winds blowing seawards, the term goes back to the early 18th century. For investments, *offshore* has been coming into increasingly common use since the early 1970s, particularly for unit trusts and interest-bearing deposits arranged in countries where there are tax advantages.

off-white *Off-white*, first used by dress designers for very pale-coloured materials, has been appropriated by interior decorators. It is an unreliable term for a colour, since there is no agreement over when 'white' becomes off-white, or how much off-white can be tinted before it is grey, pink, yellow, etc.

The expression is used in other contexts as well: people in occupations that cannot be classified as either manual or white-collar, have been called *off-white-collar* workers. There are some who call a hint of a cockney accent an 'off-white accent', which makes the term snobbish and racist.

of interest to the public See public interest . . .

often To pronounce the *t* (instead of making it rhyme with 'soften') used to be considered as vulgar as eating peas off a knife. The *t* is usually sounded in America, and heard so often now in Britain that the time may come when 'offen' will sound old-fashioned. Most current dictionaries show both pronunciations, still favouring 'offen'. People who are used to not sounding the *t* find it difficult to change the habit, although most BBC announcers now say 'often'.

oh See nought . . .; O or Oh

Oh right As if by bush telegraph, *Oh right* has spread through Britain as an all-purpose expression, at least for people under 40, of agreement, understanding and acceptance in any situation: 'We're going to Amsterdam for the weekend . . . Oh right'; 'I prefer it in a plain colour . . . Oh right'. In such contexts, *Oh right* is taking over from 'OK' and seems to be gaining ground all the time.

oil See petrol . . .

oil-slick The Torrey Canyon disaster in 1967, when 100 miles of coastline were polluted by oil, made *oil-slick* headline news. It has since become a recurring alarm signal for the environment: It is the name for the heavy coating of crude oil on the sea, whether discharged by accident or intention, moved by the wind, currents and tides, threatening beaches and destroying marine life and wild birds.

OK, OK? or **okay** The full weight of etymological scholarship has delved into the origin of this ubiquitous worldwide expression. The *OED*, which even in the 1989 edition dresses up *OK* with stops (O.K.), sees no reason to depart from the accepted wisdom that *OK* is an uneducated abbreviation of 'orl korrect', and confirms that this most successful of all Americanisms first saw the light on 23.3.1839 in the *Boston Morning Post*.

OK changes its meaning with intonation: a falling tone expresses 'I agree', 'all right', 'if you insist'. . . . A rising tone (*OK?*) asks 'Do you understand?', 'Are you ready?', 'Are you all right?', 'How do I look?'. . . . 'It's OK by me', originally a New York Yiddishism, is of course thoroughly at home now in Britain.

When used in writing as a descriptive expression to mean 'honest', 'good quality', 'competent', etc, *okay* is the usual form: an okay arrangement, an okay airline, an okay plumber.

In spite of its long history, *OK* remains conversational, not used in serious prose.

old See elderly . . .

old boy network The *old boy network* applied mostly to financial institutions, such as **merchant banks**, the Stock Exchange, and the boards of leading companies. Former pupils of public schools are 'old boys', and the old boy network was an unofficial but recognized system of preferment for the 'right' men when it came to good jobs. Before the 1960s, it was a tradition among some men working in the City of London that old school ties should be worn on Fridays. The fact that this entry is written in the past tense does not mean that the old boy network has disappeared, but to suggest that its days may be numbered.

When the London Stock Exchange was deregulated

in 1986, competence and effectiveness became the keynotes in international markets, and there has been a shake-out of 'old boys' who were not up to this and to the pressures of life at the top in the 1990s. It must be added that a survey in *The Independent* at the end of 1992 showed that banking in the City, and the *Financial Times* index of companies (see **Footsie**) still remain largely connected to the old boy network.

olde, olden and **oldie** *Olde* is a 20th-century vulgar attempt to give the word 'old' a spurious Chaucerian flavour, by people who are vaguely aware that Old and Middle English words often had a final -*e* that was sounded. There are 'olde worlde' (pron: 'oldy worldy') restaurants, with olde wooden beams, to encourage tourists to believe they are visiting Olde England.

Olden has genuine antiquity, as the expression 'olden days' is found in 15th-century writings. Nevertheless phrases such as 'in olden times' are now both affected and vague, since they give no indication of the period referred to.

In the late 19th century, *oldie* was used for an old person, but since the 1940s it has become the word for an old film, an old pop song, an old joke. . . . It has been taken up by Richard Ingrams for his magazine aimed at 'senior citizens', *The Oldie*. For people, the word *oldster* goes back to Charles Dickens. Later it dropped out of use in Britain but lived on in America. There are signs of it crossing back over the Atlantic.

Old English or **Anglo-Saxon** These are alternative names for the English language up to about the mid-12th century. The traditional name among scholars used to be *Anglo-Saxon*, and there is a professor of Anglo-Saxon at Oxford. Since the 1960s, *Old English* has become the preferred name.

Although Old English is the forerunner of the language we speak now, it is incomprehensible without special study. Here, for example, are the opening lines of the Old English epic poem *Beowulf*, which is generally dated in the 8th century and survives in a 10th-century manuscript:

Hwæt, wē gār-dena   in ʒēar-daʒum
þēod-cyninʒa   þrym ʒefrunon,
hū ðā æþelinʒas   ellen fremedon.

'What! we of the Spear-Danes of yore days,
      so was it
That we learn'd of the fair fame of kings of the
      folks . . .'
                    (from the translation by
                    William Morris and A J Wyatt)

older, oldest See elder . . .

(the) **Older Man** See Other Woman . . .

oldie See olde . . .

Old Lady of Threadneedle Street This is the affectionate sobriquet for the Bank of England. It dates from the Napoleonic wars when a cartoon portrayed the Bank of England as an old lady under attack. It is still occasionally used, or shortened to the *Old Lady*, by financial commentators when they are in an expansive mood.

(For golfers the *Old Lady* may have another meaning, as their name for the Royal and Ancient golf course at St Andrews.)

(the) Old Thunderer By the late 16th century, *thunderer* was being used for an orator able to declaim opinions with great force and passion. In the early part of the 19th century, *The Thunderer* became an admiring nickname for *The Times* newspaper. The paper is no longer published in the august-sounding Printing House Square, but down by the docks in East London, it is owned by Rupert Murdoch, an American publisher, born in Australia, and some feel that the thunder has become more distant. But the name is still used, usually now as the *Old Thunderer*, with at least some of the old respect and affection.

ombudsman The word (pron: 'OMMboodsme(r)n') was borrowed from Swedish in the late 1950s, for someone appointed to investigate complaints from the public against official bodies.

on There is a good deal to go on about the simple word *on*. To make it easier to refer to, most of the points are treated in separate entries: whether a shop is *in* Oxford Street or *on* it is dealt with under **in or on**; for whether something is *on* the table or *upon* it, see next entry; for guidelines on whether *on to* should be one word or two see **onto**. . . .

There remain a couple of other minor points: 'please phone me at 071– . . .' is often replaced now by the American idiom 'please phone me *on* . . .'. We have always done things *on* holiday, but usually *at* or *over* weekends. We can now do them *on* weekends, if we want to.

on or **upon** Some people try to use *on* and *upon* in slightly different ways. It's not worth bothering about, except to keep to certain established phrases and place-names: on no account, upon my word, Henley-on-Thames, Burton-upon-Trent. Shakespeare's birthplace has it both ways: Stratford-on-Avon, or Stratford-upon-Avon. Otherwise *on* and *upon* are interchangeable. Perhaps *upon* sounds more formal and dignified, but don't count on or upon that.

on behalf of or **on the part of** The two phrases should not be mixed up. *On behalf of* someone means in their interest or in their place: 'she is dealing with the matter on behalf of her husband'. *On the part of* relates to a quality that is attached to a person: 'the matter went wrong because of incompetence on the part of his wife'.

one Here are six points to bear in mind about the apparently simple word *one*:

1 Once you start using *one*, you are landed with it:

'One feels that travelling to other countries enlarges one's experience and gives one a better understanding of oneself'. It's wrong to change halfway: 'one feels that travelling to other countries enlarges *our* experience . . .'.

2 *One in* . . . is singular: 'one in five new businesses *fails* in the first year' (not '. . . *fail* in the first year'). The verb is controlled by *one*, not the figure that comes after.

3 *One of those* is plural, because the verb is controlled by *those*, not by *one*: 'she is one of those successful women who *are* now on the board' (not '. . . *is* now on the board').

4 *More than one* should logically be followed by a plural verb. But because of the influence of the word *one*, the usual way is to treat the phrase as singular: 'more than one woman *has* refused to attend the meeting'. Even when *more than one* stands on its own, it is still followed by a singular verb: 'more than one *has* refused . . .'.

5 '*One* of the travellers has lost *his* baggage'. But what if the traveller turns out to be a woman? See **unisex grammar**

6 *One* can have a touch of the **royal we** about it, with an implied snobbishness: in a sentence such as 'one wouldn't go to a place like that dressed in that way', *one* is another way of saying 'people like us' (see also **one of us**).

one another See **each other** . . .

on earth or **in the world** See **earth** . . .

one of us *One of us* used to be a middle-class social phrase implying that whoever it was had been to the same sort of school, did work of similar standing and in general conformed to certain kinds of social behaviour. Margaret Thatcher gave the phrase a political twist: during her long period as Prime Minister, the *one-of-us* test was loyalty to the policies of her government. *One of us* was part of Margaret Thatcher's personal style, and it was dropped by the Conservative Party after her resignation.

one-sided See **unilateral** . . .

one-upmanship See **-manship**

ongoing *Ongoing* comes in for a lot of stick: 'an overused, pretentious and totally unnecessary substitute for *continuing*, and ought to be shunned' (B A Phythian, *A Concise Dictionary of Correct English*, 1979). That is hard on a word that was already in use in the late 19th century, for *ongoing* is not as recent as most people think. E S C Weiner, an Oxford lexicographer, is more open-minded, comparing *ongoing* with 'oncoming', and considering it useful to describe something 'that goes on' (*Oxford English*, 1986). Some people find *ongoing* more direct and immediate than 'continuing': 'The ongoing problem of unemployment

. . .'. It's a matter of taste. But avoid phrases, particularly 'an ongoing situation', that have become **clichés**.

on hand See **hand**

on hold See **back burner** . . .

on-line See **off-line** . . .

on-hook *On-hook telephones, on-hook dialling* are regular terms now in telephone technology. The telephones have built-in speakers, and numbers can be dialled without lifting the handset. Only when the call is answered, do you need to stop work and pick it up.

only There are purists who deny that 'we only live once' and insist 'we live only once'. *Only*, they say, must come immediately in front of the word it refers to. **Fowler** says such pedants want to turn 'English into an exact science' (*Modern English Usage*, 1926). Everyone knows what we mean by 'I only want one glass of wine' (instead of '. . . only one glass . . .'). We can be relaxed about *only* in conversation, because our tone will make it clear what we mean. In writing, we should be more careful when there's a risk of misunderstanding. Many good writers, including Doris Lessing, Kingsley Amis, Graham Greene, Evelyn Waugh and George Orwell, are not at all fussed about placing *only* wherever it suits them: 'The captain . . . only appeared once at table' (Graham Greene), rather than '. . . appeared only once . . .'.

You must decide for yourself if you want to be punctilious about *only*, bearing in mind that the natural place for it is usually before the verb, even though it refers to another word, and 'I want only one glass . . .', '. . . appeared only once at table' sound forced.

onomatopoeia When a word approximates to the sound of what it means, that is *onomatopoeia*: **buzzwords** *buzz* around, doors *creak*, sleepers *zizz*, cats *purr*. A whole phrase can be onomatopoeic, by combining words to pick up the sound of what is intended: 'the stuttering rifles' rapid rattle' (Wilfred Owen, *Anthem for doomed Youth*, 1917).

You may have to think twice about the spelling of *onomatopoeia*, but the pronunciation rolls easily off the tongue: 'on-oh-mat-e(r)-PEE-e(r)'.

on stream (onstream) There are people who make an unwarranted fuss about *on stream* as unnecessary jargon for 'begin', 'coming into operation', 'functioning', etc. The expression goes back to the early 1930s, used in oil refineries for when oil is flowing. It seems a useful adaptation, in keeping with present-day style, for describing an operation at the moment when it gets going effectively. In business *on stream* may be used about an investment, such as a new factory or acquisition, for the point when costs are covered and it starts to produce a profit.

There are signs that *onstream* is being used increasingly as one word, a form that may well take over. The usual pronunciation puts the stress on the second part: 'onSTREAM'.

onto or **on to** The distinction between 'in to' and 'into' (see **in, into or in to**) has existed for centuries, but there has been a curious resistance to *onto* as one word. Compton Mackenzie denounced it as 'that horrid little Siamese twin of a preposition', and for a long time Oxford dictionaries refused to define it as a separate entry. The 1990 edition of the *Concise Oxford Dictionary* puts that right, conceding it has a certain usefulness, but labelling it **disp** (disputed). That label is unlikely to be justified much longer.

Onto conveys a sense of the *direction* of movement: 'the children ran onto the beach' is different from 'the children ran on the beach'. When it is impossible to use *on* alone, *on to* should always be two words: 'please pass this on to her'; 'Keep right on to the end of the road' (Harry Lauder). When movement is indicated, *onto* is an alternative: 'she climbed onto the ship'.

onward or **onwards** As a word of encouragement or command, it is *onward*: 'Onward Christian soldiers . . .'. When it is an indication of direction or time, it is *onwards*: 'we must move onwards'; 'from the time of her marriage onwards . . .'.

op art and **pop art** *Op art* (*optical art*, the term in full, is rarely used) dates from the 1960s and uses visual effects, such as discordant colours and juxtaposed geometric shapes, that dazzle and disturb the eyes.

Pop art was first used by an English art critic, Lawrence Alloway, in the mid-1950s. In his words, *pop art* takes 'mass-produced urban culture' as its subject – badges, Coke bottles, photographs from magazines, etc – to make us look at them with a new focus, and to cut across the aesthetic values of recognized art. Andy Warhol's silkscreens of soup tins and Marilyn Monroes are well-known examples.

op cit See **ibid** . . .

OPEC and **OAPEC** These are both used as **acronyms**, pronounced in the same way, but they represent different organizations. OAPEC is the Organization of Arab Petroleum Exporting Countries, formed in 1968, whose members are primarily countries in the Middle East. OPEC is the powerful Organization of Petroleum Exporting Countries, formed in 1960, a cartel which includes countries outside the Middle East, such as Venezuela and Indonesia. OPEC is much more often in the news, because its members produce most of the internationally traded oil, and it seeks to control production levels and prices, which has significant effects on world economy.

operational research Information technology, which provides government and industry with far more statistical information far more quickly than before, has made changes to the process of decision-making. Decisions that were previously matters of judgement or opinion are now subjected to a scientific approach, known to management analysts as operational research (operations research is the more usual term in America).

operator or **operative**   *Operator* is the more usual word for someone who operates a machine. An *operative* tends to be used for a skilled worker in a particular field (there is, for example, a Federation of Building Trades Operatives). Note that in America the first meaning of *operative* is for a **private eye** or a secret agent.

ophthalmologist   See optician . . .

opinion   See attitude . . .

opposite, converse, reverse or **antithesis**   *Opposite* is the all-purpose word, usually the safest one to use. The other words can have subtle or philosophical distinctions that are not often applicable to everyday use. There are a few guidelines that are helpful in deciding which alternative to use.

When *converse* is a synonym for *opposite* (a converse point of view), *opposite* is usually preferable. *Converse* is more relevant to an action: 'she often cooks dinner, but the converse is also true, since there are many times when he cooks it'.

Reverse is a general word, more pointed than *opposite*, for something that is the other way round: 'it was not a case of carelessness but the reverse, an over-attention to detail'. While *opposite* would work perfectly well in that sentence, *reverse* makes the point more sharply.

Antithesis is the strongest of all these words, since it represents the absolute opposite: 'the chairman is hesitant and indecisive, and we need the antithesis, someone who can make strong forceful decisions'.

These are not rules but points of style.

opposite *of, to* or ***from***   *Of* is preferable when *opposite* compares two nouns: 'Mary's attitude is the opposite of John's'; 'her attitude is the opposite of mine'. *To* or *from* is required when *opposite* compares two directions or positions: 'they left in the opposite direction to (or from) the one we were taking'; 'our house is on the opposite side of the road to (or from) theirs'.

opt for   See choose . . .

optician, oculist, optometrist or **ophthalmologist**   These names are confusing because, apart from anything else, the terminology changed in some ways during the 1980s.

The Opticians Act 1989 gives limited protection to the title *optician*, which is now the usual word for practitioners registered with the General Optical Council. They are not qualified doctors, and fall into two categories: an *ophthalmic optician* is qualified to test sight and supply spectacles, while a *dispensing optician* is limited to supplying spectacles against someone else's prescription.

Oculist is rarely used now, replaced by *opthalmolo-*

gist or *ophthalmic surgeon*, for a medical specialist, usually a consultant, who deals with medical and surgical treatment of eye disease and disorders.

Lastly, the American and European term, *optometrist*, has now been officially adopted in Britain as the word for an *opthalmic optician*, and some professional bodies, such as The British College of Optometrists and the Association of Optometrists, have changed their names to fit in.

As a postscript, because of 'optic', it is not uncommon for *ophthalmic* to be wrongly spelt 'opthalmic', and the pronunciation also needs to be watched: 'offTHALmic' (not 'opTHALmic').

optimal or **optimum**   These are often used wrongly and misleadingly for simply the biggest or the most: 'The optimum return is 10% pa' is simply the highest return available. *Optimum* does mean the most, but always taking into account conflicting factors involved. We should refer to *optimum return* to mean not the highest possible return but the highest return to be expected, consistent with financial security, reasonable access to capital, or whatever other factors are specified. *Optimal* means exactly the same as *optimum*, and should be used in the same way; a maximum, but taking into account other considerations.

optimistic and **pessimistic**   *Optimistic* properly describes an attitude that is part of a person's nature, an inclination to feel that things will go well, the reverse of *pessimistic*. It is commonly used about a specific case to mean 'hopeful' or 'encouraging': 'I'm optimistic that the weather will be fine tomorrow'; 'it is an optimistic sign that the opinion polls are going our way'. The same applies to *pessimistic*, which is a tendency to feel things will turn out badly. The word has become a synonym for 'not hopeful' ('I am pessimistic about the weather').

Those who care about preserving the true meaning of the word should be 'hopeful' (instead of optimistic) that this weak use of *optimistic* and *pessimistic* will be kept in check. But it is doubtful whether enough people care one way or the other. For what it is worth, most dictionaries do not yet accept these lesser meanings of the words.

optimum   See optimal . . .

optometrist   See optician . . .

or   There is the question of whether to follow items connected by *or* with a singular or plural verb. Three rules cover this:

1 When every item is singular, the verb should be singular: 'Susan or Mary or Helen *is* available to help'.

2 It is obvious that when every item is plural, the verb is plural: 'fifty men or three mechanical diggers *are* required'.

3 When items are a combination of singular and plural, the sentence reads better if the verb takes its cue from the last noun in the list: 'ten men or one mechanical digger *is* required' but 'one mechanical digger or ten men *are* required'.

-or or **-our** See -our or -or

oracy Andrew Wilkinson, a lecturer in education, coined *oracy* in his book *Spoken English* (1965) 'for general ability in oral skills'. He believed that the ability to use spoken language was not given anything like the same importance as mastering written language. *Oracy*, which is formed on the basis of 'literacy' using the Latin word for 'mouth', is included in all current dictionaries.

oral See verbal . . .

oral history A name was given to this branch of history in the late 1970s, and it will become increasingly familiar in the 21st century. An aspect of what could be called *oral history* has always existed, as spoken accounts have been passed on over generations. But this has not been verifiable evidence. This has changed, and future generations of historians will spend time listening to tape recordings as well as studying written archives.

oral sex Since the spread of **Aids**, *oral sex* has become the more understandable term, instead of the Latinate equivalents (see **cunnilingus** . . .). The Department of Health leaflet on Aids, issued in 1987, specified three forms of sexual intercourse, 'vaginal, anal and oral sex'.

orangery See conservatory . . .

orbit The word has been used since the 17th century for the path of a heavenly body, and by the 19th century it had already become extended to refer to a person's daily round of activities. Space exploration in the 1960s brought the word to the fore, as spacemen *orbited* the earth. As a result, the extended use of the word has become everyday language: 'the scheme is now in orbit'; 'after being ill for some months, she is back in orbit'.

(the) orchestra is or **are** 'The orchestra *is* about to play' but 'the orchestra *are* having their lunch'. See **collective words**

orchestrate *Orchestrate* is arranging a music score for an orchestra, and like other musical terms (**offbeat and off-key**, for example), has been adapted for use in other situations. *Orchestrate* was first intended to mean combining different elements in a harmonious way, but since the 1960s, this has given way to another meaning that has almost lost touch with the musical sense of the word. *Orchestrate* now means to arrange and plan things for the maximum effect: 'the conference was so well orchestrated that it was a great success with everyone'. In certain contexts, *orchestrate* can imply manipulation: 'the conference was orchestrated in a way that encouraged delegates to vote for the proposed changes'.

ordained or **going into the Church** This distinction was brought to light in one of John Silverlight's articles on words in *The Observer*. He was rebuked for writing about Archbishop Ramsey's previous career, before *going into the Church*. Even churchmen often describe their ordination as *going into the Church*, so John Silverlight should not have been censured too harshly. Nevertheless, as was pointed out by his critic, *baptism* is the real moment of entering or going into the Church. When men or women take holy orders, they are *ordained*.

'orDEAL' or **'ORdeal'** Both pronunciations are heard, but 'orDEAL' is the only one considered correct.

ordinary See everyday . . .

ordinary and **ordinarily** *Ordinary* in both British and American English keeps the stress on the first syllable ('AWDe(r)nery'). In Britain, the same applies to *ordinarily* ('AWDe(r)nerily'), but many people, uncomfortable with the long flight of unaccented syllables, follow the American stress pattern which puts the stress on the third syllable. But no matter how often it's heard, 'awde(r)NARily' is looked down on by some people.

organic See healthfood . . .

organization The use of *organization* for a business corporation started in America and spread to Britain in the 1960s. People would ask at conferences 'Which organization are you with?', and the answer might be IBM, *Coca-Cola*, **Xerox** . . . . The *organization man* (title of a book in the late 1950s) came into being, an executive so identified with the company that life has hardly any reality outside it.

organizer Of course an *organizer* is a person who organizes. Even the *OED* has overlooked the other meaning of the word, dating from the 1980s, which is for a loose-leaf diary-cum-personal filing system, heavy with inserts and compartments, carried about in 'executive' briefcases and handbags. **Filofax** became a generic name for these organizers (also called *personal organizers*).

Organizers are so much an alter ego for some people, that the loss of them is almost like losing personal identity, causing acute symptoms of stress.

orgasm or **climax** About the time when, according to Philip Larkin's calendar, 'sexual intercourse began in nineteen sixty-three', *orgasm* seemed to replace the word *climax* for the moment of sexual satisfaction and release in women. There is no lexicographical justification, but before then, *orgasm* was more likely to be used for men, and *climax* for women. The new equality between the sexes extended to the bed, and *orgasm* became unisex, as well as teatime conversation in the Shires. The deep-sea undertow of human sexuality came to the surface, bringing sexual terms out into the open, with new interpretations.

In 1966 Masters and Johnson published their exhaustive survey, *Human Sexual Responses*, which challenged the centuries-old male conviction that female sexual pleasure depends on the male act of penetrating the vagina as far as possible. *Vaginal orgasm* and *clitoral orgasm* became opposing terms in postfeminist sexuality. In the 1980s, research carried out by Dr Marian Dunn, Director of the Center for Human Sexuality at the State University of New York, seemed to redefine the male orgasm, suggesting it could be an intense erotic sensation not necessarily dependent on or coincidental with ejaculation. Another sexual-linguistic distinction between men and women was challenged.

orient or **orientate** Both words mean the same, originally to face or turn towards the East. If we are lost, we try to *orient* or *orientate* ourselves, that is, to find our bearings. These meanings have become extended and the fashionable use now, accepted by most dictionaries, is to say someone or something is biased in a particular direction: advertising agencies say they are client-oriented, a new model of a car claims to be oriented towards safety or safety-oriented. The longer form *orientate* is dropping out of use.

Or is it? This simple question, with its variants, *Or is she?*, *Or did he?*, etc, is an effective device, particularly in conversation, although it also works in writing, for jolting a listener or a reader out of complacency: 'That's the end of the whole matter. Or is it?'; 'Perhaps we can accept his story. Or can we?'; 'We all agree that this is a great painting. Or do we?'

Or is it? is a sharp interjection of uncertainty into something that is being taken for granted, and worth keeping in mind for an occasion when people are nodding too comfortably over something they should be thinking about.

orthopaedics Originally the medical treatment of the bones and muscles of children (*-paedics* comes from the Greek word for 'child'), *orthopaedics* has become the standard word for this branch of medicine covering patients of all ages. *Orthopaedics* is always treated as a singular noun.

Orwellian The unusual aspect of *Orwellian* is that it is used less as a description of George Orwell's (1903–50) style as a writer, more to describe the nightmare of a totalitarian society in which individuality, truth and freedom are suppressed by brainwashing. Orwell's two most well-known novels are *Animal Farm* (1945) and *Nineteen Eighty-four* (1949), which depict life under a *Big Brother is watching you* (an Orwellian slogan) regime. For the Orwellian concepts *doublethink* and *Newspeak*, see **doublespeak** . . .

-os See **-oes or -os**

Oscar *Oscars* are the gold statuettes presented at Hollywood extravaganzas and awarded by the American Academy of Motion Picture Arts and Sciences. Why Oscar? The folklore is that a member of the Academy once looked at a statuette and declared, 'My! It's just like my Uncle Oscar'. In passing, some film historians consider Oscars as Hollywood razzmatazz, a view that may be shared by Marlon Brando, who is reported to have used his Oscar as a doorstop.

In Britain, Oscar has been picked up and used for almost any kind of success: 'She gets an Oscar for her cheese soufflé!'

osmosis This technical term has proved useful in general contexts. In biochemistry, *osmosis* is the process by which one solution gradually passes through a permeable solid to be absorbed into another solution. The word is useful for describing the way in which knowledge or ideas are acquired because someone is exposed to them: 'she had taken on board many of his ideas by a kind of marital osmosis'.

(the) other place Some members of Oxford University talk about *the other place*, meaning Cambridge, and members of Cambridge University do the same in reference to Oxford, implying arrogantly that no other university exists. Members of the House of Commons talk about *the other place*, meaning the House of Lords, arrogantly implying that these are the only two places that count.

(the) Other Woman and the Older Man These are stereotyped expressions in the never-ending battle between the sexes.

A pattern for the *Other Woman* is 'the carefully coiffed beauty eating a TV dinner while waiting for the phone to ring'. In marital dramas, the Other Woman is a woman having an affair with a married man. One Other Woman describes the advantages: 'You only have quality time, not the stresses of everyday living'. Another describes the pain: 'From the first kiss I knew I was heading down a no-through road'. (Quotations are from Nancy Stein in *The Independent*.) The *Other Woman* has a ring of the past about it, when it was nearly always that way round. In the 1990s, wives leave their husbands for other men, not that anyone refers to 'the Other Man' – it would be 'another man'.

Women do talk about *the Older Man*, the image of a man from 60 to ?, who, it is said, has so much appeal to a woman 25 years or so younger. These are men 'on whom age and experience have bestowed the luxury of confidence and its natural bedfellow kindness' (Sally Brampton, *The Times*). There are two theories about the appeal of *the Older Man*. One is that some women have an eternal quest for a symbol of their father. The other is that men take so much longer to grow up, that a natural balance of maturity requires a gap of 20 to 30 years between a man and a woman. There is, in contrast, the **toy boy**.

ottoman The word comes from the Ottoman Empire, which was replaced by the state of Turkey in 1922. In British minds, an *ottoman* had a hint of the harem about it, a low upholstered seat or stool often forming a chest, not that it stops them being popular in sitting-rooms.

-our or **-or**   The American lexicographer, Noah Webster, laboured over 20 years on his *American Dictionary of the English Language*. Or rather, he *labored*, because in his simplification of spelling, he replaced the British *-our* by *-or* in most cases: *color, humor, odor*, etc – and *labor*. One or two words slipped through the net, including *glamour*, often spelt that way in America, alongside *glamor*.

The *-or* spelling sometimes jars on people accustomed to British English, but Webster had a good case etymologically, since in most of those words, the Latin root is *-or: colorem, (h)umorem, laborem, odorem*, etc. British spellings are in any case inconsistent, since when a suffix is added, the *-u-* is usually omitted and the spelling follows the American pattern: *glamorous, humorous, laborious, odorous*. . . . And to throw in a few more inconsistencies, the British have to learn exceptions, such as *colourful* but *coloration, honourable* but *honorific*. . . .

ours or **our's**   *Our's* is always wrong.

ourselves or **ourself**   *Ourselves* is the only form, as in 'we were pleased with ourselves'; 'we see ourselves as a new political party'. *Ourself* was an old-fashioned pronunciation of *ourselves*, rarely heard now. *Ourself* is also part of the **royal we** (as Queen Victoria might have said, 'We, *ourself*, are not amused').

out or **out-**   When *out* is used as a prefix, in nearly every case it forms one word, without a hyphen: outclass, outgoing, outperform, outshoot. . . . Some dictionaries make an exception for *out-patient*, (but hospitals treat it as one word) and in cases where the second word begins with a *-t* (out-talk, out-top . . .).

out and **outing**   To begin with, these were coded words among the homosexual community in America. They both became current in Britain in the early 1990s. *Outing* is the practice of revealing that well-known people are homosexuals, and *out* is the descriptive word for a person, usually well-known, who is open about homosexual preferences, the antithesis of a **closet gay**. A new American magazine called *Outweek* became famous in 1990, with a whole series of so-called *outings*. In Britain, Patrick O'Connor, interviewing Michael Tippett for *The Independent*, called him 'a famous out composer . . . who achieved an acceptance of his homosexuality'.

out or **out of**   See out of . . .

outcast or **outcaste**   The two words have different meanings. An *outcast* is rejected by society or by a group: an *outcaste* relates to the stratification in Hindu society, and is a person who does not belong to one of the four hereditary classes.

outcome   It is worth being on guard against using *outcome* to make a simple sentence sound more important: 'the outcome of the delay was losing the business', as an alternative to 'the delay made us lose the business'; 'the outcome of combining the work of both departments was saving unnecessary costs' instead of 'combining the work of both departments saved unnecessary costs'. The word is more justifiable when it is applied to the result of a long and uncertain process: 'There were many problems to overcome, but the outcome made the effort worthwhile'.

outdoors or **out of doors**   Either can be used (see out or out of).

outgoing   See extrovert . . .

outing   See out . . .

outline, summary, synopsis or **résumé**   There are distinctions here worth preserving. An *outline* is an indication of the overall form of a plan, a book or a project, sometimes prepared before the details have been worked out, and the purpose is to convey the general idea, often to get approval in principle.

A *summary* is an abbreviated version of something that includes essential detail, and the purpose is to save a reader time and trouble, or to recapitulate the main points.

A *synopsis* can cover either an outline or a summary, and is more likely to be used for a shortened version of a piece of prose or of a complete book. A synopsis usually conveys more detail than either an outline or a summary. (The plural of *synopsis* is *synopses* – pron: 'sinNOPPseez'.)

There is no difference in meaning between a *summary* and a *résumé*, and usually *summary* is to be preferred, if only because it doesn't need accents! But note that résumé (with or without accents) is the word used in America for a **cv**.

The corresponding verbs are *outline, summarize* and *synopsize*. (There is no verb for *résumé*, but if you fancy asking someone to résumé a report for you, no one should make a fuss.)

out of or **out**   In America it is normal usage to 'let the cat out the bag', but in Britain it is considered correct to let it 'out *of* the bag'. In conversation, *out* and *out of* have become interchangeable: 'she jumped out (of) the car and slammed the door'. In time, this conversational use may become standard: it is already perfectly correct to go *outdoors* as well as *out of doors*, and more usual to look out the window than out of it.

outplacement   The word *outplacement* arrived in Britain from America in the late 1980s. *Outplacement consultants*, and there are said to be about 100 in Britain, help highly paid executives who are made redundant. They are not employment agencies and do not find new jobs for their clients. Their role is partly counselling, to reassure a person dismissed from an important job that there is 'life after the sack'. Outplacement specialists show their clients how to market themselves, from preparing an impressive **cv**, to identifying the areas where they are most likely to be successful. Methods are a mixture of homespun psychology, analysis of employment opportunities and assessment of a person's value to a company.

output See input . . .

output or **throughput** *Output* suggests production, specific things that are made: the output of a factory, output of a writer ('her usual output is three novels a year'). *Throughput* can be used about industrial production in the same way but has more general applications for any kind of processing: the throughput of visa applications, the throughput of MOT tests. *Throughput* can also be used about people: for example, the throughput of the out patient department of a hospital is the number of patients treated over a specified period.

outré *Outré* (the past form of the French verb 'outrer', to overdo something) is perhaps an affected word to use in English, in place of perfectly good alternatives, such as 'in bad taste', 'going too far', 'beyond the bounds', 'over the top'.

outside or **outside of** *Outside* is preferable when it relates to a place: 'there are important collections of art outside London'; 'while her application was being discussed, she went outside the room'. In the sense of 'apart from', *outside of* is preferable: 'he has other interests outside of politics'; 'there is a spirituality about her that seems outside of her religion'. Both these are points of style.

outsider To begin with, *outsider* was a neutral word for someone outside a group. The word is still used in this way, for example for a person outside a profession or an organization, or not involved in an issue, sometimes with the suggestion that their opinion might be more valuable for that reason. The old snobbish use of the word, especially in the phrase *rank outsider*, for someone whose behaviour or social manners are beyond the pale, belongs to the past. On racecourses, an *outsider* has been used since the mid-19th century for a horse that is hardly in the running.

A new twist to the word was given when Camus's novel *L'Etranger* (1946) was translated into English under the title *The Outsider*, and by Colin Wilson's book (1956) with the same title. An *outsider* in this sense is a person, often a writer or an artist, who has a vision of life that prevents them fitting into ordinary society, and arguably gives them detached superior insight and awareness.

outstanding Look out for the two meanings of *outstanding* cutting across one another: 'There is an outstanding book we have to discuss before awarding the prize'. Is the book in question remarkable or is it the one book that still remains to be considered? When the second meaning is intended, uncertainty can be avoided by placing *outstanding* after the noun: 'There is a book outstanding that we have to discuss . . .'.

outward or **outwards** *Outward* in front of a noun, *outwards* after a noun or after a verb: 'on the outward journey', 'on the journey outwards', 'while journeying outwards'.

outworker The word is much less common than it used to be, particularly in relation to the clothing industry. At one time people did piecework in their own homes or small workshops in the East End of London, for manufacturing businesses, making buttonholes, sewing garments, etc. Another kind of outworker will become common by the end of the century: industrial **futurologists** see 'tomorrow's workplace' as the home, with the use of telecommunications enabling millions of people to become . . . **teleworkers**.

over or **over-** See **hyphens/7**

over and above See **each and every**

overall *Overall* has a place to indicate that a figure includes peripheral items: the overall length of a car would include bumpers; the overall cost would include all extras. In other cases, it is often unnecessary to use *overall*, rather than 'total', 'complete', 'general', or even no qualifying word at all: 'total sales for this product . . .', or simply 'sales for this product . . .', instead of 'overall sales . . .'; 'the general conclusion was . . .', or simply 'the conclusion was . . .', instead of 'the overall conclusion . . .'.

overheating It was during inflationary periods from the 1950s onwards that *overheating* and *overheated* were used for the first time about the economy, to describe encouraging consumer demand to build up by making credit too easily available. This led in the short term to increased employment, but also to higher prices and inflation plus overproduction, which was then followed by increased unemployment and a recession. Some economists see *overheating* as part of the **boom** and bust cycle.

overkill *Overkill* was used in America after World War II in connection with defence planning, particularly about nuclear capacity much greater than necessary for annihilating the enemy. It has become a fashionable word for any effort or protest far in excess of what the situation requires, the equivalent of the colloquial phrase 'going over the top'. In the 18th century, Pope expressed the same idea more elegantly: 'Who breaks a butterfly upon a wheel?' (*Epistle to Dr Arbuthnot*).

overlook or **oversee** Both words can have exactly the same meaning as 'supervise'. *Oversee* is usually preferable to avoid misunderstanding, for *overlook* can also have the opposite meaning, that is to ignore something, or not even notice it.

overly *Overly*, before a descriptive word, is still distinctly American, and sentences such as 'this is not overly important' do not sound at home in Britain. The simple word *too* is often the best alternative. In other cases, *over* can be suitable: 'she is too sensitive, or oversensitive' (instead of 'overly sensitive').

overtone or **undertone**   Although the words are often used interchangeably, they can imply a different quality. *Overtone* suggests a deliberate nuance beyond the surface meaning of the words: 'there was a threatening overtone in his speech to the workforce' (the suggestion is that threats were implied but not openly expressed). *Undertone* also means something not on the surface, but less deliberate, more a general feeling that can be sensed: 'there was a confident undertone in the way the figures were presented' (presumably the figures were encouraging, which led to them being presented in an upbeat way).

This distinction may need thinking about, but it is a useful one.

overview   *Overview* is shown in current dictionaries, usually without suggesting it is American usage. Yet for many people it does not seem at home in British English. For others, it is vague, usually better replaced by a more explicit word, such as 'survey', 'outline', 'review', 'broad picture', etc.

owing to   See due to . . .

own brand   *Own brand* is a marketing term that has seeped into more general use. Big retailing businesses sell products under their own name, usually at a lower price than well-known proprietary brands. In some cases, these *own brand* goods are made by the same manufacturers as proprietary brands, and packaged under *own brand* labels. The most famous own brand is *St Michael*, invoked by Marks & Spencer for the labels of anything from bras to burgundy.

own goal   Politics is like walking a tightrope, and there is an accumulation of expressions to describe inept blunders. **Banana skin** and **shoot oneself in the foot** are examples. The football expression, *own goal*, has joined the list, for an ill-considered remark or action that has a boomerang effect.

Oxbridge and **Redbrick**   *Oxbridge* is an imaginary place of learning in Thackeray's novel, *The History of Pendennis* (about 1850). The name remained waiting in the wings until about the 1950s, when *Oxbridge* became a useful term in educational contexts for setting apart the ancient universities of Oxford and Cambridge, from *Redbrick*, the collective name given to universities founded in the 20th century, where the buildings are usually built of brick, in contrast to the crumbling stone of Oxford and Cambridge colleges. *Oxbridge* is always spelt with a capital *O* (an *Oxbridge* college) but *Redbrick* as a descriptive word has a small *r* (a *redbrick* university). *Redbrick* is not usually applied to the many new universities established since World War II.

Oxford English Dictionary (*OED*)   See **dictionaries**

oxymoron   *Oxymoron* combines two Greek words with opposite meanings, 'sharp' and 'dull'. It functions as a literary term for two opposing expressions. When oxymorons reflect the contradictory nature of life they are valid: **love-hate**, for example, is a universal experience. In other cases, an oxymoron can be an absurdity, as in the common expressions 'awfully good' and 'terribly nice', or the name used in some fast food restaurants for medium-sized hamburgers – a Mini-Big. That's not only oxymoronic but moronic. (Pron: 'oksyMAWRon'.)

Oy   The 1989 edition of the *OED* graciously admits the archetypal Yiddish word *Oy* to its lexicon. We may never use the expression ourselves, but an appreciation of its multifaceted meaning is part of being worldly. For *Oy* conveys centuries of human anguish, suffering, resignation, or occasionally joy, in one poignant monosyllable.

Surprisingly, and no condescension is intended, the scholarly editors of the *OED* demonstrate they have caught the real flavour of the word by retelling a story in Leo Rosten's *The Joys of Yiddish*: Two elderly Jews were sitting on a park bench. They had sat silent and motionless for hours, lost in thought. Finally, one of them releases a long sighing *Oy!* The other one looks at him and asks, 'You're telling *me*?'

Oy should not be confused with the English 'Oi!' or 'Oy!', cockney versions of 'Hoy!', used to attract attention.

Oz   *Oz*, the sound of the truncation 'Aus' (for Australia), has become accepted in Britain, helped by the Australian airline's slogan, *Whizz to Oz*. Anthony Rose, the writer on wine, refers to 'Oz wine', and you hear dark-suited businessmen say 'I'm going to look at the market in Oz later this year'. See also **Aussie**

ozone   At one time it was fashionable to talk about going to the seaside for some *ozone* ('Breathe in the ozone, John, it's iodine,' as young John Betjeman was told – *Summoned by Bells*). It never made sense, since ozone at earth level has harmful effects, as it is produced by sunlight acting on carbon monoxide and other pollutants.

The *ozone layer*, one of the clarion calls in **green** issues, is different. This is the band of ozone in the stratosphere which protects the atmosphere of the earth from dangerous ultraviolet radiation from the sun. The threat in the 1990s is that **CFCs** and other chemicals used in refrigeration, some industries and **aerosols** are eroding the ozone layer, allowing extra ultraviolet light to reach the earth's surface. This increases skin cancers and poses risks to crops, forests and plankton, the microscopic organisms in the sea that help to sustain marine life. See also **global warming**

· P ·

pace This entry is about the Latin word, a grammatical form of 'pax' (peace), not the English word. If *pace* is to be used in English, avoid the common mistake of using it to mean 'according to'. *Pace* denotes a contrary point of view to the person whose name follows, and is the equivalent of 'with all due respect to', as a polite way of disagreeing (keeping the peace, that is): 'This picture, *pace* Dr Brown, the art historian, could not have been painted by Turner'. (That implies Dr Brown had stated it *was* a Turner.)

Either of two pronunciations can be used: 'PAYsee' or 'PAHchay' (the former is more usual).

pacemaker or **pacesetter** These are interchangeable words for someone who sets the pace for someone else to keep up with in a race or in training, or for a person who takes the lead in an enterprise: 'the marketing director is the pacesetter (or pacemaker) in the export drive'. Only *pacemaker* is used for the electronic device implanted surgically to regulate the heartbeat.

package There was a time, long ago, when the only packages were tied up with paper and string. Since the 1950s, almost the first meaning of *package* in many people's minds is for an all-in arrangement, short for the American expression *package deal*. A package can be a combined price for an air ticket, accommodation, etc for a holiday on the Costa del Sol, or an agreement over sharing political power, or a computer program complete with training manual and other supporting material. The thing about a package, in this sense, is that you cannot take a part of it, as it's usually a take-it-all-or-leave-it arrangement.

As for the word **packaging**, this has taken on, since the 1950s, a slick commercial meaning far beyond the simple wrapping up of goods (see next entry).

packaging *Packaging* began its new career after World War II as a marketing term, and has acquired more and more layers of commercial sophistication. The term now covers a whole range of skills and techniques, roping-in highly paid designers, psychologists and marketing experts, in order to encourage consumers to take a product off the shelves in supermarkets. After a new product is developed, the most important next step is *packaging*. A legendary advertising man in America once quipped, 'Don't sell the steak, sell the sizzle', the evocative **image**. *Packaging* sets out to do just that.

This concept of packaging later became extended to people. Anyone from a writer, pop star to a president or prime minister submits to packaging: the public is offered a carefully contrived presentation of the person, to encourage them to buy books or records, or to put their cross in the appropriate place on the ballot paper. This use of the word *packaging* is a cynical admission of 'selling the sizzle'.

pacts Good speakers retain a hint of the *t* sound, so that the pronunciation doesn't become 'pax'.

paean or **peon** Both words are pronounced exactly the same ('PEE-e(r)n') but the meanings are entirely different. *Paean*, from the name used for the Greek god Apollo in the Homeric hymn to his praise, has survived as the word for a song of praise or a tribute to someone. (Note that it is often wrongly spelt 'paeon'.)

Peon is a Spanish word, used in English, for a farmworker, or sometimes for a poor peasant in Latin America.

paediatric See ae or æ

pager Words can take strange roundabout routes to arrive at their present-day meaning. *Page* derives ultimately from an ancient Greek diminutive for 'boy' (there's a link with 'paediatric'). In the Middle Ages, pages served in great houses. By the 18th century, there were page-boys in hotels who ran errands. Later page-boys walked round hotels calling out the name of a person who was wanted on the telephone.

By the late 1960s, *page* moved into the electronic age: a *pager* now is a miniature radio receiver carried in the pocket or handbag. Someone dials the number on an ordinary telephone, and the person called hears a **bleep** on their pager, or with some models can read a short message in an **LCD** display on a tiny dial.

page three In the 1970s, women began to take their clothes off for photographs on page three of the *Sun*, and the publishers of that newspaper went so far as to make *Page Three* a registered name. Since then, a *page three girl* (recorded in the *OED*, no less) has become a general term for women posing provocatively, as nearly naked as allowable. Feminists object to the debasement of women, and garage mechanics from Sidcup to Solihull cut out the photographs as **pin-ups**.

painkiller See analgesic . . .

pair or **pairs** In the singular, preceded by 'a', it is clearly always *pair*: a pair of cuff-links, a pair of socks, etc. In the plural, *pairs* or *pair* can be used: two pairs (or pair) of cuff-links, half a dozen pairs (or pair) of socks, etc. *Pairs* sounds more natural in the plural and is preferable. See also next entry.

(a) **pair of is** or **are** In many cases *a pair of* can be seen as a unit or as two separate parts that come together: 'a pair of cuff-links *is* or *are* . . .'; 'a pair of trousers *is* or *are* . . .'. A *pair of scissors* is always treated as plural, and perhaps it is more natural to treat *a pair of* most other things as plural, since when *pair of* is omitted, the noun is clearly plural: 'the cuff-links *are* . . .'; 'the trousers *are* . . .'.

pajamas or **pyjamas** In America people sleep in *pajamas* and call them 'pe(r)DJAMMe(r)s'; in Britain they sleep in *pyjamas* can call them 'pe(r)DJAHme(r)s'.

palace Worrying about how to pronounce the second syllable of *palace* is not likely to keep us awake at night. Nevertheless, dictionaries are divided over it. In royal circles, it usually follows A A Milne's famous couplet and makes it rhyme with 'Alice' ('PALiss'). The more common pronunciation now follows the spelling ('PALe(r)s').

palaeo- or **paleo-** The American spelling, *paleo-*, for this Greek prefix meaning 'ancient', appears in Britain at times, but dictionaries accept *palaeo-* as the only correct form in British English.
   Palaeo- is a guide to the meaning of a number of scientific terms: *palaeobotany* (the evolution of plant life through the study of fossil plants), *palaeoclimatology* (climatic changes in ancient periods through the study of geological remains), *palaeolithic* (the early Stone Age), *palaeopathology* (disease in ancient periods through the study of early human remains).

Palestine Liberation Organization See PLO

palimony Law dictionaries do not deign to record *palimony* and the term is not recognized in British courts. It began as a slang expression in America in the 1970s, formed by combining *pal* with *alimony*, and is a useful, if arch, way of describing settlements when an unmarried couple living together separate. An MP, Teresa Gorman, believes there are nearly a million couples in Britain living together, many with children, without any legal arrangement concerning their homes and finances. When such a couple separate, they may be involved in a palimony lawsuit. The word could also apply to homosexual couples who separate.
   Although not in general use in Britain, *palimony* could become accepted as a parallel word to 'alimony', although **maintenance** is the legal term now in Britain.

pampas See grasslands

pandemic See endemic . . .

pandit See pundit . . .

panellist A *panellist* used to be someone taking part in a quiz on radio or television, but the word is now used for anyone who takes part in almost any kind of discussion programme. The spelling has two *l*s in Britain, one *l* in America.

pansy When you mean the pretty flower with velvety petals, in a variety of rich colours, that's all right. If you are still using *pansy* to mean a homosexual, you're out of date and should turn to the entry on **gay**. *Pansy* was always an insulting word in that sense.

pants See boxers . . .; trousers . . .

paparazzo This Italian word found its way into English in the 1960s and is now accepted by most current English dictionaries. A *paparazzo* (pron: 'pappe(r)RATsoh') is a photographer, ruthlessly persistent at getting photographs of celebrities, using helicopters, telephoto lenses, stopping at nothing to get a shot that could be sold for a lot of money. Day in, day out, the telescopic lenses of *paparazzi* (the plural form of the word) offer up to millions of voyeurs all over the world snapshots of off-guard moments in the lives of the rich and famous, the modern media equivalent of the old 'What the butler saw' machines on seaside piers.

papering over the cracks See quick fix . . .

paper profit With the increase in share ownership as a result of privatization issues, the term *paper profit* has moved into everyday use. When shares go up on the Stock Exchange, shareholders may gloat over how much money they have made, but it remains a paper profit until the shares are actually sold. Paper profits become losses when shares are held, and prices fall.

paper sizes *Paper sizes* became based on the metric system as part of the metrication of British industry in the 1960s. Standard paper sizes are reductions of the size known as A0, a rectangle of one square metre with sides in the proportion of 1:4, that is approx 1189 × 841mm. A1 is half that size (approx 841 × 594mm), A2 is a quarter (approx 594 × 420mm), A3, one-eighth (approx 420 × 297mm), A4 (the standard size of business notepaper), one-sixteenth (approx 297 × 210mm), and so on down to A10.
   For quantities of paper, see **quire** . . .

(above, below and *at)* **par** The stated value of a share certificate issued by a company might be £1 per share or £100 per share, or whatever value is fixed at the time of issue and printed on the certificate. When the price on the stock market goes beyond that, the shares are said to be *above par*. When the price drops below the face value it becomes *below par*. When the price matches the face value, the shares are *at par*. (See also **face value** . . . .)
   Par is a Latin word meaning equality: we can feel *below par*, meaning not quite as well as usual, or *up to par* (rather than *at par*), meaning in good form. But no

matter how well we are feeling, we do not say we're *above par*. That's left to shares.

para- Some new word formations, using the Greek prefix *para-*, have appeared since World War II. These were hyphenated to begin with but most are now treated as one word. The key to their meaning is the word *parallel*, for Greek *para* means 'beside'.

Paramedic dates from the 1960s and covers people who are not qualified doctors but have been trained to carry out certain treatments, usually in emergencies. Although *paramilitary* was in use earlier, it has become much more common since the 1960s for quasi-military movements, such as the **IRA**, which are organized like an army (hence *paramilitary uniforms*). *Paralanguage*, a term from the 1950s, covers ways of communicating other than by spoken or written language, such as intonation, gesture, **body language**. **Parapsychology** was used in the 1920s, but became fashionable during the 1960s as a more scientific name for phenomena such as telepathy and ESP.

Note that alongside the Greek prefix, there is a Latin prefix *para-* with the different meaning of 'shelter' or 'ward off'. Hence words such as *parasol*, *parachute*, *parapet*. . . .

parable See **fable** . . .

paradox See **contradiction** . . .

paragraphs At one time, the only way to give or take in information, apart from talking to people, was through written or printed words. Now most people take in more information from pictures than any other way. We have come to expect easy-going narrative, and long paragraphs can seem hard work. The tendency is for shorter and shorter paragraphs in books, newspapers and letters, with sometimes each sentence given a paragraph to itself. The result can be breathless and jerky. Longer paragraphs, like speaking more slowly, may be called for because of the seriousness and complexity of an argument, and there is no need to give in all the time to the exigencies of living in the fast lanes of the 1990s. As a general principle, when it is time to start a new train of thought, and a full stop isn't a big enough break from what has gone before, that's the moment to start a new paragraph.

paralanguage See **para-** . . .

parallel A surprising number of people have to think twice about how many *l*s there should be. A useful hint for remembering there are *two l*s in the middle is to think of *ll* being *parallel*. See also **doubling final letter** . . .

parallel pricing The term describes an unofficial form of price regulation. Manufacturers or retailers of certain products that are similar may agree to avoid competition by increasing prices by more or less the same amount. The practice of *parallel pricing* is rarely given publicity as it is usually the result of discussions behind firmly closed doors.

paramedic See **para-**

parameter *Parameter* belongs to mathematical and technical contexts, representing a constant factor or quantity in one particular case, but subject to variation in others. The extended use has a limited place for defining aspects or factors where variations apply to one instance rather than generally: 'an architect has to work within the parameters of the site, budget and purpose'. (These are fixed for one scheme but vary for others.) When factors are general rather than particular, 'limits' or 'constraints' are better words, although *parameter* has muscled in on that meaning as well, and some recent dictionaries have accepted that.

paramilitary See **para** . . .

paraphernalia *is* or *are* *Paraphernalia* is usually treated as plural when it concerns a list of items: 'You'll be surprised at all the paraphernalia that *are* required'. When it is used conversationally to describe something that is long, drawn-out and complicated, it is treated as singular, for *paraphernalia* is the equivalent of 'procedure': 'The whole paraphernalia of getting a visa *goes* on for ever!'

The origin of *paraphernalia* is curious. It came into English from a Latin legal term (derived from Greek) for the property owned by a bride in addition to her dowry, and in the 17th century it was a term for the personal possessions a married woman was entitled in law to keep as her own property. By the 18th century, *paraphernalia* was being used in much the same way as it is now, that is for a number of miscellaneous items.

parapsychology, ESP or **clairvoyance** The primary meaning of *clairvoyance* in French is clear-sightedness or shrewdness. The word was adopted into English in the 19th century for the faculty of seeing into the future, or in some other way outside normal perception. *Clairvoyance* acquired dubious associations of fairground fortune-tellers, and in the 20th century, *ESP* (used more generally than the words in full, *extrasensory perception*) was an attempt to give these apparent powers scientific credence. ESP is taken to include telepathy (seeing into another person's mind), precognition (foretelling an event that has not yet occurred) and *psychokinesis* (pron: 'syekoki-NEESis'), the movement of objects by mental concentration rather than physical means, such as making dice fall in a predetermined way.

ESP is now an established, if not altogether accepted, school of study at some universities, where it is given the more scientific name of *parapsychology*. Arthur Koestler bequeathed funds to establish a Chair of parapsychology at Edinburgh University, defining it as 'the scientific study of paranormal phenomena, in particular, the capacity attributed to some individuals to interact with their environment by means other than the recognized sensory or motor channels'.

parchment or **vellum** Except by scholars working on ancient manuscripts, neither *parchment* nor *vellum* is likely to be used now in the real sense of the words. Both words meant the skin of animals turned into writing materials, parchment usually sheepskin or goatskin, vellum usually calfskin. A *parchment* or a *vellum* was also used for the manuscript itself.

Both words are now used in the stationery trade for thick good quality paper: parchment is often **deckle-edged** and vellum particularly smooth and heavily watermarked. Not that there is any specification for *parchment* and *vellum* in the modern sense: they are no more than pretentious names for expensive notepaper.

pardon 'I beg your pardon', when a mistake has been made, such as getting someone's name wrong or pouring red wine into a glass that still has some white wine in it, is acceptable. And the same phrase can be used if you haven't heard someone properly and want them to repeat what they've said. BBC announcers use 'I beg your pardon' when they have slipped up over something. *Pardon!* (or *Pardon?*) on its own, in either situation, is considered by many people a downmarket genteelism. To say 'Pardon!' or 'Pardon me!' after a belch or a fart adds awkwardness to mischance. There are easy enough ways round all this. If you make a mistake, 'I'm sorry' does perfectly well. If you haven't heard what someone has said, 'Would you mind saying that again?' or 'I'm sorry, I didn't hear you' fit the bill. In the second situation, 'What?' is curt, 'Eh?' is testy, as bad as cupping a hand to your ear.

parent company See holding company . . .

parentheses See brackets . . .

par excellence *Par excellence* has been used in English since the late 16th century, but it should still be pronounced as if it has just arrived from Paris, that is with an acceptable French accent (roughly 'pahr-ekse(r)LAH(n)s'.

Par excellence has come to be used in two ways in English, which is sometimes confusing. One is for an outstanding example of anything good or bad: 'the chief executive is a negotiator par excellence'; 'he is considered par excellence the most boring of lecturers'. The other use is for something excellent beyond compare: 'her interpretation of Beethoven's piano sonatas is par excellence' or 'she is par excellence an interpreter of Beethoven's piano sonatas'.

parity The word has several meanings. The one that gets into the news is the relationship of *parity* to pay negotiations, expressed by trade unions. People doing one kind of work use *parity* as a justification for equal pay with people doing another kind of work considered to have similar status. *Parity* in this sense is a perceived, often imaginary, equality of one job with another.

parka We take this word for granted on labels in shopwindows selling outdoor clothes. *Parka* has been used in English for over 200 years, and is one of the few words to come into the language from Alaska, where it describes a skin jacket with a hood worn by Eskimos. *Parka* is now the name attached to any hooded coat which is below hip-length, made of windproof material.

Parkinson's law and **the Peter principle** Any job of work will take just as long as the time we are given to do it. That is *Parkinson's law*. The expression has entered English, is found in dictionaries, and has brought immortality to Cyril Northcote Parkinson, who made this shrewd observation on human nature in his book, *Parkinson's Law* (1958).

About ten years later, Lawrence J Peter made his bid for immortality with another observation on management, in *The Peter Principle* (written with Raymond Hull, 1969). The *Peter principle* operates on people working for an organization, allowing them to be promoted just beyond their level of competence, that is to a level of incompetence, at which point there is no more promotion.

parliamentarianism This *-ism* dates from the late 19th century and is often misunderstood. While a *parliamentarian* is an MP who is an expert in the procedures of parliament, *parliamentarianism* is not the study or history of those procedures. It is usually taken as the doctrine that the most satisfactory form of democracy is modelled on the British system of parliamentary government.

parlour *Parlour*, an old Chaucerian word, was where people parleyed (cf French 'parler'), a room reserved for conversation in a religious establishment. Curiously, one of its few survivals now is in *funeral parlour*, where people who are beyond conversation are prepared for burial. *Parlour games* have given way to video games, *parlourmaids* replaced by dailies (see **charlady** . . .), and in general, parlours, so beloved by seaside landladies, have become as old-fashioned as aspidistras, replaced by **sitting-rooms** or 'lounges'.

parlous As long ago as 1926, **Fowler** wrote off *parlous* as 'a word that wise men leave alone' (*Modern English Usage*). Most current dictionaries label *parlous* as archaic or humorous. It derives from the same source as 'perilous', and people still talk about a 'parlous journey', a roof being in a 'parlous condition', or someone in a 'parlous state'. But the time has come to put the word on the shelf.

parody, **pastiche**, **send-up** or **take-off** Some writers get mixed up over *pastiche* because it is used in two allied but different senses. *Pastiche* relates to the Italian word 'pasta'; in fact, 'pasticcio', Italian for a pie, was an earlier form of *pastiche* in English, and is still shown in some dictionaries. The literary and artistic meaning is for a novel, piece of music or a painting that brings together ideas and styles from different sources, a kind of creative pot-pourri: Sandy Wilson's musical comedy, *The Boy Friend*, is a pastiche of the styles of plays, novels and songs of the 1920s. But the word is often used now for a piece of literature, art or music in the style of one person or of one earlier work: in this sense, Sandy Wilson's musical *Valmouth* is a pastiche of the exotic dandyish style of Ronald Firbank's novel (1919) of the same name.

A *parody* can be used about music and art but is more often used about literature. It can also have two meanings. *Parody* can be a clever or funny imitation, done in the style of some other work: this can be intended seriously, although *parody* is more likely to be used as a literary word for a *send-up* or *take-off*, informal words, that are only used for light-hearted or satirical mimicking. Or a parody can be depreciative, suggesting a feeble, poor man's version of the real thing. It is often advisable to use an explanatory descriptive word to show which meaning is intended: 'a brilliant parody' or 'a third-rate parody', for example.

parsing See analysis . . .

parson See minister . . .

part or **portion** No one is likely to use *part* where *portion* is clearly the right word ('Would you like another portion of apple pie?'). But *portion* is often used where *part* is the normal word: 'You should read this portion of the report first'. In general, *portion* should be reserved for shares: a portion of an estate bequeathed in a will; a grant divided into portions allocated to particular needs; and, of course, a portion of apple pie, etc.

partially See partly . . .

partial to To be very *partial to* a gin and tonic (or whatever else) is perfectly in order, of course, but to express it in those words has a touch of old-fashioned gentility about it. What's wrong with 'very much liking' a gin and tonic?

partly or **partially** In most cases, *partly* is the usual word and *partially* can often sound out of place: 'the book is partly written'; 'the debt is partly repaid'; 'the decision was taken partly by the board, partly by the staff'. Some people prefer partially when it relates to a state or human faculty: 'his health is partially restored'; 'she was left partially handicapped by the accident'. But even in those examples, *partly* could be used.

partner See boyfriend; associate

parts of speech See grammatical terms

part-time When does part-time become full time? In the UK, usually an employee who is engaged to work for less than 30 hours in a week is considered to be working *part-time*. See also **job-sharing**

passed or **past** The head of a school's English department complained about a letter in *The*

Independent, regretting that a grammatical mistake had 'slipped *passed* the keenest eyes'. Clearly, as the English teacher pointed out, a second mistake had slipped *past* whoever wrote that letter.

Passed and *past* do get mixed up. *Passed* is, of course, the past form of the verb *to pass*: *past* is a descriptive word and also a noun, both relating to direction or time. The following examples keep *passed* and *past* in the right place: 'In the past (descriptive) week, I passed (verb) your window every day'; 'I have just gone *past* (direction) your window'; 'The years have passed (verb) and our love affair is long past (time)' or '. . . is in the past' (noun).

passer-by When it is hyphenated, the plural is clearly *passers-by*. Although some recent dictionaries show it as one word, the plural remains *passersby*, which looks awkward and is an argument for retaining the hyphen.

passive smoking *Passive smoking* was first used at a world conference on smoking and health in 1971, and was slow to catch on in Britain. It describes the inhalation of cigarette fumes by non-smokers. The term became familiar in 1990 when *passive smoking* was officially ruled an 'industrial accident': an asthma sufferer won a case claiming that colleagues smoking at work made her breathless. Since then, *passive smoking* has become a catchphrase, more emotive than the alternative expression, 'environmental tobacco smoke'.

passive voice See active voice . . .

pass the buck To duck responsibility by passing it on to someone else, usually higher in authority, is to *pass the buck*, an American expression from the early 1900s, now often used in Britain. The practice is, after all, universal. The British confuse *buck* with the dollar, but it has nothing to do with that. We are told it comes from the game of poker, where apparently it was traditional to pass on a penknife with a buckhorn handle to the next person, in effect passing on the deal. The legendary sign on President Truman's desk read THE BUCK STOPS HERE.

past or **passed** See passed . . .

pasta Italian restaurants (see **trattoria**) have proliferated since the 1960s, and pasta has become as familiar in Britain as roast beef and Yorkshire pudding. *Pasta* is Italian for paste, and the word covers a whole range of mixtures in different shapes – tubular, flat strips, squares, pouches, etc. Among the ones included now in English dictionaries are: *spaghetti*, which needs no explanation; *cannelloni* (pron: 'kanne(r)LOH-nee') are the large tubes filled with various mixtures; *lasagne* (pron: 'le(r)SUNye(r)') is the largest of the square flat pastas (often green because it is mixed with spinach), with filling between each layer; *ravioli* (pron: 'raveeOHlee') are small envelopes of pastry with various fillings; *tagliatelle* (pron: 'tullye(r)TELLee') are long flat strips, which in Rome and the South of Italy are called *fettuccine* (pron: 'fette(r)CHEEnee'), a name used by restaurants whose owners come from those regions. All these words are already *plural* forms so it would be a gastronomic gaffe to ask for a few more 'raviolis', or to compliment cooks on their 'cannellonis'. The singular forms are non-existent (a strand of spaghetti is not a 'spaghetto'!).

past experience and **past history** All experience is in the past, and there are no professors of past history, for all history belongs to the past. But both expressions are so common ('from past experience . . .'; 'all that is past history'), that it is pedantic to fuss about them, especially when used in conversation. English has many expressions in which there is tautological doubling-up for emphasis. In writing, there is a case for thinking twice before inserting the unnecessary word *past*, unless it is to make a point. See also **tautology** . . .

pastiche See **parody** . . .

pastor The word comes from Latin for a shepherd, and could be used for the minister of any church, although less so in the Catholic church. At one time, *pastor* was quite usual as a form of address for a vicar, but it is used much less often now. See also **minister** . . .

pâté or **terrine** Only cooks familiar with traditional French culinary terms bother to make the distinction any more between *pâté* and *terrine*. *Pâté* (French for paste) is a mixture, usually of meat or fish, pounded up to make a consistent paste. *Terrine* (French for an earthenware dish) is pâté baked in a dish. In English generally, *pâté* has become the standard word that everyone understands. *Pâté de maison* ('house pâté') used to mean pâté, home-made in the restaurant's kitchen, but don't count on that any more.

patent The old way was to make the first syllable rhyme with the name 'Pat', for *patents* registered with the Patent Office, and to say 'PAYte(r)nt' for other meanings. The tendency now is to say 'PAYte(r)nt' for all meanings, whether it is patent leather, patent medicine, registered patents, or *patent* meaning 'open' or 'obvious'.

pathos See **anticlimax** . . .

patois See **dialect** . . .

patriarchal See **fatherly** . . .

patriotism See **nationalism** . . .

patronage or **sponsorship** Both words have several meanings, but when they refer to supporting the arts or some other activity with money, there is, or should be, an underlying difference. On American television, a play or a concert may be interrupted by a bland announcer, who says something like 'And now a message from your sponsor'. What usually follows is a commercial. Sponsorship of TV programmes is growing in Britain.

Sponsorship, in the sense it is often used, has a commercial motive: whoever is paying money for a project gets publicity in return. It may be as blatant as a commercial, or the name of the company or product may be displayed where it will be caught by television cameras. Companies pay small fortunes for the privilege of sewing their logo on one sleeve of an international tennis-player's shirt.

When sponsorship occurs without obvious publicity in return, the commercial motive may be more subtle: it could be a form of conscience money from a company that feels uncomfortable about how much profit it is making, or the nature of its products, and wants to be seen to be doing good.

Patronage, in reference to the arts, is, or should be, less self-seeking, more encouragement of an artist or artistic cause for its own sake. There is a grey area in between, when a brand name is closely associated with an art exhibition, the production of an opera, a sporting event, etc, that it is difficult to see the motive as 'art for art's sake'.

pavement or **sidewalk** Logical though it is, the American word *sidewalk* has never caught on in Britain, where pedestrians walk on the *pavement*. But it hasn't always been that way. *Pavement* first meant the roadway: this was the meaning that was taken over to America on the 'Mayflower', and still remains in American English. This requires some sorting out, when policemen in London tell Americans not to park on the pavement.

pay, **salary**, **wages**, **remuneration**, **stipend** or **emoluments** In some ways, the word *pay* has cut across the social divide between *wages* for manual workers and *salaries* for professional and clerical employees. A headline, such as PAY INCREASES FOR BOSSES, applies to chairmen and chief executives: pay bargaining, pay freeze, etc are terms used for shop-floor workers. *Wages* remains a working-class word, paid to factory and part-time workers (Wages Councils are statutory bodies that make proposals about pay in certain industries), although those people are now quite likely to talk about their *pay*, the same word that a doctor or a company director might use. The term *take-home pay* can apply to everyone, meaning pay received after deduction for tax, pension contribution, etc.

Salary is perhaps not used as often as it used to be: it is usual to refer to MPs' *pay*, for example, rather than their salary. *Salary* is more of a formal word now, used sometimes to make it clear that it is paid monthly, rather than weekly.

Remuneration is especially formal and can sound pompous these days ('he gets a good remuneration', instead of 'good pay' or 'a good salary'). It has a place as a blanket term to cover pay plus the value of other benefits paid to executives and directors, such as a

company car, private medical insurance, etc. *Remuneration package* is the fashionable term now for this all-inclusive computation.

Stipend is rarely used, except for the pay or fixed allowance paid to clergymen. It is retained for *stipendiary magistrates*, paid full-time magistrates appointed from the ranks of barristers and solicitors. *Emoluments* is even more old-fashioned. In case you fancy using it as a grand word for your pay, you might remember it has very ordinary origins: it comes from an old word for grinding (compare French 'café moulu', ground coffee), and at one time probably meant the money paid to a miller for grinding corn.

pay off Whether we like it or not, the American importation, *pay off*, has partly replaced the verb 'succeed': 'The new sales policy will pay off'; 'Using road transport instead of rail has paid off'. . . .

Pay off has several other meanings which occasionally conflict with each other: when workers are sacked, they are *paid off*, given a financial settlement; if a scheme is successful in making money, it has *paid off*; in crooked dealings, to *pay off* someone is to bribe them; a ship is *paid off* when it is turned leeward, away from the wind.

As a noun, *pay-off* (hyphenated) can mean the climax or point of a story or joke, a bribe, or the final profit at the end of a business deal.

pay or **subscription television** The terms mean the same. *Pay television* is the more usual alternative for a television service that can only be received when a television set has a special decoder attached, for which a rental charge is paid.

PC (personal computer) See **desktop computer**

P/E See **price-earnings ratio**

peaceable or **peaceful** The two words are not interchangeable in all cases. *Peaceful* describes freedom from disturbance, agitation or violence: 'the protest was peaceful and no one was arrested'; 'a peaceful scene'; 'she looks peaceful sitting there, listening to music'. *Peaceable* is more often applied to someone's attitude or manner, or to a way of acting: 'he is a peaceable man, not given to fits of anger'; 'we must follow a peaceable course of action'.

peacekeeping *Peacekeeping* is the term used now in connection with the deployment of a United Nations force, known as *blue berets* or *blue helmets* (because of the caps they wear), made up of troops and supporting auxiliaries from different nations, as a buffer between warring factions in a country: UN WANTS 11,500 BLUE BERETS IN CROATIA (headline in *The Times*, 14.2.1992).

peal See **carillon** . . .

peasant *Peasant* is someone working on the land, or a farmer with a smallholding. It often implies a low

social and uneducated class. The conversational use of *peasant* as an abusive word for someone whose table-manners, for example, are rough and ready, or who is not considered up to standard culturally, has pushed the word further in that direction. It is doubtful if *peasant* can be used now in any context, other than a historical one, without suggesting an attitude between condescension and disdain.

pecking order The term arose from the observation of chickens in which an order of dominance was demonstrated by some chickens holding back, while others feed first. When this principle is extended to human society, it is much more complex. The outward signs of human pecking order, or social hierarchy, could be the way people dress, which may give them apparent authority (see **power dressing**), the houses they live in, the cars they drive, the way they speak (see **accents in speech**). See also **class**

pedantic, **pedagogic** or **didactic** For Fowler, *pedantry* was a relative word, inasmuch as one person's pedantry may be another's scholarship. But that's not the way *pedantic* is used now. For to be pedantic is to be a scholastic nit-picker who fusses over formal and academic principles, no matter how meaningless and out of touch they are. This has nothing to do with scholarship, but is often a way of showing off, or a stiff-necked refusal to change.

A *pedagogue* is an archaic word for a teacher, and if it is used at all now, it is pejorative for someone who displays learning at every opportunity.

Didactic (from the Greek word for 'teaching') is less derogatory, but usually implies a schoolmasterly attitude, someone who shows how much they know by teaching others, when it is neither called for nor asked for.

pedlar See **hawker** . . .

pee or **pence** See **pence** . . .

pee or **piss** 'The Saxon words for to urinate and to defecate', Eric Partridge maintained, 'are idiomatic and perfect English, but association and prudery put them into quarantine' (*Usage and Abusage*, 1957). It is more subtle than that: many people are not bothered about saying they're going for a *pee*, and most dictionaries consider that word no worse than 'colloquial'. But *piss*, dictionaries tell us, is a vulgar **four-letter word**. We are back with linguistic social mores.

In the 19th century, a capricious compositor on *The Times* perpetrated a notorious misprint in an account of Queen Victoria opening a new bridge. One crucial letter was changed in the report: instead of 'The Queen then *passed* over the bridge', readers were informed that Her Majesty raised the level of the waters below. The story is said to be well authenticated, although Philip Howard reports that when he was literary editor of the paper he had hunted unsuccessfully for years for a file copy of that day's edition.

In some contexts *piss* is the only word that will do:

Paul Theroux, writing about Graham Greene having never been awarded the Nobel prize, quoted another writer saying that the 'Nobel people were once again pissing on literature, as they do every year' (*The Independent*, 7.4.1991). In that comment, *peeing* wouldn't have the same effect.

peer group   *Peer group* has become standard jargon in education and sociology but it is difficult to define, because the meaning is subjective. It does not mean so much a group of people who are equals, but are perceived to be equals by members of the group. This could depend on age, apparent status, wealth or any other criterion the particular group regards as central. For this reason, *peer group* is not an expression to take for granted, but should be looked at more closely to see what measure is being used.

Peking   See Beijing . . .

pence or **pee**   When decimalization of UK currency was introduced, shopkeepers and most of their customers said *pee* instead of *pence*, to distinguish the new unit from the former one. Although BBC announcers are asked to say *pence*, many people continue to say *pee*, to remind us that things have changed since *The Times* (or a pint of milk) cost five old pence (about 2p). No stop is required after p: 10p, 50p, etc.

pendant or **pendent**   The pronunciation of both words is the same ('PENde(r)nt') and the spellings are interchangeable in all senses. *Pendant* is more common for the noun ('she wore a beautiful pendant round her neck'); *pendent* is more usual for the descriptive word (a pendent lamp).

pending   *Pending* remains a popular word in business letters: '. . . pending further information from you'; '. . . pending receipt of your cheque'. It belongs to stuffy old-fashioned **business English**, and in many cases should be replaced by 'until': '. . . until we get further information from you'.

penetration   The use of *penetration* for the sexual act between men and women is not recent: as far back as the early 18th century, the word *penetration* was linked with rape. Since the 1970s, *penetration*, in the sexual sense, is used in two other contexts. Some feminists have questioned whether penetration offers women sexual pleasure (see **orgasm**) and the spread of **Aids** has introduced the phrase 'sex without penetration'.

penis or **phallus**   Sex therapists make a distinction between *penis* for the organ in a limp state, and *phallus* for when it is erect. Otherwise, *phallus* is not a word that is used often, except in literary or classical contexts. As a descriptive word, *phallic* is used openly for an erect object seen as a symbol of potency and power, or in psychology, to describe an excessive preoccupation with the male sexual organ: you would have expected Freud's controversial observation about

women would have been called *phallus envy*, rather than *penis envy*, the name that was given to it.

pen-name   See pseudonym . . .

penny   See pence . . .

pension   See annuity . . .

Pentagon or **pentagon**   A *pentagon* is a five-sided shape or building. Give it a capital P and the security of the world depends upon it, for the *Pentagon* is the pentagon-shaped headquarters of US defence forces, built in World War II in Virginia. The word *Pentagon* is used loosely for American military policy and opinion: 'The Pentagon view is . . .'.

penumbra   See shadow . . .

peon   See paean . . .

people or **persons**   *People* is the usual word. *Persons* is sometimes preferred for a small number of people: 'only three persons applied for the job'. But there is no good reason for that, and there is nothing wrong with 'only two people turned up'.

In formal or legal contexts, *persons* has a place because it strikes a more austere note: 'the persons responsible for this outrage must be brought to justice'.

people   See race . . .

peppercorn rent   Peppercorns used to be so rare and valuable that there was a time when they could be used to pay feudal rents. When pepper became an everyday spice, no one would accept peppercorns any longer in payment of rent. Hence a *peppercorn rent* is a nominal rent of almost no value. The phrase has been misused to some extent in recent years for any rent that is considered low in relation to the property involved.

per   The Latin *per* is so common in English that it is easy to forget that we don't need to use it all the time. In some abbreviations, *per* is indispensable: *pa* and *mph* are everyday examples. But when words are spelt out in full, *per* is out of place: so much 'a year', so many miles 'an hour', for example, are preferable to per year (or per annum), per hour, etc.

Per is appropriate in Latin phrases, such as *per cent*, *per capita*, etc, and also occasionally to avoid an inconvenient repetition of *a*: 'school meals cost an average of £3 a day per child' ('a day a child' is not only awkward but is not as clear).

per annum   See previous entry

per cent or **percentage**   *Per cent* means 'in every hundred' and it should usually be preceded by a figure: '55 per cent of the voters are women'. *Percentage* is the corresponding noun, but *per cent* is also used as a noun: 'What per cent of the . . .'.

There is no point in using *percentage* without some qualification, as in 'a percentage of the voters are women'. If it is not possible to commit yourself at least to 'small' (or 'low'), or 'large' (or 'high') percentage, simply use 'some' or 'part': 'some of the voters . . .', 'part of the costs . . .'. See also **fraction** . . .

perchance   *Perchance* belongs to poetry ('To sleep: perchance to dream', *Hamlet* Act III Sc i). It is affected in everyday use: 'If perchance you're going shopping, could you get me . . .'.

perennial   See **annual** . . .

perestroika   English took *perestroika* on board soon after Mikhail Gorbachev was elected first secretary of the Soviet Communist Party in 1985. It is Russian for 'restructuring', and referred to the Soviet system and the process of converting it to a **democracy** and a **free market** economy. Like the word **glasnost**, *perestroika* (pron: 'pere(r)STROYKe(r)') will always be associated with Gorbachev, and like the man himself, is now part of history. It has earned its place in English dictionaries for, as the American Secretary of State, James Baker, observed, 'Perestroika is the most important political event this century'.

perfect   *Perfection* is an absolute quality, so in principle something cannot be *quite perfect* or *very perfect*. Nonetheless, for most of us some things seem more perfect than others, and from time to time we are content to go over the top with H E Bates' Pop Larkin and describe certain things as 'absolutely perfick' (*The Darling Buds of May*, 1958). It would be pedantic to fuss about it.

perfume or **scent**   In the see-saw of language, *scent* became a downmarket word for a perfume (it is not used in that sense in America). It was then taken up by the middle classes, while *perfume* moved downmarket. Perfume is now the usual word for most people, with *scent* an alternative to 'smell' for everyday things, such as the scent of freshly picked strawberries. *Scent* has always been a hunting word (hounds pick up the scent of a fox).

Both words have strong French connections. *Scent* relates to 'sentir', to feel (no one is sure how the *c* crept in, perhaps by association with other *sc* words, such as scene and science). *Perfume* relates to French 'fumer' (to smoke), the smell given off when something is burning. See also **aroma** . . .

perhaps   The convention of *always* putting a comma on either side of *perhaps*, in the middle of a sentence, should be thrown out of the window. Sometimes it is valid as a way of emphasizing uncertainty: 'Whether we open up the market in France or Germany is, perhaps, not as important as it seems'. At other times, the position of a single comma, one side or the other of *perhaps*, changes the meaning altogether. 'She will go to Rome perhaps, with her

lover' leaves open the possibility of her going to London, Madrid. . . . 'She will go to Paris, perhaps with her lover' leaves open the possibility of her going to Paris alone – or with someone other than her lover.

perigee   See **apogee** . . .

period or **the curse**   *The curse* used to be one of the most common expressions used by women for menstruation. Perhaps it is an echo of superstitions, fears and taboos associated with menstruation. The subject is no longer unmentionable, and women now reject any suggestion of inadequacy or incompetence because of their menstrual cycle, which was implicit in *the curse*. These days many women would not want to use that derogatory expression for a natural bodily function, referring to it instead as their *period*.

period (era)   See **age** . . .

period (stop)   See **full stop** . . .

periodic or **periodical**   Although both are interchangeable descriptive words ('this is a periodic – or periodical – problem'), the tendency now is to use *periodic* for description ('a periodic event') and *periodical* as a noun for magazines that appear, usually weekly or monthly (see also **magazine** . . .).

peripheral (computer language)   Computer technology uses *peripheral* as a noun for items that function under the control of the **central processing unit** but are not a part of it. Almost any equipment that is connected to the computer itself, usually with an **interface** adaptor, can be called a *peripheral*.

periphrasis   If instead of calling a spade a spade, you called it 'a flat or slightly concave metal implement attached to a long wooden handle', that would be *periphrasis*. For periphrasis is a roundabout way of saying something. It is not the same as a **euphemism**, a genteel or polite way of avoiding mentioning something unpleasant ('passed away' instead of 'died'), or **meiosis**, which usually expresses a positive with a negative ('not bad'). *Periphrasis* stems from a chronic aversion to simple words: an official report on conditions in Zimbabwe in early 1992 noted 'the people are facing a critical food deficit', which could be translated 'the people are hungry'.

Although it is not yet eradicated, periphrasis is not nearly as common as it used to be: for example, the notice on certain buses in London that read 'Passengers are requested not to communicate with the driver while the vehicle is in motion' has been changed to 'Please do not speak to the driver while he is driving'.

perks   Although dictionaries label *perks* colloquial or informal, the word in full, *perquisite*, is rarely used in the same sense. Sooner or later, *perks* will be promoted to standard English. It is not, after all, such a recent word, as it goes back to mid-19th century. In those days, perks were more usually minor benefits, such as free shoe-blacking for government office workers. In the 1990s, it is different: perks form a significant part of what is called the 'remuneration package', and could include a company car, low-interest mortgages, etc.

Perks can be a slightly disreputable word, sometimes used for small items taken home from a place of work, as if by right. As a result, another term has arisen – *fringe benefits* (see **fringe**).

permissive or **prescriptive (in linguistics)** These are linguistic terms used about opposing attitudes towards the English language. The *prescriptive* approach lays down the law uncompromisingly about what is good and bad English, resisting to the last changes in grammar, spelling, pronunciation and the meaning of words. The *permissive* approach seeks to be sensitive to the way the language is changing, sometimes welcoming popular usage too willingly, instead of waiting for the language itself to make a judgement in its own time.

The true path is somewhere between both points of view. If English is allowed to become a free-for-all, much would be lost, and it would be a graceless and ineffective means of communication. On the other hand, to settle down complacently is bad for a language, just as it is bad for a human being. Good writers and speakers play a part in keeping the structure of English in place, but it is a light framework supporting the language, not heavy chains that shackle it. *The Good English Guide* is an attempt to walk that tightrope.

permissiveness The preface to the book, *The Lady Chatterley's Lover Trial* (edited by H Montgomery Hyde, 1990), noted that the acquittal in 1960 of D H Lawrence's book from the charge of obscenity 'introduced the Sixties as an age of permissiveness in our morals and manners'. The poet Philip Larkin put the date three years later ('Sexual intercourse began in nineteen sixty-three'), but then he needed a rhyme for the word at the end of his next line ('Which was rather late for *me*'). *Permissiveness* has become for some people a word of abuse, symbolizing decadence, sexual perversion, homosexuality and the negation of everything that is 'good'. For others it represents a long overdue breaking down of rigid authoritarian values. Depending upon how you see it, or perhaps how old you are, the *permissive society* is an 'anything goes' society or a liberated society with more opportunities to explore human experience.

per se This is one of those Latin tags that is so unnecessary, that it brands its user as pompous, or at least old-fashioned. All *per se* (pron: 'perSAY') means is 'by itself' or 'in itself' ('This is not per se a disadvantage'). Why bother with it?

persistent See **consistent** . . .

-person or **-man** A number of compound words formed with *-man-* (chairman, mankind, spokesman,

statesman . . .) have been looked at, both in the light of the Sex Discrimination Act 1975 in Britain, and out of respect for women's expectations. There is an argument that *man* is not discriminatory: 'The prominent sense in Old English was human being' (C T Onions, *The Oxford Dictionary of English Etymology*, 1966). It is also maintained that *man* and *mankind* do not connote one sex, as they relate to that universally human attribute, the dexterous hand ('manual', 'manipulate', etc).

Etymology is one thing, but the images evoked in people's minds must also be taken into account. A pamphlet on teaching English as a foreign language, *Guidelines for the Representation of Women and Men in English Language Teaching* (1991), claims studies have shown that when *man* is used as a generic word for all humans, as it has been for centuries, 'the great majority of the people in the studies visualized only men'.

Whichever of these two points of view we adhere to, sexism will remain on the linguistic agenda for the foreseeable future. Unisex words, such as **chairperson** (or 'chair'), **spokesperson, humankind, headteacher**, are becoming standard. There are occasional problems. 'Statesperson' doesn't work, at least not yet (Simon Jenkins, when editor of *The Times*, called Margaret Thatcher a 'leading world statesman'). And Bel Mooney and other women writers have derided 'linguistic monstrosities like *herstory*'. At the same time, sensible progress is being made in reducing the undeniable masculine bias in English, although there remains a long way to go: Jenni Murray, who presents, BBC's *Woman's Hour*, has commented, 'When you marry, you are still declared "*man* and *wife*". You may think it's only semantics – I'm not so sure'. See also **sexist language** . . .

persona See **character** . . .

persona grata and **persona non grata** These Latin expressions are mostly diplomatic terms for someone who can be favourably received (*persona grata*), and for someone who is not acceptable (*persona non grata*). They are useful occasionally outside diplomacy as a formal way of indicating that a person is welcome, or not welcome. (Pron: 'pe(r)SOHna GRAHte(r)', 'nonGRAHte(r)'.)

personal See **confidential** . . .

personal computer (PC) See **desktop computer** . . .

personality See **character** . . .

personally *Personally* has an important use to make it clear that an action relates to someone *in person*: 'Deliver this letter to him personally' (that is, do not give it to anyone else); 'I shall deal with this personally' (that is, it will not be delegated). *Personally* is also useful for associating yourself with something, or making it clear that you are not involved: 'This is not just a job, I care about it personally'; 'I'll do what I can to help, although I am not personally affected'.

In many other cases, *personally* is often a pretentious intrusion: 'I personally believe . . .'; 'I don't personally enjoy . . .'; 'Personally, I would do this'. *I* is the most personal word in English and does not need propping up with *personally*.

personnel   See **human resources** . . .

persons   See **people** . . .

perspicacious or **perspicuous**   *Perspicacious* and *perspicacity* should be used about people: 'the financial director was perspicacious (or showed perspicacity)', that is showed acuteness or acumen. *Perspicuous* and *perspicuity* relate to the expression of thought: 'the financial director made a perspicuous statement about policy', that is clear and easily understood. Either way, there are simpler words available: 'shrewd', 'acute' and 'clever' in place of *perspicacious*, 'clear' and 'lucid' for *perspicuous*.

perverted   See **deviant** . . .

pessimistic   See **optimistic** . . .

(the) **Peter principle**   See **Parkinson's law** . . .

petite   See **compact** . . .

petrocurrency or **petrodollar**   The price of oil on the world's markets is quoted in US dollars: a *petrodollar* is a unit of foreign exchange linked to the US dollar and earned by exports from countries producing petroleum. *Petrocurrency* is the currency of a petroleum-exporting country, which could be vulnerable to fluctuations in world oil prices.

petrol, **petroleum** or **oil**   *Petrol* is one of the refined products, in this case specially blended with additives for use as a fuel, of the raw material *petroleum* that occurs naturally in some underground rock formations. Another name for petroleum is *rock oil* (*petro-* comes from Greek words for stone or rock), and *oil* is an alternative name for both the commodity and the industry exploiting this primary source of energy (oil wells, oilfields, oil-tankers . . .).

Oil is, of course, a general name for a variety of thick sticky liquids (olive oil, linseed oil, etc) that have nothing to do with petroleum.

phallus   See **penis** . . .

phantasy   See **fantasy** . . .

pharmacy   See **chemist** . . .

phase   *Phase* has a number of scientific and technical meanings. In a more general way, *phase* should always mark a definite point rather than an indeterminate one in a continuous process: 'the blue period was an early phase in Picasso's work'; 'the collapse of France was the end of the first phase in World War II'. The phases of the moon are a good guide to the right use of the word, referring to the changing moon at distinct points, from the first quarter to the full moon.

As a verb, *phase* follows the same meaning: to *phase in* or *phase out* something is to do it gradually, one stage at a time.

phenomenon or **phenomena**   This *phenomenon* (singular), these *phenomena* (plural). People sometimes say 'a phenomena' when they mean a phenomenon.

philanderer or **womanizer**   The words have gone through a curious development. Philandros was a name used in Greek stories for a character taking the part of a lover. In the 18th century, *philander* was an attractive verb for 'to make love', and it's a pity it has lost that meaning, although admittedly it often meant to make love casually, whenever there was an opportunity. In the easy-going relationships between men and women in the 1990s, both *philander* and *philanderer* are dated. The more likely noun now is *womanizer*, with the attendant verb, *womanize*, not often used. The disadvantage of all these words is that they can only be used about men.

-phile or **-philia**   Both suffixes are derived from 'philos', Greek for 'loving', but one describes healthy love and the other morbid love. An *Anglophile* is a person (usually not British) who loves or greatly admires everything about England and the English; an *Italophile* loves Italy, Italians, Italian food, etc; a *bibliophile* loves books. . . .

The suffix *-philia* takes us into the shadows: *Anglophilia* suggests an excessive unbalanced passion for all things English; *coprophilia* is displaying an abnormal fascination with faeces; *necrophilia* is a desire to have sex with corpses. The corresponding noun for a person adds *-c* to the word: *Anglophiliac, coprophiliac*.

Philippino   See **Filipino** . . .

philology   See **linguistics** . . .

philosophical or **philosophic**   There used to be an attempt to make some distinction between these two words, with *philosophic* related to the discipline of philosophy, and *philosophical* reflecting in a general way the calm acceptance of life you'd expect from a philosopher. Few people would recognize any differentiation now: the words are interchangeable in all contexts, with *philosophical* as the more usual form.

philosophy   See **ideology** . . .

phobia   See **mania** . . .

phoenix company   The phoenix was a fabulous bird described by the Greek historian, Herodotus, which died on a funeral pyre and rose again from its ashes. This mythological symbol of death and resurrection is brought down to earth in the business expression *phoenix company*: it is used for a private limited company which is set up with almost the same board of directors as a previous company that has gone bankrupt. The term became more current, especially with accountants, during the recession of the early 1990s.

phone, **'phone** or **telephone**   To write *'phone*, with an apostrophe dangling at the beginning, is as pedantic as writing *'bus* for 'omnibus'. Some of the latest dictionaries persist in labelling *phone* colloquial or informal, although it is the everyday word for a telephone or telephoning, and words such as *answerphone*, *phone-in*, *phone-tapping*, *phonecard*, etc are accepted as standard English by the same dictionaries. For some reason, there is still a reluctance to admit *phone* as the standard word in print: many companies prefer the formal word *telephone* on their headed paper, even though they may use **fax** for their facsimile number.

phonetic alphabets   For a note about the recognized phonetic alphabet used to represent human speech sounds, and the basic phonetic system used in *The Good English Guide*, see **International Phonetic Alphabet**.

NATO has its own *phonetic alphabet* used for spelling out, in oral communication or dictation, unfamiliar names and terms. It is useful for anyone faced with this problem:

Alpha – Bravo – Charlie – Delta – Echo – Foxtrot – Golf – Hotel – India – Juliet – Kilo – Lima – Mike – November – Oscar – Papa – Quebec – Romeo – Sierra – Tango – Uniform – Victor – Whisky – X-ray – Yankee – Zulu

phonetics or **phonology**   Professor Higgins in Shaw's *Pygmalion* defines *phonetics* as 'the science of speech'. It is in fact narrower than that, since phonetics is the scientific analysis of the *sound* of speech, the precise articulation of words by the vocal organs. *Phonology* is nearer to 'the science of speech': it is an aspect of linguistics that makes a comparative study of sound-patterns in different languages, and is taken to include intonation, pitch, style and rhythm of speaking, all of which can affect communication and meaning, but would not usually come under *phonetics*. See also **prosody**

phoney, **(phony)**, **pseudo** or **pseud**   Not accepted yet as standard English, *phoney* (*phony* in America) is useful for describing someone ('a phoney') or something ('a phoney name') that is not genuine. The origin of *phoney* is uncertain, although it is regarded as a contribution to English from Irish. Its use in America goes back at least to the beginning of the 20th century. Americans were the first to use the expression *phoney war* about the early stage of World War II, which brought *phoney* into wider use in Britain, encouraged as usual by American films.

Pseudo is the literary equivalent of *phoney*, both as a noun ('a pseudo') and a descriptive word ('a pseudo name'). Whereas *phoney* belongs to the 20th century, *pseudo* has a classical origin, taken from a Greek word meaning 'false'. *Pseud* is an abbreviation of *pseudo*, also used as a noun and a descriptive word and, like *phoney*, is regarded by dictionaries as colloquial. *Pseuds' Corner*, the feature that started in the magazine, *Private Eye*, in 1968, has given *pseud* a sharper edge, particularly for someone who puts on social or intellectual airs. Unless it is an established word (**pseudonym**, for example), *pseudo* is usually linked to other words with a hyphen: pseudo-scientific, pseudo-culture. . . .

phonezone   Few dictionaries have picked up *phonezone* yet. It appeared as part of business communication terminology in the late 1980s, and is likely to come in for increasing use. The *phonezone* is the worldwide area where communication is available by telephone. The phonezone brings most of the world almost instantly to the desks of executives, or in fact to wherever they happen to be, their cars, the aircraft they're flying in, the restaurants they're eating in . . . (see **cellphone**).

phonology   See phonetics . . .

photomontage   See collage . . .

photo opportunity   Too recent for most dictionaries to have caught up with, *photo opportunity* (or just *photo op*) is publicity jargon for an event arranged or manipulated to get a celebrity's picture in the papers or on to television screens. A leading politician is manoeuvred into the front line facing press and television photographers, looking resolute, determined, statesmanlike, or a loving family man or woman, depending on the briefing supplied by campaign managers. Photo ops are eagerly totted up by media consultants and party managers as evidence of their success in 'getting over the message'.

phrase   The grammatical definition of a *phrase* is a group of words that expresses an idea but is not a complete sentence, since it does not include a **verb**: examples are 'many a slip 'twixt cup and lip', 'a fine kettle of fish'. In fact, there is no good reason why *phrase* should not be used for any small group of words, with or without a verb: 'To coin a phrase, "I love you." '; ' "The lady's not for turning" was a political catchphrase'. See also **catchphrase**

(a) **physical impossibility**   This is a phrase that is often misunderstood. When something is a *physical impossibility*, it means it is contrary to the natural order of things: 'It is a physical impossibility that pigs could fly'. It can be used by extension to include almost anything that is against reason or common sense: 'To do the journey in less than five hours is a physical impossibility'.

The phrase is less appropriate when something is a

matter of opinion, as in 'It's a physical impossibility that she will arrive on time, as she's always late'. A physical impossibility should be demonstrably out of the question.

physician See doctor . . .

physics *is* or *are* Nouns ending in *-ics* often present this problem. See **-ics**

picketing See flying pickets . . .

pictures See cinema . . .

pidgin or **Creole** *Pidgin* is the more familiar word and people are likely to call any seemingly uneducated variant of English, *pidgin English*, although it may well be a *Creole*.

In linguistics, pidgin languages develop between people who do not speak the same main language, as a rudimentary second language with basic grammar and vocabulary. The purpose of a pidgin is everyday communication for trade, or between masters and servants. Pidgin was originally a kind of commercial jargon used in the Far East, and the word may derive from an imitation of the Chinese attempt to pronounce 'business'.

When a pidgin becomes established as a first language, the mother tongue for people, it becomes a *Creole* (pron: 'CREEohl'), usually spelt with a capital as a noun (but not as a descriptive word), because it is by then a language in its own right. A Creole is no longer a basic language just for everyday needs but has become sophisticated enough to cover a wide range of human thought. There are said to be about a hundred creole languages, relating mostly to English, French, Dutch and Portuguese, spoken by over 200 million people in the world.

For use of *Creole* for a person of mixed parentage, see **half-caste** . . .

pie See tart . . .

pie chart See bar chart . . .

pièce de résistance At enormous banquets, when one course remorselessly follows another, the traditional name for the main dish of the meal was the *pièce de résistance*. It is rarely used now, even in France: except on august occasions, the main dish of a formal meal is now more likely to be called the **entrée**. *Pièce de résistance* survives as a way of describing the most important event or happening: 'The pièce de résistance of the evening was the pianist's moving playing of the *Moonlight Sonata*'.

pied-à-terre If you have an attic in Paris or a basement in Rome, or a small flat in any town you can use from time to time, but is not your main home, there's nothing much else to call it but a *pied-à-terre* ('foot on the ground'). No English word or expression quite fits the bill. (Pron: 'pyay-dah-TAIRE'.)

pietism or **platitude** Rabbi Lionel Blue, in one of his *Thought for Today* homilies, made a distinction between a *platitude* and a *pietism*, saying that the difference is one of feeling: the first comes from the top of the head, the second from the heart. Most people do not feel this difference of meaning, for generally both words are used in a pejorative way: a *pietism* suggests a holier-than-thou sentiment, and a *platitude*, a dry observation delivered as if it were profound. Nevertheless, *pietism* can also suggest an eternal truth. The famous long-winded advice from Polonius to Laertes (*Hamlet*, Act I Sc iii) is full of platitudes ('Costly thy habit as thy purse can buy . . . Neither a borrower nor a lender be . . .'), but ends on a pietism, an expression of spiritual purpose: 'This above all: to thine own self be true'. If *pietism* is used in this way, the context should make it clear that a positive sense is intended.

pigeons See doves . . .

pigmy See pygmy . . .

pilaf or **pilau** Various spellings occur in English for this rice dish. Although the word comes from Turkish, hence associated with Middle Eastern food, some cookery books now make a distinction, using *pilaf* for Middle Eastern recipes, and *pilau* for Indian or Pakistani ones. (Pron: 'PEElaff' and 'PEElow' – second syllable rhyming with 'how').

(the) Pill In the 1960s, a reliable oral contraceptive was such a breakthrough that the *Pill* (with a capital P) transcended any brand name. It ushered in a brave new world of sexual freedom, which led Aldous Huxley to become the first writer to call it *the Pill* (*Brave New World Revisited*, 1959).

The excitement has long since died down, **Aids** has saved **condoms** from oblivion, and it seems dated now to spell the Pill with a capital. In fact, women are now more likely to call it 'a contraceptive pill', to distinguish it from other pills. See also next entry.

pill or **tablet** For a long time, *pill* was so closely associated with oral contraceptives that it was less confusing to call other pills – *tablets*. The situation has changed (see previous entry) and *pill* and *tablet* are more or less interchangeable words again.

PIN PIN is the computerized equivalent of a password. The abbreviation is so common now that a surprising number of people would hesitate before saying what the letters stand for: personal identification number. This is a number used in computer security: it is keyed in by a user at remote terminals to gain access or carry out a transaction. The most common use is for bank cash-dispensing machines.

pinchpenny See mean

pin-up The term dates from World War II, and the *OED* quotes the American magazine *Life* as one of the first to use *pin-up*, in 1941 about Dorothy Lamour. After over half a century, *pin-up* shows signs of becoming dated. A **page three** girl is the more up-to-date term, and even that is under threat: a calendar photographer, Mel Grundy, confirms that 'clients are changing from glamour to fashion and . . . we're making a definite effort to cover girls up'.

pipe or **conduit** Both words mean a tube for conveying liquids, but only engineers are likely to use *conduit*; everybody else, including plumbers, says *pipes*. When it is a tube for protecting electric wire, *conduit* is the more likely word, at least in technical contexts.

Some engineers of the old school still say 'KUNdit' or 'KONdit', following the pronunciation of the second syllable of 'circuit'. But the more usual pronunciation now follows the spelling: 'KONDyou-it'.

piped music See Muzak . . .

piteous, pitiable or **pitiful** Long ago Fowler considered these three words were too confused to be put in order. The best we can do now is to keep to a few simple rules that conform to present-day usage. *Piteous* should not be used about people, but for things that make us feel pity: a piteous cry, a piteous sight. *Pitiable* can be used both for people and for things that arouse pity: a pitiable beggar, a pitiable scene. It can also have the meaning of contemptuous: a pitiable offer, a pitiable effort. As *pitiful* can double up for all the above usages (a pitiful cry, a pitiful beggar, a pitiful offer), it is all right to use *pitiful* in all contexts.

pivotal In engineering, a pivot is a shaft on which a component turns. The application of *pivotal* in general use should follow that principle, describing a turning-point, not merely something that is important: 'the proposed budget, with its promise of increased taxation, was pivotal to the course of the election campaign'. Something can be pivotal, in that a situation goes one way or the other as a consequence, but to describe someone or something as pivotal, in an organization for example, is misapplying the word: 'central' or 'essential' are more appropriate.

place-names See **foreign place-names**

plaid See **tartan** . . .

plain See **clear** . . .

plain English Close to Whaley Bridge, on the edge of the Peak District National Park, is a white-washed building with a board outside reading: PLAIN ENGLISH CAMPAIGN.

Chrissie Maher and Martin Cutts launched their campaign in 1979 as an attack on **jargon** and obscure official language that, they said, 'left pensioners dying of cold because they couldn't understand the heating grant form'. Since then, the Plain English Campaign organizers have been employed as consultants or to run training courses for insurance companies, government departments, local authorities and professional organizations with the aim of encouraging 'clear, concise and friendly' use of the English language.

It is a good cause, especially when it is applied to functional communication, but it should be kept in its place. For language can take us far beyond the humdrum and the commonplace. Poetry does not have the obligation to be immediately clear. Sometimes we have to work to sense the imagery of a poet and the reward is an enrichment of our feelings and understanding, an aesthetic experience. The writings of mystics concern a spiritual perception of truth, which we may glimpse only in flashes of revelation. When English is used in those ways it belongs to an inner world.

Plain English belongs to the outer world of insurance policies, tax forms, statements from the government, letters from lawyers. . . . In that world, if we make others struggle to understand what we are writing or saying, we are using bad English, rotten to the core.

planned obsolescence See **built-in obsolescence** . . .

planning blight Planning is usually considered a good thing, but in the early 1960s, a new and pernicious term arose in connection with government and local planning schemes: *planning blight* can make property unsaleable, or at best saleable at a greatly reduced price, when a plan is announced to build anything nearby that would make life unpleasant for people living there (a motorway, for example, or the high-speed rail link to the Channel Tunnel).

plastic The posh pronunciation used to be 'plahstic', which now sounds affected. The usual pronunciation makes it rhyme with 'fantastic'.

plastic money 'If all the *plastic money* cards in the UK were laid end to end, they would stretch from the doors of the Bank of England to the shores of Africa' (*The Sunday Times*). Some recent dictionaries are slow to acknowledge this derisory term for credit cards, although it has been in use since the early 1980s.

Barclays Bank are said to have issued the first plastic credit card in the UK on 29 June 1966. The intervening years have seen a deluge of plastic, which reached its peak in the credit boom of the 1980s. Not only credit cards, but cash cards, cheque guarantee cards, charge cards, all of which are the same uniform size, come under the heading of *plastic money*, which prompted Midland Bank to ask in an advertisement: 'Is the amount of plastic in your wallet spoiling the cut of your designer suit?' See also **credit card** . . .; **smart card**

plastic or **cosmetic surgery** Before World War II, there were discreet clinics in Switzerland where *plastic surgeons* carried out *plastic surgery* to improve the shape of someone's nose, remove wrinkles and sagging chins, tauten drooping breasts. . . . Such operations are now called *cosmetic* surgery, leaving *plastic surgery* for the more serious work of dealing with disfigurement or facial injuries. Surgeons who perform operations to improve facial features usually prefer to call this work 'aesthetic' or 'reconstructive' surgery, as cosmetic surgery is associated with expensive private clinics for the rich. Whatever their work, the surgeons still want to be called *plastic surgeons*.

platform, podium, rostrum or **dais** Conductors of orchestras are usually described as mounting the *podium* (a podium is a platform for one person). But they might just as well mount the *rostrum*. At party conferences, leaders of political parties take their place on the *platform*, larger than a rostrum, and a general word for use in all contexts. A *dais* (pron: 'DAYiss') is another general word, especially for a low platform. *Platform* is the only one of the words extended to mean an opportunity to tell the world about a policy or point of view ('He used the broadcast as a platform for a political message'). See also **lectern** . . .

platitude See pietism . . .

Platonic or **platonic** With a capital P, *Platonic* refers to the teachings of Plato, the Greek philosopher (c429–347BC). With a small *p*, *platonic* is a corruption of Plato's concept of a reality beyond the world of the senses, and is used in a banal way for a friendship between a woman and a man without them being involved sexually, an alternative to that familiar remark by the famous to journalists, 'We're just good friends'.

An extension of the popular meaning of the word uses *platonic* almost as a synonym for **academic**, to mean theory and words rather than action: 'the declaration is purely platonic and nothing will be done about it'. It is an irreverent link with the greatest pupil of Socrates.

playbill In Britain a playbill is a poster advertising a show in a theatre, whereas in America it can also mean a theatre programme. Such show posters appear in America on *billboards* (see **hoarding** . . .).

plc See Ltd . . .

pleaded or **pled** The past form of plead is *pleaded*, except in Scotland, where *pled* is used in courts of law, and in America, where *pled* is the usual form.

Pleased to meet you See How do you do? . . .

pleasure (sexual use) Sentences such as 'He took his pleasure from her', referring to sexual intercourse, go with Victorian villains twirling moustaches. The same applies to the use of *pleasure* as a verb, meaning to give sexual gratification. Both uses of *pleasure*, still included in the latest dictionaries, would in the 1990s be greeted by a you-must-be-joking response!

plebeian A notorious word for tripping people up over the spelling, because of the *e* after the *b*. Although the ordinary people of ancient Rome were called *plebs* (cf *plebiscite*, see **referendum**), the word is now considered derogatory. (Pron. 'ple(r)BEEe(r)n'.)

plebiscite See referendum . . .

pled See pleaded . . .

plentifulness, plenitude or **plentitude** *Plenitude* is a literary or oratorical word for a fullness or an abundance. There is no such word as *plentitude*, although it is a mistake sometimes seen. The usual noun in everyday use for 'plenty' is *plentifulness*, or simply *plenty* on its own (a land of plenty).

pleonasm See tautology . . .

plimsolls or **plimsoles** Most schoolchildren in the 1990s wear **trainers** rather than *plimsolls*, which has become an old-fashioned word for canvas sports shoes with rubber soles. For anyone who lives in the past, dictionaries still include *plimsolls* and usually show, as an alternative spelling, *plimsoles*: this is a false connection with 'soles' of shoes, since *plimsoll* is said to come from Samuel Plimsoll, who introduced safety measures for merchants' ships in 1876 (the sides of the rubber soles of plimsolls reminded people of the Plimsoll line marked on the sides of ships).

PLO This is the abbreviation we hear most often in news items about efforts to establish peace in the Middle East. The polysyllabic name in full is less often mentioned: the *Palestine Liberation Organization* comprises a number of separate groups which have in common their opposition to Israel. The PLO was formed in 1964, and from the beginning has been regarded by Israel as a terrorist organization. The PLO has taken part in official peace negotiations under US sponsorship, which has given it status and a platform for expressing its point of view on television news programmes all over the world.

plonk The British expeditionary force in France during World War I came back home with a number of expressions formed out of a corruption or misunderstanding of French words. Every time we write off a wine as *plonk*, we echo the standard way of ordering a glass of white wine at a Paris bar (*Un blanc*, short for 'vin blanc'), as mispronounced all those years ago by the Tommies of the 1914–18 war.

ploughman's lunch A *ploughman's lunch*, chalked up outside pubs in the country, goes down well with tourists and people living in towns, as a healthy, rural back-to-the-land image. It is only bread, cheese and pickles, hardly enough to satisfy your average ploughman.

ploy   *Ploy* is not appropriate in a positive sense, as in 'It was a good ploy to finish everything today, so we can take tomorrow off'. The word implies cunning, or at least a clever trick in order to take advantage of someone or a situation. The origin of the word is uncertain, except that it is an old dialect word from the North of England.

PLR   Writers know what PLR stands for. Public Lending Rights is an attempt, established by Act of Parliament, which came into effect in 1983, to compensate writers and illustrators for the number of times readers borrow their books from public libraries.

plural or **singular**   Everyone knows that a singular noun is followed by a singular form of the verb, a plural noun by the plural form. Rules of grammar, like rules in life, are fine when the lines are clearly drawn, but tricky in the no man's land in between. When it's not clear-cut, here are guidelines to help decide between singular and plural forms of verbs:

1 *Two nouns linked by 'and'*   Usually these are followed by a *plural* verb: 'boys and girls *come* out to play'. When they are clearly a single unit, it is logical to use a singular verb: 'A gin and tonic *is* all I want'; 'Roast beef and Yorkshire pudding *is* obligatory for Sunday lunch'.

There is a grey area where two nouns linked by 'and' can be treated as either singular or plural: 'Law and order *is* (or *are*) on the political agenda'; 'courage and determination *is* (or *are*) required'. It is safer to use the plural form in such cases.

2 *Two nouns linked by 'or'*   There are three simple rules, which are set out in the entry for **or**.

3 *Plural nouns before a verb, followed by a singular noun after*   In most cases, it is the nouns before the verb that govern the form of the verb that follows: 'his wages *are* no more than *a token*'. (Note that 'the wages of sin *is* death', in St Paul's *Epistle to the Romans*, is archaic usage.)

4 *Two nouns linked by 'plus'*   This is a grammatical nicety. It is a common mistake to treat *plus* as the equivalent of 'and', followed by a *plural* verb (see **1** above). *Plus* is the equivalent of 'with', and should be followed by a *singular* verb: 'The minister's statement plus the latest trade figures *was* decisive in influencing voters'; 'A man and his wife *have* arrived', but 'a man plus his wife *has* arrived'.

5 *Nouns ending in -ics*   Athletics, classics, statistics, etc *is* or *are*? See entry under **-ics** (also **economics**, **ethics**, **politics**, which warrant special consideration).

6 *Collective nouns*   'Group' words such as 'government', 'company', 'family' also fall into a grey area. See **collective words** for guidance. See also **data; media**

pluralism   *Pluralism* was at one time mostly confined to ecclesiastical use, for the same cleric holding more than one benefice. It now has a much wider application in politics and society, describing minority groups retaining their separate cultural identities as part of a federalist state. James Baker, when American Secretary of State, said he welcomed 'the new pluralism in the Soviet Union'. For *cultural pluralism*, see **cultural**

plus   There are two points:

1 Should it be A plus B *is* or *are*? See **plural or singular/4**.

2 The use of *plus* as a noun, to mean an advantage, is best left to advertising jargon where it first started: 'The new model has five pluses'. In other contexts, 'benefits', 'advantages', 'improvements', 'qualities' not only sound better but are more specific.

plus-fours   See **knickers** . . .

plutocrat   *Plutocracy* attaches a Greek prefix for 'wealth' to *-cracy* derived from a Greek word for power or rule (as in democracy, aristocracy, etc). A plutocracy is a state governed by the very rich, and a *plutocrat* became a term of abuse for someone wielding power because of money. The word is more likely to be used now as a joke about anyone who seems at that moment to be well-off: 'Look at you drinking champagne – you plutocrat!'

podium   See **platform** . . .

poetess   At one of Edith Sitwell's lectures, someone asked about her work as a *poetess*. Those who were present still recall with a shudder her blazing attack on the hapless questioner. Dictionaries still dutifully list *poetess*, but it would not go down well now with a woman who writes poetry. If a woman ever gets the appointment, she will be the Poet Laureate, and might then be buried in Westminster Abbey, in Poets' Corner. See **actor; -ess forms**

poetic or **romantic**   Outside literary criticism and history, the ways *poetic* and *romantic* are used in general have something in common. Macaulay's observation, 'Perhaps no person can be a poet . . . without a certain unsoundness of mind' (*Literary Essays*), applies equally to a *romantic*. A more detailed comparison of the two words comes under the entry for **romantic**.

poetic justice   Poetic justice can work in two ways. Someone who has done something nasty unexpectedly comes a cropper as a result, instead of getting away with it. Or someone who has done something generous or kind is unexpectedly rewarded. In both cases, it is *poetic justice*.

poetic licence   See **dramatic licence** . . .

poetry or **verse**   *Verse* is literally the more down-to-earth word: it derives from Latin for a furrow made by a plough, hence a line of writing. *Poetry* is the more exalted word. A *versifier* suggests facile rhymes, popular sentimentality rather than feeling: 'There have been many most excellent poets that have never versified, and now swarm many versifiers that need never answer to the name of poets' (Philip Sidney, *The Defence of Poesy*). At the same time, *verse* is by no means a derogatory word (in *Comus*, Milton wrote of 'high immortal verse', and the divisions of a chapter in the Bible are known as verses).

Down the centuries, writers and critics have sought to define poetry: perhaps the simplest definition is 'current language heightened' (Gerard Manley Hopkins in a letter to Robert Bridges, 1879). That leaves out the capacity of poetry to communicate a vision of life. It has been described as looking through binoculars. Before you twiddle the knob, the image is blurred, but as the focus is adjusted, it becomes sharp. At its best, poetry can do that for us.

point of view, viewpoint or **standpoint** It is not worth struggling to find a subtle difference between these three expressions: they all mean exactly the same, describing a particular way of looking at something. When they are used literally, there is no problem: 'From this point of view (or viewpoint or standpoint) you can see the top of the church spire'. When they are used about general matters, they often encourage indirect, official-sounding language: 'From the financial point of view (or viewpoint or standpoint), . . .' is less out in the open than 'When it comes to money, . . .').

points of the compass See abbreviations; CAPITAL LETTERS

poker-faced See deadpan . . .

policeman See cop . . .

Politburo Since the break-up of the Soviet Union in 1991, *Politburo* (stress the first syllable: 'POLLitbyooroh') is the concern only of historians. With a small *p*, it represents the central all-powerful committee of the Communist party that forms the government of any country. But it is the word with a capital P that was most familiar in the West, as the dominant force in the former Soviet bloc. The name is an adaptation of the Russian word for a political bureau.

politic or **political** Long ago in the 16th century, *politics* was a neutral word for the principles of government (it comes from Latin through Greek from words meaning 'citizen' and 'city'). Because politics has rarely been a clean business, the word *political* has taken on dubious colouring. To say something is political suggests it is concerned with the narrow interests of a group or organization, rather than the general good (a political decision, for example, is not objective but partisan). The *internal politics* of an organization is the jockeying and intrigue for power and influence that go on behind the scenes.

Political is a straightforward word when it is used about fields of study, such as *political anthropology* (the study of forms of leadership in primitive societies),

political economy (the study of the relationship between economics and government), *political science* (an academic name for the formal study of the history and principles of governments), about which the broadcaster Alistair Cooke commented 'there could hardly be an activity less scientific than politics'. In other contexts, it is not easy to use *political* any longer, without the implication of manoeuvre and machination to gain personal or party advantage.

Politic, however, remains a neutral word, describing a decision or an action that is wise and prudent, without carrying with it the uneasy suggestion of intrigue and calculation. The *body politic* is a formal term for the state considered as a governmental organization.

politically correct The expression originated in America as a response to multiculturalism, and became the glib media term for sidestepping giving offence to people of black, Spanish, Puerto Rican origin, etc. It has been picked up by the media in Britain, as a way of giving authority to linguistic obfuscation, fudging of real issues by indirectness. For example, it is politically correct to call slums, **inner cities**, the **poor**, disadvantaged, to have token women, blacks or Asians on committees (see **statutory woman**). One publisher of children's books has instructed writers that it is 'politically correct to make mothers bus drivers, MPs, social workers instead of women staying at home'.

No matter where your heart is, it is *politically correct* to be seen to be doing, and above all saying, the right things. See also **doublespeak** . . .

politics are or **is** In most cases, *politics* is treated as singular: 'Politics *is* an uncertain business'. But when *politics* represents an attitude or preference for a political party or policy, it is treated as plural: 'What *are* his politics?'; 'Her politics on this issue *have* always been clear'.

poll *Poll* is an old word for the human head, that goes back to the 13th century. The **poll tax** demonstrated that the word is very much alive in the 1990s. Polls are part of the razzmatazz of elections, a counting of people's opinions one way or the other. The Poll (usually with a capital P) is an alternative word for the **ballot box**, the casting of votes at an election. *Poll* has doubled as a verb since the 17th century: people are *polled* to find out which way opinions are going. *Straw poll* can give a misleading impression: it latches onto the authority of the word *poll*, yet may represent the opinion of only a handful of people. See also **psephology; snapshot (survey)**

pollster See **Gallup poll**

poll tax or **community charge** Winning a political battle often depends upon winning the war of words. In the late 1980s, the Conservative government looked round for a name for the proposed replacement of the domestic rate system. 'Community' seemed a good word and 'charge' not as harsh as 'tax': *community charge* sounded fair and just. The opposition fought back: a historian among them recalled that it was the *poll tax* (**poll** in the 13th century meant a human head), a levy on every person regardless of means, that led to the Peasants' Revolt in 1381, so they made *poll tax* the battle cry against the government's proposal.

From then on members of the Conservative Party resolutely referred to the *community charge*, and the opposition to the *poll tax*. *Poll tax* was sharp and crisp for newspaper headlines, two syllables against five, so it seeped into everyone's mind. The writing was on the wall linguistically and politically. When the time came, John Cole, then BBC political editor, spoke the epitaph, summoning up another piece of 14th-century history in Britain: 'Defending the *poll tax*', he declared, 'is like defending the Black Death'. It all became politico-linguistic history in April 1993, when the tax was replaced by the *council tax*.

pollution   *Pollution* has become an all-embracing environmental term for anything that affects the health and safety of a living species. Not only does it apply to the more obvious emission of industrial pollutants, but it also includes excessive noise, from aircraft or factories, for example. The word has a central position on the political agenda in the 1990s.

Polynesian   The final syllable can have a *z* sound ('poliNEEZie(r)n') or the same sound as the *s* in 'leisure'. The former is considered preferable.

polyunsaturated   Before the 1960s, no one, other than biochemists, had heard of *polyunsaturated*. The apparent link between **cholesterol**, a fatty constituent in the blood and tissues, and heart disease, put *polyunsaturated* on the labels of culinary oils and margarines, and the focus of large advertising budgets. Even so, *polyunsaturated* is little more than a vague reassurance to overweight businessmen, for few people have more than a hazy idea of what the word means. *Polyunsaturated* describes a fat or oil that is rich in chemical bonds that unite atoms and enable the fatty content to be more readily absorbed, instead of remaining as globules of fat in the system.

poof or **pouffe**   There are so many variations in the spelling of these two words ('poove', 'pouf', etc) that it is easier to select the most usual ones and forget the rest. After all, neither word is such an important part of everyday vocabulary.

Poof (the *oo* usually has the same sound as in 'foot') is an old-fashioned derogatory slang word (in Britain, not America) for a male homosexual. *Pouffe* (the *ou* has a long sound as in '*moon*') is a thick, heavily padded cushion made to sit on like a stool.

poor and **poverty**   The *poor* are always with us (the thought is taken from *St John* 12:8) but there is a certain reluctance now to use the word. For governments and social workers, *poor* has become a four-letter word to be sidestepped with **euphemisms**, such as 'low-income groups', 'low-paid', 'deprived',

'disadvantaged', '**underprivileged**'. This does not apply to the word *poverty*, for even sociologists would hardly try to get away with 'the state of being low-paid'.

Poverty trap, a term that dates from the 1970s, is often misunderstood. It is a trap set by the system of benefits for people on very low incomes: if they earn more money, they can turn out to be worse off, because the increase in income reduces or wipes out their entitlement to State benefits.

pop or **rock**   Surprisingly, *pop* in connection with music goes back to the mid-19th century, when *pop* was slang for a popular concert with low-price tickets that people could afford, and for popular classics in contrast to chamber music. *Pop* became worldwide language after World War II, the standard term in tin-pan alley, with the television programme, *Top of the Pops*, pop albums, pop singer, pop star. . . . For cultural élitists, *pop* is often a dismissive word, on the principle that if music appeals to a mass audience, it must be commercial and superficial (see **masses**). Others see among the morass of pop music some original ideas not to be dismissed too lightly.

The term *rock music* existed in America a few years before Elvis Presley (1935–77) became famous in the mid-1950s. With Presley, *rock and roll* or *rock* was soon synonymous for most people with *pop*, used loosely about almost any music with a strong beat. For others, *rock* is a genuine part of the culture of youth, taking experimental forms in *progressive rock*, adapting folk music with the rock rhythms of Bob Dylan, to become *folk rock*. Serious newspapers have a weekly column under *Rock*, keeping *rock* for serious and interesting developments in popular music, instead of allowing *pop* and *rock* to merge.

Outside music, *pop* is more descriptive than dismissive. *Pop art* (the term dates from the mid-1950s) is accepted in national art galleries (see **op art . . .**), *pop culture*, sometimes used as an alternative to 'folk culture', can include trends in design of clothes and household objects.

pop art   See **op art . . .**

popular press   See **broadsheets and tabloids**

porcelain   See **china . . .**

pornography or **obscenity**   *Pornography* is a word to use with care, as the goalposts are not only shifting but are, according to a leading article in *The Times*, 'largely a matter of taste'. The word comes from two Greek words meaning 'prostitute' and 'writing' (compare 'calligraphy'), hence the word means literally 'the writing of prostitutes'. When it was adopted into English about the mid-19th century, *pornography* described the life and habits of prostitutes and their customers. Pornography is now taken to mean anything in pictures or words deliberately aimed at exciting people sexually. Clearly this is all in the mind, and it depends upon whose mind.

On the one hand, Mary Whitehouse, a self-appointed guardian of public morality, maintains that 'The essence of sex is that it is a private personal experience between two people' (submission to the Annan Committee on Broadcasting). On the other hand, art and literature, exploring the human situation, could hardly leave out sex and sensuality. *Lady Chatterley's Lover* is now legally literature rather than pornography. In the Musée d'Orsay in Paris, people queue up to see Manet's painting, *Déjeuner sur l'herbe*, depicting a stark naked nubile young woman lounging on the grass alongside two elegantly dressed men.

If the expression of sexuality is perceived to have style or wit, beauty or truth, most people would not call it pornography. But some will: Goya, as an old man, was summoned before a tribunal because he had painted a naked woman in bed. With certain television plays, the BBC warns viewers that some scenes are 'sexually explicit': there are people for whom that amounts to pornography.

Feminists define pornography as portraying women as sexual objects submissive to men's desires, hence the precept 'pornography is the theory, rape is the practice'. Clare Short, the Labour MP, sought as a matter of civil rights to prohibit pornography as 'the graphic, sexually explicit subordination of women'. The problem remains one of finding an agreed line in the grey area between art and literature holding a 'mirror up to nature' and crude commercial exploitation of sexual appetites.

Legal dictionaries do not usually include *pornography*, because the Law prefers the term *obscenity*, which the Obscene Publications Acts 1959 and 1964 define as 'tending . . . if taken as a whole . . . to deprave and corrupt persons who are likely to read, see or hear the matter contained and embodied in it'.

Porn is the usual conversational abbreviation for *pornography*, used in newspapers and magazines and freely in speaking, although not in formal English. *Hard-core pornography* or *hard porn* is used for words or pictures that blatantly describe or display sexual acts and perversion; *soft-core pornography* or *soft porn* is provocative rather than obscene, **nudge-nudge wink-wink** photographs.

When we use the words *pornography*, *porn* or *obscenity*, we are walking on thin ice, because they mean such different things to different people.

portentous or **portentious** *Portentous*, meaning 'of great moment', is sometimes wrongly spelt and pronounced 'portentious', because of a false association with 'pretentious'. The word 'portentious' does not exist.

porter See **doorkeeper** . . .

portfolio *Portfolio* derives from two Latin words, one for 'carry' (compare 'portable') and the other for 'leaves' (compare 'foliage'), and in the 18th century, a portfolio was a holder for keeping documents. Some current dictionaries still show this as the first meaning of the word, and it is used in that way for samples of an artist's work ('This is a portfolio of her drawings').

The most usual meaning now is an *investment portfolio*, which is the spread of investments held by an individual or a company: for example, a portfolio balanced between income and capital growth.

Portfolio is also the formal term for the office of a minister of state ('his portfolio is the Home Office') and is still current for a *minister without portfolio*, a member of the Cabinet who is not in charge of a ministry.

Note that *portfolio* is one of the *-o* words that form the plural by adding *-s* (not *-es*): *portfolios*.

porticoes or **porticos** Either. *Porticoes* is more usual.

Portland cement See **cement** . . .

posh Dictionaries consider *posh* slang or at best a conversational word. Yet it is useful in all kinds of contexts: the **broadsheets** are sometimes called the posh papers; a plummy way of speaking, a posh accent; a Rolls-Royce remains a posh car. No one knows the origin of *posh*, which first appeared at the beginning of the century. It would be nice to think it derives from the expression used for the most expensive and coolest cabins on ships to and from India ('**p**ort **o**ut **s**tarboard **h**ome'), but lexicographers shake their heads about that.

Posh is not appropriate in formal writing, so keep 'grand' or 'lordly' as standbys, although they don't have the same ring to them. Don't rely on 'classy', because that's slang too. Finally, *frightfully posh* is too *awfully posh* for words.

position See **job** . . .

positive and **negative** The old parliamentary pomposity 'The answer is in the negative' has disappeared: at Prime Minister's question time nowadays, one or other of the adversaries will snap back a terse 'No sir!' As one linguistic door closes, another opens, and *negative* has become a vague indeterminate word in all kinds of everyday contexts: 'I have negative feelings about this', 'it has received a lot of negative publicity' (instead of 'bad feelings', 'bad publicity'); 'that's a very negative attitude' (instead of 'unhelpful attitude'); 'we've made negative progress' (instead of 'no progress' or 'we've lost ground').

Positive is also overused. Usually there's a more specific and informative word available: 'happy', 'cheerful', 'hopeful' feelings; 'rapid', 'encouraging', 'good' progress, etc.

Discrimination, more often than not now a bad word, is given a U-turn with *positive discrimination*, a term used for giving preferential treatment to **under-privileged** groups in society.

positive discrimination See previous entry.

positive feedback See **feedback**

posse *Posse* smacks of shooting from the hip in the Wild West. In fact, it has a respectable English origin, short for the medieval Latin term 'posse comitatus', officially a body of men over the age of 15 in a county, leaving out peers, clergymen and the infirm, who could be summoned to keep the peace. *Posse* now seems to belong more to law enforcement in America. It is used for the body of men who are empowered by law as a force to assist the sheriff in arresting criminals or maintaining order. The Latin pronunciation survives: 'POSSee'.

possessive or **genitive case** *Genitive case* is a Latinate term which defines the relationship between certain words in a sentence. *Possessive case* is an alternative grammatical term with the same meaning, more understandable, since both terms apply to the forms of words used to denote a possessive or belonging relationship: *Mary's* letter, the *day's* work, etc. In English, the possessive (or genitive) case is formed with an **apostrophe**: the entry under that heading goes through the problems that arise. See also **case**

post See **mail** . . .

post-nuclear family See **nuclear family** . . .

pot See **cannabis** . . .

pottery See **ceramic** . . .

pouffe See **poof** . . .

pound and **sterling** *Pound* for both weight and for money are linked to the same Old English word (the money pound was originally a pound weight in silver). The *lb* abbreviation for weight and the £ sign for money derive from Latin 'libra' (the Roman pound).

Sterling, related to an Old English word for a star, arose because some Norman coins had a star on them. The word became used for coins of a prescribed weight and quality of gold and, later, of silver, hence *pound sterling*, which became the standard term for UK currency. (*Pound sterling* was superseded in the early 1990s by the new international currency code designation GBP.) *Sterling* only survives now in *sterling silver* (which must have 92.5% purity) and in phrases such as *sterling value*, *sterling worth*, echoes of faraway days when the unvarying pound sterling was the measure of all currencies. See also **LSD**

poverty See **poor** . . .

powder-room *Powder-room* doubles as the old name for the storehouse of gunpowder on board warships and as a **euphemism** for a woman's **lavatory**. In this latter sense, it originated in America but has caught on in Britain, curiously with both the grander hotels and suburban dancehalls.

power breakfast The expression belongs to the booming 1980s but it is still used, if perhaps more hesitantly. Executives living in the **fast lane** arrange meetings, usually one-to-one, over breakfast before

the official working day begins, to hammer out a deal, a contract, a takeover. The setting of a *power breakfast* is important: it must project confidence, authority and a large bank balance.

Every capital city has its power breakfast venues: in London, the Savoy Hotel and the Ritz are well up on the list. In New York, the Plaza Athenée, the Ritz-Carlton and the Peacock Alley of the Waldorf-Astoria can be singled out. In Paris, the Deux Magots in St-Germain-des-Prés is said to have the right effect. As a general rule, if you choose for a power breakfast one of the most expensive places in a city, which at the same time has an aura of luxury, tradition and worldliness, you are not likely to go wrong. And the coffee has to be beyond criticism.

power dressing In the driving 1980s, with their expansion policy and takeover deals, wearing the right suits, the right dresses, the right ties became part of 'playing to win', and the game was called *power dressing*. Research claimed that, for men, dark suits and plain or discreetly striped shirts and firmly knotted ties give an impression of serious intent, backed by knowledge and high purpose, while light-coloured suits, check shirts with the top button undone, tie loosely knotted, convey innovative talent. For the chairman of a bank, on the one hand, or a design consultant on the other, power dressing means different things.

For women, power dressing requires a carefully poised balance between looking feminine (or sexy) and at the same time authoritative and focused. Shoulder pads (their presence, their absence, their size . . .) have played a part.

power of attorney See **attorney**

pp (per pro), **for** or **for and on behalf of**
When a secretary signed a letter for her boss, she used to put *pp* (Latin 'per procurationem' – by proxy) in front of his name. That is much less common now, and it is more usual to put *for* in front of the name of someone you are signing for. *For and on behalf of* is formal legal language.

PR, **public relations** or **publicity** Thomas Jefferson used the expression *public relations* in the early years of the 19th century, so the term is older than we might think. It used to mean what it said, dealing with the public, handling complaints, making sure that people are satisfied with a service or a product, keeping in touch with the local community, in general an honest sharing of information in order to increase mutual understanding. Long since then, public relations lost its innocence. It has become almost another word for *publicity*.

There remains a difference between *PR* and *publicity*, and *advertising*. Advertising, you could say, is more out in the open, as it appears in paid-for space in publications or as commercials on radio and television. PR achieves its end by cultivating key journalists in order to get people or products written about in newspapers and magazines or shown on television. It is a rough feverish business, fighting for every possible 'column inch' in newspapers, every **photo opportunity** or **sound-bite**.

PR executives justify their fees by submitting to clients a list of all the 'free' publicity (sometimes calculated in 'column inches') they have obtained for them. PR can function in the opposite way, using contacts with the **media** to persuade the media to keep quiet about some embarrassing item of information.

Some people would consider *publicity* beneath them and would frown on the idea of *public relations*, preferring the dignity of *press secretaries* (the Queen and the Prime Minister each have one), who nevertheless appear to go about their work in much the same way as public relations practitioners, issuing press releases, photographs, etc to the media, calling press conferences, making contacts with journalists, and all the other ways of presenting their clients to the outside world in the most favourable light. Because *publicity*, for some people, is a brash commercial word, there are linguistic cover-ups to put a more civilized gloss on it.

practicable and **practical** *Practical* is always a term of praise and commendation. It suggests that something is suited in most respects for a particular purpose, and used about a person, suggests a down-to-earth problem-solving attitude: 'the scheme is practical and will overcome most of the difficulties'; 'she is a practical woman able to turn her hand to most things'.

Practicable is a neutral descriptive word meaning no more than that it is possible to do something, but not implying it is either a good or bad idea to do it: 'the scheme is practicable but will not overcome the difficulties'; 'it's practicable but that's all you can say about it'. It follows that anything that is practical is also practicable, but not necessarily the other way round: it is practicable for some people to stand on their heads to look at a painting, but that is not a practical way to appreciate a work of art.

For the distinction between the negative forms, *impracticable*, *impractical* and *unpractical*, see **impracticable** . . .

practice or **practise** This is an old linguistic chestnut, yet people still hesitate over which to use. The noun is always *practice*, the verb always *practise*: 'Practise the piano because practice makes perfect'; 'A doctor practises medicine in his practice'. It may help to remember 'device' and 'devise' which are used in correspondingly different ways. In America, there is no problem because *practice* is the usual spelling for both noun and verb (although a few people make the British distinction, some American dictionaries do not even bother to list *practise*).

pragmatic See empiric . . .

prairie See grasslands

precognition or **premonition** Both words involve a supposedly supernatural knowledge of a future event. The Latin word for knowledge is 'cognitio', and *precognition* is an inner awareness of some future happening, good or bad, without any logical explanation or rational calculation. The Latin for warning is 'monitio', and *premonition* is a supernatural foreknowledge always of some dire or tragic event. See also next entry

prediction or **prophecy** There is, or could be if it were generally observed, a useful distinction between these two words. *Prediction* should imply a statement about the future based on an examination of the present state of things plus laws learned through experience. *Prophecy* is more crystal-gazing, divine revelation, or a hunch. In everyday use, this difference is blurred.

Prophesy is the corresponding verb, often used wrongly for the noun: when we make a prophecy, we prophesy something will happen.

predominant or **predominate** *Predominate* is a verb, as in 'red predominates in the colour scheme'. *Predominant* is a descriptive word, as in 'red is the predominant colour'. Avoid the common mistake of using *predominate* as a descriptive word ('the predominate colour' instead of 'predominant colour'). Although one or two current dictionaries accept that *predominate* can be used interchangeably with *predominant*, this is often considered a mistake.

pre-empt *Pre-empt* has become a fashionable word and its range of meanings is extended. Nevertheless, *pre-empt* should always imply something being done in advance, or someone getting in first in a way that blocks another action that was planned. It should not be used, as it often is, as an alternative to 'prevent', as in 'her late arrival pre-empted them going to the theatre'.

A *pre-emptive strike* in the early stages of a war demonstrates the effective use of the word: a sudden attack is made, to destroy, for example, enemy aircraft on the ground, so they cannot be used to attack land forces. In bridge, a *pre-emptive bid* is a high bid intended to block further bidding.

prefabricated *Prefabricated* was used after World War II for the industrial building system that assembles standard components to provide factories, schools, hospitals, etc. The constructions were known as *prefabs*. The word is adapted for anything that is standardized and off the peg, lacking in individuality: there are prefabricated novels, prefabricated political speeches, prefabricated ideas, all suggesting an unoriginal assembly of different elements that have been successful in the past. See also **module** . . .

preface See foreword . . .

pregnancy discrimination The expression has arisen in the 1990s for discrimination against a woman because she is pregnant, so that she does not receive the promotion or increase in pay that she merits. A pregnancy discrimination case was brought by a woman in Scotland in 1991 and the European Court upheld the contention that pregnancy discrimination is a form of sex discrimination. An equivalent expression in America, much less dignified, is *mommy track*, which implies that women of childbearing age are given jobs with no future, because it is anticipated that they will abandon their careers to have children.

pregnant or **expectant**   Nobody says any more that a woman is 'with child'. Fewer people now say that she is *expectant*. The word *pregnant* is back again as the most normal word, although there is no need to say, as they did in the 16th century, that a woman is 'pregnant with child'.

prehistoric   *Prehistoric* is sometimes used loosely and wrongly, especially in popular journalism, to mean the period about which nothing is known. It does not mean that but a period for which there are no written records, although much might be known through the study of archaeological finds. The corresponding noun, *prehistory*, is sometimes used for archaeological studies which are not supported by written evidence. In popular everyday use, *prehistoric* can be much more recent: anything that is altogether out of date, even yesterday's joke, can be prehistoric, if someone wants to pour scorn on it.

premiere (as a verb)   Many people wrinkle their noses over *premiere* used as a verb: 'the new opera will be premiered at the Met'. This began as American usage, but is now so established in Britain that most of us, including current dictionaries, accept it, even if we prefer not to use the word that way ourselves. The grave accent over the penultimate *e* (première) is insisted on by some dictionaries but dropped in others. (Either way, the pronunciation retains a hint of the French sound: 'PREMee-air'.)

premium   The word has several uses. The most familiar is for the sum paid to insurance companies for protection against a particular risk. In general use, *premium* is any extra sum paid to buy a commodity because it is in short supply, although the phrase *at a premium*, meaning difficult to obtain because demand exceeds supply, does not always imply that an extra charge has to be paid. The Stock Exchange uses *premium* in the same way, when the market price of shares is more than their nominal or **face value**. Lastly, to put a *premium* on something is not usually financial, but an extended use of the word to say we place a special value on a person, a quality, etc ('I put a premium on his clear-sighted advice').

Premium bond, the name for the government security that is a kind of lottery, was presumably thought up by a Latin scholar at the Treasury, following Latin 'praemium' (prize or reward).

premonition   See **precognition** . . .

preparatory school   See **public school** . . .

preparedness   Although a three-syllable pronunciation is heard ('pri-PAIRD-ness'), the correct pronunciation gives the word four syllables: 'pri-PAIR-id-ness'.

prepositions   These are words, mostly short ones, that show how other words relate to each other: 'She went *to* the door . . . *into* the house . . . *up* the stairs'.

Preposition comes from Latin, meaning 'to go before', and from that stems the hackneyed worn-out rule that we must never end a sentence with *to, from, for, with, up*, or any other preposition. So there are people who insist on saying: '*At* which hotel are you staying?', '*Into* which box did you put it?', '*From* where does it come?' It sounds unnatural, and even the most cautious grammarian accepts that it is perfectly good English to end a sentence with a preposition when you want to, especially when that is the natural place for it. See also **put up with**

prepositions at end of sentences   See previous entry

prescriptive (in linguistics)   See **permissive** . . .

presently   *Presently* is an uncertain word to use because different people claim it means different things. Most of us feel comfortable about using *presently* as a slightly more urgent alternative to *soon*: 'You won't have to wait long, as the doctor will see you presently'. For some, *presently* can mean a short while ago: 'We finished dinner presently and are now having coffee'. Then there is the argument over whether *presently* can be used to mean 'at present', 'at this moment': 'We are presently having dinner'. This has long been standard usage in Scotland and also in America. It has now become so common in England ('the matter is presently under discussion'; 'she is presently writing a book about it'), that it should be accepted.

In practice, there is little scope for misunderstanding if we use *presently* to mean 'soon' or 'at present', as in the above examples. But to use *presently* about something in the immediate past ('We finished dinner presently . . .') is less familiar, and it is better to substitute 'We have just finished dinner . . .'.

The ultimate misunderstanding happened to Laurie Lee on his first day at the village school. They told him, 'Just you sit there for the present'. He was disappointed: 'I sat there all day but I never got it. I ain't going back there again!' (*Cider with Rosie*).

present participle   The grammatical term for the form of verbs ending in *-ing*: running, jumping, standing, etc.

preservation   See **conservation** . . .

preserve   See **jam** . . .

President or **president**   In the world of business, *president* is a title more commonly used in

America, usually the equivalent in Britain of managing director or chief executive. *President* is sometimes found in British companies, but usually as an honorary title given to a chairman or managing director who is particularly identified with the business, and remains involved after retirement, perhaps as a consultant or **non-executive** member of the board. Sometimes *life president* is used, when it is intended the title should be retained for the rest of a person's life.

With the present trend to use capital letters more sparingly, the president of a corporation no longer automatically rates a capital P: it is a matter of choice. A capital P still seems fitting for the President of the United States, of France or of any other state, although *The Times* has downgraded all *Presidents* to *presidents* (except in titles, such as *President Clinton*, *President Mitterrand* . . .). See also **CAPITAL LETTERS**

(the) **press** It was once the custom to refer to *the press*, meaning the national newspapers published in **Fleet Street**, as it used to be. But the term sounds old-fashioned now, except in the phrase 'to get a good or bad press', meaning good or bad publicity. Newscasters now refer to the **broadsheets** and **tabloids**, the 'papers', or the **media**.

press secretary See **PR**

pressure group Although *pressure group* dates from the 1920s, it has come into much wider use since World War II. Any group of people who get together in a concerted attempt to influence official policy is a *pressure group*. Unlike a political formation whose manifesto could embrace a wide range of national interests, a pressure group normally focuses on one particular cause, such as preventing a motorway being constructed through a village, preventing closure of a school. . . . There are *trade pressure groups* that promote the interests of certain industries to government departments. See also **lobbying**

pressurize *Pressurize* was one of the new generation of *-ize* words that many people objected to. Bruce Fraser, in his revision (1973) of Gowers' *Plain Words*, acknowledged that *pressurize* was one of the new verbs that 'cannot be gainsaid', which also applies to its extended use for people: 'she pressurized the minister to raise the matter in the House'; 'he was pressurized to accept the proposed terms'. Alternative expressions, such as 'put pressure on' and 'coerce', are available, but *pressurize* summons up a more vivid picture of the screw being put on someone.

prestigious As a descriptive word for someone or something having prestige, *prestigious* became available in the 1950s. To begin with it seemed a salesman's word to describe anything from a car to a restaurant that was good to be associated with, because it made you look rich and successful. Some people still don't like the word. But it has arrived, and there is no other convenient descriptive word with the

same meaning: a prestigious appointment, a prestigious collection of paintings, a prestigious place to live.

presume See **assume** . . .

presumptuous, **presumptious** or **presumptive** 'Presumptious' is often written and said, although it is wrong. *Presumptuous* is the correct word, pronounced with four syllables: 'preZUMP-chew-us' (not 'preZUMPshus').

Presumptive also gets mixed up with *presumptuous*, but is a different word altogether. It means there is reason for presuming something is the case, as in *presumptive evidence* (evidence based on presumption rather than facts).

pretence or **pretext** *Pretence* is to pretend something that is not true: 'They kept up the pretence of being happily married'. A *pretext* has almost the same meaning, but includes the suggestion that the pretence is used as a false excuse to do or not do something: 'She got into the security zone on the pretext that she worked there as a cleaner'.

pretty To use *pretty* in such sentences as 'he is pretty well-off', 'she is pretty clever', 'this is pretty good', etc, is normal in conversation but less appropriate in writing, where (as you can see) it can look *pretty* well out of place.

prevaricate or **procrastinate** The best of us can sometimes slip up over these two words: an article in *The Listener* commented that cold weather 'allows us to prevaricate over the spring cleaning'. It is *procrastinate* when we put something off. Remember 'Procrastination is the thief of time' (Edward Young, 1683–1765, *Night Thoughts*).

Prevaricate is almost another word for lying, but is less direct, implying evasiveness, not coming out in the open: John Cole, when BBC political editor, talked about MPs' attitude over a certain matter, commenting, 'I don't want to say "lie", but they are *prevaricating*'.

prevent There is a grammatical subtlety in the use of *prevent*. 'She will prevent *his* meeting his former wife' and 'she will prevent *him from* meeting his former wife' are grammatically impeccable. 'She will *prevent him* meeting his former wife' cuts across formal grammar. The reason is a rather tortuous differentiation between certain *-ing* forms as verbs and others as verbal-nouns (so-called gerunds).

It is questionable whether we should worry all that much about saying 'she will prevent him meeting . . .'. Similar constructions are so common now and nothing much is lost if the grammatical principle of the gerund is left quietly on the shelf. (Grammatical purists might disagree.)

preventive or **preventative** Both words exist for the same meanings. *Preventive* is taking over and sits more happily in established phrases such as *preventive dentistry* and *preventive medicine*. In passing, **condoms** used to be referred to as *preventatives*.

pre-war and **inter-war**   Not many people who would interpret *pre-war* as the period before 1914 are still alive, and it is safe to assume that it now refers to the period before September 1939. *Pre-war* is a vague description of a period: for some people it means the 1930s, for others any time from the 1920s onwards. *Inter-war* years is more precise, as it covers the period from 1918 to 1939.

We may need to be careful using these terms, as we cannot always assume that throughout the world *pre-war* and *inter-war* will be associated with World Wars I and II.

priest   This is the order of ministry in the Anglican Church above a deacon and below a bishop. It has come into particular use with the decision in 1992 to admit women into ordination in the Church of England. The term *woman priest* is used ('woman priestess' hints at pagan rites!). See also **minister. . .**

price   See **cost . . .**

price-earnings ratio   Price-earnings ratio, or P/E, as it is usually shown in the share-price columns on the financial pages of newspapers, is not always immediately understood. It takes as its basis a computation that divides the earnings of a company by the number of its common stock shares. This is then related to the current market price of the shares to give the *price-earnings ratio*. It is one of the measures of whether a particular share is good value.

prick   It is understandable that slang words for a penis should compare it to an aggressive weapon (some men even use the word 'weapon' itself). By the end of the 16th century, *prick* was commonly used, without it being especially offensive. This changed, and in the 19th century, prick was the most vulgar of all slang words for the male sexual organ. By the 1930s, it had become an insulting word to use about a person, much more offensive than the alternative word **cock**: 'Hello old cock' is a friendly, if old-fashioned, greeting from one man to another, but to call a man a *prick* invites a fight.

priest   See **minister . . .**

prima donna   It is perfectly in order to call the leading woman singer in an opera the *prima donna* (in Italian, it is literally the 'first lady'). In any other context, to call a woman (or a man, for outside the world of opera, the term is used for men as well) a prima donna is to accuse them of being temperamental, self-important and difficult to deal with.

The plural is *prima donnas*, and the *i* of *prima* should be pronounced *ee*: 'preeme(r)DONNe(r)'.

prima facie   See **a priori . . .**

'PRImarily' or **'priMARily'**   We hear 'priMARily' (stress on the second syllable) often in news programmes. This is the usual pronunciation in America, but recent British dictionaries refuse to acknowledge it as an alternative pronunciation in Britain to 'PRImarily'. Nevertheless, it is more and more common, and we have to accept the way the tide is flowing.

prime lending rate   See **bank rate . . .**

Prime Minister or **prime minister**   The practice in some newspapers now is to drop the initial capital letters: prime minister. A compromise is to use initial capitals for the current holder of the office and small letters for previous ones: 'John Major, the Prime Minister, and two former prime ministers were present'. This is a matter of taste and many people wouldn't dream of not using initial capital letters for the title of the leader of the party in government: after all, the Queen still keeps her capital Q. See also **CAPITAL LETTERS**

primeval or **primordial**   There is no discernible difference in meaning between these two words, and dictionaries use *primordial* in the definition of *primeval*, and the other way round. *Primeval* is the more usual word for the earliest ages of the world, before the appearance of man, as in primeval forests, primeval hills. (For the spelling *primaeval*, see **ae** or **æ**.)

primitive   We need to be sensitive about the use of *primitive*, because in non-specific contexts the word can carry different nuances. In some fields, it is purely descriptive. In archaeology, *primitive* is used for simple non-literate societies; in biology, *primitive* refers to an early stage of evolution; the *primitive* church is the Christian Church in early times. When it comes to art, *primitive* is often an admiring word, used about native art unaffected by self-consciousness and academic tradition (see also **naive**), or art in Europe before the Renaissance, or for the work of an unschooled painter, such as Henri Rousseau (1844–1910).

In other ways, *primitive* can be derogatory, suggesting crude, not thought out or developed: primitive ideas, a primitive approach, a primitive construction, etc.

primordial   See **primeval . . .**

principal or **principle**   Because the words sound the same, they are occasionally confused. This sentence straightens it out: 'The principal of the college believes in certain principles of teaching, which were the principal things he explained in his speech'. *Principle* is always a noun; *principal* can be a noun or a descriptive word.

print   See **engraving . . .**

printout or **hard copy**   These are interchangeable terms for the output on paper of text keyboarded into a computer system or printed out from a word-processor. Both terms also apply to printed information retrieved from a computer's **database**. See also **proofs** . . .

prison, **jail** or **gaol**   *Prison* is the standard word now in all contexts. Both *jail* and *gaol* are less often used: when they are used, *gaol*, almost unknown in America, is a variant of *jail* (both are pronounced the same). The organization is called the prison service, with the staff serving HM Prisons, and *jailer* and *goaler* have been superseded by *prison officer*.

pristine   There are people who feel strongly that *pristine* should be used in the classical sense of prim-eval, that is as it was in the beginning, free from impurity. But the word has become popular to mean something in its new and original condition (a second-hand car, for example), and by further extension to mean fresh and clean ('she left the house in pristine condition'). These other meanings have become so common that it would be pedantic to reject them any longer. They are recognized by current dictionaries, with the meaning for 'fresh' and 'clean' usually carrying a warning that not everyone accepts those definitions.

privacy   Mail-order advertisements like the Englishman's-home-is-his-castle approach and invite us to examine a product 'in the privacy of our own homes'. How we pronounce the word is up to us: most current dictionaries offer a choice between 'PRIVVasy' (first syllable rhyming with 'spiv') and 'PRYVasy' (first syllable rhyming with 'dive'). The first pronunciation is preferable in British English, the second is more American.

private   See **confidential** . . .

private eye   Presumably this began as a way of writing 'private "i" ', an American expression for pri-vate investigation agent. Raymond Chandler's hero, Philip Marlowe, the archetypal private eye, made the expression popular in Britain, and the investigative magazine, *Private Eye*, started in 1961, has given the term a political and social interpretation with a sharp edge. See also **gumshoe**

private means   People may still be said to have a 'private income', an income from investments or rents, but the expression *private means* belongs more to the 1920s than the 1990s.

private parts   This curious expression, even more curious in the 1990s when television goes in for full frontal exposure, is still used by a few older people for male or female genitals. It remains included in some recent dictionaries, but will be written off eventually as quaint.

private school   See **public school** . . .

private and **public sector**   The whole span of commerce and industry controlled by commercial organizations is in Britain called the *private sector*, and services owned and controlled by central and local government, such as education, the prison service, etc, are the *public sector*.

Since the early 1980s, attitudes towards the *private* and *public sectors* have come closer together, and senior civil servants are inclined now to use the lan-guage of marketing executives, aware of expectations from customers, running their own budgets and imple-menting innovation. In addition, some parts of public sector enterprises have been transferred to the pri-vate sector.

Perhaps an even more significant change is that there is hardly any difference any longer in attitudes between consumers of private and public sector ser-vices: in both cases, they think of themselves as cus-tomers with higher expectations, no longer willing to accept what is handed out, more aware of their rights. The Citizen's Charter, with its own minister, will bring the terms *private* and *public sectors* even closer to each other.

privatization and **denationalization**   *De-nationalization* could suggest the total transfer of a previously state-owned organization to a commercially run public limited company, answerable to its share-holders: British Telecom and British Gas are examples. *Privatization* could be limited to the transfer of part of the work of an organization, previously entirely managed by central or local government, to commercial businesses. In practice, this distinction is too subtle. In any case, *privatization*, as a word, suited the mood of the Conservative government in the 1980s, and dovetailed neatly with other phrases, such as the **private sector** and with the glorification of *private enterprise* culture.

The interpretation of the word *privatization* was hotly argued over by the political parties in the 1992 election campaign, in relation to the National Health Service. The Conservative Party angrily rejected any suggestion that the NHS was being privatized. At the same time, the opening-up to outside commercial busi-nesses of a range of non-medical hospital require-ments, such as cleaning and other domestic services, and the option for hospitals to function independently of local authorities, put privatization of the NHS on the political agenda. But the word *denationalization* was clearly not appropriate, as the NHS remained a gov-ernment responsibility.

proceeds   See **profits** . . .

process (as a noun)   How did politicians, trade unions and the international community ever manage without the word *process*? Pay-bargaining has become the pay-bargaining process, negotiating – the negotiat-ing process, talking about peace – the peace process. *Process* is an invaluable word politically, since it is non-committal: all it says is that something is being talked about, without going so far as actually happening.

process (as a verb)   Materials have been *pro-cessed* for many years. Some time after World War II, there began a sinister application of the verb *process* to human beings. People are processed when they are admitted to hospital, that is entered on computers, classified, ticketed, etc, as part of admission procedure; passengers are processed at airports, taken through various controls and formalities; in early 1991, it was announced that hundreds of thousands of Kurds crossing over the border into Iran were waiting to be processed.

No doubt *process* is a useful word in such contexts, parallel to the computer term **data processing**, but it is dehumanizing. It is mildly encouraging that those who are processing people are not called processors: so far at least, that word is kept in its place with computers and for food processors in the kitchen.

procrastinate   See **prevaricate** . . .

production line   The production line developed from the mass-production methods first used in the motor car industry by Henry Ford (see **mass-**). It describes the process that breaks down production into separate elements, which can be carried out as detached operations by a person or a group. In other contexts, *production line* describes something that is mechanical, run-of-the-mill work or ideas: 'she writes three production-line novels every year, with standardized plots and cardboard characters'.

productivity   A buzzword: everything seems to depend on *productivity*. Productivity is the measure of achievement, efficiency and competence both for a company and for an individual. Pay increases are agreed subject to *productivity agreements*, which could cover the introduction of new technology or working practices to replace wasteful methods and trade union rules.

product mix   The term is used in marketing, and shows up in business columns of newspapers. A product mix is the range of all the products made or marketed by a company, planned for diversification and profit. The term is not used in retailing for the range of products stocked by a shop.

profane or **secular**   *Profane* is a word to be careful with. It can be severely condemnatory, describing a gross violation of something that is sacred. It can also be a harmless word, classifying those things that belong outside the sphere of religion. *Profane art*, for example, is purely descriptive, a term for non-religious art. Where there could be misunderstanding, use *secular*, which can only have the purely neutral meaning of describing things that do not relate to religion (secular music, secular drama . . .).

profession   See **job** . . .

professor   At British universities, a professor is the highest ranking teacher in a particular subject, and is often the head of the relevant department or faculty. In colleges of music, professor is the traditional name for a senior teacher (a harpsichord professor). In America and other countries, professor is used more loosely. As well as an official title conferred on senior members of a faculty, it is used outside university circles for any teacher at a university: if someone is introduced as Professor So-and-so, it can be assumed it is a title that has been conferred, but if they're introduced as 'a professor', they could be any lecturer or teacher.

profile   A *profile* is, of course, used for the human face seen from either side, representing the line of the features from the slope of the forehead to the shape of the chin. In extended use, a *profile* of anything should be more than a generalization, and should include specific characteristics: 'the profile of a typical customer is a woman between 20 and 30, who has been to university or a polytechnic, earns between £15,000 and £25,000 a year . . .'.

profits, **proceeds** or **residuals**   The word *profits* is out in the open: it is how much money has been made on a transaction, the difference between cost and selling price. *Profits* may take into account expenses and operating costs (*net profits*) or may not (*gross profits*).

Proceeds is sometimes used to sidestep the commercial or money-grubbing associations of profits, particularly in connection with raising funds for a cause. *Proceeds* can be taken to mean how much money was made, the same as *profits*, but can also be the total sum received: the proceeds from the sale of a property are usually taken to mean the sum that was paid for it, without deducting the cost of the property.

Residuals can be another word for profits, or it is sometimes used as a non-committal term for the money left over in a deal, without explaining how it is calculated. In that way, *residuals* is occasionally used to be deliberately vague. In a specialized sense, *residuals* is the term for additional payments due to writers or actors for repeats of a programme on television or radio they have written or appeared in, more or less the equivalent of royalties in publishing.

prognosis   See **diagnosis** . . .

program or **programme**   The two spellings have had a roundabout history. The *-am* ending was often used before the 19th century. Later *programme* took over, departing from the pattern of words such as 'diagram' and 'telegram'. America, with the usual preference for more phonetic spelling, kept to *program*.

In the 1950s, American computer language became standard in the English-speaking world, so *program* returned to British English as the spelling for anything to do with computers. In all other contexts, Britain holds steadfastly to *programme* (theatre programme, a programme of studies, etc).

In British English, the other forms of the computer term *program* take double *-mm-*: programmed, programmer, programming. See also next entry.

programmed When a computer is *programmed*, it follows a pattern of functioning and cannot depart from it, because a computer does not have free will. This sense of *programmed* has become extended to people: when someone reacts in a predetermined way to anything, they are said to be *programmed*, that is unconscious forces and desires make their reaction inevitable. See also **brainwashing**

'PROgress' or 'proGRESS' As a noun ('we are making progress'), the stress is always on the first syllable: 'PROgress'. As a verb ('we progress a little every day'), the stress is on the second syllable: 'proGRESS'. But when a verb is followed directly by whatever is being progressed, as in 'we must progress this matter' (a usage that some people dislike), it is usual to put the stress back on the *first* syllable.

progressive See **experimental** . . .

project or **task** The noun *project* sounds serious and important so it is not surprising it has run riot in business, education and even for everyday use ('our project on Sunday is to get the garden weeded'). Schoolchildren are given projects (*project work* is an approved method of teaching students to find out things themselves); executives, writers, builders, etc all talk about 'the next project'. If you find you are using *project* too often and in trivial ways, consider that fine old 13th-century word *task* as an occasional alternative.

proles See next entry

proletariat After a very long social history, starting with Latin 'proletarius', for a Roman citizen of the lowest order, Karl Marx took possession of the word in the mid-19th century. Since the *proletariat* was the class most exploited by the capitalist system, Marx used it as a clarion call in the class struggle. *Proletariat* signified the class without property or capital. But in our society of the 1990s, with ownership of homes, videos, microwaves, etc cutting across class divisions, the word has a fusty sound to it. It is difficult to know how to use *proletariat* now, other than in a historical sense.

The late 19th-century abbreviation for *proletariat*, *proles* (made popular by George Orwell in *Nineteen Eighty-Four*) lives on, occasionally used by some people as a word of disdain for people considered unenlightened, or with stone gnomes in the front garden of their centrally-heated houses.

prone, prostrate or **supine** *Prone* and *prostrate* are lying flat, face downwards. *Prone* simply describes the position, while *prostrate* carries the idea of submission or respect. *Prone* has the additional meaning of being liable to a bad condition (see **apt** . . .). *Prostrate* can be used to mean overcome by an emotion or condition, without suggesting someone is actually lying flat: prostrate with grief, prostrate with exhaustion. . . .

Supine (pron: 'SYOOpyne') is lying face upwards, but it is a literary or formal word: doctors ask patients to lie on their backs, rather than to lie supine. If using it, do not turn *supine* upside down: it is not unknown for writers to say: 'the body lay supine, nose buried in the mud'. ('You'd have to be a contortionist to achieve that!')

pronouns *Pronouns* are those short words that save us endlessly repeating a noun: 'John looked up from John's book as John had finished reading' becomes 'John looked up from *his* book as *he* had finished reading'. Most of the time we take pronouns for granted, slipping them in as necessary. But avoid the easy mistake of using too many pronouns, so that readers or listeners lose track of who all the different 'shes', 'hes' and 'theys' are.

There is one area now that is causing problems. *Pronouns* have become a focus of masculine bias in the English language: 'Will every passenger please take care of *his* own baggage' uses the pronoun *his* to include women, whether they like it or not. See **unisex grammar**

pronunciation Pronunciation varies more than any other aspect of English. After all, the slightest change in the way we move the organs of speech changes the sound that comes out. A Lloyd James, the expert on phonetics who used to advise the BBC, said 'Speech is a jumble of noises and rhythms and tunes, whereas the printed page is what it is . . .'. Even Robert Burchfield, formerly chief editor of Oxford English Dictionaries, admits there's at least one word he pronounces differently every time he says it. It is helpful to listen carefully to news programmes on television and radio, because announcers at least try to be careful, even if only to stop other people thumping them for making mistakes.

As for social differences in pronunciation, not so much has changed since 1912, when Shaw wrote in his preface to *Pygmalion*, 'Every time an Englishman opens his mouth another Englishman despises him'. See also **accents in speech; received pronunciation**

proofs and **galleys** Writers, publishers and printers still talk about *galleys* (short for *galley proofs*) or *proofs* for the first impression used for correction of a text. The terms relate to old typesetting methods going back to the mid-17th century, when a galley was a long rectangular tray in which type was set. *Proofs* is an even older typographical term from the 16th century, for a test impression from composed type.

Typesetting is computerized now, but those grand old printing-press words, *galleys* and *proofs*, will probably remain alive as long as books are published. See also **printout** . . .

propaganda See **disinformation** . . .

propellant or **propellent** Something that propels is a *propellant*, the correct spelling for the noun.

Propellent is the descriptive word for the process of propelling, such as 'a propellent force'.

proper nouns For grammarians, *proper nouns* are opposed to 'common nouns'. It is an old Latinate grammatical term for the name of a person or place (Latin 'proprius' means 'one's very own'). *Proper nouns* are usually spelt with a capital letter: Henry, Smith, London, America. . . .

For notes on how proper nouns, as the names of people, are being used in the 1990s, see **names**. For the plural forms of proper nouns ending in *-s*, see **names ending in -s**. For capitalization, see **CAPITAL LETTERS**

property or **real estate** *Real estate* (or *real property*) is an old term in law for possessions that are immovable, land and buildings in particular. In matters of inheritance, this sets real estate apart from personal estate, which covers objects and other possessions. *Estate agent* is still the most usual name for a business selling houses, although there is an tendency now for them to be called *house agents*, which makes more sense.

In America, *real estate* is used much more in everyday language: people invest and deal in real estate, whereas in Britain they would be much more likely to use the word *property*.

prophecy See prediction . . .

proportion See fraction . . .

proposal or **proposition** In the sense of a scheme put forward, there is no perceptible difference between a *proposal* and a *proposition*. In other contexts, a proposition can mean an offer to enter into a business arrangement: 'I have a proposition to share our production facilities'; a *proposal* can be used for a more modest suggestion: 'I have a proposal for the date of our next meeting'. *Proposition* has also taken on different shades of meaning, such as 'a job to be done', that do not apply to *proposal*: there are, for example, commercial propositions, tough propositions, paying propositions, difficult propositions.

Between a man and a woman, a *proposal* is a respectable word, a formal way of asking 'Will you marry me?' There is only one use of *proposition* as a verb: when a man propositions a woman, or the other way round, it means 'Shall we go to bed together?'

proprietary name See brand name . . .

pro rata It is rather old-fashioned to use the Latin phrase *pro rata* ('according to the rate') in business letters: 'we can let you have further supplies pro rata'. Phrases such as 'at the same rate', 'at the same price', 'on the same terms' are clear alternatives.

prosody As a literary term, *prosody* is the structure of poetry, particularly its rhythm and metre. As a linguistic term, *prosody* is the stress and intonation of spoken language, an aspect of phonology (see **phonetics . . .**).

prostrate See prone . . .

protagonist The word comes in for a lot of misuse. The 'pro-' is not Latin for 'in favour of' but from Greek 'protos' meaning 'first'. A *protagonist* in Greek drama was the one leading player. By extension, the word is used for the one key person in a story or situation: 'the minister was the protagonist in the debate on European integration', that is the minister dominated it.

No one can be 'one of the protagonists', because there is only one, and the common expression 'leading protagonist' is also wrong, since a protagonist is the leading figure anyway.

Because the prefix is assumed to be Latin, the word is often taken as the opposite of 'antagonist', and is used for someone who strongly supports a cause: 'the minister is a protagonist of European integration'. This is so common, that recent dictionaries include it as one of the meanings, with a warning that this is not accepted by everyone. Even if you're not a Greek scholar, it is better to reserve *protagonist* for the key figure in something, and choose words such as 'champion' or 'advocate' for a person who supports a cause.

protectionism The word occurs especially about opposition to the European Community. *Protectionism* is a reactionary trade policy, the opposite of free trade: it is government support for an industry or an individual company by restricting or imposing heavy penalties on the import of competing products.

protégé and **protégée** Perhaps an elderly duchess might still describe her niece travelling through Italy with her as her *protégée* (the feminine form), meaning that the girl was under her protection and having her travels paid for. That's what the word means, someone under the patronage or guidance of another person. In general, the words are out of place for the independent teenagers of the 1990s. If they are used, you have to go all the way and include two acute accents.

protest *about*, *against* or ***at*** We can protest *about*, *against*, or *at* something, and it comes to the same thing. It is usually a matter of choice which word is used: 'she protested about (or against or at) the court's decision'. In American English, *protest* is often used without the help of other words ('she protested the court's decision'), but this does not sound right in British usage.

protocol *Protocol* combines two Greek words, the prefix *proto-* (first or original, compare 'prototype') and a word for 'glue'. It meant the first sheet glued to a manuscript that listed its contents. By the 17th century, *protocol* was already being used in diplomacy for the original of a document. By the 19th century, *protocol* had taken on its present meaning, a formalized order of precedence at diplomatic receptions, and hence any formality that diplomatic relations require to preserve the illusion of being civilized. Among its other uses, *protocol* is commonly found in EC directives as the term for the first draft of a treaty or other agreement worked out at a meeting and accepted.

Computer technologists, with their attitude towards computers as near-human thinking machines, picked out *protocol* as the word for the sequence of commands that enable two computers to relate to each other, which is light years from the lists of contents glued to an ancient Greek manuscript.

prototype See archetype . . .

provable or **proveable** *Provable* ('proveable' is not acknowledged as a variant spelling by most current dictionaries).

proved or **proven** You can say that something has been *proved* or *proven*, although *proved* is now the standard form, except in Scotland where courts have the right to deliver a verdict *Not proven* as a third alternative to 'Guilty' or 'Not guilty'.

provenance *Provenance* is used in specialized ways for the place of origin, in archaeology and in commentaries on literary texts. It is in the art world that *provenance* is more familiar. If you take a picture to be sold at Christie's or Sotheby's, you might be asked its provenance, a polite way of asking 'Where did you get it?' Your answer will appear in the catalogue, so it goes down better if you can name a collection or a collector as the painting's provenance, rather than saying you bought it in Portobello Road market. For the provenance of a work of art is some assurance to a purchaser of its authenticity.

proverbial Clearly *proverbial* describes anything related to a proverb: 'the proverbial slip 'twixt cup and lip'. The word has come to be used freely to mean 'taken for granted as a proverb'. So we can talk about someone's proverbial good luck. But it is distorting the meaning of the word to use it about any familiar happening, as in 'After the meeting, they went out for the proverbial business lunch'. Other words, such as 'usual' or 'habitual', would be more appropriate.

provided, **providing** or **if** We can say: 'I can come *provided* (or *providing* or *if*) you can pay my fare'. *Provided* puts a greater stress on the condition.

Provided (or *providing*) is appropriate when it introduces a condition imposed by whoever is making the statement. When it is a straightforward statement of fact or opinion, *if* is the right word to use: 'I would never have come if I had known John would be there'; 'We should have arrived on time if we had allowed longer for the journey'.

province See field . . .

Provisionals See IRA . . .

provisos or **provisoes** Some dictionaries show both as alternative spellings. Others show only *provisos*, the plural form that should be used.

proxy See mandate . . .

PS It is human to have afterthoughts and some people were always adding PS (postscript, from the Latin verb 'postscribere', to write after) to their letters. And then sometimes a PPS (a post-postscript) and so on. By that time, if there were so many afterthoughts, it would have been better to write the letter all over again.

PS seems a dated over-formal epistolary convention, although it is still used. If there is something to be added at the end of a letter, more often than not now, it is just added, without the introductory abbreviation PS: after all, if it comes after the signature, what else could it be?

Although *postscript* properly refers to something written, it is also useful in connection with a talk: 'At the end of his speech, he added a postscript'; 'Having made those points, may I add a postscript?' Only a deeply entrenched Latinist would object.

psephology The citizens of Athens in ancient Greece used to drop a pebble into an urn in order to cast their votes. In the late 1940s, a historian, R B McCallum, later Master of Pembroke College, Oxford, jokingly took the Greek word 'psephos' (a pebble) and put it together with the Greek suffix '-ology', to form *psephology*. The joke was taken seriously and *psephology* entered the language as the word for the study of election trends and statistics.

With daily opinion polls now so much a part of election cliff-hanger speculation, *psephology* has become as well-known as any other *-ology*, and during the 1992 election campaign, the BBC *Today* programme declared it had its own 'resident psephologist' to analyse the flood of polls and statistics. (Pron: 'seFOLogy'.)

pseud, **pseudo** See phoney . . .

pseudonym, **nom de plume** or **pen-name**
The French never talk about a *nom de plume*: the expression is pseudo-French, invented by the English in the 19th century for the assumed name a writer uses. In any case, *nom de plume* is as old-fashioned as 'la plume de ma tante'.

Pen-name, which arose as a literal translation of *nom de plume*, also sounds out of place in the 1990s, where so many writers sit at the keyboard of a wordprocessor. When someone chooses to write under a false name, the best word to use now is *pseudonym*. Pseudonyms (from the Greek word meaning 'false name') are not confined to writers: the word can be used about a pseudo name that anyone adopts for any reason.

In passing, the correct French expression for the same thing is 'nom de guerre' which has nothing to do with 'war' these days, but simply means an assumed name someone chooses for any purpose.

Pshaw! According to certain novelists, peppery colonels in the 8th Hussars were supposed to go red in the face and exclaim *Pshaw!* in moments of extreme anger or disgust. The word is still dutifully defined even in the most recent dictionaries, and we are solemnly warned to pronounce it 'pe(r)SHAW', although it is as obsolete as 'Golly gumdrops!'

psyche Dr Guinevere Tufnell comments that *psyche* is not used in clinical psychiatry, and is mostly confined to Jungian analysis. It comes from the Greek word for breath or life. For people who are uneasy over using the word 'soul', because of the implication of God and immortality, *psyche* may be an acceptable alternative for what Jung called 'the inmost mystery of life'. *Psyche* is indefinable: we can only glimpse its meaning, something like the essential inner quality of a human being, that transcends their psychology and intelligence. (Pron: 'SYkee'.)

psychedelic The word came to light in America in the late 1950s as part of the mind-blowing drug cult. It was formed using *psyche* (see previous entry) and means literally 'revealing the soul'. Aldous Huxley was one of the first to use *psychedelic* in connection with his experiments with the drug **LSD**, to open what he called, in the title of a book written in 1954, *The Doors of Perception*.

Psychedelic became fashionable when Timothy Leary, a former Harvard professor, started the *Psychedelic Review* in 1963. Since then, *psychedelic* has been trivialized and is used about almost anything now from jazzily coloured men's pants to deafening sound effects or startling light changes intended to shock the senses and bedazzle the mind. See also **hallucinogenic**

psychiatry, psychology, psychotherapy or **psychoanalysis** *Psychiatry* is strictly a branch of medicine, the clinical application of psychology to the treatment of mental illness. A *psychiatrist* is a qualified medical doctor. *Psychology* is the umbrella term for the general study of behaviour and the mind in human beings and animals. The qualification of a *psychologist* is not specific, although most people who use that title have a university degree in the subject, but are not medical doctors. The word is used loosely for people who work in different fields: for example, a *sports psychologist* helps contestants, such as leading golfers and snooker players, to deal with the stress involved in their sports. *Psychologist* is used even more vaguely about anyone who appears to have an understanding of human nature ('she's a good psychologist, as she knows how to talk to people in the right way').

Psychotherapy is also an imprecise term. The psychiatrist, Dr Sophia Hartland, comments that 'Psychotherapy covers many different forms of helping people to overcome mental and emotional difficulties, listening to patients a good deal, allowing them the luxury of talking through their problems, as well as using other techniques. It specifically excludes drugs and surgery'.

Psychoanalysis is a form of psychotherapy, although some practitioners would dispute that, believing their work transcends therapy. A psychotherapist or a psychoanalyst may be a qualified doctor or might have followed a non-medical course of training. The latter are sometimes known as *lay analysts*. See also **psychoanalyst . . .; cathartic**

psychic or **psychical** Both words are interchangeable in that they can be used about paranormal phenomena, such as telepathy and spiritualism. Some people prefer to use *psychical* in that sense, reserving *psychic* as the descriptive word relating to **psyche**, that is for the innermost qualities of a human being. But this is not a distinction generally recognized, and *psychic* has become the most usual word for a person who has paranormal powers, with *psychical* as the descriptive word for the powers themselves, as in 'psychical research'.

psychoanalysis See **psychiatry . . .**; also next entry

psychoanalyst, analyst or **shrink** *Psychoanalyst* is the orthodox name for a practitioner who works with patients (or *analysands*, as they prefer to call them) on a one-to-one basis, exploring their unconscious, going back to their childhood, to help them come to terms with emotional problems of the present. As psychoanalysis became more familiar, *analyst* became the usual word for a psychoanalyst.

Analysands usually have a **love-hate** relationship with their analysts, and *head-shrinker* was used in America resentfully or contemptuously as a slang name for them. In the 1960s, this was replaced by *shrink*, used more warmly. *Shrink* is equally familiar in Britain, used for analysts mostly but also for any psychiatrist, and often affectionately: the journalist Valerie Grove commented on Anthony Clare, 'For a shrink he is refreshingly sceptical of psychiatric methods'. It is unlikely that Dr Clare would have been at all offended at being called a *shrink*.

psychobabble *Psychobabble*, a word coined on the West Coast of America (where else?) in the 1970s, is a felicitous combination of the overused *psycho-* prefix and *babble*, a word for incomprehensible chatter. When people rush in to explain every slip of the tongue as a **Freudian slip**, trace every hang-up and emotional problem to some agonized childhood conflict, we are wading through the muddy waters of *psychobabble*. Dictionaries write off *psychobabble* as slang, which is a pity, because the coinage is good enough, and useful enough, to have a place in standard English.

psychokinesis See **parapsychology . . .**

psycholinguistics or **semantics** There are two ways of looking at *psycholinguistics*. One treats it as relating to the way language is acquired and to psychological aspects of linguistic behaviour. The other view of the subject is that it concerns the study of the way words interrelate with our minds and emotions. Whether we like it or not, whenever we are reading or listening, writing or speaking, we are involved in psycholinguistics: we are being affected and are affecting others, not only by what the words are saying but by their emotional charge and our unconscious associations with them. Jung called this a symbolic meaning '. . . something more than its obvious and immediate meaning. It has a wider "unconscious" aspect that is never precisely defined or fully explained'.

Semantics comes close to this second explanation of *psycholinguistics*. It is a formal name for the branch of linguistics that studies meaning in language, not so much the meanings shown in dictionaries, but the way we are affected by words, their underlying meaning. Writers and poets are alert to this other meaning, since, as Jung believed, it often carries more weight than two-dimensional dictionary definitions. Words, he wrote, 'gain life and meaning only when you take into account their relationship to the living individual' (*Man and His Symbols*).

In popular use, *semantics* and the descriptive word *semantic* are often used to mean more or less the same as 'words' and 'verbal'. If you say something may be dismissed as a 'semantic argument' or as 'only semantics', and mean a 'verbal argument' or 'only playing with words', it would be clearer to put it that way.

psychological moment   Psychologists use *psychological moment* in a clinical sense, but in general use the phrase means the most effective moment or period when something is said or done, because all the factors are just right: 'He was relaxed and quiet, so it was the *psychological moment* to tell him what has really happened'.

psychology   See **psychiatry** . . .

psychosexual   Havelock Ellis (1859–1939), who was probably the first **sexologist**, had already used *psychosexual* before the end of the 19th century. But it was only in the more open discussion of sexual matters from the 1960s onwards, that *psychosexual* became more familiar, as a term for describing the relationship between sexual desire and performance, and mental attitudes and conditioning. For example, it is now considered that impotence in men is in most cases a psychosexual problem.

psychosis   See **neurotic** . . .

psychosomatic   'Somatic', from the Greek word for body, is a descriptive word for something related to the body only: *psychosomatic* relates the body to the mind. It is used most commonly about illnesses that are brought on or aggravated by mental stress. There is a medical school of thought that believes that most diseases are 'all in the mind'.

psychotherapy   See **psychiatry** . . .

psychotic   See **neurotic** . . .

psycho- words   *Psycho-* words proliferate, as the prefix (from a Greek word for 'life' or the 'soul') is added to subjects to create new subjects. Some of these, such as *psychometrics* (using tests for measuring the functioning of the mind) and **psychosexual**, belong to specialized branches of psychology. Others, especially the word *psychological* itself, are used and misused in a confusion of meanings and non-meanings. Some of the more common *psycho-* words are covered in the preceding entries.

Note that all *psycho-* words are now formed without a hyphen.

public domain   The term *public domain* is more familiar to publishers, broadcasters and writers than to other people. It refers to the copyright of text, music and illustrations. When something is *in the public domain* it usually means it is freely available to use, the most common reason being that more than 50 years have elapsed since the death of the writer or composer. But copyright is complicated and special rules can apply in many cases. It is worth noting that while the recipient of a letter owns the letter, the writer of it owns the copyright, and it is not in the public domain.

public or **bank holidays**   When banks were dignified and august institutions, the days on which they closed were given the authority of capital letters, *Bank Holidays*, which was the usual expression for *public holidays*. Since banks have vied with each other to seem more friendly and approachable, their solemnity has dropped away, which gives the expression *bank holiday* less dignity, although it is still commonly used. The more international term, found in most diaries, etc, for Christmas Day, Boxing Day, Good Friday and so on, is *public holiday*.

public or **council housing**   *Council housing* is a peculiarly British expression, and *public housing*, a term more likely to be used in other countries, is now heard more often in Britain. It is the better term for describing houses and flats built and financed by central and local government as a social service for those who cannot afford to buy their own homes, or as a concept of social responsibility, whichever viewpoint a prevailing government might take.

public interest or **of interest to the public**   The two expressions were first placed alongside one another to make a point during the pre-election campaign of 1992 in the UK. The comparison arose over the publication of details of a short affair that Paddy Ashdown, leader of the Liberal Democratic Party, had had with his secretary. Newspapers involved claimed there was an obligation to give news about matters of *public interest*, those things that legitimately concern the public. It is possible that sooner or later there will be a Privacy Act which will attempt to draw the line between legitimate *public interest* and what is *of interest to the public*, tittle-tattle that sells newspapers but is an unwarranted intrusion on someone's life.

(the) **public is** or **are**   Generally *the public* evokes a collective image and is better followed by a singular verb: 'the public *is* entitled to know . . .'. See also **collective words**

publicity   See PR . . .

Public Lending Rights   See PLR

public relations   See PR . . .

public, private, preparatory or **independent school**   *Public school* is a peculiarly British linguistic eccentricity. In the 16th century, a public school was a grammar school endowed for educating the public. Over subsequent centuries some of these became boarding schools, charging fees to the parents of pupils. By some curious hangover, the name *public school* remained, although such schools are anything but public: they are exclusive institutions for the highly privileged.

Winchester and Eton were founded in the 14th and 15th centuries respectively. But the modern concept of the English public school started with Thomas Arnold, headmaster of Rugby from 1828 to 1842. He set new standards, not only of teaching but of discipline, the 'team spirit' and human values as part of education. Public schools became recognized as offering the best education and influence on the formation of character for boys in their care. The remark, attributed to the Duke of Wellington, that 'the Battle of Waterloo was won on the playing fields of Eton' could, by the end of the 19th century, be extended to perhaps 30 other public schools. By that time, a new caste, the *public school man*, had emerged, and 'Where did you go to school?' had become a significant social question, on which appointments to important jobs or admission to certain clubs depended.

Private schools in Britain do not have the same prestige: it is a name for any school that offers an alternative to *state schools*, the usual term now for schools that are part of the free national educational system, which were formerly called *council schools*. As the name *public school* was restricted to certain private schools for boys, the equivalent schools for girls, mostly established in the 19th century, were usually called *private schools*.

Preparatory schools are junior versions of public schools. They take pupils from about the age of 9 and are directed at 'preparing' them for the entrance examination to public schools at the age of 13. At one time it was usual to call these schools 'private schools', but parents and pupils are more likely to say *prep schools* now.

This nomenclature is in a state of flux. At the 1985 conference of headmasters of public schools, it was decided to rename them *independent schools*, because *public school* had become too much associated with snobbery and social divisiveness. The problem with this name is that 'independent' can apply to any school that is not part of the state system, regardless of its standards and background. So the name has not caught on to any extent with the parents and pupils at public schools, although the term 'public school man' is probably used more hesitantly. Most public schools now admit girls, usually at sixth-form level, but no one talks about a 'public school woman'.

Foreigners, until they are initiated, blink with bewilderment at this educational terminology, especially Americans, for whom *public schools* are any schools maintained by public funds and open to all. See also **accents in speech**

public sector   See private sector . . .

pudding   See dessert . . .

pudding wine   See dessert . . .

puerile   See juvenile . . .

pun   *Puns* are often considered feeble linguistic jokes, to be derided and avoided. Yet a clever pun can bring a smile to our lips. Even Henry **Fowler**, notorious for his severity, acknowledged that puns can be 'good, bad and indifferent'. During the 1991 Gulf War, the BBC World Service deserved a modest mark for rising to the occasion by calling its programme broadcast in the area, *Gulf Link*. Newspaper headlines make particular use of puns, more often bad and indifferent than good (for examples, see **headlines**).

punctuation   Reading books on *punctuation* is like reading books on driving a car: it is not all that much help when you find yourself doing it. The different stops (, ; : . ? !) are there to divide up the flow of words into units of meaning, and the only purpose is to help the reader to take in written language more easily. Sometimes a simple comma makes all the difference: 'When it was time to eat knives and forks were put on the table'. Slip in a comma after 'eat' and you avoid a double take.

Punctuation is part of style and worth taking seriously. Graham Greene once offered an article to *The Observer*. A note was sent to him with the proof, saying that *one comma* had been added. His secretary telephoned to say that the comma must be deleted or the article could not be published.

The style generally in the 1990s is to use fewer commas and more full stops: sentences are shorter in keeping with the faster pace of life. Many people never use a semicolon (;), a less final way of ending a sentence than a full stop; and colons (:), almost full stops but not quite, are even less used. Why not try them out occasionally, to see how they feel? A semicolon has a touch of class about it, and a colon an air of authority.

Punctuation is an inexact science, more a matter of taste and commonsense than rules. See entries for **colon and semicolon; comma; exclamation mark; full stop; question mark.**

'Stokowski wrote something on his programme and passed it across the dinner-table to the beautiful Rumanian violinist. She was confounded by the sight of one large solitary *question mark*. She sent back her reply, from a girl of twenty to a magnificent man of ninety – an *exclamation mark*.'

John Georgiadis (BBC radio)

pundit or **pandit**   These are variations (both pronounced 'PUNdit') of the same word from Sanskrit. *Pandit* is the spelling when it is the title given to a Hindu scholar, particularly someone learned in Sanskrit, Indian philosophy and law. Jawaharlal Nehru, first prime minister of independent India, was respectfully called Pandit Nehru.

In Britain, the spelling *pundit* is more often than not used in mock-seriousness or contemptuously about a so-called expert, who is either long-winded or lays down the law with more authority than they are entitled to.

punk   *Punk* has existed, with various meanings, since the beginning of the 17th century, but mostly the word is associated with the working-class youth cult of the 1970s. It was used about young people who listen to loud and aggressive rock, who demonstrated their rejection of society by wild hairstyles and outlandish clothes. The number of active punks has dwindled and the word itself, like most easy-come-easy-go words based on styles of pop music, is more now an echo from the past.

pupil   See student . . .

puppet or **marionette**   There is a technical difference: *marionettes* are jointed figures operated from above by wires attached to their limbs, while *puppets* are smaller and fit over the hand like a glove, so they can be manipulated by the fingers. In practice, *marionette* has become less used, and *puppet* tends to be the word for all types. Marionettes are often called *string puppets* to distinguish them from *glove puppets* operated directly by the fingers.

purple heart   See amphetamine . . .

purse   See handbag . . .

pussy   Dictionaries include this slang word, dating back to the 17th century at least, for a woman's genitals, but call it vulgar or coarse slang. That's as may be, and without doubt some women do object to it. But others in Britain and America find *pussy*, used in this sense, quite a friendly word, because of 'pussycat'. Between lovers, pet names for sexual organs are natural. And Emma Soames, writing in *The Sunday Times* in 1991, had no worries about reviving that popular expression from the 1960s for extra short miniskirts, *pussy pelmets*.

putt or **put**   Dictionaries usually show *put* as a variant spelling for the stroke in golf, but at the Royal and Ancient Golf Club in St Andrews they wouldn't dream of spelling it any other way than *putt*. (It's the verb and noun for the gentle stroke in golf that pops the ball into the hole or gets it nearer to it.)

put up with   When Winston Churchill read a sentence that was turned upside down to avoid ending with a preposition, he is said to have written in the margin: 'This is the sort of English up with which I will not put'. He was insisting, by exaggeration, that it is good honest English to end a sentence with 'with', 'to', 'for', 'in' or any other preposition. See **prepositions**

pygmy or **pigmy**   Most dictionaries show both spellings as alternatives, but since the Latin word (derived from Greek), meaning from the elbow to fist, is spelt with a *y*, *pygmy* is preferred.

pyjamas or **pajamas**   In Britain people sleep in *pyjamas* and call them 'pe(r)DJAHme(r)s'; in America they sleep in *pajamas* and call them 'pe(r)DJAMMe(r)s'.

pyramid selling   The term dates from the 1960s. It is a disreputable system of selling the rights to sell a particular product or service to other people, rights that are then sold on further in a series of commercial sub-lettings. On the way, the people further down the 'pyramid' incur debts to people higher up and lose out, with only the people near the top of the pyramid doing well. The term is avoided now because it rightly acquired a bad name and legislation was introduced to prevent the worst abuses.

pyrrhic victory   Expressions from classical history are notoriously misused or misunderstood, which is often a good reason to avoid them. Pyrrhus, King of Epirus, defeated the Romans in Apulia in 279BC, but with such heavy losses that he was reported to have said 'One more such victory and we are lost'. A *pyrrhic victory* has remained down the ages an expression for a victory gained at such a high price that dire consequences follow: it does not mean a victory that turns sour or goes wrong for any other reason.

Perhaps *The Times* is allowed to assume that all its readers are versed in the conflict in the 3rd century BC between the Greeks and the expanding power of Rome, and to use as the heading for a leading article on the Chancellor of Germany, KOHL'S PYRRHIC VICTORY (9.5.1992). Why should the rest of us refer to an obscure event in ancient history when we want to say that the cost of achieving something was too high? Even *The Times* leader writer would have lost nothing and would have gained in clarity to have settled for KOHL PAYS TOO MUCH.

· Q ·

qua There are people who so much enjoy using the Latin word *qua* ('in the capacity of') that they use it even when it's inappropriate. When we look at a person or a thing from different points of view, *qua* has a place, and then both or more aspects have to be mentioned: 'he is marvellous *qua* lover but hopeless *qua* husband'. To say 'I am interested in him *qua* friend' is incomplete, because it only gives one angle. It needs to be completed: 'I am interested in him *qua* friend, not as a lover'. If we are not addicted to *qua*, in nearly all contexts 'as' can be substituted, as you can see by trying it out in the above examples. (Pron: 'KWAH'.)

quadraphonic Most cars are now fitted with *quadraphonic* sound systems as standard: it is just a high-tech way of saying four speakers. The spelling is extraordinarily varied: quadrophonic, quadruphonic and quadriphonic are all found, alongside the more usual *quadraphonic*. If you want to impress people, you can say your car has *quadraphonics* or *quadraphony* (pron: 'kwodROFFany'), which are other terms for the same thing.

Quai d'Orsay The Quai d'Orsay is an embankment of the Seine in Paris where the French Foreign Office is located. Both French and English use *Quai d'Orsay* for the Foreign Office itself ('the view of the Quai d'Orsay is . . .'), just as **Whitehall** is used for the British Government ('Whitehall sources suggest . . .').

quality *Quality* has been used occasionally as a descriptive word before nouns for centuries, but some of us still stop short of using it in ways such as 'a quality car', 'quality fish and chips'. It is too conservative now to regard this use as cheap advertising jargon, because it has become general usage. Applicants for British independent television franchises were required to meet 'the quality threshold'; 'quality Sundays' is the newscasters' term for certain newspapers; quality control' was already in use in the 1930s for maintenance of standards of production.

Nowadays *quality* is used almost more often as a descriptive word than it is as a noun. But when the secretary of the University Teachers Association spoke about 'the reputation British universities have for turning out a quality product', some wrinkling of the nose was still justified.

quango *Quango* is an **acronym** imported from America in the 1960s for quasi-autonomous non-governmental organization. *Quangos* are supposedly independent bodies with statutory powers in the area they operate in. What makes people uneasy is that the government controls their finance and appoints the senior officers, so *quango* is often used in a derogatory way for rubber-stamping committees that are a waste of tax-payers' money.

quantitative or **quantitive** Both forms exist. There are linguistic arguments for preferring *quantitative*, but the awkward run of *t*s (more awkward still with *quantitatively*) has made the shorter variant *quantitive* (and *quantitively*) the more usual form.

quantity See **amount** . . .

quantum jump and **quantum leap** Everyday language adapts, uses and misuses scientific terms to suit itself. A physicist may use *quantum jump* only when talking of changes in the emission of energy in molecules, etc. But *quantum jump* and *quantum leap* have become accepted since the 1950s as a trendy way of saying a sudden and large increase or development: 'introducing this new product will bring about a quantum jump in our profits'; 'if we are to meet this challenge, there must be a quantum leap in our thinking'.

quarter days The four *quarter days* do not divide the year equally into four periods. They are arbitrary dates using certain saint's days, accepted by law, to mark the four quarters of the year, and used for dates when quarterly charges become due. In England, these are 25 March, 24 June, 29 September and 25 December. In Scotland they are different: 2 February, 15 May, 1 August and 11 November.

quarto This is a printing term for a size of paper based on folding a specified sheet into four. *Quarto* used to be the standard size of commercial writing paper, but looks old-fashioned now: since metrication the standard size of business writing paper is larger, A4 (approx 297×210mm). See **paper sizes**

quartz Quartz is a common crystalline mineral. The word is familiar now as a descriptive term in two ways. Quartz *watches and clocks* are operated by vibrations from a quartz crystal, powered by a small battery. A quartz *lamp* is a cube made from quartz filled with mercury vapour, which lights up.

quash or **squash**   *Quash* and *squash* are confusing. They both go back to the same source in Old French, linked with the current French word 'casser' (to break something or to crush stones). It is more a matter of custom which word is used in which context.

Rebellions are *quashed*, that is crushed or put down; arguments and legal judgements are *quashed*, that is cancelled out or rejected.

Fruits are *squashed* into a pulp, and passengers are *squashed* into trains. *Squash* is also used, although less commonly, in the same way as *quash* for suppressing a revolution or dismissing an argument. When it comes to deflating a person by some crushing remark, they are *squashed* rather than *quashed*.

Only *squash* can be used as a noun for a crowd of people, or for a concentrated fruit drink diluted with water (orange squash).

quasi   *Quasi*, the Latin word for 'almost', can be attached by a hyphen to other words to show that something is nearly something, but doesn't quite make it. A body can be quasi-governmental (see **quango**), quasi-official, quasi-political. Even the pronunciation hasn't made up its mind: 'KWAYzeye' or 'KWAHzee', with a preference for the former.

queen   The word *queen* (sometimes spelt *quean*) is one of the few old slang words for a homosexual that has survived (at the end of 1984, a new book about homosexuals was called *Queens*). A *queen* is usually an ageing homosexual who affects a particularly lordly manner. Paul Bailey once described, in *The Observer*, Ernest Thesiger's comment on fighting at the front in Flanders, 'My dear, the *noise*! And the *people*!', as 'a perfect example of queenly humour'.

Queen's English   Language schools in foreign countries may still specify in advertisements for teachers of English that applicants must be speakers of the *Queen's English*. You are not likely to hear the term much in Britain now, except perhaps from a few linguistic flag-wavers. The Queen's English is not so much the way the Queen speaks, but is usually taken to mean the language as spoken by the middle class in England, free from marked social or regional variations. This is more a matter of pronunciation and accent, although the aforesaid flag-wavers might well demand that it includes a severely prescriptive attitude towards English grammar.

In general, the term *Queen's English* should be avoided, because for some people it has snobbish or imperialistic undertones. The terms that scholars use are **British English**, standard English and **received pronunciation**. See also **accents in speech**

queer   At one time *queer* was the most common word, used especially by heterosexuals about homosexuals. In the 1990s, it is used so much less that it may soon be possible again for anyone to feel queer, meaning slightly ill, or to use the word for someone who is peculiar or eccentric. But wait a while, because *queer* is not yet completely out of quarantine. See also **gay**

query or **question**   As nouns, *query* and *question* are almost interchangeable. 'I have a query' suggests there is something you haven't understood: 'I have a question' can mean that as well, but also that there is something else you need to know.

As verbs, both words are sharper, usually suggesting doubt or even suspicion: 'I want to query (or question) that' implies quite strongly that you are not satisfied with what you have read or heard. Otherwise, it is better to use *question* as a noun: 'I want to ask a question about that' is a neutral request for further information.

Question arises in a number of expressions which can lead to ambiguity or misuse: see **academic** (question), **beg the question**, **leading question**, **no question** and **rhetorical question**

questionable   See **debatable** . . .

question mark   In most cases there's no problem over using *question marks*: they come at the end of a question. There are a few instances which are worth looking at more carefully.

1   When the question is indirect, a question mark at the end of the sentence is out of place: 'I am writing to ask if we can meet some time Thursday afternoon' (no question mark).

2   If a question is used as a polite way of making a request, a question mark makes it even more polite, while a full stop makes it nearer to a command: 'Would you meet me Thursday afternoon?' or 'Would you meet me Thursday afternoon.'

3   In some cases, the choice between a question mark and an **exclamation mark** changes both the meaning and intonation: 'Really?' or 'Really!'; 'Never?' or 'Never!'; 'You did that?' or 'You did that!'

questionnaire   It has become slightly affected to pronounce *questionnaire* with a *k* sound ('kestje(r)-NAIRE'), although for the time being dictionaries continue to show this as a variant pronunciation. It is better now to begin the word with a *kw* sound.

queueing or **queuing**   *Queueing* looks right but *queuing* is an alternative spelling. Dictionaries differ in their preference.

quiche   see **tart**

quick or **quickly**   *Quickly* is grammatically correct but *quick* is normal idiomatic usage, especially when it's a command: 'I don't care how it's done, but do it quick'; 'It's urgent, come quick!' In other contexts, and usually in writing, *quickly* is to be preferred. See also **slow** . . .

quick   See **fast** . . .

quick fix or **papering over the cracks**   The school of business administration at Harvard University defines *quick fix* as 'The too simple solution. The latest fad'. *Papering over the cracks* implies a cover-up, making things look good for the time being. You might get away with a quick fix, if things go your way, but papering over the cracks, in its literal sense, is a term for cheap decorating, and experience shows that cracks soon show through again.

As we would expect, *quick fix* and *papering over the cracks* are often used in and about politics, often justifiably.

quicksilver   See mercury . . .

quilt   See duvet . . .

quire and **ream**   These are both old printing terms, going back to the 15th century, for quantities of paper. *Quire* relates to the Latin word for a set of four (compare 'quarter') and was used originally for four sheets of parchment folded in half to form eight pages, a standard unit in medieval manuscripts. In printing, *quire* came to be used for 24 sheets of paper, and is now the standard term for 25 sheets, one-twentieth of a *ream*, a box or packet of 500 sheets, which is how paper is usually sold. See also **paper sizes**

quit or **quitted**   *Quit* is a 14th-century word for leaving or giving up something, and it had almost fallen into disuse in Britain, except for the legal term 'notice to quit', meaning a formal notice given to a tenant to vacate a property. But *quit* remained alive in America and came back across the Atlantic with Hollywood gangster films. It is now well-established in Britain, a sharp and brisk alternative to resign, giving up, abandoning, surrendering, etc.

Dictionaries show *quitted* and *quit* as alternative past forms, in that order. Because of American influence, the truth is that *quitted*, while correct of course, sounds formal: 'she quit the job last month' is more usual than 'she quitted the job . . .'.

quite   There is an argument for giving up the word *quite* for Lent. It conveys so many different meanings, and is often meaningless in writing, as we need to hear the intonation to know where we stand. A phrase can take on many different nuances.

When the following word is a superlative, there is no ambiguity, for *quite* intensifies the superlativeness: quite superb, quite marvellous, quite lovely. *Quite a* before a descriptive word means the same as 'moderately': 'quite a good wine'; 'quite a large flat'. . . . But *quite a* directly before a noun suggests admiration, although it is more conversational than written English: 'she's quite a pianist'; 'this is quite a restaurant'. In New York, there is usually no need to feel put out if you're told that something you've done is *quite good*, as there it is more likely to mean first-rate.

Quite or *quite so* are possibly the most noncommittal responses in the English language: they can mean almost anything from 'I agree' to 'So what?', or can be no more than a vague social comment to fill a gap in the conversation. But if we add an **exclamation mark** (Quite so!), it changes the expression to one of emphatic agreement. When Patricia Beer quoted a

remark from a book, in an article in the *London Review of Books*, 'Why have you made sex a problem? . . . Get on with it or drop it but don't make a problem of it', she commented *Quite so* (minus an exclamation mark).

***quite*, *most* and *more* excellent**   See **excellent**

quiz (as a verb)   The verb *quiz* goes back to the late 18th century, in the sense of poking fun at someone: a *quizzing-glass* was an old name for a monocle, because it could be used to give someone a funny look, and the meaning survives in *quizzical*, meaning mildly amusing, as in 'a quizzical look' for a questioning or whimsical look.

Quiz shows, which date from the early 1940s in America, have long since taken over the word, and the verb *quiz* now carries with it the implication of putting a person on the spot by asking searching questions. It's better not to use it unless that nuance is intended.

quorate and **inquorate**   These are new words, dating from the 1970s. See next entry

quorum   The word is used loosely for a sufficient number of people at a meeting to make it worthwhile, but often in a specific sense in connection with official bodies or societies, such as shareholders in companies or members of committees. Usually a prescribed minimum number at meetings is laid down by law or in the constitution of the organization, before binding decisions can be taken, or specified as a minimum proportion of the total number of members.

It is not unknown for people to show off their Latin by using the plural form 'quora'. Don't be tempted: in English, it is one *quorum*, two or more *quorums*.

A new descriptive word, dating from the 1970s, is being used more often: a 'quorate meeting' is one at which there is a prescribed quorum, and when a meeting is *inquorate* (pron: 'inKWAWrayt' or sometimes 'INkwawrayt'), there are not enough members present to consitute a quorum.

Quorum, etc begins with a *kw-* sound: 'KWAW-re(r)m' ('KAWre(r)m' is not an acceptable pronunciation).

quotation or **citation**   In the sense of reproducing the words of a short passage from a text, *quotation* is the more usual word and covers most cases. The alternative, *citation*, is appropriate when a quotation is used to back up an argument: 'the minister used two citations from his earlier speeches to demonstrate that government policy had not changed'.

Citation has the additional meanings for the mention of an individual's act of bravery in official war despatches, and for the words used to give the reasons for an honour or award.

A *quotation* or *citation* (in the sense first described) should be exactly word-for-word as it appears in the original. This does not apply to using the verb *cite* (see **quote or cite**). If words or a section are omitted, or the quotation begins in the middle of a sentence, three dots in the appropriate place is the standard way to indicate this: '. . . we shall fight on the beaches, we shall fight on the landing grounds, . . . we shall never surrender' (Winston Churchill, 4 June 1940).

Quotation has, of course, the additional meaning of an estimate of a price and, on the Stock Exchange, a current price for shares or commodities.

See also **next entry**

quotation or **quote (as a noun)** Dictionaries persist in labelling the abbreviation *quote*, for *quotation*, as colloquial or informal. Nevertheless, *quote* is so much the most usual word on news programmes ('Here are some quotes from today's newspapers'), that the word in full, *quotation*, would seem too formal. *Quote* is also the most convenient short noun for **quotation marks**, when reading aloud or dictating: see **quote/unquote**.

Except in the most formal contexts, there's no need for misgivings about using *quote* or *quotes* in place of the longer word *quotation* (the abbreviation has respectable antecedents, as it goes back to the 19th century).

quotation marks, **quotes** or **inverted commas** All three terms mean the same, single (' ') or double (" ") commas above the line. *Inverted commas* is the older term, with *quotation marks* the usual one now. *Quotes* is the everyday abbreviation, as in 'Put that in quotes please'.

Quotation marks are used in various ways, mostly to encase sentences to show they are the actual words written or spoken. Using them correctly in all cases is a daunting business, even for experienced writers. For most general purposes, the following guidelines are all you need:

1 *The position of punctuation marks relative to quotation marks*

(i) When a full stop, question mark or exclamation mark at the end of the quoted passage coincides with the end of the overall sentence, another full stop is not required.

She said, 'I love you.' (not '. . . you.'.)
She asked, 'Do you love me?' (not '. . . me?'.)
She shouted, 'Go to hell!' (not '. . . hell!'.)

(ii) When the overall sentence continues, the quoted passage is followed by a comma within the quotation marks: 'I'd like you to meet my husband,' she said, introducing a dark, good-looking man.

(iii) When punctuation properly belongs to a quoted passage, it goes within the quotation marks: 'I wonder,' she said, 'do you know Jack?' When the punctuation does not relate to the quoted passage it goes outside the quotation marks: 'I wonder', she said, 'whether you know Jack.'

(iv) When a quoted passage is a question or exclamation, and is part of a longer sentence, only include the question/exclamation mark at the end of the main sentence: 'Did you ask your husband "Why are you late for dinner"?' (Not '. . . dinner?"?') It is far better t avoid this problem where possible by rephrasing the sentence: 'Did you ask your husband why he was late for dinner?'

2 Writing what someone thinks is not usually regarded as a direct quotation, so quotation marks are not required: I wonder whether I . . . should believe him, she asked herself. (No quotation marks round: I should believe him.)

3 In print, italics are used for titles of books, operas, etc. When writing by hand, or when italics are not available, quotation marks can be used instead: 'The Satanic Verses', 'The Good English Guide', 'Carmen'. These are not required for the names of houses, pubs, hotels, etc: The Old Rectory, Rose Cottage, the Bull and Bush. Nor should they be used for brand names: 'Do you believe Persil gives you a whiter wash?'

4 It is a snobbish mannerism to put quotation marks round words or expressions to show they are downmarket or ill-educated: in Coronation Street, they eat 'meat and two veg' at 1 o'clock for their Sunday 'dinner'.

5 Single quotation marks are usual now and double ones are old-fashioned, although still required when there is a secondary quotation within the primary one: He announced, 'After the orchestra plays the overture from "Don Giovanni", there will be an interval.'

There are a number of other rules for the use of quotation marks (most of them are in **Hart's Rules**, Oxford University Press), but they are more the concern of editors and proofreaders.

quote or **cite** To *cite* a passage or comment, or to *cite* an example, is to submit it as evidence or as an illustration proving or explaining a particular point: 'I shall cite two authorities to confirm the point I have made'. Cite can also be used for presenting the factors in a situation: 'I shall *cite* all the reasons that led up to this decision'. When you *cite* something from a book or other source, a paraphrase can be used instead of the actual words: 'she cited the minister as having said that Britain must play a central role in Europe'.

We might *quote* something merely out of interest, not necessarily using it in an argument, as in the case of *cite* (see above). Or we may *quote* lines of poetry because they say what we think better than we could express it ourselves. Or, less justifiably, we might *quote* in order to show how well-read we are. In all cases, the verb *quote* assumes that the exact words in the original are used. For the accepted way of indicating that some words are omitted, see **quotation or citation**

quote (as a noun) See **quotation or quote (as a noun)**

quote/unquote *Quote and unquote* in speech is useful when reading aloud or dictating, to indicate that words or a passage are between **quotation marks**. In ordinary conversation, this convention seems clumsy: 'She said to me *quote* I am truly so grateful for the help John has given me *unquote*'. There are other ways round it: 'She said to me – and these are her actual words – I am truly so grateful . . .'.

The problem does not, of course, arise in writing, where *quotation marks* can be slipped in wherever they are required.

qv See **see** . . .

qwerty The word for the standard layout of keys on English-language typewriters and keyboards of wordprocessors and computers is known as *qwerty* ('the machine has a *qwerty* keyboard'). Why such a strange name? For once, the answer is simple and uncomplicated: it is an **acronym** formed from the first six keys on the top row of letters on keyboards, Q W E R T Y.

· R ·

r sound   See **intrusive** *r* **sound**

rabbi   There is a common misunderstanding about this Jewish title: although there are rabbis who minister the same rites as a vicar or a priest (birth, marriage, death, etc), the title has a different meaning. The first meaning of *rabbi* is still the way the name has been used in English since the 14th century: it is a man learned in Hebraic law and the *Torah*, the books of the Old Testament ascribed by tradition to Moses. In this sense, the title *rabbi* is one of respect, not necessarily a religious office.

In more general use, a *rabbi* is the minister of a synagogue and the leader of a Jewish community, carrying out a religious and social role corresponding to the work of a minister in the Church.

race or **people**   It is not always easy any longer to use *race* in a neutral way, for one of the groups of the human species that can be defined by physical characteristics, without someone picking up a discriminatory nuance. No one is put out if we refer to the *human race*, because that brings in all of us. But in some other contexts, *race* has become tainted with *racism* (see next entry). The words sound similar.

It is going much too far to suggest that the word *race* is taboo, and it is, of course, appropriate in anthropological and ethnic contexts. There are no rules, because people may react in different ways to the word. All that can be said is that *race* is now a word to watch at times, to avoid giving offence When in doubt, there is the simple alternative *people*: the Chinese people, the North African people. . . .

racism, racialism and **racial**   The arguments for distinguishing between *racialism* and *racism* are out-of-date. Both *isms* were rare before the 1930s, were not included in the original *Oxford English Dictionary*, and only in the Addenda to the later *Shorter Oxford English Dictionary* (1933). The prejudice existed (when Paul Robeson played Othello at the Savoy Theatre in London in 1930, he was unwelcome upstairs in the Savoy Hotel), but no words were commonly used to describe it.

To begin with, *racism* (pron: 'RAYsizm') was used for a biological theory that specific human characteristics and abilities are determined by race, for example that Jews tend to be especially talented as musicians, or that Afro-Caribbeans make marvellous dancers because they have natural rhythm. That is no more than a harmless generalization. But when this was extended to intelligence and cultural potential, racism became *racialism* (pron: 'RAYsherlizm'), a belief in the inherent superiority of one race over another that gives rise to prejudice and discrimination. It has been said *racism* is the theory, *racialism* the practice. Few people understand this distinction or are even aware of it. *Racism* and the corresponding word, *racist* (pron: 'RAYsist'), are now the words for hostility and prejudice of one race towards another. *Racialism* and *racialist*, still in dictionaries, are not often heard.

Racial (pron: 'RAYshal'), like the word **race**, is not in itself pejorative: 'the racial characteristics of the Anglo-Saxons'. But anything to do with *race* is such a sensitive issue that even these innocent words should be used with care (see previous entry and next entry).

racist words   There is nothing new about *racist words*. The ancient Greeks recognized an archetypal fear of people who are different, by giving it a name, 'xenophobia' (fear of strangers). And they introduced one of the first of all *racist words*, **barbarian**, for people who spoke a seemingly uncivilized language which, to the Greeks, might have sounded like the bleating of sheep ('baa-baa').

Racist words used to be taken for granted: many people in Britain used the word **wog**, for example, about almost any foreigner ('*Wogs* begin at Calais').

A glossary of racist words and other words that could give offence, published by the school of journalism at the University of Missouri, turns English into a minefield. At every turn, we apparently run the risk of treading on someone's toes. The slang verb *gyp*, for example, for swindling someone, might, we are told, offend **Gypsies**, although the origin of the word has nothing to do with them; the exclamation *Ugh!*, expressing disgust, could, it is said, offend American Indians; some people feel it is more courteous to say a person is *Jewish*, in case the word **Jew** is considered derogatory; *Asiatic* is now usually regarded as racist, only to be used in scientific and geographical contexts (see **Asian . . .**); 'nigger' brown' has disappeared from colour charts; **non-white**, used in Britain occasionally by official organizations, is offensive in South Africa as part of the language of **apartheid**; Robertson's, the marmalade makers, have had no end of trouble over their traditional symbol of a *golliwog*.

We can say all this is getting out of hand, but we are living in a multiracial society where reactions are hypersensitive to any hint of linguistic prejudice.

Everyone has an obligation to be on guard about using words and expressions that perpetuate conscious and unconscious racial prejudices. See also **black** . . .; **Caucasian**; **dago**; **half-caste** . . .; **white**

rack or **wrack** A *rack* was an instrument of torture on which a victim's limbs were progressively stretched (we still say someone is 'on the *rack*' when they are suffering great pain). The extended use is the verb *rack*, meaning to put under strain, as in **nerve-racking** or to *rack* one's brains.

Centuries ago, the *w* crept into the verb as an error, perhaps because *wrack* was an alternative for 'wreck': it survives in the phrase 'wrack and ruin' which, to confuse matters more, is shown by some dictionaries as 'rack and ruin'.

Although *wrack* remains included in most dictionaries as a variant of the verb *rack*, it is best forgotten and sooner or later will become obsolete.

For wine lovers, *racking*, taken from an old Provençal word, is drawing wines from the first casks it has been stored in into fresh casks.

racket or **racquet** It is time dictionaries stopped showing *racquet* as a variant spelling for 'tennis racket', because you'd get a very funny look at Wimbledon if you spelt it that way.

In all other senses of the word, racket is the only possible spelling, where people are kicking up a racket, running a racket to get rich quick, or in the slang expression for someone's occupation ('What's your racket?').

racking See rack . . .

racquet See racket . . .

radical *Radical* comes from Latin 'radix' (root) and so long as the word relates to that source, its meaning is clear: a *radical* solution or approach goes back to square one, the opposite to a **quick fix**.

In politics, *radical* has become a relative word, because the meaning has changed at different periods: political equality between men and women, for example, was radical in the 1920s, but accepted in the 1930s. *Radical* in politics tends now to be associated with extreme, even revolutionary socialism, although as a noun, a radical is sometimes used for any politician who argues against the party line.

Radical has been extended to cover the whole range of human thought: anything that departs from established ideas about art, education, medicine, etc is radical, without any agreement about how far-out that departure must be. Whether something is radical or not can be an attitude of mind.

radii or **radiuses** *Radii* is the more usual plural form of *radius*, but no one should argue with *radiuses*, the alternative form shown in dictionaries.

radio, **wireless** or **transistor** In 1956, according to a BBC survey, more people said *wireless*

than *radio*. That is not true in the 1990s, for *wireless* now sounds middle-aged, if not elderly. For a while *transistor* (the name for the electronic conductor that amplifies signals) became the standard word for young people. But now *radio* is the word used by nearly everybody. **Steam radio**, implying that *radio* is antiquated alongside television, has dropped out since *radio* regained so much popularity.

radiographer or **radiologist** In medicine, both names could apply to someone trained to work with X-rays. In practice, the terms are kept separate from each other. *Radiographer* is used for a trained technician who takes X-rays. A *radiologist* is a medical doctor who interprets X-rays and uses radiology to treat diseases.

radiuses See radii . . .

ragtime See jazz . . .

railway or **railroad** The steam locomotive was invented well after American independence, so railway terminology tended to go in different ways on either side of the Atlantic. For example, the 'line' in Britain is the 'track' in America, the British make 'return journeys', while Americans go on **round trips**.

Railway and *railroad* have got mixed up over the centuries. *Railroad* was already in use in 18th-century England for the rails along which something was pulled or transported. The word went out of use but survived in America, which left people thinking it was an American word in the first place.

In Britain, *railway* became, and still is, the standard term. In America, although *railroad* is more common and always used for main lines, *railway* also comes in for use, especially for local services using shorter trains.

Railroad re-entered British English as the verb, imported from America, meaning to rush an agreement through (often a Bill through parliament) without giving way to opposition.

railway buff Why *buff* for an enthusiast about railways? It recalls long-forgotten amateur firemen in New York. See **buff**.

rain check Americans have adapted this expression usefully, while the British misuse it altogether when they say, 'I'll just go outside to take a rain check', meaning to see if it's raining.

To begin at the beginning, a *rain check* at baseball was originally a ticket stub that permits someone to see another game if rain cancels a game or stops play. It is a neat two-syllable term, which the Wimbledon tennis authorities should long ago have substituted for the weighty phrase they prefer: 'Substitute ticket in the event of rain washing out play'.

Rain check is usefully adapted in the expression 'take a rain check', for an invitation you cannot accept at the time, but would like to have offered again when you're free. People also say, 'I'll take a rain check', to get out of an invitation they don't want to accept. (But what do they say when they're asked a second time?)

raincoat, mackintosh or mac   It seemed that the Scottish chemist, Charles Macintosh (1766–1843), who invented a waterproof material, would be remembered for ever, because every time it rained, people put on a *mackintosh* or a *mac* (also spelt *macintosh* and *mack*). But the words are used much less often now and may eventually die out, as most people say *raincoat*.

In the world of computers *Macintosh* and *Mac* are eponymous words in a completely different context; a *Macintosh* is a **microcomputer** made by a company called Apple, and is also known as an *Apple Mac*.

rain forest   Although *rain forests* can occur in any region where there is a pronounced rainy season, this descriptive term is usually synonymous with tropical forests, particularly in the basin of the Amazon and in Africa, Borneo and New Guinea. It became an emotive expression in the 1980s as the world woke up to the destruction of the forests, the impoverishment of the environment, and endangering species such as gorillas, orang-utans and tigers which depend on these forests for their habitat.

The poor countries of the world, where most of the rain forests are, want to exploit them commercially; the rich countries want them preserved in their pristine state. This conflict dominated the Earth Summit in Rio de Janeiro in June 1992.

raise or rise   For the use of *raise* or *rise* for an increase in pay, see **rise**. . . .

raison d'être   This is one of those foreign expressions that is useful because there is no natural equivalent in English. *Raison d'être* (French for 'reason for being') is the reason why something is there, so the *raison d'être* of a lift is to save walking up the stairs. Used about a person, *raison d'être* can mean the justification of their job in an organization, or can have the more profound meaning of a purpose for living. It should be pronounced in the best French you can muster (approx 'rayzo(hn)DETTr(e)').

rake or roué   Both words are old-fashioned names for a man who is dissolute, drinks and eats too much, seduces women and in general leads a debauched life. A *rake* is a younger man, a *roué* older. As a guide, up to 45 to 50, a man can be a rake; after that age, if he hasn't reformed, he is a roué.

rake-off   We should hesitate before using *rake-off* for a legitimate fee or commission made for negotiating a deal. For *rake-off* implies for most people an underhand arrangement to pay or receive money for one reason or another. It is a gambling expression that goes back to the late 19th century in America and probably comes from the rake used by a croupier in a gambling saloon.

Ralph   *Ralph* is one of the few names to appear as an entry in *The Good English Guide*, because there is

still a snobbish divide over how it should be pronounced. People who might think of themselves as superior in such matters, pointedly avoid sounding the *l* and say 'Rafe'. In most cases, this is a pronunciation they've picked up, rather than an awareness that 'Rafe' was the spelling in the 17th century. 'Ralf' has become the usual pronunciation, and the only one used in America.

RAM   A common computer **acronym** taken from the words random-access memory. In effect, it is the storage capacity of a computer measured in kilobytes (see **byte**). The word *random* means that any part of the data can be called up out of sequence (see next entry).

random   *Random* carries with it a mathematical and philosophical concept. Random numbers in an operation occur with equal probability and for that reason are unpredictable. At the same time, a deterministic view of life suggests that *random* is no more than a word we use because we are unable to perceive an underlying pattern, which may nevertheless exist. We need to remember this when we use the word *random*.

In statistics, a *random error* is an error that is not consistent all the way through but occurs arbitrarily, distorting results in individual tables but taken as balancing out overall.

random error   See previous entry

randy   *Randy* has been used since the mid-19th century about a man or a woman who is sexually aroused. It is still rated slang by some dictionaries, but was accepted as standard English as long ago as 1976 by the *Concise Oxford Dictionary*. *Randy* can sound indelicate, in spite of what dictionaries say, so take care where you use it. Not that there is an easy alternative, except to keep quiet about how you feel.

rank and file   Originally a military term for ordinary soldiers, footsloggers in the infantry, it has become extended to mean the general body of people in any organization. *Rank and file* is a favourite expression in reports on trade union proceedings, to refer to the mass of trade union members, as against the officials. But in the House of Commons, it would be considered disrespectful to refer to the generality of MPs as the rank and file, so political commentators fall back on 'back-benchers', which comes to the same thing.

rap   In America, *rap* (short for *rap music*) has been called the dominant force in pop music of the 1990s. *Rap* has the strong beat of rock music but the words are chanted or recited rather than sung. It defies our ideas of what a song should be, as the whole focus is on the words and the intensity of the rhythmic backing.

rape or seduction   The word, in the sense of forcing a woman to have sexual intercourse, goes back to the 15th century. The attempt to define it began in earnest in the 1980s. *Rape* comes from the Latin verb 'rapere' (seize), and the classic idea of rape is a man dragging a woman into a lonely place and demanding sex at knife-point. Far more common now is **date rape**, for surveys show the majority of rapes and attempted rapes are committed by a man already known to the woman.

The problem of defining rape has become a battle in the courtrooms. The law accepts that a woman does not lose her right to refuse sexual intercourse because she has accepted an invitation to visit a man in his flat or hotel room. In 1992 an American court rejected the contention that this implied consent when a jury found Mike Tyson guilty of rape, although Desiree Washington had visited his hotel room alone during the night. The defence lawyers introduced the term *consensual sex*, which may become a standard legal expression.

At what point does seduction end and rape begin? Or is the word *seduction*, in a sexual sense, outmoded? Encouraging a woman to drink too much or putting psychological and social pressures on her, which at one time would have been considered seduction, could now be interpreted as 'unlawful sexual intercourse with a woman who . . . does not consent to it' (the accepted definition of rape). In those terms, rape within marriage is now recognized. An American writer, Stephanie Gutman, argues that 'the word *rape* is being stretched to encompass behaviour most of us would consider innocent' (*The Independent*). It is the courts not the lexicographers who now have to draw the line between rape and seduction.

rapport It shows more linguistic savoir faire to say 'I have a rapport with her' rather than a 'good rapport'. For a 'bad rapport' is not possible, since the word implies a good, harmonious or cooperative relationship.

Although *rapport* has been used in English since the mid-17th century, the pronunciation has not become anglicized. As in French, the *t* is not sounded: 'raPAW'. Some Americans do sound the final *t*.

rapt or **wrapped** *Rapt* is the only surviving form of an obsolete verb that derived from the same source as **rape**, Latin 'rapere' (seize). But the meaning is poetic, not violent: to be *rapt* is to be carried away by an idea, a thought, a vision. We can listen with rapt attention, be rapt in thought, rapt in melancholy. . . .

Because *wrapped* has the same sound, there are examples of it being used, even by good writers, unthinkingly in mistake for *rapt*. In fact, when *wrapped* is followed by 'up' it can have a similar meaning, as an extension of the usual meaning of *wrap*, to envelop something in a material ('she is wrapped up in her work'). Otherwise, the word we want is *rapt*.

rase See raze . . .

rate of exchange See exchange rate

rather David Dabydeen, a West Indian poet and university lecturer working in England, pinpointed

rather as an 'upper-class term' (*The State of the Language*, 1990). It reaches down into the middle-class as a way of avoiding being too outspoken: 'I'm rather hungry', 'She's rather overdressed', 'This is rather good'. . . . Used in this way, *rather* seemingly softens the harshness of criticism, or modifies a comment, even if it does sound *rather* wishy-washy.

Rather! (with the stress on the second syllable: 'raTHER') is an emphatic way of saying 'Yes!', the middle/upper-class equivalent of 'Not 'alf!': 'Would you like a drink? RaTHER!' This should be left firmly in Bertie Wooster or Howard Weybridge (as Jilly Cooper calls his successor) country, where it belongs.

rationalize Be on guard against *rationalize*. It is a word that sounds reasonable, logical and fair-minded, and is used all the time in business and service organizations to justify putting us to trouble and inconvenience by closing down branches, hospitals, train services, etc, usually in the interests of making more profit.

Rationalize, in this sense, dates from the mid-1920s, and became increasingly fashionable in the 1980s. The word is also used in an equally doubtful way about people's emotions: 'Let us rationalize your fears, your being in love, your doubts . . .' is a way of saying let us bring reason to bear on emotions that are, by their very nature, irrational.

Look out for *rationalize* and don't trust it too much.

rat-race *Rat-race* appeared in America in the late 1930s as the name of a jazzy dance (compare 'jitterbug'). Within a few years it was extended as a term for the feverish activity of competitive life in business. Since then it has been extended still further for the scramble to get to the top, or merely to survive, in any activity.

People caught up in the heat and dust of the rat-race in business, politics, medicine, international organizations, etc often talk about 'leaving the rat-race', but not many of them do.

raunchy See sexy . . .

raze or **rase** *Raze* is the usual spelling of *rase*, which, although shown as a variant in dictionaries, is an older spelling now obsolete. Although *raze* means to demolish a building completely, the expression *raze to the ground* is too well established and familiar to object to the admittedly unnecessary words 'to the ground'.

razzmatazz or **razzle-dazzle** Both words are older than you might think. They go back to the late 19th century, American of course, but with different meanings to begin with: *razzmatazz* was used about an early form of jazz, and a good word for it too, and *razzle-dazzle* was a word for fun and excitement, 'having a ball'.

Both words are used now for a 'showbiz' atmosphere, over-the-top publicity used in launching new products, promoting a show, etc. *Razzmatazz* (sometimes spelt razzamatazz) is the more popular word now: it was associated particularly with the extravaganza of US elections, but would not be out of place now for elections in Britain.

Some dictionaries write off both words as slang, others accept *razzle-dazzle* as standard English and classify *razzmatazz* as colloquial, which is making such a fine point that you can hardly see it. The truth is both words are well-established and can be considered standard English to be used even in a text-book context.

R & D See **research and development**

re To use *re* instead of 'about' ('We are writing re your order . . .') is mindless **business English**. This does not apply to the legal use, where *re* is often included in the formal title of briefs and other documents.

re or **re-** See **hyphens/5**

-re or **-er** It jars on some British readers to read center, fiber, theater and similar words in American English. Yet it seems no more than a reasonable anglicization of French or Old French words. No one in Britain shudders at the spelling, for example, of *meter* when it is used to denote a measuring gauge, as in parking meter, gasometer, etc (see **metre . . .**). Nevertheless, there is no sign of the *-er* spelling in most words of this kind being accepted as an authorized variant in British English. The *-er* spelling should be retained in American proper names, such as The Kennedy Center, Washington DC.

reactionary *Reactionary* has become a value judgement of anyone who objects to change. It presupposes that all change equals progress, which evidence has disproved. *Reactionary* can also be subjective, used about someone or an attitude that opposes a change we want to bring about. When we read or hear a person or a decision described as *reactionary*, we need to look further to decide whether the word is being used about stiff-necked obscurantism or whether it is a worthwhile desire not to 'throw out the baby with the bathwater'.

read (as a noun) *Read* had appeared as a noun as far back as the early 19th century, but it was not used much until it became fashionable with reviewers from the 1960s onwards to write about a book being an interesting read, an exciting read, etc. Some dictionaries record this use as conversational, others do not list it at all. It is now common enough in serious writing to be accepted as standard: for example, a writer in *The Times Literary Supplement* questioned whether Jane Austen should be 'thought of as nothing more than a good read'.

readable See **legible . . .**

readership See **coverage . . .**

Reaganism Ronald Reagan was the first president of the United States to achieve an **-ism**.

This is all the more surprising because President Reagan was hardly noted for philosophical insight. What's more, *Reaganism* had already appeared in Britain in *The Times* during 1981, the first year of his presidency.

Defining *Reaganism* is another problem: it seems to be a concept that embraces the style of the man himself, a film-actorish way of delivering rhetoric, a near-adulation of Margaret Thatcher and the mock-scientific Reaganomics, which, among other things, described a policy of boosting the economy by seemingly limitless expenditure on defence.

Reaganism, although not *Reaganomics*, found its way into the 1989 edition of the *OED*, and both terms will have a permanent place in history books, with scholars struggling to impose a definition on them.

real In a world where so many things are not what they used to be or seem to be, perhaps people have an unconscious need for the word *real*: 'This is a real crisis'; 'This is the real truth'. . . . We can afford to be more restrained in the use of *real*, allowing pristine words, such as 'crisis' and 'truth', to stand on their own.

For the use of *real* to reassure people in descriptions (real wood, real coffee, real cotton), see **natural or real**. See also **authentic . . .**

real estate See **property . . .**

realistic and **unrealistic** These are common cover-up words. When someone wants something done cheaply, they ask for a *realistic* estimate; when a trade union leader wants a big pay settlement, he asks for a *realistic* offer. *Realistic* means whatever anyone chooses to make it mean, so don't be taken in when someone says 'I can let you have it at a realistic price'. All that applies in reverse to *unrealistic*.

really *Really* can cover a broad band of different meanings. For examples of how these can be expressed in speech and in writing, see **intonation**.

real rate of interest In calculating the rate of interest received or paid, many people do not take into account inflation. It is realistic to deduct from the quoted rate of interest the rate of inflation: the term used for the difference is the *real rate of interest*.

ream See **quire . . .**

(it stands to) reason The moment anyone says *it stands to reason*, argument and discussion are cut off, because it maintains that this is exactly how things are. It is good advice not to be browbeaten by *it stands to reason*: try asking, 'By whose reason does it stand?' See also next entry

reasonable and **unreasonable** These should be objective words based on a logical unbiased review of the facts. Both words are more often than not used in the most subjective way, and then we are in the area of what is reasonable to one person may be unreasonable to someone else, and the other way round.

Even at best, *reasonable* and *unreasonable* usually look at a situation from one angle, and it is not always the good who are reasonable and the bad who are unreasonable: 'The reasonable man adapts himself to the world; the unreasonable one persists in trying to adapt the world to him. Therefore all progress depends on the unreasonable man' (Shaw, *Man and Superman*).

(the) reason is because and **the reason why** This brings out nit-picking blue pencils. The argument is neither *because* nor *why* is necessary after *reason*: 'The reason the policy will not succeed is *because* there will be too much opposition to it'; 'The reason *why* the policy will not succeed . . .'. In both those sentences *because* and *why* can be deleted without it affecting the meaning: 'The reason the policy will not succeed is . . .'.

This is to dissect language clinically and to disregard custom and idiom. *Reason why*, in particular, is an established phrase, which **Fowler** himself used often enough (although he frowned on *reason is because*), encouraged perhaps by Tennyson ('Theirs not to reason why, Theirs but to do and die', *The Charge of the Light Brigade*).

rebut See **deny** . . .

recall, **recollect**, **remember** or **retrieve** People *recall* information that is held in their memory, and the word implies some mental effort. *Recollect* is a more reflective word (for Wordsworth, poetry was 'emotion recollected in tranquillity', Preface to *The Lyrical Ballads*), used more for past experiences, such as a love affair. *Recall* and *recollect* suggest more effort than *remember*: 'At last I have been able to recall (or recollect) what you wanted me to remember'. At the same time, all three words are often used interchangeably, although the distinction suggested offers a refinement in choosing which word fits in best.

Although computers are credited with having **memory**, they are kept in their place inasmuch as they *retrieve* data rather than recalling, recollecting or remembering it.

received pronunciation (RP) This is the style of speaking and the way of pronouncing certain words supposedly followed by educated people in southern England. RP, as it is abbreviated in linguistics, was adopted by the BBC when it was founded in 1922, and only announcers who spoke in that style were employed. There was an attempt to provide authority and regulation for RP with the BBC Advisory Committee on Spoken English (1926): the first chairman was the poet laureate, Robert Bridges, educated at Eton.

Received in the term implies an accepted standard from which all departures are variants. RP is the pronunciation used by British dictionaries as the stan-

dard. Yet at a time when some younger members of the royal family speak in a style that is not always strictly RP, when Ted Hughes, the present poet laureate, intones his poetry in a pronounced Yorkshire accent, the authority of RP has come into question.

In the 1990s, those who use the term RP should be careful about regarding it as the only, or even the best, standard of spoken English. Nevertheless, when in *The Good English Guide* a particular pronunciation is described as 'preferred', that is a reference to RP. See also **accents in speech**; **British English**; **pronunciation**; **Queen's English**

'reCESS' or 'REcess' Some speakers distinguish between the noun ('reCESS') and the verb, where stress on the first syllable sounds more natural ('REcess').

Some current British dictionaries show both stress patterns as alternatives, others insist on *first*-syllable stress for both noun and verb. The recommendation is stress on the first syllable for the noun, stress on the second syllable for the verb.

recession See **depression** . . .

recital See **concert** . . .

reckless See **feckless** . . .

reckon Most of us feel that *reckon*, in the sense of consider or think, is an **Americanism**, but it had already appeared, used in this way, in the Authorized Version of the Bible (1611). As has happened to many other words, it fell out of use in Britain but survived in America, returning across the Atlantic via Hollywood films. *Reckon* is often used this way now in British English: 'I reckon we should discuss this as soon as possible'. Some people reject it as not English: if you're criticized because you reckon it to be a good word, you can say it was used by 47 of the best scholars in Britain in the early 17th century when they retranslated the Bible.

recollect See **recall** . . .

recommended retail price (RRP) See **list price** . . .

recondite *Recondite* can be used not only for remote unfamiliar subjects or knowledge, but also about a style of writing that is difficult to penetrate, or a book or article dealing with abstruse matters.

The usual pronunciation puts the stress on the first syllable: 'REKe(r)ndyt'. You may be corrected if you put the stress on the second syllable ('riKONdyt'), although this was the earlier pronunciation, still shown by most dictionaries as an alternative.

reconnaissance The word has never been restricted to military use for a preliminary sortie to get information about the enemy or the lie of the land. It is used frequently for any expedition to obtain advance information on any kind of project in a particular area.

The pronunciation has long since been completely anglicized ('riKONise(r)ns'), and it is affected to make the last syllable rhyme with 'chance'.

record　See **disc** . . .

record-player　See **hi-fi** . . .

recourse, **resource** or **resort**　It is easy to get into a muddle over these three words, and to draw fine lines between them would be more tedious than helpful. There are three useful rules of thumb:

1　When the word comes between the verb 'have' and 'to', it should be *recourse* or *resort* (not *resource*): 'if necessary you can *have* recourse (or resort) *to* extra funds that are available for the project'. *Recourse* is more usual in this context.

2　After the word *last*, *resort* or *resource* should be used (not *recourse*): 'in the last resort (or resource), there are extra funds available for the project'. *Resort* is more usual in this context.

3　A *resource* is a means that is available for supplying needs ('the earth's *resources*' is a familiar environmental phrase), and can be used in general contexts in this sense, often in the plural: 'there are extra funds available as a resource, but when these are used up, there are no other resources'.

recto　This is a printing term that writers should be familiar with: it is the *right*-hand page of an open book and is traditionally always odd-numbered. The left-hand, even-numbered page is the *verso*. See also **double-page spread**

rector　See **minister** . . .

rectory or **vicarage**　Some parishes have *rectories*, others have *vicarages*: some people live in The Old Rectory, others in The Old Vicarage. The names preserve a historical distinction between a rector and a vicar, which no longer applies. See **minister** . . .

recycle　*Recycle* was being used in the 1920s, particularly in the oil industry for reconstituting certain materials to save costs. In the 1970s, *recycling* took off in a different direction, as one of the central environmental creeds for conserving resources and reducing the pile-up of waste materials.

Recycle is now a word to catch the eye and demonstrate environmental responsibility: everything has to be looked at to see if it is *recyclable* (the more recent descriptive word). The big supermarkets want to be seen to care and issue carrier bags with MADE WITH RECYCLED PLASTIC on them. But one of the oldest cases of recycling, still cited as the perfect example, is seen on doorsteps all over the country – the traditional British milk bottle. See also **biodegradable; green**

Red　Among many other things, the events in Eastern Europe in 1991 changed the meaning of the word *Red*, with a capital R. Before then in the West, any member of the former Soviet Union was called a

Red, if people felt that way. The Red Flag no longer flies from the Kremlin, and *Keep The Red Flag Flying* is like an old school song, a nostalgic reminder of days beyond recall.

In Britain and America, there are still people who will call anyone with left-wing political views a Red, but it is blimpish and out of touch.

Redbrick　See **Oxbridge** . . .

redecorate or **refurbish**　There is an old word 'furbish', which meant to remove rust from a sword or other weapon, and was later used about buildings. Not many people use it any more. *Refurbish*, on the other hand, has become fashionable for renovating and bringing up to date hotels, blocks of flats and other large buildings. It is usually taken to imply much more than *redecorate*, which could be no more than a couple of coats of emulsion paint.

People talk about having rooms *redecorated* rather than *decorated*, which comes to the same thing. After all, house painters don't call themselves *redecorators*.

reductionism　This is a post-World War II -ism often used to discredit an attempt to break down a complex matter into a series of A+B+C concepts. Any approach on any issue that appears to be simplistic can be called *reductionist*, just as anyone who goes in for oversimplifying causes and effects can be called a reductionist.

It has a linguistic application for a two-dimensional approach to language and **meaning**, at the other extreme from the linguistic theory of *deconstructionism*, which undermines the belief that language has any objective meaning on its own.

redundant　The word means superfluous, over and above what is required. In the 1990s, it is ominous that *redundant* is used more about people. Men and women become redundant when their jobs disappear because there is no work for them to do, or because new technology enables it to be done by fewer workers. The accompanying verb makes a difference. To be *made redundant* is to get the sack (see **dismiss** . . .); to *become redundant* is bad luck. It comes to the same thing but the latter is more face-saving.

In technology *redundant* has a positive sense: it is used about an extra component built in to take over if another component fails (see also **fail-safe**).

re-entry　In 2001, or whenever it is that space travel becomes available to passengers, *re-entry* will be a familiar word. It is the term in astronautics (see **aeronautics**) for returning through the earth's atmosphere, when spacecraft are exposed to the highest temperatures through friction.

refer　See **allude** . . .

'reFERable' or **'REFerable'**　Up to the mid-1960s, *referable* was expected to follow 'reference', with the stress on the first syllable, and moving it to the second one would have been considered uneducated. That has changed because the second-syllable stress has become standard and the only one shown in dictionaries: 'reFERable'.

referee or **umpire** They are both judges at games. It is a matter of tradition which one is used but it's not playing the game to get it wrong. It would not be keeping a straight bat to call the white-coated men presiding over a cricket pitch at Lord's or the Oval, *referees*. They are *umpires*. (Cricket also has referees, but to settle disputes off the field.) *Referee* would not go down well with strawberries and cream at Wimbledon, for *umpire* is the right word for tennis. Baseball has an umpire too, but boxing, football, hockey and rugby have *referees*.

(with) reference to We all still receive letters beginning 'I am writing with reference to . . .'. Some people even say 'I'm telephoning with reference to . . .'. The habit comes from a fear of using simple words in case they don't seem important enough. With reference to *with reference to*, there are hardly any examples in everyday communication, when 'about' doesn't do the same job a lot better, unless you are quoting a specific number for an account, insurance policy, etc. See **business English**

referendum or **plebiscite** Both words mean the same, which is offering a vote to the electorate on an important issue, such as a constitutional change or **devolution**. *Referendum* has become the standard word in British politics and is frequently used about issues such as proportional representation and **EC** treaties. *Plebiscite* (for the origin of the word, see **plebeian**) is less commonly used, usually about a general vote for the head of a state (the 1992 General Election was called by some commentators 'a plebiscite on John Major').

The Latinate plural of *referendum* is *referenda* (as with addendum/**addenda**). **Fowler** (*Modern English Usage*, 1926), most dictionaries and the leader writers in *The Times* all prefer *referendums*, but try telling that to some MPs and broadcasters, who carefully enunciate *referenda*, for fear of sounding uneducated.

referendums or **referenda** See previous entry

refined Technically, *refined* is when something is purified, with impurities eliminated. By extension, *refined* is applied to a literary style, feelings, sensibilities, but it is affected to use it about people. To say a person is refined is as bad as pronouncing it 'refayned'.

reflection or **reflexion** *Reflexion* was the earlier spelling and is still shown as a variant by some recent dictionaries. But it seems mildly eccentric now, as *reflection* has become the standard form in all the senses of the word.

reflective See contemplative . . .

reflex In its medical application, *reflex* is neurophysiological, an automatic uncontrollable response to a particular stimulus, such as the spontaneous jerk away after touching something hot, or an eyeblink at a sudden bright light, loud sound or other shock. Freud carried over the term into unconscious, equally uncontrollable mental responses to stimuli. The everyday journalistic way of putting that is a **knee-jerk** reaction.

reflexion See reflection . . .

refurbish See redecorate . . .

refusenik See -nik

'reFUTable' or **'REFutable'** The stress is now on the second syllable: 'reFUTable'. With **irrefutable**, stress on the *ref* syllable is still preferred.

refute See deny . . .

regardless or **irregardless** The suffix *-less* makes *regardless* a negative, meaning 'without regard', as in 'we shall go ahead regardless of what people say'. There is no need for the prefix *-ir*: in fact, 'irregardless', a common error, does not appear in dictionaries.

regime or **régime** The acute accent over the *e* is usually dropped now, although it is still shown as an alternative spelling in dictionaries.

There is no reason why *regime* should not be used in a favourable way, but you have to be careful because it is more often used about a government or social order that is regarded as bad: 'a corrupt regime'; 'a fascist regime'; 'overthrow the regime'. So people are inclined to react to the word in a negative way.

(in the) region of 'The price will be *in the region of* . . .' means nothing different from 'The price will be about . . .', so why use four words when one simple word will do?

regretfully or **regrettably** People may be *regretful* (have feelings of regret), and what they do or do not do may be *regrettable* (something to be regretted): 'He regretfully decided not to join us' means *he* felt sorry about it. 'Regrettably, he has decided not to join us' means *we* felt sorry about it.

rehabilitate An earlier meaning of *rehabilitate*, to reinstate a person who has lost favour or privileges, is still shown in dictionaries: in 1992 the Bomber Command Association hoped to rehabilitate the reputation of their wartime commander, Arthur Harris, by the statue erected to him in London. There is also the meaning of restoring a building. Nevertheless, the medical meaning of *rehabilitate* has largely superseded the others: this is retraining someone physically and mentally after a major operation or illness, in order to restore as far as possible normal capabilities. In this sense, rehabilitation includes physiotherapy, psychotherapy and counselling.

relate and **relationship** These words are in constant demand, a recognition that we depend on others for our wellbeing and happiness. For some people *relationship* has swept aside more precise words, such as friendship, love affair, marriage: they make do with a *relationship*. We no longer need to understand our children or our parents, so long as we *relate* to them.

The Tavistock Institute of Marital Relations sees a gradual move away from marriage as a solemn legalistic institution, and in Scandinavia there are couples who reject the standard marriage contract and write out the terms they have agreed for their *relationship*. Before the 1980s ended, the Marriage Guidance Council saw which way the linguistic wind was blowing and renamed itself *Relate*.

-related In the fast lanes of the 1990s there is a constant drive to speed up communication. As a word joined on with a hyphen, *-related* is a short cut. Instead of 'illnesses caused by stress', 'crimes caused by drink', 'negotiations about money', we have stress-related illnesses, drink-related crimes, money-related negotiations. It would be a pity to overdo this, or like any other useful linguistic device, it would degenerate into jargon.

relation or **relative** In the sense of being connected by blood or marriage, *relation* is the more usual word now, as it seems to most people a warmer word than *relative*.

relative or **comparative** See comparative . . .

relatively See comparatively . . .

relative pronouns The grammatical term for the mostly short words that take the place of a noun and enable two sentences to be joined into one: the relative pronoun *that* turns 'This is the house. Jack built the house' into 'This is the house that Jack built' (*that* takes the place of 'the house').

The relative pronouns that give most problems in use are **that or which** and **who or whom**, which (a relative pronoun) are dealt with as separate entries.

relax Leonard Bernstein called our time the *Age of Anxiety* (it is the title of his Symphony No 2), so it is not surprising that *relax* is a word in much demand. *Relax* has all but replaced the expression 'take it easy': if someone is worried or frightened, rushing more than seems necessary, we advise them to relax. If we want to seem calm about anything, we say we're completely relaxed about it. It is supposed to be a good thing to look relaxed, no matter what we're feeling inside. *Relax* has become such a desirable word that it is often forgotten that the greatest achievements come from intensity and passion, not from being **cool** or laid-back, the slang equivalent of *relaxed*.

relevant See material . . .

religion See faith . . .

relocate Business English usually seeks to sound self-important. It has been said that chief executives are paid to have big ideas and people believe that big ideas need long words. *Relocate* is one of them: head offices, factories, executives, etc are not moved from one place to another, they are *relocated*.

remember See recall . . .

remuneration See pay . . .

remuneration package See pay . . .

Renaissance, **renaissance** or **renascence** With a capital R, the *Renaissance* was the great creative movement in Europe, starting in the 14th century, that heralded the modern world. With a small *r*, it is used in a more modest way for the 'rebirth' (which is what the word means) or revival of ideas, beliefs or a fashion: '1991 saw the renaissance of the miniskirt'.

The pronunciation with the stress on the first syllable ('RENNysance') is heard in America, but British pronunciation now puts the stress on the second syllable: 'riNAYse(r)ns'. This anglicized pronunciation is usually preferred, although there are people who give a French sound to the last syllable: 'riNAYsah(n)s'.

The alternative spelling *renascence* is rarely used now and can be regarded as obsolete. That spelling should never be used for the historical period.

Renaissance man The description *Renaissance man* does not go back far. It dates perhaps from the 1970s, to describe a person who is many-sided and has many talents, not a 'Jack of all trades' but able to do a number of diverse things consummately. Above all, the expression relates to **Leonardo** da Vinci (1452–1519), artist, engineer, architect, anatomist, botanist, philosopher, innovator. In our own time, Jonathan Miller has been called a Renaissance man, as a doctor, scientist, performer, theatre director, teacher.

rendezvous *Rendezvous* has been used in English since the 16th century for a place where people meet. Over the centuries the pronunciation has become mixed up. It is half-anglicized: in the singular it is 'RONdivoo' but in the plural (also spelt *rendezvous*) it becomes 'RONdivooz'.

Unlike the word in modern French, *rendezvous* in English is also a verb. The only form that sounds natural is 'Let us rendezvous at the Café Royal'. When you get into 'rendezvouses', 'rendezvoused', 'rendezvousing' it is stretching the word to its limits. It's easier to say 'she has a rendezvous', 'they are having a rendezvous', etc. But if you fancy the other forms of the verb, they are all listed in dictionaries, as spelt out above, so you can go in for as much *rendezvousing* (pron: RONdivooing) as you like. See also **venue**

renege When someone goes back on a deal, they *renege on* the agreement. Pron: 'reNEEG' (to rhyme with 'league') or 'reNAYG' (to rhyme with 'vague'). The former is recommended.

renouncement See renunciation . . .

rent-a-mob It started with *rent-a-car* but the idea was too promising to be left at that. There are now listed in directories rent-a-bus, rent-a-chauffeur, rent-a-maid, rent-a-nanny, and the alliterative rent-a-Rolls for people who want to impress their friends.

Not listed in directories, and more sinister, is *rent-a-mob*: gangs hired or cajoled into demonstrating or committing acts of violence. The term was used by the government in the House of Commons about the anti-poll tax riots of early 1990; and William Waldegrave, Foreign Office minister at the time, called the pro-government demonstrations in Bucharest in mid-1990 *rent-a-mob*, to suggest they were not genuine.

renunciation or **renouncement** Both forms exist. *Renunciation* is so much more usual that some people will think you've made a mistake if you write or say *renouncement*.

rep See salesman . . .

repair or **fix** In Britain we get something *repaired*: in America they're more likely to get it *fixed*. See fix . . .

repairable or **reparable** Shoes and other objects that are worn out or damaged, which can be repaired, are *repairable*. If it's not possible, such things 'cannot be repaired' (the word 'irrepairable' does not exist).

Mistakes, losses, broken hearts and other non-material things are *reparable*. If that's not possible, they are *irreparable*.

Repairable is stressed on the second syllable: *repairable* and *irreparable* are stressed on the *rep* syllable.

repel or **repulse** 'Go away – you repulse me!' she cried, using the word incorrectly as many people do. *Repulse* is to drive back (as in 'repulsing an attack') or to rebuff someone by coldness or unkindness ('she was repulsed by his unfriendliness').

Repel also means to drive away (a spray to repel insects), but it can also mean to disgust someone. The woman wanted the meaning of 'repulsive' which does mean 'disgusting'. She could have cried 'Go away – you repel me!' or 'Go away – you're repulsive!' Either way, he would get the message.

repertoire or **repertory** The words both relate to the French 'répertoire' (a list or catalogue). *Repertory* is the older form in English, and goes back to the 16th century when it was used in the same way as in French. Since the early 20th century, *repertory* is used almost exclusively about the theatre, for a group of plays in rehearsal during a particular period. *Repertory theatre*, *repertory actor* were used, particularly before World War II, for permanent theatre companies, mostly outside London, which over a season mounted a different play each week ('weekly rep') or over longer periods ('fortnightly rep', 'monthly rep').

Because of television, there are few repertory theatres left. *Repertory*, long associated with run-of-the-mill provincial theatre, is kept alive as a theatrical term by the major theatre companies, for the handful of productions arranged for staging during a season. In America the terms 'stock company' (from the idea of 'stock in trade') or 'summer stock company' are used in place of *repertory*.

Repertoire is confined mostly to musicians and orchestras for the range of compositions they are able to perform. It has become extended to other items that are, so to speak, at the ready, such as a repertoire of dishes a cook can turn out to order or, ironically, the repertoire of lies or excuses that someone regularly falls back on when they're on the spot.

repetition Generally it is worth making an effort to avoid repetition of the same word in a sentence, as it lacks style and imagination: 'While the *matter* you raise is important, there are other *matters* equally important, and it does *matter* a great deal which is given priority'. The repetition of 'important' is justified for it stresses the point, but the second 'matters' could be replaced by 'issues', and the verb 'matter' could be changed to 'mean'.

Do not turn this into a slavish rule, as repetition in some cases can make a point stand out. No one would criticize '. . . we shall *fight* on the beaches . . . *fight* on the landing grounds . . . *fight* in the fields . . . *fight* in the hills . . .' (Winston Chuchill, 4.6. 1940).

See also **alliteration and assonance**

repetitious or **repetitive** Both words mean something is repeated, but the implication is different. *Repetitious* implies that the repetition is both unnecessary and boring; *repetitive* is merely descriptive, stating the fact without criticism. Ravel's *Boléro* has a strong repetitive theme which some people could find repetitious.

replace See displace . . .

replaceable or **replacable** Replaceable.

reply or **retort** *Reply* is a neutral word. *Retort* suggests that a reply is sharp, witty, angry, to the point. This applies to both words as nouns or verbs: 'she replied thoughtfully to his question'; 'he was surprised at her angry retort' (even if 'angry' were deleted, *retort* would suggest a sharp or curt reply).

reportage or **reporting** *Reporting* is the act and style of a journalist giving a news story: 'Her reporting on television news programmes is always clear and unemotional'. *Reportage* is the characteristic style in which news in general is reported: a novel or a film may be described as *reportage*, meaning that it is a straightforward unadorned piece of reporting.

repository See depositary . . .

representational (as art term) See figurative . . .

representative (as noun) See salesman . . .; congressman

representative (as descriptive word) See characteristic . . .

reproductive technology Methods of human reproduction in laboratories are giving birth not only to babies but to new words, as well as bringing formerly specialized medical and biological terms into more common use:
Embryology: the aspect of biology dealing with the formation of embryos. There is an *embryological* laboratory in the famous Bourn Hall procreation clinic in Cambridgeshire.
Flushing: the technique by which a woman acts as a living incubator. A fertile woman conceives from sperm taken from an infertile woman's partner. Within a few days the foetus is 'flushed out' and placed within the infertile woman, who later gives birth to the child.
Sperm bank: By 1984 there were twenty of these in Britain. Semen from donors is deep-frozen and made available to married and, by some clinics, to unmarried women. Semen is also stored for future use by men who are to have a vasectomy or undergo some other treatment that might result in sterility.
Surrogacy: A woman is paid a fee to be fertilized by sperm from an infertile woman's partner, and to carry and give birth to the baby. The couple then take possession of the child. There are legal and moral aspects of this that are still to be resolved.
Test-tube babies: the popular and journalistic expression for in-vitro fertilization, literally 'in glass', because fertilization is induced in a small glass dish and the resulting embryo transferred to the mother's uterus.

Republican or **republican** With a capital R, a *Republican* is a member of the Republican Party, one of the two major political parties in the US, thought of as more right wing and conservative than the Democrat Party. Ronald Reagan was a Republican president and was succeeded by George Bush, another Republican.
With a small *r*, a *republican* in Britain is an advocate of abolition of the monarchy in favour of a republican constitution. In the context of Ireland, it is someone who campaigns for the North and South to be united.

repulse See repel . . .

'REPutable' or **'rePUTable'** Because of *repute*, stressed on the *second* syllable, there are people who slip into saying 'rePUTable'. The stress is on the first syllable: 'REPutable'.

request from or **of** 'She requested it *of* him', or '. . . *from* him'? Either. But it should be a formal context before either is used in preference to 'ask of (or from)', which is the more natural expression.

require See need . . .

rescheduling Any programme or plan can, of course, be subject to *rescheduling*, that is rearranging dates. But the word has come to be particularly associated with loans from richer to poorer nations: *rescheduling debts* is a euphemistic way of saying putting off paying them.

'reSEARCH' or **'REsearch'** A few years ago there was no wavering: British scientists carried out 'reSEARCH'; in America it was optional, with both 'reSEARCH' and 'REsearch' in use.
There are signs that some of the latest British dictionaries are getting wobbly over this, showing both pronunciations as alternatives, usually with a warning that stress on the first syllable is not generally accepted. At universities on both sides of the Atlantic, 'reSEARCH' is strongly preferred. Some people try to have it both ways, saying 'reSEARCH' for the noun and 'REsearch' for the verb (or the other way round!). At the present state of play, the best advice, at least in Britain, is to keep the stress on the second syllable.

research and development (R & D) The abbreviation R & D is standard in management and industry: *research and development* applies *research* as the pure pursuit of knowledge to commercial *development*, such as new production techniques, new products, new services.
With markets becoming global, sharper competition makes innovation and improvement in products vital to profitability. That is the D side of R & D: *The Independent* commented in a leading article, '. . . however effective the R, that investment will be largely wasted if management underestimates the full complexity of the D'.

reserve currency See hard currency . . .

residuals See profits . . .

resistance *The resistance*, for a secret army in a country opposing occupying forces, came into prominent use for the underground movement in France during World War II. The word in this sense is usually felt as a judgement that it is a just struggle against tyranny, unlawful occupation and oppression. *Resistance* forces operate in a similar way to terrorists. The distinction is not one of method but of the cause: **terrorism** is evil and *resistance* is taken to be good. But which is which in a particular situation is a point of view. See also **guerrilla**

resolve or **solve** *Resolve* has a number of meanings, one of which makes it almost synonymous with *solve*: we can resolve or solve a problem, a mystery, a doubt, and it comes to the same thing. If there is a distinction, *resolve* is preferable for finding a practical way of dealing with a difficulty or a problem, while *solve* suggests finding an explanation of a mystery: 'we must resolve the dispute that is holding up production'; 'we must solve the mystery of the missing components'. There are many in-between examples where either word fits in.

resort See recourse . . .

respective and **respectively** More often than not *respective* is there just for makeweight: 'Mary, John and Helen have returned to their respective homes'. Omit *respective* and there's still no doubt about which homes they went to.

Respectively can be a clumsy way of explaining what goes with which: 'Mary, John and Helen live in London, Oxford and Cambridge respectively' is the kind of sentence that makes us look back over it to see who lives where. It could be laid on the line without using any extra words: 'Mary lives in London, John in Oxford, Helen in Cambridge'.

In a more complicated sentence, *respectively* can avoid some repetition, but it is not something to be brought out casually.

(in) **respect of** and **with respect to** If these formal phrases are to be used, *in* must be followed by *of* (*in respect of*), *with* by *to* (*with respect to*).

Unless a formal or legal style is necessary, it is usually better to replace either phrase by the simple word 'about': 'in respect of/with respect to the decision made by the committee . . .' says nothing more than 'about the decision . . .'.

respite *Respite* (a breathing-space or short period of relief) is stressed on the first syllable and the second syllable rhymes with 'spite' ('RESpyte'), or with 'spit' ('RESpit'). The first is more usual in Britain, the second in America.

responsible See accountable . . .

restaurant Whether to sound the final *t* or not to sound it, that is the question. *Restaurant* has been in English since the 19th century, for a place where meals are served. It's as English as Yorkshire pudding, which is why so many people say 'RESteront'. Some recent dictionaries give their blessing to the final *t* sound, while others won't hear of it.

Whatever they say in their private lives, BBC announcers are advised to keep the final *t* silent when they broadcast and say 'RESTora(h)n', with a slight nasal sound in the last syllable. This is the up-market pronunciation.

For a definition, see **brasserie** . . .

restaurateur According to legend, the first *restaurateur* was in Paris, some time in the mid-18th century. In a long since vanished street near the fashionable Rue du Faubourg Saint-Honoré, Monsieur Boulanger started serving soup and a few dishes on marble-topped tables. Madame Boulanger, who, we are told, was pretty and appealing, provided an extra attraction. As you would expect, there was no shortage of customers. Boulanger became the first restaurateur, the story goes on, since the Latin text on the sign outside his new establishment promised 'ego vos restaurabo' ('I will restore you').

There is no equivalent English word for *restaurateur*, unless we fall back lamely on 'restaurant-owner'. So British and American food writers and gourmets adopt *restaurateur*, giving it a half-French pronunciation: 'restere(r)TE(r)'.

In passing, to slip in an *n* ('restauranteur') is to drop a gastronomic brick.

restive or **restless** Children are restive when they won't sit still, people at a public demonstration are restive when they look as if they might turn violent, a horse is restive when it jibs at the bridle. *Restive* should imply a headstrong refusal to accept order or control.

Restless is used so often in the same contexts as *restive*, that perhaps it is a lost cause to insist on a distinction between the two words. Nevertheless, *restless* belongs more suitably to describing agitation or nervousness: we are restless, rather than restive, when we toss and turn in bed because there is something on our mind; children may be restless when they have a fever; when a horse rears up in a paddock, it's a sign that it is restless.

restrictions See censorship . . .

restrictive practices This term was first used for agreements between manufacturing companies to squeeze out competition by methods such as price-cutting or imposing conditions for supplying goods to shops. This is now controlled to some extent by the Restrictive Practices Act 1956.

The more familiar meaning of *restrictive practices* is in connection with **industrial action** by trade unions or a workforce, which interferes with the efficient running of an organization, using methods such as **go-slow** or *work-to-rule*, or opposing changes in working techniques and manning levels.

rest room See lavatory . . .

résumé See cv; outline . . .

Retail Price Index (RPI) See index

retain, consult, engage or **appoint** There is a certain professional etiquette about which word is used in which situation. See **appoint** . . .

retort See reply . . .

retreat or **withdraw** In his broadcast from Baghdad on 26 February 1991, Saddam Hussein spoke about having won a victory and ordering his forces to withdraw from Kuwait. George Bush, speaking on the steps of the White House, retorted angrily: 'Saddam is not *withdrawing* – his defeated forces are *retreating*'.

We *withdraw* in order to fight again another day; we *retreat* when we are defeated.

retrieve   See recall . . .

retrograde or **retrogressive**   As descriptive words, *retrograde* and *retrogressive* are synonymous in referring to a degenerate or deteriorating condition. *Retrograde* also serves as a noun for a person, unfairly nearly always a man for it is unusual to use the word about a woman, who is dissolute and abandoned. The corresponding verb is *retrogress*, for a situation or a person becoming retrograde or retrogressive.

reveal   See disclose . . .

revenue   See income . . .

reverse   See opposite . . .

reverse out   This printing term is more familiar now because of **desktop publishing**. An image is *reversed out* when it is reproduced in negative form, for example as white against a solid dark background.

reverse takeover   The term is appropriate when there is a merger between a large company and a small one, which for various reasons ends up with the smaller company taking over control of the whole business. See **merger**

review   See criticism . . .

review or **revue**   *Review* is the right spelling in all contexts except one: the French form *revue* was introduced into English in the late 19th century for a theatrical show composed of satirical sketches and songs.

revisionism and **revisionist**   It is fashionable, almost obligatory, for modern historians to throw overboard standard views of events in history. *Revisionism* and *revisionist*, first used dismissively in the late 19th century for a challenge to orthodox Marxist principles, have become words to put down any deviation from an established line in history, politics or almost any other subject. Because the words are generally taken to be derogatory, they should not be used when objective marshalling of evidence and corroboration of sources are sound and reliable.

revolutionary   *Revolutionary* is a strong word that describes turning upside down ideas, order, beliefs. Casual use about trivial changes ('the revolutionary hemline from Paris') is easygoing journalism, but should not be allowed to dilute the value of *revolutionary* for events and discoveries that change the world. In ordinary contexts, 'new' is a perfectly adequate alternative.

revue   See review . . .

rhetoric   The art of using language in speech and writing used to be a serious subject of study. *Rhetoric* now usually means no more than high-flown political bombast, hot air signifying nothing much. In spite of the first definition in dictionaries, which connects *rhetoric* with effective speaking, it would be misunderstood now to use the word in a good sense.

rhetorical question   A *rhetorical question* is a false question, since everyone is assumed to accept there could be only one answer: 'Don't we all know that nothing is certain except death and taxes?' People are inclined to ask rhetorical questions presumptuously, assuming that everyone agrees there could only be one answer. If that's not the way you see it, turn the rhetorical question into a real question by giving your own point of view.

rhumba   See rumba . . .

rhythmic or **rhythmical**   There is no different in meaning: both words can be used for anything in sound or movement that has a steady rhythm. *Rhythmic* has become the standard word, with *rhythmical* beginning to fall into disuse.

ribbon development   Winding roads have long been compared to ribbons, which led to *ribbon development* becoming a term in town planning. It goes back to the late 1920s for the way towns were extended by building rows of houses on the roads leading out of them.

After World War II, ribbon development became recognized as bad social and environmental planning, and the term is little used now.

Richter scale   See earthquakes

ridiculous   See absurd . . .

right bank (of rivers)   See left and right banks . . .

Right (in politics)   See Left and the Right . . .

right or **rightly**   *Right* is the normal form when it comes after the verb: 'Make sure you do it right'; 'Did I pronounce it right?'; 'He guessed right about her feelings'. No one could say *rightly* is wrong in such sentences but it would sound unnatural, as if you were on your best grammatical behaviour.

When it comes before the verb, *rightly* is usually required: 'It is rightly said that . . .'; 'He rightly decided to . . .'.

Rightly also belongs in the combination *rightly or wrongly*, whether it comes before or after the verb: 'Rightly or wrongly I have decided . . .'; 'She felt, rightly or wrongly, that . . .'. See also **wrong** . . .

right of way   In Britain, this can be a private right, under specified conditions, for certain people to walk across someone's land, or the right of the public to walk on footpaths, bridleways, etc. Note that the term is not usually hyphenated, and that the plural form is *rights of way* (not 'right of ways').

rights issue As ownership of shares becomes more widespread, terms such as *rights issue* are more familiar. It is a method of raising capital whereby a company offers shares at a price below market value to existing shareholders, usually in proportion to the number of shares already held.

rightward or **rightwards** See leftward . . .

right-wing See Left and Right in politics

rigour or **rigor** *Rigour* is the spelling of the word in everyday use, meaning harshness or strictness (the full rigour of the law). *Rigor* is the corresponding spelling in America, and also the spelling of the word as a medical term for stiffening of the body caused by a severe shock or seizure. *Rigor mortis* describes the stiffening of a body after death.

rip-off A colloquial expression that belongs to the age of inflation, and dating from about the 1970s. The difference between a *rip-off* and a fair profit is that the former is based on how much someone can charge for something and get away with it. *Rip-off* can apply to meals in restaurants, professional fees or any situation where demand outstrips supply.

rise or **raise (as nouns)** In America someone would ask for a *raise*, for an increase in pay. The usual word in Britain is *rise*, although *raise* is showing signs of edging its way in.

risk or **venture** Both as a noun and a verb, the word *venture* puts a gloss on *risk*. To risk doing something could be foolhardy, but to venture it could suggest calculation and preparation. In business, for example, an investment of capital that is highly speculative is sometimes known as *risk capital*, which frightens many people off, so there is a tendency to call it *venture capital*. It comes to the same thing but sounds, at least to some people, more prudent.

Whether you use *risk* or *venture* often depends upon whether you want people to see an enterprise as a gamble or as a worthwhile adventure. If such a proposition is put to you, it's useful to replace *venture* by *risk*, so you know where you stand.

There is one more point. Lord Rothschild, in a lecture he called 'Risk', said there is no such thing as a *risk-free* society. The word *risk* means very little until it is related to the degree of risk – is it one in a million or one in ten?

risk capital See previous entry

risqué See suggestive . . .

Ritz and **ritzy** Both words come, of course, from the *Ritz* hotels opened in Paris and London (in that order) at the turn of the century by César Ritz (1850–1918), a Swiss hotelier. *Ritz* became synonymous with luxury: for the London hotel, César Ritz imported French craftsmen to work on the Louis XVI interior, and the staircase, rotunda and spectacular Palm Court, with its over-the-top marble fountain, became legendary.

Ritz can still be used as a symbol of luxury, although the Ritz Hotel has long since adapted itself to less grandiose times: in 1991, New Zealand Airlines advertised itself as 'the Ritz of the skies'. But the word *ritzy* belongs to the charleston and flappers of the 1920s. To use it now would seem decidedly dated. See also glitzy

(the) **Riviera** See South of France . . .

road or **street** A *road* used to be a highway between towns (the London Road, the Old Kent Road . . .), and a *street* was a thoroughfare in a town where people lived. The distinction survives in terms such as *road sense*, used for a child's ability to cross roads safely, and *road test*, a test of a car's roadworthiness, as against **streetwise** for the sharpness and worldliness of life in a city. *Road works* hold up traffic, but prostitutes are said to be *on the street*, suggesting city life. We ask for the road to wherever we want to go, and it is the road to hell that is paved with good intentions.

You can always use *road* for *street* (except in specific names), but it doesn't always work the other way round: 'all roads lead to Rome', 'Which road shall I take to . . .?'

robbery See burglary . . .

robot Robot, taken from a Czech word, was first used in Karel Čapek's play *RUR* (1921), which stood for Rossum's Universal Robots, and was about a mechanical contrivance with near-human abilities and intelligence.

As machines came to take the place of workers, *robot* became a brave-new-world word of the 1930s, and then went through a period of sounding old-fashioned.

With **microchip** technology, *robot* has come back. Now when something is made by robots, the implication is that it is free from human error. The inventor, Clive Sinclair, believes that, as the Greeks and the Romans had slaves, new generations of robots will be the slaves of our time.

rock See pop . . .

rococo See baroque . . .

rodeo *Rodeo* passed into American English from Spanish for a cowboy's skills in breaking-in horses and handling cattle. We can put the stress on either the second or the first syllable: 'rohDAYoh' or 'ROHdee-oh'. The former is preferred.

role or **rôle** See accents in print and writing

rolling stock This railway term from the 1850s for engines, carriages and trucks is out of place for the high-speed trains of the 1990s. It is most likely to be used now by railway enthusiasts for steam engines.

roll-over   This is more familiar now as taxation jargon than for an extra five minutes in bed in the morning. *Roll-over* describes postponing payment of tax on gains when assets are sold, by using the money for purchasing other capital equipment.

Roman or **roman**   When used about ancient or modern Rome, a capital R is needed (Roman law, Roman roads, etc). If it is the shape of someone's nose, a capital R is also usual (a *Roman nose* is a curved beak of a nose). For the **roman numerals**, represented by letters (I, II, III, IV . . .), the capital R is optional. For the Roman alphabet (see next entry) it is a capital R, but it is *roman* for the standard upright typeface (as against sloping *italics*).

Roman alphabet   There is a great variety of alphabets in the world, with many languages such as Russian, Arabic, Chinese, Japanese, Burmese, Tibetan with individual scripts of their own. Most of the languages of Western Europe use what is still called the *Roman alphabet*, evolved by the ancient Romans for Latin, from an alphabet which can be traced back to the much older Phoenician alphabet. See also **Cyrillic** . . .

roman numerals   For all practical purposes, the cumbersome *roman numerals* using letters (I, II, III, IV, etc) were replaced in the 12th century by **arabic numerals** (1, 2, 3, 4, etc), but the Roman system is often still used in inscriptions of dates and to paginate the introduction to a book (when the lower case versions are used: i, ii, iii, iv, etc), to separate it from the main text. It is worth remembering that roman numerals are a nuisance to many people who cannot work them out beyond 39 (XXXIX). From then on, they may get into difficulties:

XL	(40)	CI . . .	(101 . . .)
XLI . . .	(41 . . .)	CC	(200)
L	(50)	CCC	(300)
LI . . .	(51 . . .)	CD	(400)
LX	(60)	D	(500)
LXX	(70)	DC	(600)
LXXX	(80)	DCC	(700)
XC	(90)	DCCC	(800)
XCI . . .	(91 . . .)	CM	(900)
C	(100)	M	(1000)

'roMANCE' or **'ROmance'**   The stress should be on the second syllable: 'roMANCE'. Stress on the first syllable is often heard, and shown by some recent dictionaries as an alternative pronunciation, but is usually considered a downmarket variant – except when the word occurs in certain pop songs.

Romanesque   See **Norman** . . .

romantic or **poetic**   The only way in which *romantic* can be used in a specific way is perhaps for the arts, especially for the movement in the late 18th century. This sought to replace the scientific rational-

ism and formality that had characterized that century by the expression of feeling and emotion. We can say poets, such as Wordsworth, Keats, Coleridge, and composers, such as Beethoven, Schubert, Chopin, belong to the romantic movement.

Outside that historical context, the nature of the word itself makes it indeterminate. It is all too often misused to describe a sentimental love story. But the word has deeper layers of meaning than that. If you are a romantic, it describes a way of looking at life that goes beyond the frontiers of common sense, into 'the deep-sea undertow of the dark and dreaming mind'. As in that line from John Tessimond's poem, *Portrait of a romantic*, the word can only be defined in romantic language, the meaning of which is half hidden, half understood. Laurence Whistler separated *romantic* from **classic**: 'The romantic is concerned with desire, and is a reaching-towards: the classic with the object of desire, and is a realization' (*The Initials in the Heart*).

If you are not a romantic, you might see it as meaning out of touch with reality, an irritating idealism or vagueness. A romantic idea could be one that is imaginative and sensitive to some people, stupid and naive to others. The meaning of *romantic* is relative to an attitude towards life, which is why it is impossible for there to be common agreement about what it signifies.

Poetic is a simpler word. When it is used, other than in relation to the nature of poetry as a form of literature, it is often a kindly description of a dreamy whimsical person or notion.

Romantic can be philosophical and psychological, and is sometimes used dismissively; *poetic*, in its nonliterary sense, is unlikely to have this deeper sense, more likely to be used lightly and indulgently.

roofs and **rooves**   Some dictionaries accept *rooves* as an alternative plural of roof, but only *roofs* is recommended, as *rooves* sounds and looks silly.

rostrum   See **platform** . . .

rotatory   Most dictionaries show the stress on the first syllable: 'ROHte(r)tery'. Most people feel more comfortable putting the stress on the second syllable: 'rohTAYTery'. It's up to you.

rouble or **ruble**   As more people go on holiday to Russia or do business with that country, the monetary unit is going to be used much more often. In Britain, *rouble* is the usual spelling, with *ruble* as the American spelling, which is the earlier form. Either way, the pronunciation is the same ('ROObe(r)l').

roué   See **rake** . . .

round   See **about** . . .

round trip   In America, a *round trip* corresponds to a British *return journey*. In Britain, a *round trip* is more likely to mean a journey following a circular route, usually stopping off at places on the way.

roup In most of Britain, we *auction* things or buy at *auctions*, but in Scotland and in some parts of Northern England, many people will use the word *roup*, both as a noun and a verb, instead of *auction* (it is usually pronounced to rhyme with 'rope').

-rous or **-erous** See -erous . . .

rouse See arouse . . .

royal (as a noun) Even the best newspapers write about 'a royal' or 'the royals' meaning members of the royal family. The use of *royal* as a noun is journalistic or conversational English and is never used officially.

Royalty Strict protocol still surrounds the way we address members of the royal family. The Queen and the Queen Mother are spoken to as *Your Majesty* to begin with, and then as *ma'am*. The word 'you' should always be replaced by '*Your Majesty*', and although there used to be a tradition about never asking the Queen a question, it is unlikely she would object nowadays to 'Would Your Majesty care for a drink?'

There are fewer problems when speaking to other members of the royal family. It is usual to address them as *Your Royal Highness* to begin with, and after that simply as *sir* or *ma'am*. In less formal situations, it is not uncommon now to use *sir* or *ma'am* when you first meet them.

royal we The expression *royal we* arose from the tradition of a King or Queen never using 'I', 'my', 'me', etc, always referring to himself or herself as *we*, *our*, *us*: Queen Victoria's characteristic way of showing her displeasure was to declare, 'We are not amused!'

The custom belongs to the past: if you listen to Queen Elizabeth at the opening of parliament, you hear her using *I* and referring to *my* government. The expression *royal we* remains to describe a supremely self-important way for a person to refer to themselves, as in that inadvertent pronouncement from the steps of 10 Downing Street: '*We* are now a grandmother'.

RP See received pronunciation

RPI The abbreviation for Retail Price Index. See index

RRP Recommended retail price. See list price . . .

rubber or **eraser** In Britain you would usually ask for a *rubber* in a stationery shop (although *eraser* would also be understood), if you wanted a small block of a substance used for rubbing out written mistakes. If you ask for a *rubber* in a stationery shop in America, you'd be likely to get raised eyebrows, because it is a common colloquial word for a condom.

rubbish (as a verb) This use of *rubbish* showed up in Britain in the 1970s, as a word meaning to criticize something severely or to reject it as nonsense. It is particularly popular with political journalists ('the Opposition rubbished the minister's claim that . . .').

To begin with people objected, letters were written to *The Times*, complaints made to the BBC. Even now, the latest dictionaries only admit *rubbish* as a verb for conversational use. It is an unnecessary fuss. Nouns in English have been more or less freely converted to verbs for centuries (see **nouns as verbs**). There is a good case for rubbishing any suggestion that *rubbish* should not be used as a verb, although remember it is a very aggressive way of dismissing something.

ruble See rouble . . .

RUC The RUC is often mentioned in the news about events in Northern Ireland. The abbreviation stands for the Royal Ulster Constabulary, which is the police force in the province.

rucksack See backpack . . .

ruddy *Ruddy* has become a mixed-up word and it is hardly possible to use it any more in its proper meaning. It goes back many centuries to Old English, and describes a red colour or someone being red in the face, out of good health rather than anger: 'Augustus was a chubby lad; Fat ruddy cheeks Augustus had' (Heinrich Hoffman, *Struwwelpeter*).

But *ruddy* became a euphemism for **bloody** (hardly a shocking word anyway now), given the 'by appointment' seal by the Duke of Edinburgh in 1956, when he used *ruddy well* in a speech. If you have a friend who has a healthy open-air complexion, and you talk about your 'ruddy friend', you can take it that nearly everyone will misunderstand you.

rude *Rude* has various meanings, one of which is about a person or a remark that is vulgar or offensive. But it's old-fashioned now to say, for example, 'He's very rude' or 'That's a rude word'. In that sense, *rude* is more or less confined to children ('Don't be rude to mummy, Johnny'). You can still use *rude* about a person or a word if you like, but it would sound stuffy and prudish to most people.

rugby or **Rugby** The game of rugby football is supposed to have originated at Rugby School in Warwickshire. For that reason many people, and even some recent dictionaries, spell the game with a capital R. The connection is too tenuous and the game too widespread to warrant this, so nearly all sports writers write *rugby*.

(work to) rule See go-slow; restrictive practices

rumba or **rhumba** Most British dictionaries show *rhumba* as an alternative spelling. But it is more correct to dance the *rumba*, which is the spelling in South American Spanish.

runner-up The term was originally used in sports, for a runner who came second in a race. It can now be used for any kind of contest, from the Olympic Games to a literary prize. The plural form is *runners-up*.

ruralization For the last two centuries in Europe, *urbanization* has been the rule, people leaving low-paid work in remote parts of the country to seek a higher standard of living in cities. Since the 1960s, there are increasing signs of the reverse process occurring, *ruralization*, people abandoning the overcrowding and high cost of living in cities for rural areas. We shall hear more of this word during the remaining years of the century.

Russia, **USSR** or **Soviet Union** See Russian and Soviet

Russian or **Cyrillic** See Cyrillic . . .

Russian and **Soviet** After 70 years of service, the name *Soviet* was finally made redundant towards the end of 1991. There was no formal ceremony as it sank into obsolescence, leaving behind considerable linguistic confusion. *Soviet* came into English when Communist rule was established in 1917: it is a transliteration of the Russian word for a council, as elected councils formed the government of the new regime. For Russians, *Soviet* originally described heroic qualities, but for the rest of the world it did service as a general descriptive word (Soviet ballet dancer, Soviet athlete, Soviet spy, etc) and as a noun (*a Soviet* was an alternative name for a Russian).

Russia (formally and long-windedly the Russian Soviet Federal Socialist Republic) remained the umbrella word in Britain and America for anyone or anything connected with the USSR. Some people were aware at the back of their minds that this ran a steamroller over Ukrainians, Moldavians, Lithuanians and people belonging to the other countries that were part of the world's largest state, but it seemed a small price to pay for a great linguistic convenience. The country as a whole was officially the USSR (the Union of Soviet Socialist Republics) or the *Soviet Union*.

The world-shaking changes in the Soviet empire in 1991 moved too fast for language to keep up, and no one knew what to call the country. Editorials in British newspapers fell back on 'what used to be the Soviet Union' or 'the former Soviet Union' but such terms were temporary stopgaps. John Major referred to 'the new Russia', without defining what that was meant to include.

By the end of 1991, it looked as if a new name was emerging for the former USSR: the *CIS*, Commonwealth of Independent States. *Commonwealth* and *independent* seemed too liberal and democratic to sit comfortably after the terrors of Stalinism and the grimness of his successors, Khrushchev and Brezhnev, and the West hesitated to take up the name CIS because the future is uncertain. From the start, the Baltic states, Estonia, Latvia and Lithuania, seceded from the alliance, Georgia was in the midst of civil war, and there is opposition from nationalist movements in some of the other countries to the dominating influence of Russia. CIS is recognized in sport. In 1992, Wimbledon tennis had a player from the CIS, there was a CIS football team (defeated 3–0 by the Scots) in the European championships and CIS athletes in the Olympics.

For many people in the West, *Russia* and *Russian* remain convenient umbrella names for the whole country and for the language. At the same time, there is growing awareness of the identity of other nations that had been submerged by the old Soviet Union, and the need to recognize Armenia, Azerbaijan, the Ukraine, Moldova (formerly Moldavia) and the others as independent sovereign states speaking their own languages. In Brussels and in other international organizations, the terms NIS (newly independent states) and FSU (former Soviet Union) are still heard, but the more reliable name now in the English-speaking world is CIS.

· S ·

s' or **s's**   See **apostrophe/1**, problem (i); **names ending in** -*s* . . .

SA   As Britain becomes more involved with Europe, we need to be familiar with the abbreviation SA. The letters stand for Société Anonyme, in many ways the equivalent of British *Ltd*. SA is used mainly for French companies but the form can also be used for companies registered in Belgium, Luxembourg and other French-speaking countries.

sabre-rattling   See **brinkmanship** . . .

saccharin or **saccharine**   *Saccharin* (pron: 'SAKerin') is the noun, white crystalline tablets or powder used as a substitute for sugar. *Saccharine* (pron: 'SAKereen') is the adjective, used to describe a sickly sweet taste or by extension anything that is cloying: a saccharine manner, a saccharine smile. . . .

sack   See **dismiss** . . .

sacred cow   The idea of a *sacred cow* comes from the Hindus who hold that animal in veneration. The expression came into use among American journalists during the early part of this century for copy that for some reason could not be changed. It is used in Britain as well now for anything that is beyond criticism, cannot be interfered with or altered, because tradition or some powers higher up would not allow it. Jonathan Glancy, writing about design in *The Independent*, called the wartime Spitfire and the E-type Jaguar *sacred cows* of British design; no one can dare to suggest that they had faults.

sacrilegious   See **irreligious** . . .

sadism   See **masochism** . . .

safe haven   See **haven**

safe sex   Before the mid-1980s, this expression could have been ambiguous, for *safe sex* belongs to the post-Aids culture: the term is used by the Health Education Council in its campaign against **Aids**. *Safe sex* is having intercourse using a condom. At the end of 1990, Durex, the leading manufacturer of condoms, responded with a new brand, a flip-top box, like a packet of cigarettes, with a seemingly handwritten name scrawled across it – *Safe Play*.

safety net   *Safety nets* are sometimes used by trapeze acrobats in a circus, to catch them if there is an accident. The term is more common now in the politics of social welfare, for built-in safeguards in the social security system to pick up those people who could not survive without some kind of support in one way or another. The euphemism for those who are left out is 'they slipped through the net'.

saga   See **epic** . . .

(it is) said that . . .   A common device in speeches, articles and conversation, usually carrying with it the implication that what is supposed to have been said is true and generally accepted. It is one of those introductory statements that brush aside objections. Don't be taken in by it: it is said that people who use this trick too often rarely know *who* it is that said *that*, and whether they are right to have said it.

Saint, **saint**, **St** or **Ste**   When we are referring to a person who has been canonized, it is always with a capital S: Saint (abbreviated to St) George. When the word is used more generally, a capital is not appropriate (saints and sinners). There is no capital in 'saint's day', nor, if we should ever use that old exclamation so beloved by schoolboy stories of the 1920s, 'My sainted aunt!'

A stop is nearly always omitted now after *St* (St John's Wood). Lastly, *Ste* is not used in English: it is the abbreviation for *Sainte*, the feminine form in French of *Saint*, which is always joined (as is *St* in French) to the name with a hyphen: Ste-Anne, Ste-Marie. . . .

(for) . . . sake   There are three rules when it is for someone's or something's *sake*:

1 When it is for the sake of someone, and their name is used, *'s* follows: for Christ's sake, for Henry's sake. . . .

2 *'s* or an apostrophe on its own follows an ordinary noun (depending on whether it is singular or plural): for the chairman's sake, for the neighbours' sake.

3 When it's a noun of more than one syllable ending in an *s* sound, neither an *s* nor an apostrophe need be used: for goodness sake, for success sake, for the policies sake. . . .

salary   See **pay** . . .

saleable or **salable**   Dictionaries show these as alternative spellings, but the fact is *saleable* is so much the rule in Britain that *salable* looks wrong, especially as dictionaries show only one spelling for *unsaleable*. *Salable* is the usual spelling in America.

salesman, **saleswoman**, **rep** or **commercial traveller** *Salesman* or *saleswoman* (a few people have tried out 'salesperson' but it doesn't seem to work) are general terms for anyone who is selling anything, although many people prefer to avoid the word: people selling houses and flats call themselves **estate or house agents**, people selling pension policies and other investments put down their occupation as 'investment consultants', people selling ideas and typescripts for books to publishers are 'literary agents'. None of them would like it if you called them salesmen or saleswomen.

A *rep* or *sales rep* (short for 'representative') is the standard term now for what used to be called a *commercial traveller* (a name that has dropped out of use), a salesman or saleswoman who travels on behalf of a company, selling its products or services.

salon or **saloon** *Salon* (French for a drawing-room), which used to be associated with grand receptions for the good and the great, has been taken over by hairdressers. The more distinguished meaning of the word is still common in France, where a salon might be an important art exhibition or a fashion show.

In Britain, a car with four doors used to be solemnly called a *saloon* car, to distinguish it from an open car. The equivalent in America was a *sedan*. Both words, as descriptions of cars, have gone down the drain. *Saloon* survives on board ship for the main lounge for passengers, and just about still exists as *saloon bar* in some pubs, which at one time marked the fading distinction between a better-appointed bar for the middle class with their gins-and-tonics, and the 'public bar' for the cloth caps with their pints of bitter. The old tradition is meticulously preserved in the mock-up of a Victorian pub, the Sir Winston Churchill, near the Arc de Triomphe in Paris: two glass doors are beautifully etched *Saloon Bar* and *Public Bar*, even if they do both lead to the same bar!

Saloon is also the word for a bar in America, but it belongs more now to the Wild West than to say the bar of the Four Seasons in Park Avenue, New York.

salve It would be rare to hear a doctor use *salve* any more as a noun, for a cream that helps a wound to heal. In that sense, *salve* belongs to the days of apothecaries.

As a verb, *salve*, in the sense of saving property, especially a ship and its cargo, from loss, is also rare, as the usual word now is 'salvage'. Which leaves only one use for this 13th-century word, which is to *salve* feelings, conscience, etc, that is to make someone feel better about what has happened. The earlier pronunciation 'sahlv' is still heard from some older people, and is shown as an alternative in some dictionaries, but it has almost given way entirely to the usual pronunciation now: 'sallv'.

salvoes or **salvos** Dictionaries allow ships to fire *salvoes* or *salvos*; the Royal Navy prefers its ships to fire *salvoes*.

same This piece of commercial jargon is regrettably still current: 'We enclose our statement which is now overdue, so we should be glad if you would settle same without delay'; 'An extra charge will be involved and we shall advise you of same'. Neither firm deserves to be paid a penny, for using *same* as a pompous substitute for 'it'.

sample See **cross-section** . . .

samurai Japanese films have made this word known in the West. A *samurai* was a member of the warrior aristocracy in Japan, fiercely arrogant and bound by a strict code of conduct. A *samurai* can now also mean any Japanese army officer. Plural is same as the singular: *samurai* (usually pron: 'SAMyooreye').

sanatorium or **sanitarium** The spellings are easily confused: it is *sanatorium* in Britain, *sanitarium* in America.

sanction A *sanction* can be imposed as a penalty or as a way of enforcing a law. As a verb, *sanction* is a formal way of giving permission: 'the governing body sanctioned his leave of absence'. Avoid using *sanction* to mean imposing sanctions or a penalty ('He was sanctioned for his absence'): the verb can only be used for giving approval.

sandwich course This is a curious way of adapting the method supposedly devised by the 4th Earl of Sandwich (1718–92) to enable him to stay at the gaming table, without breaking for a meal. *Sandwich course* dates from the 1950s as an official term for a combination of full-time education, usually at technical colleges, *sandwiched* between periods of practical experience in industry.

sang or **sung** Dictionaries used to allow the older form 'I sung a song yesterday' as well as 'I sang a song'. Recent dictionaries have dropped 'I sung' as obsolete. The two past forms now are 'I *sang* a song' and 'a song was *sung*'.

sang-froid *Sang-froid* (French for 'cold blood') is stronger than equivalent expressions in English, such as relaxed, laid back, **cool**. For *sang-froid* refers particularly to keeping calm and balanced in the face of danger or a specially demanding situation. 'Keeping your cool' means the same but is blatantly slang.

It is usual to say someone *has* or *had* sang-froid in a difficult situation, rather than 'keeping' or 'showing' sang-froid. (Pron: 'sah(n)FRWAH'.)

sank, **sunk** or **sunken** There are a number of verbs with confusing alternative past forms. *Sink* is one that people often agonize over. Here are guidelines. 'The ship *sank*' rather than 'the ship *sunk*', a form which is becoming obsolete. But 'the ship *was* *sunk*'. The older form sunken survives as a descriptive word before a noun: 'a *sunken* garden', 'a *sunken* road'. . . .

sarcastic   See caustic . . .

sari, **saree** or **sarong**   It would be offensive to an Indian woman to call her *sari* a *sarong*. *Sari* is a Hindi word that derives from Sanskrit, and the finest ones are great lengths of beautiful silk that drape elegantly round the whole body. A *sarong* is a Malay word used for a sheath-like garment hung from the hips. *Saree* is an alternative spelling shown in dictionaries, but *sari* is preferred as closer to the Hindi word.

satellite   This key word in communications in the 1990s goes back a long way, to a meaning far from the world of satellite communication systems. It derives from a Latin word for an attendant or guard, used in the 16th century for a personal retainer serving a powerful nobleman or official. Early in the 17th century, astronomy adapted this meaning, using *satellites* for the planets revolving round Jupiter, and later for any asteroid that gravitational force keeps in orbit round a larger planet.

Since World War II, *satellite* has taken off in other directions. In politics, *satellite State* was used particularly for one of the countries under the control of the former Soviet Union, evoking the original meaning of satellite. In town-planning, a *satellite town* provides accommodation and social facilities for its inhabitants, who are dependent for employment on a larger town within easy commuting distance. In computer terms, a *satellite computer* is one that processes data under the control of a larger computer installation.

It is in communication technology that the word *satellite* has really moved in. The moon, the main heavenly satellite orbiting the earth, has been joined by a number of man-made satellites which receive and transmit signals for television, telecommunication, radio, enabling us to see in Britain a test match in Australia, the President speaking on the steps of the White House, bombs hitting targets in far-off wars, at the very moment these events are taking place.

satellite dish   See dish

satisfied   See happy . . .

satsumas   See tangerines . . .

satyromaniac   See nymphomaniac . . .

sauce   See gravy . . .

Saudi   Two pronunciations are heard: 'SOWdee' (first syllable rhyming with 'cow') and 'SAWdee'. 'SOWdee' is used by the BBC and is generally preferred.

savannah   See grasslands

save   *Save* is a basic term in computer language: the input of data into a computer is impermanent until it is *saved*, that is stored on an auxiliary **disk**.

savoir faire   See know-how . . .

sawed or **sawn**   It can be either 'I have sawed the wood' or 'I have sawn . . .'. *Sawed* is the more usual for the past form of the verb, and *sawn* will eventually become obsolete. When it precedes a noun, it is *sawn* in Britain (a sawn-off shotgun), usually *sawed* in America (a sawed-off shotgun).

scab or **blackleg**   *Scab*, for a worker who refuses to take part in a strike and continues working, goes back to the beginning of the 19th century. In 1984 *scab* became one of the most abusive words in industrial relations, as it was shouted out during the year-long miners' strike, even by children, at anyone who defied the stike call.

Blackleg was first used for a worker who was brought into a factory to replace one on strike. It later became used generally for any worker who did not support a strike. Since the miners' strike, *scab* has taken over as the sharper nastier word.

scampi   See crayfish . . .

scan   As well as a number of technical and medical meanings, and the literary meaning of analysing the rhythm of verse, one meaning of *scan* is to look at something intently. Another meaning is the opposite, to look through something quickly ('She scanned the property ads looking for a flat'). Be on guard against a possible misunderstanding: 'Would you scan that report' could mean go through it carefully, but for some people it would mean – take a quick look at it.

Scandinavian   See Nordic . . .

scant   Fowler was scathing about the use of *scant* (which he considered a literary word) in everyday contexts (*Modern English Usage*, 1926): 'a scant number of shareholders turned up for the AGM'. Perhaps he was being too severe: *scant* is an old word, going back to the 14th century, but it's none the worse for that. And because it survives in some set phrases, such as 'scant regard for the truth', 'in scant supply', 'to show scant courtesy', *scant* is available when you want to stress that something is inadequate or skimpy.

scapegoat or **fall guy**   It is hard to consider *fall guy* as slang in America, since it has existed since the early years of this century, and was used during the official investigation by the Senate of Colonel Oliver North's involvement in the Iran–Contra affair. It is at home in British English, but more as an echo of the idiom of old Hollywood gangster films.

Scapegoat has much more respectable antecedents. It goes back to the mid-16th century, and is probably connected with the story in the Old Testament (*Leviticus*) of one of two goats chosen for sacrifice.

Both words mean a person who is blamed for someone else's wrongdoing or mistake. But *fall guy* carries with it the suggestion of a dupe, an easy prey to clever intrigue; whereas *scapegoat* implies victimization rather than naivety, someone being trapped in a situation beyond their control.

scarcely See **barely** . . .

scarves or **scarfs** All dictionaries show these as alternative plurals for *scarf*: some prefer one, some the other.

scenario, **script**, **screenplay** or **film-script** *Scenario* sounds Italian (which it is) and impressive, so in the early days of Hollywood it became the standard word for the script of a film. Now you hear *script* or *screenplay* in America and *filmscript* in Britain.

A more recent use (and overuse) of *scenario* is for a sequence of events in the past, or forecast for the future: 'This was the scenario that led up to the crisis', 'The scenario for what will happen next is . . .'. *Scenario* is also used pointlessly as an alternative to 'situation': 'Faced with this scenario, he had to resign'. Pron: 'seNAHrio' in Britain, 'seNAIRrio' in Hollywood. See also **nightmare scenario**

scene Actors have said for years 'It's not my scene' about a scene in a play they do not appear in. Now anyone of us can use the same expression: when there is a place or a situation we do not like or do not fit into, Ascot, for example, or a vicarage garden party, we can say 'It's not my scene'.

'Behind the scenes' is another theatrical phrase adapted to real-life situations, hyphenated as a descriptive word for confidential or secret matters: 'Some behind-the-scenes information has come our way'.

scenery See **set** . . .

scent See **perfume** . . .

sceptic *Sceptic* and its associated words are the only ones beginning with *sce-*, where the *c* is sounded: 'SKEPtic'. American English, which is more inclined towards spelling words as they are pronounced, spells it *skeptic*.

schedule There are people who tut-tut about it, but the American pronunciation, 'SKEDjool', is heard in Britain, and even respectable Oxford dictionaries show it as an alternative way of saying the word. Until the *sk-* pronunciation becomes generally accepted, it's better to stay with 'SHEDjool'.

schizophrenic It is linguistically irresponsible to use *schizophrenic* lightly, as it is sometimes, about anyone who is in two minds over what to do next. 'Undecided' or 'in two minds' are more suitable descriptions of an attitude that we all experience at times. For schizophrenia is a serious mental illness

leading to a deterioration of the whole personality. In the early part of the century, two Greek words, one meaning 'split' and the other 'mind', were linked together to form *schizophrenia*, as the name for a psychosis with a great variety of symptoms, a kind of madness in which behaviour is totally contradictory. (Pron: 'skitse(r)FRENNic'.)

schlep This Yiddish word (from German 'schleppen', to drag) means to carry heavy or cumbersome things from one place to another. *Schlep* is familiar idiom in New York, often heard in 'showbiz' circles in Britain, and now shows up (as informal usage) in sober Oxford dictionaries. A good, if incongruous, example of its use was a New York paper's comment that the Queen on her visit to America would *schlep* 95 pieces of baggage along with her (quoted by Leo Rosten in *The Joys of Yiddish*).

schmaltz Elevated to standard English by some recent dictionaries, *schmaltz*, a Yiddish word for chicken fat, is curiously listed even in the *Oxford Dictionary for Writers and Editors*. It is extended as an expressive word for anything, especially music, that is excessively sentimental and cloying. Roughly equivalent to the old-fashioned slang word 'corny' but much more colourful.

Schmaltz comes in for justifiable use in the art world, and an art critic has commented on the lucrative 'art market for schmaltz', syrupy paintings of stomach-turning sentimentality.

school See **college** . . .

science, **technology** or **technics** *Technology* has been in English since the early 17th century. Since World War II, it has become the standard word for *applied science*, an all-embracing word for scientific developments in industry and business (see also **R & D**). Outside the classroom, *science* tends to be used now mostly for research and in academic contexts. *Technics* (the word is rarely used in the singular) is an alternative word for *technology*, used perhaps more in America.

Science and *technology* are words of progress, as they have always been, but more than ever before, they are also words of apprehension at the speed of that progress. See also **mechanization** . . .

science fiction Jules Verne was writing science fiction (*Twenty Thousand Leagues under the Sea*, 1870; *Around the World in Eighty Days*, 1873), and H G Wells had written *The Time Machine* (1895) and *War of the Worlds* (1898), long before an American, Hugo Gernsback, invented the term in 1926. Now *science fiction* is a recognized form of the novel. The term is extended for use about anything futuristic and seemingly improbable ('the whole project is pure science fiction'), as a way of writing off what appear to be crazy technological ideas. But science and technology have a way of catching up and overtaking *SF*, the aficionados' term for science fiction.

scissors *Scissors*, like *trousers*, has never been turned into a singular noun. A *pair of scissors* (and *a pair of trousers*) is the only singular form. Most of us are used to it, since English has lived with this minor eccentricity since Chaucer in the 14th century.

scone The middle classes unhesitatingly pronounce *scone* as 'skon' (to rhyme with 'John'), because that's how they've been brought up, usually without knowing why. Scones originally came from Scotland, where the word was often spelt 'scon' and pronounced that way, as it still is in Scotland. The kind of people who had vicars to tea followed this pronunciation to show they knew about such things. It has remained one of the linguistic symbols of middle-class superiority ever since. (The Stone of Scone, on which Scotland's kings were crowned, is always pronounced 'skoon' to rhyme with 'moon'.)

Americans, free from such shibboleths, pronounce the word as it is spelt, 'skohn' (to rhyme with 'bone'), and many English do the same, although some people look down on them for it.

Scottish, **Scots** or **Scotch** *Scotch* is the oldest word and used to be in general use. But north of the Border, ever since the late 19th century, they have preferred to call nearly everything *Scottish*: Scottish scenery, Scottish food, etc, and *Scottish* is the accepted word to use everywhere. We should talk of *a Scotsman*, *a Scotswoman* or *the Scots* but in most other contexts, when in doubt, use *Scottish*. There is no need to ask for Scottish broth, a Scottish egg or Scottish whisky, as even the Scots are quite happy to keep *Scotch* firmly anchored to those words, to say nothing of Scotch mist (the fog-like drizzle in the Highlands).

screenplay See scenario . . .

screw The word has many meanings. The vulgar one is the slang usage that goes back at least a hundred years, as a noun or a verb meaning sexual intercourse. This is a five-letter word among the **four-letter words**, and is widely used in Britain and America. The popular Sunday newspaper, famous for reporting sexual scandals, used to be called by some people *The Screws of the World*!

scrip issue This investment term is becoming more familiar, with the increasing number of shareholders in privatized industries. *Scrip* is probably linked with 'script', something written on a piece of paper, or it is suggested it is an abbreviation for 'subscription receipt'. A *scrip issue* is a free issue of shares to existing stockholders. It is, in effect, a bonus or dividend, although this depends on whether the shares maintain their price or drop in value.

script See scenario . . .

scroll The Dead Sea Scrolls are the biblical Hebrew manuscripts dating from 250BC, discovered in the 1950s and 60s. Computer language has taken the fine 15th-century word *scroll*, for a roll of parchment, and turned it into a verb with a meaning light-years away from the work of those ancient scribes. In computer terms, to scroll is to move data or text up or down a screen in order to read the sequence or locate a section of it.

scrummage or **scrimmage** Both words are football terms and can be confusing. In rugby football, a *scrummage* is an alternative word for a *scrum* (the forwards of each team face each other, arms interlocked, heads down, and play is restarted when the ball is thrown between them). A *scrimmage* describes an interplay in American football, which starts with the oval ball on the ground pointing towards the goal.

(close) scrutiny It is hardly possible to scrutinize anything without subjecting it to *close scrutiny*. So, of course, the word *close* is not really required. Its justification is it stresses for readers the meaning of scrutiny, conjuring up a picture of someone screwing up their eyes to peer intently at something. If you need further support, the *Concise Oxford Dictionary* (1990 edition) defines *scrutinize* as 'examine with close scrutiny'.

scud The 1991 Gulf War introduced us on television to *scud missiles*, indiscriminate barrages projected from hidden sites in Iraq over Saudi Arabia and Tel Aviv in particular. Alongside its other meanings as a verb, *scud* is hesitantly emerging as a word to mean giving someone a beating, knocking them for six. Whether this new use will become established is uncertain as yet, but it must be admitted that *scud* has the right sound for this new meaning.

sculpt or **sculpture** Both words can serve as verbs for the making of pieces of sculpture. For what it is worth, a straw poll taken among a handful of sculptors shows they prefer to *sculpt* their work rather than *sculpture* it. As descriptive words, *sculpted* is more usual to describe the work of a sculptor, with *sculptured* for something that has that appearance ('sand dunes sculptured by the wind').

sculptress As many actresses prefer to call themselves **actors**, most women sculptors reject the feminine form *sculptress*. It must be added that *The Independent* dared to refer to the sculptor of the statue of Arthur Harris, wartime head of Bomber Command, as the *sculptress* of the work. Nevertheless, by the end of the century, *sculptress* will almost certainly join the ranks of authoress, poetess, etc as one of yesterday's words. See also **-ess forms**

seafood, **shellfish** or **crustacés** *Seafood* was being used in America by the mid-19th century as a word for any edible fish. About the 1960s, *seafood* started to become popular with restaurants in Britain, as a more appetizing word than 'fish', with its downmarket associations of 'fish and chips'.

Seafood is now well-established on British menus: some people use it only for *shellfish* (lobster, crab, shrimps, etc), others extend it to any fish that we eat, whether it comes from the sea or rivers.

Grander restaurants usually still prefer to head that section of their menus with the traditional word *Fish*. Gastronomic restaurants may prefer *fish* for sole, trout, salmon, etc, and the French word *crustacés* (usually given an anglicized pronunciation: 'krooSTAS-Say') for shellfish.

seance or **séance**   In English, *seance* is the usual spelling and only die-hard Francophiles insist on *séance* any more. See **accents in print**

sear or **sere**   The only spelling most of us need bother with is *sear*: it means to scorch something, or inflict acute pain or distress (seared by a tragedy), or in the kitchen, to sear meat at a very high heat so that the juices are sealed in.

The spelling *sere* is an archaic descriptive word for shrivelled by age ('in the sere and yellow' is an affected way of saying 'old'), also used sometimes by gunsmiths for the catch of a gun.

seasonable and **seasonal**   There is a fine but distinct line between these two words. 'Seasonable weather we're having' means that the weather is appropriate to the time of the year, warm days in summer, snow in winter, etc. We should only use *seasonable* when whatever it is is natural and suitable for that season of the year.

Seasonal unemployment is unemployment that usually occurs in a particular season or time of the year, soon after Christmas for example. We should use *seasonal*, not so much about natural phenomena, such as the weather, but about events that occur at a particular time or season.

The above applies equally to *unseasonable* and *unseasonal*. Weather in England is often *unseasonable*, out of place for the time of the year (snow in June, for example); *unseasonal* is an inappropriate time or period: to have a glass of whisky mid-morning is drinking at an unseasonal hour.

secondary picketing   See **flying pickets** . . .

second class   See **first class** . . .

secrecy or **secretiveness**   *Secrecy* is appropriate to information and situations, rather than to a person: 'the secrecy of these documents must be respected'; 'plans will be carried out in secrecy'. *Secretiveness* is a personal quality: 'his secretiveness over where he'd been made her suspicious'; 'because of the secretiveness of her manner, we never know what she is thinking'.

secret   See **confidential** . . .

secretary   There used to be an element of class distinction in the way *secretary* is pronounced. On the

right side of the tracks, it was given three syllables ('SEK-re-try'), and on the wrong side, four syllables ('SEK-re-terry'). Four syllables are standard in America, and are heard so often now that some current dictionaries show that pronunciation as standard in Britain. Others continue to insist on 'SEK-re-try'. It is reasonable to say now that it is a matter of taste which pronunciation is used. But gobbling the first *r* ('SEK-etry') is not acceptable.

Women, and not only feminists, are justifiably angry when a man refers to his secretary as 'my girl' ('I'll get my girl to see to it'). In the 1990s, that is offensive and out of touch.

secretiveness   See **secrecy** . . .

sect   In its origin (from Latin 'sector', to follow continually), *sect* is a neutral word for a group following a religion or a spiritual teacher. It has taken on now a predominantly negative colouring, implying the practice of antisocial or evil practices, or people under the power of a charismatic leader. This pejorative meaning has been reinforced by the media using '*sectarian* killings' in connection with Northern Ireland. While a bad meaning is not inherent in the word *sect*, we should be aware that it has acquired uneasy associations and should be careful how we use the word.

sectarian   See previous entry

section or **sector**   *Sector* used to be primarily a technical term and *section*, as well as having technical applications, was used in general contexts. Now *sector* has become standard for referring to a *section* of the economy ('the private sector', for example) or of society.

secular   See **profane** . . .

security   *Security* has been in the language since the 15th century, meaning the quality of being safe (it derives from Latin 'securitas', freedom from care), but it is now a word that is all around us. We have *security checks* at airports and going into national art museums, there are *security guards* protecting buildings, someone is deported as a *security risk* because their presence is a threat to the country, *computer security* is the protection of data stored in a computer, and the peace of the world rests with the *Security Council* of the United Nations. See also **collateral** . . .

sedative . . .   See **tranquillizer**

seduction   See **rape** . . .

see, **vide** or **qv**   All three can be used to refer a reader to another reference, another book or another section of the same book. The abbreviation *qv* stands for *quod vide* (pron: 'kwodVEEday'), meaning 'which see'. The Latin verb *vide* (pron: 'VEEday') simply means 'see'.

See . . . is the verb used in *The Good English Guide*

when readers are referred to another entry for further information. There is no good reason for using *vide*, except academic formality. The other expression, *qv*, can usually be replaced by 'refer to . . .'.

see above and **below** In a letter or a book, 'as above', 'see above', etc refer to a statement higher up the page. Such expressions can also refer to what has been mentioned on a previous page, or even two, three or more pages earlier, although that's making unreasonable demands on the reader's memory. The same applies to *below*: 'as referred to below . . .', 'the information given below . . .', etc. In such cases, it's more considerate to write 'see the previous page' or 'see page X', or summarize whatever it is, to save readers the hassle of turning to other pages.

seed-corn money This is a colourful political and industrial financial phrase borrowed from farming. Spending *seed-corn money* is using it for new projects that will 'take root and send up green shoots', leading to development of business and increased profits.

seeded and **unseeded** These are tennis terms. A strong player is *seeded*, that is placed in a special list of players to avoid leading competitors meeting each other in early matches. *Unseeded* players are not accorded that importance.

see through As a noun, *see through* is a technical term in printing for the extent to which an impression on an underlying page shows through on the next page. For the rest of us, *see through*, as a noun or a descriptive word, has a more intriguing meaning. It is said that the designer Yves Saint-Laurent introduced *see through* into modern clothes design for women with his translucent shirts, and the link between *see through* and fashion has continued ever since, restricted, for the time being, to allowing women's bodies to be revealed through diaphanous materials.

segregation *Segregation* is the term used in other countries, corresponding to **apartheid** in South Africa. It is the word for legal or social separation of racial groups, with varying degrees of severity, usually providing separate educational and public facilities. It could also include other discriminatory laws and practices.

self or **self-** *Self* can be prefixed to many words and nearly always a hyphen should be used: self-catering, self-composed, self-conscious, self-contained, self-drive, self-fulfilling, self-pity, self-sufficient, etc.

self-centred or **selfish** It is unfortunate that these words are often used interchangeably, because there is a valuable distinction. *Selfish* is thinking just of yourself and not caring about others. *Self-centred* could mean being intelligently aware of yourself, both as an individual and in relation to others. Not everyone accepts that difference of meaning, and if you say

someone is self-centred, it is more likely to be taken as a criticism.

self-fulfilling In the financial world, many prophecies are *self-fulfilling*, that is they make something happen merely by forecasting it. So much in business and investment depends upon confidence, the stock markets of the world are affected by rumours as well as facts. If enough financial experts forecast a recession and falling share prices, there is often a rush to sell shares, and prices do fall. In those terms, the prophecy is *self-fulfilling*. With the ever-increasing power of the **media**, *self-fulfilling* is coming in for more use in the 1990s.

sell by and **best before** These designations for dates are familiar to all of us now, stamped on packages containing anything from biscuits to butter. *Sell by* is clear enough: it is an instruction to staff to ensure that packets are cleared off shelves after that date.

Sell-by, hyphenated as a descriptive term, is usefully extended for more general use: an idea, proposal, scheme are said to have passed their *sell-by date* when they are no longer relevant or of use. Robert Burchfield, former editor of Oxford English dictionaries, has neatly taken *sell-by* into linguistics: a word or expression is past its sell-by date when it's no longer current and readily understood, a more lively term than the scholarly word, **archaism**.

A *best before* date is less transparent: is it a **euphemism** for 'no good after', or a sinister warning that the store abandons all responsibility for what happens to us if we eat or drink whatever it is later than the *best before* date? The sinister application of *best before* to a man or a woman has not happened, at least not yet. See also **shelf life**

seller or **vendor** In the centuries after the Norman Conquest in 1066, many Old English and Norman-French words were used as pairs, so that both sides could understand. *Seller*, from the Old English form, has remained the everyday word, with *vendor*, the French form, now only used by lawyers and estate agents as the word for the *seller* of a property. When we're buying a house, it's usual to refer to the other person as the *vendor*, but if we're buying anything else, the person behind the counter is the *seller*. Some expensive fashion shops find anything to do with selling too downmarket, so they use the modern French word for a saleswoman, *vendeuse* (pron: 'vahnDE(R)Z'). The customers (usually called **clientele**) pay all the more for the affectation.

It's curious that machines that sell articles should be called *vending*-machines rather than *selling*-machines, but language follows its own way.

sellers' market See buyers' market . . .

selling Buying and selling make the world go round, and the word *selling* now comes into a wide range of contexts. Selling goods or products has always been with us. But now we *sell* ideas, campaigns, strategies, and we *sell* ourselves. *Selling* has become an overworked word covering any act of persuasion. It is worth taking some of the load off it: instead of selling someone on an idea, we could 'convince' them; instead of prime ministers selling the nation on a policy, they could 'explain' it to them; instead of selling ourselves, we could 'make a good impression'. There's nothing wrong with the word *selling*, for as Vance Packard commented '. . . some pushing and hauling of the citizenry is probably necessary to make our $400,000,000,000-a-year economy work'. (That figure was quoted in 1957, by the way, in *The Hidden Persuaders*.) But there are other words we can use from time to time, to take the strain off *selling*.

sell short　The uninitiated are often puzzled by this expression, mostly used in dealing in stocks and shares, but occasionally about other things as well. To *sell short* is to sell things, usually shares, that you do not possess, but expect to be able to buy at a good price before you have to deliver the goods. In this way, *selling short* is a calculated gamble. But be on guard against a misunderstanding! 'To sell someone short' is to talk them down, to disparage their qualities.

semantics　See psycholinguistics . . .

semi-　See demi- . . .

semicolon (;)　See colon (:) . . .

semi-detached　We all know what *semi-detached* houses are, houses joined together down one side. During the 1980s, *semi-detached* came in for another curious use, for a married couple who live more or less separate lives. When the magazine *Harpers and Queen* reported in 1989 on a survey of married couples, they commented on 'how much time many happily-married couples are spending apart through choice'. If they can afford it, a couple might even live in separate houses: Margaret Drabble and Michael Holroyd, said to be the most celebrated literary *semi-detached* couple, live in different parts of London. *Semi-detached* has been described as 'the commitment of marriage without the curse of its routine' (Elizabeth Grice, *The Sunday Times*).

There is a sad version of *semi-detached*, which is an unhappy couple forced to share the same house, because they cannot afford to buy separate homes, trying to live apart from each other as much as possible.

seminal　Used in biological contexts in connection with semen and reproduction, *seminal* is often used more widely now to describe something that contains the seeds of future creative development: 'a seminal book', 'seminal ideas', 'a seminal speech'.

seminar　See course . . .

Semitic　Because *anti-Semitic* is discrimination against Jews, *Semitic* is often believed to have only one

meaning: Jewish. *Semitic* can be used for other peoples, Arabs and Phoenicians, for example, but the name has become so associated with the Jewish people that there could be a misunderstanding if it's used in other contexts. In linguistics, *Semitic languages* form the family of languages that includes Arabic, Assyrian, Ethiopian, among others, as well as Hebrew.

Senate　See **Congress** . . .

senator　See **congressman** . . .

send-up　See **parody** . . .

senior citizen　See **OAP** . . .

Señor, **Señora** and **Señorita**　When Spaniards are in England, do we introduce them as *Señor* Gonzalez, *Señorita* Fernandez, etc or *Mr* Gonzalez, *Miss* (or *Ms*) Fernandez? For the use of foreign courtesy titles in an English context, see **Mr, Mrs, etc or Monsieur, Frau, etc**.

sensitive or **classified**　Both words can now be used about information that could affect national, commercial or personal security. For further notes, see **classified** . . .

sensitiveness, **sensitivity** or **sensibility**　The line between these three words is not sharply defined. We are likely to talk about the *sensitiveness* of an injured part of the body, such as the sensitiveness of a leg after an operation. When it's a question of say a hand or fingers being responsive, *sensitivity* is the more appropriate word, as in the sensitivity of a pianist's fingers. *Sensitivity* and *sensitive* are also more likely to be used about someone's feelings, or of a musical performance, a situation, or for the reaction of something, such as film, to light, heat, etc.

Sensibility is not used so often. It would be convenient and logical if it meant 'full of good sense' but it doesn't, of course. It is used for the ability to feel both emotionally and physically: if a finger is badly injured, it could lose its *sensibility*, that is its sense of touch. When Jane Austen contrasted *Sense and Sensibility*, in the title of her novel, she was distinguishing between good sense and responsive feelings and emotions.

sensual or **sensuous**　Although some people use both these words in much the same way, *sensual* is usually pejorative, implying lustful indulgence in sex or excessive pleasure from food: 'She resented the sensual way he sized up her attractive figure'. *Sensuous* is a harmless word for enjoying something with one's senses: 'She loved the sensuous pleasure of swimming in a warm sea'. The distinction is worth preserving.

(length of) sentences　In creative writing the *length of sentences* is a matter of style. Short sentences go with action: long, well-written, balanced sentences can have the sonority of organ music. Straightforward functional communication is something else: long sentences embodying a number of ideas can be hard work for readers. They can get lost halfway and lose contact with the sequence of thought. The structure of sentences can make it as difficult to understand a passage as using long esoteric words. If a long sentence is necessary, at least try to put the central thought as near the beginning as possible, so readers know from the start where the sentence is leading.

Legal English is notorious for its long sentences, because lawyers are concerned that all the qualifications, conditions and exceptions are contained in a single sentence, to avoid loopholes. In fact, this is not necessary, as separate sentences can be linked by qualifying phrases such as 'As well as what has been stated . . .', 'An additional condition is . . .'. The National Consumer Council recommends lawyers to keep sentences shorter than 25 words.

Length of sentences should vary. It is a relief to a reader when several long sentences are followed by a very short one, or for that matter, a succession of short sentences is slowed down by a longer one. Remember also that it makes much more impact on a reader or listener to end a passage with a short sentence: ' "In three weeks England will have her neck wrung like a chicken." Some chicken. Some neck!' (Winston Churchill in 1941). Language, like life itself, is dull and clodhopping without rhythm.

sentiment and **sentimentality**   *Sentiment* has various meanings, but when it is contrasted with *sentimentality*, it is usually considered a true expression of feeling, sympathy, compassion and awareness of the human situation. The point at which sentiment spills over into *sentimentality* and becomes a mawkish unthinking response is a matter of opinion. James Joyce called sentimentality 'unearned emotion', a phrase that captures the idea of indulgence in emotion without paying the price of the inner struggle to comprehend it.

Sentimentality is always a pejorative word, suggesting a facile expression of emotion; *sentiment* can be reserved for the expression of genuine feeling.

separatism   See devolution . . .

sequestration   Since the Serious Fraud Office was constituted under the Criminal Justice Act 1987, *sequestration* has become a more familiar word. It is the legal term for an order by a court to commissioners, known as *sequestrators*, requiring them to take possession of an organization's or an individual's assets, wherever they may be.

sere   See sear . . .

sergeant or **serjeant**   *Sergeant* is the spelling in the army and the police. *Serjeant* survives only as legal use, in the *Common Serjeant*, a judicial officer of the City of London, who also acts as a circuit judge, the obsolete title *serjeant-at-law*, used for the highest rank in the legal profession, and *serjeant-at-arms*, formerly empowered to arrest traitors, now performing ceremonial duties, mostly in parliament.

serial or **soap opera**   The colourful satirical name *soap opera* dates from the 1930s, for radio serials in America sponsored by various brands of soap. These were traditionally family sagas, usually in half-hour episodes, each one with an emotional cliff-hanger ending. Soap operas, or *soaps*, have survived into television, popularly used in Britain as an alternative to *serial* for such long-running series as *Coronation Street* and *EastEnders*. A popular American parody of the **genre** was called – *Soap*.

serial killer   In America in the 1980s, *serial killer* replaced the more usual name 'mass murderer', for a person who commits a series of murders. The term has become familiar in Britain, mostly through well-publicized trials of American *serial killers*, such as the prostitute who in 1991 was condemned to death for killing seven middle-aged men who had hired her services.

serious or **solemn**   *Solemn* used to have a grandeur about it, a timeless transcendence of the everyday, as in, 'And all the air a solemn stillness holds' (Gray, *Elegy Written in a Country Churchyard*). *Solemn* often has a pejorative meaning now, suggesting heavy-going and dreary.

Russell Baker wrote an inspiring piece for *The New York Times Magazine*, explaining the difference between *solemn* and *serious*: he believes that jogging is solemn, poker is serious. 'Once you grasp that distinction,' he adds, 'you are on the way to enlightenment'. Among civilizations, he continued, the Roman Empire was solemn; Periclean Athens was serious. In journalism, *Playboy* is solemn; the *New Yorker* is serious. To help you get the idea, here are some more suggestions. A cheese soufflé (when it holds up) is serious; rice pudding must be *solemn*. Making love can be either serious or solemn: it all depends.

When we are serious we connect with the mainstream of human experience and feeling. When we are solemn we are out of touch and our words drag. In the 5000 or so entries in *The Good English Guide*, it must at times have lapsed into being solemn. As Russell Baker warns, it is hard to be Periclean Athens. For that matter, it's not all that easy to make a good cheese soufflé every time. It's hard to be serious. But it's always worth trying.

serjeant   See sergeant . . .

servant   See maid . . .

service   There was a good deal of fuss in the 1930s when the American use of *service* as a verb caught on in Britain. A P Herbert, MP at the time for Oxford University and a reasonable man by all accounts, fulminated against this 'foul new verb'. It was a storm in a teacup as no one thinks twice any more about asking a garage to service their car or a mechanic to service any other piece of equipment (see **nouns as verbs**).

The verb *service* has made further inroads since then, to become the institutional alternative to the verb 'serve': a local health centre, for example, is said to service a particular area. The term *service industry* has become the official name now for businesses, such as insurance, marketing, banking, catering, etc, that provide supporting facilities to other businesses, rather than manufacturing or supplying goods.

service charge See tip . . .

service industry See service

serviette See napkin . . .

session *Session* was a word mostly used in formal contexts, such as a court being *in session*, or for the meeting of an important assembly. It has now become the easygoing word for any activity: we have a long session with someone, a session at the dentist, a session with our solicitor and so on. Like all words that become fashionable, it is too often a lazy way of side-stepping the moment's thought necessary to come up with a more precise word: a 'meeting' or 'discussion' with someone, a 'treatment' with a dentist, a 'consultation' with a solicitor, or whatever other word defines what the session is about.

set, **setting** or **scenery** As a theatrical term, *set* was originally short for *stage setting*, but is now the standard word used in the theatre for the designs on the stage against which a play takes place, the painted canvas of the flats, furniture, ornaments, etc. It is more usual now to talk of the stage *set* rather than *setting*. *Set* is also the corresponding word for the designs of interior scenes of films.

Setting is used more outside the theatre to describe the general background against which anything in real life or fiction takes place: 'the setting of *Hiroshima, mon amour* was the port in SW Japan after the explosion of the first atomic bomb'. See also **context**, **framework and setting**.

Scenery belongs more to the general aspect of a landscape or the countryside, and it would sound old-fashioned to use the word for a stage set.

set-piece interview Described by a political commentator as 'a form of public torture', a *set-piece interview* is an interview on television or radio between a senior member of a political party and a more or less aggressive interviewer who is probing as deeply and uncomfortably as possible into policies, opinions, proposals, etc. The two of them sit, seemingly relaxed but not fooling anyone, facing each other for this cut and thrust contest of words, in which the interviewer aims to make the interviewee lose face. A researcher into set-piece interviews claims he has identified at least three hundred ways of *not* answering questions.

settee See couch . . .

setting See context . . .; set or scenery

settler or **settlor** A *settler* is someone who settles somewhere. *Settlor* is used only in law for a person who makes a settlement of property or of a sum of money.

set up or **set-up** We set up shop, set up a deal, set up someone financially, set up an object by placing it in a prominent position, all without a hyphen. But when it is a noun for an organization, it becomes *set-up*: 'he has organized a new set-up to handle the business'. In other contexts a set-up can mean a shady deal.

sewage or **sewerage** *Sewage* is the waste matter that has to be disposed of, and the arrangement of sewers that carries it away is the *sewerage*. To put it another way, *sewage* treatment takes place in a *sewerage* system.

sewn or **sewed** The past forms are: 'she sewed it well', 'she has sewn (or sewed) it well', 'it is well sewn (or sewed)'. Where *sewn* and *sewed* are alternatives, *sewn* is more usual.

The verb *sow*, for planting seeds, or doubts in someone's mind, has similar alternative past forms: 'she has sown (or sowed) doubts in his mind'.

sex or **gender** See gender . . .

sex or **sexuality** For the zoologist, Desmond Morris, to call the human species the sexiest of all the primates is 'a comment on the basic biological nature of the human animal' (*Manwatching*). A leader in *The Times* placed sex across the frontier of 'the most mysterious territory in human nature'. No other word in English carries such a load of yearning, fear and bewilderment, which is reflected in the sexual content of our vocabulary.

Sexuality, carrying the Latinate suffix *-ality* (the quality of being), is used at times as a less steamy alternative to *sex*: it sounds more respectable to have a discussion about *sexuality* than to talk about *sex*. A BBC radio programme in 1989 was called 'Sexuality in the Middle Ages' ('Sex in the Middle Ages' would have attracted a bigger audience!). The Church usually prefers to have an attitude towards *sexuality*, for the word does not cause the same frisson as *sex*.

sexism, **sexist** See feminism . . .

sexist language The fuss that is made about words such as **chairman**, **spokesman**, mankind, and the insistence by some women on unisex forms (*chairperson* or *chair*, *spokesperson*, **humankind**) reflects a much deeper social problem. Despite equal-pay legislation, women generally still earn less than men, and they're grossly under-represented in the professions and in parliament.

Feminists, and other women too, hope to change underlying attitudes by changing the words that reflect them. Linguistic habits are among the most difficult of all to shift and even women are divided, some feeling passionately about it, others finding the whole issue exaggerated. But the same was also true of the struggle earlier this century for votes for women. It is even more difficult with language, because masculine bias is so deeply ingrained: to take just one more example, a great painting is called an 'old master', but whatever the sex of the artist, we could hardly call it an 'old mistress'.

The best we can do is to be aware of words and expressions that could degrade or belittle women, and try to avoid them without it becoming silly. See also **-ess forms; feminine forms; -person; unisex grammar**

sex life The expression *sex life* dates from the 1920s, but it wasn't used much until the 1960s (in *Annus Mirabilis*, Philip Larkin took reasonable poetic licence to claim that sexual intercourse began in 1963, three years after the ban was lifted on *Lady Chatterley's Lover*). That's about the time when people began to talk more or less freely about their *sex life*.

By now only gynaecologists of the old school would ask their patients 'Is your sexual relationship satisfactory?' Others, who would find 'How's it going in bed?' too familiar, have no hesitation in asking 'How's your sex life?'

sexology or **sex therapy** In 1956 *The Shorter Oxford Dictionary* included sexology as an afterthought in the addenda at the back. Thanks to Alfred Kinsey, Masters and Johnson and all the others who have probed and pried into what were once dirty dark secrets, no dictionary now could leave out *sexology*. *Sexologists* carry out exhaustive research into what goes on between women and men in bed. Other sexologists treat people with sexual difficulties, and others pontificate in books on how to 'do it'. Germaine Greer described a degree in sexology at one university as 'a wonderful brew of biology, psychiatry, psychology, psychoanalysis, sociology, criminology, anthropology, education and philosophy' (*Sex and Destiny*).

Sex therapy is a clinical application of some of the mishmash of sexology. It is carried out by doctors, psychologists or other specialists in clinics and is generally regarded as respectable medical practice to help both men and women who suffer from impotence or other sexual problems.

sexual The sound in the middle can be either a *y* or a *sh*. 'SEKS-yue(r)l' is preferred.

sexual harassment See harassment

sexuality See sex . . .

sexually transmitted or **venereal diseases (VD)** *Venereal disease*, a description used since the 17th century, was the standard clinical term up to the 1970s, hardly mentioned outside hospitals and doctors' consulting rooms, or at best referred to by the abbreviation VD. *Venereal* is linked to Venus, who was the goddess identified in the Middle Ages with sin and vice, as well as in paintings and poetry with the power of love.

Venereal disease was for long associated with infection caught by men through sexual intercourse with prostitutes, and carried with it a severe social stigma. It is rare to hear the term now, as it has been largely replaced by *sexually transmitted diseases*, a more neutral term that brings in both women and men as victims.

sexuarium The *OED* has not picked up *sexuarium*, a word modelled on 'gymnasium', understandably since it is not used much outside Beverly Hills, near Los Angeles. But it has found a place in articles in British papers and inevitably in Alex Comfort's *The Joy of Sex*. A sexuarium is a room fitted out with arrangements of mirrors, lighting and sound effects, rocking chairs, grab-rings and whatever other contrivance bizarre sexual fantasies require.

sexy or **raunchy** *Sex*, from Latin 'sexus', was used in English by the 16th century for the state of being male or female. *Sexy* did not arrive until 400 years later: one authority gives 1928 as the year when it first appeared in English and defines it as 'immoderately concerned or engrossed with sex' (*Addenda* to the *Shorter Oxford English Dictionary*, 1959). But it was recorded earlier than that, in 1925, in a letter in a Paris review, suggesting that people were buying James Joyce's *Ulysses* because it was considered sexy. In the succeeding years, *sexy* has become so indispensable, that it is hard to imagine a time when the word did not exist. *Sexy* means sexually attractive to others or sexually aroused, and dictionaries now record both meanings as standard English.

Sexy is in some sense the equivalent of *erotic*, without being dressed up in Greek mythology. There is this difference: to describe a painting as *sexy* may suggest blatant excitation, whereas *erotic* implies a work of art with sexual imagery. The line between the two words may be a fine one in some cases, but using *sexy* or *erotic* about art pushes it one direction or the other.

A more recent use of *sexy* became apparent in the 1980s. The question 'Is it sexy?' meant is it different, unexpected, in tune with what people want? This new meaning has caught on, and even deans of universities talk about sexy plans for raising money, and august banking institutions openly declare they have to make finance a sexy subject. Few dictionaries have caught up with this new usage. When they do, it will doubtless be labelled 'slang' or 'informal', but it looks on the way to becoming established.

Raunchy has a more robust sexual meaning, not vulgar, but earthy and full-blooded. A classic example of *raunchiness* is Marlene Dietrich's rendition of 'See What the Boys in the Back Room Will Have' in *Destry Rides Again* (1939).

SF See science fiction

shadow or **penumbra** The main use of *penumbra* is in astronomy, particularly for the *shadow* of the moon or the Earth that is visible in an eclipse. But *penumbra* has another use, when something is only *partly* in a shadow: the distinction was made in *The Independent* when it described C E M Joad's successor in the chair of philosophy at Birkbeck College, London, as 'in Joad's shadow, or penumbra at any rate'.

Shakespearean or **Shakespearian** Both spellings are accepted for describing either the insight of Shakespeare, as revealed in his plays, or an authority on his work. Other spellings that appear are *Shaksperean* and *Shaksperian*, but these are on the fringe of acceptability. *Shakespearean* is the spelling favoured by most literary scholars.

shall or **will** Everyone has been taught something about this at school and some follow the copybook rules carefully. The English and Welsh are taught:

1 I/we *shall* and you/he/she/it *will* (simple future): 'I shall be leaving tomorrow'; 'I hope it will be ready on time'.

2 I/we *will* and you/he, etc *shall* (intention or determination): 'I will succeed whatever happens'; 'You shall do it, whatever you say'.

In Scotland, Ireland and America, 'I *will*' is normal usage for the simple future. And in his famous wartime speech of defiance, Churchill used 'we *shall*' not to express the simple future, but the utmost determination: 'We shall defend our island, whatever the cost may be . . . we shall never surrender'.

It is a confusing picture. If you know the grammarians' rules about *shall* and *will*, keep to them if that's what you prefer. Otherwise, use whichever comes naturally, remembering that the strong tendency now is for *will* to replace *shall* in all cases, especially in spoken English. To some people, 'I shall' even sounds old-fashioned. There is little doubt that purists and other defenders of the orthodox faith will wheel out their big guns to attack that advice, but it is the way some good writers and speakers deal with *shall* and *will*. In conversation, you can often sidestep the problem with *I'll*, *she'll*, etc (see **contracted forms**).

shambles The 1990 edition of the *Concise Oxford Dictionary* shows the usual meaning of *shambles*, which is for a confusion and disorder, as the first meaning of the word. But the editors label it colloquial, with the standard meaning, which is for a slaughterhouse or a bloody scene of mass killing, placed second. If the first meaning of *shambles* that comes to mind is as in the sentence, 'the whole room was in a shambles, with everything all over the place', that can hardly be considered colloquial. What's more, *shambolic*, which *is* probably more conversational than written English, never describes wholesale carnage, always a state of total disorder.

The 16th-century use of *shambles* for a slaughterhouse is falling into disuse, or is a literary form that many people are not aware of. It is still reflected in some street names, once sites of slaughterhouses.

shambolic See previous entry

shampoo This everyday word in television commercials, chemists and bathrooms was adapted for its present meaning in the mid-19th century from a Hindi word, which is why it sounds un-English. Because they look odd, we might hesitate over the other forms of the verb, which are *shampooed* and *shampooing*.

shan't See **contracted forms**

sharp or **sharply** Custom dictates which form is used:
Time: He came sharp on time; 7 o'clock sharp; look sharp about it!
Direction: Turn sharp right at the church.
Music: You played that note sharp.

In most other contexts, it is *sharply*: we speak sharply, move sharply, pull something sharply (but pull up sharp).

sharpener An early evening drink used to be called a 'shot in the arm', but publicity given to drug abuse made that slang expression dubious. A *sharpener*, said to have been introduced by the magazine *Private Eye*, has replaced it: 'Would you like a sharpener?' is the current expression among executives, especially about 6 o'clock after a hard day.

shaved or **shaven** The old past form *shaven* is obsolete except as a descriptive form: 'he had *shaved* before breakfast'; but 'he was *clean-shaved* (or *clean-shaven*)'.

Shavian At the beginning of the century, early in George Bernard Shaw's (1856–1950) career, someone, perhaps Shaw himself, used 'Shavius' as a mock-Latin adaptation of his name. He was such a towering figure in literature and thought, that *Shavian* became, and still is, a convenient descriptive word for his style, iconoclasm, wit and social insight. Later on, it even became one of the **-isms**, *Shavianism*.

she or **he** We used to be in the habit (many people still are) of using *he or she* to indicate that both sexes are referred to: 'If anyone would like to apply, would he or she please collect a form'. Some women have suggested that we should keep the balance by occasionally changing the order to *she or he*. This is dealt with under **he or she**, but only because it comes first alphabetically! See also **unisex grammar**

sheath See **condom** . . .

she'd See **contracted forms**

she'd have See **I'd have**

sheikh You never know when you might meet one these days, so remember *sheikh* should be pronounced the same way as 'shake'. In America, 'sheek' is more usual. *Sheik* is an alternative spelling but *sheikh* is preferred.

sheila There are enough Australians and New Zealanders in Britain to make us familiar with the friendly slang word *sheila*, heard **down under** (to use that quaint term from the past) for a young woman. *Sheila* is not usually intended to be derogatory, but some women take it that way.

shelf-life *Shelf-life* first applied only to the length of time a product could remain on shelves of supermarkets and still be saleable. Unlike a **sell-by** date, which usually relates to food, *shelf-life* could refer to other products for which there is a market for a certain period only.

A sinister development in the **fast lanes** of the 1990s is that *shelf-life* is now applicable to people: on the BBC *Panorama* programme, John Cole calculated 'a prime minister's shelf-life as being ten years'.

shellfish See seafood . . .

she's See contracted forms

shined or **shone** These are alternative past forms of the verb *shine*. Either can be used when it's about a light, with *shone* as more usual. *Shone* is the customary past form referring to the sun, less so for the moon in poetic contexts: 'the sun *shone* that day'; 'the moon *shined* bright that night'. This is not a fixed rule.

When it's the past form of the verb *shine*, meaning polish, only *shone* will do.

ship See boat . . .

(the) **Shires** and **county** The Shires stands for those counties of England that have or had names with the *-shire* suffix, particularly those in the South and the Midlands. But no one takes *the Shires* seriously – it is used satirically for the solid fox-hunting counties, what the Conservative Party usually means when they talk about 'the **grassroots**'. *County* has the same double-edged flavour for describing the voices, clothes and attitudes of those as to the manner born in the Shires.

shirt See blouse . . .

shit The Old English word *shit* remains indecent for many people. When you see your doctor, you can refer to your *stools* (the meaning follows the 15th-century use of *stool* for a seat containing a lavatory). If you squelch in some on the pavement, you can say 'dog mess'. You can retreat to the formality of the Latinate words 'faeces' or **excreta**, although in moments of frustration, 'Oh excreta!' would hardly relieve one's feelings. That covers most of the available alternatives.

Even four-letter words have grammatical niceties. Dictionaries show alternative past forms of the verb as either *shit* or *shitted* ('shat' is facetious): should the occasion arise, *shit* is the past form to be preferred.

Curiously, the expression *shit-scared* (meaning terrified) is not regarded as particularly indecent and is heard in interviews on the BBC without anyone pressing the panic button. There are double standards where **four-letter words** are concerned.

shock wave In physics and mechanics, a *shock wave* occurs when there is a sudden change in air pressure, caused mostly by an explosion or an aircraft travelling faster than the speed of sound. The term has become adapted for any sharp disturbance in society or an organization, or even in a group of people: 'his remark caused a shock wave at the meeting'.

shoot oneself in the foot The meaning of the expression has been turned back to front. It arose during World War I when a soldier occasionally shot himself in the foot deliberately, in order to get sick leave or to be invalided out of the army. To *shoot oneself in the foot* is now popular, particularly with political journalists, for an *unintentional* blunder. Sports writers like it as well: the *Daily Telegraph* noted that the England cricket team displayed 'an infinite capacity this summer for shooting themselves in the foot'.

shop-floor *Shop-floor*, as it is used in industrial relations, is short for 'workshop floor'. It is the collective term for the general **workforce** involved in production, as contrasted to management. The *shop-floor* is supposed to represent the opinions and decisions of the factory workers, often as interpreted by the appropriate trade union, and to some extent it has become a term of confrontation with management.

A tendency is to write *shopfloor* as one word, and that may eventually take over from the hyphenated form.

The office of *stop steward* goes back to the beginning of the century, for someone elected by the workforce as its representative with the **trade union**. See also **convener**

shop steward See previous entry

shortfall See deficit . . .

shorts See boxers . . .

short- and **long-termism** These are clumsy formations, needlessly replacing 'short-term and long-term policies'. See **-isms**

should or **would** The standard rule is, or used to be: I/we *should*, you/she/he/it *would*. This is often ignored now (see **shall or will**). *Plain Words* (1973 edition), the guide to English for civil servants, quotes a professor of poetry using *should* and *would* interchangeably, which has become almost standard practice. *Should* is used, in addition, to mean 'ought to': 'You should leave early to avoid the rush hour'.

show business (showbiz) *Show business*, and its shortened form, *showbiz* (alleged to have been coined in the mid-1940s by a man with a showbiz name,

Jack Pulaski), are straight from Broadway. Irving Berlin's song, 'There's No Business Like Show Business', carried both words over the Atlantic. They are also used now outside the theatre for anything that is difficult, goes wrong, creates a panic, keeps you working all night: people might shrug their shoulders and say, 'That's show business (or showbiz)'.

showed See shown . . .

shower See drizzle . . .

shown or **showed** These are alternative past forms of the verb *show* and either can be used. The older form *shown* remains the more usual: 'they have shown us some beautiful materials'; 'we were shown some beautiful materials'. ('They have showed us . . .', 'We were showed . . .' are not incorrect.)

shrink See psychoanalyst . . .

shut or **close** See close . . .

shuttle diplomacy *Shuttle* is a term in weaving, dating back to the 14th century, for the device that shoots backwards and forwards carrying the thread. In the 1970s it was given a new twist when Henry Kissinger, as US Secretary of State, made repeated flights to the Middle East to negotiate a truce between Israel and Syria. *Shuttle diplomacy* was born, for a diplomat or anyone else prepared to travel backwards and forwards halfway across the world to carry out negotiations.

sic The Latin word *sic* (thus, in this way) is a literary device to make it clear that a number, word or form of words is correctly quoted, even though it is unexpected. *Sic* (pronounced 'sick') is placed in brackets immediately after the words in question: 'The chairman said that a profit of £70 (*sic*) was not unreasonable in the circumstances'. More often than not, *sic* can and should be avoided, by underlining the appropriate words, putting them in inverted commas, or by adding a comment in brackets, such as '(that is the correct figure)', '(those were the actual words)', etc. Occasionally, if rarely, *sic* may be justified to inform readers that particular words were actually used and are not a misprint.

sick See ill . . .

sick joke This American slang expression, first heard on the West Coast in the 1950s, follows the American use of the word sick (see **ill** . . .), to mean physically or mentally unwell. A *sick joke* is not the kind of joke you laugh at, more a manifestation of cruelty or spite. See also **black comedy** . . .; **morbid**

side-effect or **spin-off** A *side-effect* is nearly always an unwanted and undesirable resultant effect. It was first used for the negative effects of a drug or other medication, alongside its positive therapeutic value. *Side-effect* is now extended for any unpleasant result that arises incidentally from positive action: one of the side-effects of raising interest rates in order to reduce inflation is to increase the number of people losing their homes because they can no longer afford the mortgage repayments.

Spin-off describes a good by-product or secondary benefit, often unexpected, derived from something planned for a different purpose. A journalist is flying to Paris to report on fashion shows, and on the plane she meets a man she subsequently marries. That's a spin-off! A popular children's television programme makes even more money from the spin-off of toys being sold, based on characters in the programme.

sidewalk See pavement . . .

signal-to-noise ratio *Signal-to-noise ratio* is a useful term as a measure of the efficiency of telecommunication. It is a ratio between unwanted random sound from various sources, such as electromagnetic radiation, and the intended signal which carries the information to people at the receiving end. *Signal-to-noise ratio* is a **high-tech** term for what most of us call interference.

significant other Armistead Maupin's novel, *Significant Others*, has made this expression used in America for a husband, wife or other steady relationship more familiar in Britain. It is dealt with under **boyfriend** . . . .

Signor, **Signora** and **Signorina** When Italians are in England, do we introduce them as *Signor* Clemente, *Signorina* Boldoni, etc or *Mr* Clemente, *Miss* (or *Ms*) Boldoni? For the use of foreign courtesy titles in an English context, see **Mr, Mrs, etc or Monsieur, Frau, etc.**

Sikh The pronunciation of this Indian title can rhyme with either 'seek' or 'sick'. The former is usually preferred.

silicon chip See microchip . . .

Silicon Valley *Silicon Valley* was first of all the name given to Santa Clara in California because of the concentration in that area of manufacturers of microelectronic components. It is used loosely now about any area anywhere in the world in which there is a heavy concentration of industry manufacturing components for information technology.

(take) silk See barrister . . .

silvan See sylvan . . .

simile See metaphor . . .

simple or **elementary** See elementary . . .

simple or **simplistic** *Simplistic* is sometimes used as a longer, more impressive word, where *simple* is what is meant. It derives from *simple* but does not mean the same; *simplistic* should carry with it the pejorative meaning of oversimplified, naive or even downright stupid.

simulated speech-sounds For a century or more, writers have attempted to imitate in print conversational deviations from the standard way of speaking. Policemen are made to say *Gotcher!* ('Got you!') when they lay their hands on a crook. Defiant cockneys insist 'I'm *gonna* go on doing it!'

Such devices are best left to novelists, who have to do the best they can to imitate how a character speaks. You can get into deep waters using these tricks of the trade, so most of us had better *shurrup* (first used in the late 19th-century) about it.

(living in) **sin** See **living in sin**

(Yours) **sincerely** See **letter endings**

sincerity machine The *sincerity machine* (also called the *head-up device*) was invented in America, some say for President Reagan, who first used it in Britain to speak in Westminster Hall. It is an invisible glass prompt screen, which enabled him to turn his head from side to side to look at the audience, without losing the place in the text of his speech. Some British politicians have taken to it eagerly.

sinecure Dictionaries show the first syllable as rhyming either with 'fine' or with 'pin'. The former is preferred.

single market See **EC . . .**

single parent family and **single parent child** *Single parent family* covers a number of different situations. It can mean an unmarried mother bringing up children on her own, or a widow or widower left with children, or a divorced or abandoned mother, or a divorced or abandoned father who has custody of his children.

Note that 'single parent child' is a misleading description. In most cases of divorce and separation, it is usual for both parents to want to continue to take a parental role, seeing their children regularly. To avoid misunderstanding, it is better to use the expression *single parent family* and avoid 'single parent child'.

singular or **plural** It is not always clear whether a *singular* or *plural* noun should be followed by a *singular* or *plural* verb. There are five guidelines to help you through the no man's land in between. These are explained under **plural or singular**.

Sinn Fein See **IRA . . .**

sir Before the 1960s, it was still usual for pupils at boys' schools to call the masters (and they were mostly masters in those days) *sir*. A few old-fashioned shopkeepers still use *sir* to customers. The ranks in the armed forces are obliged to use *sir* when addressing officers. Radio and television interviewers never seem to call anyone *sir*, nor do most policemen and policewomen. A prime minister will sometimes reject a request from the leader of the opposition by snapping 'No *sir!*'

It still does not seem out of place to use *sir* when speaking to a very old man, and *sir* is required when addressing male members of the Royal family (see **Royalty**). Apart from those and some other special situations, none of us know where we stand with *sir* any more, except that we don't spell it with a capital S as it used to be (except on those few occasions when we begin a letter 'Dear Sir'). By the end of the century, we can expect *sir* to be used less and less, except in prescribed and ceremonial situations. See also **Madam . . .; Mr . . .**

sirocco A *sirocco* (sometimes spelt *scirocco* but the *c* is not sounded) derives from an Arabic word and is the name given to the warm dry wind blowing from the Sahara into Sicily and southern Italy. Other regions use different names for this heavy oppressive wind; it is the *khamsin* in Egypt and Malta, for example.

sitcom *Sitcom* began as a short version, used in the television business, for **sit**uation **com**edy. The word was fashionable in America in the 1960s for light plays on television that formed part of a series. The setting was always domestic, the plot inconsequential. The same sort of programme is still shown on television in Britain and America, but the word *sitcom* is now dated and less likely to be used.

sitting-room, **living-room**, **drawing-room** or **lounge** These four terms plunge us deep into sociolinguistics. You know who and what people are from the name they give the room in their homes where they sit, talk, doze off in front of television, as against the room they have meals in.

Drawing-room, a 17th-century word, was the shortened form of 'withdrawing-room', the room the aristocracy withdrew to after dinner. Up to the 1930s, any modest house in the suburbs had its *drawing-room*, in many cases hardly ever used, except when visitors came to call. Later the word *lounge* became fashionable in the suburbs, with furniture shops selling *lounge suites* (a sofa and two matching armchairs). The middle-class look down on *lounge* as a genteelism used by upstarts (although it is perfectly in order in hotels and airports). If they abandon *drawing-room*, they switch to *sitting-room*. Estate agents have plumped for *living-room*, presumably because it is classless, even if it does suggest that other rooms are for corpses. **Parlours** have become as old-fashioned as aspidistras.

situation See **job . . .**

sixth It is careless to drop the -*s*- sound and say 'sikth' instead of 'siksth'.

sizeable or **sizable**   Most dictionaries continue to show these as alternative spellings, but the fact is that *sizeable* is so much the rule in Britain that *sizable* could look like a spelling mistake to some people. *Sizable* is the usual spelling in America.

ski   *Ski* presents no problem when it is a noun; it derives from an old Norwegian word for a snowshoe. It is the forms of the verb in English that need thinking about. The present form after 'he' and 'she' is *skis*: 'she skis down the slope'; the past form is either *ski'd* or *skied*: 'she ski'd (or skied) down the slope'. The present is *skiing*.

The British used to like to begin it with a *sh-* sound, fancying it sounded more Nordic. But everyone now accepts 'skee'.

skyscraper   In the 1880s an American architect used the vivid word *skyscraper* for the towering multi-storey buildings going up in New York and Chicago. For the next 80 years *skyscraper* meant America. Since then, most of the major cities of the world have built office blocks and hotels reaching for the skies, for the same reason as they were built in American cities: the high cost of land. *Skyscraper* is too sensational for buildings that are now familiar everywhere, and the word has been consigned to linguistic archives. See also **tower block**

slander   See libel . . .

slang   See colloquial . . .

slattern   See slut . . .

slay   See kill . . .

SLD   SLD was the abbreviation used for the Social and Liberal Democratic Party, the merger in 1988 of the Liberal Party with the Social Democratic Party. Since 1989 SLD has become obsolete, superseded by the decision to call the party the *Liberal Democrats*. Initials are not used for the abbreviation of this name. See also **liberal** . . .

sleeping partner   This used to be an expression for a person who helps a business by putting up some of the capital or acting as a consultant, but takes no day-to-day part in running it. It might still be used but generally it is old-fashioned.

sleeping rough   *Sleeping rough* can be used for spending an uncomfortable night anywhere, but its main association now is with the homeless sleeping on the streets. See also **cardboard city**

sleep together and **sleep with someone**
The most euphemistic expression for a man and a woman having sexual relations is to say they *sleep together*. It is almost as old as the hills, as there are records of the idiom in use in the 10th century. Dictionaries accept the usage: for some it remains informal or colloquial, but the *Concise Oxford Dictionary* (1990 edition) treats it as standard English for having sexual intercourse, adding the curious qualification 'especially in bed'.

The expression was challenged by Susan Crosland in *The Sunday Times*, who claimed, 'there are a hundred reasons why two people can share a bed without having sexual intercourse'. She is right, of course. Nevertheless, the no-smoke-without-fire meaning of *sleep together* is as current as ever in the 1990s, as part of gossip language.

Dictionaries do not accept *sleep around*, meaning to be sexually promiscuous, as more than conversational English. Unfair though it is, *sleep around* tends to be used much more about women than men.

Sloane Ranger   The profile of a *Sloane Ranger* went something like this: a tall, angular woman, two labradors on leads, a Range-Rover (with children's riding hats on the back seat), living within walking or easy taxi distance of Sloane Street and King's Road in London, and with an account at Harrods. The concept took off in 1982 with *The Sloane Ranger Handbook* (written by Anne Barr and Peter York), and the phrase stuck as a description of affluent self-assured people whose idea of the Third World was Bermuda and the Antilles. Although it was used mostly about women, there were male Sloane Rangers too: the magazine *Harpers and Queen* advertised 'The official Sloane Ranger men's shirt', using as a model a well set-up man whose 'spell in the Irish Guards completed the basic training for his present job as an advertising executive'.

The recession of the early 1990s has left the term *Sloane Ranger* faded and nostalgic, although you still hear it. See also **Hooray Henry**

slogan   See catchphrase . . .

slot   Programmes on television and radio are tightly packed, and public relations firms push as hard as they can to get *slots* for their clients. *Slot* is the standard word in broadcasting for anything from 15 seconds to a few minutes allotted to a politician, a writer, actor, etc in a news or discussion programme. It is indicative of the feverish scramble to be seen and heard that even celebrities queue up for a *slot*, which is the word for a narrow slit.

slow or **slowly**   As with **quick**, *slow* often replaces the correct grammatical form *slowly*. Markings on roads read SLOW, rather than SLOWLY, and workers decide to **go-slow** as a form of industrial action. In commands or very short sentences, especially following the verb 'go', *slow* is often the usual form: 'Be careful and go slow'. In most other cases, especially in writing or in longer sentences, *slowly* is the correct form to use: 'she drove slowly through the village'; 'let's go slowly until we see how things work out'.

slump   See depression . . .

slums or **inner city**   In the 1990s, there is a pulling-back from using the word *slums*, although it might still be used about shanty towns in **developing countries**. For further notes on this, see **inner city** . . .

slut or **slattern** Both words are sexist in that they are insulting and only used for women. *Slattern* is rare enough to be almost obsolete. In any case, there is hardly any difference in meaning between the words: they describe a dirty, untidy, disorderly woman, with *slut* carrying with it the suggestion of sexual wantonness.

small See **compact** . . .

smaller See **lesser** . . .

small print The expression *small print* is often used to suggest that difficult conditions in an agreement are tucked away inconspicuously. When we are advised to read the small print in a contract, it is the same as saying go through it carefully. There's nothing new in this: **caveat subscriptor** (let the signer beware) was a motto in Ancient Rome.

smart This Old English word from the 12th century hovers between being complimentary (a smart suit, a smart idea) and pejorative ('smart alec' suggests being too clever, 'a smart deal' implies unscrupulousness). *Smart* is used increasingly now as a descriptive word meaning in-the-know or **state-of-the-art** (see **smart money**; **smart card**). The 1991 Gulf War brought the most bizarre use of the word: *smart bombs* were so accurate that they could be directed into ventilator shafts.

smart card This is the name for the new generation of plastic cards. A microchip embedded in the card contains data, which can be 'read' in banks and other places where the card is used for transactions. Beyond financial dealings, there are so many potential uses for smart cards, that they are destined to become part of everyday life for all of us.

smart money A glib expression for money invested by people who are shrewd and in the know. An advertisement by financial consultants was headed 'Where should the smart money go?'

smear The 15th-century use of *smear* for discrediting a person's reputation has become political jargon. It is a *smear* when a political party spreads rumours about a rival party. If it is contrived and planned it becomes a smear campaign. Smear campaign is also used outside politics for a deliberate attempt to give someone a bad name: 'there's a smear campaign against the headteacher, suggesting he shows racial discrimination'.

The other familiar use of *smear* in the 1990s is medical, usually gynaecological: *smear* is the word most women use for a cervical smear, a scraping from a woman's cervix which is analysed to detect early signs of cancer.

smell See **aroma** . . .

smelt or **smelled** Both past forms are used: *smelt* is the usual form in Britain, *smelled* in America.

smog At the beginning of the century, **sm**oke and **fog** were combined to make *smog*, by an officer of the Coal Smoke Abatement Society. It was the name given to the thick yellowish fog in cities, notably in London. In that sense, *smog* has become an old-fashioned term since the Clean Air Acts 1956 and 1968, which banned smoky fuels within designated areas. But smog is still alive and suffocating in other cities, notably Los Angeles.

Smog is retained now for other forms of air pollution. In 1990, figures compiled by a government laboratory showed that on some days air pollution was worse in certain rural areas than in central London. This was due to low-level **ozone** acting as a major constituent of what has been called photo-chemical smog.

smokescreen words A term used by some linguistic commentators for political attempts to shroud horrors in obscure language. See **doublespeak**; (language of) **war**

smokey See **smoky** . . .

(passive) smoking See **passive smoking**

smoky or **smokey** You see *smokey* in print sometimes but it is a mistake for *smoky*, the only form shown in dictionaries.

snack *Snack*, for something light to eat, goes back to the mid-18th century, and by the early 19th century it was already being used as a verb, sometimes to mean having lunch. Now almost anything can be a snack, from a sandwich to a plastic-packaged collection of flavoured **additives**.

In the 1990s, *snack* is marking a change in family habits. Many young people are moving away from the traditional custom of eating fixed meals with the family, in favour of light casual dishes eaten at any time of the day. The fashion for snacks is reflected in the streets of cities, with an increasing number of wine and **tapas** bars, and supermarkets selling ready-to-eat light meals. This is a way of life in America, where it's called 'grazing' ('graze' was slang in the American army and prisons for eating a meal). Snacks should not be confused with **fast food**.

snapshot In the early 19th century *snapshot* began as a hunting word for a quick pot-shot at a moving target. Near the end of that century it was neatly adapted for a quick unstudied photograph. In the 1960s, the photographic use was extended for anything quick and off-the-cuff. A snapshot impression is simply a short account of a situation, not intended to be other than superficial; a snapshot survey is a survey carried out quickly among a small number of people, to give an instant indication of opinion.

snobbery or **snobbishness** English *snobbery* used to be exclusively founded on class, demonstrated by Edward VII's comment, after accepting an invitation to sail on Sir Thomas Lipton's yacht, that he was 'boating with his grocer'. That has all changed and there are now many kinds of snobbery: people are snobbish because they are rich, there is clothes snobbery (looking down on people not wearing the latest fashions), literary snobbery (reading the books that are being talked about), food snobbery (eating at the restaurants getting top accolades from food writers), wine snobbery (swirling wine endlessly round the glass and carrying out deep breathing exercises over it, before making a solemn pronouncement). *Snobbishness* could also be the word used in all such contexts, although it would be less usual.

snooze see **doze**

soap opera See **serial** . . .

sobriquet See **nickname** . . .

so-called In speech, *so-called* is a way of putting a word or a phrase in quotation marks to indicate that it is not the speaker's choice but an expression that is used: during the 1992 election campaign, for example, political commentators often referred to 'the so-called feel-good factor'. *So-called* can be used in the same way in writing, or inverted commas can be used instead: the 'feel-good' factor. *So-called* is also a way of indicating doubt about whether someone or something is genuine: 'I don't think much of this so-called burgundy'.

sociable, **social** or **sociological** A person can be *sociable*, that is enjoy being with other people; an organization, principle, problem, etc can be *social*, that is relating to people and society: social club, social worker, etc. The distinction is becoming blurred as a friendly gregarious person is often described as 'very social'.

Sociological is a scientific word describing anything related to **sociology**, the study of how societies function. For *social sciences*, see **natural sciences** . . .

social climbing The expression *social climbing* (or *social climber*) is still heard, and may well be justified at times. But with the rise of the **meritocracy** and the increasing irrelevance of the aristocracy, the catchphrase more applicable to the 1990s is **upwardly mobile**.

Socialist or **socialist** A *Socialist* (with a capital S) is a member of a socialist political party and a *socialist* is anyone who believes in a system where the people of a country own the means of production and distribution.

Socialist Party See **Labour Party** . . .

social sciences See **natural sciences** . . .

socio-economic For notes on *socio-economic*, the pseudo-scientific term marketing experts use to avoid getting caught up in class-distinction, see **class**.

sociolinguistics Language is interwoven with every aspect of human life and the human situation, which makes *sociolinguistics* a broad subject. It touches anthropology by studying the comparative use of language in different societies and communities. It is involved with sociology, studying the relation between language and social background and occupation. Deborah Tannen, a professor of sociolinguistics, has applied her subject to understanding the misunderstandings between men and women. Her book, *You Just Don't Understand*, is a study of sexual linguistics, a branch of sociolinguistics that so far has not received much attention.

sociology Sociology is the study of how societies function in different parts of the world, or the study of social problems and how to deal with them, usually within one particular country or 'socio-economic group' (see **class**). Although sociology is concerned with human beings in society, the language used by sociologists is often remote, obscured by jargon such as 'residential structures' (houses), 'adult males and females in the roles of parent' (fathers and mothers).

There is a variation in the way the second syllable of *sociology* (and its related words, *sociological, sociologists*, etc) is pronounced. It can begin with an *-s-* sound or a *-sh-* sound. In America, the *-s-* sound ('sohseeOLojee') is nearly always used, and this has become the more usual pronunciation in Britain.

sofa See **couch** . . .

soft-core pornography See **pornography** . . .

soft currency See **hard currency** . . .

soft landing The term in space technology for a spacecraft making an easy landing on its return to Earth, has been adapted for any relatively easy outcome following a drastic measure. For example, after announcing a fall in profits, a company's shares could have a *soft landing*, if the price on the Stock Exchange has only a modest fall.

soft-pedal The soft pedal on a piano is the one for the left foot that allows the pianist to play on only one string. It is one of a number of musical terms adapted for everyday life, and is used for something **low-key** not attracting much attention. *Soft-pedal* can be used as a verb ('we must soft-pedal the news') or as a descriptive word ('we must take a soft-pedal approach'). Compare **low-key**

soft sell See **hard sell** . . .

soft touch *Soft touch* is old American slang for someone it is easy to get money out of. *Soft touch* is now equally at home in Britain, labelled colloquial or informal by dictionaries, but edging its way up to standard English.

software As computer language, *software* and *hardware* go back to the early 1960s. For notes on the terms, see **hardware** . . .

soignée or **soigné** *Soignée* is feminine, *soigné* is masculine. Both words mean elegant and immaculately dressed. In practice, the word is only used about a woman (even in French, it would be unusual to describe a man as *soigné*), which means the form *soignée* is the only one we need bother with.

solar . . . As cheaper ways are discovered to convert sunlight into electrical power, we can expect *solar* (from Latin 'solaris', meaning 'of the sun') to be combined into many more compounds, alongside existing ones such as: *solar cell* (a form of battery that converts solar radiation into electricity), *solar satellite* (a satellite that converts solar energy into electrical energy and transmits it to Earth), *solar panels* (panels on the roof of a building or the side of a swimming-pool to heat houses or water), *solar bike* (a bicycle developed in 1992 and powered by solar energy). Even journalists are slow to hyphenate compound terms using *solar*, let alone to fuse them into single words.

solemn See serious . . .

solicitor See lawyer . . .

solidarity Since September 1980, when the Committee for the Defence of Workers in Poland joined with Polish trade unions under the name *Solidarity*, the word has become synonymous with working or deprived people supporting each other against management or government. That is what SOLIDARITY means when you see it defiantly spray-gunned on walls anywhere in the world.

solid-state *Solid-state* became a tag attached in the 1960s to electronic devices, especially transistor radios, although few people, other than engineers and physicists, knew what it meant. These devices used *solid* semiconductor components instead of traditional valves, making them smaller, less liable to damage and cheaper to manufacture. Shops rarely bother with labelling things *solid-state* any more, as this technical breakthrough is now taken for granted.

soliloquy See monologue . . .

solve See resolve . . .

solvent abuse or **glue-sniffing** A solvent is any substance, usually a liquid, that has the property of dissolving another substance. Most glues contain solvents which give off fumes as part of the chemical reaction. *Solvent abuse* is the formal term for *glue-sniffing*, the dangerous, addictive practice of inhaling this toxic vapour.

some When *some* is followed by a number, it is an alternative word for 'about', not for 'precisely'. It makes no sense to follow *some* by an accurate number: 'we live some 23½ miles from London' should be '. . . some 25 miles' or '. . . some 20 miles or so'.

somebody and **someone** This question keeps coming up: 'Somebody has left *his* briefcase behind'.

But what if the briefcase belongs to a woman? See **unisex grammar**

some day or **someday** The one-word version is nearly always used in America, but people often hesitate to use it in Britain. Recent dictionaries show *someday* to mean some time in the future, usually a long way off: 'We'll meet again someday, who knows when?' As two words, *some day* is more precise: 'Before we part, we'll fix some day for our next meeting'.

someplace See somewhere . . .

some time or **sometime** This is one word when it means any time ('I'll arrive sometime on Monday'), but it is better as two words when it means an unspecified period of time ('It is some time since she has seen him').

somewhat The best way the *Concise Oxford Dictionary* (1990 edition) can define *somewhat* is 'to some extent', which is open-ended. For no one is quite sure what is meant by *somewhat*. 'He is somewhat drunk' could mean a little drunk or very drunk. To lay it on the line, we'd have to say 'He is more than somewhat drunk'. There's no doubt that means the man is outrageously drunk.

somewhere or **someplace** *Someplace* is often thought of as American. But *someplace* has caught on in Britain, although it is more conversational here. *Somewhere* is the better word to use in writing.

sonata See concerto . . .

sons-in-law or **son-in-laws** *Sons-in-law*.

soon See presently

soon, **before long** or **in the not too distant future** These three expressions could indicate different degrees of delay.

Soon or *before long* imply a short period, which could be a few minutes ('Dinner will be ready soon'), or could be stretched to a few weeks ('I'll write to you *before long*'). Not that *before long* promises much; it could extend to a few months, although that is stretching the expression to its limits.

In the not too distant future is prevarication. It is too open-ended to promise anything at all: if dinner is going to be ready in the not too distant future, you might as well look for another restaurant. See also **presently**

sophisticated A few purists still insist on using this word only in its original pejorative sense of devious, not pure or genuine: this was still the primary meaning shown in the *Shorter Oxford Dictionary* (1959). Now nearly everyone uses *sophisticated*, usually with no negative implication, to mean worldly, urbane, socially poised: 'Although she is young, he was impressed by her sophisticated manner'. It is also used about something intellectual or subtle ('a sophisticated argument') or about something technologically advanced ('a sophisticated piece of equipment').

sort See kind . . .

soundscape Few if any dictionaries have picked up *soundscape*, yet the word (which parallels the word 'landscape') is in use to describe the setting of sound against which a performance or other theatrical event takes place. *Soundscape* seems to be the only word possible, where neither 'music' nor 'sound-effects' would be appropriate. For example, Siobhan Davies's ballet *Wyoming* is described on the programme as set to a *soundscape*: this is a combination of music, storm-effects, percussion and other noises given form and unity by the composer John–Marc Gowans.

South or **south** See North . . .

south or **southern** See north or northern . . .

South African English We are so familiar with South African political campaigners speaking English on television, that many people are unaware that English is the first language of little more than three million South Africans, about 10 per cent of the population. Consequently, *South African English* has come under other influences, notably Afrikaans, a language related to Dutch and Flemish, spoken by the early Dutch settlers. Afrikaners make up about 60 per cent of the white population, and Afrikaans is spoken by many blacks, particularly in the north of the country.

Although English is learned as a second language by many people in the country, it is the language most widely used for general communication. The vocabulary and the accent, marked by a clipped articulation of consonants, is strongly affected by Afrikaans.

Southern Ireland or **Eire** The various names used for different parts of Ireland can be confusing. Guidelines are given under **Ireland** . . .

South of France, **Côte d'Azur** or **the Riviera** Nowadays, you would need a monocle or lorgnettes to say you're going to the *Côte d'Azur* or *the Riviera*. Although they survived up to World War II, the expressions belong to the Edwardian period, those easygoing years before the thunderclouds of World War I darkened the scene.

Côte d'Azur and *the Riviera* disappeared with package tours and quick flights to Nice. Even the French would hardly use those names any more. As for the British, it would be affected now to say anything other than the *South of France*, a less romantic name, but at least travel agents know where you want to go.

southward, **southwards** or **southerly** See northward . . .

southwester or **sou-wester** A *southwester* is a wind blowing from the south-west: a *sou-wester* is

what you ask for when you want a waterproof hat, the kind traditionally worn by seamen because it has a flap at the back to keep water off the neck.

Soviet Union The events in the Soviet empire at the end of 1991 left behind considerable linguistic confusion, and there remains some hesitation at times over what to call the different parts of the former USSR. For notes on this, see **Russian and Soviet**.

So what? *So what?* is the most dismissive of all comments, as it writes off the value or meaning of anything. The art historian, Ernst Gombrich, once said 'There is never an answer to the question "So what?" '

sown or **sowed** See sewn . . .

space travel The vocabulary of space travel, as remarked on by Bruce Fraser in *Plain Words*, is generally refreshingly simple: *spacemen* or *spacewomen* wearing *spacesuits* are *blasted-off* from a *launching pad* in a *spaceship*, experience *weightlessness* while they set up *space stations* before returning to earth for a *splashdown*. Other new technologies, please copy!

spare parts surgery When a part of a machine is defective it is replaced by a *spare part*. Whoever thought that spare parts would ever be applied to human beings? The idea belonged to science fiction, until December 1967 when the first heart transplant operation was performed. Since then other organs from one human body have been surgically transplanted into others, and some people carry a card authorizing, in the event of their death, organs that are in good condition to be removed as 'spare parts'. The term *spare parts surgery* is not just popular journalism: it is heard in hospitals.

-speak, **-babble** or **-spiel** We can attach *speak*, with or without a hyphen, to many words to describe a particular jargon: Eurocrats converse in **Eurospeak**, wine experts talk **winespeak**, politicians use *politico-speak*.

Used as a suffix in this way, *-speak* need not be derogatory: it simply describes a specialized vocabulary used by a group of people who understand it. If we feel it is going too far, we can change the suffix to *-babble*: **psychobabble** was coined on the West Coast of America in the 1970s to describe the incomprehensible chatter of popular psychology.

Another derogatory suffix is *-spiel* (pron: 'shpeel'): this gives the resulting word the suggestion of glibness. *Spiel*, a German word, became New York Yiddish and is familiar in Britain. *Eurospiel* implies double-talk in Brussels; Michael Jones, writing in *The Sunday Times*, referred to *Neilspiel* for Neil Kinnock's answer to an awkward question, describing it as 'seamless verbal outpouring that . . . leaves one gasping for syntactical air'.

spearhead A spear is a primitive weapon, or another word for a harpoon used for hunting fish.

Ironically, *spearhead* has become a dynamic and purposeful verb to use in the most sophisticated contexts, meaning to take the lead in something: a prime minister can spearhead an attack on the opposition in an interview on television; a scientist can spearhead new research by leading a team in a laboratory.

specially See especially . . .

speechwriter *Speechwriters* are human word-processors who write speeches, mostly for presidents and prime ministers. For a long time, they were anonymous, shut away in backrooms, for politicians prefer to keep up the illusion that their speeches come straight from the heart, right off the chest. During Ronald Reagan's presidency (1981–9), speechwriters began to come out into the light. Mark Lawson, reviewing in *The Listener* a collection of Reagan's speeches, suggested he belonged to the 'High Noonan' school of rhetoric: by then it was well-known that his most famous remarks were the words of his speechwriter, Peggy Noonan, written and rewritten until they glowed with sincerity.

The next time you hear a particularly electrifying phrase coming from someone at the top, it might well have been written by a speechwriter, hired to sweat out inspiring memorable words, to be projected on to the invisible glass of a **sincerity machine**.

spelling English spelling is no joke, even for the English. Foreigners tear their hair out. In America they have gone some way towards rationalizing spelling (-*or* for -*our*, *maneuver* for *manoeuvre*, *plow* for *plough* and so on), but even the most modest reforms arouse great hostility in Britain. We are stuck with our difficult spelling and there are enough exceptions to rules to make it hardly worth learning any of them, except one: when in doubt, look it up in a dictionary. Where a dictionary lists alternative spellings, the editors prefer the first one shown. But another dictionary might reverse the order.

> Suzy, though you've studied so,
> You must take one final blow.
> Is the proper rhyme for tough
> Though, through, plough, cough, or enough?
> Hiccough has the sound of cup.
> Suzy, better give it up!

Part of a verse devised to help multinational personnel of NATO learn English (quoted by Willard R Espy in *Words at Play*).

spelt or **spelled** These are alternative past forms: *spelt* is more usual in Britain, *spelled* in America.

sperm bank See **reproductive technology**

sphere See field . . .

-spiel See -speak . . .

spilt or **spilled** We can cry over *spilt* or *spilled* milk, although it is more likely to be *spilt* in Britain, *spilled* in America.

spine An anatomical word that is usefully adapted in publishing and printing for the edge of the cover of a book on which the title, name of writer and publisher are printed so they can be read on a bookshelf.

spin-off See side-effect . . .

spinster This cold word for a woman who has never married, which often suggested unwanted and 'on the shelf', has almost dropped out of use. Unlike 'bachelor', the equivalent word for a man, *spinster* was always slightly dismissive. If we must have a term now, 'single woman' is perhaps the most acceptable.

spire or **steeple** Most people don't bother to distinguish between a spire and a steeple. As architectural terms, a *spire* is the pointed conical structure that rises from a tower or roof; a *steeple* is the tower and spire of a church as a single structure. *Steeple* is used only for churches but *spire* can be used for a tall pointed structure on any building, as in Matthew Arnold's description of Oxford: 'That sweet city with her dreaming spires' (*Thyrsis*).

spit See spat . . .

spiv *Spiv* is a slang word that belongs to the decades after World War II. It described men (*spiv* was not used for women) who exploited shortages by making money on the black market, showing off this easy money by wearing flashy clothes.

Spiv is a good word, even if it has become old-fashioned, because it sounds like what it means. Dictionaries state the origin is unknown, but the writer Bill Naughton, who made such good use of *spiv* in his stories, recalled that in those days police charge sheets were headed 'Suspected Person, Itinerant Vagabond'.

split infinitive This is the longest-running controversy in English grammar and is still alive and kicking in the 1990s. For the record, an *infinitive* is 'to' followed by a verb: 'to walk', 'to consider', 'to love', etc. When another word comes between 'to' and the verb ('to carefully consider', 'to passionately love'), that is a *split infinitive*, which to some people is as bad as eating peas off a knife: 'Listening to the 8 o'clock news on the wireless this morning, I was appalled to hear that two infinitives had been split within three minutes of each other' (letter to BBC, quoted in *The Listener*).

The Bullock Report on the teaching of English (1975) dismissed the whole business as one of the rules 'invented quite arbitrarily by grammarians in the 18th and 19th centuries'. Yet writers on English remain uneasy about giving the green light to split infinitives. In *Plain Words*, Bruce Fraser (whose attitude towards English usage was balanced and reasonable) advises against splitting 'not because you care about the taboo, but because you care about your reputation with readers'.

If you don't want to upset anyone, you will avoid *split*

infinitives. If you care more about writing good clear English, you will be prepared *to fearlessly split* any infinitive to allow words to fall naturally. Raymond Chandler asked his editor not to fuss about it: 'When I split an infinitive, godammit, it will stay split!' If that's how you feel, there's no need to split infinitives just for the sake of it: 'to' and its following verb belong to each other, and should be separated only when good sense requires it.

spoilt or **spoiled**   These are alternative past forms: *spoilt* is more natural in Britain, *spoiled* in America.

spokesman, **spokeswoman** or **spokesperson**   *Spokesperson* is a unisex word that still sounds awkward, although it is heard regularly on the radio and television and used in newspapers. Perhaps we shall get used to it one day. Until then, the alternatives *spokesman* and *spokeswoman* remain available. See also -**person** . . .

sponsorship   See patronage . . .

spontaneity   The traditional pronunciation is 'sponte(r)NEEity'. There is a marked tendency to give the stressed syllable a *nay* sound, because it's easier to say. By now, 'sponte(r)NAYity' has almost taken over as the standard pronunciation.

spoonerism   See malapropism . . .

spoonfuls or **spoonsful**   It will taste the same whether you add two *spoonfuls* or two *spoonsful* and some older dictionaries give you the choice. *Spoonfuls* is easier to say, sounds more natural, and is the only plural form in the latest dictionaries. See also -**ful**

sports psychologist   See psychiatry . . .

spot price   in **commodity** markets, the *spot price* is the price you pay on the spot, that is with no delay, in order for the title to the goods or commodities to become yours immediately.

spouse   *Spouse* is one of the oldest unisex words. It came into English as part of the invasion of Old French words after the Norman Conquest, and derives from Latin (compare modern Italian 'sposa', a bride-to-be, 'sposino', a bridegroom). *Spouse*, a convenient word that doubles for a husband or wife, is used more and more, as delegates at conferences are now women and men, who are often invited to bring their spouses.

sprang or **sprung**   Although both past forms are acceptable, in Britain we're more likely to say a boat *sprang* a leak yesterday, whereas in America, it *sprung* a leak. After the verb 'have', *sprung* is the only form anywhere (it has sprung a leak).

spritzer   *Spritzer* was coined in cocktail bars in New York in the 1960s for white wine with soda ('spritzig' is used in Germany for a wine with a slight sparkle). It caught on in London in the 1980s, first among people working in the media, who for one reason or another did not want to drink too much but wanted to order something that sounded sophisticated.

sprung   See sprang . . .

Sputnik   See -nik

spying   See espionage . . .

square   It's very middle-aged to call a dull conventional person a *square*. The current word is **nerd**.

square brackets ([ ])   See brackets

(the) **square mile**   See (the) **City**

squash   See quash . . .

St   See Saint . . .

stadiums or **stadia**   There is one BBC sports correspondent who makes a point of saying *stadia* for the plural form. Everybody else, except perhaps for a few elderly teachers of Latin, says *stadiums*.

stag (as Stock Exchange term)   See bear . . .

stagflation   See inflation

standard class   See first class . . .

Standard English   See British English . . .

standing order, **banker's order** or **direct debit**   There is no need to ponder over the difference between a *standing order* and *banker's order*, as both terms mean the same. They are written instructions to a bank where you have an account, to pay out a fixed sum of money to someone else at specified intervals, usually for instalments, subscriptions, etc. *Banker's order* is out of date, superseded by *standing order*. The amount of a standing order on a bank account can only be changed by cancelling one standing order and executing another.

Suppliers of services, such as gas, electricity, telephone . . ., are eager for us to pay them by *direct debit* through our bank account, because this allows them to vary amounts paid, without further authority from us.

standing ovation   It was during Margaret Thatcher's long tenure as prime minister that *standing ovation* became the journalistic **cliché** for a hail-the-conquering-hero reception given to leading politicians as they enter the hall of the annual party political convention. All it means is that delegates stand up and clap, adrenaline flows, and speakers eagerly tot up the number of minutes it goes on for, just as actors count the number of curtain-calls.

standpoint   See point of view . . .

star or **asterisk**   See asterisk . . .

starlight or **starlit** These are both descriptive words for a scene lit by stars, either literally or to imply glamour. You can use which one you prefer, even if Andrew Lloyd Webber's successful musical, *Starlight Express*, has edged out *starlit* in favour of *starlight*.

start See commence . . .

starter See hors-d'oeuvre . . .

Star Wars In 1977, George Lucas directed *Star Wars*, one of the most successful films ever made. In 1983, reality caught up with science fiction, and the media eagerly latched on to *Star Wars* as a melo-dramatic cliché for Ronald Reagan's *Strategic Defense Initiative*, which was designed to counteract missiles in outer space. Casper Weinberger, US Defense Secretary at the time, used it freely. Even science fiction can become outdated, and *Star Wars* seems curiously old-fashioned in the 1990s.

State or **state** Always use a capital when State refers to a nation or a political entity: the State of Israel. A small *s* is appropriate when it is unspecific or describes a general condition. New York State (specific) is one of 50 states (general) in the USA. Other examples are the State opening of parliament, a State occasion, the state of the economy.

statement See account . . .

state-of-the-art Everyone tumbles over them-selves to use *state-of-the-art*, hyphenated as a des-criptive term. To begin with, it was a restrained expression defining limits that could be reached with-out further **research and development**, suggesting there was still some way to go. Then it became a glossy **high-tech** term for the ultimate stage. In the 1980s, *state-of-the-art* caught on, as Philip Howard put it irresistibly in *Winged Words*, 'like office flu on the Friday before a Bank Holiday'.

State-of-the-art sounds impressive and forward-looking, even if it is not clear what it means. Saab cars describe their 'state-of-the-art 16-valve engine', Pana-sonic have their 'state-of-the-art video', the London Business School offer a 'state-of-the-art analysis of market forces', the YRM architectural partnership designed a 'state-of-the-art dealing room' for stock-brokers. It reached the lunatic fringe when someone from the Humane Slaughterers' Association referred to 'state-of-the-art animal handling'.

The way *state-of-the-art* is used suggests the highest level of development so far obtainable, nothing more than a fancy way of saying 'the most advanced'.

(the) **States** See America . . .

stationary or **stationery** Both words come from the same Latin source ('statio', standing still), and in the Middle Ages a *stationer* was a bookseller with a permanent station in a shop or a market, rather than a travelling salesman.

If you wrote *stationary shop*, you could claim you are harking back to the original meaning. But it would still be the wrong spelling: *stationery* is paper, pens, envel-opes, etc, while *stationary* is keeping still.

(the) **Stationery Office** See HMSO . . .

statistics *Statistics* can be a collection of numeri-cal information put together in a biased way or without clear definition of purpose ('Lies, damned lies and statistics'). Or *statistics* can be a science, subject to the proper scientific conditions of objective collection of data and accurate analysis related to a defined purpose, with absolute integrity at all stages. When you hear the word *statistics*, you have to probe deeply to find out which kind you are dealing with. Note that the only spelling for a practitioner is *statistician* (never 'statistitian').

statistics *is* or ***are*** Nouns ending in -*ics* often present this problem. See **-ics**

status *Status* is a woolly word. It used to be a person's position in society, nearly always related to family background. It is more likely to be used now in relation to a person's occupation (see **class**). *Status* is also used for personal prestige in the eyes of the public, which puts leading tennis players ahead of bishops and cabinet ministers. A bank manager might ask about someone's 'financial status', before deciding how much money could be lent to them. A more recent use of *status* is for describing the present state of something, as in 'What's the status of that report?' (that is, how is it coming along?).

A *status symbol* is even more open-ended: for some people it could be a Porsche, for others membership of the Athenaeum Club, for others a detached house with imposing wrought-iron gates. What is or is not a status symbol depends upon the values in life of the person who sees it that way.

Even the pronunciation of *status* hesitates: 'STAY-tus' or 'STATTus'. According to dictionaries, 'STAY-tus' has more *status*.

status symbol See previous entry

statutory woman As the 1980s ended, a sur-vey, *Women in Management in Great Britain*, re-vealed only eight women as directors of the UK's top hundred companies. The *statutory woman* is a con-temptuous expression, used mostly by women, for the way one or two women might be included on the boards of companies, in the Cabinet and so on, as a token concession to the ability and right of women to do many jobs as well as men can. See also **tokenism**

STD Most of us know this abbreviation used in telecommunication, but hardly any of us know what the letters stand for. Subscriber Trunk Dialling enables a caller to dial a number direct almost anywhere in the world, without going through the operator.

There is no risk of confusion with the other meaning

of STD, which is the abbreviation for **sexually transmitted disease**.

Ste　See Saint . . .

steam radio　See radio . . .

steeple　See spire . . .

steppe　See grasslands

sterile　See antiseptic . . .

sterling　See pound . . .

still lifes or **still lives**　A cat has nine *lives* but in the art world the plural of *still life* is *still lifes*.

stingy　See mean . . .

stipend　See pay . . .

stockbroker　See broker . . .

stockbroker belt　Before World War II, bowler-hatted men in black suits travelled up to London from *stockbroker belts*. The expression may still have some meaning for well-ordered residential areas, with well-maintained detached houses, within easy commuting distance of the **City**. But nowadays workers in the City are younger and could well be living in a flat in Islington or in **Dockland**, so the idea of stockbroker belts is fading out.

stomach　See belly . . .

stop　See full stop . . .

stop, **cease**, **discontinue** or **terminate**
These are four verbs for something coming to an end. *Stop* is the most general and certainly the most urgent, which is why it's often followed by an exclamation mark: Stop! *Cease* has a finality about it: when, for example, production in a factory stops, the implication is usually that it will start up again some time. But if production ceases, that sounds more final, as if the factory will close down.

Discontinue suggests breaking-off something that had been going on for a period ('after six months, she discontinued the treatment'). It is also the standard term in production for ceasing to manufacture a particular product: a line is discontinued because it is superseded by a new design.

Terminate is very formal: pregnancies are terminated, and rail travellers are used to hearing: 'We are now arriving at Euston (or wherever), where this train will now terminate'. Presumably, someone has told them to say that, instead of 'where this journey ends'.

stop off and **stop over**　Although a few people still object to these expressions as **Americanisms**, they have become standard English in Britain. They

are useful too, because *stop off* and *stop over* imply a stop at an intermediate point in a journey (*stop over* suggesting staying at least overnight), whereas to *stop* somewhere could mean the end of the journey. 'She stopped over (or off) in Paris on her way to Rome'.

stops in titles　The only punctuation marks that should be used at the end of titles, headings or subheadings are question marks or exclamation marks. Full stops should not be used: *For Whom the Bell Tolls, How Green Was My Valley?, Winner Take Nothing!*.

storey　See floor . . .

straight and **bent**　The ordinary meanings of these words present no problems. The slang meanings can get us into trouble. See **bent** . . .

straightaway　See immediately . . .

strata　See stratum . . .

strategy . . .　See tactics

stratum and **strata**　We have to stay with *strata*, the Latin plural of *stratum* ('stratums' is not an option). A more common mistake is to use *strata* for the singular form ('There is a strata . . .').

straw poll　See poll

stream of consciousness　A misleading expression devised by psychologists in the 19th century. It is more a stream of *unconsciousness*, for it describes those thoughts, feelings, fears, emotions churning around uncontrollably inside us from the moment we get out of bed in the morning. In literature and drama, *stream of consciousness* is a seemingly unintelligible monologue that makes sense at an unconscious level, revealing what is going on below the surface.

street　See road . . .

street value　*Street value* is the same as market value (see **face value** . . .), the price a buyer will pay for something, irrespective of what it is worth. But 'market value' is used about respectable items, such as shares, houses or paintings, while *street value* is used only about illicit dealings in drugs, suggesting, as is often the way, that these are sold on the street.

streetwise and **street**　*Streetwise* was an expression in the 1960s, first of all in the streets of New York, for young people who knew how to howl like a wolf in the concrete jungle. They could look after themselves, make enough money to survive in the harsh often criminal environment of a big city. *Streetwise* is used mostly for young people, quick-witted, sharp and with no illusions about life: they have *street cred*(ibility). More recently, *street* has been picked up by fashion writers for girls who look fetchingly pale and underfed, part of the apparently vulnerable young generation. They are hired to model expensively downmarket clothes, which are supposed to have that same elusive calculatedly unsophisticated quality – *street*.

strength   To give the *g* a *k* sound ('stren*k*th') is all right, according to some recent dictionaries, although it's better to hint at the *g* sound. But 'strenth' is on the wrong side of the tracks.

stricken   See struck . . .

stroke   See coronary . . .

struck or **stricken**   The past form of *strike* is *struck*, whatever the meaning: 'she struck him as hard as she could'; 'he was struck by her beauty'; 'the clock has struck 7'; 'the workforce *struck*'. . . . *Stricken* is an archaic past form, but still survives in one or two phrases, notably 'stricken with grief', 'stricken with remorse'.

student or **pupil**   Some older dons at Oxford and Cambridge are still likely to refer to their 'former pupils', which suggests someone under their academic jurisdiction ('pupillaris' in Latin describes an orphan or ward). Otherwise only schoolchildren are called pupils, but from the sixth form through all branches of higher education and professional training, they are students. Pupil nurses and articled clerks are now also all students. An exception is the law: a newly qualified barrister becomes a pupil, undergoing a period of pupillage in chambers.

Pupil may continue to decline in favour of *student*: membership of the National Union of Students is open to older school students, and writers of textbooks are fond of referring to all their readers as 'students', irrespective of age ('Physics for First Year Students'). This has something to do with appealing to a worldwide market, since *student* is the overall expression abroad.

style   *Style* in using language can mean two things, which are separate. One is what book and newspaper publishers call 'house style' (see **house**), laid down in a 'style guide'. This covers such practical things as capitalization, which alternative spellings to use (**-ize or -ise**, for example), and grammatical points, such as how far the **who/whom** rule is followed.

Since there is no equivalent for the English language of the Académie Française, which officially prescribes the style of the French language, *style* in English can vary from publisher to publisher, newspaper to newspaper, and any one of us can decide which linguistic options we prefer. The only principle we should follow is consistency within the same piece of writing.

The other meaning of *style* in language is the way a writer chooses words and puts them together, 'an unremitting never-discouraged care for the shape and ring of sentences' (Joseph Conrad, Preface to *The Nigger of the 'Narcissus'*). It is style in this sense that

sets Graham Greene apart from, say Jeffrey Archer as a writer. For as David Lodge expressed it, 'The authority of great writers rests in an authority of style'.

Outside language, there are other meanings of *style*. It is used about the way someone dresses (see **chic**), or the way they do things, from composing music, painting a picture to playing tennis. Or *style* can be how someone appears to others as human beings. *Style*, in this last sense is indefinable. Jung might have compared it to the **psyche**, Oliver Sacks believed *style* 'is the deepest thing in one's being'. This echoes George-Louis de Buffon's famous comment, 'Style is the man himself'.

subconscious   See unconscious . . .

sub judice   When a matter is *sub judice* (under consideration by a judge or a court, before a verdict is given), it is against the law to pass comment on it in the media. *Sub judice* (pron: 'subJOOdissy') can be used outside legal contexts about anything you prefer not to comment on because it is under some kind of official consideration.

subjunctive   See if I *was* . . .; mood in grammar

subliminal advertising   See brainwashing

subnormal   See abnormal . . .

subscription television   See pay television . . .

subsidence   There are two pronunciations: 'subSYEde(r)ns' or 'SUBside(r)ns', with a whisker of preference for putting the stress on the second syllable.

subsidiarity   Although *subsidiarity*, meaning the state of being a subsidiary, existed as a word, few people had heard of it until May 1992, when *subsidiarity* crept above the horizon as the latest word in the European Community. *The Times* put it in inverted commas (the 'principle of "subsidiarity" '), as if it were a new word, which it isn't. Everyone else bandied it about as if they had known the word from birth.

In European terms *subsidiarity* means devolving powers away from the **EC** to individual countries. In that sense, it is the opposite of the most controversial word in European politics, **federalism**, and it seems equally difficult to agree on what it means: Jacques Delors, as president of the EC Commission, said 'If there is somebody here who can define subsidiarity on one page, we will give you a job'. See also **devolution**

substitute   See displace . . .

subtitle   See caption . . .

suburban   In the 19th century, the idea of living in the country, with easy access to the busy commercial centre of cities, was a middle-class aspiration. *Suburban* did not have a derogatory connotation: Macaulay wrote in his *History of England* (published 1849–61) of the 'suburban residencies of our kings'. As the suburbs came to sprawl inelegantly round cities, *suburban* became synonymous with blinkered middle-class attitudes, in some ways the equivalent of *bourgeois* (see **middle class . . .**).

Suburban is still used for dull, conventional, boring. . ., although the *middle-class* meaning is outdated, since the suburbs house all manner of people. Large cities boast *inner* and *outer* suburbs, with subtle grades of distinction in **status** for each.

subway   See **underground . . .**

subway art   See **graffiti**

such as   See **like**

suede or **suède**   Only a stiff-necked pedant would continue to put a grave accent over the middle *e* in *suede*. And there are few people left who would connect *suede* with the French name for Sweden (Suède), where suede gloves first came from.

sufficient   See **adequate . . .**

suggest   See **indicate . . .**

suggestive or **risqué**   *Risqué* (pron: 'REES-kay') is French for risky and hazardous. In English, it is a tut-tut of a word for a story or remark that is mildly sexual. *Risqué* seems a quaint word to use in the permissive 1990s, when linguistic full-frontal exposure is commonplace.

Suggestive does not mean quite the same: it is used more about a story or remark that hints at a sexual meaning without coming out into the open.

summary   See **outline . . .**

summit or **IGC**   Churchill first used the mountaineers' word *summit* in 1950, when he called for 'a parley at the summit'. The word was taken up by the media, particularly for meetings on disarmament between the President of the USA and the leader of the USSR. *Summit* became associated with high drama and great expectations. By the last months of 1991, as the Soviet Union ceased to be a geo-political reality, the word *summit* lost its former association, and was freely used for the meeting of heads of governments of EC countries at Maastricht in December of that year.

Up to that time, *IGC* (intergovernmental conference) was the name for a meeting convened at top level between all members of the European Community, and remains the official term used by Eurocrats in Brussels.

In 1992 an international conference in Rio de Janeiro on the world's ecological problems was popularly called the Earth Summit.

sung   See **sang . . .**

sunk   See **sank . . .**

super   People for whom so many things are *Super!* would be surprised to learn that *super* has been in English since the 14th century. Much later, in 1903, Bernard Shaw launched the word on a new career with *Man and Superman*. It led to a never-ending flow of new *supers*: *supermarket, superpower, supersonic, superego, supergrass, supertanker* and many more, going over the top in Tim Rice and Andrew Lloyd Webber's 'Jesus Christ – Superstar'. Inevitably, *super* has become a favourite of advertising agencies, the *supersoft* option for copywriters.

Dictionaries continue to show alternative pronunciations for the first syllable of *super*: 'SOOpe(r)' or 'SYOOpe(r)'. Make the first syllable rhyme with 'soup', which nearly everyone does, and which is the only pronunciation in America.

supercede   See **supersede . . .**

superiority or **supremacy**   The words are almost identical in meaning, but *supremacy* takes *superiority* to the final stage. In December 1991, the US Secretary of State felt there was a distinction, when he said about the war with Iraq, 'We have achieved superiority but not supremacy in the air'.

superpower   The *superpowers* were taken to be the United States and the Soviet Union. The latter no longer exists, and Russia, dependent on the West for economic aid, can hardly be called a *superpower*. In this new situation, *superpower* may come to be used in an economic rather than military sense.

supersede or **supercede**   The correct spelling, take it or leave it, is *supersede* (dictionaries do not allow 'supercede'). A useful way to remember this is the meaning of the word itself, which is to supplant someone or something.

supine   This is face *up*, not face *down*. See **prone . . .**

supper   See **dinner . . .**

supremacy   See **superiority . . .**

supremo   See **generalissimo . . .**

surgery   Medical practitioners in Britain have to qualify as surgeons, which is why the room where they see patients is traditionally called the *surgery*. MPs and social workers, who would hardly know one end of a scalpel from the other, have presumptuously taken over the word *surgery* for the rooms where they see people with problems or complaints.

surrogacy   See **reproductive technology**

suspenders   More women are wearing stockings again, so the word *suspenders*, for a curious attachment with fasteners to hold them up, is back in fashion. In America, men wear suspenders, the parallel word to

British 'braces', for holding up trousers. **Fowler** deigned to comment on the whole business, disapproving of using 'suspenders' to hold up trousers, because it abandoned 'the advantage of having two names for two things' (braces for trousers, suspenders for socks!). Times have changed.

swam or **swum** It is this way round: 'I have *swum* a long way', 'I *swam* yesterday'.

swap or **swop** *Swap* can be *swapped* with *swop*. Dictionaries show them as alternative spellings.

sweetener *Sweetener* has become a derisive word, especially in political commentaries, for a financial inducement or compensation, or a kind of cover-up payment. It does not come out in the open as much as the word 'bribe', but it certainly leans in that direction. *The Times* referred to large extra sums provided by the government to help local authority costs as a 'sweetener to alleviate Tory concern over the poll tax'.

swift See fast . . .

swingeing *Swinge* is an archaic verb from Old English for flogging someone. It survives in the descriptive word *swingeing* (pron: 'SWINjing'), not used about blows but for comments and measures, especially for economies and financial cuts, that are very severe. *Swingeing* has become a popular word in politics: 'swingeing cuts in the Health Service'.

swop See swap . . .

swum See swam . . .

sylvan or **silvan** It is not every day that we use this poetic word to describe a wooded scene. Etymologically, the spelling *silvan* is correct (from Latin 'silva', a wood), but *sylvan* is usually preferred, probably because it looks more lyrical.

symbol See logo . . .

sympathetic and **unsympathetic** The primary meaning of *sympathetic* is showing compassion for someone's suffering. But even the most conservative dictionaries accept as standard English the secondary meaning, which is likeable and appealing. This is the way the French use *sympathique*, the Italians *simpatico* and the Germans *sympatisch*: about a person, a restaurant, a film, about anything they find warm and agreeable. *Unsympathetic* can be used in the opposite sense for someone or something cold and off-putting.

sympathy See empathy . . .

symptomatic See characteristic . . .

syndrome As with many fashionable words, *syndrome* is often misused, as in 'she's suffering from an anxiety syndrome'. In medicine, a *syndrome* is not a disease but a complex of symptoms pertaining to a particular malfunction. **Aids** (acquired immune deficiency *syndrome*) is an example.

The proper extended use of *syndrome* is to express a range of manifestations coming from a single cause: 'it's all part of the permissiveness syndrome', meaning different ways in which permissiveness is expressed in society.

synonym or **homonym** A *homonym* is a word with the same sound or the same spelling as another word but with a different meaning: *maid* and *made*, *May* (month) and *may* (verb). *Homograph* can be used for words with the same spelling, *homophone* for words with the same sound, but *homonym* covers both. Homonyms are linguistic curiosities of no particular importance.

Synonyms are words that have almost the same meaning, in some cases perhaps exactly the same. These are important to everyone who cares about using words well. For there are few perfect synonyms. A good relationship with words reveals different shades of meaning, just as there are shades of colour that a painter mixes on a palette to find the perfect tone. Choosing the right *synonym* gives force and subtlety to language and penetrates more deeply into a thought. *The Good English Guide* draws lines, at times very fine ones, between many apparent synonyms.

synopsis See outline . . .

syntax *Syntax* is the relationship between words in a sentence, as dictated by grammar and convention. It is not a word used often outside grammar and linguistics. Alistair Cooke, who as a young journalist served on the Advisory Committee on Spoken English set up by the BBC, once commented, 'Syntax may go to hell, so long as I sound like one man talking to another'.

synthetic See artificial . . .

· T ·

table For years we have *put our cards on the table*, when we explain exactly where we stand over anything; we have *turned the tables* on someone, when we change what was to their advantage to our advantage (an expression from the game of chess for when the board is reversed). When we *table* something, we put it on the agenda for discussion. (Note: to *table* something in America is the opposite: it removes it temporarily or indefinitely from further consideration.) Now another usage is fashionable. Governments, trade unions, corporations no longer negotiate: they *sit round the negotiating table*; instead of discussing pay settlements, management and unions *go to the bargaining table*. *Table* is now an evocative image in any kind of horse-trading situation.

table d'hôte See à la carte . . .

tablet See pill . . .

table wine The *Concise Oxford Dictionary* (1990 edition) describes *table wine* as 'ordinary wine for drinking with a meal', and in France, 'vin de table' is cheap low-quality wine. But in Britain, *table wine* was traditionally used for any wine, including the greatest wines from Bordeaux and Burgundy, to distinguish them from stronger fortified wines, such as sherry and port. The French 'vin de table' may be having some influence on the traditional meaning of *table wine* in Britain, and the term could be misleading.

tabloids See broadsheets . . .

taboo words These days all dictionaries have to include **four-letter words**, such as *shit* or *arse*. Some dictionaries label them *taboo words*, others reserve *taboo* for words the editors consider particularly offensive.

For English in the 19th century, *taboo words* were mostly sexual, but in the 20th century they have been joined by racist words. We have to be careful about words that could offend other countries and other races, and expressions that we have taken for granted as innocent are becoming taboo. We can no longer talk about **nigger** brown, for example, and we must hesitate, at least at international meetings, to describe a soldier running away from battle as taking *French leave*, or to equate *Dutch courage* with courage that has to be fortified by a drink. Some people will think all this

is going too far, but what is not taboo to us may be taboo to others. See also **racist words**

tacit See implicit . . .

tacky One meaning is slightly sticky, often used about paint before it is dry. The second meaning is more interesting, and originated in America in the 19th century, where, as a noun, *tacky* was used about a poor black in the Southern States, and from that a descriptive word meaning shabby or run-down. It was in the 1960s, that *tacky* became familiar in Britain, and continues to be a colourful word for describing anything from an idea to an object or even a person as seedy, third-rate, grotty, shoddy, nasty, in short, something you would not give houseroom to.

tactics or **strategy** These are easy to confuse. *Strategy* is broad policy, medium to long-term planning. *Tactics* are day-to-day ways of achieving the long-term plan. *Strategy* is where you are going; *tactics* are how you get there.

tactics *is* or **are** Nouns ending in -*ics* often present this problem. See **-ics**

take, fetch or **bring** See bring . . .

take or ***make a decision*** See decision . . .

takeaway *Takeaway*, which began in a modest way in the 1960s as a term for ready-prepared food you could buy and eat at home, has spread like wildfire right across the whole social spectrum. But *takeaway* is more suitable for fish and chips or a curry from your local Indian takeaway, than for a ready-cooked game pie from Harrods.

take-home pay See pay . . .

take in To *take in* someone has long meant to deceive them, but other meanings of *take in* that have come over from America have at times made the expression ambiguous. Now we can take in information, meaning to understand or grasp it, take in a film, meaning to go to the cinema, take in Madrid on our way through Spain, meaning include a visit there. But if, for example, students on a course take in environmental studies, it could mean that they have understood them, or have included them in the overall course of study. Keep an eye on *take in* in case it leads to misunderstanding in a particular sentence.

take-off See **parody** . . .

takeover See **merger** . . .

take silk See **barrister** . . .

talking up See **emphasizing** . . .

tangerines, **clementines**, **mandarins** or **satsumas** The confident labelling in supermarkets shows that someone knows the difference between these four citrus fruits, even if it is confusing for most of us. In the 19th century, small orange-coloured citrus fruit shipped from Tangier were called 'Tangier oranges', which became *tangerines*. Later, similar fruit from other countries in the Mediterranean and elsewhere were also called tangerines. *Clementines*, *mandarins* (alternatively *mandarin oranges* or *mandarines*) and *satsumas* (named after the province in Japan where the fruit was first grown) are all varieties of tangerines. If in doubt, as most people are, it could not be wrong to call this variety of fruit *tangerines*.

tangible assets See **asset**

target *Target* has become a fashionable word since World War II, used in so many ways far removed from a round board for shooting practice. There are sales targets, government spending targets, we pursue targets, reach and exceed targets. . . .

Target as a verb, in the literal sense of shooting at something, goes back to the early 19th century. In the 1940s and 50s, *target* became the *in* word in economics and business: exports are targeted to rise, government spending targeted to be cut, profits targeted to increase. . . .

It's forlorn at this stage to complain that *target* has lost all connection with its original meaning (it derives from an Old French word for a round shield): the current uses of *target* are far too useful for anyone to give them up. Note that *target* does not double the *-t-* in other forms (see examples above).

tart In the mid-19th century, *tart* was lower-class slang for a girlfriend. It was often used affectionately about a woman who was dressed up, from which may arise the expression 'get tarted up', used by either sex for putting on attractive clothes, and 'to tart up something', meaning to make it look attractive. Some years later, *tart* became the word for a prostitute, often in an endearing way, probably deriving from 'sweetheart'. Since then it has become a derogatory and abusive word for a woman who is promiscuous or sexually provocative. See also **tramp**

tart, **pie**, **flan** or **quiche** *Tart* and *pie* go back to the 14th century and are linked with medieval Latin. Over the centuries, the meanings have become separated. A *pie* is a pastry dish, usually deep, with pastry at

the bottom and covered with a crust of pastry for a lid ('When the pie was opened . . .'). The contents can be almost any kind of food, meat, fish, vegetables or fruit. A *tart* is an open pastry dish, usually with a sweet filling, less commonly savoury.

A *flan*, like a tart, is a dish made of pastry, also with the top left open, but it is just as usual for it to have a savoury or a sweet filling. Unlike a tart, a flan can also be made out of a sponge mixture (when it always has a sweet filling).

Quiche is simply the French name used in English for a flan or tart, always savoury and always made from pastry (the best-known recipe is *quiche lorraine*, traditionally with a filling of eggs, cream and bacon).

tartan or **plaid** *Tartan* is the usual word for the crisscross designs that are emblems of Scottish clans. South of the Border, some people think *plaid* is the more distinguished word for a tartan, although it's the wrong use of the word, as far as the Scots are concerned. For in Scotland, a *plaid* is a shawl in a tartan pattern wrapped round the shoulders as part of traditional highland dress for men. Pronounce it 'plad' (to rhyme with 'dad').

Tass The word was an **acronym** formed from the initials of the Russian name for the Telegraphic Agency of the Soviet Union, the source of all official news from the former USSR. It is now part of history.

taste See **attitude** . . .

ta-ta See **goodbye** . . .

tautology or **pleonasm** *Pleonasm* (pron: 'PLEEe(r)nasm') means using unnecessary words to convey a meaning: 'I saw it with my own eyes'. 'Ha!' cry the nit-pickers, 'How else could you have seen it?' Sometimes extra words add intensity to a statement. Of course, too many words are used too often, which is tedious. Yet language is not a mechanical 2+2=4 process, and some of the best writers use more words than are strictly necessary in order to convey feeling and nuances. That is not the green light to use all the words that come into our heads, and nearly everything that is written or said can be improved by cutting.

At times, the distinction between *pleonasm* and *tautology* is hardly worth making. *Tautology* is repeating the same meaning in different words, which often adds nothing but padding: 'unfilled vacancy', 'recent news', 'final upshot', and John Major's contribution, in his concern for the Kurds in Iraq, 'safe haven' (see **haven**). Once again, some seemingly unnecessary words do add a useful emphasis, or are evocative: Bernard Partridge was too severe when he wrote off as tautology (*Usage and Abusage*, 1957) expressions such as: 'appear on the scene', 'hurry up', 'just recently' and even 'twice over'. These turns of phrase are part of the language and come naturally to us.

tax or **duty** The most notorious tax in the 14th century (when it led to the Peasants' Revolt), and near the end of the 20th century (when it caused public demonstrations) was the **poll tax**. Traditionally *tax* is levied on people and *duty* charged on goods. Now *tax* usually covers nearly every form of government levy, as in *income tax, car tax, value added tax*, etc. *Death duty*, the tax on someone's property after death, was changed in 1986 to *inheritance tax*.

Duty is retained for imported goods, hence duty paid on things declared at customs, and for a tax on certain transactions, such as the sale of land and houses, and for the official registration of legal documents, for which *stamp duty* may have to be paid.

Accountants are forever quoting in taxation newsletters 'nothing can be said to be certain, except death and taxes'. Few of them know who said it: it was Benjamin Franklin in a letter written in 1789.

tax *avoidance* or *evasion* These are precise terms used in law. The classic interpretation of *tax avoidance* was in a summing-up on a case by Lord Tomlin in 1935: 'every man is entitled if he can to order his affairs so that the tax attaching . . . is less than it otherwise would be'. That is a cautious legal way of saying if you can find loopholes in the tax laws, good luck to you.

Tax evasion is something else: it is deliberately giving false information or concealing information in order to pay less tax. Both terms are used only about income tax.

tax exile A *tax exile* chooses to live in another country where there is a low level of taxation. Such countries are called *tax havens*.

tax point This is mostly a *value added tax* term. It is really tax *date*, and is the legal date at which VAT becomes payable. In practice, this is usually the date on the bill, but it could be the date on which goods are delivered.

teach-in This expression was imported in the 1960s from American universities. It is used in America and Britain for a session of lectures or discussions, usually on a controversial issue, or for an informal gathering of people who want to widen their knowledge about a subject through discussion and exchange of ideas. *Teach-in* often carries the suggestion of rebellion or defiance: participants do not merely listen passively to a lecturer, but make an active contribution. This last point is the essence of a teach-in.

(the) team *is* or *are* See **collective words**

tear gas or **CS gas** *CS gas* is sometimes referred to in news items about public disorder. It is the most common *tear gas*, causing acute eye irritation and temporary blindness, and can have a lasting effect on the eyes and lungs. CS gas bestows a sinister immortality on the two American chemists, Corson and Stroughton, who developed it in 1928.

teaser campaign We are all exposed to *teaser campaigns* at times. They are enigmatic posters or advertisements, sometimes with only one word on them, and we have no idea what they are there for. But we look at them, which is the whole point. After a period, all is revealed, and the teaser campaign is linked with a product. It is part of advertising fighting like fury for attention, since it must compete with all other advertisements, posters, and the multitudinous images that pass across our retinas.

teaspoonfuls See **-ful**

technical or **technological** Because *technological* has become such a fashionable word, it is often used when *technical* would apply. *Technical* is more practical, related to a specific mechanical or other technique, or to a skill. There may be technical problems with a piece of machinery, an artist or musician can have technical difficulties, such as problems over brushwork or the fingering of an instrument.

Technological is more scientific, relating to the study and development of engineering and applied sciences. A technical problem is something a technician can often deal with on the spot, a technological problem usually requires more research.

Technicolor Even if you don't like the American spelling of *colour*, you have to use it in *Technicolor* because that is the registered name for a particular laboratory process of colour cinematography. No one seems to mind if we use *technicolor*, with a small *t*, for dazzling vivid colours: 'she was wearing a dress in gorgeous technicolor'.

technics See **science** . . .

technique See **method** . . .

technocrat *Technocracy* was a word invented by a Californian engineer soon after World War I for the nightmare concept of technologists taking over the whole world. Technocracy would replace **democracy**, and our lives would be regulated by machines under the control of *technocrats*. *Technocracy* is not a word that is used much now, but *technocrat* has come to mean a technologist or development scientist in a position of power, perhaps as the chairman of a company or member of government. *Technocrat* suggests using science and technology to solve political and social problems, leaving out the human factor. Compare **meritocracy**.

technological See **technical** . . .

technological fix A *technological fix* is used, generally scathingly, for a two-dimensional scientific approach to a human problem. It works perfectly on the drawing-board but makes no sense in the real world, because it leaves out human nature and needs.

technology See **mechanization** . . . ; **science** . . .

teenager The first *teenagers* are now old age pensioners, for the word appeared in America in the early 1940s. *Teenager* soon crossed the Atlantic as it filled a real linguistic need. The alternative word, 'adolescent', suggests **young people** in transition between childhood and adulthood: *teenager* recognized a politically conscious group able to make its own demands on society, which is a fact of life in the 1990s.

tele- *Tele-* is the most prolific wordmaking prefix of this period. *Telescope* was one of the first *tele-* words: it goes back to Galileo (1564–1642). *Telegraph* and *telegram* are mid-18th century or earlier, and sound like it. *Telepathy* comes from the 1880s, and we are still arguing about whether it's possible.

Among the new *tele-* words, some of which are too freshly minted to get into dictionaries, are *telebooking* (see next entry), **telecommuting**, **teleconference**, *telefax* (first recorded in 1967 – see **fax . . .**), **telemarketing**, **teleprompt**, teletext, **teleworker**.

telebooking Theatre or travel tickets, restaurant tables and hotel rooms are just some of the things that can be reserved by *telebooking* through **videotext**.

telecommute *Telecommute* came over the horizon in 1990, too late to get into the new edition of the *OED*. *Telecommuting* is going to work by reaching out to pick up a telephone. **Modems** and **fax** machines have made it possible for people to work at home, receiving and transmitting work through telephone lines. The Henley Centre forecasts that by the end of the century 'almost half of all employees could telecommute for a proportion of their working week'. See also **teleworking**

teleconference or **videoconference** A *teleconference* enables people to stay in their offices, using telephone lines linked with two-way loudspeakers, and take part in a meeting with others in different parts of the country or the world. *Videoconferences* go one better, and will become commonplace by the end of the century. Instead of flying people across the world, a meeting is set up by booking time in a local *videoconference centre*. Television monitors provide a face-to-face conference with participants in different parts of the world.

telemarketing *Telemarketing* uses the telephone and **fax** to make contacts with clients. Instead of half a dozen or so calls a day, a salesman or saleswoman can make 30 or more contacts, with the cost of each contact cut to a fraction of what it used to be. Telemarketing conducted from an office or a car allows individual members of a salesforce to be instantly integrated into a national campaign, with hourly supervision by a sales manager and a **hotline** to production.

telephone See **phone . . .**

teleprompt In the theatre, the prompt sits out of sight of the audience and 'prompts' any actors who forget their lines. In a television studio, a *teleprompt*, out of view of the cameras, rolls out the script for a newscaster or presenter, who (for those not in the know) seems to have a word-perfect memory. See also **sincerity machine**

teletext See videotex(t) **. . .**

televise or **televize** Always *televise* because it is a verb formed from 'television'.

television, **TV** or **telly** These are three of the ways of referring to what the radio broadcaster Alistair Cooke calls 'the universal peeping Tom'. 'I saw it on TV' or '. . . on television' are the usual expressions. 'I saw it on the telly' is downmarket. '*On the box*', at one time almost the most usual expression, is still used but not so often now. See also **as seen on TV**.

teleworkers and **teleworking** At the time of writing, *teleworking* is not in dictionaries, but it soon will be. **British Telecom** defines teleworking as 'remote working, or **telecommuting** . . . working somewhere away from the office on either a full-time or a part-time basis, and communicating with it electronically'. In practice, this will usually be done from someone's home, but some companies will arrange local work centres covering particular areas, shared by a group of teleworkers, using **fax** machines, special business telephone lines and computers that transmit written material to the central office. Teleworkers operating from home will doubtless include a portable telephone for working in the garden on summer afternoons.

telly See television **. . .**

temperature or **fever** Earlier this century, doctors would talk about a patient having a *fever*, the correct use of the word for an above-normal body temperature. It is now often said a patient 'has a *temperature*', meaning a high temperature. That is established use, even in hospitals, although it sounds odd to say a patient 'does *not* have a temperature'! *Fever* is often taken to mean an especially high body temperature, or an illness that brings it on.

'TEMporarily' or **'tempoRARily'** It may be easier to stress the third syllable, but British dictionaries insist on 'TEMporarily' as the correct pronunciation. (The third syllable is stressed in America.)

tennis terms The ancestor of modern tennis was an indoor game that was played in France in the 13th century, known in English as 'royal tennis', corrupted into 'real tennis'. Tennis, as we know it, acknowledges its debt to that old French game by using a similar system of scoring, and adapting the French expression 'à deux' (both) as *deuce* for the score 40–all. John Silverlight in his column on words in *The Observer* took this further, claiming that *love* derives from the French 'l'oeuf' (since an egg looks like a nought). There is a better case for believing that *love* comes from the

English expression 'for love', that is for nothing ('I did it for love').

tense (grammar) *Tense* in grammar applies only to verbs and locates the action of a verb in time. There are a number of gradations of tense for different time sequences. For example, *I went, I was going, I had gone* and *I should have gone* are all forms of past tense of the verb *go*. The present and future also have a range of different tenses. See also **mood**

terminate See **stop** . . .

terrace and **townhouse** 'Semi-detached' has a suburban downmarket ring to it, so estate agents have taken up *terrace* and *townhouse* as ways of giving a fashionable snob value to Victorian workmen's dwellings in 'up-and-coming' districts of cities. 'Semi-detached' has become *end of terrace!*

terrine See **pâté** . . .

terrorism and **terrorist** *Terrorism* is so much a word of our time that it is startling to recall that *terrorist* and *terrorism* were used two hundred years ago during the most violent period (1793–4) of the French Revolution, the Reign of Terror. Since the 1960s, the words have acquired a different focus, a political problem confronting every country in the world, words that can at any time affect us personally. For terrorism, as we know it now, is indiscriminate in its choice of victims.

The Prevention of Terrorism Act 1984 defines it as 'the use of violence for political ends'. The accepted definition is that terrorism is always directed towards political advantage, not personal gain. Its sole purpose is to draw attention to a political cause by dominating the media.

The words *terrorism* and *terrorist* are loaded with predetermined judgements: the underlying cause is never allowed to be just. Terrorists have to be, by definition, a threat to civilized society and to basic human values. Conor Gearty, who wrote a book on the subject, *Terror* (1991), considered the words 'hopelessly compromised'. He left us with the question, 'Were George Washington and Oliver Cromwell terrorists?' Whether someone is a *terrorist* or a *freedom fighter* may depend upon which side you are on, or on the view taken by history. See also **guerrilla; resistance**

Tessa When John Major, as Chancellor of the Exchequer, announced in 1990 a new Tax Exempt Special Savings Account, it became overnight an **acronym** – *Tessa*. It's a scheme for earning interest on bank and building society accounts without paying tax, subject to certain limits and conditions.

test-tube babies See **reproductive technology**

testy, tetchy or **touchy** You have to work at it to separate these three words which all mean irritable.

Testy and *tetchy* seem interchangeable, with *testy* more likely to be used about someone who is old. *Touchy* is a little different, as it includes the suggestion of quick to take offence.

tête-à-tête See **face to face** . . .

text *Text* is the fashionable all-embracing term with many literary scholars, as a word for poems, plays, novels, essays, even belles-lettres. Alison Lurie, a novelist and professor of English at Cornell University, has commented (*The State of the Language*, 1990) on how the word *text* is taking over. Just as anatomical terms separate the human body from warmth, beauty and feeling, so the clinical word *text* sterilizes the passion and sweat of literature.

Text is appropriate to **information technology**, but do we want to consider *The Waste Land, Under Milk Wood* or *The Power and the Glory* as 'a set of alphanumeric characters that convey information' (definition of *text* in *Macmillan Dictionary of Information Technology*)?

TGV TGV is the abbreviation for *train à grand vitesse* (high-speed train), and the British are becoming familiar with it as part of the high-speed rail link between London and Paris. TGV have linked Paris and Lyons since 1981, and will run, as part of the new TGV network, between Paris and the entrance to the Channel tunnel. TGV, which has achieved a rail speed record of over 300mph, has become the standard for high-speed trains in Europe. Pronounce more or less as in French: 'tay-jay-vay'.

than *I* or ***me*, etc** Which is good English: 'She is richer than I' or 'She is richer than me'? The same question applies to *than she* or *than her*, etc. The argument centres on the grammatical function of the word *than*.

There are many examples of good writers and speakers using *than me, than him*, etc, and Eric Partridge, a conservative scholar, came out in favour of *than me*. Other grammarians insist on *than I, than he*. . . .

The game is hardly worth the candle and perhaps we should use whichever comes naturally. For most of us that will be *than me, than him*. . . . 'She is taller than me', 'She arrived earlier than him'. If you prefer *than I*, etc, it is better to complete the sentence: 'She is taller than I am'; 'She arrived earlier than he did'. Otherwise it can sound stilted.

In some sentences, look out for the risk of confusion: 'She loves him more than me' could mean 'She loves him more than she loves me' or 'She loves him more than I love him'. In such cases, spell it out and say what you mean.

Thanks or **Thank you** There are conventions about how we express gratitude. *Thank you* is more appreciative than *Thanks*, which can sound off-hand, unless you say *Many thanks* or *Thanks a lot. I thank* *you* is very formal, while *Thank you so much* is a shade condescending. *Many thanks* is friendly, *A thousand thanks* over the top, and *Thanks a million* is American. *Thanks awfully* sounds gushing, leaving *Thanks ever so* and *Thanking you* as decidedly downmarket.

There are also conventions about how we reply. *That's all right* is relaxed, classless and friendly. *Don't mention it* has an old-worldly courtesy about it. *You're welcome*, the usual response in America, is becoming popular in Britain. *Not at all* has a superior tone, with a hint of noblesse oblige. To reply to 'Thank you' by saying 'Thank *you*!' crosses over to the wrong side of the tracks.

that There are nine double-column pages in Fowler's *Modern English Usage* (1926) on *thatism*. One difficulty is we're often not sure whether to put *that* in or leave it out: 'I believe *that* the book *that* she has written is *that* one'. The first two *thats* could be deleted and the sentence remains good English and perfectly clear: 'I believe the book she has written is *that* one'. There are people who consider this ungrammatical, but when *that* is unnecessary for the sense or the sound, it can often be omitted, unless you want to sound formal or dignified. That's *that*.

that, which or **who** *Who* is used for people; *which* is used for things, but can *that* be used for either? Some grammarians insist there is a difference in meaning between: 'White wine that is dry goes well with fish' and 'White wine which is dry goes well with fish'. The argument is *that* is defining, specifying a *dry* white wine, rather than a sweet one, while *which* is non-defining, and assumes all white wines are dry.

This takes some working out, and since both sentences mean the same to most people, there is little point in insisting on a distinction between *that* and *which*. Bergen and Cornelia Evans summed it up fairly in *A Dictionary of Contemporary American Usage*, 'What is not the practice of most, or of the best, is not part of our common language'.

The above applies to *who*: 'Please explain it again for the women *that* came late' and '. . . the women *who* came late'. Both sentences are acceptable in practice, although 'the women *who*' sounds more natural.

On *that*, *which* or *who*, Bruce Fraser, in his revised edition of *Plain Words*, gives short sharp advice – 'Don't fuss'. But remember some people will go on fussing about it and expect you to as well.

Thatcherism Margaret Thatcher was the first prime minister to earn an -ism, perhaps because -isms were becoming more fashionable (compare **Reaganism**). *Thatcherism* is included in some current dictionaries. She, herself, believes the word is here to stay, for in an article in *Newsweek* (April 1992) she declared, 'Thatcherism will live long after Thatcher has died'.

One of the earliest references to Thatcherism was in *The Times* (24.11.79), the year of the first election victory of the Conservative Party under her leadership: the editorial commented on the 'divisiveness of Thatcherism'. That remains the keynote of the word: Thatcherism is either hated and feared or revered and blessed, depending on your viewpoint. Not that everyone is clear about what it means – Thatcherism is a combination and a confusion of style and ideology.

For some people, Thatcherism is the personal style of Margaret Thatcher, the way she speaks, the determined way she raises her chin, her regimented hairstyle, the impression she gives of absolute authority. For others, Thatcherism embraces policies such as privatization, limiting the power of trade unions, encouraging enterprise and free market forces, and opposition to unification with Europe.

If you talk or write about Thatcherism, it is as well to be aware you are using a term that will be interpreted in different ways.

the or **a** It is a compliment to call someone *the* member of parliament, *the* actor, etc, rather than *a* member of parliament, *an* actor, etc. It's more complimentary still if you pronounce *the* as 'thee' rather than 'the(r)'. For further notes on this, see **a**. . . .

theirs or **their's** *Their's* is always wrong.

theme park A *theme park* has become the commercial term for any large open space, with exhibitions, amusements, etc, focused on a particular subject. London has been called a 'historical theme park for overseas tourists'.

there- *Thereabouts, thereby, therefore* and one or two other *there-* combinations have a place, but most of the others, such as *thereafter, therein, thereinafter, thereof, theretofore, therewith*, should be used very rarely. Like wearing starched shirts or blouses, they might be justified in special circumstances. Otherwise, leave them in peace in dictionaries.

therefore *Therefore* is at best a rather heavygoing word (see previous entry). At one time, it was always preceded and followed by a comma: 'I consider, therefore, that . . .'. If there are occasions when you have to use *therefore*, the commas can at least be omitted these days in most sentences.

thesaurus A *thesaurus* (pron: 'theSAWrus') is not so much a collection of **synonyms** but lists of words and phrases that could be said to have roughly the same meaning. The limitation of a thesaurus is that it does not usually explain the different shades of meaning between the words it lists. The usual plural is *thesauruses*, but if you prefer it you can go to town and say *thesauri* (pron: 'theSAWrye').

thesis See **dissertation** . . .

the wife See **my wife** . . .

they'd have See **I'd have** . . .

they're See **contracted forms**

think or **feel** See **feel** . . .

Third Age This is said to have been coined by Charles Handy, a visiting professor at the London Business School, as his preferred alternative to 'retirement age'. The principle of the Third Age is that doors are not closing but opening to new interests and even to new careers. The Third Age has become recognized as big business: it is calculated that 40 per cent of the wealth in Britain is owned by the over-55s, and those in the know are apparently no longer calling men and women over 60 the 'crumblies', but the 'woopies' (well-off older people).

Third World The *Third World* (sometimes spelt without initial capital letters) was translated from the French, 'le tiers monde', used at a conference in 1955. ('Le tiers monde' echoed 'le tiers état' for the social class in 18th-century France other than the aristocracy and the higher ranks of the clergy.) To begin with, Third World was used specifically for countries, particularly in Africa, Asia and Latin America, not aligned with either Communist or capitalist countries. The term became used in an indeterminate, patronizing way for primitive countries in a state of poverty, dependent on agriculture and raw materials, and subject to famine. Later, another category was added, the *Fourth World*, countries that were underdeveloped but with valuable natural resources, such as oil.

The Third World was paralleled by the term *underdeveloped country*. Both terms are considered derogatory and no longer used officially. The world is now, in effect, divided between **developing countries**, once again used particularly for the countries of Africa, South America and parts of Asia, and the industrialized countries, where there is a much higher standard of living and social amenities.

though See **although** . . .

through 1 The American use of *through* to mean 'up to and including' has not caught on in Britain, although it is heard. It would be useful, as, for example, '7th through 27th January' makes it clear that the 27th is included, whereas 'the 7th to 27th' leaves it uncertain.

2 The American use of *through*, to mean finished with something, is used increasingly in Britain, particularly about relationships ('I'm through with him!'). But *through* is not often used, as it is in America, to mean someone's career is over, or that they've been sacked. British telephone operators still say, when making a connection, 'You're through', although it sometimes gives Americans a nasty turn! (See **engaged** . . .).

throughput See **output** . . .

throw or **cast** These are both Old English words going back to before the 13th century. *Cast* is now restricted to technical and particular applications: moulds are cast, actors are cast for roles, votes are cast and so are fishing lines and anchors. . . . *Throw* is the word used in most everyday contexts. In fact, where *throw* can be used, *cast* often sounds silly: 'she cast his letter into the fire'.

In other cases it is a matter of idiom which is used: the die is cast, but dice are thrown; we cast our eye over something, but throw our bonnet over the windmill.

ticks or **crosses** You would expect a *tick* to mean 'yes' and a *cross* to mean 'no'. So why do official forms require us to put a *cross* against items that are correct or relevant? A modest example of positive thinking, on tax return forms for example, is that we are now asked to put ticks, rather than crosses, in the boxes. Ballot slips at General Elections still demand a *cross* against the name of the chosen candidate, an unintentional symbol of the way a lot of people feel about politics.

tightwad See **mean** . . .

tilde (˜) A *tilde* (pron: 'TILde(r)') is the wavy line used in Spanish over an *n* to show it has a 'ny' sound, as in 'señor'. A tilde is used in Portuguese over the vowels *a* and *o* to show they are pronounced slightly through the nose. See **accents in print**

till See **until** . . .

time off or **time out** *Time off* is a British expression for a rest from work or a break from an activity, and *time out* is American for the same thing (also used for a break in a game). In 1968, a new magazine started, *Time Out*, giving news of leisure activities and entertainment in London. Since then, *time out* has slipped to British English: 'I think I'll take time out to . . .'; 'Would you take time out to work on this for me?'

time-sharing *Time-sharing* covers two meanings. The most familiar one is buying a share in a holiday home, conferring the right to use it for specified periods during the year. *Time-sharing* in computer jargon is a high-speed technique that enables expensive computer equipment to be used interchangeably by a number of operators.

times of day Even if we're reading it off a computerized digital clock, we still use the archaic 12th century *o'* form of 'of' (7 o'clock). The Latin terms, *ante meridiem* (before noon) and *post meridiem* (after noon), survive alongside the 24-hour clock system, and the only concession to the fast-approaching millennium is to allow us to drop the stops (*am* and *pm*). 12pm and 12am, as well as being illogical, are confusing: it is better to write and say *12 noon* or *12 midnight*, or simply *noon* or *midnight*.

The British prefer *a quarter to* and *a quarter past*, whereas many Americans say *a quarter of* and *a quarter after*. Either way, *tempus fugit* (Virgil's observation that *time flies*).

tin See **can** . . .

tip, **gratuity** or **service charge** Although there are some public places in Britain where there are signs reading NO GRATUITIES, it is an unnecessarily formal word for a *tip*. *Tip* was originally slang, a word for a small extra sum of money given on the side to a waiter, taxi-driver or anyone else who has rendered a service. But the word has been used in that sense since the early 18th century, and is accepted by dictionaries as standard English.

Service charge, long used in restaurants in other countries, is now common in Britain: it is the obligatory percentage added to the bill, supposedly instead of a tip, which, it is assumed, is divided among all the staff. Why is it necessary, as in other businesses the cost of labour is included in the price charged to customers? Then there is the question of whether to leave a tip in addition to paying the service charge. Such social dilemmas are outside the brief of *The Good English Guide*.

tire or tyre See tyre . . .

tissue 'TISHyou' or 'TISSyou'? The *OED* shows both pronunciations, leaning towards 'TISHyou'. But you can please yourself about it.

tit Dictionaries are funny about some words. The 1989 *Collins Concise Dictionary* regards *tit* as standard English for a nipple but slang for a woman's breast; the 1990 *Concise Oxford Dictionary* writes down *tit* as colloquial for a nipple but 'usually considered a taboo word' for a breast. *Taboo* is too severe for this harmless word, which many women use as well as men. And perhaps it is lexicographical hair-splitting for *tit* to be all right for a nipple but taboo for a breast.

titivate or titillate They do not mean the same, as some people believe. *Titivate* is standard English for the slang expression '**tart** something up'. *Titillate* is used for mild sexual stimulation, more teasing than torrid.

titles of people See ambassador; clergy; royalty

TM (Transcendental Meditation) See meditation

to There are still people who are hesitant about ending a sentence with the word *to* ('Who is it going to?'). For reassurance over this, see **prepositions**.

to a degree See degree

together with *Together with* does not combine two nouns to make a plural subject. If someone is *together with* another person, it is followed by a singular verb: 'My friend, together with her husband, *is* coming to dinner'.

toilet See lavatory . . .

tokenism This -ism was born in America in the early 1960s to describe a minimum political concession

to public pressure. It is used dismissively in Britain about such gestures as putting one woman on the board of a company (see **statutory woman**) or a black person on a national committee, or any other self-conscious gesture to avoid being accused of sexism or racism.

tomboy *Tomboy* used to be a word for a girl who showed qualities of daring and leadership. It was a word that confined women to a role that society imposed. The shift away from such attitudes has left *tomboy* as a sexist old-fashioned word that has no place in a society where women climb mountains, are cabinet ministers, leading barristers. . . .

ton or tonne *Ton* represents various units of weight, the most common of which in Britain is 20 hundredweight (2240 pounds). *Tonne* is a metric measurement and equals 1000 kilograms (approx 2205 pounds). Both *ton* and *tonne* are pronounced the same ('tun'), and if you need to indicate which is which in speech, refer to *tons* or *metric tonnes*.

tongue See language . . .

top Because it is short and sharp, journalists took to *top* for describing people in the forefront in any field (top scientists, top businessmen, etc). A few years back, the slogan 'Top people read *The Times*' gave *top* a further boost.

topless There's something **nudge-nudge wink-wink** about this word, thanks to *topless* waitresses in *topless* bars. But it's the only word we can use on beaches for women wearing **bikini** bottoms only.

tornado See blizzard . . .

tortuous or torturous These words are sometimes treated as synonymous, which they are not. They both relate to Latin 'tortus' (twisted or crooked) but are used in different ways. *Tortuous* is winding and twisted: a tortuous route, a tortuous mind. *Torturous* is something that inflicts torture: a torturous experience, torturous agony. At times there is an overlap, for driving along a tortuous road, particularly when it is icy, can be torturous.

Tory See Conservative . . .

total of . . . is or are Follow the same rules as for **number of** . . .

touchtone *Touchtone* is the telephonic term used for the musical tones that have replaced the old clicking sounds that accompanied dialling a number.

touchy See testy . . .

tough (as a verb) *Tough it out* seems to be an expression invented for Margaret Thatcher. It certainly suited her style. John Cole, political editor of the

BBC during her premiership, often used it about her approach to difficult situations. *The Sunday Times*, in a leading article, commented on her 'defiant speeches telling everybody she intends to tough it out'.

Since then, we have all taken *tough* (as a verb) on board, and when we're faced with everything collapsing all around us, anyone of us can *tough it out*.

tour de force   If you're fed up having to fall back on French expressions to convey your meaning, the best alternative to *tour de force* (feat of strength) is *masterstroke*: 'the chairman's speech was a real masterstroke'.

towards or **toward**   Either: *towards* is more usual in Britain and *toward* in America. 'Tawds' used to be the upper-class way of saying it and some people still keep to that, but 'to-wards' (two syllables and sounding the *w*) is standard now.

tower block and **high rise**   In the 1950s, when multi-storey buildings rose up as flats, offices and hotels in London and other cities, *tower blocks* and *high rise* became the accepted words for them (**skyscraper** was too much associated with American cities to be used in Britain). The term is connected particularly with local authority housing, which offered tenants a dream of luxury and modern living that was never realized.

town   See city . . .

townscape   *Townscape* goes back to the late 19th century and the word is not used much. But it is a useful term, parallel to **landscape**, for describing the visual effect of the arrangement of buildings and streets in a city.

township   *Township* has various meanings in different countries, but the one that dominates the news is for the townships in South Africa. These are urban ghettoes, built on the edge of cities, for black Africans. The most notorious group is Soweto, the townships near Johannesburg, where over a hundred people were killed during the riots in June 1976.

toy boy or **gigolo**   *Gigolo* belongs to the 1920s, when it was used for a younger man kept by an older woman as her lover. It is not an Italian word, as it sounds, but was formed from 'gigolette', an old-fashioned French word for a young woman who frequents dance halls. It is rare to hear *gigolo* now or, for that matter, the modern equivalent expression, *toy boy*.

track record   A record of performance in a race or on an athletic track was adapted some time after World War II to cover a record of achievement or failure in any other activity. If, for example, a writer has a good track record, his or her books have been successful, just as a poor track record means the opposite. Perhaps *track record*, more than the word

'record' on its own, implies a history of achievements or failures that can be used as a guide to future performance.

trade   See business . . .

trademark   See logo . . .

trade-off   In effect, *trade-off* is the business term for a compromise. A trade-off is a commercial balance between one consideration and another. If a car was as safe as technology could allow, it would cost too much for most people to buy. When it is as safe as possible, consistent with keeping the price competitive, there's a trade-off between safety and competitiveness.

trade union or **trades union**   Both forms exist. Some older trade-unionists prefer *trades union*, but *trade union* (plural *trade unions*) is usual now, except in Trades Union Congress (where *trades union* is used as the plural form).

trail (information)   See leak (information) . . .

trainers   At one time, *trainer* meant one thing, someone who trained people in sports and athletics, or trained horses. The first meaning that comes to mind now for many people, especially for the word in the plural (*trainers*), is soft **designer** boots, worn for basketball and other sports.

The word *trainers* in this sense is British and was introduced in the late 1970s. It spread like a forest fire. *Trainers* are worn by teachers, taxi drivers and trainee executives, and are standard uniform for millions of people under 30 in almost any situation.

trait   Dictionaries show two pronunciations: 'tray' or 'trayt'. Some dictionaries favour one, some the other. Some people look down on 'trayt' as uneducated, because they consider the word French: others find 'tray' affected, because it's spelt *trait*. In this linguistic no-go area, *The Good English Guide* follows the recommendation given to BBC announcers, which is that the final *t* is *not* sounded.

tramp   British and American English have fun and games with *tramp*. In Britain a *tramp* is a vagrant, someone with no home, who goes around begging (the equivalent in America is a *hobo*). *Tramp* in America corresponds to the word **tart** in Britain, a derogatory word for a prostitute or a promiscuous woman, which is what it means in the song 'That's Why the Lady is a Tramp'.

tranche   On the stock exchange, *tranche* is the word used for a section of a block of shares that is issued and paid for in stages. There is no good reason why a French word (it means a 'slice') should be used, pronounced more or less as in French ('trahnsh'). After all, we are at home talking about 'a *slice* of the action', 'a slice of the profits', as well as a slice of cake. But there it is.

tranquilllizer or **sedative** Both words are for drugs that are calming and soothing. *Sedative* is a clinical word, used in hospitals for drugs given to patients to help them relax and sleep.

Tranquilllizer has been used for over a hundred years for music and harmonious scenes that leave us in a peaceful state of mind. Since the 1950s, the word has taken on a sharper edge, the familiar name in this age of anxiety for a class of drugs (sometimes colloquially known as 'downers') prescribed, perhaps overprescribed at times, by doctors to relieve stress and tension in daily life. *Tranquilllizers* is also the name given to certain drugs used in psychiatric hospitals.

Tranquilllizer comes into non-medical contexts for something we use, or abuse, to calm ourselves: sex has been called a tranquilllizer, and food, 'the oldest tranquilllizer in the world'.

trans or **trans-** Nearly all *trans* words now appear as one word, even when it results in a double *s* (in a few words one *s* is sometimes omitted): trans-continental, transnational, transoceanic, transsexual, transship (or tranship). . . . This is the usual form, even when the second word is the name of an ocean or country: transatlantic, transpacific, etc (rather than 'trans-Atlantic', 'trans-Pacific'). One exception is the name of the longest railway in the world, the Trans-Siberian Railway.

transcendent or **transcendental** Apart from contexts in philosophy, *transcendental* connotes something beyond ordinary human experience, a surpassing of the ego and attachment to this life. The block to understanding the meaning of *transcendental* is the impossibility of knowing unless you have experienced it. For *Transcendental Meditation*, see **meditate**

Transcendent has a similar meaning but is the word to use in non-mystical contexts to mean beyond what is usual, as in transcendent importance, transcendent ability. Theologians use *transcendent* about God, for an existence that goes beyond the universe. See also **enlightenment**

transfer See **assign** . . .

'transFERable' or **'TRANSferable'** Stress on the first or second syllable has been optional for some time, with dictionaries showing preference for *first* syllable stress. This has now changed, with most dictionaries bowing to the majority, by showing only one pronunciation: 'transFERable'.

transistor See **radio** . . .

transliterate or **translate** *Translate* is straightforward: it is expressing the meaning of one language in another. *Transliterate* is representing the letters of a word in one alphabet as closely as possible using the letters of another. Russian and Greek, for example, which have their own alphabets, are usually shown in English in letters of the **Roman alphabet**, by attempting to imitate the sound. Because trans-literation can be only approximate, the adaptation of letters from one alphabet, to another can vary in differ-ent texts, so there is sometimes disagreement over how Russian names, for example, are spelt in English. Languages such as Chinese, which use characters in-stead of an alphabet, present even greater difficulties for accurate transliteration into the Roman alphabet (see, for example, **Beijing or Peking**).

transparency See **colour negative** . . .

transpire When something *transpires*, it becomes known: 'When it transpired he had been lying, he resigned'. Most books on English condemn using *tran-spire* to mean 'happen' or 'occur': 'Let's see what transpires when they meet'. This usage has existed in English for at least 150 years, and well-known writers, including Dickens, have used *transpire* in this way. Dictionaries have come round to showing 'happen' or 'occur' as one of the meanings of *transpire*, although many people still consider this unacceptable. Often the misuse of a word eventually passes into standard English and the shouting dies away. For some reason, this has not yet happened with *transpire*, so you must decide for yourself whether to follow a rule that many people have ignored for years, or to go along with the tide and use *transpire* to mean happen, occur, take place.

transport or **transportation** The usual word is *transport* (the *transport* of goods or people from one place to another), but some people prefer *transpor-tation* (the most usual word in America), and there should be no objection to this, except that it's a couple of syllables longer.

transsexual A *transsexual* is not a homosexual or a lesbian. *Transsexuality* is when a man or a woman has an irresistible psychological need to belong to the other sex, driving them sometimes to undergoing a surgical operation.

trattoria This Italian word for an eating place has been used in English since the 1830s. Since the 1960s, so many Italian restaurants have opened that *trattoria* (and the slang abbreviation *trat*) has become familiar. A *trattoria* is properly a simple restaurant, but don't bank on that any longer, as some *trats* are fashionable and expensive. Pron: 'tratte(r)REEe(r)'.

traumatic Used by doctors and psychiatrists for a severe physical or psychological injury, and by many other people for shocks of varying degrees, particu-larly about unhappy love affairs. Two pronunciations are heard: 'TRAWmatic' or 'TROWmatic' (first syllable rhyming with 'how').

treble or **triple** Some authorities lay down a complicated formula for which word is used in which contexts. The fact is, other than as musical terms when *treble* and *triple* are used in different ways, it's not worth worrying about whether you treble your efforts or triple them. If anything, *triple* is becoming more common.

trench coat *Trench coat* is an echo from World War I, when the War Office decreed that a long waterproof wrap-round coat was army uniform for officers. But it is a distant echo, for in the 1990s *trench coats* are high fashion. The designer, Jasper Conran, has displayed them in organza, other designers have used silky metallic cotton, intended, in the words of fashion writer Lisa Armstrong, 'as a sexy throw-on for evenings'. It is a long way from the battle of the Somme.

trendy Dictionaries may consider it colloquial or informal, or whatever other term they use for words that are not quite literary, but it is trendy to use the word *trendy* for the latest fashion in anything. *Trendy* often has a derogatory undertone, suggesting a self-conscious adoption of a style or manner. It survives from the early 1960s, when it was 'swinging' to be *trendy* and *trendy* to be 'swinging'.

trillion See **billion** . . .

trip In the 1960s, to *take a trip* often meant using LSD to be transported into hallucinations; an *ego-trip* was a self-indulgent exercise, which could be writing a book, making a film, or almost anything else; a *bad trip* was a disturbing emotional experience, usually associated with drugs. These extended uses of the word *trip* now seem dated, and we can once again say we're 'taking a trip' (to the seaside, etc), without any risk of being misunderstood.

triple See **treble** . . .

triumphant or **triumphal** *Triumphant* is for people and their deeds: players are triumphant when they win an important game, Oxford or Cambridge crews make triumphant gestures after winning the Boat Race. . . . *Triumphal* is more for objects or symbols celebrating a triumph: the Arc de Triomphe is a triumphal arch.

Trockenbeerenauslese See **appellation contrôlée**

troika *Troika* comes from a Russian word for 'three' and its proper meaning is a carriage pulled by three horses abreast. It is extended to provide a more forceful word than 'trio' for a group of three people forming a committee or council: during the war in Yugoslavia, it was said that the European Community dispatched a troika of foreign ministers to negotiate for a cease-fire.

trooper or **trouper** These two words get mixed up. *Trooper* is military, used for a troop-ship, or for a soldier in a cavalry regiment, who is expected to 'swear like a trooper'. Americans use *trooper* for a member of the state police.

Trouper is theatrical, for a member of a theatrical company, and by extension for a member of a team of people working together ('he's a good trouper').

(the) troubles In the late 19th century and early 20th century, *the troubles* was so much the name given to rebellions, bombings, shootings in Northern Ireland, that it was often spelt with a capital letter: *the Troubles*. Nothing has changed, and in the 1990s *the troubles* still appears in newspaper editorials about the latest outburst of violence in Ireland.

troubleshooter *Troubleshooter*, a typically vivid American word, is by now accepted as standard English in Britain. It describes anyone whose job it is to sort out political, diplomatic or industrial problems. The BBC called its programme, investigating difficulties in industry, *Troubleshooter*.

trousers or **pants** Men and women in Britain wear *trousers*; a few men like to talk about their *pants*, which can be confusing because in Britain *pants* is the usual word for underwear (see **boxers** . . .). Americans call trousers *pants*, and the underwear garment *underpants* or, more usually, *shorts*. But men and women on both sides of the Atlantic do things 'by the seat of their pants' (that is by instinct) and talk about someone 'boring the pants off them'.

trouser-suit In the days when it was still perhaps a little unusual for women to wear trousers, *trouser-suit* was the name used by women to distinguish a matching jacket and trousers from a jacket and skirt. Americans call it a *pantsuit* (see previous entry). Nowadays most women use the word *suit* for both a jacket and trousers or a jacket and skirt. In passing, changing fashions have put on the shelf the expression 'she wears the trousers', meaning a woman takes the dominant role in a relationship.

truck See **lorry** . . .

trunk call See **long-distance call** . . .

try or **attempt** *Try* is a short simple verb, more down-to-earth than *attempt*. We might *attempt* a long difficult task, but we *try* to catch a train. As a noun, *try* is more conversational than written English, so we should make *an attempt* to do something, rather than *a try*. But *a good try* is a well-established phrase, and even schoolteachers write it as a comment on an essay.

try to or **and** For many years *try and* was condemned as ungrammatical and we had to *try to* avoid it all the time. It is now usual to accept that *try and* is acceptable in speech, but less so in writing. Spoken English is influencing written English, and *try and* is so common in conversation that it's not surprising it also appears in writing. One day *try and* may become standard usage but in the meantime you would avoid criticism if you *try to* avoid it, at least in formal writing.

tsar or **czar** The title of the former emperors of Russia is extended for anyone who is the authoritative boss of a big organization. *Tsar* and *czar* are alternative spellings: although the word was originally derived from 'Caesar', *tsar* is the preferred spelling, because that is the closer **transliteration** of the Russian word. Either way, it is pronounced 'zahr'.

T-shirt The most universal garment of the second half of the 20th century had a modest beginning in the early 1920s as the American word for an undervest. In the 1950s, *T-shirts* (so-called because when spread out flat they look like a capital T) started to conquer the world. T-shirts are popular because they are cheap and comfortable, but also because they are moving posters, promoting products, clubs, singers, causes. . . . So much so, that a successful book on communication in the 1990s is called *Can You Put it on a T-Shirt?*

Turco- or **Turko-** *Turco-* is the form as a prefix relating to Turkey (a Turco-French agreement). *Turko-* is never used.

turn off and **on** In a literal sense, to turn something off is the straight opposite of turning it on. That applies to switches, taps, turning on or off a road, etc. When it comes to the extended meaning, it's more subtle. If something turns you *off*, it suggests you find it unappealing in one way or another: the smell of cooking as you enter a restaurant might turn you off, so you do an about-turn and find somewhere else to eat. But if something, or more likely someone, turns you *on*, the first meaning that comes to mind is arousing sexual excitement. As suggested above, a restaurant could turn you off, but it is unlikely to turn you on – unless the food it serves is an aphrodisiac!

turquoise *Turquoise* has been used in English since the 14th century to describe a colour that is a mixture of light blue and mid-green, but the pronunciation still hasn't settled down. Three options are available: 'TERkwoyze', 'terKWUZZ' (last syllable rhymes with 'buzz') or 'terKWAHZ'. If you're undecided, the first pronunciation is recommended.

tuxedo See **black tie** . . .

TV See **television** . . .

twee To begin with, *twee* was probably a babyish way of saying 'sweet'. It then became a word for something that is coy or arch. Even the most august dictionary now admits *twee* into standard English, not bad for baby-talk.

tycoon See **financier** . . .

typesetter, **compositor** or **typographer** A *typesetter* and *compositor* are the same, a technician who sets up or 'composes' type for printing. *Compositor* is becoming an old-fashioned word, as *typesetter* is clearly more straightforward and makes more sense in relation to computerized printing processes. The machines that set type are also called *typesetters*.

Typographers are different: they are concerned with the design of a page of type, the choice of typeface, arrangement of lines, margins, etc. In practice, a typesetter may carry out this work, which is the design rather than the technical function of typesetting. Typography is an art; typesetting a technique.

typhoon See **blizzard** . . .

typo See **misprint** . . .

typographer See **typesetter** . . .

tyre or **tire** The word may relate to *attire*, and in the 16th and 17th centuries, *tire* was the usual spelling. For a long time both spellings were used, but now *tyre* is the only one. As with other earlier forms of words, *tire* has survived as the spelling in American English.

· U ·

U and **Non-U English** In the mid-1950s, Alan S C Ross, a professor of English at Birmingham University, wrote an academic paper on linguistic indicators of the English class system. He used *U* for 'upper class' and *Non-U* for 'non-upper-class'. Although Professor Ross's paper was printed in an academic journal in Helsinki, his observations became table-talk throughout Britain, helped by Nancy Mitford taking up the idea in the book, *Noblesse Oblige* (1956).

Is it still relevant? You might hear U English at Ascot (but don't count on it) or on the playing fields of Eton or in clubs in Pall Mall (don't count on that either). Some of Professor Ross's Non-U expressions are: 'don't give up', 'it's as simple as that', 'it's just one of those things', 'I'll go along with that', 'back to square one'. But before you drop any of those, remember they are used in both Houses of Parliament, Oxford and Cambridge senior common rooms and by many cultured, educated, literary people living in Britain.

If it exists at all in the 1990s, U English is a kind of dialect of particular words, pronunciations and locutions, used or affected by certain people. It has nothing to do with the quality of words or using them sensitively or imaginatively. See also **accents in speech**, **class language**

Ulster or **Northern Ireland** The various names used for different parts of Ireland can be confusing. Guidelines are given under **Ireland** . . .

ult See **inst** . . .

ultimate *Ultimate* used to be a favourite descriptive word with advertising copywriters. It suggests that it is not possible to go any further, so 'the ultimate in luxury' goes all the way. Since then, other words have come to the forefront: a new film is more likely to be 'the greatest', a new dishwasher, television set, etc described as **state-of-the-art**. This has left *ultimate* back in the realms of theology (ultimate truths) and philosophy (ultimate analysis). In everyday contexts, *ultimate* is a **cliché**, and it's worth looking at alternatives. Here are some suggestions: foremost, front-rank, supreme, unequalled. . . .

ultra vires We hear or read this legalistic Latin expression from time to time, when actions or decisions by an organization are commented on. In certain circumstances, a person or an institution has the right to act only within powers conferred by Acts of parliament. If they go beyond those powers, such actions or decisions are *ultra vires* (beyond one's power). Pron: 'ultraVYEreez'.

umlaut See **diaeresis** . . .

umpire See **referee** . . .

un-, non- or **in-** See **in-** . . .

un- words For over a thousand years, *un-* has been prefixed to words to give them an opposite meaning. Across the centuries so many *un-* words have accumulated, that no dictionary attempts to list all of them. If you think of a useful *un-* word and cannot find it in a dictionary, that's no reason for not using it, or for assuming it has never been used before.

Writers invent *un-* words to suit themselves. Kingsley Amis described a woman with *unabundant* brown hair, the *New Statesman* used *unpublicity* about something that had escaped the attention of the media, critics call unsuccessful comedies *unfunny*, social workers avoid the nasty word 'slum' by substituting '*unfit* houses'. When it is used intelligently, the *un-* prefix is part of the continuing creativity of English, contributing different shades of meaning: to *uncomplicate* a matter, for example, is not quite the same as simplifying it.

With some *un-* words, watch out for an occasional risk of confusion between two possible meanings: 'she's undressed' could mean she has just taken her clothes off, or she has not dressed yet, which could make a significant difference!

Not un- can be useful at times to convey a nuance: 'I am not unwilling' is not quite the same as being willing. The literary term for *not un-* expressions is **meiosis**, and there are useful notes on *not un-* under that heading.

unacceptable Most dictionaries define *unacceptable* as 'not acceptable', and that's that. But the word has diplomatic and social undertones, as well as other nuances. If we say, for example, that a price is unacceptable, it is a polite, seemingly less grasping way of saying we want more money for something, or want to pay less for something we're buying. Such evasions of direct statements may help to make bargaining more friendly. For diplomats, *unacceptable* is a vague threat: it means if you don't stop doing whatever you are doing, something might be done about it. In politics, *unacceptable* is a way of demonstrating that a party wants to show it is taking a stand over an issue, although what happens next is left open.

For many people, *unacceptable* is followed by the unspoken qualifications 'to people like us', 'to right-minded people', which are loaded with undefined prejudices.

When you hear *unacceptable*, or use it yourself, look behind it for a personal conception of morality or fairness, or to see whether it is simply a word to fall back on to avoid coming out into the open.

unafraid   See **fearless** . . .

unconditional   See next entry; also **categorical** . . .

unconditional or **unconditioned**   Dictionaries show both these words as meaning not subject to conditions, with *unconditional* as the usual word for that meaning: 'an unconditional surrender'. *Unconditioned* is now usually reserved for use in a more interesting way, to mean a natural unfettered open response, free from a backlog of associations, influences and unquestioned handed-down beliefs: 'If you look at this in an unconditioned way, you will see new solutions'.

unconscious or **subconscious**   Although Freudian psychologists will distinguish between the *unconscious* and the *subconscious*, in general use, both words refer to that part of the mind we are not usually aware of, which manifests itself in dreams and influences behaviour. *Subconscious* is not heard much now, and *unconscious*, the term that Jung preferred, is used in most contexts.

Jung distinguished between the *personal unconscious*, which is described above, and the **collective unconscious**.

under or **under-**   In nearly all *under-* word formations there is no hyphen now: *underachieve, underact, undercarriage, undercover, undercut, underexpose, undermanned, undersexed.* . . . With titles, a hyphen is used: *under-secretary, under-sheriff,* etc.

underdeveloped country   See **developing country** . . .; **Third World**

underground, tube, subway or **metro**   We take the *tube* from Piccadilly, the *metro* (short for *métropolitain*) across Paris, the *subway* from Brooklyn, New York City. In London the *Underground* is the official name for the tube. Note also that *on the tube* in America means 'on television', that in Britain a subway is a pedestrian underpass beneath a busy street, and that the tube in Newcastle-upon-Tyne is the Metro.

underhand or **underhanded**   Either *underhand* or *underhanded* is used for something or somebody who is secret, devious or crooked: 'they came to an underhand arrangement'; 'she is underhand about

it'; 'he is an underhand person'. While *underhanded* could be used in all those contexts, *underhand* is the more usual word.

When it comes to games, underhand bowling (an alternative to underarm bowling) is distinct from throwing a ball by raising the arm over the shoulder. 'Underhanded bowling' could imply something else!

underlying inflation   See **inflation**

underpinning   See **foundation** . . .

underprivileged   The poor are always with us (the thought is taken from *St John* 12:8), but in the 1990s the word embarrasses us. *Underprivileged*, with its genteel polysyllables, was first used in America to cover up the uneasiness, and is now semi-official language in Britain. We are privileged when we have good health, warmth, enough to eat and so on. To be underprivileged is not to have enough of those things, that is to be **poor**.

undertaker   See **funeral director** . . .

under or **in the circumstances**   See **circumstances**

undue   Many people are not sure what *undue* means, for it has become a pompous word slipped in to sound important: 'There is no cause for undue alarm'; 'It does not require undue intelligence'. *Undue* means excessive for the circumstances. There are few occasions when it is required. To avoid sounding like a stuffed shirt, do not use *undue* unless it is really necessary, which will not be often. 'Much' or 'too much' are straightforward alternatives.

uneatable   See **inedible** . . .

uneducated   See **illiterate** . . .

unequivocal or **unequivocable**   *Unequivocal* means there is no doubt, that something is absolutely clear: 'we have to accept this unequivocal decision'. Even though you hear it sometimes in the best circles, 'unequivocable' is not in any dictionary, because there is no such word.

unification   *Unification* is primarily a political term. It made headlines in 1990 as *German unification*. By the end of that year, the Berlin Wall had come down, pieces of it sold all over the world as souvenirs, and East Germany and West Germany became reunited (see **Germany**).

unilateral or **one-sided**   *Unilateral* is an overused polysyllabic Latinate word, which goes against it. But it does have a particular meaning, and cannot always be replaced by the simpler alternative *one-sided*. A *unilateral* decision is made by one party without reference to or conditional on decisions taken by others. Such a decision could in certain circumstances be courageous and selfless. *One-sided* often has pejorative overtones, suggesting something done for one's own selfish advantage, disregarding other people. Of course, if a *unilateral* decision or action happens to be self-seeking and mean-minded, then it could well be preferable to call it *one-sided*. This does not apply to official language, which prefers the more roundabout word.

unimaginable or **unthinkable** Both words are almost interchangeable for an event that can hardly be believed or understood by the mind. *Unimaginable* is more appropriate for something that could happen in the future: 'it is unimaginable that such an old-established company would ever go out of business'. *Unthinkable* relates more to something that is actually happening or has taken place: 'it is unthinkable that such an old-established company has gone out of business'. The distinction may be too subtle for some people, but it's worth considering.

uninterested or **disinterested** This stock item in every book on English usage has almost lost its point. Either you know about it and care, or have given up the struggle. The classic distinction is this: a judge should be *disinterested*, that is, he should be impartial and not take sides. But if he is *uninterested*, he might doze off, because that would mean he is bored by the proceedings.

The earlier meaning of *disinterested* was in fact also 'not interested', so the distinction between the two words is modern. It is a useful distinction for all that. But a distinction has no value unless it is widely accepted and understood: the way it is going, the difference between *disinterested* and *uninterested* is fading out. The safer words to use now, to indicate that you are objective and not influenced by personal gain or prejudice, are 'unbiased', 'impartial', or 'have no axe to grind'. The noun, *disinterest*, has long been used for a lack of interest ('there is complete disinterest in the subject'), which must surely influence the use of the descriptive word *disinterested*.

unique *Unique* means the only one of its kind and is a so-called absolute word, like 'true'. The rules of the game are we must never write or say *very* unique or *quite* unique because there are no degrees of uniqueness. *Almost* unique is acceptable because it suggests that there are very few like it. Yet most people are happy with 'absolutely true' or even 'very true', and as good a writer as Charlotte Brontë wrote 'a very unique child'. You may decide that *unique* does not have to be as *unique* as all that, and accept *quite* unique, *very* unique, etc as expressing shades of meaning. If you decide to keep to the rules, you will use the word *rare*, except when something is truly unique.

unisex or **unisexual** The two words mean the opposite to each other. *Unisexual* dates from the early 19th century and is used in biology or botany about an organism or a plant that has the characteristics of only one sex. *Unisex* is a descriptive word that came to the surface in the late 1960s for teenage hairstyles and fashions used interchangeably by both sexes. Now *unisex* is applied right across the board to anything that does not distinguish between the sexes. In some places, separate lavatories for men and women have given way to unisex lavatories, which either can use.

In *The Good English Guide*, *unisex* is extended to language, for words such as *chairperson*, *headteacher*, etc that can apply to men and women. See also **bisexual** . . .

unisex grammar *Everybody, everyone, nobody, someone* and similar words are singular: 'everybody *is* . . .'. Such words were traditionally followed by *he* or *his*: 'Nobody has taken *his* seat yet'. The assumption that *he, his, him* include women is no longer acceptable to many people, and in advertisements for appointments could cut across the 1975 Sex Discrimination Act.

We can wear ourselves and our readers out writing **he or she** (or *she or he*) all the time. Some reference books use *s/he*, which is clumsy and cannot be read aloud. Other writers see as the way ahead using *they, them, their* as *unisex* words: 'Nobody has taken *their* seat yet'. The grammatical objection is the singular *nobody* conflicts with the plural *their*. In spite of this, *they* and *their* are taking on a plural or singular sense as required. This is not new. In the 19th century, Thackeray was writing 'Nobody prevents you, do they?' Bernard Shaw remarked 'Nobody would ever marry if they thought it over'. There are many other examples of good writers using *they, their, them* as unisex words: Kazuo Ishiguro, in *The Remains of the Day* (winner of the 1989 Booker Prize), wrote 'some fellow professional . . . would be accompanying their employer'.

At the same time, this elastic attitude towards singular and plural upsets some people a great deal. It may be possible to recast a sentence to avoid it: the example at the beginning of this entry could be rewritten '*People* have not taken *their* seats yet', although the meaning is not quite the same.

There is no universally acceptable way out of this sociolinguistic dilemma. *The Good English Guide* recommends four principles:

1 *He, him, his* should never be used to include women.

2 When it seems appropriate, *he or she, him or her*, etc (varied with *she or he*, etc) can be used, but only occasionally.

3 Where it is neither laboured nor misleading, a sentence can be rewritten to sidestep the problem.

4 In all other cases, the plural forms *they, them, their* should be used as singular unisex words, accepting with regret that some readers will shake their heads reproachfully. In a conversation on the BBC, Antonia Byatt, another Booker prizewinner (1990, for her novel, *Possession*), and Bryan Magee agreed this is the best resolution of the problem. So you will be in good company.

unisex terms See previous entry; also **actor**; **businessman** . . .; **chairman** . . .; **-ess forms**; **he or she**; **headteacher** . . .; **humankind** . . .; **-person**; **poetess**; **salesman** . . .; **sculptress**; **spokesman** . . .; **waiter.** . . . Also **feminine forms**; **sexist language**

United Kingdom, **Great Britain**, **Britain** or **British Isles** Many foreigners, and some British, are uncertain over the proper distinction between these names. To be sure of using them correctly, see **Britain** . . .

United States, **US**, **USA** or **America** See **America** . . .

universally *Universally* means everywhere or by everyone, and it makes a nonsense of the word to write 'she is universally liked by her friends'. Change it to '. . . by all her friends'.

university See **college** . . .

unlettered See **illiterate** . . .

unlisted companies See **listed companies** . . .

unmistakable or **unmistakeable** *Unmistakable.*

unmovable See **immovable** . . .

unparalleled For an easy way to remember how many *l*s there should be, see **parallel**.

unprecedented Pronounce it 'unPRESSedented', not 'unPREESedented'.

unquote See **quote/unquote** for the use of this convention in speech.

unreadable See **illegible** . . .

unsaleable or **unsalable** *Unsaleable.*

unshakeable or **unshakable** *Unshakeable.*

unsociable See **antisocial** . . .

unsocial hours See **antisocial** . . .

unsuccess See **failure** . . .

unthinkable See **unimaginable** . . .

until or **till** *Till* and *until* are interchangeable: 'I will love you till (or until) I die'. *Until* is more formal, and sounds better when it is the first word of a sentence: 'Until I die, I will love you'.

untruth See **lie** . . .

update It was some time in the late 1960s that someone got fed up with 'bringing things up to date' and decided to *update* them instead. *Update* was born as a neat crisp word in tune with **information technology**. It happened in America, as you would expect, and in no time at all we were all updating things in Britain. There are still a few people who tut-tut over the word but they might as well save their breath, for *update* is here to stay.

Update can be a noun ('Give me an update'), a verb ('Would you update these figures?'), or a descriptive word, alongside *updated* (which is more usual): 'These are the updated (or update) figures'.

up for grabs This crude expression belongs to the get-rich-quick 1980s. Crude it may be, but it has come to be used for anything that is on offer or available, even the most prestigious things. Distinguished literary prizes are described as *up for grabs*; the BBC, advertising its success at winning trophies for programmes, declared 'Of the 26 awards up for grabs, we won 21'. On the first day of the 1992 Olympic Games, we were told there were 'nine gold medals up for grabs'. This ugly phrase seems to be up for grabs about anything we want to use it for.

upfront In the 1960s, *upfront* was the go-getting word in America for money in advance. It has caught on in Britain and some current dictionaries have admitted it as standard English. It is still spelt sometimes as two words but the one-word version is likely to take over. While 'in advance' is more formal and restrained, *upfront* has a good no-nonsense ring to it: publishers pay writers an **advance**, but writers, especially younger ones, may well ask their agents to get as much money as possible – *upfront*.

Upfront has developed as a word for describing a person who is open and direct ('she's very upfront'), possibly an echo of the old expression 'having no side'.

upmarket See **downmarket** . . .

upon See **on** . . .

uppers and downers See **amphetamine** . . .; **tranquillizers**

upsetting See **disquieting** . . .

upstage See **downstage** . . .

uptight Most dictionaries give two meanings for *uptight*: tense and nervous ('she's uptight about meeting him after so long'), or starchy and conventional ('his dinner parties are so uptight and formal'). The second is the meaning of *uptight* in America, and has caught on in Britain. Both these meanings are conversational but moving towards being accepted as standard English.

up to See **down to** . . .

up-to-date or **up to date** Use hyphens when it comes before a noun (an up-to-date costing), and keep the words separate when they come after a noun (a costing that is up to date).

uptown   See **downtown** . . .

upward or **upwards**   It doesn't matter whether you point *upward* or *upwards*. Some people prefer *upward* before a noun (an upward glance) and *upwards* after a verb (point upwards), but dictionaries usually regard the words as interchangeable. Mark you, if you point *upwardly*, which is justified grammatically, you deserve to get a funny look, for general usage and grammar do not always agree.

upwardly mobile   *Social climbing* implies snobbishness and working hard at rubbing shoulders with people in a higher social class. In many ways its place has been taken by *upwardly mobile*, an expression that was needed in the 1960s. Unlike *social climbing*, it is not pejorative, as it means being carried up the social and economic scale by intelligence, ability and drive. In this way, *upwardly mobile* goes with **meritocracy**.

In 1988, Norman Tebbitt, at the time chairman of the Conservative Party, called his autobiography *Upwardly Mobile*. In 1992, as Lord Tebbitt, he became more upwardly mobile than ever.

upwards of   There is no good reason why *upwards of* ('upwards of ten people are waiting') should be used instead of *more than*. A good reason not to is that *upwards of* is less direct.

US, **USA**, **the States** or **America**   See **America** . . .

us or **we**   In certain sentences, *us* is occasionally slipped in, when the right word is *we*: 'For once, we were not as tolerant as *us* English are supposed to be'. The way to avoid this mistake is to try the sentence leaving out the word or words between *us* and the verb: clearly it has to be 'as *we* . . . are supposed to be'.

To, from, for, about are usually followed by *us*, not *we*: 'Whatever anyone says about *we* in this part of the country . . .'. The way to avoid this mistake is to try stopping the sentence after *we* or *us*, and see which fits in: clearly it has to be 'Whatever anyone says about *us* . . .'.

usable or **useable**   Some dictionaries show *usable* and *useable* as alternative spellings. Stay with *usable*, as *useable* is becoming so uncommon that many people would think it is a mistake.

usage or **use**   There is a distinction between *usage* and *use*. The *use* of anything is nothing more than its being made use of. *Usage* is the customary or regular way in which something is used. The most common error is for *usage* to become an official-sounding alternative to *use*: 'the usage of public libraries is increasing'. The proper word there is *use*. In reverse, equipment could be damaged by rough *usage*, that is the rough way it is used, rather than rough *use*. But to insist on that would be fussing too much.

Usage is commonly applied to English, describing not the use of the language all over the world for communication, but the way it is used, such as grammatical forms, pronunciation, the meaning of words and so on. An example is **Fowler**'s 'Modern English Usage'.

used to   Even experienced writers may have to stop and think about the different forms of *used to*. There is no problem when it's a straightforward statement: 'I used to walk to work'. The problems start when it is negative or asking a question.

There are two negative forms. The formal one is 'I used not to walk to work'. The more natural way, accepted by good authorities, is 'I did not (or didn't) use to walk to work'.

For asking a question, the formal sequence is 'Used you to walk to work?', 'Used you not to walk to work?', etc. Those sound as if they come out of a grammarian's English phrase book for foreigners. The natural forms, also accepted by good authorities, are 'Did you use to walk to work?', 'Didn't you use to . . .'.

Lastly, the correct contracted forms are: *usedn't to* and *didn't use to*. 'Usen't to' and 'didn't used to' are errors. Admittedly, when those forms are spoken they sound the same anyway, and they are only rarely used in writing.

user-friendly or **ergonomic**   *Ergonomic* appeared in few dictionaries before the 1950s, and *user-friendly* had not yet been coined. Taking 'economics' as a model, *ergonomics* was formed out of the Greek word 'ergon' for work. It is the study of how people interact with their environment at work and with the machinery and equipment they use, with regard to efficiency, safety and health. An ergonomic design or machine is one that takes these factors into account.

User-friendly has a similar meaning but is less scientific, and relates more to ease of use. The term was invented in America in the 1970s for computers that are easier to understand and operate, and has since been applied to almost anything from a tin-opener to a book of instructions. The art critic, Marina Vaizey, criticized museums in Paris (the Pompidou Centre and the Musée d'Orsay) for being 'definitely not user-friendly'. She meant it is difficult to find your way round them.

Ergonomy has appeared as an alternative word for *ergonomics*, but is not used often. *Ergonomic* is a high-tech **buzzword**: *user-friendly* is – *user friendly*!

users' group   When computers were fiendishly complicated and the instruction manuals written in esoteric jargon, *users' groups* were mutual-aid associations of people using the same systems. They would telephone each other to compare notes and try to resolve difficulties.

There are fewer users' groups now, although the term is still used, and as computers become more **user-friendly**, and new computer-literate (see literate) generations leave school, the idea of users' groups is retreating to the pioneer days of the past.

USM   Unlisted securities market. See **listed companies** . . .

USSR, **Soviet Union** or **Russia**   The events in the Soviet empire at the end of 1991 left behind considerable linguistic confusion, and there remains some hesitation at times over what to call the different parts of the former USSR. For notes on this, see **Russian and Soviet**.

utmost or **uttermost**   It could be that *uttermost* goes just a bit further than *utmost*, that the uttermost limits, for example, are a whisker beyond the utmost limits. This is putting a very fine point on it. In practice, the two words are interchangeable.

U-turn   On the roads, a U-turn is a 180° change of direction, often forbidden by the symbol of a U with a line through it.

U-turn has been adapted for any drastic change of mind or policy, especially in politics. The term became fashionable when Margaret Thatcher's favourite **speechwriter** came up with a popular slogan that captured her resolute inflexibility: 'The lady's not for turning'. Nor did it matter that only the literati knew it was taken from the title of Christopher Fry's play of the late 1940s, *The Lady's Not For Burning*.

U-turn is considered a derogatory term, as if a change of mind or reversal of a decision is always weak and shilly-shallying. There's no need to fall in with that, for in life, as on the roads, it could be better at times to make a U-turn than continue in the wrong direction.

· V ·

vaccinate See inoculate . . .

vaginal and **clitoral orgasm** See orgasm . . .

valuable (as a noun) You would think that a *valuable* is an object that is valuable to us. Be on guard. Valuables to an insurance company are often different from valuables to us: if you read the **small print** in a policy, you may find that *valuables* include things made of gold or silver, jewellery, works of art, but probably do not include an expensive camera, a cashmere jacket and other objects that we, ourselves, treasure as valuables.

valuable See invaluable . . .

value Oscar Wilde defined a cynic as 'A man who knows the price of everything and the value of nothing' (*Lady Windermere's Fan*, Act III). In that quotation, 'the price of everything' is the *market value*, and the 'value' is probably the *intrinsic value*. For definitions of different values, see **face value** . . .

value added In economics, *value added* (or *added value*) is doing something to raw material that makes it worth more. Virgin wool is dyed and woven into cloth, which adds value to it, more value still if people like the pattern and the colour. Value is added to wine in casks by bottling it, more value still if there's a good label on the bottle. *Value added* passed into everyday English in 1973 when Value Added Tax (VAT), already imposed in other countries in Europe, was introduced into the UK.

It is an exciting concept to think of words as the raw materials of communication. They acquire *added value* when they are put together in a way that makes people read them, listen to them, be inspired by them, moved by them or influenced by them.

value-judgement People talk readily about *value-judgements* without always being clear what they mean. A value-judgement is based on a subjective assessment of whether something is good or bad, social or antisocial, etc. *Value-judgement* often carries a pejorative implication ('That's just a value-judgement'), suggesting that it is a narrow subjective point of view. This fails to recognize that absolute objectivity is beyond the reach of most of us, so nearly all judgements are, to some extent, value-judgements.

varsity *Varsity*, as a class word for 'university', dates from the mid-19th century and should be left there, although it hasn't altogether died out. It only ever referred to Oxford and Cambridge, and survives for contests between those universities (the Varsity Boat Race), and then it sounds affected. Nowadays, even a **Hooray Henry** would think more than twice before saying his son was 'going up to the Varsity'.

vast See colossal . . .

VAT See ad valorem; value added

VATman This is the usual unofficial name for the inspector who visits businesses to check VAT returns, and it's written *VATman* (rather than 'vatman'). It is unisex: you can try 'VATwoman' or 'VATperson', if you like, but you won't score any marks for it.

VD See sexually transmitted diseases . . .

VDU (visual display unit) In computer language, a *visual display unit* (usually called a VDU) is nearly always the screen, like a television screen, which provides the visual indication of the operation going on in the computer. The term is also used for other forms of electronic visual display, such as **LCD**, liquid crystal display.

vegetarian or **vegan** Strictly, a *vegetarian* should not eat meat or fish, and would exclude dairy products. In practice, many people who call themselves vegetarians do eat fish, as well as cheese and eggs. *Vegans* (the word is a contraction of *vegetarian* and pronounced 'VEEGe(r)n') are much stricter: they exclude from their diet fish, meat and any food derived from animals, such as eggs and cheese. Some vegans extend this to clothing and would not wear anything made of leather. Someone can be a vegetarian out of taste or for health; with a vegan, it is always a moral conviction.

veldt See grasslands

vellum See parchment . . .

vending *Vend* is still included in dictionaries as a word for selling (compare French 'vendre'), but no one ever uses it. *Vending* is used only about machines that automatically dispense anything from condoms to coffee when you put the right coins into them. In passing, parking meters, which sell parking space, are not called vending-machines.

vendor See **seller** . . .

venereal diseases See **sexually transmitted diseases** . . .

venture See **risk** . . .

venture capital See **risk** . . .

venue As long ago as 1926, **Fowler** was complaining about the fashionable use of *venue* for the rendezvous or place for a meeting (*Modern English Usage*). No one listened to him, so companies still have venues for sales conferences, people have a venue for dinner, etc. There is no good reason for using *venue*, and 'place' is a simple unpretentious alternative. But if people didn't listen to Fowler, is there much point in still banging the drum?

veranda or **verandah** Either spelling will do, although *veranda* is more usual.

verbal or **oral** When Sam Goldwyn, the Hollywood film producer, said 'A verbal contract is not worth the paper it's written on', it was intended as a joke, warning people not to trust *spoken* agreements. But he used the wrong word, *verbal* instead of *oral*. Many other people make the same mistake and talk about a *verbal* agreement, meaning an agreement not written down. All agreements using words, whether in speech or writing, are verbal agreements, because *verbal* relates to the use of words. An agreement made in conversation but not written down is an *oral* agreement, just as an *oral* examination is conducted by the examiner and student talking to each other.

The misuse of *verbal* for *oral* is so widespread that it's safer to distinguish between 'a spoken agreement' and 'a written agreement'.

verbiage or **verbosity** We have all come across compulsive talkers, people who wear out everyone they meet with a deluge of words. That's *verbosity* and it's almost like an illness. It's the same in writing when people bolster their confidence or self-esteem with 'in relation to', 'with reference to', 'in respect of', 'it is appreciated that', 'it is considered advisable to bring to your attention' and thousands of other cotton-wool expressions. That is *verbiage*.

Dictionaries do not distinguish between *verbosity* for speech and *verbiage* for written language, but it's a useful distinction that can be made.

verbs It is interesting that Latin 'verbum' (a word) provides the grammatical term *verbs* for words of 'doing'. This suggests that action is the core of language. It is true that verbs give sentences drive and movement and that without them language would be

static. In fact, orthodox teaching maintains that a combination of words is not a sentence unless it includes a verb. (See also **phrase**).

Verbs are analysed into different categories, such as finite, transitive, auxiliary, etc. These terms belong to formal grammar and have little place in the process of communication, but see **mood** (**in grammar**).

verify See **cross-check** . . .

verse See **poetry** . . .

verso *Verso* is a printing term that writers should be familiar with: it is a page on the *left* of an open book that traditionally is always even-numbered. The right-hand, odd-numbered page is the *recto*. See also **double-page spread**

vertical thinking See **lateral thinking** . . .

very There is a grammatical principle that *very* belongs with adjectives or descriptive words ('*very* hot', '*very* big' . . .) and should not be used with *-ed* forms of verbs. We should say, for example, 'much used' rather than 'very used', to mean used a great deal, that someone is 'much travelled' rather than 'very travelled'. But some *-ed* forms, such as *pleased*, *tired*, *exaggerated*, are often descriptive words, rather than verbs, so there's no reason to avoid 'very pleased', 'very tired', 'very exaggerated'. . . .

Other *-ed* forms are uncertain: *disliked* and *distressed*, for example, are felt to be verbs, and some people maintain we must say or write 'much or greatly disliked' rather than 'very disliked'. . . . On the other hand, while 'very travelled' does sound wrong, 'very disliked' sounds natural. The best rule is to be aware of the problem and careful about using *very* with *-ed* forms of verbs when it seems out of place.

Because of this point of grammar, and because we are taught that *very* is used so often that it no longer has much meaning, some people make a point of writing or saying '*most* pleased', '*so* happy', '*extremely* grateful'. . . . *Very* is overused, so we should be careful, which does not mean we can never be 'very angry' or 'very much in love'. To suggest we should never use *very* is very stupid.

vessel See **boat** . . .

vest See **waistcoat** . . .

veteran See **vintage** . . .

via *Via* derives from the Latin word for a road, and should strictly be used for routes: 'we are going to Rome via Brussels'. At the same time, *via* is often extended as shorthand for 'by means of' or 'through the medium of': 'I sent it by hand, via my secretary'; 'we heard about it via a news programme on television'; 'she learned English via the BBC World Service'. This extended use has been going on for so long and is so general, that most recent dictionaries acknowledge it without comment. *Via* is a useful short word in many contexts, and there is no need for it to stay bogged down by its original meaning in Latin. Some Latinate purists will disagree but it's a lost cause.

The alternative pronunciation 'VEE-e(r)' should be avoided in favour of 'VYE-e(r)'.

viable In biology, an organism that is *viable* is one that can survive independently. It was a reasonable extension of this to talk of a subsidiary company being viable, that is able to keep going and make a profit without the support of the parent company. From this usage it became fashionable to use *viable* to mean feasible or workable ('a viable proposition'). Though this usage is disliked by some people, because the word has lost its roots in the Latin word for 'life', it is here to stay: the 1990 edition of the *Concise Oxford Dictionary* gives 'feasible' and 'practicable' as the first meaning of *viable*.

vibes To get *bad vibes* from something or somebody means to have an intuitive feeling that something is not right. This use of *vibes*, an abbreviation of 'vibrations', is a recognition of extrasensory perception (see **parapsychology**), implying that a message is coming across in a way we cannot define. No longer slang, *vibes* has moved up to colloquial usage in dictionaries.

vicar See **minister** . . .

vicarage See **rectory** . . .

vide See **see** . . .

video- More and more *video* compounds are being fused into one word: *videoconference*, *videographics*, *videophone*, *videotape*, etc. This has not yet become the overall rule, but it is likely that compounds that are still separate words (video game, **video nasty**, video recorder, etc) will become one-word terms in the next few years.

videoconference See **teleconference** . . .

videotex(t) or **teletext** *Videotex* (or *videotext*) is the generic term used for an electronic information system using a *visual display unit* (**VDU**), either broadcast or through a two-way system between computers. *Teletext* is transmitting information stored on a computer to ordinary television sets that are adapted to receive it. *Ceefax* (presumably a simplistic **acronym** for 'see facts'), for example, is the registered name for the BBC teletext system.

viewership See **coverage** . . .

viewpoint See **point of view** . . .

village or **hamlet** *Hamlet* might be used for any small cluster of houses, but there is no general agreement over when a hamlet becomes a *village*. Some people state authoritatively that a hamlet does not have a church, but in Gray's *Elegy*, 'The rude forefathers of the hamlet sleep' in the churchyard.

If in doubt, call a place a village, by far the more common word. For guidance on when a *village* becomes a *town*, see **city** . . .

For writers in America and for many in Britain, *the Village* means only one place, Greenwich Village, New York City. The Village is the equivalent in America of the Left Bank in Paris, and has a similar artistic nostalgia, that conjures up names such as Henry James, Edna St Vincent Millay, Jack Kerouac, Bob Dylan. As with the Left Bank, present-day rents are not for struggling poets and painters, but people will still talk about the Village with a certain respect for its place in the history of American literature and lifestyle.

vintage or **veteran** *Vintage* properly describes wine from a particular year (it relates to Latin 'vinum', wine). It is extended for anything from the past that is particularly good and enduring, or for a specially successful year: 'a vintage performance', 'a vintage year for breaking records'.

By general consent, a *vintage* car is one made between 1917 and 1930. A *veteran* car is one made before 1916, according to some collectors, and before 1905 according to others.

vintner See **wine merchant** . . .

violin or **fiddle** In the 14th century, *fiddle* was already a word for a stringed instrument played with a bow. But the shady meaning of *fiddle* has taken such a hold that, in spite of *Fiddler on the Roof*, we now have to say someone plays the *violin* or is a *violinist* (although *fiddle* might still be used in connection with folk music). A BBC announcer, commentating on a promenade concert at the Albert Hall, shocked listeners by announcing 'Beethoven's fiddle concerto'. An incensed musicologist telephoned to ask 'And was it played on a Stradivarius fiddle?'

Although most dictionaries consider it informal, *fiddle* in the other sense, for almost any kind of crooked deal, has almost fiddled its way into standard English.

As for 'second fiddle', it is used far away from orchestral contexts, about a person who takes a secondary role to someone else.

virago In the Middle Ages, *virago* was a word of admiration for a woman of Amazonian courage and power ('vir' is Latin for a man). The meaning deteriorated and *virago* became an abusive word for a strident ill-tempered woman. In 1973 there was an attempt to reclaim the former meaning of the word, when the Virago Press was founded, a feminist publishing company that sets out to reissue important classics by women, as well as new books by women writers about aspects of their lives.

So far, no dent has been made in the standard dictionary definition of *virago*, which remains derogatory.

virile From the 15th century, *virile* has referred to those qualities that are characteristic of men: strength, force, vigour. By the early 18th century, *virile* was being used about a man's sexual drive, which is hardly surprising since 'membrum virile' is a Latin phrase that was used in English for the penis.

Although it is a contradiction in terms, there are signs now that *virile* is slipping into use for women who are sexually potent and vital: 'She is very virile' is at present an **oxymoron**, but it is heard and read. The problem is there is no other word that is not pejorative for a woman who is highly charged sexually. All that can be said at this stage, is that *virile* is a word to watch, to see if it will eventually be accepted as a unisex description.

virtual reality (VR) *Virtual reality* is tipped to become a **buzzword**: it is already being called *VR* by people experimenting with it, and the abbreviation is likely to take over. VR uses the leading edge of **information technology** to induce hallucinations that are received as real experiences, that are *virtual reality*. Since we experience life largely through sensory perceptions, seeing, hearing, smelling, touching, when these senses are activated by technology, they are said to be indistinguishable from the experience itself.

VR uses goggles fitted with miniature television screens, gloves and other clothing with sensory fibres, all linked to a computer. This, it is claimed, is the ultimate human **interface** with technology, taking people 'virtually' anywhere they choose, from a jazz club in Paris to a battle with Martians, into sexual fantasies, all at the press of a button. The concept is a technological projection of reality that goes far beyond the escapism offered by literature and film.

virtuosi or **virtuosos** *Virtuoso* is as Italian as spaghetti, so the correct plural is *virtuosi*. But we are used to the word in English, and *virtuosos* is more natural for the plural form. Both are shown in dictionaries and either is acceptable.

virus (computers) Human terms are often connected with computer technology (**compatibility, handshaking, memory, user-friendly** . . .), a suggestion of the supposedly near-human qualities of the machines. *Virus*, associated with causing disease in living cells (see **germ**), is used for deliberate attempts to sabotage a computer. A virus is written into a piece of software (see **hardware** . . .), which 'infects' a computer when a **floppy disk** is slotted into it. This can remain dormant, programmed to take effect on a particular date, or until a particular combination of circumstances arises, when it could destroy or distort the memory in a computer by overwriting the disks.

virus See germ . . .

vis-à-vis *Vis-à-vis* is French, short for 'visage-à-visage', face to face. We do not talk about sitting *vis-à-vis*, as the French do, for in English the expression has the extended meaning of 'concerning', 'relating to': 'the

situation *vis-à-vis* our office in Birmingham . . .'. In most cases *vis-à-vis* can be, and perhaps should be, replaced by 'concerning'. (Pron: 'veez-ah-VEE'.)

visual display unit See VDU

vital statistics *Vital statistics* was originally used for the figures of births, deaths and marriages, and later for key figures connected with any other matter. This meaning was elbowed out by Hollywood, when *vital statistics* was taken over as the term for a film star's breast, waist and hip measurements. This use has become dated, leaving the expression once again available for truly vital statistics.

vitamin You can choose whether you wish to take 'VITT-amins' or 'VYTE-amins'. Both pronunciations are generally regarded as correct, unless you are a BBC announcer, in which case the recommended pronunciation is 'VITT-amins'. 'VYTE-amins' is usual in America.

viz See ie . . .

vogue words See buzzword

voicedial *Voicedial* was introduced in the 1990s for telephones activated by voice. You order the telephone to *Dial*, and then give it the number you want. A synthesized voice responds, reassuring you that the connection is being made. *Voicedial* is particularly applicable to phones in cars: even if attention is taken off the road, at least both hands can stay on the wheel.

'VOLuntarily' or **'volunTARily'** 'VOLuntarily' is more difficult to say because of the long flight of unaccented syllables, but it is worth making the effort because that is considered the correct British pronunciation.

vowel See consonant . . .

vowel-ligatures This is the term for joining *a* and *e* or *o* and *e* together (æ, œ). See ae or æ . . .

VR See virtual reality

VSOP VSOP is one of the earliest examples of **franglais**. In the Victorian and Edwardian periods, the British were the best customers for **cognac**, and when it was well aged, they called it 'very special old pale'. The French producers knew a good thing when they saw it, and put the letters VSOP on bottles of cognac over a certain age, a practice that continues, although not many cognac drinkers these days would know what the letters stand for.

vulgar, common or **coarse** Four-letter words used to be classified by dictionaries as *vulgar*. Because the word has snobbish implications, some dictionaries have switched to other terms, usually 'coarse' or 'taboo'.

Vulgar is, in fact, a harmless word that derives from Latin 'vulgus', the common people. Nor is there anything indecent about vulgar fractions. The pejorative meaning of *vulgar* comes from believing that the taste and style of the great mass of people must be rather nasty.

The problem with *common* is that it has more than one meaning: it can be cheap and nasty, or simply ordinary and everyday. It can also mean sharing something with other people. The entry under **common or mutual** offers guidelines on how to sort this out.

Coarse has a similar meaning to the pejorative sense of *vulgar* and is perhaps the more usual word now. As noted above, some dictionaries prefer it.

All three words as comments on style and behaviour could be construed as snobbish, because they suggest that whatever it is is not the way *we* would dress, speak or do something. Perhaps the words are not appropriate in the egalitarian society of the 1990s, although it must be admitted that there are circumstances when it is difficult to avoid using one or other of them.

· W ·

wages See pay . . .

waistcoat or **vest** *Waistcoats* are back in fashion, not buttoned up under a jacket but hanging loose over a shirt. In deference to traditional tailors in Savile Row, even some recent dictionaries still show the older pronunciation, 'WESke(r)t', and some younger people wearing waistcoats in the new way, flaunt that pronunciation as part of the image. The more usual pronunciation now is 'WAYscoht' (not sounding the first *t*).

Waistcoats used to be called *vests*, a word which a few elderly tailors might still use. *Vest* has remained the name for the garment in America, whereas in Britain most people assume a *vest* is an undergarment worn next to the skin (Americans call that an *undershirt*).

waiter and **waitress** Many people are hesitant nowadays to call out *Waiter!* or *Waitress!* when they want service. For one thing, most waiters and waitresses these days are more chatty than deferential, and in some grander restaurants, they aim to seem superior to the customers. It's the same in France, where to summon a waiter by calling out 'Garçon!' would no longer go down well. Yet there's no alternative word we can use. Clicking your fingers deserves to be ignored. The best we can do is to wave politely or hope to catch their eye.

There was a brief attempt to suggest *waitron* as a unisex word, but it died a death.

waive or **wave** People have been known to use *wave* when they mean *waive*. We *waive* our legal rights or a claim on someone, or an opportunity to do something, that is we give them up, or at least do not insist on them: 'She waived her right to an allowance from him'. We *wave* goodbye.

wake See awake . . .

walkabout It is piquant that *walkabout*, originally used in Australia for an Aborigine going wandering in the bush, has come to be used as the easygoing word for royalty, prime ministers and presidents putting on a democratic act by strolling among the crowds.

walkie-talkie Dictionaries classify as standard English this babyish expression for a hand-held radio receiver and transmitter.

Walkman *Walkman* is a Sony trademark. It is included in some recent dictionaries as the general word for any small cassette-player and lightweight earphones that go with a faraway look on people's faces as they walk, jog, shop in supermarkets, or do whatever else they don't want to think about. (The plural is *walkmans*, not *walkmen*.)

walk-through *Walk-through* is used in the theatre for a first rough rehearsal of a scene, so the actors can get a feeling for the rhythm, style and rapport with the other characters. It is useful in commercial presentations, sales conferences, etc, to mean the first try-out of arrangements: 'Let's have a walk-through (or let's walk it through) first, and then we'll get down to the detail'.

Wall Street Wall Street, a rather insignificant street near the New York Stock Exchange, at the lower end of Manhattan Island, more or less corresponds to the **City** in Britain. When financial experts talk about *Wall Street*, they don't mean the street in New York, but investment and financial interests in the United States in general.

want See desire . . .

(language of) war After a battle during World War II, an American colonel informed Churchill about what he called the 'body count'. Churchill turned on him angrily. 'They are dead men,' he retorted, 'the honourable dead'. During the 1991 Gulf War, a BBC correspondent commented: 'In war, truth is the first victim, the second is the English language'.

As we watch or listen to on-the-spot coverage from 'theatres of war', we learn a new language of evasiveness. Bridges, tanks, etc are *taken out*, that is destroyed. Censorship becomes *limits on media coverage*. The enemy have *offensive capability* which means they are able to fight. When that is no longer the case, underfed retreating soldiers become a *target-rich environment*. General Schwarzkopf, answering a question about the Gulf War, replied 'It's *scenario-dependent*', presumably meaning 'it depends upon what happens'. And Alistair Cooke translated for us *collateral damage*, a popular term at military press briefings, as 'civilians, old men, young men, women and children, incinerated – gone for good'. See also **friendly fire**

war See **conflict** . . .

warranty See **guarantee** . . .

(if I) **was** or **were** See **if I was** . . .

wastage or **waste** Some people think *wastage* is a formal word for *waste*. In fact it has a different meaning. A *waste* of something is when it is consumed uselessly: 'dripping taps are a waste of water'. *Wastage* is loss through legitimate use or natural causes: 'in hot weather there is a wastage of water from reservoirs through evaporation'. The same distinction works for human beings. It is a waste of well-qualified people when an organization does not make proper use of their talents: the expression 'natural wastage' has become standard in industry for the loss of employees through retirement, resignation, death or for any other reasons than dismissal.

waterfront *Waterfront* is an evocative word for the wharves, warehouses and other commercial buildings in the dilapidated district down by the docks of a city. It is a pity that *waterfront* is more an American word, not used much in Britain, where the usual name is **dockland**.

watershed If we use similes they should relate to the literal meaning of the words. *Watershed* is used for the line that separates waters where they divide to flow into different rivers or seas. The extended use of *watershed* is more than a turning-point in a situation: it is a dividing of the ways, a recognition that something has happened that will steer events away from one direction towards another. If a marriage, for example, is at a watershed, it suggests it has reached a point where the husband and wife will either resolve their difficulties, or separate.

wave See **waive** . . .

we or **us** See **us** . . .

wear and **tear** See **depreciation** . . .

weasel words *Weasel words* belong to politics and Madison Avenue, at one time famous as the home of big New York advertising agencies. They are words that hint at something without coming out in the open, words that are misleading yet keep a statement just on the right side of the law. The poet, John Tessimond, who was a copywriter, explains the craft of weasel words in his poem, *The ad-man*, who . . .

> Knows how to hide an inconvenient act
> And when to leave a doubtful claim unbacked.

Weasel words are often used by politicians, for these are words that leave escape routes open when promises are made.

weatherman See **meteorologist** . . .

Webster *Webster* to Americans is what a combination of **Fowler** and Dr Johnson (see **dictionaries**) would be to the British. Noah Webster (1758–1843) was both a lexicographer (the *American Dictionary of the English Language* was the first to provide a comprehensive study of the English used in the United States) and a grammarian. He went a long way towards standardizing American spellings. Several dictionaries under the name of Webster are in print in America, by different publishers.

we'd See **contracted forms**

we'd have See **I'd have**

wedlock *Wedlock*, as a word for the married state, is rarely used now, except in some marriage services. It has had a very long innings as an Old English word going back to the 13th century, and used by Chaucer. A P Herbert (1890–1971), a parliamentary campaigner for easier divorce laws, was one of the last to give *wedlock* popular currency, at least in a back-handed way: he called his book on the inflexibility of marriage laws – *Holy Deadlock*.

welfare *Welfare* has been used in English since the 14th century, and had become a pious word, more familiar from the pulpit than in everyday life. This changed in 1942, when the *Report on Social Insurance and Allied Services* was published (better known as the *Beveridge Report*), commissioned by Clement Attlee's post-war government. The term *welfare state* became a political concept of taking care of citizens 'from the cradle to the grave'.

In the years since then, wherever we turn we meet the word *welfare*. There are welfare centres, welfare clinics, welfare committees, welfare offices (and, of course, welfare officers). People are paid welfare benefits by welfare cheques. The word has even been given a capital W, signifying the responsibility of the State for people in need: the poor, the sick, the homeless, the unemployed, the old will talk about going for help or applying to – the Welfare.

well or **well-** When *well* compounds come before a noun, they should usually be hyphenated: a well-worn carpet, a well-thought-of book, a well-matched couple, a well-informed expert. . . . When *well* compounds come after a verb, hyphens are not usually necessary: the carpet is well worn, the book is well thought of, the couple are well matched, the expert is well informed. . . . There are some exceptions. *Well-off* is easier to read when it is hyphenated, wherever it comes in the sentence. *Well-spoken* is better hyphenated when it is about a person ('her secretary is well-spoken'), but kept as separate words when it refers to anything else ('a well spoken account of the incident').

wench This Falstaffian word once meant a maidservant. It has survived, out-of-date though it is. There are still waggish men who affectionately call women *wenches*. Some women like it, most find it offensive.

And there are 'olde worlde' restaurants on the tourist circuit that advertise their *serving wenches*, implying bosomy and saucy. It's time the word was pensioned off.

(if I) *were* or *was* See **if I was . . .**

West or **west** See **North, South, East, West . . .**

west or **western** See **north or northern . . .**

West Indian English *West Indian English* is a loose term for the language that evolved in the 17th and 18th centuries when black slaves were brought to the Caribbean. It is characterized by its sing-song intonation, with a vocabulary full of Spanish, French and American influences. Another name for it is Caribbean English, and a specific example is Jamaican Creole (see **pidgin**).

westward, **westwards** or **westerly** See **northward . . .**

wet When children wash, they often forget to dry behind their ears. *Wet behind the ears* has long been an expression for someone who is inexperienced, feeble and ineffectual. Perhaps this led to *wet* becoming jargon in British politics, under Margaret Thatcher as Prime Minister, as a dismissive word for any member of the Conservative Party who advocated caution in social and economic policies. William Whitelaw once claimed he did not know what a *wet* was, while *The Times* had it about right when it described Tory *wets* as anyone who crossed Margaret Thatcher in her aims.

Wet has lost its political force now, although it has stuck as an unfairly derogatory description of a Tory politician who advocates middle-of-the-road policies. See also **wimp**

wh- It is usual in Scotland and Ireland to pronounce the *h* in *what*, *when*, *whether*, etc ('hwat', 'hwen', 'hwether'). It became a middle-class refinement or affectation in England to do the same. Linguistic scholars have long considered the *hw* sound in southern English artificial and unjustified. At the same time, actors and BBC announcers are nearly always very careful about saying 'hwen', 'hwether', 'hwitehall' (Whitehall), etc, which has encouraged others to believe that it is uneducated to say 'wen', 'wot', 'witehall'. . . . It does sound affected to stress the *h* sound strongly, but some speakers retain a light aspiration, while others dismiss it.

If you want to go in for 'hwatting', 'hwenning', etc, old-fashioned teachers of elocution use this sentence for practice: 'Whether the weather is wet, or whether the weather is dry'. Before you work away at that, remember the trend now, rightly in the opinion of the best linguistic authorities, is to forget about *hw* and pronounce *whether* the same as 'weather', *which* the same as 'witch'.

wharves or **wharfs** While both plural forms seem to be accepted, *wharves* is so much more usual, that *wharfs* looks odd.

what *What* gives a few problems:
1 Do we pronounce it 'wot' or 'hwot'? See **wh-**.
2 Should it be 'What *is*' or 'What *are*'? There is no problem about 'What we need *is* more money'. Grammarians argue that we should also say 'What we need *is* more houses for people to live in', because *what* stands for 'the thing' which is singular. That's as may be but 'What we need *are* more houses . . .' sounds more natural. When the word relating to *what* is plural (as in 'more houses' above), both *are* and *is* are acceptable.
3 When we haven't heard something clearly, to ask 'What?' on its own is perhaps rather sharp. Is it also ill-mannered to ask 'What was that?', 'What did you say?'? If you believe it is, look up **pardon**.

what ever or **whatever** See **-ever**

whether or **if** There is, or used to be, a difference between *whether* and *if*. 'Please let me know whether you can come' meant let me know one way or the other: '. . . if you can come' meant let me know only if it is possible for you to come, otherwise don't bother. Those who like this distinction must regret that not enough people recognize it any longer for it to be reliable. To avoid misunderstanding, we have to say 'Let me know whether or not you can come' or '. . . only if you can come'.

In many statements, 'or not' after *whether* can and should be omitted as unnecessary: *whether* in the sentence 'At this stage, we do not know whether the project will succeed' already means *whether or not*. In such statements, *whether* leaves the possibility evenly balanced: *if* ('. . . if the project will succeed') suggests greater uncertainty.

wheeler-dealer See **broker . . .**

when ever or **whenever** See **-ever**

whereabouts *is* or ***are*** *Whereabouts* as a noun can be treated as singular or plural: 'her whereabouts at the time *were* (or *was*) unknown'. Although there is this option, *whereabouts* sounds more natural as a plural word.

where ever or **wherever** See **-ever**

which, who or **that** See **that . . .**

(of) which or **whose** 'The play of which the actors are all women . . .' or 'The play whose actors are all women . . .'? See **whose . . .**

which *is* or ***are*** 'Which of the five books *are* best' means which two, three or four of the books are best; 'Which of the five books *is* best' means which *one* of them is best.

which ever or **whichever** See **-ever**

while or **awhile**   Either 'he remained there *awhile*' or '. . . *for a while*', but not 'for awhile' (*awhile* means 'for a short time').

while or **whilst**   *While* and *whilst* are interchangeable, with *whilst* having a more literary ring to it. Both words properly relate to time: 'She phoned while (or whilst) you were out'. Both words are also used as an alternative to 'although': 'While (or whilst) I understand your problem, I don't think it is serious'. There is nothing wrong with this but it can sometimes lead to confusion: 'While she knows nothing about it, I expect she'll cope quite well' (The suggestion could be that if she knew more, she'd make a hash of it!) Use 'although' instead.

whirlpool   See **eddy** . . .

whisky or **whiskey**   There's more to this than you might think. You'd get into trouble in Scotland if you spelt it any other way but *whisky*. This is short for 'whiskybae', a variant of a Gaelic word for the 'water of life'. Irish *whiskey* is spelt *-ey*. The distillation made in Canada follows the Scottish spelling, *whisky*. In America the spelling is *whiskey*, which many people use wherever it comes from, although those in the know are careful to use *whisky* for the product of Scotland. Experienced drinkers who believe that only whisky distilled in Scotland is the real thing, will sometimes ask for a *Scotch*, and leave it at that.

white or **White**   We should refer to *white* people and *black* people, or *whites* or *blacks*, and avoid initial capital letters in both cases. This is a sensitive linguistic area: for additional notes, see **black; Caucasian; non-white; racist words**

Whitehall and the **White House**   Both *Whitehall* and the *White House* are used by the media as umbrella words to cover the British and American governments: expressions such as 'Whitehall sources suggest . . .', 'a White House spokeswoman commented . . .', are ways of saying that this is the attitude of the Prime Minister or the President to whatever is going on.

White Paper   See **Green Paper** . . .

whizz-kid   *Whizz* is an attempt to imitate the sound of something flashing by, and was used that way in the 17th century. Even before World War I, a *whizz* was slang for someone who is brilliant at anything (a whizz at mathematics), making a connection with *wizard*, a much older word from the 15th century. *Wizard* was linked with 'wise' and used for a sage, before it was adapted for a man with magical powers. The two meanings of *whizz* came together in *whizz-kid*, American to begin with of course, but eagerly taken up in Britain during the 'swinging sixties'.

Whizz for something flashing by must be accepted as standard English by now. *Whizz-kid* sounds slangy but is a useful term for a young man or woman who is

brilliantly successful or clever. One *z* or two, by the way.

who, **which** or **that**   See that . . .

who or **whom**   Even if you are set in your ways (one way or the other!) about *who* and *whom*, this entry may have something to offer. And it's only half a page as against **Fowler**'s three-and-a-half pages in *Modern English Usage*.

The *who* or *whom* question has become as much sociolinguistic as grammatical. Many people try to use *who* and *whom* according to the grammarians' rules in case it is thought they don't know any better. Nor are they reassured to be told that good authorities, such as Eric Partridge and, over a century earlier, Noah **Webster**, were prepared to abandon *whom* altogether.

The truth is that retaining the *who* or *whom* distinction preserves a grammatical relic and does nothing to avoid ambiguity. Philip Howard believes that *whom* by the end of the century will become 'as old-fashioned as wing-collars and corsets' (*Words Fail Me*). That's all very well, you may say, but . . .

If you believe in the grammar of *who* and *whom*, or dare not give it up for fear of what people might think, two principles are respectfully suggested:

1 Be careful not to force in *whom* in the wrong place, as many writers do, including one as good as E M Forster: 'A creature whom we pretend is here already' (*who* should have been used). Here is a useful guide, suggested by William Safire in the *The New York Times*. It works in most sentences, although there are a few exceptions. Divide the sentence into two and ask whether you use 'he' or 'him' (or 'she' or 'her'). If it's 'him' or 'her', use *whom* in the original sentence, otherwise use *who*. Two examples:

(i) The man *whom* I saw yesterday. (The man. I saw *him* yesterday.)

(ii) The woman *who* I think was here yesterday. (The woman. I think *she* was here yesterday.)

2 Avoid sounding stuffy. 'To *whom* shall I send it?', although correct, sounds over-formal in writing and downright pompous in speech. Remember that although '*Whomever* is it for?' is correct English, Oxford authorities consider it stilted and recommend that *whoever* should now be used right across the board.

If the whole subject bewilders or bores you, here is a very simple rule. *For Whom the Bell Tolls* (better known as the title of Ernest Hemingway's novel than in John Donne's poem, where it comes from) has enshrined the use of *whom* after **prepositions**, so write and say *to whom, from whom, for whom, with whom, among whom*, etc. Everywhere else, use *who*. You may be picked up for this occasionally, but the tide is going your way.

whodunit   The July 1930 issue of *American News of Books* might have seen the first appearance of the word *whodunit* (in an article by David Gordon). In the

1990s *whodunit* remains as neat a name as any for a book, play or film based on a murder story.

who ever or **whoever**   See -ever

whoever or **whomever**   Even if you are an aficionado of **who and whom**, you should think twice about writing or saying *whomever*. The Oxford English Dictionary department considers *whomever* stilted and recommends that *whoever* should now be used in all cases.

wholefood   See healthfood . . .

whom or **who**   See who . . .

whomever or **whoever**   See whoever . . .

whose or **of which**   Clearly *who* (and *whom*) must relate to people, and *which* to objects: 'the woman who has just arrived . . .'; 'the car which has just stopped . . .'. This leads some people to believe that *whose* cannot be applied to objects, which forces them into laboured sentences, such as 'the car, of which the seats are made of leather . . .'; 'the play, the actors of which are all women . . .'. There is no grammatical foundation for this rule, and all it does is make sentences obscure and pedantic. We can write: 'the car, whose seats are leather . . .'; 'the play, whose actors are all women . . .'.

wide   See broad . . .

wildcat strike   The difference between this and an unofficial strike, is that a *wildcat strike* borders on industrial sabotage: it is sudden, without discussion, usually by a group of key workers or by the whole workforce, and deliberately aimed at causing maximum disruption in order to force the management to agree to some new terms.

will or **shall**   See shall . . .

wimmin   *Wimmin*, which was at first a humorous slang phonetic representation of the word *women*, became one of the more extreme examples of feminist linguistics. The idea was to break the link with the word *men*. Some of the women who maintained a protest vigil in 1981 outside Greenham Common, the US airbase in Britain, carried placards identifying themselves as PEACE WIMMIN. The problem with *wimmin* is that it only works in print, because when you say 'women' you pronounce it *wimmin* anyway.

wimp   Although it had been heard a long time before, *wimp* emerged into popular use in America in the 1960s, and soon crossed the Atlantic. It is a noun that corresponds to *wet*, and means a weak ineffectual person. As with *wet*, *wimp* became a derisive and dismissive word for politicians, often used unfairly because their views were moderate rather than belligerent.

No one knows the origin of *wimp*: perhaps it comes from 'whimper', or a blend of 'weak' and 'simp' (an American slang word for a fool).

windfall   See bonus . . .

windfall profit   See bonus . . .

windward   See leeward . . .

wine merchant or **vintner**   What do we call places where we buy wine? *Wineshop* doesn't sound right. *Vintner*, from the Latin word for a vineyard, was the 15th-century name for a dealer in wine, and there is Vintners' Hall in the City of London. All that makes *vintner* too grand for the local *corner shop*. We are left with *wine merchant*, the most usual term. Since so many people buy their wines in supermarkets or off-licences anyway, perhaps the issue isn't all that pressing.

(names of) wines   Traditionally, regional names of wines bear initial capital letters: we drink Bordeaux, Burgundy, Sancerre, a Moselle, etc. With the present trend to use fewer **CAPITAL LETTERS**, some writers are dropping capitals from the names of wines: Joanna Simon, wine correspondent for *The Sunday Times*, not only writes about bordeaux and burgundy, but calls wines from the Loire Valley 'loires', including 'saint-nicolas de bourgueil'.

In the end, like the wines themselves, it's a matter of taste whether you drink Vouvray, Sauternes, Chianti, or vouvray, sauternes, chianti . . ., although names such as St Emilion, Saint Amour look strange without their capitals.

winespeak   The wine game is played out at dinner-tables, in restaurants and at wine-tastings. In order to keep your end up, you have to know some of the language: wine doesn't smell good – it has a *good nose*; wine is *big* or *meaty* rather than heavy, *round* or *velvety* rather than smooth, *dumb* rather than nothing special, *flabby* rather than tasteless, *corked* rather than 'off'. The best wines are *elegant* or *well-bred*. Wine can have *finesse*, a *finish*, *character* and can be *forthcoming, earthy, complex, sensuous*.

For wine writers, winespeak demands purple prose. Among examples of writers straining to express the inexpressible are 'the breeze-blown perfume of spring-time orchard flowers', and 'slightly underripe pears or the fruit near the pear skin'. (The wine in question is Condrieu, from a hillside in the northern Rhone Valley.)

If you are daunted by all this, take heart from Adrienne Lehrer, a professor of linguistics at the University of Arizona. Her paper, 'Talking About Wine' in the journal *Language*, reveals that even wine experts were unable to match descriptions of wines with the wines themselves. James Thurber gently derided the whole game in a famous caption to a cartoon, liberally sprinkling it with capital letters to make the point: 'It's a Naive Domestic Burgundy without Any Breeding. But I Think You'll be Amused by its Presumption' (*Men, Women and Dogs*).

wireless See **radio** . . .

-wise *Wise* has been tacked on to words for centuries and everyone accepts *likewise, crosswise, clockwise, otherwise* and other well-established *-wise* words. But many people object strongly to *-wise* being added to other words. It is the 'nastiest thing to have happened to the English language in recent years', according to one writer (B A Phythian, *A Concise Dictionary of Correct English*). Those are hard words about a suffix that has been used in English since the 14th century.

Admittedly, *-wise* is overused trendy jargon, but that doesn't mean it is not useful sometimes: *careerwise* is much quicker than 'in relation to my career', *moneywise* more direct than 'as far as money is concerned'. Iris Murdoch was 'in mourning *applewise*', because Cox's orange pippins were out of season.

If you use *-wise* carelessly it becomes a trendy linguistic gimmick, but occasionally *-wise* added to a word can say something quickly and effectively, as long as you remember it will make some people wince. New *-wise* words are probably not acceptable yet in serious writing.

wish See **desire** . . .

with When *with* links two nouns together, it is the noun that comes *first* which dictates whether the following verb is singular or plural: 'the *teacher* together with the children *has* arrived', but 'the *children* together with their teacher *have* arrived'.

withdraw See **retreat** . . .

withdrawn See **introspective** . . .

withhold or **withold** The double *h* may look odd but *withhold* is the correct spelling.

with it *With it* was popular slang in the 1960s for knowing what is going on, being in the swing and up to date. If you are still using it, you are certainly not *with it*.

with the exception of See **except** . . .

wog *Wog*, a slang racist name used by the British, seems to have arisen some time in the 1920s. It was first used by British servicemen and colonial administrators in a patronizing way about a dark-skinned foreigner, especially an Arab. The even more benighted view was that any foreigner was a wog: 'Wogs begin at Calais' was the blimpish slogan. No one knows the origin of the word. Some claim it is an **acronym** for 'wily oriental gentleman', but that is probably fanciful. A more likely source could be armbands said to have been worn in the 19th century by Egyptians employed by Britain, which we're told had wogs on them (working on government service).

For most people, *wog* had faded into past history of British colonialism. But memories of old insults are deep-seated, and in August 1992, *wog* was brought unexpectedly into headlines, when the Secretary-General of the United Nations gave an interview to *The New York Times*. He was asked why the British press was so critical of him. Boutros Boutros-Ghali, who is an Egyptian, replied in undiplomatic language that it was 'maybe because I'm a wog'. For some people in Britain, the word stirred uneasy feelings of chauvinistic arrogance and racism that had been slumbering below the surface.

woman See **lady** . . .

womanizer See **philanderer** . . .

womankind or **womenkind** Some dictionaries show *womenkind* as a variant form. *Womankind* is better, as it is a parallel word to 'mankind'.

wondrous or **wonderous** *Wondrous* (see **-erous** or **-rous**).

won't See **contracted forms**

wordprocessor and **wordprocessing** IBM used *word processing* in the 1960s for a typewriter that functioned with magnetic tape. Most dictionaries continue to show the terms as two words. It is beginning to show up as one word here and there, which makes sense, for who writes 'type writer'? See also **computer**

work or **oeuvre** It is perhaps pretentious to use *oeuvre* in the singular to mean a painting, a book, a composition, etc. The general word to cover all those forms is *work*: 'This work by Beethoven was written in 1805'. *Oeuvre* is useful as a word for the complete works of a writer, artist, composer, etc considered as a whole (it remains *oeuvre*, not 'oeuvres'). In this sense, *oeuvre* embraces more than 'works', implying a totality of style and achievement: 'The oeuvre of van Gogh became an enduring source of inspiration for generations of artists'. (Pron: 'ERRvr'.)

workaholic The existence of *workaholic* has a social significance. It used to be the poor who worked long hours in order to scrape together enough money to survive. The Victorian work ethic was a moral precept for the lower classes. All that has been turned on its head: *workaholic* is used about the rich and middle class who make a virtue of staying late at the office, slaving over a hot desk.

The term *workaholic* was coined in America in the 1970s, as a pejorative word suggesting a drudge who led a narrow life dominated by work. That has changed. *Workaholic* could be used now in admiration of ambitious driving people, determined to succeed. In November 1987, the Duchess of York commented in a television programme, 'It takes about 25 hours a day . . . The girls in the office insist I'm a workaholic'.

workforce To talk about the 'workers' in industry or in a factory could now be considered downgrading. The *workforce* recognizes not only the importance of the contribution made by the **shop-floor** but acknowledges the potential power of the people behind the machines in relation to management.

working class It would venture into deep waters to define the *working class* in the 1990s. The term has lost the social, economic and cultural cohesion that existed up to World War II. People in traditionally working-class occupations might now live in the same street as people working in banks, etc. They might be earning more money, travel to faraway places on holiday, and have sons and daughters at university. There could still be certain characteristics of lifestyle, social attitudes and manner of speaking, but the term *working class* no longer has the traditional homogeneity that sets it clearly apart. See also **class**

workman, **labourer** or **navvy** *Labourers* and *navvies* (originally short for navigators) used to dig the roads and railways. The terms are more or less obsolete now, and could well be taken as insults. *Workman* is the general word for any man working with his hands, no matter how rough the work might be, although building sites still have builders' labourers. See also **workforce**

work sharing See **job sharing**

workshop Since the 16th century, a workshop meant a place where things are made, worked on or repaired. Some time in the 1930s, the middle class took over the word and used it for study groups and experimental sessions, mostly in the theatre, art and music. *Workshop* has now become the standard word for any short course in any subject. Business executives attend 'communication workshops' and 'management workshops'. *Workshop* is a popular word in these contexts because it sounds more purposeful than 'class' or 'course', and suggests participation and working, rather than sitting back and listening.

work-to-rule See **go-slow** . . .; **restrictive practices**

world or **earth** See **earth** . . .

world-class *World-class* became a popular term in the 1980s in sport, for someone at the highest level of performance by world standards, as against local or national standards. *World-class* is now extended to all fields: for example, *The Independent* carried a feature on how Britain could get 'world-class schools'.

worsen See **deteriorate** . . .

worth, **worthwhile** or **worth while** When it comes before a noun, *worthwhile* is now fused into one word: a worthwhile journey, a worthwhile charity. . . . When it comes after a verb, *worth while* is better as

two words: the journey was worth while, the charity is worth while. . . . Note that *worth* is the word to use to modify a *verb*, and not *worthwhile*: 'It is worth travelling there' (not '. . . worthwhile travelling there'); 'If something is worth doing, it is worth doing well' (not '*worthwhile* doing'). See also next entry

worthwhile or **worthy** Whatever anyone says, *worthy* is slightly patronizing, a shade condescending: 'a worthy young couple' suggests they are rather dull and uninteresting. *Worthwhile* is much more wholehearted: 'a worthwhile young couple' implies that you like and admire them.

would or **should** See **should** . . .

Wow! We may regard *Wow!* as modern, rather slangy comic strip language. But it's not. *Wow*, Scottish to begin with, goes back to the 16th century, and is accepted by dictionaries as standard English. So if we are astonished by something, overwhelmed by seeing an exceptionally attractive man or a beautiful woman, taking a first sip of an unexpectedly marvellous wine, there's nothing wrong in saying *Wow!* But to say someone or something is a *wow*, meaning remarkable or a great success, belongs to the 20th century and is slang, which also applies to *wow* as a verb, meaning to astonish someone.

WPC At times, ironing out sexual discrimination in language causes confusion and resentment. Up to July 1990, WPC was the abbreviation for woman police constable. Then the prefix *woman* was officially dropped by the police, and WPCs became PCs, on a recommendation made by **equal opportunities** experts. But the W was missed. A number of the 3000 women police officers have refused to give up the prefix, saying that its omission causes confusion among both the public and the police force. There is a good possibility that WPC will return.

wrack See **rack** . . .

wrangle See **haggle** . . .

wraparound In computer language, *wraparound* has more than one meaning. The one that comes up most often is in **wordprocessing**. *Wraparound* is the built-in facility that moves words to the next line or back to the preceding line when text is inserted or deleted.

write or **write to** See **write to** . . .

write down or **off** *Write down* and *write off* are accountancy terms that are extended to everyday life. In accounts, to *write down* an **asset** is to decrease its value in stages, year by year, until it no longer appears in the assets of a company. To *write off* an item, which could be something that has been damaged or destroyed, or a debt unlikely to be paid, is to cancel the item in one go – just like writing off a car.

Outside business, a person, an idea, an activity, etc is *written down* when it is criticized as having little value. To *write off* someone or something dismisses whoever or whatever it is as worthless.

writer or **author**   As the curtain falls on the first night of a play, it is traditional for the audience to call out *Author! Author!* Nevertheless, the tendency now is for *authors* to call themselves *writers*. The Society of Authors was founded in 1884 but the more recent association is called The Writers' Guild. The same person now will often write a book, a play, a film and for television, which is why *writer* is taking over as the more usual word, although not all authors will agree, for Latinate *author* is a grander word than Old English *writer*. *The Times* sits on the fence: in one list of birthdays, it included Antonia Byatt, *writer*, Martin Amis, *author*, Brian Moore, *novelist*. When in doubt, call someone a *writer*, which is less pretentious. *Authoress* sounds silly, and don't call a writer a *pen-pusher*, unless you want to insult them.

write to or **write**   It is usual in America to say, for example, 'Please write me about it'. British English requires '. . . write *to* me . . .'. Some people in Britain have adopted the American form ('I'll write Mary about it'), but this is not felt to be good English, unless it is followed by another word: 'I'll write Mary a letter about it'.

With the verb *telephone*, it's the other way round.

Normal British usage is 'I'll telephone (or phone) Mary'. American usage includes 'to' ('I'll phone *to* Mary'), a form that is finding some favour in Britain.

wrong or **wrongly**   *Wrong* is the normal form when it comes after a verb: 'You did it wrong'; 'Did I pronounce it wrong?'; 'She guessed wrong about his feelings'. No one could say *wrongly* is incorrect in such sentences but it is less natural. Mae West's classic film was called *She Done Him Wrong*. Imagine it being called 'She Done Him Wrongly'.

When it comes *before* the verb, *wrongly* is usually required: 'It is wrongly said that . . .'; 'He wrongly decided to . . .'. *Wrongly* also belongs in the combination *rightly or wrongly*, whether it comes before or after the verb: 'She felt, rightly or wrongly, that . . .'. See also **right** . . .

WYSIWYG   Computer language has come up with one of the most bizarre **acronyms**: WYSIWYG (usually written in capitals but sometimes in small letters) stands for 'What you see is what you get', which describes a system that reproduces on a screen the layout and arrangement of text, or text plus diagrams, exactly as it will appear when printed out on paper. This enables the operator to work as designer and typesetter. Pronounce it 'WIZiwig'. But only to people who know what it means.

Xerox or xerox Chester F Carlson, a New York lawyer, invented a dry photocopying process in 1948. He combined two Greek words, *xeros* (dry) with *-graphia* (writing), and called the process *xerography*, which doesn't take a capital, any more than *photography* does. In 1952 *Xerox* was registered as the trademark for a photocopying machine using the xerographic process, and like all trademarks, *Xerox* should be spelt with a capital. It became a generic word, used for photocopying in general, with a small *x*, and some American dictionaries record it this way: 'Will you xerox this please?'; 'Look at this xerox'. The Xerox Corporation were not grateful for this free publicity, and used advertisements in *The New York Times* to remind the world that *Xerox* is a trademark and should always be spelt with a capital X.

By now the party is over. Other makes of photocopying machines are well advertised, and people are more likely now to use *photocopy* ('Will you photocopy this please?', 'Look at this photocopy').

Xmas See **Christmas** . . .

· Y ·

yang and **yin**   See **macrobiotic**

Yank   *Yankee* was used about people who lived in New England or the northern states in general. During the American Civil War, the confederate army used *Yankee* as a derogatory name for soldiers of the federal armies. By that time, the British were in the habit of using *Yankee*, and the shortened form *Yank*, for any American. When the US entered World War I, *Yank* became widely familiar in Britain, generally used with warmth.

Yank was used less in World War II. In later years, the name seemed to be fading out, although in the 1991 Gulf War, the British forces were again talking about the Yanks and the Yank radio service, which was popular with them. Nevertheless, *Yank* seems dated now as a name for an American, less likely to be used by younger people. Some Americans dislike it, but most don't care one way or the other, except in the southern states.

No one has been able to fix the origin of *Yankee*: perhaps the most likely source is 'Janke' (pron: 'YUN-ke(r)'), an old-fashioned nickname in Dutch for John.

yellow pages   The *yellow pages* (in some dictionaries with initial capital letters, as having the status of a trademark) has long been in use in America for trade telephone directories. In the late 1960s, the name was borrowed for British telephone directories, and soon became familiar: if we say 'Look it up in the yellow pages', all we mean is look it up in the trade telephone directory.

yes   You wouldn't think there would be much trouble with the straightforward monosyllable, *yes*. After all, it is an Old English word that goes back almost to the dawn of the English language. Philip Howard was one of the first to warn us that, after a millennium of signifying assent and agreement, *yes* is in danger of decline (*Winged Words*, 1988). People seem to feel that *yes* is curt and unfriendly, or dull and unimaginative. They are turning to other forms.

Since the late 19th century, *Yup* or *Yep* have been crude American alternatives that reached Britain, but never really caught on. *Yeah* followed a few years later, and is still popular with people who for some reason feel awkward about saying *yes*. OK is an old standby.

Many people now have taken to **Absolutely**, as a way of agreeing ('Isn't it a lovely day?', 'Absolutely').

That's right is standard on radio and television and with many younger people, as a transatlantic make-the-other-person-feel-good way of saying *yes*. At the bottom end of the market, *Not 'arf* held sway for many years, but is uncommon now.

We should try to preserve *yes* from extinction. Not only does this simple syllable go back to the very roots of the language, but it remains the neatest, clearest and most honest way of saying *yes*.

yeses or **yesses**   When the vote was taken, there were many more *yeses* than were expected (not *yesses*).

yesterday's words   How do we sense when words are past their **sell-by** date? Conversational language and slang date much more quickly than good written language: if you are still talking about a young couple *necking* or *spooning*, for example, or about the *old maid* who lives next door, it is high time you traded in some of your vocabulary. With many words and expressions, the balance is sensitive. Alexander Pope, writing about words in his *Essay on Criticism* (1711), left us advice that remains fresh and to the point in the 1990s:

> Be not the first by whom the new are tried,
> Nor yet the last to lay the old aside.

See also **archaisms**

Yiddish   See Hebrew . . .

yield   See dividend . . .

yin and **yang**   See **macrobiotic**

Yinglish   See Hebrew . . .

yoghurt, **yogurt** or **yoghourt**   Since the word is an adaptation of the Turkish word, it is not surprising there are variations in spelling in English. *Yoghurt* is the usual spelling, with *yogurt* as a variation. *Yoghourt* is also possible but less common. The accepted pronunciation is 'YOGGert' ('YOHgert' in America).

(between) **you and *me*** or **you and *I***   See I or me

you'd   See contracted forms

you'd have   See I'd have

you know and **you see** *You know* or *y'know* are used too often in conversation and on radio and television as meaningless stopgaps. No doubt they give whoever is speaking a split-second of time to think of what to say next. A pause would be just as good. The same applies to *you see*.

you'll See contracted forms

you name it Which sounds better: 'she brought strawberries, raspberries, cherries, altogether a whole collection of soft fruit', or 'she brought strawberries, raspberries, cherries . . . you name it'? The first sentence is a balanced expression of an idea: in the second sentence, *you name it* is no more than a mindless catchphrase.

young people, **youths** or **youngsters** The problem over these words started when *youngster* seemed to sound slightly patronizing, and the word *youth* was more associated with young men than with women. *Youths* often feature in news items about unrest and violence in **inner cities**, so the word has taken on that colouring. Faced with this dilemma, politicians, social workers, etc try to steer a middle course with the term *young people*.

The government Youth Training Scheme and its successor New Youth Training have helped to make *youth* more acceptable as a unisex word. But this has only gone so far: government advertisements for New Youth Training refer throughout to *young people*, which is the better term to use in most contexts.

See also **teenager**

young turks The Young Turks was the name of a revolutionary party in Turkey seeking to overthrow the Ottoman Empire at the beginning of the century. Established politicians like to call younger politicians who kick against a party line *young turks*. There's usually a slightly condescending and dismissive flavour to it.

you're See contracted forms

yours or **your's** Never *your's*.

Yours sincerely, etc See letter endings

you see See you know . . .

youths See young people . . .

yuppie The term that spread like wildfire in Britain and America during the second half of the 1980s is linguistic history in the 1990s. *The Times*, 21 March 1984, announced the birth of the word in New York, where it was formed from the first letters of 'young urban professional'. In Britain, where there is a more clearly defined class structure, *yuppie* became interpreted as young **upwardly mobile** professional: people from any social background, who were clever enough and single-minded enough, could move up into the big money class.

The word *yuppie* was an instant success, because it pinpointed a social phenomenon of the eighties: the cult of youth, people under 35 ruthlessly exploiting new money-making opportunities, able to handle the frantic pace of **information technology** and the new electronic money markets. For many people, *yuppie* was part-sneering, part-envious. It spawned a series of similar labels, such as *dinkies* (double income no kids) and *woopies* (see **Third Age**).

After the stock market crash in autumn 1987, *yuppie* ran out of steam. The recession of the early 1990s finished it off, as thousands of executives working for financial companies were made redundant. Although still heard, *yuppie* sounds like one of **yesterday's words**, and there is little point in using it any more, since the meaning is now too indeterminate.

-yse Unlike the suffix *-ize*, which can also be written *-ise*, *-yse* is the only accepted form for *paralyse*, *analyse* etc. (Although not etymologically justified, American English uses *-yze* for these and some other words.)

· Z ·

-z or **-zz** At one time, dictionaries showed *buz*, *fiz*, *friz*, as variant spellings of *buzz*, *fizz*, *frizz*. In the end, other forms of those words (buzzer, fizzy, frizzy) have made *buzz*, *fizz*, *frizz* the only accepted spellings. **Whiz(z)** is an exception, and most dictionaries continue to show both spellings. Lastly, in isolation, **quiz** is never 'quizz'.

zany Contrary to what some people think, *zany* is not slang but a well-established word in English, going back to the 16th century. It was first used in the theatre for a servant who had the role of a clown in Italian farces. *Zany* comes from 'Gianni', a short version of 'Giovanni', Italian for 'John', and a name used for porters. In spite of its long history, *zany* remains a lively word for anyone or anything that seems crazy, and is a more literary word than 'scatty', 'up the pole', or 'nutty as a fruit cake'.

Zen In the 1960s, people in the West began to talk casually, often unknowingly, about *Zen*, as part of the fashionable cult of **meditation**. Zen was paraded as the path to ecstasy and spiritual experience. It is a Japanese word for a religious discipline that derives ultimately from Sanskrit, and is the name of a form of **Buddhism**, known as *Zen Buddhism*. The disciplines are rigorous, using detachment and meditation to arrive at **enlightenment**.

In the mid-1970s, a bestselling book was called *Zen and the Art of Motorcycle Maintenance*: the writer, Robert M Pirsig, explained it had little to do with orthodox Zen Buddhist practice, nor was it a factual book on motorcycles. It could be described as an exploration of personal non-material values, which is what most people in the West understand by Zen in a vague uncertain way. For the experience of *Zen*, and hence the meaning of the word itself, is beyond words. The best we can do is catch half-glimpses through seemingly irrational imagery, such as a single hand clapping. In an interview for his 70th birthday, the American composer, John Cage, related this ancient spiritual discipline to a common symbol of 20th-century culture, 'two Coca-Cola bottles are both, separately, seen as the centre of the world. A different light strikes them when you look . . . The 20th century is all about seeing things that way'.

zenith See **nadir** . . .

zero See **nought** . . .

Zionism *Zionism* can be a confusing word. From a historical point of view, it could be considered obsolete, since its original meaning no longer has relevance. The term dates from 1896, a year before the first World Zionist Congress in Basle. It was the name given to the impassioned movement among Jewry to found a Jewish State in what was then called Palestine, the area between the Mediterranean and the River Jordan. When the State of Israel was proclaimed in 1948, the aims of Zionism were achieved, and its original meaning became historic.

Since then, Zionism has taken on a different significance, to describe political and financial support for the development and protection of Israel, and also as a word for the pledge by the founding fathers of that State to offer a home to any Jew in the world who applies for it.

Zip code If an American asks you for your Zip code, all they want to know is your postal code. It's short for Zone Improvement Plan.

zoology The contraction *zoo*, for 'zoological garden', leads many people to pronounce *zoology* as 'zoo-OLLe(r)jee', which may one day take over. In the meantime, it is criticized by those in the know, who pronounce it 'zoh-OLLe(r)jee', which is recommended.

zoom There is an old linguistic argument about *zoom*, that refuses to go away. It's an invented word anyway, used in the 19th century to imitate the humming sound of something flashing by. Later, it suggested the noise of an aircraft climbing up steeply at speed. Because of this, it is argued we should not use *zoom* for anything other than an upward movement. But a car racing round a circuit makes a similar noise, so no one argues with 'zoom *round*'. Zoom lenses on cameras have led to our using 'zoom *in*' for anything homing in fast from any direction, and 'zoom *out*' for enlarging the field covered by a variable focus lens. In spite of all that, some dictionaries maintain that 'zoom *down*' ('the eagle zoomed down into the valley') is as much a contradiction in terms as *dive up* would be. It seems an unnecessary fuss, but if it keeps you awake at night, let your eagles *swoop* or *dive* down into valleys.

417

zzz . . . A row of *z*s is the traditional way in comic strips to show someone is asleep or snoring. This led to *zizz* becoming a slang word for a nap during the daytime. Perhaps *zzz* . . . was suggested by **doze** and *snooze*. If you want to be more up to date, next time you take a nap, just say you're 'giving it some zeds'!

Wilhelm von Humboldt (1767–1835) was a statesman and a writer, a friend of Schiller and Goethe. He related language to spiritual energy and to the continuous evolution of humanity. These lines, taken from a translation of one of his essays, are a reminder that the last word on what is or is not *good English* can never be written:

There can never be a moment when language truly stands still, any more than there is a pause in the ever-blazing thoughts in the human mind.